T0181500

Lecture Notes in Computer Science 5611

Commenced Publication in 1973
Founding and Former Series Editors:
Gerhard Goos, Juris Hartmanis, and Jan van Leeuwen

Julie A. Jacko (Ed.)

Human-Computer Interaction

Novel Interaction Methods and Techniques

13th International Conference, HCI International 2009
San Diego, CA, USA, July 19-24, 2009
Proceedings, Part II

Springer

Volume Editor

Julie A. Jacko
University of Minnesota
Institute of Health Informatics
MMC 912, 420 Delaware Street S.E., Minneapolis, MN 55455, USA
E-mail: jacko@umn.edu

Library of Congress Control Number: Applied for

CR Subject Classification (1998): H.5, I.3, I.7.5, I.5, I.2.10

LNCS Sublibrary: SL 3 – Information Systems and Application, incl. Internet/Web
and HCI

ISSN	0302-9743
ISBN-10	3-642-02576-5 Springer Berlin Heidelberg New York
ISBN-13	978-3-642-02576-1 Springer Berlin Heidelberg New York

springer.com

© Springer-Verlag Berlin Heidelberg 2009
Printed in Germany

Typesetting: Camera-ready by author, data conversion by Scientific Publishing Services, Chennai, India
Printed on acid-free paper   SPIN: 12707218   06/3180   5 4 3 2 1 0

Foreword

The 13th International Conference on Human–Computer Interaction, HCI International 2009, was held in San Diego, California, USA, July 19–24, 2009, jointly with the Symposium on Human Interface (Japan) 2009, the 8th International Conference on Engineering Psychology and Cognitive Ergonomics, the 5th International Conference on Universal Access in Human–Computer Interaction, the Third International Conference on Virtual and Mixed Reality, the Third International Conference on Internationalization, Design and Global Development, the Third International Conference on Online Communities and Social Computing, the 5th International Conference on Augmented Cognition, the Second International Conference on Digital Human Modeling, and the First International Conference on Human Centered Design.

A total of 4,348 individuals from academia, research institutes, industry and governmental agencies from 73 countries submitted contributions, and 1,397 papers that were judged to be of high scientific quality were included in the program. These papers address the latest research and development efforts and highlight the human aspects of design and use of computing systems. The papers accepted for presentation thoroughly cover the entire field of human–computer interaction, addressing major advances in the knowledge and effective use of computers in a variety of application areas.

This volume, edited by Julie A. Jacko, contains papers in the thematic area of Human–Computer Interaction, addressing the following major topics:

- Multimodal User Interfaces
- Gesture, Eye Movements and Expression Recognition
- Human–Robot Interaction
- Touch and Pen-Based Interaction
- Brain Interfaces
- Language, Voice, Sound and Communication
- Visualization, Images and Pictures

The remaining volumes of the HCI International 2009 proceedings are:

- Volume 1, LNCS 5610, Human–Computer Interaction—New Trends (Part I), edited by Julie A. Jacko
- Volume 3, LNCS 5612, Human–Computer Interaction—Ambient, Ubiquitous and Intelligent Interaction (Part III), edited by Julie A. Jacko
- Volume 4, LNCS 5613, Human–Computer Interaction—Interacting in Various Application Domains (Part IV), edited by Julie A. Jacko
- Volume 5, LNCS 5614, Universal Access in Human–Computer Interaction—Addressing Diversity (Part I), edited by Constantine Stephanidis
- Volume 6, LNCS 5615, Universal Access in Human–Computer Interaction—Intelligent and Ubiquitous Interaction Environments (Part II), edited by Constantine Stephanidis

- Volume 7, LNCS 5616, Universal Access in Human–Computer Interaction—Applications and Services (Part III), edited by Constantine Stephanidis
- Volume 8, LNCS 5617, Human Interface and the Management of Information—Designing Information Environments (Part I), edited by Michael J. Smith and Gavriel Salvendy
- Volume 9, LNCS 5618, Human Interface and the Management of Information - Information and Interaction (Part II), edited by Gavriel Salvendy and Michael J. Smith
- Volume 10, LNCS 5619, Human Centered Design, edited by Masaaki Kurosu
- Volume 11, LNCS 5620, Digital Human Modeling, edited by Vincent G. Duffy
- Volume 12, LNCS 5621, Online Communities and Social Computing, edited by A. Ant Ozok and Panayiotis Zaphiris
- Volume 13, LNCS 5622, Virtual and Mixed Reality, edited by Randall Shumaker
- Volume 14, LNCS 5623, Internationalization, Design and Global Development, edited by Nuray Aykin
- Volume 15, LNCS 5624, Ergonomics and Health Aspects of Work with Computers, edited by Ben-Tzion Karsh
- Volume 16, LNAI 5638, The Foundations of Augmented Cognition: Neuroergonomics and Operational Neuroscience, edited by Dylan Schmorrow, Ivy Estabrooke and Marc Grootjen
- Volume 17, LNAI 5639, Engineering Psychology and Cognitive Ergonomics, edited by Don Harris

I would like to thank the Program Chairs and the members of the Program Boards of all thematic areas, listed below, for their contribution to the highest scientific quality and the overall success of HCI International 2009.

Ergonomics and Health Aspects of Work with Computers

Program Chair: Ben-Tzion Karsh

Arne Aarås, Norway
Pascale Carayon, USA
Barbara G.F. Cohen, USA
Wolfgang Friesdorf, Germany
John Gosbee, USA
Martin Helander, Singapore
Ed Israelski, USA
Waldemar Karwowski, USA
Peter Kern, Germany
Danuta Koradecka, Poland
Kari Lindström, Finland

Holger Luczak, Germany
Aura C. Matias, Philippines
Kyung (Ken) Park, Korea
Michelle M. Robertson, USA
Michelle L. Rogers, USA
Steven L. Sauter, USA
Dominique L. Scapin, France
Naomi Swanson, USA
Peter Vink, The Netherlands
John Wilson, UK
Teresa Zayas-Cabán, USA

Human Interface and the Management of Information

Program Chair: Michael J. Smith

Gunilla Bradley, Sweden
Hans-Jörg Bullinger, Germany
Alan Chan, Hong Kong
Klaus-Peter Fähnrich, Germany
Michitaka Hirose, Japan
Jhilmil Jain, USA
Yasufumi Kume, Japan
Mark Lehto, USA
Fiona Fui-Hoon Nah, USA
Shogo Nishida, Japan
Robert Proctor, USA
Youngho Rhee, Korea

Anxo Cereijo Roibás, UK
Katsunori Shimohara, Japan
Dieter Spath, Germany
Tsutomu Tabe, Japan
Alvaro D. Taveira, USA
Kim-Phuong L. Vu, USA
Tomio Watanabe, Japan
Sakae Yamamoto, Japan
Hidekazu Yoshikawa, Japan
Li Zheng, P.R. China
Bernhard Zimolong, Germany

Human–Computer Interaction

Program Chair: Julie A. Jacko

Sebastiano Bagnara, Italy
Sherry Y. Chen, UK
Marvin J. Dainoff, USA
Jianming Dong, USA
John Eklund, Australia
Xiaowen Fang, USA
Ayse Gurses, USA
Vicki L. Hanson, UK
Sheue-Ling Hwang, Taiwan
Wonil Hwang, Korea
Yong Gu Ji, Korea
Steven Landry, USA

Gitte Lindgaard, Canada
Chen Ling, USA
Yan Liu, USA
Chang S. Nam, USA
Celestine A. Ntuen, USA
Philippe Palanque, France
P.L. Patrick Rau, P.R. China
Ling Rothrock, USA
Guangfeng Song, USA
Steffen Staab, Germany
Wan Chul Yoon, Korea
Wenli Zhu, P.R. China

Engineering Psychology and Cognitive Ergonomics

Program Chair: Don Harris

Guy A. Boy, USA
John Huddlestone, UK
Kenji Itoh, Japan
Hung-Sying Jing, Taiwan
Ron Laughery, USA
Wen-Chin Li, Taiwan
James T. Luxhøj, USA

Nicolas Marmaras, Greece
Sundaram Narayanan, USA
Mark A. Neerincx, The Netherlands
Jan M. Noyes, UK
Kjell Ohlsson, Sweden
Axel Schulte, Germany
Sarah C. Sharples, UK

Neville A. Stanton, UK
Xianghong Sun, P.R. China
Andrew Thatcher, South Africa

Matthew J.W. Thomas, Australia
Mark Young, UK

Universal Access in Human–Computer Interaction

Program Chair: Constantine Stephanidis

Julio Abascal, Spain
Ray Adams, UK
Elisabeth André, Germany
Margherita Antona, Greece
Chieko Asakawa, Japan
Christian Bühler, Germany
Noelle Carbonell, France
Jerzy Charytonowicz, Poland
Pier Luigi Emiliani, Italy
Michael Fairhurst, UK
Dimitris Grammenos, Greece
Andreas Holzinger, Austria
Arthur I. Karshmer, USA
Simeon Keates, Denmark
Georgios Kouroupetroglou, Greece
Sri Kurniawan, USA

Patrick M. Langdon, UK
Seongil Lee, Korea
Zhengjie Liu, P.R. China
Klaus Miesenberger, Austria
Helen Petrie, UK
Michael Pieper, Germany
Anthony Savidis, Greece
Andrew Sears, USA
Christian Stary, Austria
Hirotada Ueda, Japan
Jean Vanderdonckt, Belgium
Gregg C. Vanderheiden, USA
Gerhard Weber, Germany
Harald Weber, Germany
Toshiki Yamaoka, Japan
Panayiotis Zaphiris, UK

Virtual and Mixed Reality

Program Chair: Randall Shumaker

Pat Banerjee, USA
Mark Billinghurst, New Zealand
Charles E. Hughes, USA
David Kaber, USA
Hirokazu Kato, Japan
Robert S. Kennedy, USA
Young J. Kim, Korea
Ben Lawson, USA

Gordon M. Mair, UK
Miguel A. Otaduy, Switzerland
David Pratt, UK
Albert "Skip" Rizzo, USA
Lawrence Rosenblum, USA
Dieter Schmalstieg, Austria
Dylan Schmorrow, USA
Mark Wiederhold, USA

Internationalization, Design and Global Development

Program Chair: Nuray Aykin

Michael L. Best, USA
Ram Bishu, USA
Alan Chan, Hong Kong
Andy M. Dearden, UK

Susan M. Dray, USA
Vanessa Evers, The Netherlands
Paul Fu, USA
Emilie Gould, USA

Sung H. Han, Korea
Veikko Ikonen, Finland
Esin Kiris, USA
Masaaki Kurosu, Japan
Apala Lahiri Chavan, USA
James R. Lewis, USA
Ann Light, UK
James J.W. Lin, USA
Rungtai Lin, Taiwan
Zhengjie Liu, P.R. China
Aaron Marcus, USA
Allen E. Milewski, USA

Elizabeth D. Mynatt, USA
Oguzhan Ozcan, Turkey
Girish Prabhu, India
Kerstin Röse, Germany
Eunice Ratna Sari, Indonesia
Supriya Singh, Australia
Christian Sturm, Spain
Adi Tedjasaputra, Singapore
Kentaro Toyama, India
Alvin W. Yeo, Malaysia
Chen Zhao, P.R. China
Wei Zhou, P.R. China

Online Communities and Social Computing

Program Chairs: A. Ant Ozok, Panayiotis Zaphiris

Chadia N. Abras, USA
Chee Siang Ang, UK
Amy Bruckman, USA
Peter Day, UK
Fiorella De Cindio, Italy
Michael Gurstein, Canada
Tom Horan, USA
Anita Komlodi, USA
Piet A.M. Kommers, The Netherlands
Jonathan Lazar, USA
Stefanie Lindstaedt, Austria

Gabriele Meiselwitz, USA
Hideyuki Nakanishi, Japan
Anthony F. Norcio, USA
Jennifer Preece, USA
Elaine M. Raybourn, USA
Douglas Schuler, USA
Gilson Schwartz, Brazil
Sergei Stafeev, Russia
Charalambos Vrasidas, Cyprus
Cheng-Yen Wang, Taiwan

Augmented Cognition

Program Chair: Dylan D. Schmorrow

Andy Bellenkes, USA
Andrew Belyavin, UK
Joseph Cohn, USA
Martha E. Crosby, USA
Tjerk de Greef, The Netherlands
Blair Dickson, UK
Traci Downs, USA
Julie Drexler, USA
Ivy Estabrooke, USA
Cali Fidopiastis, USA
Chris Forsythe, USA
Wai Tat Fu, USA
Henry Girolamo, USA

Marc Grootjen, The Netherlands
Taro Kanno, Japan
Wilhelm E. Kincses, Germany
David Kobus, USA
Santosh Mathan, USA
Rob Matthews, Australia
Dennis McBride, USA
Robert McCann, USA
Jeff Morrison, USA
Eric Muth, USA
Mark A. Neerincx, The Netherlands
Denise Nicholson, USA
Glenn Osga, USA

Dennis Proffitt, USA

Leah Reeves, USA

Mike Russo, USA

Kay Stanney, USA

Roy Stripling, USA

Mike Swetnam, USA

Rob Taylor, UK

Maria L.Thomas, USA

Peter-Paul van Maanen, The Netherlands

Karl van Orden, USA

Roman Vilimek, Germany

Glenn Wilson, USA

Thorsten Zander, Germany

Digital Human Modeling

Program Chair: Vincent G. Duffy

Karim Abdel-Malek, USA

Thomas J. Armstrong, USA

Norm Badler, USA

Kathryn Cormican, Ireland

Afzal Godil, USA

Ravindra Goonetilleke, Hong Kong

Anand Gramopadhye, USA

Sung H. Han, Korea

Lars Hanson, Sweden

Pheng Ann Heng, Hong Kong

Tianzi Jiang, P.R. China

Kang Li, USA

Zhizhong Li, P.R. China

Timo J. Määttä, Finland

Woojin Park, USA

Matthew Parkinson, USA

Jim Potvin, Canada

Rajesh Subramanian, USA

Xuguang Wang, France

John F. Wiechel, USA

Jingzhou (James) Yang, USA

Xiu-gan Yuan, P.R. China

Human Centered Design

Program Chair: Masaaki Kurosu

Gerhard Fischer, USA

Tom Gross, Germany

Naotake Hirasawa, Japan

Yasuhiro Horibe, Japan

Minna Isomursu, Finland

Mitsuhiko Karashima, Japan

Tadashi Kobayashi, Japan

Kun-Pyo Lee, Korea

Loïc Martínez-Normand, Spain

Dominique L. Scapin, France

Haruhiko Urokohara, Japan

Gerrit C. van der Veer, The Netherlands

Kazuhiko Yamazaki, Japan

In addition to the members of the Program Boards above, I also wish to thank the following volunteer external reviewers: Gavin Lew from the USA, Daniel Su from the UK, and Ilia Adami, Ioannis Basdekis, Yannis Georgalis, Panagiotis Karampelas, Iosif Klironomos, Alexandros Mourouzis, and Stavroula Ntoa from Greece.

This conference could not have been possible without the continuous support and advice of the Conference Scientific Advisor, Prof. Gavriel Salvendy, as well as the dedicated work and outstanding efforts of the Communications Chair and Editor of HCI International News, Abbas Moallem.

I would also like to thank for their contribution toward the organization of the HCI International 2009 conference the members of the Human–Computer Interaction Laboratory of ICS-FORTH, and in particular Margherita Antona, George Paparoulis, Maria Pitsoulaki, Stavroula Ntoa, and Maria Bouhli.

Constantine Stephanidis

HCI International 2011

The 14th International Conference on Human–Computer Interaction, HCI International 2011, will be held jointly with the affiliated conferences in the summer of 2011. It will cover a broad spectrum of themes related to human–computer interaction, including theoretical issues, methods, tools, processes and case studies in HCI design, as well as novel interaction techniques, interfaces and applications. The proceedings will be published by Springer. More information about the topics, as well as the venue and dates of the conference, will be announced through the HCI International Conference series website: http://www.hci-international.org/

General Chair
Professor Constantine Stephanidis
University of Crete and ICS-FORTH
Heraklion, Crete, Greece
Email: cs@ics.forth.gr

Table of Contents

Part I: Multimodal User Interfaces

Part II: Gesture, Eyes Movement and Expression Recognition

Part III: Human-Robot Interaction

Part IV: Touch and Pen-Based Interaction

Part V: Brain Interfaces

Part VI: Language, Voice, Sound and Communication

Part VII: Visualisation, Images, and Pictures

Part I

Multimodal User Interfaces

Using Acoustic Landscapes for the Evaluation of Multimodal Mobile Applications

Wolfgang Beinhauer and Cornelia Hipp

Fraunhofer Institute for Industrial Engineering, Nobelstrasse 12,
70569 Stuttgart, Germany
{wolfgang.beinhauer,cornelia.hipp}@iao.fraunhofer.de

Abstract. Multimodal mobile applications are gaining momentum in the field
of location based services for special purposes. One of them is navigation systems and tourist guides for pedestrians. In some cases, when the visibility is
limited or blind people are longing for guidance, acoustic landmarks are used
for macro-navigation rather than visual landmarks. Likewise, micro-navigation
supported by pedestrian navigation systems must comply to the user's expectations. In this paper, we present an acoustic landscape that allows the emulation
of arbitrary out-door situations dedicated for the evaluation of navigation systems. We present the evaluation capabilities and limitations of the laboratory as
well as an example of an evaluation of a pedestrian navigation system that uses
acoustic and haptic feedback.

Keywords: Acoustic landscape, test bed, pedestrian navigation, haptic feedback.

1 Introduction

User Centered Design (UCD) [1] is a widely accepted process of product development, in which specific emphasis is put on the active involvement of users at each
step of the design process. In particular, the user centered design process comprises
the iterative run through a cycle of product prototyping, real world tests with actual
users, evaluation and refined prototyping until a satisfying design has been found.
While UCD is well established as a method for the development of hardware devices
or user interfaces for software solutions, it encounters difficulties in case of other
types of applications, such as location based services, especially if those are in a premature stage.

When it comes to mobile devices and location based services, a thorough evaluation in real world outdoor tests can be hardly practicable and difficult to manage.
Ubiquitous network access is not given. The test setting is far off the development
labs. In many cases, it is impossible to maintain equal test conditions due to rapidly
changing environmental factors which are not under control. Quantitative evaluation
data might be blurred by imperfect test conditions. In the worst case, the evaluation of
premature prototypes in outdoor scenarios involving handicapped test persons might
even put them at risk.

J.A. Jacko (Ed.): Human-Computer Interaction, Part II, HCII 2009, LNCS 5611, pp. 3–11, 2009.
© Springer-Verlag Berlin Heidelberg 2009

With the Fraunhofer Interaction Laboratories, we introduce a test environment that emulates realistic outdoor conditions without the drawbacks of public space. The laboratory contains several indoor installations for testing and prototyping, one of them being a large scaled multimodal immersive environment that combines a 3D stereo projection with a novel surround sound system. The sound system allows for enhanced spatial audio perception and serves as a test bed for the development and evaluation of new interaction techniques, notably mobile applications. Within the immersive environment, ubiquitous network access is given as well as camera systems for easy evaluation and data processing, pathing the way for rapid design and short test circles.

Simple two-channel stereophony, quadrophonic or 5.1 sound systems fall short of the requirements for precise sound-based localization as introduced in the sequel. A more accurate and more flexible sound positioning is needed. The sound system presented in this paper does not deliver the quality and accuracy of high-end acoustic installations such as wave field synthesis [2], but enhances conventional multi-channel sound generation in a way that it is easy to implement and suitable for test purposes. The system is capable of emulating real-world audio conditions in a laboratory environment and creating repeatable test conditions for the evaluation of third services. This paper presents the laboratory itself and shows how the lab is used as an acoustic landscape for the development of alternative multimodal pedestrian navigation.

2 Related Work

Spatial hearing relies on interaural time difference, interaural intensity difference and head related transfer functions. Acoustic landscapes that build on these effects have been around for quite a while already. Most of previous work aimed at special audio effects. Mauney and Walker [3] introduced the idea of livable "soundscapes", and Mynatt et al. [4] introduced the term of an "audio aura". In distinction to those contributions, we focus on acoustic environments that can be used for the development and evaluation of interactive systems such as a navigation system.

The use of audio interfaces or other modalities for navigation tasks have been examined by various groups. Loomis and Klatzky [5, 6] dealt with self-orientation and related spatial orientation and multimodal spatial representations and examined their relevance for sensory substitution.

Walker and Lindsay presented a rapid prototyping tool for auditory navigation displays based on virtual reality [7]. An approach to interactive acoustic environments that are capable of streaming spatiotemporal audio data is introduced by Heimrich et al. [8].

3 The Acoustic Landscape

The idea of the lightweight acoustic landscape is to create a test environment that allows for spatial sound generation beyond stereophonic reproduction. Therefore, several independent 7.1 speaker systems are stacked on multiple layers, providing spatial perception in all three dimensions beyond psychoacoustic effects. A dedicated software controller enables the positioning of mono sounds within the laboratory area.

3.1 Installation

The physical installation of the acoustic landscape consists of two 7.1 speaker systems mounted at different height levels in a rectangular room. While the upper annulus is located at a height of $y_1 = 282$cm, the lower one raises at $y_2 = 44$cm, sandwiching the average ears' elevation. The speakers are controlled by specific software that creates a spatial sound perception. The set-up emulates a cylindrical sound space with a base radius of 256cm. Due to the given room geometry and limited fixation possibilities, an aberration from the ideal cylindrical shape is inevitable and leads to some distortion in angular sound perception. This effect can be reduced by a fine calibration of the amplifiers. An empirical evaluation has proven that satisfying results are obtained within a larger sweet spot extending close to the boundaries of the room.

The speakers deployed are conventional high-end consumer devices (GigaSet S750) that feature no special directional characteristics. The configuration leaves a rectangular experimentation space of roughly 25m². Additionally, at the right hand border, a stereoscopic display extending to the full width of the laboratory is available, making up a multimodal immersive environment.

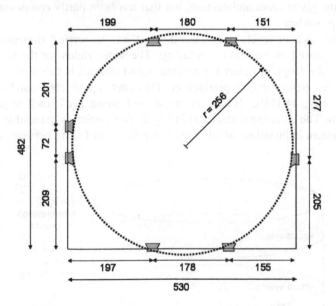

Fig. 1. The acoustic landscape consists of two 7.1 speaker systems mounted above each other (only the tweeters depicted). The set-up emulates a cylindrical sound space with a base radius of 256cm within the rectangular room. The aberration of the ideal cylindrical shape leads to some distorted angular sound perception. View from above; all dimensions are given in centimeters (cm).

3.2 Control Software

In order to put the acoustic landscape into operation, a dedicated control software was developed that makes use of the speakers beyond stereophony, quadrophony or 5.1 deployment that build on pseudoacoustic effects in order to create the impression of distance or movement. Besides the subwoofers, 14 tweeters have to be controlled in order to generate a sound composition that allows for near-reality test conditions.

One possible approach to control software would be direct control of each individual speaker. Sound samples could move along a given trajectory through the audio laboratory by hand-overs between the speakers. However, this approach is not practical, since it would require separate sound cards and amplifiers for each speaker.

The key to a simpler approach is the segmentation of the acoustic environment. Existing libraries such as OpenAL by creative labs or Microsoft DirectSoundspace ease the development of psychoacoustic effects in the periphery of the soundscape. Referring to the Fraunhofer installation, this refers to the space above and below the upper and lower plane of 7.1 systems, as well as to the outside of the cylindrical base model. Proper generation of pseudoacoustic effects requires an equidistant mounting of the speakers along the circumference of the cylinder – a requirement that is not perfectly fulfilled due to the given room architecture, but that has been partly compensated for by a calibration procedure.

In between the speaker levels, pseudoacoustic effects in vertical dimensions are eliminated and replaced by manual cross-fading. The same yields for the horizontal plane. Moreover, the Doppler Effect for moving sound sources is calculated and applied to the sounds before their reproduction. This way, up to 256 sound samples (mono-recorded *wav*, 44.1kHz, 16bit) can be moved along predefined trajectories through the room. The situation is depicted in Fig 2. The system is extensible in case a neighboring system is installed, which would require cross-fading between the two systems.

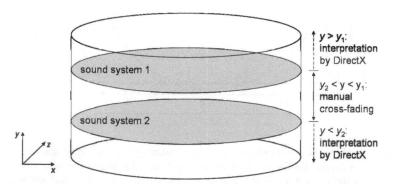

Fig. 2. Segmentation of the room with two sound systems. Human ears will usualy be located in the middle between the two planes, allowing for the most realistic sound impression.

3.3 Building an Acoustic Landscape

Usability and modularity were important aspects in the design of the user interface of the authoring tool for sound composition. The generation of a sound landscape is a two-step process. Firstly, the trajectory and playback parameters of a single sound have to be defined. This can be done graphically as shown in figure 3. A sound file is selected and its positioning in space is defined. Additionally, the dimensions of the laboratory can be altered here in order to adapt the system to new geometries. Several sound sources or trajectories can be saved as macros and can be re-used for the generation of more complex sounds.

The second step consists of the orchestration of the various sounds to a landscape. For this purpose, the preset sounds are triggered on a timeline and follow their respective trajectory. Figure 4 shows an example of an audio scene composed of 18 different sounds.

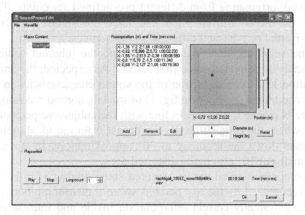

Fig. 3. User interface for presetting sounds. A trajectory through the sound space is attached to each sound source (graphical tool to the right). Alternatively, a series of co-ordinate quadruples in space and time can be defined, which are approached consecutively and in between which a linear interpolation is performed.

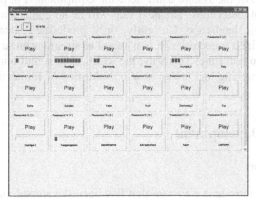

Fig. 4. User interface for composing a landscape. In the example, a landscape consisting of 18 sound sources is created.

4 Discussion

4.1 Evaluation

Currently no detailed evaluation with professional audio measurement equipment has been performed. However, an empirical study has produced some first preliminary results. The relevant criteria for the functionality of the sound landscape are the direction, where a certain sound is heard to come from and the perceived distance, where a certain sound is estimated to origin from. Moreover, it was tested how the transition of a moving sound source from the inner area of interpolated positioning to the outer area of psychoacoustic effects is perceived.

The precision in which positioned sounds are perceived respective to their set point was evaluated with a series of tests. Firstly, a test person was placed into the sweet spot, hence, in the centre of the enveloping cylinder. A sequence of pulsating sound signals was played, originating from different pre-defined set points. The test person pointed towards the direction from where she heard the sound. The series have been repeated with different persons and different sound sources.

Despite of the very inaccurate measurement and the inherent subjectivity of the procedure, the analysis delivered some first results: As expected, the anisotropy of the speaker installation leads to a distortion of the sound characteristics in horizontal dimension. In the right hand section (see fig. 1) of the lab, a good precision of about 10° angle of aperture is reached, which is in line with the subjective perception tolerance. In the left part, where the installation deviates most from the ideal cylindrical set-up, the distortion tears down the accuracy to 30° approximately. In vertical dimension, the precision remains at 10° also in the distorted area.

The perceived distance could not be captured satisfyingly so far. However, no discontinuity was recognized by the test persons when transitioning between two sound effect areas. The physically correct interpolation inside and outside psychoacoustic effects are integrated seamlessly.

4.2 Future Development

A precise evaluation of the system using acoustic equipment is in progress in order to minimize the current distortions. The next step will be an enhancement of the interactivity of the acoustic landscape. Currently, only predefined sound sources can be moved along predefined trajectories. It is planned to stream arbitrary sound sources to arbitrary positions in real time. This way, the localizable sound output could be combined with object tracking and create new possibilities of immersive interaction behavior.

5 Exemplary Development

5.1 Test Conditions

As an example, we introduce a system that has been developed and evaluated in the acoustic landscape. The exemplary development makes use of the laboratories' facilities and shows the benefits of an indoor test environment.

Navigation systems are nowadays broadly used. The use of pedestrian navigation systems is rather restricted to touristic areas or larger sports events like the Olympics. Other systems use tagging technologies like geoannotation [9]. However, these approaches based on PDA computers fail when it comes to blind people who need pedestrian navigation aids the most. In the sequel, we introduce a navigation system for the blind whose development and evaluation was supported by the creation of an acoustic landscape in the laboratory.

The acoustic landscape can be a powerful tool for the simulation of realistic test conditions, in particular in overlaying desired sound signals with unwanted background-noise. Those conditions are completely repeatable and ease evaluation procedures.

Background noise is not necessarily intrusive or distracting. It can be very informative as well. Especially for visual impaired and blind people, sounds of the personal environment of a person are valuable indicators for orientation. Especially outdoors, blinded people use the background-sound in great amount for their macro-navigation. Steady noises from distant sound sources such as the roaring of a motorway are perceived as acoustic landmarks just like a spire would de for sighted people. By contrast, micro-orientation is performed by aid of the immediate and direct environment within a short distance of a few meters. Compared to that, macro-navigation is aiming at the environment with a greater distance, e.g. the location of the next bus-station. Therefore the acoustic landscape can simulate a surrounding, which is used by blind people for the orientation in their macro-navigation. Additionally, disturbing sound sources can be blend such as the abrupt appearance of a rattling motor bike. In the sequel, two systems for blind people are tested in the acoustic landscape.

5.2 A Pedestrian Navigation System

Since the visual channel is not available, other modalities have to be found in order to create an effective navigation system for the blind. One means for accessing blind people and signaling hints for their orientation is the use of haptic interaction. Another one would be audio feeds. Haptic interaction has advantages over audio signals especially in very noisy surroundings, such as pedestrian areas or at bus-stations. Also, haptic feedback is not distracting for third people. The first test case presents the idea of haptic navigation wristbands.

The guided person wears one wristband on each arm, equipped with vibration motors, which can be controlled by a central navigation-system to direct him in the right or left direction, or to stop him in case of danger. Likewise, the person could wear a smart phone on the belt, which receives GPS information about the user's location and subsequently calculates and sends correct signals to the wristband. To enhance the accuracy, a pedometer can be integrated as well.

This wristband is very useful for blind people, when the surrounding is noisy and they cannot listen properly to an audio navigational aid. To prove this and to enhance the wristband, a noisy situation can be simulated with the help of the acoustic landscape and ensure, that in the test situation, there is always the same interfering noise, which makes audio-information less useful.

The second example represents a sound based navigation system for pedestrians. Especially for visual impaired and blind people an orientation with the help of their hearing is very important. Beside the usage of a speech-system which can tell

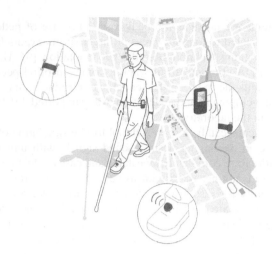

Fig. 5. The concept of haptic wristbands for pedestrian navigation. A GPS device attached to a belt receives localization data and guides the user by means of haptic stimuli transmitted by the wristbands.

information explicitly, information can be given via sounds. This can be less intrusive as speech commands because speech is intensely attention-grabbing. A continuously repeated command can be distracting and annoying, whereas a discrete sound might be much less intrusive. A comfortable short sound at this point can improve the audio-navigation system. Moreover, this idea was continued in order to improve the macro-navigation by sounds. In laboratory testing in the acoustic landscape it was found which kind of information blinds are interested in: information for orientation, safety-related information and temporary barriers like construction-sites. Furthermore, adequate sounds could be identified some of them as earcons and some as auditory icons. Earcons refer to an arbitrary melody, which were designed for information, which do not have a natural sound, like "stairs". In contrast, the auditory icons refer to reality and therefore we used for example for the information "construction work" a recording of a real construction site.

The acoustic landscape proved to be a valuable tool to test the sounds, whether the system is well heard and understood actually and not be ignored, when other sounds of the real environment are interfering. Further more it can be tested, how often and exactly when the sounds should be played in interfering situations to make sure the user received the information. Additionally it can be investigated, whether auditory icons are always useful or whether users have problems to identify, that the auditory icon is coming from the earphones and not from the real surrounding.

Ongoing developments of smart phones and personal digital assistances tend to the continuous trend of mobile usage of systems. Therefore the demand of methodology and tools for testing devices and application in a mobile situation will increase. One solution therefore will be the acoustic landscape.

Acknowledgements. We would like to thank the all contributors to the development of the acoustic landscape, in particular Frank Falkenberg and Till Issler, Jan Roehrich and Andreas Friedel. Moreover, thanks to Romy Kniewel and Brigitte Ringbauer who have been contributing decisively to the development of the pedestrian navigation system.

References

1. Norman, D.A.: The Design of Everyday Things. Perseus Books Group, New York (1990)
2. Brandenburg, K., Brix, S., Sporer, T.: Wave Field Synthesis: From Research to Applications. In: Proceedings of 12th European Signal Processing Conference (EUSIPCO), Vienna, Austria, August 7-10 (2004)
3. Mauney, B.S., Walker, B.N.: Creating functional and livable soundscapes for peripheral monitoring of dynamic data. In: Proceedings of ICAD 2004. The tenth international conference on auditory display, Sydney, Australia (2004)
4. Mynatt, E.D., Back, M., Want, R., Baer, M., Ellis, J.B.: Designing audio aura. In: Proceedings of the SIGCHI conference on Human factors in computing systems, Los Angeles, California, United States, April 18-23, 1998, pp. 566–573 (1998)
5. Klatzky, R.L., Loomis, J.M., Beall, A.C., Chance, S.S., Golledge, R.G.: Spatial updating of self-position and orientation during real, imagined, and virtual locomotion. Psychological Science 9(4), 293–298 (1998)
6. Loomis, J.M., Klatzky, R.L.: Functional equivalence of spatial representations from vision, touch and hearing: Relevance for sensory substitution. In: Rieser, J., Ashmead, D., Ebner, F., Corn, A. (eds.) Blindness, brain plasticity and spatial function, pp. 155–184. Erlbaum, Mahwah (2007)
7. Walker, B.N., Lindsay, J.: Using virtual reality to prototype auditory navigation displays. Assistive Technology Journal 17(1), 72–81 (2005)
8. Heimrich, T., Reichelt, K., Rusch, H., Sattler, K., Schröder, T.: Modelling and Streaming Spatiotemporal Audio Data. In: Meersman, R., Tari, Z., Herrero, P. (eds.) OTM-WS 2005. LNCS, vol. 3762, pp. 7–8. Springer, Heidelberg (2005)
9. Beeharee, A., Steed, A.: Minimising Pedestrian Navigation Ambiguities Through Geoannotation and Temporal Tagging. In: Jacko, J. (ed.) Human-computer Interaction: Proceedings of the 12th International Conference, HCI International 2007, Beijing, China, July 22-27 (2007)

Modeling and Using Salience in Multimodal Interaction Systems

Ali Choumane and Jacques Siroux

IRISA, University of Rennes 1, 6 rue de Kerampont, BP80518, 22305 Lannion, France
ali.choumane@gmail.com, jacques.siroux@enssat.fr

Abstract. We are interested in input to human-machine multimodal interaction systems for geographical information search. In our context of study, the system offers to the user the ability of using speech, gesture and visual modes. The system displays a map on the screen, the user ask the system about sites (hotels, campsites, ...) by specifying a place of search. Referenced places are objects in the visual context like cities, road, river, etc. The system should determine the designated object to complete the understanding process of user's request. In this context, we aim to improve the reference resolution process while taking into account ambiguous designations. In this paper, we focus on the modeling of visual context. In this modeling we take into account the notion of salience, its role in the designation and in the processing methods.

1 Introduction

A large number of current day such systems use a visual mode of communication [1, 5, 9, 10, 12]. One of the major reasons behind this use is to allow the user and the system to share their knowledge of objects through visual metaphors. Establishing and using this common universe must lead to an efficient and co-operative interaction. Each represented object disposes of visual and contextual characteristics which can impact the user's perception and interpretation during interaction. This is already showed in [6]. This makes interesting to take into account the visual impact of objects in reference resolution methods. This visual impact consists on the visual salience [6, 9]. In fact, an object is salient when it attracts user's visual attention more than others. The problem is that the system can only deal with values; hence the degree of salience of objects in visual context should be estimated to be used by the system.

In this paper, we propose a method to quantify salience and we show how the determined values can be used to resolve, in some cases, multimodal designations. We show factors which contribute to make an object more or less salient. The determination of some of these factors is based on an experimental study we have realized (other factors are already introduced in existing work [6]). These factors take into account the most relevant visual and contextual characteristics of objects. Next, we show a method for quantifying the value of each factor and for determining the final salience value of the object. We also propose pragmatics criteria for normalizing each factor.

J.A. Jacko (Ed.): Human-Computer Interaction, Part II, HCII 2009, LNCS 5611, pp. 12–18, 2009.
© Springer-Verlag Berlin Heidelberg 2009

During the interaction, the focus of attention naturally changes depending on questions and responses of user and system. Theses moves have to be taken into account; for that reason, we also propose a method for modifying salience values depending on the current request interpretation result and the initial salience values. Finally, we show how salience values are used in our system for reference resolution. They are used in gesture disambiguation process and in the processing of ambiguous definite description references.

In the following sections, we describe more closely the context of work and the problem addressed. Next, we show an experimental study concerning the influence of the visual context on the user's requests. Finally, we detail our modeling of the visual context based on the salience notion.

2 Context of Work

We are concerned with inputs of multimodal interaction systems. Our general aim consists on improving the automatic understanding process of user's input. The framework we use to analyze and validate our approach is the Georal tactile system [10]. It is a multimodal system principally used to provide information of a tourist and geographic nature. Users can ask for information about the location of places of interest (beach, campsite, château, church, etc.) by specifying a place, a zone (particular geographical or cartographical element: river, road, city, etc.). Georal has been implemented on the multiagent platform using JADE[1] middleware.

Georal offers the user the following modes and modalities:

- Oral input as well as output to the system. Users can formulate their requests and responses to the system by voice and in natural language (NL) in a spontaneous manner (no particular instructions of elocution). Some system outputs are given using speech synthesis to the user.
- Visual mode: the system displays a map of a region on the screen; this map contains a representation of the usual geographic and tourist information: cities, roads, rivers, etc. Zooming effects, highlighting, and flashing allow the system to focus the user's attention.
- Gesture mode by the intermediary of a touch screen: the user can designate elements displayed on the screen by various types of gesture (point, zone, line, etc.).

3 Reference Resolution Problem

In a user input, one of the principal problems for the system is to resolve references, i.e. to find the referent of a symbol in one modality using information present either in the same or in other modalities. In our context, the user uses the speech mode (the natural language modality) and the gesture mode to ask about information. For example, in the input *give me hotel in this city* (accompanied with a gesture on the touch screen), the system should resolve the referential expression *this city*. In this example, *this city* is matched with the single gesture. Hence, the referent of this expression is represented by the object on the map designated by the gesture.

---

[1] Java Agent DEvelopment Framework.

There are several types of referential expression (RE): those which refer to entities in the natural language (NL) history as anaphora [7], those which do not have linguistic antecedents because they are employed in first mention [11] and which refer to objects in another modality which corresponds, for example, to the visual context in the Georal system. In our context (cf. section 2), this last type of RE is produced:

– Jointly with a gesture. In this case, there are deictic REs in which the referent is the object designated by the gesture
– Without gesture. In this case, dialog becomes very important [3].

Reference resolution methods encounter several problems: In fact, the visual context, the precision of the designation activity, the nature of the desired object could lead to an ambiguous designation. The technical mechanisms used (speech recognition, linguistic processing) can also contribute to ambiguity (reference resolution problem is addressed in more details in [3, 4].

Our principal aim in this paper is to take into account the visual context to refine the processing of user's designation activities. The next section shows more details about the influence of the visual context on the designation activity and how this influence can be addressed.

4 Visual Modality and Application Objects

The visual modality for us is the context containing application objects: displayed or to be displayed[2]. In our context of work, objects are cities, rivers, roads, etc of a geographical map. User's designation activities are based on these objects and in the case of processing troubles, the objects characteristics should be taken into account.

We call CVC the Current Visual Context. It corresponds to the visual context at a given interaction situation. Hence, the CVC contains a set of objects. To allow the system to take into account the objects characteristics, these objects should be "well" modeled and encoded. Hence, we propose to assign a vector to each object. This vector contains the following attributes:

<id, label, color, form, type, size, coordinates, status, salience, nature, statusL>

In this vector, for example, *form* is the geometrical form (polyline, zone, etc.), *type* is the geographical type (city, river, etc.), *status* is a Boolean to indicate if the object is displayed or hidden, *salience* is the salience degree of the object (cf. section 5), *nature* is a Boolean to indicate if the object is *composite* or not and *statusL* is the status of the object's label (displayed or hidden). The *composition* of an object is out of the topic of this paper. In brief, an object is *composite* if it is made of at least two component objects in the CVC [2]. For example, a city is composed of a downtown and suburbs.

The characteristics' vectors are used by the methods for reference resolution [3, 4] as well as by the algorithm of salience quantification presented in the following section.

---

[2] Some objects are hidden for application reasons: screen size, dialog and contextual importance of the object.

5 Salience

An object is salient when it attracts the user's visual attention more than others. In each human-computer interaction with shared visual context, visual salience constitutes an identification criterion of the designated object [6]. To allow the system taking advantage of this fact, we should assign a salience value to each object in the visual context. The initial value of salience of an object is function of the visual and applicative characteristics of the object. In the following, we show how the salience values are computed and used.

5.1 Experiment

We have carried out an experiment aiming at observing how users phrase their requests in front of the displayed map. The objective is to determine how the user perceives the map's objects and how he or she phrases in the natural language input, the expression referring to them. In this paper, we discuss the part of the experiment which deals with the visual objects' characteristics.

The experiment consists of a simulation of interaction with the multimodal Georal system (cf. section 2). After briefly explaining the context, the user is asked to phrase a search request that believes relevant. The request should concern a specific search area communicated to the user. In the following, two user's requests from the collected corpora (translated from French language):

U1: I search for campsites near to the coast between Trebeurden and the road D21.

U2: give me hotels along the coast located between Trebeurden and the island[3].

As these requests show, the users designate a coast by using other displayed objects like the city Trebeurden, the road D21, and an island close to the coast. We note that the user was free to use any object in the neighbor of the search area to designate (a coast in the above requests).

The new point we observed in this experiment is the influence of the object label on the user attention. In fact we observed that labeled objects are more used during designation than non labeled objects. Table 1 summarizes the percentages of use of an object noted O in two steps of the experiment: in the first step (Exp1) O was not labeled and in the second one (Exp2) O was labeled.

Table 1. Percentages of use of a map's object during designation. In the first step of the experiment (Exp1) the object O was not labeled and in the second step (Exp2) O was labeled.

	Object O
Exp1 (O is not labeled)	12%
Exp2 (O is labeled)	38%

---

[3] Trebeurden is a city displayed on the map. The word « island » in the user's request concerns the only island displayed on the map.

To sum up, labeling an object makes it more salient, which must be taken into account when calculating salience scores of objects (cf. section 5.3).

5.2 Salience's Factors

The idea consists first in determining a set of salience's factors. Next, for each object in the visual context, we assign a value depending in the number of factors satisfied for this object. Two critical points in salience quantification should be taken into account: which factors are significant for the application and which quantification method should be used.

In the context of geographical information search, the topology of the map is quite complex and the number of displayed objects is high. Each object category can have several occurrences at the same time: for example, at least two rivers are displayed on the screen. Hence, only visual characteristics-based quantification method could not allow us to "isolate" an object. So, saliences' factors depend to the kind of application and we can not define a generic set of factors.

In multimodal systems for geographical information search, salience should be computed from at least the following factors: object color, size, pragmatic importance and label. In our knowledge, this last factor was never be used in previous works. The experiment we performed (cf. section 5.1) proved that labeling an object makes it more salient for the user and leads the user to designate it often more than if the object is not labeled. We have already discussed the circumstances of labeling or not an object (cf. section 4).

5.3 Salience Quantification

Given the factors defined in the previous section, we use the following algorithm for salience quantification:

If (Start of interaction) **then**
  [Initialization of saliences]
  [$f_i \in \{color, size, pragmatic\ importance, label\}]$
  For $o_j \in CVC$ **do**
    $\mid \quad S(o_j) \leftarrow \frac{1}{4}\sum_{f_i} f_i(o_j)$;
  end For
else
  [Update of saliences; this situation corresponds to the end of request processing and we dispose of the referent o_{j*}.]
  $S(o_{j*}) \leftarrow S(o_{j*}) + \alpha$;
  For $o_j \in CVC - \{o_{j*}\}$ **do**
    $\mid \quad S(o_j) \leftarrow S(o_j) - \beta$;
  end For
end If

Where f_i corresponds to the defined factors. $S(o_j)$ is the salience degree of the object o_j in the visual context. α and β thresholds are application dependent.

This algorithm takes into account the average of normalized factor values. By normalizing factors, we avoid to determine a "weight" of each factor which is not an easy task.

At the beginning of each interaction[4] we initialize the salience values. In fact, for each displayed object, we compute the values of f_i factors. Then, we normalize these values in the [0, 1] interval. Factor values are computed as described in the following:

- Color factor: The color of an object is represented in the characteristics vector (cf. section 4) using the RGB color model. The value of the color factor is equal to the luminance level computed by (R+G+B)/3.
- Size: The value of the size factor is the length or the area of the object depending on its geometric type introduced in the characteristic vector (cf. section 4).
- Pragmatic importance: The value of this factor is pre-computed depending on the tourist and historic interest of the object.
- Label: The value of this factor is 1 if the object is labeled and 0 if not. Note that the characteristic vector of an object allows the system to know at every time if the object is labeled or not.

The initial salience value of an object is the average of the computed factors after being normalized.

During the interaction, the initial salience values are modified. Hence the salience is increased for "referent" objects and decreased for other displayed objects in the CVC. This allows taking into account the interaction focus.

As mentioned above, we use salience values for reference resolution in ambiguous cases. When our methods detect ambiguous designation (this is out of the topic of this paper, [3, 4] present more details), salience values are used to help finding the object referent. For example, our method for gesture processing [4] computes a probability that a given gesture designates an object in the CVC. If several objects have close probabilities (there is ambiguity), we weight these probabilities by the salience value of each object. This allows taking into account the visual and contextual influence of represented object in the CVC.

We have implemented the salience quantification method in the Georal system. Our methods for reference resolution use salience values.

6 Conclusion and Future Work

We have proposed and described a modeling of the visual mode that allows taking into account the visual impact during interaction. This modeling is based on the visual salience notion. We presented a set of factors we use to compute the salience values. Hence we presented our experimental work that has lead to define a new salience

---

[4] An interaction is a set of requests/responses between the user and the system for the realisation of one goal.

factor: labeling an object makes it more salient and then more used by the user during designation activities. Next, we presented a simple algorithm to compute salience values of the objects in the visual context. This algorithm initializes and updates values during interaction to allow taking into account the interaction focus. We have implemented this modeling in our multimodal system. Preliminary test helped the Georal system to successfully determine the designated object in ambiguous case. We aim to lead an experiment with the Georal system to evaluate our method in natural interaction conditions.

References

1. Chai, J.Y., Hong, P., Zhou, M.X.: A probabilistic approach to reference resolution in multimodal user interfaces. In: Proc. of IUI 2004, Portugal, pp. 70–77. ACM Press, New York (2004)
2. Choumane, A.: Traitement générique des références dans le cadre multimodal parole-image-tactile. PhD thesis of university of Rennes 1, France (2008)
3. Choumane, A., Siroux, J.: Knowledge and Data Flow Architecture for Reference Processing in Multimodal Dialog Systems. In: Proceedings of the 10th ACM international conference on Multimodal interfaces, Chania, Greece, October 20-22, 2008, pp. 105–108 (2008)
4. Choumane, A., Siroux, J.: Natural Language and Visual based Gesture Disambiguation in Multimodal Communication Systems. In: Intelligent Information Systems (IIS 2008), Zakopane, Poland, June 16-18, 2008, pp. 219–228 (2008)
5. Jokinen, K., Hurtig, T.: User expectations and real experience on a multimodal interactive system. In: Proceedings of Interspeech, Pittsburgh, PA, USA (September 2006)
6. Landragin, F.: Referring to objects with spoken and haptic modalities. In: ICMI 2002, p. 99. IEEE Computer Society Press, Los Alamitos (2002)
7. Mitkov, R.: Anaphora Resolution. Pearson Education, London (2002)
8. Oviatt, S., Swindells, C., Arthur, A.: Implicit user-adaptive system engagement in speech and pen interfaces. In: CHI 2008: Proceeding of the twenty-sixth annual SIGCHI conference on Human factors in computing systems, pp. 969–978. ACM Press, New York (2008)
9. Qu, S., Chai, J.Y.: Salience modeling based on non-verbal modalities for spoken language understanding. In: ICMI 2006, pp. 193–200. ACM Press, New York (2006)
10. Siroux, J., Guyomard, M., Multon, F., Rmondeau, C.: Multimodal references in georal tactile. In: Workshop of ACL Meeting, Spain, (1997)
11. Vieira, R., Poesio, M.: An empirically-based system for processing definite descriptions. Computational Linguistics 26(4), 539–593 (2000)
12. Wahlster, W.: SmartKom: Dialogue Systems. Springer, Heidelberg (2006)

Exploring Multimodal Interaction in Collaborative Settings

Luís Duarte, Marco de Sá, and Luís Carriço

LaSIGE & Department of Informatics, University of Lisbon,
Edifício C6, Campo Grande, 1749-016 Lisboa, Portugal
lduarte@lasige.di.fc.ul.pt, {marcosa,lmc}@di.fc.ul.pt

Abstract. This paper presents an initial study of a multimodal collaborative platform concerning user preferences and interaction technique adequacy towards a task. True collaborative interactions are a missing aspect of the majority of nowadays' multi-user system on par with the lack of support towards impaired users. In order to surpass these obstacles we provide an accessible platform for co-located collaborative environments which aims at not only improving the ways users interact within them but also at exploring novel interaction patterns. A brief study regarding a set of interaction techniques and tasks was conducted in order to assess the most suited modalities in certain settings. We discuss the results drawn from this study, detail some related conclusions and present future work directions.

Keywords: Collaboration, Multimodal Interaction, Accessibility.

1 Introduction

In today's world, human beings are often regarded not as individuals, but as part of groups, communities or companies which work together towards the same goal. Group work is common in a multitude of domains such as education, therapy, business and entertainment, among others where it relies on the thoughts, decisions and work of the whole group to accomplish different tasks [5] [6]. Computer Supported Cooperative Work (CSCW) is an important research area from which several applications have emerged in order to offer technical support to group environments.

With the proliferation of unconventional ways of interacting with devices in recent years, researchers began assessing the gains and opportunities of using such technology as a substitute for more traditional interfaces. Techniques such as gesture, sound or eye-gaze interaction or the use of devices such as accelerometers, gyroscopes or bend sensors, are examples of unconventional techniques or ways of interaction [1] [2] [4]. However, despite these advances, interaction design has mainly focused individual work settings, neglecting the opportunities possibly provided by other settings, such as collaborative ones [3]. It is therefore necessary to explore novel ways of interacting in group settings as well as assessing users' behavior in such environments. Furthermore, the increased access by all kinds of individuals to technology and, more particularly, collaborative environments forces researchers to explore these interaction techniques not only to improve individuals' performance in such settings, but also to provide access and / or integrate impaired users.

J.A. Jacko (Ed.): Human-Computer Interaction, Part II, HCII 2009, LNCS 5611, pp. 19–28, 2009.
© Springer-Verlag Berlin Heidelberg 2009

As part of an ongoing project, we propose a multimodal platform, addressing both individual and co-located synchronous collaborative environments. Our approach builds on a communication engine to combine different modalities according to the users' needs, contemplating both impaired and non-impaired individuals. This engine has two main objectives: provide extendible and easy to integrate modules used to combine different input / output modalities; ensure connectivity between the different interaction devices and the target applications. This platform allows not only for single users to operate different modalities for a single task but also multiple individuals working together. We are continuously offering support to an increasing set of devices and interaction techniques in our platform in order to be used for different applications and settings: accelerometer; temperature sensor; light sensor; bend sensor; eye-tracker; speech recognizer. In this paper we present an initial study considering the adequacy and user preference of a subset of these modalities towards a set of common tasks performed both in individual and collaborative settings. Special emphasis was given to the combination of different modalities in our platform.

The paper is organized as follows: we will start by discussing some of the work in related areas; then we present our platform, the available modalities, its uses and an experiment with the available interaction techniques; finally we draw some conclusions and shed some light on our future work.

2 Related Work

In recent years there has been extensive work on developing new interaction techniques for different domains, with a focus on post-WIMP interaction and interacting by demonstration paradigms. It is important to take into consideration the impact of different modalities on how users interact with each other and also the preferences of the latter towards the former [9][11]. Jacob [1] proposes a framework for post-WIMP interfaces, focusing reality-based interaction in which users don't deviate much from the interaction patterns used in everyday life. The presented study provides an extensive source of inspiration and useful guidelines for the development of such interfaces. On a related standpoint, Magglite [12] is also a post-WIMP toolkit with which users may create graphical components and support them by providing different interaction sources and techniques. The main strength of this work is the actual separation of the interface from the interaction modalities used, which means it supports the combination of both to an extent. However, despite both works' valuable contribution, they do not cover one of the most important aspects of today's world: collaboration. None of the guidelines, conclusions and toolkits provides support towards interacting in collaborative environments. Despite being able to apply the proposed interaction techniques in cooperative settings, these would only be performed from an individual point of view within a group of persons, disregarding truly collaborative interactions that could be performed. In addition to the lack of true collaborative support, the interaction modalities employed in these works are typically centered around the use of accelerometer or gyroscope based interactions, which are somewhat mainstreamed at the present day.

Regarding the modalities studied in this paper, our intention is not the thorough evaluation of the algorithms used in speech-recognition or in eye-tracking, but rather user's comfort and preferences on using them to perform selected tasks. Nevertheless it is important to provide some examples of these modalities' uses. Speech recognition has become widespread has an attempt to reduce dependency on the keyboard and mouse duo by allowing users to input commands through voice. In more recent years it is being applied to with the same purpose on mobile devices as can be observed in [14]. Eye-tracking is an interaction technique with a respectable background work but which is slightly hindered by the high cost of the hardware to support it. In more recent years we have witnessed the growth of low-cost algorithms to allow for this kind of interaction such as the one provided by Savas [15]. Finally, the last technique approached by this paper, the use of bend sensors, has had some work in the past, but finds most of its use in the industry. Detecting if a baby-chair is in the front car seat in order to turn passenger airbag off, flexible toys, quality control or the detection of pedestrian impact in a car accident are some of the application examples of this type of sensors [16]. Concerning more academic projects, Balakrishnan has used a flexible surface to not only perform 3D modeling of surfaces on a computer but also to control camera angles [10].

Our work differs from existing ones as it focuses co-located collaborative settings and at the same time integrates novel ways of interaction into those environments, covering both gaps of the presented related work.

3 Collaborative Platform

Our collaborative platform builds up on a layered Communication Engine (Figure 1) specially tailored to act as the basis of different collaborative scenarios and applications. The main goals of this platform are: a) the reduction of the cognitive effort and time consumed setting up the network and connecting the applications between each other; b) allowing easy set up of different modules and applications in collaborative settings; c) providing a foundation on top of which synchronous collaborative applications can be built. The Session Engine is composed by three layers, which build on the functionalities of each other. The presented diagram depicts both how the layers relate to each other and how some of the components map on subsequent layers components. We will now briefly address the main components and features of the platform. For further insight on the Communication Engine, please refer to [7].

3.1 Session and Group Concepts

Our approach builds on two main concepts, both pertaining to synchronous and co-located collaborative environments: session and group. Both definitions are strictly related to their normal usage, although with a few nuances. The first is defined as a time interval during which a group of individuals exchange information through applications using the engine. This time interval is uniquely identified in our platform so that each individual may only belong to one session at a given time. Depending on the setting, sessions usually have a facilitator which is the entity responsible for sanctioning who is able to join the related session and when it starts and concludes. A group is a collection of entities that exchange data using our engine in the context of a session. A session may have several groups who are independent of each other, thus exchanging messages only between their members, despite other groups being present at the same time. An individual may simultaneously belong to more than one group (e.g. a teacher monitoring different brainstorming student subgroups).

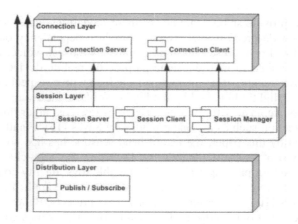

Fig. 1. Collaborative Platform Architecture

3.2 Session Server

The Server allows for the existence of multiple sessions at the same time with multiple users per session, belonging to one or more groups. This means that different groups of applications may be communicating between themselves unaware and without disruption of what is happening on other simultaneous sessions or groups. Two dynamic tables are dynamically updated regarding the available sessions and the available users for each one. Finally, the Session Server provides a simple message distribution mechanism based on the users connected to each session: when a user sends a generic data message with no specific destination, it is distributed among all users connected to his / her session.

3.3 Session Manager

The Session Manager in one of the main entities in our platform. Its first characteristic is the ability to allow the opening and conclusion of group sessions. The Manager may open a session at any time by providing and identification number or, using a friendlier approach for end-users, an adequate name. From this moment, other users may join the session and communicate with each other. As with the session start, the Manager may end the session when desired. After setting up sessions, users are expected to start joining the ones intended to them. As such, a sanctioning mechanism is provided to authorize access to users to a given session. It may happen that a user attempts to join a session he/she is not allowed to, thus the presence of the sanctioning mechanism. The Session Manager supports multiple simultaneous sessions.

3.4 Session Client

Another important entity in our platform, and the one that allows users to communicate between each other using the platform, is the Session Client. Session Clients may be used in any application in order to connect to a session, thus representing end-users in our engine. Clients may join only one session at a time, either by specifying the session's identification number or its name. Each client is identified by a name, which must be necessarily provided when joining any session.

Upon being accepted in a session, a new message distribution mechanism becomes available to the Client: either a list of destinations for the message is specified, or no destination is specified, which forces the message to be distributed among all Clients in the same session. This covers basic message exchange between users logged in the same session, allowing them to communicate between each other.

3.5 Messages

All exchanged messages in the Session Layer are built dynamically using XML tags to identify each field (e.g. operation, origin, destination, signature, body). Each message contains the identification of its sender and an operation identification number, in addition to other relevant data for the intended service. There is a specified set of operation types mostly related with session management (e.g. start of a session, end of a session) and client management (e.g. join session acceptance, leave session). The previously mentioned generic data messages do not fall into any of these categories, being able to address anything related with the session (provided the message's destination has the ability to interpret it). Messages are dynamically built, which means they only contain the necessary fields according to their operation type.

3.6 Distribution Layer

The final layer was created to provide powerful message distribution mechanisms during collaborative sessions, specifically pertaining to the group concept. The existing message exchange mechanism provides: a) client-to-manager message exchange, prior to joining a session; b) client-to-client message exchange, after joining a session; c) client-to-session message distribution, after joining a session. With these existing mechanisms, users may indeed send messages to each other, and even notify all the session's users about something relevant. However, during requirement gathering we found that in some domains it is common to create groups during collaborative sessions (e.g. during school classes, therapy session, brainstorming sessions, etc.), proving the existing mechanisms might not be sufficient for elaborate scenarios. With this in mind, we dedicated a specific module in our Collaboration Platform to more complex message management scenarios, such as the previously mentioned ones.

The Distribution Layer provides a publish/subscribe mechanism in order to support complex message exchange. Session Clients may issue subscription requests specifying the affected message type, the origin(s) of the message and an attached signature. This means that when a message reaches this layer, the distribution engine checks all subscriptions performed over the message's type and for each one it checks if the origins list contains the message's recipient and if the signature list also contains the message's signature (if available). If all conditions are satisfied, the message is forwarded to the Client who requested the analyzed subscription. With this procedure it is possible to create subgroups within a session which exchange messages only among themselves (e.g. concealing teacher message exchange from students). Note that this feature is optional over the basic one provided by the Session Server, as it only provides more complex support for message exchange.

4   Interaction Modalities

We used the Collaborative Platform described in section 3 as the foundation for the work presented in this paper. Session Client modules were integrated in small proxy applications for each of the implemented interaction modalities. These proxy applications merely process the input data coming from the interaction devices and then communicate the commands to the intended software applications through the platform. The proxy applications perform the bulk of the input processing and when a certain event is detected (e.g. selection, movement in a determined direction), a message is created through our platform that informs the target application of the triggered event. The presence of the server is necessary to ensure that more than one modality is combined with others so that we may test multimodal scenarios in co-located environments. For the study presented in this paper we used three distinct interaction modalities: eye-tracking, bend detection and speech recognition. We will now briefly describe each before addressing the study.

For the eye-tracking modality we used a software application developed by Savas [15], which is a Real-Time software for tracking human face, eyes & pupils with rotation and scale invariance property. It can also be used for blink detection, human-machine interaction (Remote device control using hand) and 2D-trajectory extraction from video sequences. The most positive aspect of this algorithm is the relative low-cost of setting it up. Contrary to the most advanced eye-tracking devices, this one only needs a computer with a simple webcam to function properly. In our case we used the eye-tracker as a pointer for on-screen pointing while detecting the blink of a single eye (right eye) for on-screen selection.

Regarding bend detection, we used four sensors from Flexpoint [16] (Figure 2a) positioned around the neck of the users as seen in Figure 2b. These bend sensors were connected to a microcontroller (Sunspot by Sun Microsystems) which forwarded relevant data about the bend degree to our applications. These sensors return a zero value when they remain in stationary position and start producing different values as they bend. We positioned them in four points around a person's neck to simulate the use of the four basic directions while manipulating objects on a screen. Note that by tilting the head backwards, the effect would be the same as pressing the UP key in a keyboard, meaning we opted to employ an inverted Y-axis for the experiment. We used the bend sensor for two different tasks: the pointing task, whose configuration is depicted in figure 2b, detects if the user intends to move the pointer up, down, left or right; the selection task, in which a bend sensor was attached to the index finger to act as a trigger – when the user pushed it, it would mean he / she wanted to select the pointed object.

The speech recognizer was implemented using the Speech SDK for C#. A set of basic words were identified to be important to be present in our test in order for users to perform the required tasks. At this stage we only used two voice commands for selection ("select" voice command) and unselecting ("undo" voice command) in the platform. More will be implemented in later stages, more specifically to allow for multiple object selection.

All applications were developed in C# using Visual Studio 2008 .NET Framework 3.5 to run on Windows Desktop environments.

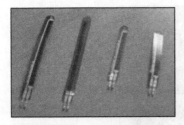 

Fig. 2. Bend Sensors and Bend Sensor Positions

5 Experiment: Pointing and Selecting

Our experiment focused on two tasks commonly performed in any environment but which may have some impact in collaborative settings: pointing and selecting items on a screen. While it may appear as a trivial task in an individual desktop computer environment, the characteristics of a collaborative environment may force it to become a more demanding task – for instance, the existence of a very large display may obstruct or hinder the interaction experience when users try to reach the upper corners of the display. The linked nature of these two tasks is one of the reasons we opted for this duo.

We used one 27'' screen with a webcam for eye-tracking, a 60'' smartboard with a webcam at its base also for eye tracking, a microphone for voice-input and a set of four bend sensors positioned according to the schema explained in the previous section. We used six subjects to our tests, all of them computer science students, thus all acquainted with traditional interaction mechanisms. None of the subjects had any type of injury or incapacity that inhibited them from testing any of the available modalities.

For the pointing task, half subjects were picked to use the bend sensors in the first place, while the other half used the eye-tracking mechanism. After clearing the task, they switched to the other modality. Half the subjects were also randomly assigned to first sit in from of the laptop and then to perform the task on the large display (again switching screens after task completion). The task required subjects to point a set of determined objects spread across the screen, similarly to typical eye-tracking calibration procedures and then to respond to a simple questionnaire using a Likert scale from 1 (harder; strongly disagree) to 5 (easier; strongly agree) addressing their preferences on the modalities tested.

Through observation of the test's results, we concluded users felt more comfortable and achieved more precise actions with the eye-tracking mechanism. The majority pointed the time spent to point objects as the main advantage of eye-tracking versus the use of bend-sensors. The bend-sensors were reported to not being accurate enough on the 27'' screen (although this may be related to how we positioned them around the necks of the users). Nevertheless two users stated it worked fairly well on the smartboard. We believe the best use of the bend sensors is, indeed, in the presence of very large displays in which information may not be easily reached using standard interaction mechanisms.

Fig. 3. Selection task using bend sensors

In the context of the selection task, we had two subjects working individually as in the first task while the remaining were paired. In this case users were asked to point a subset of objects spread across the screen and then select them using the interaction modality they were using: either voice input through the microphone or by simulating pressing a trigger by bending the sensor attached to their index finger. We used the two pairs of subjects to address how the applications worked when mixing different modalities at the same time, a scenario plausible in cooperative settings. One of the users performed the pointing task while the other performed the selection command. When the task was complete, subjects switched roles. Opposite to what happened in the first task, almost all users were enthusiastic with the use of the bend sensor as a trigger and quickly started providing suggestions of applications and games where it could be used. They praised the ability to simulate both mouse clicks using and a weapon trigger using the bend sensor. One user, however, criticized the need of having to configure a rest position for the finger and the fact that the triggering movement could start causing some pain in the fingers after several commands. Regarding the voice input modality, users referred it sometimes didn't recognize the command they were issuing. Although this may be related with the proficiency of the subjects with English language, it may be the main disadvantage of this modality compared to the bend sensor. The paired subjects were additionally asked about their opinions on having experienced cooperative interaction using different modalities. They stated it felt awkward to not have total control when completing the task as a whole and having to depend on a second person to perform it. From our observations and through the video recording, we concluded this type of interaction should be more suited for entertainment applications, such as videogames, and co-located tools for small children, in order to help them develop basic cooperation skills.

Overall subjects reacted positively to the experiment, even offering suggestions on possible applications or how to improve the interactive experience. We felt that further investigation on the positioning of bend sensors and testing different eye-tracking and voice command algorithms might even increase the degree of satisfaction of the target users.

6 Conclusions and Future Work

In this paper we presented a study regarding how users interact when a small set of different modalities are available in a collaborative context. The work, motivated by the growing need of providing truly collaborative interactions in cooperative environments, proved a positive start for developing a multimodal system for the same environments. We focused on the use and combination of an eye-tracker, multiple bend-sensors and a speech-recognizer for a set of tasks, namely on-screen pointing and item selection. Results showed that the eye-tracker is a more reliable mean to point items than the use of multiple bend-sensors (although the latter is not impractical). Although our team didn't use a sophisticated eye-tracker, the employed technique was still superior due to the quick response detecting the point where the user is looking at, although quality of the detection can be severely hindered by external conditions (e.g. room light). On the other hand, the bend sensor performed more poorly, even though we are still investigating if a more advanced sensor or a better positioning of the sensors on the user's body can improve its results. Regarding the selection task, both speech-recognition and the use of the bend-sensor as a trigger proved to be quite effective. The employed speech-recognition algorithm was praised by our testers as its accuracy proved to not hamper the intended task. The bend sensor also had good results, as the users stated it remained faithful to a button/trigger metaphor. Overall, the experience proved to be a positive start towards the development of a multimodal collaborative platform.

The future work on our platform is two folded: on the one hand we are continuously supporting more interaction modalities, namely pressure sensors, light sensitive sensors or accelerometers, so that we have a rich selection of interaction techniques suited for different tasks and for user preferences. On the other hand we are allowing the use of the platform as a building base for collaborative applications. More specifically, we are allowing students to create collaborative versions of simple applications (e.g. drawing tool, text editor) while having our collaborative platform as a functionality base. With this, we are keen on further exploring the ways users interact when they have a rich selection of modalities while in a collaborative context.

Acknowledgements

This work was supported by LaSIGE and FCT, through the Multiannual Funding Programme and individual scholarships SFRH/BD/39496/2007 and SFRH/BD/28165/2006.

References

1. Jacob, R., et al.: Reality-Based Interaction: A Framework for Post-WIMP Interfaces. In: Proceedings of CHI 2008, pp. 201–210 (2008); ISBN: 978-1-60558-011-1
2. Kwon, D., et al.: Combining Body Sensors and Visual Sensors for Motion Training. In: Proceedings of ACE 2005, pp. 94–101 (2005); ISBN: 1-59593-110-4

3. Kinns, N., et al.: Exploring Mutual Engagement in Creative Collaborations. In: Proceedings of C&C 2007, pp. 223–232 (2007); ISBN: 978-1-59593-712-4
4. Hartmann, B., et al.: Authoring Sensor-Based Interactions by Demonstration with Direct Manipulation and Pattern Recognition. In: Proceedings of CHI 2007, pp. 145–154 (2007); ISBN: 978-1-59593-593-9
5. Perry, D.: Handheld Computers in Schools. British Educational Communications and Technology Agency (2003)
6. Newman, M.: Technology in Psychotherapy: An Introduction. Journal of Clinical Psychology 60(2), 141–145 (2003)
7. Duarte, L., et al.: A Session Engine Approach for Synchronous Collaborative Environments. In: Proceedings of the 7th International Conference on Creating, Connecting and Collaborating through Computing, C5 2009, Kyoto, Japan (2009)
8. Linebarger, J., et al.: Leaving the World Behind: Supporting Group Collaboration Patterns in a Shared Virtual Environment for Product Design. Presence: Teleoperators and Virtual Environments 14(6)
9. Barthelmess, P., et al.: Human-Centered Collaborative Interaction. In: Proceedings of HCM 2006, USA (2006)
10. Balakrishnan, R., et al.: Exploring Interactive Curve and Surface Manipulation Using a Bend and Twist Sensitive Input Strip. In: Proceedings of 1999 Symposium on Interactive 3D Graphics, Atlanta, USA, pp. 111–118 (1999)
11. Bolelli, L., et al.: Multimodal Interaction for Distributed Collaboration. In: Proceedings of ICMI 2004, Pennsylvania, USA, pp. 327–328 (2004)
12. Huot, S., et al.: The MaggLite Post-WIMP Toolkit: Draw It, Connect It and Run It. In: Proceedings of UIST 2004, Santa Fe, New Mexico, USA, vol. 6, pp. 257–266 (2004)
13. Watanabe, J., et al.: Bookisheet: Bendable Device for Browsing Content Using the Metaphor of Leafing Through Pages. In: Procs. of UbiComp 2008, pp. 360–369, Korea (2008)
14. Reis, T., et al.: Multimodal Artefact Manipulation: Evaluation in Real Contexts. In: Proceedings of ICPCA, 3th International Conference on Pervasive Computing and Applications, Alexandria, Egypt, October 2008. IEEE Press, Los Alamitos (2008)
15. Savas, Z.: Trackeye: Real Time Tracking of Human Eyes Using a Webcam, http://www.codeproject.com/KB/cpp/TrackEye.aspx
16. Flexpoint Sensor Systems Inc. (FLXT). Sensory Applications, http://www.flexpoint.com/

Towards a Multidimensional Approach for the Evaluation of Multimodal Application User Interfaces

José E.R. de Queiroz, Joseana M. Fechine, Ana E.V. Barbosa,
and Danilo de S. Ferreira

Federal University of Campina Grande
Electrical Engineering and Computer Science Center – Computer Science Department
Av. Aprígio Veloso, s/n – Bodocongó, Campina Grande,
CEP 58109-970, Paraíba, Brazil
{rangel,joseana,aesther}@dsc.ufcg.edu.br,
{rangeldequeiroz,danilo.sousa}@gmail.com

Abstract. This paper focuses on a multidimensional approach for evaluating multimodal UI based upon a set of well known techniques for usability evaluation. Each technique evaluates the problem from a different perspective which combines user opinion, standard conformity assessment, and user performance measurement. The method's presentation and the evaluation analysis will be supported by a discussion of the results obtained from the method's application to a case study involving a Smartphone. The main objective of the study was to investigate the need for adapting a multidimensional evaluation approach for desktop applications to the context of multimodal devices and applications.

Keywords: Multimodal user interface; usability evaluation techniques; multidimensional approach; multimodal application.

1 Introduction

During the past two decades, a plethora of UI usability evaluation methods have been conceived. In consequence, the importance of focussing on HCI usability assessment is recognized today by academia, industry, and governments around the world. For years, users have utilized keyboards and/or mices as HCI input devices. In more recent years, a number of applications have been changing the interaction focus to multi-modal navigational cues, e.g. text + graphical/visual highlight + auditory instructions + gesture, which support a more natural interaction. Such systems whose interfaces support more than one input modality (e.g., via speech input, handwriting, gesture input, facial expressions) are known as *multimodal dialogue systems* (MDS).

In the context of such variety of I/O channels, efforts have been focused on proposing new techniques for multimodal user interface (MUI) usability evaluation. However the more evolved is the computing market toward MDS, the harder becomes for HCI evaluators to choose among the plethora of approaches for MUI usability evaluation recently proposed in the literature. It has to be taken into account that it is not a trivial task to compare between different studies, based on a number of claims made without solid statistical results. Face to these new UI features, such as dynamic

J.A. Jacko (Ed.): Human-Computer Interaction, Part II, HCII 2009, LNCS 5611, pp. 29–38, 2009.

contexts of use, mobility, and accessibility, HCI practitioners ask how effective methods, techniques and settings well known to them from previous experiences can be. And the consequent important question is if it could be possible to adapt them to MDS, by considering their distinctive features. Another question is related to whether to adopt a field or a lab approach. Although many of these issues are known to many practitioners, very little discussion is found in literature of which technique or combination of them is best suited for a specific modality and its context of use. Beyond this level of detail and for a successful choice of a methodological approach, it seems essential to know about its effectiveness, in what ways and for what purposes as well. Otherwise, he/she will expend significant effort with little payoff result.

2   Usability Assessment of MUI

It is a fact that UI are a determining factor for acceptance of interactive products. As a quality attribute, usability ables one to assess how easy UI are to use, and it can determine the difference between success and failure [1]. According to [2], usability dimensions are taken to include *effectiveness* (accuracy and completeness with which users achieve specified goals in particular environments), *efficiency* (accuracy and completeness goals achieved in relation to resources expanded); and *subjective satisfaction* (comfort and acceptability of using a system).

Despite discussing frequently to whether to adopt a field or a lab approach, it is often neglected in HCI literature effectively talking about which techniques are best suited for specific evaluation targets and their contexts of use. In order to exercise a choice of approach, this polemic subject may represents to the HCI community an equally important concern, since the efforts carried on the evaluation may not payoff if a method, technique and/or setting is not well chosen or well employed [3].

The majority of the usability studies for MUI focus on some user testing, in which user activity is monitored and/or recorded, while users perform predefined tasks. This allows the evaluator to gather quantitative data regarding how users interact with multimodal technology, which provides valuable information about usability and user experience as well. A number of types of user testing have been conducted, both in lab and in field environments, revealing user preferences for interaction modalities based on factors such as acceptance in different social contexts, e.g., noisy and mobile environments [4].

Inspection methods have also been extensively adopted, in which HCI experts rely on ergonomic knowledge to identify usability problems while inspecting the user interface. Well-known methods belonging to this category include cognitive walkthroughs (e.g., [5]), formative evaluation/ heuristic evaluation (e.g., [6]), and benchmarking approaches involving ISO 9241 usability recommendations or conformance to guidelines (e.g., [7]).

Questionnaires have been extensively administered to gather qualitative information from users, such as subjective satisfaction, perceived utility of the system, and user preferences for modality (e.g., [8]) and cognitive workload (e.g., [9]). Quite often, questionnaire use has been combined with user-testing techniques [4].

Simulation and model-based checking of system specifications have been recently used to predict usability problems, e.g. unreachable states of the systems or conflict detection of events required for fusion. A combination of task models based on concur task tree (CTT) notation with multiple data sources, such as eye-tracking data and video records has been used to better understand the user interaction [10].

A plethora of empirical studies have been carried out to determine the contribution of modalities to the user interaction, in terms of (i) understanding how usability and user acceptance is influenced by new devices and novel interaction techniques (e.g., [11][12]); (ii) showing that the perceived usability is impacted according to the kind of tasks performed (e.g., [4][13]), and according to the context of use - indoor versus outdoor conditions, mobile applications (e.g., [14]); or (iii) trying to assess the accuracy of multimodal interaction for given tasks (e.g., [15][16]).

3 The Multidimensional Evaluation Approach

The original version of the present approach was conceived for evaluating desktop application UI [17], and further adapted to evaluate the usability of mobile application UI [18]. With the aim of providing complementary results and more integrated usability information, it is based upon the premises that (i) each evaluation technique provides a different level of information, which will help the evaluator to identify usability problems from a specific point of view; and (ii) data triangulation can be used to review information obtained from multiple data sources and techniques. This resulted in a hybrid strategy which encompasses the best aspects of (i) *standards inspection*; (ii) *user performance measurement*; and (iii) *user inquiry*.

According to [2] *conformity assessment* means checking whether products, services, materials, processes, systems, and personnel measure up to the requirements of standards. For conformity assessment, the desktop version of the multidimensional approach adopts the standard ISO 9241 (*Ergonomic Requirements for Office Work with Visual Display Terminals*). In its multimodal version, and more specifically for the Smartphone case study it was found that only some parts of ISO 9241 could be applied - 14 [19], 16 [20], and 17 [21]. There are also some other standards that apply to this kind of device such as the ISO/IEC 14754 (*Pen-based Interfaces—Common gestures for text editing with pen-based systems*) [22]; ISO 9241-171 (*Ergonomics of human-system interaction — Guidance on software accessibility*) [23]; ISO/IEC 24755 (*Information technology — Screen icons and symbols for personal mobile communication devices*) [24]; ISO/IEC 18021 (*User interfaces for mobile tools for management of database communications in a client-server model*) [25]; and ITU-TE.161 (Arrangement of digits, letters, and symbols on telephones and other devices that can be used for gaining access to a telephone network, also known as ANSI T1.703-1995/1999); and ISO/IEC 9995-8:1994) [26].

In general, *user performance measurement* aims to enable real time monitoring of user activities, providing data on the effectiveness and efficiency of his/her interaction with a product. It also enables comparisons with similar products, or with previous versions of the same product along its development lifecycle, highlighting areas where the product usability can be improved. When combined with the other methods, it can provide a more comprehensive view of the usability of a system. The major change introduced in the original evaluation approach concerns the introduction of field tests as a complement to the original lab tests.

User subjective satisfaction measurement has been widely adopted as an IS success indicator, and has been the subject of a number of researches since the 1980s (e.g., [27][28]). User satisfaction diagnosis provides an insight into the level of user satisfaction with the product, highlighting the relevance of the problems found and their impact on the product acceptance. In this approach, user subjective satisfaction data are gathered from three methods: (i) *automated questionnaires* administered before and after test sessions; (ii) *informal think-aloud trials* performed during test sessions; and (iii) *unstructured interviews* conducted at the end of test sessions.

Going beyond the definition of *usability* in function of *effectiveness*, *efficiency* and *satisfaction* [7], ISO also defines that at least one indicator in each of these aspects should be measured to determine the level of usability achieved. As briefly exposed in this section, the multidimensional approach presented here meets the requirements set by ISO 9241-11 because it is used: (i) the *task execution time* as an efficiency indicator; (ii) the *number of incorrect actions*, the *number of incorrect choices*, the *number of repeated errors*, and the *number of accesses to the online/ printed help* as effectiveness indicators; and (iii) the *think-aloud comments*, the *unstructured interview responses*, and the *questionnaire scores* as subjective satisfaction indicators.

4 The Experiment: Use of Smartphone

The main objective of the study was to investigate the need for adapting a multidimensional evaluation approach for desktop applications to the context of multimodal devices and applications. Thus, the influence of (i) the context (field, mobility use), (ii) the interaction modality, and (iii) the user experience on the evaluation of multimodal devices and applications was investigated.

Mobile devices, e.g. smartphones and PDAs, can be used to implement efficient speech-based and multimodal interfaces. With the aim of investigate the influence of the context of use on usability with regard to environmental noise, three experiments were carried out in the field, for three realistic environments - *quiet*, *normal* and *noisy*. Thirty-six subjects took part in the experiment. The subjects were divided into three groups of twelve. The multimodal device chosen as the target for this study was the Smartphone *HP iPAQ 910c Bussiness Messenger* and some of its native applications.

Experiment Design
An experimental plan was drawn from the objectives of the study, and three independent variables were chosen – (i) *task context*, (ii) *user mobility*, and (iii) *user experience level* - which are not influenced by the context, the test facilitator or external factors, such as lighting, activity flow and interruptions of people. Eight dependent variables were chosen: (i) *task time*, (ii) *number of incorrect choices*, (iii) *number of incorrect actions* (incorrect decisions excluding the number of incorrect choices while performing a task), (iv) *number of repeated errors,* (v) *number of incorrect voice recognition*, (vi) *number of accesses to the help* (online help and printed one), (vii) *perceived usefulness*, and (viii) *perceived ease of use*.

Test Environment, Materials and Participants
In all test environments, all the elements (e.g., tasks, informal think aloud, unstructured interviews) were identical, only the test environment was different with regard to background noise. To minimize moderator bias, the tests were conducted with three experienced usability practitioners with 3 to 12 years of experience in usability testing. The instructions given to participants were predefined. All moderators participated in data gathering and data analysis. Statistical analysis was performed by one moderator, and revised by another one. The multimodal device used in this experiment was the *HP iPAQ 910c Bussiness Messenger* and some of its native applications. A micro-camera connected to a transmitter was coupled to the device to remotely record and transmit user-device interaction data to the lab through a wireless connection (see Fig. 1).

A remote screen capture software (*VNC*) was also used to take test session screenshots, and a web tool named *WebQuest* [29] was used as well for supporting the user subjective satisfaction measurement. *WebQuest* supports the specialist during data collection, automatic score computation, performs statistical analysis, and generates graphical results. Currently *WebQuest* supports two questionnaires: (i) a pre test questionnaire, the *USer (User Sketcher)*, conceived to raise the profile of the system users; and (ii) a post test questionnaire, the *USE (User Satisfaction Enquirer)*, conceived to raise the user degree of satisfaction with the system. The experiment setting required a wireless network. The experiments in silent and normal environments were carried out in an uncontrolled space (a typical work room). The experiment in noisy environment was carried out in an open place, characterized by the constant flow of people (a mall). In both cases, the session moderators remained with the participants, in case any explanation on the test procedure was required. Participants were selected on the basis of having previous experience with mobile devices (such as mobile phones), computers, and the Internet. They were also required to have some familiarity with the English language, since this is the language adopted in the device's user interface and in its documentation. The recruited users were divided into two groups of 12 for the tests in the quiet, normal and noisy environments (sensitive, normal and accurate sensitivities). According to their experience levels, each group was then subdivided into two subgroups. A ratio of 6 beginners to 6 intermediates was adopted.

Fig. 1. Kit to support video camera during experiment

Experimental Procedure
Observation and retrospective audio/video analysis for quantitative and qualitative data were employed. Participants were required to provide written consent to be filmed prior to, during and immediately after the test sessions, and to permit the use of their images/sound for research purposes without limitation or additional compensation. On the other hand, the evaluation team was committed to do not disclose the user performance or other personal information. According to the approach basis, the first step consisted in defining the evaluation scope for the product as well as in designing a test task scenario, in which the target problems addressed were related to the: (i) usage and interpretation of modalities; (ii) mechanisms for information input/output;

(iii) processing power; (iv) navigation between functions; and (v) information legibility. Since the test objectives focused on (i) investigating the target problems; and (ii) detecting other problems which affect usability, a basic but representative set of test tasks was selected and implemented. The test tasks consisted of (i) initializing the device; (ii) consulting and scheduling appointments; (iii) entering textual information; (iv) using the e-mail; (v) making a phone call; e (vi) using the audio player. After planning, 3 pilot field tests (*quiet*, *normal* and *noisy* environments) were conducted to verify the adequacy of the experimental procedure, materials, and environments. Aiming to prevent user tiredness, the session time was limited to 60 minutes, and the test scenario was dimensioned to 6 tasks. Thus, each test session consisted of (i) introducing the user to the test environment by explaining the test purpose and procedure; (ii) applying the pre-test questionnaire (*USer*); (iii) performing the six-task script; (iv) applying the post-test questionnaire (*USE*); and (v) performing a non-structured interview. For the participants who declared not having had any previous contact with the smartphone device, a brief explanation of the device I/O modes and its main resources was given, considering that it was not yet widely spread in Brazil at the time of the experiment.

5   Results

For summarizing conformity assessment results (see Table 1), it was computed *Adherence Ratings* (*AR*), which are the percentages of the *Applicable recommendations* (*Ar*) that were *Successfully adhered* to (*Sar*) [19]. All the ARs, excluding that one related to ISO 14745, are higher than 75%, which means successful results. As for ISO 14745, the result indicates the need to improve the input text via write recognition. Those results corroborate with the idea that the efficacy of standards inspection can be considerably improved if it is based upon standards conceived specifically for mobile devices, which could evidence more usability problems.

As for the user subjective satisfaction measurement, both questions and answers of the post test questionnaire (*USE*) were previously configured. The questionnaire was applied soon after the usability test and answered using the mobile device itself, with the purpose to collect information on the user degree of satisfaction with the device by means of 38 questions about menu items, navigation cues, understandability of the messages, ease of use functions, I/O mechanisms, online help and printed manuals,

Table 1. HP iPAQ 910c conformity with standards

Standard	#Sar	#Ar	AR(%)
ISO 9241 Part 14	66,0	72,0	91,67
ISO 9241 Part 16	31,0	34,0	91,18
ISO 9241 Part 17	54,0	57,0	94,74
ISO 14754	7,0[*]	11,0	63,64
ISO 24755	10,0[**]	17,0	58,82

[*] Not adhered recommendations in full, made small changes consistently in 4/7 points (Transcriber), 1/3 points (Letter recognizer) and 2/4 points (Block recognizer).
[**] Not adhered recommendations in full, made small changes consistently in 6 points.

Table 2. Overlay of results obtained from different techniques described above

PROBLEM CATEGORY	SI	PM	SM
Location and sequence of menu options	✓ (2)		✓ (2)
Menu navigation		✓ (1)	
Presentation of menu options	✓ (1)		✓ (1)
Information feedback		✓ (3)	✗ (3)
Object manipulation	✓ (4)		
Form filling dialogues	✓ (3)		
Symbols and icons	✓ (7)		✗ (3)
Text entry via keyboard		✓ (1)	✓ (1)
Text entry via virtual keyboard		✓ (1)	✓ (1)
Text entry via stylus (Transcriber)	✓ (4)	✓ (1)	✓ (5)
Text entry via stylus (Letter recognizer)	✓ (8)		✓ (8)
Text entry via stylus (Block recognizer)	✓ (7)		✓ (7)
Voice recognizer	✓ (2)	✓ (1)	✓ (3)
Processing power		✓ (1)	✓ (1)
Hardware issues		✓ (3)	✓ (3)
Fluent tasks execution		✓ (5)	✓ (5)
Online and offline help		✓ (2)	✓ (2)
Legend: SI – Standards Inspection. PM – Performance Measurement. SM – Satisfaction Measurement.		✓ Consistent findings. ✗ Contradictory findings.	

users' impression, and product acceptance level. With the support of the pre test questionnaire (*USer*), the user sample profile was drawn. It was composed of 20 male and 16 female users, of which 12 were *undergraduate students*, 12 *post-graduate students*, five *graduate level*, and seven *post-graduate level*. The ages varied between *18* and *55* years. They were all *right handed* and mostly (18) used some sort of reading aid (*glasses* or *contact lenses*). They also had familiarity with the English language. All of them had at least one year of *previous experience of computer systems*, and were currently using computers on a *daily* basis.

The ranges for USE normalized user satisfaction are 0.67 to 1.00 (*Extremely Satisfied*), 0.33 to 0.66 (*Very satisfied*), 0.01 to 0.32 (*Fairly satisfied*), 0.00 (*Neither satisfied nor unsatisfied*), 0.01 to -0.32 (*Fairly dissatisfied*), -0.33 to -0.66 (*Very dissatisfied*), and -0.67 to -1.00 (*Extremely dissatisfied*) [27]. The normalized user satisfaction levels achieved were 0.25 (*Fairly satisfied*), 0.32 (*Fairly satisfied*), and 0.21 (*Fairly satisfied*) for the quiet, normal, and noisy environments, respectively.

Since the multidimensional approach is based upon the triangulation of results, Table 2 summarizes the usability problem categories which were identified during the evaluation process. For each category, the number of problems identified by each technique is given. As can be seen, some of the usability problem categories were more associated to the performance measurement (e.g. hardware aspects, help mechanisms) whereas others (e.g. menu navigation, presentation of menu options) were identified by the conformity assessment.

It was possible to identify 67.6% of the problems found by other methods when combining the results from the post-test questionnaire to the comments made during the test sessions. In addition, the non-structured interviews at the end of each experiment session showed that the user opinion was in agreement (e.g., location and sequence of menu options) or disagreement (e.g., menu navigation) with the results obtained from the other two evaluation techniques. This discrepancy can originate from the users' perception of product quality, and from the perception of their own skills to perform the task.

The statistic analysis consisted of: (1) building a report with univariate statistics; (2) generating the covariance matrices for the predefined objective and subjective indicators; (3) applying the one-way F ANOVA test to the data obtained from the previous step in order to investigate possible differences; and (4) applying the Tukey-Kramer process to the one-way F ANOVA results aiming to investigate if the found differences were statistically significant to support inferences from the selected sample.

According to the results (see Table 3), the series of one-factor ANOVA showed that exists significant differences between the session's test results realized in the silent, normal and noisy environments. The Tukey-Kramer process (see Table 4) shows that the main differences are found in the comparison between the normal and noisy environments and quiet and noisy environments.

Table 3. *Quiet x Normal x Noisy* experiment results

Variable Pair	p-Value (α=0.05)		
	Quiet	Normal	Noisy
Experience x Task Time	0.226	0.007	0.146
Experience x Incorrect Actions	0.078	0.124	0.040
Experience x Incorrect Choices	0.191	0.121	0.080
Experience x Repeated Errors	0.640	0.515	0.078
Experience x Help Accesses	0.016	0.282	0.059

The results obtained from the experiment in which the multidimensional approach was applied support the original assumption that, in spite of the distinctive features of this class of devices, it is possible to adapt from the evaluation experience with conventional and multimodal devices.

Table 4. Tukey-Kramer experiment results

Variable Pair	Quiet x Normal	Quiet x Noisy	Normal x Noisy
Experience x Task Time	Not different	Not different	Different
Experience x Incorrect Actions	Different	Not different	Different
Experience x Incorrect Choices	Not different	Not different	Different
Experience x Repeated Errors	Not different	Not different	Not different
Experience x Help Accesses	Not different	Different	Not different
Experience x Incorrect Voice Recognition	Not different	Different	Different

6 Final Considerations

From the data analysis it became evident that certain problem categories are better found by specific techniques, as shown in Table 2. The analysis of the pre-test and post-test questionnaires and the informal interviews showed that familiarity with the English language, domain knowledge and computer literacy, which characterize the user experience level, have significant influence on the user performance with multimodal devices and applications. Physical characteristics of the device affected the user performance and the data gathering during the experiment. Outdoors, in ambient light and higher noise level conditions, the screen's legibility was reduced as well as the accuracy level of the voice recognizer was affected. According to the user's opinion stated during the informal interview, the kit to support video camera did not interfere with the task execution, but the majority decided to lay the device down during task execution. As for the entry of text information, the users showed a preference for the on-screen keyboard instead of virtual keyboard and handwriting recognition feature such as *Block Recognizer, Letter Recognizer,* or *Transcriber* to enter text. Based on their comments, as well as on the informal interview, it was concluded that writing long messages is very cumbersome both using the virtual keyboard and using the handwriting recognition application.

The individual user preference was for the modality touchscreen combined with graphical interaction, aided by the use of the stylus. Handwriting recognition and voice recognition features had influence in the test results, especially regarding to the time of completion of the task.

From the application of the multi-layered approach, the data gathered and analyzed support the initial assumption that minor adaptations in the traditional evaluation techniques and respective settings are adequate to accommodate the evaluation of the category of multimodal devices and application targeted by this study.

References

1. Nielsen, J.: Usability engineering. Academic Press, Boston (1993)
2. ISO 9241-11. Ergonomic requirements for office work with visual display terminals (VDTs)—Part 11: Guidance on usability. International Organization for Standardization, Geneva, Switzerland (1998)
3. Turnell, M.F.Q.V., de Queiroz, J.E.R., Ferreira, D.S.: Multilayered Approach to Evaluate Mobile User Interfaces. In: Lumsden, J. (ed.) Handbook of Research on User Interface Design and Evaluation for Mobile Technology, IGI Global, vol. 1, pp. 847–862 (2008)
4. Jöst, M., Haubler, J., Merdes, M., Malaka, R.: Multimodal interaction for pedestrians: an evaluation study. In: Riedl, J., Jameson, A., Billsus, D., Lau, T. (eds.) Proc. IUI 2005, San Diego, pp. 59–66. ACM Press, New York (2005)
5. Blandford, A., Hyde, J.K., Curzon, P., Papatzanis, G.: EMU in the car: evaluating multimodal usability of a satellite navigation system. In: Graham, N., Palanque, P. (eds.) DSVIS 2008, pp. 1–14. Springer, Heidelberg (2008)
6. Taib, R., Ruiz, N.: Evaluating Tangible Objects for Multimodal Interaction Design. In: Proc. OZCHI 2005, Narrabundah, Australia, pp. 1–4 (2005)
7. Bach, C., Scapin, D.: Ergonomic criteria adapted to human virtual environment interaction. In: Rauterberg, M., Menozzi, M., Wesson, J. (eds.) Proc. INTERACT 2003, Zurich, Switzerland, pp. 880–883. IOS Press, Amsterdam (2003)
8. Kaster, T., Pfeiffer, M., Bauckhage, C.: Combining speech and haptics for intuitive and efficient navigation through image database. In: Oviatt, S. (ed.) Proc. ICMI 2003, pp. 180–187. ACM Press, New York (2003)
9. Trevisan, D.G., Nedel, L.P., Macq, B., Vanderdonckt, J.: Detecting interaction variables in a mixed reality system for maxillofacial-guided surgery. In: SBC Symposium on Virtual Reality (SVR 2006), Belém do Pará, pp. 39–50. SBC Press, Brazil (2006)
10. Paternò, F., Santos, I.: Designing and developing multi-user, multi-device web interfaces. In: Calvary, G., Vanderdonckt, J. (eds.) CADUI 2006. Kluwer Academics Publishers, Dordrecht (2006)

11. Bowman, D., Gabbard, J., Hix, D.: A survey of usability evaluation in virtual environments: Classification and comparison of methods. Presence: Teleoperators and Virtual Environments 11(4), 404–424 (2002)
12. Nedel, L., Freitas, C.M.D.S., Jacob, L., Pimenta, M.: Testing the use of egocentric interactive techniques in immersive virtual environments. In: Rauterberg, M., Menozzi, M., Wesson, J. (eds.) Proc. INTERACT 2003, pp. 471–478. IOS Press, Zurich (2003)
13. Dybkjær, L., Bernsen, N.O., Minker, W.: Evaluation and usability of multimodal spoken language dialogue systems. Speech Communication 43, 33–54 (2004)
14. Baille, L., Schatz, R.: Exploring Multimodality in the Laboratory and the Field. In: Lazzari, G., Pianesi, P. (eds.) Proc. ICMI 2005, pp. 100–107. ACM Press, New York (2005)
15. Balbo, S., Coutaz, J., Salber, D.: Towards automatic evaluation of multimodal user interfaces. Intelligent User Interfaces, Knowledge-Based Systems 6(4), 267–274 (2003)
16. Holzapfel, H., Nickler, K., Stiefelhagen, R.: Implementation and evaluation of a constraint-based multimodal fusion system for speech and 3D pointing gesture. In: Sharma, R., Darrell, T. (eds.) Proc. ICMI 2004, pp. 175–182. ACM Press, New York (2004)
17. De Queiroz, J.E.R.: Abordagem Híbrida para avaliação da usabilidade de interfaces com o usuário. Tese de Doutorado, UFPB, Brazil. 410 p. (in Portuguese) (2001)
18. Turnell, M.F.Q.V., de Queiroz, J.E.R., Ferreira, D.S.: Multilayered Approach to Evaluate Mobile User Interfaces. In: Lumsden, J. (ed.) Handbook of Research on User Interface Design and Evaluation for Mobile Technology, IGI Global, vol. 1, pp. 847–862 (2008)
19. ISO 9241-14, Ergonomic requirements for office work with visual display terminals (VDTs) —Part 14: Menu dialogues. ISO, Geneva, Switzerland (1997)
20. ISO 9241-16, Ergonomic requirements for office work with visual display terminals (VDTs)—Part 16: Direct manipulation dialogues. ISO, Geneva, Switzerland (1999)
21. ISO 9241-17, Ergonomic requirements for office work with visual display terminals (VDTs)—Part 17: Form filling dialogues. ISO, Geneva, Switzerland (1998)
22. ISO/IEC 14754, Information technology—pen-based interfaces—common gestures for text editing with pen-based systems. ISO, Geneva, Switzerland (1999)
23. ISO 9241-171, Ergonomics of human-system interaction – Part 171: Guidance on software accessibility. ISO, Geneva, Switzerland (2008)
24. ISO/IEC 24755, Screen icons and symbols for personal mobile communication device. ISO. Geneva, Switzerland (2007)
25. ISO/IEC 18021, Information technology— user interfaces for mobile tools for management of database communications in a client-server model. ISO, Geneva, Switzerland (2002)
26. ITU-T E.161. Arrangement of digits, letters and symbols on telephones and other devices that can be used for gaining access to a telephone network. International Telecommunications Union-telecommunications, Geneva, Switzerland (2001)
27. Bailey, J.E., Pearson, S.W.: Development of a Tool for Measuring and Analyzing Computer User Satisfaction. Management Science 29(5), 530–545 (1983)
28. Aladwani, A.M., Palvia, P.C.: Developing and validating an instrument for measuring user-perceived Web quality. Information & Management 39, 467–476 (2002)
29. De Oliveira, R.C.L., De Queiroz, J.E.R., Vieira Turnell, M.F.Q.: WebQuest: A configurable Web Tool to prospect the user profile and user subjective satisfaction. In: Salvendy, G. (ed.) Proc. HCI 2005, vol. 2. Lawrence Erlbaum, Mahwah (2005) (U.S. CD-ROM Multi Platform)

Multimodal Shopping Lists

Jhilmil Jain, Riddhiman Ghosh, and Mohamed Dekhil

Hewlett-Packard Labs, 1501 Page Mill Road, Palo Alto CA 94304
{jhilmil.jain,riddhiman.ghosh,mohamed.dekhil}@hp.com

Abstract. In this paper we present a prototype for creating shopping lists using multiple input devices such as desktop, smart phones, landline or cell phones and in multimodal formats such as structured text, audio, still images, video, unstructured text and annotated media. The prototype was used by 10 participants in a two week longitudinal study. The goal was to analyze the process that users go through in order to create and manage shopping related projects. Based on these findings, we recommend desirable features for personal information management systems specifically designed for managing collaborative shopping lists.

Keywords: shopping lists, images, text, video, audio, mobile, web.

1 Introduction

We define "intent" as any stage in the shopping cycle that typically starts with a generation of an impulse or a need for a product and ends in a purchase. This process can be broken down into the following intent levels - Level 1: impulse or need; Level 2: research, advice seeking; Level 3: price comparison; and Level 4: decision to buy. Please note that these levels are not linear, for example level 2 and 3 can occur in parallel and iterative multiple times. An impulse to explore a product might be created when a user is flipping through a magazine or if a product is recommended by a co-worker; similarly a need to buy a product might arise when a user wishes to accomplish a particular goal. For

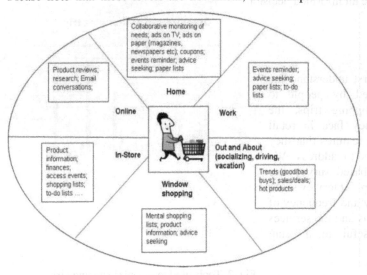

Fig. 1. Locations and types of information consumed

J.A. Jacko (Ed.): Human-Computer Interaction, Part II, HCII 2009, LNCS 5611, pp. 39–47, 2009.
© Springer-Verlag Berlin Heidelberg 2009

example, Jane is a teenager who bought her first car and noticed that she would save a lot of time while driving if she had a GPS system. Jane now enters the first level of the intent cycle. She asks her friends and family for recommendations and also searches online for a GPS that is within her price range, or visit various retail stores to test the look and feel of the product or to get expert advice; these activities shift her into level 2. This is followed by price comparisons online to determine a trustworthy store which has the best price, shifting her into level 3. Levels 2 and 3 are performed iteratively and are usually intertwined until level 4 (i.e. decision to buy a particular brand/make of a GPS) is reached.

As the above example illustrates, the task of shopping is: a) complex, requiring multiple decisions b) collaborative, involving advice and permission seeking, c) social, involving experiential and recreational aspects [6], [9]. Shopping tasks span various locations (e.g. home, store, work etc.), involve multiple touch points (e.g. online, discussions with friends and family, mobile etc.), and tools (e.g. to-do lists, email, SMS, social networking websites, reminders etc.). Figure 1 illustrates the type of information and locations of these intents that the user would like to capture Systems that require consumers to track and report their shopping intent in a structured manner are not very successful [10]. This motivates the use of systems that will allow for unobtrusive or casual capture of shopping related intents using suitable modalities.

The main issues that we want to address in this space are: a) capturing intent in multiple places/locations; b) using existing technology and devices with minimal user effort to capture and access information, c) managing different levels of intent; and d) converting intention to behavior or action. There are three types of intention-action gaps [2]: physical - not being in the right place (how can the   consumer record an intent if no access to their desktop is available or if they need to capture an impulse which will be acted upon once they are in the store); awareness - not the current focus of attention (how can intent be recorded if the consumer is driving or is in a meeting); and informational - insufficient information (how can advice from friends and family be collected to make an informed decision).

2 User Survey

Our goal was to first understand the common tools used by people to organize their shopping trips, the frustrations that they face in retail stores, and missing features that they would like retailers to address. We conducted a Web-based survey and multiple follow-up interviews to identify the severity and frequency of shopping frustrations and the services that would be useful in a retail environment.

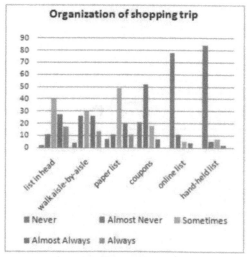

Fig. 2. Tools used to organize shopping trips

There were 69 respondents, of whom 54% were female and 46% were male. 70% were primarily responsible for shopping, and 32% had children in their household. We found that shopping trips for most consumers are usually unorganized, especially for commodity items. Figure 2 details the popularity of various tools used for organizing shopping trips by the participants in our survey.

It was observed that most participants (44%) usually make a mental note of things that need to be purchased (27% answered almost always and 17% answered always) or they walk down aisle-by-aisle in the retail store to determine items to be bought (26% answered almost always, 13% answered always).

These results are in line with Thomas's study on list making behaviors of grocery shoppers [8]. Our study also indicated (as expected) that since most shoppers are unorganized, forgetting what they came to buy was rated as one of the top 5 shopping frustrations.

3 Our Solution

We implemented a solution that enables the creation of shopping lists using different modalities or formats such as structured text, audio, still images, video, unstructured scribbles and annotated media (i.e. annotating images, video frames etc.). The lists can be created from three primary sources: 1) using a toolbar on the Web when users have access to a computer, (fig. 3 and 4) or 2) using any phone (landline or cell phone) by dialing into a number and leaving an audio message when users do not have access to the Web on the phone, or 3) by downloading a mobile client on their PDAs and accessing the service using the data network provided by the cellular carrier or any wireless network (fig. 5). These multimodal shopping lists are made accessible via the Web on any desktop (fig. 6) or mobile phone (fig. 7).

Fig. 3. Closeup of the browser toolbar

3.1 Interaction Details

Users can install a Web browser toolbar (fig. 3). During this process, the user is required to choose a username and password to use the service from a Web browser, and a phone number to use the service from a landline or cell phone. To add an item to the shopping list from the Web, the user needs to highlight the product details (this could be in the form of text, image, audio or video clip) on the Web page (fig. 4) and click on the relevant list name (e.g. "To Buy"). Behind the scenes, a request is sent to the Web server with the Web page URL and the date and time of the capture. There are no restrictions on the type of information (i.e. text/image/audio/video) or the website – thus any information from any website can be added to the shopping list. Users can collaboratively add to the same shopping list on the Web by using the same login information. Similarly, other intents such as researching an item, permission/advice seeking, reminder to buy item for a particular events, etc. can be added to the respective lists named – Research, Ask, and Events.

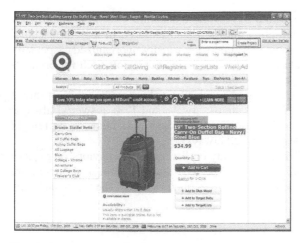

Fig. 4. To capture information (such as text and images) from the web highlight relevant information and click on the list name to add it to the list. Here we are adding to the "To-Buy" list.

Fig. 5. Mobile client to capture shopping information from hand-helds

Audio input from a phone can be added to the list by calling a predefined phone-number to record a voice message. Our system extracts keywords from the audio and adds it to the original recorded audio, along with the date and time information.

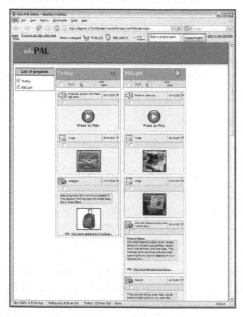

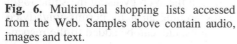

Fig. 6. Multimodal shopping lists accessed from the Web. Samples above contain audio, images and text.

Fig. 7. Multimodal shopping list accessed from a mobile phone

Still images, audio and video based information are added via MMS using preexisting software on the cell phone. The email send from the phone is parsed such that the multimedia file, date, time (and optionally text) information is extracted and added to the appropriate list (the list name is the subject of the email). Alternatively, users can download and install a mobile client to add multimodal information to the shopping lists (fig 5).

The user can access the aggregated multimodal lists from any Web enabled device – on the desktop (fig. 6) or on the mobile device (fig 7).

4 Longitudinal Study and Findings

Ten users were asked to install and use the system to create lists via the Web and phone while maintaining a diary to record their thoughts and observations in a week long longitudinal study. Five of the participants were married and five were single; age distribution was fairly uniform (20s – 3; 30s – 2; 40s – 3; 50s – 2.) On an average, the participants shopped for groceries 1-2 times a week, browsed or shopped online 4 times a week; and shopped in retail stores 2 times a week. Before using our system, participants were using tools like kitchen whiteboards, post-it notes, paper lists, SMS, and email to create shopping lists.

During the week long study, a total of 255 entries were made by all 10 users. 187 entries were made on the Web and 68 entries (approximately 30%) were made from a phone. At the end of the week long study we conducted one-on-one in-depth interviews with each participant that lasted between 60-90 minutes and also asked them to complete a usability questionnaire. The interviews and participant diaries were analyzed inductively using the grounded theory approach to generate design guidelines. Using this approach, we first discovered the key components, and then identified a number of categories and concepts, as well as interrelations between each of them using coding and sorting. The grounded theory analysis identified multiple key experiential categories as described below:

Highlight and add to list
This technique of adding items to a list was extremely popular. On day 2 of use, one user said: *"added items to the cart quickly, like second nature now. [I now] know to highlight more text like price, stuff that will help me with making a decision"* .Another user said: *"I thought I had to highlight the item and then drag and drop it to the list. As soon as I realized that I can just click the list name to add the item I was thrilled."* This mechanism provides a flexible and intuitive way to select and capture information of choice. The primary purpose of the toolbar was to allow users to add items to their shopping list that they intended to purchase at the store. Interestingly the toolbar was used for various other "unintended" purposes as well.

Comparison shopping
One of the most popular uses of our toolbar was in the form of product and price comparison from various websites. Comparison websites like PriceGrabber.com, BizRate.com, NextTag.com, etc. extract product prices from pre-configured websites that cannot be customized by users. Our toolbar helped users highlight and capture product details they were considering from any website and allowed them to prune the information on demand. *"It served as my personal customizable Froogle [1]"*

Collaborative shopping
The next popular use was to create collaborative lists. At the time of the experiment, multiple users could share the login information in order to add items to the same list.

One of our participants was the primary person responsible for weekly shopping chores in a family of four. Other family members would use email for communication whenever they thought of something to be bought. She kept a centralized list that she would update whenever a new request was made. She asked her family members to use the toolbar instead for a week and said: *"It [the toolbar] really made life easier for me – saved me a lot of time and reduced confusions"*.

Another participant used the toolbar to find a birthday gift for her niece and she said: *"It would be nice to share it [shopping list] with my sister since she is also looking for gifts for my niece (her daughter). Last night I showed her some of the things I found (from memory) but it would be nice to share the list."*

This example illustrates that sharing of lists is a very important aspect. In the next version, we plan to add features that will allow sharing the whole or parts of the list with family/friends in real time without having to share login information. We will also have the capability using which the list owner can identify the user that added a particular item.

Organizing shopping

"[I am] finding it [toolbar] an extremely useful tool for organizing my web shopping... especially the panic, last minute b-day shopping where I move from site to site at about 100 mph. Usually I just rely on memory... I can spend a lot of time trying to remember and retrace my steps". We observed that when users started with level 1 of their intent cycle, they rarely knew what structure their activity would take. Our toolbar was intentionally designed to be flexible and light weight so that items of interest can be quickly collected in an unstructured way and organized as the list evolves. As we move forward more sophisticated features are required to manage the lists once they are collected. We will highlight these in the section on discussions.

Editing and modifying list

One of our participants, an administrative assistant, used the toolbar to track items that were left after an office event. Initially she created a list of the items that she bought for the event, and at the end of the event she edited the list to remove the items that were consumed. She said: *"After an event I have no way of tracking and communicating [to other admins] that I have 5 cases of soda remaining that can be used for future events"*. This example illustrates the need to have functionality for editing and modifying lists.

Repeatable lists

"We use the same things for various events" .One of the participants mentioned that products used for similar events remain unchanged; yet for every event they had to make a new list. Using this toolbar she created a "master list" that was printed and shared with other admins. When they are planning a new event for the first time, they are able to simplify the process by using items from the master list to initiate a new list. This example demonstrates the need of creating repeatable lists or templates for events. These templates serve as a starting point and provide a structure to the activity being planned.

Re-finding information

The toolbar allows users to save items they are currently interested in or are currently tracking. The toolbar was used to re-find information that users had looked at a while ago. After using the tool for 4 days one user said: *"I am at the point where I am ready to make a decision about what to buy. I really like having this list. I had totally forgotten some of the things I had selected earlier in the week! I know I would not have written this stuff down, I may have bookmarked some but I am hesitant to bookmark short-term stuff because it clutters bookmarks and requires cleaning up later (which I often don't do)."*

The organization of the bookmarks is different from the information collected by the toolbar. Users spend significant amount of effort to create and maintain their bookmarks, where as there seems to be a low commitment to the upkeep of the information captured from the toolbar and its more "throw-away". This is due to the fact that the toolbar serves a different purpose than bookmarks and the information captured is transient, and re-finding is more short-term. This could be the reason that prevents users from adding retail related information to the browser bookmarks.

Wish list

One of our participants used the toolbar to create a wish list of clothing by capturing text and images from online fashion magazines and forums with the primary purpose of finding affordable versions on her next shopping trip. She said: *"I have a word file in which I copy and paste the images and description of the clothes that I am interested in, and the website URL from which I copied them – this is so much work, and I always have to remember to email the file to myself so that I can access anywhere."*

The ease of collecting text and images from the website, allowed her to form an initial estimate of clothes that she was interested in and she could later use this initial list to make additional decisions. It was important for her that the system could tolerate the collection of non exact items that she could use for interpretation and that the shopping list served more as a point of inspiration than a definitive list.

Research for consumers with special needs

A few of our participants or their family members had special needs (e.g. allergies to peanuts, vegan diet). Due to this they had to research each item before purchasing it from a store. They would typically go to pre-determined websites to conduct this research. Though they liked the ability of collecting related information about a product in a centralized location, the system could in future provide features to help them determine if a product is suitable for their needs by partially automating the process – e.g. extract ingredients information and flag the items which contain peanuts in the ingredients.

Reminder

Participants used the toolbar for creating location based "to-do" items – e.g. *"get quarters for laundry from Albertsons, mail letters"* by adding free-form notes to the Web shopping list. These reminders were not necessarily related to the products on the shopping list and provided the users with a low-effort mechanism of customizing the lists. This flexibility and free-form capture of the toolbar is important since it is difficult to predict what the lists will be used for.

Audio

The users typically used the audio interface while they were driving or when they were in a "hands-busy" and "eyes-busy" environment. 30% of the messages were sent via the phone, even though a few steps were required to login before the users could leave an audio message. We believe that this could be a much higher number if users could leave a message by one-touch dialing.

Most users had not expected the system to extract keywords from audio, and were pleasantly surprised. On an average, the system takes about 2-3 minutes to extract keywords from the audio message and populate the shopping list. Most users felt that this response time was satisfactory even though recognition/extraction was not accurate 100% of the time.

The audio part of the system was very useful for product comparison purposes, though the login and dialog management were tedious. Some users sent voice reminders of prices of products (e.g. multigrain bread at Albertsons was $2.50 and at Trader Joe's was $3.45) in order to compare them at a later stage.

"It would be nice to type in notes or suggestions about what I am looking for. Some businesses don't have a web site or don't list their products on their web site, but I know they are a good places to buy... like Mervyns (good HelloKitty stuff) and a Japanese store that has good Japanese character toys. The phone allows me to do this, so I will add these when I can connect". This example illustrates the need for creating free-form notes that users can use as reminders or for sharing their recommendations.

A drawback of using a third party solution for implementing audio capture was the lack of customization of instructions on how to use to use the system. Since we intentionally did not provide instructions on how to use the system to mimic a real life situation where users may not read manuals, two of the ten participants did not realize that they could leave a voice message with multiple product names in the same message. We believe that this issue could have been resolved if the "greeting" message of the audio piece was customized with this fact.

Most consumers typically do not use the Web to shop for commodity items. This could be the reason why the toolbar interface of the system was not used much for adding grocery items to the shopping lists (approx. 1%) and approximately 90% of items added from the phone were grocery items.

5   Related Work

There have been other efforts to assist users to capture purchase information to be used in a retail environment. The Domisilica [5] project proposes a refrigerator with a network connection and attached display to display and record shopping lists among other things. However such "computationally enhanced" devices are out of reach of the common customer in the real world. Also, we feel that refrigerators, even if they were computationally enhanced, would not be able to support ubiquitous, pervasive and timely capture of shopping intent. It differs from our system which uses commodity hardware and software.

Sellen et al. from HP Labs describe concepts for a reminder service targeted towards working parents, where reminders or notifications are delivered to parents inside a car [7]. This system differs from ours as the only inputs it affords for reminder creation are either "offline" at a computer, or by typing on a handheld.

PlaceMail [4] is a location-based reminder service. We find the following important differentiating factors between this system and ours: The system requires a GPS (which does not work indoors) enabled cell phone with a wireless "data" connection between a user cell phone and the system for data transfer. Our system works with both a regular POTS phone and any cell phone, and uses the cellular/telco carrier to interact with the system rather than a "data" connection. Also, using a cell phone on Placemail requires a user to login by typing on the cell phone before it can create reminders. Moreover, creating a reminder involves specifying time/location (translated to latitude/longitude). We feel this requires significant effort by the user and the interaction with the system is not through natural interfaces. This is in fact reflected in the results of their study where over 86% of users preferred their web interface to creating reminder lists, with only 6% using their cell phone interfaces. Another area of differentiation is that in PlaceMail no information is extracted from the audio reminder, whereas in our system information extracted from intent lists serves the purpose of a "hint" about information contained in the audio. PlaceMail is also unable to support collaborative creation and access to lists, as their primary means of delivery is personal cell phones (a device that is typically not shared amongst users).

6 Conclusions

Shopping is a collaborative and social activity and tools that are successful in this domain need to extend beyond just capturing and sharing on the Web (like Google Notebook [3]). Since an impulse to buy can be created at any time and anywhere, and users may not have access to their PCs to capture this impulse, we believe that using multiple devices and integration of multiple modalities is needed to ease the process.

Our longitudinal study revealed that shopping is mostly goal-oriented. Users want to complete a certain goal (e.g. find an affordable birthday gift, buy food for potluck dinner), and they don't necessarily have a particular structure of search in mind when they start. Thus the "highlight-and-click-to-add" feature of the web toolbar, and the availability of multiple modalities for adding items to the list provided a suitable degree of flexibility to the users and was extremely easy to learn.

Acknowledgments

We are grateful to all the participants of the user study. We would like to thank Kenton O'Hara for his insightful comments on our longitudinal study findings.

References

1. Froogle. Google product search, http://www.google.com/products
2. Gershman, A.V., McCarthy, J.F., Fano, A.E.: Situated Computing: Bridging the Gap between Intention and Action. In: Proc. ISWC 1999, pp. 3–9. IEEE Press, Los Alamitos (1999)
3. Google Notebook, http://www.google.com/notebook
4. Ludford, P., Frankowski, D., Reily, K., Wilms, K., Terveen, L.: Because I Carry My Cell Phone Anyway: Functional Location-Based Reminder Applications. In: Proc. CHI 2006, pp. 889–898. ACM Press, New York (2006)
5. Mankoff, J., Abowd, G.D.: Domisilica: Providing Ubiquitous Access to the Home. Technical Report GIT-GVU-97-17, GVU Center, Georgia Institute of Technology (1997)
6. Miller, D.: A Theory of Shopping. Cornell University Press, Ithaca (1998)
7. Sellen, A.J., Hyams, J., Eardley, R.: The everyday problems of working parents: implications for new technologies. Technical Report HPL-2004-37, Hewlett-Packard Labs (2004)
8. Thomas, A.: Grocery shopping: list and non-list usage. Marketing Intelligence & Planning 22(6), 623–635 (2004)
9. Underhill, P.: Why We Buy: The Science Of Shopping. Simon & Schuster, NY (2000)
10. Wolfinbarger, M., Gilly, M.: Shopping Online for Freedom, Control and Fun. California Management Review 43(2), 34–55 (2001)

Value of Using Multimodal Data in HCI Methodologies

Jhilmil Jain

Hewlett-Packard Laboratories
1501 Page Mill Road, MS#1203
Palo Alto, CA 94304 USA
jhilmil.jain@hp.com

Abstract. In this paper, I will discuss two HCI methodologies, diary study and affinity diagramming, that were carried out using multimodal data such as images, audio, video, annotated media along with the traditional use of text. I will discuss a software solution that was developed at HP Labs to conduct a multimodal diary study using three touch points: PCs, mobile devices and any type of landline/cellular phone. This will be followed by a discussion on how Microsoft StickySorter software was used to conduct multimodal affinity diagramming exercises.

Keywords: multimodal diary study, multimodal affinity diagrams, audio, video, images, text, free-hand notes, annotated media.

1 Introduction

Diary study is a methodology that asks participants to keep a diary, or journal, of their interactions with a computer system (e.g. interactions with a digital reading device) or a process (e.g. nurses record entrics to uncover inefficiencies in their processes). Participants are typically required to record in real time the date and time of an event, where they were, any significant events or problems during their use of a system, and their reactions or thoughts [1]. The diary study methodology is useful when you cannot directly observe users or when you want to observe behavior over an extended period of time. It also allows users to track their own progress without a researcher standing over their shoulder. But one of the main problems with diary studies is that participants often forget to record entries or are selective in reporting.

Text based diaries do not allow for dynamic self documentation or naturalistic capturing in mobile situation. Researchers have acknowledged this problem and have created voice-mail based diaries [2], photo diaries [3], combination of photo and audio diaries [4], and combination of texting (SMS), photo and audio diaries [5]. It was found that while these may be suitable for a certain type of user study, these approaches still lack a variety of modes of expression and touch points to capture diary entries. Also, once diaries are captured, suitable means of organizing and viewing of diaries by participants or HCI researchers, and subsequently tools for aiding the analysis of diaries are still missing or are not well integrated.

Researchers conducting studies to observe mobile behavior [6] or group behavior [7] have respectively observed the need for a methodology that allows flexibility of

J.A. Jacko (Ed.): Human-Computer Interaction, Part II, HCII 2009, LNCS 5611, pp. 48–57, 2009.
© Springer-Verlag Berlin Heidelberg 2009

expression from one or more devices, and one that allows seamless collaborative creation of the diary by multiple participants.

To address these issues, I propose using multimodal diaries that allow entries to be made in multiple formats and from various touch points. I hypothesize that these will be ideal for the studying user interactions and behaviors in the following scenarios:

- Multiple locations – e.g. shopping lists created at home, at work, when the user is out and about
- Various touch points – e.g. accessing bank accounts or information on the Web, ATM, or using mobile device
- Collaboration – e.g. creating a travel plan with friends and family
- Time line specific – e.g. using Web or mobile devices for trouble shooting activities
- Complex processes – e.g. planning, organizing, scheduling and orchestrating an event such as corporate events or wedding planning
- Iterative processes – e.g. using Web or mobile devices for real time visual analysis of data
- Online research/web activity
- Mobile activity

In section 2, I will describe a multimodal diary solution that was developed at HP Labs. Please note that at the time of writing this paper, this solution was not yet used by researchers to conduct a formal user study.

Affinity diagramming is a methodology that is used to create hierarchy of observations such that they can be grouped into trends. This enables us to uncover tools, terminology, methods, strategies used by the participants [1]. Traditionally, text-based notes are used for conducting affinity diagramming. For analyzing multimodal diaries, I have extended the affinity diagrams to contain audio, video and still images as well such that richer data sets can be easily analyzed and grouped while preserving the context of creation. In section 3, I will discuss how I used Microsoft StickySorter [8] to conduct multimodal affinity diagramming exercise.

2 Multimodal Diary Study

At HP Labs, a multimodal diary solution was implemented that enables the capturing of diary elements using different modalities or formats such as structured text, audio, still images, video, unstructured scribbles and annotated media (i.e. annotating images, video frames etc.). By using the annotation feature, users can add position-based audio, video, images or text annotation on top of an image.

Diary entries can be recorded from three primary sources:

1) On the PC, by using a web browser toolbar (fig. 1 and 2),

2) On any phone (landline or cell phone), by dialing into a number and leaving an audio message (when users do not have access to the Web on the phone), or

3) On any mobile device, by downloading a mobile client on their PDAs and accessing the service using the data network provided by the cellular carrier or any wireless network (fig. 3 and 5) or by using the MMS (Multimedia Messaging Service) service.

These multimodal diaries can be accessed, edited and organized via the Web on any PC (fig. 6) or mobile phone (fig. 4).

2.1 Capturing Diary Entries

Participants need to install a Web browser toolbar (fig. 1) to record entries from their PCs. During this process, the participant is required to choose a username and password to use the service from a Web browser, and a phone number to use the service from a landline or cell phone.

To record an entry from the Web, the participant needs to simply highlight the information, (this could be in the form of text, image, audio or video clip) on the Web page (fig. 2) and click on the relevant diary name (e.g. "BBQ Grill"). Behind the scenes, a request is sent to the Web server with the Web page URL and the date and time of the capture. There are no restrictions on the type of information (i.e. text/image/audio/video) or the website – thus any information from any website can be added to the diary.

Audio entries from a phone can be added to the diary by calling a predefined phone-number to record a voice message. In the backend, the solution extracts keywords from the audio and adds it to the original recorded audio, along with the date and time information of the recording.

Fig. 1. Closeup of the browser toolbar that allows users to capture diary entries from the Web

Fig. 2. To capture information (such as text and images) from the web, highlight relevant information and click on the diary name to add it. In this figure, the image and the text on the right to it are being highlighted such that they can be added to a diary.

Fig. 3. Mobile client for capturing diary entries from handhelds

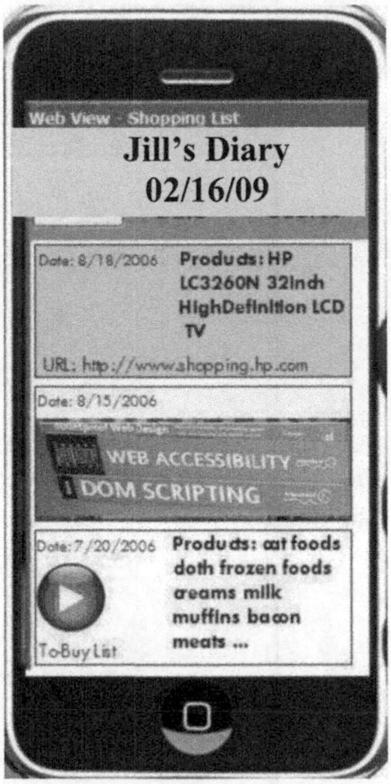

Fig. 4. Diary entries can be viewed on mobile devices as well

Fig. 5. Example of multimodal annotation tags: positional (video, audio and structured text) and non-positional sketching added on a still image by a user

Fig. 6. Multimodal diaries can be accessed and organized via a Web based service. Samples diaries in the figure contain audio, images and text based.

Using the mobile client, participants can additionally annotate still images or video frames by using multimodal tags (fig. 5). These tags consist of: structured text (entered via the mobile device keyboard), free-hand notes (written on the screen using the stylus/finger), audio, and video. Each of these types of tags are position based, that is if added on coordinate x=10, and y=25, their position is retained. A non-positional tag, such as sketching on the image itself is also available. Using both positional and non-positional tags, participants have the capability to easily capture rich contextual data.

The participants can access the aggregated multimodal diary from any Web enabled device – on the PC (fig. 6) or on the mobile device (fig 4). Participants can even collaboratively add to the same diary by using the same login information (from the PC) or mobile number (from the phone). Additionally, participants can even right click on the diary and share it with one or more people.

Still images, audio and video entries can be created via MMS by using preexisting software on the cell phone. For using this option the participants must have a data plan on their mobile device from their network providers. The MMS message sent from the phone is parsed by out backend solution such that the multimedia file, date, time (and optionally text) information is extracted and added to the appropriate diary. The requirement is that the diary name is the subject of the MMS message.

Alternatively, participants can download and install a mobile client to add multimodal information to the diary (fig 3). To use the mobile client, participants can either use their network provider's data plan or any wireless connection or Bluetooth connection. The HP multimodal diary solution's mobile client is network agnostic.

2.2 Managing and Organizing Diary Entries

Entries captured from the Web or the phone can be tagged. Each entry can have one or more tags such that notes can be sectioned into categories for easy organization. These tags can be created by the participant of the study to categorize the entries. Purely text based entries (like in a traditional diary study) can also be made from the Web or a mobile phone.

For all entries made from the Web, the date, time and URL are automatically captured. Similarly, all data captured from the mobile phone is automatically tagged with date and time stamp, location stamp (using GPS information), and all voice mails have a date and time stamp as well. Participants of the diary study no longer have to worry about recording the date and time of entries.

All diary entries can be easy sorted based on time, input format (e.g. audio, video, images etc.) and tags.

Each entry is treated as a block in the diary and can be moved from one diary to another or re-ordered within each diary using a simple drag-and-drop operation. Double clicking on the note allows the user to edit them. Notes can be deleted and cloned as well.

The solution also allows users (participants of the study or the researchers) to select one or more entries of the diary for publishing them in various formats (e.g. pdf, word). Any multimodal entry type (e.g. images, video, audio, text) can be included in the published document (fig. 7). For audio entries, keywords from the file are extracted and displayed on the document. For video entries, key-frames from the file are extracted and displayed on the document. There are a number of parameters available for customizing the layout of the document: number of columns, include data source of the entry, organize entries by time or tags etc.

2.3 Implementation Details

The Web toolbar extension was implemented for the Firefox browser. Regular POTS (plain old telephone service) or Cellular carrier was used for connection between the customer and the system, over any phone line. An audio-blogging website was used to capture audio lists and Dragon Naturally Speaking was used for speech to text conversion. Any MMS enabled cell phone can be used to send images to the system. SQL Server 2005 was used as the database to store intent. Microsoft IIS was used as the web server to host shopping list interfaces on the Web. Apache Tomcat was used as the web server to host the sign-up interface, sign-in interface, toolbar extension, diary interface on the PC and phone, and all updates made to the diary database. All software was implemented using Microsoft .NET 2.0 framework.

Fig. 7. One or more multimodal items from the diary can be chosen by the participant or the HCI researcher to be published in various formats such as pdf. Various templates for formatting are also available.

3 Multimodal Affinity Diagramming

Using this solution, researchers can organize and categorize the diaries as they see fit and subsequently they can automatically generate .CSV (comma separated values) files that can be opened and modified using Microsoft Excel. The .CSV file is automatically generated to contain the following entries since my goal was to conduct the affinity diagramming exercise using Microsoft StickySorter:

- *Text (Field 1)* – text entered by the diary participant. For audio entries, this field contains the keywords extracted from the file. For the rest of the formats, this field contains any textual annotations added by the participant.
- *Hyperlink* – If the note is an audio, video or an image, the source of the file is automatically added such that clicking on the note in StickySorter will open the file.

- *Tag* – the categories/tags that were created by the participants.
- *Touch point* – location where the entry was created. For Web entries, it contains the URL of the website from where the information was collected and for mobile entries, it contains the GPS location (latitude and longitude). If a database of latitude and longitude with corresponding address was created by the researcher, then this field contains the address details.
- *Creator* – name or identification of the participant that create the entry
- *Date Created* – date of diary entry
- *@X Position and @Y Position* – these will be filled in by the Microsoft Sticky-Sorter when researchers organize the notes on the display.
- *@Note Color* - these will be filled in by the Microsoft StickySorter when researchers create note hierarchies. By default, all notes are created "Yellow".
- *!Group* – name of the group that the note will be assigned to (e.g. in figure 8, two out of the four notes have been assigned to the group "Multimodal Diary")
- *@Note ID* - automatically filled in by Microsoft StickySorter.

Figures 8 and 9 show screen shot of an example .CSV file created by the solution.

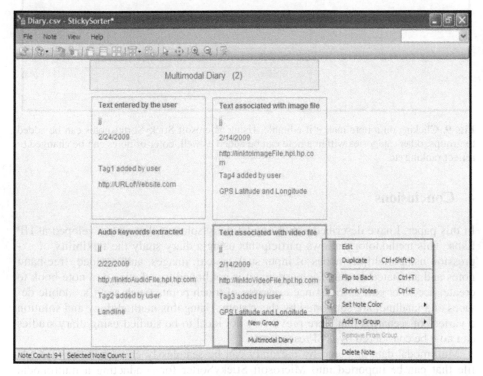

Fig. 8. Screen shot of Microsoft StickySorter displaying the .CSV file create by the solution. Four sample notes have been created, representing four entries created by a participant. Top left displays a text entry, top right displays an image entry, bottom left displays an audio entry and bottom right displays a video entry.

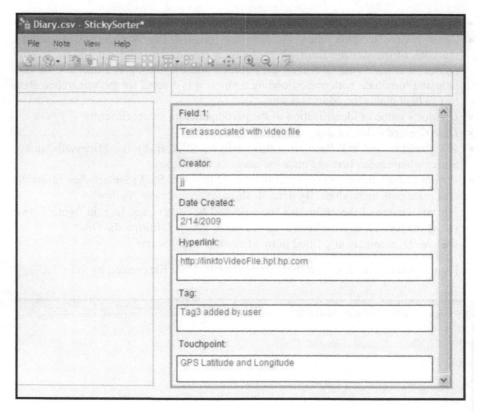

Fig. 9. Clicking on a note makes it editable. Using Microsoft StickySorter notes can be added to groups, other categories within a note can be added as well, color of notes can be changed to reflect ranking etc.

4 Conclusions

In this paper, I have described a multimodal diary solution that was developed at HP Labs. This methodology allows participants using a diary study the flexibility of expression using multiple modes of input such as text, images, audio, video, free-hand notes and annotated media. The participant is not bound to a device or a note-book to create, access or edit entries since a variety of touch points (such as PCs, mobile devices and landline) are supported by the system. Using this methodology and solution a variety of scenarios that were previously not ideal to be studied using diary studies can now be considered by HCI researchers.

Multimodal data gathered by the diary can be seamlessly converted into a .CSV file that can be imported into Microsoft StickySorter for conducting a multimodal affinity diagramming exercise.

The next steps of this project are to recruit HCI researchers to conduct multimodal diary studies using this tool, such that it can be further enhanced. More research is required to develop methodologies for analyzing qualitative multimodal data that is captured over time and requires to be compared over a time period.

Acknowledgments. I would like to thank Catherine Courage for providing helpful feedback on initial drafts, Riddhiman Ghosh for developing the RSS feed for the voice mail feature of the solution, and my managers Mohamed Dekhil and Meichun Hsu for sponsoring this project.

References

1. Kuniavsky, M.: Observing the User Experience: A Practitioner's Guide to User Research. Morgan Kaufmann, San Francisco (2003)
2. Palen, L., Salzman, M.: Voice-mail diary studies for naturalistic data capture under mobile conditions. In: Proceedings of the 2002 ACM Conference on Computer Supported Cooperative Work. CSCW 2002, New Orleans, Louisiana, USA, November 16 - 20, 2002, pp. 87–95. ACM, New York (2002)
3. Van House, N.A.: Interview viz: visualization-assisted photo elicitation. In: CHI 2006 Extended Abstracts on Human Factors in Computing Systems, CHI 2006, Montréal, Québec, Canada, April 22 - 27, 2006, pp. 1463–1468. ACM, New York (2006)
4. Carter, S., Mankoff, J.: When participants do the capturing: the role of media in diary studies. In: Proceedings of the SIGCHI Conference on Human Factors in Computing Systems, CHI 2005, Portland, Oregon, USA, April 02-07, 2005, pp. 899–908. ACM, New York (2005)
5. Brandt, J., Weiss, N., Klemmer, S.R.: Txt 4 l8r: lowering the burden for diary studies under mobile conditions. In: CHI 2007 Extended Abstracts on Human Factors in Computing Systems, CHI 2007, San Jose, CA, USA, April 28 - May 03, 2007, pp. 2303–2308. ACM, New York (2007)
6. Sohn, T., Li, K.A., Griswold, W.G., Hollan, J.D.: A diary study of mobile information needs. In: Proceeding of the Twenty-Sixth Annual SIGCHI Conference on Human Factors in Computing Systems, CHI 2008, Florence, Italy, April 05 - 10, 2008, pp. 433–442. ACM, New York (2008)
7. Hyldegård, J.: Using diaries in group based information behavior research: a methodological study. In: Proceedings of the 1st international Conference on information interaction in Context, Copenhagen, Denmark, October 18 - 20, 2006. IIiX, vol. 176, pp. 153–161. ACM, New York (2006)
8. Microsoft StickySorter,
   http://www.officelabs.com/projects/stickysorter/Pages/
   default.aspx

Effective Combination of Haptic, Auditory and Visual Information Feedback in Operation Feeling

Keiko Kasamatsu[1], Tadahiro Minami[2], Kazuki Izumi[2], and Hideo Jinguh[2]

[1] Tokyo Metropolitan University, 6-6, Asahigaoka, Hino, Tokyo, Japan
[2] Kanazawa Institute of Technology, 3-1, Yatsukaho, Hakusan, Ishikawa, Japan
kasa@neptune.kanazawa-it.ac.jp

Abstract. This research designed the means to offer the haptic feedback to the touch panel by producing the pen-shaped vibratory device. The task performance and the feeling of push touch using this device was experimented by the sensory evaluation. The psychological effects concerning the difference in the feeling of push touch and the acceptance of the device was evaluated by giving the haptic feedback compared with the visual and the auditory feedback. As a result, not only the haptic sense but also the effectiveness of two or more sensory integration was taken as an operation feeling. The goodness of the operation feeling was confirmed the improvement by a clear impression and comprehensible feedback. It is thought that the goodness of operativeness by the vibratory stimulation is connected with the sensibility such as the feeling of comfortable and security.

Keywords: feeling of push touch, haptic feedback, psychological effects.

1 Introduction

There are some products of the information transmission that uses the vibrating alert of the cellular phone and the vibration of alarm clock. These are often used in a limited situation of presence of the vibration under the situation set beforehand. And, these are not often distinguished depending on the kind of the vibration. The improvement of a further usability is expected by adding sense of touch information. It can propose the quality composition in which the mind is moved by adding the element that promotes positive use "I want to use it" and "It is pleasant" and "It is possible to use it naturally" in addition to the satisfaction in the usability. The vibratory stimulation is not a supplementary role of the information transmission and is used as the main role. This promotes an improvement of the usability and positive use. Then, it is necessary to examine the relation to vibration pattern and human sensibilities. The product using the touch panel is widely widespread now as the operation machines such as ATMs and information terminals. This has been a focus of attention as an interface that takes the place of the mouse and the keyboard on the computer.

There are a lot of advantages in the touch panel for the operator. For example, the combination with Graphical User Interface (GUI) can have a variegated function, and the change in the function is easy. There are a lot of advantages in the touch panel for the user. For example, it is possible to operate by touching the operation object

J.A. Jacko (Ed.): Human-Computer Interaction, Part II, HCII 2009, LNCS 5611, pp. 58–65, 2009.
© Springer-Verlag Berlin Heidelberg 2009

directly, and to operate it intuitively. However, there are the following problems in the touch panel. It is not easy to recognize whether it was possible to input it accurately because feedback to the input is poor. It is difficult for the optically-challenged people to operate it, because the recognition of the controlling elements depends on the visual contents. When the button is pressed in the real world, the visual, auditory, and haptic feedback can be obtained. However, the button displayed on the touch panel cannot obtain these feedbacks unlike the button in the real world. The visual and the auditory feedback are presented in the touch panel product used now. For example, animation into which the color of the button changes and the button dents and operation sound has been reproduced when the button displayed in the touch panel is pushed. However, there is little case to present the tactile feedback in a current touch panel.

The researches on the touch panel and the sense of touch pen have been a focus of attention. Forlines and Balakrishnan [1] evaluated the direct input using tabletPC and stylus, and the indirect input using CRT monitor and stylus. The differences by presence of haptic and visual feedback were analyzed by selection time, error rate, and Fitts' law. Lee et al. [2] produced the Haptic Pen with pressure-sensitive tip which was simple and low cost. Kyung et al. [3] developed the Ubi-Pen II, a pen-shaped haptic interface and presented empirical studies on Braille, button, and texture display.

In this research, A pen-shaped vibratory feedback device was produced, and the system that offered the haptic feedback when the touch panel was used was designed. The task performance examined and the feeling of push touch using this device was experimented by the sensory evaluation. The psychological effects concerning the difference in the feeling of push touch and the acceptance of the device were evaluated by giving the haptic feedback compared with the visual and the auditory feedback.

2 Pen-Shaped Device with Haptic Feedback

This pen-shaped device is simple, low cost and easy control. A pen-shaped device with built-in voice coil motor (VCM, Audiological Engineering Corp.) was made as a device to present the haptic stimulation (Fig. 1). Feedback to the operation can be given to the finger by touching the touch panel with this pen. The high response can be expected of VCM compared with the vibrating motor like the DC motor used for the vibration function of the cellular phone. Moreover, there is no influence on the

Fig. 1. The pen-shaped device with haptic feedback

vibration time by inertia, and the control of the vibration of various strength and the frequencies etc. is easy. The size of the pen-shaped device was 150mm in length and 18mm in diameter. The parameter of the vibration as haptic information prepared the amplitude, the frequency, the presentation timing, and the vibration duration.

The experiment system was made by using Visual Studio.Net. The image processed based on the picture image of ten keys was displayed at the center of the screen. When each button of ten keys is pressed, this system can present the haptic, auditory, and visual feedback. The presence of feedback can be switched respectively independently. It is possible to input it by operating each button of ten keys displayed on the display with a pen-shaped device with haptic feedback. The input characters are displayed in the textbox in the upper part of ten keys.

3   Experimental Methods

The mode of expression of the feeling of push touch with a pen-shaped haptic device in addition to a past visual and auditory in the device was examined, and evaluated. The experiment participants were ten men of 21~23 years old.

3.1   Measurement of Vibration Differential Threshold on Pen-Shaped Device with Haptic Feedback

The differential threshold of the vibratory stimulation in the pen-shaped haptic device was requested by the method of limits. As a result, the differential threshold of the vibration was 13.1Hz.

3.2   Feedback Stimuli

The vibratory stimuli were five conditions of 100, 180, 200, 220, 260Hz. When the button was pressed, the vibration was presented. The auditory stimulus was the sound of pushing the key.

3.3   Experimental Task

The experiment accomplished the figure input task for ten minutes. Ten figures a trial were input as early as possible, and the task was done continuously for ten minutes. The image of ten keys was displayed on the touch panel, and each button of 0~9 of ten keys was made to touch with a pen-shaped device.

3.4   Measurement Indices

The operation time and the error rate on a trial as measurement indices were measured. The evaluation items concerning the feeling of push touch were 14, and evaluated it by seven stage method.

3.5   Procedures

The figure displayed on the touch panel was input touching with the pen-shaped device. After the operation to each stimulus had finished, the operation feelings to the stimulation were evaluated. First, the experiment of the effect of five stimuli of 100~260Hz was conducted, and the stimulus with the best evaluation and performance was examined. Afterwards, three kinds of haptic stimulation and two kinds of auditory stimulus were selected, it experimented on five combination conditions as shown on Table1, and feeling of push touch was evaluated.

4   Results

The best frequency was examined as task performance and feeling of push touch among five of 100~260Hz vibratory stimuli. The error was excluded and mean operation time was requested as operation time. As a result, it was the longest in the vibratory stimulus of 100Hz at operation time, and shortest in 220Hz(Fig.2). The error rate was highest in the vibratory stimulus of 180Hz, and about 3% in other stimuli(Fig.3). The result of the evaluation concerning the feeling of push touch is as shown in Fig.4. The evaluation with 200Hz and 220Hz were high, and the evaluation of 100Hz had lowered. The analysis of variance was to examine the difference between five stimuli. As a result, there were significant differences at 5% level in "clearly", "pleasantly", "comfortable", "texture", "expectation", "feeling of luxury", "feeling of push touch", "reality", "easiness", "discrimination", "user-friendliness". As a result of the multiple comparison, significant differences were recognized between 100Hz and 200Hz, 100Hz and 220Hz.

Table 1. The combination conditions of vibratory and auditory stimuli

Conditions	Vibratory stimuli			Auditory stimuli
	220Hz	100Hz	no	
A	○	-	-	○
B	○	-	-	-
C	-	○		○
D	-	○	-	-
E	-	-	○	○

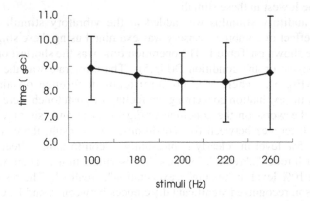

Fig. 2. Operation time on five vibratory stimuli

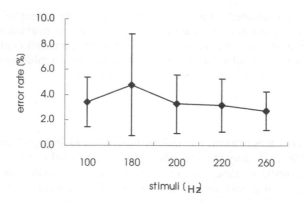

Fig. 3. Error rate on five vibratory stimuli

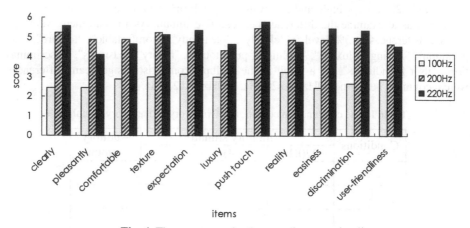

Fig. 4. The sensory evaluation on vibratory stimuli

Therefore, it was suggested that the vibratory stimulus of 220Hz was a haptic feedback to be able to work comfortably. The evaluation of the vibratory stimulus of 100Hz was the lowest in these stimuli.

Next, the auditory stimulus was added to the vibratory stimuli of 220Hz and 100Hz. The effect of combined sensory was examined using these stimuli. The used conditions are shown on Table 1. The operation time was the shortest on the condition C, and the longest on the condition D(Fig.5). The error rate was the highest on the condition D(Fig.6). There was no significant difference on any conditions. The results of the evaluation concerning the feeling of push touch were the best on the condition A, the worst on the condition D(Fig.7). The analysis of variance was to examine the difference between five conditions. As a result, there were significant differences at 5% level in "clearly", "pleasantly", "comfortable", "feeling of luxury", "feeling of push touch", "relief", "easiness", "discrimination". There were significant differences at 10% level in "texture", "expectation", "reality". The results of the multiple comparison recognized significant differences between A and D, C and D.

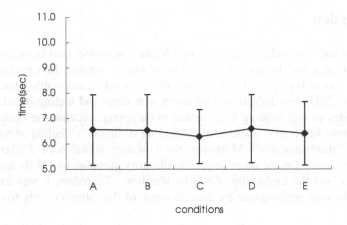

Fig. 5. Operation time on vibratory and auditory stimuli conditions

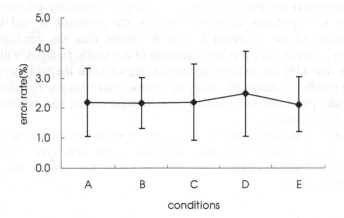

Fig. 6. Error rate on vibratory and auditory stimuli conditions

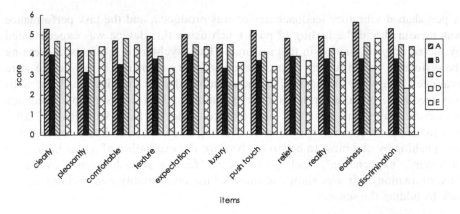

Fig. 7. The sensory evaluation on vibratory and auditory stimuli conditions

5 Discussion

The best vibratory stimulus as feeling of push touch was examined from respect of the task performance and the sensory evaluation. It was shown that the vibratory stimulus of 220Hz was a haptic feedback to be able to work comfortably. The vibratory stimulus of 220Hz was judged as a vibration with clear and feeling of luxury, and it was suggested to feel pushing by clearness to be strong, because the evaluation of it was high score in "clear", "expectation", "feeling of luxury", "feeling of push touch", "easiness", "discrimination". Moreover, the vibratory stimulus of 220Hz had high task performance. On the other hand, the vibratory stimulus of 100Hz had low task performance and the evaluation of feeling was low. Therefore, it was suggested to influence the task performance by the difference of the vibration only for the haptic feedback.

Multimodal integration adding the auditory stimulus to the haptic feedback of vibratory stimulation brought the effect on the task performance and the sensory evaluation. Multisensory integration has the possibility of improving the comfort in task. There was no significant difference between the condition B and C, however, the evaluation of the condition C was the better than the condition of B on every items. This showed that the evaluation of the tactile feedback with a not good evaluation that adds the auditory stimulus is higher from the best tactile feedback. There is a possibility that multisensory integration with a not good precision feedback become more preferable than excellent simple feedback on task performance and a psychological evaluation.

There was no influence for the occurrence of error though the multisensory integration tended to have a negative influence at the task speed. However, the improvement of easiness and clarity was taken by the sensory integration as a psychological effect.

6 Conclusion

A pen-shaped vibratory feedback device was produced, and the task performance was measured and the feeling of push touch using this device was experimented by the sensory evaluation in this research. The psychological effects concerning the difference in the feeling of push touch and the acceptance of the device were evaluated by giving the haptic feedback compared with the visual and the auditory feedback. As a result, he vibratory stimulus of 220Hz was a haptic feedback with comfortably and good task performance. The vibratory stimulus of 220Hz was judged as a vibration with clear and feeling of luxury, and it was suggested to feel pushing by clearness to be strong, because the evaluation of it was high score in "clear", "expectation", "feeling of luxury", "feeling of push touch", "easiness", "discrimination". It was shown to improve the comfortably and performance in task by adding the sense.

References

1. Forlines, C., Balakrishnan, R.: Evaluating Tactile Feedback and Direct vs. Indirect Stylus Input in Pointing and Crossing Selection Tasks. In: CHI 2008 Proceedings Tactile and Haptic User Interface, pp. 1563–1572 (2008)
2. Lee, J.C., Dietz, P.H., Leigh, D., Yerasunis, W.S., Hudson, S.E.: Haptic Pen: A Tactile Feedback Stylus for Touch Screens. In: Proceedings of the 17th annual ACM symposium on User interface software and technology, vol. 6, pp. 291–294 (2004)
3. Kyung, K., Lee, J., Park, J.: Haptic Stylus and Empirical Studies on Braille, Button, and Texture Display. J. Biomedicine and Biotechnology 2008, Article ID 369651 (2008)

Multi-modal Interface in Multi-Display Environment for Multi-users

Yoshifumi Kitamura, Satoshi Sakurai, Tokuo Yamaguchi, Ryo Fukazawa,
Yuichi Itoh, and Fumio Kishino

Graduate School of Information Science and Technology
Osaka University
kitamura@ist.osaka-u.ac.jp

Abstract. Multi-display environments (MDEs) are becoming more and more
common. By introducing multi-modal interaction techniques such as gaze,
body/hand and gestures, we established a sophisticated and intuitive interface
for MDEs where the displays are stitched seamlessly and dynamically according to the users' viewpoints. Each user can interact with the multiple displays as
if she is in front of an ordinary desktop GUI environment.

Keywords: 3D user interfaces, CSCW, graphical user interfaces, perspective
correction.

1 Introduction

A variety of new display combinations are currently being incorporated to offices
and meeting rooms. Examples of such displays are projection screens, wall-sized
PDPs or LCDs, digital tables, desktop and notebook PCs. We often use these multiple displays simultaneously during work. Thus, MDEs are becoming more and more
common. We expect to work effectively by using multiple displays in such environments; however, there are important issues that prevent users from effectively
taking advantage of all the available displays. MDEs include displays that can be at
different locations from and different angles to the user; as a result, it can become
very difficult to manage windows, read text, and manipulate objects. Therefore, it is
necessary to establish a sophisticated interface for MDEs where the displays are
stitched seamlessly and dynamically according to the users' viewpoints, and a user
can interact with the multiple displays as if she is in front of an ordinary desktop
GUI environment.

Therefore, we propose a system that includes multi-modal interaction techniques
utilizing multiple displays. The multi-modal interactions such as gaze inputs, finger
gestures, make tasks more comfortable and intuitive. Moreover, they can be used
for detecting context of the environment, so that it provides a perspective-correct
GUI environment for viewing, reading, and manipulating information for each
MDE user.

J.A. Jacko (Ed.): Human-Computer Interaction, Part II, HCII 2009, LNCS 5611, pp. 66–74, 2009.
© Springer-Verlag Berlin Heidelberg 2009

2 Previous Work

2.1 System Utilizing Multi-Display Environments

Research on computer systems that use several displays has been active for more than 30 years. Early systems focused on the optimization of collaborative processes, and provided personal displays for individual users and large displays for shared use [1]. Newer systems provide more flexible interfaces that integrate combinations of displays as tabletops, personal displays, and large vertical displays [2, 3, 4, 5, 6]. These MDEs typically provide graphical interfaces based on standard WIMP paradigms, perhaps with extended features such as new techniques for cross-display operation [2, 4, 7], novel techniques to manipulate objects [6] and replication techniques to access proxies of distant content from more accessible locations [7, 9]. The geometry that these systems use is mostly inherited from the desktop monitor interface - that is, rectangular elements that assume the user is perpendicular to all displays.

2.2 Multi-modal Interfaces

People communicate with others using multi-modalities in every-day life. Especially we effectively use non-verbal communication channels such as body/hand gestures, eye contacts, and so on. Therefore, many efforts have focused on multi-modal interfaces and non-verbal interfaces.

Voice input has been one of the hot topics since voice commands are effective when combining with other modalities like the gestures [10]. Schmandt proposed a system which adapts the user's complex demands by analyzing his voice [11]. In another example, voices are used as sound signals including information of loudness, pitch and so on [12].

Non-verbal inputs are also used from early years. Bolts et al. proposed a system allowing the users to create and edit figures by using both the gestures and the voice commands [10]. Similarly, the Finger-pointer proposed by Fukumoto et al. supports gestural commands of hands [13].

There are many examples using gaze inputs as another representative type of the non-verbal interactions. MAGIC pointing [14] supports the selections of icons by using gaze information with the cursor. Gaze-Orchestrated Dynamic Windows [15] and EyeWindows [16] allow users to select a window by staring for a while. Although the gaze inputs include some errors, some experimental report that the users can select objects more quickly with the gaze inputs than the mouse.

As described above, the multi-modal interactions have favorable possibility as human-computer interfaces. However, there is no research focusing on the multi-modal interfaces in MDEs.

3 Multi-Display Environment

3.1 Seamless Use of Multiple Displays

We propose a multi-display environment that combines several displays as if they were part of one large virtual GUI environment. The proposing environment defines a virtual plane which is perpendicular to the user as a virtual large display. GUI objects (e.g. windows and cursors) on the virtual plane are projected onto the real displays. As a result, wherever the user's viewpoint is, the user observes GUI objects (cursors and windows) without distortion; just as if they were perpendicular to the user. Even if a GUI object extends to several displays, the user observes it continuously beyond the boundaries of the displays.

Fig. 1. An example of multi-display environment

Figure 1 shows an example of MDE. When the user's viewpoint or some of the displays move, the environment detects these movements with 3D motion sensors and updates the display immediately to maintain the relationship. In the environment, the user controls the cursor on a virtual sphere around the user, so that the cursor can move seamlessly between displays. Also, the user can interact with the multiple displays not only from a certain specific computer, but also from all computers in the environment.

3.2 Middleware Architecture

MDEs can be composed of displays with different characteristics (e.g. resolution, size) located in any position and at different angles. These heterogeneous arrangements present specific interface problems: it is difficult to provide meaningful transitions of cursors between displays; it is difficult for users to visualize information that is presented on oblique surfaces; and it is difficult to spread visual information over multiple displays. Therefore, we proposed middleware architecture designed to support a new kind of perspective-aware GUI that solves the aforementioned problems. Our interaction architecture combines distributed input and position tracking data to generate perspective-corrected output in each of the displays, allowing groups of users to manipulate variety of applications from current operating systems across a large number of displays.

A *3D server* (a dedicated 3D server machine with specific 3D server software) keeps track and processes three-dimensional information of positions and orientations of the users' viewpoints and mobile displays measured through 3D motion sensors. The positions and orientations of user viewpoints and displays are measured by 3D motion sensors that are processed in the 3D server software to calculate the positions and orientations of the GUI objects on the virtual plane. This information is subsequently sent to the client software that runs in each of the client machines.

The system uses an independent *application server machine* that runs actual applications and sends the graphical data to the client machines. The software that carries out the functions of broadcasting the graphical data and receiving input from the client software instances is called the *application server software*.

In addition to presenting the graphical output of applications the system needs to be able to feed user input to these same applications. Users manipulate regular mice and keyboards that are connected to the client machines in order to interact with the applications shown in any display. The client software sends all inputs to the 3D server software, and then the 3D server software relays the inputs to the corresponding windows according to the positions and orientations of the GUI objects in the environment. When the cursor is on top of a window, the 3D server software transfers the cursor inputs to the application server software. For the consistency of the input/output flow, the keyboard inputs on the client machines are sent to the application server software through the 3D server software. In this way, the inputs on all client machines are appropriately processed through the network. Details of each type of software are described in [17].

3.3 Perspective-Aware Features

In MDEs, there are a variety of displays' and users' arrangements so that the users observe the displays at diverse relative positions and postures. If a display is oblique to a user the visibility of information is severely reduced. Moreover, if information extends to multiple displays, part of the information might not be visible, and will consequently be very difficult to interpret. To solve these problems, the system uses the Perspective Window and the Perspective Cursor.

3.3.1 Perspective Window

The Perspective Window provides an optimal view of information in MDEs [18]. They display the same kind of contents as traditional 2D windows (e.g., a web browser or a text processor) but offer extra features derived from the perspective-aware capabilities of the system. Main difference between regular windows and the Perspective Window is that the latter provide optimal visibility to the user regardless of the angle of the display. The windows are rendered using a virtual plane that is perpendicular to the user in the center of the window, and then projected onto the display as shown in Figure 2. If a window is displayed across more than one surface

Fig. 2. Perspective corrected windows

Fig. 3. Window across displays

simultaneously, perspective can help reduce fracture as shown in Figure 3. The perspective windows also help reduce representational disparity since the perspective distortion that affects windows located in different displays is eliminated, making comparisons among their contents easier.

When the viewpoint move measured by a 3D motion sensor. At this time, windows and cursors stay attached to a pixel in a display through an anchor situated in the top left corner of these GUI objects. Their shapes and orientations vary if the display or the user moves, but the objects will remain attached to the same physical point in the display.

When multiple displays are placed at different locations and angles, it can be difficult for people to work with the displays. We investigated the benefit of perspective in multi-display environments [18]. In a controlled experiment that compared perspective windows to flat windows on five basic interaction tasks we found that when using perspective windows, performance improved between 8% and 60%, depending on the task. Our results suggest that where 3D positional information can be obtained, using perspective information in the design of multi-display environments offers clear user benefits.

3.3.2 Perspective Cursor

The system uses the Perspective Cursor as a cross-display user control [19]. Each user manipulates a cursor that is displayed in the user's color. Perspective halos of the same color of the cursor are used to indicate the position of the cursor when it is between displays. Perspective cursor works as follows. The 3D position coordinates of the head of the user is measured and at the same time, a 3D model of the whole environment is maintained, with the actual position of all the screens. The model, together with the point-of-view coordinate of the user's head, lets us determine which displays are contiguous in the field of view, something very different to displays actually being contiguous in 3D space. The position and movement of the pointer are calculated from the viewpoint of the user, so that the user perceives the movement of the pointer across displays as continuous, even when the actual movement of the pointer considered in three dimensional space is not. The pointer travels through the empty space to get from one display into the next. Actually, the cursor can be in any position around the user, even if there is no display there to show graphical representation of the cursor. Figure 4 shows an example movement of the perspective cursor.

Fig. 4. Perspective cursor   **Fig. 5.** Perspective halo

There are not many environments in which the users are completely surrounded by displays, meaning that users might lose the pointer in non-displayable space. The solution that we implemented is a perspective variant of halos [20]. Figure 5 shows the perspective halo from the user's viewpoint. Halos are circles centered on the cursor that are big enough in radius to appear, at least partially, in at least one of the screens. By looking at the displayed part of the circle, its position and its curvature, the users can tell how far and in which direction the perspective cursor is located. When the cursor is barely out of one display, the displayed arc section of the halo is highly curved, showing most of the circle. If the cursor is very far away, the arc seen will resemble a straight line.

4 Multi-modal Interface

In MDEs, users' workspace is much larger than traditional ones. As a result, the users' tasks often become more difficult and time-consuming. For example, a user needs to move mouse for long distance in order to click a desired target object when it is located far from the current position of the cursor. Moreover, users might lose the cursor when it goes to a gap between displays. In these situations, interactions using gaze inputs show much effectiveness. For example, Figure 6 shows a cursor-motion and a window-jumping to the position where the user stares. It prevents the user from losing the cursor and the window. These interactions reduce the user's load of manipulating the pointing devices for long distance. Besides, the gaze inputs can be effectively used for several other purposes. For example, a particular gaze movement can be registered as often-used actions.

In the system, we use the head direction of the user in addition to the gaze input. Figure 7(a) shows a device for detecting gaze, and (b) shows a device for detecting head direction of a user which consists of two 3D positional trackers. In addition, it supports gestural interactions. Figure 8 shows an example in which one of the users moves a window to the position pointed by his finger. This contributes efficiency in collaborative tasks; for example, a user can take another's notice to the position pointed by the finger with moving an object. Other interactions like voice commands are also effective. We can easily expect that the combinations of these multi-modal interactions will improve the effectiveness and intuitiveness of the tasks. For example, the user can give a command with the voice inputs while indicating the object or the position of the command by the finger gestures. Users can select these options according to their preferences, tasks, attitudes, and so on.

In the system a user can also use ordinary interactions devices such as mice according to her preference. These are still useful for tasks which require accurate paintings.

The perspective windows can be used by multiple users. In this case, the system needs to know which point-of-view to optimize for, i.e., who the owner of the window is. Therefore, the system implements an implicit mechanism for assigning windows to users through the user's attention detected from the user's head directions and the gestures. When the user's head directs to a window for a while, the system interprets that he is working or interested in the window. At this time, the system corrects perspective distortion of the window for him automatically. Figure 9 shows an example in which the system is correcting the window gazed by the user. Similarly,

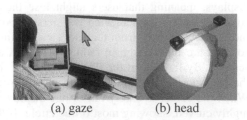

<table>
<tr><td>(a) gaze</td><td>(b) head</td></tr>
</table>

Fig. 6. Cursor-motion and window jumping caused by gaze input

Fig. 7. Gaze and head tracking devices

Fig. 8. Window-motion by finger pointing

Fig. 9. Perspective correction using gaze input

when the system detects the finger pointing, it adapts the perspective correction. The owner can be changed explicitly by clicking the window with the cursor too.

5 The Prototype

The prototype system was demonstrated at SIGGRAPH Asia Emerging Technologies [21]. As shown in Figure 10, many participants easily understand future possibilities of MDEs through our interactive demonstration. Multi-modal interactions were

Fig. 10. Snapshots of people enjoying our demo at SIGGRAPH Asia

presented using their head positions, directions, and finger gestures. They could also use seamless interaction across multiple displays using the Perspective Window and the Perspective Cursor. Besides, they could experience the automatic and dynamic perspective adaption according to the positions and movements of their viewpoints, their heads' directions, and finger gestures.

6 Summary and Future Work

In this paper we described a system that includes multi-modal interaction techniques utilizing multiple displays. The multi-modal interactions such as gaze inputs, finger gestures, make tasks more comfortable and intuitive. Moreover, they can be used for detecting context of the environment, so that it provides a perspective-correct GUI environment for viewing, reading, and manipulating information for each MDE user.

The MDE technology with multi-modal interface is one of the key technologies to establish future ambient information environment. In an ambient information environment, such explicit instructions as commands are not required. The environment is expected to identify the situation and give necessary information. In such an environment, a multitude of sensors will be installed. The environment is required to comprehensively evaluate the information obtained from these sensors and accurately identify the situation in real time. Various types of information presentation devices will also be installed. The environment will give appropriate people appropriate information by adequately combining these devices depending on the situation.

Acknowledgements

This research was supported in part by and Microsoft Institute for Japanese Academic Research Collaboration and "Global COE (Centers of Excellence) Program" of the Ministry of Education, Culture, Sports, Science and Technology, Japan.

References

1. Kraemer, K.L., King, J.L.: Computer-based systems for cooperative work and group decision making. ACM Computing Surveys 20, 115–146 (1988)
2. Biehl, J.T., Bailey, B.P.: ARIS: an interface for application relocation in an interactive space. In: Proceedings of Graphics Interface (GI), pp. 107–116 (2004)
3. Myers, B.A., Stiel, H., Gargiulo, R.: Collaboration using multiple PDAs connected to a PC. In: Proceedings of ACM Conference on Computer Supported Cooperative Work (CSCW), pp. 285–294 (1998)
4. Prante, T., Streitz, N.A., Tandler, P.: Roomware: computers disappear and interaction evolves. Computer 37, 47–54 (2004)
5. Rekimoto, J.: A multiple device approach for supporting whiteboard-based interactions. In: Proceedings of Conference on Human Factors in Computing Systems (ACM SIGCHI), pp. 344–351 (1998)
6. Rekimoto, J., Saitoh, M.: Augmented surfaces: a spatially continuous work space for hybrid computing environments. In: Proceedings of Conference on Human Factors in Computing Systems (ACM SIGCHI), pp. 378–385 (1999)

7. Hinckley, K., Ramos, G., Guimbretiere, F., Baudisch, P., Smith, M.: Stitching: pen gestures that span multiple displays. In: Proceedings of the Working Conference on Advanced Visual Interfaces (AVI), pp. 23–31 (2004)
8. Khan, G., Fitzmaurice, D., Almeida, N., Burtnyk, N., Kurtenbach, G.: A remote control interface for large displays. In: Proceedings of ACM Symposium on User Interface Software and Technology (UIST), pp. 127–136 (2004)
9. Tan, D.S., Meyers, B., Czerwinski, M.: WinCuts: manipulating arbitrary window regions for more effective use of screen space. In: Extended Abstracts on Human Factors in Computing Systems (ACM SIGCHI), pp. 1525–1528 (2004)
10. Bolt, R.A.: Put-that-there: voice and gesture at the graphics interface. In: Proceedings of Conference on Computer Graphics and Interactive Techniques (ACM SIGGRAPH), pp. 262–270 (1980)
11. Schmandt, C., Hulteen, E.A.: The intelligent voice-interactive interface. In: Proceedings of Conference on Human Factors in Computing Systems (ACM SIGCHI), pp. 363–366 (1982)
12. Igarashi, T., Hughes, J.F.: Voice as sound: using non-verbal voice input for interactive control. In: Proceedings of ACM Symposium on User Interface Software and Technology (UIST), pp. 155–156 (2001)
13. Fukumoto, M., Mase, K., Suenaga, Y.: Finger-pointer: a glove free interface. In: Posters and Short Talks of Conference on Human Factors in Computing Systems (ACM SIGCHI), p. 62 (1992)
14. Zhai, S., Morimoto, C., Ihde, S.: Manual and gaze input cascaded (MAGIC) pointing. In: Proceedings of Conference on Human Factors in Computing Systems (ACM SIGCHI), pp. 246–253 (1999)
15. Bolt, R.A.: Gaze-orchestrated dynamic windows. In: Proceedings of Conference on Computer Graphics and Interactive Techniques (ACM SIGGRAPH), pp. 109–119 (1981)
16. Fono, D., Vertegaal, R.: EyeWindows: evaluation of eye-controlled zooming windows for focus selection. In: Proceedings of Conference on Human Factors in Computing Systems (ACM SIGCHI), pp. 151–160 (2005)
17. Sakurai, S., Itoh, Y., Kitamura, Y., Nacenta, M., Yamaguchi, T., Subramanian, S., Kishino, F.: A middleware for seamless use of multiple displays. In: Graham, T.C.N., Palanque, P. (eds.) DSV-IS 2008. LNCS, vol. 5136, pp. 252–266. Springer, Heidelberg (2008)
18. Nacenta, M., Sakurai, S., Yamaguchi, T., Miki, Y., Itoh, Y., Kitamura, Y., Subramanian, S., Gutwin, C.: E-conic: a perspective-aware interface for multi-display environments. In: Proceedings of ACM Symposium on User Interface Software and Technology, pp. 279–288 (2007)
19. Nacenta, M., Sallam, S., Champoux, B., Subramanian, S., Gutwin, C.: Perspective cursor: perspective-based interaction for multi-display environments. In: Proceedings of Conference on Human Factors in Computing Systems (ACM SIGCHI), pp. 289–298 (2006)
20. Baudisch, P., Rosenholtz, R.: Halo: a technique for visualizing off-screen object. In: Proceedings of Conference on Human Factors in Computing Systems (ACM SIGCHI), pp. 481–488 (2003)
21. Sakurai, S., Yamaguchi, T., Kitamura, Y., Nacenta, M., Itoh, Y., Fukazawa, R., Subramanian, S., Kishino, F.: M3: Multi-modal interface in multi-display environment for multi-users. In: ACM SIGGRAPH Asia Emerging Technologies (2008)

Reliable Evaluation of Multimodal Dialogue Systems

Florian Metze[1], Ina Wechsung[2], Stefan Schaffer[2], Julia Seebode[2],
and Sebastian Möller[2]

[1] School of Computer Science, Carnegie Mellon University, Pittsburgh, PA 15213
[2] Deutsche Telekom Laboratories, TU Berlin, Ernst-Reuter-Platz 7, Berlin, Germany
fmetze@cs.cmu.edu

Abstract. Usability evaluation is an indispensable issue during the development
of new interfaces and interaction paradigms [1]. Although a wide range of reliable usability evaluation methods exists for graphical user interfaces, mature
methods are rarely available for speech-based interfaces [2]. When it comes to
multimodal interfaces, no standardized approach has so far been established. In
previous studies [3], it was shown that usability questionnaires initially developed for unimodal systems may lead to unreliable results when applied to multimodal systems. In the current study, we therefore used several data sources
(direct and indirect measurements) to evaluate two unimodal versions and one
multimodal version of an information system. We investigated, to which extent
the different data showed concordance for the three system versions. The aim
was to examine, if, and under which conditions, common and widely used
methods originally developed for graphical user interfaces are also appropriate
for speech-based and multimodal intelligent interfaces.

Keywords: usability evaluation methods, multimodal interfaces.

1 Introduction

Ever since the appearance of the "put-that-there" paradigm [4], multimodal user interfaces have been a subject of intensive scientific study in the human-computer interaction (HCI) community, and systems have been developed with a wide range of research foci [e.g. 5,6] and for a variety of applications [7,8]. Successful development
and deployment of a multimodal interface requires proven performance of the underlying component modalities. Evaluation of a multimodal user interface therefore
generally includes technical evaluation of individual components, to gather so-called
indirect data [9]. This is usually relatively easy to do and reliable, in the sense that
results can be reproduced, and, to some extent, predicted.

On a more abstract level, systems are usually evaluated with respect to their usability. HCI literature provides a wide range of methods to measure usability. Most of
them were developed to evaluate unimodal graphical user interfaces (GUIs). Parameters used for usability measures include *direct* data, collected directly from users,
often through questionnaires, and indirect data like for example log-files containing
task duration or performance data. Since all these parameters are measuring at least
roughly the same concept, namely usability, they would be expected to show high
correlations between them.

J.A. Jacko (Ed.): Human-Computer Interaction, Part II, HCII 2009, LNCS 5611, pp. 75–83, 2009.
© Springer-Verlag Berlin Heidelberg 2009

Multimodal interfaces between man and machines however cannot adequately be evaluated by using performance metrics originally developed for individual modalities only (e.g. word error rate or bandwidth), as humans cannot directly perceive these system properties, but unfortunately usability evaluation of multimodal interfaces has shown deficiencies in the past. In particular, it is unclear if methods well established for unimodal systems can provide valid and reliable results for multimodal systems and if preference for a certain modality can be correlated with measurable variables.

In earlier work, we observed that standardized questionnaires are not suitable for usability evaluation of multimodal systems, as there was only little agreement between the results measured with different questionnaires [3,10]. Concerning unimodal systems, a meta-analysis conducted by Nielsen and Levy [11] showed that performance and predicted preference are indeed correlated. Similar results were reported by Sauro and Kindlund [12], who found positive correlation between satisfaction (direct data) and time, errors and task completion (indirect data).

However, several studies reported opposing findings: Krämer and Nitschke [13] showed that user ratings of multimodal interfaces are not affected by increased intuitivity and efficiency. Möller [14] could not find correlation between task duration and user judgements when evaluating speech dialogue systems. Also, Frøkjær and colleagues [15] could not find correlation between user ratings and efficiency. Results from a meta-analysis by Hornbæk and Lai Chong-Law [16] showed that the user's experience of the interaction (direct data) and indirect data differ considerably from each other or show even negative correlations.

In view of the studies mentioned above, it seems necessary to use both kinds of data in usability evaluation, in order to obtain reliable results. Developing methods for usability evaluation of multimodal systems can only be done by validating within data types (e.g. validation across questionnaires), but also between data types (e.g. comparing indirect and direct results). The purpose of this paper is therefore to analyze, which questionnaire relates most to objective data and to investigate if the results are consistent with our earlier findings.

2 Method

2.1 Participants and Material

Thirty-six German-speaking individuals (17 male, 19 female) between the age of 21 and 39 (M=31.24) took part in this study of a multimodal system, which was originally available as a touch-only system, and then extended with speech input. Half of the participants were familiar with the touch-based system and thus considered as experts. The other eighteen participants were novices. They had no prior experience with the system.

The system tested is a wall mounted information and room management system operable via a graphical user interface with touch screen, speech control and a combination of both. The output is always given via GUI. The users performed six different tasks with the system (cf. Table 1).

Table 1. Description of tasks and required interaction steps

Task	Description	Minimum # of interaction steps required	
		Speech	Touch
T1	Show main screen	1	1
T2	Show 18. floor	1	1
T3	Search for employee	3	6
T4	Search for room	2	1 to ∞*
T5	Show event screen	1	1
T6	Show room for event	1	1

* If the room was accidentally booked at the time of the test, the task was solvable with one click. Otherwise a systematic search overall rooms was necessary.

To collect user ratings, the AttrakDiff questionnaire [17] was used in its original form. In addition the **S**ubjective **A**ssessment of **S**peech **S**ystems **I**nventory (SASSI) questionnaire [18] was used in a modified form, as shown in Table 2.

2.2 Procedure

Each individual test session took approximately one hour. Each participant performed the tasks in three blocks, one for every system version. At the beginning of each block, participants were instructed to perform the tasks with a given modality.

After each block, they were asked to fill out the AttrakDiff questionnaire [17] and a modified SASSI [18] questionnaire (cf. Table 2), in order to rate this version of the system. In order to balance fatigue and learning effects, the sequence of the unimodal systems was randomized in the first two blocks. In the third block,

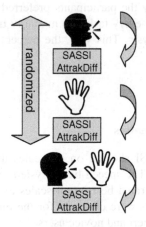

Fig. 1. Test sequence of touch, speech, and multimodal tests

Table 2. Modified and excluded SASSI items

Speech (original)	I sometimes wondered if I was using the right word
Touch (modified)	I sometimes wondered if I was using the right button
Multimodal (modified)	I sometimes wondered if I was carrying out the right action
Speech (original)	I always knew what to say to the system
Touch (modified)	I always knew which button to use
Multimodal (modified)	I always knew which action to carry out
Speech (original)	It is clear how to speak with the system
Touch (modified)	It is clear how to interact with the system
Multimodal (modified)	It is clear how to interact with the system
Excluded	The system is pleasant
	The system is friendly

participants could freely choose the interaction modality, and test the multi-modal system, before again filling out the SASSI and the AttrakDiff to rate the multimodal system (Figure 1).

The subscales for each questionnaire were calculated according to the instructions in the relevant handbook [17,18]. Furthermore for the SASSI an overall scale was calculated based on the mean of all items.

All negatively-poled items were re-coded, to ensure that higher values always indicate better ratings.

Furthermore, video, audio and log data were recorded during the sessions. As a measure of efficiency task duration was assessed via log-files and was, for each system version, summed over all tasks.

To analyze which modality the participants preferred, log-data of the multimodal test block was annotated. For every task, the modality used first to perform the task was selected for further analysis. This way, the percentages of modality preference per task have been computed.

3   Results

3.1   Direct Data - Questionnaires

Ratings on SASSI: The SASSI showed on all scales differences between all three system versions (cf. Table 3). The speech-based system was rated worst on all scales. The touch-based system was rated best on all scales except the speed scale. On the speed scale the highest ratings were observed for the multimodal system. No differences were found between expert and novice users.

Table 3. Ratings on SASSI subscales

Scale	System	Mean	SD	F (df)	p (part. eta^2)
Accuracy	Touch	2.99	0.46	128.86 (2,68)	.000 (.791)
	Speech	1.18	0.53		
	Multimodal	2.20	0.79		
Likeability	Touch	3.16	0.40	139.22 (2,68)	.000 (.804)
	Speech	1.78	0.58		
	Multimodal	2.95	0.65		
Cognitive Demand	Touch	2.87	0.60	116.68 (2,70)	.000 (.769)
	Speech	1.25	0.57		
	Multimodal	2.52	0.78		
Annoyance	Touch	2.72	0.46	79.16 (2,70)	.000 (.693)
	Speech	1.73	0.50		
	Multimodal	2.58	0.68		
Habitability	Touch	2.64	0.85	62.70 (2,68)	.000 (.648)
	Speech	1.22	0.57		
	Multimodal	2.44	0.78		
Speed	Touch	1.90	0.33	5.34 (2,70)	.007 (.132)
	Speech	1.81	0.47		
	Multimodal	2.10	0.35		
Global Scale	Touch	2.70	0.36	180.25 (2,70)	.000 (.837)
	Speech	1.49	0.37		
	Multimodal	2.45	0.55		

Ratings on AttrakDiff: The AttrakDiff questionnaire revealed differences between all three systems versions: On the scale measuring pragmatic qualities the touch-based system got the highest ratings, the speech-based system got the lowest. On the scale hedonic quality-stimulation the multimodal and the speech-based system received higher ratings than the touch-based system. Regarding hedonic qualities-identity the touch-based and the multimodal system were rated better than the speech-based. On the attractiveness scale the touch-based was rated better than the multimodal and the speech-based system. The detailed results are given in Table 4. Again, novices and experts showed no differences.

3.2 Indirect Data – Performance Data

Task Duration: Participants needed least time to solve the tasks when using the multimodal system *(F(2,68)=185.02, p=.000, part. eta^2=.845)*. Means and standard deviation for each system version are given in Fig. 2. No differences were found between experienced and inexperienced users.

Table 4. Ratings on AttrakDiff subscales

Scale	System	Mean	SD	F (df)	p (part. eta^2)
Pragmatic Quality	Touch	1.19	0.75	93.79 (2,66)	.000 (.740)
	Speech	-0.87	1.01		
	Multimodal	0.76	1.12		
Hedonic Quality - Stimulation	Touch	0.54	0.93	15.38 (2,68)	.000 (.311)
	Speech	1.03	0.68		
	Multimodal	1.21	0.79		
Hedonic Quality - Identity	Touch	0.82	0.78	12.84 (2,68)	.000 (.274)
	Speech	0.24	0.70		
	Multimodal	0.83	0.92		
Attractiveness	Touch	1.15	0.80	47.53 (2,68)	.000 (.583)
	Speech	- 0.06	0.87		
	Multimodal	0.92	0.99		

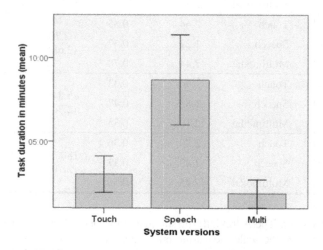

Fig. 2. Overall task duration for all three modalities

Modality Preference: Over all tasks, speech as input modality (52.3%) was slightly more preferred than touch (47.7%). A detailed analysis showed that modality preference was strongly determined by task characteristics: Users tended to prefer the modality most efficient (in terms of required interaction steps) for the specific task. The tasks T3 and T4 could be solved with less interaction steps when using speech. For both tasks speech was preferred more frequently than touch. For all other tasks either no differences were shown, or touch was preferred (cf. Table 5).

Table 5. Modality usage (percentages) by tasks

Task	Speech	Touch	χ^2	p	N
T1	50.0	50.0	.000	1.000	36
T2	22.2	77.8	11.110	.001	36
T3	75.0	25.0	9.000	.004	36
T4	83.3	16.7	16.000	.000	36
T5	57.1	42.9	.714	.500	35
T6	26.5	73.5	5.770	.024	34

3.3 Comparison of Direct and Indirect Data

Correlations between Scales Measuring Efficiency and Task Duration: Over all systems the scales measuring constructs related to efficiency were correlated with task duration. Significant negative correlations were observed between efficiency related scales and task duration. The highest correlation was shown for the AttrakDiff scale "pragmatic qualities". However significant correlations between the questionnaire ratings and task duration could only be found over all systems but not for the single system versions (cf. Table 6).

Table 6. Correlation (Pearson's r) between scales measuring efficiency and task duration ($*p<.01; **p<.05$)

Scale	Task Duration
SASSI Speed (N=107)	-.217*
AttrakDiff Pragmatic Qualities (N=105)	-.520**
AttrakDiff Attractiveness (N=104)	-.344**

Comparison between Modality Usage and Questionnaire Rating: The speech-based system was rated worst on all questionnaire scales except for one of the AttrakDiff scales ("hedonic quality – stimulation"). Furthermore task duration was longest with the speech-based system. Nevertheless, when interacting with the multimodal version speech was used more than touch or equally frequently used as touch to solve four of the six tasks.

4 Discussion

In the present study questionnaire ratings (direct data) partly matched the task duration (indirect data). As in a previous study [3], the AttrakDiff scale pragmatic qualities showed the highest agreement with task duration data. Thus this scale measures the construct it was developed for. A similar conclusion can be drawn from the SASSI results: Ratings on the speed scale matched the task duration data. However, correlations were only observable over all system versions but not for every single version.

Furthermore the actual usage behaviour was hardly affected by the perceived quality (questionnaire ratings). Modality preferences and usage behaviour were strongly influenced by task characteristics. The most efficient modality (in terms of fewest necessary interaction steps) was chosen first. If the number of necessary interaction steps was the same for both modalities, either the touch system was preferred or no differences were observable. Since touch is more common it can be assumed that participants were more familiar with this modality. So possibly the usage of speech as input modality would increase as a function of practice.

In summary, the questionnaires showed correlations with the task duration measures but are not useful as a predictor of actual modality usage. Thus the current results are consistent with our earlier findings: Questionnaire initially developed for unimodal systems are not necessarily the best choice for the evaluation of multimodal systems. As in our previous studies [3,10] the current results point to the AttrakDiff as the most suitable questionnaire and thus as a proper basis for the development of new methods .

References

1. Sturm, J.: On the usability of multimodal interaction for mobile access to information services. PhD thesis, Radboud University Nijmegen, Nijmegen, The Netherlands (2005)
2. Larsen, L.B.: Assessment of spoken dialogue system usability - what are we really measuring? In: Eurospeech 2003, pp. 1945–1948 (2003)
3. Naumann, A., Wechsung, I.: Developing Usability Methods for Multimodal Systems: The Use of Subjective and Objective Measures. In: Proceedings of the International Workshop on Meaningful Measures: Valid Useful User Experience Measurement (VUUM), pp. 8–12 (2008)
4. Bolt, R.A.: "Put-that-there": Voice and gesture at the graphics interface. In: Proceedings of the 7th Annual Conference on Computer Graphics and interactive Techniques (1980)
5. Cohen, P.R., Johnston, M., McGee, D., Oviatt, S., Pittman, J., Smith, I., Chen, L., Clow, J.: QuickSet: multimodal interaction for distributed applications. In: Proceedings of the Fifth ACM international Conference on Multimedia (1997)
6. Martin, J., Buisine, S., Pitel, G., Bernsen, N.O.: Fusion of children's speech and 2D gestures when conversing with 3D characters. Signal Process 86, 12 (2006)
7. Perzanowski, D., Schultz, A.C., Adams, W., Marsh, E., Bugajska, M.: Building a Multimodal Human-Robot Interface. IEEE Intelligent Systems 16(1), 16–21 (2001)
8. Thalmann, D.: The virtual human as a multimodal interface. In: Proceedings of the Working Conference on Advanced Visual interfaces (2000)
9. Möller, S., Engelbrecht, K.-P., Kühnel, C., Wechsung, I., Weiss, B.: Evaluation of Multimodal Interfaces for Ambient Intelligence. In: Aghajan, H., López-Cózar Delgado, R., Augusto, J.C. (eds.) Human-Centric Interfaces for Ambient Intelligence. Elsevier, Amsterdam (2009)
10. Wechsung, I., Naumann, A.B.: Evaluation Methods for Multimodal Systems: A Comparison of Standardized Usability Questionnaires. In: André, E., Dybkjær, L., Minker, W., Neumann, H., Pieraccini, R., Weber, M. (eds.) PIT 2008. LNCS (LNAI), vol. 5078, pp. 276–284. Springer, Heidelberg (2008)

11. Nielsen, J., Levy, J.: Measuring usability: Preference vs. performance. Communications of the ACM 37, 4 (1994)
12. Sauro, J., Kindlund, E.: A method to standardize usability metrics into a single score. In: Proc. CHI 2005. ACM Press, New York (2005)
13. Krämer, N.C., Nitschke, J.: Ausgabemodalitäten im Vergleich: Verändern sie das Eingabeverhalten der Benutzer? [Output modalities in comparison: Do they change user's input behaviour?]. In: Marzi, R., Karavezyris, V., Erbe, H.-H., Timpe, K.-P. (Hrsg.) Bedienen und Verstehen. 4. Berliner Werkstatt Mensch-Maschine-Systeme, VDI-Verlag, Düsseldorf (2002)
14. Möller, S.: Messung und Vorhersage der Effizienz bei der Interaktion mit Sprachdialogdiensten [Measuring and predicting efficiency for the interaction with speech dialogue systems]. In: Langer, S., Scholl, W. (eds.) Fortschritte der Akustik - DAGA 2006. DEGA, Berlin (2006)
15. Frøkjær, E., Hertzum, M., Hornbæk, K.: Measuring usability: are effectiveness, efficiency, and satisfaction really correlated? In: Proc. CHI 2000. ACM Press, New York (2000)
16. Hornbæk, K., Law, E.L.: Meta-analysis of correlations among usability measures. In: Proc. CHI 2007. ACM Press, New York (2007)
17. Hassenzahl, M., Burmester, M., Koller, F.: AttrakDiff: Ein Fragebogen zur Messung wahrgenommener hedonischer und pragmatischer Qualität [A questionnaire for measuring perceived hedonic and pragmatic quality]. In: Ziegler, J., Szwillus, G. (eds.) Mensch & Computer 2003. Interaktion in Bewegung. B.G. Teubner, Stuttgart (2003)
18. Hone, K., Graham, R.: Subjective assessment of speech-system interface usability. In: Proceedings of Eurospeech 2001, vol. 3 (2001)

Evaluation Proposal of a Framework for the Integration of Multimodal Interaction in 3D Worlds[*]

Héctor Olmedo-Rodríguez, David Escudero-Mancebo,
and Valentín Cardeñoso-Payo

ECA-SIMM Laboratory, Universidad de Valladolid. Campus Miguel Delibes s/n. 47014
Valladolid, Spain
{holmedo,descuder,valen}@infor.uva.es

Abstract. This paper describes a multimodal architecture to control 3D avatars with speech dialogs and mouse events. We briefly describe the scripting language used to specify the sequences and the components of the architecture supporting the system. Then we focus on the evaluation procedure that is proposed to test the system. The discussion on the evaluation results shows us the future work to be accomplished.

1 Introduction

One of the most interesting applications of Spoken Technologies (ST) is the implementation of multimodal interfaces [1]. Voice can be useful in different practical scenarios like mobile terminals or entertainment and training applications where ST complements graphical interaction. ST potentially increases the immersion capacities making the 3D world interaction easier (hands free, naming objects out of vision field, etc.). Despite of the spectacular growth on 3D and ST research and development, the state of art on multimodal applications that combine 3D and Dialog Systems (DS) is still characterized by a small number of prototypes. Although there are proposals for the standardization of multimodal systems, existing prototypes seems ad-hoc solutions focussing on reduced fields and with limited application (except visual speech applications). Here we present a proposal that combines 3D and DS. We have created a platform for developing applications based on 3D virtual worlds, including a language named XMMVR to specify scenes and interaction, allowing multimodal interaction driven by spoken dialogue.

The evaluation of the framework is the main concern of this paper. The evaluation is a challenge because the state of the art on 3D systems mainly focuses on the quality of the graphics and very few on the quality of the interaction. We present a procedure that is based on the methodology presented in [2]. We defend the compliance of a guideline that includes graphic, vocal and multimodal metaphors of interaction.

This paper first presents the XMMVR language. Next the architecture required to interpret XMMVR documents is described. Then, we present our evaluation proposal with a guideline of metaphors compliance and we end with the conclusions and future work.

---

[*] This work has been partially financed by the research project of the Junta de Castilla y León VA077A08.

J.A. Jacko (Ed.): Human-Computer Interaction, Part II, HCII 2009, LNCS 5611, pp. 84–92, 2009.
© Springer-Verlag Berlin Heidelberg 2009

2 XMMVR Language and Platform

We briefly present the scripting language and platform for the integration of multimodal interaction in 3D worlds already described in [3].

2.1 XMMVR Language

The eXtensible markup language for MultiModal interaction with Virtual Reality worlds or XMMVR is a markup language to specify 3D scenes, behaviors and interaction. Each world is modelled by an XMMVR element, using the cinematographic event driven movie metaphor. It is a hybrid markup language because it embeds other languages as VoiceXML [4] or X+V [5] for vocal interaction and X3D [6] or VRML [7] for describing the 3D scenes. The XML files that comply with the XMMVR DTD include links to the necessary programs and files needed to run the specified 3D world.

Figure 1 shows the structure of an XMMVR document. Any *xmmvr* element is formed by a cast of *actors* named *cast* and a sequence of scenes named *sequence* determining the temporal evolution of the world. The element *context* is reserved for future use.

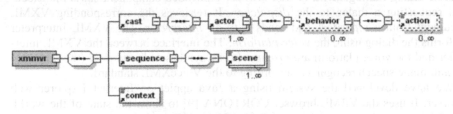

Fig. 1. Elements of the XMMVR language

Each *actor* of the cast is an element with graphical appearance described in a VRML file and a *behavior* that specifies the user interaction. Each behavior is defined as a pair *<event, list of actions>*. The actions are executed when a *condition* is met. The user is considered a member of the audience. He or she is able to interact with the actors of the world though is not considered as an actor of the world.

The user generates events using the graphical interaction *GUI* or the vocal interaction *VUI*. There are also system events to define the interaction with other actors of the world (*ACT* events) or to interact with the system (*SYS* events). The list of actions is a set of actions to be run when the event occurs. The actions can be of GUI, VUI, ACT or SYS type. GUI actions modify the graphical appearance of the 3D World. VUI actions are dialogs. ACT actions are messages sent between actors. SYS actions are the navigation between scenes.

The *sequence* element schedules the *scenes* of the world. By defect the scenes are displayed in the same order as they are written in the document. SYS events and actions allow to navigate among scenes by changing the sequential default order. At least one scene must be defined in the xmmvr world. Interaction is only possible if at least one actor is defined.

According to these premises, a DTD [8] has been defined so that it is possible to develop multimodal applications by writing a XML file that complies with the XMMVR DTD. 3D scenes, actors, its behavior and the interaction with the user are defined in the same markup file. This file is used by the system architecture to run the application as will be described next.

2.2 XMMVR Platform

We have created a framework to develop multimodal HCI applications where the flow of the interaction in 3D environments is driven by spoken dialogs. To build an application using our framework the developer has to specify the virtual world, the sequence of dialogues and the list of actions to be triggered when the events are generated by the users.

One of our goals was to build a multimodal web application, so we have developed a system embedded in a web navigator. Dialogs are programmed using VoiceXML and 3D scenes and actors are described in VRML. We have developed a world manager to schedule the actions to be performed in the 3D world using a Java applet. In the following sections we describe how the spoken interaction is carried out and how the system manages the overall 3D world behavior.

Speech dialog management. A web browser embedded component starts the execution requesting a dialog to the *dispatcher*. It retrieves the corresponding VXML document from a *repository* and sends it to an *interpreter*. The VXML interpreter performs the dialog using the *voice platform*. The interface between the VXML interpreter and the voice platform are *prompts* (to be synthesized) and *field* (the output of the automatic speech recognizer) according to the VoiceXML standard.

We have developed the system using a Java applet on Internet Explorer web browser. It uses the VRML browser CORTONA [9] to show the state of the world. The GUI interaction is based on the EAI API [10]. We use a servlet in an Apache Tomcat server to feed the vocal browser of our dialogue system. We created our own VXML interpreter that uses the Ibervox ATLAS voice platform [11]. As the vocal components are distributed over different severs, multimodal applications can run in a conventional PC with audio and the appropriate browsers.

Management of the 3D world. The required components that make the 3D world react to events are shown in figure 2. The VUI events are dispatched by the *Spoken dialog manager* and the GUI events are typically generated by clicking the 3D elements. The system obtains the information about the 3D scenes and the actors from the XMMVR document. The same document specifies the behavior of the actors as pairs *<event, list of actions>* and links to the VRML document that specifies the 3D scene and actors. The left side of the figure 2 shows the relationship between two XMMVR actors named actor A and actor B and two 3D VRML elements named node A and node B. In response to the events, the system makes changes in the nodes, according to the specifications of the XMMVR document.

The first stage of the system is the *Event scheduling* task, where events are queued and multiplexed in a number of parallel queues (in this case four queues, but this parameter is programmable). Each queue is attended by the corresponding thread, and this allows the concurrent execution of actions in the scene. The threads access a hash

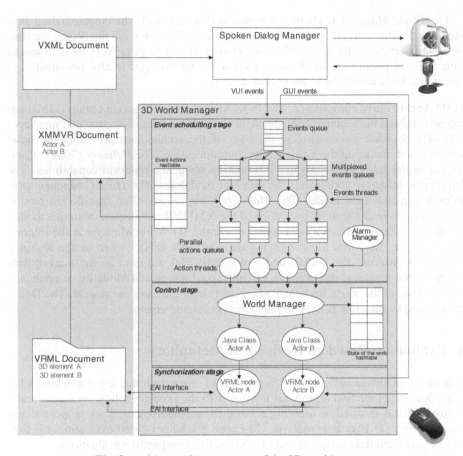

Fig. 2. Architectural components of the 3D world manager

table that contains the actions corresponding with the events, as described in the XMMVR document. If any of the actions is not elemental, the thread is responsible to decompose it, producing a new queue of elemental actions ready to be run by the *World manager* in the next stage. We have programmed an *Alarm manager* to enter anti-actions that eliminate several actions to be cancelled when exceptional events occur (alarms).

Each 3D VRML element has two associated Java Classes: Control and Interface. Control executes elemental actions and interacts with the corresponding variables of the *State of the world hash table* and Interface manipulates the graphics of the 3D node. Between the Interface Java Class and the 3D nodes there is an interface (*synchronization stage* in figure 2) that is responsible to use the EAI to manipulate the VRML elements and to receive the GUI events and forward them to the system input. In the figure 2, the node A is manipulated through the Java Class Interface Actor A. The difference between the node A and the node B is that node B can potentially send GUI events such as a mouse click on the 3D VRML node B.

The *World Manager* reads the elemental actions and calls the corresponding Java Methods. Furthermore, it updates the *State of the world hash table* that stores the state of the properties of the world. The information of this hash table is used to assign values to the parameters of the Java methods. The manager is also responsible to update this table according to the executed actions.

MMI Architecture compliance. The W3C Multimodal Interaction Group (MMI) has recently defined the required components for a multimodal architecture and interfaces [12]. The *Runtime Framework* is the core of the architecture providing the basic structure and managing the *Constituents* communication. The *Delivery Context Component* of the framework provides information about the platform capabilities. The *Interaction Manager* coordinates the different modalities. The *Data Component* provides a common data model. The *Modality Components* offer specific interaction capacities. There is a straight projection of the XMMVR architecture onto this model: our Runtime Framework is a Java applet where the 3D World Manager is the Interaction Manager; the XML file complying the XMMVR DTD is used as the Runtime Framework markup; the VRML and VoiceXML files are used as the markup language for the graphical interaction/scene and vocal interaction Modality components; and the State of the world hash table plays the role of the Data component. The Delivery Context Component is to be implemented in future versions.

3   Evaluation Based on Revision of Metaphors

Evaluation on virtual environments is still a field of research that lags far behind what is needed. In [2] we find a proposal to cope with the problem following a systematic approach that is inspired on usability engineering methodologies. They propose to use four iterative: (1) User task analysis, (2) Expert guidelines-based evaluation, (3) Formative user-centered evaluation and (4) Summative comparative evaluations.

User task analysis is the process of identifying a complete description of tasks, subtasks, and methods required to use a system, as well as other resources necessary for user(s) and the system to cooperatively perform tasks.

Expert guidelines-based evaluation (heuristic evaluation or usability inspection) aims to identify potential usability problems by comparing a user interaction design—either existing or evolving—to established usability design guidelines.

Formative user-centered evaluation is an empirical, observational evaluation method that ensures usability of interactive systems by including users early and continually throughout user interaction development.

Summative comparative evaluation is an empirical assessment of an interaction design in comparison with other maturing interaction designs for performing the same user tasks.

The XMMVR language is suppose to permit to specify the interaction the tasks that the user is expected to perform. Our intention was the language to impose the tasks that the user can do with the system including visual and vocal interaction. The language has been designed as result of the task analysis. We present in this paper the heuristic evaluation of the language and architecture to cope with the expected situations. The procedure to build the guideline was to review the interaction metaphors found in the bibliography related with graphical, vocal and multimodal interaction. In the following subsections, we review the guideline and we comment on the XMMVR capabilities to comply with them.

3.1 Graphical Interaction

Graphical interaction based on mouse and keyboard as known nowadays, is supported by the model of events and actions predefined in behaviours. In the project CONTI-GRA [13] two fundamental metaphors are defined, five structural metaphors and five navigational metaphors. Besides of these metaphors, **transportation of objects** is used as an interaction metaphor on some virtual worlds where some tools or interface elements can be used on several action spaces.

3.1.1 Fundamental Metaphors
There are basically two fundamental metaphors:
Theatre metaphor (tm): User has an static position and a point of view where world changes around. Inside of this metaphor we could consider the movie metaphor that could be a variation of the theatre metaphor.
Locomotion metaphor (lm): User has a dynamic position and will be translated through a structure.

3.1.2 Structural Metaphors
Structural metaphors are based on physical localizations:
Rooms: Can be considered as parts of both fundamental metaphors (tm, lm) and are applied on areas like virtual entertainment, education or electronic commerce.
Revolving stages: Are characteristical examples of the theatre metaphor (tm), because the user's point of view keeps constant.
Buildings with floors, corridors, levels: Are typical examples of the locomotion metaphor (lm).
Space stations, molecules, bubble-nets: Belong to the locomotion metaphor (lm).
Urban metaphors: Are examples of the locomotion metaphor (lm).

3.1.3 Navigational Metaphors
Navigational metaphors are based on different ways of movement (lm). Most known are:
Elevator / hydraulic ramp: Due to its lineal movement, they support *sequential tasks*.
Track vehicle / train: *Two directions* are possible with this sequential metaphor in most of the cases.
Cable railway / slide: Sequential metaphor with one way where an only strict sequence of visited action spaces is allowed.
Flying chair / carpet: Belongs to the group of parallel metaphors because user can fly to more than one or two action spaces.
Tele-Portage / "Beam me up": Despite of disorientation, it is an appropriate metaphor for completely free structures and allows the election of several destination spaces.

We think our proposal is able to implement every described graphical metaphor despite of being based in the theatre metaphor. Structural metaphors are quickly developed with our solution: metaphor of "rooms" can be developed assigning the *scene* element to every room defined in the application; metaphor of "revolving stages" could be solved assigning the element *scene* to each of the stage as well; in the cases of "buildings", "space stations" and "urban" the solution could be the same delimiting the building, space station or urban in several levels that could be our *scenes*.

Navigational metaphors will be implemented with great effort in graphical design. We will assign every element of these metaphors to element *actor* of our language. Thus, metaphor the elevator could be an *actor* moving over floors (element *scene*) resulting a combination of a navigational metaphor (elevator) and a structural metaphor (building).

3.2 Vocal Interaction

Oviatt [14] points out the need for restricted language by the limitations of the dialogue systems to understand the natural language and the need for feedback to adapt the language to new situations or state changes. The use of VoiceXML imposes restricted dialogues and it also allows feedback.

McGlashan [15] distinguishes four vocal interaction metaphors:

Proxy: The user can take control of various agents in the virtual world and thereby interacts with the virtual world through them; for example, painter, paint the house red!

Divinity: The user acts like a god and controls the world directly; for example, Let the house be red!

Telekinesis: Objects and agents in the virtual world can be dialogue partners in their own right; house, paint yourself red!

Interface Agent: The user communicates with an agent, separate from the virtual world, which carries out their spoken commands.

The system is prepared to resolve Proxy and Interface Agent metaphors because the dialogues are vinculated to the different *actors* through the *behaviour* element. Nevertheless, the use of the Proxy metaphor should demand the availability of a VoiceXML interpreter with different voices to associate to the different agents to play.

Telekinesis and *Divinity* metaphors will be simulated using an *actor* without graphical appearance responsible to dialogue with the user and to interact with the rest of agents through *ACT type events*.

3.3 Cooperation between Modalities

There are five basic types of cooperation between modalities as said in [16]:

Transfer: Part of the information produced by a modality is used by another modality.

Equivalence: Both types could treat the same information.

Specialization: A determinated type of information is always processed by the same modality.

Redundancy: The same information is processed by both modalities.

Complementarity: Different parts of information are processed by each modality but have to be combined.

Transfer is guaranteed by keeping a *context* in the XMMVR language and in the *World manager* of the architecture (*hash table State of the World*). One of the modalities can provoke the execution of an action that modifies the value of these context variables and this information be used by the other modality. *Complementarity* can also be programmed using the context of the XMMVR language. *Equivalence* also can be done because the sequence of *actions* can be executed as a consequence of a vocal or graphical event. *Specialization* is responsiveness of the programmer of scenes that can delegate determinated task to one or other modality. By last, *Redundancy* is the most problematic case. When both modalities introduce information referred to the same locking situations can be done because actions can be executed concurrently. This is predicted with the inclusion of the element *Alarm manager* expected to be able to cancel actions from the queues. Nevertheless, there are situations that will need the architecture to be modified, such as dialogue cancellations when graphical introduces redundant information.

4 Conclusions and Future Work

The definition of the XMMVR language shows that it is possible to write scripts to specify virtual worlds with multimodal interaction based on symbolic commands. The use of this language brings modularity, resulting on single development cycles and improving the possibilities to reuse or to standardize components. We have implemented an architecture supporting this language and we have illustrated its use with an example consisting on a 3D scene with two active nodes.

Our proposal is to build a generic platform for the development of VR applications with multimodal interaction. The platform is expected to allow the specification of 3D movies based on different multimodal interaction metaphors. This makes possible the development of applications for specific areas where multimodality could be a great support to ease the interaction in fields such as entertainment applications, educative games or handicapped people interfaces.

We have presented the evaluation methodology we follow relating it with the one presented in [2] On the one hand we have identified several interaction metaphors and types of cooperation between them. On the other hand we have evaluated the capabilities of our solution to implement every interaction metaphor and every kind of cooperation. The result is that our system is capable to implement every interaction metaphor and almost every cooperation between modalities.

As future work, we will develop applications based on our framework to do a formative user-centered evaluation of our framework and finally a Summative comparative evaluation according to [2].

Another challenging future work has to do with the components of architecture and the need to move to public domain tools and libraries. We expect to replace the Cortona by another browser capable to interpret X3D abandoning EAI API by SAI API [17]. We are testing FreeWRL [18] or XJ3D [19] that can be executed on platforms as Debian Linux. Also we are developping the presented framework to work over an Adobe Shockwave Player [20] based platform. Concerning to vocal browsers, open source solutions are still difficult to find in nowadays state of art.

References

1. Jaimes, A., Sebe, N.: Multimodal human-computer interaction: A survey. In: IEEE IW on HCI & ICCV 2005 (2005)
2. Gabbard, J.L., Hix, D., Swan II., J.E.: User-Centered Design and Evaluation of Virtual Environments. IEEE Computer Graphics and Applications (1999)
3. Olmedo-Rodríguez, H., Escudero-Mancebo, D., Cardeñoso-Payo, V., González-Ferreras, C., González-Escribano, A.: Conceptual and practical framework for the integration of multimodal interaction in 3D worlds. In: New Trends on Human Computer Interaction. Springer, Heidelberg (in press)
4. VoiceXML Forum. Voice eXtensible Markup Language, http://www.voicexml.org (revised at June 2008)
5. XHTML+Voice Profile 1.2, http://www.voicexml.org/specs/multimodal/x+v/12/spec.html (revised at December 2007)
6. Extensible 3D (X3D), http://www.web3d.org (revised at June 2008)
7. Hartman, J., Wernecke, J.: The VRML 2.0 Handbook. Silicon Graphics (1994)
8. XMMVR DTD, http://verbo.dcs.fi.uva.es/~holmedo/xmmvr/xmmvr.dtd
9. CORTONA, http://www.parallelgraphics.com/products/cortona/ (revised at June 2008)
10. Phelps, A.M.: Introduction to the External Authoring Interface, EAI. Rochester Institute of Technology, Department of Information Technology, http://andysgi.rit.edu/andyworld10/gallery/archives/vrml/media/eaiclass.doc (revised at December 2006)
11. ATLAS IBERVOX, http://www.verbio.com (revised at June 2008)
12. Multimodal Architecture and Interfaces, http://www.w3.org/TR/mmi-arch (revised at June 2008)
13. CONTIGRA, http://www.contigra.com/ (revised at October 2008)
14. Oviatt, S., Cohen, P.: Multimodal interfaces that process what comes naturally. In: Com. of the ACM (2000)
15. McGlashan, S., Axling, T.: Talking to Agents in Virtual Worlds. In: UK VR-SIG Conf. (1996)
16. Martin, J.C.: TYCOON: Theoretical and software tools for multimodal interfaces. AAAI Press, Menlo Park (1998)
17. SAI, Scene Access Interface, http://www.xj3d.org/tutorials/general_sai.html (revised at June 2008)
18. FreeWRL, http://freewrl.sourceforge.net (revised at June 2008)
19. XJ3D, http://www.xj3d.org (revised at June 2008)
20. Adobe Shockwave Player, http://www.adobe.com/products/director/ (revised at January 2009)

Building a Practical Multimodal System with a Multimodal Fusion Module

Yong Sun[1,2], Yu (David) Shi[1], Fang Chen[1,2], and Vera Chung[2]

[1] National ICT Australia
Level 5, 13 Garden Street, Eveleigh NSW 2015 Australia
[2] School of Information Technologies, J12
The University of Sydney, NSW 2006 Australia
yong.sun@nicta.com.au

Abstract. A multimodal system is a system equipped with a multimodal interface through which a user can interact with the system by using his/her natural communication modalities, such as speech, gesture, eye gaze, etc. To understand a user's intension, multimodal input fusion, a critical component of a multimodal interface, integrates a user's multimodal inputs and finds the combined semantic interpretation of them. As powerful, yet affordable input and output technologies becoming available, such as speech recognition and eye tracking, it becomes possible to attach recognition technologies to existing applications with a multimodal input fusion module; therefore, a practical multimodal system can be built. This paper documents our experience about building a practical multimodal system with our multimodal input fusion technology. The pilot study has been conducted over the multimodal system. By outlining observations from the pilot study, the implications on multimodal interface design are laid out.

Keywords: Multimodal system design, practical multimodal system, multimodal input fusion.

1 Introduction

A Multimodal User Interface (MMUI) allows input and/or output to be conveyed over multiple modalities. Empirical data shows that an MMUI is easy for people to use because the interface is more natural and intuitive. It is preferred by users for many applications, such as map-based military and transport planning. Driven by powerful, yet affordable input and output technologies currently becoming available, such as speech recognition and eye tracking, a functional MMUI becomes more attainable than it used to be. To understand a user's intension conveyed through multiple modalities, Multimodal Input Fusion (MMIF) integrates multimodal inputs recognized by signal recognizers and derives combined semantic interpretations from them. With a flexible and portable MMIF technique that can adapt to other types of input modalities, it is possible to attach recognition technologies to existing systems and build a multimodal system. And the building process can be low-cost and time-saving. We propose an open MMIF approach termed PUMPP (Polynomial Unification-based Multimodal Parsing Processor) in [7] that can handle two parallel input strings. An approach termed THE HINGE has also

J.A. Jacko (Ed.): Human-Computer Interaction, Part II, HCII 2009, LNCS 5611, pp. 93–102, 2009.

been proposed to understand MMIF result and trigger a system action in [6]. In an attempt to develop a plug-and-play MMIF technique, and an economic and practical MMUI, a tentative multimodal system is built based on the MMIF techniques previously developed. Its recognition components are all off-the-shelf products and its application background is a pre-existing system. These pre-developed systems, which can be calibrated/adjusted individually and integrated with very few re-adjustments, enable us to concentrate on how to economically link these pre-developed systems together with our MMIF techniques both in cost and time. This paper reports how the tentative multimodal system is built and a pilot study over it. Implications found in the experience are also discussed.

2   The MMIF Technologies Applied in the System

Because all related MMIF technologies have been documented in the previous papers, an overview of them is outlined here.

PUMPP [7] is used for MMIF in the tentative multimodal system. It accepts multimodal inputs during a multimodal turn. A multimodal turn refers to an opportunity or segment that comes successively to a user to express his/her meaning to a system in multimodal human computer interaction. The multimodal inputs accepted by PUMPP are recognized by recognizers from multimodal signals a user utters. An atomic unit recognized by a signal recognizer is termed as a symbol. A complete set of symbols recognized from multimodal input signals during a multimodal turn consists of a multimodal utterance. Because the tentative system uses speech and eye gaze as input modalities, the inputs of PUMPP in multimodal system are speech symbols and gesture symbols which belong to a multimodal utterance as demonstrated in Fig. 1.

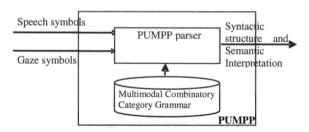

Fig. 1. The architecture of PUMPP

The internal of PUMPP parser has been introduced in [7], and it is not related to particular applications. Multimodal utterances that are legitimate in a multimodal interface are defined in multimodal combinatory category grammar; therefore, the multimodal combinatory category grammar is closely related to applications. In multimodal combinatory category grammar, most language information are condensed in lexical rules, therefore, this kind of grammar is mildly context-sensitive [8].

Although the semantic interpretation generated by PUMPP is represented in hybrid modal logic [4], which is a systematic semantic representation framework, the semantic interpretation still needs to be understood by a specific application. Intuitively, understanding MMIF result is mapping a semantic interpretation to a function of an application. A mapping mechanism termed as THE HINDGE that accepts semantic interpretation in hybrid modal logic has been proposed in [6]. As shown in Fig. 2, THE HINGE is configured with a triggering condition to event table for an application. This table defines which triggering event should be generated under which condition. When PUMPP sends THE HINGE an MMIF result, THE HINGE finds a triggering condition compatible with the semantic interpretation in the MMIF result, and generates a triggering event corresponding to the triggering condition.

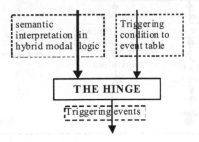

Fig. 2. The input and output of THE HINGE

3   The Tentative Multimodal System

3.1   Origin of the Multimodal System and Its Functions

There is an MPML3D (Multimodal Presentation Markup Language 3D) [5] player. It is a player that can deliver presentations described by scripts in MPML3D. In the presentations, life-like animated agents act in the role of virtual presenters that convey information with their multimodal expressiveness such as voice, gesture and body motion in a convincing and entertaining way.

Although the player has powerful multimodal presentation capability, it can only accept input from traditional keyboard and mouse. We attach speech recognition and eye tracking to it and try to enable its multimodal input capability.

The player running with a script is used as the background application. Based on it, a tentative multimodal system is built. In the tentative multimodal system, two animated agents introduce two MP3 players to a user, then, a user can ask questions regarding these two MP3 players with his/her speech and eye gaze. His/her eye gaze is used to select entities that he/she queries about.

3.2   Overview of the Multimodal System

Fig. 3 delineates the components in the tentative multimodal system and the relationships between them. A user's speech is caught by a Mic. and recognized by VoiceIn[TM] speech recognizer from Fonix [3]. The speech recognizer is running as a standalone thread. It is configured to recognize words and phrases defined as possible input in the tentative multimodal system.

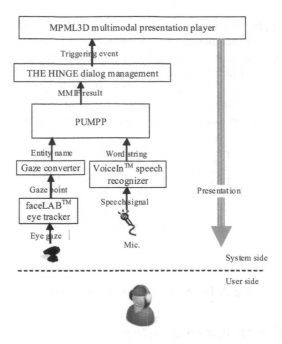

Fig. 3. The overview of the tentative multimodal system

A user's eye gaze is tracked by the faceLAB™ eye tracker, a commercial product from Seeing Machine [9]. The gaze converter accepts gaze points tracked by faceLAB™ eye tracker, deduces gaze points to the entity being gazed on, and provides the name of the entity as eye gaze input to PUMPP. The faceLAB™ eye tracker runs on an independent computer and sends tracked coordinates to the gaze converter. The eye gaze converter shares the location information of entities displayed on a screen in a presentation with the MPML3D player.

PUMPP, running as an independent thread, accepts a user's speech and eye gaze input and derives semantic interpretation of them. THE HINGE sends a triggering event to the MPML3D player according to the semantic interpretation received. To be compatible with input method of MPML3D player, keyboard and mouse, the triggering event is sent out as simulated combinations of key strokes.

Although the speech recognizer needs to be configured for an application and the eye tracker needs to be calibrated for each user, those are not very related to our MMIF techniques. We focus on what needs to be done to fit our MMIF techniques in a practical multimodal system in this paper.

3.3 Preparing a Multimodal Combinatory Category Grammar for PUMPP

Writing a multimodal grammar for PUMPP follows the guide in [2]. The following lexical rule of a PUMPP multimodal grammar illustrates the key concepts and tags.

```
<family closed="true" pos="PDet" name="PDet">
  <entry name="Primary">
    <complexcat>
      <atomcat type="np">
        <fs id="2">
          <feat val="3rd" attr="pers"/>
          <feat attr="index">
            <lf>
              <nomvar name="X"/>
            </lf>
          </feat>
        </fs>
      </atomcat>
      <slash mode="*" dir="/"/>
      <atomcat type="n">
        <fs id="2">
          <feat attr="num">
            <featvar name="NUM:num-vals"/>
          </feat>
          <feat attr="index">
            <lf>
              <nomvar name="X:appliance"/>
            </lf>
          </feat>
        </fs>
      </atomcat>
      <slash mode="^" dir="/"/>
      <atomcat type="n">
        <fs id="3">
          <feat attr="num">
            <featvar name="NUM:num-vals"/>
          </feat>
          <feat attr="index">
            <lf>
              <nomvar name="Y"/>
            </lf>
          </feat>
        </fs>
      </atomcat>
      <lf>
        <satop nomvar="X:sem-obj">
          <diamond mode="det">
            <nomvar name="P:proposition"/>
            <prop name="[*DEFAULT*]"/>
          </diamond>
          <diamond mode="ref">
            <nomvar name="Y"/>
          </diamond>
        </satop>
      </lf>
    </complexcat>
  </entry>
  <member stem="this"/>
</family>
```

The above fragment defines a category for a lexical family, and word "this" is one of its members. Each category has syntactic description and semantic description. The semantic description is encapsulated by "<lf> ... </lf>", and syntactic description is above semantic description. The syntactic description says the functor category is "np(pers:3rd)/*n/^n". Because both the final "np" and the first "n" have the same feature ID "<fs id="2">", the final "np" can inherit the all attributes of the first "n". Semantic description is in hybrid modal logic. The semantic interpretation of final "np" is X, the semantic interpretation of first "n" is X as well and the second "n" has semantic "Y". The semantic description specifies that the semantic interpretation of the final "np" has property "Det", whose value is the stem of a member of this category family, and property "Ref" whose value is the semantic interpretation of the second "n". More information about hybrid modal logic can be found in [1]. In the multimodal grammar designed for the tentative multimodal system, there is no information to mark out which modality a symbol should be uttered from. This strategy makes the exchange of modalities possible because a symbol is legal to be uttered from either speech or eye gaze in the tentative multimodal system.

After all lexical rules of input symbols in a multimodal system are defined, MMIF results of a multimodal utterance can be determined by PUMPP. Fig. 4 illustrates an MMIF result. It contains the final category, syntactic information and semantic information.

The semantic information is represented in hybrid modal logic. A hybrid logic formula can be formed using both *logical and operator* "^" and the *satisfaction operator* "@". A formula @A(p) states that the formula *p* holds at the state *A*. For example, "@X0(<num> sg)" in Fig. 4 means property *num* is "sg" at state X0. A *nominal* is used to refer a state. The combination of these formulas fully describes semantic information. The semantic information in an MMIF result is regarded as the semantic interpretation of a multimodal utterance.

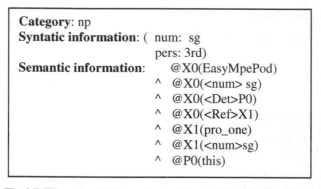

Fig. 4. The MMIF result of "this one" plus "EasyMP3Pod" selected by eye gaze

3.4   Configuring the Triggering Condition to Event Table for THE HINGE

After an MMIF result is derived by PUMPP, its semantic information is sent to THE HINGE module for dialog management. The multimodal utterances acceptable to the tentative multimodal system are in command and control style. Within the system, a user issues a multimodal command, and the system performs a function/action in responding to the command. Because multiple similar multimodal commands may result in the same system action, there is a multiple to one relation between multimodal commands and a system function. To implement the multiple to one mapping between MMIF results and a system function, the common constituent of the semantic interpretations of these multiple similar commands are defined as the triggering condition for a system function.

```
    @E_1(how)
^   @E_1(<body>X_3)
^   @E_1(<mod>X_2)
^   @X_2(<mod>big)
^   @X_3(<pat>question)
^   @X_3(<Arg>X_7)
^   @X_5(EasyMP3Pod)
^   @X_7(storage)
^   @X_7(<mod>X_5)
```

Fig. 5. A triggering condition in THE HINGE

THE HINGE keeps a table listing pairs of triggering condition and the event to trigger the function. Fig. 5 illustrates a triggering condition. It is also represented in hybrid logic. Intuitively, a triggering condition separates a function in a system from others; and the collection of the separated functions should cover all functions in a system. This idea is illustrated in Fig. 6.

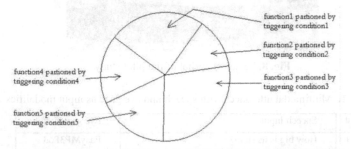

Fig. 6. A set of functions in a system partitioned by trigger conditions

4 A Pilot Study over the Tentative Multimodal System

4.1 Setup of the Pilot Study

In the pilot study, there is a virtual sales scenario where a team of two 3D animated agents present two MP3 players (EasyMP3Pod and MP3Advance) to a user. A user is seated in front of the monitor screen to communicate with the system, as shown in Fig. 7. All the components, except faceLAB™ eye tracker, of the system described in section 2 are running on a Dell Precision computer. The faceLAB™ eye tracker is running on an HP notebook computer. It communicates with Gaze converter through local network. As shown in Fig. 8, there are 6 entities in the screen for a user's eye gaze to select.

Fig. 7. The pilot study setup

Fig. 8. Screen snapshot of the pilot study

Table 1. Multimodal utterances with speech and eye gaze as input modalities

#	Speech Input	Eye gaze fixation
1	How big is its storage	EasyMP3Pod
2	How big is its storage	MP3Advance
3	How many songs can it hold	EasyMP3Pod
4	How many songs can it hold	MP3Advance
5	How many songs can this powerful one hold	MP3Advance
6	How many songs can this advanced one hold	MP3Advance
7	Does this simple one have an FM tuner	EasyMP3Pod
8	What functions does this big one come with	MP3Advance
9	What is the storage medium of this easy one	EasyMP3Pod
10	What is the storage medium of this simple	EasyMP3Pod
11	Does this lovely one have a screen	EasyMP3Pod
12	Does this lovely one have a screen	MP3Advance
13	How many buttons does it have	EasyMP3Pod
14	How many buttons does it have	MP3Advance

To evaluate the performance of the tentative multimodal system, 10 subjects, 8 males and 2 females aging from 20 to 40, were recruited. Most of them are not native English speakers. They are asked to interact with the system with pre-scripted multimodal utterances about the two MP3 players, listed in Table 1. Each subject was asked to interact with the system with all multimodal utterances for 3 times. At the beginning of the study with a subject, the faceLAB™ eye tracker is calibrated for the subject.

4.2 Results and Discussion

Out of 10 subjects, only the data from 9 was usable, since one user had difficulty comprehending the tasks, such that he could not achieve the goals of the task. Surprisingly, more than 90% utterances issued by a user were correctly understood by the system that was indicated by a correct response by the system. After a subject tried the multimodal system, he/she was asked to design two questions about the information in the presentation. We found that most of the questions could not be understood by the system.

These observations imply that a practical multimodal system is possible when a user's utterance is constrained within a certain scope. Otherwise, the user's utterances will not be understood by the system. Because any multimodal system is designed for a certain function or purpose, the multimodal utterances understandable to a multimodal system have to concentrate on a certain domain. When this fact is considered, a multimodal system can be re-defined as a system which a user can use utterances in a certain domain to communicate with. Facing a multimodal system, users often do not know which utterances are legitimate to it. As shown in Fig. 9, there are mismatches between the set of multimodal utterance understandable to a multimodal system and the set issued by users. There should be some facilities to constrain utterances users may issue, and make the utterances issued by a user fall in the multimodal utterance set understandable to a multimodal system.

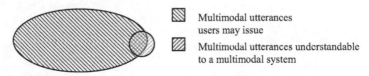

Fig. 9. Mismatches of two set of utterances in an MMUI

5 Conclusion and Future Work

This paper details the process building a practical multimodal system with our MMIF techniques. A practical multimodal system can be built by linking off-the-shelf recognition products and an existing application with PUMPP and THE HINGE. The works that need to be done to build the system have been enumerated.

Through the observation from the pilot study, we can conclude that a practical multimodal system with certain functions is attainable. The pilot study also reveals that the set of multimodal utterances a user may issue does not match or even far exceeds the set of multimodal utterances a multimodal system can support. Therefore, a functional multimodal system should be able to constrain the multimodal utterances a user may issue. The closer these two sets overlap, the better the satisfaction index of a multimodal system will be. How to constrain a user's input in a multimodal interface can be a research issue.

References

1. Baldridge, J., Kruijff, M.G.: Coupling CCG and Hybrid Logic Dependency Semantics. In: 40th Annual Meeting of the Association for Computational Linguistics (ACL), Philadelphia (July 2002)
2. Bozsahin, C., Kruijff, M.G., White, M.: Specifying Grammars for OpenCCG: A Rough Guide. The OpenCCG package (2006), http://openccg.sourceforge.net/
3. http://fonixspeech.com/
4. Kruijff. G. M.: A Categorial Modal Architecture of Informativity: Dependency Grammar Logic & Information Structure. Ph.D thesis, Charles University, Prague, Czech Republic (2001)
5. Nischt, M., Prendinger, H., Andre, E., Ishizuka, M.: MPML3D: a Reactive Framework for the Multimodal Presentation Markup Language. In: Gratch, J., Young, M., Aylett, R.S., Ballin, D., Olivier, P. (eds.) IVA 2006. LNCS, vol. 4133, pp. 218–229. Springer, Heidelberg (2006)
6. Sun, Y., Prendinger, H., Shi, Y., Chen, F., Chung, V., Ishizuka, M.: THE HINGE between Input and Output: Understanding the Multimodal Input Fusion Results In an Agent-Based Multimodal Presentation System. In: CHI 2008 extended abstracts on Human factors in computing systems, Florence, Italy, April 2008, pp. 3483–3488 (2008)
7. Sun, Y., Shi, Y., Chen, F., Chung, V.: An Efficient Unification-based Multimodal Language Processor in Multimodal Input Fusion. In: 19th Australasian conference on Computer-Human Interaction: Entertaining User Interfaces, Adelaide, Australia (November 2007)
8. Steedman, M.: The Syntactic Process. MIT Press, Cambridge (2000)
9. http://www.seeingmachines.com/

Modeling Multimodal Interaction for Performance Evaluation

Emile Verdurand[1,2], Gilles Coppin[1], Franck Poirier[2], and Olivier Grisvard[1,3]

[1] Institut Télécom; Télécom Bretagne; UMR CNRS 3192 Lab-STICC
Technopôle Brest-Iroise CS 83818,
29238 Brest, France
{emile.verdurand,gilles.coppin,
olivier.grisvard}@telecom-bretagne.eu
[2] UBS; VALORIA; Campus de Tohannic, Bât. Yves Coppens, BP 573
56017 Vannes, France
franck.poirier@univ-ubs.fr
[3] THALES Aerospace; Radar & Warfare Systems

Abstract. When designing multimodal systems, the designer faces the problem of the choice of modalities to optimize the system usability. Based on modeling at a high level of abstraction, we propose an evaluation of this choice during the design phase, using a multi-criteria principle. The evaluation focuses on several points of view simultaneously, weighted according to the environment and the nature of the task. It relies on measures estimating the adequacies between the elements involved in the interaction. These measures arise from a fine decomposition of the interaction modalities.

Keywords: modeling, evaluation, modality, context adequacy, interaction language, multimodal interaction.

1 Introduction

Usability is one of the fundamental issues in designing human-system interaction. This issue becomes critical when the systems' complexity increases, for instance in the defense area (e.g. airborne maritime surveillance) or in the medical domain (e.g. assisted surgery). For the time being, users must often carry out tasks under heavy constraints, possibly in critical environmental conditions, while remaining able to handle secondary tasks, such as interacting within a team. In this context, multimodality can allow for more natural and efficient interactions. However, in order to design multimodal human-system interaction on a rational and motivated basis, it is crucial to focus on predicting the usefulness and usability of the modalities, or of their combination, in the context of use. Otherwise, multimodality may not be used [15].

Most of the currently used evaluation methods of multimodal applications are based on empirical analysis that test interaction performances on prototypes or final versions of the system. The major drawback of empirical approaches is a potentially high development cost, notably because of their lack of predictive analysis capabilities [16].

Of course, many analytical methods are proposed in the literature, but one must notice that most of them only offer a restricted choice amongst a limited set of relevant

J.A. Jacko (Ed.): Human-Computer Interaction, Part II, HCII 2009, LNCS 5611, pp. 103–112, 2009.

modalities. Furthermore, they do not allow for predictive evaluation of the real conditions of use of multimodal interaction.

The purpose of this paper is to propose such an approach for predictive evaluation of multimodal interaction, based on some existing models that we propose to extend and federate in a global one. First, we present a brief state of art of the modeling approaches dedicated to evaluation. Then we present our model and we introduce some measures devoted to assessment of the adequacy of modalities to the context of use.

2 Interaction Modeling and Evaluation

Human-machine interaction modeling has given rise to a rich and diverse literature open to many various objectives. Before focusing on models and current needs specifically related to evaluation, we present a brief survey of some existing models, to better situate our work.

2.1 Interaction Models

Interaction models describe different mechanisms implemented to set a dialogue between a user and a system. One can classify these models according to the point of view they favor: some are "task centered" (with cognitive or behavioral modeling), others are "interaction objects centered", and others again are "input / output devices centered" or "interaction situation centered". We shall not elaborate on the first three categories that focus on limited parts of the interaction and thus do not allow for a global analysis such as we aim to achieve[1].

Some models, presenting a global vision, come from different interaction paradigms. We can cite, in relation to the hybrid interaction paradigm, the ASUR notation [8]. It helps describing the various facets of interaction of a user with a mixed system (interaction paradigm for augmented reality / augmented virtuality) and facilitates the exploration of solutions. In the context of interaction with mobile and wearable devices, we can also mention the constraints model presented by Bürgy & Garrett [5] which is based on the one hand on constraints arising from the situation and the activity, and on the other hand on constraints arising from the tasks, the environment, the application, the user and the device.

Finally, in relation to the multimodal interaction paradigm we can cite the model presented by Bouchet [4] for multimodal interaction. It proposes to model the input interaction modalities and their possible compositions, in a global framework for multimodal interaction including task, user and environment modeling. The major limitation of these models is that they are essentially oriented towards the choice of modalities (or modality combinations) in the design phase without evaluative justifications. Some models try to tackle interaction in a predictive way but, as we will see in the next section, in a limited manner.

2.2 Interaction Models Dedicated to Evaluation

Among "restricted" interaction models dedicated to evaluation, we can mention models of the "Goals Operators Methods Selection" family [10]. The goal that the user

---

[1] See [1] for more information.

wants to achieve is split into sub-goals that can be achieved with adequate methods consisting of an operators series (corresponding to actions). Evaluation is conducted on a limited number of measures (task execution time, procedure learning time for NGOMS, error number). When confronted to the complexity of the phenomena involved in the current systems, these models become increasingly complex as shown in EPIC [12] for example. One of the main critics of these methods relates to the time needed to learn and use them.

Besides, even when models try to consider the global interaction situation, they do not seem to be adequate with an evaluative approach. Thus the approach in [5] is criticized on the coarse granularity of the constraint definition and on the fact that only some specific interaction devices are supported. The approach presented in [13] is not intended to assess a specific interaction task between the system and the users, but mainly the way the task can be carried out along with the interaction device in a wearable computing interaction paradigm.

Actually, it seems there is no work on models that would consider the overall situation of interaction dedicated to a predictive evaluation within the framework of a multimodal interaction paradigm. As such, existing models may suffer from one or several of the following defaults:

- The lack of global modeling of the interaction situation: the users and the environment are frequently missing;
- The lack of relevant human factor consideration: the task nature is not taken into account;
- An insufficient description of interaction modalities, that does not allow for their representation in an uniform way and the implementation of an appropriate evaluation;
- An insufficient number of evaluation criteria used to address the complexity of the interaction situation;
- A superficial interaction evaluation (e.g. completion time): it would be profitable, for a predictive evaluation (or *a priori* evaluation), to address the causes of poor performance, such as the quality of the relations between the elements interacting within the global system.

3 Multimodal Interaction Model

Our model's main objective is to assess the interaction quality allowing the designer to refine the interaction solutions envisioned or make choices among them[2]. We present in the following paragraphs the foundations of our model, and then describe more in details the entities that compose it.

3.1 Overview and Foundations

We use the term *interaction* to designate a mediated communication activity between a user and a system, characterized as a sequence of information and/or action

---

[2] Our approach registers in the context of both MDE and HCI areas [17] with promising results illustrating the relevance of such approaches. Models developed in model driven design methods can be completed and used in a predictive evaluation phase.

exchanges. Interaction is modeled through the description of the user, the application (interactive task and domain concept), the environment and of course the interaction modalities. This approach federates existing specialized approaches such as of Bouchet [4], Nigay [14] and Beaudouin-Lafon [2], that we complete to provide the grounds for evaluation.

We illustrate in figure 1 how an interaction can be decomposed. The user performs a task (e.g. *file selection*) acting on one or several domain objects (e.g. selection indicator, an attribute of the file : *"is selected"*) amending the internal state of the system. The user manipulates an interaction modality (e.g. *a trackball associated with a pointer*), or a combination of modalities, and interacts with the device using an interaction language (e.g. *movement language in the plan*). Then, the new system internal state is expressed through an output modality or a combination of output modalities and perceived and interpreted by the user[3].

The entities of the model are expressed along three different abstraction levels, usually identified in the literature, namely: semantic level, articulatory level and physical level (*cf.* figure 1).

3.2 Entities of the Model

We will focus mainly on the two main sub-parts of the modeling which are more directly related to our predictive evaluation goal: the interaction modality on the one hand and the environment on the other hand. The application and the user, modeled along with both his/her physical and cognitive capabilities, will not be described here.

Interaction Modality. Classically, an interaction modality is defined as a couple (d, l), with d an interaction device and l an interaction language [14]. Another definition is given in the context of instrumental interaction [2] as "a mediator or a transducer in

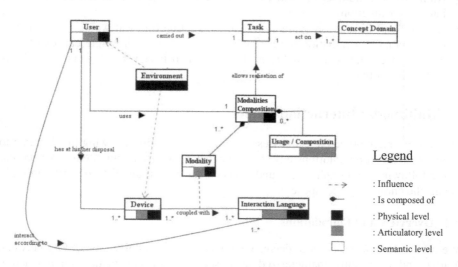

Fig. 1. Global and schematic presentation of the model

---

[3] For simplicity reasons, output interaction is not represented on figure 1.

both directions between the user and the domain objects (...) the instrument is composed of a physical part, the input device and a logical part, the instrument representation at software level and on the screen".

Our definition aims at associating these approaches and enabling the representation of a broad homogeneous set of possible modalities, allowing for the evaluation of the adequacy of modalities to the context of use. The main composing elements of our model are (see Figure 2):

- The *physical device*: a real world object allowing for information transmission to the computing system (e.g. a microphone);
- The *logical device:* a tool that, combined with information provided by the physical device, allows for the manipulation of objects or domain concepts. For input, it is usually an entry processing algorithm (e.g. a voice recognition engine for the vocal modality);

- The *interaction language* (or representational system) is a "structured system of signs that provides a function of communication between the human and the computer system" [14] (e.g. constrained natural command language for surveillance systems).

We decompose the interaction language into three levels of abstraction:

- *High level* or *semantic interaction language*: it consists of meaning units conveyed by the physical level and expressed in a structured manner by the logical level. It subsumes the two other levels (physical and logical) and because it is inseparable from them, it is expressed through them;
- *Intermediate level* or *logical interaction language*: this language expresses the structure of the information expression conveyed by the modality, and it is constituted by well-constructed interaction concepts (see definition hereafter).

We define the interaction concepts (see Figure 2) as abstract, generic elements. They can be of event type (with an action dimension), object type or state type, allowing to designate or to represent domain concepts which are precise object or event instances.

- *Low level* or *physical interaction language*: this language covers all the physical actions that convey sense and that can be applied to the physical interaction object or the user input mode (see Bellik's definition [3]). Thus, for a mouse selection, the physical interaction language will be the manual movements applied in the plan on the mouse, and the pressure and click carried out. In the case of the vocal modality, the voice or the sound waves indirectly manipulate the microphone physical device.

Representations of interactions concepts (see Figure 2) are instances of the physical interaction language. The properties characterizing these representations are physical (properties of the sensors and the effectors of interaction modalities). They can be spatial (positions, distances between reference objects, movement, objects size, etc.), or intensity nature (such as volume, color, strength in haptic, etc.). These properties are independent of the information conveyed during the task, but characterize the conveyor.

We will see that the breakdown of the interaction language following these abstraction levels, when associated to the environment description, allows for the representation in one framework, assessable, of various interactions.

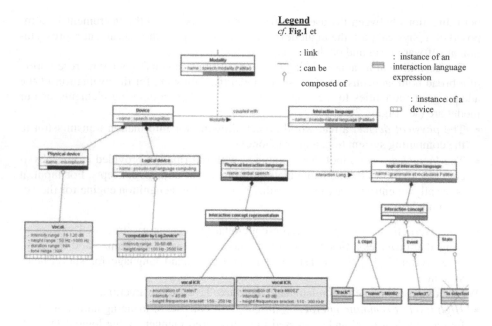

Fig. 2. Modeling of an interaction modality

Environment. We consider the concept of *environment* as close to the broad interaction context definition used by Bellik [3]. Environment is any information relating to a being, an object, a place or a state modification deemed relevant to influence the relations between the user and the system's interaction modalities. We do not define and model the environment in an exhaustive manner, but through all the elements having a significant influence on the user sensitive abilities and the physical input devices.

From the previous descriptions of the modeling of interaction modalities and the environment, it is now possible to set up some measures which allow to compare the level of adequacy of a modality to the task to be performed, among others, and thus to predicatively assess the different design choices[4]. We describe these elements in the next section.

4 Evaluation Method

Traditional approaches focus mainly on the evaluation of results, with the limits we mentioned previously (see 2.3). We propose to tackle the evaluation question through another angle; we focus on the cause of potentially poor interaction performance: the nature of the relations between the elements involved in the interaction. We propose adequacy measures based on properties characterizing the elements of the model.

---

[4] Our evaluation method is limited, until now, to the comparison of modalities two-by-two through some measures. Modality combination effect evaluation is carried out with more traditional ergonomic rules. We think that it is possible to define adequacy measures based on a large number of these rules.

4.1 A Global Approach

Our approach is in the same line as the existing works of Karsenty [11] and Beaudouin-Lafon [2]. The first distinguishes four classes of modality choice determinants (the task-modality link, a subjective performance evaluation function, the initial preferences, and the user experience). The second presents an approach providing a mean for interaction techniques comparison, introducing the concepts of instrument properties that are at the origin of our own adequacy notion. We propose to generalize this comparison mean, and consequently to lay down the problem differently in assessing adequacy of the overall configuration to the task. Our goal is thus to identify discriminating criteria of modality characteristics allowing to carry out a task in a optimal manner, in function of the user capacities and the environment. This assessment is done through a set of compatibility measures working at different levels of abstraction (semantic, articulatory and physical).

4.2 Adequacy Measures

Characteristics allowing to set up measures. Our adequacy measures rely on some characteristics attached to the model's entities or to elementary components constituting these entities. An interaction device is thus decomposed into a physical device and a logical device, and these two components are – besides others – characterized by their respective degrees of freedom. One can either define the level of effort required for a mental task through three possible values. Thus, the relative effort to an mental interaction task could be estimated by the designer to *medium* for selecting an item in three imbricate sub-menus but to *low* for elocution with a vocal modality. Many of these characteristics or properties are present in the literature [4], [6] and [7], and are used in design frameworks.

Abstraction Levels. We propose to classify the identified adequacy measures according to the three levels of abstraction mentioned previously. We present briefly these three sets of measures.

Top Level Measures – Semantics. These measures[5] allow for indicating adequacy between the expression power of entities implied in the interaction and the semantic level required by the task and the interaction language. They focus notably on the metaphorical intensity highlighted by Fishkin [9], the purpose nature or expressive capacities of the language.

Intermediate Level Measures – Articulatory. Adequacy measures[6] at this level are used to characterize the quality of relationships between entities in different dimensions. These dimensions, briefly mentioned above, group together properties that characterize modeling elements and are used as resources during the interaction.

---

[5] M^1_S = f(metaphorical intensity, user expertise), M^2_S = f(metaphorical homogeneity), M^3_S = f(grounding, anaphoric references, feedback), M^4_S = f(goal nature, modality).

[6] M^1_A = f(spatial relationship, temporal relationship), M^2_A = f(logical device dimensions, physical device dimensions), M^3_A = f(operator expertise level, language expertise level), M^4_A = f(solicited cognitive capacities, required of interaction language), M^5_A = f(mental efforts ratio: craft mental task - interaction).

One measure incorporates the *integration degree* presented in [2] initially designed for graphical modality. It is defined as the ratio between the number of degrees of freedom (also called dimensions) of the physical device (PD) and the number of dimensions of the logical device (LD) useable with the interaction language.

Another measure concerns the "expertise" homogeneity. The expertise level of the user should be similar to the required expertise level of the interaction language. To relate it to the Cognitive Load Theory [18], we can consider that this measure expresses the adequacy of the user mental schemas with the interaction language used.

Low Level Measures – Physic. Adequacy measures[7] at this level focus on the relationship between the user physical abilities and the physical device precision capabilities, for input as well as output. Through these measures we are also interested in the precision required from the device by the interaction language.

Measures Weighting. Generally speaking, an interaction modality is not good or bad, it can be assessed according to a goal to reach. Therefore, the adequacy measures, alone, do not allow for a meaningful evaluation and should be considered along with the task to achieve. We propose to describe every task with its characteristics "speed", "reliability", "effort" and "required satisfaction" mentioned by Karsenty [11]. All the adequacy measures are representative, in whole or partly, of one or more of the above characteristics. Thus, we can weight every measure with the importance of these characteristics for the task achievement. This weighting allows to meaningfully aggregate measures in a single evaluation indicator.

4.3 Validation

We have started to validate our approach with the results of interviews obtained during a classic empirical evaluation campaign on a prototype of a multimodal maritime surveillance system. The evaluation aimed at showing the contributions of multimodality when compared to a functionally equivalent mono-modal system. We have compared the theoretical results of our predictive evaluation method to the results of the interviews. We have modeled, for a designation task, three different input interaction modalities (vocal, trackball, trackball and vocal combination). We have applied the adequacy measures described in this paper, considering a neutral environment and two different types of tasks (and consequently two different weighting values for measurement): one task with a high reliability and low required effort, the other with a significant required execution speed. The trends observed are compatible with the forecast which can be made out of our modeling.

5 Conclusion

We propose an interaction model of multimodal systems, laid down on several levels of abstraction, describing the entities involved in multimodal interaction and

---

[7] M^1_P = f(user physical capacities, device physical capacities), M^2_P = f(characteristics « interaction concepts – logical / physical device », user modes characteristics), M^3_P = f(implementation quality of logical device, confidence factor of physical data, effort), M^4_P = f(channel size, quantity of information to transmit, amplitude).

characterizing them by their properties. This detailed description allows us to carry out a predictive evaluation of multimodal interaction performance and to identify its main characteristics and mechanisms.

Taking into account the available resources gives us the possibility to study both inter and intra-device relations and the overall transmission of information. This evaluation is simultaneously performed along several points of view, weighted according to the environment and the task nature. Among the three criteria – descriptive, evaluative and generative – allowing for the evaluation of the quality of the interaction modeling, we have chosen to emphasize the evaluative, contrary to traditional methods which favor the design phase and consequently the generative one.

We plan to conduct experiments focused on a more formal validation of the approach in order to highlight its contributions. The objective, in the end, is to offer an assisting decision tool guiding the designer in his/her preliminary choice of a multimodal configuration during the design of the system.

References

1. Appert, C.: Modélisation, Évaluation et Génération de Techniques d'Interaction. PhD Thesis. Paris: Université Paris Sud (2007)
2. Beaudouin-Lafon, M.: Instrumental interaction: an interaction model for designing post-WIMP user interfaces. In: Proceedings of the SIGCHI conference on Human factors in computing systems. ACM Press, The Hague (2000)
3. Bellik, Y.: Présentation Multimodale de l'Information. HDR. In: LIMSI-CNRS. Paris: Université d'Orsay Paris-Sud (2006)
4. Bouchet, J.: Ingénierie de l'interaction multimodale en entrée. Approche à composants ICARE. PhD Thesis. Grenoble Université Joseph-Fourier - Grenoble 1 (2006)
5. Bürgy, C., Garrett, J.H.J.: Situation-aware Interface Design: An Interaction Constraints Model for Finding the Right Interaction for Mobile and Wearable Computer Systems. NIST Special Publication (2003)
6. Coutrix, C., Nigay, L.: Interagir avec un objet mixte: Propriétés physique et numérique. In: IHM 2007, Paris (2007)
7. Dubois, E., Gray, P.: A Design-Oriented Information-Flow Refinement of the ASUR Interaction Model. In: Engineering Interactive Systems (EHCI-HCSE-DSVIS 2007), IFIP, Salamanca, Spain (2007)
8. Dubois, E., et al.: Un modèle préliminaire du domaine des systèmes mixtes. In: IHM 2004 Namur, Belgium (2004)
9. Fishkin, K.P.: A taxonomy for and analysis of tangible interfaces. In: Personal Ubiquitous Computing, vol. 8, pp. 347–358. Springer, Heidelberg (2004)
10. John, B.E., Kieras, D.E.: Using GOMS for User Interface Design and Evaluation: Which Technique? ACM Transactions on Computer-Human Interaction 3, 287–319 (1996)
11. Karsenty, L.: Les déterminants du choix d'une modalité d'interaction avec une interface multimodale. In: ERGO-IA 2006 (2006)
12. Kieras, D.E., Wood, S.D., Meyer, D.E.: Predictive engineering models based on the EPIC architecture for a multimodal high-performance human-computer interaction task. ACM Press, New York (1997)
13. Klug, T., Mühlhäuser, M.: Modeling Human Interaction Resources to Support the Design of Wearable Multimodal Systems. In: ICMI 2007. ACM, Nagoya (2007)

14. Nigay, L.: Modalité d'interaction et multimodalité. Université Joseph Fourier, Grenoble (2001)
15. Oviatt, S.: Ten myths of multimodal interaction 42(11), pp. 74–81 (1999)
16. Oviatt, S., Coulston, R., Lunsford, R.: When do we interact multimodally? cognitive load and multimodal communication patterns. In: Proceedings of the 6th international conference on Multimodal interfaces. ACM Press, State College (2004)
17. Sottet, J.-S., et al.: A Model-Driven Engineering Approach for the Usability of Plastic User Interfaces. In: Engineering Interactive Systems, Salamanca, Spain (2007)
18. Sweller, J., Van Merrienboer, J.J.G., Paas, F.G.W.C.: Cognitive Architecture and Instructional Design. Educational Psychology Review 10(3), 251–296 (1998)

Usability Evaluation of Multimodal Interfaces: Is the Whole the Sum of Its Parts?

Ina Wechsung[1], Klaus-Peter Engelbrecht[1], Stefan Schaffer[1], Julia Seebode[1], Florian Metze[2], and Sebastian Möller[1]

[1] Deutsche Telekom Laboratories, TU Berlin
Ernst-Reuter-Platz 7, 10587, Berlin
[2] InterACT center, Carnegie Mellon University,
Pittsburgh, PA
Ina.wechsung@telekom.de

Abstract. Usability evaluation of multimodal systems is a complex issue. Multimodal systems provide multiple channels to communicate with the system. Thus, the single modalities as well as their combination have to be taken into account. This paper aims to investigate how ratings of single modalities relate to the ratings of their combination. Therefore a usability evaluation study was conducted testing an information system in two unimodal versions and one multimodal version. Multiple linear regression showed that for overall and global judgments ratings of the single modalities are very good predictors for the ratings of the multimodal system. For separate usability aspects (e.g. hedonic qualities) the prediction was less accurate.

1 Introduction

Since human communication is multimodal in nature multimodal systems are expected to provide adaptive, cooperative and flexible interaction [1]. By providing multiple communication channels such systems are assumed to support human information processing by using different cognitive resources [2, 3].

But making a system multimodal by just adding a further modality to a unimodal system might not necessarily lead to improvement [4]. A higher cognitive load due to more degrees of freedom may be the result [5]. Furthermore, the different modalities may interfere with each other [5]: When presenting identical information via two modalities (e.g. reading and listening to the same text simultaneously) a synchronization problem can occur [6]. Moreover, if different modalities refer to the same cognitive resources task performance may decrease [3].

Apparently, usability evaluation of multimodal systems is a complex issue. The single modalities as well as their combination have to be taken into account. Established procedures usually cover only specific modalities [e.g. 7,8] and evaluating multimodal systems by combining weighted judgements of single modalities is difficult [9].

In the current study an information system is evaluated in two unimodal versions and one multimodal version. The aim is to investigate how user ratings of the single modalities relate to the rating of the multimodal system.

J.A. Jacko (Ed.): Human-Computer Interaction, Part II, HCII 2009, LNCS 5611, pp. 113–119, 2009.
© Springer-Verlag Berlin Heidelberg 2009

2 Method

2.1 Participants and Material

Thirty-six German-speaking individuals (17 male, 19 female) between the age of 21 and 39 (M = 31.24) took part in the study.

The system tested is a wall-mounted information and room management system controllable via a graphical user interface (GUI) with touch input, via speech input and via a combination of both. The output is always given via GUI.

2.2 Procedure

The users performed six different tasks with the system. To collect user ratings the AttrakDiff questionnaire [10] was used.

Each test session took approximately one hour. Each participant performed the tasks with each system version. Participants were instructed to perform the tasks with a given modality. After that, they were asked to fill out the AttrakDiff in order to rate the previously tested version of the system. This was repeated for every modality. In order to balance fatigue and learning effects the order of the systems was randomized. After that, the tasks were presented again and the participants could freely choose the interaction modality. Again the AttrakDiff had to be filled out to rate the multimodal system.

The 4 AttrakDiff sub-scales comprising 7 items each (*pragmatic quality, hedonic quality-stimulation, hedonic quality-identity, attractiveness*) were calculated according to [10]. Furthermore an overall scale was calculated based on the mean of all 28 items. All questionnaire items which were negatively poled were recoded so that higher values indicate better ratings.

To analyze which modality the participants preferred when using the multimodal system version, the modality chosen first to perform the task was annotated. This way, the frequencies of modality usage were assessed.

3 Results

3.1 Rating for Different System Versions

The results show differences between the three versions of the system for all Attrak-Diff scales. For the scale *pragmatic qualities* the touch-based version was rated best and the voice control version worst (F $(2,66)= 93.79$, p=.000, eta^2=.740). For both hedonic scales the multimodal version was rated best. Regarding *hedonic qualities-stimulation* (F$(2,68)=12.84$, p=.000, eta$^2= .274$) the speech version received the lowest ratings. For *hedonic qualities-identity* the touch-based version was rated worst (F $(1.65, 55.99)=15.35$, p=.000, eta^2=.311)[1].

The *attractiveness scale*, the AttrakDiff scale covering pragmatic as well as hedonic qualities, showed the lowest ratings for the speech-based version (F$(1.51$,

---

[1] Greenhouse-Geisser-correction was applied to control for violation of the sphericity assumption.

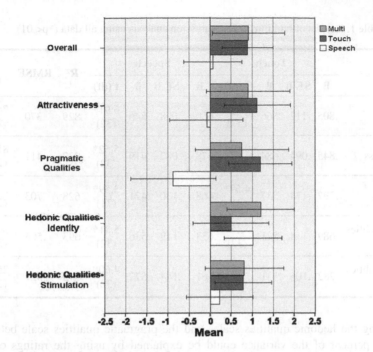

Fig. 1. Ratings on AttrakDiff overall scale and AttrakDiff subscales for all system versions. Error bars display one standard deviation.

51.22)= 47.53, p=.000, eta²=.583)[1] and highest ratings for the touch-based version. Regarding the overall scale, the scale based on the mean of all items, the speech-based version was rated worse than the touch-based and multimodal systems versions. The touch-based version and the multimodal version were rated equally good.

Differences between male and female user were not observable.

3.2 Relationship between Uni-and Multimodal Judgments

To investigate if and how the ratings of the unimodal system versions relate to ratings for the multimodal system version stepwise multiple linear regression analysis was conducted for each sub-scale and the overall scale. The judgments assessed after the interaction with the unimodal systems version were used as predictor variables, the judgments collected after interacting with the multimodal system version were used as the response variable.

The results show that for the attractiveness scale and the overall scale the judgments of the unimodal system are very good predictors of the judgments of the multimodal version. For both regression analyses the beta–coefficients were higher for the judgments of the touch-controlled version of the system. This is in line with the modality usage for the multimodal system: Touch-input was used more frequently. Thus the overall and global judgments of the multimodal system should be more influenced by the interaction with the touch-input.

Table 1. Results of multiple linear regression analysis using all data (*p<.01)

Scale	Touch				Speech				R²	RMSE	F (df)
	B	SE B	β	t (df)	B	SE B	β	t (df)			
Overall	.805	.112	.566	0.21* (32)	.680	.098	.546	6.91* (32)	.829	.370	74.94* (2,31)
Attractiveness	.845	.094	.684	9.02* (32)	.478	.087	.419	5.52* (32)	.837	.411	81.99* (2,32)
Pragmatic Qualities	.797	.174	.537	4.57* (31)	.468	.130	.421	3.59* (31)	.628	.703	26.19* (2,31)
Hedonic Qualities Stimulation	.689	.134	.521	5.13* (32)	.633	.119	.536	5.31* (32)	.693	.508	36.05* (2,32)
Hedonic Qualities Identity	.282	.106	.331	2.66* (32)	.661	.144	.572	4.60* (32)	.612	.527	25.24* (2,32)

Regarding the hedonic qualities scales and the pragmatic qualities scale between 61 and 69 percent of the variance could be explained by using the ratings of the unimodal systems as predictors of the ratings for the multimodal system. The beta–coefficients of speech were higher than those of touch for both hedonic scales, therefore the rating of speech had a larger impact on the multimodal system judgment than the judgment on touch

A 10 fold cross validation was conducted to test for overfitting effects. For the *attractiveness scale* and the overall scale R² is still around .8 indicating a good fit. For the other scales the overfitting effects were larger, resulting in the worst accuracy for *hedonic qualities-identity*. Except for the pragmatic scale the models with beta-coefficients in line with the actual usage were more stable. The detailed results are given in Table 2 and visualized in Figure 2.

Table 2. Results of multiple linear regression analysis using 10 fold cross validation (*p<.01)

	Overall	Attractiveness	Pragmatic Qualities	Hedonic Qualities Stimulation	Hedonic Qualities Identity
R²	.799	.805	.539	.607	.391
RMSE	.384	.431	.754	.572	.615

For the models with lower R², we also analyzed the ad-hoc assumption that the best- (*pragmatic qualities*, both hedonic scales) or worst-rated (*hedonic qualities-identity*) modality might determine the judgment of the multimodal system. However taking the maximum or minimum judgment as a predictor into a regression function did not produce a higher accuracy (s. Table3).

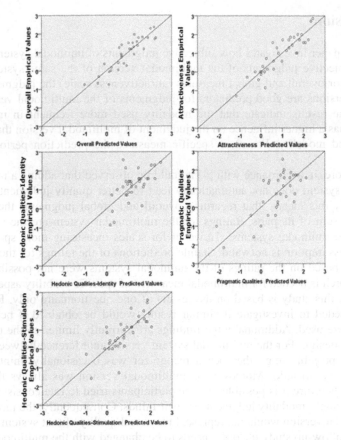

Fig. 2. Scatter plots for predicted values (after 10 fold cross validation) and empirical values

Table 3. Results of multiple linear regression analysis using the maximum or minimum judgement as predictor

Scale	Max (Touch, Speech)				R²	RMSE	F (df)
	B	SE B	β	t(df)			
Pragmatic Qualities	1.002	.190	.688	5.37* (32)	.474	.823	28.81* (1,32)
Hedonic Qualities Stimulation	.944	.189	.657	5.01* (33)	.432	.705	25.09* (1,33)
Hedonic Qualities Identity	1.006	.143	.774	7.01* (33)	.598	.509	49.19* (1,33)
Scale	Min (Touch, Speech)				R²	RMSE	F (df)
	B	SE B	β	t (df)			
Hedonic Qualities Identity	.560	.117	.640	4.79* (33)	.410	.617	22.95* (1,33)

4 Discussion

The current paper investigates how subjective judgments of unimodal system versions relate to subjective judgments of the multimodal version of the same system. It was shown that for overall and global measures (attractiveness scale) the judgments of the unimodal versions are good predictors for judgments of the multimodal version. Additionally the results indicate that the modality used more frequent in multimodal interaction has a higher influence on the judgment of multimodal version than the less frequent used modality. For more specific measures the prediction performance is lower.

Furthermore, in accordance with [4] it could be observed that adding a modality to a unimodal system does not automatically lead to better quality judgments. For the present study this means, that regarding overall and global judgments the whole is actually the sum of its parts. Ratings for the multimodal system are the sum of the ratings of the unimodal systems. However for scales measuring more specific constructs this assumption is not valid: Stabile predictions of the ratings for the multimodal systems based on the ratings of the unimodal systems were not possible. Hence further research is needed for multimodal measures of specific usability aspects.

Moreover this study is based on the results of one questionnaire only. Further research is needed to investigate if similar results would be obtained if performance measures were used. Additionally the findings are currently limited to the tested system and test design. For the multimodal system version interference between the modalities was possible (e.g.: the speech recognizer was occasionally unintentionally switched on by off-talk). Moreover the multimodal version was always the system tested last. Therefore it is possible that the participants tried to rate consistently, adding up their single-modality judgments in their minds. Consequently, the judgments of the multimodal version would not represent the actual quality of that system.

So, in a follow-up study the order needs to be changed with the multimodal system version tested first.

References

1. Chen, F.: Designing Human Interface in Speech Technology. Springer, New York (2005)
2. Baddeley, A.D., Hitch, G.J.: Working memory. In: Bower, G. (ed.) The psychology of learning and motivation, pp. 47–89. Academic Press, New York (1974)
3. Wickens, C.D.: Multiple resources and performance prediction. Theoretical Issues in Ergonomics Science 3, 159–177 (2002)
4. Oviatt, S.L.: Ten myths of multimodal interaction. Communications of the ACM 42(11), 576–583 (1999)
5. Schomaker, L., Nijtmans, J., Camurri, A., Lavagetto, F., Morasso, P., Benoît, C., Guiard-Marigny, T., Le Goff, B., Robert-Ribes, J., Adjoudani, A., Defée, I., Münch, S., Hartung, K., Blauert, J.: A Taxonomy of Multimodal Interaction in the Human Information Processing System. A Report of the ESPRIT Project 8579 MIAMI. NICI, Nijmegen (1995)
6. Schnotz, W., Bannert, M., Seufert, T.: Towards an integrative view of text and picture comprehension: Visualization effects on the construction of mental models. In: Otero, J., Graesser, A., Leon, J.A. (eds.) The Psychology of Science Text Comprehension., pp. 385–416. Erlbaum, Mahwah (2002)

7. Kirakowski, J.: The software usability measurement inventory: background and usage. In: Jordan, P. (ed.) Usability Evaluation in Industry, pp. 169–177. Taylor & Francis, London (1996)
8. Hone, K.S., Graham, R.: Towards a tool for the Subjective Assessment of Speech System Interfaces (SASSI). Nat. Lang. Eng. 6(3-4), 287–303 (2000)
9. Beringer, N., Kartal, U., Louka, K., Schiel, F., Türk, U.: PROMISE: A Procedure for Multimodal Interactive System Evaluation. In: Procs of the Workshop Multimodal Resources and Multimodal Systems Evaluation, Las Palmas, Gran Canaria, Spain, pp. 77–80 (2002)
10. Hassenzahl, M., Burmester, M., Koller, F.: AttrakDiff: Ein Fragebogen zur Messung wahrge-nommener hedonischer und pragmatischer Qualität. In: Ziegler, J., Szwillus, G. (eds.) Mensch & Computer 2003, Interaktion in Bewegung, pp. 187–196. B.G. Teubner, Leipzig (2003)

Part II

Gesture, Eyes Movement and Expression Recognition

An Open Source Framework for Real-Time, Incremental, Static and Dynamic Hand Gesture Learning and Recognition

Todd C. Alexander[1], Hassan S. Ahmed[2], and Georgios C. Anagnostopoulos[1]

[1] Electrical and Computer Engineering,
Florida Institute of Technology,
Melbourne, Florida USA
talexand@fit.edu, georgio@fit.edu
[2] Electrical Engineering, University of Miami,
Miami, Florida USA
h.ahmed@umiami.edu

Abstract. Real-time, static and dynamic hand gesture learning and recognition makes it possible to have computers recognize hand gestures naturally. This creates endless possibilities in the way humans can interact with computers, allowing a human hand to be a peripheral by itself. The software framework developed provides a lightweight, robust, and practical application programming interface that helps further research in the area of human-computer interaction. Approaches that have proven in analogous areas such as speech and handwriting recognition were applied to static and dynamic hand gestures. A semi-supervised Fuzzy ARTMAP neural network was used for incremental online learning and recognition of static gestures; and, Hidden Markov models for online recognition of dynamic gestures. A simple anticipatory method was implemented for determining when to update key frames allowing the framework to work with dynamic backgrounds.

Keywords: Motion detection, hand tracking, real-time gesture recognition, software framework, FAST corner detection, ART Neural Networks.

1 Introduction

User experience in human-computer interaction can be dramatically improved by allowing users to interact in more natural and intuitive ways. The problem is that there is no single efficient, robust, and inexpensive solution to recognize static and dynamic hand gestures, consequently interfaces maybe be less natural or intuitive.

Visualizing and interpreting hand gestures the way humans are able to, will provide many new ways to interact with computers. Already applications such as sign language recognition [1] and [2], touch-less computer interaction [3] and [4], and behavior understanding [5] have demonstrated why bare hand computer interaction plays an important role in emerging consumer electronics.

Solutions used in the past to improve tracking and recognition include using gloves or markers [6], or using more expensive hardware such as infrared cameras [7].

J.A. Jacko (Ed.): Human-Computer Interaction, Part II, HCII 2009, LNCS 5611, pp. 123–130, 2009.
© Springer-Verlag Berlin Heidelberg 2009

Gloves and markers require setup and mandatory calibration, resulting in a less natural user experience. Infrared cameras improve the robustness in regard to dynamic backgrounds; however, the costs of these cameras prevent them from being widely adopted.

The Gestur framework developed in this research provides a foundation for creating new, and improving existing, applications that depend on hand gesture recognition, by providing a framework that depends on minimal hardware and software resources, and the ability to operate in a vast range of conditions.

In the rest of the paper, we examine the Gestur framework and its components in Section 2. Finally, Section 3 provides a summary of our work and a discussion about some of Gestur's key characteristics.

2 Gestur

Gestur is an open-source software framework designed and developed for software developers wishing to incorporate static and dynamic hand gesture recognition into their applications. Developers have access to the framework via its application programming interface, which provides abstractions for capture, calibrating, tracking, training, and classification in hand gesture recognition. Unlike previous libraries and toolkits [8] and [9], Gestur is primarily focused on real-time hand gesture recognition.

2.1 Software Architecture

Gestur is written in the C# programming language [10] and runs on the Microsoft.NET framework utilizing the DirectShow API [11]. DirectShow exists as an unmanaged[1] framework thus in order to utilize it an unofficial managed wrapper[2] called DirectShow.net [12] was employed. The main children namespaces outlined in Fig. 1 are:

- Capture: works closely with DirectShow to allow any video capture device that supports the Windows Driver Model to be used as an input device.
- Calibration: retrieves parameters that other framework components need to perform their job reliably and efficiently—for e.g. the finger tip radius to use in FAST corner detection.
- Tracking: searches and keeps track of objects of interest, namely the hand.
- Learning: allows training the framework for subsequent recognition and classification.
- Utility: provides many image processing methods to assist other objects in the framework.

The majority of components present in Gestur are polymorphic in design allowing programmers to replace any component with an alternative. The framework is also fully open source making code distribution, review, and issue tracking convenient for interested developers.

---

[1] Gestur runs on Microsoft.NET—a managed framework, hence memory management is done automatically. DirectShow is written in native C++ which does not provide any garbage collection.

[2] DirectShow.net facilitates the interoperability between the managed and unmanaged domains.

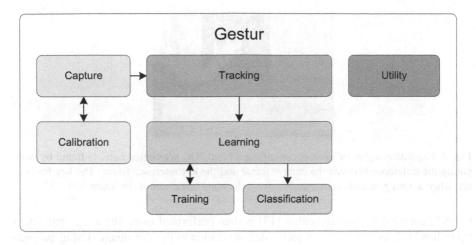

Fig. 1. Software architecture of the Gestur framework. Main components interact with each other as indicated by the arrows. Utility provides general purpose image processing methods.

2.2 Hand Detection

Human beings are constantly in motion, and when about to perform a static or dynamic gesture some degree of motion is expected. Using a two frame difference, as illustrated in Fig. 2, the areas containing motion can be easily identified. The result is a binary image containing potential areas where the hand may be located, called candidate regions of interest.

Fig. 2. Example of a previous, current, and the two-frame difference of the previous and current in A, B, and C, respectively. The two-frame difference identifies regions in which motion occurred.

The amount of motion being experienced also dictates, when the key/reference frame should be updated. This approach allows the framework to anticipate when to expect a hand gesture. The setting of this reference frame is very important for obtaining an outline of the hand as in Fig. 3.

Every candidate region presented by the two-frame difference is investigated as a number of sub-images[3] as shown in Fig. 3. The Fast Accelerated Segment Test

---

[3] The dimensions used for each sub-image is determined during calibration.

Fig. 3. Candidate region of interest containing a hand. The segmented hand is found by computing the difference between the current frame and the key/reference frame. The key frame is set, when a hand gesture is anticipated to avoid the hand being part of the frame.

(FAST) corner detection algorithm [13] is then performed using the suggested finger tip radius [14], as well as the object's size in relation to the sub-image. Using geometric constraints of a typical hand [15], feedback is provided on whether or not the sub-image contains a hand.

2.3 Static Gestures

Once the hand has been detected and tracked, a variety of elementary, easy to compute, geometric features are extracted to determine whether a gesture is being performed (gesture detection) and, finally, to recognize the type of gesture. The rotation-, translation-, scale-, and reflection-invariance of these features was mandated to ensure robust and computationally efficient recognition. The features used with the default classifier are the number of fingers and the angle formed between the centroid of the finger tips and the forearm, illustrated as A in Fig. 4.

Static gestures are learned and, subsequently, recognized by a semi-supervised Fuzzy ARTMAP (ssFAM) neural network [16-18]. ssFAM is a neural network architecture, which is built upon Grossberg's Adaptive Resonance Theory (ART). It has the ability to learn associations between a set of input patterns and their respective class/label, which then can be utilized for classification purposes. The ssFAM network clusters training patterns into categories, whose geometrical representations are hyper-rectangles embedded in the feature space. Each time a test pattern is presented a similarity measure is computed to determine, which of the discovered categories it belongs too. Via this mechanism, it also has the ability to discover, if completely new information is being presented to the network. This is the case, when a given test pattern does not fit the characteristics of any of the categories that the system has learned so far. This mechanism is useful in our application so that irrelevant or ambiguous gestures are appropriately ignored.

An additional, important quality of ssFAM (and of ART-based classifiers) is the fact that the network is able to learn incrementally and, therefore, is ideal for online learning tasks. In our framework of gesture recognition this is a highly desirable feature, as it will allow our system to add new gestures or to accumulate additional knowledge about already learned gestures in an online fashion.

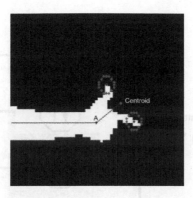

Fig. 4. Features used for classifying static gestures: number of finger tips, and the angle, A, between the centroid of the finger tips and the forearm. These features are rotation-, translation-, scale-, and reflection-invariant.

Finally, the fact that ssFAM is capable of organizing its acquired knowledge by forming categories in a semi-supervised manner, allows the system to generalize well, when attempting to learn gestures.

2.4 Dynamic Gestures

The movement of the hand conveys important information about the message users are trying to communicate. This information is represented by the moving hand's trajectory, which can be expressed as a stream of primitive movements. Because of the success of Hidden Markov Models (HMM) in applied recognition of symbol sequences [19], HMMs comprise the default classifier used in Gestur for dynamic hand gesture recognition.

After the hand is detected, the center of the palm is computed and tracked. The trajectory is sampled from the beginning of the gesture until its end and a sequence of motion primitives is established, as shown in Fig. 5. This stream is fed to a bank of HMMs, where the most likely dynamic gesture is labeled as the sequence of primitives that best fit the model.

The main challenge with classifying dynamic gestures this way is accurately identifying the beginning and end of the gesture. In Gestur, the beginning is indicated, when a hand containing a recognized static gesture is present and has moved some minimum distance. The end of the gesture is marked, when the hand comes to a stop.

Furthermore, on-line recognition of dynamic hand gestures via HMMs was made possible through utilization of an optimized version of the Viterbi algorithm [20]. Additionally, movement can only be in one of eight directions—up, down, left, right or a combination of vertical and horizontal—hence this architecture remains efficient and facilitates incremental learning [21], since new gestures are often extensions of already learned models.

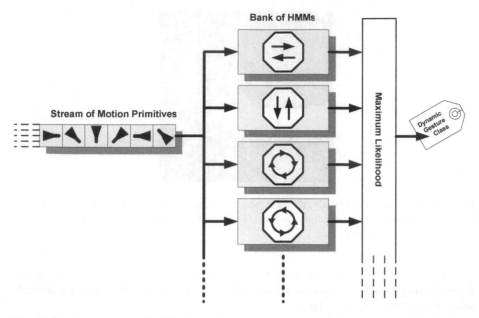

Fig. 5. Dynamic gesture classification subsystem. A stream of simple motion primitives is forwarded to a bank of HMMs, each of which is specialized to recognize a specific dynamic gesture. The dynamic gesture is labeled according to the model reporting the maximum likelihood of having generated the observed sequence.

3   Discussion

Gestur provides an easy way for any software developer to quickly develop event driven applications involving hand gesture recognition. It provides robust detection and tracking in almost every situation in the home, office, conference room, etc. with ample light present. The framework is also resilient to background changes through anticipatory key frame updating. Gestur utilizes the DirectShow API to allow any image processing operations supported by the hardware to be performed on the hardware instead of having to implement such operations in software.

As a result we have been able to successfully use Gestur to produce an application that controls Microsoft® PowerPoint presentations, whereby users indicate to the computer the direction to advance slides, terminate a presentation, or any other action initially configured. This application also shows how static and dynamic gestures can replace computer events traditionally triggered through the use of hands, a keyboard, and a mouse. In this application we were able to classify six static, and five dynamic gestures, with an overall recognition rate of 76%.

Furthermore, Gestur was designed and developed with the goal of providing a lightweight, practical, and robust framework to further research in the area of hand gesture recognition. The polymorphic design of the framework allows users to experiment with different components making it possible to study various machine learning techniques as they relate to online static and dynamic hand gesture recognition.

Acknowledgements

The authors would like to thank the National Science Foundation for funding much of the fundamental research through Grant No., 0647018 and 0647120. Also, Todd Alexander wishes to acknowledge partial support by the National Science Foundation under Grant No. 0717674. Any opinions, findings, and conclusions or recommendations expressed in this material are those of the author(s) and do not necessarily reflect the views of the National Science Foundation.

References

1. Vogler, C., Metaxas, D.: A framework for recognizing the simultaneous aspects of american sign language. Computer Vision and Image Understanding 81, 358–384 (2001)
2. Fang, G., Gao, W., Ma, J.: Signer-independent sign language recognition based on SOFM/HMM, Recognition, Analysis, and Tracking of Faces and Gestures in Real-Time Systems, 2001. In: Proceedings of the IEEE ICCV Workshop on RATFG in RTS, p. 90 (2001)
3. von Hardenberg, C., Berard, F.: Bare-hand human-computer interaction. In: Proceedings of the 2001 workshop on Perceptive user interfaces, pp. 1–8 (2001)
4. Rainer, J.M.: Fast hand gesture recognition for real-time teleconferencing applications. In: International Workshop on Recognition, Analysis and Tracking of Faces and Gestures in Real-time Systems, pp. 133–140 (2001)
5. McAllister, G., McKenna, S.J., Ricketts, I.W.: Hand tracking for behaviour understanding. Image Vision Computing 20, 827–840 (2002)
6. Keskin, C., Erkan, A., Akarun, L.: Real time hand tracking and 3d gesture recognition for interactive interfaces using hmm. In: Kaynak, O., Alpaydın, E., Oja, E., Xu, L. (eds.) ICANN 2003 and ICONIP 2003. LNCS, vol. 2714. Springer, Heidelberg (2003)
7. Breuer, P., Eckes, C., Muller, S.: Hand Gesture Recognition with a Novel IR Time-of-Flight Range Camera—A Pilot Study. In: Gagalowicz, A., Philips, W. (eds.) MIRAGE 2007. LNCS, vol. 4418, pp. 247–260. Springer, Heidelberg (2007)
8. Lyons, K., Brashear, H., Westeyn, T., Kim, J., Starner, T.: GART: The gesture and activity recognition toolkit. In: Jacko, J.A. (ed.) HCI 2007. LNCS, vol. 4552, pp. 718–727. Springer, Heidelberg (2007)
9. Westeyn, T., Brashear, H., Atrash, A., Starner, T.: Georgia tech gesture toolkit: supporting experiments in gesture recognition. In: Proceedings of the 5th international Conference on Multimodal interfaces. ICMI 2003, pp. 85–92. ACM, New York (2003)
10. Hejlsberg, A., Wiltamuth, S., Golde, P.: C# Language Specifcation. Addison-Wesley Longman Publishing Co., Inc., Boston (2003)
11. Microsoft DirectShow,
    http://msdn.microsoft.com/en-us/library/ms783323VS.85.aspx
12. DirectShow.net Library, http://directshownet.sourceforge.net/
13. Alkaabi, S., Deravi, F.: Candidate pruning for fast corner detection. Electronics Letters 40, 18–19 (2004)
14. Angel, E., Morrison, D.: Speeding up bresenham's algorithm. IEEE Computer Graphics and Applications 11, 16–17 (1991)
15. Jerde, T., Soechting, J., Flanders, M.: Biological constraints simplify the recognition of hand shapes. IEEE Transactions on Biomedical Engineering 50, 265–269 (2003)

16. Grossberg, S.: Adaptive pattern classification and universal recoding, II: feedback, expectation, olfaction and illusions. Biological Cybernetics 23, 187–202 (1976)
17. Anagnostopoulos, G., Georgiopoulos, M., Verzi, S., Heileman, G.: Reducing generalization error and category proliferation in ellipsoid ARTMAP via tunable misclassification error tolerance: Boosted ellipsoid ARTMAP. In: Proc. IEEE-INNS-ENNS Int'l Joint Conf. Neural Networks (IJCNN 2002), vol. 3, pp. 2650–2655 (2002)
18. Anagnostopoulos, G., Bharadwaj, M., Georgiopoulos, M., Verzi, S., Heileman, G.: Exemplar-based pattern recognition via semi-supervised learning. In: Proceedings of the International Joint Conference on Neural Networks, vol. 4, pp. 2782–2787 (2003)
19. Makhoul, J., Starner, T., Schwartz, R., Chou, G.: On-line cursive handwriting recognition using hidden Markov models and statistical grammars. In: Proceedings of the Workshop on Human Language Technology, Human Language Technology Conference, Plainsboro, NJ, March 08 - 11, 1994, pp. 432–436. Association for Computational Linguistics, Morristown (1994)
20. Zen, H., Tokuda, K., Kitamura, T.: A viterbi algorithm for trajectory model derived from HMM with explicity relationship between static and dynamic features. In: Proceedings of ICASSP 2004, pp. 837–840 (2004)
21. Cavalin, P., Sabourin, R., Suen, C., Britto, A.: Evaluation of incremental learning algorithms for HMM in the recognition of alphanumeric characters. Pattern Recognition (2008)

Gesture-Controlled User Input to Complete Questionnaires on Wrist-Worn Watches

Oliver Amft[1,2], Roman Amstutz[1,3], Asim Smailagic[3], Dan Siewiorek[3], and Gerhard Tröster[1]

[1]Wearable Computing Lab., ETH Zurich, CH-8092 Zurich, Switzerland
[2]Signal Processing Systems, TU Einhoven, 5600 MB Einhoven, The Netherlands
[3]Carnegie Mellon University, Pittsburgh, PA 15213, USA
{amft,troester}@ife.ee.ethz.ch, {asim,dps}@cs.cmu.edu

Abstract. The aim of this work was to investigate arm gestures as an alternative input modality for wrist-worn watches. In particular we implemented a gesture recognition system and questionnaire interface into a watch prototype. We analyzed the wearer's effort and learning performance to use the gesture interface and compared their performance to a classical button-based solution. Moreover we evaluated the system performance to spot wearer gestures and the system responsiveness. Our wearer study showed that the watch achieved a recognition accuracy of more than 90%. Completion times showed a clear decrease from 3 min in the first repetition to 1 min, 49 sec in the last one. Similarly, variance of completion times between wearers decreased during repetitions. Completion time using the button interface was 36 sec. Ratings of physical and concentration effort decreased during the study. Our results confirm that wearer training state is rather reflected in completion time than recognition performance.

Keywords: gesture spotting, activity recognition, eWatch, user evaluation.

1 Introduction

Gesture-based interfaces have been proposed as alternate modality for controlling stationary computers, e.g. to navigate in office applications and play immersive console games. In contrast to their classic interpretation to support conversation, gestures are understood in this area as directed body movements, primarily of arms and hands, to interact with computers. Gesture-based interfaces can enrich and diversify interaction options as in gaming. Moreover, they are vital for computer access by handicapped, such as enabled by sign language interfaces, and for further applications and environments where traditional computer interaction methods are not acceptable.

Mobile systems and devices are a primary field concern for such alternate interaction solutions. While the above cited stationary applications demonstrate the applicability of directed gestures for interaction, future mobile solutions could

J.A. Jacko (Ed.): Human-Computer Interaction, Part II, HCII 2009, LNCS 5611, pp. 131–140, 2009.

profit from deployment of gesture-based interfaces in particular. Currently, mobile systems lack solutions that minimize user attention or support access for users with specific interaction needs. Hence, gestures that are directly sensed and recognized by a mobile or wearable device are of common interest for numerous applications.

In this work, we investigate gesture-based interaction using a wrist-worn watch device. We consider gestures as an intuitive modality, especially for watches, and potentially feasible for wearers that cannot operate tiny watch buttons. To this end, it is essential to evaluate the wearer's performance and convenience while operating such an interface. Moreover, the integration of gesture interfaces into a watch device has not been previously evaluated. Resource constraints of wrist-worn watch devices impose challenging restrictions regarding processing complexity for embedding a gesture recognition solution into watch devices.

Consequently, this paper provides the following contributions:

1. We present a prototype of an intelligent wrist-worn watch, the eWatch, and demonstrate that a recognition procedure particularly designed for gesture spotting, can be embedded into this device. The recognition procedure consists of two stages to spot potential gestures in continuous acceleration data, and classify the type of gesture. Feasibility of this recognition procedure was assessed by an analysis of the implementation requirements.
2. We present a user study evaluating the wearer's performance in executing gestures to complete a questionnaire that was implemented on the watch as well. In particular, we investigated recognition accuracy and wearer learning effects during several repetitions of completing the questionnaire. Moreover, we compared the time required to complete the questionnaire using the gesture interface to a button interface.

As this work evaluates gesture-based interaction regarding both, technical feasibility and user performance, it provides an novel insight into the advantages and limitations of gesture interfaces. We believe that these results are generally relevant for gesture-operated mobile systems.

Section 2 discusses related works and approaches to develop intelligent watches, gesture-operated mobile devices, and recognition procedures for gesture spotting. Subsequently, Sections 3 and 4 briefly present the watch system and the embedded gesture recognition procedure, respectively. The user study and evaluation results are presented in Section 5. Section 6 concludes on the results of this work.

2   Related Work

Wrist-worn watches have been proposed as truly wearable processing units. A pioneering development was the IBM Linux Watch [1]. Besides time measurement, various additional applications of wristwatches have been identified and brought to commercial success. This includes sports and fitness monitoring and support watches as, e.g. realized by Polar (www.polar.fi/en/) and Suunto (www.suunto.com). With the Smart Personal Object Technology(SPOT)[2], consumer watches become broadcast news receivers. Similarly, wristwatches have been used as a mobile phone (www.vanderled.com) or for GPS-navigation (www.mainnav.com). Besides the frequent button-based control, wristwatches have been equipped with touch-sensitive displays (www.tissot.ch) to improve interaction. No related work was identified that investigated gesture-based interaction for wristwatches as it is proposed in this paper.

Gesture recognition has been investigated for various applications in areas, such as activity recognition and behavior inference [3,4,5], immersive gaming [6,7], and many forms of computer interaction. In this last category, systems have been proposed to replace classical computer input modalities. A review on the various applications was compiled by Mitra and Acharya [8]. In this work, we focus our discussion on related approaches in gesture-operated mobile devices. Moreover, we provide a coarse overview on established gesture recognition and spotting techniques.

2.1 Gesture-Operated Mobile Devices

Gesture spotting and recognition based on body-worn sensors has primarily used accelerometers to identify body movement patterns. These sensors are found in many current mobile phones. However, due to the constraint processing environment of watches, their interfaces had classically been restricted to simple button-based solutions. Consequently, gesture interfaces for watches have not been extensively investigated.

Recent investigations started to address the implementation challenge of gesture interfaces onto mobile devices, beyond simple device turning moves. Kallio et al. [9] presented an application using acceleration sensors embedded in a remote control to manage home appliances. Their work was focused on confirming the feasibility for classifying different gestures using hidden Markov models (HMMs). Recently, Kratz and Ballagas [10] presented a pervasive game that relied on gestures as input recognized on mobile phones.

2.2 Gesture Spotting

Various algorithms have been proposed for spotting and classifying gestures. While the first task relates to the identification of gestures in a continuous stream of sensor data, the second task deals with the discrimination of particular gesture types. The recognition procedure must be capable of excluding non-relevant gestures and movements. For the spotting task various methods have been presented that cope with the identification problem, e.g. [11,12,5]. We deploy in this work an approach related to the work of Lee and Kim [11]. The authors have used the Viterbi algorithm to preselect relevant gestures. For the classification task, many works have proposed HMMs, e.g. [11,5]. For the implementation presented this work we followed this approach by deriving individual HMMs for each gesture class and used a threshold model to discriminate non-relevant movements.

3 Watch System and Embedded Questionnaire

We used in this investigation an intelligent watch prototype, the eWatch. Figure 1 shows the device running a questionnaire application. The eWatch consists of a ARM7 processor without float-point unit, running with up to 80 MHz. A detailed description of the system architecture can be found in [13]. In this work, we used the MEMS 3-axes accelerometer that is embedded in the eWatch, to sense acceleration of the wearer's arm and supply the recognition procedure with sensor data.

Fig. 1. eWatch prototype running a questionnaire application

The questionnaire was chosen as an evaluation and test application to verify that the gesture recognition procedure achieves an user-acceptable recognition rate. Moreover, we used the questionnaire to stimulate the wearer to perform alternating gestures during the interface evaluation in Section 5.

The questionnaire application was designed to display a question on the left side of the watch screen and provides four answer options on the right side to choose from. In order to respond to the question, the wearer had to perform at least one "select" gesture for each question. This gesture would choose the highlighted answer and advance to the next question dialog. When the wearer intended to choose a different answer than the currently selected one, "scroll-up" and "scroll-down" gestures could be used to navigate between possible answers. Figure 2 shows the individual gestures considered in this evaluation. The "scroll-up" and "scroll-down" gestures can be described as outward and inward (towards the trunk) rotation movements of the arm. The "select" gesture consisted of raising and lowering the arm two times.

Fig. 2. Gestures used to operate the eWatch device: "scroll-up", "scroll-down", and "select"

These gestures were selected empirically out of 13 different gestures repeatedly performed by nine test persons. The gestures were chosen based on initial tests of the recognition procedure, as detailed in Section 4 below, and according to qualitative feedback of the test persons. The reliable spotting and classification were however given priority, since we considered an accurate operation as most essential design goal.

Although related gesture recognition evaluations considered far larger gesture sets successfully, e.g. in the work of Lee and Kim [11], we expected that additional gesture options would be confusing for the wearer. In addition, a larger set of gestures may require longer training times for the user.

4 Watch-Based Gesture Spotting

In order to evaluate gesture-based interaction for a wristwatch, we developed and implemented a recognition procedure into the eWatch device. We briefly summarize the design and implementation results here, which indicate the feasibility of the gesture recognition approach.

4.1 Gesture Recognition Procedure

The recognition procedure consists of two distinct stages: the spotting of relevant gestures that are used to operate the questionnaire, and the classification of these gestures. The first stage has to efficiently process the continuous stream of sensor data and identify the gestures embedded in arbitrary other movements. Due to this search, this task can have a major influence on the processing requirements. The second stage evaluates the selected gestures and categorizes them according to individual pattern models. The deployed procedure is briefly summarized below.

For the spotting task in this work, we extracted the dominating acceleration axis, defined as the axis with the largest amplitude variation within the last five sampling points. The derivative of this acceleration was used in combination with a fixed sliding window to spot gestures. Individual discrete left-right HMMs for each gesture were manually constructed, with six states for the scroll gestures, nine states for the select gesture. A code-book of 13 symbols was used to represent the derivative amplitude in strong/low increase/decrease for all acceleration axes and rest, for small amplitudes. The Viterbi algorithm was used to calculate the most probable state transition sequence for the current sliding window. The end of a gesture was detected if the end state in an HMM was reached in the current window. Using this end-point, the corresponding gesture begin was determined. Based on these preselected gestures, a HMM-based classification was applied. A gesture was classified to the HMM achieving the maximum likelihood value. Moreover, the gesture was retained only if the likelihood value exceeded that of a threshold HMM. The threshold HMM was derived according to [11]. If more than one gesture was detected in one sliding window, the one with larger likelihood was retained.

4.2   Watch Implementation

Our implementation of the gesture recognition procedure used the eWatch base system for managing hardware components. A CPU clock of 65 MHz was used. Acceleration data was sampled at 20 Hz. The HMMs required a total memory of approximately 3.75 KB.

Our analysis showed a processing time below 1 ms for each HMM at a sliding window size of 30 samples. The total gesture recognition delay was below 2.7 ms for the entire procedure. This delay remains far below delays that could be noticed by the user. These results confirm the applicability of the recognition method.

Our empirical analysis of the gesture recognition performance showed that the "scroll-down" gesture perturbed the overall recognition performance. By restricting the interface to "scroll-up" and "select" gestures, we improved robustness, while simplifying the interface. The questionnaire application was equipped with a wrap-around feature, in order to select each answer option by just using "scroll-up". Our subsequent user evaluation, as detailed below, confirmed that this choice did not restrict the users in operating the application.

5   User Evaluation of Gesture and Button Interfaces

We conducted a user study to evaluate the feasibility of the gesture-operated interface and to assess the user's performance, perception, and comfort using a gesture interface. In particular, we investigated recognition accuracy and wearer learning effects during several repetitions of completing the questionnaire. Finally, we compared the time required to complete the questionnaire using the gesture interface to a classic button interface.

5.1   Study Methodology

Ten students were recruited to wear the eWatch and complete the questionnaire in four repetitions. Five users from non-technical background were included in order to analyze whether expertise with technical systems would influence performance or ratings.

The users performed the evaluation individually. Initially, they watched a training video demonstrating the handling of the watch and the gestures. If they had further questions, these were resolved afterwards. Subsequently, the users attached the watch and performed four repetitions of a questionnaire asking for eight responses. This questionnaire was designed to indicate a particular answer option for each question, which the users were asked to select. With this protocol, the number of gestures performed by each user was maintained comparable.

For each repetition of the questionnaire the completion time was measured. Each gesture execution, conducted gesture, and result was logged by an observer. In addition, the recording sessions were videotaped using a video camera installed in the experiment room. The camera was positioned over the head of the users at the side of the arm, where the watch was worn. In this way, the video captured scene, gestures performed by the user, as well as the response shown at the watch screen when users turned the watch to observe the result. This video was later used as a backup for the experiment observer to count correct gesture performances.

After each repetition users completed an intermediate paper-based assessment questionnaire, assessing their qualitative judgment of convenience to use the system, rating their personal performance, physical effort, concentration effort, and performance of the system. After all repetitions were completed, the users completed additional assessment questions. These questions were intended to capture general impressions of the gesture interface.

Physical effort was assessed by asking the question: "How tired are you from performing the gestures?". A visual analog scale (VAS) was used with 1 (not tired at all) to 10 (very tired). Concentration effort was assessed with the question: "How much did you have to think about how the gesture has to be performed?". A VAS with 1 (not at all) and 10 (very much) was used.

After all repetitions using the gesture interface, the users were asked to complete the same watch questionnaire application once more using an eWatch with a button interface. Finally, the users were asked to rate the gesture and button-based interfaces based on their experience made in the evaluation.

5.2   User Study Results

The recognition accuracy was evaluated by comparing the user-performed gestures and reactions to the eWatch screen feedback. Figure 3 shows the average accuracies for each questionnaire repetition and both gestures: "scroll-up" and "select". Accuracy was derived here as the ratio between recognized and total performed gestures. From these average accuracy results, no clear learning effect

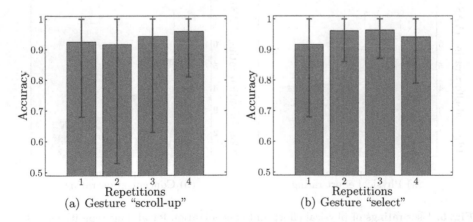

(a) Gesture "scroll-up"   (b) Gesture "select"

Fig. 3. Average recognition accuracies for all four repetitions of the study using the gesture interface. Error bars indicate minimum and maximum recognition performances individual users.

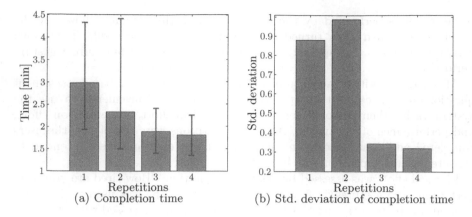

Fig. 4. Average user completion times for all four repetitions of the study using the gesture interface. Error bars indicate minimum and maximum times for individual users.

can be observed. Large initial accuracies above 90% indicate that the initial the user training, before starting the evaluation allowed the users to acquire a good skill in performing the gestures. Overall, the accuracies remained above 90% for all repetitions, while individual performances for "scroll-up" increased during the last three repetitions. The drop in the performance for "select" might have been caused by the fact that this gesture required more effort to be performed. Consequently, users may have become tired.

A clear trend can be observed from the questionnaire completion times shown in Figure 4. Both absolute time required, as well as the std. deviation for all

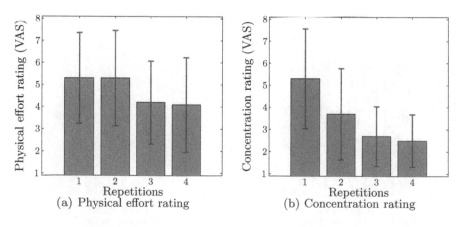

Fig. 5. User ratings of physical effort and concentration for all four repetitions of the study using the gesture interface. Error bars indicate std. deviations for individual users. The ratings were obtained using a VAS from 1 (low effort) to 10 (high effort). See Section 5 for a detailed description.

users decreased during the study, reaching a minimum in the last repetition. This result shows that completion time can indicate user accommodation to the gesture interface and improved training state.

Furthermore, we assessed the completion time for the button interface. Average completion time was here $\sim$36 sec, with a std. deviation of $\sim$2.5 sec. In comparison to the last repetition using the gesture interface, which was performed immediately beforehand, a three times lower completion time can be observed. As the gesture recognition and watch reaction time was confirmed to be not noticeable to the user, this difference can be entirely attributed to time required to perform the gestures.

Figure 5 shows the results from the user ratings on VAS between 1 (low effort) to 10 (high effort). The average ratings of physical effort and concentration decreased over all repetitions. Only three users reported an constant or increasing physical effort to perform the gestures. These results support our assumption of an improvement in the user training state during the repetitions.

6   Discussion and Conclusions

Our investigation confirmed that a gesture interface deployed into a watch device is a feasible approach to replace classic button-style interaction. The evaluations performed in this work indicate that a gesture interface requires training, even for a very limited number of gestures. Consequently even after four repetitions of the questionnaire application considered in this work, we observed an improvement in the user performance.

This user training state was not clearly reflected in an improvement of gesture recognition accuracy. However, the completion time needed to achieve the task was found in this study to be directly related to the training. Hence, with improved training state users required less time to perform the gestures. This improved training state was confirmed by user ratings of required physical effort and concentration on the task. Both metrics decreased during repetitions of the questionnaire application.

Our gesture-based interaction concept did not meet the low completion times of a comparable button-based solution. This observation was confirmed by final user ratings for a personally preferred interface. Nine out of ten users preferred the button-based interface. While our study was successful to evaluate the gesture interface itself, we expect that this disadvantageous rating for the gesture-based interaction can be explained by the questionnaire task and setting chosen for this investigation. Users were asked to perform the task, without further constraints in an isolated lab environment. Although this was a useful methodology for this evaluation stage, we expect that gesture-based interaction, can be a very vital alternative in particular applications and contexts. Several potential applications exist, in which buttons cannot be used, including interaction for handicapped individuals that cannot use small buttons as well as interaction in work environments, where the worker cannot use hands or wears gloves. These vital application areas and user groups should be considered further, based on the successful results obtained in this work.

References

1. Narayanaswami, C., Raghunath, M., Kamijoh, N., Inoue, T.: What would you do with a hundred mips on your wrist? Technical Report RC 22057 (98634), IBM Research (January 2001)
2. Goldstein, H.: A dog named spot (smart personal objects technology watch). IEEE Spectrum 41(1), 72–73 (2004)
3. Ivanov, Y., Bobick, A.: Recognition of visual activities and interactions by stochastic parsing. IEEE Transactions on Pattern Analysis and Machine Intelligence 22(8), 852–872 (2000)
4. Kahol, K., Tripathi, K., Panchanathan, S.: Documenting motion sequences with a personalized annotation system. IEEE Multimedia 13(1), 37–45 (2006)
5. Junker, H., Amft, O., Lukowicz, P., Tröster, G.: Gesture spotting with body-worn inertial sensors to detect user activities. Pattern Recognition 41(6), 2010–2024 (2008)
6. Bannach, D., Amft, O., Kunze, K.S., Heinz, E.A., Tröster, G., Lukowicz, P.: Waving real hand gestures recorded by wearable motion sensors to a virtual car and driver in a mixed-reality parking game. In: Blair, A., Cho, S.B., Lucas, S.M. (eds.) CIG 2007: Proceedings of the 2nd IEEE Symposium on Computational Intelligence and Games, April 2007, pp. 32–39. IEEE Press, Los Alamitos (2007)
7. Schlömer, T., Poppinga, B., Henze, N., Boll, S.: Gesture recognition with a wii controller. In: TEI 2008: Proceedings of the 2nd international conference on Tangible and embedded interaction, pp. 11–14. ACM, New York (2008)
8. Mitra, S., Acharya, T.: Gesture recognition: A survey. IEEE Transactions on Systems, Man, and Cybernetics, Part C: Applications and Reviews 37(3), 311–324 (2007)
9. Kallio, S., Kela, J., Korpipää, P., Mäntyjärvi, J.: User independent gesture interaction for small handheld devices. International Journal of Pattern Recognition and Artificial Intelligence 20(4), 505–524 (2006)
10. Kratz, S., Ballagas, R.: Gesture recognition using motion estimation on mobile phones. In: PERMID 2007: Proceedings of the 3rd International Workshop on Pervasive Mobile Interaction Devices, Workshop at the Pervasive 2007 (May 2007)
11. Lee, H.K., Kim, J.H.: Gesture spotting from continuous hand motion. Pattern Recognition Letters 19(5-6), 513–520 (1998)
12. Deng, J., Tsui, H.: An HMM-based approach for gesture segmentation and recognition. In: ICPR 2000: Proceedings of the 15th International Conference on Pattern Recognition, September 2000, vol. 2, pp. 679–682 (2000)
13. Maurer, U., Rowe, A., Smailagic, A., Siewiorek, D.: eWatch: A wearable sensor and notfication platform. In: BSN 2006: Proceedings of the IEEE International Workshop on Wearable and Implantable Body Sensor Networks, Washington, DC, USA, pp. 142–145. IEEE Computer Society Press, Los Alamitos (2006)

UbiGesture: Customizing and Profiling Hand Gestures in Ubiquitous Environment

Ayman Atia, Shin Takahashi, Kazuo Misue, and Jiro Tanaka

Graduate School of Systems and Information Engineering, Department of Computer
Science, University of Tsukuba, Japan
ayman@iplab.cs.tsukuba.ac.jp, {shin,misue,jiro}@cs.tsukuba.ac.jp

Abstract. One of the main challenges of interaction in a ubiquitous environment is the use of hand gestures for interacting with day to day applications. This interaction may be negatively affected due to the change in the user's position, interaction device, or the level of social acceptance of a specific hand gesture. We present UbiGesture as architecture for developers and users who frequently change locations while interacting in ubiquitous environments. The architecture enables applications to be operated by using hand gestures. Normal users can customize their own hand gestures when interacting with computers in context-aware ubiquitous environments. UbiGesture is based on combining user preferences, location, input/output devices, applications, and hand gestures into one profile. A prototype implementation application for UbiGesture is presented. Then a subjective and objective primary evaluation for UbiGesture while interacting in different locations with different hand gesture profiles is presented.

Keywords: Ubiquitous environment, Hand gesture profiles, Context aware services.

1 Introduction

Human hand gestures are an intuitive way for humans to express their feelings and to interact with several objects in daily life. Hand gestures can be used as a tool for interacting with different applications like media player, presentation viewer...etc. Interaction can be done through predefined hand gestures; however it is difficult to fit all users or enabling users to customize their own hand gestures. The interaction can be affected negatively if the use's change position, interaction device, or application or all of them together. There are two other parameters that can have direct impact on users so that they change their hand gesture pattern. First is the position of the user while customizing his hand gesture. A predefined hand gesture, such as moving the elbow towards the body in a standing position, will be difficult to do when the user is sitting down on a sofa or sitting at a table because of the limited space. Second is the social implication of the hand gesture; some hand gestures may scare, annoy, or disturb other people. For example, user A is sitting on a sofa beside person B. If user A moves his or her arm towards person B (someone A knows), Person B might become annoyed and interpret the gesture as a minor interruption. A more complex reaction

J.A. Jacko (Ed.): Human-Computer Interaction, Part II, HCII 2009, LNCS 5611, pp. 141–150, 2009.
© Springer-Verlag Berlin Heidelberg 2009

might occur if there is no relationship between people such as in a public space. Such a gesture may scare the other person. The main idea behind UbiGesture is to provide users with enough appropriate hand gesture profiles for any given situation. The system enables users to define and store their hand gestures using single training hand gesture templates inside a ubiquitous environment context. The context includes the user's location, interaction device, application, and defined application functions. The UbiGesture system helps developers to operate their applications with hand gestures. There is no need for developers to understand the details of hand gesture recognition algorithms or user profiling details. The UbiGesture system was built using inexpensive resources, which benefits the usability and availability of the system.

The rest of this paper is divided into sections discussing related work, UbiGesture architecture, primary evaluation, and conclusion and future work.

2 Related Work

The study of gesture recognition with a presentation viewer application was shown in [1]. They show an active region for starting and ending gesture interaction. Also they point out that gestures can be useful in crowded or noisy situations, such as in a stock exchange or manufacturing environment. Head and hand gestures have been used for limited interactions as demonstrated in [2]. They point out the problem of learning gestures and show the importance of customization. Kurze et al. presented personalization of multimodal applications as a design approach [3]. They focus on implicit and explicit customization of systems according to a user's preferences. Kawsar et al. presented customizing the proactive applications preferences in a ubiquitous environment [4]. They present customization in many levels of artifact, action, interaction, and timing preferences. Customizing a tilt rest hand gesture in eight directions has been discussed in our previous work [5]. We compared interactions with remote displays using three methods and user-customized tilt hand gestures. The users' shows increase in accuracy and time to hit targets when they were allowed to customize their hand gestures.

There are many studies that focus on reusing current applications and interfaces in context-aware environments. Nakajima proposed a model for displaying a GUI on multiple output devices [6]. He/She also developed a way for selecting devices according to a user's location. Ronkainen et al. studied the usability of hand gestures in different ubiquitous environments [7]. They conducted a survey on the social implications of hand gestures in public spaces. Moreover, they present a tap gesture for interacting with mobile devices as a type of socially acceptable hand gesture. They point out that there are gestures that are perceived as being threatening in public spaces. Hand-gesture positions were determined from our previous results gathered by Ayman et al. [8]. They show that the position of hand gestures could affect the accuracy and speed of interaction with an interface for entering text.

The information technology revolution in the last ten years had a direct impact on the size and performance of wireless sensors. Some of these sensors have been used for inferring the context of user and providing ubiquitous services. Recently, there have been many multifunction sensors that have been embedded in small devices [9] [10]. The problem of these small sensors is their short battery life and their high cost. UbiGesture uses wii remote as an interacting device in ubiquitous environments. The Wii [11] remote controller has been suggested as an interaction device for entertainment purpose and some music and art applications [12] [13].The main advantage of the Wii remote is its embedded 3D-accelerometer and optical sensor that is used for motion and position tracking. The Wii remote acceleration range is ±3 G and has been used in many studies for hand-gesture recognition [14] [15].

3 UbiGesture Architecture

The UbiGesture system is used for profiling hand gestures of users depending on the context parameters they exists in. In this research an inexpensive Bluetooth infrastructure was used because this technology is now embedded in most hand held devices. Sanchez et al. used this technique for commercial advertising based on location [16]. Fig. 2. shows an overview of the UbiGesture system. There is a need for different level of users to operate the UbiGesture system (administrator, developer, and regular users). An administrator's main role is managing resources and granting permissions to each user. A developer enables his or her application to be customized by defining keyboard shortcuts or application programming interfaces (APIs). A regular user has to define his or her gesture profile and store it in the network.

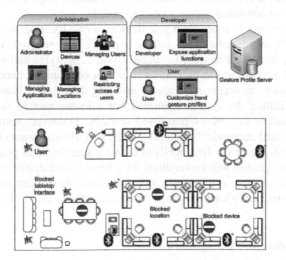

Fig. 1. UbiGesture system overview and Bluetooth infrastructure in office prototype

UbiGesture was built using four main modules each module is responsible for some functions. Fig. **2.** shows the system architecture modules of UbiGesture.

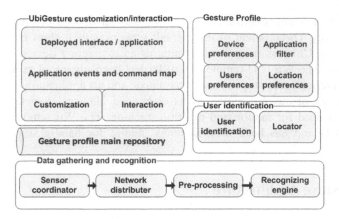

Fig. 2. UbiGesture System architecture

3.1 User Identification Module

UbiGesture assumes that there is a Bluetooth location manager server "Locator" in each location, which was a low-specification desktop PC with a Bluetooth dongle. The locator hosts an application that reads a user's identification by continuously searching for a user's device's media access control (MAC) address within a 30-second interval. Each user may have one or more identification devices such as a hand held mobile device or a Bluetooth sensor. The locator grants access to users for specific devices in one location and it logs the user's entrance and exit time from the location. Whenever users exist in location covered area, it flags a message for all the permitted devices to download the user gesture profile.

User can have access to more than one device in one location; hence, authentication is required "User identification" before a device can be used. Interaction with devices is usually initialized using a keyboard, mouse, or stylus and touch panel. We believe that hand gestures could be similar to someone's unique hand-written signature, by which a user can access a device by entering their device hand gesture signature. In the UbiGesture the system administrator asks the user to define his or her personal hand gesture to control permitted devices. However, sometimes devices could have predefined authentication hand gestures. If the user wants to use a plasma display, for example, he or she first needs to create a specific hand gesture for starting this device; another gesture will be required for a large screen display and so on.

If there are two or more users in one place and both have been granted access to the same device, the User identification module locks the device to be used with only a single user.

3.2 Data Gathering and Recognition

The user has to press the Wii remote's "A" button to start recording a gesture and release the button to stop the recording. Hand gesture h can be represented as a sequence of accelerometer sensor readings. A reading at time t can be represented as $A(t)=\{a_{xt},a_{yt},a_{zt}\}$. A sensor coordinator connects the Wii remote, a human-computer interface, and a locator module. The locator module receives readings from the Wii

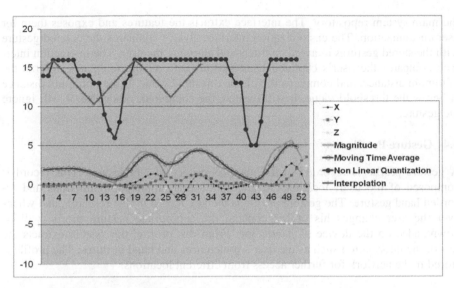

Fig. 3. The analysis of a gesture that entails the shaking of the hand gathered from wii remote

remote and sends them using Transmission Control Protocol/Internet Protocol (Tcp/Ip) to the appropriate authenticated device "Network distributer". On each device there is an application for receiving the data and checking data appropriate receiving order. The collected data pass into three levels of preprocessing for the gathered signal to obtain better recognition of the hand gesture. Fig. **3.** shows the analysis of a gesture that entails the shaking of the hand.

The core of the recognition engine was built using a slightly modified DP-Matching algorithm for recognizing users' hand gestures. The cost function of the algorithm has been calculated as Euclidean distances between two 3d vectors, as shown in Equation 1, where $p_{\{x,y,z\}}$ is one of the accelerometer readings of a user's hand gesture and $q_{\{x,y,z\}}$ is the accelerometer readings inside the list of stored template hand gestures.

$$\text{Cost}= \sqrt[2]{\left(p_x - q_x\right)^2 + \left(p_y - q_y\right)^2 + \left(p_z - q_z\right)^2} \tag{1}$$

The minimum value between a user's hand gesture and all stored template gestures is calculated. The result value should be less than the threshold value, which depends on the sensitivity of the application.

3.3 UbiGesture Customization/Interaction

We have designed two prototype applications, one for customizing hand gestures and the other for using defined hand gestures with developer's applications. The command map translates the gesture commands into application understandable events. In the current version of UbiGesture, a hand gesture is translated into keyboard-shortcut sequences. Each keyboard shortcut sequence is mapped to an interface or application function. The application developer has to list all application functions and features in the main system repository. The interface extracts the features and exposes them for user customization. The customization interface always compares the entered gesture with the stored gestures to avoid conflicts and alarming the user. The interaction interface compares the user's captured hand gesture with all the templates, returns the minimum distance, and compares it with the threshold value. If the minimum distance is below the threshold value, it will execute the command; otherwise, it will ignore the gesture.

3.4 Gesture Profile

A gesture profile is recorded in the main repository of UbiGesture. This record is composed of the user, location, device, application, application functions and recorded hand gesture. The gesture profile is the key record in this research, and whenever the user changes his or her context, the appropriate gesture profile will be downloaded on the device of interaction. From this profile, the system extracts the rest of the information such as the user's preferences and hand gestures. The profile is stored in the network for further access from different locations.

4 Primary Evaluation

For a primary evaluation, we ran experiments with three volunteers. All volunteers were between the ages of 20 and 25, and all were computer science specialists. The customization of hand gestures, which depends on location, its effect on the error recognition rate, and interaction speed, was tested. In addition, we studied the effect of imposing position and social parameters on users interacting with predefined hand gestures. A test bed was established using two Bluetooth location-discovery PCs in two different rooms. The first room (Room A) had a large display screen and a three-seater sofa. The second room (Room B) had a large display screen only (see Fig. 4.).

Voluntccrs used their cellular phones as an identification device. A prototype application for image manipulation was developed using Microsoft C\# and Windows Presentation Foundation. Table 1 shows the application's 20 functions. Predefined hand gestures for those functions were set to cover complex, simple, different

Fig. 4. User positions in Room B (left) and Room A (right)

Table 1. Application functions and gesture patterns

Function Name	Gesture pattern	Function Name	Gesture pattern	Function Name	Gesture pattern
Zoom in all pictures		Zoom camera out		Move camera up	
Zoom out all pictures		Take picture		Move camera down	
Start PTZ camera		Rotate image		Zoom camera in	
Show image	Double Shake	Crop image		Browse down	Shake +
Close application		Black white		Browse left	Shake +
Move camera right		Save captured image, close		Browse right	Shake +
Move camera left		Browse up	Shake +		

geometrical shapes and entailed handshake gestures. These different shapes enable users to imagine what hand gesture he or she can customize using his or her hands.

4.1 Experimental Setup

The administrator granted permission for volunteers to access Rooms A and B, access the big display screen in both rooms, and run the photo application on both devices. The administrator also set a default authentication gesture to start the devices. The developer made all the applications accessible by keyboard shortcuts. For example, to open an image in full view, volunteers select an image by pressing the keyboard arrows and "v". To zoom in, he presses "z", to zoom out, "o", and so on. The Administrator stored the application functions and their corresponding keyboard shortcuts in the main repository. The volunteers were asked to perform two sequences of hand gestures. The first sequence was to browse images, view in full view, rotate, crop, and add black and white effects. The second sequence was to capture an image using a pan tilt zoom (PTZ) camera and save it.

The first experiment involved a full sequence of pre-defined hand gestures. The volunteers were asked to do the experiment in two positions; standing and sitting on the sofa. We put a border between each sofa seat to simulate the presence of another person. The volunteers should not touch this border during the experiments.

The second experiment was to test the UbiGesture on the customization of hand gestures per location. A volunteer customized his hand gestures for browsing images in a sitting position in Room A, (Customization Scenario 1). Then we asked the volunteer to customize his hand gestures for capturing a picture in a standing position in Room B (Customization Scenario 2).

4.2 Results and Discussion

The volunteers were asked to enter 22 gestures in sequence (one session), and they had to make three sessions per experiment, for a total of 198 hand gestures. We measured the average number of hand gestures to finish scenario 1 and 2 (Fig. **5.**5a) and the average interaction time (Fig. **5.**5b).The results show that using customized hand gestures reduces the interaction time and number of hand gestures by an average of 47 percent.

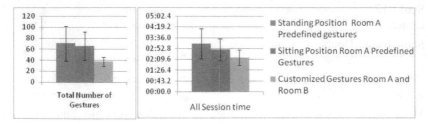

Fig. 5. (a) Average total number of gestures per session, (b) Average time to finish session

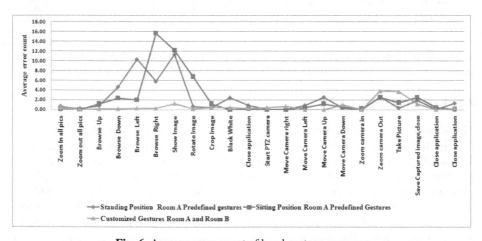

Fig. 6. Average error count of hand gesture sequence

Table 2. Volunteers' satisfaction results for UbiGesture system

Question	Average
Was it easy to interact using predefined hand gestures in a standing position?	1.67
Was it easy to interact using predefined hand gestures in a sitting position?	2.33
Was the customization easy?	2.67
Was it easy to interact using customized hand gestures in a sitting position?	4.33
How many times did you touch the sofa border?	4

The average time needed to customize the hand gestures for Customization Scenarios 1 and 2 was 3 minutes and 20 seconds. When using the predefined hand gestures in the sitting position and interacting with the application, we observed that the volunteers hit the borders or left the seat many times to gesture. In real situations, these gestures may annoy others close by. Also it was remarked that the volunteer sometimes failed to perform the predefined hand gestured towards lower body. Fig.6 shows the average error counts to execute the sequence of hand gestures. The peek seen in Average error count of hand gesture sequence6 for gesture "Browse Right" using a predefined hand gesture and in a sitting position, explains how hard it was for the volunteer to gesture.

The volunteer tried to avoid touching the border nearest to him, so he failed in completing the gesture. When the volunteer was able to customize this gesture, the error rate and time dramatically decreased. When the volunteers completed all the experiments, we asked them to answer a short questionnaire by giving a score from 1 to 5 (5 meaning very good). The results are listed in **Table 2**. We received comments from the volunteers about the need for a GUI feedback showing the pattern of the customized gestures. Sometimes the volunteers forgot the pattern of the gesture they made and requested to re-customize the gesture.

5 Conclusion and Future Work

We developed the UbiGesture system, which profiles a user's gestures according to specific parameters. The system was built using inexpensive resources making it more available to more users. The system also enables developers to add hand gestures to their applications in a few easy steps. The end users can customize their hand-gesture profiles depending on the context, which gives them more flexibility and intuitive interaction. Moreover, we also proposed a solution for starting devices in a shared-resource ubiquitous environment. Using two-handed gestures is a more intuitive way in human interaction. We need to evaluate the usability of UbiGesture by running different scenarios and test beds. We proposed user adapted-systems; however, we need to address concerns about system-adapted hand gestures in which a system recommends a suitable gesture for users depending on the context.

References

1. Baudel, T., Beaudouin-Lafon, M.: Charade: remote control of objects using free-hand gestures. Commun. ACM 36, 28–35 (1993)
2. Keates, S., Robinson, P.: The use of gestures in multimodal input, pp. 35–42 (1998)
3. Kurze, M.: Personalization in multimodal interfaces, pp. 23–26 (2007)
4. Kawsar, F., Nakajima, T.: Persona: a portable tool for augmenting proactive applications with multimodal personalization support, pp. 160–168 (2007)
5. Ayman, A., Takahashi, S., Tanaka, J.: Coin Size Wireless Sensor Interface for Interaction with Remote Displays, pp. 733–742 (2007)
6. Nakajima, T.: How to reuse existing interactive applications in ubiquitous computing environments?, pp. 1127–1133 (2006)

7. Ronkainen, S., Hakkila, J., Kaleva, S., Colley, A., Linjama, J.: Tap input as an embedded interaction method for mobile devices, pp. 263–270 (2007)
8. Ayman, A., Takahashi, S., Sato, D., Tanaka, J.: Evaluating interaction with Popie using coin size wireless sensor, pp. 4-17–4-18 (2008)
9. SunSpot, http://www.sunspotworld.com/
10. Ubisense, http://www.ubisense.net/
11. Wii Remote, http://www.nintendo.com/wii
12. Bruegge, B., Teschner, C., Lachenmaier, P., Fenzl, E., Schmidt, D., Bierbaum, S.: Pinocchio: conducting a virtual symphony orchestra, pp. 294–295 (2007)
13. Lee, H.-J., Kim, H., Gupta, G., Mazalek, A.: WiiArts: creating collaborative art experience with WiiRemote interaction, pp. 33–36 (2008)
14. Shirai, A., Geslin, E., Richir, S.: WiiMedia: motion analysis methods and applications using a consumer video game controller, pp. 133–140 (2007)
15. Schlomer, T., Poppinga, B., Henze, N., Boll, S.: Gesture recognition with a Wii controller, pp. 11–14 (2008)
16. Sanchez, J.-M., Cano, J.-C., Calafate, C., Manzoni, P.: BlueMall: a bluetooth-based advertisement system for commercial areas, pp. 17–22 (2008)

The Gestural Input System for Living Room Digital Devices

Wen-Shan Chang and Fong-Gong Wu

Department of Industrial Design, National Cheng Kung University, 1,
Ta-Hsueh Road, Tainan, Taiwan 70101, Taiwan
Michelle33.tw@yahoo.com.tw

Abstract. The focus of this research is to help users learn gesture symbols through semantic perception. With the semantic perception as the basis, qualitative and quantitative analysis will be conducted to analyze digital homes – as exemplified by the gesture symbols in the 3D space of the living room in order to deduce the design principles of different perceptive semantics. Samples of the case studies will be constructed in accordance with this design principle. Inspections and assessments will also be conducted to demonstrate the accuracy and feasibility of this principle. The findings in this research shall serve as reference for the design of interfaces and gesture recognition systems in the comprehensive surrounding. It shall also serve as the design standard for relevant future designs that involve semantic perception and design gesture symbols.

Keywords: home audiovisual multimedia, gesture recognition, gesture symbol, cognition.

1 Introduction

At present, many input devices are available in the market and input techniques are improving by the day. The existing gesture input recognition techniques include: DataGlove and HMM 3D gesture recognition (CMU), Video Camera, and Data-Driven Clustering in gesture recognition (MIT Media Lab, 1995). As the recognition efficiency increased, their usage also became more extensive. They are also gradually applied in our daily lives. Gesture inputs differ from those of hardware inputs as gesture inputs do not pass through other interfaces, making them more intuition-driven and human. However, since they are more difficult to learn, users often feel frustrated or confused the first time they use them. At the moment, a number of researchers have expressed their intent to help users learn through cognition. (Lin Jing, 2006) Based on the users' cognition of 2D symbols and in-depth researches on the present symbology and related applications [1], in this research, the existing gesture input technology shall serve as the basis, and the various home appliance commands in the living room will be integrated based on traditional semantic cognition. Through analysis, they will be converted into gesture symbols in the 3D space. The gesture symbol language in the space will be redesigned, and the users' cognition, recognition, response time, and preference level of 3D space gesture symbols will be probed into.

J.A. Jacko (Ed.): Human-Computer Interaction, Part II, HCII 2009, LNCS 5611, pp. 151–160, 2009.
© Springer-Verlag Berlin Heidelberg 2009

2 Literature Review

2.1 Visual Cognition

When we see the form of an object, we start to associate it with other things through our sense of 'sight', 'touch', 'smell', 'sound', and 'taste.' Among these senses, associations of image through the sense of sight are the most evident. Baxter (1995) proposed that human visual message processing could be analyzed in two stages. The first stage is the rapid scanning of the overall visual image to obtain the 'form' and 'shape of the image.' This process is fast and not laborious. The second stage of overall visual image processing involves attention given to details of visual components. The visual cognition process in the first stage is prioritized in terms of the overall image. One feature is that the object we see is integral rather than components of the visual image. It is prioritized over the attention-based second stage.

This priority signifies that the visual image obtained in the first stage tends to dominate or affect the visual cognition process in the second stage. Seeing the 'details' of the object, the initial visual image stays in the mind. If we want to look at other images, we must take our eyes off the image we were looking at, close our eyes, or pay attention to other matters. Once a new image pops up, the attention will lead us to engage in detailed recognition of tasks. Users' performance is enhanced though the design displayed, which allows the users to attain information while completing the visual search. Apparently, the 'meaning' of the information can be sent out through visual search. In the visual method, meanings are frequently sent out through our perception ability. Based on these reasons, the interactions between perception ability and interpretation will become more and more important in design displays in the future. Therefore the learning design in this research will allow users to obtain the visual images and related information. Moreover, through cluster classifications, the users will be able to deduce the types of correlations between images and functions.

In turn, it will help the users understand the meaning of individual graphics in the cluster including reduced work loads and enhanced visual search and comprehension.

2.2 Gesture Prototyping

Although attempts have been made to search for ways to recognize graphics independently, the overlapping between perception and recognition has become more and more evident. Many interfaces form image clusters through clustering and designating locations. In addition, research findings show that clustered graphics not only helps users find suitable functions, they also rapidly and effectively allow users to learn about the correlation between graphic functions. In the aspect of perception, it is perceived that the addition of colors and frequently used shapes in conveying messages is rather important. All these are indications of the extensive use of frequently used visual methods when graphics are developed or spread through languages. Therefore, designers need to have the ability to effectively observe these frequently used methods. Although it is true that not all traditional designs are good, it is still an issue to consider. Martha (2006) proposed that the graphic model setup was rather important because it served as basis in design. Users may start to recognize graphics from the graphic prototype to alter the complex and tiny details. The design elements of the graphic prototype tend to lessen the load of the users while learning and assist them to strengthen their memory in terms of cognition.

2.3 Real-Time Fingertip Tracking

An infrared video camera is used to detect the temperature of the fingertip and locate the position of the fingertip. The advantages of using the infrared video camera are that it is not subject to effects of background colors and the brightness of the surrounding light. It accurately positions the fingertip under the normal body temperature range. The principle of fingertip tracking surveys is the position of the previous image based on the fingertip. A Kalman Filter is used to predict the position of the fingertip in a particular image. This process is adopted to distinguish the location of each fingertip. The distinguished fingertip tracking data detected is able to assemble more gesture symbol arrays than the traditional palm tracking.

The symbolic gesture recognition is the same as most gesture recognition systems in which the graphic gesture recognition system adopts the Hidden Markov Model (HMM). The two factors for HMM inputs to recognize fingertip tracking include: (1) No. of fingertip tracking; and (2) 16 discontinuous encodings used to describe the average direction of fingertip shifts.

2.4 Intelligent Home Information Appliances

The origin of the 'IA' concept is dated back to 1978. Jef Raskin, a computer engineer of Apple that created the name 'Macintosh', had suggested the term 'Information Appliance' at the time. Raskin established Information Appliance Inc. in 1982. On the other hand, with regard to the concept of 'Information Appliance, IA, Sondre Bjella wrote in 'The Intelligent Home of 2010' in 1987 that there will be an internet gateway in every future home. It connects to the external telecommunication network and provides home telecommunication functions. It connects internally to the home devices to monitor the home appliances. Due to information and electronic technology advancement, this concept has gradually become a reality. Man's information applications are now complex and versatile. In IA related discussions, it is often defined as a 'PC-based intelligent home device.' Some people also call it the internet application platform-based internet appliance or IA (digital appliance). Simply, it is defined as information-based home appliances. As the demand for global intelligent home appliances grows, all home appliances will be integrated in the intelligent home network in the future. The management platform will connect the external service networks. According to a research report on In-Stat cited by Industrial Technology Research Institute, 448,000 units of smart appliances were sold around the globe in 2002. It is speculated that 3,810,000 units will be sold by 2007. The annual compound growth rate from 2002 to 2007 is 53.4%. Due to technological advancements, home appliances have become prevalent. The information-based home appliance industry and the electronic-based and information-based products will result in the intelligent living system's becoming an important part of home living facilities. The development of living application technologies that are humanity-based, user-friendly, and convenient will be the trend of the future.

3 Research Planning

This research is divided into two stages, lexical analysis experimentation and gesture symbol design. In lexical analysis related experiments, the commands of audiovisual devices frequently used in home living rooms will first be collected. Subsequently, a usability assessment will be conducted to select the final commands. The selected commands will then be clustered to choose the final 9 functional clusters and 6 product commands in the experiment. After integrating the results above, the theories, principles and current development technologies stated in review literatures as well brainstorming and expert discussions will be adopted to construct new gesture symbols. Finally, they will be compared with the simulated actual use conductions. The results will be evaluated for analysis and discussions. The advantages, disadvantages, and effects of the new gesture symbols will be summarized to provide reference for gesture recognition researchers and interface design staff.

3.1 Lexical Analysis Experiment

In this research, the collection of vocabularies and usability survey analysis within the scope of the research will first be conducted. The research scope and framework will then be narrowed and confirmed. First, the frequently used audiovisual home appliances in living rooms will be surveyed to find out their prevalence, i.e., command function surveys. The use instructions of the 7 products will serve as reference, and the listed command names will be classified. Then, the 57 subjects who have had over 3 years home input system use (34 males and 23 females) will be requested to collect and compile the home input device commands. Among the various home digital devices, the usability questionnaire allows us to further derive at the commands used by most people.

In the usability survey undertaken by the subjects, the subjects are asked in the questionnaire to choose 5 commands in order of frequency of use. These 5 commands are rated on a scale of 1-5. The command of higher use is selected. In the questionnaire survey, representative products are first selected. Select 6 products with the highest use frequency and importance. As to product function, select the representative commands in order of their scores.

3.2 Command Clustering

After selecting the commands, since the product types and commands are complex, they need to undergo command simplification to reduce the load of the user during learning. After that, command clustering will then be conducted. The various basic types and norms obtained from previously compiled literature data and semantic analysis discussions will be adopted along with the 10 design experts in undergoing new gesture symbol command clustering. (Target group members – those that have had over 4 years of design background and have received professional training in design education)

Table 1.

Name	Function	Name	Function
Function 1	Switch, receive/disconnect	Function 9	Menu, emergency mode, mode switch
Function 2	Play, dial	Product 1	Image display
Function 3	Number input	Product 2	T.V.
Function 4	Pause, hold, timer	Product 3	Telephone
Function 5	Stop, eject	Product 4	Light
Function 6	Frequency (left/right), redial	Product 5	Door
Function 7	Amplifier,call,beep	Product 6	Air-conditioning
Function 8	Fast/slow.motion, frequency (up/down), volume,brightness, temperature (high/low),wind speed (fast/slow),wind direction (left/right)		

Lexical clustering consists of 6 products (image display, T.V., telephone, light, door, air-conditioning, etc.) and 9 command functional clusters. (switch, play, number input, pause, eject, frequency (left/right), amplifier, fast/slow motion, menu, etc.) shall serve as reference for design in future researches. It is also of great referential value for converting commands into gestures.

3.3 Gesture Symbol Design

In the gesture symbol design stage, word-concept association and brainstorming are adopted. In order to demonstrate how users detect and assess the issues, they are required to incorporate their design concept or features in the descriptive text. The users' feelings are gathered to assess design features and concepts. By means of collective idea formulating, the users brainstormed for different ideas. The 10 design experts undergo the design of new gesture symbols in this research. (Target group members: those that have had over 4 years of design background and have received professional training in design education)

3.4 Symbol Analysis Assessment

In the gesture analysis and assessment stage, the gesture command symbols obtained and distributed previously are based on the current technologies and one's understanding and analysis of the products. In addition, all the lexical associations obtained in the pre-test and various suggestions shall also serve as important references. They are regarded as the 'meaning' of commands to the users. The gesture symbols that are more difficult to implement technically are deleted or combined if they are identical. Finally, the gestures are divided into two groups, single-handed gestures and two-handed gestures. The 72 single-handed gestures and 76 two-handed gestures make up the 148 formulated ideas.

3.5 Semantic Differential Ratings/Symbol and Set Preferences

After analyzing and assessing the symbols, compile the gesture symbols and conduct a Semantic Differential Ratings/Symbol and Set Preferences. Through the Semantic Differential Ratings/Symbol and Set Preferences, the subjects' preference level for the gesture symbols will be found, which shall serve as reference in determining the gestures and designing the symbols. After compiling the analysis, a subjective assessment on the gesture symbols is conducted. A total of 41 subjects filled out the questionnaire. The scores range from 0-6. The questionnaire covers the gesture design pictures and association design elements. The gesture symbols with higher scores are selected to undergo significance analysis. After the Semantic Differential Ratings/Symbol and Set Preferences, the results obtained by the experts, and the objective factors such as recognition difficulties due to limitations of technology will be taken into consideration to determine the final single-handed and two-handed gesture design system.

4 Experimental Analysis

Foley [4] believes that the quality of the graphic interface design can be assessed through three main criteria including: response time–the users' time spent to complete a task; recall rate–the recall ratio of the user's completing a certain task; and preference–the users' preferences during use. Zwaga [21] expounded two factors, experience and age, and the effects they have on the subjects when assessing the graphics. Cued Response Assessment is the assessment method adopted. The cued response matrix places the illustrations and their respective meanings on the upper and lower part of the questionnaire arrayed in random numbers. The subjects are then asked to fill in the meanings they know below the illustrations. The results are then made into a cued response matrix. In the matrix, the numbers of subjects who answer correctly are recorded on the boxes corresponding to the X-axis (graphic) and Y-axis (meaning of the graphic) and the rest are subjects who have given wrong answers. This shall serve as reference for assessing the cued response of the graphics assessed. If the rate of correct answers is high, the graphic cued response is said to be low; on the contrary, if the rate of correct answers is low, the graphic cued response is said to be high. This research probes into the recall rate through Symbol Identification Test. The cued responses are assessed through cued response tests, and the user' preference of use is found through Semantic Differential Ratings/Symbol and Set Preferences.

4.1 Experimental Method

1. Cued Response Tests: after reading the symbols, the subjects select the gesture commands believed to be the most suitable matches (placed on the same page) to test the cued response.
2. Symbol Identification Tests: All gesture commands are arrayed randomly. The subjects are asked to demonstrate the gesture symbol expressed. The operation error rate and response time are then measured.

3. Semantic Differential Ratings/Symbol and Set Preferences: at the end of the symbol identification tests and cued response tests, fill out the subjective scales to find out the users' preferences.

Ritu (1996) proposed that in order for users to understand the functions of the information system, a good pre-education mode has to be found because the users' software interfaces eventually become a fixed set of operation behaviors (single-handed mode) when using related software in the future. Thus, in reference to related literatures, a set of gesture learning methods are set up including the learning mode and the learning content.

1. ERI Method (Zhai & Kristensson, 2003): Learners must demonstrate the actions to strengthen the learners' memory provided that correct symbols are not displayed. If the learner demonstrates the correct symbols, they will appear twice after determining the order. If the correct symbols cannot be demonstrated, the original order of array will continue.
2. Top-Down Method (Lee & Zhai, 2004): The collective visual space of the alphabet and memory technology establishes an array familiar with the commands. It is more favorable than repeated training. The teaching procedures set up in accordance with the literatures, the screen images and verbal explanations are adopted. The subjects take on the teaching processes in two experiments. The experiment is carried out in two sessions with three tests for each experiment conducted one day apart. The experiment is completed in a span of three days.

4.2 Teaching Content of Gestures

1. Concreteness: Clearly inform the subjects regarding the implications of the gestures. (Gilhooly & Logie, 1980; Paivio et al, 1968)
2. Semantic distance: Describe the correlation of gesture semantics and graphic functions. Semantic linking fosters a closer relationship between commands and graphics. (McDougall et al, 1999)
3. Complexity: Inform the subjects regarding the detailed constituents and complexity of the gestures.

5 Experimental Results

Cued Response Tests: After the second cued response test, the recognition rates for single-handed and two-handed are both 92% or higher. After learning for the second time, remarkable improvements are shown as compared to the first experimental results.

Symbol Identification Tests: In terms of the operation error rate in accordance with the second experiment, in the single-handed shows a P value of 0.267 based on the results of the 'Chi-Square Test'. In other words, the error frequencies of single-handed and two-handed show no significant differences. In terms of the response time in accordance with the results of The Mann-Whitney U Test, the 15 gesture symbols of the observed values, after the average time of the 30 samples of the original observed values are converted into classes, the classes of the single-handed average time total 212.00. The average value of the classes is 14.13. The classes of the two-handed average time total 253.00. The average value of the classes is 16.87. The P value is 0.412, showing that no significant differences exist between the average time of single-handed and two-handed.

Semantic Differential Ratings/Symbol and Set Preferences: Based on the results of The Mann-Whitney U Test, the 15 gesture symbols of the observed values, after the 30 samples of the original observed values are converted into classes, the P value is 0.683. In other words, there are no significant differences in preference level between single-handed and two-handed.

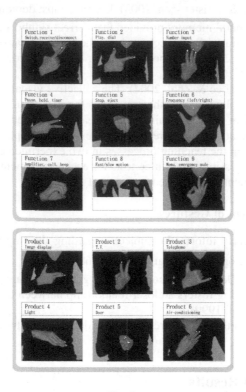

Fig. 1.

6 Conclusion and Recommendation

The single-handed and two-handed designs show no significant differences in terms of assessment results. All the gesture commands have reached the applications of a set of public label symbols stated in the public sign design standard operation procedures of the International Organization for Standardization. (ISOTC 145/SCI) The ISO recommends that a correct recognition rate of 67% or higher be reached. However, discussions can be conducted on the subjects' opinions and the operation conditions. Among the 24 subjects, 7 expressed that out of the single-handed and two-handed gestures, the two-handed gestures are preferred, 15 subjects prefer single-handed, 2 subjects expressed no preference over single-handed or two-handed gestures. Among the users that prefer single-handed gestures, the reasons that attribute to this preference include: single-handed gestures are easier to remember and are more convenient as the commands can be demonstrated with one hand. It is intuition-based that the gestures can be memorized using symbols. The actions are so 'cool' that they require no extra actions. The design logics of two-handed gestures have less uniformity. Among the subjects that prefer two-handed gestures, the reasons that attribute to this preference include: they find it more difficult to relate to single-handed gestures. They do not know what to do with the other hand. When matched with actions, they are able to comprehend and remember the gestures. The design disparity is also greater and the gesture variations are more versatile. On the other hand, single-handed commands are less 'friendly.'

Although single-handed and two-handed gestures show no significant differences in the experimental results, after the experiment and expert discussions, the single-handed gestures are believed to have higher development potentials than two-handed gestures in the future. Single-handed gestures have limitations in terms of the design of actions. Nevertheless, convenience will remain an important factor for future gesture designs. In single-handed commands, the actions of function 5, function 7, and function 3 with 0 in number are more similar. Confusions are likely to result in recognizing them. Overtly similar gesture symbol designs should therefore be avoided during designing.

Furthermore, 'the effects on culture and language' are also an important factor. Take this research for instance, the switch function of the T.V. and telephone is expressed as 'ON/OFF' in English, but in Chinese, it is translated as 'to open', 'to play', etc. There are misunderstandings and confusions in cognitive integrations. Future researches may probe into whether or not semantic cognitions differ in countries of different languages and cultures. Also, the concept of gesture inputs not only enhances the convenience in life, the use rights of minority groups such as the visually impaired, verbally impaired, and seniors have to be taken into consideration with more care and creative ideas. Finally, the inclusion of this user group as test subjects will make the research more comprehensive and user-friendly.

References

1. Christian, A.S., Tombre, K.: Architectural Symbol Recognition Using a Network of Constraints. Pattern Recognition Letters 22(2), 231–248 (2001)
2. Fisher, J.: Testing the Effect of Road, Traffic sing Information Value on Driver Behavior. Human Factors 34, 231–237 (1992)
3. Fiske, J.: Introduction to Communication Studies (1995) ISBN 9573225204
4. Foley, J.D., Wallace, V.L., Chan, P.: The Human Factors of Computer Graphics Interaction Techniques. IEEE Computer Graphic and Application 4, 13–48 (1984)
5. Gittins, D.: Icon-based Human-Computer Interaction. International Journal of man-Machine Studie 24, 519–543 (1986)
6. Horton, W.: The Icon Book Visual Symbols for Computer Systems and Documentation. John Wiley & sons, Inc., Chichester (1994)

7. Neilson, J.: Top Ten Mistakes in Web Design. Sunsoft Distinguished Engineer (1996); Caplan, S.: Using focus groups methodology for ergonomic design. Ergonomic 33(5), 527–533 (1990)
8. Neilson, J.: Usability Engineering, pp. 97–155. Ap Professional Press, California (1993)
9. Nespoulous, J.L., Perron, P., Lecours, A.R.: The Biological Foundations of Gestures: Motor and Semiotic Aspects. Lawrence Erlbaum Associates, Hillsdale (1986)
10. Nordin, A. (ed.): Taxonomy and phylogeny of Buellia species with pluriseptate spores (Lecanorales, Ascomycotina). In: Symb. Bot. Ups., vol. 33(1), pp. 1–117 (2000)
11. Oka, K., Sato, Y.: Real-Time Fingertip Tracking and Gesture Recognition University of Tokyo Hideki Koike University of Electro-Communications, Tokyo (2002)
12. Piaget, J.: Construction of reality in the child. Routledge & Kegan Paul, London (1954)
13. Schlenzig, J., Hunter, E., Jain, R.: Vision based gesture interpretation using recursive estimation. In: Asilomar Conference on Signals (1994)
14. Starner, T.: Visual Recognition of American Sign Language Using Hidden Markov Model, Master's Thesis, MIT Media Laboratory (February 1995)
15. Starner, T.: Visual recognition of American Sign Language using Hidden Markov Models. Master's thesis, MIT Media Lab (July 1995)
16. Turing, M., Hannemann, J., Haake, J.M.: Hypermedia and Cognition: Design for Comprehension. Communications of the ACM 38, 57–66 (1995)
17. Wallschlaeger, C.: Basic Visual Concepts and Principles for Artists, Architects and Designers, Times Mirror Pte Ltd. (1996)
18. Weimer, D., Ganapathy, S.K.: Interaction techniques using hand tracking and speech recognition. Multimedia interface design, 109–126 (1992)
19. Whitaker, L.A., Sommer, R.: Perception of Traffic Guidance sing Containing Conflicting Symbol and Direction Information. Ergonomic 29(5), 699–711 (1986)
20. Wickens, C.D., Hollands, J.G.: Engineering Psychology and Human Performance, 3rd edn., pp. 513–550. Prentice-Hall Inc., Englewood Cliffs (2000)
21. Zwaga, H.J., Boersema, T.: Evaluation of a set of Graphic Symbols. Applied Ergonomic 14(1), 43–54 (1983)

Touchless Interaction-Novel Chances and Challenges

René de la Barré, Paul Chojecki, Ulrich Leiner, Lothar Mühlbach,
and Detlef Ruschin

Fraunhofer Institute for Communication Technologies,
Heinrich-Hertz-Institut, Einsteinufer 37
10587 Berlin, Germany
{Rene.de_la_Barre,Paul.Chojecki,Ulrich.Leiner,Lothar.Muehlbach,
Detlef.Ruschin}@hhi.fraunhofer.de

Abstract. Touchless or empty-handed gestural input has received considerable attention during the last years because of such benefits as removing the burden of physical contact with an interactive system and making the interaction pleasurable. What is often overlooked is that those special forms of touchless interaction which employ genuine gestures – defined as movements that have a meaning – are associated with the danger of suffering from the same drawbacks as command based interfaces do, which have been widely abandoned in favor of direct manipulation interfaces. Touchless direct manipulation, however, is about to reach maturity in certain application fields. In our paper we try to point out why and under which conditions this is going to happen, and how we are working to optimize the interfaces through user tests.

Keywords: interaction, touchless, direct manipulation, gestures, hand tracking, user experience.

1 Touchless Interaction through Hand Movements

The topic of this paper is touchless interaction between humans and artificial systems, which takes place with the help of new interaction devices. Interaction devices are the units that can either execute or sense interactive behavior. For example in gaze controlled computing both the human eyes, for which the relevant behavior is their line-of-sight change, and the gaze tracker employed to monitor the eyes' movements, are interaction devices. Interaction is said to be touchless if it can take place without mechanical contact between the human and any part of the artificial system, which means that for example the interaction with a Wii through its wireless controller is not touchless. Touchless interaction can be multimodal, in which case the interactive behavior produces simultaneous events in the visual modality (color, form, or position change), in the auditory modality (speech, sounds) or in the olfactory modality (odors). In the following, however, we will be concentrating on form and position changes of the user's hands as relevant events in touchless interaction.

Such hand movements should not be equated with gestures. The proper classification of manual behavior into gesture and non-gesture helps to distinguish between two types of touchless interaction, which correspond with the well-known dichotomy between direct and indirect manipulation introduced by Shneiderman [1].

J.A. Jacko (Ed.): Human-Computer Interaction, Part II, HCII 2009, LNCS 5611, pp. 161–169, 2009.
© Springer-Verlag Berlin Heidelberg 2009

According to a distinction made by Cadoz [2], hand movements can be of three different kinds, which the author had termed *semiotic, ergotic*, and *epistemic* (quoted after Mulder [3]). The semiotic kind of hand movements is used to convey meaning, the ergotic kind is used to change the state of the physical environment, and the epistemic kind is performed to feel the environment and thus to gain knowledge.

As far as gestures are concerned, a consensus seems to be emerging about what kind of behavior should count as gesture, which Kendon [4] formulated in the following way: *"'Gesture' we suggest, then, is a label for actions that have the features of manifest deliberate expressiveness"*. This means that a gesture is a body movement which is being performed with the perceivable intention to express something. According to this definition hand gestures are clearly a subclass of semiotic hand movements. Hence those movements are ruled out as gestures which are either performed to serve some practical goal, i.e. the ergotic movements, or to explore the world, i.e. the epistemic movements. Another important subclass of semiotic movements, which is, however, not of interest here, consists of the involuntary movements that are considered meaningful by observers, like trembling as a symptom of strain.

2   Interaction Styles

2.1   Direct Manipulation

Shneiderman in his already mentioned article tried to identify a common denominator of several then new and exciting user interfaces, which did not rely on written command input. From diverse examples ranging between screen-based text editors, interactive maps, and video games he concluded that this common denominator was what he termed direct manipulation. Through mentioning an article by Nelson about "the design of virtuality" [5] Shneiderman made clear that the alleged directness is often only based on "a representation of reality that can be manipulated". One of his examples for such a representation was the dragging of a document icon onto a printer icon to produce a hardcopy of the document which that icon represented.

The notion of directness may be misleading, because it only refers to the subjective impression gained from the interaction. Direct manipulation resembles what in engineering is called control, where a manipulated variable influences a controlled variable, and the controlled variable is fed back to provide information that can be used to readjust the manipulated variable. Due to the plasticity of human sensory-motor coordination an impression of directness occurs not only when the turning of a steering wheel causes car wheels to turn but also when the hand moves a mouse or a pen and thus causes a screen cursor to move. Furthermore in the discussed computer-oriented examples the user manipulates only signs, even though an illusion of influencing some kind of represented reality may occur.

The main point we would like to make from this review of direct manipulation is that the human behavior in this mode is always either ergotic or epistemic. Even if only signs are manipulated the interactive behavior serves to change some perceivable state but not to express something. An example for epistemic movements is the head motion performed to look around objects. Such head motions can be used to directly manipulate an interactive imaging system, which reacts to the motion by producing a perspective change of the rendered the image.

2.2 Indirect Manipulation

The true opposite of direct manipulation is not the use of command lines as Shneiderman suggested, but rather what could be termed *communication based interaction*. The reason for this claim is that the basic distinction which underlies Shneiderman's dichotomy is the one between "do it yourself" and "have the machine do it" approaches, as the title of one of his later articles ("Beyond intelligent machines: Just Do It!") [6] seems to confirm. However, commands can also be issued nonverbally through pointing and clicking. To use f.i. a "delete" button is certainly a command, and it is difficult to see why Shneiderman classified such actions as direct manipulation. Furthermore many of the messages exchanged during indirect manipulation are not commands in a strict sense. This is especially true for messages like "error", which are issued by the interactive system and which in most cases are only informative. However, it is also debatable whether the human input consists of nothing but commands. Compare for example the y/n feedback that many applications request.

Therefore indirect manipulation in principle comprises any type of interactive behavior that can be interpreted as a speech act in the sense of Searle [7], i.e. as an assertion, declaration, question, promise and so on, amongst which commands are just one example. Because speech acts are the minimal units of communication, indirect interaction could be properly termed communication based.

3 Hand Movement Types and Interaction Styles

As was explained above direct manipulation is generally performed through ergotic or epistemic movements. This remains true when the interaction happens in a touchless way. Imagine for example a hypothetical kind of Squash gaming application, in which a ball is shown to move and bounce from a virtual wall via computer animation and the players in front of the screen are acting as if they were hitting a real ball with their open palms. Because the palms are tracked through computer vision, information about their movements can be used to influence the animation of the ball, and thus the players can "directly" manipulate the ball.

By contrast we can consider a kind of hand movements that contain a meaning to trigger a response from a system. An example could be the formation of a thumbs-up hand configuration to operate a light switch. With that movement a human can communicate to a system that he wants it to switch the light on. Given the above definition, such a deliberately produced semiotic movement is a gesture. Therefore indirect, or communication based, manipulation correspond with gesture based interactions, whereas all direct manipulation interfaces correspond with interactions based on nongestures.

This leads to an important conclusion. As interface designers, when we are faced with the decision whether we should incorporate gestures into the available repertoire of interactive behavior, we should be aware that any of the classical arguments against indirect manipulation interfaces also hold concerning gesture based interfaces. One of these arguments is the necessity to memorize arbitrary communication rules. This concerns even gestures that are considered to be highly plausible, because most of the words used for written commands are also highly plausible and can nevertheless be confused (c.f. "purge", "remove", or "delete" to destroy a digital entity).

Features of (verbal or non-verbal) speech acts such as intuitivity, plausibility, familiarity are usually more helpful for recognition than for recall.

4 The Naturalness of Hand-Based Interaction

Sometimes it is claimed that gesture based interaction is highly natural [8], [9] and should be therefore preferred. With a loose definition of gesture, which does not distinguish true gesture from meaningless hand movements, this claim might be justifiable. However, for true gestures the naturalness claim points to a visionary far future. The idea behind it is that of the computer as artificial human, which in its most extreme form envisages the computer to interpret facial expressions, looking behavior, spoken language, gestures and so on. With such artificial humans around the real humans would no more need to adapt themselves to the machines. Unfortunately with the current state of the art special knowledge and skills are as yet necessary for successful human-machine interaction, for which gestural type is a good example.

Individuals without disabilities use gestures almost exclusively in combination with speech. The co-speech gestures are syntactically and semantically integrated with the verbal utterance (c.f. McNeill [10]) in a way that is not yet completely understood, and their interpretation is virtually impossible, if the accompanying words are unknown. Furthermore most of the gestures are uncoded, i.e. their meaning can only be inferred and not be looked up in a lexicon. In real human machine interaction this complex way of communicating must be replaced with the use of primitive artificial sign languages, about which Cassel [11] wrote, *"I don't believe that everyday human users have any more experience with, or natural affinity for, a 'gestural language' than they have with DOS command"*. An illustration of such a "gestural language" is the pen-based gesture inventory built into Microsoft's Windows Vista SDK [12], because the same gestures could also be employed in a touchless interface. In this inventory for example the "insert" command can be evoked by drawing a triangle.

5 Reasons for Touchlessness

The previous discussion relates to touch-based as well as to touchless interaction forms, but what are the special benefits of touchless user interfaces?

The conditions under which touchless or "free-form" (c.f. Saffer [13]) interactions seem to have advantages as compared with touch based interfaces include:

- Sterile environments or clean rooms: Usually, surfaces that are touched have to be made aseptic after being used. As an example, when using touch screens in operating rooms for controlling medical devices, the screens usually are covered with transparent plastic films, which have to be changed after each operation. When using touchless interaction technologies, effort, time and money can be saved.
- Vandalism-prone environments: When using cameras or similar devices for sensing fingers, hands, eyes etc. from a certain distance, it is possible to place the display device and the sensor at vandalism-proof places, e.g. behind glass walls. Among other things, this can be a useful solution for information systems at public places or for interactive store window displays.

- Co-located shared use: Interactive systems that are jointly used by a group of persons and therefore employ more distantly located large displays, f.i. in a class or lecture room.
- Placing and moving objects in three dimensions: If a task requires to move a (real or virtual) object in all three dimensions it will be easier or more convenient to use a touchless user interface, provided that it has the capability to scan a finger or hand position in x, y, and z. Such operations can be necessary - among other things - in construction tasks.
- Eventually contact-free interaction can be more suitable than contact-based interaction in cases of fleeting use, i.e. when there is extremely little time to seek, grasp and comprehend a system's input devices. These systems can be screenless, such as doors and lights in public spaces, conveyor transport systems, service robots etc.

Apart from the above examples that have been chosen on rather rational grounds there will exist cases in which the main advantage of touchless manipulation resides in the emotional sphere (c.f. [14]) or at the "visceral level", as Norman calls it [15].

Even if a touchless interactive system does not work easier, faster, more error-proof etc. than a touch-based counterpart people may nevertheless like it more and experience more fun with it. How that could be exactly explained has not yet been sufficiently investigated. Our hypothesis is that the main factor is a sense of wizard power users might gain by controlling a scene from a distance without having to touch it, an interaction style which might be called "direct manipulation by mystic means".

6 Research at Fraunhofer HHI

6.1 Interaction Concepts

For the cases in which touchless interaction is beneficial we have been developing solutions at the Fraunhofer HHI, and we have been restricting ourselves to direct manipulation interfaces as much as possible. However, in systems that incorporate more than one function, a means must be provided to switch between these functions, and it is a proven practice to employ menus or command buttons for this purpose. This means to mix up elements of direct and communication based interaction in the same user interface. The main reason why this mixture works so well is the utilization of the *menu principle*, through which the possibility of arbitrary input is replaced with a limited choice from available items.

A touchless nonverbal method to choose from a menu consists of two components, namely an addressing mechanism and an action signal, which are equivalent to pointing and clicking, respectively, in mouse based interactions. With our implementation of a touchless addressing mechanism the user can move a fingertip through the air in a predefined virtual frame and thus control a screen cursor. The virtual frame is defined through calibration of a vision based hand tracker, which can be located either above or below the hand. In our experience this frame is most conveniently placed in a fronto-parallel plane in the usual human gesture space, which is located in chest height.

To trigger the action it is necessary to define a suitable gesture. For the sake of robustness we aimed at using a simple behavior of a single finger and thus to circumvent the recognition of hand configurations. After some trial and error we were left with two candidates, amongst which we needed to decide on an experimental basis, namely

1. staying on a point, i.e. the finger or the cursor must be held over an interactive element for a minimum dwell time to start an action associated with that element (Fig. 1 left part), and

2. movement across a z-threshold, i.e. positioning the cursor over an element and then moving the finger over some distance towards the display (Fig. 1 right part). This resembles the pushing of a button in the air.

In our experiment with 20 subjects we used an interactive element in the form of a graphically represented button, and we investigated five dependant variables that are suitable to indicate the relative usability of the two candidate gestures to activate the button. Those dependent variables were

1. the learning/exploration time till the subjects felt to master the gesture subsequent to a verbal instruction
2. the precision of addressing the button during its activation
3. the minimal button size the subjects felt to be acceptable for each gesture
4. the subjective satisfaction with each kind of gesture
5. the task completion time for addressing and activating a button.

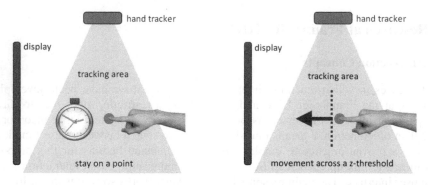

Fig. 1. Illustration of button activation by staying on a point (left) and movement across a z-threshold (right)

We found that there was a significant advantage (statistically and otherwise) for the staying on a point variant in the first four variables (Fig. 2), with task completion time, once the gesture had been learned, being the same.

As a result of these experiments we now normally employ staying on a point as an action signal in our touchless systems. We are also using the described single finger based interaction for direct manipulation. Thus touchless dragging, zooming, rotating and painting are easily possible. However, our research is ongoing, because we feel that in future comparisons slightly different z-movements might score better as an activation signal or as a grabbing action.

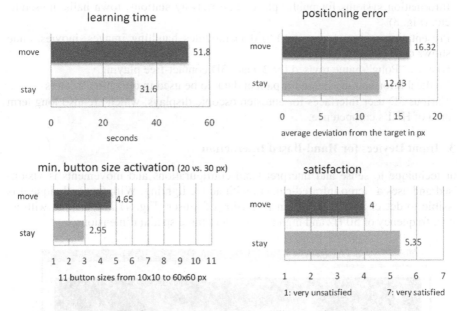

Fig. 2. Result of the gesture usability experiment

6.2 Application Scopes

Based on the mentioned scenarios that are advantageous for touchless interaction, Fraunhofer HHI has been developing various prototypes. They are used both as demonstrators on fairs or exhibitions and as testbeds for usability studies and further technology concepts [16]. Commercially available appliances include

Fig. 3. The iPoint Explorer, a touchless information system

- Information systems for public places like railway stations, town halls, museums etc. (Fig. 3)
- Presentation system for up to 120 data modules handling images, movies, slide shows or 3D objects
- Historic "Pong"-game revised for 2D and 3D contact-free playing
- Medical information system for patient data, to be used in operating theaters
- Various 3D user interfaces for autostereoscopic displays, which are also long term area of HHI's competence.

6.3   Input Devices for Hand-Based Interaction

Our technique to sense and interpret hand configurations and movements is vision-based and uses a stereo infrared-camera with active lighting. With that technique it is possible to detect and track all ten fingertips of a user (Fig. 4) in real-time with an image frequency of 50 Hz and high resolution in three spatial dimensions.

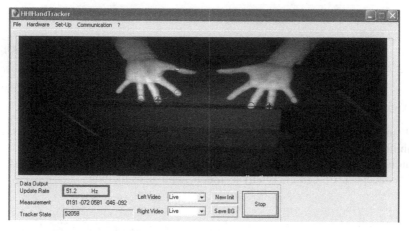

Fig. 4. Administrative user interface of Fraunhofer HHI hand tracker. Control image shows 10 detected fingertips

A number of measures like discarding static backgrounds have been contributing to the tracker's robust performance. Potential problems are the limited range of the active lighting and interfering objects in the camera's field of view that could be mistaken for fingers.

Several alternatives to our approach have been suggested in the literature or are already available on the market. Those include ultrasound position measurement devices, electrical field sensing devices, and time-of-flight depth cameras. The first two of these solutions cannot be used to recognize forms, and currently it is impossible to realize multitouch interaction with them. Therefore both are only suitable as finger mice, with three degrees of freedom, though. Electrical field sensing requires the placement of antennae near the user's hand, and some implementations of this principle require the user to stand on a metal ground plate. The time-of-flight principle is promising, but commercially available devices seem as yet to suffer from poor resolution, and the price tag of higher resolving units that are on the development roadmaps can be expected to be considerably higher as that of stereo cameras. Furthermore it remains to be seen how their performance is affected by objects in the field of view, the depth of which is mismeasured due to their problematic light reflection properties (either strong scattering or strong reflection).

Altogether the emerging techniques will soon offer useful, usable and fascinating forms of touchless interaction, but it is still necessary to carefully compare them with each other in terms of accuracy, reliability, and costs.

References

1. Shneiderman, B.: Direct manipulation: A step beyond programming languages. IEEE Computer 16(8), 57–69 (1983)
2. Cadoz, C.: Les réalités virtuelles. Dominos, Flammarion (1994)
3. Mulder, A.: Hand gestures for hci. Technical report, Hand Centered Studies of Human Movement Project, Simon Fraser University (1996)
4. Kendon, A.: Gesture: Visible Action as Utterance. Cambridge University Press, New York (2004)
5. Nelson, T.: Interactive systems and the design of virtuality. Creative Computing 6(11), 56–62 (1980)
6. Shneiderman, B.: Beyond intelligent machines: Just Do It! IEEE Software 10(1), 100–103 (1993)
7. Searle, J.: Speech Acts. Cambridge University Press, New York (1969)
8. de la Barré, R., Pastoor, S.: Conomis, Ch., Przewozny, D., Renault, S., Stachel, O., Duckstein, B., Schenke, K.: Natural Interaction in a desktop Mixed Reality environment. In: 6th International Workshop on Image Analysis for Multimedia Interactive Services WIAMIS 2005 (2005)
9. Varona, J., Jaume-i-Capó, A., Gonzàlez, J., Perales, F.J.: Toward natural interaction through visual recognition of body gestures in real-time. Interacting with Computers 21(1), 3–10 (2008)
10. McNeill, D.: Gesture and thought. University of Chicago Press, Chicago (2005)
11. Cassel, J.: A Frameworkfor gesture generation and interpretation. In: Cipolla, R., Pentland, A. (eds.) Computer Vision for Human-Machine Interaction, pp. 191–215. Cambridge University Press, New York (1998)
12. Application Gestures and Semantic Behavior (Windows),
    http://msdn.microsoft.com/en-us/library/ms704830(VS.85).aspx
13. Saffer, D.: Designing Gestural Interfaces. O'Reilly, Sebastopol (2008)
14. Norman, D.A.: Emotional Design: Why We Love (Or Hate) Everyday Things. Basic Books, New York (2004)
15. Hassenzahl, M.: Hedonic, emotional, and experiential perspectives on product quality. In: Ghaoui, C. (ed.) Encyclopedia of Human Computer Interaction, pp. 266–272. Idea Group, Hershey (2006)
16. Heinrich-Hertz-Institut - Department Overview,
    http://www.hhi.de/en/departments/
    interactive-media-human-factors/department-overview/

Did I Get It Right: Head Gestures Analysis for Human-Machine Interactions

Jürgen Gast[1], Alexander Bannat[1], Tobias Rehrl[1],
Gerhard Rigoll[1], Frank Wallhoff[1],
Christoph Mayer[2], and Bernd Radig[2]

[1] Department of Electrical Engineering and Information Technology,
Institute for Human-Machine Communication
[2] Computer Science Department,
Chair for Image Understanding and Knowledge-Based Systems

Technische Universität München
80290 Munich, Germany

Abstract. This paper presents a system for another input modality in a multimodal human-machine interaction scenario. In addition to other common input modalities, e.g. speech, we extract head gestures by image interpretation techniques based on machine learning algorithms to have a nonverbal and familiar way of interacting with the system. Our experimental evaluation proofs the capability of the presented approach to work in real-time and reliable.[1]

1 Motivation

Multimodal communication ways are becoming more important for a robust and flexible human-machine interaction in everyday surroundings. Therefore, our objective is to introduce a communication channel providing a natural and intuitive way of simple nonverbal communication. It emulates a common way of showing agreement / disagreement via head gestures, like it is known from human-human dialogs.

Due to its simplicity and omnipresence in every-day life, this contributes to making dialog systems more efficient.

2 Use-Cases

As already mentioned above, head gestures are present in numerous situations. Until now, we have integrated the recognition system in two human-machine interaction scenarios. In the following sections, we will present these two implementations.

---

[1] All authors contributed equally to the work presented in this paper.

J.A. Jacko (Ed.): Human-Computer Interaction, Part II, HCII 2009, LNCS 5611, pp. 170–177, 2009.

2.1 CoCoMate

Our first area of application is the automated coffee machine "CoCoMate" (Cognitive Coffee Machine) with a pan-tilt camera to facilitate interactions in the visual domain. In Picture 1, the system architecture of our coffee machine is depicted. The user can order various styles of coffee via speech input. This scenario facilitates dialog structures with several user confirmations to questions such as "Would you like to have an espresso?". These confirmations are mostly designed to have a simple yes or no structure. The answers of the user are recognized via speech or head gestures (here: nodding or shaking). Especially in noisy environments (here: grinding coffee beans) the state-of-the-art speech recognition is currently not robust enough to extract the uttered confirmation correctly. Therefore, the additional gesture communication channel can be exploited as complementary information source to deliver the desired semantic information of the user.

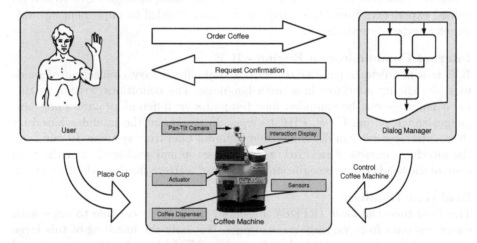

Fig. 1. Controlling CoCoMate: User interacts via a dialog system, which controls the ordering process and the actuators of the machine

2.2 Service Robot

The second implemented use-case is a more wide-spread application scenario concerning human-machine interaction situated in a household (see [1]). A service robot (for more details and examples please refer to [2]) is assisting the human in his daily tasks, e.g. bringing dishes, setting the table, etc. Therefore, the human has to communicate with the robot. To avoid unintended robot actions, it is very important for the human to know, if the robot got the right command. For accomplishing this degree of security, the dialog structure is designed in the following manner, that every action has to be confirmed by the user. This confirmation can be retrieved via an audio-based command, in this case a commercial speech recognizer software is applied. Additionally, the head of the service robot [3] is equipped with two firewire cameras following the user. One of these cameras is used within the head gesture detecting process.

3   System Overview

The system can be easily adapted to different human-machine dialogs, because the hard- and software requirements are very low. For the integration of the results obtained by the head gesture analysis, many interface modules are imaginable.

3.1   Interfaces

Many different kinds of interfaces are thinkable to constitute the interface between the head gesture software module and the dialog manager. Due to several gained experiences from other projects, we have decided to implement two different interface approaches:

Internet Communication Engine - ICE
ICE is a middleware (similar to SOAP) that allows easy connection of modules by defining interfaces in a meta language. The definitions written in this meta language can be compiled into templates in different programming languages ranging from C++, PHP to Java. Furthermore the modules based on these interfaces can run distributed on different operating systems. In our case, the interface consists of `initialize`, `start`, `stop` and `getResults` methods to control the head gesture recognition process and retrieve the desired information.

Real-time Database
The Real-time Database (RTDB) presented in [4,5,6] is capable to cope with enormous data from varying sensor inputs. Not only the handling of this large amount of data is accomplished easily by the RTDB, but also the processing of these data is done in real-time with a low processing overhead. The original area of application of the Real-time Database was situated in cognitive autonomous vehicles, where the database manages all sensor inputs to keep the vehicle on track.

The RTDB processes objects that can be created and updated by input modules, also called *writers*. In addition to the actual input data, these *writers* have to submit information about the time the data was acquired. Thereby, it is possible for the RTDB to synchronize the data coming in asynchronously from multiple sources and at different sampling rates. Output modules (called *readers*) wait for new objects to process them. In the here presented system, a simple camera-writer and reader is used for the head gesture recognition tool.

As a further advantage of the RTDB, the data stream of the camera-writer can not only be used for on-line head gesture recognition, but can also be recorded to deliver training input for the classification modules.

3.2   Dialog Manager

The controlling unit of the dialog (e.g. when the user is ordering a coffee) is based on a finite state machine (FSM). This dialog manager is responsible for acquiring high-level information and its semantic interpretation gained from sensor modules performing low-level operations. For example: When a human response via head gestures is expected, the dialog manager adjusts the camera on the face of the communication partner under consideration. High-level operations executed by the dialog manager comprise the switching between the states, depending on the currently available sensor inputs.

3.3   Head Gesture Analysis

Referring to the survey presented in [7], this task can be split into three subtasks. First, the location of the face is estimated in the image and a model fitting algorithm provides a face model parameterization. Then, features are extracted that describe the image content. Finally, machine learning techniques derive high-level information.

Face Model fitting

First, the face of the human interaction partner has to be located and extracted from the video data delivered by the RTDB. Therefore, a face detector basing on the well-known Viola Jones approach [8] is utilized to obtain possible locations of human faces. These hypothesis are validated using a model based on skin color [9,10]. In case that more than one validated human face is present in the scene, our first approach is to select the face, which surface surpasses all others in size. Having these information at hand, it is now possible to adjust the pan-tilt camera to focus the user's face in the center of the image plane immediately. As a next step, the generic model of a humanoid face has to be fitted to the one of the current dialog partner.

We integrated an implementation of the algorithm of Viola et al. [11]. A 3D-model forms an abstractions of the visible person's real world face and describes its properties by a parameter vector. In order to extract high-level information, model parameters have to be estimated, describing the face within a given image best. Model fitting solves this task and is often addressed by minimizing an objective function that evaluates, how well a model parameterization fits the processed image.

In contrast to other approaches, the objective function of our method is learned rather than being manually designed. This approach is constituted on general features of ideal objective functions [12]. The main idea behind this applied method is that if the function used to generate training data is ideal, the function learned from the data will also be approximately ideal. Additionally, we provide the learning algorithm with a large number of image features, which characterize the image content. In contrast to humans, the machine learning algorithm is capable to consider this vast amount of data and select the most descriptive features to build the calculation rules of the objective function. This provides both, good runtime performance and high precision.

Feature Extraction

In the second step, descriptive features are extracted, that characterize the displayed head gesture. This step is accomplished by extracting pose information from the fitted rigid 3D face model.

The small amount of model parameters provides a short computational time resulting in real-time capability. Five model parameters – in-plane transition of the face and the three rotation angles – are considered to train a classifier for the recognition of head gestures. Yet, instead of using the absolute parameter values of single images, we calculate the transitional and rotational speed of the face from temporal parameter changes.

Classification

In the third step, the head gesture, performed by the person visible, is obtained from the extracted features.

The feature values gained from the model-fitting process are now analyzed with a continuous Hidden Markov Model (HMM). The HMM was trained from the image data of fourteen different persons performing three basic types of head gestures (nodding, shaking and neutral). Two sequences per test person and head gesture have been captured.

Continuous Hidden Markov Models serve this purpose well for several reasons. First, they inherently consider temporal dynamics of the training data and the test data. Since head gestures are also inherently dynamic, HMMs model their characteristics well and therefore provide profound classification results. Second, HMMs compensate changes in the speed of the performed head gesture during recognition. Therefore, head gestures that are performed slower or faster than depicted in the training data are also recognized. Both advantages allow the HMM to consider temporal aspects, although the data is presented image vice. Therefore, the temporal aspects do not have to be modeled by the designer, for instance via sliding windows.

4   Evaluation

Finally, an experimental evaluation of the recognition system was conducted. This evaluation has the classification accuracy of the Hidden Markov Model under investigation. The reliability of the gained results of the HMM has a crucial impact on the entire human-machine-communication process. This is especially entailed in the reactions of the human user towards the machine, how naturally the communication is perceived and how comfortable he is feeling about using the presented dialog system. Therefore, a six fold cross validation has been conducted to prove the robustness and reliability as well, see Table 1.

For this purpose, we divided the recorded data into six disjunct sets. One of these sets was taken to constitute the testing set and the five remaining sets were used to build the HMM-model. This procedure was conducted six times and the arithmetic mean value of the obtained results can be seen in Table 1. The number of states J of the Hidden Markov Model ranges from four to seven.

Table 1. This table presents recognition rates of our HMM trained with four to seven states. The results are obtained from a 6-fold cross validation.

	Sequence Label		
Classified As	Shaking	Neutral	Nodding
Shaking	**94%**	5%	0%
Neutral	16%	**77%**	7%
Nodding	0%	22%	**78%**
Mean error rate	17.00%		

a) classification result with four states

	Sequence Label		
Classified As	Shaking	Neutral	Nodding
Shaking	**100%**	0%	0%
Neutral	11%	**89%**	0%
Nodding	0%	6%	**94%**
Mean error rate	5.67%		

b) classification result with five states

	Sequence Label		
Classified As	Shaking	Neutral	Nodding
Shaking	**100%**	0%	0%
Neutral	6%	**88%**	6%
Nodding	0%	6%	**94%**
Mean error rate	6.00%		

c) classification result with six states

	Sequence Label		
Classified As	Shaking	Neutral	Nodding
Shaking	**100%**	0%	0%
Neutral	6%	**94%**	0%
Nodding	6%	6%	**88%**
Mean error rate	6.00%		

d) classification result with seven states

Again, the above described six fold cross validation was also applied to determine the recognition accuracy. The best results are achieved for $J = 5$, which can be seen in Table 1, showing the mean error rate and additionally an overview of the accuracy values.

5   Conclusion and Future Work

In this paper we introduce head gesture recognition as a simple and robust communication channel for a human-machine interaction. Due to the following three reasons, the results of the implemented system show high potential of this interaction method. First, this method is similar to the human-human interaction of showing agreement and disagreement (head nodding and head shaking). Second, the system is capable to extract head gestures in real-time with a low resource usage. Third, the learned objective function as well as the gained HMM can be replaced with a more sophisticated version without necessitating further modifications on the head gesture recognizer module.

Future work will lay stress on extending the area of robust applications towards real-life scenarios (lighting conditions, multiple points of view, etc.). Additionally, it is foreseen to integrate facial expressions into the classification process.

Acknowledgment

This ongoing work is supported by the DFG excellence initiative research cluster *Cognition for Technical Systems – CoTeSys*, see www.cotesys.org for further details and information. At first, we want to mention here Stefan Sosnowski, the constructor of the EDDIE head [3]. He was a great support for the realization of this project, and he always helped us with words and deeds. The authors further acknowledge the great support of Matthias Göbl for his explanations and granting access to the RTDB repository. In addition, we want to thank all our partners within our CoTeSys-Projects for the fruitful discussions and implementation work to make our visions and ideas become reality.

References

1. Beetz, M., Stulp, F., Radig, B., Bandouch, J., Blodow, N., Dolha, M., Fedrizzi, A., Jain, D., Klank, U., Kresse, I., Maldonado, A., Marton, Z., Mösenlechner, L., Ruiz, F., Rusu, R.B., Tenorth, M.: The assistive kitchen — a demonstration scenario for cognitive technical systems. In: IEEE 17th International Symposium on Robot and Human Interactive Communication (RO-MAN), Muenchen, Germany (2008) (Invited paper)
2. Homepage of Institute of Automatic Control Engineering (LSR), Technische Universität München, Munich,
   http://www.lsr.ei.tum.de/research/research-areas/robotics/
   murola-the-multi-robot-lab

3. Sosnowski, S., Kuhnlenz, K., Buss, M.: EDDIE - An Emotion-Display with Dynamic Intuitive Expressions. In: The 15th IEEE International Symposium on Robot and Human Interactive Communication. ROMAN 2006, University of Hertfordshire, Hatfield, United Kingdom, September 6-8, 2006, pp. 569–574 (2006)
4. Goebl, M., Färber, G.: A real-time-capable hard- and software architecture for joint image and knowledge processing in cognitive automobiles. In: Intelligent Vehicles Symposium, pp. 737–740 (June 2007)
5. Stiller, C., Färber, G., Kammel, S.: Cooperative cognitive automobiles. In: Intelligent Vehicles Symposium, pp. 215–220. IEEE, Los Alamitos (2007)
6. : Thuy, M., Göbl, M., Rattei, F., Althoff, M., Obermeier, F., Hawe, S., Nagel, R., Kraus, S., Wang, C., Hecker, F., Russ, M., Schweitzer, M., León, F.P., Diepold, K., Eberspächer, J., Heißing, B., Wünsche, H.J.: Kognitive automobile - neue konzepte und ideen des sonderforschungsbereiches/tr-28. In: Aktive Sicherheit durch Fahrerassistenz, Garching bei München, April 7-8 (2008)
7. Pantic, M., Rothkrantz, L.J.M.: Automatic analysis of facial expressions: The state of the art. IEEE Transactions on Pattern Analysis and Machine Intelligence 22(12), 1424–1445 (2000)
8. Viola, P., Jones, M.: Rapid object detection using a boosted cascade of simple features. In: Conference on Computer Vision and Pattern Recognition1, pp. 511–518 (2001)
9. Soriano, M., Huovinen, S., Martinkauppi, B., Laaksonen, M.: Skin Detection in Video under Changing Illumination Conditions. In: Proc. 15th International Conference on Pattern Recognition, Barcelona, Spain, pp. 839–842 (2000)
10. Vezhnevets, V., Sazonov, V., Andreeva, A.: A survey on pixel-based skin color detection techniques. In: Proc. Graphicon 2003, pp. 85–92 (2003)
11. Viola, P., Jones, M.J.: Robust real-time face detection. International Journal of Computer Vision (2004)
12. Wimmer, M., Stulp, F., Pietzsch, S., Radig, B.: Learning local objective functions for robust face model fitting. IEEE (PAMI) 30(8) (2008)

Interactive Demonstration of Pointing Gestures for Virtual Trainers

Yazhou Huang and Marcelo Kallmann

University of California, Merced
{yhuang6,mkallmann}@ucmerced.edu

Abstract. While interactive virtual humans are becoming widely used in education, training and delivery of instructions, building the animations required for such interactive characters in a given scenario remains a complex and time consuming work. One of the key problems is that most of the systems controlling virtual humans are mainly based on pre-defined animations which have to be re-built by skilled animators specifically for each scenario. In order to improve this situation this paper proposes a framework based on the direct demonstration of motions via a simplified and easy to wear set of motion capture sensors. The proposed system integrates motion segmentation, clustering and interactive motion blending in order to enable a seamless interface for programming motions by demonstration.

Keywords: virtual humans, motion capture, interactive demonstration.

1 Introduction

The motivation of this work is to develop new algorithms and techniques to achieve effective virtual assistants that can interact, learn, train, assist and help people to execute tasks, with the potential to provide assistance, deliver training and education, etc. In general, there are two main approaches for synthesizing gestures for interactive virtual humans: 1) the first approach produces high quality gestures with pre-defined keyframe animation either hand-crafted or by motion capture (*mocap*) [1] [2]. These systems are then able to reproduce the available motions according to the given goals, context and speech. The final result is usually very realistic; however motions cannot be easily reused in new scenarios. 2) The main alternative is to algorithmically synthesize the needed motions, such as in the VHP [3] and MAX [4] systems, however achieving less realistic results.

This paper proposes a framework that attempts to capture the advantages of both approaches. We employ parameterized motion blending techniques [5] in order to achieve realistic results which can be adapted and parameterized, and we also take into account on-line motion demonstrations for the interactive modeling of new gesture motions. To test our framework we present in this paper our prototype system for demonstration of pointing gestures. Pointing was chosen because of its importance: besides being one of the earliest forms of communication used by humans it serves several purposes: it guides the attention of the listeners or viewers, assigns meanings and labels to locations and objects, etc [6]. Our framework can be easily adapted to

J.A. Jacko (Ed.): Human-Computer Interaction, Part II, HCII 2009, LNCS 5611, pp. 178–187, 2009.
© Springer-Verlag Berlin Heidelberg 2009

other demonstrative gestures for instance for describing characteristics (weight, size, etc), for showing how actions should be performed, or for expressing qualitative characteristics needed to perform actions. The main characteristic explored in this work is the fact that the end-effector trajectory and/or final location are the most important aspects in demonstrative gestures.

The proposed framework also presents a new gesture modeling paradigm based on interactive motion demonstrations. Our framework can be seen as an imitation-based approach [7] [8] and is especially relevant for controlling and programming tasks for humanoid agents [9] [10] [11] [12] [13]. It also represents a natural approach to human-computer interaction by analogy to the way humans naturally interact with each other. This paper describes our first results towards achieving an intuitive interface based on low cost wearable motion sensors for programming and customizing demonstrative gestures.

2 System Overview

Our framework models each demonstrative gesture with a cluster of example gestures of the same type but with variations for the different locations being demonstrated. In the pointing gestures modeled in this work the different locations are the locations being pointed at. For example a gesture cluster for a certain way of pointing consists of several examples of similar pointing gestures but each pointing to a different location. Gestures in a cluster are time-aligned in order to allow correct blendings and Inverse Kinematics corrections to be performed for computing a final gesture motion able to achieve given specific target pointing locations. This process is referred here as *Inverse Blending*.

We have also developed for our system a *gesture vest*, for achieving a mocap-based human-computer interface for on-line motion demonstrations. Example motions can be demonstrated interactively and converted to new examples to be added in the database, in order to enable the interactive customization of gestures. This interactive interface allows seamless user interactions for programming gestures. Our overall system is depicted in Figure 1.

The system maintains a gesture database on-the-fly by storing selected demonstrations from the gesture vest. The database can also be initialized with basic gestures. The virtual character can then reuse the demonstrated motions in order to point to any

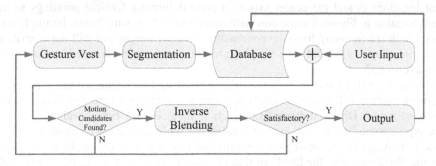

Fig. 1. System overview

desired location and the resulted motion will exhibit the same characteristics of the demonstrated examples. If suitable candidate example motions are not available in the database, or if the user is not satisfied with the aspect of the output motion, new demonstrations can be interactively given by the user via the gesture vest. The system can therefore learn user-specific (pointing) tasks in different scenarios through on-line demonstrations, and at the same time preserve the characteristics of the demonstrated motions as much as possible.

The next section describes our inverse blending algorithm for pointing gestures, and section 4 presents our *gesture vest* interface built specifically for this work.

3   Inverse Blending of Pointing Gestures

After a collection of similar pointing motion segments is acquired, they will form a gesture cluster G stored in the database. Let m_i be one motion segment in G. Each motion is represented as a sequence of frames and each frame is represented with the position of the root joint and the rotations of each other joint in the character skeleton. The system then computes the stroke time t_i of m_i and determines the position p_i and orientation q_i of the character's hand in global coordinates at time t_i by Forward Kinematics, with the orientation q_i being represented in quaternion format. Each segment m_i is then time-warped such that all motions have their stroke times and durations the same. The stroke time is in particular addressed here due its main importance for parameterizing demonstrative gestures, and in particular pointing gestures.

A motion blending mechanism is then employed for computing new gesture motions for achieving new targets at the stroke point. We use a traditional blending scheme of the type $m_b(w_1, \ldots, w_n) = \sum B_i(w_i) m_i$ to interpolate examples from G, where B_i are normalized kernel functions whose values depend on the weight coefficients w_i. The challenge is to determine the weight values which will lead to stroke locations as close as possible to the (p,q) target. A typical approach is to adjust the kernel functions B_i in order to best address the parameterization and spatial constraints [14] [5]. However pre-computation of the weights is required making this approach less suitable for interactive systems and in any case it is not possible to guarantee precise placements. Therefore, in order to achieve hand placements with precise control, we also employ Inverse Kinematics (IK) corrections.

We first determine the blending weights according to the distances between the wrist locations p_i and the center axis of a cone delimiting feasible pointings to the target location p. Figure 2 illustrates such a cone in yellow wire frame. Example motions which are far away from the cone will get a zero weight and will not contribute to the blending result. Once the weights are computed, a first blended motion m_b is then determined.

Motion m_b will produce a pointing motion pointing to a location nearby the target but most likely it will not be precisely pointing to the target. Correction iterations are then performed. Different iterative correction methods are being evaluated in our prototype system and we are currently using a simple correction mechanism as follows. Let (p_b, q_b) be the wrist joint position and orientation at the stroke time of motion m_b. We then adjust the hand position p_b in order to achieve the fingertip precisely pinpointing the goal, obtaining a new position p'_b. Next, we use the position and orientation (p_b',q_b) as a IK goal for producing a new arm posture precisely pointing the target. We use a fast analytical IK solver [15] which allows specifying the swivel angle of the final arm posture to be the same as the swivel angle observed in the stroke posture of m_b. The solved IK posture will therefore precisely point the target and at the same time will be very similar to the blended posture due to the enforcement of the original q_b and the swivel angle. The blending weights are then adjusted during a few iterations in order to get new a blended motion with a stroke posture closer to the solved IK posture. When finished, a final correction with IK is performed in all the frames of the motion to compute the final precisely correct pointing motion. First the stroke posture is corrected by the posture computed by the IK and then decreasing correction values are propagated along all the previous and subsequent frames of the motion in order to achieve the final pointing motion. See Figure 3 for some obtained examples. In this way, blending is guiding IK to be more "human-like", while IK is guiding blending to get closer to the precise pointing. As the algorithm iterates, the blended posture approaches the IK solution, given that enough example motions are available.

Note that a suitable solution may not be found in several cases: when positions are not reachable within the desirable error, when there are no sufficient example gestures in the database, etc. The user will then need to interactively demonstrate new gestures

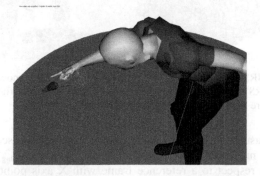

Fig. 2. A cone is used to delimit the region of feasible pointings. The shown posture represents one example pointing posture that will receive a high blending weight as it is close to the cone.

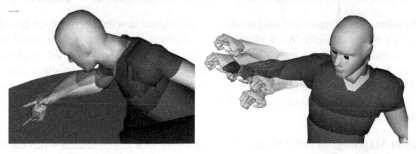

Fig. 3. Left: comparison between a posture obtained with blending (in transparence) and the same posture after IK correction. Right: precise pointings are achieved after the IK correction.

to be included in the cluster until an acceptable result is obtained. This overall combined approach will result in an effective system for gesture modeling and synthesis.

4 Wearable Motion Capture Vest

We have built a wearable motion capture vest for achieving a suitable human-computer interface for our system. The interface uses five InnaLabs AHRS sensors [16] to capture the orientation changes of performer's spine, head and a full arm. In addition, a 5DT data glove is used to capture hand shapes, and a Nintendo Wii remote controller is used for providing basic instructions (record, play, delete, etc) during demonstration of new example gesture motions. As illustrated in Figure 4, the sensors are attached on a detachable sleeve, in the form of an easy-to-wear gesture vest. The vest is connected to a computer via wired USB-RS 485 converters, optionally connected to a wireless USB hub.

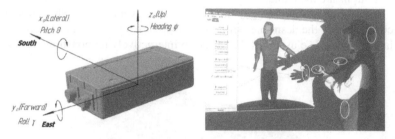

Fig. 4. Left: miniAHRS m2 sensor used in our system. Right: Our mocap vest, with a data glove and 5 miniAHRS sensors placed on spine, head, right upper-arm, right forearm and right hand. The locations are highlighted with yellow circles.

Each sensor measures its orientation in global coordinates based on triaxial gyro, accelerometer and magnetometer. Each measured rotation $q_{reading}$ is represented in quaternion form in respect to a reference frame with X axis pointing South, Y axis pointing East, and Z axis pointing upwards, as shown in Figure 4-left. The maximum update rate is 120 Hz in quaternion mode. These commercially-available sensors provide good results but different sensors and technologies can also be used [17] [18].

Calibration: The sensors use magnetometers to acquire absolute orientation based on the earth's magnetic field. We perform an initial orientation calibration by standing in a T-pose facing North to match the zero-rotation of the sensor with the negative X pointing North, as shown in Figure 5(2). Since the sensors can be in slightly different positions every time the performer wears the vest, a calibration is done before each new capture session. The calibration will record a reference rotation q_{calib} for each sensor.

Skeleton Mapping: In order to map the sensed rotations to our skeleton representing the character to be animated we have to transform the rotations to suitable frames in local coordinates. First we transform $q_{reading}$ to a Z-up coordinate system, producing a rotation compatible with the sensor's native coordinate system (Z-up, see

Figure 4-left). In this way, for example, a rotation $q_{reading}$ along South axis will produce the corresponding quaternion rotation $q_{Z\text{-up}}$ along X axis after applying the calibration quaternion. Rotation $q_{Z\text{-up}}$ is obtained with:

$$q_{Z-up} = q_{reading} \cdot q_{calib}^{-1} \cdot$$

The virtual character we're using follows a Y-up coordinate system as shown in Figure 5(1). In order to drive our character, we use pre-rotations and post-rotations that transform the rotation from miniAHRS Z-up coordinate to our Y-up coordinate:

$$q_{Y-up} = q_{preRot} \cdot q_{Z-up} \cdot q_{postRot},$$

where q_{preRot} is 120° rotation along axis (-1, 1, 1) in quaternion form that rotates the character from the Y-up frame to the Z-up frame (see Figure 5). Rotation $q_{postRot}$ produces the opposite rotation which is -120° rotation along same axis (-1, 1, 1).

Before applying $q_{Y\text{-up}}$ to character's joints, it has to be transformed to local coordinates. The joint structure of our character is shown on the right side of Figure 5. Every time the character's skeleton is updated with the sensed values, the rotation of each joint in global coordinates is computed by Forward Kinematics, i. e., by recursively multiplying the local rotations of all parent joints, starting at the root joint. Global rotations can then be transformed to local coordinates with:

$$q_{local} = q_{parent}^{-1} \cdot q_{Y-up},$$

where q_{local} is the final rotation to be sent to the joint being mapped and q_{parent} is it's parent rotation in global coordinates.

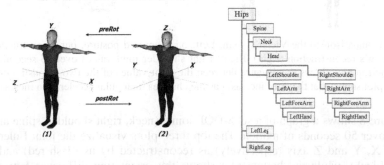

Fig. 5. Left: the different coordinate systems. Right: character structure.

Quality Evaluation: We have compared the results achieved by our mocap vest against results recorded with the Vicon optical-based motion capture system, which captures positions in global coordinates with precision generally better than 4 millimeters. We have captured motions simultaneously with the two systems, wearing our mocap vest underneath the Vicon suit with the reflective markers placed following the suggestions in Vicon's manual. The sensor readings were acquired at a rate of 30 frames per second and were directly mapped to our skeleton. We used Vicon Blade software to fit the same skeleton used by our system to the optical markers, and we initialized the reconstruction with identical initial poses. The global reference frame of Vicon's reconstruction was also transformed to be the same as in our system. Since our mocap vest does not capture lower body motions, the performer maintained the waist at the initial position. Although neither reconstruction is perfect, Vicon matches the original motions visibly better, thus we treat it as ground truth in our comparison analysis. Evaluation is done by comparing the rotations for a set of corresponding joints on both skeletons.

The left side of Figure 6 shows one frame of a 85-seconds range-of-motion capture with the right arm covering most of its reachable space. Our reconstruction is shown on the left and Vicon's on the right. The left side of Figure 7 shows the trajectories of the right hand joint along a portion of the captured motion, with our reconstruction marked with red, and Vicon's marked with blue. The plots are different views from the same motion frame. Vicon's reconstruction matches the original motion slightly better as it captures more joints than our vest, though our vest is able to better reconstruct subtle motions such as slight wrist flicks and more precise head orientation as shown in Figure 6-left (note that our current vest does not capture the left arm, which is kept in its initial configuration).

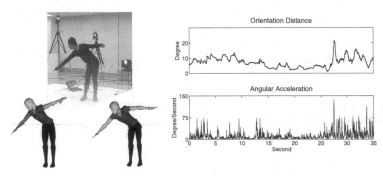

Fig. 6. Comparison to the Vicon system. Left: one captured posture, our reconstruction (left) and Vicon's reconstruction (right). Right: right shoulder joint values over 35 seconds of motion. The top plot shows the distance between the joint values of the two reconstructions. The bottom plot shows that the error increases as the changes in angular acceleration increases.

Figure 8 shows a graph of a set 3-DOF joints (neck, right shoulder, spine and right hand) over 50 seconds of motion. The top three plots visualize the joint Euler angles (along X, Y and Z axis respectively) as reconstructed by us (dash red) and Vicon (solid black), while the bottom plot shows the orientation difference between our reconstruction and that of the Vicon system. The orientation difference is introduced by computing the quaternion distance [19] of a pair of corresponding joints (between us and Vicon) defined as:

$$\theta = \arccos(q_1 \cdot q_2).$$

As can be seen from the plots, the orientation differences are generally below 10°~20°. Joint rotations from our mocap system could mostly follow that of Vicon, except for some motion periods where the difference becomes slightly larger, in particular when angular acceleration of the motion greatly increases or decreases (see Figure 6-right). This is due to the characteristics of the miniAHRS sensor as the orientation sensing relies more on gyroscope and accelerometer to achieve fast responses when angular acceleration increases, and depends more on magnetometer when motion becomes slow to then give fairly accurate readings.

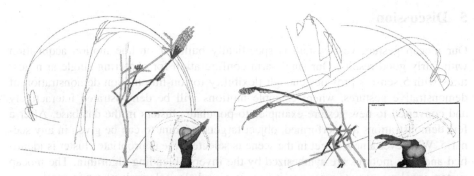

Fig. 7. Trajectories of the right hand joint with our reconstruction (marked in red) and Vicon's (marked in blue). The two plots are different views of same motion frame.

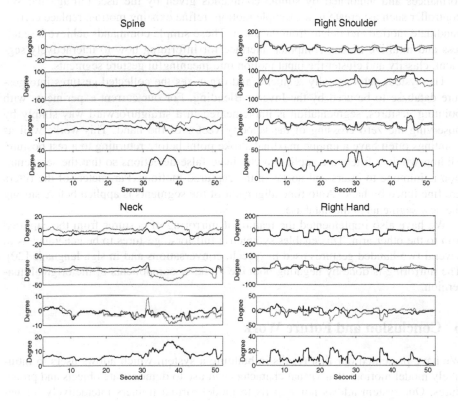

Fig. 8. Euler angle plots for a set of 3-DOF joints (neck, right shoulder, spine and right hand) over 50 seconds of motion. The top three plots compare joint Euler angles as reconstructed by us (dash red) and Vicon (solid black). The bottom-most plot shows the orientation difference between the two reconstructions.

5   Discussion

Our mocap gesture vest system is specifically built for on-line motion acquisition with fairly good results. Our single-arm configuration for capturing single arm gestures with 5 sensors provides enough flexibility for on-line motion demonstration of demonstrative gestures, where example motions will be demonstrated interactively and converted to new gesture examples to populate clusters in the database. After a few demonstrations are performed, object targets to point to can be given in any scenario. Whenever a new target in the scene is selected, the appropriate cluster is identified and new motions are synthesized by the inverse blending algorithm. The mocap system is robust, easy to wear, intuitive to use, and also relatively cheap in cost.

The motion stream produced by the sensors is continuously monitored during performances and annotated by simple commands given by the user through the Wii controller such as: create new example motion, refine existing motion, replace current candidate motion and delete from database. These simple commands achieve a seamless and intuitive human-computer interface for informing how to interactively segment, classify and cluster the input motion into meaningful gesture segments.

The system automatically segments and organizes the collected gestures into gesture database to be used by the Inverse Blending. For our current experiments with pointing gestures, segmentation is implemented in a straightforward way simply by observing the zero crossing of the velocity vector of the hand. This works well as pointings often have a unique maximal stroke point before returning to a rest posture. Sliding-window filters are applied to eliminate false detections so that the segmentation is immune to jitters and noises in the captured motions. Parameters of the filters are fine tuned by hand. Auto time-alignment of the segments is applied before storing the new segments in the database.

We have also implemented the feature of mirroring of gestures from the captured arm to the other arm. This enables symmetric full-torso gestures to be generated as in several two-handed gestures used in speech, conversations and in sign language [20]. The mirroring is done by negating both the x and w components of the original quaternion.

6   Conclusion and Future Work

We have presented our first results in building a system which allows users to intuitively model motions that virtual characters can use to demonstrate objects and procedures. Our system allows non-experts to model virtual trainers interactively for generic training and educational applications.

As future work, we are exploring several improvements and extensions, for instance: an improved inverse blending solver and the integration of locomotion in order to enable the character to also move around the objects being demonstrated.

Acknowledgements. This work was partially supported by NSF Award CNS-0723281 and a CITRIS seed project.

References

1. Gebhard, P., Michael Kipp, M.K.T.R.: What are they going to talk about? towards life-like characters that reflect on interactions with users. In: Proc. of the 1st International Conf. on Tech. for Interactive Digital Storytelling and Entertainment, TIDSE 2003 (2003)
2. Thiebaux, M., Marshall, A., Marsella, S., Kallmann, M.: Smartbody: Behavior realization for embodied conversational agents. In: Seventh International Joint Conference on Autonomous Agents and Multi-Agent Systems (AAMAS) (2008)
3. Noma, T., Zhao, L., Badler, N.I.: Design of a virtual human presenter. IEEE Computer Graphics and Applications 20(4), 79–85 (2000)
4. Kopp, S., Wachsmuth, I.: Model-based animation of co-verbal gesture. In: Proceedings of Computer Animation 2002, pp. 252–257 (2002)
5. Rose, C., Bodenheimer, B., Cohen, M.F.: Verbs and adverbs: Multidimensional motion interpolation. IEEE Computer Graphics and Applications 18, 32–40 (1998)
6. Kita, S.: Pointing: A foundational building block of human communication. In: Kita, S. (ed.) Pointing, Where Language, Culture, and Cognition Meet. Lawrence Erlb. Ass., NJ (2003)
7. Breazeal, C., Buchsbaum, D., Gray, J., Gatenby, D., Blumberg, D.: Learning from and about others: Towards using imitation to bootstrap the social understanding of others by robots. Artificial Life 11, 1–2 (2005)
8. Schaal, S., Ijspeert, A., Billard, A.: Computational approaches to motor learning by imitation. The Neuroscience of Social Interaction 1431, 199–218 (2003)
9. Suleiman, W., Yoshida, E., Kanehiro, F., Laumond, J.P., Monin, A.: On human motion imitation by humanoid robot. In: 2008 IEEE International Conference on Robotics and Automation (ICRA), pp. 2697–2704 (2008)
10. Olenderski, A., Nicolescu, M., Louis, S.: Robot learning by demonstration using forward models of schema-based behaviors. In: Proceedings of International Conference on Informatics in Control, Automation and Robotics, Barcelona, Spain, pp. 14–17 (2005)
11. Nicolescu, M.N., Mataric, M.J.: Natural methods for robots task learning: Instructive demonstration, generalization and practice. In: Proc. of the 2nd Internat. Joint Conf. on Autonomous Agents and Multi-Agent Systems (AAMAS), Melbourne, Australia (2003)
12. Ramesh, A., Mataric, M.J.: Learning movement sequences from demonstration. In: Proceedings of the International Conference on Development and Learning (ICDL), pp. 302–306. MIT, Cambridge (2002)
13. Billard, A., Mataric, M.J.: Learning human arm movements by imitation: Evaluation of a biologically inspired connectionist architecture. Robotics and Autonomous Systems 37(2-3), 145–160 (2001)
14. Mukai, T., Kuriyama, S.: Geostatistical motion interpolation. In: SIGGRAPH 2005: ACM SIGGRAPH 2005 Papers, pp. 1062–1070. ACM, New York (2005)
15. Kallmann, M.: Analytical Inverse Kinematics with Body Posture Control. Computer Animation and Virtual Worlds (CAVW) 19(2), 79–91 (2008)
16. Innalabs miniAHRS m2 user's manual (2008)
17. Vlasic, D., Adelsberger, R., Vannucci, G., Barnwell, J., Gross, M., Matusik, W., Popovic, J.: Practical motion capture in everyday surroundings. In: SIGGRAPH 2007: ACM SIGGRAPH 2007 papers, p. 35. ACM, New York (2007)
18. Slyper, R., Hodgins, J.: Action capture with accelerometers. In: 2008 ACM SIGGRAPH / Eurographics Symposium on Computer Animation (2008)
19. Hanson, A.J.: Visualizing Quaternions. The Morgan Kaufmann Series in Interactive 3D Technology, pp. 248–249. Morgan Kaufmann, San Francisco (2005)
20. Xiong, Y., Quek, F., McNeill, D.: Hand gesture symmetric behavior detection and analysis in natural conversation. In: IEEE Internat. Conf. on Multimodal Interfaces, p. 179 (2002)

Anthropometric Facial Emotion Recognition

Julia Jarkiewicz, Rafał Kocielnik, and Krzysztof Marasek

Polish-Japanese Institute of Information Technology
Koszykowa 86, 02-008 Warszawa, Poland
{julia.jarkiewicz,rafal.kocielnik,kmarasek}@pjwstk.edu.pl

Abstract. The aim of this project is detection, analysis and recognition of facial features. The system operates on grayscale images. For the analysis Haar-like face detector was used along with anthropometric face model and a hybrid feature detection approach. The system localizes 17 characteristic points of analyzed face and, based on their displacements certain emotions can be automatically recognized. The system was tested on a publicly available database (Japanese Female Expression Database) JAFFE with ca. 77% accuracy for 7 basic emotions using various classifiers. Thanks to its open structure the system can cooperate well with any HCI system.

Keywords: emotion recognition, facial expression detection, affective computing.

1 Introduction

Effective computer image analysis was always a great challenge for many researchers. Tasks, usually quite simple for humans, such as object or emotion recognition proves to be very complicated in computer analysis.

Among the main problems are susceptibility to varying lightning conditions, color changes and differences in transformation. Effective detection of human faces is one of the greatest problems in image analysis. Therefore it is even more challenging to efficiently and effectively localize features of a face in analyzed image and to relate them to expression of emotions.

Hereby work is actually an attempt to create a computer system able to automatically detect, localize and recognize facial features. Sought features are, in this case, characteristic points placed in selected locations on human face model. The locations and distances between them change during facial expressions.

There are many, more or less effective solutions capable of detecting or recognizing faces, however only a few comprehensive and effective solutions exist connecting all those features together and, at the same time, able to cooperate with an emotion recognition system. The work is largely based on solutions presented in [1], [2], [3]. As our test-bed the JAFFE database [4] was used. It consists of 213 grayscale 256x256 pixels photos of 10 Japanese woman faces showing 6 basic emotions (fear, sad, angry, happy, surprised, disgust) each in 3 variants and one neutral face. Low resolution, grayscale only photos form a challenge even for advanced techniques.

J.A. Jacko (Ed.): Human-Computer Interaction, Part II, HCII 2009, LNCS 5611, pp. 188–197, 2009.
© Springer-Verlag Berlin Heidelberg 2009

2 Face Detection

Before any attempt to detect facial features can be made, a precise position of a face must be determined. Number of approaches exists that address this task, see [3] for complete description. The one used for this work is presented below.

2.1 Cascade Haar-Like Feature Classifier

Solution uses Haar-like features based on a very simple Haar function:

$$H(t) = \begin{cases} 0 \ for \ t < 0 \\ 1 \ for \ 0 \leq t \leq 0,5 \\ -1 \ for \ 0.5 \leq t < 1 \\ 0 \ for \ t \geq 1 \end{cases} \tag{1}$$

The method works in different scales. For the sake of performance, the analysis begins at the highest scale and when the template is found, the region nearby is searched again in a more precise scale. This makes the detection a coarse to fine approach. The process is repeated until the most precise scale is reached. The method is one of the most popular thanks to its effectiveness and efficiency [2]. This is because of three main characteristics:

Cascade classification – The whole classification process is divided into stages that follow one another, greatly saving processing power and increasing efficiency.

Fig. 1. Haar-like image masks and their placement on analyzed image (after [7])

Image masks (weak Haar-classifiers) and boosting – each of the stages in cascade is a separate complex classifier based on boosting (Adaboost) [9] in the form of a decision tree with at least two leaves. The final determination is made based on the so called Haar-like features. The Haar-like features are in fact simple image masks that have been designed to find different features of the image like lines, corners, etc. The extended set of such masks is presented in Fig. 1.

Usage of integral image –for detection of objects in different locations a sliding widow technique is used. Finding objects in different sizes, was solved by usage of integral image which allows to resize classifier rather than the image itself [2].

The implementation of the algorithm used in this work is a part of the *OpenCV* [5] free image processing library. The results of the face localization are shown in Fig. 2.

Fig. 2. Examples of face localizations (*JAFFE database and Internet*)

2.2 Face Normalization

Currently two types of normalization are used by the system: illumination and geometrical normalizations.

Illumination normalization is in use at various stages of processing, beginning with normalization for the whole image and then followed by normalization for identified regions containing facial elements. Plain histogram equalization but also histogram matching and Retinex method [6] are used in different areas of this work.

Geometrical normalization is used in order to scale, crop or rotate a face. In this work only rotation and cropping of the face is performed since scaling could introduce some lose of the details that are important for precise feature detection.

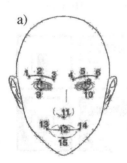 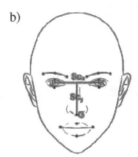 

Fig. 3. Normalization of anthropometric distances: a) localization of points, b) angle normalization, c) distances computed

As can be observed in Fig. 2 faces are localized quite imprecisely and without information about rotation. For the next stages of the analysis it is a key feature to locate the face as precisely as possible, since this allows for correct placement of all face elements. In order to correct inaccuracies and acquire information about the rotation of the face a geometrical normalization based on eye center positions has been added. Although its length can vary for different faces, the perpendicular line placed in the geometric center between eyes almost always sets the face's symmetry axis (Fig. 3b). The very final information provided is the rotation of the face, which can be determined by measuring the angle between eye centers (Fig. 3b).

3 Localization of Characteristic Points in a Face

Anthropometry is a section of biology which deals with measuring human body and its parts. The authors of [1] have created the anthropometric model of human face measuring 300 facial en face images of more than 150 people originating from different parts of the world. The model can be used for localizing facial elements based on positions of eye centers. In Fig. 3a) localization of basic points is shown. They describe well face features which change during emotions' expression.

3.1 Localization of Eyes

For use with anthropometric model eye centers need to be localized very precisely. Unfortunately, most of the methods give location of the pupil rather than the eye center itself. The real difficulty starts when eye is half-shut or closed.

To meet all the requirements and deal with the aforementioned problems a Haar-like feature classifier has been used once again, trained this time specifically to detect left and right eye separately following [8].

Eye localization based on Haar-like features has numerous advantages (ability to operate on grayscale images, ability to detect eyes even if they are not fully open, resistance to changeable lightning conditions, effortless usage and efficiency). Initial attempts to use this method revealed some difficulties. In most cases detection process gives a number of possible candidate positions for one eye. Although several candidates are provided, the correct one is always among them. It has also been spotted that the correct localization of face itself is limited to the rotations of about ±30°. Consequently, there is no need to look for eyes in the whole face area.

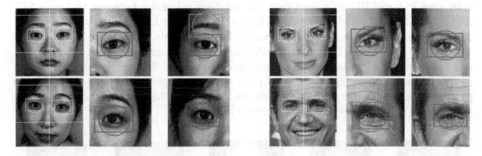

Fig. 4. Eye localization with usage of limited search space (*JAFFE database and Internet*) in *white* – final eye positions (white circle and rectangle), limiting regions (white lines) *in gray* – candidates for eyes inside limiting region

As shown in Fig. 4, in most cases, usage of limiting regions eliminates the problem of ambiguous localization. The limiting regions have been chosen to cover all the possible locations of eyes for every detected rotation of face. Further improvement can be achieved using a cost function which prefers best-matching candidates or/and those with smallest angle between left and right eye.

Since, at this stage, eye center positions are already known, face can be normalized geometrically. For this purpose the angle between eye centers must be determined and used for face rotations (Fig. 5).

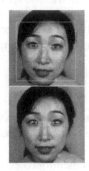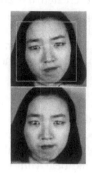

Fig. 5. Images before (*upper panel*) and after (*lower panel*) the corrective rotation based on the angle between eye centers (*JAFFE database and Internet*)

3.2 Localization of Characteristic Regions in a Face

The placements of face and eye centers are known at this stage. Furthermore, the face is already rotated to eliminate the initial rotation. The anthropometric face model is then used to localize remaining facial elements (mouth, eyebrows, nose).

According to the model [1], statistical proportions between certain distances on ordinary human face remain generally constant. Thus, areas of locations of points P2, P5, P11 and P12 (Fig. 3a) can be estimated based on the distance between centers of both eyes P16 and P17 as a shift from the geometrical center between two eyes SC_x (Fig. 3b). After the middles of facial elements have been localized it is necessary to define the size of the regions surrounding those elements. A distance between eye centers P16 and P17 has been used for this purpose. The sizes of regions were defined as to contain the element in every possible deformation. The rectangle surrounding mouth is, in this case, quite large and may, when the mouth is closed, contain large parts of face or even the surroundings of the face itself. The facial element rectangles for different facial expressions are presented in Fig.6.

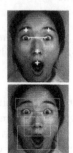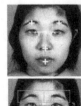

Fig. 6. Localization of face elements based on anthropometric model (*JAFFE database and Internet*)

Because of the mentioned variations in facial expressions it has been decided that an additional stage of refinement for mouth and nose needs to be added. In those two cases the more precise localizations of elements are determined using specially trained Haar-classifiers as described in [8].

3.3 Localization of Characteristic Points in a Face

Having the isolated regions containing facial elements like eye, nose, mouth and eyebrows it is now possible to find 17 characteristic points selected specifically to represent facial mimic as fully and as economically as possible (Fig.3). For maximal efficiency a hybrid approach is used - every facial element is analyzed in different, individually designed way ensuring the best usage of its characteristics.

3.3.1 Analysis of Nose

Two points, placed in the centers of nostrils, need to be found. Nostrils are two very contrasting, dark circular or elliptical areas. The detection of nostril center points is done by filtration that is able to separate dark circular areas from the brighter background. Here a LoG (Laplacian of Gaussian) filter is used [3]. To make the process immune to different size of nostrils, the filter size is changed and the operation is repeated several times. Nostril central points are found by localizing local maxima and then performing verification based mainly on anthropometric conditions. To further improve the result horizontal Sobel filter is used to visualize nose ending line. The final decision is taken based on a specially formed goal function constructed from all the aforementioned information.

3.3.2 Analysis of Mouth

The mouth is probably the most changeable element of face. At first, the image contrast is adjusted in order to make the mouth darker and the surrounding skin brighter. After this the two points placed in the mouth corners are looked for. Two properties are used in this search. Firstly, these points are usually placed in strong image corners. Secondly, between mouth corners, irrespective of the state of the mouth, always exists a dark "valley". This darker area can be strengthened using a horizontal Sobel filter. The candidates for corners are obtained as a result of search for strong image corners in the mouth image and then verified based on the properties mentioned above. Having the mouth corners localized it is possible to define the middle part of the mouth and look for outer points of the lips. Here own procedure is used. The image is inverted and binarized with a threshold calculated using an iterative procedure. The contour is further analyzed. Two points located on the mouth contour and having the x coordinates exactly in the middle between the corners are chosen. From those two, the one having the highest y coordinate value is set as the lower lip point, and the other one is chosen as the upper lip point.

3.3.3 Analysis of Eyes

As a result of eye analysis 4 points should be localized. Two in the eye corners, which are localized first, and another two in the middle of eyelids. In the first stage the intensity of eye image is adjusted to make the eyelids more apparent. The image is then converted to a binary version using iteratively calculated threshold [3]. The areas obtained this way are surrounded by contours using 8-connected contour [11]. The largest contour is further analyzed to choose the outer and inner corner. To deal with misleading shadows in eye corners, the locations are checked against additional anthropometric conditions and if they are not met additional mechanism is used which uses localization of strong image corners. Having the locations of corner points already found, the search for middle eyelid points begins. The eye contour is divided to three parts. Points in the middle part with maximal vertical distance between them are chosen. Those are then verified against anthropometric conditions and further corrected if needed using the mechanism described in [12].

3.3.4 Analysis of Eyebrows

Three points are found for each eyebrow. In the first stage the image colors are inverted as to make eyebrows bright areas on dark background (in most cases). The facial hair that may be inside the region is eliminated by subtracting average background illumination image form the original one. In order to obtain this image morphological operation of opening is used with elliptical structuring element of as much as 10 pixels. Further, the image contrast is increased based on the pixels' cumulative distribution. Then using the Otsu's method [13], the binary image is obtained. The uniform areas in the image are approximated using the 8-connected contour algorithm [11]. The eyebrow contour, which is usually the largest one with its width greater than height, is further analyzed. The inner and outer eyebrow points are chosen first. Then the x coordinate of middle point is calculated as the average of the x coordinates of the aforementioned points. Y coordinate is retrieved as the top-most one. The identified points are checked against anthropometric conditions including the angles and distances between them and corrected if needed.

3.4 Test Results

On average for the JAFFE database the precision of automatic localization of all 17 points used in further emotion analysis was 2.63 pixels (computed as distance to reference hand labeling) or 95,58% (ratio of distance between automatic and hand-labeling divided by the distance between the eyes).

4 Data Normalization for Emotion Detection

In the recognition of emotions the distances between anthropometric points are used with assumption that they change during facial expression of emotions (Fig. 3c). Two types of data normalization are used to obtain person-independent and photo-independent classification of emotions.

Normalization of features [3] – is necessary because perception of emotions is influenced by differences in face proportions. To achieve this average neutral face is generated from all of the faces in the training set belonging to the class labeled as neutral. Feature vector of this face is then subtracted from every face in the data set.

Normalization of data space - it is similar to scaling and fitting the critical features of two photos (nose, eyes, mouth, eyebrows) in a way that would cause them to overlay with as much accuracy as possible. 100% accuracy is not possible for two different photos, however, it is possible to manipulate any photo in such a way that the regions of eyes, brows and nose will overlay with any other photo. This type of normalization ensures that the photographs in the set do not have to be normalized with respect to position and size of the face.

Normalization of data space is done by averaging two distances between the faces that serve as horizontal and vertical scale factors for every set of face points. First of those distances is one between the two eye centers, while the other connects the averaged eye center to the central point between the nostrils.

5   Classification of Emotions

In experiments recognition of 7 basic facial expressions was tested (fear, sad, angry, happy, surprised, disgust, neutral). For classification of emotions three types of classifiers were used as well as two methods of averaging the results - voting and weighted average.

First of the used classifiers is a 15xQx7 RBF Neural Network [10], chosen for its ease of training as well as a good data fit. Q is a variable number, which depends on the exact data used to train the network. The hidden layer of the network is in fact composed of seven independent subnets, each of them responsible for one of the recognized emotions. Isolation of subnets helps with selection of weights and makes recognition of each emotion a separate task. Neurons' activation function is modeled as:

$$N = exp\left(-\sum_{i=1}^{M} \frac{(x_i - c_i)^2 w_i}{2r^2}\right) \qquad (2)$$

where M is the number of features, c is a vector of neuron centers, w is a vector of neuron weights and r is radius of a particular neuron.

The network is trained by adding a new neuron for each averaged emotion of each face in the training set. For every incorrectly recognized sample a new neuron is added until all emotions are recognized correctly. Every neuron center is trained by averaging features of all samples that it should recognize, that is the samples of a particular emotion belonging to a particular face that the neuron was created for.

The radius for every neuron is trained by averaging the distances from all the other neurons in the subnet that the neuron belongs to. This spreads the influence of a particular subnet over the entire space in which the emotion recognized by that subnet could hypothetically appear, according to the training data set. Because RBF networks are linear in their weights it was possible to train it by using the SVD algorithm, without having to restore to time-consuming on-line training. In addition to the RBF network, two other classifiers were used: Naive Bayes Classifier and KNN. It was observed that various classifiers tended to classify emotions incorrectly for different samples. Combining them all together boosted the overall accuracy of emotion classification. This is especially evident for the weighted average method.

5.1 Results and Discussion

The system performs generally well even on automatically labeled data (Table 1 and 2). Please note that best results are obtained for weighted combination of KNN and RBF network. It confirms good generalization ability of RBF network needed for unknown face, while KNN is good for known faces, where exact matching is preferred.

Table 1. Data sets used in experiments

Name of data set	# photos (faces) in test data set	# photos (faces) in training data set
known face	70 (10)	143 (10)
unknown face	22 (1)	191 (9)

Table 2. Percentage of correct facial emotion recognition, [1]KNN size set to 1 for known faces, 11 for unknown; [2]KNN and RBF network only; [3]YM face from JAFFE used as unknown

name of data set	points extraction	Bayes	KNN[1]	RBF network	weighted average[2]	voting
known face	automatic	52.85%	71.42%	65.71%	**74.28%**	75.71%
	manual	64.28%	85.71%	75.71%	**90.00%**	87.14%
unknown face[3]	automatic	54.54%	63.63%	86.36%	**81.81%**	72.72%
	manual	63.63%	86.36%	77.27%	**86.36%**	81.81%

6   Conclusions and Future Plans

Needless to say, there is still room for improvement, especially for the part of the task that deals with classification. Better results can be expected if:

- rotation along Y axis is compensated for (the face is seen not perfectly en face)
- the number of neurons is reduced based on face similarity
- Mahalanobis distances are used instead of Euclidean
- the way in which expressions are classified is changed to allow for the use of different tools for different types of faces (known, unknown)

The facial emotion recognition system has been modified to allow for on-line usage. The feature detection part uses optical flow [14] to track locations and the classifier displays the scores of all 7 facial expression types. The implementation is able to work in real time for 320x240 15 frames/s videos on ordinary PC, without optimization. Further planned modification is to use color information for more precise location of the anthropometric points, computational load optimization and use of higher image resolutions. The system can be easily incorporated into any HCI framework.

Almost 200 years ago Charles Darwin pointed out the importance of emotional expression as part of human communication. Advances in computer vision and technology allows for emotional human-computer interaction. Our preliminary results show that use of anthropometric features eases the task of facial emotion recognition, the points can be precisely located and they contain enough information for recognition of seven basic facial emotional expressions.

References

[1] Sohail, A.S.M., Bhattacharya, P.: Detection of Facial Feature Points Using Anthropometric Face Model. In: Damiani, E., et al. (eds.) Signal Processing for Image Enhancement and Multimedia Processing. Springer, Heidelberg (2007)

[2] Viola, P., Jones, M.J.: Robust Real-Time Object Detection. In: Second International Workshop on Statistical and Computational Theories of Vision - Modeling, Learning, Computing and Sampling, Vancouver, Canada (2001)

[3] Sohail, A.S.M., Bhattacharya, P.: Support Vector Machines Applied to Automated Categorization of Facial Expressions. In: Prasad, B. (ed.) Proceedings of the 3rd Indian International Conference on Artificial Intelligence IICAI 2007, Pune, India, December 17-19 (2007) ISBN 978-0-9727412-2-4

[4] The Japanese Female Facial Expression (JAFFE) Database, http://www.kasrl.org/jaffe.html

[5] OpenCV Wiki-pages, http://opencv.willowgarage.com/wiki/

[6] Jobson, D.J., Rahman, Z., Woodell, G.A.: A multiscale retinex for bridging the gap between color images and the human observation of scenes. IEEE Transactions on Image Processing 6(7), 965–976 (1997)

[7] Lienhart, R., Maydt, J.: An Extended Set of Haar-like Features for Rapid Object Detection. In: Proceedings of the International Conference on Image Processing. IEEE, Los Alamitos (2002)

[8] Castrillón-Santana, M., Déniz-Suárez, O., Antón-Canalís, L., LorenzoNavarro, J.: Face And Facial Feature Detection Evaluation (2008), http://gias720.dis.ulpgc.es/Gias/Publications/visapp-2008-1.pdf

[9] Freund, Y., Schapire, R.E.: A decision-theoretic generalization of on-line learning and an application to boosting. Journal of Computer and System Sciences 55(1) (1997)

[10] Oukhellou, L., Aknin, P.: Optimization of Radial Basis Function Network for Classification Tasks. In: Neurap 1998 IV International Conference on Neural Networks and their Applications, Marseille (1998)

[11] Ritter, G.X., Wilson, J.N.: Handbook of Computer Vision Algorithms in Image Algebra. CRC Press, Boca Raton (1996)

[12] Kuo, P., Hannah, J.M.: An Improved Eye Feature Extraction Algorithm Based on Deformable Templates. In: IEEE International Conference on Image Processing, Genova, Italy, pp. 1206–1209 (2005)

[13] Otsu, N.: A Threshold Selection Method from Gray Level Histograms. IEEE Trans. Systems, Man, and Cybernetics 9(1), 62–66 (1979)

[14] Bouguet, J.-Y.: Pyramidal Implementation of the Lucas Kanade Feature Tracker. Intel Corporation, Microprocessor Research Labs (2002)

Real-Time Face Tracking and Recognition Based on Particle Filtering and AdaBoosting Techniques

Chin-Shyurng Fahn, Ming-Jui Kuo, and Kai-Yi Wang

Department of Computer Science and Information Engineering
National Taiwan University of Science and Technology
Taipei, Taiwan 10607, Republic of China
csfahn@mail.ntust.edu.tw

Abstract. In this paper, a real-time face tracking and recognition system based on particle filtering and AdaBoosting techniques is presented. Regarding the face tracking, we develop an effective particle filter to locate faces in image sequences. Since we have considered the hair color information of a human head, the particle filter will keep tracking even if the person is back to the line of sight of a camera. We further adopt both the motion and color cues as the features to make the influence of the background as low as possible. A new fashion of classification architecture trained with an AdaBoost algorithm is also proposed to achieve face recognition rapidly. Compared to other machine learning schemes, the AdaBoost algorithm can update training samples to deal with comprehensive circumstances, but it need not spend much computational cost. Experimental results reveal that the face tracking rate is more than 97% in general situations and 89% when the face suffering from temporal occlusion. As for the face recognition, the accuracy rate is more than 90%; besides this, the efficiency of system execution is very satisfactory, which reaches 20 frames per second at least.

Keywords: face tracking, face recognition, particle filter, AdaBoost algorithm.

1 Introduction

Face detection and tracking in an image sequence is a key problem in the research of human computer interaction. The purpose of face recognition is to endow computers with the same ability of identifying a person by analyzing his/her face images. Foresti et al. proposed a face tracking system which applied the Kalman filter [6]. Their system consists of three face detection methods, including outline analysis, skin color detection, and principal component analysis (PCA). After the face is located, the associated image is fed into the Kalman filter. However, the outline analysis depends on the goodness of the change detection algorithm. Additionally, the skin color detection is confined to the quality of illumination conditions, and the eigenface method is settled by the number of face images to be trained. An et al. also completed a face tracking system using a simple linear Kalman filter [2]. There two critical problems in this proposed method, lighting condition change and the number of clusters in the k-means clustering, are not solved yet. The development of face recognition is more and more advanced in the past twenty years. Most of these researches try to take the

J.A. Jacko (Ed.): Human-Computer Interaction, Part II, HCII 2009, LNCS 5611, pp. 198–207, 2009.
© Springer-Verlag Berlin Heidelberg 2009

features which are robust enough to represent different human faces. One method that combined the techniques of PCA, Fisher's linear discriminant analysis (LDA), and radial basis function was realized to increase the successful rate of face recognition [5]. Another PCA-based method combined with moment invariants was proposed for varied-pose face recognition [12].

In this paper, we intend to develop a face tracking and recognition system for detecting and recognizing human faces in image sequences acquired in real environments. In the face detection, we adopt an improved temporal difference method which needs no additional morphological image processing to find moving objects speedily. Regarding the face tracking, we apply a particle filter to locate faces in an image sequence. Besides the reduction of the computational load, we utilize a fixed threshold to avoid the degeneracy problem and exploit both color and motion cues to make the influence of the cluttered background as low as possible. In the face recognition, a new architecture is built to achieve the fast classification of human faces. During the face tracking process, we will capture the face region and fed its features derived from the wavelet transform into a strong classifier which is trained with an AdaBoost algorithm. And a bottom-up hierarchical classification structure is devised for multi-class face recognition. Fig. 1 shows the flowchart of our face tracking and recognition system.

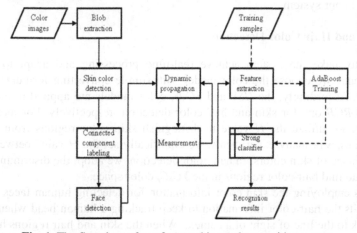

Fig. 1. The flowchart of our face tracking and recognition system

2 Face Detection

In this section, we introduce a feature invariant method to detect human faces in image sequences. First, the change detection is adopted to find moving blobs that are the possible locations of objects. Then an enhancement process is required to improve the detected blobs because the object's shape cannot be extracted exactly by change detection [10]. To achieve this, we mainly use temporal differences to detect moving objects [4], and the scene containing no moving object will not be further processed.

2.1 Change Detection and Blob Extraction

The result of temporal differences shall be a binary image in order to segment moving objects from the background. There are two commonly used manners for getting the blobs. One is to choose an appropriate threshold to differentiate moving objects from the background in a scene and then carry out morphological image processing. Another way is to conduct motion analysis [8]. The first step in the latter approach is to compute the absolute values of the differences in a neighborhood (typically 9×9 pixels) surrounding each pixel. When the sum of the absolute values called accumulated difference is beyond a predetermined threshold T_d, we classify the center pixel as part of a moving object. The threshold T_d is typically set at 1.5 times of the temporal noise standard deviation, which can be alternately set by a certain multiple of the number of pixels in the neighborhood. By applying the threshold to the accumulated difference rather than a single pixel difference, we gain two following benefits. First, the T_d can be expressed more precisely. Second, the neighborhood processing has an effect similar to the morphological operation "dilation." This is useful to fill small gaps occurring in the area where a moving object has resembling pixel values to the background. Through many experiments, we find the above-mentioned technique to be very effective for a wide variety of cluttered background scenes, which is employed for blob extraction in our system.

2.2 Skin and Hair Color Detection

In order to make the system achieve real-time processing and adapt to most of environments, we choose the color model with simple converting formulas and low sensitivity. Accordingly, the *HSV* and *YC_bC_r* color models are applied to replace the traditional *RGB* one for skin and hair color detection, respectively. For locating human faces, we utilize the *H* value to distinguish skin color regions from non-skin color regions. Via many experiments, we empirically set the *H* value between 3 and 38 as the range of skin colors. In hair color detection, we adopt the discriminant functions [14] to find hair color regions in the YC_bC_r color space.

Besides employing the skin color information for detecting human faces, our system exploits the hair color information to keep tracking a human head when the person is back to the line of sight of a camera. When the skin and hair regions have been detected, the morphological operation "opening" is then conducted to eliminate the noise such as isolated pixels.

2.3 Connected Component Labeling

After the previous processing, the outcome is a binary image where the white pixels stand for skin and hair regions. Thus, we should determine each pixel-connected region individually, and then perform face region verification on these candidates to validate face locations. We resort to the linear-time connected component labeling technique which is proposed by Suzuki et al. for completing the components to be eight-connected [16].

2.4 Face Region Verification

Once we have obtained connected components, we will focalize on the search of a skin color region whose circumscribed box is possessed of the maximum probability to cover the face of a person according to geometrical features; for instance, the center of mass, box dimensions, and aspect ratio.

If the box dimensions are too small with respect to the size of the blob of a person, or the box is found in a position that is too low comparatively to the normal position of a head, then the box is thrown away. Because the height of a human face is mostly greater than its width, we utilize the aspect ratio to determine the face region; that is, we discard the box with the height smaller than the width. Besides this, according to the experiments of some literature, the height of a human face is usually smaller than 2.2 times of the width. Therefore, we prescribe (1) to locate probable face regions.

$$B_H > B_W \text{ and } B_H < 2.2 B_W \tag{1}$$

where B_H and B_W are the height and width of the circumscribed box of a skin color region. Finally, we select the maximum box as the human face from the remaining boxes after the above verification step is completed. Since we cope with each moving object in an image, it is reasonable for finding the maximum box.

3 Face Tracking

The goal of target tracking is that once the system has detected moving objects, it keeps analyzing their movements and trajectories to get the locations in real time. At present, there are many tracking algorithms proposed by researchers. Among these tracking algorithms, the Kalman filter [17] and particle filter [15] are applied extensively. Through rigorous evaluation, we employ the particle filter to effectively attain face tracking in our developed system. The following elaborates how we utilize a particle filter to implement face tracking. It is composed of four main stages, including propagation, observation, selection, and estimate.

3.1 Propagation

Suppose a target found at time step t-1 is represented by a rectangular window and the state of the target is defined as:

$$s_{t-1} = \left\{ x_{t-1}, y_{t-1}, B_{x_{t-1}}, B_{y_{t-1}} \right\} \tag{2}$$

where (x_{t-1}, y_{t-1}) is the center of the window; $B_{x_{t-1}}$ and $B_{y_{t-1}}$ symbolize the width and height of the window, respectively. The sample set consisting of N particles should be predicted by a dynamic model. To generate a particle, the dynamic function is established by a random model as shown in (3):

$$\begin{cases} x_t = x_{t-1} + \Delta x_t \\ y_t = y_{t-1} + \Delta y_t \end{cases} \text{ and } \begin{cases} B_{x_t} = B_{x_{t-1}} + \Delta B_{x_t} \\ B_{y_t} = B_{y_{t-1}} + \Delta B_{y_t} \end{cases} \tag{3}$$

where Δx_t, Δy_t, ΔB_{x_t}, and ΔB_{y_t} are computed by use of a Gaussian distribution at time step t.

3.2 Observation

In the observation model, we first consider the color cue to describe the target by the method proposed in [15], instead of using a color histogram [11]. To deal with the clutters arisen from skin-colored objects in the background, we further employ the motion cue in the observation model to overcome the limitation of the individual cue. Since we are interested in the motion of skin and hair color regions, we subtract the skin and hair color image of the target found at time step t-1 from that of a particle generated at time step t to obtain the skin and hair color difference image which acts as the observation of the motion cue. Accordingly, this method can track moving objects in dynamic backgrounds. For each particle, the likelihood of the box bounding the face is estimated by color and motion cues in the rectangular window.

We observe that when the face moves rapidly; that is, the velocity of the moving face is high, the motion cue is obvious. It means such an observation of the motion cue is more reliable. On the other hand, when the movement is slow, we can weigh particles mainly by the observation of the color cue. Therefore, we take a linear combination of color and motion cues to characterize their contributions of importance, which is represented by

$$M = (1-\lambda)\cdot M_c + \lambda\cdot M_m \tag{4}$$

where M_c and M_m are the color and motion cues, respectively, and λ is proportional to the velocity of a moving face that yields

$$\lambda = k\cdot\sqrt{\dot{x}^2 + \dot{y}^2} \tag{5}$$

with a normalization factor k such that λ is ranged from zero to one. In the above equation, $\dot{x}$ and $\dot{y}$ stand for the velocities in the horizontal and vertical directions, individually. Then the likelihood of each particle is specified by a Gaussian distribution with zero mean and variance.

3.3 Selection

Assume that we have to select N particles to track the target. At first, we draw the particles with the weights greater than or equal to a predefined threshold T_w, and compute the sum of these weights that are acquired from the likelihood of each particle at the previous stage. The remaining particles with the weights less than T_w are set to be zero. Thus, we employ (6) to determine how many particles with the same weight $\pi^{(i)}$ should be selected from the i-th particle.

$$C_i = \left\lfloor \left(\pi^{(i)}/W \right)\cdot N \right\rfloor \quad \text{with} \quad W = \sum_{i=1}^{N} \pi^{(i)} \tag{6}$$

where W is the sum of the modified weights of the particles. Ultimately, we choose the particle with the highest weight to be the predicted result as the desired target at time step t.

4 Face Recognition

Through the face tracking procedure, we have received the face image that is then fed to the face recognition procedure. To begin with, we apply the image normalization to make the sizes of face images be the same. The brightness of the images will be also adjusted for diminishing the lighting effect. After that, we subsequently conduct feature extraction to obtain the feature vector of a face image. Then it can be used to discriminate the identity of a person. In advance of accomplishing this, we should collect face images as training data. The feature extraction methods include the eigenface [5], wavelet transform [1], averaging [9], and so forth. Herein, we adopt the Haar wavelet transform for extracting features, and then employ an Adaboost algorithm to recognize human faces.

4.1 Preliminary Processing

To raise the recognition rate, we should have adaptive pre-processing for reducing the differences among various images such as the faces taken in different sizes or illumination conditions. For the consideration of computational load, we prescribe the image size of 40×60 pixels used in our developed system.

The brightness change of an image is on a global scale under the varied conditions of illumination; that is, when the lighting becomes dark, the average gray value of this image will be small, and vice versa. Therefore, we utilize such a property to adjust the gray level of each face image and let the average value be 128. Given an image with n pixels, we make use of (7) to adjust all the grey levels of constituting pixels.

$$I_{modified} = (128 - I_{ave}) + I_i \quad \text{with} \quad I_{ave} = \sum_{i=1}^{n} I_i / n \tag{7}$$

where I_i represents the gray level of the i-th pixel.

4.2 The AdaBoost Algorithm

Boosting is a general method for improving the performance and extending the capabilities of any learning algorithm. The AdaBoost algorithm was proposed in the literature of computational learning theory in 1996 [7]. The weak classifier is the core of an AdaBoost algorithm. Each weak classifier produces the answer "yes" or "no" for the particular features of the subjects to be recognized. The AdaBoost algorithm is flexible because it can be combined with any classifier, such as the K-nearest neighbor, linear discriminant analysis (LDA), Naive Bayes, support vector machine (SVM), and neural network. Here, we adopt Classification & Regression Trees (CARTs) as the structure of a weak classifier trained with the AdaBoost algorithm[3].

4.3 Our AdaBoost-Based Multi-classifier

In the face recognition procedure, we do not use all the information received from the Haar wavelet transform executed on a face image. If the dimensions of the original information are n, we can first perform a sorting operation on the information. And then select l larger values ($l \leq n$) to constitute the feature vector. The number of l is determined by accumulating the larger values until the amount is just greater than

0.95 times of the sum of all values. This is in terms of the more significant information that are mainly required. The smaller values may be the noise, which are dropped to reduce the error rate. Thus, the training and recognition time can be economized.

Since the AdaBoost algorithm we exploit is a binary classifier, we further develop a bottom-up hierarchical classification structure for multi-class face recognition. This structure has a good property that we can update the model locally by training only new added data, without modifying the whole model trained before. Fig. 2(a) shows a classifier M_1 that recognizes persons α and β. When we put in another person γ to be recognized, we just construct the classifier M_2 by taking persons α and β as the negative samples and person γ as the positive sample as shown in Fig. 2(b). Hence, we can utilize this structure to carry out the face recognition of more than two classes.

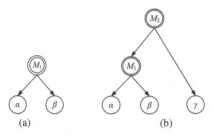

Fig. 2. Illustration of classifier expansion: (a) binary classifier; (b) ternary classifier from expanding (a)

5 Experimental Results

Table 1 lists both the hardware and software that are used for the development of our face tracking and recognition system to demonstrate the effectiveness of the proposed methods. The experimental results comprise two parts: 1) face tracking using a particle filter; 2) face recognition using an AdaBoost algorithm.

Table 1. The Developing Environment of Our Face Tracking and Recognition System

Hardware	Software
CPU: Pentium 4 3.2GHz	Tool: Borland C++ Builder 6.0
RAM: 512MB	MATLAB 7.2
Camera: Logitech Quick-Cam Pro 4000	Operating System: Microsoft Windows XP

5.1 The Results of Face Tracking

The types of test image sequences are roughly classified into three kinds: the front face (Type A), the back side (Type B), and the temporal occlusion (Type C). Each type has three different image sequences, and we will complete five tests on each of them. In these experiments, we use 30 particles to track faces in each frame.

Fig. 3 illustrates part of the tracking results obtained from an image sequence of Type B. From this figure, we can see that the person back to the line of sight of a camera is still correctly tracked. Notice that there are some skin color regions around the head in the background, but our algorithm can track it effectively because the motion cue is employed in the particle filter.

(a)   (b)

Fig. 3. Part of the tracking results indicated by green rectangles: (a) thirty possible locations; (b) the mostly possible location of a human face

Table 2. The Comparison among the Conventional, Mean Shift, and Our Methods

Measurement	Conventional particle filter	Mean shift	Our proposed method
Avg. execution time (each frame)	51 ms	28 ms	18 ms
Avg. frame rate (frames per second)	16	25	37
Number of particles	100	30	30
Avg. accuracy rate (Type A)	92.2%	99.5%	99.0%
Avg. accuracy rate (Type B)	90.3%	98.1%	97.2%
Avg. accuracy rate (Type C)	81.9%	90.6%	89.7%

What follows compares the performance of our proposed tracking method to those of the conventional and mean shift embedded particle filters [15]. From Table 2, we can observe that our method is superior to the other two methods in both the execution time and frame rate, but the accuracy rate of the mean shift method is slightly better than ours. In general, the tracking accuracy of the face with temporal occlusion is lower than those of the other two types. This is because that when the object is moving to the front of a face, the particles are usually predicted on the arm or the hand which are also the skin color regions. On the other hand, the false alarms and miss rates of face tracking for Types A and B are produced by ill illumination, complicated backgrounds, and so on.

5.2 The Results of Face Recognition

In the following experiment, there are three subjects to be recognized, and each of them has 150 samples. Fig. 4 illustrates some of our training samples, where the faces may be panned from −30° to 30° and tilted from −10° to 10° when taking pictures. The features of these training samples are obtained from the two-level Haar wavelet transform. And the size of each wavelet face image is 10×15 pixels.

In this experiment, we employ 5-fold cross-validation to estimate the accuracy of different system models. Finding out the optimal numbers of tree nodes and training iterations are in order to avoid over-fitting simultaneously. From the model estimation, we can see that the best performance is achieved with the AdaBoost algorithm for a 24-split CART. The detailed experimental data and its associated analysis are recorded in Table 3. For each subject, we choose 150 face images from some video samples, and select the same number of face images of other subjects as the test data. The recognition result received from the strong classifier is a confidence. If this confidence is within a certain range which approaches zero, we will sort out the subject as "Others."

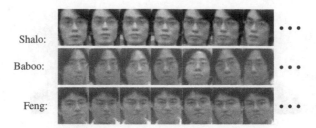

Fig. 4. The sample faces used for training the classifier

Table 3. The Face Recognition Results of the Three Subjects

Subject	Shalo	Baboo	Feng	Other	Avg. Accuracy rate	Avg. execution time
Shalo	137	8	4	1	91.3%	26 ms
Baboo	0	136	12	2	90.7%	43 ms
Feng	0	12	136	2	90.7%	45 ms
Other	5	7	4	134	89.3%	45 ms

6 Conclusions

In this paper, we have developed a face tracking procedure that is able to detect and locate human faces in image sequences acquired in real environments, followed by a face recognition procedure using a strong classifier trained with an AdaBoost algorithm. The particle filter in our face tracking procedure can use fewer particles to maintain multiple hypotheses than the conventional particle filters do, so the computational cost is greatly decreased. When applying the particle filter to face tracking, a manner based on the fusion of color and motion cues is employed to reliably measure the likelihood of each particle. The skin and hair color models are adapted to deal with color variation during the face tracking.

We realize weak classifiers using the CARTs, which are integrated into a strong classifier automatically by means of the AdaBoost algorithm. Then the face image is to be recognized through the authentication of the strong classifier where we predefined a threshold to determine whether the corresponding person is in our identified member list. Experimental results reveal that our approach is preferable to the conventional particle filters when it is applied to face tracking. As for the face recognition, compared with the other machine learning methods such as an SVM [13] and a neural network [5], the AdaBoost algorithm does not employ a complicated computational technique under the prerequisite that the accuracy of face recognition is close to each other. It not only takes less training time than the other machine learning methods do, but also maximizes the margin that separates a pair of classes. Thus, we can update the training samples to handle different situations, but need not spend much computational cost.

Acknowledgements

The authors would like to thank the National Science Council of Taiwan for her support in this work under Grant NSC94-2218-E011-012.

References

1. Acharyya, M., Kundu, M.K.: Document image segmentation using wavelet scale-space features. IEEE Trans. on Circuits and Syst. for Video Tech. 12(12), 1117–1127 (2002)
2. An, K.H., et al.: Robust multi-view face tracking. In: Proc. of the IEEE Int. Conf. on Intell. Robots and Syst., Edmonton, Alberta, Canada, pp. 1905–1910 (2005)
3. Breiman, L., et al.: Classification and Regression Trees. Chapman and Hall, New York (1984)
4. Chen, K.Y., et al.: Design and implementation of a real-time pan-tilt visual tracking system. In: Proc. of the IEEE Int. Conf. on Control Appli., Glasgow, Scotland, pp. 736–741 (2002)
5. Er, M.J., et al.: Face recognition with radial basis function (RBF) neural networks. IEEE Trans. on Neural Net. 13(3), 697–710 (2002)
6. Foresti, G.L., et al.: Face detection for visual surveillance. In: Proc. of the 12th IEEE Int. Conf. on Image Anal. and Process. Mantova, Italy, pp. 115–120 (2003)
7. Freund, Y., Schapire, R.E.: Experiments with a new boosting algorithm. In: Proc. of the 13th Int. Conf. on Machine Learning, Bari, Italy, pp. 148–156 (1996)
8. Graf, H.P., et al.: Multi-modal system for locating heads and faces. In: Proc. of the 2nd Int. Conf. on Automat. Face and Gesture Recogni., Killington, Vermont, pp. 88–93 (1996)
9. Huang, Y.C.: A hierarchical face recognition system. Master Thesis, Dept. of Inform. Eng. and Comput. Sci., Feng Chia Univ., Taichung, Taiwan (2003)
10. Jang, L.S.: Detection and tracking of human in dynamic scenes. Master Thesis, Dept. of Elect. Eng., Tatung Univ., Taipei, Taiwan (2003)
11. Nummiaro, K., et al.: An adaptive color-based particle filter. Image and Vision Comput. 21(1), 99–110 (2003)
12. Phiasai, T., et al.: Face recognition system with PCA and moment invariant method. In: Proc. of the IEEE Int. Symp. on Circuits and Syst., Sydney, Australia, vol. 2, pp. 165–168 (2001)
13. Qin, J., He, Z.S.: An SVM face recognition method based on Gabor-featured key points. In: Proc. of the 4th Int. Conf. on Machine Learning and Cybern, Guangzhou, China, pp. 18–21 (2005)
14. Song, K.T., Chen, W.J.: Face recognition and tracking for human-robot interaction. In: Proc. of Int. Conf. on Syst., Man, and Cybern, Hague, Netherlands, pp. 2877–2882 (2004)
15. Song, X.Q.: Real-time visual detection and tracking of multiple moving objects based on particle filtering techniques. Master Thesis, Dept. of Comput. Sci. and Inform. Eng., Nat. Taiwan Univ. of Sci. and Tech., Taipei, Taiwan (2005)
16. Suzuki, K., et al.: Linear-time connected-component labeling based on sequential local operations. Comput. Vision and Image Understand 89(1), 1–23 (2003)
17. Welch, G., Bishop, G.: An introduction to the Kalman filter. Tech. Report TR 95-041, Dept. of Comput. Sci., Univ. of North Carolina, Chapel Hill, North Carolina (2004)

A Real-Time Hand Interaction System
for Image Sensor Based Interface

SeIn Lee[1], Jonghoon Seo[1], Soon-bum Lim[2], Yoon-Chul Choy[1],
and TackDon Han[1]

[1] Dept. Of Computer Science, Yonsei University,
134, Sinchon-dong, Seodaemun-gu
{sipkjy,jonghoon.seo,ycchoy,hantack}@yonsei.ac.kr
[2] Dept. Of Multimedia Science, Sookmyung University,
52 Hyochangwon-gil, Yongsan-gu,
Seoul, Korea
sblim@sookmyung.ac.kr

Abstract. Diverse sensors are available in ubiquitous computing of which resources is inherent in environment. Among them, image sensor acquires necessary data using camera without any extra devices, which is a different aspect
from other sensors. It can provide additional services and/or applications by using a location of code and ID in real time image. Focusing on this, Intuitive interface operating method in ubiquitous computing environment that has plenty
of image codes is suggested. GUI using image sensor was designed, which
works real-time interactive operation between user and the GUI without any
additional button or device. This interface method recognizes user's hand images in real-time by learning them at a starting point. The method sets interaction point, and operates the GUI through hand gestures defined previously. We
expect this study can be adopted to augmented reality area and real time interface using user's hand.

Keywords: HCI, Hand interface, Hand interaction, Augmented Reality.

1 Introduction

In 2008, Microsoft's Bill Gates emphasized the importance of convenient interfaces
using the phrase "second digital decade."[1] However, there are many inconveniences
with the interface. Input inconvenient and lacking in intuition, thus necessitating
additional learning. In contrast, the second digital decade interfaces need to be more
intuitive, user-friendly, and convenient to use. We suggest an interaction system that
satisfies the needs for future ubiquitous computing environment. Various information
and applications can be used in ubiquitous computing environment. The ubiquitous
computing environment is assumed for the study, in which digital information used
has a 2d image code form. We are considering image sensor based real time and real
environment service or application under the environment. This is a kind of
augmented reality (AR) approach. In this paper, as a method to interact with GUI in
AR environment, we present a system that directly uses user's hand.

J.A. Jacko (Ed.): Human-Computer Interaction, Part II, HCII 2009, LNCS 5611, pp. 208–215, 2009.
© Springer-Verlag Berlin Heidelberg 2009

2 AR Interaction Analysis

Depending on the interaction modes used, augmented reality interfaces can be classified into tangible user interface (TUI) based method, control device based method, or hand based methods. There are diverse control devices available, with the keyboard and the mouse being the most common. Examined here is an example of AR utilization in a hand-held device that employs the touch screen and tablet pen based interface, which is lately gaining increased application.

The method most easily and often used for AR interface is the TUI based interface. In general, the TUI utilization method employs as the physical tool for interaction, a 2D image marker based on an image processing marker recognition method. When this is done, the marker is either attached to a stick or made so that it can be hand-held in order to prevent the marker's image part from being occluded [2,3,4,5,6]. Or in certain situations, a special TUI [7] is created. When an image marker is used, since the decoding algorithm of the marker is already established, construction of additional physical user interface is convenient and easy. However, if the marker is occluded during interaction, the feedback from the marker is lost, and thus there is a constraint of not having any part of the marker occluded during operation. Furthermore, since the decoding of one ID is done by one marker, in order to carry out complex manipulations, the number of TUI has to be increased by a corresponding amount. This creates a shortcoming in that the interaction becomes uncomfortable and manipulation unnatural. The non-vision based, specially produced TUI can resolve this to some extent, but it cannot be easily built since from production to interaction it requires special devices.

The touch screen based method [8,9,10,11], with a 2D interface familiar to general users, makes easy manipulation possible. But if it is used in mixture with the AR environment, confusion occurs in interaction. While the elements for UI augmentation utilize real environment resources, the user's manipulations take place in the device's 2D screen. Therefore, it only serves the role of receiving information inherent in the environment without any interaction with a physical medium, and the virtual object, rather than being directly controlled, is indirectly manipulated.

There are various forms of interaction using the hand within the AR environment. There is the method of using a special device like a glove [12], and as in [13], there is the occlusion based method using occlusion of the marker in an image. The manipulation method using the shadow of a hand on a touch creen was also employed, as shown in [11]. These methods employ the hand and at the same time require other resources in addition to the hand. In contrast, the most natural and simple method is the vision based method which directly uses just the hand. The vision based method is employed in [14]. This method, however, only utilizes the single, most prominently recognized finger and thus additionally requires a control panel for manipulation, which tends to diminish intuitiveness.

Focusing on intuitiveness and naturalness, we created a gesture interaction system through a vision based recognition method. This uses natural and familiar gestures employing just the hand without a TUI or supplementary devices. A detailed explanation of our method will be given in Chapter 3.

3 Personal Hand Interface System

We are considering developing an application that augments service or GUI using 2D image sensors afterwards. As preparatory research for the proposal, this paper researched technology that recognizes hands using neural network and uses them interactively.

3.1 System Processing

The system operates as shown in Figure 1. When the program is first run, it goes through the learning process of extracting user's hand information. Through it a neural network is composed and the process moves to hand recognition stage. In the hand recognition stage, the individual user's hand is recognized and then, in the gesture recognition stage, gestures are discerned based on hand shapes. Afterwards, interaction is carried out according to changes in the gestures.

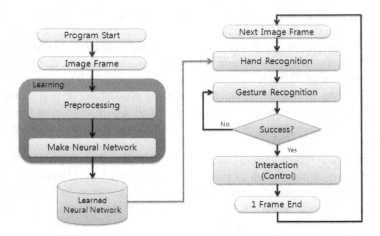

Fig. 1. The processing architecture

3.2 Learning

In the learning stage, the features of a user's hand are identified and a neural network is established. To find the features, when the user places a hand on the circular mark at the center of the picture as shown in Figure 2(a), the R, G, B, H, S, V, Y, Cb, Cr color tones of the circular mark area are extracted. The RGB model is the basic system model, the HSV model is good for detecting changes in color tones, and because the YCbCr model is good for accurately sorting out luminance and chrominance, it is mainly used for skin color modeling.[9]

The characteristics thus extracted are used to learn a neural network. Figure 2(b) shows the structure of a neural network realized in the system, and it is composed of an input layer which inputs nine types of color value averages from user's hand, a two column hidden layer made up of 30 neurons, and one output neuron. The system was taught to make the output neuron converge to zero.

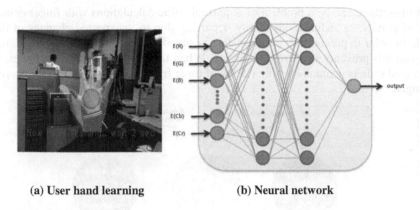

(a) User hand learning	(b) Neural network

Fig. 2. Learning stage via (a) user's hand learning image (b) neural network model

3.3 Hand Recognition

Once learning is completed, the recognition stage is carried out. From the image, candidate areas deemed to be the skin color area are identified through the average and standard deviation of Y, Cb, Cr, H elements. Based on the silhouette pixel number k from the user hand data extracted during the learning stage, among the candidate areas, objects that are too small or too big are judged to be noise and eliminated.

From all the objects left on the screen, the color values that match those from the learning stage are obtained and their average is calculated. Then the neural network produced from the learning stage is recalled, and the resulting value of each object is tested. Because the system was taught to make the resulting value of the output neuron converge to zero in the learning stage, from among the objects that have been tested, the one with the resulting value approaching closest to zero is judged to be user's hand.

Fig. 3. Hand recognition stage {binary, noise reduced, neural network value attached} images

3.4 Gesture Recognition

The hand image area and centroid coordinates were obtained, and the radius was established according to the area ratio. Then the hand is explored along a circle to confirm the number of fingers and tip points in the hand are selected. While processing images in real-time, there can be a problem of abnormal value calculations with finger count, center of gravity, or radius momentarily occurring due to unexpected changes in the images. In order to prevent this, another state is added into the middle of the changing states, and this prevents error from occurring. When the number of fingers changes, if the changed state is maintained with a delay of three frames, then the state is registered as changed.

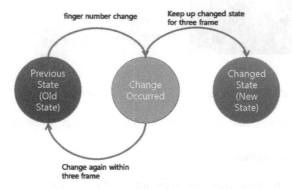

Fig. 4. Gesture state change graph

3.5 Interaction Design

There are a total of six gesture types that users can use. To enable the user to easily learn the operating method, in considering the gestures we sought natural motions or familiar motions of a common interface such as "Grasp" and "Click" of Table 1. Table 1 presents the gesture descriptions.

	1 Finger	Click	2 Finger	Grasp	5 Finger	Fist
Interaction	• Object select	• Confirm selection	• Object select • Drag release	• Dragging • Confirm selection	• Predefined event	• Predefined event
Example						

Fig. 5. Design of gestures

4   User Study

To evaluate the constructed system, the test participants were required to fill out a survey after using the system. Seven users, ages 25 to 30, participated in the test. In order to aid users to make comparative evaluations, the testing was done with the additional inclusion of the TUI based and touchscreen methods. The tasks required of the participants were scaling, rotation and translation, the basic manipulations for 3D

Table 1. The detailed description of the three interactions used in the experiments

	TUI based	Hand Gesture based	Touchscreen based
Tools	Cube type TUI	User's hand	Tablet pen Touch screen
Interaction method	Dialing interaction(TUI) Image marker changing	Hand Gesture	Touch by tablet pen and press Right button
Description	Rotate L/R: turn the TUI Scale P/M: turn the TUI Translate: move the TUI Change manipulation: marker switch	Rotate L/R: grasping gesture or click gesture and move Scale P/M: grasping gesture or click gesture and move Translate: grasp gesture and move or click gesture and move Change manipulation: five finger gesture	Rotate L/R: touch and move Scale P/M: touch and move Translate: touch and move Change manipulation: right button

objects. The details are presented in table 1. After verbally explaining to the participants how to do the manipulations, they were requested to do the test right away.

4.1 Usability Survey and Result

The participants were each requested do the same task employing 3 methods and then fill out the survey. The survey included six items of evaluation: easy to learn, intuitiveness, naturalness, immersion, accuracy of control, and preference. We surveyed the user response by employing seven interval scale items—1 for "very low," 2 for "low," 3 for "little low," 4 for "medium," 5 for "little high," 6 for "high," and 7 for "very high." The results are shown in Figure 6.

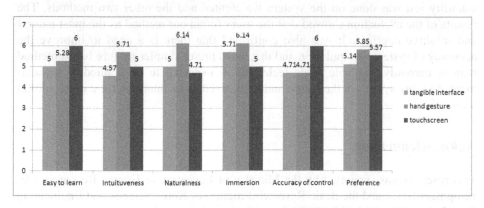

Fig. 6. Result of the survey(avg)

4.2 Discussion

First, regarding the question of manipulation accuracy, the users gave the highest evaluation to the touch screen method. The respondents considered manipulation to be relatively difficult in the remaining two methods. It appears that this was due to the difference in 3D and 2D interfaces as well as the existing experience of the users. Since all the participants had experience of using a touch screen, it was the method most familiar to them. Hence it required less supplementary instructions for learning how to use it. The other two methods, based on observing the users, showed that although they listened to the instructions, their manipulations were awkward at the start and gradually improved as time passed.

Next, the participants were asked how intuitive and natural each method was, and they gave the highest evaluation to the hand gesture method. They found there was no feeling of incongruity with this method since part of the body was directly used and the gestures were easy. The TUI method was not difficult, but they responded that using only a marker made it difficult to intuitively infer the method of use. The touch screen was found to have relatively less natural feeling.

As for immersion, the participants gave the lowest evaluation to the touch screen and positive marks to the other two methods. This is due to the difference in interaction space: for the TUI method and the hand gesture method, manipulation takes place directly in the physical space photographed as an image and the feedback occurs simultaneously; whereas, for the touch screen, the manipulation takes place in a 2D screen, but the interaction with the virtual object occurs in a real-time image (physical space).

5 Conclusion and Future Works

In order to enable users to natural control an enhanced GUI this paper researched a technology that recognizes hands and, with it, analyze gestures and provide interaction. Finally, evaluation criteria were presented and comparative evaluation using a usability test was done on the system we created and the other two methods. The results of the evaluation showed that the users found our method as the most natural and intuitive interface. It was also confirmed that there is a need to improve the accuracy of system manipulation and that users prefer simpler gesture based method than is currently available. This technique is expected to be applied to an augmented reality system in the future and be utilized as its interface for a more natural interaction.

Acknowledgement

This research was supported by the Ministry of Education & Human Resources Development BK21 and the Basic Research Program of Korea Science and Engineering Foundation (R01-2005-000-10898-0 / R01-2008-000-20849-0).

References

1. Gates, B.: World to enter 'second digital decade' - Times Online,
   http://technology.timesonline.co.uk/tol/news/tech_and_web/
   article3144255.ece
2. Lee, G.A., Nelles, C., Billinghurst, M., Kim, G.J.: Immersive authoring of Tangible Augmented Reality applications. In: International Symposium on Mixed and Augmented Reality, pp. 172–181 (2005)
3. Kim, L., Cho, H., Park, S.H., Han, M.: A Tangible User Interface with Multimodal Feedback. In: Schmorrow, D.D., Reeves, L.M. (eds.) HCII 2007. LNCS, vol. 4565, pp. 94–103. Springer, Heidelberg (2007)
4. Zhou, Z., Cheok, A.D., Chan, T., Pan, J.H., Li, Y.: Interactive Entertainment Systems Using Tangible Cubes. In: Australian Workshop on Interactive Entertainment (IE 2004), pp. 19–22 (2004)
5. Billinghurst, M., Kato, H., Poupyrev, I.: Tangible Augmented Reality. International Conference on Artificial Reality and Telexistence (ICAT) Tutorial (2004)
6. Moore, A., Regenbrecht, H.: The Tangible Augmented Street Map. In: International Conference on Artificial Reality and Teleexistence (ICAT), pp. 249–250 (2005)
7. Sinclair, P., Martinez, K.: Adapting Information Through Tangible Augmented Reality Interfaces. In: UbiComp 2004 (2004)
8. Mooser, J., Wang, L., You, S., Neumann, U.: An Augmented Reality Interface for Mobile Information Retrieval. In: International Conference on Multimedia and Expo (ICME), pp. 2226–2229 (2007)
9. Wagner, D., Schmalstieg, D.: First Steps Towards Handheld Augmented Reality. In: 7th International Conference on Wearable Computers (ISWC 2003), pp. 127–135 (2003)
10. Wilson, A.D.: PlayAnywhere: a compact interactive tabletop projection-vision system. In: UIST 2005, pp. 83–92 (2005)
11. Wagner, D., Pintaric, T., Ledermann, F., Schmalstieg, D.: Towards massively multi-user augmented reality on handheld devices. In: Gellersen, H.-W., Want, R., Schmidt, A. (eds.) Pervasive 2005. LNCS, vol. 3468, pp. 208–219. Springer, Heidelberg (2005)
12. Dorfmüller-Ulhaas, K., Schmalstieg, D.: Finger tracking for interaction in augmented environments. In: International Symposium on Augmented Reality, pp. 55–64 (2001)
13. Lee, G.A., Billinghurst, M., Kim, G.J.: Occlusion based Interaction Methods for Tangible Augmented Reality Environments. In: International conference on Virtual Reality continuum and its applications in industry, pp. 419–426 (2004)
14. McDonald, C., Roth, G.: Hand Based Interaction in Augmented Reality. In: IEEE International Workshop on Haptic Audio Visual Environments and their Applications (HAVE 2002), pp. 55–59 (2002)

Gesture-Based Interface for Connection and Control of Multi-device in a Tabletop Display Environment

Hyunglae Lee[1], Heeseok Jeong[2], Joongho Lee[3], Ki-Won Yeom[3],
and Ji-Hyung Park[3]

[1] Department of Mechanical Engineering, Massachusetts Institute of Technology, USA
hyunglae@mit.edu
[2] Game Development Center, NHN Corporation, Korea
heesuk0@naver.com
[3] Intelligence and Interaction Research Center, Korea Institute of Science and Technology,
Korea
{yap153,pragman,jhpark}@kist.re.kr

Abstract. In this paper, we propose a gesture-based interface for connection and control of multiple devices in a ubiquitous computing environment. With simple selection and pointing gestures, users can easily control connections between multiple devices as well as manage information or data between them. Based on a robust gesture recognition algorithm and a virtual network computing technology, we implemented this concept in an intelligent meeting room consisting of a tabletop, interactive wall displays, and other popular devices such as laptops and mobile devices. We also performed a preliminary user study in this environment, and the results show the usability of the suggested interface.

Keywords: Gesture-based interface, multi-device connection.

1 Introduction

In today's ubiquitous computing environment, we are exposed to various types of computing devices such as desktops, laptops, and mobile devices. While dealing with these devices, any user might have had the experience of wasting time in managing connections and controlling the device. Solving the connection problems in using multiple computing devices, ranging from the above-mentioned ones to emerging devices such as tabletops and interactive surfaces, has become an important issue in HCI research.

In this paper, we propose a novel gesture-based interface to eliminate the cumbersome processes in connection and control of multiple devices in a tabletop and interactive surface environment. With simple selecting and pointing hand gestures, users can easily connect the tabletop with the surrounding wall screens. In addition, this interface enables users to connect their personal devices, ranging from a laptop to a mobile device, with public ones, such as wall screens or a tabletop display. After connection has been established, users can control the connected device using the controlling device or transmit data by selecting the data and pointing to the connected device.

J.A. Jacko (Ed.): Human-Computer Interaction, Part II, HCII 2009, LNCS 5611, pp. 216–225, 2009.

A robust hand and fingertip detection algorithm and a virtual network computing technology are integrated to realize this concept. We implemented the suggested interface in an intelligent meeting room consisting of a tabletop, three interactive wall displays, several laptops, and mobile devices. A preliminary user study in this environment showed that the suggested interface enables users to easily manage connections between multiple devices, and to intuitively handle data.

2 Related Works

There have been several studies on virtual connections of multiple devices in a tabletop and interactive surface environment. Here, a virtual connection means a network connection between physical devices which allows users to control one device while using another one as if two are physically connected. There are several researches [19, 24] and commercial software supporting virtual connections [5, 17, 25], even though most of them are specially designed for remote PC connections.

i-Land [23] extends the collaboration environment to public devices including a tabletop to wall screens. However, it only supports the transportation of whole documents from the tabletop to wall displays. *Table-centric space* system [7] enables moving objects from the tabletop to the wall screens by introducing the concept of "World in Miniature (WIM)." MultiSpace [13] is a similar example consisting of a tabletop display and wall screens. The user can send the data to the wall screen or laptop by dragging it onto an appropriate portal located in the corner of the tabletop display. Although the above two systems provide new interfaces between the tabletop and wall screens, users might feel inconveniences in matching correspondences between several WIMs or portals and multiple screens. *i-Room* [3] is another example supporting virtual connections of multiple devices for efficient collaborations. Although *PointRight* [4] in this environment allows a single mouse and keyboard to control multiple screens, there still exists the inconvenience in interfacing devices.

Over the last decade, there have been many researches done on the virtual connecting of multiple devices through natural and intuitive means as well as researches on the direct manipulation of remote information. Rekimoto proposed a pen-based interface called *Pick-and-Drop* [22] which allows a user to pick up an object on one device and drop it on the other one as if the two were physically connected. *Slurp* [9] is similar to the *Pick-and-Drop* interface except it uses an eyedropper instead of a pen. *That one there* [6] interface uses tags and a gesturepen for data sharing. A user can transmit data by pointing the gesturepen to the device with a tag. *Sync Tap* [20] and *Touch-and-Connect* [26] enables virtual connections by pressing a button synchronously and touching the device, respectively. A virtually connected medium called *tranStick* [1] was also suggested that functions as a virtual wire. Users can easily establish, change, and close connections between devices using a pair of *tranSticks* with the same identifier. *Gaze-Link* [2] is another intuitive means of virtual connection in which a user can establish a virtual connection over a network by looking at the target through a camera on his/her computer. Rekimoto also proposed a new interface called *FEEL* [21] by introducing a nearfield communication channel such as RFID or infrared communication technology. A user can establish a wireless connection by bringing two devices closer together.

Although there are several advantages in using physical media, closeness, touch, and gaze information, users might feel uncomfortable whenever moving to near the devices to establish network connections. In addition, there exist inconveniences in carrying the devices. On the other hand, in our approach, users need not move near to the device or carry any special device in their hands for network connections. We formerly suggested a new interface concept called Select-and-Point in [8]. In this paper, we fully implemented the concept and extended the Select-and-Point interface to multiple devices, including laptops and mobile devices, in the tabletop and interactive wall displays environment.

3   System Description

The suggested interface provides users with a simple and intuitive interface and interaction style in connecting and controlling multiple devices through a simple selecting and pointing gesture. Users can easily establish, change, and close network connections between devices by selecting the device of interest and pointing to the other one. After a connection has been established, users can control the connected device using their own device as if the two are physically connected. In addition, users can easily transmit data by pointing to the connected device after selecting the data to send. We implemented the interface successfully by combining a virtual network computing technology and a robust hand-gesture recognition algorithm.

3.1   System Configuration

The system consists of three parts: a presence server, a controlling peer, and a controlled peer. The architecture of the system is described in Fig. 1.

The presence server consists of a connection management module, a gesture recognition module, and a networking module. The connection management module takes charge in handling the network connections that enables virtual network connections between multiple devices based on the Internet Protocol Address, port number, and ID number of each device. The gesture recognition module analyzes vision information from cameras to interpret users' hand gestures. The networking module is commonly used in the presence server, controlling peer, and controlled peer to transmit or receive data between them.

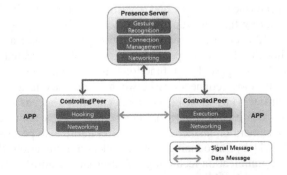

Fig. 1. System architecture of the suggested interface

The controlling peer is installed on the controlling device and the controlled peer on the device to be controlled by the controlling peer. For example, when a user controls the interactive wall screen using his/her laptop, the controlling peer and controlled peer is embedded in the laptop and the wall screen computer, respectively. The hooking module in the controlling peer detects users' input events such as keyboard inputs, mouse events, or file selections. The execution module in the controlled peer generates input events such as keyboard or mouse, and executes the file transferred from the controlling peer.

A protocol consists of signal messages and data messages. Signal messages are messages related to connections and disconnections between the presence server, controlling peer, and controlled peer. Data messages are transmitted between the controlling peer and controlled peer, and carry information to operate the connected device. Message types used in the system are described in Table 1.

Table 1. Message types used in the protocol

Type	Message Description
Registration/ Termination	Register a new controlled peer to a presence server or terminate existing registration
Control-ready	Ready message from a controlling peer to a presence server to control the selected device
Selection	Message from a controlled peer to a presence server to notify the device selection
Address	Message from a presence server to a controlling peer to inform IP address and port number of the device to be connected
Connection Complete/ Termination	Message from a controlling peer to a presence server to inform the completion / termination of network connection
Keyboard	Message from a controlling peer to a controlled peer to transmit keyboard events
Mouse	Message from a controlling peer to a controlled peer to transmit mouse events
File	Message from a controlling peer to a controlled peer to transmit the selected file information

Network connections are independent from the type of device and each device can be either controlling or controlled (see Fig. 2). In general, personal devices ranging from laptops, to PDAs, to mobile phones are connected with shared devices such as interactive wall screens or electronic boards. The system also supports simultaneous connections. For example, three keyboards can be simultaneously connected to one display to be controlled.

The entire network is based on asynchronous communication to minimize blocking during data transmission.

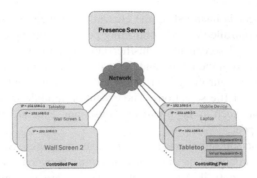

Fig. 2. Support of multiple device connections

3.2 Bare-Hand Gesture Recognition

The bare-hand gesture recognition is essential to implement the suggested interface. Here, bare-hand means that no devices are attached to the user and the user uses his/her hands as an input device. First, we introduced an adaptive background subtraction method to extract the foreground from the dynamically changing background. From the separated foreground, we extract the skin areas by using color information in RGB and HSV color space. Considering that each hand region has a certain size, we eliminate skin pixels that do not contain small circular area. All filtered skin areas are then grouped into several clusters. Then, we check the movement of each cluster by calculating optical flows around each cluster. Clusters whose image velocity is higher than the threshold value are considered as a hand candidate. Among hand candidates, we finally extract hand areas with simple geometric filters that characterize the hand. While scanning the contour of the circle around the center point of each hand candidate with radius bigger than hand size, exactly two intersection points should be encountered or no intersection points exist. Fingertips can be also easily detected from the positions of the hands with a circular shape filter similar with the one used in hand detection. We can easily calculate the direction a user is pointing based on the detected position of hand and fingertip, and also recognize the user's command gestures with Hidden Markov Model algorithm. We used a USB webcam or a network camera in implementation, and the suggested algorithm runs at a full frame rate (30Hz) that satisfies real-time interactions. Details of these concepts, as well as each operation of the hand and fingertip detection algorithm, will be described in a future publication.

4   Implementation in a Tabletop Display Environment

The suggested interface is implemented in an intelligent meeting room called "Intelligent and Responsive Space (IRS) [10, 11]." The IRS, which mainly consists of a tabletop display and three surrounding wall screens, is set up for efficient collaborative works such as team meetings or seminar presentations. Laptops and other mobile devices can be used in this environment. In addition, we installed a pan-tilt-zoom IP camera at the center of the ceiling of this environment to recognize users' hand gestures.

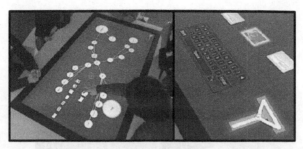

Fig. 3. The tabletop system in the IRS (Left: tabletop display; right: virtual keyboard and "T" icon)

Our tabletop is built as a horizontal table with a 55 inch LCD unit and an infrared LED touch panel supporting high-resolution images of 1920 x 1080. Users can manipulate this system with the fingers. This system also provides command icons called "interactive callout icons" and a virtual keyboard for the ease and diversification of information handling. Users can create command icons and control the system by drawing the shape of icons, each of which has a specific meaning to represent the user's intention. To implement the suggested interface in this environment, we introduced an T-shaped icon which means "ready for a new virtual network connection." The tabletop system, virtual keyboard, and an example of interactive call out icons are shown in Fig.3.

The surrounding wall screens were installed to extend the information sharing space and support effective collaboration.

The suggested interface enables users to easily connect and control devices of interest between the tabletop, wall screens, laptops, and mobile devices. Several examples of multiple device connection and control are given below.

First, a user can connect the tabletop with one of the wall screens through a simple selecting and pointing gesture. After creating the T-shaped icon, the user attaches this icon to the virtual keyboard to be used. This is the selecting process in the tabletop. With a pointing gesture, the indicated wall screen and the virtual keyboard with mouse touchpad are connected over the network. Visual and sound feedbacks notified the success of the connection (see upper right of Fig.4), and the user is able to control the contents of the wall screen with the virtual keyboard on the tabletop as if these two devices were physically connected. The user can also send the file on the tabletop display to the wall screen just by selecting the file of interest and pointing at the wall screen. With this operation, the file on the tabletop is transmitted to the wall screen and executed there. The device connection and file transmission are shown in Fig.4.

The interface can be used in the same way in other devices, except selecting operations change accordingly. Because we cannot select a keyboard and mouse or files on laptop or mobile device without a touch panel, we suggested an additional interface by adding Select functions to the Windows shell menu. With the right click of a mouse, the user can find a file select menu or a keyboard/mouse connection menu. Fig.5 shows Select operations in a laptop (without a touch panel) and mobile device (with a touch panel).

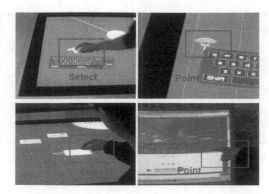

Fig. 4. Device connection(upper) and file transmission(lower)

Fig. 5. Select operations in the laptop and touch sensitive mobile device (left: laptop without touch panel; right: UMPC with touch panel)

After selecting the input device or data either by click or touch, the user can connect his/her own device with the indicated device with the same pointing gesture.

5   User Study

We performed a preliminary qualitative user study in the above-mentioned environment to verify our expectation that the suggested interface would improve users' interaction in a multiple device environment.

A total of twelve subjects (8 males, 4 females) recruited within the Korea Institute of Science and Technology participated in the experiment. The age distribution was from early twenties to late thirties. All of them have used and were familiar with popular computing devices. In contrast, most participants had little or no exposure to the tabletop and interactive wall displays.

We conducted three sets of experiments for each participant. Before the main experiments, we asked each participant to "send one picture file on the tabletop to one of wall screens" without any information about the suggested interface. We then explained the concept of the suggested interface to all participants for a few minutes and then carried out the main experiments. Three experiments, each of which consists of several tasks, were designed so that the participants would be exposed to different applications. Of course, each participant was trained for about 15 minutes on how to use the devices in the experimental environment – the tabletop system, Windows shell menu of laptop, and media player of UMPC.

In Experiment 1, the participant was asked first to create a virtual keyboard and mouse and to connect them to one of wall screens. The participant was then asked to transmit a presentation file on the tabletop to the connected wall screen, and modify some part of the file using the connected virtual keyboard and mouse. Finally, the participant was asked to control the presentation slide with bare-hand gestures. Experiment 2 is similar to Experiment 1 except it used the laptop instead of the tabletop to connect to and control the wall screen. The participant was asked to send the word file on his/her laptop to the wall screen and modify it with the laptop. In Experiment 3, the participant was first asked to play the video clip on his/her UMPC. The participant was then asked to pause the video clip on his/her UMPC, and resume it on one of wall screens. For this experiment, we specially developed a media player that enables resuming the multi-media file transmitted from the other device at the position the user has paused.

After these experiments, we asked each participant the following simple questions: 1) how easy was it to understand and use the suggested interface?; 2) how would you prefer the suggested interface to the existing interface and method?; and 3) what are the problems of the suggested interface if any exist?

In the pre-experiment, all of participants only selected the file and could not proceed any further. However, with a hint about using hand gestures, three participants exactly performed selecting and pointing gestures. In the main experiments all of the participants easily understood the concept of the interface, and all but one participant completed several tasks in the three experiments successfully without failure in connecting devices and controlling the data. Ten of the twelve participants preferred the proposed method to the traditional ones of using physical cables, e-mail/FTP, and mass storage devices. Two participants gave comments about the suggested interface: "It could also be a cumbersome process to setup several programs in each device to use the interface," and "Doing hand gestures in a public space makes me a little bit uncomfortable." Experimental results indicate that first-time users can easily use the suggested interface with brief explanations about the concept.

6 Conclusion and Future Works

The suggested gesture-based interface enables users to manage connections and handle information data intuitively and naturally in a multiple device environment. We fully implemented the suggested interface in an intelligent meeting room consisting of a tabletop, interactive wall displays, and other popular devices such as laptops and mobile devices. From the results of the user study, we knew that the concept of the suggested interfaces in different types of devices is easily accepted by users. Although there are a few comments concerning the use of the interface, we hope that this interface and the possible following works can significantly improve users' interaction with multiple devices in tabletop and interactive surface environments.

We are now working on combining this interface with various types of command gestures to easily handle information data and control devices. As one experiment participant suggested, we are also considering extending the suggested interface to control every day machines, such as home electronics and appliances. Finally, we plan to conduct extensive user studies to better understand the issues and problems in using the gesture-based interface in a ubiquitous environment.

Acknowledgments. This research was funded by Korea Institute of Science and Technology.

References

1. Ayatsuka, Y., Matsushita, N., Rekimoto, J.: Gaze-Link: A New Metaphor of Real-World Oriented User Interface. IPSJ Journal 42(6), 1330–1337 (2001)
2. Ayatsuka, Y., Rekimoto, J.: tranSticks: physically manipulatable virtual connections. In: Proc. CHI 2005, pp. 251–260. ACM Press, New York (2005)
3. Borchers, J., Ringer, M., Tyler, J., Fox, A.: Stanford interactive workspaces: a framework for physical and graphical user interface prototyping. IEEE Wireless Communications 9, 64–69 (2002)
4. Citrix's ICA, http://www.citrix.com/technology/icatech.htm
5. Everitt, K., Shen, C., Ryall, K., Forlines, C.: MultiSpace: Enabling Electronic Document Micro-mobility in Table-Centric, Multi-Device Environments. In: Proc. TableTop 2006, pp. 27–34 (2006)
6. Iwasaki, Y., Kawaguchi, N., Inagaki, Y.: Touch-and-Connect: A Connection Request Framework for Ad-Hoc Networks and the Pervasive Computing Environment. In: Proc. IEEE International Conference on Pervasive Computing and Communications, pp. 20–29 (2003)
7. Johanson, B., Hutchins, G., Winograd, T., Stone, M.: PointRight: Experience with Flexible Input Redirection in Interactive Workspaces. In: Proc. UIS 2002, pp. 227–234 (2002)
8. Kova, J., Peer, P., Solina, F.: Human skin color clustering for face detection. In: Proc. IEEE EUROCON 2003, vol. 2, pp. 144–148 (2003)
9. Lee, H., Jeong, H., Lee, J., Yeom, K., Shin, H., Park, J.: Select-and-Point: A Novel Interface for Multi-Device Connection and Control based on Simple Hand Gestures. In: Extended Abstract. CHI 2008, pp. 3357–3362. ACM Press, New York (2008)
10. Letessier, J., Bérard, F.: Visual tracking of bare fingers for interactive surfaces. In: Proc. UIS 2004, pp. 119–122 (2004)
11. Lucas, B., Kanade, T.: An iterative image registration technique with an application to stereo vision. In: Proc. Imaging understanding workshop, pp. 121–130 (1981)
12. Microsoft Corporation, Remote Desktop Protocol (RDP), Features and Performance White Paper (2000)
13. Miller, R., Myers, B.: Synchronizing clipboards of multiple computers. In: Proc. UIS 1999, pp. 65–66 (1999)
14. Park, J., Yeom, K., Lee, J.: Intelligent and Responsive Spaces: Integrated Design of Ambient Physical Spaces and Information Spaces. Korean Journal of Information Society 26(3), 15–25 (2008)
15. Park, J., Yeom, K., Ha, S., Park, M., Kim, L.: An Overview of Intelligent Responsive Space Technology in Tangible Space Initiative. In: Fishkin, K.P., Schiele, B., Nixon, P., Quigley, A. (eds.) PERVASIVE 2006. LNCS, vol. 3968, pp. 223–232. Springer, Heidelberg (2006)
16. Rabiner, L.: A Tutorial on Hidden Markov Models and Selected Applications in Speech Recognition. Proc. IEEE 77(2), 257–286 (1989)
17. Rekimoto, J.: Pick-and-Drop: A Direct Manipulation Technique for Multiple Computer Environment. In: Proc. UIST 1997, pp. 31–39 (1997)
18. Rekimoto, J., Ayatsuka, Y., Kohno, M.: SyncTap: An Interaction Technique for Mobile Networking. In: Proc. Mobile HCI 2003, pp. 104–115 (2003)

19. Rekimoto, J., Ayatsuka, Y., Kohno, M., Oba, H.: Proximal interactions: A direct manipulation technique for wireless networking. In: Proc. INTERACT 2003, IFIP, pp. 511–518 (2003)
20. Richardson, T., Stafford-Fraser, Q., Wood, K., Hopper, A.: Virtual Network Computing. Journal IEEE Internet Computing 2(1), 33–38 (1998)
21. Streitz, N., Tandler, P., Muller-Tomfelde, C., Konomi, S.: i-LAND: An Interactive Landscape for creativity and Innovation. In: Proc. CHI 1999, pp. 120–127. ACM Press, New York (1999)
22. Swindells, C., Inkpen, K., Dill, J., Tory, M.: That one there! Pointing to establish device identity. In: Proc. UIS 2002, pp. 151–160 (2002)
23. Viola, P., Jones, M.: Rapid object detection using a boosted cascade of simple features. In: Proc. CVP 2001, pp. 511–518 (2001)
24. Wigdor, D., Shen, C., Forlines, C., Balakrishnan, R.: Table-centric interactive spaces for real-time collaboration. In: Proc. AVI 2006, pp. 103–107 (2006)
25. X Window System, http://www.opengroup.org/tech/desktop/x/
26. Zigelbaum, J., Kumpf, A., Vazquez, A., Ishii, H.: Slurp: tangibility spatiality and an eye-dropper. In: Proc. CHI 2008, pp. 2565–2574. ACM Press, New York (2008)

Shadow Awareness:
Bodily Expression Supporting System with Use of Artificial Shadow

Yoshiyuki Miwa[1], Shiorh Itai[1], Takabumi Watanabe[1], Koji Iida[1],
and Hiroko Nishi[2]

[1] Waseda University, 3-4-1, Ohkubo, Shinjuku-ku, Tokyo, Japan
miwa@waseda.jp, itai@fuji.waseda.jp, takabumi@fuji.waseda.jp,
koji.e-da@suou.waseda.jp
[2] Toyo Eiwa University, 32, Miho-cho, Midori-ku, Yokohama, Kanagawa, Japan
hiroko@toyoeiwa.ac.jp

Abstract. As a supporting means for self-creating bodily expression, shadow media system was developed with which shadow is artificially deformed into diverse forms and such deformed shadow can be displayed on a screen without separating it from the own body. With the system, it was found that the awareness was established inside the body via deformed shadows; therefore it can support an improvised creation of the images. Furthermore, by the subject-object inseparable interaction through shadows, co-creation of images with others was encouraged. Accordingly, it was indicated that this media system is promising and effective to support co-creative expression and shows its potential applicability as a creative archive technology to connect to past people.

Keywords: Bodily Expression, image, awareness, co-creation, shadow media.

1 Communicability and Bodily Expression

For expanding the communicability of each individual, the following two things are considered essential; (I) you should respect and accept other people's expression as an equivalent value as yours, and its irradiation should be taken inside yourself, and (II) "bodily sensitivity" with which a new awareness on your and other's existence will be created by the reflection of the expression. When the equivalence of expression is secured, diverse expression with personality can be extracted from each individual by the so-called "function of open body" which are supported by bodily sensitivity; so that the "*Ba*" of encounter might be created [1-4]. At the same time, in the co-creative expression [5], a new image will be co-created with the other person while sensing reflection of your own expression pre se, by the "function of open body". With this manner, the impromptu and self-consistent expression can make advance in simultaneous and complementary manner without any interruptions.

Based on what has been described above, in the present study aiming on expanding the communicability, it should be pointed out that expressing self should sense the reflection of own expression, and this supports creation of new image. For approaching this aim, we turned our attention to be ontologically inseparable between body

J.A. Jacko (Ed.): Human-Computer Interaction, Part II, HCII 2009, LNCS 5611, pp. 226–235, 2009.
© Springer-Verlag Berlin Heidelberg 2009

and shadow. This study will also investigate possible method with which, a clear awareness can occur or body itself can be expanded by visualizing the reflected expression which was normally sensed inside yourself as an expression by your own shadow. Moreover, this study will examine possible methods for a shadow expression for perpetually spinning expression by continuous image creation. Furthermore, "creative archive expression method of "*Ba*" will be investigated. This will allow current people to encounter past people beyond time and space by re-displaying other person's past expression recorded with use of shadows. The last purpose was aimed to acquire design guidelines for media technology which can support the communicability and co-creative expression. There are none previous works on technologies using shadow as an embodied media expect our works [6] and [7].

2 Ontological Inseparability of Shadow

2.1 Structure of System

In this study, as discussed in more detail below, bodily expression was intended to be extracted by the free deformation of own shadow. For achieving this task, the system for creating artificial your own shadow is necessitated. Fig.1 shows the system structure as well as creation process. In the developed system, the thermal vision camera for obtaining human image is installed at the Backspace as a virtual light source. With this virtual light source, shadow artificially produced by PC is then displayed from participant's standing position. With this system, thermal distribution image of human obtained from the thermal vision camera is sent to PC. The areas of floor surface and

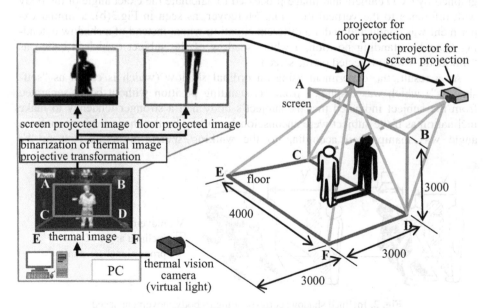

Fig. 1. System configuration

screen in thermal distribution image area are designate as two rectangular shapes, and floor projected image as well as screen projected image were produced. Moreover, by binarization of these thermal images, these images were converted to shadow images and further performed with projective transformation to map these images in the projection space. OpenCV was utilized to paste and display images load into PC and for image processing of shadows. Lastly, these two shadow images are projected by a projector for screen surface projection which is installed at the Back surface of the screen and a projector for floor projection which is installed at the ceiling. By the structure mentioned above, shadow created by PC can be projected coordinately from participant's standing position. Moreover, it was verified that artificially created shadow can be projected in 15[fps]. The following experiments were conducted using this system.

2.2 Body, Moved by Shadow

Firstly, authors had performed the following experiments on simple walking movements in order to investigate the ontological relationship between body and its shadow. Subjects are 10 males (age range: 22 - 30 years old). Subject was asked to be moved parallel with the screen. Furthermore, he was asked to walk Back and forth along 3.6 m distance with his preferable walking speed. During their walking, as seen in Fig.2, each subject's shadow (whose speed was proportional to the subject's walking speed) was inclined toward to his walking direction, and inclination angles of subject's body as well as his shadow were measured and recorded. For experiments, red LEDs were installed at subject's chest and waist. These movements were photographed by CCD camera and image-processed to calculate the exact angle of the body with reference to the vertical direction. Moreover, as seen in Fig.3(b), a similar experiment was conducted under a different situation when, instead of a shadow extending from his standing position, a whole shadow of the subject (which is called as "silhouette") was projected on the screen.

As a result, the experiment using an ordinal shadow (which is called as "self-shadow") which was displayed from his standing position without being separated from the subject indicated that the subject's body had a stronger tendency to make inclination as if the subject were unconsciously pulling by the shadow whose inclined angle was manipulated according to the walking speed, in comparison to the

V ; movement speed
□ ; inclined angle of shadow
k ; proportional constant

Fig. 2. Inclined shadow, corresponding to body movement speed

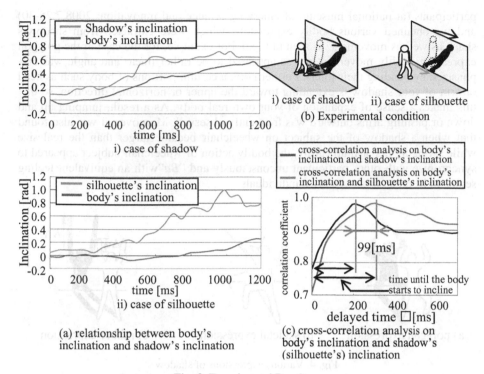

Fig. 3. Experimental Results

silhouette tests. One typical example of results is shown in Fig.3. More interested, it was found that the time when body started to make inclination using the self-shadow was 100ms earlier than that using the silhouette. This characteristic difference suggests that there are two types of functions – function for unconscious reaction and conscious (cognitive) reaction –, and former type of function precede appearance of latter type of function. This implies the characteristic of the self-shadow, which is originated from ontologically inseparable relationship between body and shadow, and a similar phenomenon should not be realized with a body image on mirror (or mirror image) which is ontologically separated from own body. In other words, human can unconsciously position his existence in actual field by his own shadow.

2.3 Metamorphosis of Body Sensation by Deforming Self-shadow

If we employ ontologically inseparable relationship between body and shadow as described above, it is expected that bodily expression can be extracted in correspondence to the deformed mode by artificially deforming your own shadow. As seen in Fig.4, we have developed several software for generating polygonized shadow (polygon expression), showing shadow with lines (skeleton expression), or extending the shadow of one part of the body in accordance to its body part's moving speed (rubber expression), which were installed in the above system. Several image examples of shadow are demonstrated in Fig.5. These systems were experienced by general participants (at national museum of emerging science and innovation; 2008.7.25-30) and we obtained various bodily expressions which were extracted from shadow's shape as well as movement, as seen in Fig.6. For example, for the case of the polygon expression, bodily movement per se appeared to be rather linear and angle was emphasized by bending their joints. Furthermore, a certain portions of body such as head or arm of your shadow is extending toward the upper or horizontal direction, so that this makes a sense of expansion of your own real body. As a result, jumping up and down or pushing arms outward was frequently observed. Moreover, it was also found that when a shadow of the subject on wheelchair became larger than the real size while swinging his arm upwardly, the bodily action of wheelchair subject appeared to synchronize with other participant unconsciously and "Ba"with an equivalent feeling seems to be created between two individuals.

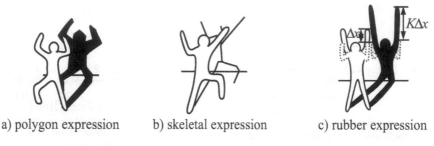

a) polygon expression   b) skeletal expression   c) rubber expression

Fig. 4. Various expressions of shadow

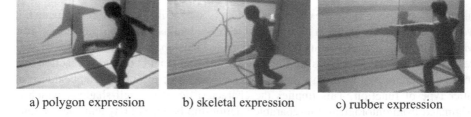

a) polygon expression   b) skeletal expression   c) rubber expression

Fig. 5. Example of shadow expression

a) polygon expression   b) skeletal expression   c) rubber expression

Fig. 6. Creation of bodily expression by various shadow expressions

3 Self-creation of Expression by Shadow Image

The previous results can be understood by the thought that the feeling in gap generated between your own body and unexperienced shadow might create the bodily
awareness, and it is furthermore hypothesized that the body kept its expression in
order to accept such feeling in gap. If our assumption is correct, it can be expected
that each subject can open their bodies by respective expression through their shadows and they can create "Ba" of encounter, being accompanied with mutual bodily
awareness. However, since such gap is defined by designers' preference for this case,
the restriction caused from the system is strong and the thus image has a tendency to
be fixed. As a result, a reflection of expression (with which body sensation as well as
existence sensation could be jeopardized) might be unidirectional. In order to solve
this problem, it seems to be crucial for participants involved in the system to self-
create the gap per se. In other words, a development of novel expression software
with self-referentiality is urgently required. By the self-creating shadow image using
such software, gap between your body and shadow can be eliminated, and a new gap
can be generated at the same time. In fact, this software can create an expression by
the circulation between body and shadow.

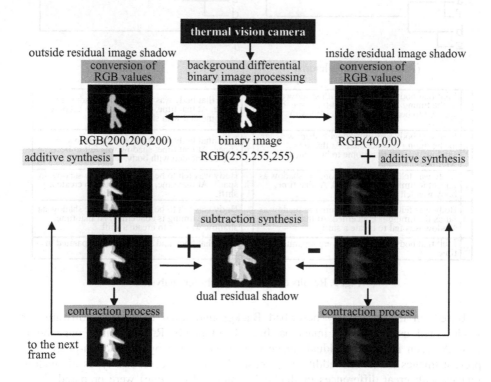

Fig. 7. Generation algorithm for dual residual shadow

Fig. 8. Bodily expression using dual residual shadow

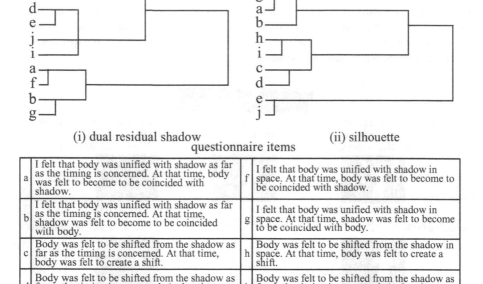

(i) dual residual shadow   (ii) silhouette
                    questionnaire items

a	I felt that body was unified with shadow as far as the timing is concerned. At that time, body was felt to become to be coincided with shadow.	f	I felt that body was unified with shadow in space. At that time, body was felt to become to be coincided with shadow.
b	I felt that body was unified with shadow as far as the timing is concerned. At that time, shadow was felt to become to be coincided with body.	g	I felt that body was unified with shadow in space. At that time, shadow was felt to become to be coincided with body.
c	Body was felt to be shifted from the shadow as far as the timing is concerned. At that time, body was felt to create a shift.	h	Body was felt to be shifted from the shadow in space. At that time, body was felt to create a shift.
d	Body was felt to be shifted from the shadow as far as the timing is concerned. At that time, shadow was felt to create a shift.	i	Body was felt to be shifted from the shadow as far as the timing is concerned. At that time, shadow was felt to create a shift.
e	I felt that body and shadow were separated in time.	j	I felt that body and shadow were separated in space.

Fig. 9. Results of hierarchical cluster analysis

Based on the previously described Background, dual expression software for shadow with use of residual image has been developed by R. Okiyama of our laboratory. As seen in Fig.7, residual image can be generated by contraction-processing present images made with additive synthesis. For this process, two types of shadow images with great differences in shadow's color (RBG value) were prepared. Then this software performed the above processing to respective image, and, at the final stage, the dual residual shadow was generated by subtraction synthesis of these two residual image shadows. Here two cases are demonstrated; I) outside residual image shadow (with large RBG value), showing a sharp reaction to variations on bodily movements, and (II) inside residual image shadow (with small RBG value), showing a slow reaction to the m. Since each residual image possesses different contrast, experiment subject can feel a boundary appeared at inside and outside residual image shadows and the boundary defined at outside residual image shadow and system space as a temporal and spatial gap. As a result, this makes the subject feel to have competing bodily expansion and contraction. The feature of bodily expression using the present software is demonstrated in Fig.8. Among many comments, the followings are typical; "I felt as if I wanted to continue to move." "There was a sense of relief as well as a sense of unity." "Time sensation has been varied." "Changes and movements of mind can be sensed." Hence, it was noticed that diverse expression can be spun along with creating images.

Furthermore, we conducted a questionnaire survey with regard to temporal and spatial gap between shadow and body. Obtained results were subjected to the hierarchical cluster analysis by Ward method, as seen in Fig.9. In Fig.9, for comparison purpose, results on the silhouette tests are also shown. Several points should be noticed. By the dual residual shadow, two situations - a situation where body and shadow are unified in time-and-space and inseparable, and another situation where body and shadow have a gap or are separated – form two large clusters which divides all items in two. Namely, in the case of the dual residual shadow, it can be speculated that relationship between body and shadow circulate among inseparable and separable situations, and this circulation make it possible to create new expression constantly. Moreover, results on the dual residual shadow show that a pair of time and space forms nearest cluster in the items about unity, so that it can be also suggested that, when subjects feel body and shadow unified, time and space can not be separated inside the subject mind. On the other hand, when subject feel time and space separated, the subject can sense the separation of the time and space which are taking place inside the subject's mind, and feel that shadow create such a gap. From these results, in the case of the dual residual shadow, expression can step by step advance by dual situations – inseparable feeling of time and space in the case of unification between shadow and body, separable feeling of time and space in the case of separation between shadow and body-. This furthermore indicates that the "*Ba*" (space) can be varied by subject's expression, and new expression can be created at the "*Ba*" (space) if such a thing is felt as a gap. Moreover, space and time which construct the expression can be self-created by complementary and circulating manner by the unifying the body and shadow and gap via the double shadow, just like the similar situation where time providing the Base for the expression can advance by time-difference in ever-changing expression.

4 Creative Archive of "*Ba*" with Use of Shadow

The present authors have previously developed "Communication System of "*Ba*" (WSCS)" which employs the shadow as your own agent and we have reported that, by reproducing past actual field by the shadow, we can position our existence together with the past people's shadow in past actual field [6]. However, since it is principally impossible for us to have an interaction with people's shadow, we could not

Shadow of the past person here

Fig. 10. An example of archive in case of dual residual shadow usage

accomplish a creation of context of *"Ba"* by playing with past people. Hence, in order to overcome this problem, the present authors examined the creative archive expression of *"Ba"* which can integrate the bodily expression of past people and current people in subject-object inseparable manner. As a result, it is hypothesized that current people can position past people in the same stage (*"Ba"*) by not making the direct interaction between past and current people's shadow, but creating an another shadow image enveloping partner's shadow through the mutual bodily expression. This requires that shadow has different dual function. One is subject-object inseparable function. The other is subject-object separable function. Then, we tried to apply the previous dual residual shadow. A part of results is presented in Fig.10. In this figure, current people dance with past people's shadow by re-displaying the recorded past people's shadow. Among many comments, the followings are typical; "Although I was firstly very confused, later on, breath of shadow and *"Maai"* entered into me and started to feel "we are unified." "Although I only moved very awkwardly by forcing to adjust to the other people, later on I felt that I can dance more freely unconsciously and I found some joyful moment when I noticed that we danced in prefect harmony."

When respective shadows of past and current people are expressed with dual residual shadow, participants feel that the outside residual image precedes the inside residual image. As a result, is can be considered that a unique expression - with which the current people behaves as if he anticipates the movement of the past people - was extracted from the present people. In other words, the outside residual image has a subject-object inseparable function. Through this function, the expression of the current people can be unified with that of the past people in complementary and simultaneous manner, so that the current people can be apparently related to the past people and position himself in their mutual common *"Ba"*. Namely, the present authors consider that, by an occurrence of an apparent co-creative expression with the past people, the current people can continue to self-create his expression while the current people is grasping past people's mind and past people's context of expression to some extent.

5   Toward Supporting the Image Creation for Bodily Expression

The dual residual shadow is characterized by utilizing the differences between outside and inside residual image processing, and creating the temporal and spatial gap at their boundary by bodily movements; therefore, body being inseparable from its shadow is felt as if the outside shadow appears to advance in time (or anticipate the future) than the inside shadow. In other words, changes in inside shadow is sensed and recognized as a mental gap which changes by sensing the reflection of self expression, and on the other hand, the outside shadow's changes are sensed as an existence gap of self bodily expression. The expression can be constantly created in such a way that such explicit double gap is integrated as an original function for connecting outside and inside of the body. The fact that majority of experiment subjects had comments on projecting his mind to shadow might suggest that reflection of expression is circulated between shadow and yourself by encountering the shadow, and *"Ba"* where you might had a conversation with the shadow is created. By the single display of the residual shadow or dual shadow having previously fixed boundary between inside and outside shadow, we have received comments "There was some sort of restriction." "I did get any positive imagination." These comments suggest us that it appears to be important for boundary of *"Ba"* to renew autonomously by the bodily expression, in order to set free the time-and-space restriction for expression and support constantly the image creation. Moreover, the interaction of the bodily expression via the duality of shadow like the dual residual shadow can promote the co-creation of images and can be effective for supporting the co-creative expression. Furthermore, it was indicated that dual residual shadow shows its potential applicability as a creative archive technology to connect to past people.

Acknowledgments. This research was partially supported by Grant-in-Aid for Scientific Research (S), 18300044, from Japanese Ministry of Education, Science, Sports and Culture. This research also has been conducted under the project "Generation and Control Technology of Human-Entrained Embodied Media" and is supported by CREST of JST. We would like to express our sincere thanks to our graduate students, K. Haga, R. Okiyama, H. Watanabe for their assistants.

References

1. Shimizu, H.: The Thoughts of "Ba": Creative Stage of Life (in Japanese). Universitey of Tokyo Press (2003)
2. Shimizu, H., Kume, T., Miwa, Y., Miyake, Y.: Ba and co-creation (in Japanese). NTT Publishing (2000)
3. Miwa, Y., Nishi, H.: Communicability support for "Ba" of encounter - a trial on functional relationship and existence relationship with bodily expression. In: Proceedings of Human Interface symposium, pp. 889–892 (2008) (in Japanese)
4. Nishi, H., Noguchi, H., Yoshikawa, K., Hattori, M.: How can we apply three-dimensional computer graphics to creative physical expression? In: Proceedings of Human Interface symposium, pp. 137–140 (2008) (in Japanese)
5. Miwa, Y., Itai, S., watanabe, T., Nishi, Y.: Communicability and co-creative expression. In: Proceedings of SI 2008 (2008) (in Japanese)
6. Miwa, Y., Itai, S., Sakurai, D., Hasegawa, S.: Shadow arts-communication -System supporting communicability for encounter among remote groups. In: Smith, M.J., Salvendy, G. (eds.) HCII 2007. LNCS, vol. 4558, pp. 84–94. Springer, Heidelberg (2007)
7. Miwa, Y., Ishibiki, C.: Shadow Communication: System for embodied interaction with remote partners. In: Proceedings of CSCW 2004, pp. 467–476 (2004)

An Approach to Glove-Based Gesture Recognition

Farid Parvini, Dennis McLeod, Cyrus Shahabi, Bahareh Navai,
Baharak Zali, and Shahram Ghandeharizadeh

Computer Science Department
University of Southern California
Los Angeles, California 90089-0781
{fparvini,mcleod,cshahabi,navai,bzali,shahram}@usc.edu

Abstract. Nowadays, computer interaction is mostly done using dedicated devices. But gestures are an easy mean of expression between humans that could be used to communicate with computers in a more natural manner. Most of the current research on hand gesture recognition for Human-Computer Interaction rely on either the Neural Networks or Hidden Markov Models (HMMs). In this paper, we compare different approaches for gesture recognition and highlight the major advantages of each. We show that gestures recognition based on the Bio-mechanical characteristic of the hand provides an intuitive approach which provides more accuracy and less complexity.

1   Introduction

Gestures are destined to play an increasingly important role in human-computer interaction in the future. Humans use gestures in their everyday communication with other humans, not only to reinforce the meanings that they convey through speech, but also to convey meaning that would be difficult or impossible to convey through speech alone. Hence, to make human-computer interaction truly natural, computers must be able to recognize gestures in addition to speech. Furthermore, gesture recognition is a requirement for the virtual reality environments, where the user must be able to manipulate the environment with his/her hands.

Closely related to the field of gesture recognition is the field of sign language recognition. Because sign languages are the primary mode of communication for many deaf people, and because they are full-fledged languages in their own rights, they offer a much more structured and constrained research environment than general gestures. While a functional sign language recognition system could facilitate the interaction between deaf and hearing people, it could also provide a good starting point for studying the more general problem of gesture recognition.

As an example, American Sign Language (ASL) is a complex visual-spatial language that is used by the deaf community in the United States and English-speaking parts of Canada. ASL is a natural language and it is linguistically complete. Some people have described ASL and other sign languages as 'gestural' languages.

J.A. Jacko (Ed.): Human-Computer Interaction, Part II, HCII 2009, LNCS 5611, pp. 236–245, 2009.
© Springer-Verlag Berlin Heidelberg 2009

ASL includes two types of gestures: static and dynamic. Static signs are the signs that according to ASL rules, no hand movement is required to generate them. All ASL alphabets excluding 'J' and 'Z' are static signs. In contrary to the static signs, dynamic signs are the ones which their generation require movement of fingers, hand or both.

One of the most challenging issues in gesture recognition is the ability to recognize a particular gesture made by different people. This problem, often called *user-dependency*, rises from the fact that people have different ergonomic sizes, so they produce different data for the same gestural experiment.

As a solution device manufacturers suggest *Calibration*, which is the process makes the generated data as identical as possible.

Another relevant challenge in gesture recognition is device-dependency. That is the generated data by two different devices for the same experiment are completely different. In this paper, we compare three different approaches that are used for static sign language recognition. In our current implementations we only considered the static signs and dynamic sign detection is not supported by any of these three implemented systems.

While the accuracy is one of the aspects that we consider when comparing these approaches, we also consider other characteristics that can affect the accuracy and may favor one of these approaches for a specific application (e.g. user-independency and extensibility).

The remainder of this paper is organized as follows. Section 2 discusses the related work. We present each approach along with its strengths and limitations in Sections 3, 4 and 5, respectively. The results of our comparative experiments are reported in Section 6 . Finally, Section 7 concludes this paper and discusses our future research plans.

2   Related Work

To date, sign recognition has been studied extensively by different communities. We are aware of two major approaches: Machine-Vision based approaches which analyze the video and image data of a hand in motion and Haptic based approaches which analyze the haptic data received from a sensory device (e.g., a sensory glove).

Due to lack of space, we refer the interested readers to [6] for a good survey on vision based sign recognition methods. With the haptic approaches, the movement of the hand is captured by a haptic device and the received raw data is analyzed. In some studies, a characteristic descriptor of the shape of the hand or motion which represents the changes of the shape is extracted and analyzed. Holden and Owens [8] proposed a new hand shape representation technique that characterizes the finger-only topology of the hand by adapting an existing technique from speech signal processing. Takahashi and Kishino [9] could recognize 34 out of 46 Japanese kana alphabet gestures with a data-glove based system using joint angle and hand orientations coding techniques. Newby [10] used a "sum of squares" template matching approach to recognize ASL signs. Hong et. al [7] proposed an approach for 2D gesture recognition that models each gesture as a Finite State Machine (FSM) in spatial-temporal space.

More recent studies in gesture recognition have focused on Hidden Markov Model (HMM) or Support Vector Machines (SVM). While these approaches have produced highly accurate systems capable of recognizing gestures [15], we are more concerned about important characteristic of approaches such as extensibility and user-dependency rather than only the accuracy.

3   Neural Network Approach

Neural networks are composed of elements, called neurons, which are inspired by biological nervous systems. The elements operate in parallel and form a network, whose function is determined largely by the connections between them.

The main reason for Neural Network popularity is that once the network has configured, it forms appropriate internal represender and decider systems based on training examples. Since the representation is distributed across the network as a series of interdependent weights instead of a conventional local data structure, the decider has certain advantageous properties:

- recognition in the presence of noise or incomplete data
- pattern generalization

3.1   Strengths and Limitations of the Neural Network Approach

Neural networks are very popular in these types of classification applications for their simplicity. Some of the advantages of neural networks are listed here:

1. No calibration is required
2. A trained neural network would recognize an unknown input sign very fast
3. Our experiments proved that with sufficient data, this approach produces very good results
4. With their current popularity, ready-to-use neural network packages are readily available, so there is almost no time spent on implementing the system.

Neural networks have some drawbacks, too:

1. A large amount of labeled examples are required to train the network for accurate recognition
2. If a new gesture is added or one is removed, more accuracy can achieved by re-training the whole system.
3. Neural networks can over learn, if given too many examples, and discard originally learned patterns. It may also happen that one bad example may send the patterns learned into the wrong direction. This or other factors, such as orthogonality of the training vectors, may prevent the network from converging at all.

4. Neural networks tend to consume large amount of processing power, especially in the training phase.
5. The major problem in utilizing neural networks is to understand what the network had actually learned, given the ad-hoc manner in which it would have been configured.
6. There is no formal basis for constructing neural networks, the topology, unit activation functions, learning strategy and learning rate. All these should be determined by trial and error.

4 Multi-layer Approach

The Multi-Layer Approach, originally proposed in [1] combines template matching and neural networks, so it benefits from both approaches. By layering, the system achieves device independency and extensibility, two important properties that most other systems lack.

4.1 Strengths and Limitations of the Multi-layer Approach

Since this approach also uses neural networks, it has some of the drawbacks listed in 3.1, which are not repeated in this section.

Advantages of this approach can be summarized as the following:

1. No calibration is required
2. For a trained system, recognizing an unknown input sign is fast
3. Our experiments show that when we have limited number of data sets for training the neural networks, this approach behaves more accurately than a single layer neural network
4. Since the neural networks have limited number of inputs, training of the system (38 neural networks) takes much less time than training a single layer general-purpose neural network
5. Extensibility is another important feature; to add a new sign, it is not necessary to redefine and retrain the networks as it is in the single layer neural network. The postural templates are supposedly sufficient for defining all the simple postures required for ASL. Hence, we only need to add a gestural template to the system for the new sign. Even if a new postural predicate needs to be defined, we only need to map required sensors to a new predicate in the first layer, define a new postural predicate and train only the new corresponding neural network, and define the new gestures. Nothing in the rest of the system needs to be changed.
6. The application layer, or the gestural template layer, is device independent. The system can work with different types of haptic or visual devices only by some modifications in the first two layers.
7. The first two layers are also application independent, so that when the postures are detected in the second layer, any application can use this clean semantic description of hand for their own purpose.

As it is mentioned before, this system has some of the drawbacks of single layer neural networks as well as the followings:

1. When the number of training sets increased to 18 sets, both single layer neural network and GRUBC approaches behaved more accurately than the Multi-Layer Framework. Although we only represent our results for one training set vs. 18 training sets for each approach, we tested the system with different number of sets and it appears that somewhere between 1 and 18 this approach achieves its maximum accuracy.
2. Using multiple neural networks and combining them with template matching makes implementation of the system somehow complicated.

5   GRUBC: Gesture Recognition by Utilizing Bio-mechanical Characteristics

Gesture recognition by utilizing bio-mechanical characteristics, proposed in [2] is inspired by the observation that all forms of hand signs include finger-joint movements from a starting posture to a final posture. We utilize the concept of 'range of motion' from the Bio-Mechanical literature at each joint to abstract the motion and construct a signature that represents the signature.

Due to lack of space, we refer the interested readers to [2] for detailed process of constructing the signatures.

Registration which is the core of this approach is completely different from 'training' in the following aspects:

- In contrast to 'training' that requires several sets of data, we require one set of samples (one sample for each sign) to completely register all signs.
- While having more signers register each sign will potentially increase the accuracy, there is no direct relationship between the number of registered signs and accuracy, as is in the training.

5.1   Strengths and Limitations of GRUBC

Based on our observations and the primary results of our experiments, this approach benefits from the following advantages:

1. User-independency, which implies that the registration can be done by any signer without having impacts on the overall accuracy.
2. Device independency which allows the registration to be done with another device or even without any sensory device. The reason is that the information we require to register a sign is the relative movements of the sensors, if this information can be provided by another device or even without using sensory device, we can still register the sign.
3. No calibration (a must in most traditional approaches) is required prior to data gathering from different users.

4. This approach is extensible, i.e. new signs can be recognized just by registering them and there is no requirement to train the system all over again.
5. While the focus of this approach is on the problem of classification, it has a broader applicability. With classification, each unknown data sample is given the label of its best match among known samples in a database. Hence, if there is no label for a group of samples, the traditional classification approaches fail to recognize these input samples. For example, in a virtual reality environment where human behavior is captured by sensory devices, every behavior (e.g., frustration or sadness) may not be given a class label, since they have no clear definition. This approach can address this issue by finding the similar behavior across different users without requiring to have them labeled.

On the other hand, the shortcomings of this approach can be listed as follows:
1. As we was mentioned before, the core of this approach is based on the signature matching of an unknown sign and the registered signs. If two signs have similar signatures (e.g. ASL alphabets R and U), this approach fails to differentiate them.
2. To match two signatures, we used two approaches:
   (a) We could recognize two signatures identical if their distances are less than a threshold (ε). In this approach, the threshold should be defined and we assume the value is application dependent.
   (b) Two signatures are identical, if they are the nearest-neighbors. In this approach, two signatures may be recognized identical while they are very far and completely different due to the fact that no other match could be found.

6   Performance Results

In this section, we present results of the experiments conducted to compare performance of three gesture recognition approaches in recognizing the ASL static signs.

6.1   Experimental Setup

For our experiments, we used CyberGlove [16] as a virtual reality user interface to acquire data. CyberGlove is a glove that provides up to 22 joint-angle measurements.

We initiated our experiments by collecting data from 19 different subjects performing static signs ('A' to 'Y', excluding 'J') from a starting posture while wearing the glove. We assured the same starting posture for all the experiments. For each sign, we collected 140 tuples from the starting posture to the final posture, each including 22 sensor values.

While each sign was made by a transitional movement from a starting posture to a final posture, we conducted the experiments in a way that the last 40 tuples of each experiment belong to the static sign and do not include any transitional movement.

During our preliminary experiments, we discovered due to the limited number of sensors in the CyberGlove, it is not capable of capturing all the finger positions associated with every ASL alphabet. Hence, it cannot be used to differentiate some alphabets regardless of the approach.

For example, H and K are just different in some wrist rotation that is not captured by the glove.

Another example is R and U, as there are not enough sensors in the glove to capture the relationship between the index and middle fingers which is essential to differentiate R from U. Thus we left the signs H & R out of our experiments. For some data files, complete sensor values are not captured for some lines. We also excluded all the data lines which did not have all 22 sensor values.

For each approach, we conducted two different sets of experiments: Leave-One-Out and Keep-One-In. With the Leave-One-Out approach, all the data sets are used in training except one, which is used for testing. The same test is conducted 19 times, each time with a different set of data used for testing, until all the data sets are tested. The reported results for this set of experiments are the average of all 19 sets.With Keep-One-In approach, which is the opposite of the Leave-One-Out, only one data set is used for training the system, and the remaining 18 sets are used for testing. There again, we repeated this set of experiments 19 times, each time a different data set used for training and the remaining 18 sets for testing. The reported result of this set of experiments is again the average of all the 19 experiments. For the experiments both neural network frameworks used similar setups and experimental approaches.

Single-Layer Neural Network Experimental Setup. In these sets of experiments, we used a feed-forward, back propagation neural network from the MATLAB [17] neural network toolbox. This network has one hidden layer with 20 neurons. The input layer has 22 neurons (each for one sensor) and there are 22 neurons (one for each sign) in the output layer. The set of experiments conducted are exactly as explained above.

Multi-Layer Experimental Setup. In this approach, in addition to the training set, there is also a tuning set. Although we followed the same guidelines to run the experiments as single-layer neural network approach, because of this difference we had to divide the training sets into two parts.

For the first set of experiments, Leave-One-Out, when 18 sets are used in training and one in testing, we tested two different setups; in the first one, we used 9 data sets for training, 9 other data sets for tuning the networks and the 19th set for testing the system (9-9-1 setup). In the second setup for Leave-One-Out, we used 18 sets for training the networks, and used the same 18 sets for tuning the networks and the last set for testing (18-18-1 setup).

In the second sets of experiments, which were Keep-One-In, one set is used for training and the same set is used for tuning the system, and then system is tested on all the remaining 18 data sets (1-1-18 setup). As in 7.2.1, all these experiments are repeated 19 times, each time for a different subject.

GRUBC Experimental Setup. We repeated two sets of aforementioned experiments with GRUBC as we did for the neural network and multi-layer, except we did not have the training phase for this approach. The other dominant difference between the experiments of neural network and GRUBC is that in the former case, the data used to train the system was a preprocessed data, including statistical calculated data, e.g. min, max and average, while with GRUBC, only the raw data was used for registration. We conducted the Leave-One-Out experiment (i.e., registered with 18 sets and tested with the remaining set) and repeated it 19 times. We then conducted Keep-One-In experiment (i.e., registered with one set and tested with the remaining 18 sets) and repeated it 19 times.

Alphabet	Neural Network	Neural Network	Multi-Layer	Multi-Layer	Multi-Layer	GRUBC	GRUBC
A	89.47%	29.83%	78.95%	84.21%	58.78%	94.44%	78.00%
B	100%	42%	100%	100%	92%	94%	78%
C	57.89%	23.98%	73.68%	89.47%	39.33%	83.33%	56.00%
D	84.21%	40.06%	89.47%	89.47%	69.11%	94.44%	72.00%
E	94.74%	36.55%	100.00%	94.74%	62.00%	88.89%	78.00%
F	100%	45%	100%	100%	81%	94%	83%
G	68.42%	22.52%	42.11%	57.90%	42.56%	55.56%	44.00%
I	89.47%	35.97%	84.21%	73.68%	73.22%	94.44%	89.00%
K	78.95%	23.98%	94.74%	100.00%	56.94%	72.22%	67.00%
L	73.68%	39.77%	42.11%	52.63%	41.28%	88.89%	72.00%
M	89.47%	29.24%	63.16%	52.63%	47.72%	83.33%	72.00%
N	73.68%	33.92%	42.11%	26.31%	58.11%	61.11%	39.00%
O	63.16%	26.90%	57.89%	47.37%	38.44%	55.56%	33.00%
P	94.74%	22.52%	84.21%	89.47%	19.11%	83.33%	78.00%
Q	78.95%	32.75%	68.42%	47.37%	39.11%	50.00%	17.00%
S	84.21%	36.84%	89.47%	68.42%	57.61%	94.44%	72.00%
T	57.89%	21.93%	21.05%	5.26%	27.72%	83.33%	67.00%
U	57.89%	21.05%	15.79%	5.26%	34.78%	88.89%	72.00%
V	84.21%	30.99%	15.79%	10.53%	59.44%	61.11%	39.00%
W	100%	26%	100%	100%	93%	100%	100%
X	84.21%	35.67%	0.00%	0.00%	41.32%	94.44%	83.00%
Y	94.74%	52.05%	94.74%	94.74%	72.11%	94.44%	89.00%
AVERAGE	**81.82%**	**32.24%**	**66.27%**	**63.16%**	**54.75%**	**82.32%**	**67.18%**
	Training set : 18	Training set : 1	Training set : 9 Tunining set : 9	Training set : 18 Tunining set : 18	Training set : 1 Tunining set : 1	Registration: 18	Registration: 1
	Testing set : 1	Testing set : 18	Testing set : 1	Testing set : 1	Testing set : 18	Testing set : 1	Testing set : 18
	Repeating: 19	Repeating: 19	Repeating: 19	Repeating: 19	Repeating: 19	Repeating: 19	Repeating: 19

Fig. 1. Comprehensive result for two sets of experiments

6.2   Experimental Results and Observations

In this section the results of the experiments are listed, followed by the explanation regarding the differences between the results of the two sets of experiments and our observations. In each set of experiments, the results are represented after averaging the results of each sign across all users. The average results of static ASL alphabet signs in each set of experiments and each approach are shown in Table 1.

In the Leave-One-Out set of experiments, the single layer neural network approach had the overall accuracy of 81.82% while in the multi-layer approach, the accuracy for 9-9-1 setup was 66.27% and 63.16% for 18-18-1 setup respectively. We achieved the overall accuracy 82.32% for GRUBC approach, which was the maximum accuracy among all the approaches and setups.

For the Keep-One-In set of experiments, the overall accuracy for the Single layer neural network approach was 32.24%. The multi-layer approach showed 54.75% for the 1-1-18 setup and in GRUBC approach, the accuracy was 67.18%.

In the single layer neural network method, the results of the second experiments, Keep-One-In experiments, have degraded due to the fact that the neural network's training set is composed of input patterns together with the required response pattern as we mentioned earlier. If we don't provide the network with proper and adequate training set, the learning process will not complete. As a result, when we train the network with one subject and then test with the remaining 18, the accuracy will drop.

For the multi-layer approach, since the 38 neural networks in the second layer are specifically trained for a simple posture and the range of input data is very limited, they can behave more accurately than the general neural network when the training set is very small.

For the GRUBC approach, higher accuracy in Leave-One-Out is explained as follows: When registering each sign by 18 different signers, the error rises from having different sizes will be compensated a lot, i.e. the chance of having the signs registered with a similar hand is much higher. The second factor is that since the variety of registered signs is wider, the possibility of finding a similar sign in the registered signs is higher. If we consider each alphabet a point in 'n' dimensional space (in this case 'n' is equal to 22), we call each experiment a correct recognition if the unknown sign is the nearest neighbor of its matched alphabet, meaning that the unknown gesture (representing the point in 22-dimensional space) is a correct recognition if its nearest neighbor is its identical alphabet (e.g. nearest neighbor of 'a' is 'a'). In the second set of experiments, we have 18 similar points around the data representing the unknown gesture, so the possibility of its nearest neighbor being the matched sign is much higher.

7   Conclusion and Future Works

In this paper, we compared different major approaches for recognizing static hand gestures and high-lighted the significant advantages of each approach. We also compared the results and showed while 'Gesture Recognition based on Biomechanical Characteristic' provides higher accuracy, it addresses detecting the similar hand gestures without having them labelled, a problem that most traditional classification methods fail to address

We plan to extend this work in two directions. First, we intend to extend our technique to recognize complex dynamic signs.

Second, we would like to show that in general, utilizing any other characteristic which defines the system on a higher level or abstraction rather than data layer (e.g. Bio-mechanical characteristic) provides both higher accuracy on result and less dependency on the data gathering process.

References

1. Eisenstein, J., Ghandeharizadeh, S., Golubchik, L., Shahabi, C., Yan, D., Zimmermann, R.: Device Independence and Extensibility in Gesture Recognition. In: IEEE Virtual Reality Conference (VR),LA, CA (2003)
2. Parvini, F., Shahabi, C.: Utilizing Bio-Mechanical Characteristics For User-Independent Gesture Recognition. In: International Workshop on Biomedical Data Engineering (BMDE 2005), Tokyo, Japan (April 2005)
3. Su, S.A., Furuta, R.K.: VRML-based representations of ASL fingerspelling. In: Proceedings of the third international ACM conference on Assistive technologies
4. Emran, S.M., Ye, N.: Robustness of Canberra Metric in Computer Intrusion Detection. In: Proceedings of the IEEE Workshop on Information Assurance and Security (2001)
5. Van der Weken, D., Nachtegael, M., Kerre, E.: Some New Similarity Measures for Histograms. In: Proceedings of ICVGIP 2004, 4th Indian Conference on Computer Vision, Graphics and Image Processing, Kolkata, India (December 2004)
6. Wu, Y., Huang, T.S.: Vision-Based Gesture Recognition: A Review. In: Braffort, A., Gibet, S., Teil, D., Gherbi, R., Richardson, J. (eds.) GW 1999. LNCS, vol. 1739, p. 103. Springer, Heidelberg (2000)
7. Hong, P., Huang, T.S., Turk, M.: Constructing finite state machines for fast gesture recognition. In: International Conference on Pattern Recognition (ICPR 2000) (2000)
8. Holden, E.J., Owens, R.: Representing the finger-only topology for hand shape recognition. Machine Graphics and Vision International Journal (2003)
9. Takahashi, T., Kishino, F.: Hand gesture coding based on experiments using a hand gesture interface device. SIGCHI Bul (2003)
10. Newby, G.B.: Gesture Recognition Using Statistical Similarity
11. Murakami, K., Taguchi, H.: Recognition using Recurrent Neural Networks. Human Interface Laboratory, Fujitsu Laboratories LTD
12. Boehm, K., Broll, W., Sokolewicz, M.: Dynamic Gesture Recognition Using Neural Networks; A Fundament for Advanced Interaction Construction. In: SPIE Conference Electronic Imaging Science and Technology, San Jose, CA
13. Harling, P.A.: Gesture Input using Neural Networks. University of York, Heslington, York
14. Reese, N.B.: Joint Range of Motion (2001) ISBN 0721689426
15. Yang, J., Xu, Y.: Hidden Markov Model for Gesture Recognition. institution = Robotics Institute, Carnegie Mellon University
16. Immersion Corporation, http://www.immersion.com
17. Mathworks Corporation, http://www.mathworks.com

cfHMI: A Novel Contact-Free Human-Machine Interface

Tobias Rehrl, Alexander Bannat, Jürgen Gast, Gerhard Rigoll,
and Frank Wallhoff

Department of Electrical Engineering and Information Technology,
Institute for Human-Machine Communication
Technische Universität München
80290 Munich, Germany

Abstract. In this paper we present our approach for a new contact-free Human-Machine Interface (cfHMI). This cfHMI is designed for controlling applications – instruction presentation, robot control – in the so-called "Cognitive Factory Scenario", introduced in [1]. However, the interface can be applied in other environments and areas of application as well. Due to its generic approach, this low-cost contact-free interface can be easily adapted to several independent applications, featuring individual menu-structures, etc. In addition, the modular software architecture facilitates the upgrades and improvements of the different software modules embedded in the cfHMI.[1]

1 Motivation

Our objective for the implementation of this contact-free Human-Machine Interface is the following: Due to appearing demands and constraints as a consequence of the industrial surroundings in the "Cognitive Factory Scenario", a new form of a HMI was required. The current state-of-the-art of HMI [2,3,4] is not well suited for the factory design encountered in the "Cognitive Factory Scenario".

In general, the present and in particular the future forms of industrial assembly require a holistic approach to tackle the challenges appearing in the interaction between humans and developing (cognitive) robots. Therefore, the cfHMI can be a module for a more pleasant interaction, because of its flexibility and adjustability to the production task as well as to the current working step. Additionally, it provides for the certain amount of safety and secure handling needed in industrial factory surroundings. A modular architecture concept is a further objective of the cfHMI, because this kind of concept relieves the software-module development and improvement. Besides, the in this paper introduced cfHMI features three major underlying conceptual foundations: flexibility in presentation, secure handling of system operations and adaptability in the displayed menu-structure.

---

[1] All authors contributed equally to the work presented in this paper.

J.A. Jacko (Ed.): Human-Computer Interaction, Part II, HCII 2009, LNCS 5611, pp. 246–254, 2009.

2 Hardware Setup

As mentioned above, the here introduced cfHMI requires only a small amount of hardware, this characteristic facilitates the integration of this system in various surroundings. A typical standard PC is sufficient for executing all vision-based computations for the cfHMI. A simple webcam delivers the raw video data as input for the image-processing steps. For this purpose, a webcam is mounted above the workbench to survey the menu interaction scene, besides a projection unit is attached in the vicinity of the webcam. Via this projection unit the interaction menu is displayed on the workbench. The borders of the projected interaction menu are constituted via two black markers. These markers have a rectangular form, which is beneficial for the vision-based processing steps.

3 System Overview

Our approach for the cfHMI is based on a modular concept, where different software modules process different tasks. Following this concept, it is necessary to define a clear and simple interface for these software modules. However, in turn, a huge advantage of this concept is that these software modules can be readily replaced with a more sophisticated and improved version, without any further modifications at the remaining software modules. In addition, with this approach a high-degree of flexibility and portability of the system to other areas of application comes along.

We have subdivided the system into two major components: menu-design and image-processing.

3.1 Menu-Design

The design of the interaction menu of the cfHMI is splited into two domains. In the first domain, the structure of the menu and basic depiction features are defined. The second domain is concerned with the underlying logic of the functions incorporated in the interaction menu.

Menu Structure

The menu structure of the cfHMI can be defined with an XML-based configuration file. Generally, the main characteristics of the menu are set up in the XML-file: color, amount of interaction buttons, label-text and associated function calls.

This choice of XML to design the structure of the menu has the following reasons: First, XML has a simple and coherent structure, and thus the creation and adaption of the menu structure can be easily implemented. Second, the syntax underlying in the XML is coming up to meet a menu structure with its different menu points and sub-menus.

Menu Functions

Different menu functions (e.g. timers) are implemented in the computer programming language python. Because of its simplicity and reduced syntax, the multi-paradigm programming language python is used to implement varying menu functions. A further point for the implementation of the menu functions in python is the reason, that python supports OpenCV [5] constituting the foundation for the implementation of the image-processing operations.

3.2 Image-Processing

Many tasks for the cfHMI are situated in the visual domain, therefore, OpenCV is used for the image-processing, because many standard and high-level computer vision techniques are implemented in this open source library. As a starting point for the image-processing, the two black markers have to be located. Besides, the hand of the user has to be detected and the interactions with the projected menu have to be interpreted to trigger the corresponding menu commands. Another problem treated with OpenCV is the transformation of the positions of the two black markers into suitable coordinates for the projection unit.

Marker Localization

As mentioned above, two black rectangular markers constitute the indicators for the boundaries of the display region of the menu. In Figure 1, a schematic setting of the markers and the resulting menu plane is depicted. The before mentioned markers are indicated as "Upper Marker" and "Lower Marker". As a starting point, a simple thresholding operation is performed to exclude image elements, having a brightness above a certain limit. After this pre-segmentation step, a typical filter operation embedded in OpenCV, the famous Canny Filter [6] is applied to detect the edges and corners occurring in the image, delivered of the top-down-view camera monitoring the interaction scene from above. As the subsequent step, the obtained contours from the filter operation are evaluated. A-priory knowledge about the characteristics of the two markers – geometric

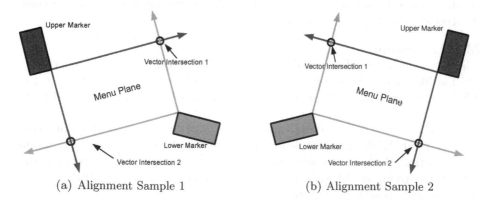

(a) Alignment Sample 1   (b) Alignment Sample 2

Fig. 1. Menu Plane

features – assists in the verification process of possible marker candidates constituted by the gained contours. After completion of the pre-processing steps, only the two markers are visible in the processing image and the marker localization can begin.

At first, the two centers of gravity of the two markers are determined. Afterwards, for each marker the inner border point is extracted. If the upper marker is left of the lower marker: The upper border of the menu is the lower right corner of the upper marker, and the lower border is the upper left corner of the lower marker, see Figure 1(a). Vice-versa, if the upper marker is right to the lower marker: The upper border of the menu is the lower left corner of the upper marker, and the lower border is the upper right corner of the lower marker, see Figure 1(b). However, only two corner points of the interaction menu are determined by the markers. Thus, the remaining corners have to be computed. For this computation, the angle of the principal component of the upper marker is necessitated.

To calculate the missing two corners of the menu, two simple vector intersections need to be computed, marked as "Vector Intersection 1" and "Vector Intersection 2" in Figure 1.

Coordinates Transformation

For a contact analog displaying of the cfHMI, it is necessary to establish a relation between the coordinates of the image obtained by the webcam and the table projector coordinates. Therefore, a serial projection of three points is used to calculate the mathematical dependencies between the two different coordinate systems to acquire the homogeneous transformation matrix H. The reference points are statically set up to cover the entire workspace in the webcam image. In the next step, these points are displayed with the table projection unit. Afterwards in the calibration phase of the system, the user has to select the projected points in the webcam image. The webcam coordinates are stored into an internal vector array.

After having clicked on all three points, the mathematical dependencies between the projector and the webcam coordinate systems are then calculated and as a result, the transformation matrix H, containing information about the rotation R, translation T and some shearing S between both systems, is stored into a text file. A fourth acquired point is afterwards reverse calculated and then displayed to be able to verify the gained resulting precision of the transformation process.

Hand Localization and Hand Interaction

For the hand localization process, the four obtained corner points of the interaction menu are utilized to set up a region of interest (ROI) and therefore reducing the computational requirements as well as decreasing false positives. In the next step in this ROI, a skin-color filter method [7,8] is applied to extract possible hand candidates. Afterwards, non-linear filter operations are used to remove noise and little speckles in the resulting filter mask. We made the following constraint, that all hand-based interaction within the ROI have to be performed orthogonal to the horizontal borders of the cfHMI (e.g. we assume that the pointing finger is parallel aligned to the vertical borders). In practice, these constraints are neither disturbing the overall usage of the system, nor reducing the joy of use.

For reducing the complexity and enhancing the reliability in the hand gesture extraction process, we introduced a rotation invariant working image (riwi). This so-called "riwi" is obtained by performing a rotation via the principal component axis angle of the upper marker around the center of the interaction menu on the resulting image of the filter operation.

Having the hand information available, the hand gestures can be analyzed depending on the current state of the interaction menu. All available gestures are depicted in Figure 2 and are explained in the following. In the starting process and to unlock the interaction menu, a closed hand (see Figure 2(a)) has to hover above the interaction menu. For activating menu functions and menu navigation, a pointing gesture (see Figure 2(b)) has to be performed. A moving hand (see Figure 2(c)) from the right vertical border to the left vertical border will trigger the menu locking, if the gesture is performed rectangular to the verticals and has a certain velocity. The first and the second hand gesture interaction are basing on a template matching algorithm, whereas the third gesture utilizes optical flow for the detection process [9].

(a) Closed hand for un-   (b) Pointing gesture.   (c) Wiping gesture.
locking the menu.

Fig. 2. Hand gestures to be recognized by the presented system

4   Menu Interaction

In general, the menu interaction process between the user and the cfHMI can be subdivided into three main operations: initialization / unlocking, navigation / function control and locking.

As a requirement for the menu interaction, two black markers are needed. Both markers constitute the limiters for the display region. To introduce the required flexibility in displaying the menu, the corner-points – set-up by the above described markers – can be adapted in real-time. With this feature, it is possible to relocate the displayed menu within the region observable by the top-down-view camera and also covered by the projection unit. As a further system-characteristic, the size of the menu can be on-line rescaled – within a certain allowed surface size, predetermined by the layout of the designed menu-structure – by simply moving the markers freely on the active surface. By analyzing the principle component of the anchor marker ("Upper Marker"), a rotational angle for the displayed menu can be set, cf. Section 3.2.

4.1 Initialization / Unlocking

The first step for enabling the interaction with the cfHMI is the following: The closed right hand (see Figure 2(a)) has to hover above the starting screen for a certain amount of time, i.e. two seconds, to unlock the menu. This procedure has also to be performed by the user, if the menu is in the locked state. The reasons for this initialization and unlocking procedure are the following: To avoid unintended interaction and to reduce the amount of information currently available on the workbench (cf. screen saver).

4.2 Navigation / Function Control

The pointing gesture (see Figure 2(b)) has to be performed by the users hand to activate the navigation in the interaction menu as well as to enable/disable menu functions. The exact position for the selection of a menu field is determined by the tip of the right index finger. The selection of the menu function incorporated by a certain field is confirmed via two feedback channels: acoustical and visual. A short audio signal provides the user a feedback for activation of a certain field, besides this field is also highlighted by color change of the borders of the field.

4.3 Locking

The locking operation is applied to set the menu from the active interaction mode to standby mode. Here, we use the evaluation of the optical flow above the cfHMI to trigger this function (see Figure 2(c)). In addition, this procedure is also accompanied by audio feedback. The purpose for this operation is comparable to the unlocking procedure. The user can actively choose to deactivate the system interaction and therefore avoid unintended usage of the presented cfHMI (cf. keypad locking in cellular phones).

Furthermore, in context of an industrial application, a worker using this presented system could accidentally activate functions in an unsafe situation, e.g. by laying his hand on the active surface while performing his assembly task, therefore, a further safety-feature is implemented. For preventing such activations, the system is equipped with an automatic keylock-procedure: If the unlocked and operational system remains inactive for a certain amount of time, the cfHMI will switch to the initial locked state.

5 Area of Application

Up to now, two different areas of application have been developed for cfHMI. The first area of application is an interface for a robot control (see Figure 3(a)). With

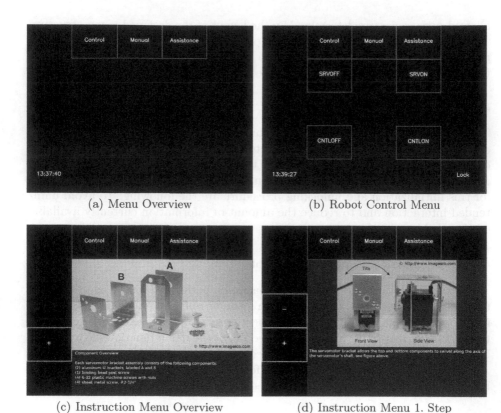

(a) Menu Overview

(b) Robot Control Menu

(c) Instruction Menu Overview

(d) Instruction Menu 1. Step

Fig. 3. Overview of the Projected Interaction Menu

this unit, it is possible to communicate simple control commands to the robot. The second area of application is an assisting presentation of the instruction for a hybrid assembly, where the human manufactures in cooperation with an industrial robot a given product. This hybrid assembly resembles the setup of the CoTeSys Project *Joint Action of Humans and Industrial Robots (JAHIR)* presented in [10].

5.1 Robot Control

The industrial robot manipulator arm controlled by the cfHMI is a Mitsubishi robot RV-3SB. The robot manipulator arm has six degrees of freedom and can lift objects with a maximum weight of three kilograms. A radius of 0.642 m around the robot's trunk composes the accessible and manipulable workspace of the robot. Its tool point is equipped with a force-torque-sensor and a tool-change unit.

The current version of the robot control unit is capable to communicate four different commands towards the robot (see Figure 3(b)). It is possible to control the robot arm in four directions (up, down, left, right), however, this set of commands can be easily extended.

The instantaneous communication between the robot and cfHMI is implemented via a direct network access of the menu computer on the robot control unit.

5.2 Assembly Instruction

In the context of an industrial manual assembly station, the here presented cfHMI was also integrated. In this scenario, the purpose for the menu interaction system is to display assembly instructions, as depicted in Figures 3(c) and 3(d). The advantage of the cfHMI is the flexibility in the location and scale of the menu. With this setup, the worker can decide where to project the assembly instructions (location as well as rotation). The cfHMI is used as a browser interface towards the assembly instructions, where the instruction steps can be shifted through forwards as well as backwards. Furthermore, the user can set up the degree of displayed information, allowing him to choose the preferred amount of details for the current assembly step.

6 Conclusion and Future Work

A first technical realization of the cfHMI has been integrated in a scenario occurring in the "Cognitive Factory". The system has not achieved its ultimate state, and there are still some domains, where improvements can be made. Nonetheless, the presented approach offers high potential to be integrated in a new form of a multimodal human-robot interaction scenario as an additional input modality.

At the current state, the interaction with cfHMI is limited to button selection and simple gestures. As a next step, it is imaginable to incorporate a large set of hand gestures for the menu interaction. In addition, it is thinkable that to a certain degree the trajectory of the human hand can be repeated by the robot arm for "Programming by Demonstration".

A further starting point for improvement is the integration of the cfHMI software-architecture into the real-time database, see [11,12,13]. This framework, as foundation for the cfHMI, facilitates the integration in a multimodal interaction scenario.

Acknowledgment

This ongoing work is supported by the DFG excellence initiative research cluster *Cognition for Technical Systems – CoTeSys*, see www.cotesys.org for further information and details.

We want to thank all our partners within our CoTeSys-Projects for the fruitful discussions and implementation work to make our visions and ideas become reality.

References

1. Zäh, M.F., Lau, C., Wiesbeck, M., Ostgathe, M., Vogl, W.: Towards the Cognitive Factory. In: Proceedings of the 2nd International Conference on Changeable, Agile, Reconfigurable and Virtual Production (CARV), Toronto, Canada (July 2007)
2. Jaimes, R., Sebe, N.: Multimodal human computer interaction: A survey, pp. 15–21 (2005)
3. Goodrich, M.A., Schultz, A.C.: Human-robot interaction: A survey. Foundations and Trends in Human-Computer Interaction, 203–275 (2007)
4. Chouvardas, V.G., Miliou, A.N., Hatalis, M.K.: Tactile display applications: A state of the art survey. In: Proceedings of the 2nd Balkan Conference in Informatics, pp. 290–303 (2005)
5. Bradski, G., Kaehler, A.: earning OpenCV: Computer Vision with the OpenCV Library. O'Reilly Press, Sebastopol (2008)
6. Canny, J.: A computational approach to edge detection. IEEE Trans. Pattern Anal. Mach. Intell. 8(6), 679–698 (1986)
7. Soriano, M., Huovinen, S., Martinkauppi, B., Laaksonen, M.: Skin Detection in Video under Changing Illumination Conditions. In: Proc. 15th International Conference on Pattern Recognition, Barcelona, Spain, pp. 839–842 (2000)
8. Vezhnevets, V., Sazonov, V., Andreeva, A.: A survey on pixel-based skin color detection techniques. In: Proc. Graphicon 2003, pp. 85–92 (2003)
9. Lucas, B.D., Kanade, T.: An iterative image registration technique with an application to stereo vision, pp. 674–679 (1981)
10. Lenz, C., Nair, S., Rickert, M., Knoll, A., Rösel, W., Bannat, A., Gast, J., Wallhoff, F.: Joint Actions for Humans and Industrial Robots: A Hybrid Assembly Concept. In: Proc. 17th IEEE International Symposium on Robot and Human Interactive Communication, Munich, Germany (2008)
11. Goebl, M., Förber, G.: A real-time-capable hard- and software architecture for joint image and knowledge processing in cognitive automobiles. In: Intelligent Vehicles Symposium, pp. 737–740 (June 2007)
12. Stiller, C., Färber, G., Kammel, S.: Cooperative cognitive automobiles. In: Intelligent Vehicles Symposium, pp. 215–220. IEEE, Los Alamitos (2007)
13. Thuy, M., Göbl, M., Rattei, F., Althoff, M., Obermeier, F., Hawe, S., Nagel, R., Kraus, S., Wang, C., Hecker, F., Russ, M., Schweitzer, M., León, F.P., Diepold, K., Eberspächer, J., Heißing, B., Wünsche, H.-J.: Kognitive automobile - neue konzepte und ideen des sonderforschungsbereiches/tr-28. In: Aktive Sicherheit durch Fahrerassistenz, Garching bei München, April 7-8 (2008)

Fly! Little Me: Localization of Body-Image within Reduced-Self

Tatsuya Saito and Masahiko Sato

Tokyo University of the Arts
2-5-1 Shinko, Naka-ku, Yokohama
Kanagawa 231-0001 Japan
+81.45.210.9297
{tatsuyas,sato}@gsfnm.jp

Abstract. In conventional interface design, manipulated objects are visually represented and an actor of manipulation is a user's physical body. Although it is a bodily contact between the user and the virutla objects, these virtual objects are detached from the user's physical body and are usually operated as target objects through an interface device. We propose a new type of embodied inter-action based on visual-somatosensory integration to evoke localization of a user's body-image within a visual object on a screen. The major difference be-tween conventional interation and the proposed framework is whether the cen-ter of the user's body-image is localized within the screen or outside of the screen. When the user's body-image is outside of the screen, manipulation of screen objects is transitive action, or target operation under a subject-object structure. In contrast, when the user's body-image is localized within a screen object, the operation of the object becomes intransitive action and the user op-erates the screen object as if he moves a part of his body. Although object ma-nipulation as intransitive action indeed has a history as long as interface design itself, it has not yet been exposed to thorough inspection. To qualitatively ana-lyze intransitive manipulation and effect of body-image localization, which we think is a core factor, we implemented an interactive system based on several proposed design principles and exhibited the system at a gallery opened for the public to collect qualitative evidences on the effect.

Keywords: Embodied Interface, Spatialized Display, Localization of Body-Image, Visual somatosensory Intergration. Categories and Subject Desciptors: H.5.2 [User Interfaces]: Evaluation/methodology, Interaction styles, User-centered design. General terms: Performance, Design, Experimentation, Secu-rity, Human Factors, Theory.

1 Introduction

We began with fundamental questions: what it is to manipulate intangible virtual objects whether it is textual, graphical or tangible, how it differs from physical objects and what types of new manipulation can be realized by a new mode of interaction. Manipulation conventionally is a *transitive* action that mediates between a user, or a subject, and an object being manipulated by the user. However, on close inspection, manipulation in

J.A. Jacko (Ed.): Human-Computer Interaction, Part II, HCII 2009, LNCS 5611, pp. 255–260, 2009.
© Springer-Verlag Berlin Heidelberg 2009

digital media can be considered in two ways: transitive action and intransitive action (Fig.1). In case of controlling a virtual charactor on a screen using a game-pad interface, the controlled charactor can be either an object of manipulation being controlled by a user or a subject engaged in intransitive action such as jumping, runing and attacking enemies. Although the transition from the transitive to the intransitive is often unconscious, a user often feels very vivid bodily sensations in intransitive action even in technologically mediated environment. We, as a game player, often experience feeling of falling when the virtual charactor jumps from a high. There are highly fluid structures between a user and what is graphically represented and manipulated in an interactive environment. Even in case of conventional interface devices such as a mouse, the *proximal* object, or a mouse device, recedes from our awareness and the *distal* object, or a mouse cursor, vividly feels being a part of our body[1]. In neuro-physiology, this *out-of-body experience* is called localization of body-image. In majority of interface studies, emphasis is on interaction as transitive action and how we can make it more efficient by adapting new interfaces and interaction methods. Although interaction as intransitive action has not been paid much attention, it is another pivotal aspect in designing innovative interaction. The major difference between the transitive and the intransitive is where to locate a user's body-image or the self. Therefore, the prime issue in designing intransitve interaction is how we can extend a user's body-image and accomodate it within a virtually representaed entity on a screen.

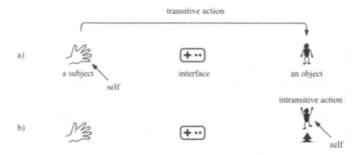

Fig. 1. Modes of interaction: the transitive and the intransitive in controlling a virtual self

We also expect that a result of this study turn out to be a effective experimental playground for brain science and neuro-physiology. Body-image and self-identification in visual media such as recorded monitor image of oneself and virtually controllable avators in virtual environments are becoming major topics in the fields. Although our physical body is thought to be identical to the boundary of our body-image or *the self*, a number of experimental evidences have shown that our *the self* does not simply fit into the boundary of bodily skin in some cases of disorder due to brain injury and congenital defect. Usually, experiments on these cases are done in closed lab environment and a method for inspection and expected results are also limited. Intending to extend human experience, interactive media can cast a light onto questions such as how our body-image can be extended and what the *self* really is. Going beyond merely phenomenological predications, we take an approach to pragmatically design interactive systems to clarify necessary conditions to evoke the body-image localization and its potential rolls in interactive systems.

2   Principles

We started with enumeration of several design principles that are   considered to be necessary-and-satisfactory conditions to evoke localization of body-image within an external visual representation in a screen-based interactive systems: *Action, Synchronization, Feedback, Representation, Display*. Some of the proposed factors are already being studied in related fields mainly in physiological studies.

Table 1. Five principles for intransitive interaction

Principle	Effect
Action	kinesthetic quality
Synchronization	self-identification within virtual representation
Feedback	perception of the law defining the behavior of the virtual environment and the virtual self
Representation	extension/reduction of the virtual self
Display	spatialized representation of the virtual self

2.1   Action

A user is involved in an interactive system through his unconscious and/or conscious action. And, even extremely symbolical actions such as clicking, dragging or pointing with a finger are always accompanied by a specific kinesthetic sensation based on human muscular system. This bodily sensation gives a particular somatic quality to visual images responding to the user's actions. This somatic quality often is something that can only be described as *such-and-such feeling* at best and never became a subject of scrutiny under clear articulation. However, interaction is not viable without a user's action and the quality of the action determines the quality of interactive experiences. This is the starting point.

2.2   Synchronization

Coordination between a user's actions and visual responses is a next important factor. We human beings are capable of distinguishing what belongs to or is part of ourselves and what is not. Any signals changning simulnaniously with one's movement are perceived to be belonging to oneself in various modalities[2]. We are highly sensitive to visual images that move syncronically to our body movements just as a figure of oneself in a monitor image, a mouse cursor o n a computer screen and simply one's shadow moving on the ground. There is a series of studies on self-recognition in video images and also in other media based on other modalities[3]. It has been verified through a number of experiments utilizing various interactive instruments that syncronization of a visual signal largely contributes to perception and extension of one's body image[4]. In interactive systems as well, simultaneous perceptual stimulation and a user's motor-action contributes to vivid bodily awareness of what environmental change belongs to the user.

2.3 Feedback

A unignorable challenge for designing interactive experiences is to design experiences not possible in the real world and not only to mimic it with high fidelity. Not only being synchronized with a user in movement, the visual representation of the user has to behave in a certain way depending on the principles and models of the virtual environment. A user perceives the conditions and dimensions of the environment by an action and feedbacks to the action[5]. Therefore, to build a virtual environment to allow fascinating bodily experience, it is indispensable to think of how to design the feedback and how to make the virtual environment with vivid the actuality.

2.4 Representation

To engage a user in an interactive system through localization of a body-image, a virtual representation of the user has to be visually shown on a screen in some form. The representation does not necessarily have to be photo-realistic. Just as shown in studies on biological motion, we can detect even primitive representation such as points and lines as belonging to or a part of ourselves[6].

2.5 Display

The act of seeing is not a mere ocular phenomenon. It is rather an embodied act engaging a whole body. There are modes of *looking* that define spatial relationship such as *looking-down* and *looking-up*. Even with static visualization such as paintings and photos, it is always a matter of consideration how to deploy the displays. We see things in spatialized configuration. *Display* includes a certain kind of mechanism or format for viewing that forces a viewer to take a certain body posture or physical movements. *Display* also defines *Action* as mentioned earlier by prescribing kinesthetic constraints of human body.

3 Design

In this study, through verification of the above proposed principles, we aimed at creating bodily sensations that we have never experienced in reality. Feeling of flying is a

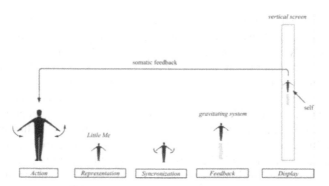

Fig. 2. A design plan for Fly! Little Me

bodily sensation that we humans have always been dreaming of and yet we cannot experience in the real life. It should be a very distinctive sensation just as we experience in a dream. We set up realization of the feeling of flying as an immediate goal for a further study.

4 Realization

We utlized a camera vision system to implement the design plan and named the system *Fly! Little Me*. When a user moves his arm like a bird, the camera vision system detects the movement by calculating the difference of the width of the silhouette between frames. A small silhouette of the user of 10 inches height (*little me*) is projected on a 20 foot-long vertical screen and moves toward the ceiling at a speed proportionally to the user's movement speed.

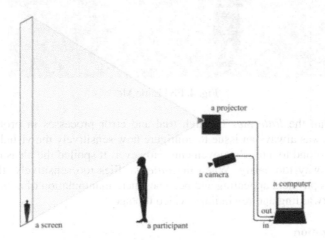

Fig. 3. The system diagram of the installation

5 Results

We installed *Fly! Little Me* at a show titled *Transform yourself*[1] and had 20,000 visitors. Most of the visitor's impression was that they vividly experienced feeling of floating in the air and enjoyed the novel sensation. Some visitors told that it feels like flying in dreams. That was a quite interesting testimony implying how wide varieties of bodily sensations it is possible to evoke in intransitive interaction.

6 Discussions

6.1 Controllability

Visitors felt frustration before getting the hang of how to fly and enthusiastically moved their arms. This emotional response shows that their body-image is deeply

---

[1] NTT InterCommunication Center [ICC] Kids program 2008 - *Transform Yourself.*

Fig. 4. Fly! Little Me

localized within the *little me*. Through trial and error processes in prototyping the installation, it was always an issue to configure how sensitively the visual representation should respond to a user's movements. However, It spoiled the pleasure when the *little me* flies way too easily. When the *little me* flies too sensitively, the response suddenly loses physical appealing and becomes mere manipulation of a moving image just as fast-forwarding and rewinding a video footage.

6.2 Spatialization

The effect of spatialized representation on the long portrait-oriented screen was substantial. When the *little me* reaches at the ceiling, a viewer leans backward to see it. The motor-sensation and the muscle tension strongly contributed to the *being- up-in-the-air* feeling. This was a evidence to prove the significance of *Display*.

References

1. Polanyi, M.: The Tacit Dimension. Routledge, London (1966)
2. Blakemore, S.-J., Wolpert, D.M., Frith, C.D.: Central cancellation of self-produced tickle sensation. Nature Neuroscience 1(7), 635–640 (1998)
3. Botvinick, M., Cohen, J.: Rubber hands "feel" touch that eyes see. Nature 391, 756 (1998)
4. Ramachandran, V.S., Rogers-Ramachandran, D.C., Cobb, S.: Touching the phantom. Nature 377, 489–490 (1995)
5. Gibson, J.J.: The Ecological Approach to Visual Perception. Houghton Mifflin, Boston (1979)
6. Johansson, G.: Visual perception of biological motion and a model for its analysis. Perception and Psychophysics 14, 201–211 (1973)

New Interaction Concepts by Using the Wii Remote

Michael Schreiber, Margeritta von Wilamowitz-Moellendorff, and Ralph Bruder

TU Darmstadt, Institute of Ergonomics, Petersenstr. 30,
64287, Germany
{schreiber,bruder}@iad.tu-darmstadt.de, m.wilamowitz@gmx.de

Abstract. The interaction concept of the video game console Nintendo Wii has created a furor in the interface design community due to its intuitive interface: the Wii Remote. At the Institute of Ergonomics (IAD) of the Darmstadt University of Technology, several projects investigated the potential of interaction concepts with the Wii Remote, especially in nongaming contexts. In a first study an interactive whiteboard according to [1] was recreated, modified and evaluated. In this case, the Wii Remote is not the human-machine-interface but the sensor that detects an infrared emitting (IR) pencil. A survey with 15 subjects was conducted in which different IR pencils were evaluated. In a second study the potential of a gesture based human-computer interaction with the help of the Wii-Remote according to [2] was evaluated by using a multimedia software application. In a survey with 30 subjects, the Wii gesture interaction was compared to a standard remote control.

Keywords: Wii Remote, Wii, gesture based interaction, interactive whiteboard.

1 Introduction

Since the introduction of the video game console Nintendo Wii, researchers all over the world have been inspired by its human machine interface: the Wii Remote. A main feature of the Wii Remote is its motion sensing capability and its resulting intuitive handling. Furthermore, all sensor data can be readout and processed by computers having a Bluetooth interface. Due to these capabilities, an easy adaption of this interface to other use cases is possible and thus, the controller has become very popular for alternative human computer interfaces.

Reference [1] presented, inter alia, software for the tracking of fingers, using an LED array, reflective tape and the infrared camera of the Wii Remote. In this case, the Wii Remote is not directly the human-machine-interface, but the sensor (the Wii Remote is positioned on top or under the screen that is used for the tracking) that detects the infrared (IR) light, which is reflected by the tape on the fingers. This setup enables users to interact with their computer simply by waving their hands and fingers in the air. In addition to the finger tracking, [1] provided a program to track the position of the user's head, with the help of modified goggles that are equipped with IR LEDs on both sides. These IR emitting sources

J.A. Jacko (Ed.): Human-Computer Interaction, Part II, HCII 2009, LNCS 5611, pp. 261–270, 2009.

were then tracked via the infrared camera of the Wii Remote. By rendering the images on the screen depending on the position of the user's head, it transforms a display into a 3D virtual environment.

Another software application that is provided by [1] is the "Low-Cost Multi-point Interactive Whiteboards Using the Wiimote" that can turn every screen or projector into an interactive interface. In addition to the Wii Remote, users need an IR pencil, which is no more than a pencil with an IR LED on the tip and an on/off switch. This device was rebuilt at the IAD and the IR pencil was ergonomically optimized and tested. The functionality of this device will be discussed in section 3.

Reference [3, 4] used the Wii Remote as a navigation device to inspect volumetric medical data coming from Magnetic Resonance Imaging (MRI) or Computer Tomography (CT), to enhance the performance of clinician tasks. They also combined this tangible interaction with speech recognition. Furthermore, a control of simulated avatars was developed such as the bird character of [5], who demonstrated that the Wii Remote interface provides a better and more immersive control in comparison to joysticks. Reference [2, 6] presented a gesture interaction library (WiiGee) for the Wii Remote based on Hidden Markov Models that is available via the World Wide Web. This software was adapted and used at the IAD to develop a gesture based interaction for a Media Center application. This study will be presented in detail in section 4. Another approach for gesture recognition was shown by [7], who presented the game Wiizards, where the user can execute charms by gesturing with the Wii Remote. A different gaming application was shown by [8], who integrated the controller into a multi-wall virtual reality theatre (similar to a cave), by using a multiple sensor bar setup.

The Wii Remote has also been used in the field of arts and music. The virtual conducting of an orchestra was done by [9]. Tempo and volume of the orchestra's performance are influenced by the motion recognition of the Wii Remote. Reference [10] used the Wii Remote as the input device to capture movement data together with the playback of musical stimuli to score the degree of synchronization between the presented music and the motion of the subject. In the project WiiBand, [11] explored an application where three interactors collaboratively created music using Wii Remotes (e.g. horizontal motions of the Wii Remote alters the pitch of a sound, vertical motions the volume).

In additional to all research projects with the Wii Remote, some research only adapted the interaction concept of the Wii. Reference [12] showed a Wii-like interaction with mobile phones for large public game screens where the phones become game controllers for multiplayer games. In addition to the Wii Remote, the hardware add-on Nintendo Balance Board[1] was used as a device for a virtual reality input by [13] (e.g. for 3D rotation in a desktop visualization application or for navigating a map in a personal VR station).

---

[1] In addition to the Wii remote, Nintendo presented in 2007 a new input controller, the balance board. The board contains multiple pressure sensors that are used to measure the user's center of balance in order to process an input command.

2 The Wii Remote

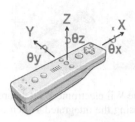

Fig. 1. Wii Remote - the main controller of the video game console Wii

The Wii Remote [14] (fig. 1) is a wireless electronic interaction device of the video game console Wii, which uses the Bluetooth standard for data transmission and is thus cable free. All sensor data can be readout and processed by every computer with a Bluetooth interface. A main feature of the Wii Remote is its motion sensing capability and its resulting intuitive handling. The controller has a 3- axis accelerometer, which can be used to determine relative x, y and z movements and due to the effects of gravity a determination of the current rotation status is also possible. Furthermore the Wii Remote has 9 buttons including a directional pad and a trigger control (located on the bottom side and operated with the index finger) as input controls. A speaker and limited haptic (rumble) feedback is provided by the controller as output signals to the users.

3 Wii Whiteboard

All presented developments in this section are based on the idea of the "Low-Cost Multi-Point Interactive Whiteboards Using the Wiimote" by [1].

The visualization of ideas, concepts and opinions is needed in many different working environments such as meetings, school lessons or workshops. Depending on the room setup and the number of participants, tangible utilities such as flip charts, black- and whiteboards or electronic devices like overhead projectors are suitable options. Nonetheless, these tools lack the possibility to save the developed ideas and notes directly to the computer and make them become easily interchangeable and sharable, something becoming more and more important. A device that combines the advantages of an intuitive handling of tangible utilities and the advantage of a direct digital recording (e.g. for backup of all notes or special software utilities) are interactive whiteboards. These devices connect a computer and a projector to a touch-sensitive display, where users control the computer using a pencil or finger. The main benefit of these systems is that users can user their mental models and skills of the handling of conventional pencils or pieces of chalk even without any experience in dealing with computers.

3.1 Interactive Whiteboard

In addition to prototypes in research laboratories [15] and commercial solutions [16] starting at several hundred dollars, [1] proposed a low cost alternative by using the Wii Remote. For the realization of this low cost interactive whiteboard the software of [1], a computer with a Bluetooth interface, a Wii Remote ideally with an appropriate mounting (e.g. tripod), a data projector, and an IR pencil are needed. In the general setup, the infrared camera of the Wii Remote points at a projected screen to detect the IR point that is emitted by the IR pencil. Through the calibration software of [1], a

Fig. 2. Three versions of an IR LED Pencil for the operation of the Wii electronic Whiteboard. Pen v1.0 and pen v1.1 are using LED and a switch. Pen v2.0 is using the integrated switch on the tip of the pencil.

relation of the IR source and the mouse position on the screen is possible. All movement of the pencil on the projected image (e.g. on the screen or wall) is linked with the position of the mouse. As mentioned in section 1, this whiteboard was rebuilt at IAD and the IR pencil was re-engineered. The software was not modified. At the end of the design process, three IR pencils were created and are shown in fig. 2. Pen v1.0 and pen v1.1 are simple versions of an IR pencil consisting of a shell of a board marker, IR LEDs (one LED for pen v1.0 and 3 LEDs for pen v1.1) and a button to turn the LED on. Both prototypes have a serious disadvantage. The interaction is not equal to real pencils, because of the frequent activation of the IR source, which had to be turned on and off constantly when writing and clicking. In the case of writing block letters, users have to push and release the on/ off button at least one time for every letter (e.g. to write the word "Hello" users have to push and release the on/off button 7 times - 3 times for the capital H and 1 time for every remaining letters).

The main requirement for the development of pen v2.0 was a more pencil-like handling to make the interaction more intuitive and simple. The design team came to the decision to put the on/ off button on the tip of the IR pencil. Due to this advancement, every time the IR pencil is touching the screen, the electric circuit is closed and the LED turns on. The result of the development process is shown in fig. 2 (image on the right). Since the on/ off button is on the tip of the pencil, the LEDs have to be moved elsewhere. In the solution of IAD, the LEDs are arranged in a circle around the on/ off button on the tip of the pen.

3.2 Exploring the Usability of Pen v1.1 and Pen v2.0

For the evaluation of the capability and efficiency of the electronic whiteboard, one of the simple IR pencils (pen v1.1) and the improved IR pencil (pen v2.0) were evaluated in a usability study. In the experiment, the subject had to perform typical operations of a workshop. 15 subjects (mean=28.4 years; SD=5.6 years) took part in this experiment, where nine subjects tested pen v1.1 and six persons the improved version (pen v2.0).

Before the experiment started, the subjects were asked to fill in a questionnaire with general questions about their experience and qualification with electronic devices. Afterwards the subjects were briefed on the functionality of the Wii electronic whiteboard and the software Jarnal, which is an open-source application for note taking, sketching and annotating a document with which they had to work during the

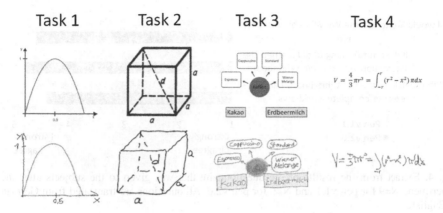

Fig. 3. Upper Line: Four different tasks given to the subjects during the study. Lower line: Example of the result of the drawings/writings of one subject with the pen.

experiment. Then the subjects received a written introduction with precise instructions for every task. The whole experiment contained several different tasks such as drawing (e.g. a graph or a cube), handwriting (e.g. an equation) and writing with the screen keyboard. Examples of the drawing and handwriting tasks are shown in fig. 3 on the top. At the bottom of the figure the result of the task for one subject is displayed. After the subjects completed all tasks, they were asked to use the IR pencil to save their documentation. Afterwards the subjects were verbally interviewed and requested to fill in a questionnaire about their impressions when interacting with the Wii Whiteboard. For the investigation of such new concepts, not only the efficiency and effectiveness of interaction is essential, but also the satisfaction with the design, the joy of use and the customer's inherent need to develop themselves have an impact on perceived quality of products.

Therefore, the subjects filled in the AtrakDiff [17, 18], a questionnaire about different quality aspects of products (e.g. electronic devices) with the feature of separating the pragmatic from the hedonic quality. The pragmatic and hedonic quality is measured by a specific value with a rating between 1 and 7, whereas 7 is the best and 1 is the worst and can be defined as follows [18]:

> ***Pragmatic Quality (PQ)***
>
> *Shows product usability. Can the user achieve his goals with the product?*
>
> ***Hedonic Quality (HQ)***
>
> *Indicates to what extent the functions of a product enhance the possibilities of the user, stimulate him or communicate a particular identity (e.g. by creating a professional, cool, modern or any other impression).*

3.3   Results of the Usability Experiment of the IR Pencils

After the subjects had finished the experiment, they filled in the AttrakDiff to measure hedonic and pragmatic quality of the Wii Whiteboard with pen v1.1 and pen v2.0. Additionally, a questionnaire was given to the subjects concerning the interaction

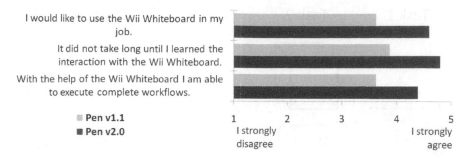

Fig. 4. Extract from the results of the questionnaire that was given to the subjects after the experiment. N=9 for pen v1.1 and N=6 for pen v2.0. All questions are translated from German to English.

with the Wii Whiteboard. Three exemplary questions are shown in fig. 4. One can see that for the interaction with both pens the rating is at a medium to high level. The subjects who tested pen v1.1 agreed with the statement that they would like to use it in their job and they expect that they can execute complete workflows with it. Furthermore, they confirmed that it did not take long to learn how to use and interact with it. Due to the refinements to pen v2.0, the assessment of interaction with the Wii Whiteboard was improved to ratings that are close to "I strongly agree" on all of the scales.

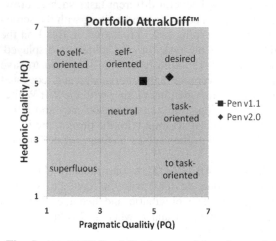

Fig. 5. AttrakDiff Portfolio for pen v1.1 and pen v2.0. N=9 for pen v1.1 and N=6 for pen v2.0.

The results of the Attrak-Diff are shown in fig. 5 with the help of the portfolio presentation that is used to visualize the relation between pragmatic and hedonic quality of the product. The hedonic quality of both pencils were in the upper area; their results showed values of 5.11 for pen v1.1 and 5.26 for pen v2.0 with a range between 1 and 7, where 7 was the best and 1 was the worst. The pragmatic quality of pen v1.1 was only in a medium area, and achieved a value of 4.59 (the rating was also arranged from 1 to 7, where 7 is the best). With the improvements of pen v2.0, the pragmatic quality was increased to 5.57. The simplified interaction by putting the on/off switch on the tip of the pen led to an increase in the usability and utility of the product. This also explains the higher satisfaction in the other questionnaire.

4 Wii Gesture Recognition

Gesture recognition applications are becoming more and more popular in the field of human computer interaction. In addition to character recognition on tablet computers or palms, which have already entered the mass market, hand and finger gestures also extend their range of use, especially in research projects (e.g. for the operation of in-vehicle infotainment systems [19, 20] or remote control of robots [21]). Furthermore, a few products with finger and hand gestures have entered the market, such as the iPhone. However, the gesture recognition is not a new type of interaction. Already in the 1980s, [22] demonstrated a media room where users could interact with a wall-like screen and [23] showed the potentials of gesture interaction with a DataGlove, which was also equipped with piezo actuators for tactile feedback. Since Nintendo released its Wii, a low cost device is on the market that provides programmers with the hardware to implement gesture recognition algorithms. In a study at the IAD, the potential of a gesture based human-computer interaction with the help of the Wii Remote was evaluated by using a multimedia program. The Wiigee gesture recognition algorithms of [2, 6] were used for the implementation and matched to relevant Windows applications. Those algorithms are based, as many other approaches for gesture recognition [24, 25, 26], on Hidden Markov Models, a statistical tool for modeling a wide range of time series data.

4.1 Exploring the Usability of Wii Gesture Recognition

For the exploration of the usability and the aspects of joy of use while interacting with the Wii gesture recognition, an experiment was conducted, where subjects had to perform different tasks in a Media Center[2] application with both the gesture recognition and a standard remote control.

Fig. 6. Example of gestures input in the Media Center. Top: upward stroke of the Wii Remote to navigate one step higher in the navigation menu.

The navigation though this program is normally done by a remote control, mouse, or the keyboard of a computer. For the navigation in the Media Center, the user mainly needs a directional pad (up, down, right, or left), a button to enter or to confirm, a "back" button, and a "play" button. In the gesture recognition interaction, these buttons were replaced by motions of the Wii Remote, e.g. to navigate one step to the right in the Media Center menu, users had to perform a motion with the Wii Remote to the right (compare fig. 6 bottom). These movements/gestures are derived from a prior study with 20 subjects.

30 subjects (mean=24.2 years, SD=3.9 years) participated in the study. At the

---

[2] A Media Center is an application designed to serve as a home-entertainment system that might include pictures, music tracks, music videos, television channels, movies, etc.

beginning, an introduction was given regarding the use of the standard remote control and the Wii remote gestures as well as time to practice (with) both of them. Then everyone had to fulfill a series of common Media Center tasks, such as navigate to a predetermined music track, check the temperature for today in the weather forecast or search for a specific picture in the picture database. The subjects had to complete the series of tasks with the common remote control and similar tasks with the gesture based Wii Remote. Hidden Markov models were used for the gesture recognition, which implies that the gesture must be trained either by the subject or by the experimental conductor. Due to the training time of such gestures, they were predefined by the conductor. Nonetheless, in a small supplementary study, with five subjects, the potential of individual trained gestures was investigated. Subjects filled in the AttrakDiff [18] and the System Usability Scale (SUS) [27] questionnaires for the evaluation of both interfaces after they finished the tasks.

4.2   Results of the Wii Gesture Recognition

The results of the AttrakDiff show on the one hand that the hedonic quality is significantly higher for the Wii Remote gesture application than for the standard remote control. The subject visibly enjoyed the interaction through gestures. But on the other hand, the pragmatic quality and the score of the SUS, with a result of 73.8, showed

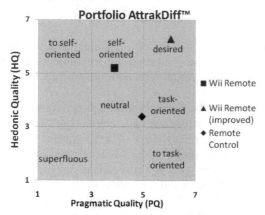

the advantages of the standard remote control (in comparison to the Wii Remote with a score of 53.25). The main reason for this result is probably the high amount of misinterpretations of the not self-trained gestures. In the supplementary study with five subjects, which was conducted after the main study, the potential of individual trained gestures was investigated and it turned out that misinterpretations could be highly reduced. Thereby, the pragmatic quality was enhanced as is shown in fig. 7 as Wii Remote (improved). Thus, the type of gesture training has a major

Fig. 7. AttrakDiff Portfolio for the Wii Remote gesture recognition with pre trained gestures (Wii Remote), the Wii Remote gesture recognition with subject trained gestures (Wii Remote improved) and a standard remote control (Remote control). N=30

impact on the perceived quality of the interaction concept. For a future gesture based Media Center, the gestures should therefore be self-trained. The training of the system is to be done once at the beginning, taking about 15 minutes and then the system will improve its recognition during usage. This should ensure a highly desired, fun provoking and usable interaction.

5 Conclusion

The literature review and both projects that were conducted at IAD show the potentials of the Wii Remote for existing low cost interaction concepts. Most of the aforementioned Wii applications do not achieve the quality of commercial solutions (e.g. electronic whiteboards). However, it was shown that with small improvements (e.g. from pen v1.1 to pen v2.0 of the IAD electronic whiteboard), usability engineers are able to considerably improve the usability of those prototypes and make them nearly equal to the quality of commercial applications, with lower costs. Not only existing ideas could be emulated with the Wii remote, but also new ideas, such as the gesture control of a media center, were surveyed by the IAD, giving new exciting opportunities. Further research and developments might be necessary, but the potential for a future application is foreseeable. Another essential aspect of doing research with the Wii Remote is the power to create new ideas and stimulate research. This is due to two major reasons. First, the possibility to access the sensor data of the Wii Remote. This makes it easy to adapt the interface to all kinds of applications that were programmed all over the world. And second, most of the developed applications are available via the World Wide Web and can be downloaded, modified and experienced by everybody. This is creating a powerful network with researchers and amateurs from all over the world being inspired, sharing their ideas about the Wii Remote and creating a new community to develop a part of the interaction of tomorrow.

References

1. Johnny Chung Lee Wii Projects,
   http://www.cs.cmu.edu/johnny/projects/wii/
2. Schlömer, T., Poppinga, B., Henze, N., Boll, S.: Gesture Recognition with a Wii Controller. In: Second International Conference on Tangible and Embedded Interaction, pp. 11–14. ACM Press, New York (2008)
3. Gallo, L., De Pietro, G., Coronato, A., Marra, I.: Toward a Natural Interface to Virtual Medical Imaging Environments. In: The Working Conference On Advanced Visual Interfaces, pp. 429–432. ACM Press, New York (2008)
4. Gallo, L., De Pietro, G., Marra, I.: 3D interaction with Volumetric Medical Data: Experiencing the Wiimote. In: ACM International Conference on Ambient Media and Systems, ICST, Brussels (2008)
5. Shiratori, T., Hodgins, J.K.: Accelerometer-based User Interfaces for the Control of a Physically Simulated Character. In: International Conference on Computer Graphics and Interactive Techniques. ACM Press, New York (2008)
6. Wiigee, A.: Java-based gesture recognition library for the Wii remote (2008),
   http://www.wiigee.org/
7. Kratz, L., Smith, M., Lee, F.J.: Wiizards: 3D Gesture Recognition for Game Play Input. In: FuturePlay 2007, pp. 209–212. ACM Press, New York (2007)
8. Schou, T., Gardner, H.J.: A Wii Remote, a Game Engine, Five Sensor Bars and a Virtual Reality Theatre. In: 19th Australasian conference on Computer-Human Interaction, pp. 231–234. ACM Press, New York (2007)
9. Bruegge, B., Teschner, C., Lachenmaier, P., Fenzl, E., Schmidt, D., Bierbaum, S.: Pinocchio: Conducting a Virtual Symphony Orchestra. In: International Conference On Advances In Computer Entertainment Technology, pp. 294–295. ACM Press, New York (2007)

10. Demey, M., Leman, M., De Bruyn, L., Bossuyt, F., Vanfleteren, J.: The Musical Synchrotron: Using Wireless Motion Sensors To Study How Social Interaction Affects Synchronization With Musical Tempo. In: 8th International Conference on New Interfaces for Musical Expression, p. 372. ACM Press, New York (2008)
11. Lee, H.-J., Kim, H., Gupta, G., Mazalek, A.: WiiArts: Creating collaborative art experience with WiiRemote interaction. In: 2nd International Conference on Tangible and Embedded Interaction, pp. 33–36. ACM Press, New York (2008)
12. Vajk, T., Coulton, P., Bamford, W., Edwards, R.: Using a Mobile Phone as a "Wii-like" Controller for Playing Games on a Large Public Display. International Journal of Computer Games Technology (2008)
13. De Haan, G., Griffith, E.J., Post, F.H.: Using the Wii Balance Board as a Low-Cost VR Interaction Device. In: ACM symposium on Virtual reality software and technology, pp. 289–290. ACM Press, New York (2008)
14. Nintendo Wii, http://www.nintendo.com/wii
15. Cuypers, T., Schneider, J., Taelman, J., Luyten, K., Bekaert, P.: Eunomia: Toward a Framework for Multi-touch Information Displays in Public Spaces. In: 22nd British HCI Group Annual Conference, pp. 31–34. British Computer Society, Liverpool (2008)
16. SMART Board,
    http://www2.smarttech.com/st/en-US/Products/SMART+Boards/default.htm
17. Hassenzahl, M., Burmester, M., Koller, F.: AttrakDiff: Ein Fragebogen zur Messung wahrgenommener hedonischer und pragmatischer Qualität. In: Ziegler, J., Szwillus, G. (eds.) Mensch & Computer 2003 Interaktion in Bewegung. B.G. Teubner, Stuttgart (2003)
18. AttrakDiff, http://www.attrakdiff.de/en/Home/
19. Althoff, F., Lindl, R., Walchshäusl, L.: Robust Multimodal Hand- And Head Gesture Recognition For Controlling Automotive Infotainment Systems. VDI-Berichte Nr. 1919, 187–205 (2005)
20. Zobl, M., Geiger, M., Schuller, B., Rigoll, G., Lang, M.: A Realtime System for Hand-Gesture Controlled Operation of In-Car Devices. In: 4th International Conference on Multimedia and Expo, pp. 541–544. IEEE Press, New York (2003)
21. Fong, T., Conti, F., Grange, S., Baur, C.: Novel interfaces for remote driving: gesture, haptic and PDA. SPIE Telemanipulator and Telepresence Technologies VII (2000)
22. Bolt, R.A.: "Put-that-there": Voice and gesture at the graphics interface. In: 7th International Conference on Computer Graphics and Interactive Techniques, Seattle, pp. 262–270 (1980)
23. Zimmerman, T.G., Lanier, J., Blanchard, C., Bryson, S., Harvill, Y.: A Hand Gesture Interface Device. In: SIGCHI/GI conference on Human factors in computing systems and graphics interface, pp. 189–192. ACM Press, New York (1987)
24. Hofmann, F., Heyer, P., Hommel, G.: Velocity Profile Based Recognition of Dynamic Gestures with Discrete Hidden Markov Models. In: International Gesture Workshop on Gesture and Sign Language in Human-Computer Interaction. Springer, London (1997)
25. Wilson, A.D., Bobick, A.F.: Parametric Hidden Markov Models for Gesture Recognition. IEEE Transactions on Pattern Analysis and Machine Intelligence 21(9), 884–900 (1999)
26. Chen, F.-S., Fu, C.-M., Huang, C.-L.: Hand gesture recognition using a real-time tracking method and hidden Markov models. Image and Vision Computing 21(8), 745–758 (2003)
27. Brooke, J.: SUS: a "quick and dirty" usability scale. In: Jordan, P.W., Thomas, B., Weerdmeester, B.A., McClelland, A.L. (eds.) Usability Evaluation in Industry. Taylor and Francis, London (1996)

Wireless Data Glove for Gesture-Based Robotic Control

Nghia X. Tran, Hoa Phan, Vince V. Dinh, Jeffrey Ellen, Bryan Berg, Jason Lum,
Eldridge Alcantara, Mike Bruch, Marion G. Ceruti, Charles Kao, Daniel Garcia,
Sunny Fugate, and LorRaine Duffy

Space and Naval Warfare Systems Center, Pacific (SSC Pacific)
53560 Hull Street, San Diego, CA 92152-5001
{nghia.tran,hoa.phan}@navy.mil,
dinhvv@spawar.navy.mil, jeffrey.ellen@navy.mil,
bberg@spawar.navy.mil, jason.lum@navy.mil,
eealcant@ucsd.edu,
{michael.bruch,marion.ceruti,charles.kao}@navy.mil,
{daniel.garcia10,sunny.fugate,lorraine.duffy}@navy.mil

Abstract. A wireless data glove was developed to control a Talon robot. Sensors mounted on the glove send signals to a processing unit, worn on the user's forearm that translates hand postures into data. An RF transceiver, also mounted on the user, transmits the encoded signals representing the hand postures and dynamic gestures to the robot via RF link. Commands to control the robot's position, camera, claw, and arm include "activate mobility," "hold on," "point camera," and "grab object."

Keywords: Communications, conveying intentions, distributed environment, gestures, human-computer interactions, human-robot interactions, military battlefield applications, non-verbal interface, robot, wireless data glove, wireless motion sensing.

1 Introduction

Robots are becoming increasingly useful on the battlefield because they can be armed [5] and sent into dangerous areas to perform critical missions. Controlling robots using traditional methods may not be possible during covert or hazardous missions. A wireless data glove was developed for communications in these extreme environments where typing on a keyboard is either impractical or impossible [2]. This paper reports an adaptation of this communications glove for transmitting gestures to a military robot to control its functions.

Novel remote control of robots has been an active area of research and technology, especially over the past decade. (See, for example [1, 4, 5, 6, 7, 9, 10]) For example, a wearable, wireless tele-operation system was developed for controlling robot with a multi-modal display [5]. Remotely controlled robots have been used in environments where conditions are hazardous to humans [4]. Gestures were used to control a flying manta-ray model [1]. A glove apparatus was used to control a wheelchair using robotic technology [7].

J.A. Jacko (Ed.): Human-Computer Interaction, Part II, HCII 2009, LNCS 5611, pp. 271–280, 2009.
© Springer-Verlag Berlin Heidelberg 2009

2 Talon Robot

The Talon US Army robot [5], (Figure 1) serves several purposes from mine detection and removal to attack missions on battlefields. Civilian applications can include the assessment of unstable or hazardous areas. The Talon robot can negotiate a variety of terrain with its tank-track mobility system. It is equipped with surveillance devices, a pan-and-tilt camera, and a general-purpose robot arm. The original control method includes joysticks, mechanical switches, and push buttons housed in a large, heavy case.

3 Data-Glove Operation

The data glove (Figure 1) has motion sensors (e.g., accelerometer, gyros, and magnetic bend sensors) on the back of the hand and on the fingertips to provide information regarding motion and orientation of the hand and fingers. Bend sensors detect finger postures whereas the gyros detect hand rotations. In a similar application, flying robots have been controlled using wireless gloves with bend sensors [1].

With Talon robot and control module the data-processing unit on the glove reads and analyzes the sensor data and translates the raw data into control commands equivalent to those produced by the Talon robot's joystick and switch. Then the data-processing unit sends the commands to the Talon's controller wirelessly via radio frequency. The Talon controller assembles all commands from the data glove and

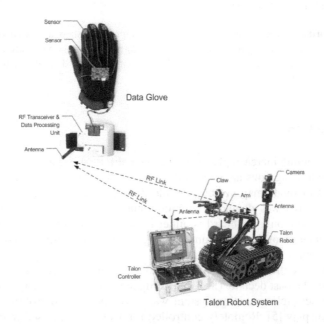

Fig. 1. Data glove (Patent pending NCN 99084; SN 12/325,046)

other sources into a package and sends them to the robot for execution. This architecture has the advantage of allowing traditional control of the robot as well as conforming to the robot's existing interface.

For some applications the data glove can control the Talon directly without using the controller. For other applications, data-glove information can be translated into data to a PC via an RF-receiving station where the data-glove information is translated into data compatible with devices such as a mouse or game pad and transferred to the PC's USB input device. The receiving station can interface to software for the Multiple-Operational Control Unit (MOCU), which is used to control the Talon and other robots.

4 Human Factors

Translating glove data into robot control commands based on gross motor skill and fine motor skill human hand provides granularity not possible with uniform control mechanisms, such as a joystick. For example, gross hand motion is translated into commands controlling coarse motions of the robot, whereas fine motion of fingers is translated into more precise motion control. Orientation and motion sensors on the back of the data glove, shown in Figures 1 and 2, provide gross motion information of hand postures and dynamic gestures used to control characteristics such as speed and direction, operation of the arm, and rotation of the camera mount. Bend sensors mounted on the glove's fingertips measure the fine motion of the fingers. That information is used as a reference to control the precision of the Talon claw's aperture. The fine motion of the fingers also can be used to control other high-resolution operations such as the focus-and-zoom lens of the robot's camera.

The data glove gives users an intuitive sense of control, which facilitates learning the robotic operation. The glove also frees users to observe video and audio data feedback and the environment rather than focusing on the control mechanism, resulting in a more effective overall operation. The data glove does not need pivot-reference station points such as mechanical joysticks. Moreover, the data glove does not require the user to stay in contact with the Talon controller module. The user may move during control operation, and therefore, can operate the robot in various situations and positions. For example, the user can lie prone to maintain covertness, which offers a low-profile advantage on the battlefield.

Figure 1 also depicts the sensor circuit board that is mounted on the back of the glove, the wires that connect it to the sensors on the fingertips, as well as the RF transceiver and data-processing unit that the user wears on the forearm. The glove and processing unit are light and flexible enough so that they do not cause physical fatigue. The apparatus is not difficult to hold and it does not impede the user's motion. This aspect of the apparatus enables the user to concentrate on the control aspects of the robot and that task that the robot is performing.

The user can interact with the robot in a manner that requires either line-of-sight proximity to the robot, or a screen display of the output from the camera mounted on the robot, as shown in Figure 1. This method of interaction is different from eye-gaze based interaction [12], because the computer system does not track the user's eye motion. However, the wireless-glove interaction is similar to eye-gaze-based interaction because neither method of computer interaction requires the use of a mouse.

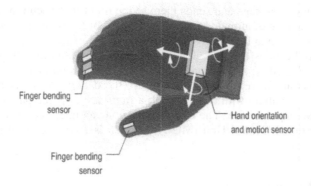

Fig. 2. Data glove sensor layout

Figure 2 shows an X-Y-Z axis of the whole hand, which is used as a reference for finger motions in general. The three types of sensors, listed above in section 3,detect relative finger motion and hand motion about this three-axis system. Three-axis micro-electromechanical systems (MEMS) accelerometers and gyroscopes have been used for wireless motion sensing to monitor physiological activity [3], [8], [11].

5 Data-Translation Methods

The data-glove processing unit reads and processes sensor data. Before data are sent to the robot, they are converted into machine language for robot control. Three basic methods are applied to convert hand motion and positions of the hand and fingers into computer-machine language inputs. These three different methods are depicted in Figures 3, 4, and 5.

Figure 3 shows how the thumb is used as an OFF/ON switch. Even though the sensor on the thumb provides fine resolution of position, translation software defines the sensor data range as two values, OFF or ON, depending on the angle between the thumb and the wrist. This operation of thumb provides the digital logic value "0" or "1" as input to controller. Electrical OFF/ON switches are used for critical robotic operations, such as such as shooting triggers, selecting buttons, and activating emergency switches.

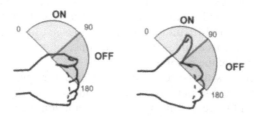

Fig. 3. Thumb operated as OFF/ON switch

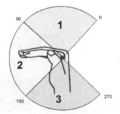

Fig. 4. Three regions of fingers positions

For some applications, the motion and positions of hand and fingers, needs to be divided into more than two regions. Figure 4 shows finger positions divided into three regions: region 1 from 0-90 degrees, region 2 from 90-180 degrees, and region 3 from 180-270 degrees. The wide range required for each region acts as a noise filter, filtering out natural hand and finger shaking of different users. This operation is coded into the numeric values of "1," "2," and "3." The code values provide an effective method to define hand and fingers positions, and therefore, define hand postures.

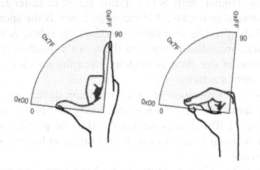

Fig. 5. Index finger operated as a potentiometer

For applications requiring precision control, the full resolution of the sensor is used. In Figure 5 above, the motion of index finger provides an 8-bit data range of values from 0 to 255 (0x00-0xFF). This operation is analogous to operation of a potentiometer. This angular vibrational motion can be used to control the gap of the robot's claw or zoom as well as the focus of the camera, etc.

6   Command Gestures for Talon Robot

Given the sensor arrangement and data- translation methods, the authors devised the following control language specifically for Talon Robot operation, which incorporates all of the most frequently used Talon commands.

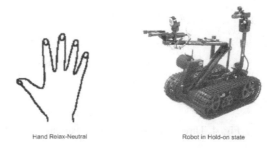

Hand Relax-Neutral   Robot in Hold-on state

Fig. 6. Command 1 - Hold-on

Command 1 (Figure 6) - Hold-On: Opening the hand in a neutral-relax position is interpreted as hold-on state. This command will cause the Talon to retain current commands and stop receiving new commands. This also allows the hand time to relax or can be used as an intermediate state between commands.

Command 2 (Figure 7) - Mobility: The palm forms a vertically oriented fist as though it were holding a joystick. Rotating the hand left or right causes the robot to turn left or turn right. Higher degrees of rotation result in faster robot turning rates. Bending the hand forward or backward at the wrist controls the speed of the robot. A higher degree of bending results in a faster speed of the robot. A thumb pointing-up gesture acts as a brake, immediately bringing the robot's speed to zero as soon as possible. Thus, the motion of the glove is modeled after the joystick in which a potentiometer controls the robot's actions.

Previously, wireless teleoperation of an exoskeleton device was used to control a mobile robot's kinematics [4]. The robot in this study had two arms was designed to follow human motion [4]. The data glove described in the present work not only controls the robot's translational kinematics and a robotic arm but it also controls a camera mounted on the robot.

Command 3 (Figure 8) - Camera control: The hand forms the symbol for "VIEW" or "EYE" in American Sign Language. Gross hand panning left or right, i.e. a rotation about the Z-axis is translated into a panning-motion command to the robot's camera.

Bending the hand around the X-axis translates into a tilting motion command. The fine-grained angle of the index and middle fingers control the zoom of the camera's lens. For example, a gesture to open the hand, i.e. straightening the index and middle finger, makes the lens zoom out whereas the retraction of the index and middle finger towards a fist-like posture causes the lens to zoom in.

Command 4 (Figure 9) - Arm and claw control: This command is similar to command 3. The gross motion of hand around the X, Y, and Z axes is translated into commands to control the tilt, rotation, and pan of robot's arm respectively. The Bending the thumb and the index finger on the glove controls precisely the gap of the claw. As one might expect, widening the gap between the thumb and the index finger of the glove also widens the gap of the robot's claw. To grasp an object remotely, the glove allows the user to close the hand of the glove, thus narrowing the gap of the claw after the arm has been moved into the appropriate position near the object.

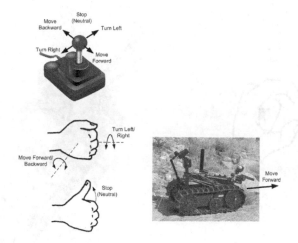

Fig. 7. Command 2 – Mobility

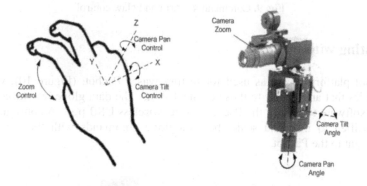

Fig. 8. Command 3 - Camera control

These commands were selected because the user's hand performs a motion very similar to the one the robot's camera and claw perform. Thus, the system of commands is more intuitive, easier to learn, and easier to remember than some arbitrary system in which the robot's motion does not track user's hand closely.

The following is an explanation of how the user tells the glove which mode of operations to use. When the user wants to widen the robot's claw, pick up an object, then focus the camera on that object, the following method is used to convey the command sequence to the robot. The user performs the posture-pause command that tells the robot to keep the current position of claw. Then the user performs the exit command to exit current claw control command state to hold-on state. When the robot is in the hold-on state, the user performs the posture-camera-control command to enter the camera-control state from the hold-on state. Thus, using one hand, the glove can control multiple robot operation commands at the same time. However, in case of ambiguity among hand postures that may cause robot perform undesired operation, the user must operate one command at a time. The software program defines the command states that require user to perform the hand posture to enter and exit a specific control-command state.

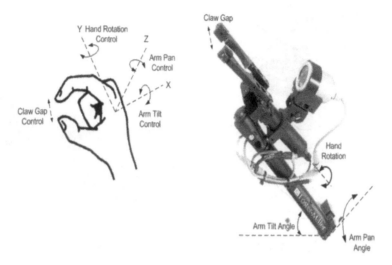

Fig. 9. Command 4 - Arm and claw control

7 Testing with Pacbot

The robot platform that was used for testing was a Pacbot, (Figure 10), which has capabilities that are similar to those of the Talon. The data glove interfaced with the MOCU software to control the Pacbot via PC wireless USB port. A configuration file was modified to map and scale the data-glove commands with the data that the MOCU sent to the Pacbot.

Fig. 10. Pacbot

8 Directions for Future Research

A future data glove will have an input-filtering algorithm to minimize unintended commands originating from noises that produce shock and vibration, which can perturb the natural motion of the hand and fingers. This upgrade also will make the glove more robust in the battlefield environment, which is characterized by loud noises, shock, and vibration from gunshots, bombs, and low-flying aircraft.

Another future modification will be for the robot to transmit haptic signals to the glove, thus creating a tactile image of an object as the robot's claw narrows its gap around the object, thus simulating the feel of the object in the user's hand. This could enable better handling of fragile items as well.

Acknowledgements

The authors thank the Defense Threat Reduction Agency, the Office of Naval Research and the Space and Naval Warfare Systems Center, Pacific, Science and Technology Initiative for their support of this work. This paper is the work of U.S. Government employees performed in the course of employment and no copyright subsists therein. This paper is approved for public release with an unlimited distribution. The technology described herein is based in part on the "Wireless Haptic Glove for Language and Information Transference," Navy Case No. 99084; Serial no. 12/324,046, patent pending.

References

1. Ballsun-Stanton, B., Schull, J.: Flying a Manta with Gesture and Controller: An Exploration of Certain Interfaces in Human-Robot Interaction. In: Sales Dias, M., Gibet, S., Wanderley, M.M., Bastos, R. (eds.) GW 2007. LNCS, vol. 5085. Springer, Heidelberg (2009),
   http://it.rit.edu/~jis/IandI/GW2007/
   Ballsun-Stanton&SchullGW2007.pdf
2. Ceruti, M.G., Dinh, V.V., Tran, N.X., Phan, H.V., Duffy, L.T., Ton, T.A., Leonard, G., Medina, E.W., Amezcua, O., Fugate, S., Rogers, G., Luna, R., Ellen, J.: Wireless Communication Glove Apparatus for Motion Tracking, Gesture Recognition, Data Transmission, and Reception in Extreme Environments. In: Proceedings of the 24th ACM Symposium on Applied Computing (SAC 2009), Honolulu, March 8-24 (2009)
3. Fong, D.T.W., Wong, J.C.Y., Lam, A.H.F., Lam, R.H.W., Li, W.J.: A Wireless Motion Sensing System Using ADXL MEMS Accelerometers for Sports Science Applications. In: Proc. of the 5th World Congress on Intelligent Control and Automation (WCICA 2004), vol. 6, pp. 5635–5640 (2004),
   http://ieeexplore.ieee.org/stamp/
   stamp.jsp?arnumber=1343815497/&isnumber=29577
4. Jeon, P.W., Jung, S.: Teleoperated Control of Mobile Robot Using Exoskeleton Type Motion Capturing Device Through Wireless Communication. In: Proceedings of the 2003 IEEE/ASME International Conference on Advanced Intelligent Mechantronics (AIM 2003), July 20-24, 2003, vol. 2, pp. 1107–1112 (2003)

5. Jewell, L.: Armed Robots to March into Battle. In: Transformation United States Department of Defense (December 6, 2004),
   `http://www.defenselink.mil/transformation/articles/`
   `2004-12/ta120604c.html`
6. Lam, A.H.F., Lam, R.H.W., Wen, J.L., Martin, Y.Y.L., Liu, Y.: Motion Sensing for Robot Hands using MIDS. In: Proceedings of the IEEE International Conference on Robotics and Automation (ICRA 2003), Taipei, September 4-19, 2003, pp. 3181–3186 (2003),
   `http://ieeexplore.ieee.org/stamp/`
   `stamp.jsp?arnumber=1225497&isnumber=27509`
7. Potter, W.D., Deligiannidis, L., Wimpey, B.J., Uchiyama, H., Deng, R., Radhakrishnan, S., Barnhard, D.H.: HelpStar Technology for Semi-Autonomous Wheelchairs. In: Proceedings of the 2005 International Conference on Computers for People with Special Needs (CPSN 2005), Las Vegas. CSREA Press, June 20-23 (2005)
8. Sadat, A., Hongwei, Q., Chuanzhao, Y., Yuan, J.S., Xie, H.: Low-Power CMOS Wireless MEMS Motion Sensor for Physiological Activity Monitoring. IEEE Trans. on Circuits and Systems I: Regular Papers 52(12), 2539–2551 (2005)
9. Seo, Y.H., Park, H.Y., Han, T., Yang, H.S.: Wearable Telepresence System using Multimodal Communication with Humanoid Robot. In: Proceedings of ICAT 2003. The Virtual Reality Society of Japan, Tokyo, December 3-5 (2003)
10. Seo, Y.H., Park, H.Y., Han, T., Yang, H.S.: Wearable Telepresence System Based on Multimodal Communication for Effective Teleoperation with a Humanoid. IEICE Transactions on Information and Systems 2006 E89-D(1), 11–19 (2006)
11. Shinozuka, M., Feng, M., Mosallam, A., Chou, P.: Wireless MEMS –Sensor Networks for Monitoring and Condition Assessment of Lifeline Systems. In: Urban Remote Sensing Joint Event (2007),
    `http://ieeexplore.ieee.org/stamp/stamp.jsp?arnumber=04234451`
12. Sibert, L.E., Jacob, R.J.K.: Evaluation of Eye Gaze Interaction. In: Proceedings of the ACM SIGCHI Conference on Human Factors in Computing Systems (CHI 2000), pp. 281–288 (2000); The Hague Amsterdam. CHI Letters. 2(1), 1–6 (April 2000)

PALMbit-Silhouette:
A User Interface by Superimposing
Palm-Silhouette to Access Wall Displays

Goshiro Yamamoto, Huichuan Xu, Kazuto Ikeda, and Kosuke Sato

Graduate School of Engineering Science, Osaka University
1-3 Machikaneyama, Toyonaka 560-8531, Japan
{goshiro,iamxhc,k-ikeda}@sens.sys.es.osaka-u.ac.jp
sato@sys.es.osaka-u.ac.jp

Abstract. In this paper, we propose a new type of user interface using palm-silhouette, which realizes intuitive interaction on ubiquitous displays located at far from user's location or interfered in direct operation. In the area of augmented reality based user interface, besides the interface which allows users to operate virtual objects directly, the interface which lets users to interact remotely from a short-distant location is necessary, especially in the environment where multi-displays are shared in public areas. We propose two gesture-related functions using the palm-silhouette interface: grasp-and-release operation and wrist rotating operation which represent "selecting" and "adjustment" respectively. The usability of proposed palm-silhouette interface was evaluated by experiment comparison with a conventional arrowhead pointer. We studied and concluded the design rationale to realize a rotary switch operation by utilizing pseudo-haptic visual cue.

Keywords: user interface, shadow, pseudo-haptic.

1 Introduction

Many recent studies of a user interfaces on wall-sized display environment discussed about how to augment large workspaces with mixed reality technology or advanced large-sized screen display technology[1]. In such wall display environments, as shown in Fig. 1, overcoming the difficulties to avoid directly touch virtual objects which are generated by projectors or large-scale displays and sometimes not preferable to be directly touched, and enhancing the intuitiveness of distant-access-interface are one of key issues to increase the usability and practical value of such studies.

In this paper, firstly we will discuss the metaphor of a shadow which is a cast of user's own hand and acts as an interface to connect the worlds of real and virtual. Then, we will introduce an experimental user interface of palm-silhouette casting for wall display environments and involving hand-gesture recognition methods. The proposed system, PALMbit-Silhouette, realizes a distant user interface which lets user to move an icon among distributed wall-based displays

J.A. Jacko (Ed.): Human-Computer Interaction, Part II, HCII 2009, LNCS 5611, pp. 281–290, 2009.

Fig. 1. User interfaces are categorized into two classes in wall interactive display environments; Type 1(left): users operate with directly touch; Type 2(right): a user operates from a not-reachable place

with natural hand gestures. Experiments with a prototype system showed that it enabled users to interact seamlessly with virtual objects in augmented distributed display environments[2,3]. The system interface also lets a user to adjust volumes by a gesture of rotation around his/her wrist joint. We also focus on the pseudo-haptic physiological phenomenon which makes a user feel something like touch sensation by visualizing different patterns of shadow projected. A shadowing users' palm is internally processed and a corresponding artificial shadow is actually projected like a real shadow. Therefore the user identifies it as his/her own body movement[4]. This paper describes experimental results of the cognitive effects of a controlled artificial movement in shadow representation.

2   Related Work

Some projection techniques have been studied, many of which focused on direct access through physically touching objects[5,6,7]. In a distributed display environment, it is possible that a user cannot physically reach the display which is far from his/her location or which may be interfered in direct operation. In order to solve this problem, we proposed an intuitive interface using the metaphor of the shadow. Since Pavani found that shadow is recognized as owner's physical extension[8], users may utilize their shadows as interfaces, feelings as if the shadows would be the part of owner's body.

VIDEOPLACE[10] is the shadow-based interaction technique which not only projects silhouette but provides artistic expression of shadows by processing the image data and adding various graphical effects. However, still there is a difficulty for user to understand the correspondence between the generated artificial shadow and users' own body in the experimental environment. In our proposed interface, the artificial shadow is designed to be projected at the same location of the real shadow, utilizing shadow as a metaphor, and generating the feeling of correspondence between the generated artificial shadow and users' own body.

In some researches, Virtual Shadow[9] and Shadow Reaching[11] are utilized together with hand gestures to realize shadow interfaces, which could provide users intuitive operation by displaying natural shadows. The biggest disadvantage of these systems is that a hand shadow is covered by a body shadow since they require a light source behind user. Therefore, users can hardly operate naturally in front of the display. In our proposed system, we focus only on the hand shadow and aim to provide a user-friendly interface by displaying only palm-silhouette.

3   Silhouette Interface

Shadow is a common physical phenomenon where there is a point light source. We utilize shadow's characteristics in our user interface to access and interact with distributed-displays which are not directly or physically accessible by user, as shown in Fig. 2. With it, this interface could be intuitive since our daily experience so that its mental model is integrated.

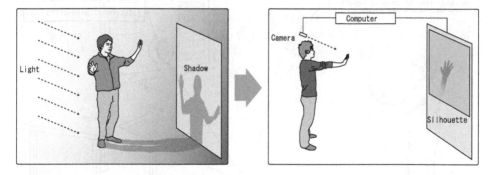

Fig. 2. Accessing wall displays that located where users cannot touch directly; left: physical shadow; right: artificially generated silhouette

In this paper, "silhouette" is defined as an artificial replacement of the shadow which shares some of the same characteristics of the real shadow. There are four major advantages of the silhouette user interface: First, a user does not need to handle and operate by hand any external pointing devices like a mouse or a trackball, though it is necessary to set a camera to recognize a user's hand position. Second, user can identify easily his/her own silhouette by the shadow movement from a distributed-display environment even where there are multiple number of users and several similar silhouettes, since the shadow and the computer-generated silhouette corresponding to the body movement based on the real shadow itself causes a natural and intuitive visual feedback. Third, it is a natural phenomenon that the shadow and its corresponding silhouette represent the user's body itself on distant surface, so silhouette interface is suitable for intuitive user interface of a remote operation. Finally, the computer-generated silhouette does not block visual information projected by optical projectors or generated by large-scale display like the real shadow since the transparency of the silhouette can be adjusted to superimposing.

Silhouette has some other useful visual properties than transparency. With graphical image combined, silhouette can be changed in some expressions: change of not only light-dark tone but also color or texture, scale change in arbitrarily defined environment, layer structure. Moreover, silhouette can also be intentionally deformed and modified in motion pattern. These features will be introduced into details in the following chapters.

We take the advantages of the above palm-silhouette characteristics to realize a distant interaction system for 10-foot user interface on wall displays. Figure 3 shows the conceptual idea of human-computer interaction with the proposed interface. On the other hand, since the displayed figure is not the real shadow but the artificial one, there may cause a processing lag which makes users feel unnatural.

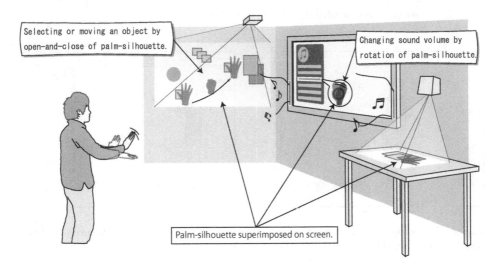

Selecting or moving an object by open-and-close of palm-silhouette.

Changing sound volume by rotation of palm-silhouette.

Palm-silhouette superimposed on screen.

Fig. 3. Conceptual configuration of palm-silhouette interface; user is able to operate selecting or adjustment control with one's own silhouette

4   System Configuration

We propose a novel interface system with new intuitive accessing method by palm-silhouette display and hand gesture recognition. As shown in Fig. 4, the system consists of three elements: a camera and a projector and a screen. User's hand is captured by the camera and processed for gesture recognition. Palm-silhouette image is projected to the screen. The two operation functionalities we implemented in the system includes "selecting" and "adjustment" which are achieved by capturing palm-silhouette in real time. The detailed description about these operations is mentioned in the next section.

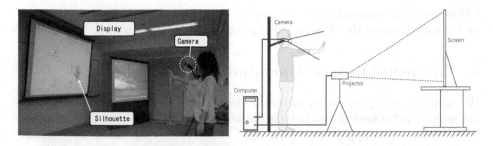

Fig. 4. System overview; left: experimental setup; right: system configuration

4.1 Two Types of Operations

Currently the proposed interface supports two operations: selecting and adjustment in Mac OS X and Windows XP. First, the selecting operation enables users to select an object on a display without using any pointing devices. This operation is implemented with grasp-and-release gesture based on the result of a preliminary experiment. Through this experiment, we found that test subjects accessed to an object on a display screen by grasping hand action. We confirmed that users could naturally move their own silhouette onto objects. We apply grasp-and-release operation for access a virtual object.

Second, adjustment operation enables some basic functions such as volumes control or rotary switch. The rotation movement is one of possible parameters by the joint rotation of our body. The controllable joint positions we could use for adjustment operation are: shoulder, cubital region, wrist and finger. There are the advantages and drawbacks for each joints. Requiring users of body movement such as rotation in the shoulder joint is likely to leads users fatigue. On the other hand, recognizing small changes in hand posture makes image processing complicated. Therefore, we decided to use the rotation in wrist, since its rotation does not require large movement which gives physical burden. Also, we applied the wrist rotation to adjustment operation such as controlling continuous quantity and multi-step selection.

4.2 Image Processing

A palm-silhouette is projected onto the screen by the projector after capturing and processing hand motion images. The processing is performed in three consequent steps: recognition of hand region on captured images, analyzing hand gesture and tilt parameter, creating CG images of palm-silhouette. First, the system acquires color images from the camera. Using skin color extraction, it makes captured color images be binarized as hand region. Second, some necessary parameters are calculated from the binary images. To detect palm-silhouette position on the screen, it finds the center of palm with excepting wrists or arms region from the binary images. The system also detects hand posture for select operation and calculates palm sway parameter for adjustment operation. Finally,

CG image of the palm-silhouette is generated in correspond to these parameters, and it superimposes the silhouette image on screen or PC desktop.

5   Grasp-and-Release Operation

We design grasping operation so that a virtual object can be operated by closing users' hand where the object on the screen and the half-transparent palm-silhouette are overlapped with each other. Also, release operation is designed so that the object can be released when users open their hand. Figure 5 shows grasp-and-release operation sequences. Like how we handle real objects by our hands in the real world, we can operate virtual objects by our palm-silhouette. We evaluated of grasp-and-release operation in following experiments.

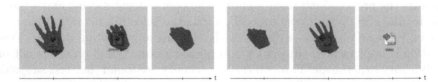

Fig. 5. Grasp-and-release operation by closing and opening hand through palm-silhouette; left: Grasp operation; right: Release operation

5.1   Experiment 1: Usability Evaluation in Displaying Palm-Silhouette

We agree that users may recognize the pointing location by looking at his/her own palm-silhouette in the same way of a cursor pointer indication. The most important advantage of using silhouettes to be expremirated, is that users can confirm the transition between opening and closing their palm. In order to understand the effect of the difference between visual information which users get through using both the conventional arrowhead pointer and the palm-silhouette, we conducted following experiments.

Test subjects are asked to perform the following task by both arrowhead pointer and palm-silhouette respectively. The task is "to replace four icons, two of which are located on the right half (Group A) and rests are on the left half (Group B), so that icons in Group A goes on the left and those in Group B does on the right."

Subjects are 16 students in the total males and females who major in the computer science in their twenties and are asked which visualization they feel to operate easily.

Results showed that subjects' answers to be the question which palm-silhouette or arrowhead pointer to be used easily; 91% "palm-silhouette," 3% "arrowhead pointer," and 6% neither. Also users gave following positive feedbacks:

- Silhouette lets a user understand operations intuitively.
- Since silhouette gives palm states such as opening and closing, it is easy to adjust how to grasp.

We obtained a finding that operativeness has been improved through the visual feedback in palm states such as opening and closing because visualizing the palm-silhouette is expressible of the shape variation according to the palm movement operation.

5.2 Application

We created an application in which users can move arbitrary icons on a conventional computer desktop in the same way users move real objects on the real desktop. Users can access GUI objects a the computer desktop through the silhouette. With image processing, proposed system recognizes hand gesture in each frame: the hand is recognized as open when the system identifies five fingers, the hand is recognized as close when the system does no finger. Real time gesture recognition realizes virtual object selection and movement function.

Even in the environment where are several computers and several displays, it is easy that users grab and move the virtual objects visually and intuitively by using networking systems. This enables seamless data transfer among multiple displays by using consistent operation in distributed-display environment.

6 Wrist Rotating Operation

In this section, we will describe how to realize adjustment function by palm rotation for both continuous operation such as volume control and descrete multi-step function such as rotary switch.We used hand the following hand gestures in our system for adjustment operation as shown in Fig. 6. It is easy to enable functions such as a tuning-knob operation, however such continuous operation provides user with monotonous haptic feeling because a user is not actually touching the object.To realize multi-step rotary type adjustment, we included visuo-tactile operation, which lets a user feel the resistance on one's hand by imposing movement restrictions on palm-silhouette. The following experiments show how to design rotary operation using palm-silhouette.

In one of experiments, we make the virtual shadow rotation angle larger than actual hand rotation angle as shown in Fig. 7. By such processing, a user perform rotation operation in relatively larger range with relative less body effort. We designed the virtual rotation angle range within an acceptable range within which user will not have feeling of incompatibility. We assume that it makes a user operating in range of large rotation angle with small rotation hand gesture easily. Through the experiment, the suitable ration of rotation angle stretch parameter was confirmed about 1.5. Also, we have confirmed that suitable hand gesture rotation range is about 80-degree.

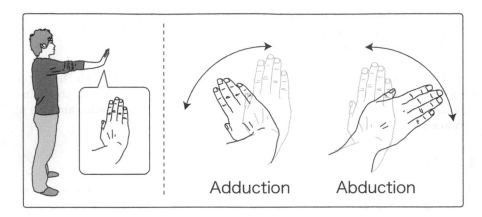

Fig. 6. Hand rotation around a wrist joint point

We also studied how many points can be selected by rotary-switch like discrete operation as shown in Fig. 8. Multi-step control can be realized by discretizing of movement of palm-silhouette which is supposed to match the actual rotation of hand palm continuously in a natural way if there is no physical resistance. By discretizing virtual shadow's movement into steps, users can have visuo-tactile feeling of resistance and they can feel that they are actually operating a rotary switch. It is necessary to find out the minimum value of width of tuning angle quantum with which a user can realize they are doing discrete adjustment operation. Through the experiment of finding a width of tuning angle quantum, we confirmed that the minimum value is about 5-degree, so it is possible to build up about 40 points of discrete adjustment. Also, the results show that silhouette movement with large width of angle quantum have a risk of recognizing as a response delay.

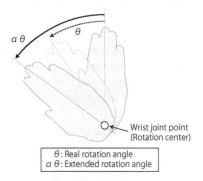

Fig. 7. Angle expansion that palm-silhouette rotation angle is more stretched than real hand one

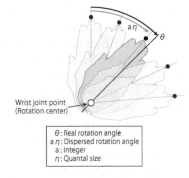

Fig. 8. Discrete palm rotary motion to select from multi-step control like rotary switch

7   Conclusion

In this paper we introduced a novel user-interface which let user to execute intuitively access interfaces which are far from user's location or which may be interrupted in direct operation, especially in multi-display environments. Shadow is used as the ideal interaction metaphor to connect real and virtual worlds. The "shadow" called in the proposed system, may occlude visual contents shown on display or projected by an optical projector because it is computer-generated artificial shadow, which we call "silhouette" in this paper. Such silhouette is generated from a hand image which is captured by a camera installed on user's arm. As users can move the artificial shadow naturally in real time, they could feel that the computer-generated silhouettes were their own shadow experiments. We proposed two gesture-related functions; "selecting" function by grasp-and-release operation and "adjustment" function by wrist rotating operation. We evaluated that the usability of proposed interface comparing a arrowhead pointer. Through another experiment, we studied and concluded a design rationale to realize a rotary switch operation with utilizing pseudo-haptic visual cue.

Shadow is a natural phenomenon occurring where there is a light source, no special training is needed to control it extended through our daily experience.

In the future, we will build a extended silhouette interface for targeting multi-user case. We will also evaluate the usability of wearable silhouette implementation of interface. Artificial shadow could connect the real and virtual worlds. We believe this human-computer interaction technique based on shadow metaphor can be applied to useful many practical domains.

References

1. Czerwinski, M., Robertson, G., Meyers, B., Smith, G., Robbins, D., Tan, D.: Large Display Research Overview. In: CHI 2006 extended abstracts on Human factors in computing systems, pp. 69–74 (2006)
2. Ni, T., Schmidt, G.S., Staadt, O.G., Livingston, M.A., Ball, R., May, R.: A Survey of Large High-Resolution Display Technologies, and Applications. In: Proc. of IEEE Virtual Reality Conf., pp. 223 236 (2006)
3. Hutchings, D.R., Czerwinski, M., Meyers, B., Stasko, J.: Exploring the Use and Affordances of Multiple Display Environments. In: Workshop on Ubiquitous Display Environments at UbiComp (2004)
4. Lécuyer, A., Burkhardt, J.M., Etienne, L.: Feeling Bumps and Holes without a Haptic Interface: The Perception of Pseudo-Haptic Textures. In: Proc. of the SIGCHI Conf. on Human Factor in Computing Systems, pp. 239–246 (2004)
5. Wellner, P.: Interacting with Paper on the Digitaldesk. ACM Communication 36(7), 87–96 (1993)
6. Koike, H., Sato, Y., Kobayashi, Y., Tobita, H., Kobayashi, M.: Interactive Textbook and Interactive Venn Diagram. In: Proc. of the SIGCHI Conf. on Human Factor in Computing Systems, pp. 121–128 (2000)

7. Wilson, A.: Playanywhere: A Compact Tabletop Computer Vision System. In: Proc. of the ACM UIST Symp., pp. 83–92 (2005)
8. Pavani, F., Castiello, U.: Binding Personal and Extrapersonal space through body shadows. Nature Neuroscience 7(1), 14–16 (2004)
9. Xu, H., Iwai, D., Hiura, S., Sato, K.: User Interface by Virtual Shadow Projection. In: SICE-ICASE Int'l Joint Conf., SA14-1, A0897 (2006)
10. Krueger, M.W., Gionfriddo, T., Hinrichsen, K.: VIDEOPLACE – An Artificial Reality. ACM SIGCHI Bulletin 16(4), 35–40 (1985)
11. Shoemaker, G., Tang, A., Booth, K.S.: Shadow Reaching: A New Perspective on Interaction for Large Displays. In: Proc. of the ACM UIST Symp., pp. 53–56 (2007)

Potential Limitations of Multi-touch Gesture Vocabulary: Differentiation, Adoption, Fatigue

Wendy Yee

User Centric, Inc.
2 Trans Am Plaza Dr, Ste 100,
Oakbrook Terrace, IL 60181 USA
wyee@usercentric.com

Abstract. The majority of gestural interactions in consumer electronics currently represent "direct" gestures related to the direct manipulation of onscreen objects. As gestural interactions extend beyond consumer electronics and become more prevalent in productivity applications, these gestures will need to address more abstract or "indirect" actions. This paper addresses some of the usability concerns associated with indirect gestures and their potential limitations for the typical end-user. In addition, it outlines a number of considerations for the integration of abstract gestures with productivity workspaces.

Keywords: Interaction design, multi-touch, software design, gestures.

1 Introduction

With the advent of the iPhone, Surface, and other consumer-oriented multi-touch devices, gestural interactions have become an increasingly common mode of interacting with software environments [1]. Since gestures tap into a very basic part of the human syntax [2], these gestural interactions may be an especially appropriate way to make technology accessible to a broader audience.

The majority of gestural interactions in consumer electronics currently represent "direct" gestures related to the direct manipulation of onscreen objects, such as the standard "dragging" action used to move onscreen objects on the Apple iPhone and Microsoft's Surface table. As gestural interactions extend beyond consumer electronics and become more prevalent in productivity applications, these gestures will need to address more abstract or "indirect" actions, such as acting on a group of onscreen objects or navigating through an information hierarchy. This paper addresses some of the usability concerns associated with indirect gestures and their potential limitations for the typical end-user. In addition, it outlines a number of considerations for the integration of abstract gestures with productivity applications.

2 Review of Current Criteria for Effective Gestures

Gestural interaction has its roots in the 1980s and 1990s [3], but has become increasingly mainstream with the integration of gesture recognition with operating systems

J.A. Jacko (Ed.): Human-Computer Interaction, Part II, HCII 2009, LNCS 5611, pp. 291–300, 2009.
© Springer-Verlag Berlin Heidelberg 2009

[4, 5], including applications supported by recent-model 2008 MacBooks with multi-touch trackpads [6, 7]. Although gestural manipulation of items and files have been commercially available through iGesture keypads [8] and graphic design tablets that recognize direction and stroke pressure [9], gestural interactions have not yet achieved integration with the daily activities associated with typical productivity applications (e.g., writing, analyzing data in spreadsheets, manipulating images, editing video).

Across existing literature [10, 11, 12, 13, 14], five major criteria are thought to contribute to the effectiveness of gestural interactions:

A. **Provide a high degree of interaction context:** The application or system interface should make it clear to the user that gestures can be used. From the user perspective, gestures should be obvious and intuitive in the context of relevant tasks.

B. **Allow users to gesture with minimal effort:** Effective gestures should be simple to perform and should not require unusual dexterity.

C. **Use appropriate metaphors:** Gestures should have a logical relationship with the application functionalities that they represent, both in the type of movement and type of interaction with objects that they are acting on.

D. **Be designed for repetitive use and minimal muscle stress:** Given the repetitive nature of most activities associated with productivity, consumer, and gaming applications, gesture fatigue is likely to be a common issue among end-users.

E. **Facilitate accurate recognition by the application**: In the ideal world, gestures would be sufficiently unambiguous to applications so that minor variations of the same gesture can be recognized by software as having the same function. In addition, applications would ideally recognize completely different gestures with a minimum of false-positives or cross-positives.

These criteria have been especially relevant when gestures have been used to replace basic navigation and selection actions that were formerly associated with point-and-click selections (mouse and trackpad) or game controller/joystick selections (gaming systems). Here, they represented "direct" gestures with one-to-one correlation to vector-based movement (e.g., length of the gesture determines the extent of the software action, such as zooming) or single-movement-to-object associations (e.g., dragging a photo across the screen). This direct type of interaction has benefited consumers by reducing their learning curve and focusing their attention on direct interactions with the digital representations of objects.

Now, however, gesture vocabularies are poised to expand beyond basic navigation tasks into productivity applications. Indirect or "abstract" gestures are increasingly common and can now be used to initiate, manipulate, and complete activities that are not associated with direct one-to-one visual representations [15]. For example, the "three-finger swiping" gestures allows users of recent-model MacBooks to gesture on their trackpads and rapidly advance through documents. A related "four-finger swiping" gesture allow users to quickly locate an open window or to hide all windows

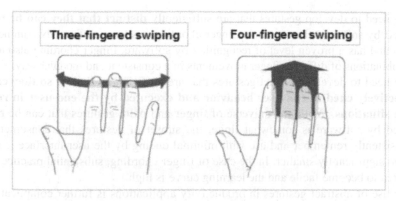

Fig. 1. Examples of indirect gestures on recent-model MacBook trackpads. Source: Apple Support Article HT3211 (February 20, 2009).

without clicking on any specific target. Neither of these indirect gestures require the user to select an object before taking action.

3 Potential Limitations of Using Gestures in Productivity Applications

By their nature, abstract gestures can be more difficult for users to discover and adopt. For example, Fingerworks has developed gestures that will allow users to initiate and execute abstract actions using different combinations of multi-finger gestures and movements [8], which Apple has incorporated into a multi-touch gesture library [16].

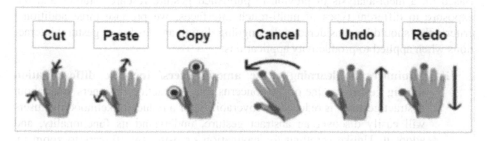

Fig. 2. Finger chords from the Fingerworks gesture keymap for editing. Source: http://www.fingerworks.com/gesture_keymap.html

There are also additional commercial examples of abstract multi-touch gestures that can be used to trigger contextual menus and navigate between and within applications [17, 18]. These are typical events associated with productivity applications.

The relationship between abstract gestures such as finger chords and the requirements of multi-touch gestural interactions is an interesting one because it reflects basic tensions between the need to satisfy two potentially disparate requirements:

- The need to develop gestures that are sufficiently **distinct that they can be recognized by software.** For example, finger chording has been sufficiently commercialized and has a proven level of recognition by software. Finger chording also allows combinations of different finger movements in a consistent and modular way.
- The need to develop abstract gestures that are sufficiently **distinct so they can be effectively cued in end-user behavior and executed by the end-user in repetitive situations.** While the universe of finger and palm gestures that can be recognized by software is somewhat finite, the subset of gestures that consumers can consistently remember and use with minimal cueing by the user interface is likely to be significantly smaller. In the case of finger chording, substantial practice is required to become facile and the learning curve is high.

The use of abstract gestures in productivity applications is further complicated by the likelihood that gestures are likely to occur on a larger physical scale due to the size of multi-touch displays (multi-touch tablet screens, laptop screens, and monitors). To accommodate the space between objects and the general screen real estate, gestures may no longer be limited to finger spans.

Eventually, there will need to be workable guidelines outlining abstract gestures that are intuitive and ergonomic for the end-user but also distinct enough to facilitate recognition by the system. Although the visual user interface context is critical for helping users understand what they can do when faced with abstract tasks, there are obvious limitations for cueing abstract gestures.

4 Additional Criteria for Usable Gestures in Productivity Applications

Based on a meta-analysis of previously published gesture research studies and our exposure to different types of multi-touch interfaces, we propose three additional criteria that should be considered in the ongoing design and testing of gestural interactions when applied to productivity applications:

F. **Minimize the learning curve among users/ increase differentiation among gestures:** One of the concerns that interaction designers have about abstract gestures is reduced discoverability, or a reduced likelihood that users will easily discover an abstract gesture, understand its functionality, and adopt it. Unlike scrolling for navigation or using two fingers to zoom in, there is a much weaker causal (and visual) association between (for example) three-fingered swiping and page navigation. Although abstract gestures have been compared to right-clicking - which also has some discoverability issues - the potential variety of abstract gestures is likely to increase the learning curve much more than right-clicking. (Most mice and trackpads only have one right button but gestures are theoretically limited only by flexibility.)

G. **Cue efficient gestures:** There are currently a limited number of gesture-related UI cues used to prompt users' movements in multi-touch environments. For example, partial-height rows at the top and/or bottom of touchscreen lists and menus are often used to let the user know than they can scroll further up or down the list. On the Surface table, onscreen items or areas that can recognize physical objects (such as a tagged glass or tagged mobile device) will appear to pulsate or glow and will display a simacrulum of the target object. However, these cues typically rely on one-to-one correlations between an onscreen object and the use of a single gesture.

The use of one-to-one gestures may be too repetitive since multiple instances of the same gesture may be required to sort, select, or organize multiple items. Instead, a good gesture ecosystem should help the user identify gesture "shortcuts" and prevent the user from making needless repetitive gestures. If the user should be using a more efficient gesture, there should be consistent cues that alert them to this option.

H. Focus abstract gestures on finger movements: Although full-hand gestures that involve movement of entire hand and forearm might be useful for extending the specific actions, these gestures require more physical effort that limited-range finger movements. Repetitive use of full-hand gestures (where the entire hand moves) is likely to lead to unnecessarily arm fatigue. There may be cases where large-scale gestures may more accurately map to an action type than a small-scale gesture (such as dragging fingertips across a screen to navigate to a new area of a map), but repetitive use of this gesture may be counterproductive. This argues for representation of large-scale actions using equivalent gestures with finger movements.

5 Gestural Considerations

Our hypothesis is that applying these additional usability criteria would yield a more cohesive and self-evident set of abstract gestures in productivity applications. To facilitate further discussion in the interaction design and research community, we suggest the following specific points for the three criteria discussed earlier.

5.1 Minimize Learning among Users and Increase Differentiation among Gestures

- **Examine the gesture ecosystem for an application:** We urge our colleagues in interaction design, HCI, and software development to think of multi-touch gestures as part of a clearly defined "ecosystem" of gestures. As with all ecosystems, the presence of redundant gestures or gesture-related UI elements can make it difficult for the overall ecosystem to thrive.
- **Evaluate and test related gestures:** Are gestures that are not related to one another sufficiently distinct? Can the user differentiate between related gestures and non-related gestures?

- **Apply consistent semantic guidelines to gestures:** Does the overall approach to the design of gestures reflect a consistent approach?
  - For example, are sweeping gestures used for large group selections while small, nudging gestures are used to move single items? Or are small circular movements to bring up context menus vs. large circular movements to act on a group of objects?
  - Full-hand gestures may be best reserved for actions that represent a definitive starting or stopping action. Body language associated with broad gestures suggests that broad strokes should be reserved for formal transitions or actions with a certain degree of completion.
- **Increase discoverability by focusing on the design of the user interface:** The visual cues used to prompt gestures needs to be self-explanatory and provide abundant affordances for prompting and confirming gestures.
  - Well-designed visual cues and affordances in the interface will help users better understand the context, which will in turn help them select the appropriate set of gestures for a set of items or tasks.
  - Users will gauge their success with a gesture interface based on the overall behavior of the interface and its responses to gestures.
  - Based on observations made during user research studies, gestural interfaces that provide **visual and audio cues** for abstract gestures are more likely to be discovered, such as:
    - Solid visual metaphors for relationships (groups, linkages)
    - Affordance for navigating between different views of the same object sets (grouped or sorted by date, name or another attribute)
    - Self-evident and persistent modes for canceling an action and/or undoing the immediate previous action
    - Indication of the type of gestural action initiated
    - Indications of which items can be acted on (or not)
    - Indications of which items are selected (or not).

5.2 Design Efficient Gestures to Increase User Adoption

- Ensure the extensibility of gestures:
  - Make sure that an abstract gesture can be applied to a single item as well as multiple items, regardless of the size of the group of items
  - Separate different types of gestures for initiating new events
  - Support navigation gestures for non-visible items (or navigation access via a preview of items)
- **Select the mode of gesture interaction (with menus or without menus):** The use of abstract gestures will typically require increased context which might take the form of onscreen confirmations and/or controls. For example, depending on an interaction design team's gesture philosophy, one of the following approaches might be used to act on a group of files.

Option A: Close out the task using an indirect gesture.

Fig. 3. Use of a direct gesture to select files, followed by use of a fictional indirect gesture to close out the task (upload the selected files)

Option B: Close out the task with an indirect gesture (right hand) while simultaneously using a screen control (left hand) to confirm the selection and prevent the gesture from being applied in error.

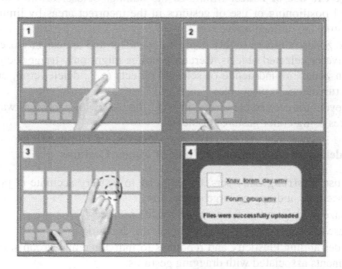

Fig. 4. Use of a direct gesture to select files, followed by **simultaneous** use of an onscreen control and a fictional indirect gesture to close out the task

Option C: Select and group items using direct gestures, then close out the task with screen controls.

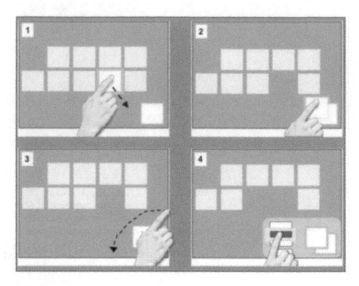

Fig. 5. Use of direct gesture to select and group files, followed by use of onscreen controls to close out the task

- **Leverage the use of zones:** Minimize the number of user errors caused by the accidental positioning or use of gestures in the incorrect areas by limiting recognized gestures to defined active zones:
  - Active zones could be highly context-dependent and appear in close proximity to active or selected objects. Certain gestures might only trigger actions occurring in zones around active or selected objects (e.g., delete, crop, erase, apply filter, run macro, replace, etc)
  - To prevent unrecoverable errors, provide the user with persistent ways to undo gestures using either gestures or menus.

5.3 Considerations: Maximize the Value of Finger Gestures

- **Play to users' strengths:** Users' fingers tend to be very accurate at pointing and are less accurate at dragging large object sets.
  - Optimize more gestures for pointing-related accuracy.
  - Increase error margins for gestures involving dragging.
  - Consider adding elasticity and rebounds to individual and group selections and movements associated with dragging gestures.
- **Do not assume gestures need to scale:** Allow users to act on a group of items by using smaller scale finger gestures once that group is selected. In other words, gestures do not need to be "to scale" once a group selection is made - regardless of the "size" of the group.

6 Evaluating Gesture Ecosystems

We would argue that (a) the strength of gestural interactions is derived from the overall functionality and usability of a complete gesture set and (b) these "gesture ecosystems" are subject to the same enduser expectations for consistency and usability. Given the relatively new state of commercial gestural interactions, it is reasonable to expect that these interactions (both the gestures and the UI context for gestures) will take decades to evolve, similar to the way point-and-click GUIs have evolved over the last twenty years.

The only data-based way to evaluate the effectiveness of multi-touch gestures in productivity applications is to test potential gestures with users at different stages of interaction design and development. The usability adage to "test early and test often" is definitely applicable to the design and development of gestural interactions.

We anticipate that major technology organizations already have specific plans to formalize their own distinct flavors of gestural interactions. Given the supposed advantages of intuitiveness and self-evidency (and discoverability) of gestural interactions, we urge all interaction designers to consider the additional usability criteria for abstract gestures we have discussed in this paper when designing both direct and indirect gestures for productivity applications.

References

1. Green, K.: Touch screens for many fingers. Technology Review, January 18 (2007), http://www.technologyreview.com/computing/18079/
2. Goldin-Meadow, S.: The resilience of language: What gesture creation in deaf children can tell us about how all children learn language, p. 262. Psychology Press, New York (2003)
3. Buxton, B.: Multi-touch systems I have known and loved, http://www.billbuxton.com/multitouchOverview.html
4. Apple iPhone User Guide (2008), http://manuals.info.apple.com/en_US/iPhone_User_Guide.pdf
5. Microsoft: Introduction to Windows Touch, http://download.microsoft.com/download/a/d/f/ adf1347d-08dc-41a4-9084-623b1194d4b2/Win7_touch.docx
6. Apple: MacBook Air and MacBook Pro (early 2008): Useful keyboard and trackpad tips and shortcuts. Support article HT1115, http://support.apple.com/kb/HT1115
7. Apple: MacBook: Using the trackpad Support article HT3211. kb/HT3211, http://support.apple.com/
8. Fingerworks iGesture Keypad, http://www.fingerworks.com/userguides.html
9. Wacom, http://www.wacom.com
10. Keates, S., Robinson, P.: The use of gestures in multimodal input. In: FACM SIGACCESS Conference on Assistive Technologies archive. Proceedings of the third international ACM conference on Assistive Technologies, pp. 35–42 (1998)
11. Hummels, C., Staplers, P.J.: Meaningful gestures for human computer interaction: Beyond Hand Posters. In: Proceedings of the 3rd International Conference on Automatic Face & Gestures Recognition (FG 1998), pp. 591–596. IEEE Computer Society Press, Los Alamitos (1998)

12. Nielsen, M., Storring, M., Moeslund, T.B., Granum, E.: Procedure for developing intuitive and ergonomic gesture interfaces. Technical Report CVMT 03-01 (2003)
13. Karam, M., Schraefel, M.C.: Investigating user tolerance for errors in vision-enabled gestural interactions. In: Proceedings of the working conference on Advanced Visual interfaces table of contents, 225–232 (2006)
14. Pavlovic, V., Sharman, R., Huang, T.: Visual Interpretation of Hand Gestures for Human-Computer Interaction: A Review. IEEE Transactions on Pattern Analysis and Machine Intelligence 19(7), 677–695 (1997)
15. Saffer, D.: Designing Gestural Interfaces, 1st edn. O'Reilly Media, Sebastopol (2008)
16. Elias, J.G., Westerman, W.C., Haggerty, M.M.: Multi-Touch Gesture Dictionary. US Patent Application 20070177803 (2007)
17. Perceptive Pixel, http://www.perceptivepixel.com
18. Tse, E., Shen, C., Greenberg, S., and Forlines, C.: Enabling Interaction with Single User Applications through Speech and Gestures on a Multi-User Tabletop. Advanced Visual Interfaces (AVI) (2006)

Part III

Human-Robot Interaction

A Multimodal
Human-Robot-Interaction Scenario:
Working Together with an Industrial
Robot

Alexander Bannat[1], Jürgen Gast[1], Tobias Rehrl[1],
Wolfgang Rösel[2], Gerhard Rigoll[1], and Frank Wallhoff[1]

[1] Department of Electrical Engineering and Information Technology,
Institute for Human-Machine Communication
[2] Faculty of Mechanical Engineering,
Institute for Machine Tools and Industrial Management

Technische Universität München
80290 Munich, Germany

Abstract. In this paper, we present a novel approach for multimodal
interactions between humans and industrial robots.

The application scenario is situated in a factory, where a human
worker is supported by a robot to accomplish a given hybrid assembly
scenario, that covers manual and automated assembly steps. The robot
is acting as an assistant as well as a fully autonomous assembly unit.

For interacting with the presented system, the human is able to give
his commands via three different input modalities (speech, gaze and the
so-called soft-buttons).[1]

1 Introduction

In general, the cooperation between humans and industrial robots is emerging
more and more in ongoing research fields, concerning human machine interaction
as well as industrial safety requirements.

The here presented work is part of such a research group and aims to integrate
industrial robots in human-dominated working areas using multiple input modalities to allow a true peer-to-peer level of collaboration. Thus, a smart working
environment for joint-action between a human and an industrial robot is to be
designed as an experimental setup consisting of various sensors monitoring the
environment and the human worker, an industrial robot, an assembly line sup-
plying the manufacturing process with material and tools, and a working table.
The long term goal of this project is to form an umbrella for so-called "Cognitive
Factories", where the new kind of cognitive systems abolish the currently used
static and inflexible technical systems. A first approach for our realization of this
long-term goal is presented in [1].

---

[1] All authors contributed equally to the work presented in this paper.

J.A. Jacko (Ed.): Human-Computer Interaction, Part II, HCII 2009, LNCS 5611, pp. 303–311, 2009.
© Springer-Verlag Berlin Heidelberg 2009

This paper is organized as follows: In the next section, a motivation for our presented multimodal approach towards intuitive and robust human-robot-interaction is given, followed by a description of the demonstrator set-up. A detailed explanation of our system architecture is lined out, succeeded by some first results. Finally, the next planned steps are shortly sketched and close this paper.

2   Motivation

As mentioned above, our long-term goal is to establish the so-called "Cognitive Factory" as the manufacturing concept for the 21st century. Here we present a small slice of our concept, constituting a foundation for a multimodal communication between a human and a robot (see Figure 1), which is flexible, robust and most appropriate for hybrid assembly. Furthermore, by utilizing more than two input modalities, we introduce redundancy in the communication channel to compensate failures in general or the total loss of an interaction modality. For the maximization of this redundancy, our interaction framework is constituted on three different channels (eyes, voice and hands). This approach does not only ameliorate the redundancy but also the diversity of possible communication ways. Therefore, consider the case, two input modalities basing on the same human interaction method (e.g. the human hand) can be blocked by a complex task requiring this interaction method (e.g. the work piece must be held with both hands). Having three input modalities basing on the three channels, the interaction between the human and the robot can be significantly shaped into a more natural, robust and intuitive way.

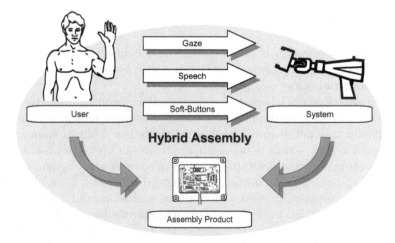

Fig. 1. Hybrid Assembly: Exploiting three independent communication channels for accomplishing a given construction task for a human worker and an assisting industrial robot

3 Set-Up Description

In the following two sections the hardware set-up as well as the assembly product will be described in detail. However, the main focus in this two sections will not be laid on the assembly process, which will be given in the Section 5.

3.1 Hardware Set-Up

In Figure 2 the demonstrator set-up is depicted. As it can be seen, the worker is wearing a head-mounted microphone as well as eye-tracking glasses. The industrial robot manipulator arm used in the scenario is a Mitsubishi robot RV-6SL. It has six degrees of freedom and can lift objects with a maximum weight of six kilograms. Its workspace lies within a radius of 0.902 m around its body. Its tool point is equipped with a force-torque-sensor and a tool-change unit. Furthermore, the robot is able to change the currently installed gripper by itself at a station, depicted on the left side of the table in Figure 2. The station features four distinct kinds of manipulators performing specific operations:

- two finger parallel gripper
- electronic drill
- camera unit for automatic observations
- gluer

These manipulators give the robot the capabilities of being able to solve entirely different tasks, like screwing and lifting.

The workbench has an overall workspace of approximately 0.70 square meters. A global top-down view camera is mounted above the workbench. This device has the overview over the entire work-area and makes it possible to watch the actions on the workbench and locate objects on the surface. Additionally, a PMD

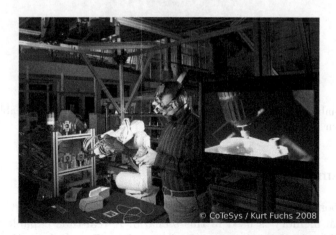

Fig. 2. Hybrid assembly station: tool station, robot arm (with electric drill) and assembly-table

range sensor is mounted above the workbench for providing depth information of the scenery.

For bringing information into the worker's field of view, a table projector is also installed above the workbench. This device projects information directly onto the surface of the workbench. With this modality, it is possible to show contact analog assembly instructions and system feedbacks.

Moreover, flexible interaction fields can be displayed to communicate with the system (see Section 4.3).

3.2 Assembly Product Description

The product constructed in the hybrid assembly scenario is a high frequency transmitter, as it can be seen in Figure 3. The following parts are required for the construction of this high frequency transmitter:

– *One base plate:* The base plate delivers the foundation for the hybrid assembly on which all remaining construction parts will be mounted on.
– *One electronic part:* The electronic part is an inlay, which has to be mounted into the base plate.
– *One wiring cable:* The wiring cable has to be plugged into the electronic part. It needs to be put into the designated cable line on the base plate.
– *One plastic cover and four screws:* With the four screws, the plastic cover is mounted on top of the base plate to protect the inlay against influences from the environment, like dust and dirt.

Fig. 3. Assembly product: a base plate, one electronic part, a wiring cable, a plastic cover and four screws

4 System Overview

As a backbone for the integration and fusion of the three input modalities, a short term memory is used in this scenario. A real-time capable framework processes all kinds of data streams (Real-Time Data Base [2,3,4]). Here, the data streams constituted by the three input modalities have very diverse features.

These differences appear especially in the sampling rates of sensory sources and losses of data packets. Another reason, why the Real-Time Data Base (RTDB) is used, is the following: The RTDB can process asynchronous data streams in real-time and allows a best match access to these streams, so that a high-degree of data coherence is achieved for further processing.

Three different modules capture the required data for the processing: First, the gaze-module captures the current human gaze vector via the EyeSee Camera [5] and the result is stored into the RTDB. Second, the speech module transmits the raw audio data into the RTDB and last, the soft-buttons module displays different buttons onto the workbench and returns the button status to the RTDB (selected/not selected).

4.1   Human Gaze

The first channel in this scenario is human gaze. Therefore, the worker has to wear eye-tracking glasses, enabling the system to extract the gaze information. The perceived information consists of the intersection of the gaze trajectory and the workbench surface. As a result of this sensor device, the actual 2D-coordinates in the table plain are transmitted into the RTDB. The update rate of this position data is approximately about 120 frames per second.

Having the actual position of the worker's gaze on the workbench, the system is now capable to provide the worker with important information directly in his current field of view.

Besides with having the gaze point, a new kind of human-machine interaction is now available: control by gaze. The gaze point can be used to select certain sensitive fields either by fixating these over a certain period of time or choose the desired function with gaze and confirm the selection with a further modality. This input can then be used to initiate several system functionalities, e.g. to browse through an assistant assembly instruction system, like presented in [6]. This form of interaction is especially suited for situations where hands-free interaction is needed and the environment does not allow reliable speech recognition.

4.2   Speech Input

As known from many human-human interaction scenarios, speech is a common and favored communication channel. Thus, speech constitutes the main interaction method in our scenario (as our second channel). Therefore, a speech recognition software is integrated into the framework.

The raw audio data is captured with a head-mounted microphone in PCM-standard format. This data stream is delivered via the RTDB towards the speech recognition engine, which in turn writes the recognition results with their corresponding confidence back into the RTDB-buffer.

So far, the recognition is based on phonemes. This enables the system to detect predefined command words, which can be defined in a Backus-Naur Form [7].

This grammar can be adapted during runtime according to the current task. Thus, to the actual state-of-the-art of speech recognition software, it is situated to use command language instead of natural language. Because the complexity of the speech recognition is drastically reduced by applying a command-word structure and, therefore, a high acceptable recognition rate is accomplished. Furthermore, command-word-based recognition software is also able to cope with different users more efficiently. The complex training process of natural speech recognition software is not necessary in the used set-up.

4.3   Button Interface

The third channel is our concept of the so-called Soft-Buttons. With a Soft-Button it is possible to control a function associated with a certain sensitive field. The content and appearance of this field, as well as its position, can be adjusted at run-time according to the desired user-preferences with respect to the current available space on the workbench for displaying. Therefore, in a certain area reserved for human-system interactions, fields are projected onto the workbench with a table-projection unit mounted above the workspace.

The system is capable of detecting whether the worker's hand is within a sensitive area or not, therefore a vision based hand-detector is applied. A skin color model, like presented in [8], delivers the foundation for the hand-detector module. Furthermore, the Soft-Buttons can be selected via exploiting the above introduced human gaze information.

The free distribution of the sensitive fields on the workbench allows an ergonomic interface design and an optimal workspace usage. Due to the fact that the information is directly displayed into the worker's field of view, there is no need for him to shift his attention from his current task towards a monitor. This modality decreases disturbances in the workflow.

5   Preliminary Assembly Process

The assembly process of the product described in Section 3.2 is depicted in Figure 4. The first interaction – initiated via Soft-Button/Speech Command – between the human and the robot is the supply of the worker with the base plate. Having the required work pieces available at hand, the worker starts to teach in a glue-line (see Figure 4.a). The track of the glue-line on the base plate is taught with *Programming by Demonstration* (PbD). This is done by tracking a colored pointer. Therefore, a color-based image segmentation is performed on the output frame of a top-down-view camera, mounted above the workbench.

The result is then used to locate the green tip of the pen, now visible as a binary-coded plane in the filtermask. The motion of this object in the image plane is analyzed and transformed into the world-coordinate-system. While the line is perceived, its trajectory is on-line projected back onto the work piece as a direct feedback for the worker. On completion of this step the robot changes

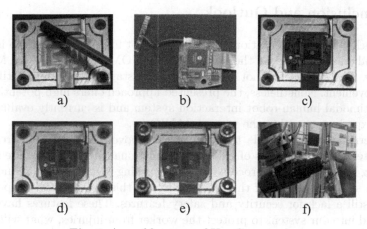

Fig. 4. Assembly steps of Use-Case product

its tool device from the gripper to the gluer according to the next step in the work plan. After the PbD, the robot protracts the glue on the work piece. Via transforming these gained world-coordinates into the robot-coordinate-system, the industrial robot is now able to exactly repeat this motion trajectory and perform the gluing-operation autonomously.

As per assembly instructions the robot reaches out for the electronic parts. Therefore, a fully automated tool change operation is performed by the robot, thus, exchanging the currently mounted gluer towards gripper. The following assembly of the electronic parts (see Figure 4.b) require fine motor skills. Therefore, the next step is solely done by the human. In spite of the fact that the robot does not give any active assistance in this assembly step, the system supports the worker via presenting the manufacturing instructions for the insertion of the electronic parts into the base plate (see Figure 4.c and 4.d).

After the worker has acknowledged the completion of the current step via Soft-Button (third channel) or a speech based command (second channel), the robot fetches the four screws for the final assembly step. While the worker is pre-fitting the screws in the designated mount ports (see Figure 4.e), the robot retrieves the automatic drill device from the tool changer station. The velocity of the drill is adjusted to the contact pressure of the work piece against the drill (see Figure 4.f). The more pressure is applied, the faster the drill goes. As soon as the human recognizes that the screw is fixed – the rattling noise of the slipping clutch – he will loosen the former conducted pressure. This modality allows for an intuitive screwing behavior of the system.

The final step requires the worker to acknowledge the completion of the screwing operation via speech command or Soft-Buttons. The system will go into the init state and the whole assembly process can be again started for the next production turn.

6   Conclusion and Outlook

A first technical implementation of a human-robot interaction scenario is introduced and was exhibited at the trade fair "AUTOMATICA 2008" in Munich, Germany. The system has not reached its final stage and it shows still room for improvement. Nonetheless, the presented approach offers high potential for a new multimodal human-robot interaction system and is currently evaluated by human experiments within the project JAHIR [9].

Furthermore, it is possible to produce the above described high frequency transmitter – this product is of course non functional. At this stage, we showed a working hybrid assembly process – human working together with an industrial robot. In spite of the fact of the functionality of this new form of cooperation, there is still a lack for security and safety features. These features have to be integrated into our system to protect the worker from injuries, what will be the next task in our research.

As a further field of improvement, the EyeSee Camera mentioned in Section 4.1 does not allow a noninvasive gaze recognition because of the eyetracking glasses and the required wiring. Therefore, a remote gaze tracking system is currently developed at our institute for enabling an undisturbed and naturalistic workflow.

Acknowledgment

This ongoing work is supported by the DFG excellence initiative research cluster *Cognition for Technical Systems – CoTeSys*, see www.cotesys.org for further details. The authors further acknowledge the great support of Matthias Göbl for his explanations and granting access to the RTDB repository.

References

1. Zäh, M.F., Lau, C., Wiesbeck, M., Ostgathe, M., Vogl, W.: Towards the Cognitive Factory. In: Proceedings of the 2nd International Conference on Changeable, Agile, Reconfigurable and Virtual Production (CARV), Toronto, Canada (July 2007)
2. Goebl, M., Färber, G.: A real-time-capable hard- and software architecture for joint image and knowledge processing in cognitive automobiles. In: Intelligent Vehicles Symposium, pp. 737–740 (June 2007)
3. Stiller, C., Färber, G., Kammel, S.: Cooperative cognitive automobiles. In: Intelligent Vehicles Symposium, pp. 215–220. IEEE, Los Alamitos (2007)
4. Thuy, M., Göbl, M., Rattei, F., Althoff, M., Obermeier, F., Hawe, S., Nagel, R., Kraus, S., Wang, C., Hecker, F., Russ, M., Schweitzer, M., León, F.P., Diepold, K., Eberspächer, J., Heißing, B., Wünsche, H.J.: Kognitive automobile - neue konzepte und ideen des sonderforschungsbereiches/tr-28. In: Aktive Sicherheit durch Fahrerassistenz, Garching bei München, Garching bei München, April 7-8 (2008)
5. Bardins, S., Poitschke, T., Kohlbecher, S.: Gaze-based Interaction in various Environments. In: Proceedings of 1st ACM International Workshop on Vision Networks for Behaviour Analysis VNBA 2008, Vancouver, Canada (2008)

6. Bannat, A., Gast, J., Rigoll, G., Wallhoff, F.: Event Analysis and Interpretation of Human Activity for Augmented Reality-based Assistant Systems. In: IEEE Proceeding ICCP 2008, Cluj-Napoca, Romania, August 28-30 (2008)
7. Naur, P.: Revised Report on the Algorithmic Language ALGOL 60. Communications of the ACM 3(5), 299–314 (1960)
8. Soriano, M., Huovinen, S., Martinkauppi, B., Laaksonen, M.: Skin Detection in Video under Changing Illumination Conditions. In: Proc. 15th International Conference on Pattern Recognition, Barcelona, Spain, pp. 839–842 (2000)
9. Lenz, C., Nair, S., Rickert, M., Knoll, A., Rösel, W., Bannat, A., Gast, J., Wallhoff, F.: Joint Actions for Humans and Industrial Robots: A Hybrid Assembly Concept. In: Proc. 17th IEEE International Symposium on Robot and Human Interactive Communication, Munich, Germany (2008)

Robotic Home Assistant Care-O-bot® 3
Product Vision and Innovation Platform

Birgit Graf, Christopher Parlitz, and Martin Hägele

Fraunhofer IPA, Nobelstr. 12, 70569 Stuttgart, Germany
{Birgit.Graf,christopher.parlitz,
martin.haegele}@ipa.fraunhofer.de
www.care-o-bot.de

Abstract. The development of a mobile robot to assist people in their home is a long term goal of Fraunhofer IPA. In order to meet this goal, three generations of a robotic home assistant "Care-O-bot®" have been developed so far. As a vision of a future household product, Care-O-bot® 3 is equipped with the latest industrial state-of-the art hardware components. It offers all modern multimedia and interaction equipment as well as most advanced sensors and control. It is able to navigate among humans, detect and grasp objects and pass them safely to human users using its tray. Care-O-bot® 3 has been presented to the public on several occasions where it distributed drinks to the visitors of trade fairs and events.

Keywords: robotic home assistant, Care-O-bot, product vision, navigation, manipulation, object learning and detection, safe human-robot interaction, fetch and carry tasks.

1 Introduction

Inspired by movies and television series, people have for a long time been dreaming of intelligent robots accompanying them in their daily lives and taking over unpopular and strenuous tasks. Such robots would not only be an enormous help to support the independence of elderly and handicapped people. Similar to domestic appliances, entertainment and IT systems they could contribute to enrich everybody's daily life.

The development of such a mobile robot able to assist persons in their home is a long term goal of Fraunhofer IPA. In order to meet this goal, three generations of Care-O-bot® prototypes have been developed so far: Care-O-bot® I was built more than 10 years ago: in 1998 – when the idea of building robots for applications outside of industrial environments was still new [11]. It consists of a mobile platform with a touch screen, able to navigate autonomously and safely in indoor environments, communicate with or guide people. Three robots based on the same hardware platform and control software as Care-O-bot® I were installed in March 2000 for constant operation in the "Museum für Kommunikation Berlin" where they autonomously move among the visitors, communicate to and interact with them [3].

Care-O-bot® II (Fig. 1, middle), built in 2002, is additionally equipped with a manipulator arm, adjustable walking supporters, a tilting sensor head containing two cameras and a laser scanner [4]. The manipulator arm, developed specifically for the

J.A. Jacko (Ed.): Human-Computer Interaction, Part II, HCII 2009, LNCS 5611, pp. 312–320, 2009.
© Springer-Verlag Berlin Heidelberg 2009

robot, provides the possibility of handling typical objects in a home environment. A hand-held control panel is used for instructing and supervising the robot. In addition to the mobility functions already solved in Care-O-bot® I, the second prototype was able to execute simple manipulation tasks autonomously and could be used as an intelligent walking support.

Some major difficulties made it impossible to further proceed with the Care-O-bot® II platform towards long term installations in public and home environments: First of all, the platform was too big and the differential drive system not flexible enough to navigate in narrow home environments. Even more crucial was the concept of interacting and passing objects to and from human users with the robotic arm. By tilting its sensor head and recording the corresponding laser scanner data, Care-O-bot® II was able to generate a 3-dimensional image of the environment and plan collision free arm motions accordingly. However, as taking the 3-D scan took some time and was only executed once, the robot was not able to react dynamically to changes in the environment taking place after the 3-D scan had been taken. Therefore, a more suitable concept for safely passing objects to and from humans was required and was one of the main targets when designing the next Care-O-bot® generation.

Care-O-bot® 3 was built in 2008 and is equipped with the latest state-of-the-art industrial components including omnidirectional drives, a 7 DOF redundant manipulator, a three finger gripper and a flexible interaction tray that can be used to safely pass objects between the human and the robot. Its moveable sensor head contains range and image sensors enabling autonomous object learning and detection and 3-D supervision of the environment in real time. Care-O-bot® 3 was designed accordinag to an overall concept suitable for a product vision, combining technological aspects with a compact and user friendly design.

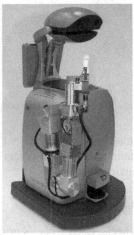

Fig. 1. Care-O-bot® I, II and 3

2 Care-O-bot® 3 Hardware

2.1 Safe Human-Robot Interaction

The primary interface between Care-O-bot® 3 and the user consists of a tray attached to the front of the robot, which carries objects for exchange between the human and the robot. The tray includes a touch screen and retracts automatically when not in use.

The basic concept developed was to define two sides of the robot (Fig. 2): One side is called the 'working side' and is located at the back of the robot away from the user. This is where all technical devices like manipulators and sensors which can not be hidden and need direct access to the environment are mounted. The other side is called the 'serving side' which is where all physical human-robot interaction takes place. The concept behind using the tray to interact with the user is to reduce possible users' fears of mechanical parts by having smooth surfaces and a likable appearance [8]. On the technical side, it is much easier to ensure collision free interaction with the static tray than with a robotic arm moving freely in 3-D-space. As the locations where the robot autonomously grasps objects, e.g. in the kitchen, can be supervised by stationary sensors, moving the arm in the vicinity of humans can be avoided.

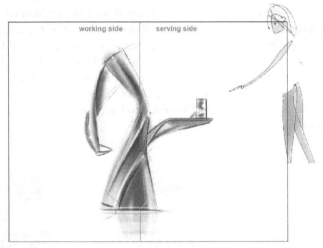

Fig. 2. Care-O-bot® 3 interaction concept

Using these described interaction concept, Care-O-bot® 3 enables the safe executing of fetch and carry tasks and thus provides the potential to operate a mobile, manipulating robot safely in public environments.

2.2 Mobility and Manipulation

Care-O-bot® 3 is driven by four wheels. Each wheel's orientation and rotational speed can be set individually. This omnidirectional drive system enables advanced movements and simplifyes complete kinematic chain (platform-manipulator-gripper) control. The wheeled drive was preferred to legged locomotion because of safety (no risk of falling) and stability during manipulation. The base also includes the Li-ion battery pack for the robot, laser scanners and a PC for navigation tasks. The size of the base is mainly determined by the required battery space. Nevertheless, the maximal footprint of the robot is approx. 600 mm and the height of the base is approx. 340 mm.

The torso sits on the base and supports the sensor carrier, manipulator and tray. It contains most of the electronics and PCs necessary for robot control. The base and torso together have a height of 770 mm.

The manipulator is based on the Schunk LWA3, a 7-degrees-of-freedom (DOF) light-weight arm. It has been extended by 120 mm to increase the work area so that the gripper can reach the floor, but also a kitchen cupboard. The arm is connected to a 7-DOF Schunk Dexterous-Hand with tactile sensors in its finger making advanced gripping possible. Special attention was paid to the mounting of the arm on the robot torso. The result is based on simulations for finding the ideal work space covering the robot's tray, the floor and area directly behind the robot following the 'two sides' concept developed. Since the manipulator has a hollow shaft no external cables are needed.

The sensor head carries high-resolution firewire stereo-vision cameras and 3-D time of flight cameras, enabling the robot to identify, to locate and to track objects and people in 3-D. These sensors are mounted on a 4 DOF positioning unit allowing the robot to direct its sensors to any area of interest.

Fig. 3 shows Care-O-bot® 3 without covers and gives an overview of the single hardware components.

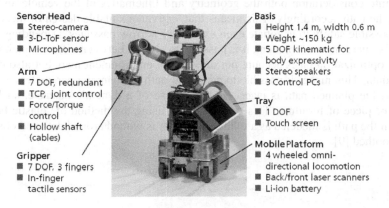

Sensor Head
- Stereo-camera
- 3-D-ToF sensor
- Microphones

Arm
- 7 DOF, redundant
- TCP, joint control
- Force/Torque control
- Hollow shaft (cables)

Gripper
- 7 DOF, 3 fingers
- In-finger tactile sensors

Basis
- Height 1.4 m, width 0.6 m
- Weight ~150 kg
- 5 DOF kinematic for body expressivity
- Stereo speakers
- 3 Control PCs

Tray
- 1 DOF
- Touch screen

Mobile Platform
- 4 wheeled omni-directional locomotion
- Back/front laser scanners
- Li-ion battery

Fig. 3. Care-O-bot® 3 Hardware Components

3 Fetch and Carry Task Execution

The dependable execution of fetch and carry tasks provides the basis for a large number of assistive tasks in home environments. Fetch and carry tasks usually consist of the following components:
1. Accept user command
2. Move to target position
3. Locate desired object

4. Grasp object
5. Bring object to user

In order to execute the single steps, the following key technologies need to be solved: safe navigation among humans, object learning and detection, and object manipulation. The solutions implemented and used on Care-O-bot® 3 will now be described in further detail.

3.1 Navigation

Localization. In order to plan its actions, the mobile robot should know its current location at any time. The localization of Care-O-bot® 3 is based on two principles. Firstly, the current position and orientation of the vehicle is estimated by coupled navigation and mathematical integration of the travelled route. Where exclusive use is made of odometric information, however, small errors are unavoidable and these add up over time. Therefore, additional use is made of environment sensors, specifically the laser scanners attached to the front and rear of the robot, in order to detect significant environment features such as walls or poles. These features are checked against their reference positions, which are stored in a global environment map. Finally, the position of the robot is calculated in relation to the detected environment features.

Path Planning and Path Modification. Path planning allows a mobile robot to find a continuous trajectory from a given start configuration to a target configuration [6]. The previously learned environment map is used as the basis for planning, the planner taking into consideration both the geometry and kinematics of the vehicle and optimizing the path accordingly. This means that – given a suitable design of the vehicle – it is possible safely to negotiate even extremely narrow passages. Depending on the vehicle's operating environment, it is possible to choose between different planners.

Path optimization takes account not only of the environment map, but also current sensor data. This makes it possible to adapt the path to changing parameters, e.g. if a point on the planned path is inaccessible because of a dynamic obstacle, such as a person or piece of furniture. This task is solved using the method of "elastic bands", in which the path is modeled as a rubber band that is wound around detected obstacles and smoothed [9].

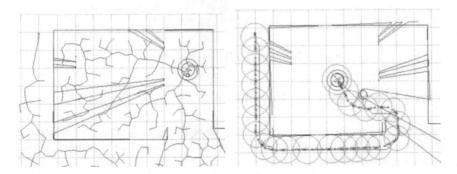

Fig. 4. Example for a probabilistic path planner (left), smooth and collision free path leading around an obstacle after path modification with elastic bands (right)

Motion Control. This component controls the smooth and efficient movement of the vehicle along the planned path. The realized software modules allow the control of a variety of vehicle kinematics from simple differential drives to omnidirectional wheels.

The control system for Care-O-bot® 3 is split in three hierarchical levels: The first level is the trajectory-tracking controller, which keeps the robot on its path. Then follows a controller instance that coordinates the four wheel modules and a third instance for each individual wheel module. The representation of the robots motion state is based on reformulating the ICM [1], similar the method proposed by Thuilot, D'Andréa-Novel and Micaelli [13].

3.2 Object Learning and Detection

In order to grasp an object, the robot must first be able to detect and locate it in the environment. By combining a range imaging sensor [12] with a color camera it is possible to upgrade conventional 2-D recognition processes from traditional grey- and color-image processing into 3-D recognition processes. To achieve this, a special calibration between the sensors is used in order to compute an approximate color image, the pixel coordinate system of which is brought into alignment with that of the depth-image camera. In the resulting "shared image" not only the color value, but also the distance of the respective neighborhood point is known for each pixel in the image (Fig. 5).

The recognition algorithm is based on scale invariant feature transform (SIFT) descriptors that are recorded for each object and fed into a learning algorithm (one-class Support Vector Machine, SVM) [7]. Using the data of the range imaging sensor, specific feature points can be segmented from the background. A region in space is effectively masked out in the color image of the scene using the range measures for the corresponding pixels in the range image.

New objects are taught to the robot by placing them in front of the sensors and by recording the relevant SIFT-key-points for the object [5]. Fig. 6, left displays the teaching of new objects using the proposed range segmentation. The right three images of Fig. 6 illustrate the learning process and resulting representation of an object: Several images of the object are recorded and for each the feature points are detected. In a second step, the feature points of all images are fused into a "feature point cloud" which again can be used to detect and compute the position of the object in a given scene.

Fig. 5. Depth image of a scene (left) and corresponding shared image (right)

Fig. 6. Spatial segmentation for object learning (left), side view of an object, detected feature points and corresponding feature point cloud (right three images)

3.3 Manipulation

Based on the data from the range imaging sensor and the identified location of the object to be grasped, a collision free trajectory for moving the manipulator to the detected object can be computed. To solve this, the robot and scene are modeled using »oriented bounding boxes« (OBBs) [2]. For the robot a distinction is made between static components (e.g. the robot's torso) and dynamic components (e.g. its manipulators). The dynamic components are mapped by articulated models which are updated with each robot movement. The model of the scene is obtained by generating corresponding OBB models from the point cloud obtained by the range sensor. The obstacle model is used as the basis for online collision monitoring. The algorithm consists of two main phases: determination of potentially colliding objects by a rough distance check based on the velocity vectors of all moving parts, and subsequent elaborate collision tests for all objects in the determined potential colliding sets [10]. Fig. 7, left shows the velocity vectors of a moving arm, Fig. 7 middle and right show the successful detection of potential collisions.

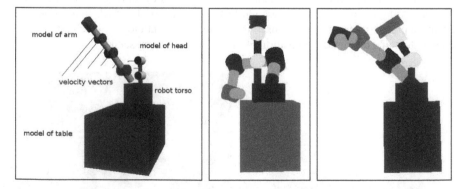

Fig. 7. Model of Care-O-bot® 3 standing in front of a table, lines indicate velocity vectors of moving parts (left). Detection of potential collisions between different parts of the robot illustrated in red color (middle, right).

In the next step, the collision detection algorithm is coupled with a path planner. On the basis of the current robot configuration, the path planner calculates a collision-free path to the target configuration. The entire obstruction model is again used as the basis for the path search, with the result that the determined path is guaranteed to be collision-free with respect to both the robot's itself and also its environment.

4 Public Presentations of Care-O-bot® 3

After its first public presentation at AUTOMATICA fair in June 2008 in Munich, Care-O-bot® 3 has been displayed successfully at several occasions such as the opening of the Fraunhofer inHaus in Duisburg and the Science Night in Vienna in November 2008. Care-O-bot® 3 showed its abilities to dependably grasp bottles from a shelf, place them on its tray, and hand them to the visitors. In Vienna, more than 100 bottles were passed to the visitors in one night. In March 2009 two Care-O-bot® 3 systems were displayed at CeBIT 2009 in Hannover where they presented themselves and their capabilities to the visitors in a multimedia show.

Fig. 8. Care-O-bot® 3 presentations at AUTOMATICA fair (left) and in Vienna (middle, right)

References

1. Connette, C., Pott, A., Hägele, M., Verl, A.: Control of a pseudo-omnidirectional, non-holonomic, mobile robot based on an ICM representation in spherical coordinates. In: IEEE Conference on Decision and Control (December 2008)
2. Gottschalk, S., Lin, M.C., Manocha, D.: OBBTree: A hierarchical structure for rapid interference detection. In: Computer Graphics. Annual Conference Series, vol. 30, pp. 171–180 (1996)
3. Graf, B.: Dependability of Mobile Robots in Direct Interaction with Humans. In: Prassler, Erwin (eds.) Advances in Human-Robot Interaction, pp. 223–239. Springer, Berlin (2005) (Springer Tracts in Advanced Robotics - STAR 14)
4. Graf, B., Hans, M., Schraft, R.D.: Care-O-bot II – Development of a Next Generation Robotic Home Assistant. Autonomous Robots 16(2), 193–205 (2004)

5. Kubacki, J., Baum, W.: Towards Open-Ended 3-D Rotation and Shift Invariant Object Detection for Robot Companions. In: Institute of Electrical and Electronics Engineers Intelligent Robots and Systems / CD-ROM: Proceedings IEEE/RSJ International Conference, Beijing, China, October 9-15, 2006, pp. 3352–3357. IEEE Press, Piscataway (2006)
6. Latombe, J.-C.: Robot Motion Planning. Kluwer Academic Publishers, UK (1996)
7. Pontil, M., Verri, A.: Support vector machines for 3-D object recognition. IEEE Trans. Pattern Anal. Mach. Intell. 20(6), 637–646 (1998)
8. Parlitz, C., Hägele, M., Klein, P., Seifert, J., Dautenhahn, K.: Care-O-bot 3 - Rationale for human-robot interaction design. In: ISR 2008: 39th International Symposium on Robotics International Federation of Robotics, Seoul, Korea, October 15-17, 2008, pp. 275–280 (2008)
9. Quinlan, S., Khatib, O.: Elastics bands: Connecting Path Planning and Control. IEEE Transactions on Robotics and Automation (1993)
10. Reiser, U., Volz, R., Geibel, F.: ManIPA: A flexible Manipulation Framework for Collision Avoidance and Robot Control. In: ISR 2008: 39th International Symposium on Robotics International Federation of Robotics, Seoul, Korea, October 15-17, pp. 407–411 (2008)
11. Schraft, R.D., Schaeffer, C., May, T.: The Concept of a System for Assisting Elderly or Disabled Persons in Home Environments. In: Proc. of the 24th IEEE International Conference on Industrial Electronics, Control& Instrumentation (IECON), Aachen, Germany, vol. 4 (1998)
12. Oggier, T., et al.: An all-solid-state optical range camera for 3-D real-time imaging with sub-centimeter depth resolution SwissRangerTM. Proceedings of the SPIE 5249(65) (2003)
13. Thuilot, B., D'Andréa-Novel, B., Micaelli, A.: Modeling and feedback control of mobile robots equipped with several steering wheels. IEEE Transactions on Robotics and Automation 12(3), 375–390 (1996)

Designing Emotional and Interactive Behaviors for an Entertainment Robot

Yo Chan Kim[1], Hyuk Tae Kwon[1], Wan Chul Yoon[1], and Jong Cheol Kim[2]

[1] Department of Industrial and Systems Engineering,
Korea Advanced Institute Science and Technology (KAIST),
Daejeon, Korea (305-701)
yochan82@gmail.com, jehdeiah@kaist.ac.kr, wcyoon@kaist.ac.kr
[2] Advanced Technology TFT, Future Technology Laboratory, KT,
17 Woomyeon-dong, Seocho-gu, Seoul, Korea
jckim07@kt.co.kr

Abstract. In the process of developing an entertainment robot, Mon-e, we represented the robot's emotional and interactive behaviors in the form of scripts. A unified model was established to manage all the different scripts. We designed the personality profile to possess two dimensions of criteria for script selection. Emotion variable was introduced to create a variety of robot behavior according to the context. Reinforcing mechanisms of the personality profile and the emotion variable were developed.

Keywords: Human-Robot Interaction, Script-based Robot Behavior, Robot Personality, Robot Emotion, Service Robots.

1 Introduction

With the development of many types of personal service robots, researchers have been studying human-robot interactions. These studies have focused on the performance and safety of interfaces or actuators. However, it is also important to study how and when the many types of robot behaviors should be organized and presented to users. These issues can be resolved by analyses of tasks performed by robots and humans.

An entertainment robot, considered as a type of personal service robot, should behave like a human or in such a manner that users can predict it actions [1]. The actions of a robot must be understandable so that users can attribute its actions to rational causes. This proposition is related to another contention that holds that entertainment robots should have a diverse range of behaviors. When presented with a single stimulus, a human can react with several different expressive methods; hence, a robot can be expected to behave as a human. An entertainment robot should be able to present its own behavioral styles according to its individual personality in the manner similar to individuals behaving in different ways with each coherent trait.

In the process of developing an entertainment robot Mon-e (Fig. 3 shows its appearance), emotional or interactive behaviors were designed and they were applied to the robot by using several interfaces and actuators [2]. The appearance of the robot is similar to that of a monkey. It can move in every direction using three wheels and can

J.A. Jacko (Ed.): Human-Computer Interaction, Part II, HCII 2009, LNCS 5611, pp. 321–330, 2009.

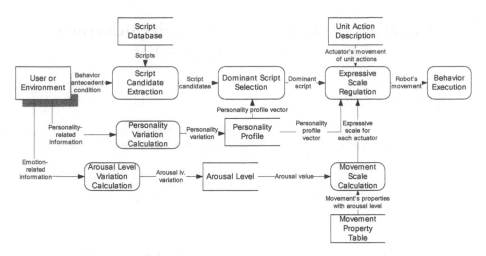

Fig. 1. Information flow diagram of the proposed system. The rounded rectangles, arrows, and rectangles with one side open represent primary processes, flows of information, and databases, respectively. The robot behavior management model is depicted at the upper part of this figure. The middle and lower parts show the variation process of personality profile and emotion state.

actuate its head and tail. Furthermore, it can change colors in some parts of its body and emit sounds through a speaker. The robot can recognize some noises, light, body heat, and touch and can measure its orientation on the basis of the principles of angular momentum. To diversify the interactive behaviors that utilize the abovementioned functions, several models developed on the basis of psychological studies on personality and emotion were established.

2   Robot Behavior Management Model

In order to realize robot behaviors, many robot planning and action selection skills have been introduced (the approaches are explained in [3]). The proposed model for the robot can not only show reactive behaviors according to specific situations but also exchange answers and questions with a user while maintaining the contextual knowledge of the actions. These interactive and reactive behaviors should be presented by using several styles according to the traits of the robot.

In this study, the scripts of robot behaviors are written and utilized in order to demonstrate the interactive behaviors [4]. In the scripts, the robot's behaviors are mapped to various situations, and many action procedures with their personality level are written for each behavior. By using such scripts, the behavior management model selects and executes the robot's response. This approach allows for the behaviors of the robot to become more reliable and allows the designer to modify or add behaviors easily.

The overall system configuration is depicted in figure 1. When an event that corresponds to the conditions described in a script database occurs, the system extracts the corresponding scripts, which are known as script-candidates. The script-candidates are evaluated on the basis of the personality profile and the script personality level.

Each script candidate is assigned a weight, and a script is eventually selected by means of a weighted random selection process. Before the execution of the script, the system determines the detailed scale and velocity of each action by referring to an emotion model.

3 Personality

Personality can be defined as the distinctive and characteristic patterns of thought, emotion, and behavior that define an individual's personal style of interaction with physical and social environments [5]. A robot's personality may provide useful affordance, providing users with a method to model and understand robot behavior [6]. Several researchers have emphasized that personality is a key factor in human-robot interactions [7,8]. Fong classified five common personality types used in social robots: Tool-like, Pet or creature, Cartoon, Artificial being, and Human-like [6]. However, even within a robot that has one of the personality types, there may exist various personality patterns; hence, we focus on finding dimensions that connote the various patterns. For further understanding of the personality, we must review personality researches on a human who is a user and model of a social robot.

3.1 Human Personality

Many approaches are adopted to explain human personality as several traits [9,10,11,12,13]. Cattell obtained sixteen personality factors by using questionnaires and factor analyses [9]. Eysenck introduced the PEN model [10], and Myer proposed the Myer-Brigg model [11]. However, many researchers agree that the five traits or dimensions provide an almost accurate description of human personality. Costa and McCrae's Five Factor Model [12] and Goldberg's Big-Five Model [13] adopt different methods for naming and interpretation; both the methods can be described by an abbreviated word: OCEAN [5].

– Openness (intelligent, imaginative, flexibility)
– Conscientiousness (helpful, hard-working)
– Extraversion-introversion (sociable, outgoing, confidence)
– Agreeableness (friendliness, nice, pleasant)
– Neuroticism (emotional stability, adjusted)

In particular, dimensions of extraversion and agreeableness are close to interpersonal traits [14] and are similar to two axes (dominance and friendliness) of interpersonal theory [15].

3.2 Robot Personality

Robotics researchers have defined personality on the basis of various concepts. These concepts can be roughly divided into the type-style of personality, as images specified by the user or developer, and the parameter-style of personality, as variables affecting robot behavior styles. Severinson-Eklund et al. regarded personality as a property that humans obtain from a robot's embodiment, motion, manner, and developed Cero character [16]. Edsinger et al., by using a similar definition of personality, attempted to realize a socially inviting personality by a robot's face [17]. Iida et al. set three cases of responsive behavior patterns for the robot's face, such as the follower and selfish types [18]. Yoon et al. presented personality types on the basis of emotion (anger, timid, enjoyable) and developed synthetic characters for each type [19].

Many approaches that employ the parameter-style of personality are based on the trait theory of human personality. Okuno et al. used personality to define the attention control of multi-talk by using the interpersonal theory [20]. Miwa et al. developed a human-like head robot and applied three dimensions of the five factor model [21]; they divided personality into sensing personality, which indicates how a stimulus works for the robot's emotion, and expression personality, which indicates how the emotion works for the robot's expression. While proposing a robot's framework (called as Tame), Moshkina and Arkin utilized all the dimensions of the five factor model to influence emotion, mood, and ultimately attitude [22]. Lee et al. used three dimension of the Big-five model as the tendency associated with motivation, homoeostasis, and emotion of artificial creatures [23]. For developing a robot for hands-off therapy, Tapus and Matataric considered personality as a key element that decides socially interactive behaviors [8]. They applied an extroversion-introversion level, one dimension of the Eysenck's Pen model.

For establishing the personality model, the established model should fulfill the following demands. Robot behaviors that originate from different personalities should be significantly realized and distinguished by the user. Furthermore, the model should be useful for the purpose of developing a robot. Variables of personality should be presented with consideration of the robot's expression capability.

Entertainment robots will be more affective if they can deliver diverse personalities according to user preference. Some researches have shown that a user's understanding about a robot's personality or behavior styles depends on the user's personality, gender, and age [8, 24]. Goetz and Kiesler revealed that user preference about robot personality relies on the purpose of robot applications [25].

When implementing OCEAN dimensions as the robot personality, it is not suitable to apply every dimension. Each difference within extraversion or agreeableness, which are interpersonal traits among OCEAN dimensions, is relatively easier to be distinguished by the user. However, the other three traits are difficult to be applied [20], and the difference in each trait may not be relatively useful for service robots. For example, a user who employs a robot that has a lazy and emotionally unstable personality may attribute the robot's behaviors to troubles of the system. Reeves and Nass insist that two principal factors responsible for the intermediate agent's personality are dominance and friendliness [26]. Hence, in this research, we assume that the developing robot is conscientious, emotionally stable, and intelligent and has many different levels of extraversion and agreeableness.

Two traits (extraversion and agreeableness) are applied to each robot's personality profile and scripts personality level. In the personality profile, there exist two variables, which range from −1 to 1. Each variable refers to a personality level of the robot (extraversion, agreeableness). In the script database, each script has a pair of personality levels. Each level receives one value among −1,0,1, indicating whether the content of each script is extravert, neutral, or introvert and disagreeable, neutral, or agreeable.

3.3 Personality Variation

Personality can be changed by accumulated experience. Thus, a personality variation process is instituted. The personality variation process allows for the robot behavior to change continuously. The robot personality profile can be changed on the basis of three factors (figure 2 depicts relationships between the three factors and vectors on a coordinates). The first factor is termed "inherent disposition." The inherent disposition refers to the tendency to become a particular personality profile independently of the user input or situational issues. The second factor is termed "manual setting." The user can select the robot's personality through a control panel. The last factor is the reinforcement from the robot's incoming information. For example, rude user behaviors such as shaking or overthrowing the robot can cause the robot to become disagreeable. Additionally, some attentive user actions such as hugs make the robot agreeable. Related rules and equations are developed for this process.

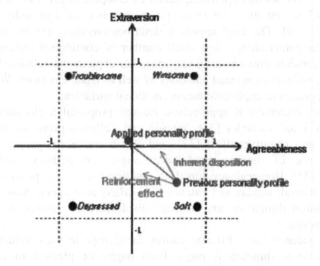

Fig. 2. The personality profile can be represented as a vector on a two-dimensional plane. The personality is changed by manual settings (one of the four points such as winsome, soft, etc.), reinforcement effect, and inherent disposition.

4 Emotion

Most interactions between entertainment robots and users are emotional interactions. A robot's reactions are related to simulating how the robot feels during a recognized situation. Hence, social robots require the capability of expressing and inducing emotions to interact with users plausibly and reliably [27]. Because a script-based behavior model is used, a pre-scripted database contains data indicating how the robot reacts to situations or human emotions. The robot does not interpret situations or understand human emotions autonomously, but it shows emotional interactions by following the contents of an appropriate script. Abundant script-databases and personality profiles allow diverse emotional interaction.

The script-based behavior model has some limits. The model cannot diversify behavior in conformity to a robot's emotion state. Emotions are continuously affected by the lapse of time as well as particular events, although, in this approach, a robot's emotional behavior discretely changes with some events represented in scripts. To overcome these problems, this paper presents an emotional parameter which varies robot behaviors according to time and events.

4.1 Arousal Variable

In spite of brisk researches on emotion, there still exist many arguments on how emotions arise and how emotions are classified [28]. There are three major hypotheses to classifying emotions. The first hypothesis is that emotion can be categorized by some basic emotion [29]. In this approach, changes in emotion can be described by some production rules. The second approach, called as component process theory, denies the existence of basic emotion and argues that emotions consist of underlying, more elementary units [30]. The final approach describes emotions not by listing them separately but as points along some small number of continuous dimensions [31]. This approach presents conceptual dimensions that explain the relationship among emotions, and it reflects compound emotions as well as basic emotions. We come up with the final approach to apply continuous emotional variables.

As one of the dimensional approaches, Russell proposed a circumplex model with two dimensional variables [31]. Watson and Tellegan proposed two axes of positive affect and negative affect [32], and Smith and Scott proposed a three-dimensional space of pleasure-displeasure, attentional activity, and personal agency/control [33]. Breazeal developed an emotion robot to express emotion by dimensions of arousal, stance, and valence [34]. Many researchers have mentioned attention or arousal dimension and pleasure-displeasure or valence dimension as principal dimensions.

Arousal and valence have different causes for change in their values. Emotion variations in valence dimensions range from happy or pleased to annoyed or frustrated, and the main factor of the variance is cognitive appraisal about particular situations. Breazeal states that valence is associated with how much the stimulus is relevant and pleasant intrinsically and how much the stimulus is directed to the robot's goal. It does not appear easy to quantify the appraisal of valence. Therefore, in the robot behavior management model, valence-related information of a robot's expression is included in the contents of the script database.

On the other hand, arousal variables can take emotion values ranging from exited or astonished to tired or sleepy. Arousal variables depend on lapse of time. Furthermore the arousal state evoked from an irrelevant event affects interpretation of events that are emotionally both positive and negative [35,36]. One of the examples is that men on a wobbly bridge feel more attractive to a female interviewer as compared to men on a sturdy bridge. This result implies that an arousal state can have an effect on further emotional states, whatever the cause of the arousal. On the basis of the above results, arousal is a useful variable for the behavior management model.

4.2   Variation of Arousal Value and Its Function

Breazeal proposed effective appraisals as intensity of stimulus, relevance of stimulus, intrinsic pleasantness, and goal directness, and he stated that arousal was related to intensity and relevance [34]. We added the activity level of robot movement as the cause of arousal.

- Intensity of stimulus: strong stimulus increases the arousal level (e.g., loudness of sound and intensity of light or user's touch)
- Relevance of stimulus: specific stimulus increases or decreases the arousal level (e.g., confrontation of an obstacle, user's calling, and robot's falling down)
- Robot's movement: a large number of movement increases the arousal level (e.g., actuating tail, head, or body)

These factors vary the arousal level according to a related rule, and the level is deactivated as time passes. The decay process follows an exponential function.

$$\text{Arousal}_t = (\text{Arousal}_{t-1} + \text{Arousal}_{event}) \times k^{t\_event} \tag{1},$$

where k denotes the decay constant; t, the current time; t_event, the time passed from stimulus; Arousal_t, the current arousal value; and Arousal_event, the value added due to the three factors. The Arousal value ranges from positive to negative and determines the range and velocity of movements about the action being executed. Examples are shown in table 1.

Table 1. The scale of each actuator moves according to the arousal value. When the arousal value has a number that lies between the columns of this table, the scale is calculated by using a proportional expression.

Part		Arousal: 0	Arousal: 1	Arousal:-1
Head	-Angle range	0°~15°	0°~20°	0°~12°
	-Velocity	2 cm/s(100%)	2.5 cm/s(150%)	1 cm/s(50%)
Color remaining period		0.5 s(100%)	0.3 s(80%)	1 s(200%)
Moving velocity		10 cm/s(100%)	15 cm/s(150%)	5 cm/s(50%)
Tail	-Angle range	0°~30°	0°~45°	0°~15°
	-Velocity	30°/s(100%)	60°/s(200%)	6°/s(20%)

5   Implementation

The proposed models and established variables were implemented onto a 3D graphic simulator and onto the Mon-e robot platform (the snap shot is shown in figure 3). The 3D graphic simulator was developed for efficiently examining the diversity and understandability of behaviors evoked from the behavior management model.

We wrote many different scripts by using a script exploration method [37]. When the simulators perceived a particular environment, the behavior management model selected a proper dominant script according to values of extraversion and agreeableness. For example, when a user turns on the robot having a winsome personality, it sings songs and dances. When the user turns on the robot having a depressed

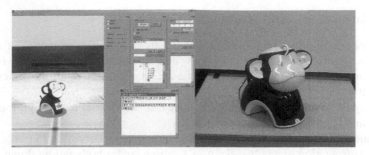

Fig. 3. The 3D graphic simulator (*left*) and Mon-e robot platform (*right*)

personality, it just displays a starting screen. After selecting the dominant script, the management model determines the velocity and scale of each motion in line with the arousal level, and it then sends motion commands to an execution module. As some situations were inputted to a simulator or robot platform, the arousal level or personality profile was varied by a few degrees.

6 Conclusion

In this paper, to demonstrate emotional and interactive behaviors of a robot, we proposed several models and variables. We investigated psychological researches and robotic results associated with personality and emotion. The established models were implemented on to a graphic simulator and Mon-e robot platform. As part of future studies, using several types of user test, we will validate and improve the practical effects of the proposed system.

Existing researches on the robot's emotional behaviors have focused on how to make the robot's behavior human-like or animal-like so that the robot's behaviors can be modeled on the basis of motivational factors such emotion, drives, or homeostasis [38,34,23]. We introduced an approach to show diverse behaviors on a robot's personality in order to create affective services or behaviors of entertainment robots. The behavior management model that uses scripts is effective to manage highly complex interaction procedures. For example, when a user turns on a robot, the robot can ask some recommendable services, obtain the user's response, and execute a service in accordance with the user's response. Several scripts in the model allow the robot to react to several responses. The behavior management model has an advantage that designers or users can easily modify and add scripts. If a system to support writing scripts is developed, the modification will be more enhanced.

Acknowledgments

This research was supported by the "KT RoboLab at KAIST" programs funded by KT in Korea.

References

1. Kim, Y.C., Kwon, H.T., Yoon, W.C., Kim, J.C.: Scenario Exploration and Implementation for a Network-Based Entertainment Robot. In: Khong, C.W., Wong, C.Y., Niman, B. (eds.) 21st International Symposium Human Factors in Telecommunication: User Experience of ICTs, pp. 239–246. Prentice Hall, Malaysia (2008)
2. World Design market_seoul,
   http://www.seouldesignmarket.org/EN/seoul_d_firms/
   seoul_d_firms_end_end.php?id=325&page=3
3. Murphy, R.: An Introduction to AI Robotics. MIT Press, Cambridge (2000)
4. Kim, Y.C., Yoon, W.C., Kwon, H.T., Kwon, G.Y.: Multiple Script-based Task Model and Decision/Interaction Model for Fetch-and-carry Robot. In: The 16th IEEE International Symposium on Robot and Human interactive Communication, pp. 815–820. IEEE Press, Los Alamitos (2007)
5. Smith, E.E., Nolen-Hoeksema, S., Fredrickson, B.L., Loftus, G.R.: Atkinson and Hilgard's Introduction to Psychology. Wadsworth (2002)
6. Fong, T.W., Nourbakhsh, I., Dautenhahn, K.: A survey of socially interactive robots. Robotics and Autonomous Systems 42, 143–166 (2003)
7. Nakajima, H., Morishima, Y., Yamada, R., Brave, S., Maldonado, H., Nass, C., Kawaji, S.: Social intelligence in a human-machine collaboration system: Social responses to agents with mind model and personality. Journal of the Japanese Society for Artificial Intelligence 19(3), 184–296 (2004)
8. Tapus, A., Matarić, M.J.: User Personality Matching with a Hands-Off Robot for Post-stroke Rehabilitation Therapy. In: Siciliano, B., Khatib, O., Groen, F. (eds.) The 10th International Symposium on Experimental Robotics. Springer Tracts in Advanced Robotics, vol. 39, pp. 165–175. Springer, Heidelberg (2008)
9. Cattell, R.B.: The description of personality: Principles and findings in a factor analysis. American Journal of Psychology 58, 69–90 (1945)
10. Eysenck, H.J.: Dimensions of personality: 16, 5 or 3? Criteria for a taxonomic paradigm. Personality and Individual Differences 12, 773–790 (1991)
11. Myers, I.: Introduction to Type. Consulting Psychologists Press, Palo Alto (1998)
12. Costa, P.T., McCrae, R.R.: Age differences in personality structure: A cluster analytic approach. Journal of Gerontology 31, 564–570 (1976)
13. Goldberg, L.R.: The structure of phenotypic personality traits. American Psychologist 48, 26–34 (1993)
14. John, O.P., Srivastava, S.: The Big-Five Trait Taxonomy: History, Measurement, and Theoretical Perspectives. In: Pervin, L.A., John, O.P. (eds.) Handbook of personality: Theory and research. Guilford University Press, New York (1990)
15. Wiggins, J.S.: A psychological taxonomy of trait-descriptive terms: The interpersonal domain. Journal of Personality and Social Psychology 37, 395–412 (1979)
16. Severinson-Eklundh, K., Green, A., Huttenrauch, H.: Social and collaborative aspects of interaction with a service robot. Robotics and Autonomous Systems 42, 223–234 (2003)
17. Edsinger, A., O'Reilly, U.M., Breazeal, C.: Personality through faces for humanoid robots. In: Proceedings 9th IEEE International Workshop on Robot and Human Interactive Communication, pp. 340–345. IEEE Press, Los Alamitos (2000)
18. Iida, F., Tabata, M., Hara, F.: Generating Personality Character in a Face Robot through Interaction with Human. In: Proc. of 7th IEEE International Workshop on Robot and Human, pp. 481–486. IEEE Press, Los Alamitos (1998)

19. Yoon, S., Blumberg, B., Schneider, G.E.: Motivation Driven Learning for Interactive Synthetic Characters. In: Proceedings of the fourth international conference on Autonomous agents, pp. 365–372. ACM, New York (2000)
20. Okuno, H.G., Nakadai, H., Kitano, H.: Realizing Personality in Audio-Visually Triggered Non-verbal Behaviors. In: Proceedings of the 2003 IEEE International Conference on Robotics and Automation, pp. 392–397. IEEE Press, Los Alamitos (2003)
21. Miwa, H., Takanishi, A., Takanobu, H.: Experimental Study on Robot Personality for Humanoid Head Robot. In: Proceedings of the 2001 IEEE/RSJ International Conference on Intelligent Robots and System, pp. 1183–1188. IEEE Press, Los Alamitos (2001)
22. Moshkina, L., Arkin, R.C.: On TAMEing Robots. In: IEEE International Conference on Systems, Man and Cybernetics, pp. 3949–3959. IEEE Press, Los Alamitos (2003)
23. Lee, C.H., Lee, K.H., Kim, J.H.: Evolutionary Multi-Objective Optimization for Generating Artificial Creature's Personality. In: IEEE Congress on Evolutionary Computation, pp. 2450–2455. IEEE Press, Los Alamitos (2007)
24. Woods, S., Dautenhahn, K., Kaouri, C., Boekhorst, R., Koay, K.L.: Is this robot like me? Links between human and robot personality traits. In: 5th IEEE-RAS International Conference on Humanoid Robots, pp. 375–380. IEEE Press, Los Alamitos (2005)
25. Goetz, J., Kiesler, S.: Cooperation with a Robotic Assistant. In: Conference on Human Factors in Computing Systems, pp. 578–579. ACM, New York (2002)
26. Reeves, B., Nass, C.: The Media Equation: How People Treat Computers, Television, and New Media Like Real People and Places. Center for the Study of Language and Inf. (2003)
27. Cañamero, L.D., Fredslund, J.: I Show You How I Like You-Can You Read it in My Face? IEEE Transactions on Systems, Man and Cybernetics, Part A 31, 454–459 (2001)
28. Kalat, J.W., Shiota, M.N.: Emotion. Wadsworth Publishing, Belmont (2006)
29. Ekman, P., Davidson, R.J.: The nature of emotion: Fundamental questions. Oxford University Press, New York (1994)
30. Ortony, A., Turner, T.J.: What's basic about basic emotions? Psychological Review 97, 315–331 (1990)
31. Russell, J.A.: A circumplex model of affect. Journal of personality and social psychology 39, 1161–1178 (1980)
32. Watson, D., Tellegan, A.: Toward a Consensual Structure of Mood. Psychological Bulletin 98, 219–235 (1985)
33. Smith, C.A., Scott, H.S.: A componential approach to the meaning of facial expressions. In: Russell, J.A., Fernández-Dols, J.M. (eds.) The Psychology of Facial Expression, pp. 229–254. Cambridge University Press, New York (1997)
34. Breazeal, C.: Designing Sociable Robots. MIT Press, Cambridge (2002)
35. Schachter, S., Singer, J.: Cognitive, social, and psychological determinants of emotional state. Psychological Review 69, 379–399 (1962)
36. Dutton, D.G., Aron, A.P.: Some evidence for heightened sexual attraction under conditions of high anxiety. Journal of Personality and Social Psychology 30, 510–517 (1976)
37. Go, K., Carroll, J.M.: Scenario-Based Task Analysis. In: Diaper, D., Stanton, N. (eds.) The handbook of task analysis for human-computer interaction, pp. 117–134. LEA, London (2004)
38. Arkin, R.C., Fujita, M., Takagi, T., Hasegawa, R.: An ethological and emotional basis for human–robot interaction. Robotics and Autonomous Systems 42, 191–201 (2003)

Emotions and Messages in Simple Robot Gestures

Jamy Li[1], Mark Chignell[1], Sachi Mizobuchi[2], and Michiaki Yasumura[3]

[1] Interactive Media Lab, Department of Mechanical and Industrial Engineering, University
of Toronto, 5 King's College Road, Toronto, M5S 3G8, Canada
jamy.li@utoronto.ca, chignell@mie.utoronto.ca
[2] Toyota InfoTechnology Center, 6-6-20 Akasaka, Minato-ku, Tokyo 107-0052, Japan
sa-mizobuchi@jp.toyota-itc.com
[3] Interactive Design Lab, Faculty of Environment and Information Studies, Keio University,
5322 Endo, Fujisawa, Kanagawa, Japan
yasumura@sfc.keio.ac.jp

Abstract. Understanding how people interpret robot gestures will aid design of
effective social robots. We examine the generation and interpretation of gestures in a simple social robot capable of head and arm movement using two
studies. In the first study, four participants created gestures with corresponding
messages and emotions based on 12 different scenarios provided to them. The
resulting gestures were then shown in the second study to 12 participants who
judged which emotions and messages were being conveyed. Knowledge
(present or absent) of the motivating scenario (context) for each gesture was
manipulated as an experimental factor. Context was found to assist message
understanding while providing only modest assistance to emotion recognition.
While better than chance, both emotion (22%) and message understanding
(40%) accuracies were relatively low. The results obtained are discussed in
terms of implied guidelines for designing gestures for social robots.

Keywords: Human-Robot Interaction, Gestures, Social Robots, Emotion.

1 Introduction

Modern robots are used not only for performing physical tasks, but also as social
partners—pets (e.g., Sony's AIBO), domestic helpers (iRobot's Roomba), healthcare
assistants (RIKEN Japan's Ri-Man) and emotional companions (PARO and MIT's
Kismet and Leo). Thus traditional human-robot interaction (HRI), such as mechanical
manipulation for teleoperation, is being supplemented with social human-robot interaction. Many authors have subsequently called for better design of robots capable of
engaging in meaningful social interactions with people (e.g., [1], [2]). This new breed
of robots is called socially interactive robots [2] or social robots [1].

The use of gestures has been identified as crucial to the design of such robots [2]. Research on robot gestures is required because: 1) few guidelines exist for the design of
robotic gestures; 2) previous research in HRI that have investigated robotic gestures
covered gesture creation but did not convincingly evaluate people's understanding of
those gestures; and 3) studying gesture understanding is key to improving human-robot
interaction for many robots that have limited ability for speech and facial expression.

J.A. Jacko (Ed.): Human-Computer Interaction, Part II, HCII 2009, LNCS 5611, pp. 331–340, 2009.
© Springer-Verlag Berlin Heidelberg 2009

The goal of this research is to investigate two research questions: First, what types of information do robot gestures convey to people? Second, how do contextual characteristics affect how well this information is conveyed? The studies reported below used a simple robot (Fig. 1) and focused on movements made with the head and arms only. This allowed the properties of gestures to be examined in the absence of the distracting effects of speech and facial expressions.

Fig. 1. Participant manipulating robot bear used in this study

2   Literature Review and Hypotheses

2.1   Gesture in Interpersonal Communication

Gestures are synchronized with speech and therefore closely linked to human cognition and communication [3]. Argyle [4] characterized social communication in terms of dialogues involving successive rounds of coding (gesture creation) and decoding (gesture interpretation). Many authors have identified and classified different roles for gestures during interpersonal communication (e.g., [4, 3]). The following sections review work on communication of emotions and messages, as well as the effect of contextual information on the coding-decoding process.

2.2   Communication of Emotions

Emotions play an important role in human communication and have a strong tendency to be affected by body motion. For example, people can be emotionally engaged when watching dance performances. Previous research suggests that emotions can be identified in videos of body gestures without speech or facial expressions using standard recognition tasks such as selection from a list of emotions [4]. Emotions are also identifiable with point-light animations of arm movement [5], body movement [6] and paired conversations [7], although recognition rates are sometimes low. However, DePaulo and Rosenthal [8] found that using facial expression to judge emotion resulted in much higher accuracy than either body or tone of voice—suggesting that although body gestures in isolation may be used to judge emotion, people tend to rely on facial expression as the key indicator of emotion. It is therefore of interest to ask whether in the absence of an expressive face robots can still convey emotions using simple head and arm gestures.

Relevant research literature includes examples of robots using gestures to show emotions: Mizoguchi et al. [9] employed ballet-like poses of a mobile robot; Scheeff et al. [10] used smooth motions for a teleoperational robot ("Sparky"); and Marui et al. [11] used the same robot bear employed in this study to look at how participants used head and arm movements to convey emotion. However, these earlier studies investigated the creation of emotion-conveying gestures, whereas the research reported here focused on whether people could in fact understand the emotions that robot gestures were supposed to convey. Based on social responses observable with interpersonal gesture communication, the authors hypothesized that subjects would also be sensitive to emotional gestures of robots.

- H1: Gestures viewed in isolation will be able to communicate emotional content.

2.3 Communication of Messages

Experimental evidence supporting the idea that gestures in isolation convey semantic, non-emotional information have shown that some gestures have conventionalized or emblematic meanings ("thumbs up" or "raised fist", for example) [12] and that body movement assists communication through provision of redundant information [13]. When gestures are communicated with speech, people tend to judge meaning based on what they hear rather than what they see [14]—indicating that in both emotion and message communication with other humans, gestures may guide interpretation only in a supporting role. Nevertheless, when gestures are viewed in isolation, viewers are able to identify the correct interpretation but only slightly better than chance [15].

The use of movement of technological entities to convey semantic meaning has been investigated mostly through embodied conversational agents. Cassell [16] described humanoid computer agents such as a virtual real estate agent capable of human-like movements to support conversational speech. However, many of today's robots are not able to employ speech, so it is of interest to investigate whether in lieu of verbal communication, the gestures of such agents are able to convey meaning.

- H2: Gestures viewed in isolation will be able to communicate semantic content.

2.4 Situational Context

Research in social psychology has shown that in human-to-human communication, the perceived meaning of a gesture depends on its social context [3, 4]. A raised hand, for example, has different meanings in a classroom environment versus in a setting of greeting friends. For emotional content, Clarke et al. [7] found that knowledge of social context aided perception of emotion in point-light body movement videos. Similarly, gestures convey semantic meaning more reliably when they are associated with semantic content [15]. Although this is typically done with accompanying speech, we predict that situational context in the form of a narrated scenario will also provide the semantic content needed to improve identification.

- H3: Knowledge of situational context will improve understanding of both emotional and semantic content in gestures.

3 Methodology

The methodology employed was based on a pair of experiments: a first study in which participants created a corpus of robot gestures and a second in which a different set of participants viewed those gestures.

3.1 Study 1

3.1.1 Apparatus
The robot used for this study had the form and size of a traditional teddy bear. It was developed at the University of Tokyo as an IP phone system called "Robot-PHONE" [17]. The bear had six motors (two in the head and two in each of the arms) that allowed it to move its head and each of its arms both vertically and laterally. It could perform movements such as nodding its head and waving its arms, but it was unable to move its torso and did not have elbows. Its movements were recorded by a Sony Vaio laptop PC with Windows XP, connected via USB, for later playback.

3.1.2 Participants
Four participants (two female, two male) ranging in age from 21 to 35 (mean 25) were recruited from within the Keio University community. The study was conducted at the Shonan Fujisawa Campus located near Tokyo. The participants did not have previous experience with robotic bears. Participants had relatively neutral attitudes toward the social influence of robots (M=15.4, SD=5.4, where 15 was the midpoint) and toward emotional interaction with robots (M=7.3, SD=4.5, where 9 was the midpoint) according to the Negative Attitudes toward Robots Scale [18].

3.1.3 Procedure
In the first study, four participants created a gesture for each of 12 scenarios presented as one or two sentences of text (Table 1). A translated excerpt of the Japanese instructions is as follows: "First, listen to the scenario. Pretend that you are in this scenario. Then, pretend that you see the bear robot. Create a gesture that the bear will make. The gesture must try to convey a message and/or emotion to you."

Participants were given time to practice the gesture before recording it, to review the gesture created and to re-record if they were dissatisfied with their result. They were asked to write the message and/or emotion that they wanted to be conveyed.

3.2 Study 2

3.2.1 Apparatus
This experiment was conducted on a Sony Vaio laptop PC with Windows XP. Participants viewed robot gestures as animations on the RobotPHONE software interface and as Quicktime videos of the bear robot performing each gesture (Fig. 3).

Table 1. List of Scenarios

1. You have just returned home.
2. You are in the living room watching TV. You laugh at a funny show.
3. You reach your hand to the bear to pick it up.
4. You pat the bear's head.
5. You have been working at your desk for a long time. You yawn.
6. You take your clothes off.
7. You start eating dinner.
8. You say "goodnight" to the bear.
9. You start crying.
10. You start playing music on your computer.
11. You are sitting at your computer and working.
12. You start drinking a beer.

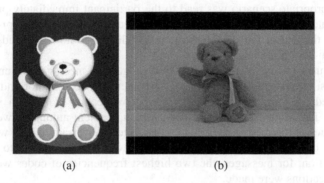

(a)   (b)

Fig. 3. Participants viewed each gesture either under as a software animation (a) or as a video of the bear robot (b)

3.2.2 Participants

Twelve participants (three female, nine male) ranging in age from 18 to 60 (mean 26) were recruited from the Keio University population, as in Study 1. All Study 1 participants were excluded from participating in Study 2. Participant had moderate attitudes towards both social influence of robots (M=15.4, SD=5.2) and emotional interaction with robots (M=8.44, SD=2.39).

3.2.3 Procedure

In the second study, participants were shown each of the 48 gestures created in Study 1 and attempted to identify the message and emotion being conveyed by each gesture from lists of possible messages and emotions. These lists were coded by two investigators and one translator from the written descriptions given by the gesture authors (i.e. Study 1 participants). It is important to note that while the scenarios provided influenced message creation, they did not necessarily define those messages: for example, given the scenario "You start drinking a beer", different participants generated a diverse set of messages such as: "Don't do that!", "Good job" and "That looks delicious." Participants were asked to rate lifelikeness of the gesture, how much they liked the gesture and their degree of confidence in the correctness of the emotion and message that they had assigned to the gesture. While making judgments they were allowed to replay gestures as often as desired.

The study was structured as a fully within-subjects experiment with two factors: medium and context. Both factors were balanced in a within-subjects design across the study with the ordering of experimental conditions being randomized for each participant. For medium, two conditions were used: in one condition an animated version of the gesture was shown as a software avatar ("animation") and in the other a video of the bear robot was shown ("robot") (shown in Fig. 3). This factor was included to test whether results would be mediated by the medium in which the gesture was displayed—i.e. would results differ between a 3D animation (similar to an embodied conversational agent) versus a 3D video of an actual robot. We used video recordings instead of a co-present robot because earlier studies of human gestures typically showed viewers videos of gestures rather than co-present actors, and to ensure that all participants saw exactly the same gestures. Context had two conditions: either the appropriate scenario was read to the participant immediately preceding the gesture ("context"), or else information about the scenario was not provided ("no context"). At the end of the session, participants discussed how they judged the gestures in a semi-structured interview.

Two measures of successful transmission of gesture message and emotion were used. The first represented the amount of agreement between author and viewer and was calculated by comparing the author's written meaning with each viewer's selected codes. The second represented consensus agreement among viewers (referred to as "inter-viewer" agreement). For emotions, inter-viewer agreement was based on the frequency of the most selected code among viewers without regard to the author's intended emotion; for messages, the two highest frequencies of codes were used because two selections were made.

Table 2. List of Messages and Emotions

Messages		Emotions
I want to ask a question	I want more	I am happy
Good job	Please touch me	I am interested
Welcome home	Let's play	I love you
Take care of me	You seem tired	I am confused
What happened?	No	I am embarrassed
I'm bored	Don't do that	I am sad
It's stupid	That looks delicious	I am feeling awkward
I don't understand	It's okay	I am angry
I want to shake hands	Good night	I am surprised
I want to be hugged	I'm hungry	
Thank you		

4 Results

Hypotheses 1 and 2 were supported. Gestures viewed in isolation carried both emotional and semantic information. The ability of people to detect intended emotions was assessed in the following way. First the 432 emotion judgments were scored as either correct or incorrect based on whether or not the selected emotion agreed with the emotion that had been attached to the gesture by its author (trials without a designated emotion were excluded). Next a binomial test was used to see if the observed proportion of correct responses (22%) was greater than the one in ten (10%) correct responses that would have been expected by chance alone. Using the Z approximation to the binomial test as implemented in SPSS, the proportion of correct emotion responses was found to be significantly greater than chance (p<.001) although fully 78% of the emotions were not judged correctly. Thus our expectation that the emotions associated with gestures would be judged relatively poorly, but still better than chance, was confirmed.

Of the 432 message judgments 176 (40%) were correct (i.e., agreed with the author's intended message). As assessed by a binomial test, this proportion was significantly greater (p<.001) than the two out of 21 (9.5%) correct responses that would have been expected by chance alone (since there were 21 message options in total and participants were asked to choose two of them per gesture).

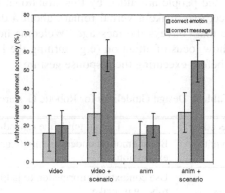

Fig. 4. Emotion and message agreement accuracy versus experimental condition. Contextual information improves accuracy. Error bars show 95% confidence intervals.

Hypothesis 3 was supported. Two-way repeated measures analysis of variance (ANOVA) was conducted with medium and context as within-subjects factors. Situational context improved both message and emotion identification accuracy. Context had a significant main effect on author-viewer message agreement, $F(1,11) = 93.849$, $p < .001$, and a borderline significant main effect on author-viewer emotion agreement, $F(1,11) = 4.46$, $p = .058$. Fig. 4 shows how the experimental conditions affected the accuracy of identifying the correct message and emotion. For messages (dark bars), participants were able to identify the gesture author's intended message more accurately when situational context was provided (M = 56.5%, SD = 3.85%) versus when it was excluded (M = 20.1%, SD = 1.31%) in both media. Similarly for emotions (light bars), context improved emotion recognition (M = 26.7%, SD = 3.61%) compared with no context (M = 15.2%, SD = 3.48%). There was no main or interaction effect of medium. No effect of context was found on participant ratings of identification confidence, although in post-study interviews subjects reported judging gestures to be easier when the scenario was provided.

5 Discussion and Design Guidelines

While this research is a first step in the systematic study of the interpretation of simple robot gestures and should be seen as exploratory, three tentative design guidelines can be inferred (Table 4). First, there is a need to boost emotion understanding when interacting with social robots. This can be done by adding facial expressiveness, limiting the number of possible emotions to be considered or including statements of emotion either in words or non-speech sounds (e.g., chuckling for happiness). Second, social robots should employ contextual information when deciding which gestures to express to users, since users will be using similar information in decoding a robot's actions. As an example, a robotic pet may consider the time of day, lighting conditions, movement in its environment and the number of people around it to decide whether it should employ gestures indicative of excitement or boredom. A third design guideline is that the context in which gestures of social robots occur should be made clear to users, since people are aided by this situational knowledge. A robotic companion, for instance, may make a verbal remark about a door being opened and then execute a gesture that conveys the message "Welcome home." Alternatively, a robot can gesture to show locus of attention (e.g., turning the head or pointing at the agent it is reacting to) before executing the response gesture.

Table 4. Design Guidelines for Robotic Gestures

Experimental result (decoding)	Design guideline (encoding/decoding)
Gestures in isolation do not convey emotion well	Boost emotion understanding (e.g. by including vocal expression)
Context improves gesture understanding	Use contextual information to help decide what gestures robot will make
	Ensure context in which robot is gesturing is made known to user

6 Scope and Limitations

One of the challenges in carrying out research on human-robot interaction is that many possible types of robots can be studied. This research uses a relatively simple robot to establish a baseline or lower bound for the types of gestural interpretation that are possible and to facilitate easy manipulation that would allow untrained individuals to create gestures, thus avoiding the need to program robotic movement. While our results are directly applicable only to social robots that are limited to arm and head movements such as the one used in our studies, we expect that the gesture design guidelines proposed above may be generalizable to more sophisticated robots. However, this expectation will need to be tested through future inquiry into how gestures of more complex robots are interpreted.

A further limitation of this study is that we used only four authors who had no special training in developing gestures for robots. Thus our results are likely to provide a low estimate of the type of interpretability achievable with a simple social robot. It is possible that the people we asked to create gestures were not very skilful and that "experts" could in fact create much more interpretable and lifelike gestures. However, trained individuals were not used to create gestures in this study because it was unclear what expertise was needed (e.g., psychology, puppetry, drama). Further, using amateurs reflects current practice whereby robot gestures are created by engineers without formal experience in gesture creation and reflects the intended use of the RobotPHONE (where lay users gesture to each other via the robot).

7 Conclusion

This paper explored the novel area of gesture understanding in human-robot interaction. The results from this study demonstrate that even gestures of a simple social robot capable of arm and head movement only can convey emotional and semantic meaning. How well viewers are able to decode a gesture's intended meaning is found to be improved with knowledge of the gesture's situational context.

The issue of how to create gestures—and who should create them—is particularly important for designers of social robots. Since puppeteers have extensive experience in creating expressive gestures with movements of dolls that typically have little if any variability in facial expression, it is recommended that future research examine whether or not puppetry experience is beneficial in creating effective robot gestures.

While Hollywood visions of human-like androids may come to pass at some point in the future, it seems likely that social robots will continue to have limited capabilities for the foreseeable future, making it important that simple gestures be expressive and meaningful. The results of this research provide reason to believe that, in the absence of full artificial intelligence, it should still be possible for designers to use gestures as interface elements to support interacting naturally with robots.

Acknowledgements. We thank Ryo Yoshida for valuable research and translation assistance in carrying out the studies, the iDL lab, our experimental participants and JSPS and NSERC for funding.

References

1. Breazeal, C.: Toward sociable robots. Robotics and Autonomous Systems 42, 167–175 (2003)
2. Fong, T., Nourbakhsh, I., Dautenhahn, K.: A survey of socially interactive robots. Robotics and Autonomous Systems 42, 143–166 (2003)
3. McNeill, D.: Gesture and Thought. The University of Chicago Press, Chicago (2005)
4. Argyle, M.: The Psychology of Interpersonal Behaviour, 5th edn. Penguin Books, London (1994)
5. Montepare, J., Koff, E., Zaitchik, D., Albert, M.: The use of body movements and gestures as cues to emotions in younger and older adults. Journal of Nonverbal Behavior 23(2), 133–152 (1999)
6. Pollick, F.E., Paterson, H.M., Bruderlin, A., Sanford, A.J.: Perceiving affect from arm movement. Cognition 82, B51–B61 (2001)

7. Clarke, T.J., Bradshaw, M.F., Field, D.T., Hampson, S.E., Rose, D.: The perception of emotion from body movement in point-light displays of interpersonal dialogue. Perception 34(10), 1171–1180 (2005)
8. DePaulo, B.M., Rosenthal, R.: The structure of nonverbal decoding skills. Journal of Personality 47(3), 506–517 (1979)
9. Mizoguchi, H., Sato, T., Takagi, K., Nakao, M., Hatamura, Y.: Realization of expressive mobile robot. In: Proceedings of the International Conference on Robotics and Automation, pp. 581–586 (1997)
10. Scheeff, M., Pinto, J., Rahardja, K., Snibbe, S., Tow, R.: Experiences with Sparky: A social robot. In: Proceedings of the Workshop on Interactive Robot Entertainment (2000)
11. Marui, N., Matsumaru, T.: Emotional motion of human-friendly robot: Emotional expression with bodily movement as the motion media. Nippon Robotto Gakkai Gakujutsu Koenkai Yokoshu 23, 2–12 (2005)
12. Sidner, C., Lee, C., Morency, L.-P., Forlines, C.: The effect of head-nod recognition in human-robot conversation. In: Proc. of ACM SIGCHI/SIGART conference on HRI, pp. 290–296 (2006)
13. Bartneck, C.: eMuu—an emotional embodied character for the ambient intelligent home. Ph.D. dissertation, Technical University Eindhoven, The Netherlands (2002)
14. Krauss, R.M., Morrel-Samuels, P., Colasante, C.: Do conversational hand gestures communicate? Journal of Personality and Social Psychology 61, 743–754 (1991)
15. Krauss, R., Chen, Y., Chawla, P.: Advances in experimental social psychology. In: Zanna, M.P. (ed.) Advances in Experimental Social Psychology, vol. 28, pp. 389–450. Academic Press, San Diego (1996)
16. Cassell, J.: Embodied conversational interface agents. Commun. ACM 43(4), 70–78 (2000)
17. Sekiguchi, D., Inami, M., Tachi, S.: RobotPHONE: RUI for interpersonal communication. In: CHI 2001: Extended Abstracts, pp. 277–278 (2001)
18. Nomura, T., Suzuki, T., Kanda, T., Kato, K.: Altered attitudes of people toward robots: Investigation through the negative attitudes toward robots scale. In: Proc. AAAI 2006 Workshop on Human Implications of Human-Robot Interaction, pp. 29–35 (2006)

Life with a Robot Companion:
Video Analysis of 16-Days of Interaction with a Home Robot in a "Ubiquitous Home" Environment

Naoko Matsumoto[1,*], Hirotada Ueda[2], Tatsuya Yamazaki[3], and Hajime Murai[4]

[1] Graduate School of Information Science and Electrical Engineering, Kyushu University, 744 Motooka Nishi-ku Fukuoka 819-0395 Japan
matsun@valdes.titech.ac.jp
[2] Faculty of Computer Science and Engineering, Kyoto Sangyo University, Motoyama, Kamigamo, Kita-Ku, Kyoto-City 603-8555 Japan
ueda@cc.kyoto-su.ac.jp
[3] Universal City Group, National Institute of Information and Communications Technology, 3-5 Hikaridai, Seika-cho, Soraku-gun, Kyoto 619-0289 Japan
yamazaki@nict.go.jp
[4] Department of Value and Decision Science, Tokyo Institute of Technology, 2-12-1 Ookayama Meguro-ku Tokyo 152-8552 Japan
h_murai@valdes.titech.ac.jp

Abstract. This paper examines human-robot interaction within a home environment over the course of a 16 day-long experiment. Its purpose is to describe the human cognitive activities involving a symbiotic robot with dialogue interface within domestic settings. The participants were a couple in their 60's. Analysis of video data indicates that (a) the participants continuously used the robot's dialogue interface, and persevered within this despite the performance of the voice recognition system (b) the participants checked out the robot's function as a tool and gradually came to regard the robot as a companion, (c) fixed instruction expressions increased the use of the dialogue interface for the light controls, while the participants employed both the dialogue interface and the remote controller for the TV and light controls.

Keywords: home robot, ubiquitous environment, dialogue interface, life experiment, video analysis.

1 Introduction

In the near future, daily human-robot interaction in assigning tasks and enjoying conversations will be common within domestic settings. What kind of phenomena might we expect within homes from long-term human-robot interactions?

Several studies have observed long-term interactions between humans and robots. For instance, the seal-like robot Paro was introduced into a care house for one month, and was found to increase the social interactions of the aged people and to have beneficial effects on their health [1]. The humanoid robot Robovie (which speaks

---

* Affiliated with Kyushu University until December, 2008.

J.A. Jacko (Ed.): Human-Computer Interaction, Part II, HCII 2009, LNCS 5611, pp. 341–350, 2009.
© Springer-Verlag Berlin Heidelberg 2009

English) was immersed in a Japanese elementary school for 18 days and the English abilities of the students improved [2]. Similarly, the social robot Qrio was immersed in a kindergarten for five months, with results suggesting that toddlers treated the robot as a peer rather than a toy at the end of the period [3]. Although these three studies provide minute descriptions concerning the quality of long-term human-robot interactions, the activation times for the robots were limited to a numbers of hours each day / week, because those studies were conducted at public institutions. It is difficult to observe human attitudes toward a robot that is activated for 24 hours each day, and, because of privacy issues, it is even more difficult to observe the "daily life" human-robot interactions within domestic settings.

The present project seeks to analyze daily human-robot interactions within a domestic setting. We analyze the conversation log recorded by the robot's voice recognition system. During the early stage of the study, the participants interacted with the robot as a tool for some tasks, but they gradually became more accustomed to the home robot [4]. In an interview, the participants expressed attachment emotions towards the robot; "I wanted to go home early because the robot is there" [5]. Such comments suggest that the participants came to simultaneously regard the robot both as a tool and as a companion. We propose the concept of "companion model[1]" for the psychological behaviors toward symbiotic robots [4].

However, there are errors with voice recognition systems[2]. Accordingly, in the present paper, we analyze video data and aim to describe the human cognitive activities involved when using the dialogue interface of home robots. The dialogue interface is easy for everyone to operate. In the future, dialogue interfaces will be effective and realistic interfaces for home robots. Investigating this kind of emerging phenomenon can provide interesting insights into how human communicate with symbiotic robots within real home environment, notwithstanding the case study nature of the present study with a limited number of participants.

2   The Design of the Experiment

This section explains about the "Ubiquitous Home" environment, the home robot, the participants, and the instructions provided.

2.1 Ubiquitous Home and the Home Robot Phyno

As a so-called home of the future, the Ubiquitous Home has been built by the National Institute of Information and Communications Technology in Japan. The layout of the Ubiquitous Home is 2LDK (2 rooms in addition to a living-dining room and a kitchen) (Figure 1).

---

[1] With the passage of time, the participants construct a psychological model concerning the functions and abilities of the symbiotic robot (cf. device model), while simultaneously seeking a psychological role for the robot on the assumption of a mind within the robot (cf. theory of mind). Thus, the participants regarded the robot both as a tool and, at the same time, as a companion (companion model).

[2] According to a previous study [5], the robot system was able to achieve a 60% recognition rate for participant utterances, when the participants talked to the robot.

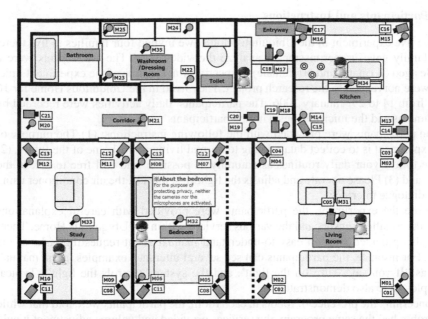

Fig. 1. The layout of the Ubiquitous Home and positions of the installed cameras, microphones, and robots

All the cameras and microphones are located in the ceiling. In order to protect the participants' privacy, the cameras and microphones on the bedroom and bathroom were not activated.

▬ Ceiling camera   🔍 Ceiling microphone   🐧 Phyno robot

The purpose of the house is to provide a testing ground for the ubiquitous domestic environment [6]. In order to collect information and to present various forms of multimedia content to residents, there are many networked cameras, microphones, displays, speakers, RFID system, and some small visible robots in the Ubiquitous Home. Residents are totally free to come and go as they please 24 hours a day, undisturbed by the presence of researchers, and so can live as if they were living in a normal apartment.

The robot in the Ubiquitous Home is called "Phyno" (Figure 2). Phyno is 25cm in height and does not walk. In the Ubiquitous Home, there is a total of five robots in each room. All the robots are equipped with voice recognition and synthesis systems, and an infant-like voice. The robots were activated for 24 hours each day, and provide residents with multiple services, such as TV

Fig. 1. Phyno

program recommendations (living room), providing recipes (living room and kitchen), and a reminder service (entrance). The robot's dialogue strategy is to repeat any words uttered by a user that are not part of its known vocabulary (e.g. "What is abc? ("abc" is the repeated part)). This strategy provides the user with feedback about the limitations with the vocabulary database, which helps them to understand the robot's dialogue function [7].

2.2 Participants and Instructions

For the live experiment in the Ubiquitous Home, we invited four families to live there. One family gave us permission to analyze the video data. The participants were a couple aged 64 (male) and 60 (female), respectively at the time of the experiment time, who were not related to the research project. They lived in the Ubiquitous Home for 16 days, from 14 to 29, January 2006. The participants' daily activities were recorded by the cameras and the microphones with the participants' consent.

The participants were provided with the following instructions: (1) The purpose of this experiment is to collect data relating to normal living in the home of the future, (2) Please follow your daily routines as naturally as possible, and feel free to talk to the robot, and (3) Please operate and adjusts the lightings, the TV, the air conditioner using robot dialogue interface.

Before the experiment, the participants were provided with careful explanations about the installed sensors and the various services within the Ubiquitous Home. There were also provided with an easy-to-understand manual about requesting tasks of the robot. For instance, the participants can see several utterance examples in the manual, such as "If you say 'Turn on the light', and the system controls the light". Typical examples were also demonstrated.

Concerning the presence of robots in each room, the participants were told that while each robot had the same program, the services provided and volume adjustment would vary depending on the room. In order to observe the participants' cognitions towards the five robots, no further information about the robots was provided.

3 Video Analysis

The experimental data analyzed is available to the public [8].

3.1 Video Data

Daily activities in the Ubiquitous Home were recorded by a total of 17 ceiling cameras with the motion JPEG format of 5 frames per sec. At the same time, a total of 25 ceiling microphones recorded the sounds with the MP3 format of 64kbps.

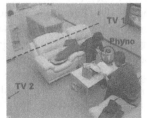

In total, the image and voice data consisted of approximately 1,671 GB. In this study, we analyze data recorded in the living room, selecting one ceiling camera (C02 in Figure 1) and one microphone (M31 in Figure 1). After extracting sections where the participants were in the living room (Figure 3), the video data was produced to synchronize the image data with the

Fig. 3. The experimental setting in the living room. The living room is extends from the dashed line.

voice data. The video data consists of approximately 37.2 GB. All the utterances by the participants and the robot within the living room were transcribed for the 16-day period.

3.2 Lengths of Stays in the Living Room

Table 1. Lengths of stays in the living room and other information

Day		h:m:s	visitors
1	Sat	10:39:28	daytime
2	Sun	9:57:00	
3	Mon	16:17:50	daytime
4	Tue	7:12:40	
5	Wed	18:59:15	daytime
6	Thu	14:27:21	daytime
7	Fri	13:37:32	
8	Sat	7:01:12	evening
9	Sun	9:44:47	
10	Mon	15:49:40	daytime
11	Tue	9:16:14	
12	Wed	17:10:55	daytime
13	Thu	9:46:43	evening
14	Fri	13:14:18	
15	Sat	7:46:43	daytime
16	Sun	6:01:05	daytime
Total		187:02:43	

* System down on the 9th day.

The male (husband) went to work on the weekdays and the female (wife) spent a great deal of time in the Ubiquitous Home. The total time that the participants spent in the living room was 187:2:43 (h:m:s) (average; 11:41:25 / day). Table 1 shows the lengths of stays in the living room and visitor information. During the daytime, the wife's friends visited and, in the evenings, sometimes their family (their son's family) visited the house. We did not include visitor utterances in the analysis. The system was down on the ninth day.

4 Analysis Results and Discussion

Before the experiment, the participants were not provided with explanation concerning all vocabularies that the robot can recognize, so they had to discover which vocabulary items could be recognized by the robot during the experimental period. The dialogue interface in the home robot substitutes for a traditional TV remote control and light switch, and also provides new services. The instruction provided to the participants asked them to use the robot's dialogue interface whenever the system was running, but it is interesting to examine whether the participants would diligently follow the request to keep using the robot's dialogue interface that would sometimes make recognition errors in a real domestic environment.

This paper focuses on examining (a) human cognitions when probing the new functions of the home robot, (b) human efforts with the dialogue interface, and making (c) a comparison in terms of usage between the dialogue interface and the remote controller.

4.1 Exploring the Robot's Functions

In order to examine how the participants explored the new functions of the robot and the new words that the robot could recognize, we exclude from the analysis situations where the participants conformed to the instructions provided. The analysis utilized the voice data obtained from the microphone in the living room.

Exploration Examples. For example, when the system failed to recognize the utterance "please turn down the volume", the participants paraphrased this saying "please make the sound smaller". Similarly, when the robot was printing out a retrieved recipe, it failed to recognized the utterance "please copy it", so the participant then tried other words, such as "printer", "print" and "please print". As an example of applying instructions from the manual, the phrase of "please turn off the air conditioner" was paraphrased as "please turn off the stove". When the participants requested the robot to retrieve a recipe, they tried an applied dialogue of "please teach dinner". In another case, they paraphrased "arigato" (thank you in Japanese) as "thank you". The participants also tried new words. For example, during recipe retrieving, they asked the robot "Is there another (recipe)?". While in another situation, the participants tested the robot's recognizable vocabulary, by asking "How's your feeling? ... 'feeling', can you understand the word 'feeling'?". Through trial and error, the participants identified some aspects of the robot's actions; for instance, they discovered the robot is equipped with a repeat function, and that that an apology is the robot response to loud sounds.

Changes in the Quantity of Function Explorations over Time. In total, there were 76 explorations over the 16-day experimental period. Figure 4 presents the frequencies of these explorations as a bar graph. The frequencies of such explorations gradually decrease. During the first day, the participants wanted to communicate in the manner shown in the provided manual, but the voice recognition system did not function well. Accordingly, the participants tried some new words that were not in the manual, and also varied their pronunciations.

Changes in the Quality of Function Explorations over Time. Explorations for the robot's tasks employing the dialogue interface can be categorized into two types: (a) Explorations of task performance functions (including the voice recognition function) and (b) Explorations of communication functions (such as greetings and responses). Figure 4 presents the frequency changes as a line graph. Although the frequency of task requests was high during the first day, these gradually decreased. Having achieved a certain level of understanding about the robot's communication vocabulary, there were no communication explorations during the period from Day 13 to Day 16. While the participants initially explored the robot's functions as a device, they gradually came to explore its functions as a companion. This shift indicates their construction of the "companion model" [4].

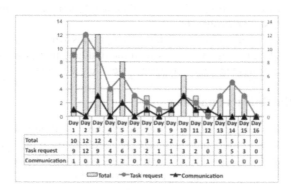

Fig. 4. Explorations Frequencies for Robot Functions Employing the Dialogue Interface

4.2 Efforts in Using the Robot's Dialogue Interface

In this section, we discuss the participants' efforts to utilize the robot's dialogue interface. Although the participants are instructed to use the dialogue interface, most attempts at voice recognition by the system were not successful straightaway. Recognition errors were due not only be daily noises, but also to the participants' lack of experience with voice recognition systems. It has been reported that participants learn to use appropriate utterances over time when employing voice recognition systems [5]. How did the participants persevere with the voice recognition system?

The analysis results identified 774 attempts (48.375 trials / day in Table 2) employing the dialogue interface. Figure 5 presents the numbers of attempts until the voice operation was successful, as well as the numbers of attempts until the participants gave up during the 16-day period. Apart from Day 8, the participants would make at least four attempts irrespective of whether they were successful or gave up. Through the 16 days of the experiment, the participants continuously and eagerly persevered in using the dialogue interface.

There are two reasons why the participants persevered in their efforts to employ the dialogue interface. One reason is the instruction provided to the participants to use the robot dialogue interface. Another reason seems to be an attachment emotion towards the robot. In an interview with the participants [5], they would comment about the state of the robot after using the dialogue interfacing, saying things such as "it is more fun to use the robot than the remote controller" and "the robot's voice is like a little kid's and it is so cute". Moreover, such positive evaluations concerning the robot's reactions after voice operation could be observed in the video data.

Table 2. Frequencies of Task Request Attempts Employing the Dialogue Interface

Day	1	2	3	4	5	6	7	8	9	10	11	12	13	14	15	16	Total
Trial	37	54	77	32	66	71	33	19	16	77	54	55	58	35	42	48	774

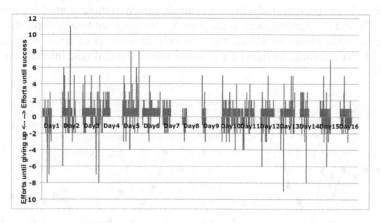

Fig. 5. Perseverance in Efforts to Attempt Task Requests Using the Dialogue Interface: Until Successful versus Until Giving-up

4.3 Usage Comparison with Remote Controller

The Ubiquitous Home has two types of interfaces for the lighting, the TV, and the air conditioner control; namely, the dialogue interface and a remote controller. In the video analysis, the remote controllers for the lighting and the TV were clearly visible. In the present analysis, voice data obtained from the living room was analyzed.

Figure 6 and Table 3 present the usage frequencies for both the dialogue interface and the remote controls for lighting and the TV. In their daily lives, people do not adjust the lighting so frequently, and there are relatively limited ways in which such instruction can be expressed, such as "turn on / off the light". We can assume that the participants tended to use the dialogue interface because it has appropriate instruction expressions.

On the other hand, the frequencies for using the dialogue interface of TV were high on Days 1 and 2. However, usage of the remote controls was much higher from Day 3 to Day 7, and from Day 8, the frequencies for using the dialogue interface and for using the remote controls were fairly similar (Figure 6). The remote controller was used when the participants were flicking through the channels for a program they wanted to watch. There were no set instruction expressions for controlling the TV. For example, various expressions could operating the TV, such as "turn the TV on", "I want to watch TV", and "yesterday's TV, please". There was also much variety in terms of selection expressions, such as "change the program", "I want to watch channel 1", "change to program A", and "Please show me the recommended comedy". This variety of expressions was a factor reducing the robot's voice recognition rates, and, in turn, might have had a negative impact on the participants' motivations to use the dialogue interface.

According to Matsumoto et al. [9], there are two points that encourage users to persevere in their efforts to use dialogue communication with the robot through the dialogue interface in requesting tasks (e.g., TV control, light control); (a) the existence of alternative tools, such as the remote control, and (b) the quantity of the instruction expressions. In the present study, there was an alternative remote control (or switch) for both the TV and the lighting, and so the participants were not totally dependent on the dialogue interface alone. However, the relatively limited set of fixed instruction expressions for controlling the lights did promote use of the dialogue interface to operate the lights.

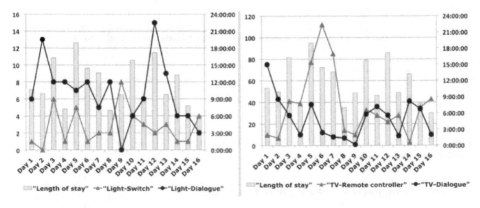

Fig. 6. Usage comparison for the dialogue interface and the remote controller for lighting (upper) and TV (lower) control

Table 3. Usage Frequencies for the dialogue interface and the remote control

Day		1	2	3	4	5	6	7	8	9	10	11	12	13	14	15	16	Total
Light	D	6	13	8	8	7	8	5	8	0	4	6	15	9	4	4	2	107
	R	1	0	6	1	5	1	2	2	8	4	3	2	3	1	1	4	44
TV	D	75	43	28	10	38	12	8	7	1	29	36	28	9	41	34	10	409
	R	10	7	41	39	77	112	85	14	10	33	28	22	28	3	35	43	587
Total		97	85	119	71	160	176	106	36	19	89	73	68	80	49	74	60	1147

*D: dialogue interface, R: remote control.

5 Conclusion

This paper has focused on the dialogue communications between humans and robots during a 16-day real-life experiment within the "Ubiquitous Home" environment. The participants were a couple of their 60's. Video analysis results indicate that the participants made continuous use of the robot's dialogue interface over the whole 16-day period. They patiently persevered in attempting to use the robot's voice recognition system and restated task requests many times.

During the early stage of the experiment, the participants explored the robot's functions, testing to see what words the robot could recognize. With the passage of time, the participants gradually began to regard the robot more as a companion and sought to use words that were more conversational in nature with the robot.

In the experiment, there was an alternative to controlling the TV and the lighting through the dialogue interface in the form of remote controllers for the TV and the lights. In terms of operating the TV and lights, the participants made use of both methods. However, the more limited range of set instruction expressions seems to have increased the use of the dialogue interface when adjusting the lighting.

Although the present study only analyzes the data for two participants (the one couple), the study is significant in that it utilizes and analyzes data obtained from an almost natural living environment. Thus, the results can provide interesting insights concerning how to study actually humans living with dialogue robots.

Acknowledgement

We would like to thank Dr. Terry Joyce for his helpful comments. This work was supported by "The Kyushu University Research Superstar Program (SSP)", based on a budget from Kyushu University allocated under the President's initiative.

References

1. Wada, K., Shibata, T.: Living with Seal Robots- Its sociopsychological and Physiological Influences on the Elderly at a Care House. IEEE Transactions on Robotics 23(5), 972–980 (2007)

2. Kanda, T., Hirano, T., Eaton, D., Ishiguro, H.: A Practical Experiment with Interactive Humanoid Robots in a Human Society. In: Third IEEE International Conference on Humanoid Robots (Humanoids 2003) (2003)
3. Tanaka, F., Cicourel, A., Movellan, J.R.: Socialization between Toddlers and Robots at an Early Childhood Education Center. Proceedings of the National Academy of Sciences of the USA (PNAS) 104(46), 17954–17958 (2007)
4. Matsumoto, N., Ueda, H., Yamazaki, T., Tokosumi, A.: A Companion Model for Symbiotic Robots: A Life Experiment in the Home Ubiquitous Environment. Journal of Human Interface Society 10(1), 21–36 (2008) (in Japanese)
5. Matsumoto, N., Ueda, H., Yamazaki, T., Tokosumi, A.: The cognitive characteristics of communication with artificial agents. In: Joint Third International Conference on Soft Computing and Intelligent Systems and Seventh International Symposium on Advanced Intelligent Systems (SCIS & ISIS 2006), pp. 1269–1273 (2006) CD-ROM
6. Yamazaki, T.: Human Action Detection and Context-aware Service Implementation in a Real-life Living Space Test Bed. In: Second International IEEE/Create-Net Conference on Testbeds and Research Infrastructures for the Development of Networks and Communities (TridentCom 2006) (2006)
7. Kobayashi, K., Ueda, H., Satake, J., Chikama, M., Kidode, M.: Real-life Experiments of the Dialogue Robot in the Home Ubiquitous Environment and an Evaluation of the Dialogue Strategy. Transactions of Information Processing Society of Japan 48(5), 2023–2031 (2007)
8. OpenWare Page regarding the Ubiquitous Home of NICT,
   http://univ.nict.go.jp/past_pj/disco/index-e.html
   (retrieved December 4, 2008)
9. Matsumoto, N., Ueda, H., Yamazaki, T.: Efforts for a Dialogue Interface Communication with a Symbiotic Home Robot. In: Proceedings of the Twenty-third Fuzzy System Symposium, pp. 567–571 (2008) (in Japanese)

Impression Evaluation of a Conversational Robot Playing RAKUGO

Akihiro Ogino, Noritaka Moriya, Park Seung-Joon, and Hirotada Ueda

Kyoto Sangyo University,
Motoyama, Kamigamo, Kita-Ku, Kyoto-City, Japan
{ogino,moriya,parksj41,ueda}@cc.kyoto- su.ac.jp

Abstract. The purpose of this paper is to detect a comfortable strength and timing of gestures of the robot for people. This paper describes the evaluation of individual impressions concerning RAKUGO of the traditional Japanese comic storytelling that is performed by a conversational robot. This paper shows that the gestures of the robot like professional actor of RAKUGO give smart and mature impressions to people than exaggerated gestures. In order to detect a tendency of impression based on individual personality, this paper also describes a relation between the individual impression to the gesture of the robot and Transactional Analysis that is one of psychology. We detect that there is a correlation between their impression to the gesture and their personality.

1 Introduction

Recently, a conversational robot has been attempted to use for an interface of an intelligent system to help people to search information or to understand emotion and feeling of them [1][2][3].

The conversational robot affects on a state of people's mind when it has been conversation with them. For example, a nod of robot causes the pull-in effect between voices of people and physical actions of the robot. People that have lived together with a robot for 2 weeks get to like the robot. The people get to notice the little difference of the robot action and have emotional reaction to the robot [4]. An avid action of the robot raises a tolerance level of people when the robot failed to recognize the voice of them. A direction in a robot's head and a timing to move it affect smoothness of conversation between a person and a robot [5]. We think that a conversational robot should have a skill to talk and listen to people and have ability to encourage and calm people. In order to make the robot, we have to clarify how a robot gets confidence as a partner from people.

In order to detect a comfortable strength and timing of gestures of the robot for people, this paper describes an evaluation about individual impressions concerning RAKUGO in which a conversational robot performs. The RAKUGO is the traditional Japanese art of comic storytelling that features humor everyone can enjoy. The robot performed two kinds of RAKUGO, which are different timings and gestures with almost same words, to 31 examinees. In order to detect a tendency of impression based on individual personality, this paper also describes a relation between an individual impression to the gesture of the robot and a personality based on Transactional Analysis that is one of psychology [6].

J.A. Jacko (Ed.): Human-Computer Interaction, Part II, HCII 2009, LNCS 5611, pp. 351–360, 2009.
© Springer-Verlag Berlin Heidelberg 2009

2 Experiment

A robot that is used for this experiment is Phyno shown in Fig.1. The Phyno is an interactive conversational robot that is 25 cm of length and does not move but has 3 degree of freedom in his head, 1 degree of freedom in his arms and 1 degree of freedom in his body. This robot can perform gestures, which are programmed by a user, and can speak words by a voice of a boy.

Fig. 1. Phyno is an interactive conversational robot that is 25 cm of length and does not work but has 3 degree of freedom in his head, 1 degree of freedom in his arms and 1 degree of freedom in his body. This robot performs gestures and speaks words by a boy's voice.

Fig.2 has shown a story of RAKUGO that are performed by the robot in this experiment. In this a RAKUGO story, a boy in a temple, a quack doctor and an explainer appears. The robot acts the three persons with three different voices and a direction of a head and a body.

> Explainer: A boy was running and knocked against a doctor. The doctor catches the boy and raises his hand and then is about to beat him.
>
> A boy: Please stop being about to swat me by your hand. I would like to be kicked by your foot than to be swatted by your hand.
>
> A Doctor: Why do you ask me such a thing?
>
> A boy: I can survive even if kicked by your foot. However, I cannot survive if your hand treats me.

Fig. 2. The story of RAKUGO by which the robot performed

In this experiment, we define the robot's gestures about the body, head and arms in order that the robot performs the RAKUGO based on the following policies:
- The robot changes the direction of the body to perform three persons, respectively.
- The robot actively expresses emotions, which can be expressed by the head and body movement, by gestures.

We define the robot gestures of two versions that are different from movement and timings. The version A is defined by a student that does not know RAKUGO well. The version B is made about the same to a professional actor of RAKUGO by arranging a story and gestures of the robot. The story of version B is became simpler than version A of it. The gestures of the robot also are faster and less than version A of it.

We evaluate individual impressions about the two types of RAKUGO, by Semantic Differential (SD) that is a method to measure the individual impression with diversity [7]. In SD, the respondent is asked to choose where his or her position lies, on a scale between two bipolar adjectives, such as Good-Bad. We use 9 words, which are shown on Table.1, and the scale of -3 to 3 in order to measure impression of people by the SD method.

Table 1. Two bipolar adjectives for Semantic Differential method in this Study

Adjective Pair	
Humorous	Humorless
Stupid	Smart
Lovable	Hateful
Relevant Tempo	Irrelevant Tempo
Immature	Mature
Friendly	Unfriendly
Warm	Cool
Inactive	Active
Inferior	Superior

3   Result

We investigated impressions of 31 examinees, which are 27 men and 4 women, concerning two type of RAKUGO that are performed by the Phyno. The Fig.3 shows the average and standard deviation about every impression of 31 examinees. The upper and lower figure of Fig.3 is respectively impressions concerning version A and version B.

The Fig.3 indicates that the average evaluations concerning "Humorous" and "Lovable" are a both high degree in version A and B. We suppose that a factor of the result is an adorable design of the robot. We guess that an exaggerated gesture gives impressions to people that the robot is childlike because the average of evaluation concerning "Immature" and "Inferior" is high in version A. We also think that a little gesture and simple story gives an impression to people that the robot is clever because the average of evaluation of the version B concerning "Stupid" and "Inferior" is lower and "Fast" is higher than the version A.

In order to make sure that there are difference about impressions of people between version A and B, we hypothesize that examinees give good points concerning impressions to the version B than version A. We test the hypothesis by one-sided Wilcoxon's signed rank sum test.

- H_0: There are not difference between version A and B.
- H_1: The version B is better (not better) than version A.

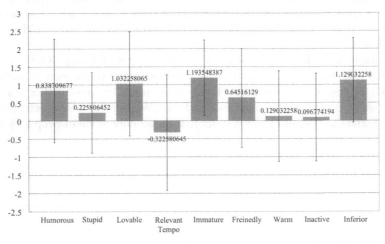

Average and Standard Deviation of Impressions about Version A

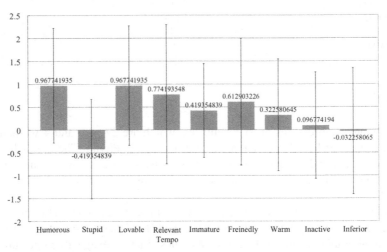

Average and Standard Deviation of Impressions about Version B

Fig. 3. The upper figure is the average and standard deviation about impressions in 31 examinees concerning version A by which a student, who does not know RAKUGO well, defined. The dark bars show the average of 31 examinees about each impression. The line shows the standard deviation of 31 examinees about each impression. The lower figure is the average and standard deviation about impressions in 31 examinees concerning version B that was made about the same to a professional actor of RAKUGO by arranging a story and gesture.

There is a significant difference in "Stupid-Smart", "Relevant-Irrelevant", "Immature-Mature" and "Inferior-Superior". From the result of the test, examinees feel impressions that version B is more smart, relevant tempo and mature than version A.

However, the Fig.3 shows that there are differences about impressions felt from gestures of the robot between individuals because a large standard deviation indicates that the data are far from the mean. We guess that there are the examinees that are sensitive to gestures of the robot and the other examinees that react to exaggerated gesture of the robot, in this experiment. Therefore, we try to classify 21 examinees, who agreed to do the psychology test, by their personality using Transactional Analysis (TA). The TA is an integrative approach to the theory of psychology and psychotherapy and was developed by US psychiatrist Eric Bern. The TA divides people to 3 divisions (5 subdivisions) as shown Table.2.

Table 2. The Ego-State (Parent-Adult-Child, PAC) model in Transactional Analysis

Ego-State	Ego-State (Subdivisions)	Explanation
Parent	CP: Critical Parents	This state acts according to faith and does not change their sense of value.
	NP: Nurturing Parents	This state is caring and concerned and offers unconditional love, calming them when people are troubled.
Adult	A : adult	This state is comfortable with self and considers based on a fact and judges it.
Child	FC: free child	This state acts according to their desire and feelings.
	AC: adapted child	This state controls their feelings and reacts to the world around them and changes themselves to fit in.

Table 3. The classifcation of examinees based on the result of Transactional Analysis

Group	Number of Group		Average and Standard Deviation of				
			CP	NP	A	FC	AC
1	7	Ave	2.43	1.71	1.85	2.57	2.57
		SD	0.53	0.48	0.38	0.53	0.53
2	7	Ave	2.00	2.86	3.00	1.29	3.00
		SD	0.00	0.38	0.00	0.49	0.00
3	7	Ave	1.43	2.29	1.57	1.57	2.00
		SD	0.53	0.76	0.53	0.53	0.82

Table 4. The eignvalues, associated percentage of variance and cumulative percentage of variance, in Principal Component Analysis for Group 1

Group 1 - Version A				Group 1 - Version B			
Component	Eigen value	Associated Percentage of Variance	Cumulative Percentage of Variance	Component	Eigen value	Associated Percentage of Variance	Cumulative Percentage of Variance
1	6.47	39.86	39.86	1	14.92	65.13	65.13
2	4.72	29.04	68.90	2	3.77	16.47	81.60

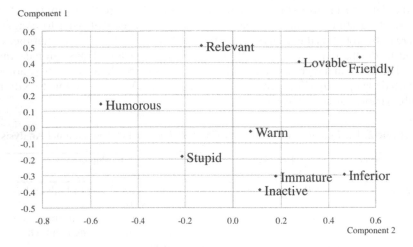

Group 1 – Version A

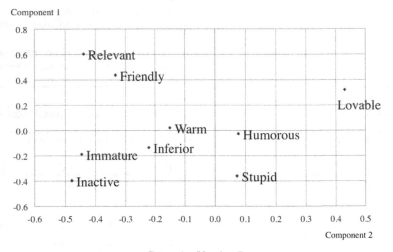

Group 1 – Version B

Fig. 4. The eigenvectors of Principal Component Analysis for group 1 on the map composed by component 1 and 2

Table 5. The eignvalues, associated percentage of variance and cumulative percentage of variance, in Principal Component Analysis for Group 2

	Group 2 - Version A				Group 2 - Version B		
Com po- nent	Eigen value	Associated Percentage of Variance	Cumulative Percentage of Variance	Com po- nent	Eigen value	Associated Percentage of Variance	Cumulative Percentage of Variance
1	6.07	50.00	50.00	1	5.53	41.17	41.17
2	2.72	22.44	72.44	2	4.45	33.13	74.30

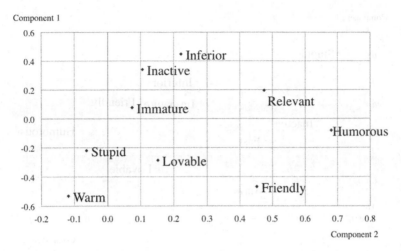

Group 2 – Version A

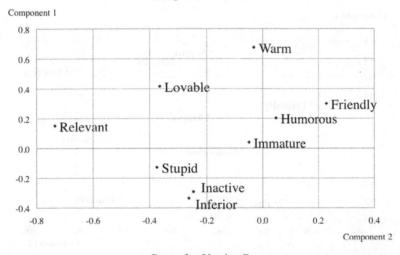

Group 2 – Version B

Fig. 5. The eigenvectors of Principal Component Analysis for group 2 on the map composed by component 1 and 2

Table 6. The eignvalues, associated percentage of variance and cumulative percentage of variance, in Principal Component Analysis for Group 3

Group 3 - Version A				Group 3 - Version B			
Com po- nent	Eigen value	Associated Percentage of Variance	Cumulative Percentage of Variance	Com po- nent	Eigen value	Associated Percentage of Variance	Cumulative Percentage of Variance
1	5.99	42.51	42.51	1	5.64	46.29	46.29
2	3.10	22.00	64.52	2	3.23	26.46	72.75

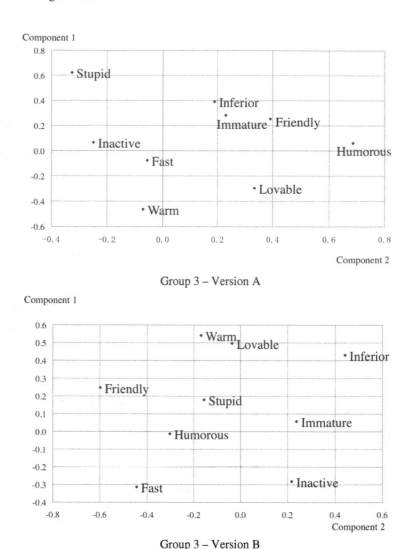

Fig. 6. The eigenvectors of Principal Component Analysis for group 3 on the map composed by component 1 and 2

We classified 21 examinees by similarities of a grade of indexes based on the TA result. The grade of each index of TA is the scale of 1 to 3. The Table 3 shows the average and standard deviation of a grade of five indexes concerning the groups.

The group 1 is lower about the A and NP index than other indexes. The type of group 1 is that a sense of obligation and responsibility and a criticism mind are high. It is also that the consideration for others is strong. The group 2 is lower the FC index than other index. The type of group 2 is that they are the gloomy person and are stubborn and strict and are obedient for the boss. The group 3 is that the NP and AC index are high and the

A and CP index are low. The type of group 3 is that they are kind to a person, and do their best for others.

The Table 4 and Fig.4 indicate impressions of the group 1. This group that is considerate for others shows a friendly attitude to the both gesture type of the robot. This group feels "Lovable", "Relevant Tempo" and "Friendly" concerning the version B of smart gestures than the version A of exaggerated gestures.

The Table 5 and Fig.5 indicate impressions of the group 2. This group that is the stubborn and strict has feelings of inferior and inactive concerning the version A of the robot. However, this group shows the attitude of "Warm" and "Lovable" to the version B of a simple story and smart gestures.

The Table 6 and Fig.6 indicate impressions of the group 3. This group that is kind and does their best for others feels small children to the version A of the robot because they show a high rate about "Stupid", "Immature" and "Inferior" on the map. This group feels also childish to the version B because rates of "Warm", "Lovable" and "Inferior" are high.

In the result of analysis, we detect that there is the difference of impressions among people concerning the gesture or timing of the robot. We also find that there are a correlation between the type of TA and a tendency of evaluations of impressions.

4 Conclusion

We experimented to detect a comfortable strength and timing of gestures of the robot for people by an analysis of individual impressions concerning RAKUGO to which the robot performed. A result of this experiment indicates that the gestures of the robot like professional actor of RAKUGO give smart and mature impressions to people than exaggerated gestures. Therefore, we have found that impressions of people are changed by gestures and timings of the conversational robot.

We also examined an individual personality using Transactional Analysis that was one of psychology. We compared and analyzed their impression to their personality to detect a difference of impressions to gestures of the robot based on individual personality. We have detected that three groups that are classified by the TA have a tendency in gestures of the robot. There is also a correlation between a type of the TA and evaluations of impressions.

In a future, we try to predict a type of people by a reaction to gestures of a robot and change a gesture and timing of the robot. We try to adapt an interaction strategy of a robot to people in order that the people can use the robot comfortably.

Reference

1. Tsuyoshi, T., Yosuke, M., Tomotada, I., Tetsunori, K.: A Conversational Robot utilizing Facial and Body Expressions. In: 2000 IEEE International Conference on System, Man and Cybernetics, pp. 858–863. IEEE Press, New York (2000)
2. Shibata, T., Inoue, K., Irie, R.: Emotional Robot for Intelligent System - Artificial Emotional Creature Project. In: 5th IEEE International Workshop on Robot and Human Communication, pp. 466–471. IEEE Press, New York (1996)

3. Bennewitz, M., Faber, F., Joho, D., Schreiber, M., Behnke, S.: Towards a Humanoid Museum Guide Robot that Interacts with Multiple Persons. In: 5th IEEE-RAS International Conference on Humanoid Robots, pp. 418–423. IEEE Press, New York (2005)
4. Hirotada, U., Michihiko, M., Masaki, C., Junji, S., Akihiro, K., Kenzabro, M., Masatsugu, K.: Human-Robot Interaction in the Home Ubiquitous Network Environment. In: 12th International Conference on Human-Computer Interaction, pp. 990–997. Springer, Heidelberg (2007)
5. Akiko, Y., Keiichi, Y., Yoshinori, K., Matthew, B., Michie, K., Hideaki, K.: Precision Timing in Human-Robot Interaction: Coordination of Head Movement and Utterance. In: The 26 annual SIGCHI conference on Human factors in computing systems. ACM, New York (2008)
6. Berne, E.: Games People Play – The Basic Hand Book of Transactional Analysis. Ballantine Books, New York (1964)
7. Osgood, C.E., Suci, G., Tannenbaum, P.: The measurement of meaning. University of Illinois Press, Urbana (1957)

Performance Assessment of Swarm Robots

E. Oztemel[1], C. Kubat[2], O. Uygun[2], T. Canvar[2], T. Korkusuz[2], V. Raja[3],
and A. Soroka[4]

[1] Marmara University, Eng. Fac., Dept. Of Ind. Eng., Göztepe Campus, Istanbul
[2] Sakarya University, Eng. Fac., Dept. Of Ind. Eng., Esentepe Campus, Sakarya
[3] University of Warwick, Warwick Manufacturing Group, Warwick, UK
[4] Cardiff University, Manufacturing Engineering Center, Cardiff, UK

Abstract. Swarm intelligence is the emergent collective intelligence of groups
of simple autonomous agents which are autonomous subsystems that interact
with their environment. This paper presents a performance evaluation system
for swarm robots. The model proposed includes a set of performance assessment criteria and performance assessment and monitoring system. The
proposed approach is developed for swarm robots developed for health system
responsible for delivery, guidance, monitoring, recognition, and delivery which
a project in European 6th Framework Research Program and carried out by several European nations.

Keywords: swarm robots, performance assessment.

1 Introduction

Swarm intelligence is the emergent collective intelligence of groups of simple
autonomous agents which are autonomous subsystems that interact with their environment, which probably consists of other agents, but act relatively independently
from all other agents [8]. IT is important to point out the concept of swarm here as it
provides several advantageous over being a single agent performing certain functions.
By creating swarm of robots for example, it may be possible to assign a very complex
set of tasks to a set of robots capable of performing collective and cooperative actions.
As clearly pointed out by Kassabalidis, *et al.* [7], swarm intelligence, as demonstrated
by natural biological swarms, has numerous powerful properties desirable in many
engineering systems. In addition, new paradigms for designing autonomous and scalable systems may result from analytically understanding and extending the design
principles and operations exhibited by intelligent biological swarms. A key element of
future design paradigms will be emergent intelligence – simple local interactions of
autonomous swarm members, with simple primitives, giving rise to complex and intelligent global behaviour.

Swarm intelligence boasts a number of advantages due to the use of mobile agents
and stigmergy [7]. These are;

- *Scalability*: Population of the agents can be adapted according to the network size.
  Scalability is also promoted by local and distributed agent interactions.
- *Fault tolerance:* Swarm intelligent processes do not rely on a centralized control
  mechanism. Therefore the loss of a few nodes or links does not result in catastro-
  phic failure, but rather leads to graceful, scalable degradation.

J.A. Jacko (Ed.): Human-Computer Interaction, Part II, HCII 2009, LNCS 5611, pp. 361–367, 2009.
© Springer-Verlag Berlin Heidelberg 2009

- *Adaptation:* Agents can change, die or reproduce, according to network changes.
- *Speed:* Changes in the network can be propagated very fast, in contrast with the Bellman-Ford algorithm.
- *Modularity:* Agents act independently of other network layers.
- *Autonomy:* Little or no human supervision is required.
- *Parallelism:* Agent's operations are inherently parallel.

Detailed information about swarm intelligence and their possible characteristics can be found in [1, 3, 4, 10] However, designing a self-organizing swarm robot is not a trivial task. From an engineering perspective, the design problem is generally decomposed into two different phases: (i) the behaviour of the system should be described as the result of interactions among individual behaviours, and (ii) the individual behaviours must be encoded into controllers [5]. Robots are designed to perform specific behaviour. Performance of the robot is assessed in accordance with the capability of performing intended function as effectively as expected. The scope of this Paper is to provide a general framework to indicate basic issues regarding performance assessment and possible implications.

Although there have been many studies on swarm intelligence, there is little information in the literature on a set of criteria to evaluate a swarm intelligence. Rybski et al. [9] showed how the performance is affected by the number of robots working in the same area, the distribution of the targets the robots are searching for, and the complexity of the environment as the environmental factors. Liu and Passino [8] mention to make an evaluation based on the flexibility, which is essentially a robustness property. They proposed measures of fault tolerance and local superiority as indices. They compared two swarm intelligent systems via simulation with respect to these two indices. Similarly, Banks *et.al.* [3] identified five basic principles that could be used to identify swarm intelligence especially for Unmanned Air Vehicles (UAVs) as follows;

- **Proximity.** All swarm members should be able to perform elementary space and time computations. That is an attempt to compute an immediate course of action that will have the highest likelihood of achieving the group goal.
- **Quality.** The swarm members should be able to respond to quality measures with respect to the attainment of their individual goals.
- **Diversity of Response.** The swarm should not excessively commit its resources in a manner that would leave it vulnerable.
- **Stability.** This principle is important, because an unstable swarm, that is one that changes its behaviour too often, is inefficient.
- **Adaptability.** All the swarm members should be able to switch to a different mode of operation, but only when there is a sufficient return on investment.

Xie *et al.* [11] studied optimizing semiconductor devices by self-organizing particle swarm in their studies. The testing on benchmark functions and an application example for device optimization with designed fitness function is used to assess the performance of the swarm behaviour. Baldassarre et.al. [2] presented a robust solution to a difficult coordination problem that might also be encountered by some organisms, caused by the fact that the robots have to be capable of moving in any direction while being physically connected. And they assess performance of moving capability of moving as quickly as possible and as fast   straight as possible, avoiding obstacles, and approaching a light target. Fukuda et al. [6] try to make an evaluation of swarm intelligent system based on the flexibility, which is essential, a robustness property. They proposed measures of fault tolerance and local superiority as indices. The approaches implemented in these studies are rather application depended. There is a need for a general framework for creating a swarm robot assessment system. This paper presents such a framework which will be implemented in assessing the performance of swarm robots responsible for cleaning, surveillance, monitoring, delivery and guidance in a hospital.

2 Proposed Performance Evaluation Model

Figure 1 indicates the architecture and components of proposed evaluation system. This system is mainly developed for IWARD and European 6th Framework Research Program developed for Intelligent Robot Swarm for Attendance, Recognition, Cleaning and Delivery.

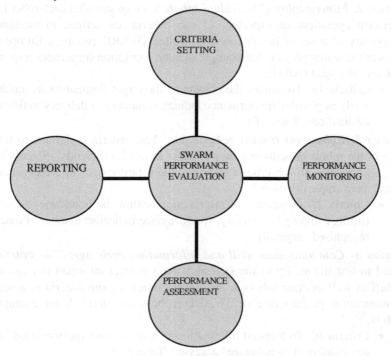

Fig. 1. Elements of performance evaluation system of swarm robots

3 Criteria Setting

In order to be able to measure and quantify the performance of swarm robots, a set of criteria needs to be set up. There could be two types of criteria mainly;
• General criteria
• Domain specific criteria

A set of performance criteria so called indicators are defined taking the following aspect into account.

- **Feasibility**: Performance indicators should be feasible in terms of cost, risk, technology and social possibilities.
- **Manageability**: Performance indicator should be targeted at specific functions which can be easily carried out without violating operational rules.
- **Usefulness:** Performance indicators should be targeted on the functions that provide certain benefit(s) to the user
- **Acceptability:** Performance indicators should not create any objection by the users.
- **Necessity:** Performance indicator may be targeted on the desired function which may not also directly related to end user but is needed to perform user related activities

Based on these aspects, a set of general criteria are defined as the following.

- *Criterion 1: Functionality of individual robots* to make sure that each robot is able to perform operations as expected. 15 sub criteria are defined to measure the functionality of a set of health robots so called IWARD robots, a European 6th framework research project. An example of such a criterion for a robot responsible to deliver an object could be
  - Criteria 1a- To deliver the objects to the target destination as much correctly as possible (performance indicator: number of delivery to the wrong destinations, Target: 0)
- *Criterion 2: Robustness (robust behaviour):* This criteria is defined to test the ability of the robots to perform allocated tasks as much efficiently, effectively and robust as possible. 16 sub criteria to assess the robustness of IWARD robots are defined, an example of which is
  - Criteria 2f- Detection of *intervention* within the boundaries of sensors (lifting / tipping / tampering) (performance indicator: number of cases unrecognised, target: 0)
- *Criterion 3- Communication skill and information exchange:* This criterion is defined to test the ability to transmit and share correct information required by the staff as well as other robots at the correct times. 12 sub criteria to assess the communication performance of IWARD robots are defined, an example of which is;
  - Criteria 3d- To transmit information in a secure way (performance indicator: number of unauthorized accesses, Target: 0)
- *Criterion 4- Timeliness and responsiveness:* This criterion is defined to test the ability to perform the tasks on time. The following example can be a good indicator for robot performance. 10 sub criteria is designed for IWARD robots for this criterion. An example of a sub criteria is;
  - Criteria 4b- Preventing time delays in robots' schedules assigned to the robot (performance indicator: average amount of time delays; Target: 0 min)

- *Criterion 5- Synchronization:* This criterion is defined to test the ability to perform joint actions on time between the robot and other robots, staff and patients. 6 criteria is defined for IWARD robot synchronisation.
  - Criterion 5g- Ability to work together with other robots (Performance indicator: tester's assessment, Target: Tester's assessment)
- *Criteria 6- Swarm intelligence*: This criterion is defined to test the ability to perform intelligent (swarm) behaviour of the robot. IWARD robots are assessed with 14 sub criteria for this.
  - Criterion 6h- Capability of mutual decision making (performance indicator: satisfying pass criteria, Target: to be defined during design)

Similar examples can be derived for the following criteria which were identified for swarm robots to assure their performance for their intended functions.

- *Criteria 7- Reliability:* This criterion is defined to test the ability to perform reliable actions. IWARD robots are assessed with 6 sub criteria for reliability.
- *Criteria 8- Usability*: This criterion is defined to test the extent to which a product can be used by specified users to achieve specified goals with effectiveness, efficiency and satisfaction in a specified context of use. 10 criteria is defined for IWARD robots for assessing usability.
- *Criteria 9- Accessibility:* This criterion is defined to test the ability to access that the information is available to the widest possible users.

There could be some domain specific performance criteria related to the activities and users of the swarm robots. For IWARD robots especially end-user comfort and psychological effects on the patients and hospital staff are considered along this line.

4 Performance Monitoring and Assessment

Once the set of criteria is defined, they are monitored during the operations of robots. A coloureds scheme can be implemented on a grid indicating performance gaps. There could be a coloured scheme indicating the level of compliance as given below.
- Green colour- respective criteria are fully satisfied
- Blue colour- respective criteria are partially satisfied
- Red colour - respective criteria are not implemented

Figure 2 indicates a performance grid which is designed to monitor the performance of swarm robots. A fully green performance grid indicates an ideal well performing set of robots. Note that Figure 2 only shows criteria listed above. The actual grid will have all criteria with respect to all robots.

Figure 2 indicates that robot 1 has some problems in transferring the information in a secure way. Similarly, Robot 2 has problems with corporate decision making.

To be able to define the colour of the grid for a specific robot for specific criteria an assessment form is designed. It includes a set of facts and questions to be filled out by the assessor which will yield to the colour of the grid. Each assessment sheet is designed based on a scenario defined by the development team to indicate all implications of the domain with respect to delivery, recognition, guidance, cleaning etc.

Performance indicators	Robots		
	R1	R2	**R3**
Criterion 1a			
Criterion 2f			
Criterion 3d			
Criterion 4b			
Criterion 5g			
Criterion 6h			
Criterion ..			
Criterion ..			
Criterion ..			
.....			

Fig. 2. Performance grid

5 Conclusion

This paper presented a performance evaluation system which is developed to assess the performance of swarm robots. A set of criteria is defined based on through an extensive domain analysis and a well defined procedure to make sure that each criteria is acceptable to the users and measurable as well as assuring benefits of the swarm system.

The system is developed for IWARD (Intelligent Robot Swarm for Attendance, Recognition, Cleaning and Delivery) project. The IWARD robots are developed and in the stage of integration. Once the system is integrated and ready to use, then it will be tested and performance of the robots will be identified through implementing the criteria recommended.

There have been several scenarios defined to test the functionality of the robot. An assessment sheet is developed for each scenario. The assessment sheet includes a set of questions and observations to be filled out. These are defined using the set of criteria explained above. Each criteria is detailed down to some measurable and observable statements and facts. Once the robots are assessed based on these facts the colour of respective criteria for each robot will be defined and performance grid will be filled out. This will clearly indicate performance gaps which could then be fixed before hacving the robots in operation.

References

1. Baldassarre, G., Domenico, P., Nolfi, S.: Coordination and Behaviour Integration in Cooperating Simulated Robots (2004),
   http://laral.istc.cnr.it/baldassarre/publications/2004BaldPa
   riNolf-InteConfSimuAdapBeha-CoorBehaInteInSimuRobo.pdf

2. Baldassarre, G., Parisi, D., Nolfi, S.: Distributed Coordination of Simulated Robots Based on Self-Organisation, Institute of Cognitive Sciences and Technologies, National Research Council (ISTC-CNR) (2005),
   http://laral.istc.cnr.it/baldassarre/publications/2005BaldPa
   riNolf-ArtiLife-DistCoorInSimuRoboBaseOnSelfOrga.pdf
3. Banks, A., Vincent, J., Phalp, K.: Particle swarm guidance system for autonomus unmanned aerial vehicles in an air defence role. The journal of Navigation 61, 9–29 (2008)
4. Bayındır, L., Şahin, E.: A review of studies in Swarm Robotics. Turk. J. Elec. Engin. 15(2) (2007)
5. Dorigo, M., Trianni, V., Şahin, E., Grob, R., Labella, T.H., Baldassarre, G., Nolfi, S., Deneubourg, J.-L., Mondada, F., Florena, D., Gambardella, L.M.: Evolving Self-Organizing Behaviors for a Swarm-bot (2004),
   http://www.idsia.ch/~luca/swarmbot-control.pdf
6. Fukuda, T., Funato, D., Sekiyam, K., Arai, F.: Evaluation on flexibility of swarm inelligent system. In: Proceedings of the 1998 IEEE International Conference on Robotics and Automation, May 16-20, vol. 4, pp. 3210–3215 (1998)
7. Kassabalidis, I., El-Sharkawi, M.A., Marks, R.J., Arabshahi, P., Gray, A.A.: Swarm intelligence for routing in communication networks (2001),
   http://ieeexplore.ieee.org/stamp/stamp.jsp?arnumber=00966355
8. Liu, Y., Passino, K.M.: Swarm Intelligence: Literature Overview (2000),
   http://www.ece.osu.edu/~passino/swarms.pdf
9. Rybski, P., Larson, A., Lindahl, M., Gini, M.: Performance Evaluation of Multiple Robots in a Search and Retrieval Task. In: Workshop on Artificial Intelligence and Manufacturing (1998)
10. Takemura, Y., Sato, M., Ishii, K.: Toward realization of swarm intelligence mobile robots. International Congress Series, vol. 1291, pp. 273–276 (2006)
11. Xie, X.-F., Zhang, W.-H., Bi, D.-C.: Optimizing Seöiconductor Devices by Self-organizing Particle Swarm. In: Congres on Evolutionary Computation–CEC, Oregon, USA (2004)

A Robotic Introducer Agent Based on Adaptive Embodied Entrainment Control

Mutsuo Sano[1], Kenzaburo Miyawaki[1],
Ryohei Sasama[2], Tomoharu Yamaguchi[2], and Keiji Yamada[2]

[1] Osaka Institute of Technology, Fuculty of Information Science and Technology
1-79-1 Kitayama, Hirakata City, Osaka, Japan
{sano,miyawaki}@is.oit.ac.jp
[2] NEC Corporation, C&C Innovation Research Laboratories
8916-47 Takayama-Cho, Ikoma, Nara, Japan
{r-sasama@cp,yamaguchi@az,kg-yamada@cp}.jp.nec.com

Abstract. The necessity for the individual and the individual's tying in real space increases while the age of piece progresses. The robot is requested in that and it is requested what role be able to be played. Here, we pursue the research on the robot design to expand and to promote the group conversation. It proposes the technique to advance the conversation of couple 1 of the first meeting smoothly as the first stage. Especially, it is confirmed that nonverbal interactions are more important than language interactions by a lot of researches so that the individual and the individual may tie. We newly define the communications activity based on embodied entrainment, and propose the method to control the behavior of the robot dynamically according to the state of communications. The active control method uses interaction timing learning which depends on nonverbal communication channels. Our mechanism selects an appropriate embodied robotic behavior by changing the communication strategy based on the state transition of an introduction scene, and increases the communication activity measured by sensing data. The action timing is learned and controlled by a decision-tree. As the result, the real agent robot could control communication situations similarly to a human. We became "Yes" by the evaluation value of 82% for the question that communications had risen as a result of doing the questionnaire survey to 20 university students. Moreover, familiarity became a first meeting introduction robot with "Yes" for the question about whether being possible to have it by the evaluation value of 85%. Therefore, the effectiveness of this proposal technique was verified. Finally, the possibility that the circle of communications can be expanded to N person's group is discussed based on this result.

Keywords: Embodied Entrainment Nonverbal Communication Robotic Introducer Agent, Group communication, Human's Action Learning.

1 Introduction

Recently, the necessity for an individual mind and the mind's tying in real space increase in the human society while the age of piece progresses. What is the role

J.A. Jacko (Ed.): Human-Computer Interaction, Part II, HCII 2009, LNCS 5611, pp. 368–376, 2009.
© Springer-Verlag Berlin Heidelberg 2009

that the robot that has the sociality can be accomplished in that? We pursue the robot design to expand the circle of communications at the same time as smoothly doing the group conversation by a home space and a public space, etc. Humans communicate with each other via many channels, which can be categorized into verbal and nonverbal. It has been confirmed that the nonverbal communication channels, such as an intonation, an accent, a gaze, a gesture, nodding or an emotional expression, encourage synchronization, embodied entrainment and a friendship [1]–[7]. Watanabe et al. [8] has investigated such a robotic agent, which includes embodied entrainment. The research has developed the speech-driven interactive actor, the Inter Actor, which could predict an appropriate timing of a nod and a gesture with voice information of a communication partner. Kanda et al. [9] [10] adopts a joint gaze function to a robot and has investigated more adaptive robot through design-based approach. However, we cannot find so many researches about an adaptive embodied entrainment, which aims to increase group communication activity by real time feedback on a situation of the group communication. This paper presents adaptive control of the embodied entrainment using learning of interaction timing in group communication. The control mechanism is based on communication activity measurement and uses nonverbal communication channels effectively. First of all, we start from the research that the robot supports the case with a first meeting couple 1 mutually shown in Fig.1, and install the system into a robotic introducer agent and confirm its effectiveness. In this paper, we show our robotic agent design. Next, we explain our method for adaptive control of embodied entrainment and show an experimental result of our method. Finally, the effectiveness is verified according to result of the questionnaire, and the N person's development with the group communications is discussed.

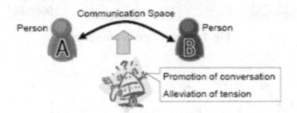

Fig. 1. Introducer robot of a first meeting couple

2   Basic Strategy to Promote Group Conversation

Fig. 2 shows our robot agent. The purpose of this introducer agent is support of conversations of 2 participants who have not known each other. For the purpose, we designed various basic strategies of agent behaviors. The details of the behaviors are as follows. (Fig.3)

1. Leading utterances

The agent asks a question to participants for establishment of a binary reliable relation between herself and each participant.

2. Gaze lead

For transmission of information of a participant A to the other participant B, the agent moves her gaze to A and asks him/her about the information. After that, the agent leads A's gaze to B to accord A's gaze and B's gaze.

3. Gaze distribution

When all participants talk each other, the agent moves her gaze to them equally.

4. Synchronizing nod

The agent adjusts her nod timing to participants' nod.

5. Dynamically Synchronizing

Synchronizing method is dynamically changed according to the state of two persons as follows.

a) Natural synchronizing to a listener

When the listener listens and tunes to the talker by the nod and the back-channel feedback operation, the robot tunes it according to listener's timing to pile up the communication space further.

b) Synchronizing to a speaker to invite the other participant to the conversation

When the listener is not tuning it to talker's timing, the robot tunes to talker's rhythm while turning one's gaze to the listener, invites the listener's tune, and creates the rhythm of the communications space.

Fig. 2. Robotic Introducer Agent

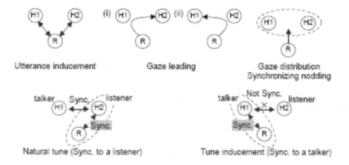

Fig. 3. Basic strategies to promote group conversation

3 Adaptive Control of Embodied Entrainment

3.1 Macro Strategy to Promote Group Conversation

We think about the state transition model to promote the group conversation by using the basic strategies. It establishes a rapport by grounding process, and communications of the group are activated by enhancement process in Fig.4. We segmented an introduction scene into 5 states based on preliminary observations. The agent moves among these states according to the situation of the participants' communication. Fig.4 shows the 5 state transitions. The details of the states and the agent behaviors are as follows.

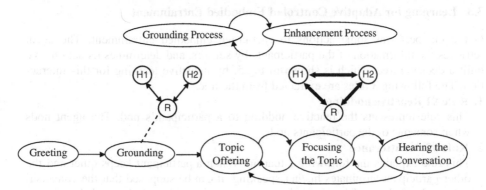

Fig. 4. Macro strategy and state transition of an introduction scene

3.2 Communication Activity Measurement and the State Transition Condition

The robot agent monitors the situation of participants' communication, and estimates the current state on Fig.4. For the estimation, we define the communication activity measurement. The agent calculates the activity in every time slice. It is defined by the average of speech power, gaze direction, and gaze corresponding degree of both. When it satisfies a condition of a state transition, the agent moves to the next different state, which is directed by the transition.

Next we show the behaviors at each state.

1. Greeting

The agent introduces himself and offers a brief explanation of the situation. Then, she simply introduces the participants' name.

2. Grounding

In this state, the agent tries to make a reliable relationship between the robot and each participant. For this, the agent cites the participants' profile and asks simple questions to them. It aims to entrain them in to the rhythm of the robot by using the strategy of utterance leading. Here, the robot assumes that it knows the data of the hobby etc. of the person who is introduced.

3. Topic Offering

This state encourages conversations between the participants. The agent offers the information and profiles about a participant to the other participant, or asks a simple question to the participants in order to make a favorable situation for conversations of the participants. By such behaviors, the agent controls the participants' gaze to make them communicate face to face each other.

4. Focusing on a Specified Topic

In this state, the agent tries to join in a conversation of the participants. The agent focuses on a topic, which was offered at the previous state, Topic Offering.

5. Hearing Conversations

After a success in making a close and friendly relationship between the participants, the agent keeps hearing their conversations quietly. In this state, the agent nods and looks at a speaker using basic embodied entrainment strategies, with a proper timing.

3.3 Learning for Adaptive Control of Embodied Entrainment

Our agent performs some actions to encourage embodied entrainment. The agent retrieves the information of the participants by sensors, and determines its action. We built a decision-tree, which is shown in Fig.5, by inductive learning for this interaction. The following 3 rules are extracted from the tree.

1. Rule #1 Reactive nodding

This rule represents the reactive nodding to a participant's nod. The agent nods when someone of the participants nods.

2. Rule #2 An utterance

This rule explains the following situation. When a participant keeps quiet and the other participant terminates his/her speaking, it can be supposed that the conversation got into a break. Therefore, the agent recognizes this situation and she offers a topic to avoid silence.

3. Rule #3 An utterance and a nod to a participant's speech

This rule is very similar to the Rule #2 but represents the situation that a participant stopped his/her utterance without terminating his/her speech. In this situation, the agent speaks in 70% probability and nods in 30%. The criterion to determine

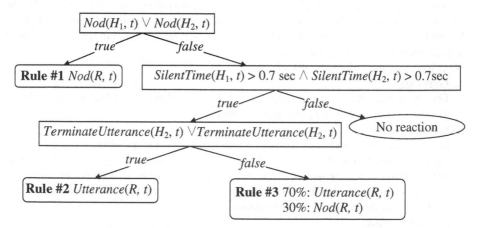

Fig. 5. Decision tree for embodied entrainment

whether a participant terminated his/her utterance or not, depends on the final part of the utterance. We extract the final part by Japanese morphological analysis.

4 Experiments

4.1 Experimental System

Information of current situation is recognized by the situation cognitive system which is composed of voice recognition, voice power detection, gaze detection and nodding detection. After that the interaction generator retrieves the information, and determines the agent behavior with the participants' profiles.

4.2 Sensing Environment

Detection modules in the cognitive system retrieve raw sensor data and extract the participants' state and action. The details of each module and sensors are listed below.

1. Gaze Detection

Multiple cameras are used for this module. We set 2 cameras for each participant. Each camera detects the participant's face, and the gaze detector estimates that the participant is turning his/her gaze to the camera, which can detect the participant's face.

2. Nodding Detection

We set acceleration sensors to the participants' head, and measure the movement of heads. Based on the movement, this module detects his/her nodding.

3. Voice Recognition, Voice Power Detection

A pin microphone is set on each participant.

4.3 Experimental Result

Fig.6 shows an experiment with our introducer agent. We asked 2 participants to talk each other during 6 minutes. The participants had never known each other. In this situation, we checked whether our method could control the agent behavior appropriately.

Fig.7 plots the $Eval(t)$ and the state transition of a communication situation. $Eval(t)$ is the communication activity degree at time slice, and is defined as follows.

$$E(t) = \sqrt{\left(\alpha * \frac{PA(t)}{PA(ave)}\right)^2 + \left(\alpha * \frac{PB(t)}{PB(ave)}\right)^2 + \left(\frac{1}{\beta} Gw\right)^2}$$

(1)

$$Eval(t) = \frac{E(t) + Eval(t-1)}{2}$$

$PA(t)$ or $PB(t)$ denotes the speech power of person A or B at time t, and $PA(ave)$ or $PB(ave)$ is the average of $PA(t)$ or $PB(t)$. Gw shows the probability (%) of gaze

Fig. 6. Experiments with the agent

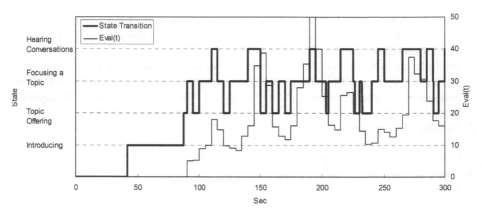

Fig. 7. *Eval(t)* and state transition

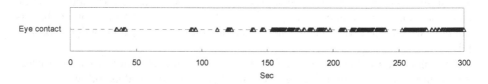

Fig. 8. Participants' eye contact

corresponding. α and β are a weighting factors. Then we define *Eval(t)* as the average of *E(t)* on the time axis.

We can see an appropriate movement of the state and the *Eval(t)* on the graph. Fig.8 shows a frequency of participants' eye contact. We could also observe the situation that the participants had intensified friendship through many natural conversations, which had been led by our agent.

We did the questionnaire survey to 10:20 university students. As a result, a negative evaluation was not at all, and became 82% for the question that communications had risen by the evaluation value in which four or more was converted by 100% by the evaluation value of five stage average. Against the first meeting introduction robot and familiarity was confronted to the question about whether being possible to have it, and moreover, a negative evaluation was not at all, and became 85% by the evaluation value in which four or more was converted by 100% by the evaluation value of the stage average. Thus, the effectiveness of this proposal technique was verified by the questionnaire survey.

5 Future Works

The mechanism of the group communications activation of couple 1 proposes with this paper can be enhanced also to N person's group communications basically. However, an important point is to have to select the strategy for activation appropriately in enhancing responding to group member's personality. It doesn't mediate in consideration of the character though a hobby each other and the concern, etc. are understood beforehand and communications were supported in the actual experiment. For instance, it might be effective to have the person with a high communications skill to the group of the facile personality the coupling. Moreover, the scene that mediates communications is not only a first meeting. We assume application to the home for the aged and the waiting room, etc. shown in Figure 9, and are researching the framework to activate the group communications. The number also of cases to shut one's mind voluntarily increases for the elderly person, and the achievement of the heart proxy that the robot ties to the mind the mind in real space is requested.

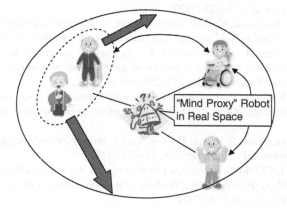

Fig. 9. Enhancing of activation of N person's group communications to research

6 Conclusion

We proposed the mechanism of the group communications activation of couple 1. We showed the control mechanism of adaptive embodied entrainment and implemented the mechanism and installed it into the real robotic introducer. The effectiveness of our proposal was confirmed by the communication experiments and the questionnaire survey. This mechanism was based on the communication activity measurement, and the learning of timing for the nonverbal actions such as gaze, nodding or back-channeling. In the aspect of embodied action control, the system selects the most appropriate action, which is suitable to each communication state, such as greeting, grounding, offering topics, focusing the topic and hearing a conversation. Add to the action control, the proper changes of a speaker and a listener increased the communication activity degree. We focused on the gaze lead, gaze distribution and synchronizing nod for the embodied action. The timing of robotic actions and utterances was based on the rules, which was extracted from a decision-tree built through induction learning of human behaviors. We installed our control system into the introducer robot and tested it on the communication experiments. As the result, the agent could control the communication situation similarly to the human.

We start to enhance this method to N person's group communications schema. And we will apply it to the application of the home for the aged and the waiting room.

References

[1] Matarazzo, J.D., Weitman, M., Saslow, G., Wiens, A.N.: Interviewer influence on durations of interviewee speech. Journal of Verbal Learning and Verbal Behavior 1, 451–458 (1963)
[2] Webb, J.T.: Interview synchrony: An investigation of two speech rate measures in an automated standardized interview. In: Pope, B., Siegman, A.W. (eds.) Studies in Dyadic Communication, pp. 115–133. Pergamon, New York (1972)
[3] Kendon, A.: Movement coordination in social interaction: Some examples described. Acta Psychologica 32, 101–125 (1970)
[4] Condon, W.S., Sander, L.W.: Neonate movement is synchronized with adult speech: interactional participation and language acquisition. Science 183, 99–101 (1974)
[5] Bernieri, F.J., Reznick, J.S., Rosenthal, R.: Synchrony, pseudosynchrony, and dissynchrony: Measuring the entrainment process in motherinfant interactions. Journal of Personality and Social Psychology 54, 243–253 (1988)
[6] Takeuchi, Y., Katagiri, Y.: Emotional feedback by synthesized voice and facial expressions. In: Proccedings of the 3rd international conference of cognitive science, pp. 697–698 (2001)
[7] Kojima, H., Nakagawa, C., Yano, H.: Can a robot empathize with people? International Journal of Artificial Life and Robotics 8, 83–88 (2004)
[8] Watanabe, T.: E-COSMIC: Embodied Communication System for Mind Connection. In: Proc. of the 13th IEEE International Workshop on Robot-Human Interactive Communication (RO-MAN 2004), pp. 1–6 (2004)
[9] Kanda, T., Ishiguro, H., Ono, T., Imai, M., Maeda, T., Nakatsu, R.: Development of 'Robovie' as platform of everyday-robot research, The transactions of the Institute of Electronics. Information and Communication Engineers. D-I J85-D-I(4), 380–389 (2002)
[10] Kanda, T., Ishiguro, H., Imai, M., Ono, T.: Development and Evaluation of Interactive Humanoid Robots. Proceedings of the IEEE (Special issue on Human Interactive Robot for Psychological Enrichment) 92(11), 1839–1850 (2004)

Robot Helps Teachers for Education of the C Language Beginners

Haruaki Tamada, Akihiro Ogino, and Hirotada Ueda

Faculty of Computer Science and Engineering, Kyoto Sangyo University
Kamigamo Motoyama, Kita-ku, Kyoto, Japan
{tamada,ogino,ueda}@cc.kyoto-su.ac.jp

Abstract. In this paper, we propose a learning support framework for teacher and learners that achieves the following three requirements: (A) to use unaware system, (B) to support the teacher for educating learners, and (C) to support learners for solving assignments. Based on the proposed framework, we implemented a system using a robot which supports learners.

Keywords: Robot, the C language, human/robot interaction.

1 Introduction

Recently, the interaction of human and robot is very important research topics, because robots will be generalized and human and robot interaction will become hot.

In this paper, we propose a framework of educational support for programming beginners, which is a one of application of human and robot interaction. The beginning of programming learner usually makes errors such as a syntax error (missing semicolon and unmatched brackets) and linkage error (misspell of symbol names). The compiler and the linker present message for fixing errors. However, the beginner almost cannot understand the message, because actual causes are too far from causes the beginner thinks.

For example, Figure 4 shows error messages from compilation of source code of Figure 4. Missing semi-colon on declaration statement (line number 3 on Figure 4) causes those errors. The beginner could not understand what an actual cause in six lines of message is.

Meanwhile, it is rare case that the programming education is conducted one-on-one. Generally, one teacher lectures a few dozen students. Therefore, it is difficult for the teacher to comprehend the understanding of each student and to know the weak point and/or specialty point of each student. Additionally, it is also difficult for the teacher to show the understanding of student in real time. The teacher can only infer the understandings of students from reaction of them.

The one of goals of this work is to support the teacher by giving information of statistics of errors and this information would be factors of inferring student's understanding. The other goal is to support students for solving assignments by translating compilation messages. Using the proposed framework, the robot would support student who troubled in simple errors, hence, the teacher can apply oneself for teaching the perspective of issues and the solution of complex error. Moreover, the robot is different with teaching assistant and needs no human cost.

J.A. Jacko (Ed.): Human-Computer Interaction, Part II, HCII 2009, LNCS 5611, pp. 377–384, 2009.
© Springer-Verlag Berlin Heidelberg 2009

This paper is organized as follows: Section 2 addresses requirements of proposed framework. In Section 3, we describe the design to implement requirements. In Section 4, we describe how to implement the proposed framework. In Section 5, we describe a scenario of the proposed framework. In Section 6, we review existing approaches of human and robot interaction. Finally, in Section 7, we summarize our paper.

2 Framework Requirements

In this section, we present three requirements for the proposed framework. Specifically, the requirements are: (A) to use unaware system, (B) to support the teacher for education of learners, and (C) to support learners to solve of assignments. These requirements are intended to implement in any learning support system.

2.1 (A) To Use Unaware System

The one of goal of proposed method is to support learning of programming beginners. Because beginners do not understand operations for programming, it is difficult for beginners to distinguish between the work for programming and the work for using a learning support system. Therefore learners are confused when we let a learner be conscious of the use of the learning support system. Then the efficiency of learning would be greatly decreased. Hence, the proposed system must be unconscious of using from programming learners.

The architecture of the proposed system must not have the special interface such as a web interface, and a special command. Beginners only learn the work of programming and use only usual interfaces.

2.2 (B) To Support The Teacher for Educating Learners

The proposed system supports education by showing the statistics information of the data based on actions of the learner. A teacher needs to educate many things to learners. Also, the teacher usually wants to change the level of education by understanding of learners. However, understanding of learners generally can measure in only particular opportunity such as exam, and report.

Teacher can suppose the understanding of the learner by being shown the data based on actions of the learner in real time. Therefore, the level of education can be altered based on shown data.

For example, if many learners finish an assignment by taking hints of the assignment, the teacher could open the new assignment. On the other hand, if not, the teacher could explain the assignment, or give more hints.

2.3 (C) To Support Learners for Solving Assignments

The practical course is that the learner tries to solve given assignments by making trial and error. Unfortunately, the beginning of programming learner makes many mistakes because of misunderstanding and incomprehension of compilation error messages. Thereby, the learner might give up the programming.

This requirement is for holding a learning motivation of learners. For this, the proposed framework introduces a game element to increase the learning efficiency [2], applauds the learner to elicit the appetite for learning.

3 Design of the Proposed Framework

Figure 1 shows an overview of the proposed framework. In the practical course, the teacher usually gives assignments to learners. Learners try to solve given assignments, and teacher educates some techniques through assignments. The proposed framework supports education of teacher and solving assignments of learners, which are surrounded by the dotted oval of the figure.

3.1 Programming Environment

To construct unaware system of use, we must exclude unnecessary processes on a normal assignments solution cycle. Moreover, a learner can use same interface in both the house and our practical course. We exploit Mac OS X for programming environment. Since Mac OS X provides UNIX tools, the C compiler and the Java compiler as default, it is more than acceptable for learning environment of programming.

Besides, an environment to use laptop (MacBook) owned by students in the practical course was constructed and deployed from April 2008 in our university. The environment use NetBoot service of Mac OS X server which enables to boot client PC from server-side disk image. The laptop PC booted from server-side image is running as fully managed PC even if the laptop PC is owned by the student. Features of this environment are described as follows.

- Each learner owns MacBook privately and he/she can set up unique configuration.
- If the learner does not have a laptop for repair, he/she can use the spare laptop.
- In this environment, the laptop PC of learner is booted from server-side disk image and it would be fully managed.
- We can use commercial software such as Mathematica and MATLAB because the OS is booted from our managed disk image. In this environment, OS and various applications can be lent like library. We call this environment OSSP (Operating System Service Provider).

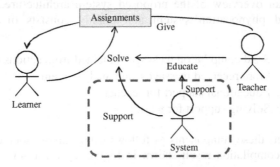

Fig. 1. Overview of Proposed Framework

3.2 Statistics of Compilation Error of Learners

In this work, we focus on the compilation of source code in actions of the learner for educational support. The programming beginner does not have enough knowledge to fix the compilation error. Therefore, he/she cannot understand compilation errors and does not read them. That is, to fix compilation errors is hard task for programming beginners.

The teacher wants to comprehend the condition of the learner in each situation for more effective education. Therefore, we collect error messages of compilation of learners. Collected compilation errors are automatically categorized and summarized. The resultant data is presented to the teacher.

3.3 Robot: Supporter of Learners

We apply the robot for supporting learners to give a clue of a solution of assignments. We control the robot for gesturing by corresponding actions of the learner (e.g. failure of compilation). Additionally, we provide game elements to the system by giving many movement patterns to the robot. Thus, we induce learner to interest in the robot.

We choose Phyno as the robot [3]. Phyno is child robot, which modeled a 3 years old child, and is designed to perform pretty gesture. The cuteness of the gesture makes the learner trying to find out various gestures.

Table 1. Properties of the learner which are sent with compile message

Property Name	Description
UserId	User name for distinction of learners
CompilerVersion	The version of the compiler for switch the compile message parser.
CommandLine	Command line which is executed by the learner.
IpAddress	IP address of the learner for locating the learner's scat

4 Implementation

4.1 Phynocation System

Figure 2 shows an overview of the proposed system architecture. The proposed system is named phynocation system and mainly consists of following four components.

- Component I: Send compilation messages obtained from actions of learner.
- Component II: Store received messages, and analyze them.
- Component III: Educational support for teacher.
- Component IV: Solving support for learners.

This paper explains these components as follows using sample source code shown in Figure 4 and its compilation result shown in Figure 4 by gcc 4.0.1 on Mac OS X 10.5.6.

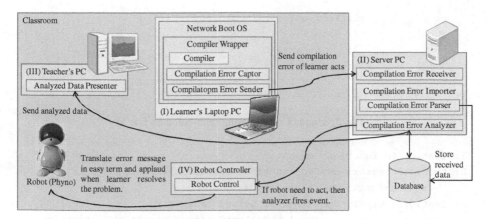

Fig. 2. Overview of Architecture of the Proposed System

4.2 Component I: Send Compilation Messages Obtained from Learner's Action

This component hooks compile action of a learner and captures a result of compiler. The ``Learner's Laptop PC'' is this component in Figure 2. This component sends whole messages shown in Figure 4 and also sends information of the learner to a server. Main properties of the learner are shown in Table 1, which shows name and description.

To execute above sequence unconsciously, we constructed a wrapper of the compiler. In our practical course, every learners boot OS from network in one's laptop. When the learner is in house, he/she boots OS from local hard disk of one's laptop. Since the component is installed in NetBooted OS image, the learner can try to solve assignments in the house and our practical course both same interface[1].

4.3 Component II: Store Received Messages and Analyze Them

Sent the compile result from Component I are received this component which is ``Server PC'' shown in Figure 2. Then, this component parses the compile result and stores it to the database. Next, the compile result is analyzed for categorization of error type.

In message parsing phase, at first, a compile result is divided in each line because the compile result usually contains multiple types of error. For instance, in Figure 4, 5 types of error message are reported. Each message has 4 types of attributes, which are file name, line number, error type, and error message. We store those attributes and properties from component I to the database.

After storing, an analyzer will be performed, which is composed of following Component III and Component IV.

4.4 Component III: Educational Support of Teacher

This component aims to present a statistics data of learners for educational supports to teacher, which is ``Compilation Error Analyzer'' of ``Server PC'' and ``Teacher's

---

[1] Note that NetBooted OS is ordinary in our university, because every practical courses use it.

```
1: #include <stdio.h>
2: main(){
3:    int answer
4:    answer = 3 + 5;
5:    printf("answer=%d\n", answer);
6: }
```

Fig. 3. Sample Code (missing semi-colon on line 3)

```
1: test.c: In function `main':
2: test.c:3: error: nested functions are disabled, use
   -fnested-functions to re-enable
3: test.c:3: error: syntax error before `answer'
4: test.c:4: error: `answer' undeclared (first use in this function)
5: test.c:4: error: (Each undeclared identifier is reported only once
6: test.c:4: error: for each function it appears in.)
```

Fig. 4. The Compilation Result of Figure 3

PC" in Figure 2. This analysis mainly shows overall trend of learners. Typical analyses are as follows.

- Frequency of each error types.
- Frequency of error types per unit time.

4.5 Component IV: Solving Support of Learners

This component also analyzes information of learners. The difference from Component III is to analyze individual-focused statistics. This component is ``Compilation Error Analyzer'' of ``Server PC'' and ``Robot Controller'' in Figure 2.

When a learner failed to compilation of specific number of times, the robot translates the result of compilation and shows a solution with endearing gesture. Then, if the error was fixed in next compilation time of the learner, the robot praises him/her. We expect to achieve the motivation of the learner by praising them.

5 Framework Scenario

Typical scenario of the proposed framework is shown in Figure 5. At first, (1) the teacher explains assignments, then (2) learners try to solve given assignments. In solving, learners would compile the source code. (4) The proposed framework collects compilation data of learners and (5) analyze them. Next, (6) the proposed framework presents a statistics of errors of learners. (7) The teacher gives hints of assignments to learners by taking the statistics of errors of learner. Also, (9) the proposed framework controls the robot for (10) translating the compilation error and giving a clue of solution. (8, 11) Learners try to fix errors by getting hints or the clue of solution. Finally, when learners fix errors, (12) the robot praises them.

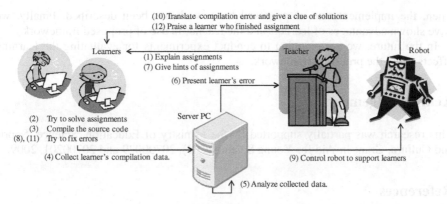

Fig. 2. Scenario of Proposed Framework

Advantages for learners to use this framework
Without the proposed framework, learners might not get hints and they would need much time to solve an assignment. Using the proposed framework, because a hint and a clue are provided when the learner fails in an assignment, they can try more assignments in a unit time. To solve many assignments is deepened an understanding of programming of learners and would increase educational effects.

Advantages for the teaches to use this framework
The teacher can know the statistics of errors of learners in real time. It can become the factor for measuring the understanding of learners. Thereby, the teacher can educate of programming along the understanding of learners in real time.

Moreover, the robot helps learners made mistake by a simple error. Hence, the teacher can dedicate himself/herself to education of essential issues of programming.

6 Related Works

Sartatzemi et al. reported the research of teaching the programming fundamentals to Greek secondary school student using LEGO Mindstorms technology [5, 6]. The C language is the very important position in programming languages. We cannot avoid studying it.

A human have a friendly feeling to a robot by its gesture and manner of speaking even if the robot makes uniform response [1]. Therefore, in this work, we use this result to induce interest of students.

7 Conclusion

In this paper, we have proposed the framework of educational support system as one of application of human and robot interaction. At first, in our proposed framework, we have presented three requirements: (A) to use unaware system, (B) to support the teacher for education of learners, and (C) to support learners to solve of assignments.

Then, the implementation of proposed framework has been described. Finally, we have shown advantages of learners and the teacher in use of proposed framework.

In the future, we are planning to conduct experiments for evaluating the learning effects using the proposed framework.

Acknowledgements

This research was partially supported by the Ministry of Education, Science, Sports and Culture, Grant-in-Aid for Young Scientists (B), 20700029 and 20700201, 2009.

References

[1] Matsumoto, N., Ueda, H., Yamazaki, T., Tokosumi, A.: The cognitive characteristics of communication with artificial agents. In: Proc. Joint 3rd International Conference on Soft Computing and Intelligent Systems and 7th International Symposium on advanced Intelligent Systems (SCIS & ISIS 2006), September 2006, pp. 1269–1273 (2006)
[2] Feldgen, M., Clua, O.: Games as a motivation for freshman students to learn programming. In: Proc. of 34th Annual Frontiers in Education, 2004. FIE 2004, pp. 11–16 (2004)
[3] Ueda, H., Chikama, M., Satake, J., Sato, J., Kidode, M.: A prototyping of a dialog interface robot at the ubiquitous-home. In: IPSJ Ubiquitous Computing Systems (UBI) Information Processing Society of Japan (IPSJ), March 2005, vol. 2005, pp. 239–246 (2005)
[4] Apple Computer Inc.: Netboot and Network Install,
http://www.apple.com/server/macosx/netboot.html
[5] Sartatzemi, M., Dagdilelis, V., Kagani, K.: Teaching Programming with Robots: A Case Study on Greek Secondary Education. In: Bozanis, P., Houstis, E.N. (eds.) PCI 2005. LNCS, vol. 3746, pp. 502–512. Springer, Heidelberg (2005)
[6] The LEGO Group, Mindstorms Education,
http://www.legoeducation.jp/mindstorms/

An Interactive Robot Butler

Yeow Kee Tan, Dilip Limbu Kumar, Ridong Jiang, Liyuan Li, Kah Eng Hoe,
Xinguo Yu, Li Dong, Chern Yuen Wong, and Haizhou Li

Institute for Infocomm Research, 1 Fusionopolis Way, #21-01, Connexis, Singapore 138632
{yktan,dklimbu,rjiang,lyli,kehoe,xinguo,ldong,cywong,
hli}@i2r.a-star.edu.sg

Abstract. This paper describes a novel robotic butler, developed by a multi-disciplinary team of researchers. The robotic butler is capable of detecting and tracking human, recognize hand gestures, serving beverages and performs dialog conversation with guest about their interests and their preferences; and providing specific information on the facilities at Fusionopolis building and various technologies used by the robot. The robot employs an event driven dialogue management system (DMS) architecture, speech recognition, ultra wideband, vision understanding and radio frequency identification. All these components and agents that are integrated in the DMS architecture are modular and can be re-used by other applications. In this paper, we will first describe the design concept and the architecture of the robotic butler. Secondly, we will describe in detail the workings of the speech and vision technology as this paper mainly focuses on human-robot interaction aspects of the social robot. Lastly, this paper will highlight some key challenges that were faced during the implementation of speech and vision technology into the robot.

Keywords: speech recognition, gesture recognition, robot and dialog management system.

1 Introduction

Recently, research in social robotic has become prominent in the interactive robot development. Despite its importance, little progress has been made in interactive robot development due to the complicated process and intersection of research field such as robotics, human-robot interaction, signal processing and cognitive science. Numerous social robotics exist today, but to the best of our knowledge none of them offer a similar service to the one described in this paper. The service robotic system that offers the closest service might be Robovie [1]; a robot intended to perform duties related to a museum guide capable of interacting with visitors via hand gestures and possesses the capability to recognize speech and RFID tags. Robovie was deployed in a science museum and guest commented that they face difficulty in conversing with the robot, which the author suggested the speech recognition engine employed was unable to work as expected in open environment. The RFID tag wore by the visitors contain personal information such as

J.A. Jacko (Ed.): Human-Computer Interaction, Part II, HCII 2009, LNCS 5611, pp. 385–394, 2009.

the name, age and birthday of the visitor. The RFID tag allows the robot to greet visitors by their name. Robovie was also deployed in a shopping area [2], where it uses passive-type RFID reader and floor sensors to provide robust tracking of people's position. The uses of passive-type RFID and floor sensors create a symbiosis relationship where each technology's capability compliments each other's weaknesses.

2   Hardware and Software Architecture of the Robotic Butler

The hardware configuration of the robotic butler includes a Pioneer P3-DX™ mobile base, a wheel based powered by DC motors with a differential drive that allows 2 degree of freedom (X-Y). The mobile base is also equipped with bumper, ultrasound and laser sensors. The laser sensor is also used for path planning and environment mapping purposes. The navigation module is able to guide the robotic butler autonomously to reach the waypoint(s) safely and approach detected persons. The aesthetic casing of the robotic butler was constructed using a carbon fiber composite. The tray on the robotic butler consists of LED lights that will light up when the pressure sensor detects a wine glass on it. The tray is also equipped with motion sensors to detect any intrusion into the tray area. Any intrusion detected will cause the mobile base to stop moving immediately to prevent any possible collision. Radio frequency identification (RFID) reader was installed on the chest section of the robotic butler, which gives the best performance due to the ideal position to scan for RFID tags wore by the guests. Three Mini-ATX boards (Intel® Core ™2 Duo Processor 2GHz and 1GB DDR2 RAM) are installed to perform the required processing of speech recognition, vision understanding, RFID, navigation and machine control. To acquire auditory signals, a far-talk microphone array (Acoustic Magic, Voice Tracker™) is fixed on top of the robot's head. The head section of the robot also holds a stereoscopic camera (Videre Design, STOC-C) to capture live video feed needed by the vision understanding module. AT&T Natural Voices voice pack (UK English - Charles) that runs on Microsoft SAPI 5.1 text-to-speech engine was installed in the robotic butler to allow the robot to speak. Meanwhile the Abacus speech recognition engine was integrated to allow the robotic butler to recognize user's speech input. Each module (e.g. speech and vision) interacts directly to the central server through TCP/IP socket messages. The ultra wideband (UWB) reader is installed at the operating site and is connected to a PC that calculates the position of the UWB transmitter installed on the robotic butler's head. The robot's location is transmitted to the central server on the robot at every three seconds through wireless connection for autonomous navigation. In addition to that, based on the input/signals fired by each respective module, the central server determines the action to be performed. The central server is a script-based dialog state machine, where the series of actions to be carried out is all written in a script-like manner. This allows developers to change the parameters or the actions accordingly without the need to re-compile and software code.

Hardware	Description
Far-talk Microphone Array (Acoustic Magic)	To acquire speech input to perform speech recognition process.
Stereoscopic Camera (Videre Design)	To track human and their gestures.
Ultra-Wideband (UWB) Transmitter	To transmit localization data to the UWB reader to perform real-time and accurate localization.
Audio Speakers (LACie's USB Speaker)	Text-to-speech output to allow an interactive conversational dialog between the human and the robot.
Radio Frequency Identification (RFID) reader	To read the RFID tags worn by the guest.

Fig. 1. The appearance of the robotic butler and hardware configuration

3 Abacus Speech Recognition

The Abacus is a multilingual, speaker-independent phonetic engine able to recognize continuous sentences or phrases. It supports both Large Vocabulary Continuous Speech Recognition (LVCSR) and Backus-Naur Form (BNF) grammar-based speech recognition. Developers can create dialogue grammars and vocabulary easily for applications through a set of Software Development Kit (SDK) Application Programming Interface (API). The active vocabulary can be as large as 64000 words, which provides great flexibility for variety of multimedia or telephony applications. The speech recognizer is a frame-synchronous HMM-based recognizer, employing 3-state HMM to model context dependent tri-phones. Each of these states has a mixture of 16 Gaussians. Abacus uses n-gram statistical language model to support LVCSR. In grammar mode, Abacus supports BNF grammar and VXML grammar definition. It allows the developers to build a dialogue context using simple grammar, such as word list, or complex one as in conversational speech. The result parser outputs n-best recognition results with semantic parsing results, word confidence score and time stamps, which provides great flexibility for application development. The Robotic Butler uses a grammar-based approach to perform speech recognition. The grammar consists of 1444 combinations of words/sentence (e.g. "Fusion World", "I would like to know more about Fusion World". Each dialogue session will use a common or a different grammar that consists of a set of possible words spoken by the user. Speech recognition result will be further evaluated for any possible keywords that invoke the robot to perform an action. If more than one keyword appears, the robot will clarify which actions to be taken. Through such approach, verbal commands spoken in any order/manner will be interpretable by the dialog manager to carry out a particular task. On top of the base model trained, an additional of 10,430 spoken utterances equivalent to 372 minutes of speech utterance was recorded using the far-talk micro-phone array and used to adapt the acoustic model. The voice activity detection algorithm is based on signal-Noise spectral distance in multiple Mel-frequency bands. The algorithm is performed in short-term Fast-Fourier Transform (FFT) domain with a frame length of 32ms and frame shift of 8ms. The noisy Short-time Fast Fourier transform (STFFT) spectrum is smoothed by moving average and then is transformed in specific Mel-frequency bands. The reference noise average levels in specific Mel-frequency bands are first estimated during the first 0.25 second and later being updated in non-speech frames. The decision of speech or noise for each frame is based on a logistic operation derived from its distances to the corresponding reference noise levels in that specific frequency bands.

4 Dialog Management System

The Dialog Management System (DMS) [3] is one of the key modules in the system configuration of social robot as speech technology provides intuitive, flexible, natural and inexpensive means of communication. In terms of interaction, spoken dialog is the prominent modality for the social robot. Despite the seamless integration with other modules, the dialog system must be responsive in humanoid manner and can be evolved based on the context and task domain. To address these needs on spoken dialog system, an event driven dialog system architecture is proposed. A template-based cum rule-based language generation paradigm is proposed to render the

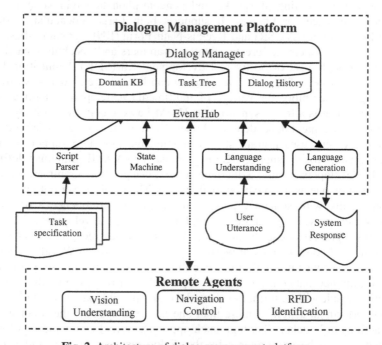

Fig. 2. Architecture of dialog management platform

interaction. Three levels of error recovery strategy are employed to address different types of errors. The architecture of dialog management platform is shown in fig. 2. Functionally, the dialog management platform is comprised of script parser, state machine, language understanding, language generation and an event hub. The entire system structure is supported by a data management module, which manages the dialog task tree, domain/context database and keeps track the dialog history. The event hub stands in the centre of the whole system to manage different kinds of messages so that various modules and agents are able to cooperate and synchronize seamlessly to perform different functions as a social mobile robot.

5 Human Detection and Gesture Recognition

The tasks for vision module are the perception of humans around in the view and recognize the hand gesture of a person asking for service when the robot is moving around, as well as tracking the guest when approaching him to serve the drinks even in the crowded scenarios with temporal occlusions of the guest by other persons. Hence, the vision module has two main functions: (a) human detection and tracking; and (b) hand gesture recognition. In this system, a novel method for robust human detection and tracking from the mobile robot is developed and deployed. The method

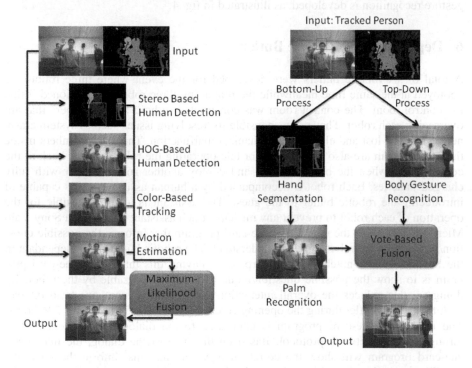

Fig. 3. Illumination of human detection and tracking

Fig. 4. Illumination of hand gesture detection

integrates the stereo-based human detection, HOG-based human detection, color-based tracking, and motion estimation under a Maximum-Likelihood based fusion framework, as illustrated in fig. 3. Our previous method of stereo-based human detection based on scale-adaptive filtering [4] is adopted in this system. It is improved by a MAP (Maximum A Posterior) based approach for human segmentation. An efficient strategy of perspective constrained human detection is proposed. Using HOG-based human detector, we can detect potential humans in the view with only 200 detection windows, compared with 200,000 detection windows required for conventional approaches. Our previous DCH (Dominant Color Histogram) based multiple person tracking algorithm [5] is adopted in this system. A novel Maximum-Likelihood based fusion framework is proposed and applied in this system to integrate the stereo-based human detection, HOG-based human detection, DCH-based human tracking, and motion estimation to achieve robust human detection and tracking in real-world environments. The human detection rate is increased to 94%, compared to 86% by state-of-the-art human detection methods, and the errors of tracking humans through complex occlusions is reduced to 1/4 compared with existing tracking methods on the evaluation data sets from real-world tests. The system is very robust to cluttered environments and crowded scenarios. Once a human is detected, the hand gesture recognition is performed. To be adaptive to humans of various distances to the robot, an innovative method to fuse the bottom-up hand segmentation and top-down body-gesture recognition is developed, as illustrated in fig. 4.

6 Deployment of Robotic Butler

A total of six robotic butlers were developed for the event where three robots are deployed at the same time meanwhile the remaining three robots are stationed inside the control room. The control room was constructed to hold team members that are overseeing each robot. They are responsible for resolving issues such as system crash, network signal lost and electronic/mechanical malfunction. The team members inside the control room are also responsible for tele-operating the robotic butler back to the control room when the battery is low and deploy another robotic butler with fully charged batteries. Each robot is accompanied by a human assistant that is capable of introducing the robotic butler to the guest. The assistant is also responsible for the operation of each robot to prevent any mishaps. Each assistant also carry a Sony Vaio Micro PC that holds the interactive cue-card program that informs the possible question/request that the robot is able to understand. The robotic butler is not dependant to the handheld micro-notebook. The purpose of having this interactive cue-card program is to show the possible question/request that is recognizable by the robot. By doing so, this reduces the overall interaction time allowing more guests to interact with the robotic butler during the opening ceremony, which only lasted for 2 ½ hours. The interactive cue-card program is connected to the dialog management system through TCP/IP network protocol. Based on the state of the dialog, the interactive cue-card program will show the correct images and text that inform the guest the possible topics that the robot understands. A guest is able to get robot's attention by waving their hands. Once the vision understanding module detects a human, the vision module sends a "wave detected" message and the central server will request the vision module to acquire the coordinates and angle of the person who was waving. The coordinate received by the central server allows the navigation module to move to the correct location. The robot will stop in front of the guest based on the distance estimated by the human-tracking module using the stereoscopic camera. The robotic butler was programmed to stop one meter away from a human, a distance that most of the robotic butler team member found appropriate while interacting with the robot. Once it reaches the destination, the robot will start the speech dialog by checking the script in the dialog management system. Based on the script, appropriate speech will be generated by the text-to-speech module. Next, the guest will have to speak the verbal command, which will be recorded by the far-talk microphone array and speech processing process will be executed. Based on the speech recognition result, the dialog management system will then check the required state/signal that it needs to transmit to the central server. The central server will then inform the related module to perform the actions accordingly. During the speech interaction mode, the robotic butler utilizes the laser sensor to detect the presence of the guest within the operating vicinity. This is achieved by detecting whether there is an obstacle, in this case a person's leg within an area of 15 degrees, the frontal position of the robotic butler. If the laser sensor detected no obstacles, the central server will send a signal to the speech module to end the conversation and the robot will resume moving around the area to scan for possible waving gesture.

7   Issues Faced during the Development and Deployment of the Robotic Butler

7.1   Batteries for the Microphone and Audio Speaker

When the far-talk microphone array was installed onto the robotic butler, the audio recorded by the microphone consist an audible static noise. Further exploration into this problem pinpointed to the central battery system that is found that the voltage is "noisy". As the audio speaker was drawing power from the same battery system, a soft humming sound can also be heard when no audio is being played. To address this issue, a lithium ion battery pack was purchased to supply power to the microphone and the speaker.

7.2   Interference Generated by the RFID Reader

In the early design of the robotic butler, RFID was intended for two purposes. To identify the guest using RFID and to detect the guest is still in front of the robot. Preliminary testing on the robotic butler has shown the whenever the RFID is in scanning mode, the audio equipments will output/record a beeping sound. Such interference susceptibly affects the performance of the speech recognition and the speech dialog. Though the interference was reduced using shielded cable and aluminum foil, the microphone and audio speaker was still affected. Hence the use of RFID to detect user's presence was replaced with the use of laser sensor to track the guest's leg as described in section 6.

7.3 Design of the Head Section

During the implementation stage of the microphone array onto the robotic butler, the team faces challenges of sound reverberation within the robotic head, which greatly affect the performance of the speech recognition engine. To address this issue, the internal section of the robotic head was wrapped with sound proofing material and the placement of the microphone was moved closer to the mesh surface of the robotic head.

7.4 Speed of the Robot Affecting Vision Understanding Module

Based on the testing of the mobile base with a speed of 0.5 meter per second, such movement speed affects the performance on the human detection and gesture recognition. The speed of the mobile base was tested and it was found that 0.2 meter per second was acceptable.

7.5 Data Storage

The use of the compact flash (CF) card as hard disk for speech processing and vision understanding was found to be unacceptable due to speed and reliability issues. To address this issue, the CF card was then replaced by Integrated Drive Electronics (IDE) hard disk for notebook.

8 Discussions

Unlike Robovie as reported in [2], the robotic butler is able to detect a guest's intention to interact with the robot through a simple wave from a distance. During the opening ceremony event, such action was found to be acceptable and guests imply that such method is similar to how human get other's attention. However as the robot is turning to reach the next waypoint, there are incident where the guest waving but the robot's camera is out of sight. Some of the guest thought the robot is ignoring them. The performance of the speech recognition was found to be acceptable and the guests were surprised that the robot is capable of recognizing their request, which was spoken in a full sentence (E.g. Tell me more about Fusion World). An experiment of several speakers requesting the robot to explain certain facilities in Fusionopolis using a spoken English sentence shows the Abacus speech recognition system is able to achieve a correct alarm rate of 82%. During the event, it was also found that the guest is skeptical about holding the interactive cue-card. The reason was unknown but we suspect they are afraid of dropping the equipment. During the interaction, the guest relies on human assistant to explain on how to interact with the robot. During the event, it can be observed that some of the guests have difficulty hearing what the robot is trying to say due to the noisy background noise even though the speaker volume was set to the highest. The use of the RFID to obtain guest's details also increase the interactivity of the dialog and the guest are impressed that the robotic butler is able to greet them by their names, able to play their favorite music and talk about their favorite actor, movie, sports team and player. While developing the robotic butler, it is found that a preliminary study to determine the hardware (e.g. microphone, audio interface, camera and sensors) to be integrated onto the robot should be carried out early in the project. This allows the researchers/engineers and product designer to have a common understanding of the hardware/software requirements (E.g. position and the dimension of the camera and far-talk microphone array). At the end of this study, the product designer will have the sufficient information to design a robot within the requirements set upon by the hardware/software. Meanwhile the researchers/engineers will have to work using the resources as discussed. In addition to the challenges faced by the robotic butler as discussed in section 7, they are other issue that a robotic platform using speech recognition should take note of. During the event, there are occurrences where the robot is waiting for speech input from the guest however he/she might be talking to someone else instead to the robot. In such scenario, the voice activity detection will detect a speech but it was unable to determine whether the speech it heard is intended to the robot or to someone else. The inability to determine the recipient of the speech input will cause the robot to response even though the speech was not intended to the robot. Future work will include devising a solution that combines speech processing and vision understanding to perform attention-directed speech dialog that intends to address this issue. The combination of vision and speech can also further enhance the speech input. For example the work carried out by [6] integrates vision and speech to provide a robot the ability to find a speaker, tracking the speaker's face and focus its attention to the speaker who is talking to it and by doing so they are able to purify the speech signal. Though it is possible to place various sensors in the environment to acquire various data to improve the robot's capability and efficiency (e.g. [7]), the social robotic research team in Institute for Infocomm Research is concentrating their effort to develop robotic platforms that is employs only sensors, which it carries. Such effort removes the need to integrate various sensors (camera, microphone and pressure sensors) in the environment, user's privacy is not intruded all the time and the robot possesses characteristics/capabilities that depict a real human being.

9 Conclusions

We have developed an interactive robotic butler that employs various technologies such as speech recognition, gesture recognition, Radio Frequency Identification (RFID) and ultra-wideband (UWB). The robotic butler was successfully deployed in the Fusionopolis Opening Ceremony and the use of gesture recognition and speech recognition for human-robot interaction received positive remarks from the guests.

10 Future Work

We are currently developing a far-talk microphone array using a series of small microphones that can be placed impose fewer constraints (E.g. can be placed on a surface with curvature). The development of such far-talk microphone array system also allows the team to have full control over the microphone to perform various signal-processing processes such as speech enhancement and voice activity detection. The team is also working on sound localization and vision-based technology to detect human's gaze attention and lip movement that allows the robot to perform attention-directed speech dialog.

References

1. Masahiro, S., Takayuki, K., Hiroshi, I., Norihiro, H.: Interactive Humanoid Robots for a Science Museum. IEEE Intelligent Systems 22(2), 25–32 (2007)
2. Kenta, N., Taichi, T., Masahiro, S., Takayuki, K., Hiroshi, I., Norihiro, H.: Integrating Passive RFID tag and Person Tracking for Social Interaction in Daily Life. In: 17th IEEE International Symposium on Robot and Human Interactive Communication, Germany (2008)
3. Ridong, J., Yeow Kee, T., Haizhou, L., Chern Yuen, W., Dilip Kumar, L.: Development of Event Driven Dialogue System for Social Mobile Robot. In: Global Congress on Intelligent Systems (2009)
4. Liyuan, L., Yingting, K., Shuzhi, G., Weiming, H.: Stereo-based Human Detection for Mobile Service Robots. In: International Conference of Automation, Robotics, and Computer Vision, vol. 1, pp. 74–79 (2004)
5. Liyuan, L., Weiming, H., Irene, G., Ruijiang, L., Qi, T.: An Efficient Sequential Approach to Tracking Multiple Objects Through Crowds for Real-Time Intelligent CCTV System. IEEE Trans. System, Man, Cybernetics-Part B 38(5), 1254–1269 (2008)
6. Kai-Tai, S., Jwu-Sheng, H., Chi-Yi, T., Chung-Min, C., Chieh-Cheng, C., Wei-Han, L., Chia-Hsing, Y.: Speaker Attention System for Mobile Robots Using Microphone Array and Face Tracking. In: IEEE International Conference on Robotics and Automation (2006)
7. Hirotada, U., Michihiko, M., Masaki, C., Junji, S., Akihiro, K., Kenzabro, M., Masatsugu, K.: Human-Robot Interaction in the Home Ubiquitous Network Environment. In: Jacko, J.A. (ed.) HCI 2007. LNCS, vol. 4551, pp. 990–997. Springer, Heidelberg (2007)

Part IV

Touch and Pen-Based Interaction

A Study on Fundamental Information Transmission Characteristics of an Air-Jet Driven Tactile Display

Takafumi Asao[1], Hiroaki Hayashi[2], Masayoshi Hayashi[2],
Kentaro Kotani[1], and Ken Horii[1]

[1] Faculty of Engineering Science, Kansai University,
3-3-35 Yamate-cho, Suita, Osaka, Japan
{asao,kotani,khorii}@iecs.kansai-u.ac.jp
[2] Faculty of Engineering, Kansai University
{sa7m402,gh50075}@edu.kansai-u.ac.jp

Abstract. There are many people with impaired vision as well as hearing. Tactile displays can be useful to such people for communicating by means of characters and shapes. Many devices for tactile displays such as oscillators and electrocutaneous stimulators have been developed. However oscillators have two drawbacks: physical stress tends to build up in actuators because of long term exposure to oscillations, and they may transmit erroneous information because of unstable contacts between magnetic pins and the skin. Moreover, electrocutaneous stimulators cause discomfort to the user. In this study, we have developed a tactile information presentation technique that uses air jet stimulations and tactile phantom sensations induced by a complex combination of tactile perceptions. The tactile display can transmit information to the skin without physical contact and is free from the restriction of pitch size. In this paper, we have examined its fundamental information transmission characteristics.

Keywords: Tactile Display, Air Jet Stimulation, Phantom Sensation.

1 Introduction

In Japan, there are 20,000 people with impaired vision as well as hearing [1]. Tactile displays can be useful to such people for communicating by means of characters and shapes. In order for the tactile displays to be widely accepted, it has been established that the type of actuators and the pitch size of the actuators are major factors to be considered while designing tactile displays [2][3].

Selecting the appropriate type of actuator for transmitting accurate tactile information has been considered to be a challenge. Many devices such as oscillators and electrocutaneous stimulators have been developed that serve as the principle mechanism of tactile displays. It has been reported that oscillators, however, have two drawbacks: physical stress tends to build up in these actuators because of long term exposure to oscillations [4], and they may transmit erroneous information because of unstable contacts between magnetic pins and the skin [5].

Electrocutaneous stimulators have been reported to induce pain [4]. These stimulators require physical contact between the actuators and the skin; thus, they

J.A. Jacko (Ed.): Human-Computer Interaction, Part II, HCII 2009, LNCS 5611, pp. 397–406, 2009.
© Springer-Verlag Berlin Heidelberg 2009

are prone to interference [6]. Consequently, though these actuators have an advantage in that the coupling between the actuators and the skin provides instantaneous tactile information, they also have a disadvantage that they cause discomfort to the user.

Selecting the appropriate pitch size is important for the effective transmission of information. For improving the transmission efficiency, some researchers have attempted using actuators with a high spatial density [3][7], and others have attempted invoking tactile apparent motions [8][9][10]; however, these techniques have been ineffective in overcoming the above mentioned problems, thus far.

In this study, we have developed and demonstrated a tactile information presentation technique that uses air jet stimulations and tactile phantom sensations (PSs) [11] induced by a complex combination of tactile perceptions. Tactile displays that employ air-jet stimulations can be used to present noncontact stimuli so that safety as well as non-interference is assured [6]. Therefore, this presentation technique can potentially compensate for the above mentioned drawbacks to some extent.

A tactile PS is a combination of sensations that is evoked by a stimulus at a certain location where no stimulus is indeed present. This phenomenon typically occurs at a specific location of the skin when two stimuli are provided to the skin at a specific distance from each other. It has been reported that the location of the PS shifts depending upon the ratio of intensities between the two real stimuli; therefore, the location of the PS can be changed by controlling the intensities of the two stimuli. This controllability of the location of the stimulus implies that a limited number of actuators can be used to provide PS-based stimuli at many locations. This leads to a high efficiency in density of stimulus actuators for a tactile display by applying PS-based stimuli.

Thus, the tactile display that uses air-jet stimulations and PS-based stimulus presentation technique can transmit information to the skin without physical contact and is free from the restriction of pitch size. In this study, we have developed a noncontact tactile display and have examined its fundamental information transmission characteristics.

2 Noncontact Tactile Display Using Air-Jet Stimulations

The stimulus presentation unit of our noncontact tactile display consists of 25 nozzles (HB-U1/8VV-00D3, Spraying Systems, Japan) arranged in a 5 × 5 matrix (see Fig. 1(a) for the unit). A schematic diagram of the tactile display is shown in Fig. 2. Compressed air supplied by an air compressor (EC1430H2, Hitachi Koki) is emitted from the nozzles. The amount of air supplied is controlled by using a digital electro-pneumatic regulator (EVD-1900-P08 SN, CKD) and a precision regulator (RP2000-8-08-G49PBE, CKD). The pressure level is controlled with a resolution of 1.0 kPa. A digital I/O board (PCI-2726C, Interface) is used for transmitting control signals from a PC to determine the pressure level in each nozzle.

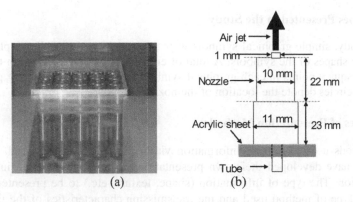

Fig. 1. Noncontact 5 × 5 tactile display. ((a) side view of the stimulus presentation unit, (b) internal structure of the nozzle).

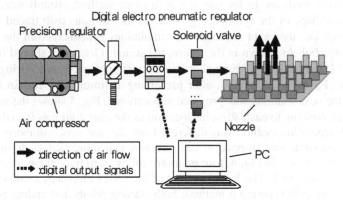

Fig. 2. Schematic diagram of the tactile display

3 PS Generation Scheme and Presentation Patterns

In this study, PSs were generated by using a 3-point simultaneous stimulus presentation pattern. In previous studies [12][13], it was reported that PSs were clearly evoked when mechanical and electrical stimulations were presented by using a 3-point simultaneous stimulus presentation pattern designed on a planar surface. According to a study conducted on the optimum conditions required for the generation of PSs [14], the location of each PS was assumed to be the median point of the weighted intensities of the stimuli at three adjacent locations.

4 Experiment

An experiment was conducted to evaluate the information transmission characteristics of the proposed tactile display.

4.1 Shapes Presented in the Study

In this study, simple graphical symbols were presented via the tactile display. Fig. 3 shows the shapes of the symbols. A total of eight shapes were selected. In the figure, the black square points in each graphical symbol denote the PS generating points and the white circles denote the location of the nozzles.

4.2 Types of Presentation Methods

The methods used to present information via tactile displays are varied. Many researchers have developed their own presentation methods for effective information transmission. The type of information (shape, texture, etc.) to be presented may restrict the type of method used and the transmission characteristics of the tactile display. In this study, three presentation methods were tested for their preciseness in transmitting tactile information: They were one-stroke drawing, path separation, and vertex emphasis methods. In the one-stroke drawing method, stimuli were presented by tracing the shape of the symbol. Fig. 4 shows the stimulus path traced in the case of a trapezoid, i.e., the exact sequence of stimulations generated from the nozzles to present the symbol. As shown in the figure, the stimulus locations shifted in the order 1 through 11 and back to 1. Note that stimuli were not presented during transition between two PS locations, that is, after presenting a stimulus for certain duration at location 1, the next stimulus was provided at location 2. Fig. 5 shows the set of active nozzles corresponding to each stimulus location as the trapezoid was traced.

The path separation method was different from the one stroke drawing method in that air jet emission was stopped at each corner, indicating that each straight path deviated at the corners. In Fig. 4, four paths are followed to trace the trapezoid: 1 to 4, 4 to 7, 7 to 9, and 9 to 1. The basic concept of the vertex emphasis method was similar to that of the path separation method; both starting points and ending points were emphasized to recognize the path easily. While a no-stimulus interval was used to indicate the vertex location in the path separation method, stimuli with a high intensity were used to indicate the vertex locations in the vertex emphasis procedure. The intensity of the stimulus generated at each corner was determined from the inner angle of two paths intersecting at that corner. The intensities of the stimuli in the case of the vertex emphasis method were set according to the following equation:

$$I = \theta + 350 . \tag{1}$$

$$\text{Where} \qquad I : \text{Intensity of stimulus [kPa]}$$
$$\theta : \text{Inner angle between two paths [°]}$$

According to this equation, if two paths intersect at an inner angle of 90°, the stimulus intensity at the vertex becomes 440 kPa.

In all the methods, the duration of stimulus presentation ranged from 100 ms to 500 ms, as determined by each subject prior to the experiment so that the stimuli could be perceived very clearly. The optimum duration of stimuli presentation was different for each individual.

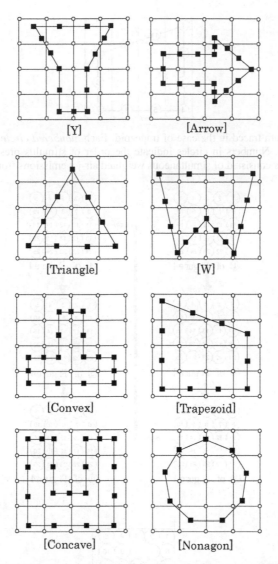

[Y]   [Arrow]

[Triangle]   [W]

[Convex]   [Trapezoid]

[Concave]   [Nonagon]

Fig. 3. Shapes of graphical symbols presented in the study. Note that all PS generating points (*black squares*) are linked for the purpose of legibility. No tracing stimuli were presented between two PS generating points throughout the experiment.

4.3 Sequence of Events during Experiment

Fig. 6 shows the sequence of events followed during the experiment. Two trials, each consisting of a set of stimuli corresponding to a shape, were carried out in the following manner. A set of stimuli were presented in the first trial. After the second set of stimuli was presented, the subjects identified the shapes as perceived by them. The subjects had been notified of the list of graphical symbols visually, but not tactually, prior to the experiment. Table 1 summarizes the other experimental conditions.

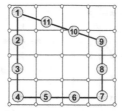

Fig. 4. Stimulus path traced in the case of trapezoid. Each *numbered circle* corresponds to the location of the PS. Numbers in circles indicate the order of stimulus presentation. Each PS-generating stimulus consisted of simultaneous weighted air-jet emissions from three nozzles.

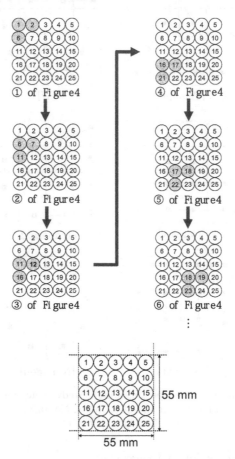

Fig. 5. Set of active nozzles corresponding to each stimulus location as the trapezoid is traced. Air-jet stimulations were emitted from the shaded nozzles to generate the PSs. The exact locations of the PS are shown in Fig. 4. Intensity of the air-jet for each nozzle was different from each other, based on the weighted midpoint to generate PS at designated position. This figure shows the exact arrangement of the nozzles in the tactile display developed in this study.

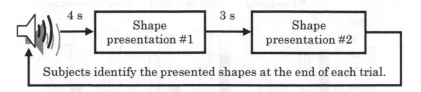

Fig. 6. Sequence of events during each trial

Table 1. Experimental Conditions

Subject	Five healthy males
Body location for the stimulus presentation	Center of the palm
Distance between the skin and nozzle	5 mm
Total intensity of the 3-point air-jet stimulations	350 kPa
Presentation duration	100–500 ms, adjusted according to the optimum duration for each subject
Number of presentation methods	3
Number of shapes presented	8
Number of trials in a block	4

5   Results and Discussion

Fig. 7 shows the correct responses rates along with the average correct response rates of each subject for the three different presentation methods. Fig. 8 shows the correct response rates categorized by shape. As shown in Fig. 7, the correct response rate was the highest in the case of the path separation method. The path separation method appeared to be the most effective tactile stimulus presentation method within the range of the experimental conditions. On the other hand, the one-stroke drawing and vertex emphasis methods were not as effective. Subjective responses revealed that the shapes were not perceived clearly when stimuli were presented by the one-stroke drawing method. The edge information was distorted in the case of the one-stroke drawing method, and the loss of information resulted in low correct response rates. In the case of the vertex emphasis method, the subjects responded that the intensities of the air-jet stimuli presented at the vertices were sometimes very high and they obscured the tactile information of the adjacent locations. Identifying each path separately is important to be able to interpret a symbol accurately, and the vertex emphasis method offers an advantage in this aspect; however, depending on the intensity of the stimulus, the stimulus itself may obscure the location information of the adjacent feature.

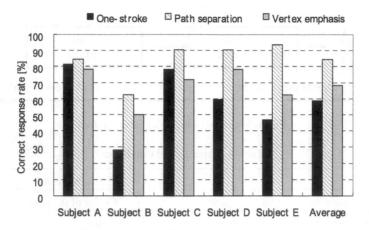

Fig. 7. Correct response rate of each subject

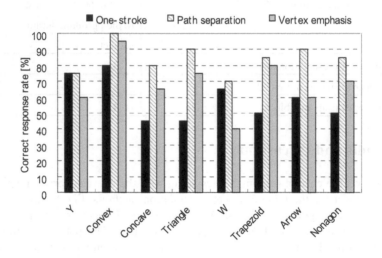

Fig. 8. Correct response rates categorized by shape

Wake et al. [15] evaluated correct response rates by using a 17 × 17 pins TVSS (television substitution system). In their experiment, the subjects were visually impaired and the number of shapes to be identified was increased on the basis of the subjects' performance. First, five shapes were randomly presented by using the TVSS, and after the subjects analyzed the first experimental block, the number of shapes was increased to eight by adding three new shapes. The subjects then analyzed this second experimental block consisting of eight different shapes. By the end of the seventh experimental block, the number of shapes was increased to 17. The average correct response rate was 80.0% in the case of the first experimental block, and it ranged from 78.6% to 87.5% in the case of subsequent blocks. Our study, on the other hand, was different from their study in terms of the type of actuators used (pins were used in their study), type of symbols presented, number of subjects, location of stimulus presentation (entire back region was used in their study), etc.; therefore, the results of the two studies cannot be compared quantitatively. However, the trends of the two studies in terms of the subjects' performances were rather similar, especially in the case of the path separation method when the average correct response rate in our study was 84.38%. With regard to the spatial resolution of the tactile display, a 5 × 5 actuator matrix was used in our study, which was considerably smaller than that used by Wake et al. [15] (17 × 17), implying that PSs can compensate for a large number of actuators. This presents the possibility of transmitting tactile information by the proposed PS-based technique.

6   Conclusion

In this study, we developed the noncontact tactile display that uses air-jet stimuli to present information of two-dimensional shapes by the PS-based technique. Although the number of subjects was limited, the correct response rate was 58.75% in the case of the one-stroke drawing method; 68.13%, vertex emphasis method; and 84.38%, path separation method. The subjective response data obtained during the experiment has provided the basis for further studies. For example, the intensity of a stimulus may affect the clear recognition of a vertex as well as cause unclear perception of location information around the stimulus. In general, the possibility of transmitting information by using the developed tactile display was confirmed and the fundamental information transmission characteristics of the tactile display were studied. Future researches will focus on finding the optimum distance for PS generation and improving the stimulus presentation methods.

Acknowledgment

This study was supported by JSPS Kakenhi (20370101) and Research for Promoting Technological Seeds (11-003) from JST.

References

1. Fukushima, S.: Person with Visual and Hearing Impairment and Normalization. Akashi Publisher, Tokyo (1997)
2. Yamamoto, A.: Actuator Technologies for Tactile Interfaces, J. Society of Instrument and Control Engineers 47(7), 578–581 (2008)
3. Morizono, T., Yamada, Y., Arai, K., Umetani, Y.: A Study on the Pin Pitch of Tactile Display Devices with Pins Arrayed in a Matrix Form for Displaying Surfaces without Roughness. Trans. Virtual Reality Society of Japan 6(3), 235–237 (2001)
4. Asonuma, M., Matsumoto, M., Wada, C.: Direction Indicating Method by Presenting Tactile Stimulation to the Face. Trans. Human Interface Society 8(4), 65–74 (2006)
5. Cohen, J.C., Makous, J.C., Bolanowski, S.J.: Under Which Conditions Do the Skin and Probe Decouple During Sinusoidal Vibrations? Exp. Brain Res. 129(2), 211–217 (1999)
6. Suzuki, Y., Kobayashi, M.: Air Jet Driven Force Feedback in Virtual Reality. IEEE Computer Graphics and Applications 25(1), 44–47 (2005)

7. Ohka, M., Koga, H., Miyaoka, T., Mitsuya, Y.: Virtual Lattice Texture Presentation Using a Tactile Mouse Featuring a Fine Pin Array. Trans. Japan Society of Mechanical Engineers 71(711), 3174–3180 (2005)
8. Mizukami, Y., Uchida, K., Sawada, H.: Tactile Transmission by Higher-level Perception Using Vibration of Shape Memory Alloy Thread. Trans. Information Processing Society of Japan 48(12), 3739–3749 (2007)
9. Saida, S., Shimizu, Y., Wake, T.: Computer-Controlled TVSS and Some Characteristics of Vibrotactile Letter Recognition. Perceptual and Motor Skills 55, 651–653 (1982)
10. Ide, H., Uchida, M., Yokoyama, S.: Character Trainer Aid for the Blind by Using Sensor Fusion. J. Robotics Society of Japan 12(5), 672–676 (1994)
11. Bekesy, G.V.: Neural Funneling Along the Skin and Between the Inner and Outer Hair Cells of the Cochlea. J. Acoustical Society of America 31(9), 1236–1249 (1959)
12. Tanie, K.: Study on Electrocutaneous Information Transmission. Report of Mechanical Engineering Laboratory 106(105) (1980)
13. Mann, R.W.: Force and Position Proprioception for Prostheses. In: Peter, H., Roland, K., Robert, M., Ingemar, P. (eds.) The Control of Upper-Extremity Prosthesis and Orthoses, pp. 201–219. Charles C Thomas Publisher, Illinois (1974)
14. Ueda, S., Uchida, M., Nozawa, A., Ide, H.: A Tactile Display used Phantom Sensation with Apparent Movement Together. IEEJ Transactions on Fundamentals and Materials 127(6), 277–284 (2007)
15. Wake, T., Simizu, Y., Yamasita, Y.: Exercising Process with Visual Substitution Machine. In: Sensory Substitution Symposium, vol. 1, pp. 59–69 (1975)

VersaPatch: A Low Cost 2.5D Capacitive Touch Sensor

Ray Bittner and Mike Sinclair

Microsoft Research
One Microsoft Way
Redmond, WA 98052, USA
{raybit,sinclair}@microsoft.com

Abstract. Capacitive input devices are becoming increasingly prevalent in consumer devices. This paper presents the hardware and algorithms for the low cost implementation of a capacitive 2.5D input device. The low cost and low power consumption of the device make it suitable for use in portable devices such as cellular phones. The electrical properties used are such that the pre-existing snap dome technologies in such devices can be used as capacitive sensing elements, further reducing the cost and size impact of the capacitive sensor.

Keywords: 2D Pointing, Capacitive Sensing, Interface, Low Cost, Low Power.

1 Introduction

Capacitive sensing is becoming a hot topic in embedded devices; currently popularized by Apple's iPod and iPhone. In this paper, we will describe a very cost effective technique for producing a two and a half dimensional capacitive touch sensor. The sensor will give absolute X-Y position, as well as some useful pressure information that can be used to emulate button presses and/or provide a simplistic Z coordinate.

The basic circuit used for capacitive sensing is illustrated in Figure 1. The capacitive sense pad is connected to a large pullup resistor and a GPIO pin on the microcontroller. The object is to measure the capacitance between a finger, or other pointing device, and the sense pad. As a finger approaches the sense pad, the capacitance at the sense pad increases. This change in capacitance is measured by using the GPIO to first ground the sense pad, and then tri-state it (change it to be an input). A timer

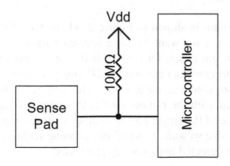

Fig. 1. Sensing Circuit Instance

J.A. Jacko (Ed.): Human-Computer Interaction, Part II, HCII 2009, LNCS 5611, pp. 407–416, 2009.
© Springer-Verlag Berlin Heidelberg 2009

inside the microcontroller then measures the amount of time needed for the total capacitance attached to the GPIO to charge and register as a logical 1. The time elapsed is an indication of the combined capacitance of the sense pad, the GPIO pin and the rest of the circuit. The characteristic voltage curve of such a circuit follows the typical exponential curve for capacitive charging, resulting in a non-linear relationship between timer counts and actual time elapsed, but it is sufficient for our purposes. This is similar to what is discussed in [1]. The value of the pullup resistor allows the designer to optimize the circuit for more sensitivity (higher values) or more noise immunity (lower values). A value of 10MΩ is shown, but a wide range of values are possible depending on the application.

The system is exceedingly inexpensive because all that is required is a single microcontroller with multiple available GPIO pins, one resistor per sense pad, and the sense pads themselves. The sense pads can be fabricated in etched copper or other conductor directly on the circuit board for the cheapest possible implementation. The conductors used for the sense pads do not need to be very low resistance because the pullup resistor is of very high value. This suggests many possible materials and modalities for use of the basic principle.

We have used a Texas Instruments MSP430 as the microcontroller. These processors are useful because of the very low leakage current exhibited by their GPIO pins; less than 50nA as specified in the datasheet [1]. The low leakage current allows a large value pullup resistor to be used, which increases the effective resolution of the timer reading. Other processors could be used, but we have found the MSP430 to be exceptional in this regard. Further, this entire application was made to work in the Flash-based MSP430F2011, which currently has a list price of $0.80 in 100 unit quantities. It is generally known that this price can be much lower in higher quantities; particularly if a production ROM part is chosen. Since the microcontroller is at least 90% of the cost of the system, its cost can be used as an estimated implementation cost.

The average current needed is less than 40μA at 3.3V at with a 16 MHz clock, owing to the low power capacitive sensing method, and the low power performance of the MSP430. Lower power consumption is possible by lowering the operating voltage or sampling frequency, but the choice of operating voltage is often a cost issue in consumer devices, and 3.3V is a reasonable choice in today's technology.

2 Sense Pad Design

The PCB electrode layout is shown in Figure 2 where E1...E9 are the sensing electrodes. With this solution we want to use a low-cost microcontroller which usually means one with a low pin count. Of course, if dozens of pins (and electrodes) were available with which to construct the sensor, 2D finger sensing would be much easier since the electrode size could be made small with respect to the finger size and the sensing would not alias with the sample size of the electrode. In our implementation, the finger size (the size of the finger pad in contact with the sensing surface) is on the order of the electrode size so some form of anti-aliasing technique is required for sub-sample positions to be detected and properly processed.

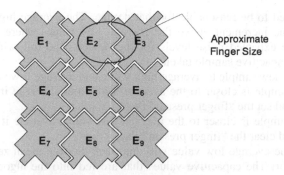

Fig. 2. Anti-Aliased Electrode Layout

In the imaging world, anti-aliasing is usually accomplished with a 2D anti-aliasing filter placed over the sensor which effectively blurs the boundary between pixels. We used a ragged pattern on the PCB to create anti-aliasing in our design. Figure 2 shows this pattern, which creates a 'blurring' or a smooth transition of capacitances between the electrodes.

The device is built by connecting each pad-resistor pair to a single microcontroller as shown in Figure 1. The microcontroller firmware cycles through the ground, tri-state, sense logic 1 cycle as described above. In the prototype device, the microcontroller's internal clock rate is 16MHz, and all 9 sense pads are connected to inter-rupt-capable GPIOs, allowing precise and repeatable timing within the firmware.

3   Mean Zero Value Calculation

The coordinate calculation algorithm requires a known zero reference capacitance for each sensor, which will be termed the mean zero value. This mean zero value is the summation of timing delays in the firmware, plus the inherent capacitance of the sensing pin and the PCB design. Calculation of the mean zero value must be done per pin, per design, and possibly per device instance since each design and sensing chip will be slightly different, and because these values change with device aging and environmental effects. To combat these problems, an adaptive algorithm was devel-oped to calculate the mean zero value at run-time per pin in each device.

The problem is to find a value as close as possible to the true mean zero value in the presence of noise during normal use. Difficulties are encountered since the sensors may be covered by an object that registers as a high capacitance such as a pen or thigh, or someone may be attempting to use the device. What is needed then is an algorithm that can make successive approximations of the true mean zero value while classifying sensed capacitive events. We have developed an algorithm for this task called the Method of Split Averages.

Two running averages are kept for each capacitive sensor. One of these, the aver-age high value, represents an average of all the readings that are believed to have been taken when a capacitive event is registered. The average low value is the average of all readings that are believed to have been taken when no capacitive stimulus was present. At initialization, the average low value may be set to zero, or to some value that is considered to be reasonable for that device. The average high value is initialized to be some increment above the average low value, where the increment is greater than the expected noise levels for the device. The following steps are then performed per capacitive sample taken:

1. Compare the new sample to average high value and average low value.
2. If the new sample is closer to the average high value, average it into the average high value and set the "finger present" flag.
3. If the new sample is closer to the average low value, average it into the average low value and clear the "finger present" flag.

Over time, the average low value will approach the true mean zero value for that capacitive sensor. The capacitive values that are fed into the algorithm are already pre-averaged to some small extent, rather than using the raw readings. This helps the algorithm in the discrimination process in a noisy environment. The raw capacitive values are averaged using an exponential filter, using the shift and add method, so that the memory and processing requirements are manageable in a microcontroller environment. Typically, the initial averaging window is over two to four values at a sampling rate of 80 Hz.

The window length used for the algorithm's average high and average low values is longer. If this window too short, then the two averages will track noise spikes and finger events too closely. If the window is too long, the averages will not correct themselves quickly enough at initialization or in the event that a long series of abnormal readings occurred. We have found that a shift by 12, giving an averaging window of approximately 4096 values, works well.

In a production environment, the initialization values for the average high value and average low value may be standardized across all devices based on values that are found to be generally applicable to the system at hand. This will reduce the initial calibration time so that it should not be noticeable to the end user.

The "finger present" flag is used to trigger the coordinate calculation algorithm, and may also be used to implement capacitive button press detection. Finally, the difference between the average high value and average low value is the dynamic range of the capacitance reading, which is a concept that will be used later.

4 Memory Saving Technique

Microcontrollers typically have a very small amount of RAM and as presented the Method of Split Averages would require two separate running sums to be kept for each sensor pad. Each running sum is likely a 24-bit or 32-bit quantity; requiring significant space when multiplied by the number of sensor pads. The number of bytes required is equal to the number of pads multiplied by the width of the sums times two.

If the dynamic range of the pads may be assumed to be roughly similar, then significant memory may be recovered by maintaining only a single average dynamic range for all of the sensor pads and eliminating the average high value completely. In that case, a separate average low running average is kept for each sense pad, and then a single common average dynamic range is kept for all of them. This reduces the memory needed by nearly a factor of 2. In practice, the assumption of similar dynamic range turned out to be a good one for our applications and so this optimization was used.

5 Coordinate Calculation Algorithm

A 3x3 sensor array will be used as an example, but the method scales to larger sensor grids as well. Figure 3 shows a logical view of the capacitive array and not necessarily the exact dimensions or pad shapes used in a real design. The goal of the algorithm is to produce X-Y coordinates in the range of 0 to 1, so that these can be multiplied by a scaling factor to achieve whatever integer range is desired.

In order to generate the 0 to 1 fractional scale, each row and column of the array is assigned a weight. Intuitively, the columns would be assigned weights 0, 0.5 and 1, as would the respective rows, representing the desired range of output values. However, a weight of 0 is problematic because when used as a multiplicative factor it will zero out the contribution of that row or column in the final result. For that reason, a value of 1 is added to all weights, making the range 1 to 2, which is what is depicted in Figure 3. The added 1 can be subtracted back out later.

The calculation of the X-Y coordinates uses these weights in a weighted average to give far more resolution than the apparent 3x3 array. The X position is given by:

$$X = 1 * \frac{\Sigma_i C_{i,0}}{C_{Total}} + 1.5 * \frac{\Sigma_i C_{i,1}}{C_{Total}} + 2 * \frac{\Sigma_i C_{i,2}}{C_{Total}} - 1 \tag{1}$$

Where $C_{i,j}$ represents the adjusted capacitance value from the associated pad and C_{Total} is the sum of all the adjusted capacitances. As can be seen, the summation multiplies the weight of each column by the fractional contribution of that column to the total capacitance measured. The -1 on the right had side adjusts the output range back down to a 0 to 1 fractional scale. The resulting X value may be multiplied by any scaling factor, such as 256, to obtain a useful integer range. By carefully performing all summations and multiplications before any divisions, floating point math may be avoided. A power of 2 scaling factor further simplifies the amount of code needed. As an example, the formula may be rewritten as:

$$X = 256 * \frac{\Sigma_i C_{i,0} + 3 * \frac{\Sigma_i C_{i,1}}{2} + 2 * \Sigma_i C_{i,2}}{C_{Total}} - 256 \tag{2}$$

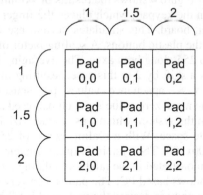

Fig. 3. Row/Column Weight Assignment

The corresponding unscaled equation for the Y coordinate is:

$$Y = 1 * \frac{\sum_j c_{0,j}}{c_{Total}} + 1.5 * \frac{\sum_j c_{1,j}}{c_{Total}} + 2 * \frac{\sum_j c_{2,j}}{c_{Total}} - 1 \tag{3}$$

Except in this case, the sums are computed across the rows. By using the proportional contribution from each pad, rather than absolutes, the weighted average avoids problems with moment to moment sensing differences such as humidity, temperature, the actual distance between the finger and the sense pads, etc.

Note that this same method may be used for other array dimensions by assigning more intermediate weights to the rows and columns of the array. For example, if a 4x4 grid is desired, then starting weights of 0, 0.33, 0.66 and 1 could be used.

A larger grid may be desired in the case where the finger size of the user is smaller than the size of a sense pad. In that case, the algorithm may not have enough capacitive contribution from adjacent pads to give sufficient resolution. In that case, larger array dimensions may be needed to make the size of the sense pad commensurate with, or smaller than, the size of the user's finger.

The algorithm expects the dynamic range of all pads to be roughly equal under a given set of conditions. This translates to making the sensing pads all have roughly the same surface area. Though, even if they are not, the disparity could be adjusted by individual pad weights.

6 Experimental Results

In order to show the effectiveness of this approach, we placed the device on a precision stepper table and used a brass finger as the pointing device. The stepper table was moved in 0.1" increments in both X and Y. At each step, the finger remained stationary briefly while sample data was collected at the rate of 80 samples per second. The finger was electrically connected it to the operator, but was not grounded through any other path. In practice, we have found that a real finger performs better than the brass one, but this provides a worst case scenario. The individual sensor pads measured 0.545" square from point to point, and the overall 3x3 pad measured 1.4" square from point to point.

The left hand graph of Figure 4 shows the results of skimming the finger across the top of the plastic keys on the keypad, which places the finger 0.060" off of the top of the sensors on the circuit board. This simulates normal use most closely, where the finger is in contact with the plastic buttons. A scaling factor of 256 was used, giving a nominal response of 0 to 255 along both axes. The averaging being applied on a sample by sample basis uses a shift by 2 in this case, resulting in a moving average window over approximately 4 capacitance values per sensor. The slower moving averages used to track the mean zero value for each pad used a shift by 12.

There is some noise in the system, which was characterized by a standard deviation of 2.16 in XY coordinate space. With a scaling factor of 256, this gives a true XY resolution of roughly 100x100. The system is quite useable as a pointing device in this state, as we have demonstrated in the lab by emulating a serial mouse and using it to drive a Microsoft Windows based PC. The pad is also very responsive with shift by 2 averaging, and if lower noise is desired the pad would still be very useable if a shift by 3 or 4 were employed. Also evident is the fact that the device was rotated slightly clockwise when the samples were taken.

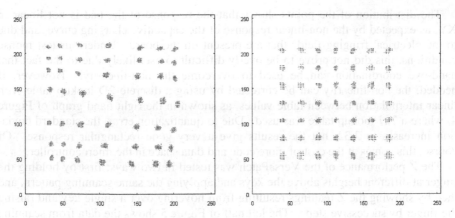

Fig. 4. XY sample data at keypad surface, before linearization (left), after linearization (right)

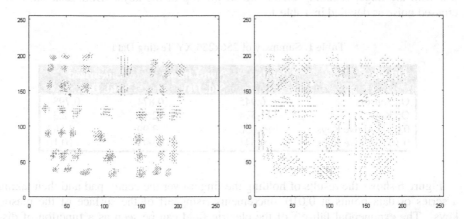

Fig. 5. XY sample data, 0.050" above keypad (left), 0.100" above keypad (right)

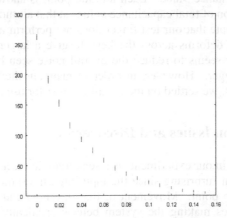

Fig. 6. Z sample data from key surface in 0.010" increments

The distribution of the points shows that the response of the pad is not linear in XY, as expected by the non-linear response of the capacitive charging curve, and due to the electrical fringing fields that are present on the board. Under our test mouse conditions, this did not prove to be overly difficult to use; likely due to the fact that hand-eye coordination can be used to overcome the non-linearity. However, if needed, the non-linearity can be corrected by using a discrete 2D lookup table with linear interpolation between table values, as shown in the right hand graph of Figure 4, where a 7x7 lookup table was used. Due to quantization error, the standard deviation increases to 2.32, but the results give a very good rectangular response. Of course, this comes at the cost of more code and data space in the microcontroller.

The Z performance of the VersaPatch was tested in two ways; first by holding the finger at different heights above the keys and applying the same scanning pattern, and then by showing the Z readings resulting from hovering over a single key and raising the finger by successive steps. The left half of Figure 5 shows the data from scanning the finger 0.050" higher off of the keypad. The right half of Figure 5 shows the same test with the finger scanning 0.100" off of the top of the keys. Both tests show increased noise as detailed in Table 1.

Table 1. Summary of 256x256 XY Testing Data

Altitude	# Points	Non-Linear Std. Dev.	Linearized Std. Dev.
On Sensors	6,945	0.874	0.7983
On Keys	11,574	2.16	2.32
0.050" Above Keys	9,050	3.99	4.592
0.100" Above Keys	9,541	6.993	10.10

Figure 6 shows the results of holding the finger over the center pad and then taking a series of data points at 0.010" increments rising off of the surface of the plastic keys. The exponential fall off of the electric field can be seen as a function of distance. The X axis shows height above the plastic keys in inches, and the Y axis shows the total capacitance value. Each altitude point is shown as a vertical bar to indicate the distribution of total capacitance values at that altitude.

It is important to note that our test finger does not perform as well as a real finger because a real finger deforms across the keys to give a larger cross sectional area. Also, body chemistry seems to reduce the overall noise seen by the sensor as compared to the brass finger. However, in order to maintain the best repeatability and accuracy in placement, we settled on the metallic finger for use as a stylus.

7   Implementation Issues and Discoveries

The main issue noted in our experiments is a sensitivity to electrical noise in the power system. This is not surprising since the input high threshold of the GPIO pin determines the detection point. Movement of that threshold causes fluctuations in the capacitive timer values making the system behave erratically. However, we have found that a linear regulator will negate local power supply noise issues.

The system is also somewhat sensitive to PCB layout issues, and best results will be obtained when the traces from the sensing pads are run over a ground plane on the PCB. Our experience is that using wire wrap wire to connect the sense pads to the microcontroller will make the system unusable due to electrical noise.

The C_{Total} quantity can be used for emulated button presses, as well as fairly coarse grain finger altitude detection. Although, the Z detection falls off quickly with the electric field as a function of $1/r^2$.

The fact that the conductor used for the sense pads can be of relatively poor quality has suggested the use of clear conductors overlaid directly on a display to allow for finger based device navigation. This is something that we have not experimented with as yet, but will be the subject of future investigations.

An implementation possibility that we have explored is the use of snap domes as the capacitive sensing element. These are commonly found in electronic devices, such as cellular phones, mounted on the PCB beneath the plastic buttons that the user sees. The snap domes make electrical contact for the switch, as well as producing the audible click and tactile feedback that is normally expected. Since these domes are metallic, the device can be built so that each dome is at the center of one of the sense pads shown in Figure 2, and the dome becomes part of the sense pad. The same algorithms described transform the normal keypad into a gesture or cursor positioning device at very little cost, while maintaining button functionality as normal. In our design, the dome electrically "hides" the normal button down contact under the dome so that it does not interfere with the capacitive sensing. The button down contact is grounded so that when activated, the sense pad appears to be stuck to ground, which is captured as a timeout by the firmware and reported as a button press. We have implemented this in a prototype device and have found it to work quite well.

8 Prior Work

A Texas Instruments application note describes the use of an MSP430 microcontroller to implement a capacitive touch slider [1]. The mean zero value is established in a somewhat similar way, but the method employed does not attempt to track the dynamic range of the capacitance values. Also, the methods discussed only work for a 1D capacitive sensor strip, rather than creating a 2D pad.

The most complete reference for capacitive sensing that we are aware of is a book by Baxter [2]. That book details a large number of circuits and measurement techniques and is a very good reference.

A relaxation oscillator based capacitive measurement circuit has been proposed by van der Goes, et. al., [7], and is believed to be at the heart of many commercial capacitive sensing devices. By using the capacitance of interest to vary the frequency of an oscillator, frequency measurements allow detection of changes in capacitance of less than 100aF. While the sensitivity of that method is startling, a custom ASIC was needed to realize it. We have found our method to have sufficient sensitivity for practical use as an input device, while still using an off the shelf microcontroller.

In [4], a technique is discussed for measuring small capacitances where the small capacitance to be measured is repeatedly charged and then switched in parallel with a larger capacitor of known value. The number of switches needed to charge the large capacitor gives the size of the smaller capacitor. The added circuit complexity of that method would add to the overall cost of the solution as compared to the RC method proposed in this paper, both in terms of components and pins on the microcontroller.

References

1. Albus, Z.: PCB-Based Capacitive Touch Sensing With MSP430. Texas Instruments Application Report SLAA363A, Dallas, TX (2007), http://www.msp430.com
2. Baxter, L.K., Herrick, R.J.: Capacitive Sensors: Design and Applications. IEEE Press Series on Electronics (August 1, 1996)
3. Dietz, Paul, A.: Pragmatic Introduction to the Art of Electrical Engineering, Parallax, Rocklin, CA (1999), http://www.stampsinclass.com
4. Geiger, R., Allen, P.: VLSI: Design Techniques for Analog and Digital Circuits. McGraw-Hill, New York (1990)
5. Sinclair, M.J., Hinckley, K.P., Kajiya, J.T., Sherman, N.C.: Capacitance Touch Slider. US Patent #7,158,125, Issued, January 2 (2007)
6. Texas Instruments: MSP430x20x1, MSP430x20x2, MSP430x20x3 Mixed Signal Microcontroller, Dallas, TX (2007), http://www.msp430.com
7. Van der Goes, F.M.L., Meijer, G.C.M.A.: Novel Low-Cost Capacitive-Sensor Interface. IEEE Transactions On Instrumentation And Measurement 45(2), 536–540 (1996)

From Implicit to Touching Interaction by Identification Technologies: Towards Tagging Context

Jose Bravo[1], Ramon Hervas[1], Carmen Fuentes[1,2], Vladimir Villarreal[3],
Gabriel Chavira[4], Salvador Nava[4], Jesus Fontecha[1], Gregorio Casero[1],
Rocio Peña[1], and Marcos Vergara[1]

[1] MAmI Research Group, Castilla La Mancha University, Spain
[2] General Hospital of Ciudad Real, Ciudad Real, Spain
[3] Technological University of Panamá, Panamá
[4] Faculty of Engineering, Autonomous University of Tamaulipas, México
{jose.bravo,ramon.hlucas}@uclm.es, mcfuentesg@gmail.com,
Vladimir.villarreal@utp.ac.pa, {gchavira,snava}@uat.edu.mx

Abstract. Intelligent environments need interactions capable of detecting users and providing them with good-quality contextual information. In this sense we adapt technologies, identifying and locating people for supporting their needs. However, it is necessary to analyze some important features in order to compare the implicit interaction, which is closer to the users and more natural, to a new interaction by contact. In this paper we present the adaptability of two technologies; Radiofrequency Identification (RFID) and Near Field Communication (NFC). In the first one, the interaction is more appropriate within intelligent environments but in the second one, the same RFID technology, placed in mobile phones, achieves some advantages that we consider to be an intermediate solution until the standardization of sensors arrives.

Keywords: Ambient Intelligence, NFC, Touching Interaction, Location-based Services.

1 Introduction

Ubiquitous Computing paradigm and, most recently, Ambient Intelligence (AmI), are the visions in which technology becomes invisible, embedded, present whenever we need it, enabled by simple interactions, attuned to all our senses and adaptive to users and contexts [1]. A further definition of AmI is as follow: *"Ambient Intelligence refers to an exciting new paradigm of information technology, in which people are empowered through a digital environment that is aware of their presence and context sensitive, adaptive and responsive to their needs, habits, gestures and emotions"*.

This vision and the three pillars concerned in it, Ubiquitous Computing, Ubiquitous Communications and Natural Interfaces, promote a shift in computing from the traditional desktop computer to a lot of devices placed around us, offering services. In this sense, it is essential to adapt technologies as inputs to the context, allowing the user not to ask the computer explicitly for what he/she needs. The idea of creating intelligent environments requires unobtrusive hardware, wireless communications,

J.A. Jacko (Ed.): Human-Computer Interaction, Part II, HCII 2009, LNCS 5611, pp. 417–425, 2009.

massively distributed devices, natural interfaces and security. Thus, by introducing intrusiveness technologies into daily objects and by embedding interaction in daily actions, it is possible to feel in an intelligent environment.

To attain this vision, it is fundamental to analyze some definitions of context. In [2], A. Dey defines this concept as "any information that can be used to characterize the situation of an entity. An entity is a person, place, or object that is considered relevant to the interaction between a user and an application, including the user and application themselves". This author also defines context awareness as the "context to provide relevant information and/or services to the user, where relevancy depends on the user's task".

In order to design context-aware applications it is necessary to observe certain types of context-aware information as being more relevant than others: identity-awareness, location-awareness, time-awareness, activity-awareness and objective-awareness are essential. All these types of awareness answer the five basic questions ("Who", "Where", "What", "When" and "Why"), which provide the guidelines for context modelling. This kind of information allows us to adapt or build the technology that needs to be dispersed throughout the environment and to model the human behavioural support.

Once the context and their important features are defined, it is time to study new interaction forms proposing the approach to the user by means of more natural interfaces. At this point we have to talk about Albrecht Schmidt and his concept of Implicit Human Computer Interaction (iHCI) [3][4]. It is defined as follows:

"iHCI is the interaction of a human with the environment and with artefacts, which is aimed to accomplish a goal. Within this process the system acquires implicit input from the user and may present implicit output to the user"

Schmidt defines implicit input as user perceptions interacting with the physical environment, allowing the system to anticipate the user by offering implicit outputs. In this sense the user can concentrate on the task, not on the tool as Ubiquitous Computing Paradigm proposes.

The next step that this author proposes is that of Embedded Interaction in two terms. The first one embeds technologies into artefacts, devices and environments. The second one, at a conceptual level, is the embedding of interactions in the user activities (task or actions) [5]. With these ideas in mind, our main goal is to achieve natural interaction, as the implicit interaction concept proposes.

Our idea of the adaptability of sensorial capabilities is through Identification technologies as specialized sensorial capabilities. With these, the idea of natural interfaces is possible and the implicit inputs and the proactive aspect could be guaranteed [6,7]. To achieve just that, we have adapted RFID technology. Users only have to wear RFID tags, embedding interaction into daily activities. At the moment, we perceive the context awareness by the "who", "when" and "where" aspects, thereby obtaining "what"[8,9]. However, some disadvantages have to be addressed. For example, the cost of infrastructures is high. Moreover, the places for readers and antennas are fixed in the environment. Finally, the context responsibility identifying people, their profiles and the services allowed for everyone is an important factor to be considered when making intelligent environments.

For this reason we have adapted the recent NFC (Near Field Communications) technology, which is RFID combined with mobile phones. In NFC, the process, communication and storage capabilities are added to the identification by RFID through a reader placed into the mobile phones. This technology requires an interaction by contact achieved by bringing the mobile phone near to an NFC tag, reader or another mobile phone. Even though this is a weakness when compared to the implicit interaction that RFID offers, other advantages have to be addressed. For instance, the cheaper cost of infrastructure, the mobility compared to the fixed places for devices and the responsibility of the "when" aspect, which in this case is a user dependability, are significant in accomplishing an intermediate solution for building intelligent environments[10,11]. At this moment, it is important to talk about the idea of "tagging context". By placing tags through the context, users can interact with the environment, seeking to meet their need by means of a simple touch. In this sense we have structured 1-Kb Mifare tags containing information about the environment by means of identifying and running applications automatically, by touching. To do that we are tagging users, places, objects and interaction with public displays.

We have adapted this technology in some solutions for education, healthcare, shopping areas and public administration contexts. In all of these, the "when" responsibility, the mobility, the running of applications by contact and the simple infrastructure of tagging context are important features that have to be considered, at least, as an intermediate and quick solution.

Under these lines we present an introduction to the RFID and NFC technologies. Then, we present our proposal of tagging context by using the NFC technology in three different contexts: an Alzheimer's day centre, hospital wards nursing care and a proposal for managing documents in public administrations. Finally, conclusions resume these ideas.

2 Identification Technologies

2.1 RFID

In RFID systems there are basically two elements, tags or transponders, which consist of a microchip that stores data, and an antenna (coupling element), and readers or interrogators which emit radio waves and receive signals back from the tag. The "interrogation" signal activates all the tags that are within its reach. RFID systems are classified as active and according to the kind of tag used. Readers have a frequency of operation and are usually divided into three basic ranges: Low (125Khz.), High (13.56 MHz), which is the standard one, and Ultra High Frequency (UHF). Depend of frequencies, different distances can be detected. From a few centimetres to some hundred meters are possible to read tags.

Using this technology it is possible by embedding it into daily objects and embedding interaction into daily actions, we perceive the context-awareness by the "who", "when" and "where" aspect obtaining "what". Typical services by identification are Access, Location, Inventory and so on, but we are interested in the Visualization service. With it, we try to offer information to the user in some parts of a mosaic. This way requires no user interaction according with the Ubiquitous Computing idea about not intrusion. Figure 1 (left) shows the typical RFID devices: computer, reader, antenna and tag.

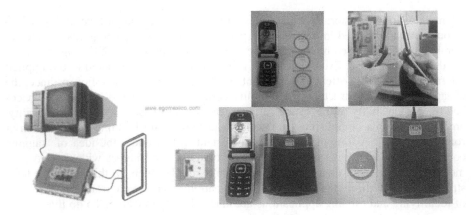

Fig. 1. RFID & NFC devices

2.2 NFC

NFC is a new short-range wireless connectivity technology developed by Philips and Sony in 2002. It is a combination of RFID and interconnection technologies. NFC uses a high frequency band of up to 13.56 MHz, with a data transmission speed of 424 Kbits/s and a reach of 10 cm. NFC systems consist of two elements, the Initiator that controls the information exchange and the Target that responds to the requirement of the initiator.

In an NFC system, there are two modes of operation: active and passive. In the active one, both devices generate their own field of radio frequency to transmit data (peer to peer). In the passive one, only one of these devices generates the radiofrequency field, while the other is used to load modulation for data transfers. In Figure 1 three types of NFC devices can be seen. Mobile phone Nokia 6131 which is reader-enabled, Mifare tags with 1Kb storage and readers. In addition, all operation modes are shown: mobile phone-tag, mobile phone-mobile phone, mobile phone-reader and reader-tag. See figure 1 (right).

3 Tagging Context: Some Examples

3.1 Alzheimer Day Centre

Alzheimer's disease is a neurodegenerative illness where the patient displays cognitive impairment and behavioural disorders. Alzheimer's patients may be admitted to a day centre to give respite to their relatives and to improve their own quality of life. These centres are organized as a set of rooms for rehabilitation, therapy, crafts, audio-visual displays and a dining room. In these, a great variety of activities (physical, cognitive, social, etc.) are devised according to the patients' needs and disease level. To achieve this, a professional team of physicians, physiotherapists, assistants, psychologist, etc., is needed and a large supply of auxiliary equipment is required for interventions.

Fig. 2. Personalized Information and Therapy Support

In these kinds of centres, when a caregiver notices a patient incident, he or she needs to stop doing their job, leave their patients with another caregiver, and write the incident in a notebook manually. There are many clinics and centres which follow this protocol, causing numerous problems. These include the interruption of day to day work, lack of formalism and the impossibility of searching for the information and generating accurate reports for physicians at a later date.

In order to solve this problem we have formalized all kind of incidents making a classification by activity. Then, we are now able to offer a form to the user so that he/she can add the incidents to the system in a consistent way. It means, by using the NFC technology tagging patients, activities, places and other things like the display interaction as therapy support. Only by touching the patient and incident tag in each activity it is possible to transfer de desired information to other caregiver, physicians or relatives. See figure 2 (left).

In the therapy activity we propose a simple interaction to get information about each patient from the server. In the case below, with just the activity and the patient tag involved, it is possible to visualize on a public display an exercise to test memory. The exercise is contained within the server, which then sends it to a display thanks to a wireless video sender. This device can offer different data: video, voice, text, etc. Also, the corresponding exercise structure is given, only, touching tags. All the data about each patient is accessible to relatives who are introduced to the appropriate centre web site. For that, some advice is offered in order to find the best type of memory information. It can be seen on figure 2 (right).

3.2 Hospital Wards Nursing Care

Some authors argue that a great percentage of a nurse's work corresponds to management of information (22%). This takes up time that could otherwise be used for caring, so technological adaptability seems to be needed towards solving this problem by reducing that percentage. At the same time, this adaptability has to consider the visualization of information, which is very important in a hospital context. For that, our proposal consists of placing tags on the patients' wrist, beds, rooms, medication and displays. In addition, nurses use NFC- enabled mobile phones and public displays, aiming to reduce the time taken to manage the patient's nursing record with the simple touch Patient Nursing Record. Finally, the visualization of information completes our proposal for the management of information for nursing in a hospital ward.

Figure 3 shows the cycle for nursing with an NFC-enabled mobile phone. In the top left, the contact between two mobiles is displayed, a contact which makes the shift change possible when a new nurse comes into the hospital ward. The schedule is transmitted from the nurse on duty to the mobile phone of the incoming nurse, along with all the information needed. The next step, on the right, presents a J2ME application for managing nursing tasks. There are two modes of operation with this application: by task or by schedule (time). In the first one, the nurse chooses the task required from the menu and, in the second one we may observe the shift schedule that was mentioned before, which controls the entire process by the touching of tags. The third step shows different information that can be stored in tags. There are five types: patients' wrists, rooms (there could be more than one patient), beds, medications and interaction tags.

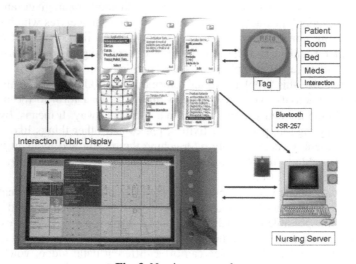

Fig. 3. Nursing care cycle

In our proposal for tagging a hospital ward, the patient tag contains all the information needed for nursing, which means, drugs prescribed & their doses, blood/urine tests (control of requests for these), diets, wound dressings, data monitoring and the contraindications of the medication. The tag on the bed can contain useful data of a patient such as identification, blood/urine tests pending and their diet. The room tag contains the patient's/patients' identification. This information shows the schedule for the room at that particular time. The tags for medication store specific information for everyone, along with support for the control of their administration and corresponding preparation in the nurse's cabinet. Finally, the interaction tags provide a simple way for visualizing and managing information.

The fourth step, below right, shows the nursing server. It is a PC connected by the data base for patients and contains the Nurse Patient Record. All the information managed in the patient room is transmitted by Bluetooth or NFC Reader. The first one can be done by touching the tags next de PC display and, the second one, by touching an NFC reader connected to the PC. We consider this a very appropriate way to manage the Nurse Patient Record, which at the same time avoids complicated interactions and reduces the time nurses spend on managing information.

Finally, a visualization service completes this cycle. In this, nurses manage the information for patients by just the interaction with tags placed on the public display. Collaboration between nurses in the shift change is also possible. We have placed four tags for interaction next to the public display. Another tag for supporting the identification control is also needed. This one allows each nurse to take control of the display.

3.3 Public Administration

In this section we describe the context, that is, an example of public administration: a city council through a scenario. Also, the simple proposed architecture is explained.

Peter has hurry this morning because he has to arrange some documents that will be present in the city council. Also, he has to be at 10h for an important meeting 20 km. distance from there. He arrives at 8.45 at council reception asking to the receptionist about the process to payment fees for an authorization for improvement of his house. Worker says Peter that he has to go to the third floor and look for the desk number four. Then, in the desk, an auxiliary give Peter a form giving him information about the improvement and, also, some documents are required. It means that, after getting these documents, Peter has to back to the council, filling this form and, in a few days is going to receive a notice about the council decision.

With this technology it is possible to realize the process mentioned before more easily and quickly. For that people have to introduce the citizen profile into the mobile phone. It consists in personal data concerning to obligation of citizens, e. g. date and place born, address, house and car references, taxes, and so on. This data have to be stored into the mobile phone adequately. The reason is the matching process between data profile and the form requirements. This fact make needed a standardization of public administrations but, we think it is not difficult because there is a powerful mechanism to define formal vocabularies in order to reduce the ambiguity.

In figure 4 we show the process described into the scenario. In a point of information the user obtain the information about the place that he has to go and the corre spondent form. This place is a desk with some tags, each one run an application for the required document. Next, this form is automatically filled with the information enclosed into the user profile. After that and, only passing the mobile phone next to the reader, the filled form is transmitted to the database. In a few days, the user will receive the document in the mobile phone by GPRS or attached to an e-mail.

Finally, to complement this kind of processes, we have implemented a variety of mobile-desktop applications. With these, each user exchange information from and to the PC, printer or visualization devices. These applications help users to obtain the information adequately into a display or paper. Additionally, it is a simple mode to carry out all kinds of documents and exchange then in public administration processes.

424   J. Bravo et al.

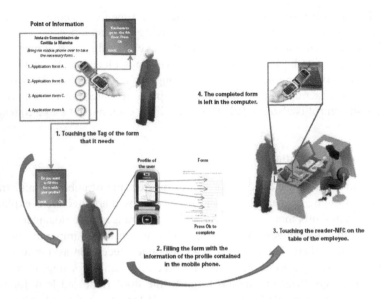

Fig. 4. NFC filling form process

4 Conclusions

We have adapted two similar technologies. However, the NFC one offers us an unexpected approach of thinking about the interaction in intelligent environments and, at the same time. For that, a new way of receiving services from it appears. In this paper we have presented this approach through three different contexts. In them, we have tagged the environment adequately trying to minimize the user interaction: only a touch is needed.

References

1. ISTAG, Scenarios for Ambient Intelligence in 2010 (February 2001),
   http://www.cordis.lu/ist/istag.htm
2. Dey, A.: Understanding and Using Context. Personal and Ubiquitous Computing 5(1), 4–7 (2001)
3. Schmidt, A.: Implicit Human Computer Interaction Through Context. Personal Technologies 4(2&3), 191–199 (2000)
4. Schmidt, A.: Interactive Context-Aware Systems. Intering with Ambient Intelligence. In: Riva, G., Vatalaro, F., Davide, F., Alcañiz, M. (eds.) Ambient Intelligence (2005)
5. Schmidt, A., Kranz, M., Holleis, P.: Interacting with the Ubiquitous Computing – Towards Embedding Interaction. In: Smart Objects & Ambient Intelligence (sOc-EuSAI 2005), Grenoble, Francia (2005)
6. Bravo, J., Hervás, R., Sánchez, I., Chavira, G., Nava, S.: Visualization Services in a Conference Context: An approach by RFID Technology. Journal of Universal Computer Science 12(3), 270–283

7. Bravo, J., Hervás, R., Chavira, G.: Ubiquitous Computing at classroom: An approach through identification process. Journal of Universal Computer Science 11(9), 1494–1504
8. Bravo, J., Hervás, R., Chavira, G., Nava, S.: Towards disappearing Interaction: An Approach through RFID. In: The 2nd International Conference on Intelligent Environments, Athens, Greece, Julio (2006)
9. Bravo, J., Hervás, R., Chavira, G., Nava, S.: Modeling Contexts by RFID-Sensor Fusion. In: The Workshop on Context Modelling and Reasoning (CoMoRea 2006) at the 4th IEEE International Conference on Pervasive Computing and Communication (PerCom 2006), Pisa, Italy, March 13-17 (2006)
10. Bravo, J., Hervás, R., Chavira, G., Nava, S.: Adapting Technologies to Model Contexts: Two approaches through RFID & NFC. In: The Second International Conference on Digital Information Management (ICDIM 2007), Lyon, France (October 2007)
11. Bravo, J., Hervás, R., Chavira, G., Nava, S.W., Villarreal, V.: From Implicit to Touching Interaction: RFID and NFC Approaches. In: IEEE Conference on Human System Interaction (HIS 2008), Krakrow, Poland (May 2008)

VTouch: A Vision-Base Dual Finger Touched Inputs for Large Displays

Ching-Han Chen and Cun-Xian Nian

National Central University, Computer Science & Information Engineering Department,
No.300, Jhongda Rd., Jhongli City, Taoyuan County 32001, Taiwan
pierre@csie.ncu.edu.tw, yalight@hotmail.com

Abstract. In this work, we present a complete architecture to implement a dual touch function for large sized displays. The architecture includes the hardware device and the software algorithm. The system has lower cost and smaller size than previous works for large sized display. And the proposed approach eliminates the requirement of special hardware. The system can be plugged to a normal display and change the display to equip the dual touch function. At the final of this paper, we give an experiment to demonstrate the system and show its usability.

Keywords: Human-computer interaction, dual touch screen, multi-touch screen, user interface.

1 Introduction

To touch and manipulate data on screens directly without any intermediary device provides more convenient and instinctive using experience to the user. There are several implements of multi-touch displays, but most current techniques need special hardware for the touching ability. For instance, spatially segmented antennas to sense the changes in electronic capacity are employed in [1], [2] and projected electronic capacities are used in iPhone [3]. Another approach proposed in [4] uses a frustrated total internal reflection (FTIR) device to detect the fingers optically. Moreover, current implements are either still too experience or too bulky for widespread adoption especially to large displays.

This work proposed a vision-base system to achieve the dual fingertip touching ability for large displays. This system eliminates the need of special hardware. It only employs two cameras with wide-angle lens and applies image processing techniques to detect the fingertip touched on the display. It can be mounted on a general monitor and turn it to a touch screen. It is cheap and thin compared with previous works.

With this system, user can manipulate the screen directly with their one or two fingertips. For examples, a dual touché display can be installed on a museum wall to be a versatile screen. The user can drag, zoom or rotate photos on the screen by their fingertips, or play two people interacted games on the screen.

J.A. Jacko (Ed.): Human-Computer Interaction, Part II, HCII 2009, LNCS 5611, pp. 426–434, 2009.

2 Approach

In the main idea, there are two cameras to capture the two scenes above the surface of the display. Then, the system applies the detection algorithm to detect whether there is any object touched the display. If there is any object touched the display, it will compute the coordinates of the objects on the display. The following are the detail descriptions of hardware and software in this system, respectively.

2.1 Hardware Device

The major components are two cameras in the hardware mechanism. The two cameras are installed on the two cutting edges of the display and the optical axis of each camera is parallel with the surface of the display. For capturing the full scene above the surface of the display, the wide-angle lenses are employed. Besides, there is a set infrared rays (IR) LED modules at the side of each camera. The IR LED provides light source when the environment is dark. A thin border which can absorb infrared rays is appended on the display. The border is to reduce environmental interferences and make the system more robust. Fig. 1 shows the illustration of the hardware device.

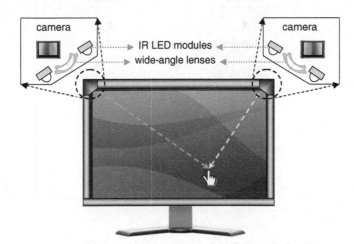

Fig. 1. Two cameras with wide-angle lenses are on the top-left and top-right corner of the display. The IR LED modules are at the side of the camera. The optical axes of cameras and IR LED are all parallel to the surface of the display. The display is surrounded by a thin border which can absorb the infrared rays.

2.2 Software Algorithm

When the two cameras capture a set of scenes, the system receives the left and right images from the cameras and applies the algorithm on the images to achieve the touch ability of the screen. The algorithm detects whether there is any object touched on the display. If so, it calculates the coordinate of the object. The main procedure of the algorithm can be separated to four stages and they are image pre-processing, locating

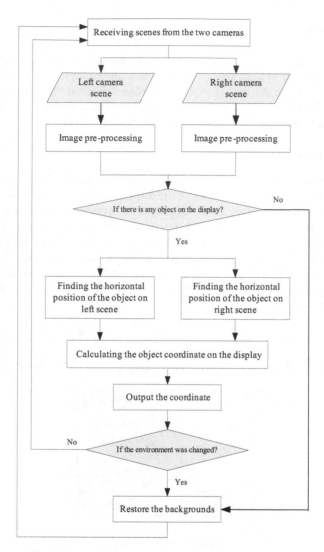

Fig. 2. Overall flowchart of the algorithm in the system

coordinate, object tracking, and restoring background. Fig. 2 shows the procedure of the algorithm and following is the detail descriptions for each stage.

For the camera, it can capture a full size image. However, the lens axis of the camera is parallel with the surface of the display. We can detect whether any object touched the display by the intersection between the screen surface and the surrounding. The intersected region is small and thin in the full image. This reduces size of data needed to process and enhance the performance. The red rectangle in fig. 3 is the region used in our system implementation.

Fig. 3. The red rectangle is the region is the intersection of screen surface and the surrounding and it is applied to our algorithm

Image Pre-processing. In this stage, a serial image processing procedure is applied on the two received scenes. It includes the color transformation, subtracting background, image median filter, image bi-level, horizontal image profile converter, and equalization. Fig. 4 shows the flowchart and the sample images of each step of the image pre-processing.

The camera sensor can capture color images, but we lose most color information of the captured image due to the IR filter. The captured images are looked like the source image in Fig. 4. For the reason, the color transformation in image pre-processing simply translates the received images to gray level images. The gray level image is easier and faster to process. Then, we take the current image to subtract the background image, and we can get a clear image to identify if there is object touched the display. The background image is stored at the system initialization. For reducing the noise, which may be produced by camera or environmental interference, a median filter is employed. In the next, we project the image to a horizontal image profile which counting how many bright pixels in each column of the image. Subsequently, we equalize the horizontal image profile to smooth it. The equalization replaces each

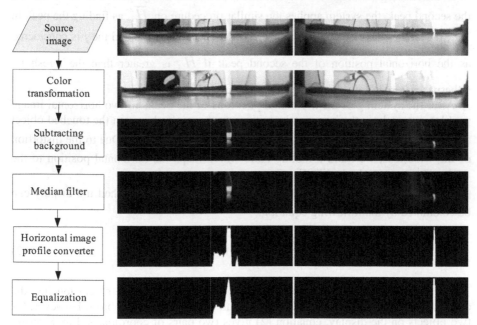

Fig. 4. The flowchart of the image pre-processing and the corresponding sample images of each step

element in the horizontal image profile with the average value of near the elements. The equalization can be expressed as the following equation.

$$\overline{H}_i = \frac{1}{k}\sum_{j=1}^{k} H_{i-j+k/2} \tag{1}$$

Where H_i is the value of the ith element in original horizontal image profile and $\overline{H}_i$ is the value of the ith element in the equalized horizontal image profile, and k is the degree of equalization. The degree of equalization decides the degree of smooth.

Locating Coordinate. After image pre-processing, the system detects whether there is any peak in the two horizontal image profiles. If so, it finds out the horizontal positions of the peaks in the two horizontal image profiles. Fig. 5(b) is the procedure of finding the peaks and Fig. 5(a) is the sample images of the procedure. At the beginning of the procedure, it searches the element $\overline{H}_i$ with the maximum value in the horizontal image profile $\overline{H}$ which got from image pre-processing. If $\overline{H}_i$ is greater than the threshold, the i is considered as the horizontal position of the peak in $\overline{H}$. If not, the system considers there is no peak exists. In other words, it represents there is no object touched the display. After the first peak is found, the system eliminates the decreasing region from the ith element in $\overline{H}$, and the residual horizontal image profile is $\overline{H}'$. To find the second peak, the system applies the similar procedure on $\overline{H}'$ as finding the peak in $\overline{H}$. It searches the element $\overline{H}_j$ with maximum value in $\overline{H}'$, and the j is considered as the horizontal position of the second peak if $\overline{H}_j$ is greater than the threshold. Otherwise, there is considered only one peak existed in $\overline{H}$.

After the system gets the horizontal positions of the peaks in two horizontal image profiles, it translates the horizontal positions to the angles between the touched object and the two cameras. The angles are as the θ_1 and θ_2 in Fig. 6. Due to the distortion of the wide lens, we build a lookup table which maps the horizontal position to the angle. The mapping looks like Fig. 7.

With having the θ_1 and θ_2, the coordinate of the object touched the display can be calculated by the following equation.

$$x = \frac{W \tan \theta_2}{\tan \theta_1 + \tan \theta_2}, \quad y = x \tan \theta_1 \tag{2}$$

In equation (2), the W is the width of the display. If only one object touched the display, the x and y in equation (2) is the result coordinate of the object. However, for two objects on the display, equation (2) gives two pairs of coordinates. Fig. 8 shows the diagram. The correct coordinates of the two objects are among the two pairs of coordinates. To solve the problem, this system adopts the object tracking technique to eliminate the false coordinate and output the true one.

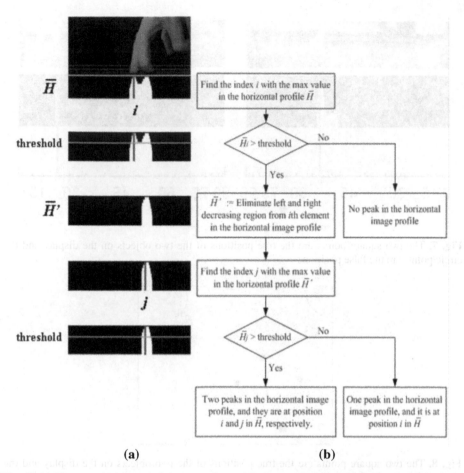

(a)   (b)

Fig. 5. (a) The sample images of the procedure of finding peaks. (b) The flowchart of the finding peaks.

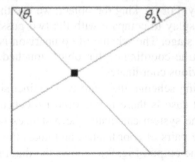

Fig. 6. The square point is the location of the object touched the display. The system can calculate the coordinate of the location with the two angles θ_1 and θ_2.

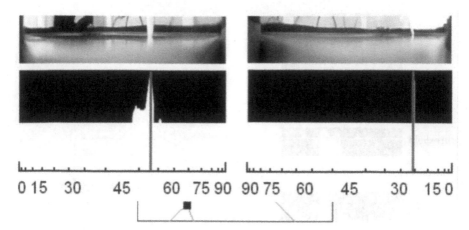

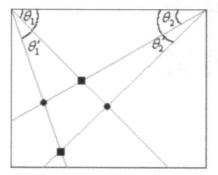

Fig. 7. The two square points are the true positions of the two objects on the display and the circle points are the false positions

Fig. 8. The two square points are the true positions of the two objects on the display and the circle points are the false positions

Object Tracking. The object tracking is used when the system detects there are two object touched the display. For tracking the object, we use the previous coordinate of the object touched the display to compare with the two possible pairs of coordinates which got from previous stage. The scheme of comparison is to select the closer pair of coordinates to be the true coordinates that object touched. The closer pair has the shorter distance with previous coordinates.

With this object tracking scheme, there are two distinct situations need to be handled separately. The first case is there is one object touched the display in previous detection. In this case, the system calculates the distances between previous coordinate and the two possible pairs of coordinates, and takes the pair of coordinates with the shortest distance as the output. Fig. 9(a) shows the diagram of this case. The second case is there are two objects touched the display in previous detection. For this case, the system calculates the distances between previous pair of coordinates and the two possible pairs of coordinates, and select the pair of coordinates has shorter distance as the output. Fig. 9(b) is the diagram of this case.

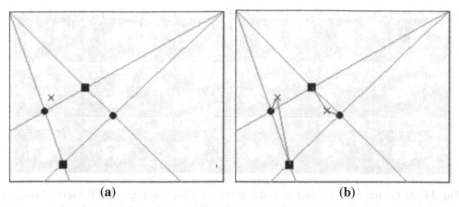

(a)   **(b)**

Fig. 9. (a) The circle points and square points are two possible pairs of coordinates, and the cross point is previous coordinate. The circle point is closer to the cross point, so the circle points are selected as the output. (b) The red and blue lines are the two distances between two possible pairs of coordinates and previous pair of coordinates. The length of red line is shorter, so the circle points are selected as the output.

Restoring Background. In the system, the changes of the environment will affect the accuracy of the object detection. The changes of the environment may come from the changes of light, the moves of the display, camera noises and so on. To overcome these interferences, the system measures the changes of the environment and decides to whether restores the background scenes in the end of the algorithm.

The scheme of measurement is to count how many columns have a great change. The comparison is based on the background image and current image. A column is considered has a great change if there are many pixels changed in this column. If a lot of columns are counted to the changed columns, then the system replaces the background image with current image, and uses the new background to process.

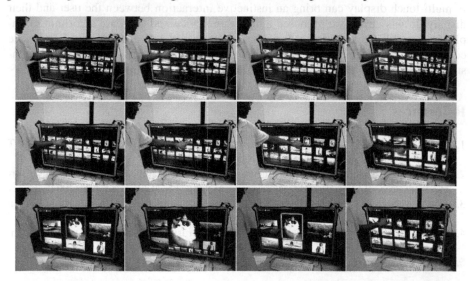

Fig. 10. The user scrolled the pohoto wall by one finger and selected a interested photo

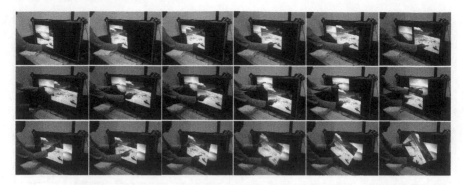

Fig. 11. At the top row, the user moved a photo with his one finger. At the second row, he moved the two photos simultaneously with his two fingers. The last row is the rotation of the photo with his two fingers.

3 Experimental Results

Two experimental results with this system are given in this section. The fist one is the manipulations of PicLens [5] which is a photo viewer application. In this experiment, it shows the ability of single touch. Fig. 10 is serial images of the demonstration. The second one is to show the ability of dual touch. The second one demonstrates the move, scale and rotation on photos with two fingertips. Fig.11 shows serial images of the second demonstration.

4 Conclusion

A multi-touch display can bring an instinctive interaction between the user and their display. In this paper, we proposed a hardware device and software algorithm to implement a dual touch for large displays. It improves the disadvantages of expensive cost and bulk, and eliminates the requirement of special hardware. We have demonstrated the system with some applications and vilified the usability of the system.

References

1. Dietz, P., Leigh, D.: DiamondTouch: a multi-user touch technology. In: Proc. of UIST 2001, Orlando, FL, pp. 219–226. ACM, NY (2001)
2. Rekimoto, J.: SmartSkin: an infrastructure for freehand manipulation on interactive surfaces. In: Proc. of SIGCHI 2002, Minneapolis, MN, pp. 113–120. ACM, NY (2002)
3. Hotelling, S., Strickon, J.A., Huppi, B.Q.: Multipoint touchscreen. U. S. Patent Application 20060097991 (2006)
4. Han, J.Y.: Low-cost multi-touch sensing through frustrated total internal reflection. In: Proc. of UIST 2005, Seattle, WA, pp. 115–118. ACM, NY (2005)
5. [Online] PicLens, http://www.cooliris.com/

Overview of Meta-analyses Investigating Vibrotactile versus Visual Display Options

Linda R. Elliott[1], Michael D. Coovert[2], and Elizabeth S. Redden[1]

[1] U.S. Army Research Laboratory, U.S. Army Infantry Center, Fort Benning, Georgia
[2] University of South Florida, Tampa, Florida
{linda.r.elliott,elizabeth.redden}@us.army.mil,
m.coovert@gmail.com

Abstract. The literature is replete with studies that investigated the effectiveness of vibrotactile displays; however, individual studies in this area often yield discrepant findings that are difficult to synthesize. In this paper, we provide an overview of a comprehensive review of the literature and meta-analyses that organized studies to enable comparisons of visual and tactile presentations of information, to yield information useful to researchers and designers. Over six hundred studies were initially reviewed and coded along numerous criteria that determined appropriateness for meta-analysis categories. Comparisons were made between conditions that compared (a) adding a tactile cue to a baseline condition, (b) a visual cue with a multimodal (visual and tactile) presentation, and (c) a visual cue with a tactile cue. In addition, we further categorized within these comparisons with regard to type of information, that ranged from simple alerts and single direction cues to more complex tactile patterns representing spatial orientation or short communications.

Keywords: Tactile, Visual, Display, Interface, Design, Military, Army, Attention management, Spatial orientation, Navigation, Communication.

1 Introduction

Recent reviews [26, 45] provide comprehensive information with regard to several different tactile and haptic devices and discuss the characteristics of these devices that affect perception and localization. In contrast, we present the results of a meta-analysis of 64 studies that address the question- does a tactile cue actually enhance task performance?

To allow for reasonable comparisons, experimental data were limited to one kind of tactor (vibrotactile) and were organized according to its informational and task purpose.

First, we distinguished three types of visual-tactile comparisons. (e.g., did the experiment conditions substitute a visual cue with a tactile, add a tactile cue providing new information to a "baseline" condition, or add a tactile cue that provides the same information as the visual cue in multimodal fashion). Merely knowing that people can perceive tactor arrays and patterns is not sufficient—our focus was on performance and effectiveness. We expected, and found, that efficacy also depends on the purpose for which the tactors are used and how the tactile information is integrated with other

J.A. Jacko (Ed.): Human-Computer Interaction, Part II, HCII 2009, LNCS 5611, pp. 435–443, 2009.

information cues. Our review is distinguished from others by our focused but specific scope-- the establishment of an organizational framework which enables systematic and the quantitative comparisons enabled by meta-analytic methods.

1.1 Approach

Table 1 lists the studies included in our meta-analyses and describes the organization of our approach. We distinguished studies according to type of information represented by the tactile or visual cues. Thus, we categorized them by: a) tactile cues for alerts (attention management), b) tactile cues for direction (e.g., navigation and targeting), c) tactile cues for orientation, and d) tactile cues for communications. Comparisons were also limited to studies that compared cues that were accurate and reliable, which excluded some interesting studies regarding levels of reliability, trust, and performance.

Table 1. Index of Studies included in Meta-analyses, organized by Study Framework

Studies included in Baseline Versus Vibrotactile Comparisons by Information Type	
Alarms	Hammeed et al., 2006; Ho et al., 2007; Hopp et al., 2005; Moorhead et al., 2004; Scott & Gray, 2008
Direction	Bloomfield & Badler, 2007; Chen & Terrence, 2008; Davis, 2007; Dorneich et al., 2006; Elliott et al., 2006; Glumm et al., 2006; Hammeed et al., 2007; Lindemann et al., 2003; Lindeman et al., 2005; Murray et al., 2003; Tan et al., 2003
Spatial Orientation	Aretz et al., 2006; Chiasson et al., 2002; Diamond et al., 2002; McGrath et al., 2004; Raj et al., 2000; Small et al., 2006; Tripp et al., 2007; van Erp et al., 2002; van Erp et al., 2003; van Erp et al., 2006
Studies included in Visual Versus Visual & Vibrotactile Comparisons by Information Type	
Alarms	Calhoun et al., 2002; Calhoun et al., 2004; Calhoun et al., 2005; Forster et al., 2002; Hopp et al., 2005; Krausman et al., 2007; Moorhead et al., 2004; Sklar & Sarter, 1999
Direction	Bloomfield et al., 2007; Elliott et al., 2007; Latham & Tracy, 2002; Tan et al., 2003; van Erp et al., 2002
Spatial Orientation	Chiasson et al., 2002; Eriksson et al., 2006; McKinley & Tripp, 2007; van Erp et al., 2007
Studies included in Visual Versus Vibrotactile Comparisons by Information Type	
Alarms	Calhoun et al., 2002; Forster et al., 2002; Hammeed et al., 2007; Krausman et al., 2005; Scott et al., 2008; Sklar et al., 1999; van Erp et al., 2004
Communication	Brewster & King, 2005; Ho et al., 2001; Pettitt et al., 2007;
Direction	Bloomfield et al., 2007; Cholewiak et al., 2006; Davis, 2006; Elliott et al., 2006; Elliott et al., 2007; Glumm et al., 2006; Hammeeed et al., 2006; Lindeman et al., 2003; Savick et al., 2008; van Erp et al., 2002; van Erp et al., 2004
Spatial Orientation.	McKinley, 2007; Small, 2006.

1.2 Method

Literature Search
The following databases were used in the literature search: Association for Computing Machinery (ACM), Institute of Electrical and Electronics Engineers (IEEE), IngentaConnect, PsycInfo, Web of Science, Defense Technical Information Center (DTIC), and Cambridge Scientific Abstracts (CSA). Next, a seven-year retrograde hand-search was conducted on the table of contents for the following journals and conference proceedings: Human Factors, Human Computer Interaction, Military Psychology, Eurohaptics, Society of Industrial and Organizational Psychology, and Institute of Electrical and Electronics Engineers. We also reviewed references cited in relevant articles. To be included, studies needed to have performance criteria, as opposed to ratings of workload or user feedback. . Studies were reviewed to ensure manipulations were reasonable (e.g. not counterintuitive) and reliable. We did not include studies with special populations that are not generalizable (e.g., deaf, blind) or studies based on less than four subjects. Many articles that were eligible for inclusion lacked the necessary statistics (e.g., standard deviations). In such cases, the primary and/or secondary authors were contacted via e-mail or telephone (when possible) to obtain the needed statistics for study inclusion. This was particularly challenging for repeated-measures (within-subject) designs, because many studies do not report any paired statistics (e.g., paired correlation, paired t-test, etc.), especially when an overall F test statistic is not significant. For some studies in which data were not available, we estimated a paired correlation of .3 to .5, utilizing the more conservative estimate if there was a difference in overall effect size [3, 21]; Borenstein, personal communication, February, 2008). Studies were entered into a web-based bibliographic reference database [(Coovert, Walvoord, Elliott, & Redden, 2008). This database can be accessed on request by contacting the lead author of this paper.

Calculation of Effect Sizes
A random effects model [25] was used for the analyses, as variance is assumed to stem from study-level sampling error in addition to subject-level sampling error. Random effects models are considered more conservative because they account for variance stemming from study characteristics as well as sampling error, which typically result in wider confidence intervals. The analyses were conducted using the procedures of [21] as applied in Comprehensive Meta-analysis (CMA) 2.0 [3], that assigns weights to studies based on degree of precision associated with the effect size. We did not apply further corrections (e.g., for restriction of range, unreliability) that are relevant to issues such as personnel selection test validation [25]. While corrections can increase effect size, these data are not suited for such corrections. Consequently, our results and conclusions are conservative with regard to effect size and significance.

2 Results

2.1 Three Types of Comparisons

Baseline versus Tactile Comparison. Table 1 lists the studies used for baseline versus tactile (B vs. T) studies (N – 26 studies). B vs. T studies assessed the effectiveness of tactile cues when added to a baseline condition. Many experiments that compared a tactile cue with a visual or audio cue also included a baseline condition. Thus, we were able to find a larger number of experiments for this comparison category. Despite the large pool of initial studies, many studies were screened out. Most studies in this category were based on simulation and VR-based situations. However, [15]and [14] assessments were based on actual land navigation (and secondary tasks) in the field. Performance measures varied, but most reflected some type of speeded performance (e.g., reaction time, time to navigate, time to visually search, number of targets or icons found in speeded situations, etc.).

For B vs.. T comparisons, almost all studies favored the tactile condition. Hedge's g, which represents the overall effect size across all studies, was 1.03 (SE 0.144) and was significant at p = .00, in favor of the tactile cue condition. There was a consistent strong effect favoring the tactile condition across most studies and thus a high probability that tactile cues can improve performance when added as an alert, direction, or orienting cue. Analyses were then run with subgroups divided by type of information. All subgroup analyses were significantly in favor of the tactile condition, for alerts (g = 1.59; s.e. = 0.355, $p = 0.00$), direction cues (g = 0.911, s.e. = 0.210, $p = 0.00$), and spatial orientation cues (g = 1.13, s.e. = 0.248, $p = 0.00$).

<u>Visual versus Tactile Comparison.</u> Table 1 lists the studies used for visual versus tactile (V vs. T) cue conditions. V vs. T studies compared tactile cues to visual cues presenting the same information for the same purpose. For studies in this review, visual and tactile alerts or direction cues have been compared for a variety of tasks, including simple reaction time or visual search tasks (e.g., [18]) simulated driving and/or targeting tasks ([12]; [19]; [38], [39]; [48]; [47], complex cockpit, UAV, or command simulations ([5]; [20; 22; 28; 32; 40; 41] communicating information [4], localization from dense multi-tactor displays [10] land navigation in the field [15, 16] and orienting in virtual environments [2].

Overall Hedge's g was 0.597, SE = 0.217, with $p = 0.006$, in favor of tactile cues over visual cues. Results for studies using tactile cues as alerts were mostly in favor of tactile cues. For alerts, Hedge's g was 1.809 (s.e. = 0.451, $p = 0.00$). For studies in which tactile cues were used to communicate information, Hedge's g was 2.291 (s.e. = 0.612, $p = 0.00$) in favor of tactile cues. Most studies compared visual and tactile direction cues, albeit for different purposes. For this category, Hedge's g was -0.203 (s.e. = 0.294, $p = 0.50$), indicating strong differences among studies with regard to visual versus vibrotactile effect. There were only two studies that compared visual and tactile cues for spatial orientation and neither was significant (Hedge's g = 0.02, s.e. = 0.70, $p = 0.98$).

<u>Visual versus Visual-Tactile Comparison.</u> Table 1 lists the studies used to compare visual cues to a combination of redundant visual and tactile cues (V vs. VT). V v VT studies compared a multimodal presentation of visual and tactile cues representing the same information, to conditions consisting of only visual cues. This category appears similar to the B v T comparison, but is distinguished by the multimodal and redundant nature of the VT condition. Studies included simple reaction time or tracking tasks [18; 34] to more complex situations such as communications (driving [2; 48], complex cockpit or C3 simulations [6, 7; 24; 28; 40], land navigation [16], tele-operation

in VR environments [29], more advanced tactile arrays for spatial orientation in flight [9; 17; 45] or localization of a dense array of tactors [42].

Overall Hedge's g was 0.89, s.e. = 0.155, p = 0.000, in favor of multimodal cueing over visual-only cueing when analyzed across all studies. Results for studies using tactile cues as alerts were mostly in favor of tactile cues, with g = 0.412 and p = 0.08. For alerts, Hedge's g was 1.08 (s.e. = 0.236, p = 0.00), also in favor of the multimodal presentation. For studies in which multimodal cue patterns were used to convey direction information, the multimodal presentation was again favored, with Hedge's g = 0.635 (s.e. = 0.26, p = 0.01). Studies that compared visual versus visual-tactile cues for orientation had an overall Hedge's g of 0.93 (s.e. = 0.339, p = 0.00), also in favor of the multimodal presentation.

3 Discussion

Meta-analysis was used to assess effectiveness of tactile cues across a range of task demands. Results were consistent with Wicken's multiple resource theory [50, 51], which predicts that distribution of information across sensory channels can result in better performance when one channel is overloaded. Tactile cues were found to be particularly helpful when added to provide additional information, such as alerts, direction cues, and spatial information. Multimodal presentation of both visual and tactile cues that represent the same information, was also significantly associated with better performance.

Adding tactile cues to support performance. Overall results showed a consistent and overwhelming positive result for tactile cues, particularly when tactile cues were added to support an existing task, rather than replace a visual information cue. When tactile cues were added to a baseline task, all subgroup analyses were significant, for alerts, direction cues, and spatial orientation cues. There were no studies in this comparison category that used tactile cues for communication. Tactile cues were found to be very effective when used to manage attention and to support tasks such as visual search, navigation, driving, targeting and piloting.

Effectiveness of multimodal cues. Tactile cues were also effective overall when used in a multimodal presentation, favoring the multimodal over visual when analyzed across all studies. Results for studies using multimodal cues as alerts were mostly in favor ofmultimodal cues,. Subgroup analysis for direction cues was also significantly in favor of the multimodal condition. Additionally, studies that compared visual versus visual-tactile cues for orientation favored a multimodal presentation though it should be noted this finding is based on only three studies.

Replacing visual cues with tactile cues. Results for studies that compared a tactile to a visual presentation of the same information favored the tactile presentation; however, there was much more variation among these studies. Results for studies using tactile cues as alerts were mostly in favor of tactile cues. Studies in which tactile cue patterns were used to convey information also favored the tactile presentation, although it should be noted that this finding is based on only three studies. There was only one study that compared visual and tactile cues for spatial orientation so the results in this category are tentative. While tactile cues were found to be associated with better performance, designers should instead consider a multimodal presentation that combines visual and tactile cues, rather than using tactile information to replace an existing visual cue.

Strength of findings. A potential shortcoming of meta-analysis, in general, is incomplete data. Quite a few studies that met preliminary experimental criteria with regard to measures, manipulation, and process, did not report complete data. In those cases we strived to contact authors and request data. This issue is made more difficult in that some journals appear to encourage authors to provide graphs but not repeat the numbers in text or tables, leaving the reader to interpolate means from relatively small graphs. Often, indicators of variance or confidence intervals are not reported. In addition, F tests are often reported for multiple groups, but there is no reference to planned or follow-up paired comparisons. Also, detailed results (means, variance, t or p values) are often not reported for non-significant results, leaving the reader with perhaps a graph and the assurance that p was not significant. Thus, we urge readers and editors to please ensure basic statistics (means, variances, N) are provided, and some indication of paired comparison (paired correlation, paired t-test) when the experiment is a repeated-measures design, which is commonly used in human-factors evaluations.

Although we urge researchers to report these results, the impact of incomplete data for these analyses is not likely to change the results or conclusions. The aggregated effect size for each comparison was very high. Classic fail-safe N tests for each comparison indicate that the results are very robust. The algorithm for the Fail-Safe N involves computing a combined p-value for all studies in the analysis, and then determining how many additional studies with (an average) z (reflective of effect size) of zero would be required to yield a non-significant p-value. That is, how many studies with non-significant effects must be added to make the overall meta-statistic non-significant. Here, the fail-safe N ranged from to 353 to 1855 non-significant studies that would have to be added to change current conclusions.

In summary, we provide a comprehensive description of experiments assessing the efficacy of tactile, specifically vibrotactile, cues. In order to better distinguish when and why tactile cues should be considered, we differentiated between comparison types in our analysis. Results show overwhelming evidence for the effectiveness of tactile cues when added to a task situation to guide and direct attention or to support spatial orientation. Results were also consistently positive for multimodal applications. Although overall results favored replacing visual cues with tactile cues, the variation among studies indicates the need for careful consideration by interface designers of task demands and cue characteristics.

References

References included in the meta-analysis are marked with an asterick *

1. *Aretz, D.T., Andre, T.S., Self, B.P., Brenaman, C.A.: Effect of tactile feedback on Unmanned Aerial Vehicle Landings. In: Proceedings of the Interservice /Industry Training, Simulation, and Education Conference (I/ITSEC), paper 2849 (2006)

2. *Bloomfield, A., Badler, N.I.: Collision avoidance using vibrotactile arrays. In: Proceedings of the IEEE Virtual Reality Conference, Charlotte, NC, March 10-14, pp. 163–170 (2007)
3. Borenstein, M., Hedges, L., Higgins, L., Rothstein, H.: Comprehensive meta-analysis, Version 2.0: A computer program for research synthesis. Biostat, Englewood (2005)
4. *Brewster, S., King, A.: The design and evaluation of a vibrotactile progress bar. In: Proceedings of the First Joint Eurohaptics Conference and Symposium on Haptic Interfaces for Virtual Environment and Teleoperator Systems, 0-7695-2310-2/05. IEEE, Los Alamitos (2005), http://www2.computer.org/portal/web/csdl/doi/10.1109/WHC.2005.127
5. *Calhoun, G., Draper, M., Ruff, H., Fontejon, J.: Utility of a tactile display for cueing faults. In: Proceedings of the Human Factors and Ergonomic Society 46th Annual Meeting, pp. 2118–2122. Human Factors and Ergonomic Society, Santa Monica (2002)
6. *Calhoun, G.L., Fontejon, J., Draper, M., Ruff, H., Guilfoos, B.: Tactile and aural redundant alert cues for UAV control applications. In: Proceedings of the 48th Annual Meeting Human Factors and Ergonomics Society, pp. 137–141. Human Factors and Ergonomic Society, Santa Monica (2004)
7. *Calhoun, G.L., Ruff, H.A., Draper, M.H., Guilfoos, B.J.: Tactile and aural alerts in high auditory load UAV control environments. In: Proceedings of the Human Factors and Ergonomic Society 49th Annual Meeting, pp. 145–149. Human Factors and Ergonomic Society, Santa Monica (2005)
8. *Chen, J., Terrence, P.: Effects of tactile cueing on concurrent performance of military and robotics tasks in a simulated multitasking environment. Ergonomics 51(8), 1137–1152 (2008)
9. *Chiasson, J., McGrath, B., Rupert, A.: Enhanced situation awareness in sea, air, and land environment. In: Proceedings of NATO RTO Human Factors & Medicine Panel Symposium on Spatial disorientation in military vehicles: Causes, consequences and cures, La Coruña, Spain, pp. 1–10 (2002); No. TRO-MP-086
10. *Cholewiak, R., McGrath, C.: Vibrotactile targeting in multimodal systems: Accuracy and interaction. In: Proceedings of the 14th Symposium on Haptic Interfaces for Virtual Environment and Teleoperator Systems, pp. 413–420 (2006)
11. *Davis, B.: Effects of visual, auditory, and tactile navigation cues on navigation performance, situation awareness, and mental workload (Technical Report No.ARL-TR-4022). Aberdeen Proving Ground, MD: Army Research Laboratory (2007)
12. *Davis, B.: Effect of tactical navigation display modality on navigation performance, situation awareness, and mental workload. In: Proceedings of the Human Factors and Ergonomics Society Annual Meeting, pp. 2089–2093. Human Factors and Ergonomics Society, Santa Monica (2006)
13. *Diamond, D.D., Kass, S.J., Andrasik, F., Raj, A.K., Rupert, A.H.: Vibrotactile cueing as a master caution system for visual monitoring. Human Factors & Aerospace Safety 2(4), 339–354 (2002)
14. *Dorneich, M., Ververs, P.I., Whitlow, S., Mathan, S.: Evaluation of a tactile navigation cueing system and real-time assessment of cognitive state. In: Proceedings of the Human Factors and Ergonomics Society 50th Annual Meeting, pp. 2600–2604. Human Factors and Ergonomic Society, Santa Monica (2006)
15. *Elliott, L.R., Redden, E., Pettitt, R., Carstens, C., van Erp, J., Duistermaat, M: Tactile Guidance for Land Navigation. Technical Report ARL-TR-3814. Aberdeen Proving Ground: Army Research Laboratory (2006)
16. *Elliott, L., Duistermaat, M., Redden, E., van Erp, J.: Multimodal guidance for land navigation (ARL Technical Report No. ARL-TR-4295). Aberdeen Proving Ground: Army Research Laboratory (2007)

17. *Eriksson, L., van Erp, J., Carlander, O., Levin, B., van Veen, H., Veltman, H.: Vibrotactile and visual threat cueing with high G threat intercept in dynamic flight simulation. In: Proceedings of the Human Factors and Ergonomics Society 50th Annual Meeting, San Francisco, pp. 1547–1551. Human Factors and Ergonomic Society, Santa Monica (2006)
18. *Forster, B., Cavina-Pratesi, C., Aglioti, S.M., Berlucchi, G.: Redundant target effect and intersensory facilitation from visual-tactile interactions in simple reaction time. Experimental Brain Research 143(4), 480–487 (2002)
19. *Glumm, M., Kehring, K., White, T.L.: Effects of Tactile, Visual and Auditory Cues about Threat Location on Target Acquisition and Attention to Visual and Auditory Communications (Technical Report No. ARL-TR-3863). Aberdeen Proving Ground, MD: Army Research Laboratory (2006)
20. *Hameed, S., Ferris, T., Jayaraman, S., Sarter, N.: Supporting interruption management through informative tactile and peripheral visual cues. In: Proceedings of the Human Factors and Ergonomics Society 50th Annual Meeting, pp. 376–380. Human Factors and Ergonomic Society, Santa Monica (2006)
21. Hedges, L.V., Olkin, I.O.: Statistical methods for meta-analysis. Academic Press, Inc., San Diego (1985)
22. *Ho, C., Reed, N., Spence, C.: Multisensory in-car warning signals for collision avoidance. Human Factors 49, 1107–1114 (2007)
23. *Ho, C., Nikolic, M., Sarter, N.: Supporting timesharing and interruption management through multimodal information presentation. In: Proceedings of the Human Factors and Ergonomics Society 45th Annual Meeting, pp. 341–345. Human Factors and Ergonomic Society, Santa Monica (2001)
24. *Hopp, P.J., Smith, C.A.R., Clegg, B.A., Heggestad, E.D.: Interruption management: The use of attention-directing tactile cues. Human Factors 47(1), 1–11 (2005)
25. Hunter, J.E., Schmidt, F.L.: Methods of meta-analysis: Correcting error and bias in research findings, 2nd edn. Sage, Thousand Oaks (2004)
26. Jones, L., Sarter, N.: Tactile displays: Guidance for their design and application. Human Factors 50(1), 90–111 (2008)
27. *Krausman, A., Pettitt, R., Elliott, L.: Effects of redundant alerts on platoon leader performance and decision making (Technical Report No. ARL-TR-3999). Aberdeen Proving Ground, MD: Army Research Laboratory (2007)
28. *Krausman, A., Elliott, L., Pettitt, R.: Effects of visual, auditory, and tactile alerts on platoon leader performance and decision making (Technical Report No. ARL-TR-3633). Aberdeen Proving Ground, MD: Army Research Laboratory (2005)
29. *Latham, C., Tracey, M.: The effects of operator spatial perception and sensory feedback on human-robot teleoperation performance. Presence 11(4), 368–377 (2002)
30. *Lindeman, R.W., Sibert, J.L., Mendez-Mendez, E., Patil, S., Phifer, D.: Effectiveness of directional vibrotactile cuing on a building-clearing task. In: CHI 2005: Proceedings of the SIGCHI conference on human factors in computing systems, Portland, Oregon, USA, pp. 271–280 (2005)
31. *Lindeman, R.W., Yanagida, Y., Sibert, J.L., Lavine, R.: Effective vibrotactile cueing in a visual search task. In: Proceedings of the Ninth IFIP TC13 International Conference on Human-Computer Interaction (INTERACT 2003), Zurich, Switzerland, September 1-5, pp. 89–96 (2003)
32. *McKinley, R.A., Tripp Jr., L.D.: Multisensory cueing to improve UAV operator performance during landing. In: 78th Annual Scientific Meeting Aerospace Medical Association, New Orleans, LA, May 14-18 (2007)
33. *McGrath, B., Estrada, A., Graithwaite, M., Raj, A., Rupert, A.: Tactile situation awareness system flight demonstration final report (Technical Report No. USAARL 2004-10), Pensacola, FL, Naval Aerospace Medical Research Laboratory (2004)

34. *Moorhead, I., Holmes, S., Furnell, A.: Understanding multisensory integration for pilot spatial orientation (Technical Report No. SPC 03-3048), Farmborough, UK. QunetiQ Ltd. (2004)
35. *Murray, A., Katzky, R., Khosla, P.: Psychophysical characterization and tested validation of a wearable vibrotactile glove for telemanipulation. Presence 12(2), 156–182 (2003)
36. *Pettitt, R., Redden, E., Carstens, C.: Comparison of army hand and arm signals to a covert tactile communication system in a dynamic environment (Technical Report No. ARL-TR-3838). Army Research Laboratory, Aberdeen Proving Ground, MD (2006)
37. *Raj, A.K., Kass, S.J., Perry, J.F.: Vibrotactile displays for improving spatial awareness. In: Proceedings of the Human Factors and Ergonomics Society Annual Meeting, pp. 181–184. The Human Factors and Ergonomics Society, Santa Monica (2000)
38. *Savick, D., Elliott, L., Zubal, O., Stachowiak, C.: The effect of audio and tactile cues on soldier decision making and navigation in complex simulation scenarios (ARL Technical Report No. ARL-TR-4413). Human Research and Engineering Directorate, Army Research Laboratory, Aberdeen Proving Ground, MD (2008)
39. *Scott, J.J., Gray, R.: A comparison of tactile, visual, and auditory warnings for rear-end collision prevention in simulated driving. Human Factors 50(2), 264–275 (2008)
40. *Sklar, A., Sarter, N.: Good Vibrations: Tactile feedback in support of attention allocation and human-automation coordination in event-driven domains. Human Factors 41(4), 543–552 (1999)
41. *Small, R., Keller, J., Wickens, C., Socash, C., Ronan, A., Fisher, A.: Multisensory integration for pilot spatial orientation (Technical report No AFRL-HE-WP-TR-2006-0166). Wright-Patterson Air Force Base OH: Air Force Research Laboratory Human Effectiveness Directorate (2006)
42. *Tan, H., Gray, R., Young, J., Traylor, R.: A haptic back display for attentional and directional cueing. Haptics-e 3(1) (2003), http://www.haptics-e.org
43. *Tripp, L., Warm, J., Matthews, G., Chiu, P., Bracken, B.: +Gz Acceleration loss of consciousness: Use of G-suit pressurization and sensory stimulation to enhance recovery. In: Proceedings of the Human Factors and Ergonomics Society 51st Annual Meeting, pp. 1296–1300. Human Factors and Ergonomic Society, Santa Monica (2007)
44. van Erp, J.: Tactile displays for navigation and orientation: Perception and behavior. Mostert & Van Onderen, Leiden (2007)
45. *van Erp, J., Erriksson, L., Levin, B., Carlander, O., Veltman, J., Vos, W.: Tactile cueing effect on performance in simulated aerial combat with high acceleration. Aviation, Space, and Environmental Medicine 78(12), 1128–1134 (2007)
46. *van Erp, J.B.F., Groen, E., Bos, J., van Veen, H.: A tactile cockpit instrument supports the control of self-motion during spatial disorientation. Human Factors 48(2), 219–228 (2006)
47. *van Erp, J.B.F., Jansen, C., Dobbins, T., van Veen, H.A.H.C.: Vibrotactile waypoint navigation at sea and in the air: two case studies. In: Proceedings of Eurohaptics, pp. 166–173. Technische Universität, München (2004)
48. *van Erp, J.B.F., Meppelink, R., van Veen, H.A.H.C.: A touchy car (Report No. TD-2001-0358). TNO Human Factors Research Institute, Soesterberg (2002)
49. *van Erp, J., Veltman, J., van Veen, H.: A tactile cockpit instrument to support altitude control. In: Proceedings of the Human Factors and Ergonomics Society 47th Annual Meeting, pp. 114–118. Human Factors and Ergonomic Society, Santa Monica (2003)
50. Wickens, C.: Multiple resources and mental workload. Human Factors 50(3), 449–454 (2008)
51. Wickens, C.: Multiple resources and performance prediction. Theoretical Issues in Ergonomics Science 3(2), 159–177 (2002)

Experimental Study about Effect of Thermal Information Presentation to Mouse

Shigeyoshi Iizuka[1] and Sakae Yamamoto[2]

[1] NTT Network Service Systems Laboratories
9-11 Midori-Cho 3-Chome, Musashino-Shi, Tokyo, 180-8585 Japan
shigeiizuka@gmail.com
[2] Tokyo University of Science
1-14-6 Kudan-kita Chiyoda-ku, Tokyo, 102-0073, Japan
sakae@ms.kagu.tus.ac.jp

Abstract. Despite the many types of telecommunication systems that have been developed, it can still be hard to convey various types of information expressively to a remote partner. Our research focuses on the use of variations in temperature to represent information expressively. We developed a mouse device with thermal capabilities; the device becomes warmer or colder to a user's palm when the user clicks "thermal" photographic images on a computer screen. Each image has an associated thermal value. In this paper, we report the results of an evaluation of the thermal performance of the device. We also report results from a preliminary experiment that determine how the thermal expression affects a user's impression of images.

Keywords: thermal information, thermal mouse, warm sense, cold sense, pair comparisons.

1 Introduction

Now, by development of the communication means using the computer, various information can be communicated. However, since the information only on characters or images is communicated in many cases, it is difficult to communicate the user's feeling or delicate textures of objects efficiently. It is thought that the more two or more feeling channels are used simultaneously, the more the communication interface is user friendly, and an actual feeling increases. Therefore, it is considered to support communication like perusal or choice, etc. of the information in everyday life, to use various consciousnesses positively. In the Web communication, we depend for the great portion of information acquisition on vision. So, it is considered to be good to use consciousness information other than the vision in the senses in complement. Then, in communication using the computer, we are studying giving an actual feeling more to information and supporting communication of informational perusal, choice, etc. by presentation of warm and cold feeling, as one way with which vision information is compensated. In this paper, we show the experiment which checked the influence which thermal information presentation has on user's subjectivity evaluation by presenting warm and cold feeling information through a mouse in addition to the presentation (vision) information on a computer screen.

J.A. Jacko (Ed.): Human-Computer Interaction, Part II, HCII 2009, LNCS 5611, pp. 444–450, 2009.

2 Presentation Method of Thermal Information

As a method of complementing vision information by presentation of warm or cold feeling information, we considered the presentation to the skin. Since the thermal information presentation to the skin is modality different from vision or hearing, it has the advantage that a user can perceive a certain contents also in viewing and listening. That is, without barring the user's activity, it becomes possible that the user is made to aware existence of the related information on the contents under viewing and listening or present auxiliary information. We focused on "mouse" used in many cases, using generally at the time of computer operation as a device which people touch, and contacting a palm. We decided to use the presentation method through a mouse of thermal information as addition information on vision information. Hereafter, the outline and architecture are shown.

2.1 Outline

We made a mouse, which the function to perform scan of XY plane of a computer screen and two button inputs are as it is, by equipping with a peltiert device the portion which a palm's touches, and can present the user under computer use thermal information (Fig. 1). The peltiert device with which the mouse was equipped gets warm or cold by a user clicking the contents (picture etc.) itself or area, such as picture (a part of etc.) which was shown on the computer screen and to which warm and cold feeling information were given. The user perceives thermal information in a part of the palm in contact with the peltiert device (Fig. 2). Thus, as for the mouse, thermal information presentation function was added, without spoiling the function of the mouse as an input device itself. And while the mouse is the general-purpose device which can be used only by USB connection, the presentation information to a user can be added without increasing the device with which a user is made to newly equip.

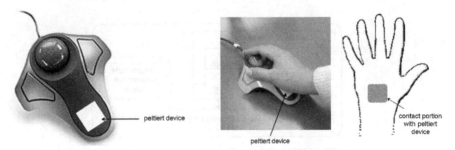

Fig. 1. Appearance of Mouse   **Fig. 2.** Usage

2.2 Hardware Composition

The hardware composition of a mouse is shown in Fig. 3. The mouse was connected with PC by USB and the inside of the mouse case is equipped with all the mechanisms in which thermal information are generated. In addition to the usual mouse mechanism, the inside is equipped with the 2 port USB hub and USB parallel

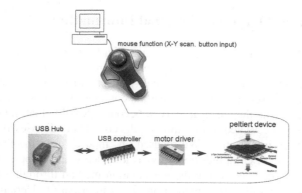

Fig. 3. Hardware Composition

controller IC, a motor driver IC, and a peltiert device. Control of temperature change and heating or cooling can be performed by adjusting the quantity and the direction of the current which controls the peltiert device. The control information on thermal information is sent to Controller IC through USB hub, the peltiert device is driven by carrying out PWM (Pulse Width Modulation) control of the motor driver, and thermal information presentation are realized. Since these are mounted using the space inside the case of a trackball mouse, as shown in Fig. 1, the appearance is still the usual mouse except being equipped with a peltiert device, and operability is also still the usual mouse.

2.3 Software Modules

The module composition inside the inside of a mouse and PC is shown in Fig. 4. The usual mouse function is maintained as it is by the "operation input part." And it has "the drive part (motor driver)" and "the heat transfer part (peltiert device)" as a

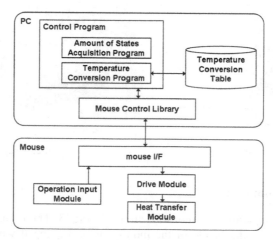

Fig. 4. Modules

presentation mechanism of thermal information. In the PC side, the "amount of states acquisition program" which distinguishes that the contents or the area where thermal information were given was clicked based on the mouse control information received from a mouse control library and the "temperature conversion program" changed into the information which controls heating or cooling from the information attached to the clicked contents or the area based on the "temperature conversion table" are possessed.

3 Experiment

This chapter shows the purpose and method in detail about an experiment which checks the influence of the user's subjectivity evaluation by thermal information grant using Scheffe's Paired Comparison performed for the picture of dish.

3.1 Purpose

It is thought that people know experientially about the suitable temperature of each dish, therefore, and that even if they do not actually put it into their mouth, by feeling temperature, the impression over the picture of the shown dish changes. We thought that, in communication using the computer, it complements the main vision information that a user perceives in the palm warm or cold feeling information as an amount of states which the dish has in addition to a picture of the dish as the vision information shown on the screen, and it changes the user's impression over the information shown on the computer screen, and leads to playing the role which supports the selection. Then, we determined to conduct an experiment which checks whether user's subjectivity evaluation is affected by presenting warm or cold feeling information to the user's palm without making it an actual temperature about the picture of the dish shown on the computer screen.

3.2 Method

We conducted an experiment that had users evaluate subjectively (looks delicious or not) of the picture of the dish shown on the computer screen and warm or cold feeling information perceived from the mouse. A picture list of the shown dish is shown in Fig. 5. Three steps of temperature conditions (warm, usual, and cold) were set

pizza   ramen noodles   salad

yogurt   orange juice   cake

Fig. 5. Picture List for Experimen

up to each of 6 pictures. It carried out each with 11 men/women of 20s. To a participant, only 1 picture of food (drink) is first shown on a computer screen, and he/she perceives warm or cold feeling information by clicking the picture. Then, the same picture with different temperature is shown and he/she clicks. And he/she entered the result which compared them in the reply paper shown in Fig. 6. All participants carried out all trial. The pictures of the food (drink) were randomly showed for every

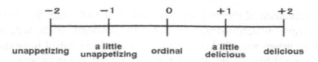

Fig. 6. Evaluation Scale

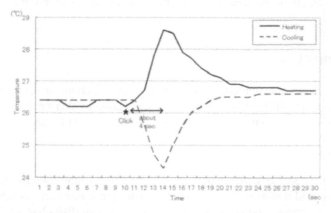

Fig. 7. Temperature Change at the time of Heating and Cooling

participant. In addition, about the mouse used for this experiment, the size of a peltiert device was 3cm×3cm, impression voltage to an element per 12V, and for 1 second is made to turn on electricity per control. Actually, each surface temperature change at the time of heating and cooling control was shown in Fig. 7. In heating and cooling control, the temperature rise and descent have reached the peak (about 2°C) after about 4 seconds from a control start (click). (Average value of temperature change was +2.26°C (SD:0.13) at the time of heating control and -2.12 °C (SD:0.19) at the time of cooling control as a result of measuring heating and cooling control 5 times)

4 Result

We analyzed using the result of ten persons except 1 person considered to have not felt a stimulus almost. As an experiment result, the yardstick which has arranged the coordinates of each stimulus for every presentation picture is shown in Fig. 8.

From this result, it can be said that, about the dish (ramen noodles, pizza) generally eaten at a temperature higher than ordinary temperature, there is a significant effect which a user feels delicious rather than the case (ordinary temperature) where sympathy news is not given in warm feeling information grant. On the other hand, about the dish (salad, yogurt, cake, orange juice) with which is eaten deliciously generally made into a temperature lower than ordinary temperature, when cold feeling information is presented, it is significantly effective in user's feeling delicious rather than the case (ordinary temperature) where cold information is not given. Moreover, in all except a cake, it has also cleared that the user's evaluation changes to feeling not delicious rather than the case of ordinary temperature by being presenting thermal information contrary to original suitable temperature. From these results, it turns out with warm or cold feeling information perceiving through a palm, even if it is the same picture that user's subjectivity evaluation is affected.

5 Conclusion

In communication using the computer, in order to support communication of informational perusal, choice, etc. by presentation of warm and cold feeling, as one way with which vision information is compensated, we conducted an experiment which checks whether user's subjectivity evaluation is affected by presenting warm or cold feeling information to the user's palm through the mouse which we developed about the picture of the dish shown on the computer screen. As a result, it can be said that, about the dish generally eaten at a temperature higher than ordinary temperature, there is a significant effect which a user feels delicious rather than the case (ordinary temperature) where sympathy news is not given in warm feeling information grant. On the other hand,

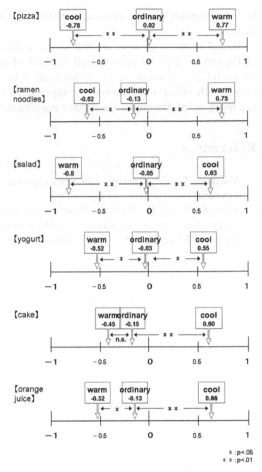

Fig. 8. Result of Experiment

about the dish with which is eaten deliciously generally made into a temperature lower than ordinary temperature, when cold feeling information is presented, it is significantly effective in user's feeling delicious rather than the case (ordinary temperature) where cold information is not given. And it turns out with warm or cold feeling information perceiving through a palm, even if it is the same picture that user's subjectivity evaluation is affected.

By the way, it is said that the temperature consciousness characteristic of a palm changes with parts (Sako, 2007). About the tactile sense, it is already known that sensitivity of the fingertip is sharper than a palm (Matsuda, 2000). Also about thermal sense, if the tendency of the tactile sense in a palm and the same tendency are seen, a fingertip will be too considered that sensitivity is sharp compared with a palm. Because the mouse made as an experiment this time mounted thermal information presentation function using the space inside the case of a trackball mouse, a palm portion was equipped with the peltiert device, it is thought that there is the necessity of thinking over again also about the part made perceiving. Furthermore, it is also considered that the contact surface product sensitivity of thermal information presentation part differs.

Based on these viewpoints, and while acquiring knowledge about the optimal form of the device and the presentation method of thermal information, we aim to realize the technique of supporting communication by presentation thermal information as a way which vision information is compensated and to continue to give an actual feeling more to information on computer communication.

References

1. Matsuda, T.: The foundation of consciousness psychology. Baifukan, Tokyo (2000) (in Japanese)
2. Sako, K., Horio, H., Wada, C.: Development research of the tactile sense display using the temperature stimulus. In: Proceedings of the 66th Convention of Virtual Reality Society of Japan, 3D2-1 (2007) (incl. CD-ROM) (in Japanese)

Preliminary Study on Vibrotactile Messaging for Sharing Brief Information

Teruaki Ito

The Institute of Technolgy and Science
The University of Tokushima
2-1 Minami-Josanjima, Tokushima 770-8506
Japan
ito@me.tokushima-u.ac.jp

Abstract. Ubiquitous computing is spreading as a post-desktop model of human-computer interaction, in which information processing is thoroughly integrated into everyday objects and activities. This study focuses on the vibrotactile signals for sharing and feeling the brief information among several users. The information here is limited to brief information which does not include detailed information but does cover the rough idea of the content of the information, so that the data size of the information can be kept very small. This paper presents a prototype device for vibrotactile messaging called VIBRATO. Then it shows the experimental results regarding VIBRATO message under different conditions and clarifies how to use VIBRATO effectively for understanding vibrotactile messages. The simple vibration alert used in a silent mode of mobile phones does not fully exploit the potential of vibration as a means of communication. This experiment shows how to exploit this potentiality of vibration.

Keywords: Vibrotactile message, brief information, ubiquitous computing, human interface.

1 Introduction

As a post-desktop model of human-computer interaction, ubiquitous computing is spreading, where information processing is thoroughly integrated into everyday objects and activities. For example, RFID is one of the technologies to develop an environment for ubiquitous computing. RFID is also evolving as a major technology enabler for identifying and tracking goods and assets around the world. Applications of RFID include access control for people, access control for vehicles, manufacturing automation, logistics and distribution, retail, maintenance, product security and many more. It can help hospitals locate expensive equipment more quickly to improve patient care, pharmaceutical companies to reduce counterfeiting, and logistics providers to improve the management of moveable assets.

RFID is spreading everywhere and information supply from RFID will possibly become continuous and seamless in the near future. Under these circumstances, portable devices such as mobile phone or PDA are often used to obtain information from RFID tags. Various kinds of FRID readers are available on the market. CF card type

J.A. Jacko (Ed.): Human-Computer Interaction, Part II, HCII 2009, LNCS 5611, pp. 451–460, 2009.
© Springer-Verlag Berlin Heidelberg 2009

readers are very portable and often used for PDA. RFID reader could be embedded to mobile phones in the future. The small screen of the visual display on mobile phone is often insufficient due to the limited screen space, or inappropriate, such as when the device is in a pocket but requires the user's attention. Therefore it is importance to consider using alternative modalities through which information can be presented.

Vibration is often used as an alert to give a simple buzz to users to inform incoming calls or messages, or to upcoming calendar appointments. Manufacturers have recently started to go beyond these simple alerts in their products. However, the simple vibration alert used in a silent mode of mobile phones does not fully exploit the potential of vibration as a means of communication. This study focuses on the vibrotactile signals for sharing and feeling the brief information among several users.

Section 2 presents an idea for vibrotactile messaging, which is called VIBRATO (VIBRATion infOmation). A prototype system of VIBRATO was designed and implemented as a form of stick, which sends a signal by gesturing and receiving a signal by vibration. Section 3 shows the experimental results regarding the recognition rates of gesturing message under different conditions and discusses how to use VIBRATO effectively for understanding vibrotactile messages. The prototype is designed to embed vibration motors into its grip. However, it is still under study to implement as one of the functions of the stick. Therefore, experimental study was conducted using a wrist band type of prototype which is presented in Section 4. This section discusses how to exploit this potentiality of vibration. Then some concluding remarks will be given in Section 5.

2 VIBRATO User Interface

It has been stated that standard phone vibration motors may not be suitable for communicating complex information, as they do not offer subtle control due to their limited bandwidth and high latency. Some research is under study to develop a set of distinguishable vibrotactile message which could be used to customize incoming call alerts. However, vibrotactile messaging for sharing information still open issues. The goal of this study is to develop a new vibrotactile media for sharing information which will be delivered from ubiquitous devices, such as RFID system. The information here is limited to brief information which does not include detailed information but does cover the rough idea of the content of the information. In this way, the data size of the information can be kept very small in the vibrotactile messaging.

This study proposes an idea of prototype device for vibrotactile messaging, which is called VIBRATO (VIBRATion infOmation). The device is designed as a stick shape, composed of two modules, which are signal sending module and message display module. Considering the use of vibrotactile interface device by senior people, who are not fully enjoying the benefit of ubiquitous network computing due to the hurdle of IT interface, the prototype was designed as the form of stick which can be often carried around by senior people. However, it could be implemented as one of the other personal-use items such as a mobile phone, an umbrella, wrist watch, etc if the target user is somewhere else. The signal sending module uses gesture of the user to transmit a signal. The message display module uses vibration to display the incoming message. For both modules, the objective is not to transmit the content of the message itself but rather an identification signal, from which the user can easily recognize the contents from the context.

Figure 1 shows the signal sending function when a user is making a gesture to send a message to the system. The acceleration sensors embedded in the stick generate the data of gesturing, which is transmitted to the system and recognized the meaning of the message.

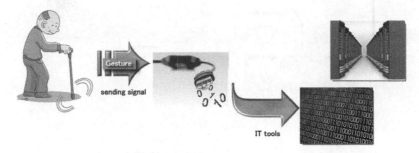

Fig. 1. VIBRATO as an input device by sending signals by gesture

Figure 2 shows the vibrotactile message display function of VIBRATO. The vibro-tactole display generates vibration to the user who holds the device. In this way, the user can feel the message delivered by the system.

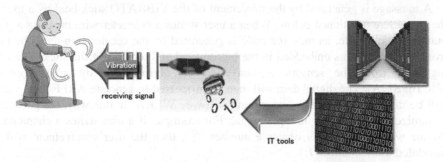

Fig. 2. VIBRATO as an information display device by generating vibration

Both of these modules will be embedded to the stick interface in the final stage. However, since this is a preliminary stage of the research, each module is now under implementation as separate modules. The input module of VIBRATO is under study as the form of stick, which will be described in Section 3. However, the vibrotactile message display is under study as the form of wrist strap and used in the experiment described in Section 4.

3 VIBRATO Message Sending Module

3.1 Message Sending Experiment

This section presents the VIBRATO message sending module, which was implemented as the form of stick. Figure 3 shows the process flow of message sending

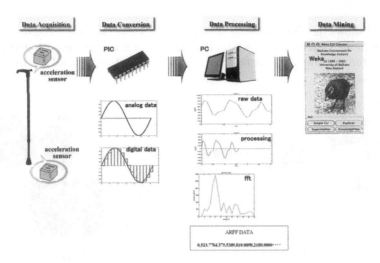

Fig. 3. Message generation procedure of VIBRATO

procedure including data acquisition, data conversion, data processing, and data mining.

A message is generated by the movement of the VIBRATO stick held by a user in the procedure mentioned below. When a user writes a character with pressing a push button at the handle, its message code is generated by the acceleration data obtained from the two sensors embedded in the bottom-end and top-end of the stick. The analog data from the sensors is converted as digital data by microprocessor (PIC16F877A). The digital data will then be processed to generate ARFF data, which will be taken care of by the data mining software WEKA. In this way, the gesture is recognized to be used as an input signal. For example, if a user writes a character in the air with the stick, for example number "7", then the user's movement will be translated as the number 7.

The feasibility of this message sending module using a gesture was tested in the experimental study. Figure 4 shows the overview of this experiment. Five examinees joined the experiment. Each examinee writes one of the nine numbers from zero to nine using the VIBRATO stick in three postures; namely, writing towards the floor in stand-up posture, writing towards the front of the body also in stand-up posture and writing on the floor surface in sitting down posture as shown in Figure 5.

As shown in Figure 4, six examinees performed all 10 numbers from zero to nine for ten times in each number, and 600 raw data sets were collected. 300 data sets were selected from 600, and used as training data sets for neural network training in WEKA. The remaining 300 data sets were used as test data sets and given to this trained neural network to see how the number can be recognized. No detailed instruction was given to the five examinees. They just wrote numbers in their own style.

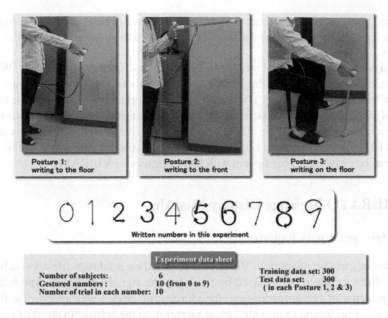

Fig. 4. Message sending experiment in three different postures

3.2 Results and Discussions

Figure 5 shows the results of experiments in three postures. Since this experiment is in the preliminary stage, the number of subjects is not enough to come to a conclusion. However, some comments can be given from the observation of the experiments.

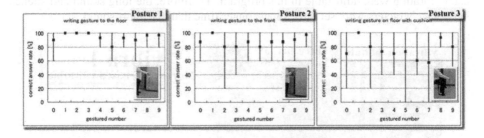

Fig. 5. Message recognition results of VIBRATO in three different postures

No detailed instruction was given to the subject to write numbers. Therefore, the subjects wrote numbers in their own style. The score differs in each person, but the average correct recognition rate in Posture 1 is 80% or higher. The correct recognition rate in Posture 2 is lower than Posture 1. From our observation, the reason of this deterioration was caused by G-forces. For comparison, writing on the floor was also tested because it would be comfortable for a person sitting on a chair to write numbers by contacting the bottom-end of the stick to the floor. The correct recognition rate of

Posture 3 was very low, which was never improved even if different types of the surface conditions were used because of the vibration noise caused by the surface contact.

As a result, the downward writing in Posture 1 provided the best result. When the examinee writes numbers in the air in Posture 3, it should also mention that the same kind of results as in Posture 1 was obtained. As opposed to the ubiquitous devices such as PDA, this stick interface of VIBRATO does not come with the input keypads or any explicit input interface. Therefore, it is not suitable to input complex message with VIBRATO. However, a single character such as a number tested in this experiment can be provided to the system with hand gestures of VIBRATO.

4 VIBRATO Message Display Module

4.1 Message Display Experiment

The idea of message display in VIBRATO is based on a vibrotactile approach, which means that a message is displayed by the vibration signals. Since this module is still in the position of preliminary stage, the vibrotactile device was attached to the wrist band type of prototype to provide a clear vibration to the subject in stead of embedded in the VIBRATO stick. Therefore, this section describes the idea based on the wrist band type of prototype.

The device was designed and implemented using a simple circuit of PIC16F877A with small vibration motors as shown in the upper-left corner of Figure 6. A test program was implemented to convert a character set to vibration pattern in two modes. One mode is Morse code-based conversion or *vibra 1*, which convert a character set to a Morse code set. For example, a single "F" is converted to ". . - .". , whereas a character set "NO" is converted to "-. ---". The length of vibration and interval time of each vibration were adjustable in this program. Therefore, the long sound and silence between characters were set three times longer time than the short sound.

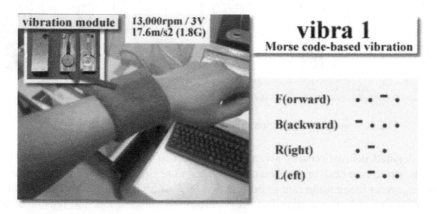

Fig. 6. Vibra 1: Morse code-based vibration

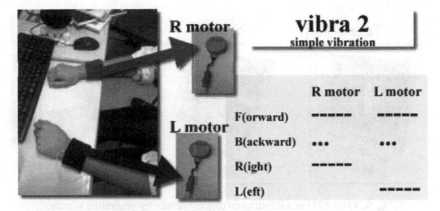

Fig. 7. Vibra 2: simple vibration with two motors

The other mode, or *vibra 2* is a simple pattern-based conversion using a pair of vibration motors. For example, a character "F" standing for "Forward", switches on both motors to generate a short vibration "-----" simultaneously. The pattern can be any meaning based on the local rule. To validate this module, an experiment was conducted using a maze navigation problem. The experiment was conducted by five pairs of examinee and instructor. The examinee is given a blank form with indicated the start and goal cells only as shown in Figure 8.

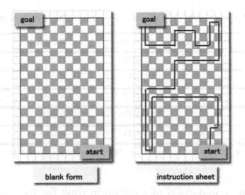

Fig. 8. Blank form and instruction sheet for the navigation experiment

The instructor is given an instruction sheet with a route from the start cell to the goal cell as shown in the right hand side of Figure 8. The examinee is given an instruction for navigation, starting from the start cell heading towards the goal cell by the instructors navigation. The instruction is given by VIBRATO display module in two modes. For comparison of performance, text instruction, symbol instruction and audio instruction were also given to each examinee.

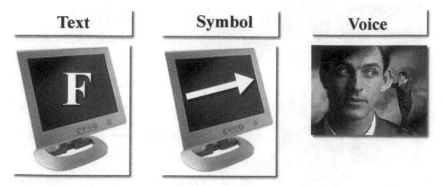

Fig. 9. VIBRATO as a information display device by generating vibration

4.2 Results and Discussions

Prior to the experiment, a pre-experiment was given to the five examinees to see if they could recognize the difference in different pattern of vibration without difficulty. Table 1 shows the summary of correction ratio. As show in this table, all 5 examinees (A-E) could tell the difference between ate/tea, yes/no, ate/tea/ai, and yes/no/ok/ng. A mistake was recognized in ok/ng in subject A. The vibration instruction given in the experiment was one of the single characters, namely "F", "B", "L", or "R". Therefore, it was confirmed that the vibration instruction in *vibra 1* was correctly understood by all the examinees in the experiment.

Table 1. Correction ratio (%) to distinguish the different patterns

	ate/tea	ok/ng	yes/no	ate/tea/ai	yes/no/ok/ng
A	100	66	100	100	100
B	100	100	100	100	100
C	100	100	100	100	100
D	100	100	100	100	100
E	100	100	100	100	100

ate: .- - . tea: - . .- ai: .- .. ok: --- -.- ng: -. --. yes: -.-- . ... no: -. ---

Figure 10 show the comparison of navigation time for the five examinees (A-E). This figure shows that the navigation time in *vibra 1* was twice as longer as the other instruction media. However, the message was understood by all the examinees in all of these five media. Especially, *vibra 2* gives direct instruction showing clearly which way to go in the maze panel, according to the comments from the examinees.

If the conventional media, such as audio & visual is not suitable, vibration media provides an alternative method of communication. Suppose a user cannot look into the visual display to read information due to concentrating on something else, audio or vibration information can be an alternative display. A detailed instruction or information cannot be understood by vibration message only. However, brief information on which this study focuses, such as the one presented in this experiment, can be

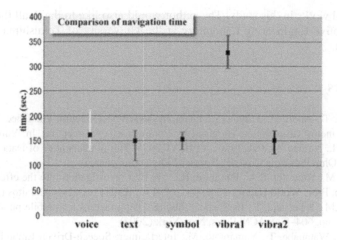

Fig. 10. VIBRATO as a information display device by generating vibration

feasible in a vibrotactile way. Direct instruction with two motors such as *vibra 2* showed better performance in this experiment. However, it can only provide a specific combination of meaning in message. Morse code-based vibration can provide more general framework of message. It can deliver not only the single character but also even a sentence. However, there are many issues to be solved to use the Morse code-based vibration for general users who are not familiar with them. It should be pointed out that VIBRATO examinees could distinguish the difference of vibration message even if they do not know if "..-." stands for "f" in Morse code.

5 Concluding Remarks

This paper proposed the idea of vibirotactile message for brief information. Using the prototype system, this paper presented the way to send and receive information by a vibrotactile manner. The simple vibration alert used in a silent mode of mobile phones does not fully exploit the potential of vibration as a means of communication. This experiment shows how to exploit this potentiality of vibration.

For future work, this study will extend the use of VIBRATO to multiple of people, receiving information, for example from RFID tags in a simultaneous way. When the number of people receives the signals, those people not only share the information but also may share the same atmospheres. Reviewing the result of experiments based on the test environment of VIBRATO system, this study will work on the usability of vibrotactile interfaces and would like to propose a direction into which the potential of vibration can be exploited as a means of communication in the near future.

Acknowledgement

The author would like to acknowledge Mr.Takashi Niwa, Mr. Naoki Nishioka, and Mr. Kouhei Oshima of the University of Tokushima for their assisting with the experimental works in this study. The author would also like to thank all the members of Collaborative Engineering Laboratory at the University of Tokushima to support this research.

References

1. Amemiya, T., Ando, H., Maeda, T.: Phantom-DRAWN: Direction Guidance using Rapid and Asymmetric Acceleration Weighted by Nonlinearity of Perception. In: Yamaguchi, K., Motoda, H., Numao, M. (eds.) Proc. of ICAT 2005. The fundamentals of Data Mining, pp. 201–208. Ohm Pulishing Co. Ltd., Tokyo (2006) (in Japanese)
2. Brown, L.M., Brewster, S.A., Purchase, H.C.: A first investigation into the effectiveness of tactons. In: Proc. World Haptics 2005, pp. 167–176. IEEE Press, Los Alamitos (2005)
3. Brown, L.M., Kaaresoja, T.: Feel who's talking: Using tactons for mobile phone alerts. In: CHI 2006, pp. 604–609. ACM Press, New York (2006)
4. Nagai, H., Watanabe, T., Yamamoto, M.: InterPointer: Speech-Driven Embodied Entrainment Pointer System. In: Proceedings of the 2005 International Conference on Active Media Technology (AMT 2005), pp. 213–218 (2005)
5. Minamizawa, K., Kamuro, S., Kawakami, N., Tachi, S.: A Palm-worn Haptic Display for Bimanual Operations in Virtual Environments. In: Ferre, M. (ed.) EuroHaptics 2008. LNCS, vol. 5024, pp. 458–463. Springer, Heidelberg (2008)
6. Tsukada, K., Yasumrua, M.: ActiveBelt: Belt-type Wearable Tactile Display for Directional Navigation. In: Davies, N., Mynatt, E.D., Siio, I. (eds.) UbiComp 2004. LNCS, vol. 3205, pp. 384–399. Springer, Heidelberg (2004)
7. Uesaka, Y.: Introduction to MATLAB programming. Makino Shoten (2000) (in Japanese)
8. The University of Waikato,
   http://www.cs.waikato.ac.nz/~ml/weka/index.html

Orientation Responsive Touch Interaction

Jinwook Kim, Jong-gil Ahn, and Heedong Ko

Korea Institute of Science and Technology, Imaging Media Research Center,
P.O.Box 131, Cheongryang, Seoul 130-650, Korea
{jwkim,hide989,ko}@imrc.kist.re.kr

Abstract. A novel touch based interaction method by use of orientation information of a touch region is proposed. To capture higher dimensional information of touch including a position and an orientation as well, we develop robust algorithms to detect a contact shape and to estimate its orientation angle. Also we suggest practical guidelines to use our method through experiments considering various conditions and show possible service scenarios of aligning documents and controlling a media player.

Keywords: Touch Interaction, Interaction techniques, Touch direction, Touch orientation, Tabletop, Media player controller.

1 Introduction

We introduce a novel touch based interaction method by use of orientation information of a touch region. We observe explosive interests on touch based interaction due to recently introduced hardware and software [1,2,3,4,5]. They are focused mostly on detecting positions of multiple points of the contact. Our motivation is to use higher dimensional information for touch interaction not restricted to two-dimensional positions only. Fig.1 shows consecutive images of a single contact shape during the touch interaction. Note that the center of contact shape changes little compared to its relative orientation angle, which means that an orientation angle of the touch gives us a new independent axis of interaction information.

We present how to detect the touch and retrieve a contact shape using computer vision methods followed by robust estimation of an orientation angle of the approximated elliptical shape of the contact. Also we suggest practical guidelines for our method through experiments considering various conditions. Finally we enumerate possible interaction scenarios using our methods.

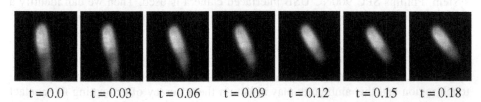

t = 0.0   t = 0.03   t = 0.06   t = 0.09   t = 0.12   t = 0.15   t = 0.18

Fig. 1. Images of a contact area during the touch interaction

J.A. Jacko (Ed.): Human-Computer Interaction, Part II, HCII 2009, LNCS 5611, pp. 461–469, 2009.
© Springer-Verlag Berlin Heidelberg 2009

2   Related Works

There have been tremendous researches to rotate things in computer applications using traditional input peripheral devices such as a mouse, a key-pad, a stylus pen, and so on. Compared to manual manipulation of physical objects, most of the work however lack in enough degrees of freedom and are difficult to achieve relevant feedback information during the manipulation.

In this case, automatic alignment of the things can be useful. InfoTable [22] rotates an item of interest automatically to align the item with display boundaries near to a user. STARS [15] and ConnecTable [17] introduce similar functions of automatic rotation of objects. In several tabletop display systems, the "corner to rotate" method has been used and proved its usefulness. Kruger et al. [18] presented the RNT algorithm to rotate digital objects using a physically based model.

Recently touch interaction using bare fingers gathers explosive interests and is used in many touch input and display systems such as DiamondTouch [4], SmartSkin [9], and DViT [11]. Rotation of the objects in touch based interaction becomes more important especially in multiple users tabletop environments [2,12,13,14] because users expect the system to support intuitive manipulation methods by using their hands and fingers only. Matsushita et al. [21] proposed the dual touch method using two fingers which is one of the most popular methods to rotate objects. Recently Microsoft [2] announced a rotation technique using only one finger but details on the algorithms and performance have not been published officially yet.

3   Orientation Responsive Touch Interaction

While most of the touch interaction methods are point based, the proposed interaction method uses additional orientation information. We first identify a contact region between a finger and the touch interface followed by estimating the contact shape to achieve orientation information. Then the orientation angle can be used to rotate objects or other subsystems requiring the orientation information. In this section we investigate how to detect a touch area, to retrieve the contact shape and to estimate an orientation angle of the shape.

3.1   Touch Detection

To detect an event of touch interaction, we use MTmini package [3] which is a software framework to expedite a development of multi touch applications. A camera inside a box can capture the silhouette of hands and fingers of touch (Fig.2). In our system, Phillips SPC 900NC USB interfaced camera is used. Then we can identify a region of contact and generate the corresponding grayscale intensity image.

3.2   Contact Shape Retrieval

A grayscale intensity image acquired previously is very blurry to identify an exact touch region and this ambiguity may affect on the accuracy of estimating the contact shape. To this end, we convert a grayscale intensity image (Fig.3(a)) into a binary

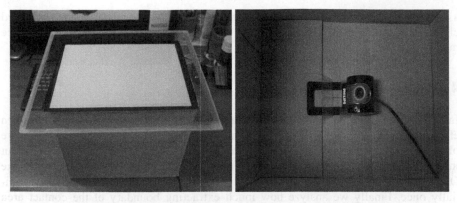

Fig. 2. MTmini

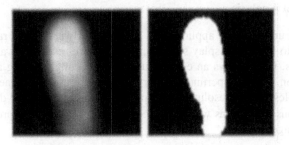

Fig. 3(a). Grayscale image (b) Binary image

image (Fig.3(b)) by Otsu's method [6]. The method assumes that the image to be thresholded contains two classes of pixels (e.g. foreground and background) then calculates the optimum threshold separating those two classes so that their combined spread (intra-class variance) is minimal.

As shown in the Fig.3, the input grayscale image can be segmented into two regions clearly. One possible problem is that Otsu's method is computationally intensive to be applied each of the input images every frame. However the threshold level changes little in a controlled working environment as ours. Thus the value can be computed once in the initialization step and be reused without any update afterward. Section 4.2. refers the reader to details on the observation.

3.3 Orientation Estimation

Given a set of points on a boundary of the contact shape, we estimate an orientation angle by assuming an elliptical shape of the contact boundary. Let $p_i = \Re^2$ be the ith point on the boundary. We translate all the points so as that the centroid of the shape is located at the origin. Then we compute a covariance matrix $X = \sum (p_i - p_c)(p_i - p_c)^T$, where p_c is the centroid of the shape represented as a column vector. Finally a rotation matrix indicating how much the approximated ellipse is rotated can be computed using the polar decomposition of the covariance matrix X [8].

4   Experimental Results

In this section, we experiment the proposed method in various conditions to draw an efficient combination of the algorithms according to target hardware and software platforms. First we examine consistency of the results in various resolutions of input images. Second we compare an accuracy of an estimated orientation angle when the Otsu's method is applied every frame and when the threshold value is computed initially once. Finally we analyze how much extracting boundary of the contact area affects on the orientation angle estimation.

4.1   Resolution Analysis

To verify that our method is applicable to various hardware setups ranging from mobile interfaces to tabletop display systems, we compare results on various resolutions of input images. Fig.4 shows an estimated orientation angle during a short period of touch interaction. In this experiment, binary images are used. Our method works very robustly regardless of the resolution of input images. Note that the difference among tests with various resolutions was measured less than 2° during approximately 45° of orientation change in total.

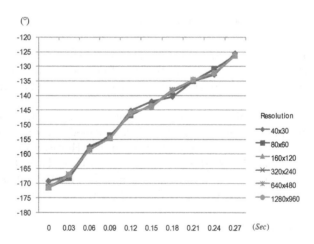

Fig. 4. Orientation angle estimated using various resolutions of input images

4.2   Application of Otsu's Method Analysis

Our method requires converting a grayscale intensity image into a binary image. The conversion process can be done using the Otsu's method which might be expensive

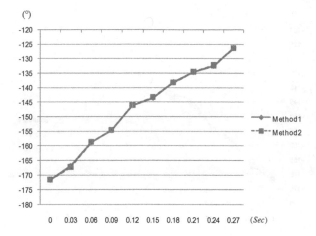

Fig. 5. Orientation angle estimated changing the Otsu's method conditions.

for mobile interfaces equipped with a low computational power. Hence we examine whether the threshold level should be updated every frame.

In the method 1, we perform Otsu's method every frame and the method 2 compute the threshold level once in an initialization step and reuse the value without any update afterward. As shown in the Fig.5, two methods show very close results because illumination conditions and touch patterns change little in our hardware setup. Hence the method 2 is preferable considering computational costs.

4.3 Boundary Extraction Analysis

When estimating a touch orientation angle, our basic assumption is that a boundary shape of the contact region is elliptical, which means that our algorithm requires extracting boundary pixels from the binary image. However the orientation is invariant to the scale of the image and therefore considering all the pixels inside the contact region not only the boundaries does not affect the orientation estimation much. Hence it is desirable to eliminate the unnecessary process of extracting boundaries if possible.

Fig. 6. (a) Intensity image.   (b) Binary image.   (c) Boundary image.

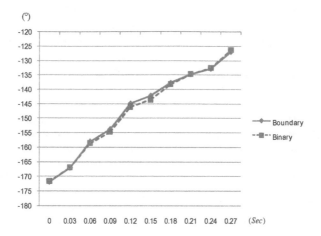

Fig. 7. Orientation angle estimated using boundary image and binary image

In this sense, we compare results of applying Canny's edge detection algorithm [7] to achieve the boundary and considering all the pixels in the contact region. As shown in the Fig.6, the maximum difference was measure less than 1.5° and we can safely skip the process of extracting a boundary of the binary image.

5   Service Scenarios

We propose two service scenarios using the proposed orientation estimation method. The first one is to align documents in a tabletop display system and the second is to control widgets in a media player on small touch interfaces.

5.1   Document Alignment

Assume that multiple users share a common tabletop environment where several objects representing documents, media and images are located arbitrarily as shown in Fig.8. Possibly the object may not be aligned according to the user's viewing direction. This typical situation decreases user's affordance especially in reading documents like news papers [20].

While one of the most popular methods to orient the objects in touch interfaces is multiple contact points based, the proposed method can be used to reorient the objects using only one finger. Fig.9 illustrates the scenario. Arguably using only one finger is preferable in many applications.

5.2   Media Player Controller

One more example of the orientation responsive touch interaction is controlling widgets in media players. Slider controls and buttons to adjust a volume or fast forward the media shown in Fig.10(a) can be replaced by the proposed interaction method. In small touch interfaces, touch based slider control widgets can be cumbersome because

Fig. 8. Documents and media arbitrarily located on a tabletop display

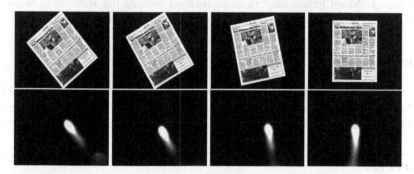

Fig. 9. Changing an orientation of a document for a better alignment

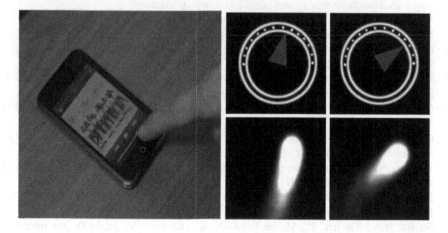

Fig. 10 (a). Slider controller widget. (b) Dial widget using orientation responsive touch interaction method.

the working area of touch is too small and a minute control of the widgets is required. However our method is robust to small area of touch with the limited resolution of the captured touch image and hence is very intuitive to use. Fig.10(b) shows a dial widget using our method. Users can control minutely the control value. Also our method does not require a user to scroll the finger across the touch interface and therefore fits well to small form factored devices.

6 Conclusion

We propose a novel orientation responsive touch interaction method. Since our approach can estimate a contact orientation as well as a position, users can enjoy contents in a new interaction style. Our technique can be applied only when images of the contact shape are available. However many of the existing hardware setups for touch interaction can generate such an image data of the contact. Also computationally expensive image processing procedures required to acquire a robust contact shape should be minimized when applied to mobile devices equipped with a low computational power. Nevertheless the proposed method introducing more dimensions for interaction information suggests us a variety of orientation sensitive interactions.

Acknowledgements

This work was supported by the IT R&D program of MKE/IITA [2009-F-033-01, Development of Real-time Physics Simulation Engine for e-Entertainment] and by Korea Institute of Science and Technology (KIST) through the Tangible Web Project.

References

1. Apple iPod touch, http://www.apple.com/ipodtouch
2. Microsoft Surface, http://www.microsoft.com/surface
3. MTmini package, http://ssandler.wordpress.com/MTmini
4. Deitz, P., Leigh, D.: DiamondTouch: a multi-user touch technology. In: Proceedings of UIST 2001, pp. 219–226. ACM Press, New York (2001)
5. Han, J.Y.: Low-cost multi-touch sensing through frustrated total internal reflection. In: Proceedings of UIST, pp. 115–118. ACM Press, New York (2005)
6. Otsu, N.: A threshold selection method from gray-level histograms. IEEE Trans. Systems, Man, and Cybernetics 9(1) (1979)
7. Canny, J.F.: A computational approach to edge detection. IEEE Trans. Pattern Analysis and Machine Intelligence 8(6) (1986)
8. Higham, N.J.: Computing the polar decomposition with applications. SIAM J. Scientific and Statistical Computing 7(4) (1986)
9. Rekimoto, J.: SmartSkin: An Infrastructure for Freehand Manipulation on Interactive Surfaces. In: Proc. CHI 2002, pp. 113–120 (2002)
10. Streitz, N.A., Tandler, P., Muller-Tomfelde, C., Konomi, S.: i-LAND: An Interactive Landscape for Creativity and Innovation. Proc. CHI 1999, 120–127 (1999)

11. SMARTTech.: Digital Vision Touch Technology. White Paper (2003),
    http://www.smarttech.com/dvit/
12. Shen, C., Lesh, N., Forlines, C., Vernier, F.: Sharing and Building Digital Group Historie.
    In: Proc. CSCW 2002, pp. 324–333 (2002)
13. Shen, C., Lesh, N.B., Moghaddam, B., Beardsley, P.A., Bardsley, R.S.: Personal Digital
    Historian: Use Interface Design. In: Proc. CHI 2001 Extended Abstracts, pp. 29–30 (2001)
14. Shen, C., Everitt, K.M., Ryall, K.: UbiTable: Impromptu Face-to-Face Collaboration on
    Horizontal Interactive Surfaces. In: Dey, A.K., Schmidt, A., McCarthy, J.F. (eds.) Ubi-
    Comp 2003. LNCS, vol. 2864, pp. 281–288. Springer, Heidelberg (2003)
15. Magerkurth, C., Stenzel, R., Prante, T.: STARS – a ubiquitous computing platform for
    computer augmented tabletop games. In: Extended Abstract of UbiComp 2003, pp. 267–
    268. Springer, Heidelberg (2003)
16. Shen, C., Vernier, F., Forlines, C., Ringel, M.: DiamondSpin: An extensible toolkit for
    around-the-table interaction. In: Proceedings of CHI 2004, pp. 167–174. ACM Press, New
    York (2004)
17. Tandler, P., Prante, T., Müller-Tomfelde, C., Streitz, N., Steinmetz, R.: ConnecTables: dy-
    namic coupling of displays for the flexible creation of shared workspaces. In: Proceedings
    of UIST 2001, pp. 11–20. ACM Press, New York (2001)
18. Kruger, R., Carpendale, S., Scott, S.D., Tang, A.: Fluid integration of rotation and transla-
    tion. In: Proc. CHI, pp. 601–610. ACM Press, New York (2005)
19. Hancock, M.S., Vernier, F., Wigdor, D., Carpendale, S., Shen, C.: Rotation and translation
    mechanisms for tabletop interaction. In: Proc. Tabletop, pp. 79–86. IEEE Press, Los
    Alamitos (2006)
20. Koriat, A., Norman, J.: Reading Rotated Words. Journal of Experimental Psychology.
    Human Perception and Performance 11(4), 490–508 (1985)
21. Matsushita, N., Ayatsuka, Y., Rekimoto, J.: Dual touch: A two-handed interface for pen-
    based PDAs. In: ACM UIST Symposium on User Interface Software and Technology, pp.
    211–212 (2000)
22. Rekimoto, J., Saitoh, M.: Augmented surfaces: a spatially continuous work space for hy-
    brid computing environments. In: Proceedings of CHI 1999, pp. 378–385. ACM Press,
    New York (1999)
23. http://www.youtube.com/watch?v=_wHQKbME39k

Representation of Velocity Information by Using Tactile Apparent Motion

Kentaro Kotani[1], Toru Yu[2], Takafumi Asao[1], and Ken Horii[1]

[1] Graduate School of Engineering, Kansai University
3-3-35 Yamate-cho, Suita, Osaka 564-8680, Japan
{kotani,asao,khorii}@iecs.kansai-u.ac.jp
[2] Faculty of Engineering Science, Kansai University
3-3-35 Yamate-cho, Suita, Osaka 564-8680, Japan
sa8m405@ipcku.kansai-u.ac.jp

Abstract. The objective of the study is to evaluate whether use of apparent motion can be an effective presentation method for velocity information. Ten subjects participated in the experiment where they perceived apparent motion generated by air-jet and they controlled the speed of the moving object on the PC screen to express their perceived velocity. As a result, perceived velocity decreased significantly as the ISOI was increased. Perceived velocity changed with the duration when the ISOI was between 30–70 ms and when apparent motion was provided. Duration only affected perceived velocity when apparent motion is provided to the subjects. In conclusion, apparent motion generated by stimuli can be effectively used to transmit precise velocity information tactually.

Keywords: Apparent motion, Velocity, Tactile perception, Air-jet.

1 Introduction

Recently, tactile interfaces, which are user interfaces that employ tactile perception for input/output, have been the focus of an increasing number of studies [3]. Tactile-interface design guidelines that help optimize the characteristics of human tactile perception have not yet been fully developed. Hayashi, et al. [4] indicated that the fundamental characteristics of tactile-interface design are not properly understood; very few studies have been performed on the mechanics of velocity perception in order to establish design guidelines.

Studies associated with velocity perception are very few compared to studies pertaining to pattern representation and texture perception in tactile displays. Moreover, studies dealing with velocity perception have focused on the fundamental characteristics of the ability to discriminate velocity in response to tactile stimuli, i.e., advanced studies have not been conducted on the manner in which people perceive velocity in response to a discrete set of stimuli under the skin.

In this study, we examined the use of apparent motion as a medium for filling the gaps between spatially separated stimuli generating velocity information. Tactile apparent motion is defined as a perceptual phenomenon; in this phenomenon, a person receives a pair of stimuli separated by a certain duration but perceives the motion of a

J.A. Jacko (Ed.): Human-Computer Interaction, Part II, HCII 2009, LNCS 5611, pp. 470–478, 2009.
© Springer-Verlag Berlin Heidelberg 2009

single stimulus from the location of the first stimulus presentation to the location of the subsequent stimulus presentation [5].

Apparent motion has been extensively studied by researchers in the field of visual science. Some of these studies focused on modeling the perception of apparent motion [1][2][6][9]. These studies have evaluated the applicability of Kolers's equation [8] for estimating perceived velocity. The results of these studies indicated that while the equation attempts to approximate the changes in perceived velocity on the basis of the inter-stimulus onset interval (ISOI) and the distance between two stimuli, the values obtained by using the equation deviated significantly from the actual perceived velocity of visual apparent motion, which is determined experimentally. At present, using Kolers's equation to estimate tactile velocity perception directly appears to be difficult. Moreover, no detailed studies have been performed on using Kolers's equation to determine the tactile perception of velocity by considering the duration of the stimuli, which has been found to affect the perceived velocity.

The literature review revealed that it is necessary to study the changes in perceived velocity generated by different types of apparent motion by considering various parameters in order to understand the mechanism of perceived velocity better. The objective of this study is to evaluate whether use of apparent motion can be an effective presentation method for velocity information. We also quantitatively evaluated the manner in which perceived velocity changed with the duration of the stimuli and the ISOI; it has been suggested that the duration of the stimuli can be potentially used to characterize perceived velocity in the general apparent motion paradigm.

2 Methods

2.1 Subjects

Ten subjects, recruited from the university community, participated in the study. All the subjects were right handed and consented to participating in the study.

2.2 Apparatus

Figure 1 shows the experimental setup used in our study. Pressurized air was generated by an air compressor and delivered using solenoid valves. Air pressure was regulated using a series of electropneumatic regulators.

A computer program was developed especially for determining the subjects' perceived velocity by means of a cross-modality matching method. A screenshot of the computer program is shown in figure 2. The top–left part of the display area shows a red circle representing a moving object that moves upward, as shown in the figure. Control icons are located on the right-hand side and the bottom of the screen. They were used for changing the velocity of the object such that the velocity perceived through tactile stimuli was identical to that represented by the movement of the object. The diameter of the object was 6.4 mm (0.3° in terms of visual angle). The computer program was able to simulate the speed of he moving object over a range of 0.35 to 150.05 cm/sec with a resolution of 0.35 cm/sec.

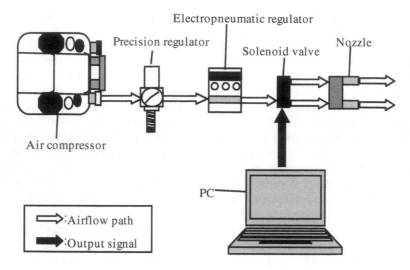

Fig. 1. Experimental setup

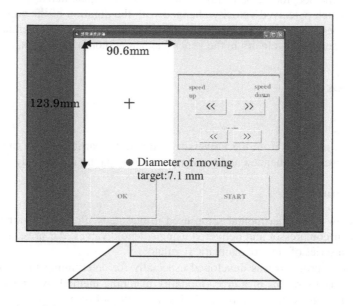

Fig. 2. Screenshot of the computer program used for measuring perceived velocity by using the cross-modality matching method

2.3 Experimental Procedure

The intensity of the air-jet stimuli was controlled at 150 kPa, and the stimuli were applied to the center of the left palm. Responding to the stimuli, the subjects controlled the speed of the moving object on the PC screen by using the keyboard.

Figure 3 shows the posture of the subjects during the aforementioned task. Each subject sat in an adjustable chair and placed his/her right hand over the computer mouse. The height of the seat was adjusted such that the eye level of each subject was at the same height as the center of the display showing the moving object, indicated by the symbol "+" in figure 2. The distance between the eyes and the display was set to approximately 650 mm; however, the subjects were allowed to sit comfortably by moving their backs and heads, sitting forward, or leaning backward to some extent. The subjects used earplugs and headphones in order to be completely isolated from the noise generated during air-jet emission, so that the possibility of guessing the velocity on the basis of the sound intensity of the pressurized air was eliminated. The location of stimulus presentation (i.e., the center of the subjects' palms) was immobilized by placing the subjects' hands on a clay base molded to the shape of the hand.

Fig. 3. A subject performing trials

2.4 Data Analysis

The subjects completed the velocity estimation tasks for 42 stimuli–set patterns. Each pattern was applied over six trials, yielding a total of 252 trials. Different combinations of the stimuli characteristics (duration and ISOI) were used to create different patterns. These patterns were classified into two groups on the basis of the results of a pilot study indicating the clarity of perception of apparent motion. The patterns were thus classified because we were primarily concerned with studying the effect of apparent motion on the accuracy of the velocity perception. Tables 1 and 2 summarize the stimuli patterns and the experimental conditions used in this study, respectively.The values of perceived velocity obtained by using the cross-modality matching method were analyzed using a two-factor model ANOVA (Duration and ISOI were used as the factors.). Scheffe's multiple-comparison test was conducted as a post hoc test. The experimentally determined perceived velocity was compared with the perceived velocity estimated from Kolers's equation [8], which is defined as follows.

$$v = s \,/\, \text{ISOI} . \tag{1}$$

Table 1. Stimuli sets used in the experiment

Duration [ms]	ISOI [ms]	
	Clear apparent motion	Unclear apparent motion
50	30, 50, 70	100, 150, 200
70	30, 50, 70	100, 150, 200
100	30, 50, 70	100, 150, 200
120	30, 50, 70	100, 150, 200
150	30, 50, 70	100, 150, 200
170	30, 50, 70	100, 150, 200
200	30, 50, 70	100, 150, 200

Table 2. Experimental conditions

Subject	Ten healthy males
Number of stimulus sets	42
Number of trials in a block	6
Distance between stimuli	30 mm
Order of presentation	Random
Distance between the subject's skin and the nozzle	5 mm
Nozzle diameter	1.0 mm
Location of stimulus presentation	Center of the palm
Direction of stimulus presentation	From palm to the distal part of the middle finger
Force generated by the air jet	7 gf

Where v: perceived velocity generated by a pair of continuously applied tactile stimuli, and s: physical distance between the locations of the first and subsequent stimuli along the motion path.

3 Results

Table 3 summarizes the results of the ANOVA of perceived velocity. The duration ($F_{6, 2471} = 10.08$, $p < .01$) and the ISOI ($F_{5, 2478} = 86.82$, $p < .01$) as well as their interaction term ($F_{30, 2478} = 1.77$, $p < .01$) were found to be statistically significant. Figure 4 shows the change in the velocity perception with the duration of the stimuli sets. The results of the multiple comparison test are denoted by the symbol "*" in figure 4. For any given duration, the perceived velocity decreased as the ISOI increased. The trend was more apparent when the duration was short, i.e., when apparent motion was clearly perceived.

Figure 5 shows the difference between the experimentally determined perceived velocity and the velocity estimated from Kolers's equation. Under the chosen experimental conditions, Kolers's equation approximately fitted our results when the ISOI was 50 ms. When the ISOI was less than 50 ms, the equation overestimated the perceived velocity. Conversely, the equation underestimated the perceived velocity when the ISOI was more than 50 ms. Moreover, it is noteworthy that the relative difference between the experimental results and estimated values was nearly constant when apparent motion was not clearly generated.

Figure 6 shows the change in velocity perception with the ISOI of the stimuli sets. The figure clearly shows that for an ISOI of 30, 50, and 70 ms, the perceived velocity decreased as the duration decreased when the tactile stimuli generated clear apparent motion. However, when apparent motion was not generated, the perceived velocity did not change significantly with the duration. For example, the perceived velocity decreased by 25% (from 85 to 65 cm/s) when stimuli were applied for longer durations with an ISOI of 30 ms, while the perceived velocity remained almost constant or even increased when stimuli were applied for longer durations with an ISOI of 200 ms.

Table 3. Analysis of variance of perceived velocity

Source	Sum of Squares	DF	Mean Square	F	p-value
Duration	30909.69	6	5151.62	10.08	0.000
ISOI	221928.65	5	44385.73	86.82	0.000
Duration * ISOI	27087.22	30	902.91	1.77	0.006
Error	1266859.45	2478	511.24		
Total	1546785.01	2519			

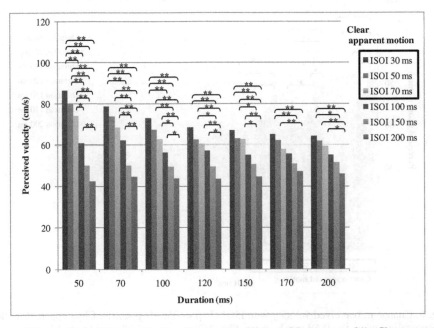

Fig. 4. Change in perceived velocity with duration (*: p < .05; **: p < .01). Clear apparent motion was perceived when the ISOI was between 30 and 70 ms (range indicated by the box).

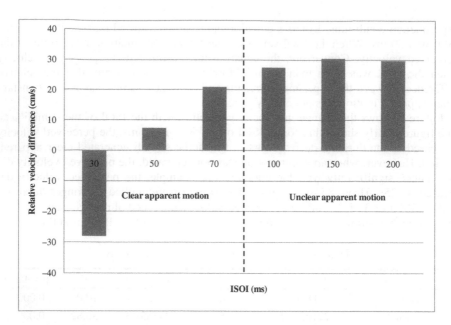

Fig. 5. Change in the experimentally determined perceived velocity and perceived velocity estimated from Kolers's equation with the ISOI. The clarity of the apparent motion perceived by the subjects is also indicated in the figure.

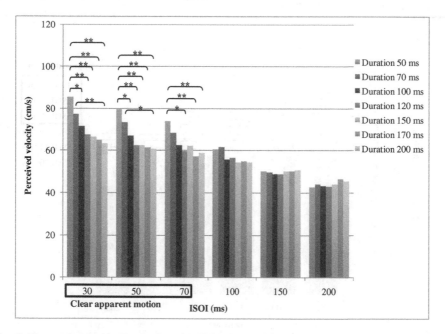

Fig. 6. Change in perceived velocity with ISOI (*: $p < .05$; **: $p < .01$). Clear apparent motion was perceived when the ISOI was between 30 and 70 ms (range indicated by the box).

4 Discussion

4.1 Effects of ISOI on Perceived Velocity

Perceived velocity decreased significantly as the ISOI was increased. This occurred regardless of the duration within the range we tested. This behavior was found to be consistent with that of the perceived velocity estimated by using Kolers's equation. However, the results shown in figure 5 reveal that Kolers's equation underestimated perceived velocity in all cases except when ISOI was 30 ms. Thus, Kolers's equation does not appear to reflect the experimentally determined perceived velocity generated using tactile apparent motion. Furthermore, the results of Scheffe's multiple comparison test revealed that the perceived velocity did not differ significantly unless the ISOI was at least 30–40 ms and the duration of the stimuli was short. These results suggested that Kolers's equation should be modified to include the interaction terms of duration and ISOI in order to render it more precise.

4.2 Effects of Duration of Stimuli on Perceived Velocity

As shown in figure 6, perceived velocity changed with the duration when the ISOI was between 30–70 ms and when apparent motion was provided. The results of the multiple comparison test performed under these conditions suggested that in some cases, the perceived velocities decreased significantly as the duration increased. This suggests that Kolers's equation was not accurately fitted to the empirical results and that besides the distance and ISOI, duration affects the determination of perceived velocity significantly. Giascha et al. (1989) also reported similar trends in visual apparent motion. They conducted an experiment to determine perceived velocity generated by visual apparent motion by means of parameter estimation by sequential testing (PEST). They suggested that the determination of perceived velocity was related to neuronal activities in the primary visual cortex. In the primary visual cortex, neurons sensitive to higher velocities ("high-pass cells") are activated by processing stimuli with higher velocities, whereas neurons sensitive to lower velocities ("low-pass cells") are activated by processing stimuli with lower velocities. Studies on tactile apparent motion are very few compared to those on its visual counterpart; thus, the mechanism underlying the construction of velocity perception is yet to be defined. Kohli, et al. [7] investigated the characteristics of tactile apparent motion generated by using vibrotactile devices. They used three levels of ISOI (fast: 64 ms; medium: 110 ms; and slow: 190 ms) with a constant duration of 100 ms. The effect of duration on velocity perception was not considered in their study. On the basis of the experimental results obtained in this study, we conclude that a neurophysiological mechanism similar to that pertaining to perceived velocity might be suitable for processing tactile perception as well.

When non-AM stimuli are applied, the perceived velocity did not change with the duration. Therefore, it can be concluded that duration only affects perceived velocity when apparent motion is provided to the subjects. This suggests that use of apparent motion can help transmit precise velocity information by tactile stimulus presentation.

5 Conclusion

Perceived velocity was found to decrease when the durations of the stimuli increased, as long as apparent tactile motion was provided. Apparent motion generated by stimuli can be effectively used to transmit precise velocity information tactually.

Acknowledgements

This study was supported by JSPS Kakenhi (20370101) and Research for Promoting Technical Seeds (11-003) from JST.

References

1. Castet, E.: Apparent speed of sampled motion. Vision Research 35(10), 1375–1384 (1995)
2. Giaschia, D., Anstis, S.: The less you see it, the faster it moves: Shortening the "on-time" speeds up apparent motion. Vision Research 29(3), 335–347 (1989)
3. Hafez, M.: Tactile interfaces, applications and challenges. The Visual Computer 23(4), 262–267 (2007)
4. Hayashi, S., Watanabe, J., Kajimoto, H., Tachi, S.: Study on motion after effect in tactile sensation. Trans. VR Soc. Japan 11(1), 69–75 (2006) (in Japanese with English abstract)
5. Higashiyama, A., Miyaoka, T., Taniguchi, S., Sato, A.: Tactile and Pain. Brain publication (2000) (in Japanese)
6. Koffka, K.: Principles of Gestalt Psychology (International Library of Psychology). Routledge & Kegan Paul PLC (1935)
7. Kohli, L., Niwa, M., Noma, H., Susami, K., Yanagida, Y., Lindeman, R., Hosaka, K., Kume, Y.: Towards effective information display using vibrotactile apparent motion. In: Proceedings of the 2006 IEEE Symposium on Haptic Interfaces for Virtual Environment and Teleoperator Systems, pp. 445–452 (2006)
8. Kolers, P.: Aspects of Motion Perception. Pergamon Press, Oxford (1972)
9. Yonemura, T., Nakamizo, S.: Effects of pursuit eye movement and stimulus factors on perceived velocity of 'sigma-movement. Vision 16(4), 209–221 (2004) (in Japanese)

Tactile Spatial Cognition by the Palm

Misa Grace Kwok

Keio Research Institute at SFC
5322 Endo Fujisawa-shi Kanagawa, 252-8520, Japan
grace@sfc.keio.ac.jp

Abstract. The purpose of this research is to determine tactile spatial cognition characteristics through basic experiments. Two experiments were conducted: 1) distinctiveness of geometrical figure recognition, 2) haptic spatial recognition. As for the results, difference characteristics between visual spatial cognition and tactile spatial cognition were detected. The vertically direction is more accurate and easier to understand than horizontally direction to recognize spatial information.

Keywords: tactile, spatial recognition, palm, vertical direction.

1 Introduction

Many numbers of system or devices, which are presenting distance information or spatial information, are existed around the world. There are many experiments and researches about 'visual cognitive distance' or 'visual spatial recognition', however, there are only small numbers of fundamental experiment and research using tactile sense or haptics. The researches of haptic spatial recognition or cognitive distance are represented by researches for "Tactile Maps". "Tactile Maps" are the map for the blind. It is embossed or written in Braille, thus the user can get necessary information of the map tactually. "Tactile Maps" are usually used by the blind. Almost every "Tactile Maps" in Japan are very difficult to understand their meanings. The reasons for these difficulties are: 1) "Tactile Maps" have many shapes, so the user gets confused to correctly recognize; 2) "Tactile Maps" usually make a point to the landmark, therefore the user often receives wrong distance information; 3) Almost every "Tactile Maps" do not be designed basis on human tactile characteristics and tactile recognition. In 2007, JIS T0922:2007, which was titled 'Guidelines for older persons and persons with disabilities – Methods of displaying tactile guide maps' was established [1]. However, these guidelines are difficult to use for designing tactile Maps, because of which these guidelines were created basis on existing tactile maps. The creators of existing tactile maps converted the visual maps to the tactile maps only; therefore they had not carried out tactile or haptic basic experiments to find out the human tactile or haptic characteristics.

In recent years, with the developments in Internet and the researches of Virtual Reality, tactile or haptic interactive devices or systems, such as iPod Touch (Apple Inc) or "Virtual Reality Meshing of Touch Glove" [2], are creating for the sighted people, not only for the blind people. Some of these devices and systems are designed basis

J.A. Jacko (Ed.): Human-Computer Interaction, Part II, HCII 2009, LNCS 5611, pp. 479–485, 2009.
© Springer-Verlag Berlin Heidelberg 2009

on basic tactile or haptic experiments or researches. However, there are only little numbers of basic researches [3].

In this research, two basic tactile experiments were carried out for finding out the characteristics on human tactile spatial recognition.

2 Experiment 1: Geometrical Figure Recognition

The purpose of this experiment is to determine the threshold of recognizing fundamental patterns. The figure recognition is one of the most important factors for understanding human tactile spatial recognition.

2.1 Stimuli

1 mad quadrate figure and 10 mad rectangle shaped figures were used (see table 1). All stimuli presented in the experiments were made of styrene paper. Each stimulus presented for tactile shape identification was pasted in the center of an A-3 size drawing paper to provide a uniform feel of the materials.

Table 1. Stimuli (mm)

Stimuli		X	Y
name	type		
A	Rectangle	19	102
B	Rectangle	24	81
C	Rectangle	29	67
D	Rectangle	34	57
E	Rectangle	39	50
F	Quadrate	44	44
G	Rectangle	49	40
H	Rectangle	54	36
I	Rectangle	59	33
J	Rectangle	64	31
K	Rectangle	69	28

2.2 Subjects

The experiment was conducted on 20 sighted subjects (10 men and 10 female) of 23 to 65 years of age. The subjects wore an eye-mask to prevent seeing the materials during the experiment.

2.3 Procedure

The experimenter placed the stimulus pasted on the drawing paper in front of the subject, instructed the subject to feel the pattern freely with their dominant hand. The subjects touched the stimuli, then described the stimuli's shapes as "quadrate" or "rectangle" orally. As for the presentation of the stimuli, "The Constant Method" was used. The experimenter recorded each reaction time, and the reproduced stimuli's shape.

2.4 Results and Discussion

As for the results, there was no significant difference on the results of reaction time. However, on the rating of subjects' answered "Quadrate", noteworthy characteristics were found. The stimulus A, B, C, D, and E were vertically long rectangles, and the stimulus G, H, I, J, and K were horizontally long rectangles. On the vertically long rectangles' situation, there was significant difference between stimulus D and E. Meanwhile, on the horizontally long rectangles' situation, there was significant difference between stimulus G and H. Thus, the vertically long rectangles were easier to recognize than the horizontally long rectangles for human beings.

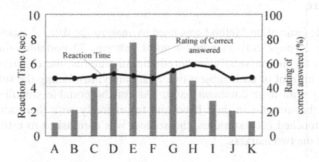

Fig. 1. Result of experiment 1: The correct answer for the stimulus F was "Quadrate", and the correct answers for the other stimuli were "Rectangle"

3 Experiment 2: Tactile Spatial Recognition

The purpose of these experiments was to determine the characteristics of distance recognition using tactile figures. On these experiments, make them clear that cognitive spatial recognition (hereinafter referred to as "The Spatial Recognition") and embodied knowledge of distance perspective (hereinafter referred to as "The Embodied Knowledge") characteristics using tactile sense.

3.1 Stimuli

The stimuli presented to the subjects were uniform boxes (10-cm width, 20-cm length, and 2-cm height) of styrene boards to which two styrene paper markers (5-cm width, 1-cm length, and 0.2-cm height) were affixed, separated from one another by distances ranging from 1-cm to 14-cm at intervals of 1-cm; thus stimuli of 14 discrete distances served as experimental stimuli (see figure 2).

3.2 Subjects

The experiments were conducted on 20 sighted subject (10 male and 10 female) ranging from 23 to 65 years of age. The subjects wore an eye-mask to prevent seeing the materials during touching to the stimuli.

Fig. 2. Stimuli

3.3 Procedure

The Magnitude Estimation Method was used to analyze the data. 2 types of presentation manners; 1) physically-anchored stimuli patterns, 2) portable stimuli patterns were used. As for the physically-anchored stimuli patterns, the experimenter placed each stimulus in front of each subject twice randomly, instructing the subjects to feel stimulus freely with their dominant hand. As for the portable stimuli patterns, the subjects held the stimulus in their hand and felt it freely with their dominant hand. After having touched each stimulus, the subject was then asked to estimate the distance between the two markers.

On The Spatial Recognition Situation
First, the subject touched the reference stimulus; the distance length between 2 bar markers were set at 5-cm, with wearing eye-masks for 3 minuets. The subject memorized the distance of the reference stimulus as 10. Secondly, the presenter presented the stimulus randomly one at a time to the subject. The subject touched the stimulus and represented a distance as a number based on The Magnitude Estimation Method. The experimenter recorded subjects' oral representation.

On The Embodied Knowledge Situation
First, the subject touched the reference stimulus; the distance length between 2 bar markers were set at 5-cm, with wearing eye-masks, and walked 9 meters to memorize the distance between 2 bar markers and the distance walked, without wearing eye-masks. 10 minuets later, the presenter presented the stimulus randomly one at a time to the subject. The subject touched the stimulus with wearing eye-masks, then took off the eye-masks and represented a distance by walk. The experiments were carried out at about 60 meters straight sidewalk in Shonan Fujisawa Campus, Keio University for ensuring the subjects' safe. The experimenter measured the subjects' distance walked and recorded them.

3.4 Results and Discussion

As for the results, there were significant different characteristics between the cognitive distance and the cognitive distance walked. On the Spatial Recognition situation, there were no significant different characteristics between the physically-anchored stimuli manners and the portable stimuli manners. The cognitive distance's magnitude showed a little right side up curve. On the physically-anchored stimuli manners, the

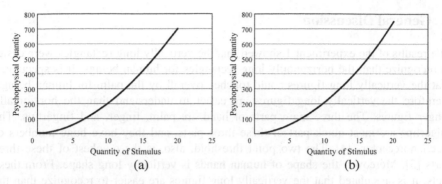

Fig. 3. Results of the Spatial Recognition Situation: (a) The results of physically-anchored stimuli manners, (b) The results of portable stimuli manners

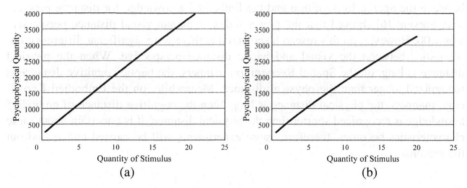

Fig. 4. Results of the Embodied Knowledge Situation: (a) The results of physically-anchored stimuli manners, (b) The results of portable stimuli manners

power index was 1.8121. From the power index, equation 1 was found. On the portable stimuli manners, the power index was 1.8336. From the power index, equation 2 was found.

$$R-3.0507*S^{1.8121} \tag{1}$$

$$R=3.1024*S^{1.8336} \tag{2}$$

On the Embodied Knowledge manners, the cognitive distance's magnitude showed a little right side down curve. On the physically-anchored stimuli manners, the power index was 0.9305. From the power index, equation 3 was found. On the portable stimuli manners, the power index was 0.8323. From the power index, equation 4 was found.

$$R=222.1777*S^{0.9305} \tag{3}$$

$$R=270.6450*S^{0.8323} \tag{4}$$

4 General Discussion

The results of the experiment 1 showed that the vertically long rectangles were easier to recognize than the horizontally long rectangles for human beings. It is speculated that the vertically long figures could touched overall by the palm for human beings, therefore the vertically long figures are easier to understand than the horizontally longer figures. The three main parts of hand are palm, finger, and fingertips. The fingertips are most quick part of these three parts, and they have huge numbers of mechanoreceptors [4]. The two point threshold, also, is the quickest of these three parts [5]. Moreover, the shape of human hands is vertically long shape. From these facts, it is speculated that the vertically long figures are easier to recognize than the horizontally long figures.

As for the results of the experiment 2, there are significant different characteristics between the Spatial Recognition and the Embodied Knowledge for distance perspective. Stevens [6] showed that the power index of human visual distance perspective was 1.00. However, on this research showed that there were significant different characteristics between the visual and haptic distance perspective. When the physical distance is long, on the Spatial Recognition manners, the haptic cognitive distance is recognized longer than the physical distance. Meanwhile, on the Embodied Knowledge manners, the physical distance is long, then the cognitive distance of embodied knowledge is recognized shorter than the physical distance. It is uncertain about these characteristics becomes, therefore, more experiments will be carried out to find out the reasons.

5 Conclusion

In conclusion of this research, the vertically long figures are easier to understand and could presented distance information correctly than the horizontally long figures. For comparison, 16 acquired blind subjects (7 man and 9 women, 27 to 48 years of age. All the blind subjects suffered from sight-restriction after they were over 18 years old and had been trained how to recognize by tactile ability) were carried out the same experiment as Experiment 1. As for the results, the horizontally long figures were easier and faster to understand than the vertically long figures for the blind subjects. It was found that the sighted subjects and the blind subjects have different haptic characteristics, therefore, the product designers have to select correct data or information for creating the products.

References

1. JIS T0922. Guidelines for older persons and persons with disabilities – Methods of displaying tactile guide maps (2007)
2. Virtual Reality Meshing of Touch Glove. Virtual Reality Laboratory, State University of New York at Buffalo, http://www.vrlab.buffalo.edu/

3. Kwok, M.G.: Nine basic experiments of Haptic Interactions. In: Proceedings of Accessible Media (2006)
4. Carmon, A.: Stimulus contrast in tactile resolution. Perception & Psychophysics 3(4A), 241–245 (1968)
5. Weinstein, S.: Intensive and extensive aspects of tactile sensitivity as a function of body part, sex, and laterality. In: Kenshalo, D.R. (ed.) The Skin Senses. Thomas, Springfield, Illinois (1968)
6. Stevens, S.S.: A metrics for the social consensus. Science 151, 530–541 (1966)

A Study on Effective Tactile Feeling of Control Panels for Electrical Appliances

Miwa Nakanishi[1], Yusaku Okada[2], and Sakae Yamamoto[3]

[1] Chiba University, Graduate School of Engineering, Division of Design Science,
Yayoi 1-33, Inage, Chiba, Japan
m.nakanishi@faculty.chiba-u.jp
[2] Keio University, Faculty of Science & Technology, Department of Administration
Engineering, Hiyoshi 3-14-1, Kohoku, Yokohama, Japan
okada@ae.keio.ac.jp
[3] Tokyo University of Sciencve, Faculty of Engineering, Department of Management Science,
Kagurazaka 1-3, Shinjuku, Tokyo, Japan
sakae@ms.kagu.tus.ac.jp

Abstract. This study focuses on the fact that tactile factors, compared to visual factors, have not been effectively applied to enhance the usability of control panels. It also evaluates the effectiveness of allocating a rough/smooth feeling to the surface of each button in a control panel according to its operational function. The first experiment reveals relationships between some of the impressions concerning the operation of electrical appliances and the rough/smooth feeling when touching the surface of buttons. Moreover, it provides specific information on what degree of roughness/smoothness should be applied to what types of functional buttons. The second experiment demonstrates that the usability of control panels can be enhanced by providing a rough/smooth feeling to each button, considering suitability with respect to operation impressions. In addition, results indicate that users may feel discomfort when the rough/smooth feeling does not correspond to operation impressions.

Keywords: Tactile feeling, operation impression, control panel.

1 Introduction

An overwhelming majority of human interfaces for controlling electrical appliances are control panels composed of a set of buttons or keys. Because they are very easy to manipulate and can be placed in a compact space, such control panels are expected to continue to find wide use.

Usually, the surfaces of all buttons/keys on a control panel are made of the same material, and the "control feeling," that is, the stimulus when we touch buttons/keys, is simple and uniform. Therefore, distinguishing between buttons/keys on a control panel greatly depends on visual factors such as labels and colors. For example, the button to start an appliance is typically colored green and the button to stop it is colored red so users can intuitively distinguish them [1]-[8]. (The color scheme may be different in different cultures.) However, whether users can always look at buttons/keys in the correct operational sequence depends on situations.

J.A. Jacko (Ed.): Human-Computer Interaction, Part II, HCII 2009, LNCS 5611, pp. 486–495, 2009.
© Springer-Verlag Berlin Heidelberg 2009

Another technique to help distinguish buttons/keys is by providing a tactile factor represented by a point or bump on the surface [9][10]. This is applied in several electrical appliances such as TV remote controls, lighting switches, and car audio systems. Although the point on the surface can help users distinguish a button or key, it cannot necessarily supply meaning, such as what the key does or what the operation results in.

Thus, compared with visual factors, tactile factors have not yet been effectively applied to enhance the usability of control panels. In addition to focusing on this point, the present study discusses effective methods to apply tactile factors to control the interfaces of electrical appliances.

In a previous study, we conducted research whether users typically associated particular tactile feelings with specific impressions, as they may associate particular colors with specific impressions [11]. We found that cool/warm and rough/smooth feelings on the surface of buttons/keys are related to impressions concerning degrees, such as big/small or bright/dark. This suggests that properly designed cool/warm and rough/smooth feelings on the surface of buttons/keys help users intuitively understand the meanings of operations, and increase cognitive satisfaction.

Based on the above prospects, in this study, we validate the relationship between impressions that particularly concern the operation of electrical appliances and a rough/smooth feeling, which is comparatively easy to apply to a button/key surface. Furthermore, we experiment with how the rough/smooth feeling on a button/key surface affects users' cognitive experience. Our aim is to clarify whether tactile feelings on button/key surfaces that suit operation impressions can enhance control panel usability.

2   Experiments on the Relationship between the Rough/Smooth Feeling and Operation Impressions

The aim of this experiment was to determine users' impressions concerning the operation of electrical appliances and to clarify the relationship between these impressions and the rough/smooth feeling users' experience when they touch buttons/keys on a control panel. In the following experiments, button/key surfaces were provided different roughness/smoothness using sandpaper of different grades.

2.1   Pilot Study

The relationship between the degree of response or sensation of a sensory organ and the intensity of the stimulus is approximately logarithmic. Therefore, we first conducted the following pilot study to determine the relationship between the degree of the rough/smooth feeling when users touched buttons and the physical roughness/smoothness as quantified by the fineness of the sandpaper's grains (F). Nine grades of sandpaper were prepared (F = 40, 80, 120, 150, 180, 220, 280, 320, 400; a larger number indicates smoother sandpaper). Sandpapers of different grades were attached to the surface of two buttons (Fig. 1), which were placed in a half-open box (Fig. 2) so that the button surfaces were not visible. Subjects (9 students, 18–23 years old) placed a hand into the box and alternatively touched the two buttons with a forefinger. Next, they marked how much rougher (or smoother) the upper button was than the lower button on a line marked −3 to +3 (Fig. 3). Each subject evaluated all

Fig. 1. Different grades of sandpaper attached to the surface of different buttons

Fig. 2. Half-open box including the control panel

Fig. 3. Scaled line used to evaluate how rougher or smoother the upper button is compared to the lower button

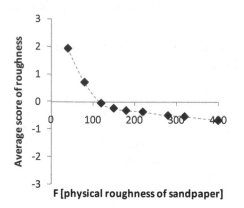

Fig. 4. Relationship between physical roughness and sensitive roughness.

combinations of the nine grades of sandpaper in randomized order. We analyzed the data using Scheffe's paired comparison and obtained the result shown in Fig. 4. The horizontal axis corresponds to the F values (physical roughness of sandpaper) and the vertical axis corresponds to the average roughness score. We could confirm that the rough/smooth feeling is approximately expressed by the logarithm of the F value. From the result, we chose five grades of sandpaper (F = 40, 80, 180, 280, 400) so that the difference in the rough/smooth feeling between each pair is about the same, and performed the following experiment to clarify the tionship between operation impressions and the rough/smooth feeling.

2.2 Experimental Method

We surveyed the methods in which buttons/keys are included in the control panels of popular electrical appliances, and compiled operational impressions as word pairs (e.g.,

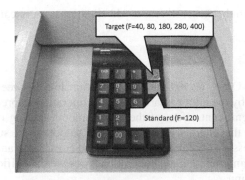

Fig. 5. Upper button with target sandpaper and lower button with standard sandpaper

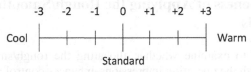

Fig. 6. Scaled line used to evaluate subjects' response on touching the target button compared to the standard button

Table 1. Thirty types of operation impressions

Impression (Word pair)
Stop / Start
Below / Above
Reduce / Increase
On / Off
Close / Open
Dark / Light
Cool / Warm
Receive / Send
Weak / Strong
Low / High
Backward / Forward
Small / Big
Stable / Swing
Back up / Proceed
Positive / Negative
Extract / Insert
Slow / Fast
Near / Far
Light / Heavy
Put / Get
Cancel / OK
Pull / Push
Shorten / Extend
Tumble / Raise
Behind / Front
Manual / Automatic
Short / Long
Release / Catch
Left / Right
Cut / Connect

Start/Stop). Furthermore, we removed extremely lized impressions and combined more common ones, finally selecting 30 types of operation (Table 1). In the experiment, the abovementioned five sandpaper grades were used as the evaluation target, and another grade of sandpaper (F = 120) was used as the evaluation standard. A "target" sandpaper and the standard one were attached to the buttons (Fig. 5). Subjects (20 students, 21–25 years old) first touched the standard button and then the target button with a forefinger. Next, they evaluated the impression that came to their mind on touching the upper button, and how intuitive the association was compared to when touching the lower button, and scored each line on −3 to +3 scale. For example, if they felt warm more strongly when they touched the upper button than when they touched the standard button, they gave a positive score to the cool/warm line, as shown in Fig. 6. We did not let subjects know which grade of sandpaper was attached to the target button they were touching. However, we did not place the buttons inside a box but

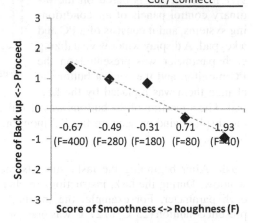

Fig. 7. Relationship between the rough/smooth feeling and the Back up/Proceed impression

allowed the subjects to observe them because, in real-world situations, users can generally see the control panel.

2.3 Results

We analyzed the data using ANOVA to examine the relationship between the rough/smooth feeling as quantified by the pilot research and each operation impression. As an example, Fig. 7 shows a significant effect of the rough/smooth feeling on the Back up/Proceed impression. From this chart, we can see that the smoother the surface of the button, the stronger the impression of "Proceed." We applied correlation analysis to the other operation impressions, and found that 21 operation types were significantly correlated to the rough/smooth feeling.

3 Experiments on Effectiveness of Applying the Rough/Smooth Feeling to Control Panels

The aim of this experiment was to examine whether allocating the rough/smooth feeling to each button in accord with the operation impressions enhances control panel usability.

3.1 Method

Experimental Systems. Focusing on 4 of the 21 operation types that have a significant correlation to the rough/smooth feeling, we assembled a simple control panel that included functional buttons corresponding to these impressions as an experimental system. Its design is based on the ordinary control panels of air conditioning systems, and it consists of a PC and a keypad. A display window visualizing each parameter was presented on the PC monitor, and the control buttons to change them was replaced by the keypad.

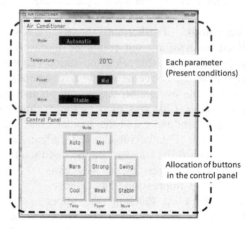

Fig. 8. Display window on PC monitor

The allocation of the buttons was also presented on the PC monitor. Fig. 8 shows the display window seen on the PC monitor, and Fig. 9 shows the allocation of the buttons.

Task. After beginning the task, subjects monitored the information in the display window. During the task, instructions to change a parameter appeared to the right of each parameter. For example, the instruction to change the temperature from the present condition (25°C) to 27°C was presented, subjects were required to correctly and quickly operate the control panel and completely change the parameter according to the instruction. The experimental air conditioning system then ran at the automatic mode

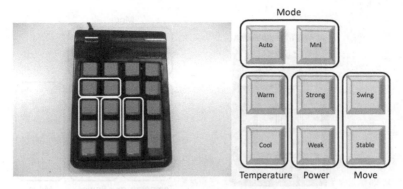

Fig. 9. Allocation of buttons

normally. Thus, subjects had to switch the mode from automatic to manual before changing a parameter, and also had to switch the mode back from manual to automatic afterward. For example, when the abovementioned instruction was given, they touched the "Mnl" button to switch the m ode, touched the "Warm" button twice to shift the temperature up to 27°C, and touched the "Auto" button to switch the mode again. The duration of a task was set at 180 [s]. During a task, instructions were provided six times. The timing of the instructions was random, but the intervals were set at more than 20 [s].

Experimental Conditions. We prepared the following three conditions.
(C-1) Use a control panel with buttons that all felt the same:
    Subjects performed the task using a control panel in which the same seals were applied to the surface of every button, so that they experienced the same tactile feeling whichever key they touched.
(C-2) Use a control panel with buttons that had rough/smooth feelings corresponding to operation impressions:
    Based on the result of the first experiment described in section 2, a rough/smooth feeling corresponding to operation impressions was allocated to each button. Specifically, two grades of sandpaper (F = 40, 400) were attached to the surface of two different buttons to shift a parameter in different directions so that the rough/smooth feeling corresponded to the impressions of the directions. For example, in the case of the

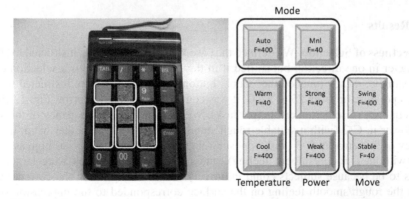

Fig. 10. Allocation of rough/smooth feeling that suits operation impression (C-2)

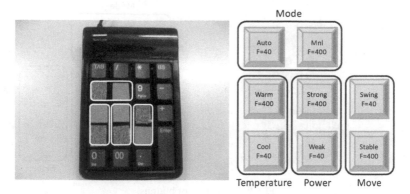

Fig. 11. Allocation of rough/smooth feeling that is opposite to each operation impression (C-3)

"Warm" and "Cool" buttons to change the temperature, the rougher button (F = 40) was attached to the former, and the smoother button (F = 400) was attached to the latter. Fig. 10 shows which grade of sandpaper was allocated to which button in this condition.

(C-3) Use the control panel with buttons that had rough/smooth feelings opposite to the operation impressions:

In contrast to C-2, rough/smooth feelings that did not correspond to operation impressions were allocated to each button. For example, in the case of the "Warm" and "Cool" buttons to change the temperature, the smoother button (F = 400) was attached to the former, and the rougher button (F = 40) was attached to the latter. Fig. 11 shows which grade of sandpaper was allocated to which button in this condition.

Other. Subjects were 12 students, 20–25 years old. After they understood the procedures of the task and practiced it, they performed the task once per condition. To eliminate the order effect, we managed their trial order carefully. Moreover, we adjusted the temperature and light to keep the experimental environment comfortable. We recorded all the actions that subjects performed during the task. We also conducted a recollection test in which subjects were required to write down what instructions were given, the order of the instructions, and what operations they performed to accomplish each of them one minute after they finished each task.

3.2 Results

Correctness of Selection. We defined the case where subjects were instructed to shift a parameter in one direction but shifted it in the opposite direction as a selection error. For example, if they touched the "Cool" button although they were instructed to shift the temperature up from 25 to 27°C, it was counted as a selection error. Fig. 12 shows the frequency of selection errors (per task). We can see that the frequency of this error was lower in C-2 (with a suitable rough/smooth feeling). On the other hand, the frequency of this error in C-3 (with opposite rough/smooth feeling) was as high as that in C-1 (without a rough/smooth feeling), and individual differences were large. This seems to be because subjects could intuitively and naturally select the correct button when the rough/smooth feeling on the surface corresponded to the impression of the

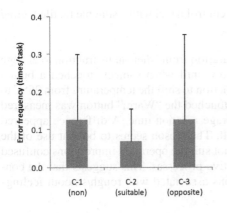

Fig. 12. Frequency of the selection error (per task)

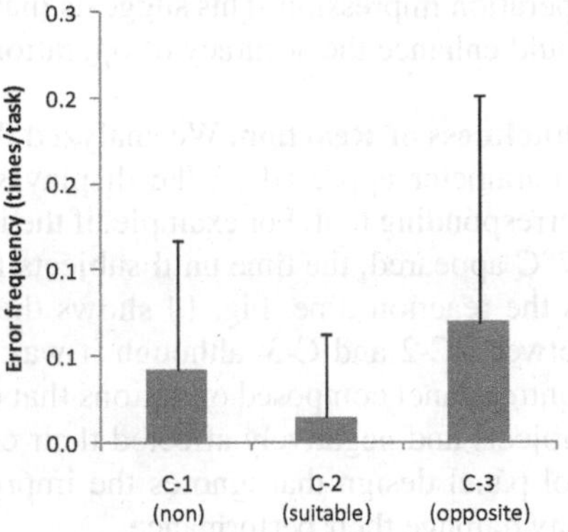

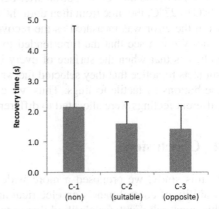

Fig. 13. Frequency of the adjustment error (per task)

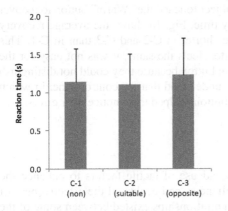

Fig. 14. Average reaction time

Fig. 15. Average recovery time

direction in which they shift a parameter. This suggests that the control panel design that considered the impressions associated with tactile feelings was effective in helping subjects correctly select buttons.

Accuracy of Manipulation. We defined the case where subjects manipulated a button too many times in changing a parameter as an adjustment error. For example, if they shifted the temperature to exceed 27°C by carelessly touching the up button more than twice, although they were instructed to increase the temperature from 25°C to 27°C, it was counted as an adjustment error. Fig. 13 shows the frequency of adjustment errors (per task). We can see that the frequency of this error was lower in C-2 than in other conditions. On the other hand, the frequency of this error was particularly high in C-3. This seems to be because subjects could have a detailed realization of the operation when they were touching the button with a rough/smooth feeling that suited the operation impression. This suggests that the control panel with a suitable tactile feeling could enhance the accuracy of operation.

Quickness of Reaction. We analyzed the duration from when an instruction to change a parameter appeared on the display window until when subjects touched a button corresponding to it. For example, if the instruction to shift the temperature from 25°C to 27°C appeared, the time until subjects first touched the "Warm" button was measured as the reaction time. Fig. 14 shows the average reaction time. A difference appeared between C-2 and C-3, although it was small. The reason seems to be that use of the control panel composed of buttons that did not suit the operation impressions confused subjects and negatively affected their cognitive processes. This suggests that the control panel design that ignores the impressions associated with rough/smooth feelings may damage their performance.

Quickness of Recovery. We analyzed the duration from when the abovementioned selection error occurred to when subjects touched the correct button. For example, if a subject touched the "Cool" button after being instructed to increase the temperature from 25°C to 27°C, the time from then until the subject touched the "Warm" button to recover from the error was measured as the recovery time. Fig. 15 shows the average recovery time. We can see that the time tended to be shorter in C-2 and C-3 than in C-1. This indicates that when the surface of every button feels the same, it was not easy for the subjects to notice that they selected the wrong button because they could not distinguish the buttons by tactile feelings. Thus, we can understand that the control panel in which different feelings were allocated to different buttons helped them notice their errors.

4 Conclusion

In this study, we proposed a more widespread use of tactile factors to enhance the usability of control panels on electrical appliances, and evaluated the effectiveness of this approach. First, we clarified that certain relationships existed between some of the impressions concerning the operation of electrical appliances and the rough/smooth feeling experienced in touching the surface of buttons. Moreover, we obtained specific information on what degree of roughness/smoothness should be attached to what type of functional buttons. Second, we found that the usability of the control panel was enhanced by allocating the rough/smooth feeling to each button considering the fit with the operation impressions. On the other hand, we pointed out that users might feel discomfort and confusion when rough/smooth feelings on the surface of the buttons did not correspond to the operation impressions.

Acknowledgement

The authors wish to thank Takehiro Okubo who received the Bachelor's degree in 2007 from Tokyo University of Science and Kazuki Omori received the Master's degree in 2009 from Keio University.

References

1. ISO 17398: Safety colours and safety signs – Classification, performance and durability of safety signs (2004)
2. ISO 7010: Graphical symbols – Safety colours and safety signs – Safety signs used in workplaces and public areas (2003)
3. ISO 3864-1: Graphical symbols – Safety colours and safety signs – Part1: Design principles for safety signs in workplaces and public areas (2002)
4. ISO 3864-2: Graphical symbols – Safety colours and safety signs – Part2: Design principles for product safety labels (2004)
5. ISO 3864-3: Graphical symbols – Safety colours and safety signs – Part3: Design principles for graphical symbols for use in safety signs (2006)
6. Nakano, Y.: Outline of the revision of JIS Z 9101 (Safety colours and safety signs-Design principles for safety signs in workplaces and public areas): Global harmonization by conforming to ISO 3864-1: 2002 (IDT), IEICE technical report 106(86), 5–8 (2006)
7. Baek, S., et al.: KANSEI-Based Image Retrieval Associated with Color. Fuzzy Logic and Applications 3849, 326–333 (2006)
8. Sungyong, H., et al.: Searching Color Images by Emotional Concepts. In: Shimojo, S., Ichii, S., Ling, T.-W., Song, K.-H. (eds.) HSI 2005, vol. 3597, pp. 361–365. Springer, Heidelberg (2005)
9. Øvstedala, L., Lidb, I., Lindlanda, T.: How to evaluate the effectiveness of a tactile surface indicator system? In: Vision 2005 - Proceedings of the International Congress, vol. 1282, pp. 1051–1055 (2005)
10. Ward, T.: Designing Consumer Product Displays for the Disabled. In: Proceedings of the 34th Annual Meeting Human Factors Society, vol. 1, pp. 448–451 (1990)
11. Nakanishi, M., Yamamoto, S.: What Images are Evoked by Tactile Feeling? In: Proceedings of the Workshop on Tactile and Haptic Interaction For Designing Control Interfaces Taking Tactile Feeling into Consideration, pp. 22–29 (2007)

Facilitating the Design of Vibration
for Handheld Devices

Taezoon Park[1], Jihong Hwang[2], and Wonil Hwang[3]

[1] School of Mechanical and Aerospace Engineering,
Nanyang Technological University Singapore 639798
tzpark@ntu.edu.sg
[2] Department of Die and Mould Design
Seoul National University of Technology, Seoul, South Korea
hwangjh@snut.ac.kr
[3] Department of Industrial and Information Systems Engineering
Soongsil University, Seoul, South Korea
wonil@ssu.ac.kr

Abstract. Vibrations are actively used both to supplement the multi-modal interactions and to deliver information independently. Especially, vibration is adopted as a feedback for touch-screen type interfaces for cell phone because touch-screen interface lacks the tactile feedback. However, how to effectively design vibration is not being investigated yet although different types of vibration is used according to its application area. This study summarizes the characteristics of vibrations especially in the view point of human perception, and covers a couple of attempts to composing vibrations currently used. Finally, a suggested design for developing software tools which facilitates the design of effective vibrations is presented as a conclusion.

Keywords: Vibration, Haptics, Vibration composer.

1 Introduction

Haptics is gaining more and more attention both as an independent communication channel and a supplementary medium for fortifying the effect of visual or audio effect. [10] Vibrations are used as a substitute for the ring tone in the environment where the auditory feedback is limited. Recently, tactile feedback is widely adopted especially for mobile devices. As the technology advances the mobile phone is becoming the portable tool for communication, information retrieval, and also entertaining device. Since the form factor of handheld device is inherently limited, building an effective user interface for covering extended capabilities of mobile phone becomes more and more challenging. After the introduction of the touch screen interfaces on mobile phone, the lack of tactile feedback has become a serious usability issue, which encourages the use of vibration feedback as a substitute for the tactile feedback of mechanical button [1][3]. On the other hand, force feedback and vibration feedback has been used in the virtual reality field to reinforce the auditory and visual effects. For example, force and vibration feedback is helpful to understand 3D structures, comprehend force fields, and perceive complicated shapes, which is mostly used in immersive virtual reality system. Especially, game industry has actively been

J.A. Jacko (Ed.): Human-Computer Interaction, Part II, HCII 2009, LNCS 5611, pp. 496–502, 2009.
© Springer-Verlag Berlin Heidelberg 2009

adopting tactile feedback on developing vivid effects on video games. Although the vibration is spreading fast as new communication channel, there has not been an effective authoring tool for the vibration introduced. In this study, a model for designing vibration is proposed considering both the physical characteristics of vibration and the human perception of the vibration together.

2 Research Backgrounds

In the literature, the mechanical characteristics of vibration are presented to better understand the innate nature of vibration in a physical viewpoint. Human perception of vibration follows which includes the sense of touch and especially for the vibration. Although the physical characteristics of vibration are very similar to sounds, the perceptual characteristics of human should be reconfirmed to apply findings regarding the sound to the vibration.

Variables influencing human responses to vibration can be categorized as extrinsic and intrinsic variables. Extrinsic variables are mainly related to the characteristics of vibration itself, whereas intrinsic variables are related with human. [2]

2.1 Physical Characteristics of Vibration

Extrinsic variables represent physical characteristics of vibration, which is similar to sound. Representative extrinsic variables are magnitude, frequency, direction, waveform, and duration. The magnitude of vibration can be measured by the acceleration or displacement, and the frequency is measured by the number of pulses per a second. The direction of vibration can be arbitrary. Lateral motions along the x, y, and z axis in Cartesian coordinate combined with rotations produce six axes of potential movement. [6] According to the waveform, vibration can be classified into a number of subgroups. If the future form of vibration is predictable, in other words, the future form of vibration is determined by the history, it is considered as deterministic, and if the future wave form is unpredictable, the vibration is termed as random. Furthermore, deterministic vibration can be subdivided into periodic and non-periodic by its repeatability. If the same cycle repeats, the vibration is called as periodic, but if the vibration occurs as one cycle at a time, it is treated as non-periodic. [2] However, vibrations in practice are mostly random, and random vibration can be subdivided into stationary and non-stationary by the motion's statistical properties. If the statistical properties of the vibration changes over time, it is considered as non-stationary, otherwise it is treated as stationary. [6]

2.2 Human Perception of Vibration

Intrinsic variables include the body configuration, age, gender and experiences, all of which is related with human who experience the vibrations. The perception and influence of vibration could be different by personal characteristics.

According to the magnitude, the effect of vibration to human body could be different, which changes the primary concern of the research. For the low magnitude vibrations, issues of refinement and perception are important, whereas discomfort, performance, and health problems are main concern for high magnitude vibrations.

For the low magnitude vibrations, the human perception of stimuli is studied by the psychophysical method. In order to design effective interface, the threshold, just noticeable differences (JND), and perceived subjective equality have been investigated. Weinstein (1968) measured the two-point discrimination threshold on the whole body, and found out the sensitive spot is lips and fingertips. Verillo (1963) found that the frequency and contact area influences the sensitivity to vibratory stimulus if the contact area is larger than 0.02 cm2. According to his research, the absolute sensitivity to vibration shows U-shaped curve, which has maximum value around the frequency of 250 Hz.

Summers et al. (1997) attempted to use vibrotactile stimuli as a communication channel which supplements the lip reading process of people who have problems in hearing. Their finding about the human's perception of vibration as an information channel showed that it is not suitable for delivering large amount of information through vibration. This implies that vibration would be more suitable for supplementing different modalities, such as visual or auditory in order to deliver information. Also, representing the current mood or implying the atmosphere of the current context would be potential area of applications for vibration. However, these kinds of affective aspect of vibration are relatively ignored. An experimental study showed that hedonic dimensions of vibration could be classified as softness and comport. [8]

2.3 Tools for Designing Vibration

There have been a couple of attempts to provide software interface for authoring vibration for mobile devices and force and vibration feedback game controller in the commercial area.

Mobile phone has limited ability of generating vibrations when compared to tactile feedback gaming devices. Nokia proposed to use MIDI sequencer for designing ringtones with vibration support. They included an optional method for vibration control using MIDI messages. Since vibrations of most cell phones are fixed frequency and amplitude, only turning on and off is the only control that is allowed. The note on message turns vibration on and the note off message turns off. Vibration channel is monophonic and only one note can be rendered at a time [7]. As the full screen touch phones are being introduced, vibration feedback is actively adopted to provide tactile feedback. Vibrations on mobile phone usually rely on the vibration motor, which generates vibrations with an eccentric rotating mass. Because the vibration is only controlled by the rpm of the motor, the magnitude and frequency is confounded. In other words, high frequency vibration has high magnitude. Ryu et al. (2007) proposed a vibration editor which profiles the magnitude of the vibration, and generates smooth form of vibration by changing the control point of the profile.

Gaming device has more capability of generating various vibrations. Since conventional game pad uses two actuators with different eccentric rotating mass for generating vibrations, it is possible to overlapping two different vibrations together. Although the frequency and magnitude of the vibration is also correlated, various effects can be generated by combining waveforms. Without the vibration authoring tool, vibration should be generated program code, which makes it difficult to design vibrations iteratively. Immersion (2006) has implemented the development environment for designing vibrations for video game consoles. Immersion Studio, the authoring tool used for designing vibration, provides abilities to change waveform, magnitude, and direction. Microsoft Force Editor also provides functionality for designing force and vibration feedback. Basic functions are similar to Immersion Studio, which provides pre-built waveforms and ability to change details about the vibration.

3 Suggested Model

Since the perceptual characteristics of vibration are not thoroughly investigated yet, it is hard to design the effective design tool for the vibration. However, for the sound and music that have similar physical trains, theories and tools are developed for professionals like musician, composer, and even for the general public. This study proposes a exemplary tool for designing vibrations that can be used for handheld devices including mobile phone, joystick, and gamepad by introducing two concepts of envelope editing and rhythm/melody.

3.1 Attack, Decay, Sustain, and Release (ADSR)

Attack, decay, sustain, and release is used mostly for the electric musical instruments, which is introduced to simulate mechanical instruments. The volume of the sound produced changes over time when playing mechanical musical instrument, and their envelope profile is different from instrument to instrument. For instance, when playing a pipe organ, it generates a constant volume note, but when playing a piano, it generate large sound when the hammer hits the string and dies away. The definitions of each parameter are presented below. (see Figure 1) [13]

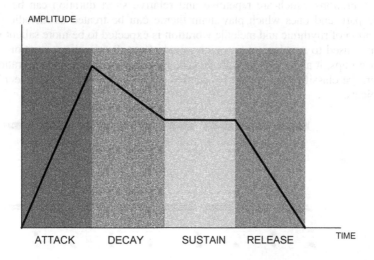

Fig. 1. The change of amplitude envelope according to attack, decay, sustain, and release

- Attack: Time taken to reach full volume after the sound is activated.
- Decay: Time taken for the sound to drop to the sustain level after the initial peak.
- Sustain: Time taken for the "constant" volume after decay until the note is released. This parameter specifies a volume level rather than a time period.
- Release: Time taken for the sound to fade when a note ends. Often, this time is very short.

Vibrations can be also designed with four parameters suggested above. By modifying those characteristics, basic set of vibration could be build up like the musical instrument sets. Furthermore, the real vibration can be captured by measuring the vibration profile itself. This captured vibration set is to be used as a single vibration unit, and full score of vibration could be built by combining those unit vibrations.

3.2 Rhythm vs. Melody

One of the categorization methods for classifying musical instruments is melody vs. rhythmic instrument. Rhythmic instruments are drum, bass, and most of percussion instrument, and melodic instruments are violin, cello, and most of winds. Melodic instrument has a set of pitches, which make a main theme of the music, and Rhythmic instrument keeps the beats. Periodic and consecutive play of a note is considered as a rhythm even the pitch of the note is different in the case of bass. The music score for drum is somewhat different from the generic score for melodic instruments. Typical drum set includes 5 pieces composed of bass drum, tom-tom drums, snare drum, cymbal and hi-hat cymbal, each of which as different pitch. Drum score presents plays for those different drums on a musical sheet by arranging different drums from top to bottom according to its pitch (see Figure 2). For example hi-hat, which generates highest pitch, is arranged on the top line, followed by tom-tom, snare, floor-tom. The bass drum is located at the bottom line. [3]

Similarly, vibration can be divided into melody and rhythm by the perception of the human. Vibrations which are repetitive and relative short duration can be named as rhythmic part, and ones which play main theme can be treated as melodic part. The classification of rhythmic and melodic vibration is expected to be more salient when the vibration is used to supplement music or sound effect. By dividing vibrations into two different groups, it also could contribute to help the task of composing vibration effect. However, the classification should be verified by psychophysical experiment with human subjects.

Fig. 2. Example drum score used for band performance

3.3   Suggested Design of Vibration Composer

Based on the literatures and implementation for vibration authoring, a prototype of
Vibration composer is suggested, which facilitates the design of various vibration
effects. (see Figure 3)

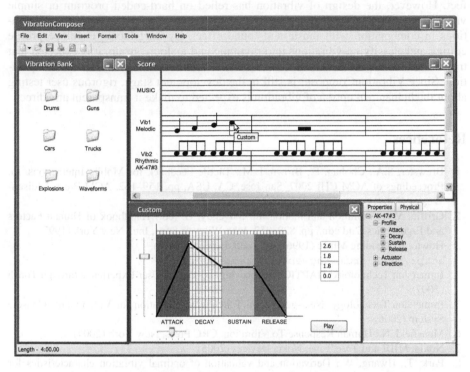

Fig. 3. Screenshot of vibration composer

Vibration composer has three basic windows; vibration library, vibration score, and
envelope editor. Vibration library is provided on the left panel, which contains pre-
build sets of vibrations to simulate sound effect, music instrument, and also basic
wave forms like square, saw tooth, sinusoidal, and triangular. User defined vibration
is can be registered on the library set as a customized vibration set. The specific parameters of customized vibrations are designed by the envelope editor window located on the bottom. In the envelope editor, user can change attack, delay, sustain, and
decay by putting on number directly or moving the slide bars at the bottom and side.
Designed vibration can be played by attached devices like gamepad for the refinement
and test. In the main window, midi sequencer type vibration score is provided to
combine different sets of vibrations including music and sound effect. By providing
music and wave editor, the synchronization of audio and haptic stimulus can be obtained easily. Multiple channel of vibration is supported to organize vibrations as
melodic and rhythmic parts. Also, assigning multiple channels to one actuator is also
supported to make an overlapping effect.

4 Conclusion and Future Directions

Multimodal interaction becomes more and more important for handheld devices because the limited bandwidth of audio and visual communication. Vibrations work both as a separate communication channel and a supplemental effect with audio effect. However, the design of vibration has relied on hard-coded program or simple visual editor. This study suggests an exemplary design of an authoring tool for vibrations in combination with music and sound effect. By introducing envelope profile editing and classifying vibrations into rhythmic and melodic group, it is expected that the vibration designer can easily make and edit vibration effect by direct manipulation. Since VibrationComposer is still in the development stage, rigorous user testing about the human perception of vibration is expected to make it transparent and direct.

References

1. Brewster, S.A., Chohan, F., Brown, L.M.: Tactile Feedback for Mobile Interactions. In: Proceedings of ACM CHI 2007, San Jose, CA, USA, pp. 159–162. ACM Press Addison-Wesley (2007)
2. Griffin, M.J.: Vibration and motion. In: Salvendy, G. (ed.) Handbook of Human Factors and Ergonomics, 2nd edn., pp. 828–857. John Wiley & Sons, Inc., New York (1997)
3. Howie, T.: Reading Music (1996) (accessed, February 2008),
   http://www.drummingweb.com/reading.htm
4. Immersion Technology: HAPTICS: Improving the Mobile User Experience through Touch (2007)
5. Immersion Technology: Next-generation TouchSense Vibration for Video Game Console System (2006)
6. Mansfield, N.: Human Response To Vibration. CRC Press, New York (2004)
7. Nokia: MIDI and True Tone. Nokia Devices (2005)
8. Park, T., Hwang, W.: Derivation and validation of optimal vibration characteristics for pleasure and attention: implication for cell phone design. In: Proceedings of HCI International 2005, Las Vegas, NV (2005)
9. Ryu, J., Jung, J., Kim, S., Choi, S.: Perceptually Transparent Vibration Rendering Using a Vibration Motor for Haptic Interaction. In: Proceedings of the IEEE International Symposium on Robot & Human Interactive Communication (RO-MAN), pp. 310–315 (2007)
10. Summers, I.R., Cooper, P.G., Wright, P., Gratton, D.A., Milnes, P., Brown, B.H.: Information from time-varying vibrotactile stimuli. The Journal of the Acoustical Society of America 102(6), 3686–3696 (1997)
11. Verrillo, R.T.: Effect of contactor area on the vibrotactile threshold. Journal of the Acoustical Society of America 35, 1962–1966 (1963)
12. Weinstein, S.: Intensive and extensive aspects of tactile sensitivity as a function of body part, sex, and lterality. In: Kenshalo, D.R. (ed.) The skin senses. Thomas, Springfield (1968)
13. Wikipedia: ADSR envelope (2008) (accessed, February 2008),
   http://en.wikipedia.org/wiki/ADSR_envelope

Interaction Technique for a Pen-Based Interface Using Finger Motions

Yu Suzuki, Kazuo Misue, and Jiro Tanaka

1-1-1 Tennodai, Tsukuba, Ibaraki, 305-8573, Japan
{suzuki,misue,jiro}@iplab.cs.tsukuba.ac.jp

Abstract. Our research goal is to improve stylus operability by utilizing the human knowledge and skills applied when a user uses a pen. Such knowledge and skills include, for example, the way a person holds a pen to apply a generous amount of ink to draw a thick line with a brush pen. We propose a form of interaction, Finger Action, which uses input operations applying such knowledge and skills. Finger Action consists of five input operations: gripping, thumb tapping, index-finger tapping, thumb rubbing, and index-finger rubbing. In this paper, we describe Finger Action, a prototype pressure-sensitive stylus used to realize Finger Action, an application of Finger Action, and an evaluation of the practicality of Finger Action.

Keywords: Pen-based Interface, Finger Motion, Pen Grip, Pressure Sensor.

1 Introduction

Much research has been done on the application of pre-existing human knowledge and skills for human-computer interaction (HCI) technology [1]. An advantage of these approaches is that they enable people to operate computers after a modest amount of learning or training. We believe that such an approach is important to further the development of HCI technology.

Many people have used a pen from a young age and the pen is one of their favorite tools. We think that a pen-shaped interface stylus is one of the best forms of interface because a stylus is similar to a real pen and its use takes advantage of existing human knowledge and skills. However, the current stylus does not offer high operability because it does not fully utilize the freedom allowed by a pen. The input information used with the current stylus consists of only coordinates indicating where the tip is on a display contact, the pressure applied to the tip, and ON/OFF as selected with a barrel button.

The purpose of our research has been to improve the operability of the pen-based interface. Previously, we studied use of the positions and postures of the stylus in the air [2]. In this research, we observed the behaviors of people when they used pens, and found that most made intricate finger motions when using a pen. These finger motions can be considered acquired knowledge and skills related to pen use, and we think there are other knowledge and skills concerning pen use in addition to those we have observed. We call this kind of knowledge and skills "pen-experience".

J.A. Jacko (Ed.): Human-Computer Interaction, Part II, HCII 2009, LNCS 5611, pp. 503–512, 2009.

In our current work, we have tried to use pen-experience to improve pen-based interfaces. In this paper, we examine whether we can use finger motions to operate a pen-based interface and how such finger motions can be applied.

2 Related Work

The purpose of our research is to improve stylus operability. Our approach is to use pre-existing human knowledge and skills. In this section, we clarify the position of our research by introducing related work from two aspects: that of research having the same goal as our research and that of research aimed at applying pre-existing human knowledge and skills.

2.1 Research Aimed at Improving Stylus Operability

Other research aimed at improving stylus operability has been done by various researchers.

Compared to mouse-click operations, stylus tapping operations are difficult to do correctly. Therefore, research has been done to develop circular rather than linear menus. Hopkins developed PieMenu [3] as a menu interface which enables easy operation with a stylus. Other menu interfaces which use a circular menu like PieMenu include Marking Menu [4] and FlowMenu [5].

An interaction technique called "crossing" was proposed as a way to invoke commands by using a stylus when operating GUIs [6]. While it is difficult to correctly tap a small target with a stylus, it is easy to cross a target when the stylus is in contact with the display. Crossing takes advantage of this ease.

Smith et al. focused on the difficulty of operating a scroll bar with a stylus, and their research was aimed at improving stylus operability in this regard [7, 8]. They developed a tool which recognizes a clockwise gesture on the display. When using this tool, a user can scroll anywhere on the display.

The approach of these studies was to find ways to overcome the difficulty of tapping a small area with a stylus. In contrast, our approach is based on pre-existing human knowledge and skills.

2.2 Research Using Pre-existing Human Knowledge and Skills

Tangible Bits [9], proposed by Ishii et al., can be understood as the application of pre-existing human knowledge and skills. One concept underlying Tangible Bits is the coupling of bits and atoms in a way that allows a person to apply pre-existing knowledge and skills.

Mohler et al. developed an interaction technique for moving through virtual space by walking on a treadmill [10]. While a user can use a mouse or joystick as a means to move through virtual space, the user has to train operations before using them. By applying walking actions to moving through virtual space, a person can move through virtual space without any training because it is based on moving through real space by walking.

Rekimoto proposed using the tilt of devices as an interaction method for small display devices [11]. For example, a user can change the viewpoint in a map browser by tilting the device. Such control is intuitive to the user because it follows physical laws understood by the user.

Depth perception in virtual 3D space is represented on 2D display by using atmospheric colors, fog, shadows and so on [12]. These techniques rely on the user's knowledge that distant objects look blurred.

These studies have attempted to apply pre-existing human knowledge and skills to interfaces of VR, AR and small devices. In contrast, we aim to apply them to a pen-based interface.

3 Proposed Interaction Technique

3.1 Using Pen-Experience

A benefit of applying pre-existing human knowledge and skills to HCI is that a user can use a computer with minimal learning or training. The pen-based interface imitates the use of a real pen and paper and uses pen-experience for operations. Therefore, the user can use a pen-based interface without having to learn how to operate the interface.

By focusing on the pen and typical human actions when using one, we found that there are other pen-experiences. For example, when drawing thick lines with a fude-pen[1] , the user applies more pressure to make more ink come out of the pen. This small change in the amount of power applied to the fingers is rarely used in pen-based interfaces. We aim to improve the stylus operability by using such actions based on pen-experience.

3.2 Finger Action

There are various finger motions related to pen-experience. To be used as input operations of a pen-based interface, these motions must meet two conditions: be simple for the user to perform and not physically strain the user. The following motions satisfy these two conditions:

A) A motion to more strongly grasp the stylus grip
B) A motion to lightly tap the grip with the thumb
C) A motion to lightly tap the grip with the index finger.

Other motions are also physically possible, such as rubbing motions. Although these are not always incidental motions when using a pen, we also experimentally tested two other motions:

1. A motion to rub the grip with the thumb
2. A motion to rub the grip with the index finger.

We call these five motions finger actions (Fig. 1). Finger actions can be broadly classified into three motions: (A) gripping, (B) tapping, and (C) rubbing. Tapping and

---

[1] A *fudepen* is a kind of brush pen. Because a *fudepen* is made from soft material, the user can change the amount of ink applied and the line thickness by applying more or less pressure.

rubbing can each be separated into two types: (1) thumb motion and (2) index-finger motion. We refer to these as (B-1) thumb tapping, (B-2) index-finger tapping, (C-1) thumb rubbing, and (C-2) index-finger rubbing. The interaction technique we have established based on these actions for a pen-based interface is called Finger Action.

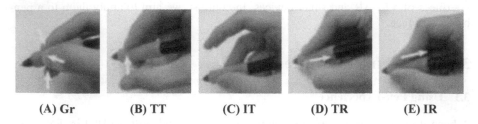

(A) Gr   (B) TT   (C) IT   (D) TR   (E) IR

Fig. 1. Five motions of Finger Action: (A) – (E) respectively show gripping, thumb tapping, index-finger tapping, thumb rubbing, and index-finger rubbing

4   Development of a Pressure-Sensitive Stylus

We have developed a pressure-sensitive stylus that enables a user to use Finger Action. In this section, we describe this stylus.

4.1   Requisite Data to Realize Finger Action

A human uses three fingers to control a pen (the thumb, index finger and middle finger), so the pressure-sensitive stylus must be able to detect these three fingers. In other words, we need to be able to sense the three points where these fingers make contact with the stylus grip. In addition, to apply the rubbing operation with either the thumb or the index finger, we have to ensure the stylus can sense the vertical movement of these two fingers.

4.2   Pressure-Sensitive Stylus

Figure 2 shows the pressure-sensitive stylus. We use FSR402[2] pressure sensors to detect pressure applied to the stylus grip. The stylus is equipped with five of these sensors, each with a diameter of about 18 mm. A sensor's electrical resistance decreases as the applied pressure increases. We used two of the sensors for the thumb, two for the index finger, and one for the middle finger. We use a PIC-BASIC microcomputer to read the sensors' output, and the gripping power is analyzed in real time. The time resolution when reading out sensor values is 200 ms.

A user does not need any special instruction to use the pressure-sensitive stylus because the sensors are placed where a person naturally holds a pen.

---

[2] Interlink Electronics, Inc.

Fig. 2. Pressure-Sensitive Stylus

5   Evaluation of Effectiveness

Gripping, thumb tapping, index-finger tapping, thumb rubbing, and index-finger rubbing are common actions when a person actually uses a pen, are simple to do, and are physically easy to perform. To determine whether these actions are suitable for input operations, though, we did an experiment to investigate the usefulness of Finger Action as a pen-based interface.

5.1   Outline of the Experiment

In the experiment, we measured the ease of the actions for users and the physical strain imposed upon the user when performing the actions.

The experiment consisted of two tasks. In task 1, participants did operations while concentrating on performing the five input operations. A few seconds after the experiment began, a short trigger sound was presented. The participants were to do an input operation when hearing the sound. The sound was presented ten times in each trial with the time interval randomly varied between 3-6 seconds. The interval variation was to prevent the participants from guessing the timing of the trigger. Each participant performed this trial five times for each input operation, so in task 1 a participant performed every input operation fifty times.

In task 2, participants did the same operations as in task 1 while drawing characters, a picture, or something similar. That is, participants did the trial independently in task 1, but they did the trial while doing other work in task 2. After finishing tasks 1 and 2, the participants completed a questionnaire where they evaluated the operability of the stylus and the physical strain of using it on a scale of one to five. (A score of 5 indicated the best operability or the least strain and a score of 1 indicated the worst operability or the heaviest strain.)

There were eight participants: seven males and one female. Because none of the participants were familiar with Finger Action, we spent five minutes explaining how to use Finger Action. The participants then practiced all of the actions a few times. Each task in the experiment took about twenty minutes, and there was a break between the two tasks.

We evaluated the ease of the actions according to the average measured time for each operation and the questionnaire responses, and evaluated the physical strain according to the questionnaire responses.

5.2 Results

We show the mean time needed to perform each input operation and the standard deviation in Fig. 3, and the questionnaire results in Fig. 4.

First, we consider the ease of each action. In some cases, sensing errors or participants' operation errors did not allow the participants to perform the intended actions. Such errors are not included in these results.

Human cognitive processing and the processing time of the prototype system affected the results. Human cognitive processing begins with recognition of a stimulus through a perception system, which is followed by analysis of the detected signal's meaning through the cognitive system, and then transmission of an action to be taken to the motor system. In our experiment, this processing sequence took 300-400 s [13]. As mentioned, the time resolution in our prototype system when reading out sensor values is 200 ms. When the system detects tapping or rubbing, the average delay is 200 ms because the system uses two contiguous values. Therefore, we considered a good result to be 500-600 ms for gripping and 700-800 ms for tapping or rubbing.

In the task 1 results, the mean value for gripping slightly exceeded 600 ms and for tapping it slightly exceeded 800 ms, so the amount of delay was acceptable. In the questionnaire results, the scores for the operability of gripping and tapping exceeded the midpoint score of 3, indicating that gripping and tapping were easy actions to perform independently.

Comparing the task 1 results to the task 2 results, we see that the average delay times were 100-200 ms longer for task 2 for all operations. In task 2, the participants had to switch from their current work to another type of work to perform the required finger action, and this probably is the reason for the greater delay. The questionnaire results again showed that the average response for the operability of the gripping and tapping operations exceeded the midpoint score of 3. Therefore, although the time for

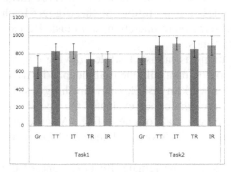

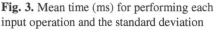

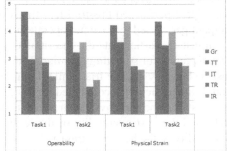

Fig. 3. Mean time (ms) for performing each input operation and the standard deviation

Fig. 4. Questionnaire results

operation was about 100 ms to 200 ms longer than when performing the gripping and tapping operations independently, the operations were easy to perform.

Next, we consider the physical strain. The average questionnaire responses for gripping and tapping exceeded 3.5 in both task 1 and task 2. Therefore, gripping and tapping operations can be done without undue physical strain when performing the operations either independently or dependently.

Last, we consider the number of input errors (Fig. 5). There was a big difference between the average number of input errors in tasks 1 and 2 for all operations. A t-test at a 5% significance level for the average number of input errors showed a significant difference for tapping (thumb tapping: p=0.0002, index-finger tapping: p=0.0021). Therefore, the number of input errors is likely to increase when performing the tapping operation while doing other work.

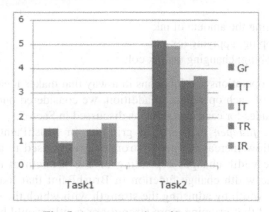

Fig. 5. Average number of input errors

To summarize the results, gripping and tapping appear to be useful operations whether work is being done independently or dependently. However, many operation errors are likely to occur when a user performs the tapping operation while also doing other work. This might be because the user has to lift his/her finger off the stylus to perform the tapping. We propose a way of mapping between Finger Action and the operations of applications: gripping should be mapped as an operation which can be done while the user is engaged in another operation at the same time, while tapping should be mapped as an operation which can be done independently.

Improving the rubbing operability will be part of our future work.

6 Application of the Pressure-Sensitive Stylus

We developed a paint tool, BrushPaint, as an application of the pressure-sensitive stylus. When using BrushPaint, a user can interact with a computer in a way that is like using a real pen. In this application, we assigned each of the gripping, tapping and rubbing operations to a specific function:

Fig. 6. BrushPaint screenshot

- Gripping: changing the amount of ink
- Index-finger tapping: applying ink
- Index-finger rubbing: changing the ink color

We mapped the operations and functions in a way that makes it easy for the user to imagine the result of each operation. In addition, we considered our findings regarding the users' aptitudes for each operation, as discussed in Sect. 5.

We applied the *fudepen* metaphor to gripping in BrushPaint. When using a *fudepen*, the ink flow increases when a stronger grip is used to apply more pressure, so the stroke width changes depending on the strength of the grip. We implemented a stroke width change function in BrushPaint that likewise allows the user to change the width by adjusting the strength with which the stylus is gripped. We also considered that gripping more strongly or gently would be easy for a user to do.

We similarly applied the brush pen metaphor to index-finger tapping. When a user taps a brush which has a lot of ink, the ink drops onto the paper, and the amount of dropped ink changes depending on the tapping strength. When the user taps the pressure-sensitive stylus, some ink drops onto the virtual canvas, and again the amount of dropped ink depends on the tapping strength. The distance from the stylus to the dropped ink changes randomly. We also considered that fewer tapping operation errors are likely to occur when the operation is performed independently.

We assigned an ink changing function, which might be the most frequently used function, to the index-finger rubbing operation. The hue of the ink changes at a constant rate every time index-finger rubbing is done.

In general paint tools, a user has to use menu operations even if the intended operation is very simple. However, the use of Finger Action in BrushPaint allows the user to use three functions without resorting to menu operations. In general, since menu operation using a stylus is awkward, Finger Action should make operations with a stylus much easier.

7 Conclusion and Future Work

In this paper, we have proposed a novel interaction technique, called Finger Action, that is based on pen-experience. Pen-experience means a user's pre-existing knowledge and skills concerning the use of a pen. Finger Action consists of five input operations: gripping, thumb tapping, index-finger tapping, thumb rubbing, and index-finger rubbing. We developed a pressure-sensitive stylus equipped with pressure sensors to realize Finger Action. Using the pressure-sensitive stylus, we did an experiment to evaluate the usefulness of Finger Action as input operations for the stylus. We found that while gripping and tapping are useful, rubbing does not work well in the current implementation. In addition, we introduced BrushPaint, an application of the pressure-sensitive stylus.

As our future work, we plan to refine the pressure-sensitive stylus, and then conduct an experiment comparing Finger Action with other stylus interaction techniques.

Acknowledgment. This study was supported in part by the Global COE Program on "Cybernics: fusion of human, machine, and information systems."

References

1. Jacob, R.J., Girouard, A., Hirshfield, L.M., Horn, M.S., Shaer, O., Solovey, E.T., Zigelbaum, J.: Reality-Based Interaction: A Framework for Post-WIMP Interfaces. In: Proceedings of the SIGCHI Conference on Human Factors in Computing Systems (CHI 2008), pp. 201–210 (2008)
2. Suzuki, Y., Misue, K., Tanaka, J.: Pen-based Interface Using Hand Motions in the Air. The IEICE Transactions on Information and Systems E91-D(11) (2008)
3. Hopkins, D.: The Design and Implementation of Pie Menus. Dr. Dobb's Journal 16(12), 16–26 (1991)
4. Kurtenbach, G., Buxton, W.: The Limits Of Expert Performance Using Hierarchic Marking Menus. In: Proceedings of the SIGCHI Conference on Human Factors in Computing Systems (CHI 1993), pp. 482–487 (1993)
5. Guimbreti´ere, F., Winograd, T.: FlowMenu: Combining Command, Text, and Data Entry. In: Proceedings of the 13th Annual ACM Symposium on User Interface Software and Technology (UIST 2000), pp. 213–216 (2000)
6. Accot, J., Zhai, S.: More than dotting the i's - Foundations for crossing-based interfaces. In: Proceedings of the SIGCHI Conference on Human Factors in Computing Systems (CHI 2002), pp. 73–80 (2002)
7. Smith, G.M., Schraefel, M.C.: The Radial Scroll Tool: Scrolling Support for Stylus- or Touch-Based Document Navigation. In: Proceedings of the 17th Annual ACM Symposium on User Interface Software and Technology (UIST 2004), pp. 53–56 (2004)
8. Schraefel, M. C., Smith, G., Baudisch, P.: Curve Dial: Eyes-Free Parameter Entry for GUIs. In: Proceedings of the SIGCHI Conference on Human Factors in Computing Systems (CHI 2005), pp. 1146–1147 (2005)
9. Ishii, H., Ullmer, B.: Tangible Bits: Towards Seamless Interfaces between People, Bits and Atoms. In: Proceedings of the SIGCHI Conference on Human Factors in Computing Systems (CHI 1997), pp. 234–241 (1997)

10. Mohler, B.J., Thompson, W.B., Creem-Regehr, S.H., Willemsen, P., Herbert, L., Pick, J., Rieser, J.J.: Calibration of Locomotion Resulting from Visual Motion in a Treadmill-Based Virtual Environment. ACM Transactions on Applied Perception (TAP) 4(1) (2007)
11. Rekimoto, J.: Tilting Operations for Small Screen Interfaces. In: Proceedings of the 9th Annual ACM Symposium on User Interface Software and Technology (UIST 1996), pp. 167–168 (1996)
12. Bowman, D.A., Kruijff, E., LaViola, J.J., Poupyrev, I.: 3D User Interfaces: Theory and Practice. Addison Wesley Longman Publishing Co., Inc. (2004)
13. Okada, K., Nishida, S., Kuzuoka, H., Nakatani, M., Shiozawa, H.: Human Computer Interaction. Ohmsha, Ltd. (2002) (in Japanese)

A Basic Study of Sensory Characteristics toward Interaction with a Box-Shaped Interface

Noriko Suzuki[1], Tosirou Kamiya[1,2], Shunsuke Yoshida[1], and Sumio Yano[1]

[1] National Institute of Information and Communication Technology
ATR Cognitive Information Science Laboratories,
2-2-2 Hikaridai, Seika-cho, Soraku-gun, Kyoto, 619-0288, Japan
{nrk_szk,tkamiya,shun,yano.s}@nict.go.jp
[2] Osaka University, Aomatani-higashi, Minoo City, Osaka, 562-002, Japan

Abstract. Our research focuses on the sensory characteristics of interacting with a novel box-shaped interface device for facilitating transfer of a digital object to another person. Such findings are important for constructing an ultra-realistic communication system with shared reality. This paper presents two kinds of pilot studies: (I) **graspability** of a box-shaped interface device through controlling feedback timing from the device, and (II) **the sense of possessing a modality** in information transfer between two devices. Both psychological and behavioral evaluation results suggest that graspability increases more from feedback of the device just after grasping it than from that just before grasping it. Furthermore, psychological evaluation results suggest that a touch-and-move method, i.e., the receiver of feedback changes precisely from one user to the other after touching the two devices, increases the sense of possessing a modality more than does a touch-and-copy method, i.e., both users simultaneously receive feedback after touching.

Keywords: Sensory characteristics, Box-shaped interface device, Ultra-realistic communication system, Graspability, Sense of posessing a modality, Behavioral evaluation, Psychological evaluation.

1 Introduction

In everyday life, many people often grasp some object and move it to a new location, or pick up it from a shelf and examine it from all angles. They also hand over an object to another person, or circulate it among friends. In the case not of a real object but a virtual 3-D object, how do people feel about its graspability? How do people feel about the sense of handing it over to another?

Some multi-sided display device has been developed for supporting natural interaction between people via a digital object (e.g., [7,5]). These devices have the capability to facilitate grasping an object or handing it over to another person. However, little research has focused on the basic way of examining a designer's concept using a handheld digital device.

The authors are working on the Ultra-realistic Communication System Project of the National Institute of Information and Communication of Japan (NICT).

J.A. Jacko (Ed.): Human-Computer Interaction, Part II, HCII 2009, LNCS 5611, pp. 513–522, 2009.
© Springer-Verlag Berlin Heidelberg 2009

The project aims at constructing a system for embodied interaction with remote partners through multi-modality techniques, i.e., 3-D images, 3-D audio, olfaction and the tactile senses. As a way to improve the reality of interaction, our research focuses on facilitative factors of handing over digital objects via a physical interface device, i.e., the graspability or sense of possessing the virtual 3-D object by using a box-shaped interface device.

This paper examines whether people's impressions and behaviors are affected by (I) feedback timing from a device and (II) the information transfer technique used between two devices. First, a pilot study is conducted to investigate the relationship between the graspability of a device and the feedback timing from the device. We compare the following feedback timings: (a) feedback from the device just before grasping, and (b) that just after grasping it. Second, a pilot study is conducted to investigate the facilitative factors of the sense of possessing a modality in information transfer between two devices. We compare the following information transfer techniques: (a) touch-and-copy method, i.e., both users simultaneously receive feedback after touching the two devices, and (b) touch-and-move method, i.e., the receiver of feedback changes precisely from one user to the other after touching. These studies were conducted with a within-participants design by using a simple box-shaped interface device with three kinds of simple modalities of information: light, sound, and vibration (size:

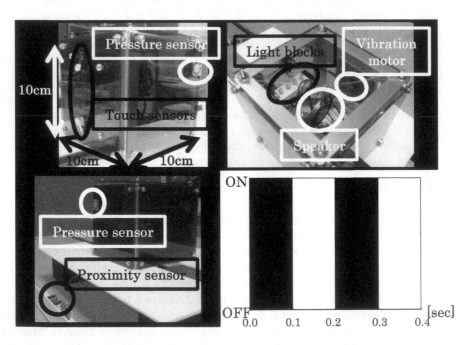

Fig. 1. A box-shaped interface device with sensors (upper and bottom left) and motors in the device (upper right), on and off patterns of output signals from motors in the device (bottom right)

10 x 10 x 10 cm, Fig. 1). The preliminary results were analyzed by two methods: psychological and behavioral evaluations.

2 Related Works

2.1 Manipulating Virtual Objects

In the research field of virtual reality, most conventional studies have tried to implement a manipulation method of virtual objects by hand as an extension of the metaphor of our everyday hand activity. The "Put-That-There" system [2] and the concept of "Direct Manipulation" [9] are typical examples. They developed methods for manipulating virtual objects on a screen by physical actions, i.e., pointing gesture [2] and selection by mouse, joystick, touch screen, etc. [9] instead of typing. Their approach has been applied to a system for manipulating virtual objects by grasping with a virtual hand [10,11]. In seeking a method of tactile feedback from an object, tangible manipulation by using physical objects has been developed [13,4]. Multi-sided handheld display devices have enabled us to view 3-D images and to manipulate them [7,5]). These conventional studies have come close to the ability to manipulate physical objects in the real world. However, little attention has been given to the feedback timing from an interface device for facilitation of grasping the device. This paper examines the relationship between the graspability of the device and the feedback timing from the device.

2.2 Handing over Virtual Objects

In the research field of computer-supported cooperative work, most conventional studies have tried to develop a structure for handing over or sharing digital objects among participants in a remote area. Conventional studies on sharing and exchanging data have started from referencing a common database [3]. This has been applied to multi-media/multi-point communication systems by using a broadband network [1]. Ubiquitous computing techniques or wireless network technologies have enabled digital information transfer among different mobile devices [8,12]. However, these approaches have lacked a sense of handing over objects among participants, although the sense of sharing or transferring digital data was satisfied. This paper examines the relationship between the sense of possessing modality from the device and the information transfer technique.

3 Experimental Settings

Two box-shaped interface devices were constructed for two pilot experiments. Both devices have the following specifications:

Size: 10 x 10 x 10 cm (width/depth/height).
Input sensors: The devices has the following input sensors:

1. **Proximity sensor:** for detecting the approach of a hand.
2. **Pressure sensor:** for detecting grasping by a finger.
3. **Touch sensor:** for detecting contact between two devices.

Output modalities: The devices has the following output modalities:

A. **Audio:** Beep sounds are output from a center speaker of the device. Frequency range: 2.8 kHz to 7.7 kHz (695 Hz overtone spectrum distribution), sound pressure level: 52 dB measured by Bruel & Kjaer 223 BZ7100, microphone: 4190-L-001.

B. **Light:** While light is output from ten light blocks on both sides of the device. In total 170 candela measured by MINOLTA LS-100.

C. **Vibration:** Vibration is output from two coin-type vibration motors on both sides of the device.

Figure 1 (bottom right) shows on and off temporal patterns of output modalities from the device.

Controller and data logging: Lego Mindstorm RCX.

4   Experiment I: Graspability of a Box-Shaped Interface Device

First, we conducted a preliminary experiment to examine the facilitative factors of grasping (i.e., **graspablity** of) a box-shaped interface device by controlling feedback timing. The reason for this is that most of the conventional studies related to this issue have given little attention to the following points:

(1) Feedback from the device just before grasping; instead, previous studies were sensitive to response delay.
(2) Interaction with partner via physical objects; instead, previous studies used a large screen or a desktop-sized display.

Prediction: A box-shaped interface device giving feedback just before it is grasped may facilitate both human grasping behavior and psychological impressions.

Setting: A box-shaped interface device having audio/light/vibration feedback modalities and equipped with a proximity and a pressure sensor (Fig. 1).

Instruction: A participant stood in front of the box-shaped interface device. S/he was instructed to reach for the box on the table, grasp it, and then pull back her/his hand. S/he answered a post-trial questionnaire.

Conditions: Seven kinds of conditions (2 feedback timings x 3 modalities + 1 control condition).

Feedback timings: The following types of feedback were output.

(a) **JBG:** Just before grasping, the device acts as a proximity sensor to detect the approach of a hand (Fig. 2 (upper)).

(b) **JAG:** Just after grasping, the device acts as a pressure sensor to detect the stress of a finger (Fig. 2 (bottom)).

Participants: Twelve people.

Measurements: Two measurements were taken.

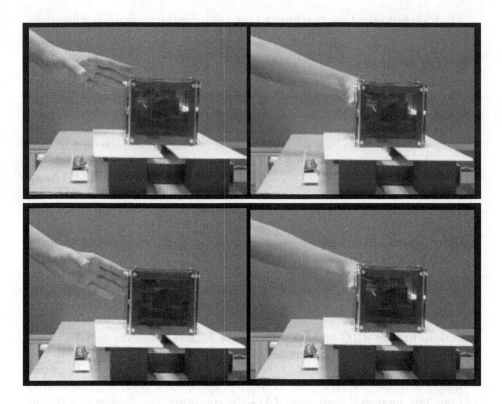

Fig. 2. Graspability: (a) Feedback from the device just before grasping (**JBG**, upper) and (b) feedback from the device just after grasping (**JAG**, bottom) for outputting light modality

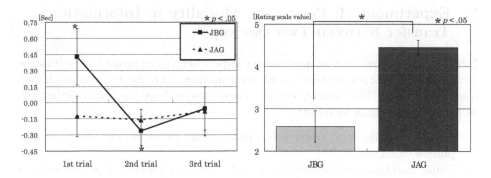

Fig. 3. Results of experiment I: Duration between timing detection of a proximity sensor and that of a pressure sensor (left), Psychological evaluation of relationship between the participants' reaching behavior and feedback from the box-shaped interface device (right)

1. **Psychological evaluation:** A post-trial questionnaire using a five-point scale.
2. **Behavioral evaluation:** Logging the durations between timing detection of proximity sensor and that of pressure sensor.

Results: Figure 3 (left) shows a time series variation of the behavioral evaluation for the duration between timing detection of a proximity sensor, just before grasping (**JBG**), and that of a pressure sensor, just after grasping (**JAG**). These durations were used to calculate the difference from the average duration from the proximity sensor to the pressure sensor of each participant. There was a significant tendency in **JBG** condition among the three trials ($F(2, 11) = 2.88$, $p = .07$) as a result of full factorial ANOVAs using within-subject factors. Subsequently, multiple comparisons using Fisher's PLSD test indicated significant longer to the average duration of 1st trial than that of 2nd trial ($p < .05$). On the other hand, there was no significant difference in **JAG** condition. As a result of multiple comparisons, we found that the 1st trial in **JBG** condition was larger than the 2nd trial.

Figure 3 (right) shows the psychological evaluation of the relationship between the reaching behavior of the participants and the feedback from the device. There was significant difference between **JBG** and **JAG** conditions ($t = -4.42$, $p < .05$).

Discussion: The **JBG** condition may have caused hesitating behavior from participants, especially in the first trial. In the **JBG** condition, it may be difficult to find the relationship between the reaching behavior of the participants and the feedback from the device. From these results, **graspability** may have increased more from **JAG** the condition, i.e., feedback of the device just after grasping, than from the **JBG** condition, i.e., feedback just before grasping.

5   Experiment II: Possessing Modality in Information Transfer between Two Devices

Next, we conducted another preliminary experiment to examine the facilitative factors of possessing a modality in information transfer between two box-shaped interface devices. Specifically, we had these motivations for investigating the factor of possessing a modality:

(1) Using a simpler and easier information transfer techniques than cellular phones or PDAs.
(2) Using direct-contact between two devices, not metaphorical action such as [8,12].
(3) Comparing performances with the same device as well as the same modality, not different ones such as [6].

Prediction: An information transfer technique that feedback are transferred perfectly from one to another user may facilitate both impression and behavior of possessing a modality of the her/his own device.

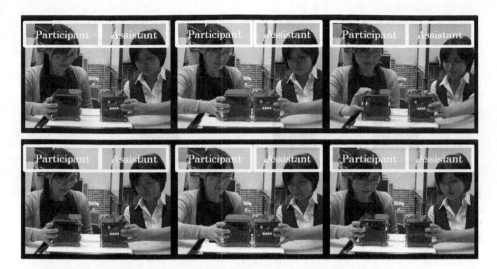

Fig. 4. Information transfer: touch-and-copy method (**TCM**, upper) and touch-and-move method (**TMM**, bottom) for outputting light modality

Setting: Two box-shaped interface devices with the same modality as in Experiment I. Furthermore, a touch sensor was incorporated in the device for participants (Fig. 1).

Instruction: A participant sat next to an assistant of the experimenter in front of two box-shaped interface devices. First, the assistant grasped the device on the left. Second, the participant grasped the device on the right, moved it to the interface of the assistant, put the two devices together, and then moved the right device back to its original position.

Conditions: Seven kinds of conditions (2 information transfer methods x 3 modalities + 1 control condition).

> **Information transfer technique:** Feedback from the box-shaped interface of the participant was output, just after touching the two interfaces together, by a touch sensor detecting their contact. At that time, feedback from the interface of the assistant:
>
> (a) **TCM:** Continued outputting after the two devices made contact (touch-and-copy method) (Fig. 4 (upper)).
>
> (b) **TMM:** Stopped outputting after the two devices made contact (touch-and-move method) (Fig. 4 (bottom)).

Participants: Twelve people.

Measurements: Two measurements were taken:

> 1. **Psychological evaluation:** A post-trial questionnaire using a five-point scale.
> 2. **Behavioral evaluation:** Logging the duration of contact between two devices with a touch sensor.

Results: Figure 5 (left) shows the psychological evaluation of the sense of possessing or sharing a modality for both the touch-and-copy method (**TCM**),

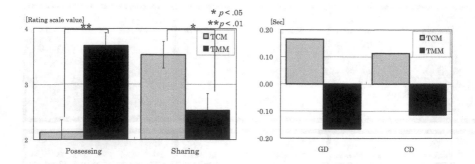

Fig. 5. Results of experiment II: Psychological evaluation between touch-and-copy method (**TCM**) and touch-and-move method (**TMM**) (left), duration of grasping the device by pressure sensor (**GD**) of participants and duration of contact by a touch sensor (**CD**) under the two information transfer techniques (right)

and the touch-and-move method (**TMM**). There were significant differences between **TCM** and **TMM** (sense of possessing the modality: t = 2.659, p < .05, sense of sharing the modality: t = -4.34, p < .01).

Figure 5 (right) shows duration of grasping the device by pressure sensor (**GD**) and duration of contact between two devices by a touch sensor (**CD**). These durations were used to calculate the difference from the average duration in the touch sensor of each participant. There were no significant difference in either the **TCM** or the **TMM**.

Discussion: The **TMM** may increase **the sense of possessing a modality**, while the **TCM** may increase the sense of sharing. These results suggest that the users of the multi-sided handheld display device may prefer to select the touch-and-move method for indicating that the contents of the device are to be transferred or presented as a gift to another person. On the other hand, the users of the device may prefer to select the touch-and-copy method for indicating that these contents are to be moved or copied to another person.

6   Discussion

The above preliminary results have some practical implications for the interface design of a handheld cube-shaped device:

Graspability of a box-shaped interface device: Feedback from the device when grasping might have facilitated either grasping behavior or the positive relationship with reaching behavior. Feedback of the device just before grasping might make the users hesitate to grasp the device. In other words, graspability may be increased more from feedback of the device just after grasping it than from feedback just before grasping it.

Sense of possessing a modality in information transfer between two devices: The touch-and-move method, i.e., the receiver of feedback changes precisely from one user to the other after touching two devices, might increase the sense of possessing a modality. The users of the multi-sided handheld display device may thus prefer to select this method to indicate transferring possession of the device's contents or presenting these contents as a gift to another person. On the other hand, the touch-and-copy method, i.e., both users simultaneously receive feedback after touching, might increase the sense of sharing the modality. The users of the device may prefer to select this method to indicate simply moving or copying the contents to another person.

7   Conclusions

In this paper, we focused on the sensory characteristics of interacting with a box-shaped interface device. These sensory characteristics perceived by people were investigated as a fundamental aspect of facilitating the transfer of a digital object to another person at a remote location via the box-shaped interface device. We examined how people were affected in their psychological impressions and behaviors from (I) feedback timing from a device and (II) the information transfer technique between two devices. We analyzed the experimental data through log data from sensors for behavior and psychological evaluation. From these pilot studies, we obtained the following findings:

- Graspability of a box-shaped interface device might be facilitated by the device outputting feedback just after the user grasps it.
- The sense of possessing the contents of the device might be increased when the contents are transferred "perfectly" from the device of one user to that of the other user, after touching two devices.

We confirmed that feedback timing from the device and the information transfer technique between two devices affect the impressions or behavior of people, even though the device outputs simple modalities, i.e., beep sounds, white light and vibration.

As future work, the authors will investigate the human sensory characteristics in interaction between interface devices and people. For example, we will examine the sensitivity to time by controlling the feedback delay from the device. Furthermore, we will study the sense of possessing a modality in interaction between the box-shaped interface device and a large screen.

We will apply these findings to the actual design of multi-sided interface devices such as [5].

Acknowledgement

The authors would like to thank Dr. Naomi Inoue, Dr. Hiroshi Ando and Dr. Robert Lopez-Gulliver for their continuous support and advice in this work. The authors also thank Ms Naho Orita for her technical support.

References

1. Addeo, E.J., Gelman, A.D., Dayao, A.B.: Personal multi-media multi-point communication services. In: IEEE Proc. of Grobecom, pp. 53–57 (1988)
2. Bolt, R.A.: Put-That-There": voice and gesture at the graphics interface. In: ACM SIGGRAPH, pp. 262–270 (1980)
3. Greif, I., Sarin, S.: Data sharing in group work. ACM Transactions on office information systems 5(2), 187–211 (1987)
4. Ishii, H., Ullmer, B.: Tangible Bits: towards seamless interfaces between people, bits and atoms. In: CHI 1997, pp. 234–241 (1997)
5. Lopez-Gulliver, R., Yoshida, S., Yano, S., Inoue, N.: gCubik: a cubic autostereoscopic display for muitiuser interaction: grasp and group-share virtual images. In: ACM SIGGRAPH 2008 (133) (2008)
6. Ogawa, K., Ono, T.: ITACO: Constructing an emotional relationship between human and robot. In: IEEE RO-MA 2008, pp. 35–40 (2008)
7. Poupyrev, I., Newton-Dunn, H., Bau, O.: D20: Interaction with multifaceted display devices. In: ACM CHI 2006, pp. 1241–1246 (2006)
8. Rekimoto, J.: Pick-and-drop: a direct manipulation technique for multiple computer environments. In: ACM UIST 1997, pp. 31–39 (1997)
9. Shneiderman, B.: Direct manipulation: a step beyond programming languages. IEEE Computer 16(8), 57–69 (1983)
10. Sturman, D., Zeltzer, D., Pieper, S.: Hands-on interaction with virtual environments. In: ACM UIST 1989, pp. 19–24 (1989)
11. Takemura, H., Kishino, F.: Cooperative work environment using virtual workspace. In: CSCW 1992, pp. 226–232 (1992)
12. Yatani, K., Tamura, K., Sugimoto, M., Hashizume, H.: Information transfer techniques for mobile devices by "toss" and "swing" actions. In: IEEE WMCSA 2004, pp. 144–151 (2004)
13. Wellner, P.: The digitalDesk calculator: tangible manipulation on a desk top display. In: ACM UIST 1991, pp. 27–33 (1991)

TACTUS: A Hardware and Software Testbed for Research in Multi-Touch Interaction

Paul Varcholik, Joseph J. Laviola Jr., and Denise Nicholson

Institute for Simulation & Training
University of Central Florida
Orlando, Florida
pvarchol@ist.ucf.edu, jjl@cs.ucf.edu, dnichols@ist.ucf.edu

Abstract. This paper presents the TACTUS Multi-Touch Research Testbed, a hardware and software system for enabling research in multi-touch interaction. A detailed discussion is provided on hardware construction, pitfalls, design options, and software architecture to bridge the gaps in the existing literature and inform the researcher on the practical requirements of a multi-touch research testbed. This includes a comprehensive description of the vision-based image processing pipeline, developed for the TACTUS software library, which makes surface interactions available to multi-touch applications. Furthermore, the paper explores the higher-level functionality and utility of the TACTUS software library and how researchers can leverage the system to investigate multi-touch interaction techniques.

Keywords: Multi-Touch, HCI, Touch Screen, Testbed, API.

1 Introduction

The pending proliferation of multi-touch technology, which allows interaction with a surface through multiple simultaneous points of contact and from multiple concurrent users, has the potential to radically change Human-Computer Interaction. However, unless the research community can answer fundamental questions about optimizing interface designs, and provide empirically driven guidelines, the technology can become just another I/O modality looking for a purpose. Unfortunately, there is limited availability of hardware and software to support this research. Thus, investigators must overcome a number of technical challenges to develop a multi-touch platform before they can begin research in this area.

Through an extensive literature and state-of-the-art review, an analysis of the requirements for a multi-touch research platform revealed two categories of components: those essential for basic multi-touch research; and secondary components necessary for extensive investigation and longer-term research projects. These components, listed in Table 1, emphasize a low-cost, do-it-yourself approach.

A multi-touch platform is made up of two primary components: a physical interaction surface, and a software system for collecting and interpreting points of contact. The hardware and software systems each require significant investments of time and effort to construct. While advances in hardware and multi-touch software

J.A. Jacko (Ed.): Human-Computer Interaction, Part II, HCII 2009, LNCS 5611, pp. 523–532, 2009.

infrastructure provide interesting research opportunities themselves, they are a barrier
to entry for researchers who want to focus on higher-level interface issues or the development of novel applications.

This paper presents the TACTUS Multi-Touch Research Testbed, a hardware and
software system for enabling research in multi-touch interaction. A detailed discussion is provided on hardware construction, pitfalls, design options, and software architecture to bridge the gaps in the existing literature and inform the researcher on the
practical requirements of a multi-touch research testbed. This includes a comprehensive description of the vision-based image processing pipeline developed for the
TACTUS software library, which makes surface interactions available to multi-touch
applications. Furthermore, the paper explores the higher-level functionality and utility
of the TACTUS software library and how researchers can leverage the system to
investigate multi-touch interaction techniques.

Table 1. Essential and Secondary Components for a multi-touch research platform

Essential Components	Description
Multi-touch surface	Constructed using commercial-off-the-shelf hardware and requiring near zero pressure to detect an interaction point
Software Hit-Testing	Ability to determine the presence and location of each point of surface contact; supporting at least four users
Software Point Tracking	Identifying a continuous point of contact and reporting its velocity and duration
Secondary Components	
Application Programming Interface (API)	A software system upon which multiple multi-touch applications can be developed
Multi-Platform Support	The ability to access multi-touch interaction data from different computing environments (e.g. languages, OS's, etc.)
Reconfiguration	Modifying the software system without recompilation
Software Service	Allowing multiple applications to access multi-touch interaction data simultaneously, including over a computer network
Presentation-Layer Independence	Isolating the multi-touch interaction data from the system to graphically present such data, allowing any GUI to be employed when developing multi-touch applications
Mouse Emulation	Support for controlling traditional 'Window, Icon, Menu, Pointing Device' interaction through a multi-touch surface
Tangible Interfaces	The ability to detect and interact with physical devices placed on or near the multi-touch surface
Customizable Gesture System	Support for training arbitrary multi-touch gestures and mapping them to software events

2 Related Work

In 2001, Deitz presented the Mitsubishi *DiamondTouch* [1], a front-projection, multi-
touch system that uses an array of antennas to transmit identifying signals that are
capacitively coupled through a user. The *DiamondTouch* is fairly expensive,

compared to a do-it-yourself approach, and users will occlude the front-projection display as they interact with the system.

In 2005, Han presented work on constructing low-cost multi-touch surfaces using Frustrated Total Internal Reflection [2]. Much of our hardware is a derivative of Han's work. However, while Han's paper presented a starting point for building low-cost multi-touch surfaces, it left out some of the details necessary to reliably construct a multi-touch platform.

In 2004, Wilson introduced *TouchLight* [3] and in 2007 Microsoft announced the Microsoft Surface [4] – an exciting development for bringing multi-touch technology closer to the consumer market. While a preliminary release of Microsoft Surface started in Spring 2008, there is still limited availability of this platform.

Both the *DiamondTouch* and the Microsoft Surface have commercial APIs for developing applications for their products. However, use of these software packages is largely dependent on the acquisition of their associated hardware. A few open-source multi-touch libraries exist, including: Touchlib [5], reacTIVision [6], and BBTouch [7]. These support various operating systems and programming environments, and vary in feature set and ease-of-use.

Much more work exists on the development of multi-touch hardware technology and associated software as in [8-10]. Our efforts build upon these achievements and offer a low-cost, full-featured multi-touch research testbed.

3 Multi-Touch Hardware

Although there are a variety of multi-touch designs, we believe that Frustrated Total Internal Reflection (FTIR) technology offers a robust and affordable hardware solution. FTIR surfaces share a set of common components: 1) An optical waveguide for conducting infrared (IR) light, 2) A supporting structure for holding the waveguide, 3) An IR sensing camera, 4) A projector and diffuser, 5) An IR emission source, 6) A computer. Our design is pictured in Figure 1. For the optical waveguide, we've chosen a 32"x24", ½" thick sheet of clear acrylic. The dimensions of the surface match the 4:3 aspect ratio of most modern, short-throw projectors. The supporting structure for the acrylic is a 37" high table and includes a 6" wide border around the waveguide, for placing materials (or resting elbows) that will not interact with the surface. The IR camera and projector are placed below the acrylic, and are contained within the table. This design supports collaboration with up to four seated or standing users. The IR camera is a Microsoft LifeCam VX-6000, a commercial-off-the-shelf webcam that has been modified to allow IR light while filtering visible light. The projector is a Mitsubishi XD500U-ST short-throw projector, capable of producing a 60" diagonal from only 33" away. The diffuser is a sheet of Rosco Gray 7mm thick PVC, rear-projection material. For IR emission we chose a set of 32 Osram 485 LEDs. These are split into 4 chains (connected in parallel) of 8 LEDs (connected in serial) running to a common 12V power supply. Lastly, we've chosen a small-footprint MicroATX computer for operating the multi-touch surface software.

Fig. 1. Multi-Touch Hardware Design

Several of these components are discussed in more detail below.

Acrylic Waveguide & Infrared LEDs. Acrylic has optical properties conducive to Total Internal Reflection [2]. It's also quite durable, inexpensive, and can be manufactured in a number of sizes. Thickness is a consideration at large dimension, as pressure on the surface causes the acrylic to noticeably deflect. At 32"x24" we found a ½" thick sheet of acrylic to be a nice compromise between rigidity and cost.

When placing the LEDs around the acrylic, the primary concerns are providing enough light and fully distributing that light within the waveguide. We initially drilled 5mm wide depressions, into the acrylic edges, to house the LEDs. This works quite well, and does not require polishing the acrylic edge to introduce light into the waveguide. A drawback to this approach is that the LEDs are semi-permanently affixed to the acrylic. Working with the acrylic (for example, to pour on a silicone rubber compliant surface) often requires removing the LEDs. In our final design, we chose to surround the acrylic with LEDs, equally spaced, and abutting the acrylic edges. Again, we found that polishing the acrylic edges was not required. The choice of 8 LEDs per side is more than sufficient for our surface size, given their 40-degree viewing angle. In fact, we found quite reasonable results with only two adjacent edges lit. To determine if enough light is being introduced into the waveguide, point the IR camera at an edge opposite to the illumination. The camera should detect a solid bar of IR – the light escaping the edge. If this bar of light is segmented, or significantly varies in intensity, then the illumination is not being fully distributed throughout the waveguide and additional LEDs are required.

Projector & Diffuser. Short throw projectors, capable of displaying large images from very close distances, have become increasingly available in recent years. A short throw is necessary for maintaining small table depth. If the multi-touch system has no depth requirement (e.g. a wall-display) then a traditional projector can help reduce cost. Strictly speaking, a traditional projector, with a system of mirrors for increasing focal length, can be used in a depth-limited multi-touch surface. However, this adds complexity to the hardware design.

The diffuser is the surface upon which the projected image will be displayed. Aside from the choice of materials, a chief concern for the diffuser is its placement – either above or below the waveguide. Placing the diffuser below the waveguide causes a slight disparity (of the thickness of the waveguide) between the interaction surface and the projected display. Furthermore, a pliable diffuser material, placed below the waveguide, will sag, deforming the projected image if not otherwise supported. Moreover, the diffuser may absorb some of the IR light passing through it. While this is a benefit for reducing ambient IR light, the diffuser will also absorb some of the light being reflected through FTIR when placed below the waveguide. For these reasons, we suggest placing the diffuser above the waveguide. This approach also protects the waveguide from scratches and oils from the users' fingers. Unfortunately, placing the diffuser above the waveguide negatively impacts the coupling between the users' fingers and the waveguide, decreasing the light reflected through FTIR. A material, placed between the diffuser and the waveguide, is required to improve coupling and thereby increase the amount of IR light directed to the camera while decreasing the force necessary to reflect it.

Compliant Surface. A finger makes an imperfect connection with acrylic. Micro airgaps form between the user's fingers and the waveguide and maintain the original acrylic-to-air interface, thus supporting Total Internal Reflection. Moistening fingertips or pressing firmly on the surface can improve coupling, but these are not viable long-term solutions. A coupling material is required to permit low-force, high-quality surface interaction.

After much trial-and-error, we settled on a 1mm thick layer of SORTA-Clear 40 – a translucent silicone rubber – placed between the acrylic and the diffuser. SORTA-Clear 40 is a liquid that, when mixed with its catalyst, will cure at room temperature into a firm (40A Shore hardness) material that provides very good coupling with limited hysteresis. However, mixing the rubber with its catalyst creates air bubbles, which will cause considerable noise in the captured image. Placing the mixed rubber into a vacuum chamber can help remove these bubbles, but there is limited time before the material begins to cure, and the pouring and smoothing process will reintroduce some air. Placing the entire surface into a vacuum, after the material has been poured, may be the best option for removing bubbles – if a large enough vacuum chamber is available. We found good results, in mitigating air bubbles, simply by keeping the thickness of the rubber very small (e.g. <=1mm) and by pouring and smoothing slowly and deliberately. Applying a small amount of heat, from a hair dryer or heat gun, can help remove any stubborn bubbles before the rubber cures.

While pre-cured layers of rubber are available, we found them difficult to adhere to the acrylic without introducing a large number of air pockets. Pouring the silicone rubber directly onto the surface produced the best results.

4 Software Framework

The chief function of the TACTUS software library is to collect and interpret multi-touch surface input. The core components of the library do not specify how this data is used or displayed. Thus, the library is presentation-layer independent and graphical user interface (GUI) systems such as Windows Presentation Foundation (WPF), Windows Forms (WinForms), and Microsoft XNA can all be used to develop front-end applications that utilize the multi-touch framework. To support various presentation systems, the TACTUS software framework maintains two modes of data communication: polling and events. Traditional WinForms applications use events to communication object information; whereas polling is more common for simulations or video games, where input devices are continuously queried.

4.1 Image Processing

At the core of the software, is an image processing system that converts raw camera data into points of interaction. The image processing system runs in its own software thread, and captured frames are sent through the processing pipeline depicted in Figure 2.

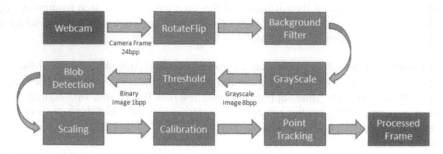

Fig. 2. Image processing pipeline

Processing begins by capturing an image from a video source – a Microsoft DirectShow compatible device. The camera's device enumeration, frame rate, and resolution are specified through the framework's XML configuration file. The *RotateFlip* step transforms the image vertically and horizontally, as specified in the configuration file, orienting the image to match the projector.

During initialization, the software library captures a set of frames, while the surface is quiescent, and combines them to form a background image. The *Background Filter* step subtracts this background image from the active frame, thus removing noise from the image. Noise originates from ambient infrared light, "hot-spots" produced by the projector, oils and debris on the waveguide and compliant surface, and from light unintentionally escaping the waveguide. The TACTUS software library allows the user to recapture the background image at any time and does not force the restart of the image processing system to compensate for a dynamic lighting environment.

Most webcams capture images in color, typically at 24 bits per pixel (bpp). The *Grayscale* action converts a color frame to grayscale (8bpp). This step can be removed if the camera natively captures images in grayscale – the format required for the subsequent *Threshold* filter, which further isolates pixel values to black or white (fully *on* or fully *off*). Pixels below the configurable threshold value are treated as *off* and pixels above as *on*. The resulting 1bpp black & white image is sent to the *Blob Detection* process, which groups neighboring *on* pixels into *blobs*. Blobs are the regions of the image that we consider for potential points of surface interaction. The blob detector filters out blobs below a minimum width and height, as specified in the configuration file.

Scaling adjusts the dimensions of the image to correspond to the resolution of the image projected onto the multi-touch surface. The *Calibration* step then adjusts for differences between the interaction surface, projector, and the camera that create discrepancies between the points touched on the surface and the location of those points in the camera frame. By sampling points at the four corners of the surface, we can construct a transformation matrix and generate a lookup table with the corrected location for every point of interaction. This table can be serialized, and the resulting file specified in the XML configuration for automatic loading by the framework.

The final phase of the image processing pipeline is *Point Tracking*, which takes the detected, scaled, and calibrated blobs and abstracts them into *FtirPoint* objects. An FtirPoint object has attributes including: a globally unique identifier (GUID), location, timestamp, bounding box, speed, direction, and duration. Each FtirPoint represents a single point of interaction with the surface, and it is this data that is most useful for multi-touch applications. With the location and bounds of an FtirPoint we can perform hit testing – testing an area on the screen for an interaction point – through simple rectangle intersection. The point tracking process also labels each FtirPoint with a GUID that is maintained as long as the interaction point is present. To track a point across frames, we again perform rectangle intersection between the previous and current frame's FtirPoints. Points that intersect are considered the same point, and differences in location and time are used to calculate the point's speed, direction, and presence duration. Detected points that do not intersect with previous points are assigned a new GUID. This process allows points to split and merge, and enables gestural interaction with the surface. However, the performance of this technique is tied to the quality of the camera and the compliant surface.

The purpose of the compliant surface is to improve coupling between the user's fingers and the waveguide. If that coupling is poor, the user's fingers will "stutter" across the surface, and will not continuously reflect IR to the camera. The gaps between images would cause the point tracking system to re-label what would otherwise be the same point. The framework provides a stutter-correction system that tracks points within a time-window for label reuse. Tracked points that become absent from a camera frame are transferred to a "pending disposal" collection for a user-configurable time (250 millisecond default). Newly detected points are matched against this collection, again through rectangle intersection, before they are assigned a new GUID. In this fashion, the framework will reconstitute a point that becomes briefly disconnected from the surface. Stutter mitigation, however, does not address a camera with a slow frame rate. If the user's fingers move across the surface faster than the camera can track, the software library will label the points as disconnected. Future work on the library will attempt to address this through point prediction.

Exiting the image processing pipeline is the set of currently detected FtirPoints. Figure 3 shows a camera frame as it is passed through the image processing pipeline. Specifically, the figure displays: the raw camera frame (a), the background filtered image (b), the threshold image (c), and the fully processed FtirPoints displayed on the multi-touch surface (d).

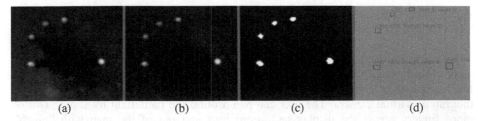

(a)   (b)   (c)   (d)

Fig. 3. A camera frame passed through the image processing pipeline: raw camera frame (a), background filtered (b), threshold (c), processed points (d)

4.2 Framework Features

While the image processing system forms the heart of the TACTUS software framework, there are a number of additional features that can aid in the creation of multi-touch applications including: multi-platform communication, 2D/3D graphics, pen/writing-style interaction, and gesture recognition.

The TACTUS software library is built on two open-source libraries: the Bespoke Open Sound Control Library (OSC) [11] and the Bespoke 3DUI XNA Framework [12]. OSC is an open, lightweight, message-based protocol that enables, for example, multi-touch data to be transmitted over a network. The Bespoke 3DUI XNA Framework is a software library for enabling research in game development and 3D user interaction (3DUI). The TACTUS software framework employs this library as a presentation layer for multi-touch applications; allowing games and simulations to be constructed with multi-touch input.

Another interesting feature of the TACTUS software system is its support of pen/writing-style interaction. Pen-style computing refers to human-computer interaction through the digital representation of ink or writing, typically input through a computer stylus [13]. Ordinarily, pen-computing is single-touch – where input is collected from only one location at a time. This is a degenerate case of multi-touch, where we constrain the input and treat interaction points as digital ink. The TACTUS software library collects ink data into *Stroke* objects which can be used for 2D recognition. TACTUS provides a machine-learning system for training and classifying stroke data based on work by Rubine [14].

5 Case Studies

The TACTUS software library has been utilized in the creation of many multi-touch applications, and across a variety of domains. This section discusses four projects built with the framework, pictured in Figure 4: SurfaceCommand (a), InkDemo (b), Waterfall (c), and the TACTUS mouse emulator (d).

(a)   (b)   (c)   (d)

Fig. 4. Multi-Touch applications: SurfaceCommand (a), InkDemo (b), Waterfall (c), and the TACTUS mouse emulator (d)

SurfaceCommand is a multi-touch demonstration styled after real-time strategy games. Built using the Bespoke 3DUI XNA Framework, with the TACTUS multi-touch extensions, SurfaceCommand presents a 3D battlefield viewed through an orthographic virtual camera. The user can pan around the battlefield by sliding two or more fingers across the display and zoom into and out of the map with "pinch" gestures – a motion whereby two interaction points are moving in roughly opposite direction, either toward or away from each other. Spaceships within the battlefield can be selected and moved about the map with single interaction points; and multiple ships can be selected and deselected with mode buttons along the bottom of the display. This simple application explores techniques that could be used within a real-time strategy video game and was developed in just four days.

InkDemo, pictured in Figure 4b, demonstrates the pen-style interaction of the TACTUS framework. Stroke data is collected when the user provides only a single point of interaction. As the user slides a finger across the display, simple block-style lines are generated to visualize the underlying stroke data. A set of strokes can be labeled and committed to the TACTUS symbol recognition system. With a sufficient number of training samples, the user can then classify an unlabeled set of strokes.

Our third application, Waterfall, is an example of multi-platform communication and the rapid development capability of the TACTUS software system. The application is a fluid-dynamics demonstration, where simulated water flows down an inclined surface and can be perturbed by multi-touch surface interaction. Users interact with the water to form "dams" with their hands and fingers. The simulation was developed in C++ and rendered with the OGRE game development platform [15]. The multi-touch input was serialized via Open Sound Control, as described in section 4.2, and received by the simulation using an open-source C++ OSC implementation. The integration effort took only three days from start-to-finish.

The last example demonstrates the TACTUS mouse emulator – an application that allows the use of a multi-touch surface to control traditional, mouse-driven Windows applications. The mouse emulator associates a set of gestures with common mouse commands, as listed in Table 2.

Table 2. Mouse emulator gesture mappings

Function	Gesture Description
Left Click	Quick tap on the surface with one finger.
Left Click (alternate)	While holding down a finger, tap another finger to the left side of the first.
Drag	Perform a Left Click (alternate) but do not release the left side press. Drag both fingers to the destination and release.
Right Click	While holding down a finger, tap another finger to the right side of the first.
Double Click	Tap two fingers at the same time.
Mouse Wheel Scroll	While holding down a finger, drag another finger vertically and to the right side of the first. Dragging up scrolls the mouse wheel up and vice versa.
Alt-Tab	While not a mouse command, the Alt-Tab command is a useful Windows feature that switches between applications. To perform an Alt-Tab, hold down a finger and drag another finger horizontally above the first. Dragging to the left moves backward through the list of active applications and dragging to the right moves forward.

Figure 4d shows the emulator in use with the commercial video game *Starcraft* by Blizzard Entertainment. This popular real-time strategy game is controlled through the mouse and keyboard; but using the TACTUS mouse emulator, one can play Starcraft through a multi-touch surface. Videos of these, and other TACTUS demonstrations, can be found at http://www.bespokesoftware.org/.

6 Conclusions

In summary, while multi-touch technology has generated considerable excitement and offers the potential for powerful new interaction techniques, the researcher must overcome a significant obstacle for entry into this field – obtaining a multi-touch hardware and software research platform. Few commercial options exist, and there are deficiencies in academic literature on constructing such a platform. This paper describes the requirements of a multi-touch research system and presents TACTUS, a hardware and software testbed that enables research in multi-touch interaction. The testbed discussed offers insight into the construction of a robust, low-cost multi-touch surface and the development of an extensible software system for the rapid creation of multi-touch applications.

This work is supported in part by the National Science Foundation under award number DRL0638977.

References

1. Dietz, P., Leigh, D.: DiamondTouch: A Multi-user Touch Technology. In: 14th ACM Symposium on User Interface Software and Technology, pp. 219–226. ACM, New York (2001)
2. Han, Y.J.: Low-cost Multi-touch Sensing through Frustrated Total Internal Reflection. In: 18th ACM Symposium on User Interface Software and Technology, pp. 115–118. ACM, New York (2005)
3. Wilson, A.: TouchLight: An Imaging Touch Screen and Display for Gesture-based Interaction. In: 6th International Conference on Multimodal Interfaces, pp. 69–76. ACM, New York (2004)
4. Microsoft Surface, http://www.microsoft.com/surface/
5. TouchLib, http://nuigroup.com/touchlib/
6. Martin, K., Ross, B.: reacTIVision: A Computer-vision Framework for Table-Based Tangible Interaction. In: 1st International Conference on Tangible and Embedded Interaction, pp. 69–74. ACM, New York (2007)
7. BBTouch, http://code.google.com/p/opentouch/
8. Davidson, P., Han, J.: Synthesis and Control on Large Scale Multi-touch Sensing Displays. In: The 2006 Conference on New Interfaces for Musical Expression, pp. 216–219. IRCAM, Paris (2006)
9. Kim, J., Park, J., Kim, H., Lee, C.: HCI (Human Computer Interaction) Using Multi-touch Tabletop Display. In: PacRim Conference on Communications, Computers and Signal Processing, pp. 391–394. IEEE Press, New York (2007)
10. Tse, E., et al.: Enabling interaction with single user applications through speech and gestures on a multi-user tabletop. In: Proceedings of the working conference on Advanced visual interfaces. ACM, New York (2006)
11. The Bespoke Open Sound Control Library,
    http://www.bespokesoftware.org/osc/
12. The Bespoke 3DUI XNA Framework,
    http://www.bespokesoftware.org/3dui/
13. Bowman, D., Kruijff, E., LaViola, J., Poupyrev, I.: 3D User Interfaces: Theory and Practice. Addison Wesley, Reading (2004)
14. Rubine, D.: Specifying gestures by example. In: International Conference on Computer Graphics and Interactive Techniques (1991)
15. Torus Knot Software. OGRE - Open Source 3D Graphics Engine,
    http://www.ogre3d.org/

Low Cost Flexible Wrist Touch UI Solution

Bin Wang, Chenguang Cai, Emilia Koskinen, Tang Zhenqi, Huayu Cao, Leon Xu,
and Antti O. Salo

Nokia Inc., Research Center (Beijing)
No.5 Dong Huan Zhong Lu, BDA, Beijing, China 10017
{bin.6.wang,ext-chenguang.cai,emilia.koskinen,ext-huayu.cao,
leon.xu,antti.o.salo}@nokia.com

Abstract. Wrist device is an interesting and convenient user interaction method between a user and a mobile communication device. This paper presents a low cost flexible wrist device user interaction solution based on flexible touch screen technology. We mainly focused on the 2 aspects: one is the user study to understand what requirements of the wrist UI the users demand; and another is how to realize the specific UI solutions that the users demand. Base on user study report from NRC Helsinki and Beijing, we adopt 3x3 matrix resistance touch panel module and 2-color flexible LCD module as the user interaction hardware solution.

Keywords: Wrist UI, resistance touch panel, accessory, user study.

1   Introduction

Wrist UI device is an interesting and convenient user interaction method between a user and a mobile communication device. The device is connected with mobile phone via Bluetooth to display contents of user's mobile phone and remotely control mobile phone, such as making a phone call with a Bluetooth headset, read a message while the mobile phone is inconvenient to reach. Our major research efforts are currently targeting the "touch user interface" of wrist device as an accessory of mobile phone into current mobile environment; we call it "wrist touch UI". Nowadays, people are more and more desired to ubiquitous calculating, no matter in office, gym, at home, or on the street according to different mobile lifestyles.

And developers and researchers are trying to find out appropriate end device or technologies forms which are fitting to different occasions in the last decade. Prof. Joe Paradiso and his team of the MIT Media Lab have made a sensor component network prototype of 16 sensors that are integrated with a wireless transmitter and mounted onto a shoe (expressive footwear) [1].

IBM, Fossil, Inc. Timex Datalink, Hitachi, Panasonic Computer Solutions Company, they also take effort into wearable computer development. Arcom Control Systems offers the ZYPAD, a wrist wearable touch screen computer with GPS, Wi-Fi and Bluetooth connectivity and which can run a number of custom applications. [2]

Chandra Narayanaswami, M. T. Raghunath who come from Wearable Computing Platforms, IBM TJ Watson Research Center, developed a smart watch which

J.A. Jacko (Ed.): Human-Computer Interaction, Part II, HCII 2009, LNCS 5611, pp. 533–541, 2009.

equipped a package of powerful processor and memory system, coupled with a ultra high-resolution display and wireless communication, year 2000. [3]

Gábor Blaskó, Franz Coriand and Steven Feiner, developed a set of interaction techniques that assume that the wrist-worn computer and projector are equipped with position and orientation sensors, in addition to a touch-sensitive built in screen, further more, study the interaction design by this way. [4]

But we are trying another way to the mobile calculating which takes use of current mobile phone and makes this system cheaper. Our solution is developing a wrist device linked to mobile phone. The wrist UI device has not powerful processor and big memory chips, it just sends the input demands and output results from mobile phone, and leaves the heavy computing task to mobile phone, or in other case, to PC and net work server.

We choose resistive touch screen as the interaction implement which has multitouch function. The touch screen is made of a resistive multi-touch panel and a flexible dichromatic LCD. The touch panel comprises 3x3 matrix which maps to 9 touch buttons.

Following the result of user studies (easy touching, no physical keys, and graphical user interface, flat UI structure, etc.) and low cost touch screen technological solution, the 3x3 graphic UI is the suitable view. Every icon matches the pattern, which is like the virtual key on the display. So, users can just press the icon on the display directly with finger to get the all functions of the wrist device with such low resolution touch panel. The following use cases could be the reference. When user does a physical exercise, he (she) could conveniently monitor his mobile phone status without missing incoming call and messages. On another case, user could also do a simple control functions to his (her) laptop, such power on, getting email, shut down, etc.

2   User Study to the Fist Version of Wrist Device

By the end of year 2007, Nokia Research Center (Beijing) has developed the first version of wrist UI without touch panel, Shown in fig. 1.

Transparent TPU lens

Flexible LCD module

Fig. 1. The first version of wrist UI device

Using a preliminary mockup of flexible wrist device which was based on the existing wrist devices and our earlier internal studies, we conducted two 12-person user studies, one in Helsinki (Finland) and another in Beijing (China). The user studies include the following main aspects: 1) the size of the device, 2) the flexibility of the device, 3) the user interaction method, and 4) the functionality needed for the device.

2.1 User Study in Helsinki

Emilia Koskinen, our colleague in Helsinki site, finished a paper prototype user study in Finland. She interviewed 12 participators individually who came from company internal employees. There were six males and six females participating. Their age varied from 22 years to 45, average age being 31 years All the participants were very familiar with using a mobile phone; all of them have used mobile phone for over 5 years. At the moment 7 of the participants use a wristwatch and five do not.

She showed user 4 paper prototypes as fig. 2., The "c" device is our test device.

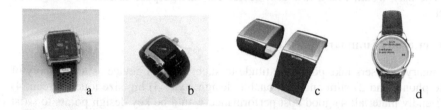

Fig. 2. The paper prototypes, "c" device is our test prototype

In Emilia Koskinen's report, feedback is as follow:

1. the users commented that wrist UI device would be very useful for them and it would bring a solution for many real life situations that they are struggling with when they mobile phone isn't easily within reach, such as sporting, shopping, expo sight-seeing (noisy and crowed), etc.;

2. The users took positive attitude to the wrist UI device. The users who already wear wrist watch think it would add value than wrist watch, and those who have no wrist watch think such idea is attract them to try also;

3. Most important thing in the design is that the display is large enough that all incoming information is easily accessible;

4. Most of users mentioned design should not like traditional wrist watch, and further fore, should be fashionable and non-cheap looking;

5. 7 users out of 12 said that they would prefer touch screen to operate their wrist device. And the users stressed that in this case the UI should be very simple and easy to use, and the screen should be large enough to touch;

6. 5 users told that small buttons would be better and more appropriate to use, but too many buttons is fussy.

2.2 User Study in Beijing

We have also done a user study in Beijing. We interviewed 6 people and show this version wrist device to them and ask users' feedback. Generally speaking, there are 2 issues about device size and screen mostly mentioned by users:

In our study, we used brain-storming and focus group to conduct the user studies. From our study, we obtained these major observations:

1. The users feel that the smaller of the width of the wrist device, the larger enough display, the better the user experience;

2. The users demand a more convenient user interaction method such as touch panel which is viewed more ergonomic than the currently existing keypad plus regular display solution;

3. The users like the flexible and soft feeling of the wrist device which is regarded more comfortable and humane;

4. The users have selected a unique group of functionality for the wrist electronic device which is neither a traditional watch nor a wrist phone, but a flexible and convenient wearable UI accessory between the users and their mobile phones;

5. The user would like a low cost device for this purpose instead of a high end gadget.

2.3 User Study Summary

In summary: 1) users take positive attitude to such wrist UI device as a accessory of mobile phone, and 2) slim and fashionable design style; 3) big size touch screen; 4) skin friendly material; 4) good cost performance would be key design points to wrist UI device as a accessory of mobile phone from the user study reports from Helsinki and Beijing NRC.

3   Low Cost Flexible Touch Panel

Based on the above mentioned user studies, touch UI, as a directional UI, is a friendlier UI for wrist device. As the users requested, this flexible wrist display is used as an accessory of the mobile phone, in which the users can interacting with the mobile phones for incoming phone calls, SMS message, and calendar alarms, as well as other functions without manipulating the mobile phones. And furthermore, the low cost is an important factor for the touch screen.

As one of the key enable for the flexible wrist device UI solution, a low cost flexible resistive touch panel was developed. Currently there are a lot of touch panels which are based on different technologies (such as capacitive, resistive, surface sound wave, infrared, etc.) [5]. However, all of these touch panels need specific driving algorithm and IC to control. A low cost touch panel solution is presented without specific driving algorithm and IC required based on the conventional resistive touch panel.

Specifically, our resistive touch panel consists of three layers, upper layer, isolating layer and bottom layer. Upper layer and bottom layer are transparent conductor layers, respectively cut into several strips. Because of the limitation of input/output ports, each transparent conductor layer is cut into three strips. While the strips of upper layer are perpendicular to strips of bottom layer, nine sections are determined, as illustrated in Fig. 3. Normally, the resistive touch panel needs a specific driving method and IC [6]. But in our solution, the nine sections can act as nine keys on display, be scanned using key scanning method and circuits. So this touch panel can be directly connected with the digital input/output pins of the engine chip, no special driver integrated circuit and algorithms are required. And this kind of touch panel has not requirement of resistance ratio for the transparent conductor. These make cost lower. The layers of the touch panel are manufactured by flexible transparent conductor film, which make the touch panel flexible, can be bent.

Fig. 3. The structure of the low cost flexible touch panel

4 The Second Version of Wrist UI Device

Base on the above user studies reports and technology solution, we designed the second version wrist UI device, as fig. 4. The structure section of display part is shown as fig. 5

Fig. 4. The second version wrist UI design and working sample

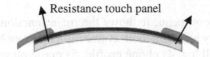

Fig. 5. The structure section of display

On this case, we use the 2 color LCD module from Citizen Display Co.LTD., the active area is 31mmx35mm, and the resolution is 132 x 176-dot LCD.

4.1 User Interface Layout Design

Considering of the size of the screen and low cost principle, we think 3x3 matrix touch button screen UI would be efficient for user. We thought, it could show the icons on the boot menu as many as we expected meanwhile the individual button's size is big enough fitting to user's forefinger.

In Emilia Koskinen's report, we got the pie chart of the features that use most want on such wrist UI device, shown as fig. 6, the figure is the number of people who mentioned he/she want this function.

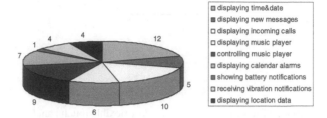

Fig. 6. Features pie chart

Considering this result, we developed the UI spec version. According to the UI spec, we design the "stand by" as following, fig. 7, the stand by screen shows the date and time. On this view, we take use of the multi touch function. As shown fig.7, user could press and hold 2 screen keys to unlock the screen.

Fig. 7. Stand by views

The fig. 8 is the boot menu, it shows the main functions which come from user study result: 1) battery and Bluetooth connection (with mobile phone) status indication; 2) contact; 3) call log; 4) phone profile; 5) music player; 6) SMS; 7) agenda.

Fig. 8. Boot menu view: graphic UI icons and 3x3 matrix touch buttons

Some other sub menus and events views are shown as following fig. 9.

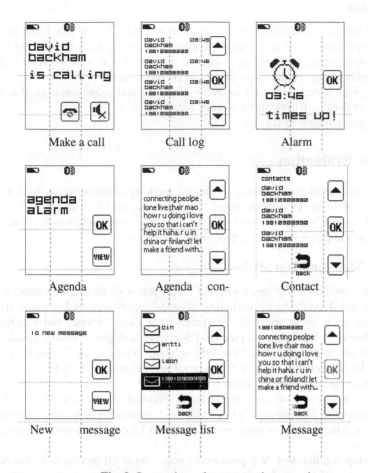

Fig. 9. Some other sub menus and events views

Fig. 10. Display font library

4.2 Fonts Design

Because of the low cost consideration, the resolution (132x176) of this LCD is not high, and some program issue (it's hard to display font dot by dot), we can not take use of current free-copyright fonts, we decide to develop a new font library for this LCD, try to display characters as many as we can on this screen.

We set 6x8 pixel matrix as a unit to every character and punctuator, so that the software engineer is easy to code them as same size blocks.

The font library is shown as fig. 10.

5   Final User Evaluation

After we done the second version wrist UI device working demonstration, we took a user evaluation of it in December 2008. The purpose is to evaluate the cost-performance of some advanced technology and user interaction solution from user's sight, and then, to enlighten the next step of Wrist UI device.

5.1   User Candidates and Test Method

8 user candidates are Nokia Beijing's internal employee. 4 of them are female, 4 of them are male, and 4 come from marketing & sales department and 4 come from R&D department. all of them are in the age range from 26 to 35 years old 4 of them have bachelor degree, 1 has master degree, and 3 have PhD degree. General speaking, the users have been good educated, have OK or good incoming in China, they are young but not old, and sensitive to new things, professional area or daily life.

The test methods include interview and focus group.

First step, we interviewed all users individually, showed the demo to them and let them try by themselves. The purpose is to test the first impression to wrist UI from the users, mainly to get the reflection from user to the wrist UI concept without manufacturing quality issue.

The second step is home test. We gave every user a wrist UI device, a Nokia N82 mobile phone and a Bluetooth headset to use at home and office. In the middle of home test we invite users back to lab and take a focus group user feedback collection.

And the last step is final interview to get the feedback of using, further more, comments.

5.2   User Evaluation Results

General speaking, the feedback in the first interview is positive:

1. "easy to take with", "light weight", "make call leaving mobile phone in bag or pocket" are most often mentioned. 1 user think touch panel is a good operation interface instead of physical key.

2. but users mentioned some issues that they expect: more soft belt, more sensitive touch panel, colorful display with backlight, more game or entertainment applications, one-hand operation, more Bluetooth connection distance, share a charger with mobile phone, longer battery life, and 1 user complain that too many devices to take (mobile phone, wrist UI device and Bluetooth headset)

3. 5 persons hold positive attitude to wrist UI, 2 negative and 1 no feeling

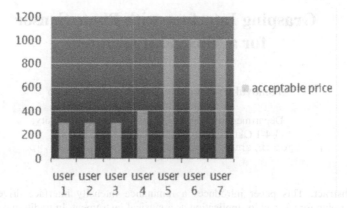

Fig. 11. Acceptable price (RMB) from users

4. The fig. 11 shows the price of such wrist UI device is acceptable to them to buy one.

5. "time & date", "massager", "calendar alarm" are the top3 indispensible items. Media controller; phone call, display mobile phone's information: power, signal strength indicate, call log and phone contact also are mentioned as necessary features

6. "detect physical information: cardiac rhythm and blood pressure", "functions base on RFID", "GPS function" are the top3 "most worthy to have" items, game is also a recommended item.

6 Conclusion

Wrist watch-like device is an instant interaction implement comparing to mobile phone, PDA and laptop PC. People could easily access such portable IT device by flicking their wrist. And since such UI device could be worn around wrist, there is not lot of chances to lose it.

Based on our user studies and developed technology solution, Low cost flexible wrist touch UI solution could potentially provide a novel and ergonomic UI solution between the users and their mobile communication devices.

References

1. Paradiso, J., Hsiao, K., Hu, E.: Interactive Music for Instrumented Dancing Shoes. In: Proc. of the 1999 International Computer Music Conference, October 1999, pp. 453–456 (1999)
2. http://en.wikipedia.org/wiki/Wearable_computer
3. Narayanaswami, C., Raghunath, M.T.: Application design for a smart watch with a high resolution display. In: IEEE 4th International Symposium on Wearable Computers, October 2000, pp. 7–14 (2000)
4. Blaskó, G., Coriand, F., Feiner, S.: Exploring Interaction with a Simulated Wrist-Worn Projection Display. In: IEEE 9th International Symposium on Wearable Computers, October 2005, pp. 2–9 (2005)
5. http://www.elotouch.com/Products/detech2.asp
6. http://www.cypress.com/?docID=2147

Grasping Interface with Photo Sensor
for a Musical Instrument

Tomoyuki Yamaguchi and Shuji Hashimoto

Department of Applied Physics, Waseda University,
3-4-1 Okubo, Shinjuku,Tokyo, 169-8555, Japan
{gucci,shuji}@shalab.phys.waseda.ac.jp

Abstract. This paper introduces a luminance intensity interface driven by grasping forces, and its application as a musical instrument. In traditional musical instruments, the relationship between the action and the generated sound is determined by the physical structures of the instruments. Moreover, the freedom of the musical performances is limited by the structures. We developed a ball-shaped interface with handheld size. A photo diode is embedded in the translucent rubber ball to reacts to the grasping force of the performer. The grasping force is detected as the luminance intensity. The performer can use the ball interface only by grasping directly but also by holding to the environmental light or shading it by hands. The output of the interface is fed to the sound generator and the relationship between the performer's action and the generated sound is determined by the instrumental program to make the universal musical instrument.

Keywords: Grasping interface, Illumination control, Ball-shaped interface, Musical performance.

1 Introduction

Musical instrument is a device to translate human body motion to sound. In traditional musical instruments, the relationship between the performer's action and the generated sound is determined by the physical structures of the instruments. Moreover, the freedom of the musical performances is limited by the structures. Most of digital musical instruments which have interfaces imitating traditional instruments have the same limitations, although they are easy to play for the users who have experienced with traditional musical instruments. On the other hand there have been reported a lot of new music systems that utilize a haptic interface, a video and motion capture devices to create music according to human gesture and body movement [1]-[13].They introduce various types of sensing techniques to detect human motion, and the measured body movements are mapped to music or sound. One example is a magnetic based motion capture system [14]. Especially, a video-to-music system has been emphasized with the aim of investigating how to associate natural gestures with sound/musical features for interactive performance, for example [9][15] [16] [17]. Thus the advanced information technology has proposed a variety of new ways of music creation and performance to make people free from the physical limitations by providing different abilities on music creation.

J.A. Jacko (Ed.): Human-Computer Interaction, Part II, HCII 2009, LNCS 5611, pp. 542–547, 2009.
© Springer-Verlag Berlin Heidelberg 2009

In this paper, we present a new type of grasping interface that detects the user's grasping and handling actions by luminance intensity for musical performance. Our goal is to realize a new interface that has the following features: 1) wireless communication, 2) handheld size, 3) intuitive operation.

Several approaches have been proposed to make handheld interfaces. Beatbug [18] is a bug-shaped musical controller. Although this instrument is similar to the mouse, it does not use wireless communication. GrapMIDI in our previous study [19], [20] is ball-shaped for easy handing and the material is silicon rubber. The ball-shape is one of the popular shapes for the interface of digital sports in the last few years. Sugano et al. [21] proposed "SHOOTBALL". This interface is not considered to apply the musical instrument though the ball is equipped with some sensors to detect the impact caused by users. BouncingStar [22] is also ball-shape. This is based on wireless technology and includes infrared and full-color LEDs and an acceleration sensor. It is well protected against shocks and bounces by using silicon rubber. The color and flushing speed of the LEDs inside the ball change in relation to the acceleration data. Although this device can illuminate, it does not receive the light signal. Moreover, the ball without digital devices is used for a lot of sports such as baseball, volleyball, and basketball etc. We are interested in the feature of the ball-shape that can be applied for a lot of applications. Therefore, we also employ the ball-shape for the interface of the musical instrument.

Fig. 1. Prototype of the proposed grasping interface

2 Structure of the Proposed Interface

Figs. 1 and 2 show a prototype of the proposed interface, the overview of the proposed system, respectively. The main body of the proposed interface consists of a rubber ball, a Bluetooth wireless module, a photo diode, LEDs, a PIC (Peripheral Interface Controller) and a battery (9.0 V). All electronics devices are enclosed in the rubber ball which represents translucent and hollow. In the rubber ball, the Bluetooth wireless module, the photo diode, the PIC, and the battery are deposited on the substrate. This substrate is fixed by urethane sponge inside the rubber ball. Moreover, LEDs are bonded interior the rubber ball. The specification of the rubber ball is as follows: diameter 152 mm, weight 245 g, material PVC (Polyvinyl Chloride). User grasps this interface, and then performs the control of the instrument by the grasping force.

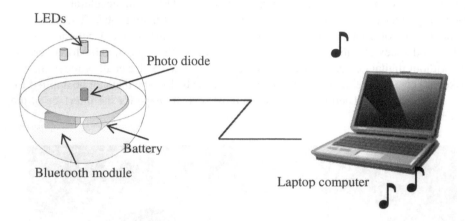

Fig. 2. Overview of the proposed system

3 Operation Procedures

When the rubber ball change its shape due to the grasping force of user, the distance between the photo diode which is embedded in the inside and LEDs varies as shown in Fig. 2. Consequently, the signal which depends on the grasping performance is obtained by the output value from the photo diode (i.e. illumination intensity varies). This output signal is inputted to the laptop computer as digital signal via Bluetooth wireless module.

Usually in the musical performance, the user contacts the musical instruments directly. On the other hand, there are some musical instruments like Theremin that can be performed without physical contact. Although the proposed interface can achieve the performance by detecting the grasping forces via the intensity of illumination, the proposed interface is able to perform using the difference of the illumination from outside of the ball because it is made of translucent rubber-ball. Therefore, it is expected that users can achieve a musical performance like Theremin performance to extend the degree of freedom of the performance style.

Fig. 3 illustrates the different styles of performance using the proposed interface as a musical instrument. Figs. 3.1 to 3.3 show the directly grasping performance. Users are able to perform the music by their hands or fingers actions. Figs. 3.4 and 3.5 show another styles by bouncing and throwing, respectively. In the case of the bounding and the throwing, the intensity of illumination varies according to the changed shape of the interface by the impact of bounding or catching. Figs. 3.6, 3.7, and 3.8 show the cases to use the ambient light such as a desk lamp. Especially, the case shown in Fig. 3.8 is similar to Theremin case where the user performs without contact.

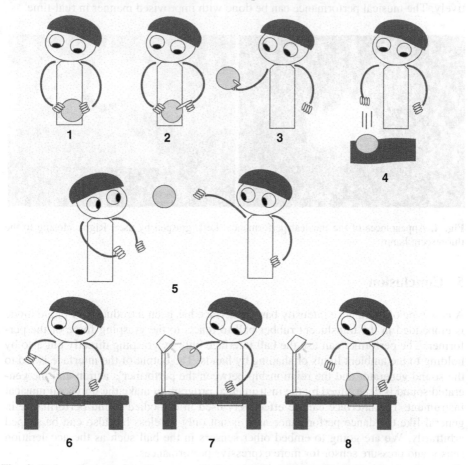

Fig. 3. Styles of musical performance. 1) Grasping by both hands, 2) Pushing by finger, 3) Grasping by one hand, 4) Bounding, 5) Throwing, 6) Lamp comes close to interface, 7) Interface comes close to lamp, 8) Shade the light by hand.

4   Application for Musical Instrument

We examined the musical performance by using the developed grasping interface with a photo sensor. We use the fluorescent lamp as an environmental light, and perform the experimental music in indoor room.

In this experiment, the user controls the musical scale depending on the grasping force and the positional relation between the environment light and the developed interface. Although the relationship between the action and the generated sound is determined by the physical structures of the instrument in the traditional musical instruments, the relationship in the proposed interface as a musical instrument is able to be set freely.

Fig. 4 shows the appearances of the musical performance when the proposed interface is used. Left and Right figures of Fig. 4 correspond to Fig. 3.1 and 3.7, respectively. The musical performance can be done with improvised manner in real-time.

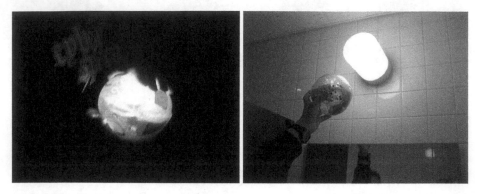

Fig. 4. Appearances of the musical performance. Left: grasped by user, Right: closing to the fluorescent lamp.

5 Conclusion

A new type of luminance intensity based interface has been introduced. A photo diode is embedded in the translucent rubber ball to reacts to the grasping force of the performer. The performer can use the ball interface only by grasping directly but also by holding to the ambient lights or shading by hands. The output of the interface is fed to the sound generator and the relationship between the performer's action and the generated sound is determined by the instrumental program to make the universal musical instrument. The interface can be effectively used in embodied sound performance in general like the dance performance as it is not only wireless but also can be shaped arbitrarily. We are going to embed other sensors in the ball such as the acceleration sensor and pressure sensor for more expressive performances.

Acknowledgments

This work was supported in part by a Waseda University Grant for Special Research Projects(B) No.2008B-094; the "Global Robot Academia," Grant-in-Aid for Global COE Program by the Ministry of Education, Culture, Sports, Science and Technology, Japan; and CREST project "Foundation of technology supporting the creation of digital media contents" of JST.

References

1. Boie, B., Mathews, M.V., Schloss, A.: The radio drum as a synthesozer controller. In: Proc. ICMC, pp. 42–45 (1989)
2. Rubine, D., McAvinney, P.: The videoharp. In: Proc. ICMC, pp. 49–55 (1988)
3. Keane, D., Gross, P.: The midi baton. In: Proc. ICMC, pp. 151–154 (1989)
4. Chabot, X.: Performance with Electronics. In: Proc. ICMC, pp. 65–68 (1989)
5. Cook, P.R.: A Meta-Wind-Instrument Physical Model, and a Meta-Controller for Real Time Performance Control. In: Proc. ICMC, pp. 273–276 (1992)
6. Tanaka, A.: Musical technical issue in using interactive instrument technology with application to the BioMuse. In: Proc. ICMC, pp. 124–126 (1993)
7. Siegel, W., Jacobsen, J.: Composing for the Digital Dance Interface. In: Proc. of ICMC, pp. 276–277 (1999)
8. Paradiso, J.: The Brain Opera Technology: New instruments and gestural sensors for musical interaction and performance. Journal of New Music Research 28, 130–149 (1999)
9. Camurri, A., Hashimoto, S., Ricchetti, M., Ricci, A., Suzuki, K., Trocca, R., Volpe, G.: EyesWeb - Toward Gesture and Affect Recognition in Dance/Music Interactive Systems. Computer Music Journal 24(1), 57–69 (2000)
10. Wanderley, M., Baffer, M. (eds.): Trends in Gestural Control of Music CD-ROM. IR-CAM, Paris (2000)
11. Jordà, S.: Interactive Music Systems for Everyone: Exploring Visual Feedback as a Way for Creating More Intuitive, Efficient and Learnable Instruments. In: Proc. of the Stockholm Music Acoustics Conference (SMAC 2003), pp. 1–3 (2003)
12. Kaltenbrunner, M., Geiger, G., Jordà, S.: Dynamic Patches for Live Musical Performance. In: Proc. of the 4th Conference on New Interfaces for Musical Expression (NIME 2004), pp. 19–22 (2004)
13. Morita, H., Hashimoto, S., et al.: A Computer Music System that Follows a Human Conductor. IEEE Computer 24(7), 44–53 (1991)
14. Paradiso, J., Hsiao, K.Y., Hu, E.: Interactive Music for Instrumented Dancing Shoes. In: Proc. of ICMC, pp. 453–456 (1999)
15. Ng, K.C.: Sensing and Mapping for Interactive Performers. Organized Sound. Organized Sound 7, 191–200 (2002)
16. Nakamura, J., Kaku, T., Hyun, K., Noma, T., Yoshida, S.: Automatic Background Music Generation based on Actors' Mood and Motions. The Journal of Visualization and Computer Animation 5, 247–264 (1994)
17. Lyons, M., Tetsutani, N.: Facing the Music: A Facial Action Controlled Musical Interface. In: Proc. of CHI, pp. 309–310 (2001)
18. Weinberg, G., Aimi, R., Jennings, K.: The Beatbug Network - A Rhythmic System for Interdependent Group Collaboration. In: Proc. of NIME 2002, pp. 106–111 (2002)
19. Sawada, H., Onoe, N., Hashimoto, S.: Sounds in Hands -A Sound Modifier Using Datagloves and Twiddle Interface. In: Proc. ICMC1997, pp. 309–312 (1997)
20. Hashimoto, S., Sawada, H.: A Grasping Device to Sense Hand Gesture for Expressive Sound Generation. J. of New Music Research 34(1), 115–123 (2005)
21. Sugano, Y., Ohtsuji, J., Usui, T., Mochizuki, Y., Okude, N.: SHOOTBALL: The Tangible Ball Sport in Ubiquitous Computing. In: ACM ACE 2006 Demonstration Session (2006)
22. Izuta, O., Nakamura, J., Sato, T., Kodama, S., Koike, H., Fukuchi, K., Shibasaki, K., Mamiya, H.: Digital Sports Using the "Bouncing Star" Rubber Ball Comprising IR and Full-color LEDs and an Acceleration Sensor. In: SIGGRAPH 2008 New Tech. Demo (2008)

Part V

Brain Interfaces

Ensemble SWLDA Classifiers for the P300 Speller

Garett D. Johnson and Dean J. Krusienski

University of North Florida
Jacksonville, FL 32224
dean.krusienski@unf.edu

Abstract. The P300 Speller has proven to be an effective paradigm for brain-computer interface (BCI) communication. Using this paradigm, studies have shown that a simple linear classifier can perform as well as more complex nonlinear classifiers. Several studies have examined methods such as Fisher's Linear Discriminant (FLD), Stepwise Linear Discriminant Analysis (SWLDA), and Support Vector Machines (SVM) for training a linear classifier in this context. Overall, the results indicate marginal performance differences between classifiers trained using these methods. It has been shown that, by using an ensemble of linear classifiers trained on independent data, performance can be further improved because this scheme can better compensate for response variability. The present study evaluates several offline implementations of ensemble SWLDA classifiers for the P300 speller and compares the results to a single SWLDA classifier for seven able-bodied subjects.

1 Introduction

A brain-computer interface (BCI) is a device that uses brain signals to provide a non-muscular communication channel [16], particularly for individuals with severe neuro-muscular disabilities. The P300-event related potential is an evoked response to an external stimulus that is observed in scalp-recorded electroencephalography (EEG). Based on multiple studies in healthy volunteers [7], and initial studies in persons with physical disability [9][12][15], the P300 speller has potential to serve as an effective communication device for persons who have lost or are losing the ability to write and speak.

Many classification techniques have been investigated for the P300 Speller [1][2][6][8][13]. Several of these studies indicate that simple linear classifiers perform as well or better than more complex nonlinear classifiers for discriminating the P300 response. Recent work on ensemble linear classifiers shows the potential for further performance improvements [10]. The study uses an ensemble of linear classifiers trained on independent data using support vector machines (SVM). It has been shown that linear classifiers trained using stepwise linear discriminant analysis (SWLDA) can perform favorably compared to training using SVMs [8]. The objective of the present study is to investigate whether an ensemble of SWLDA classifiers offers any performance advantages over a single SWLDA classifier for the P300 speller by evaluating several offline implementations of ensemble SWLDA classifiers and comparing the results to a single SWLDA classifier for able-bodied subjects.

J.A. Jacko (Ed.): Human-Computer Interaction, Part II, HCII 2009, LNCS 5611, pp. 551–557, 2009.
© Springer-Verlag Berlin Heidelberg 2009

The P300 Speller. The P300 Speller described by Farwell and Donchin [5] presents a 6 x 6 matrix of characters as shown in Figure 1. Each row and each column are intensified; the intensifications are presented in a random sequence. The user focuses attention on one of the 36 cells of the matrix. The sequence of 12 flashes, 6 rows and 6 columns, constitutes an Oddball Paradigm [4] with the row and the column containing the character to be communicated constituting the rare set, and the other 10 intensifications constituting the frequent set. Items that are presented infrequently (the rare set) in a sequential series of randomly presented stimuli will elicit a P300 response if the observer is attending to the stimulus series. Thus, the row and the column containing the target character will elicit a P300 when intensified, because this constitutes a rare event in the context of all other character flashes. With proper P300 feature selection and classification, the attended character of the matrix can be identified and communicated.

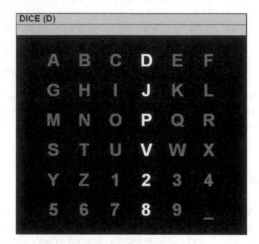

Fig. 1. The 6x6 matrix used in the current study. A row or column intensifies for 100 ms every 175 ms. The letter in parentheses at the top of the window is the current target letter "D." A P300 should be elicited when the fourth column or first row is intensified. After the intensification sequence for a character epoch, the result is classified and online feedback is provided directly below the character to be copied.

2 Data Collection

The data were collected by the Wadsworth Center BCI Laboratory in accordance with New York State Department of Health Institutional Review Board.

Participants. Seven able-bodied people (six men and one woman ages 24-50) were the participants in this study. The participants varied in their previous BCI experience, but all participants had either no or minimal experience using a P300-based BCI system.

Task, Procedure, and Design. The participant sat upright in front of a video monitor and viewed the matrix display. The task was to focus attention on a specified letter of the matrix and silently count the number of times the target character intensified, until a new character was specified for selection. All data was collected in the copy speller mode: words were presented on the top left of the video monitor and the character currently specified for selection was listed in parentheses at the end of the letter string (see Figure 1). Each session consisted of 8-12 experimental runs; each run was composed of a word or series of characters chosen by the investigator. The rows and columns were intensified for 100 ms with 75 ms between intensifications. One character epoch (i.e., one trial) consisted of 15 intensifications of each row and column. Specifically, the classification was performed after every row and column has been intensified 15 times. Each session consisted of 36 character epochs, equivalent to 6480 stimuli (row/column intensifications). A single session, lasting approximately one hour, per participant was collected per day over several weeks.

Data Acquisition. The EEG was recorded using a cap (Electro-Cap International, Inc.) embedded with 64 electrodes distributed over the scalp, based on the International 10 – 20 system [14]. All channels were referenced to the right earlobe, and grounded to the right mastoid. The EEG was bandpass filtered 0.1 – 60 Hz and amplified with a SA Electronics amplifier, digitized at a rate of 240 Hz, and stored. All aspects of data collection and experimental procedure were controlled by the BCI2000 system [11].

3   Response Classification

Responses were collected from the 8 ear-referenced channels shown in Figure 2. The channel selection and data preprocessing are based on results found in [7]. For each of the 8 channels, 800-ms segments of data following each intensification were extracted. The segments were then moving average filtered and decimated to 20Hz. The resulting data segments were concatenated by channel for each intensification, creating a single feature vector for training the classifiers.

Several ensemble classification schemes were investigated, where each linear classifier in the ensemble was trained using Stepwise Linear Discriminant Analysis (SWLDA) [3]. SWLDA is a technique for selecting suitable predictor variables to be included in a multiple regression model that has proven successful for discriminating P300 Speller responses. A combination of forward and backward stepwise regression was implemented. Starting with no initial model terms, the most statistically significant predictor variable having a p-value < 0.1, was added to the model. After each new entry to the model, a backward stepwise regression was performed to remove the least significant variables, having p-values > 0.15. This process was repeated until the model includes a predetermined number of terms, or until no additional terms satisfy the entry/removal criteria. In this case, the final discriminant function was restricted to contain a maximum of 60 features [7].

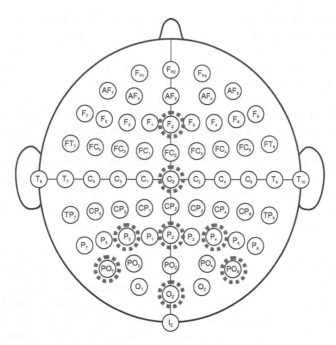

Fig. 2. The electrode montage used in the current study [8]. The 8 electrodes selected for analysis are indicated by the dotted circles.

The ensemble classifiers used for this study consist of N linear classifiers, each independently trained using SWLDA. For each subject, the first session of data was used to train the ensemble classifier. This session's data was divided into N equal, non-overlapping segments, where each segment was used to train an individual classifier in the ensemble. The ensemble classifiers were evaluated using the 4 subsequent sessions for each subject. For a given set of test data, each classifier in the ensemble independently evaluates the inner product of its respective SWLDA weights and the feature vector corresponding to each response, forming N scores, one for each classifier. The resultant score for each intensification response was generated as a weighted sum of the N individual classifier scores. The predicted matrix symbol was determined as the maximum of the sum of resultant scores for the respective row and column intensifications, respectively:

$$predicted\ row = \max_{rows}\left[\sum_{i_{row}}\sum_{n=1}^{N} w_n \cdot x_{i_{row}}\right] \tag{1}$$

$$predicted\ column = \max_{columns}\left[\sum_{i_{column}}\sum_{n=1}^{N} w_n \cdot x_{i_{column}}\right] \tag{2}$$

The following values of N were evaluated: $N = [1, 2, 4, 6, 9, 12]$. In addition, three schemes for weighting the individual classifiers in the ensemble to produce the single classification score were investigated: a simple average of the N classifier scores (AVG), weighting each classifier score by its respective accuracy on the training data (ACC), and using only the maximum output of all classifiers as the resultant ensemble score: i.e., all other classifiers are weighted by zero (MAX). The coefficients for each of these weighting schemes were also determined using the same training set used for training the SWLDA classifiers.

4 Results

The performance, averaged across subjects, of the various combinations of number of classifiers in the ensemble and classifier weighting methods is shown in Figure 3.

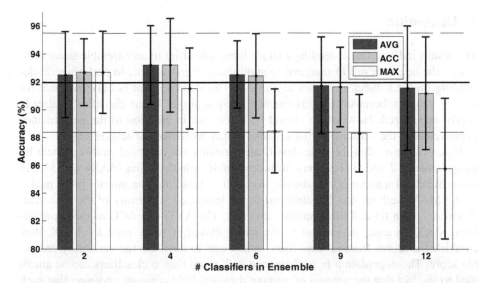

Fig. 3. The figure shows the classification accuracy, averaged across subjects, for the number of classifiers in the ensemble (2, 4, 6, 9, 12) and the three classifier weighting methods (AVG, ACC, MAX). The solid line indicates the average baseline performance using a single SWLDA classifier, with the dotted lines indicating the standard error. The error bars also indicate the standard error for each method.

A balanced one-way ANOVA on the accuracy across subjects after 15 intensifications did not reveal a statistically significant difference between any of the methods. The maximum classification accuracy achieved by an ensemble SWLDA classifier method for each of the seven subjects is compared to the accuracy achieved by a single SWLDA classifier in Table 1.

Table 1. For each subject, the table lists the baseline performance (± standard deviation across test sessions) using a single SWLDA classifier and the best performance achieved by an ensemble SWLDA classifer method. The numbers following the method abreviation indicate the number of classifiers in the ensemble. Note that multiple ensemble classifier methods resulted in the same performance results.

SUBJECT	BASELINE	BEST	METHOD
A	93.75 ± 7.3	94.44 ± 6.42	AVG6, ACC6
B	71.84 ± 6.27	81.28 ± 10.32	ACC4
C	93.75 ± 5.73	95.14 ± 4.74	AVG2,4,6; ACC2,4,6
D	98.61 ± 1.6	98.61 ± 1.6	AVG2, ACC2, MAX2
E	97.92 ± 2.66	99.3 ± 1.39	MAX2
F	89.83 ± 3.77	89.91 ± 5.75	MAX4
G	97.92 ± 2.66	97.92 ± 2.66	*All except* MAX4,6,9,12

5   Discussion

The results indicate that extending a single linear classifier to an ensemble linear classifier scheme can result in marginal to significant improvements in performance, depending on the subject as shown in Table 1. The improvement is only marginal for several subjects because the performance using a single linear classifier is already nearly maximized. However, it should be noted that in addition to the performance improvements, the variance across sessions is also decreased for several subjects.

Figure 3 shows that the best classification results are achieved in this context by using between 2 and 6 classifiers in the ensemble, which all but MAX4 and MAX6 perform better on average than the single classifier baseline. The inferior performance of the MAX methods can be attributed to the increased variability of the individual classifiers when trained using smaller data sets. The AVG and ACC methods outperform MAX because, in contrast to the single classifier score used for MAX, they combine the scores from all classifiers, which acts to decrease the variability ensemble score. The degradation in performance with more than 6 classifiers can be attributed to the fact that the amount of training data was held constant, meaning that each individual classifier is trained on proportionally less data as the number of classifiers increases. Because P300 classification often remains stable over time [7], additional training data can be used to create a larger ensemble that can potentially better account for response variance.

Based on related P300 Speller classification studies [8][10], it is presumed that similar results would be attained using classifier training methods other than SWLDA. When employing a single classifier, it is straightforward to construct an ensemble in this fashion to potentially improve performance. By using the AVG or ACC method, an equivalent single classifier can be realized via the linear combination of the ensemble classifiers using the respective classifier weights. This is not possible with the MAX method because the computation of the maximum classifier output does not allow for the individual classifiers to be combined linearly.

References

1. Blankertz, B., Müller, K.R., Krusienski, D.J., Schalk, G., Wolpaw, J.R., Schlögl, A., Pfurtscheller, G., Millán, J.R., Schröder, M., Birbaumer, N.: The BCI Competition III: Validating Alternative Approaches to Actual BCI Problems. IEEE Transactions on Neural Systems and Rehabilitation Engineering 14(2) (2006)
2. Bostanov, V.: BCI competition 2003-data sets Ib and IIb: feature extraction from event-related brain potentials with the continuous wavelet transform and the t-value scalogram. IEEE Trans. Biomed. Eng. 51, 1057–1061 (2004)
3. Draper, N., Smith, H.: Applied Regression Analysis, 2nd edn., pp. 307–312. John Wiley and Sons, Chichester (1981)
4. Fabiani, M., Gratton, G., Karis, D., Donchin, E.: Definition, identification, and reliability of measurement of the P300 component of the event-related brain potential. Advances in Psychophysiology 2, 1–78 (1987)
5. Farwell, L.A., Donchin, E.: Talking off the top of your head: Toward a mental prosthesis utilizing event-related brain potentials. Electroenceph. clin. Neurophysiol. 70, 510–523 (1988)
6. Kaper, M., Meinicke, P., Grossekathoefer, U., Lingner, T., Ritter, H.: BCI competition 2003-data set IIb: Support vector machines for the P300 speller paradigm. IEEE Trans. Biomed. Eng. 51, 1073–1076 (2004)
7. Krusienski, D.J., Sellers, E.W., McFarland, D.J., Vaughan, T.V., Wolpaw, J.R.: Toward Enhanced P300 Speller Performance. Journal of Neuroscience Methods 167, 15–21 (2008)
8. Krusienski, D.J., Sellers, E.W., Cabestaing, F., Bayoudh, S., McFarland, D.J., Vaughan, T.M., Wolpaw, J.R.: A Comparison of Classification Techniques for the P300 Speller. Journal of Neural Engineering 3, 299–305 (2006)
9. Nijboer, F., Sellers, E.W., Mellinger, J., Jordan, M.A., Matuz, T., Furdea, A., Mochty, U., Krusienski, D.J., Vaughan, T.M., Wolpaw, J.R., Kubler, A.: A Brain-Computer Interface (BCI) for People with Amyotrophic Lateral Sclerosis (ALS). Clinical Neurophysiology 119, 1909–1916 (2008)
10. Rakotomamonjy, A., Guigue, V.: BCI Competition III: Dataset II – Ensemble of SVMs for BCI P300 Speller. IEEE Trans. Biomedical Engineering 55(3), 1147–1154 (2008)
11. Schalk, G., McFarland, D.J., Hinterberger, T., Birbaumer, N., Wolpaw, J.R.: BCI2000: A general-purpose brain-computer interface (BCI) system. IEEE. Trans. Biomed. Eng. 2004 51, 1034–1043 (2004)
12. Sellers, E.W., Donchin, E.: A P300-based brain-computer interface: Initial tests by ALS patients. Clin. Neurophysiol. 117, 538–548 (2006)
13. Serby, H., Yom-Tov, E., Inbar, G.F.: An improved P300-based brain-computer interface. IEEE Trans. Neural Syst. Rehabil. Eng. 13, 89–98 (2005)
14. Sharbrough, F., Chatrian, C.E., Lesser, R.P., Luders, H., Nuwer, M., Picton, T.W.: American Electroencephalographic Society guidelines for standard electrode position nomenclature. J. Clin. Neurophysiol. 8, 200–202 (1991)
15. Vaughan, T.M., McFarland, D.J., Schalk, G., Sarnacki, W.A., Krusienski, D.J., Sellers, E.W., Wolpaw, J.R.: The Wadsworth BCI Research and Development Program: At Home with BCI. IEEE Transactions on Neural Systems and Rehabilitation Engineering 14(2) (2006)
16. Wolpaw, J.R., Birbaumer, N., McFarland, D.J., Pfurtscheller, G., Vaughan, T.M.: Brain-computer interfaces for communication and control. Clin. Neurophysiol. 113, 767–791 (2002)

The I of BCIs:
Next Generation Interfaces for Brain–Computer Interface Systems That Adapt to Individual Users

Brendan Allison[*]

Institute for Automation, University of Bremen, Otto Hahn Allee NW1,
28359, Bremen, Germany

Abstract. Brain-computer interfaces (BCIs) have advanced rapidly in the last several years, and can now provide many useful command and control features to a wide variety of users--if an expert is available to find, assemble, setup, configure, and maintain the BCI. Developing BCI systems that are practical for non-experts remains a major challenge, and is the principal focus of the EU BRAIN project and other work. This paper describes five challenges in BCI interface development, and how they might be addressed with a hypothetical easy BCI system called EZBCI. EZBCI requires a new interface that is natural, intuitive, and easy to configure without expert help. Finally, two true scenarios with severely disabled users highlight the impact that EZBCI would have on users' lives.

Keywords: Brain-computer interface; Brain-machine interface; BCI; BMI; expertise; nonexpert; interface; adaptive; reliability; usability; flexibility; assistive technology; smart homes; realworld; EZBCI.

1 Recent Progress and Emerging Challenges

The principal goal of brain–computer interface (BCI) research has been providing communication to persons with motor disabilities so severe that they prevent communication through other means. Hence, the main focus of many research groups has been addressing fundamental challenges, such as getting a BCI to work at all [1], [2], [3], getting it to work outside of the laboratory [4], [5], [6], or getting it to work with patients [7], [8]. Indeed, the very theme of the second international BCI conference in 2002 was "Moving Beyond Demonstrations."

Helping patients should and will remain very important. Due to the success of BCI research so far, however, the most helpful research directions are changing. It is no longer so impressive to demonstrate that a simple BCI might allow one specific function, most of the time, for some patients, as long as a PhD student from the local BCI research lab can find, assemble, customize, and maintain the BCI system. The goal of proving that a BCI can provide a function to a user has been attained; the next challenge is getting any BCI to reliably provide any function for any user.

---

[*] The author is now with a new institution: the Laboratory of Brain-Computer Interfaces, Institute for Knowledge Discovery, Graz University of Technology, Krenngasse 37, 8010 Graz, Austria. He can be reached at allison@tugraz.at

J.A. Jacko (Ed.): Human-Computer Interaction, Part II, HCII 2009, LNCS 5611, pp. 558–568, 2009.
© Springer-Verlag Berlin Heidelberg 2009

The reader is assumed to have a basic familiarity with BCIs; reviews can be found elsewhere [9], [10], [11]. Recent developments include:

- Different BCI approaches have been further investigated with severely disabled users in home and other real world environments [12], [13], [14], [15], [16].
- Crucial parameters have been identified and explored [17], [18], [19], [20], [21], [22], [23], [24].
- New BCI applications have been validated, such as control of a robotic arm [24], [25], neural prosthesis [6], [26], mobile humanoid robot [27], Smart home [28], and virtual [15] or real [29], [30] wheelchair;
- BCIs have proven useful as communication systems for broader user groups than previously recognized [14], [31], [32].
- BCI have been explored as tools for rehabilitation of stroke, psychopathy, autism, addiction, and attentional disorders [9], [33], [34], [35], [36], [37].
- New software tools within the BCI2000 framework have greatly reduced the time and inconvenience of developing and using new BCI applications [38].
- The promising possibility of combining multiple BCIs has begun to be addressed [9], [31], [32], [39], [40].
- More realistic, immersive interfaces have been used with different BCI systems [3], [15], [41]. Leeb and colleagues compared an immersive VR environment to a conventional, mundane setting and found that the VR environment yielded reduced training time, fewer errors, and more motivated and happy subjects.

Despite this piecemeal progress, BCI systems are still predominantly inflexible, difficult to use, unreliable, and unavailable to nearly all people who need them. They are seen primarily as research tools with limited practical function that might only be useful to some people with very severe physical disabilities. BCIs are typically accessible only via research laboratories that are seeking research subjects, and expert assistance is necessary for initial configuration, daily operation, maintenance, and updating. BCIs would be far more practical to much larger populations if they could easily identify and adapt to the needs, desires, and abilities of each individual user and operate effectively each day with little or no oversight. That is, what users need most are not additional laboratory studies or offline simulations, but working BCIs--ideally suited to each user--that operate reliably in home environments with minimal support.

Figure 1 below highlights the challenges and potential solutions inherent in developing a BCI system that is practical for nonexperts. The term "EZBCI" is hereby introduced to describe this hypothetical easy BCI system. Panel A shows an individual who wishes to interact with the environment. The person can receive information from the environment, but is not able to reciprocate or control the environment. Assistive Technology (AT) tries to bridge this ability gap by restoring the ability to send messages or commands. Panel B shows how modern BCI systems bridge this gap. The user's EEG activity is translated into signals that might control a monitor or device. These systems only exist in laboratories, require expert assistance, and allow control of only individual devices. Panel C shows how EZBCI will address the need for a practical BCI that can control many applications.

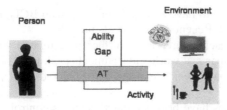

a) The ability gap that AT tries to address.

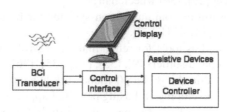

b) Emerging BCI solution in laboratories.

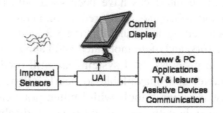

c) Desired solution in an EZBCI system.

Fig. 1. Panel A shows the ability gap facing many users that assistive technology addresses. Panels B and C show how conventional BCIs and a hypothetical EZBCI system bridge this gap. The acronym "UAI" refers to the Universal Application Interface, discussed in the text. This figure is adapted from [42], which itself adapted a figure from [43].

Figure 2 below presents a more detailed representation of how EZBCI must address four accessibility gaps in modern BCIs. The panel on the left presents the current accessibility of BCI components. Four accessibility gaps are represented by the image of the scientist wearing the ubiquitous white lab coat. These reflect tasks that currently require expert assistance. The leftmost gap reflects the need for a trained caretaker to prepare the subject for each session of BCI use. An expert must also identify and purchase the correct equipment. The second accessibility gap is signal processing: an expert is needed to configure relevant parameters. The third accessibility gap is applications: even with expert help, users can only use the application developed by a local research group. The fourth accessibility gap, in operating protocol, has two components. First, users do not have any choice of mental strategy, and second, expert help is required to provide even limited customization of stimulus parameters. The third and fourth gaps have question marks to reflect that, even with expert help, very few applications and operating protocols are available.

The panel on the right depicts accessibility after EZBCI is developed. The first accessibility gap requires a much easier setup process. The necessary equipment must be easy to purchase from established European manufacturers without expert help. Instead, an untrained caretaker could apply the cap to users with severe disabilities, and other users could setup the system without help. The second accessibility gap requires providing software that identifies and implements the correct parameters and enables improved performance even in noisy or unstable settings. The third and fourth accessibility gaps are addressed through the Intuitive Universal Interface (IUI) discussed in more detail below.

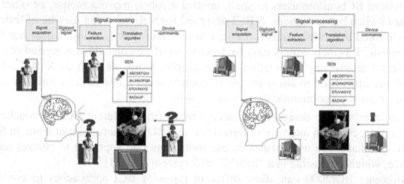

Fig. 2. BCIs today and tomorrow. The left panel shows the four accessibility gaps that currently impair BCI accessibility, and the right panel shows how this would change with the development of a practical BCI system such as the hypothetical EZBCI.

Two recently funded projects within the EU aim to improve BCIs by addressing these challenges. The TOBI (Tools for Brain-Computer Interaction) project, developed by Jose Millán and colleagues across twelve institutions, has identified four application areas where BCI assistive technology can make a real impact for people with motor disabilities:

- Communication & Control
- Motor Substitution
- Entertainment
- Motor Recovery

The BRAIN (BCIs with Rapid Automated Interfaces for Nonexperts) project, developed by the author and colleagues in seven institutions, has three RTD goals:

- New sensor systems to detect brain activity without requiring electrode gel
- Automated software to determine the best signal processing parameters and BCI approach for each user
- An Intuitive User Interface (IUI) that allows users to easily switch between applications

BRAIN and TOBI are only two examples of projects aimed at developing better interfaces or other components for BCIs. The text, ideas, and figures used here are meant to present major challenges in BCI research rather than issues specific to any grant proposal or research team. The author and colleagues hope that this article and associated discussion provide new contacts, ideas, and collaborations.

While improved sensors, signal processing tools, and rehabilitation are important, this article focuses primarily on issues relating to the interface component of BCIs. There has been relatively little attention to HCI issues within BCI research, especially during early BCI research efforts, since attention was focused on simply getting a BCI to work. The work that has been done has focused on issues like the role of feedback or the timing of stimulus presentation [3], [44], [45]. Important questions (and hence challenges) within BCI interface development remain:

1. How can a single integrated BCI system allow users to control a variety of applications and smoothly switch between them?

Modern BCIs allow users to spell, control a robot, move a mouse, or other tasks, but not switch between them. A BCI designed for web browsing may be of little value to a disabled user who wants to move a wheelchair, pour a drink, adjust her bed, or play music. It is increasingly easy to develop interfaces that allow a myriad of devices to control almost any application. For example, protocols such as X10, Zigbee, or UPnP are often used to allow people to control smart home devices through conventional or assistive communication systems [46].

2. Can interfaces be designed that accept input from different BCI approaches? For example, could an interface designed for an ERD BCI accept input from an SSVEP BCI? What if the user wishes to use more than one approach to control an interface, which is possible in a "hybrid" BCI system [9], [31]?

Although BCI2000 can allow different types of BCI approaches to control the same application, this opportunity has been mostly ignored. Only one study has even compared different BCI approaches within users, and this work used different interfaces [10]. A Universal Remote Control (URC) system or Windows driver need not even know what type of BCI produces an input signal.

3. How can BCI interfaces adapt to the needs, abilities, desires, and usage histories of individual users?

Ideally, BCIs should be adjustable via three means. First, BCIs should try to learn what's best for each user and adapt accordingly. Second, BCIs should allow users to manually configure the system as desired. Third, it should also be easy for friends, family, carers, or other third persons to make adjustments based on user requests.

4. How can BCIs incorporate HCI concepts designed around low bandwidth input?

One article proposed combining a BCI with DASHER [47], but did not do so. The Hex-O-Spell BCI system developed by the Berlin group [48] is an excellent but rare example of a novel and straightforward interface developed specifically for BCIs. Automated error correction is another technology that has only begun to be explored with BCIs [49], [50]. No BCIs work with the T9 text entry system, advanced word or sentence completion (such as in the WordsPlus software system developed with eye trackers), or other potentially helpful HCI innovations. Again, some of this functionality is possible in BCI2000, but has not been explored.

5. How can BCIs best exploit the graphical user interface (GUI) concept?

Identifying and launching applications or sending specific commands should seem easy and natural. Interfaces should be easy to customize so users can attain goals easily and have the information they need without feeling overwhelmed.

2 Building an Intuitive Universal Interface (IUI) for BCIs

Many companies and research groups have spent tremendous resources over many years to develop conventional operating environments that are straightforward, intuitive, flexible, and easy to learn, use, and customize without expert help. If the five questions above were rephrased around a Windows operating system, considerable progress would be apparent. Users can very easily control different applications and switch between them. Control is possible via a keyboard, mouse, trackball, voice control, or various assistive devices such as an EMG, eye tracker, or sip-and-puff switch. Users can manually customize various parameters and/or allow Windows to adapt to common actions, such as by placing commonly selected applications in the Start menu. Windows offers support for persons using low bandwidth interfaces in various ways. The GUI has come a very long way.

Similar progress is needed within BCI research before BCIs can mature as a practical means of communication--for disabled or healthy users. Figure 3 below presents the IUI, which aims to address these five challenges within BCI systems.

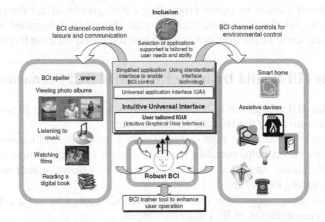

Fig. 3. The Intuitive Universal Interface (IUI) includes a front end called the Intuitive Graphical User Interface (IGUI) and back end called a Universal Application Interface (UAI). Dr. Gaye Lighthody from the University of Ulster developed this figure for the BRAIN grant.

The front end of the IUI is the Intuitive Graphical User Interface (IGUI). The IGUI will include one consistent, familiar display that allows users to perform certain tasks or switch applications. The IGUI will use a flexible architecture and display that adapts itself to each user's abilities, desires, and needs, and/or can be modified by the user. Some users may dislike cluttered displays, while others might prefer displays with information such as the ambient temperature, battery power of medical or other devices, any noisy or bad electrodes, or activity present on security cameras. The IGUI will adapt to each user's abilities by increasing image sizes for those with poor vision, prompting users with memory deficits, providing a BCI trainer if desired, etc.

Addressing these varied user needs requires allowing customization of the applications needed, the sequence of the operations used for control, and the interface. The IUI should support a plug and play type interface and methodology that will support such customization with limited effort and no outside support.

The back end is called the Universal Application Interface (UAI) and will translate the user's requests into meaningful commands to different applications. The UAI will use established wired and wireless interface technologies. By using these well developed standards, the IUI will open up a world of new devices without extensive new development. The IUI must minimize work for the user, who will typically be unfamiliar with BCIs and may present other challenges such as mild dementia, poor computer literacy, poor vision, or limited patience.

The IUI should recognize and integrate relevant context. The IUI, like any good interface, should not allow users to open a window or door that is already open, turn on a light that is already on, move a wheelchair into a wall, launch a movie that is already playing, or navigate toward a clearly erroneous URL. This context awareness requires bidirectional communication between the UAI and other applications.

Unlike prior BCIs, the IUI will accept input from different BCI approaches. A user who has poor SSVEP activity, finds flickering lights annoying, could instead use ERD activity for control. Users could also combine different BCI approaches to improve usability, bandwidth, or accuracy [9].

The IUI will not exist in isolation. On the contrary, progress in related challenges such as improved sensors or signal processing could greatly affect the options available within the IUI. Further, these technologies should be integrated with the IUI, tested across different target user groups, and revised based on their feedback.

3 How the IUI Would Improve Realworld BCI Scenarios

How would the IUI change the BCI usage experience from the user perspective? Consider the status quo along the five challenges above:
1. An expert is required to get even one application working. Adding another application requires expert help, possibly from a different research group. To switch between applications, an expert or trained user must change numerous parameters and re-launch the BCI system.
2. No BCI can accept input from more than one BCI approach, nor a combination of them, nor a combination of BCI and other input.
3. Customizing a BCI interface also requires an expert.
4. BCIs do not use helpful technologies common in other low bandwidth interfaces.
5. Most BCIs have a simple, clunky interface that requires instruction.

Below are two true stories of recent efforts to provide BCIs for patients, followed by hypothetical improvements that could result from EZBCI. Again, emphasis is placed on interface improvements:

Dr. A is in his early 50s and runs a neuroscience research lab. He has late stage ALS, with some remaining gaze control. Experts at the Wolpaw lab developed a P300 speller that the patient has used for about 2-6 hours per day for over two years. The Wolpaw lab gave him the necessary hardware and a license to BCI2000 software. The Wolpaw lab identified the processing parameters, and provides periodic support. Dr. A requires a caretaker to assist with daily electrode cap preparation and cleaning. Although Dr. A can use an eye tracking system, he prefers the BCI because it is easier to use, faster, and produces less fatigue [14].

One day, Dr. A informed the Wolpaw lab that his system was no longer working. An expert was sent to fix the problem. It turned out that Dr. A had unintentionally sent a combination of key strokes that caused the display to shift beyond the range of the monitor. Hence, whenever the system was launched, no display was visible. The expert repaired this problem and the system worked again.

While this is a modern BCI success story, there is much room for improvement. With EZBCI, assistance would still be needed with cap preparation due to the patient's motor disabilities. However, this process would be much faster and easier, and feasible for an untrained career. Software would automatically find the best parameters. The IUI would not allow unwanted functions such as repositioning the display. Dr. A would be able to easily customize his speller, such as by changing the number of items in the display (the BCI's vocabulary), speed or intensity of flashes, or size of the letters. He could incorporate word or sentence completion. He might add new selections to the speller matrix such as commonly spelled phrases, and/or the system could automatically develop and periodically propose such suggestions.

Most importantly, Dr. A. would also be able to control other applications, either with a similar interface or a different IGUI that he could customize. For example, if Dr. A liked the P300 speller, he could have a similar system in which the classic "Donchin matrix" contained not letters or words but commands to a smart home device, wheelchair, or movie player. Or, he could choose a different type of display to control these devices, perhaps with P300 and/or other activity. Some of this functionality is currently available within BCI2000, but only via expert help.

Mr. B was a stockbroker living near Atlanta, Georgia. In March 2005, he was mostly locked in due to ALS and had moderate gaze control. He was very active via a gaze based spelling system called WordsPlus, and traveled to the US Congress and successfully pushed for Medicare changes to aid severely disabled patients. In spring 2005, his gaze control rapidly declined. He contacted Prof. Melody Moore through friends in the local assistive technology community. Prof. Moore and colleagues (including the author) developed an SSVEP BCI system that allowed Mr. B to send about 4 bits per minute via a 1D cursor movement system. This system was used for testing within the lab and could not allow meaningful communication. Work with Mr. B halted when the author left the lab.

The IUI would have allowed Mr. B to perform useful tasks with his BCI, instead of only validating the possibility of future functionality. There were no other fundamental challenges to overcome with Mr. B. He could generate a signal and effect control, but no tools existed to translate those control signals into meaningful outputs. BCI users who can move a cursor in one dimension can select letters or other items from a menu [14], control bed position or make other medical requests [52], control a wheelchair [30], or perform other tasks.

In conclusion, the BCI research community has attained some important early goals, such demonstrating proof of concept and validating BCIs as practical communication tools for patients who need them. Emerging challenges include reducing the demand for expert assistance and improving customizability and flexibility. The proposed suite of next generation BCI interface and application control tools, called IUI, would allow nonexpert users to control a variety of applications via a friendly, intuitive, and adaptive display. The IUI could greatly expand the usability and flexibility of any existing BCI system and thereby help develop BCIs into practical communication and control systems. These interface developments, combined with improvements to other components of BCIs, could move the EZBCI system from a hypothetical proposal to an available, complete communication system for severely disabled users and much broader groups.

Acknowledgments. Some material herein presents ideas from the BRAIN grant (EU FP7 224156). The author was lead author and Program Manager for BRAIN. The Project Coordinator of BRAIN is Prof. Axel Graeser, and the BRAIN grant was developed under the Marie Curie project BRAINROBOT. The author wishes to thank Sara Carro-Martinez and Drs. Gaye Lightbody, Paul McCullagh, Maurice Mulvenna, Gary Garcia, Bernhard Graimann, and for their help with the BRAIN proposal, Jin Jing for assistance with formatting, and Dr. Gerwin Schalk for details of challenges with Dr. A.

References

1. Farwell, L.A., Donchin, E.: Talking off the top of your head - toward a mental prosthesis utilizing event-related brain potentials. Electroencephalogr. Clin. Neurophysiol. 70, 510–523 (1988)
2. Wolpaw, J.R., McFarland, D.J., Neat, G.W., Forneris, C.A.: An EEG-based brain-computer interface for cursor control. Electroencephalogr. Clin. Neurophysiol. 78, 252–259 (1991)
3. Pfurtscheller, G., Brunner, C., Leeb, R., Scherer, R., Müller-Putz, G., Neuper, C.: Graz brain-computer interface. In: Graimann, B., Allison, B.Z., Pfurtscheller, G. (eds.) Brain-Computer Interfaces: Non-invasive and Invasive Approaches. Springer, Heidelberg (in press)
4. Allison, B.Z., Moore, M.M.: Field validation of P3 BCI under adverse field conditions. In: Society for Neuroscience Conference, vol. Program No. 263.9, San Diego (2004)
5. Lalor, E.C., Kelly, S.P., Finucane, C., Burke, R., Smith, R., Reilly, R.B., McDarby, G.: Steady-state VEP-based brain-computer interface control in an immersive 3D gaming environment. EURASIP J. Appl. Signal Process, 3156–3164 (2005)
6. Pfurtscheller, G., Müller-Putz, G., Scherer, R., Neuper, C.: Rehabilitation with brain-computer interface systems. IEEE Computer Magazine 41, 58–65 (2008)
7. Birbaumer, N., Ghanayim, N., Hinterberger, T., Iversen, I., Kotchoubey, B., Kubler, A., Perelmouter, J., Taub, E., Flor, H.: A spelling device for the paralysed. Nature 398, 297–298 (1999)
8. Pfurtscheller, G., Müller, G.R., Pfurtscheller, J., Gerner, H.J., Rupp, R.: 'Thought'–control of functional electrical stimulation to restore hand grasp in a patient with tetraplegia. Neurosci. Lett. 351, 33–36 (2003)
9. Allison, B.Z., Wolpaw, E.W., Wolpaw, J.R.: Brain-computer interface systems: progress and prospects. Expert Rev. Med. Devices 4, 463–474 (2007)
10. Birbaumer, N., Cohen, L.G.: Brain-computer interfaces: communication and restoration of movement in paralysis. J. Physiol. 579, 621–636 (2007)
11. Graimann, B., Allison, B.Z., Pfurtscheller, G.: An introduction to brain – computer interface (BCI) systems. In: Graimann, B., Allison, B.Z., Pfurtscheller, G. (eds.) Brain-Computer Interfaces: Non-invasive and Invasive Approaches. Springer, Heidelberg (in press)
12. Kübler, A., Nijboer, F., Mellinger, J., Vaughan, T.M., Pawelzik, H., Schalk, G., McFarland, D.J., Birbaumer, N., Wolpaw, J.R.: Patients with ALS can use sensorimotor rhythms to operate a brain-computer interface. Neurology 64, 1775–1777 (2005)
13. Kübler, A., Mushahwar, V.K., Hochberg, L.R., Donoghue, J.P.: BCI Meeting 2005 - Workshop on clinical issues and applications. IEEE Trans. Neural. Syst. Rehabil. Eng. 14, 131–134 (2006)
14. Vaughan, T.M., McFarland, D.J., Schalk, G., Sarnacki, W.A., Krusienski, D.J., Sellers, E.W., Wolpaw, J.R.: The Wadsworth BCI research and development program: At home with BCI. IEEE Trans. Neural. Syst. Rehabil. Eng. 14, 229–233 (2006)
15. Leeb, R., Friedman, D., Müller-Putz, G.R., Scherer, R., Slater, M., Pfurtscheller, G.: Self-Paced (Asynchronous) BCI Control of a Wheelchair in Virtual Environments: A Case Study with a Tetraplegic. Comput. Intell. Neurosci. 79642 (2007)

16. Nijboer, F., Sellers, E.W., Mellinger, J., Jordan, M.A., Matuz, T., Furdea, A., Halder, S., Mochty, U., Krusienski, D.J., Vaughan, T.M., Wolpaw, J.R., Birbaumer, N., Kubler, A.: A P300-based brain-computer interface for people with amyotrophic lateral sclerosis. Clin. Neurophysiol. 119, 1909–1916 (2008)
17. Blankertz, B., Müller, K.R., Krusienski, D.J., Schalk, G., Wolpaw, J.R., Schlogl, A., Pfurtscheller, G., Millán, J.D.R., Schroder, M., Birbaumer, N.: The BCI competition III: Validating alternative approaches to actual BCI problems. IEEE Trans. Neural. Syst. Rehabil. Eng. 14, 153–159 (2006)
18. Blankertz, B., Losch, F., Krauledat, M., Dornhege, G., Curio, G., Müller, K.R.: The Berlin brain-computer interface: accurate performance from first-session in BCI-naive subjects. IEEE Trans. Biomed. Eng. 55, 2452–2462 (2008)
19. Allison, B.Z., Pineda, J.A.: Effects of SOA and flash pattern manipulations on ERPs, performance, and preference: Implications for a BCI system. Int. J. Psychophysiol. 59, 127–140 (2006)
20. Durka, P.J.: Time-frequency microstructure and statistical significance of ERD and ERS. Prog. Brain Res. 159, 121–133 (2006)
21. Krusienski, D.J., Sellers, E.W., McFarland, D.J., Vaughan, T.M., Wolpaw, J.R.: Toward enhanced P300 speller performance. J. Neurosci. Meth. 167, 15–21 (2008)
22. Müller, K.R., Tangermann, M., Dornhege, G., Krauledat, M., Curio, G., Blankertz, B.: Machine learning for real-time single-trial EEG-analysis: From brain-computer interfacing to mental state monitoring. J. Neurosci. Meth. 167, 82–90 (2008)
23. Pfurtscheller, G., Solis-Escalante, T.: Could the beta rebound in the EEG be suitable to realize a brain switch? Clin. Neurophysiol. 120, 24–29 (2009)
24. Sellers, E.W., McFarland, D.J., Vaughan, T., Wolpaw, J.: The Wadsworth non-invasive brain-computer interface research program. In: Graimann, B., Allison, B.Z., Pfurtscheller, G. (eds.) Brain-Computer Interfaces: Non-invasive and Invasive Approaches. Springer, Heidelberg (in press)
25. Vora, J.Y., Allison, B.Z., Moore, M.M.: A P3 brain computer interface for robot arm control. Society for Neuroscience Abstract 30, Program No. 421.19 (2004)
26. Müller-Putz, G.R., Pfurtscheller, G.: Control of an electrical prosthesis with an SSVEP-based BCI. IEEE Trans. Biomed. Eng. 55, 361–364 (2008)
27. Bell, C.J., Shenoy, P., Chalodhorn, R., Rao, R.P.N.: Control of a humanoid robot by a non-invasive brain-computer interface in humans. J. Neural. Eng. 5, 214–220 (2008)
28. Guger, C., Holzner, C., Groenegress, C., Edlinger, G., Slater, M.: Control of a smart home with a brain - computer interface. In: Fourth International BCI Workshop and Training Course, pp. 339–343. Verlag der Technischen Universitaet Graz, Graz (2008)
29. Cincotti, F., Mattia, D., Aloise, F., Bufalari, S., Schalk, G., Oriolo, G., Cherubini, A., Marciani, M.G., Babiloni, F.: Non-invasive brain-computer interface system: towards its application as assistive technology. Brain Res. Bull. 75, 796–803 (2008)
30. Galán, F., Nuttin, M., Lew, E., Ferrez, P.W., Vanacker, G., Philips, J., Millán, J.D.R.: A brain-actuated wheelchair: Asynchronous and non-invasive brain-computer interfaces for continuous control of robots. Clin. Neurophysiol. 119, 2159–2169 (2008)
31. Allison, B.Z., Graimann, B.: Why use a BCI if you're healthy? IEEE Intell. Syst. 23, 76–78 (2008)
32. Allison, B.Z.: Towards ubiquitous BCIs. In: Graimann, B., Allison, B.Z., Pfurtscheller, G. (eds.) Brain-Computer Interfaces: Non-invasive and Invasive Approaches. Springer, Heidelberg (in press)
33. Scherer, R., Mohapp, A., Grieshofer, P., Pfurtscheller, G., Neuper, C.: Sensorimotor EEG patterns during motor imagery in hemiparetic stroke patients. International Journal of Bioelectromagnetism 9, 155–162 (2007)

34. Daly, J.J., Wolpaw, J.R.: Brain-computer interfaces in neurological rehabilitation. Lancet. Neurology 7, 1032–1043 (2008)
35. Pineda, J.A., Brang, D., Hecht, E., Edwards, L., Carey, S., Bacon, M., Futagaki, C., Suk, D., Tom, J., Birnbaum, C., Rork, A.: Positive behavioral and electrophysiological changes following neurofeedback training in children with autism. Research in Autism Spectrum Disorders 2, 557–581 (2008)
36. Kouijzer, M.E.J., de Moor, J.M.H., Gerrits, B.J.L., et al.: Long-term effects of neurofeedback treatment in autism. Research in Autism Spectrum Disorders 3(2), 496–501 (2009)
37. Birbaumer, N., Sauseng, P.: BCIs in neurorehabilitation. In: Graimann, B., Allison, B.Z., Pfurtscheller, G. (eds.) Brain-Computer Interfaces: Non-invasive and Invasive Approaches. Springer, Heidelberg (in press)
38. Mellinger, J., Schalk, G.: BCI2000: A general purpose software platform for BCI research. In: Graimann, B., Allison, B.Z., Pfurtscheller, G. (eds.) Brain-Computer Interfaces: Non-invasive and Invasive Approaches. Springer, Heidelberg (in press)
39. Pineda, J.A., Allison, B.Z., Vankov, A.: The effects of self-movement, observation, and imagination on mu rhythms and readiness potentials (RP's): toward a brain-computer interface (BCI). IEEE Trans. Rehab. 8, 219–222 (2000)
40. Geng, T., Gan, J.O., Dyson, M., Tsui, C.S., Sepulveda, E.: A novel design of 4-Class BCI using two binary classifiers and parallel mental tasks. Comput. Intell. Neurosci. 5 (2008)
41. Pineda, J.A., Silverman, D.S., Vankov, A., Hestenes, J.: Learning to control brain rhythms: making a brain-computer interface possible. IEEE Trans. Neural. Syst. Rehabil. Eng. 11, 181–184 (2003)
42. Mason, S.G., Bashashati, A., Fatourechi, M., Navarro, K.F., Birch, G.E.: A comprehensive survey of brain interface technology designs. Ann. Biomed. Eng. 35, 137–169 (2007)
43. Cook, A., Hussey, S.: Assistive technologies: Principles and practice. Elsevier, New York (2002)
44. McFarland, D.J., Sarnacki, W.A., Wolpaw, J.R.: Brain-computer interface (BCI) operation: optimizing information transfer rates. Biol. Psychol. 63, 237–251 (2003)
45. Neuper, C., Scherer, R., Wriessnegger, S., Pfurtscheller, G.: Motor imagery and action observation: modulation of sensorimotor brain rhythms during mental control of a brain-computer interface. Clin. Neurophysiol. 120, 239–247 (2009)
46. Martin, S., Kelly, G., Kernohan, W.G., McCreight, B., Nugent, C.: Smart home technologies for health and social care support. Cochrane Database Syst. Rev. 13 (2008)
47. Wills, S.A., MacKay, D.J.C.: DASHER - An efficient writing system for brain-computer interfaces? IEEE Trans. Neural. Syst. Rehabil. Eng. 14, 244–246 (2006)
48. Müller, K.R., Tangermann, M., Dornhege, G., Krauledat, M., Curio, G., Blankertz, B.: Machine learning for real-time single-trial EEG-analysis: From brain-computer interfacing to mental state monitoring. J. Neurosci. Meth. 167, 82–90 (2008)
49. Buttfield, A., Ferrez, P.W., Millán, J.D.R.: Towards a robust BCI: error potentials and online learning. IEEE Trans. Neural. 14, 164–168 (2006)
50. Ferrez, P.W., Millán, J.D.R.: Error-related EEG potentials generated during simulated brain-computer interaction. IEEE Trans. Biomed. Eng. 55, 923–926 (2008)
51. Friedrich, E.V., McFarland, D.J., Neuper, C., Vaughan, T.M., Brunner, P., Wolpaw, J.R.: A scanning protocol for a sensorimotor rhythm-based brain-computer interface. Biol. Psychol. 80, 169–175 (2009)
52. Kaiser, J., Kubler, A., Hinterberger, T., Neumann, N., Birbaumer, N.: A non-invasive communication device for the paralyzed. Minim. Invasive Neurosurg. 45, 19–23 (2002)

Mind-Mirror: EEG-Guided Image Evolution

Nima Bigdely Shamlo and Scott Makeig

Swartz Center for Computational Neuroscience, Institute for Neural Computation,
University of California, San Diego, USA
{nima,scott}@sccn.ucsd.edu

Abstract. We propose a brain-computer interface (BCI) system for evolving
images in real-time based on subject feedback derived from electroencephalography (EEG). The goal of this system is to produce a picture best resembling a
subject's 'imagined' image. This system evolves images using Compositional
Pattern Producing Networks (CPPNs) via the NeuroEvolution of Augmenting
Topologies (NEAT) genetic algorithm. Fitness values for NEAT-based evolution are derived from a real-time EEG classifier as images are presented using
rapid serial visual presentation (RSVP). Here, we report the design and performance, for a pilot training session, of a BCI system for real-time single-trial
binary classification of viewed images based on participant-specific brain response signatures present in 128-channel EEG data. Selected training-session
image clips created by the image evolution algorithm were presented in 2-s
bursts at 8/s. The subject indicated by subsequent button press whether or not
each burst included an image resembling two eyes. Approximately half the
bursts included such an image. Independent component analysis (ICA) was
used to extract a set of maximally independent EEG source time-courses and
their 100 minimally-redundant low-dimensional informative features in the time
and time-frequency amplitude domains from the (94%) bursts followed by correct manual responses. To estimate the likelihood that the post-image EEG contained EEG 'flickers' of target recognition, we applied two Fisher discriminant
classifiers to the time and/or time-frequency features. The area under the receiver operating characteristic (ROC) curve by tenfold cross-validation was
0.96 using time-domain features, 0.97 using time-frequency domain features,
and 0.98 using both domain features.

Keywords: human-computer interface (HCI), brain-computer interface (BCI),
evolutionary algorithms, genetic algorithms (GA), electroencephalography
(EEG), independent component analysis (ICA), rapid serial visual presentation
(RSVP), genetic art, evolutionary art.

1 Introduction

Recent advances in Evolutionary Algorithms have lead to the introduction of methods
for evolving images based on human feedback [15]. These methods present a succession of images to a user who rates each image on how closely it resembles an imagined target picture. These user fitness ratings are exploited to evolve the sequence of
pictures towards the imagined target. An example of such a system is Picbreeder

J.A. Jacko (Ed.): Human-Computer Interaction, Part II, HCII 2009, LNCS 5611, pp. 569–578, 2009.
© Springer-Verlag Berlin Heidelberg 2009

(picbreeder.com), a collaborative web application for evolving pictures. Although these evolutionary methods can be quite successful in maximizing fitness, they are limited by the speed at which humans can provide fitness-value feedback and the amount of feedback they can generate before becoming fatigued.

Several brain-computer interface (BCI) systems for broadening user feedback performance in image processing tasks have been developed in last few years (Bigdely-Shamlo et al. [3] and Sajda et al. [8], [13], [14]). These interfaces use a rapid serial visual presentation (RSVP) paradigm to present a stream of image 'clips' drawn from a larger search image at high presentation rates (about 12/s). Subjects look for clips containing a set of predefined target types (e.g., airplanes or helipads) among the clips presented in the stream while EEG signals are recorded and analyzed in near-real time to detect dynamic brain signatures of target recognition. These signatures are used to find the image clip in the sequence in which the subject spotted a target feature.

Basa et al. [1] proposed an EEG-based genetic art evolution algorithm based on evaluation of 'interestingness' of each image. They trained SVM classifiers on EEG and an array of other physiological measures recorded during exposure to emotion-inducing images. In test sessions, their classifiers were able to distinguish positive and negative emotions elicited by genetic art images, produced without subject online feedback, with 61% accuracy.

Here we propose a real-time EEG-based system for evolving images based on subject feedback produced by EEG classifier output during an RSVP stream of generated images. Bursts of images generated by an image evolution algorithm are presented to the subject. Images resembling the targeted or 'imagined' image elicit some level of target response which may be recognized by the EEG classification algorithm, generating feedback to the image evolution algorithm guiding the generation of the next RSVP images. This process is repeated continuously until the images in the RSVP stream wholly or mostly resemble the 'imagined' image with adequate detail and accuracy. At that point, the presented images would 'mirror' the original target image in the mind of the viewer.

2   Methods

2.1   Training Experiment

In previous work [3], we demonstrated online EEG classification to detect 'flickers of recognition' associated with spotting a target feature in a sequence of images displayed using rapid serial visual presentation (RSVP) at a rate of 12 images per second. Here, we report initial training session results of individualized EEG-based classification of images in an RSVP sequences that resemble an imagined target, here "two eyes facing the subject." We propose that the derived classification model or one like it can be used in on-line test sessions to drive image evolution of imagined pictures.

In the training session, EEG and manual responses were recorded as the subject viewed the RSVP sequence. Fig. 1 shows a trial timeline. After fixating a cross (left) for 1 s, the participant viewed a 2-s RSVP image burst (presentation rate, 8 images per sec), and was then asked to indicate, by pressing one of two (yes/no) finger buttons, whether or not he/she had detected an image resembling the imagined (two-eyes) target among the burst images. Half of these bursts included a two-eyes image. Visual error/correct feedback was provided after each burst. The training session was comprised of 467 RSVP bursts organized into 52 9-burst bouts with a self-paced break after each bout. In all, each session thus included 253 (~3%) two-eyes and 7219 (~97%) not-eyes image presentations. No burst contained more than one target (two-eyes) image.

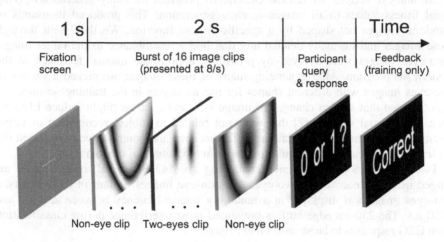

Fig. 1. Time-line of each RSVP burst. Participant response feedback ('Correct' or 'Incorrect') was delivered only during Training sessions (rightmost panel).

2.2 Stimuli

We used a modified version of the GeneticArt program written in Delphi by Mattias Fagerlund [6] to create images used in the training session. It generates gray-scale images produced by a Compositional Pattern Producing Network (CPPN) [17] evolved using the NeuroEvolution of Augmenting Topologies (NEAT) algorithm [16]. The CPPN used in the experiment is a network of Gaussian function nodes connected by a directed graph. The input to each node is the sum of values from input connections weighted by connection weights. The output of each node is sent via output connections to other nodes in the network. The function of the network is to generate a gray-scale image. Its final output is a matrix of light intensities at each pixel of the output image. To generate an image, the light intensity at each pixel is calculated by providing values indicating the (x,y) location of the pixel in the image ($\in$ [0,1]) and its distance to the center of the image.

The topology of the CPPN network (its connections, connection weights, and node types) is evolved by the NEAT algorithm. Each new generation of images is created by applying genetic operators (mating, mutation…) to the individual images (or image pairs) in the previous generation based on their received fitness values. NEAT begins by evolving simple (low node- and connection-count) networks, gradually creating more a complex network that produce higher received fitness values. By starting the search from a low-dimensional space, NEAT increases the chance of finding a desirable solution by preventing the problems associated with searching in a high dimensional space (many nodes and connection weights). In our case, the network starts with simple shapes and can increase the amount of visual detail in later image generations.

We used two sets of two-eyes and not-eyes images generated by the network in previous behavioral pilot sessions to prepare the stimuli for the training session. To create non-eye images, we ran the GeneticArt program for many generations giving equal fitness values to all images in each generation. This produced thousands of 'random' images not shaped by a specific fitness function. We then went through these images and manually deleted any that had a resemblance to the target image. Two-eyes images were evolved by providing appropriate manual feedback to the GeneticArt program. After generating many of these images, we picked a variety of two-eyes images with different shapes for use as targets in the training session. We hypothesized that sudden changes in image size and contrast might induce EEG responses to visual surprise [7] that were not related to subject recognition of target resemblance. To minimize variations in feature size and contrast, we normalized the center of mass location and angular momentum magnitude of the images.

Two-second RSVP bursts, each containing 16 (547x343 pixel) images, were arranged using the normalized two-eyes and non-eye images. In half of these bursts, a two-eyes image was displayed at a randomly selected latency between 250 ms and 1750 ms. The 250-ms edge buffers prevented most interference during classification from EEG responses to burst onsets and offsets.

2.3 Experimental Setup

RSVP bursts were presented at a rate of 8 images per second and synchronized with EEG and behavioral data collection using our custom *DataRiver* interactive stimulus presentation and data recording suite (A. Vankov). Events corresponding to image display, image type (two-eyes or not-eyes), and subject post-burst manual responses were recorded synchronously with EEG into a single file. EEG was recorded using a BIOSEMI Active View 2 system with 128 electrodes mounted in a whole-head elastic electrode cap with a custom near-uniform montage across the scalp and bony parts of the upper face. Computer data acquisition was performed via USB using a customized acquisition driver at a sampling rate of 512 Hz. In this pilot experiment, we recorded one hour of data from one (28-year old male) subject.

2.4 Data Preprocessing

Preprocessing of training session data was performed in the Matlab environment (Mathworks, Inc.) using EEGLAB [5] functions and data structures. The scalp channel data were first high-passed using an FIR filter above 2 Hz. Two channels containing invalid EEG signals were then removed. The rest of the EEG data were then re-referenced from the Biosemi active reference to average reference. EEG data epochs from 1.5 s before burst onset until 2 s after (2-s) burst offset were extracted from the continuous EEG and concatenated. Data epochs were then decomposed using extended-infomax ICA [2][10] [11] [12] to obtain 126 maximally independent

components (ICs), spatial filters separating EEG sensor data into maximally temporally independent processes, most appearing to predominantly represent the contribution to the scalp data of one brain EEG or non-brain artifact source, respectively.
Bursts followed by a correct subject response (438 of 467, ~94%) were used for classifier training and cross-validation.

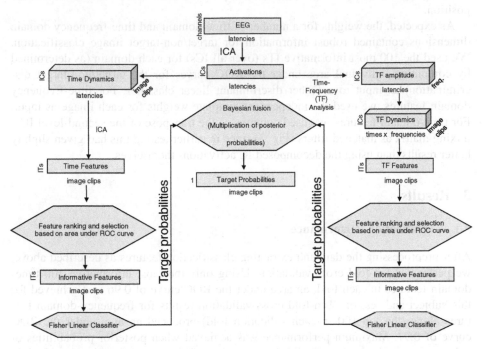

Fig. 2. Flowchart of the classifier system. Both (left) temporal activity patterns (phase-locking
following stimulus onsets) and (right) event-related changes in spectral amplitude are used by
the classifier (center). [From N. Bigdely Shamlo et al., IEEE Transactions on Neural Systems
and Rehabilitation Engineering, 2008].

2.5 Image Classification

We used methods described previously [3] for classifying image responses as target
(two-eyes) or non-target (not-eyes). Fig. 2 summarizes the classification process. We
exploited information from both time-domain and frequency-domain features of EEG
signals following image presentations. Time-course templates were selected by a
method that involved performing, for every IC, a second-level deconvolutive ICA
decomposition on the time-domain IC activation following image presentations. To
do this, for each IC we constructed matrices (of size 410 lags by 6570 images) by
concatenating columns consisting of lagged IC activation time series in the 800 ms
following each image presentation. Applying principal component analysis (PCA), we
then reduced the rows of this matrix to 50. A second-level ICA was then performed
on the dimension-reduced matrix to find 50 independent time course templates (IT$_{TCs}$)
for each IC. These features form a natural spatiotemporal decomposition of the EEG

signal with low interdependency, making them natural candidate features for an EEG classifier. Time-frequency amplitude ITs (IT_As) were found by decomposing the single-trial spectrograms of the IC activations following image onsets, vectorizing these, then concatenating them into a large (frequencies × latencies, images) matrix that was reduced to its first 50 principal dimensions by PCA before second-level ICA decomposition.

As expected, the weights for a number of time-domain and time-frequency domain dimensions contained robust information for target/non-target image classification. We used the 100 most informative ITs (over all ICs) for each domain (as determined by computing individual area under the ROC curves for the target/non-target discrimination) as input to a Fisher discriminant linear classifier. For time-frequency domain features, we used the independent template weights for each image as input. For time-domain features, we used columns of the transpose of the second-level ICA mixing matrix as matched filters (Fig. 3) since in earlier testing this had given slightly better results than using the decomposed IC activations themselves.

3   Results

3.1   Classification Performance

After preprocessing the data and extracting classification features as described above, we performed ten-fold cross-validation. Using only the most informative 100 time-domain features in each fold, an area under the ROC curve of 0.96 was achieved for this subject and session. Ten-fold cross-validation results for frequency-domain features alone (the top 100 in each validation fold) produced an area under the ROC curve of 0.97. Maximum performance was achieved when posterior probabilities of being a target obtained from the time-domain and frequency-domain classifiers in each validation fold were combined using naive Bayesian fusion (i.e., when the two probabilities were multiplied). In this case, the area under the ROC curve was 0.98.

3.2   EEG 'Flickers' of Target Recognition

Both time-domain and frequency-domain contain information regarding EEG signatures of target detection. To investigate the information content of sources used in the classifier, we calculated the ten-fold cross validation area under ROC for individual ICs. All independent templates (ITs) for each IC were used in the manner described in Fig. 2.

Equivalent dipole sources for ICs were then localized using Spherical Four shell (BESA) model and components with residual variance less than 0.2 were selected. Fig. 3 shows these dipoles in the standard MNI head space. Both size and color of each dipole reflect the amount of information relevant to target detection, measured by the area under ROC of the single-IC classifier. Most likely Brodmann areas associated with dipole locations, identified using the Talairach Client [18], are displayed on the most informative IC dipole spheres.

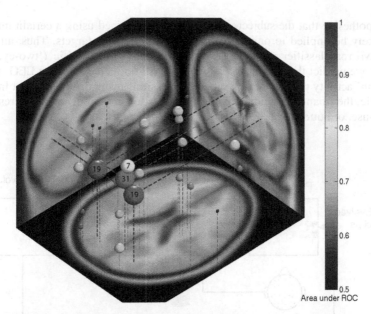

Fig. 3. Equivalent dipoles for subject ICs with low (< 0.2) dipole model residual variance. The color and size of each dipole sphere shows the relative amount of information about target classification in the IC activation. Numbers on the most informative (red-yellow) dipole markers indicate the Brodmann area most probably associated with the dipole location (BA19, BA31, etc.).

The most informative IC (Fig. 3) required a dual-symmetric dipole model with source areas located in or near BA 19, a secondary visual cortical area associated with visual processing, specifically, higher order visual processing involving object recognition and movement sensing [19]. Another informative IC was located in or near the precuneus (BA 31). Activity in this area is associated with attentional processes, including shifts of attention between object features [4]. A third most target-information bearing IC was located in or near right BA 7 (superior parietal lobule), an area associated with visual-spatial processing and use of spatial imagery. Note, that the most informative areas involved responses peaking 200 ms and more after target image onsets in higher regions of the brain visual system hierarchy, areas known to be involved in visual target recognition. A number of medial and frontal area sources (light blue balls in Fig. 3) also contributed information via later potentials that maximally projected to the frontal scalp.

4   Discussion

4.1 The Proposed Mind-Mirror System

The pilot training session we report here is the first step in creating the proposed Mind-Mirror system. Further system development involves testing the use of classifier output online for image evolution (Fig. 4). Based on our initial RSVP studies [3], we hypothesize that the subject-specific classifier trained using a certain image target can likely be applied to online evolution of other image targets. Thus, although the Mind-Mirror classifier reported here was trained on a specific ('two-eyes') target image, we predict that during test sessions it will correctly detect an EEG 'target recognition' activity pattern for this subject in sessions using different target images. For example, the (manually guided) evolution algorithm can produce images resembling a car, house, or butterfly.

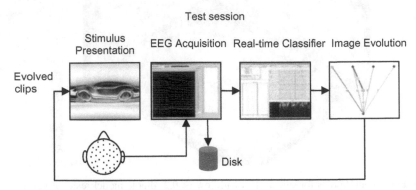

Fig. 4. Schematic of the proposed Mind-Mirror system in intended operation. Here, the subject is imagining an image of a sports car. EEG target recognition signals fed to the image evolution algorithm from the real-time EEG classifier continually shape the evolution of the image sequence to resemble more and more closely the subject's imagined car image. In the test session, the subject observes RSVP image bursts produced by the image evolution algorithm. If subject detects an image with some resemblance to imagined picture, it will be reflected in a high target probability value output of the EEG classification algorithm. These values are then sent to the image evolution program to evolve a new generation of images, which are then displayed in the next RSVP burst. This establishes a feedback loop, shown in Fig. 3 (right), which favors image features resembling the imagined target picture. After the subject views many bursts, the system may consistently generate a 'mirror image' of the image the subject has been mentally imagining. By eliminating the need for subject manual feedback in the Mind-Mirror system, its speed and user convenience might be increased.

Despite the near-perfect image classification obtained by our method in this session, several factors could limit the success of the derived EEG model in guiding online image evolution. The EEG features used by the classifier might be attenuated, altered, or even absent in response to early sequence images that only vaguely resemble the image target, or in response to later target-like images presented more frequently than one target per burst. Such feature changes could degrade image classification and evolution performance in early and/or later stages of image evolution. To avoid these pitfalls, the training session images might better resemble early- or later-stage image evolution sequences. Solutions for several practical issues for online classification related to dealing with session-to-session shifts in the electrode montage, novel within-session artifacts, and channel drop-outs have been described in our earlier RSVP paper [3].

Based on the strong recent acceleration of technical, business, and popular interest, appears that applications of EEG-based human-computer interaction are just beginning. Very likely, the best uses for EEG in brain-computer interfaces should be those that respect the natural brain functions associated with the features used for interaction. The proposed Mind Mirror exemplifies this by making use of EEG features that constitute the complex EEG 'flicker of recognition' that immediately follows recognition of a sought visual target. The Mind Mirror system, if sufficiently robust, might be used as a game, to create art, or using a somewhat different image evolution algorithm, to guide production of a face image resembling a suspect as recalled by a witness in a criminal investigation.

References

1. Basa, T., Go, C., Yoo, K., Lee, W.: Using Physiological Signals to Evolve Art. In: Rothlauf, F., Branke, J., Cagnoni, S., Costa, E., Cotta, C., Drechsler, R., Lutton, E., Machado, P., Moore, J.H., Romero, J., Smith, G.D., Squillero, G., Takagi, H. (eds.) EvoWorkshops 2006. LNCS, vol. 3907, pp. 633–641. Springer, Heidelberg (2006)
2. Bell, A., Sejnowski, T.: An Information Maximization Approach to Blind Separation and Blind Deconvolution. Neural Computation 7, 1129–1159 (1995)
3. Bigdely-Shamlo, N., Vankov, A., Ramirez, R., Makeig, S.: Brain Activity-Based Image Classification From Rapid Serial visual Presentation. IEEE Transactions on Neural Systems and Rehabilitation Engineering 16(4) (2008)
4. Cavanna, A.E., Trimble, M.R.: The precuneus: a review of its functional anatomy and behavioural correlates. Brain 129, 564–583 (2006)
5. Delorme, A., Makeig, S.: EEGLAB: an open source toolbox for analysis of single-trial EEG dynamics including independent component analysis. J. of Neuroscience Methods 134(1), 9, http://sccn.ucsd.edu/eeglab
6. DelphiNEAT GeneticArt program, http://www.mattiasfagerlund.com/DelphiNEAT/
7. Einhuser, W., Mundhenk, T.N., Baldi, P., Koch, C., Itti, L.: A bottom-up model of spatial attention predicts human error patterns in rapid scene recognition. J. of Vision 7(10), 1–13 (2007)
8. Gerson, A., Parra, L., Sajda, P.: Cortically-coupled computer vision for rapid image search. IEEE Transactions on Neural Systems and Rehabilitation Engineering 14(2), 174–179 (2006)
9. Lee, T., Girolami, M., Sejnowski, T.J.: Independent Component Analysis Using an Extended Infomax Algorithm for Mixed Subgaussian and Supergaussian Sources. Neural Computation 11(2), 417–441 (1999)
10. Makeig, S., Bell, A.J., Jung, T.-P., Sejnowski, T.: Independent component analysis of electroencephalographic data. In: Touretzky, D., Mozer, M., Hasselmo, M. (eds.) Advances in Neural Information Processing Systems, vol. 8, pp. 145–151 (1996)
11. Makeig, S., Enghoff, S., Jung, T.P., Sejnowski, T.J.: A natural basis for efficient brain-actuated control. IEEE Trans. Rehabil. Eng. 8, 208–211 (2000)
12. Makeig, S., Jung, T.P., Bell, A.J., Ghahremani, D., Sejnowski, T.J.: Blind separation of auditory event-related brain responses into independent components. Proc. Natl. Acad. Sci. USA 94, 10979–10984 (1997)
13. Parra, L.C., Christoforou, C., Gerson, A.D., Dyrholm, M., Luo, A., Wagner, M., Philiastides, M.G., Sajda, P.: Spatio-temporal linear decoding of brain state: Application to performance augmentation in high-throughput tasks. IEEE Signal Processing Magazine 25(1), 95–115 (2008)

14. Sajda, P., Gerson, A., Parra, L.: High-throughput image search via single-trial event detection in a rapid serial visual presentation task. In: Proc. 1st Inter. IEEE EMBS Conf. on Neural Engineering, Capri Island, Italy (2003)
15. Secretan, J., Beato, N., D'Ambrosio, D.B., Rodriguez, A., Campbell, A., Stanley, K.O.: Picbreeder: Evolving Pictures Collaboratively Online. In: Proc. Computer Human Interaction Conf (CHI), 10 Pages. ACM Press, New York (2008)
16. Stanley, K.O.: Evolving Neural Networks through Augmenting Topologies. Evolutionary Computation 10(2), 99 (2002)
17. Stanley, K.O.: Exploiting Regularity Without Development. In: Proc. AAAI Fall Symposium on Developmental Systems, 8 pages. AAAI Press, Menlo Park (2006)
18. Talairach Client, http://www.talairach.org/client.html
19. Worden, M.S., Foxe, J.J., Wang, N., Simpson, G.V.: Anticipatory biasing of visuospatial attention indexed by retinotopically specific alpha-band electroencephalography increases over occipital cortex. J. Neurosci. 20, RC63 (2000)

BEXPLORER: Computer and Communication Control Using EEG

Mina Mikhail, Marian Abdel-Shahid, Mina Guirguis, Nadine Shehad,
Baher Soliman, and Khaled El-Ayat

Computer Science and Engineering Department, American University in Cairo,
New Cairo Campus: The American University in Cairo, P.P. Box 74 New Cairo 11835,
Egypt
{minamohebn,m.abdelshahid,mina.gb,bahers}@gmail.com,
{n_shehad,kelayat}@aucegypt.edu

Abstract. Humans are able to communicate in many rich and complex ways, with each other, or increasingly, with digital devices. A brain-computer interface (BCI) is a direct neural interface and a communication pathway between the human brain and an external device such as a computer or artificial limb. With such an interface, a severely handicapped person, such as an Amyotrophic Lateral Sclerosis (ALS) patient, with severe muscle disorder may still communicate and even control their environment relying solely on his brain activity. The system introduced detects EEG signals arising from various eye-blinking activities and applies the results to control various popular computer applications. Using BCI2000 as a platform, the system allows handicapped patients to communicate with a computer and initiate various computer commands, send instant messages, and even browse the web. The application also enables the user to communicate using mobile phone SMS messaging.

Keywords: BCI, ALS, electroencephalography (EEG), blink artifact, assistive technology, Human computer interface (HCI), information transfer rate, classification.

1 Introduction

The rapid development in technology has enriched humanity with various channels of communication. However, even with this variety of choices, some individuals are still deprived from benefiting from this technological improvement. Handicapped and totally paralyzed people are still locked in, lacking communication with the outside world.

One of the main applications of the Brain Computer Interface (BCI) is to assist people with severe motor disabilities to communicate and control their environment. Patients who have Amyotrophic Lateral Sclerosis (ALS) are in need of such technology. ALS is a chronic, progressive neurodegenerative disease marked by gradual degeneration of the nerve cells in the central nervous system that control voluntary muscle movement [5]. The occurrence of ALS is thought to be consistently around 1-2 per 100,000 people per year [1]. The objective of the Brain Computer Interface (BCI) system discussed in this work is to enrich the lives of such patients by giving

J.A. Jacko (Ed.): Human-Computer Interaction, Part II, HCII 2009, LNCS 5611, pp. 579–587, 2009.

them control over their environment and helping them with their communication needs.

The developed system uses Eye-blink artifact signals to control a variety of computer actions. This is accomplished by classification of the user's EEG signals to detect eyelid movements. The developed application BEXPLORER uses these classified signals as control signals for performing the various computer commands. Using BEXPLORER, the user can browse computer files, watch a photo gallery, watch movies, play music, write text and browse PDF files. Moreover, the user can send SMS messages from a cell phone and communicate with the outer world by writing and sending email, browsing the internet, and chatting with other BEXPLORER users as well as normal users. Section 2 of the paper discusses related works, followed by a system overview of BEXPLORER in section 3. Signal processing and classification is discussed in section 4. BEXPLORER is described in section 5. Experimental results are given in section 6, followed by a computer vision comparison and finally a conclusion in sections 7 and 8.

Contributions of this work are signal processing, classification and a companion application that detects and classifies eye-blink and eye-lid movements and translates these into popular computer communication commands such as editing, emailing, browsing and messaging. The system uses eye-blink information instead of rejecting them. The application framework allows the user to control his computer environment and communicate with the outside world. A key advantage of BEXPLORER is noise tolerance; subject head movements and unintentional eye blinks are tolerated thus lessening eye fatigue symptoms.

2   Related Works

Numerous approaches concerning hands-free human-computer interaction have been developed in the past years. The introduction of BCI research added more to these approaches. HaMCoS, which stands for "Hands-free Mouse Control System", is one of these approaches. It uses intentional muscle contraction to control computer action. The system combines EEG with EMG as input signals [6]. It was designed to be an extension of the Windows® operating system enabling persons, who cannot use their hands, to operate a computer.

HaMCoS captures the difference in potential resulting from temporal sequences of contractions using a forehead sensor which senses user brow muscle contractions. The detected contractions are divided into two categories: single contractions (SC's) and double contractions (DC's). The first refers to a contraction after an "idle activity", while the second happens if the user issues another intentional contraction within a time period.

The subject is presented with four buttons in the four directions. The processing module changes the cursor position or issues a click at the current position of the cursor. The same HaMCoS system was later used to efficiently control a wheel chair [6].

3   BEXPLORER System Overview

BEXPLORER uses artifacts generated from Eye-Blink and eye lid movements as a basis for controlling various computer commands. Following the 10-20 system for EEG recording, electrodes placed at positions Fz and Cz are used as input channels to the signal processing module with the right mastoid used as a reference channel. Recording was performed from 8 channels for experimental purposes and it was determined that the two channels mentioned above were sufficient for controlling the final application.

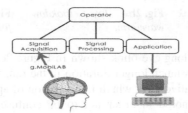

Fig. 1. BEXPLORER System Overview

BEXPLORER uses a standard BCI system architecture as shown in Figure 1. The main building blocks of the system are Data acquisition, Signal Processing and Application modules. To acquire EEG brain signals, the g.MobiLAB, biomedical amplifier and A/D converter, from g.TEC was used.

BCI2000 system was used as our main software platform, and provides a convenient interface between the hardware used and the application [2,9]. BCI2000 is a flexible modular open source BCI platform that can be used by BCI researchers and developers. The signal acquisition module is connected to g.MobiLAB and reads the digitized EEG brain signals at a 256 sample per second rate.

Two modules were added to control BEXPLORER, a processing module and an application module. The processing module detects three types of eyelid movements. The application module receives the classification results using BCI2000.

4   BEXPLORER Signal Processing and Classification

To control BEXPLORER, we need to detect the intended user actions from the user's EEG signals and translate them into control inputs to the application. We experimented with three different eyelid movement signals and verified them on ten different subjects. The three signals are shown in Figures 2a, 2b and 2c.

The first signal is an intentional short eye-blink signal shown in Figure 2a. It is characterized with a positive peak with amplitude greater than 15 uV. The peak can be observed for a number of samples ranging from 7 to 63 samples, each sample being 3.9 ms in duration.

The second signal type used is downward eye movement shown in Figure 2b. It has a negative peak that is less than -15 uV and lasts for more than 30 samples. A positive peak follows the negative peak with duration of around 64 samples. The positive peak is rejected by the classification algorithm so that it is not recognized as an eye blink.

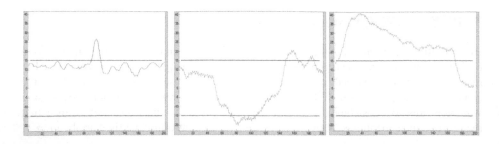

Fig. 2a. *Normal eye blink waveform.*   **Fig. 2b.** *Eye lookdown waveform.*   **Fig. 2c.** *Long eye blink waveform.*

The third signal is the long eye blink shown in Figure 2c. It is similar to the short eye blink. However, it has much longer duration in the range of 90 to 158 samples. It is also followed by a negative peak which has duration of approximately 64 samples. This negative peak is ignored in order not to be confused with a downward eye movement.

The classifier attempts to detect positive peaks greater than 15 uV or negative peaks less than -15 uV. After the peaks disappear, the number of peaks is checked in order to determine the type of signal. If a short eye blink is classified, a state of 1 is sent to the application. If a long blink is classified, a state of 2 is sent to the application and the classifier ignores the following 64 samples to avoid misclassification of this negative peak as an eye movement. Finally, if a negative peak greater than 30 samples is classified, a state of 3 is sent to the application and the classifier ignores the next 64 samples to avoid misclassification as an eye blink.

Unintentional blinks are rejected in classification because their signal amplitudes are less than 15 uV. This feature reduces eye fatigue since it is virtually impossible for any subject to avoid unintentional eye blinks when seated for long hours in front of a computer screen. This results in an easy to use application.

5   BEXPLORER Application

As mentioned above, three different Eye-blink artifact signals are used to control BEXPLORER, short blink, long blink and downward eye movement.   A severely handicapped user of BEXPLORER would initially need some assistance with electrode cap montage, connecting the electrodes and starting the BCI2000 platform and BEXPLORER application. Once this is accomplished, the user has control over the application.

5.1   BEXPLORER Browser

When the application is initiated, the BEXPLORER Browser page shown in Figure 3a appears. The page includes all the drives on the computer and a side application menu. The application side menu is accessed by a downward eye movement signal. As for the browser part, every 600ms one of the drives is highlighted. The user can choose to open a certain drive by blinking once when the drive is highlighted.

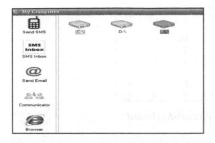

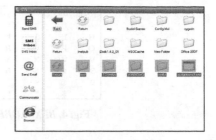

Fig. 3a. BEXPLORER Browser

Fig. 3b. Folders and Files with 3rd row highlighted

After opening a drive, all folders and files in that drive appear. Since the number of items that appear may be large, each row in the list is highlighted one row at a time every 600ms as shown in Figure 3b. The user chooses a row by blinking when the row is highlighted. Each item in the selected row is then highlighted, one item at a time, and the user selects a file or folder by blinking when its icon is highlighted.

When the user opens a file, BEXPLORER checks its extension and a corresponding sub-application is activated. BEXPLORER supports many types of files including images, videos, music, text files and PDFs.

5.2 BEXPLORER Multimedia Tools

The system enables the user to view images and videos. The image viewer sub-application is activated whenever an image file type is selected. The user can view the next image by performing an eye blink, rotate the image by performing a long blink and exit the viewer by performing a long blink.

As for the B_Media Player, the user can open music or video files. The user is allowed to play, pause, control the sound volume and change the state to full screen of the selected media file. This sub-application is intended as an entertainment application to the handicapped user. By default the file is opened in full screen mode. The user can change the full mode by performing an eye look down. When the full screen mode is changed and a menu appears that contains some commands: play/pause, volume up, volume down and full screen. By default, play/pause command will be highlighted. The user can perform an eye blink to select the highlighted command or perform an eye look down to change the highlighted command or a long blink to terminate the application.

5.3 BEXPLORER Collaboration Tools

The system also, provides the user with the ability to read and edit files. The first sub-application of this category is the B_PDF Viewer which is activated when the user selects a PDF. The B_PDF enables the user to scroll down the document using an eye look down or scroll up using an eye blink.

The second sub-application of this category is the B_Text Editor. The text editor is activated when text files are selected and allows the user to read and edit text. A virtual keyboard is used for text entry as shown in Figure 4. The keyboard consists of a

SPACE	DEL	TAB	SEND	CLEAR	.	,	RET
A	B	C	D	E	F	G	RET
H	I	J	K	L	M	N	RET
O	P	Q	R	S	T	U	RET
V	W	X	Y	Z	1	2	RET
3	4	5	6	7	8	9	RET
0	@	-	_	:	(	)	RET
;	$	*	!	+	?	=	RET

Fig. 4. *BEXPLORER's Virtual-Keyboard*

2D matrix of letters in which the rows are highlighted in red one by one every 600ms as. When the user selects a certain row, each letter in the row is highlighted every 600ms. When the user selects a letter, it is written in the text box in the cursor position. Letter selection requires only two blinks.

5.4 BEXPLORER Communication Tools

BEXPLORER enables the user to communicate and interact with the outer world by enabling the user to send emails, SMS, chat with other users and access the web.

Text entry uses the previously described keyboard. An email address text box appears so the user can address the recipient. In SMS mode the user types in the recipient's number and the message. To send SMS, the computer is connected to a mobile phone with a cable or wireless connection. BEXLORER enables the user to open the mobile phone inbox and check for new messages. When opening the application, the first message in his inbox is displayed. He can blink to proceed to the next message in his inbox. To close the application, the subject makes a long blink.

BEXPLORER also, enables the user to chat with other users. The BEXPLORER IM is similar to the popular IM chatting application, tailored to a handicapped BEX-PLORER user. It is implemented using open source Jabber® IM technology and is based on Gmail accounts provided by Google™. After the user logs in, the user is provided with a list of online contacts. Names on the list are sequentially highlighted every 600ms and a selection made with an eye-blink. A chatting window is opened containing the same keyboard and the user can then type and view messages. The IM exchange can be with a normal or another handicapped user. A long blink will close the application and return to the BEXPLORER's main browser again.

Finally, the user is given the ability to surf the web. When the user selects the web browser icon from the side menu, a keyboard appears so that user can enter the navigation address. The user can tab between the links on the web page by using downward eye movement and can select a certain link by making an eye blink. The main disadvantage of this browser is that if there are a lot of links in the website, it will be exhausting for the user to tab among the links.

6 Experimental Results

Our applications are divided into two categories. In the first category of applications, action is initiated by the user without intervention from the system. In the second category of applications, the user reacts to a given stimulus. Typically these applications require the subject to type something to the screen or browse different system files. We focused our measurements on the latter applications.

In order to verify that our signal processing and applications will work fine on different subjects and on both genders, we tested our system on 10 subjects between 18 and 60 years of old. Out of the 10 subjects, 2 were females and 8 were males. Most of the subjects had little or no familiarity with the system. Familiarity with the system includes the whole experience starting from wearing the cap and electrodes for EEG measurements up to knowing the places of the characters in the virtual keyboard. The subjects were asked to type three different sentences, "Hello", "Thank you very much", and "Love makes the world go round." Sentences were chosen with different lengths to test typing speed. The time taken by the subjects to type the sentences was recorded in Table 1. The third, fourth and fifth columns represents that time taken by each subject to type the sentences "Hello", "Thank you very much", "love makes the world go round" respectively. The average typing speed in characters/sec. is also shown.

It is noted that system familiarity contributed to faster typing rates as expected. The achieved results are quite promising with further improvements possible. The application can clearly be expanded with more vocabulary added to provide additional application control signals. The system is easy to use because it tolerates unintentional user blinking and alleviates eye fatigue. Also, the technique itself doesn't require any training and can work for any subject. Furthermore, subject typing accuracy and speed improved as the user got used to the interface of the application. This is partly due to the user getting more familiar with keyboard positions and spending less time searching for the desired character. We managed to reach an accuracy of 100% for detecting the user blink, long blink and downward eye movement.

Table 1. Application Performance on different subjects

#	Familiarity	Sentence 1		Sentence 2		Sentence 3	
		Total time	Av. Speed	Total time	Av. speed	Total time	Av. speed
1	2 weeks	0:21	0.24 char/sec	1:23	0.23 char/sec	1:50	0.26 char/sec
2	3 or 4 days	0:20	0.25 char/sec	2:20	0.135 char/sec	4:08	0.12 char/sec
3	3 or 4 days	0:23	0.21 char/sec	1:52	0.17 char/sec	2:16	0.213 char/sec
4	3 or 4 days	0.35	0.14 char/sec	2:13	0.143 char/sec	3:48	0.127 char/sec
5	1 or 2 times	0:24	0.2 char/sec	2:12	0.144 char/sec	4:14	0.114 char/sec
6	1 or 2 times	0:35	0.14 char/sec	3:20	0.095 char/sec	6:00	0.08 char/sec
7	1 or 2 times	0:20	0.25 char/sec	2:33	0.124 char/sec	3:16	0.148 char/sec
8	1 or 2 times	0:29	0.17 char/sec	2:22	0.133 char/sec	3:50	0.126char/sec
9	1 or 2 times	0:25	0.2 char/sec	2:51	0.11 char/sec	3:47	0.128 char/sec
10	1 or 2 times	0:50	0.1 char/sec	3:05	0.1 char/sec	4:48	0.1 char.sec

BEXPLORER can be compared with the Dasher project [10], at the University of Cambridge. DASHER is a human–computer interface for entering text using continuous or discrete gestures using eyetracking device, a headmouse or other hardware devices. DASHER efficiently converts bits received from the user into text, and has been shown to be a competitive alternative to existing text-entry methods. Users steering DASHER with a mouse can write at 25 words per minute. Similar rates have been reported using DASHER with eyetracking hardware. DASHER is proposed in [10] as well-matched to the low bit-rate, obtained from brain–computer interfaces (BCIs).

The research reported in [4] integrates DASHER text-entry with a BCI system using neural signals instead of gestures. Users were able to type small words like "Hello" at a speed of 0.125characters/second with an accuracy of 100%, while faster typing rates resulted in higher error rates. Typing short phrases like "thank you very much" and "love makes the world go round" was done at an average speed of 1.25 words/minute [4]. This can show that the typing speed of BEXPLORER is better than that of DASHER.

BEXPLORER can also, be compared with P300 speller BCI. P300 spellers have been reported with 7-8 characters / minute typing speeds compared with 14 characters /minute for BEXPLORER [3]. 100% typing accuracy is assumed since the typing rates measured already account for correction of typing mistakes. It should be noted that while eye-blink based control achieves higher typing speeds than a P300 speller BCI and higher typing accuracy, it requires some muscle control. Pure BCI systems rely only on EEG signals and no muscle control which may be needed for certain severely handicapped users.

7 BEXPLORER vs. Computer Vision

BCI and Computer vision / eye tracking are two very different approaches. They are complementary in the sense that BCI relies on brain signals whereas Computer vision requires eye muscle control for gaze direction. For example, a patient with complete muscle impairment cannot control his eye gaze. Many eye tracking systems use voice activated commands, unlike BCI which relies only on EEG [7].

The main disadvantage of using EEG based BCI technology is the long set up time. Each experiment takes around thirty minutes. BCI environment is also uncomfortable as the user has to wear an electrode cap. A key advantage of BEXPLORER is noise tolerance. Subject head movements and unintentional eye blinks are tolerated. On the other hand, computer vision has some disadvantages as mentioned in [8]. It is very difficult to distinguish between voluntary acts and involuntary acts. This problem is known as "Midas Touch" Problem. Also, eye tracking algorithms deteriorates over time due to the drift effect caused by changes in eye characteristic over time. Also, the presence of glasses affects the efficiency of the computer vision algorithms. Finally, computer vision is affected by the quality of the lighting source.

8 Conclusion

BCI systems use neural EEG signals as a basis for communication. They are proposed as a promising means for severely handicapped patients to communicate and control their environment. A current limitation of BCI systems is the information transfer rates.

Eye-Blinking artifacts are usually filtered in BCIs since the scalp signals produced by eye-blink may obscure required EEG activity. Instead of rejecting eye-blink activity, the developed system, BEXPLORER, uses Eye-blink artifact signals to control a variety of computer actions. EEG classification is used to detect eyelid movements. BEXPLORER allows user control over common applications such as browsing computer files, watching a photo gallery, watching movies, playing music, text editing and browsing PDF files. Moreover, the user can send SMS messages from a cell phone, write and send email, browse the internet and chat with other BEXPLORER users as well as non-BEXPLORER users. Ten subjects form different genders and ages were asked to test our system. The results show that even with little training, users achieved 14 characters / min typing rates including typing corrections. The system is easy to use, tolerates unintentional user blinking and helps reduce eye fatigue. It is proposed for use by handicapped users as a fast, easy, to use computer interface. Videos of the system can be found at:
http://www.cs.aucegypt.edu/~elayat/bci/

References

1. ALS Therapy Development Institute (ALSTDI) Glossary,
   http://www.als.net/als101/glossary.asp
2. BCI 2000, http://www.bci2000.org
3. Donchin, E., Spencer, K.M., Wijesinghe, R.: The mental prosthesis: Assessing the speed of a P300-based brain-computer interface. IEEE Trans. Rehab. Eng. 8, 174–179 (2000)
4. Felton, E.A., Lewis, N.L., Wills, S.A., Radwin, R.G., Williams, J.C.: Neural Signal Based Control of the Dasher Writing System. In: 3rd International IEEE Conference on Neural Engineering CNE 2007, pp. 366–370 (2007)
5. Felzer, T., Freisleben, B.: Controlling a computer using signals originating from muscle contractions. In: Proc. METMBS 2002, vol. 2, pp. 336–342. CSREA Press (2002)
6. Felzer, T., Freisleben, B.: HaWCoS: the hands-free wheelchair control system. In: Proceedings of the ACM SIGCAPH Conference on Assistive Technologies, Edinburgh, Scotland, pp. 127–134. ACM Press, New York (2002)
7. Karpov, A., Ronzhin, A., Nechaev, A., Chernakova, S.: Multimodal system for hands-free PC control. In: 13th European Signal Processing Conference EUSIPCO 2005, Turkey (September 2005)
8. Kumar, M., Paepcke, A., Winograd, T.: EyePoint: Practical Pointing and Selection Using Gaze and Keyboard. In: Proceedings of the SIGCHI Conference on Human factors in computing systems (CHI 2007), pp. 421–430. ACM Press, New York (2007)
9. Schalk, G., McFarland, D.J., Hinterberger, T., Birbaumer, N., Wolpaw, J.R.: BCI 2000: A general-purpose brain-computer interface (BCI) system. IEEE Trans. Biomed. Eng. 51(6), 1034–1043 (2004)
10. Wills, S.A., David, J.C.: MacKay: DASHER - an efficient writing system for brain-computer interfaces? IEEE Transactions on Neural Systems and Rehabilitation Engineering 14(2), 244–246 (2006)

Continuous Control Paradigms for Direct Brain Interfaces

Melody Moore Jackson, Rudolph Mappus, Evan Barba, Sadir Hussein,
Girish Venkatesh, Chetna Shastry, and Amichai Israeli

Georgia Tech BrainLab
School of Interactive Computing MC 0760
Georgia Institute of Technology
85 Fifth St NW, Atlanta GA 30308 USA
{melody,cmappus}@cc.gatech.edu, ebarba3@gatech.edu,
{sadir,chetna,amichai}@gatech.edu, gvenkatesh3@mail.gatech.edu

Abstract. Direct Brain Interfaces (DBIs) offer great possibilities for people
with severe disabilities to communicate and control their environments. However, many DBI systems implement discrete selection, such as choosing a letter
from an alphabet, which offers limited control over certain tasks. Continuous
control is important for applications such as driving a wheelchair or drawing for
creative expression. This paper describes two projects currently underway at the
Georgia Tech BrainLab exploring continuous control interface paradigms for an
EEG-based approach centered on responses from visual cortex, and functional
near Infrared (fNIR) imaging of the language center of the brain.

Keywords: Direct Brain Interfaces, Brain Computer Interfaces, Continuous
Control, SSVEP, functional near Infrared imaging.

1 Introduction

Direct Brain Interfaces (DBI) have been demonstrated to restore communication and
environmental control to people whose severe motor disabilities prevent them from
using traditional input technology such as switches or mice [17]. Although research in
DBI systems holds immense promise, they are typically slow, error prone, and tedious
to learn [20]. The control that can be implemented with a DBI ranges from discrete
selection, with either a "touch screen" direct selection paradigm, or an indirect selection from a group of items (such as selecting an icon with a mouse), to continuous
control paradigms such as moving a pointer in a 2- or 3-dimensional space. Much of
the work on DBIs to date has focused on discrete selection as the target task [11][15].
While discrete selection is essential to restoring communication, for example, selecting "yes" or "no" or selecting letters to spell, discrete selection is very awkward for
tasks such as driving a wheelchair or moving a cursor on a screen. The more complex
and rich control provided by continuous paradigms merit study in order to improve
the bandwidth of DBI communication.

J.A. Jacko (Ed.): Human-Computer Interaction, Part II, HCII 2009, LNCS 5611, pp. 588–595, 2009.

1.1 Continuous Control

A *continuous control* DBI performs a proportional mapping of inputs to outputs. Compared to a discrete control DBI which functions essentially as an n-ary switch, a continuous control is similar to a dial or throttle; it allows for the question: "how much?" rather than simply: "which one?" The gradual or proportional component of continuous control makes it much more suited to activities that require precision, such as turning a wheelchair or pressing the pedals in accelerating an automobile. In DBIs, continuous control is often implemented as positional control, which dynamically maps or transforms the outputs of continuous brain signal processing into a series of relative positions in space. Two dimensional continuous positional control interfaces are used to move a cursor on a screen or to implement drawing or navigating tasks. They can also be used for selection by positioning a cursor over an icon and holding for a specified interval (a "dwell" selection). Continuous positional control interfaces have been implemented for a variety of DBI approaches, including implanted cortical electrodes [9][13][8][2], and EEG-based DBIs [19][21]. However, continuous control has not been fully explored for tasks beyond moving a cursor for indirect selection. This paper describes ongoing work in the Georgia Tech BrainLab studying and characterizing continuous control paradigms for two very different brain imaging approaches: EEG-based evoked response in visual cortex, and hemodynamic response as measured by functional Near Infrared (fNIR) imaging.

2 Continuous Control with Visual Evoked Potentials

The best performance reported to date for a DBI is 68 bits (more than eight characters) per minute [3][6], significantly higher than the average DBI performance of 24 bits per minute [20]. This DBI approach, based on an evoked response called Steady-State Visual Evoked Potentials (SSVEP), employs electroencephalogram (EEG) electrodes on the scalp over the visual cortex and requires little or no training. Accuracy of SSVEP-based DBIs is reported at over 95% [1]. This combination of factors makes SSVEP-based systems the most promising DBIs currently available. SSVEP is an *evoked response*, meaning that it is a reaction in the brain to an external stimulus. SSVEP changes can be detected via scalp EEG electrodes over the visual cortex of the brain in response to visual stimuli. Typically, the visual stimuli consist of a set of LEDs or images on a computer screen flashing at distinct constant frequencies, such as 10, 12, and 15 Hz [12]. As a DBI user attends to a particular stimulus, signals in the visual processing centers of the brain (directly beneath the electrodes) will oscillate at an identical frequency to the stimulus. Signal processing techniques can then determine which selection the user wishes to make based on which frequency is prominent in the EEG. SSVEP studies have shown that subjects have been able to differentiate 48 distinct simultaneous frequencies [6]. SSVEP DBIs have been used for communication [16], environmental control [6], immersive gaming [10][7] and have even been incorporated into wearable systems [18]. However, these systems implement SSVEP DBIs for discrete control, identifying the dominant frequency over a specific time bin. The control interfaces are typically simple selection paradigms; none of them implement continuous control, which entails calculating dynamic shifts in dominant frequency in real-time. Trejo et. al [19] report studies of continuous control of cursor movement using SSVEP.

In most previous studies of SSVEP systems, control depends on a simple discrete selection paradigm, such as choosing between "yes" or "no," or choosing from a set of targets. This paradigm is very similar to the functionality of a touch-screen – the user directly selects a desired item. Discrete-selection DBIs based on SSVEP have been proven to be effective and accurate, but they are limited in the types of control that they can provide, such as selecting letters for spelling or choosing a channel on a television. However, they do not work well for continuous tasks such as drawing, moving a cursor on a screen, or driving a wheelchair. An SSVEP-based continuous DBI would significantly increase the range of applications and tasks, refine the granularity of control, and improve reliability in DBI systems.

2.1 Continuous SSVEP-Based Game Controller

The eventual goal of this work is to drive a power wheelchair with proportional control. However our initial testbed is a "first-person shooter" style computer game based on a 3-D virtual world. The user can navigate through the world, and can "shoot" at targets, by focusing on one of four flashing stimuli on the periphery of the computer screen. The stimuli, in the form of flashing checkerboxes, represent different actions that the user can make. The checkerboxes to the right and left are for turning left and right respectively. The checkerbox towards the top of the screen is for moving forward and the one towards the bottom of the screen is for shooting. This design represents hybrid control; the three "positioning" stimuli are used to implement continuous, proportional control, while the "shooting" stimulus is used to implement discrete control (to "fire"). Figure 1 below illustrates the rendered 3D scene with the target in the middle of the screen.

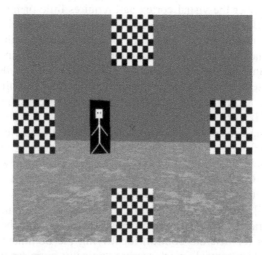

Fig. 1. Virtual world for first-person shooter game

2.2 SSVEP Classifier

Our initial work has shown that users can increase and decrease the amplitude of their SSVEP by intensifying their focus on a particular stimulus. We developed a classifier which performs Non-parametric Bayes Classification to identify the dominant (highest amplitude) signal frequency, which the classifier outputs as one of four classes. We then modulate a continuous control channel based on the amplitude of the brain signal at that frequency, until it drops below a threshold (indicating the user is no longer attending to the stimulus). This approach of classifying the dominant frequency in visual cortex provides discrete control, but we have used an interpolation mechanism to make the control of the game appear continuous. The classification process that we are using in this game outputs a decision every half a second; the classifier analyzes the signal read from the amplifier during a 500 millisecond time window and outputs data identifying the dominant frequency. Without any interpolation it would appear that the user's first-person avatar moves only during discrete time intervals (depending on the settings for the classifier parameters which affect the time lapse between messages sent to the game module). We interpolated movement over a time interval of 500 milliseconds. That is, when the game module receives a classification decision to move in a particular direction from the classifier, it acts on the decision and moves the avatar in that direction in small increments over the next 500 milliseconds, instead of making a large instantaneous move as soon as it receives a decision from the classifier. Using this technique the user perceives that the avatar is being controlled continuously.

2.3 Continuous Control SSVEP Pilot Study

We are currently conducting a pilot study with 24 able-bodied users to refine the continuous control paradigm and to improve the classifier. We are using a 16-channel G.Tec bioamplifier; the SSVEP signals are recorded from electrodes O1 and O2 on the standard 10/20 system. We sample at 256 Hz, and employ an FFT function to transform the signals into a frequency domain representation. The users participate in an initial calibration where their responses to stimuli at different frequencies are measured. Then we run the 6 trials for the experiment, each with different settings. For each trial, the game consists of 10 rounds of play. In each round the target is placed at a different predetermined location. These 10 different positions are the same for each trial. Each round lasts for 45 seconds, unless the user manages to shoot the target before this time, in which case the next round begins immediately. The 10 positions to be used are chosen such that all the 3 stimuli are equally tested. The accuracy of the interface for each trial is calculated and compared. We are still collecting data and improving the interface; initial results show accuracy above 50% with no training (chance is 10%).

3 Continuous Control Based on Hemodynamic Response

We are also studying continuous control paradigms for another DBI approach based on functional near infrared (fNIR) spectroscopy. fNIR is a multi-wavelength optical spectroscopy technique that can assess temporal progression of brain activity through the measurement of hemodynamic changes. We are performing this study with the OTIS fNIR imaging device developed by Archinoetics Inc. [5]. The OTIS apparatus contains a sensor consisting of an infrared light source and a light detector that receives light after it has interacted with the tissue. Based on the amount of infrared light that is reflected to the detector, the OTIS can determine the amount of oxygen in the blood in a particular region of the brain. We are currently positioning a single emitter/detector over Broca's area, over the left inferior frontal gyrus (in a right-dominant subject) as shown in Figure 2. The subject performs language-based mental tasks such as sub-vocal counting or silent singing to activate the brain in that area.

Fig. 2. The placement of the OTIS emitter/detector over Broca's area in a right-dominant subject

The user task for this study is two-dimensional line drawing. In order to test the users' control, we implemented a guided task paradigm in which the users trace simple letter shapes, as shown in Figure 3. To implement the two-dimensional drawing paradigm with a single fNIR sensor, we enforce some constraints on the location of the current drawing point and make some initial assumptions. First, the point always starts in the middle of the drawing pane. Second, the starting state of the drawing point is assumed to draw straight down from the midpoint. Both the rate of drawing as well as the curvature of the line is a function of the input observations of the fNIRS device, the lower the fNIR activation, the more curved the line. For example, if a user wishes to draw a straight line, he or she performs language-oriented tasks such as sub-vocal counting to raise the hemodynamic response. To allow the line to curve, the user focuses on nonsense syllables such as "la, la, la" very slowly, or to perform cognitively orthogonal tasks such as mental rotation of a shape, which has the effect of reducing the hemodynamic response in Broca's area.

Fig. 3. Letter template for guided drawing task

We are currently performing a pilot study of the drawing task with able-bodied participants. The goal of the experiment is to trace a letter in the drawing pane. A letter template is placed in the background of the drawing pane to indicate to subjects which stimulus to draw. Participants are asked to perform activation tasks in order to draw a straight line, and deactivation tasks to draw a curved line. The initial state of the line direction is always down. The starting activation state is augmented using an initial bias. For instance, for letter C, the activation bias was toward curvature initially; then the user must straighten the line, then let it curve again. We calculate accuracy (error) by the amount of deviation of the letter drawn by the participant from the prepared template of the letter that is displayed to the participant on the screen. The deviation is quantified by the Root Mean Square (RMS) of the distances of the sample points in the trial alphabet from the corresponding points in the template. The RMS values that we obtained in our study also serve as a direct indication of the difficulty of the task with higher values for alphabets with more number of transitions (from a curve to a straight line or vice versa). We plan to complete this pilot study with ten able-bodied subjects and two subjects with motor disabilities.

4 Conclusions and Future Work

For the millions of people with severe motor disabilities [4], the power to navigate and control devices and appliances unaided throughout their own home environment has the potential to significantly improve quality of life, for themselves and also for those charged with their care. The tasks inherent in real-world home living environments represent a unique and vital set of problems for researchers as well as for people with severe disabilities [14]. Continuous control represents a powerful mechanism that enables many application possibilities in real-world environments. Proportional continuous control represents a powerful paradigm shift for the field of biometric interfaces, and could fundamentally improve assistive technologies for people with severe motor disabilities. We hypothesize that continuous control, and hybrid continous/discrete control, will significantly increase the range of tasks, granularity of control, and reliability of output in DBI systems. We plan to complete our fundamental studies of continuous paradigms for both evoked response (SSVEP) and hemodynamic response (fNIR) based BCIs, and apply the results to improve quality of life for people with severe motor disabilities.

Acknowledgments. This work is funded by the National Science Foundation CISE/IIS Human Centered Computing program under award number IIS-0705679 (Ephraim Glinert, Program Manager) and by the CISE/IIS CreativeIT program under award number IIS-0745829 (Mary Lou Maher, Program Manager). The authors would like to express our gratitude to the NSF for their support for this research.

References

1. Beverina, F., Palmas, G., Silvoni, S., Piccone, F., Giove, S.: User Adaptive BCIs: SSVEP and P300 Based Interfaces. PsychNology. 1(4), 331–354 (2003)
2. Black, M.J., Bienenstock, E., Donoghue, J., Serruya, M., Wu, W., Gao, Y.: Connecting Brains with Machines: the Neural Control of 2D Cursor Movment. In: First International IEEE EMBS Conference on Neural Engineering, March 20-22, pp. 580–583 (2003)
3. Cheng, M., Gao, X., Gao, S., Xu, D.: Design and implementation of a brain-computer interface with high transfer rates. IEEE Transactions on Biomedical Engineering 49, 1181–1186 (2002)
4. Christopher Reeve Paralysis Foundation (2003), http://www.crpf.org
5. Downs, H., Downs, T., Robinson, W., Nishimura, E., Stautzenberger, P.: A New Approach to fNIR: the Optical Tomographic Imaging Spectrometer. In: Schmorrow, D. (ed.) Foundations of Augmented Cognition. Routledge, New York (2005)
6. Gao, X., Xu, D., Cheng, M., Gao, S.: A BCI-based environmental controller for the motion-disabled. IEEE Trans. Neural Syst. Rehabil. Eng. 11(2), 137–140 (2003)
7. Green, C.S., Bavelier, D.: Action video game modifies visual selective attention. Nature 423(6939), 534–537 (2003)
8. Hochberg, L.R., Serruya, M.D., Friehs, G.M., Mukand, J.A., Saleh, M., Caplan, A.H., Branner, A., Chen, D., Penn, R.D., Donoghue, J.P.: Neuronal ensemble control of prosthetic devices by a human with tetraplegia. Nature 442(7099), 164–171 (2006)
9. Kennedy, P., Bakay, R., Moore, M., Adams, K., Goldthwaite, J.: Direct Control of a Computer from the Human Central Nervous System. IEEE Transactions on Rehabilitation Engineering 8(2) (2000)
10. Lalor, S., Kelly, C., Finucane, R., Burke, R., Reilly, G., McDarby, G.: Steady State VEP Brain-Computer Interface control in an Immersive 3-D Environment. EURASIP Journal on Applied Signal Processing 2005(19), 3156–3164 (2005)
11. Mason, S., Moore Jackson, M., Birch, G.: A General Framework for Characterizing Studies of Brain Interface Technology. Annals of Biomedical Engineering 33(11), 1653–1670 (2005)
12. Middendorf, M.S., McMillan, G., Calhoun, G., Jones, K.S.: Brain-computer interfaces based on the steady-state visual-evoked response. IEEE Trans. Rehabil. Eng. 8(2), 211–214 (2000)
13. Moore, M., Kennedy, P., Mankoff, J., Mynatt, E.: Nudge and Shove: Frequency Thresholding for Brain Signal Control. Accepted to SIGCHI 2001, Seattle Washington (March 31 - April 4, 2001)
14. Moore, M.: Real-World Applications for Brain-Computer Interface Technology. IEEE Transactions on Neural Systems and Rehabilitation Engineering 11(2) (June 2003)
15. Moore Jackson, M., Mason, S., Birch, G.: Analyzing Trends in Brain Interface Technology: a Method to Compare Studies. Annals of Biomedical Engineering 34(5), 859–878 (2006)

16. Mueller-Putz, G., Scherer, R., Brauneis, C., Pfurtschellar, G.: Steady-state visual evoked potential (SSVEP)-based communication: impact of harmonic frequency components. Journal of Neural Engineering 2, 123–130 (2005)
17. Neumann, N., Hinterberger, T., Kaiser, J., Leins, U., Birbaumer, N., Kubler, A.: Automatic processing of self-regulation of slow cortical potentials: evidence from brain-computer communication in paralysed patients. Clinical Neurophysiology 115(3), 628–635 (2004)
18. Piccini, L., Parini, S., Maggi, L., Andreoni, G.: A Wearable Home BCI System: Preliminary Results with SSVEP protocol. In: Proceedings of the 27th Annual Conference of the Engineering in Medicine and Biology Society (September 2005)
19. Trejo, L., Rosipal, R., Matthews, B.: Brain-Computer Interfaces for 1-D and 2-D Cursor Control: Designs using Volitional Control of the EEG Spectrum or Steady-State Visual Evoked Potentials. IEEE Transactions on Neural Systems and Rehabilitation Engineering 14(2) (June 2006)
20. Wolpaw, J.R., Birbaumer, N., McFarland, D.J., Pfurtscheller, G., Vaughan, T.M.: Brain-computer interfaces for communication and control. Clinical Neurophysiology 113, 767–791 (2002)
21. Wolpaw, J.R., McFarland, D.J., Vaughan, T.M., Schalk, G.: The Wadsworth Center Brain-Computer Interface (BCI) Research and Development Program. IEEE Transactions On Neural Systems and Rehabilitation Engineering 11(2) (June 2003)

Constructive Adaptive User Interfaces
Based on Brain Waves

Masayuki Numao, Takayuki Nishikawa, Toshihito Sugimoto, Satoshi Kurihara,
and Roberto Legaspi

The Institute of Scientific and Industrial Research, Osaka University
8-1 Mihogaoka, Ibaraki, Osaka 567-0047, Japan
numao@sanken.osaka-u.ac.jp

Abstract. We demonstrate a method to locate relations and constraints between a music score and its impressions, by which we show that machine learning techniques may provide a powerful tool for composing music and analyzing human feelings. We examine its generality by modifying some arrangements to provide the subjects with a specified impression. This demonstration introduces some user interfaces, which are capable of predicting feelings and creating new objects based on seed structures, such as spectrums and their transition for sounds that have been extracted and are perceived as favorable by the test subject. This paper proposes to define knowledge components for the seed structure.

1 Introduction

Music is a flow of information among its composer, player and audience. A composer writes a score that players play to create a sound to be listened by its audience. Since a score, a performance or MIDI data denotes a section of the flow, we can know a feeling caused by a piece of score or performance. A feeling consists of very complex elements, which depend on each person, and are affected by a historical situation. Therefore, rather than clarifying what a human feeling is, we would like to clarify only musical structures that cause a specific feeling. Based on such structures, the authors constructed an automatic arrangement and composition system producing a piece causing a specified feeling on a person.

The system first collects a person's feelings for some pieces, based on which it extracts a common musical structure causing a specific feeling. It arranges an existing song or composes a new piece to fit such a structure causing a specified feeling.

The authors have developed an inductive logic programming (ILP) system that acquires rules describing personal feelings for musical pieces[5, 1]. They analyze the description and find some knowledge components written as a rule set. Since variables are introduced in ILP, it has to search a huge space of variable combinations. By introducing knowledge components, its search space becomes comparable to that of attribute-based learners, such as decision tree learners or neural networks.

Most machine learning methods can not learn a relation between elements from data. Structures and relations are necessary to acquire language or symbolic representations, such as a musical score and a structural formula in chemistry. However, since there are

J.A. Jacko (Ed.): Human-Computer Interaction, Part II, HCII 2009, LNCS 5611, pp. 596–605, 2009.
© Springer-Verlag Berlin Heidelberg 2009

combinatorial number of relations between elements, learning of a relation often causes explosion of search space. Although ILP assumes proper limited search spaces to overcome this difficulty, it depends on each application domain.

The authors are using FOIL[4] to acquire structural description of musical scores. Its programmer experimentally learns that it is easy to assign variables without searching for the variable space, since the rules have some patterns. This paper proposes a method to separate such patterns from the learning algorithm, and describe them.

2 Extracting Structures in Musical Scores

We address the problem of determining the extent by which emotion-inducing music can be modelled and generated using creative music compositional AI [5]. Our approach involves inducing an affects-music relations model that describes musical events related to the listener's affective reactions and then using the predictive knowledge and character of the model to automatically control the music generation task. We have embodied our solution in a Constructive Adaptive User Interface (CAUI)[3] that re-arranges or composes a musical piece based on one's affect.

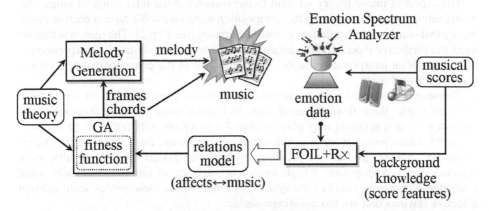

Fig. 1. The learning architecture

The learning architecture is shown in Fig. 1. The relational model is induced by employing the inductive logic programming paradigms taking as inputs the musical score features and the ESA-provided emotion data. The musical score features are represented as definitions of first-order logic predicates and serve as background knowledge to the induction task. The next task employs a genetic algorithm (GA) that produces variants of the original score features. The fitness function of the GA fits each generated variant to the knowledge provided by the model and music theory. Finally, the CAUI creates using its melody-generating module an initial tune consisting of the GA-obtained chord tones and then alters certain chord tones to become non-chord tones in order to embellish the tune.

In order to obtain a personalized model of the coupling of emotional expressions and the underlying music parameters, it is vital to: (1) identify which musical features (e.g., tempo, rhythm, harmony, etc.) should be represented as background knowledge, (2)

Frame *features*		Chord *features*	
Tempo	adagio, lento, andante, moderato, allegretto, allegro, presto, larghetto	Key	As, B, Cis, D, Fis, G, A, H
		Tonality	dur (major), moll (minor)
Rhythm	2/2, 2/4, 4/4, 6/8	Root	I, II, III, IV, V, VI, VII
Melodic instrument	piano, sax (soprano or tenor)	Form	5th, 7th, 9th
Accompaniment	piano, guitar	Inversion	zero, 1, 2, 3
Key	As, B, Cis, D, Fis, G, A, H	Semi-own	present, absent
Tonality	dur (major), moll (minor)	Secondary dominant	II, IV, V, VI, absent
Cadence	complete (or authentic), half, other	Special variations	Neopolitan 6th, sus4, absent
		Function	tonic, dominant, subdominant

Fig. 2. Basic aspects of music theory

provide an instrument to map the features to identified emotion descriptors, (3) logically represent the music parameters, and (4) automatically induce the model. Although the influence of various features has been well studied, the task of the CAUI is to automatically find musical structure and sequence features that are influential to specific emotions.

The aspect of music theory relevant to our research is the interaction of music elements into patterns that can help the composition techniques. We have a narrow music theory that consists of a limited set of music elements (see Fig. 2). The reason is that we need the predictive model to be tractable in order to perform controlled experimentations and obtain interpretable results. The definitions of the concepts can be found in texts on music theory.

Fourteen (14) musical piece segments were prepared consisting of four pieces from classical music, three from Japanese Pop, and seven from harmony textbooks. The amount of time a segment may play is from 7.4 to 48 seconds (an average of 24.14 seconds). These pieces were selected, albeit not randomly, from the original 75 segments which were used in our previous experiments. Based on prior results, these selected pieces demonstrate a high degree of variance in emotional content when evaluated by previous users of the system. In other words, these pieces seem to elicit affective flavours that are more distinguishable.

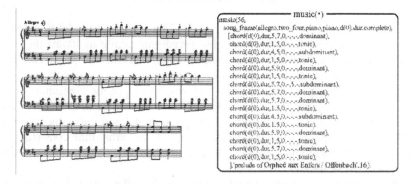

Fig. 3. Representation of a score

The background knowledge of the CAUI are definitions in first-order logic that describe musical score features. The language of first-order logic, or predicate logic, is known to be well-suited both for data representation and describing the desired outputs. The representational power of predicate logic permits describing existing feature relations among data, even complex relations, and provides comprehensibility of the learned results. Score features were encoded into a predicate variable, or relation, named *music(•)*, which contains one *song_frame(·)* and a list of sequenced *chord(•)* relations describing the frame and chord features, respectively. Fig. 3 shows the *music(•)* representation ('-' means NIL) of the musical score segment of the prelude of Jacques Offenbach's Orpheé aux Enfers.

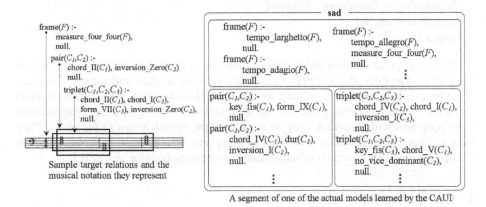

Fig. 4. A segment of a set of rules that are supposed to stimulate a sad feeling

The CAUI needs to learn three kinds of target relations or rules, namely, *frame(•)*, *pair(•)* and *triplet(•)*, wherein the last two represent patterns of two and three successive chords, respectively. These rules comprise the affects-music relational model. Fig. 4-left, for example, shows structural information contained in the given sample relations and the actual musical notation they represent. Fig. 4-right shows a segment of an actual model learned by the CAUI that can be used to construct a musical piece that is supposed to induce in one user a sad feeling.

In the following section, we explain the learning algorithm of FOIL and introduce a new target relation, namely, *chords(•)*, which is a generalization of *pair(•)* or *triplet(•)*, and represents a successive chord sequence with an arbitrary length.

3 FOIL

The following is the algorithm of FOIL.

Algorithm 1 FOIL
Initialize $H \leftarrow \varphi$
Remaining ← Positive(Examples)
repeat

```
C ← R(X1,X2, ...) :-
repeat
    Literals ← all possible literals in BK
    for all L in Literals do
      C' ← add L to the right-hand side of C
      calculate Gain(C')
    end for
    C ← C' with the best Gain
    until notCover(Negative(Examples),C)
  H ← H ∪ C
  Remaining ← Remaining - Covered
  until |Remaining|=0
  output H
```

This is a popular separate and conquer rule learning algorithm. When the literal does not contain variables, the number of candidate *Literals* is small and we use this algorithm for rule learning in data mining applications. However, in ILP the literal contains variables, whose number of combinations is quite large. Although human programmers write programs with variables, they do not search the combinations of variables. They have a library of programming patterns or components to construct a large program. This paper proposes a method to introduce programming components to ILP.

4   Components for Musical Scores

To learn structures in musical scores the authors introduce *frame(A)* to describe overall characteristics of the score *A*, and *chords(A)* to describe a sequence of chords in the score. The definitions of *frame(•)* can be translated into a decision tree with some attributes, since it uses only one variable.

The definitions of *chords(•)* contain some variables describing structure in a chord sequence. They have some patterns and are compositions of the following clauses with those in the appendix:

```
(1)  chords(A)  :- chords2(A, B).

(2)  chords2(A, B)  :-
         has_chord(A, B, C),

         key(C),
         moll-or-dur(C),
         chord(C),
         form(C),
         inversion(C),
         root_omission-or-not(C),
         semi_own-or-not(C),
         vice_dominant(C),
         augment_chord-or-not(C),
```

```
        change(C),
        additional(C),
        function(C),
        chords3(A, B).
```

(3) chords3(A, B) :- next_to(A, B, D), chords2(A,D).
(4) chords3(A, B). % don't care

The predicate has_chord(A,B,C) represents that a musical piece A contains a chord B, whose structure is C. The predicate next_to(A,B,D) represents that in a musical piece A the successive chord of B is D. In clause (2) the literals from key(C) to function(C) represent features of chord structure C to be replaced by the right hand side of a clause in the appendix to obtain a rule. For example, key(C) is replaced by key_c(C), key_cis(C), key_d(C), etc. When key(C) is replaced by the empty right hand side of 'key(C).% don't care' in the appendix, the feature key(C) is removed from the rule.

To replace a literal in a clause with the right hand side of another clause, the literal is unified with the left hand side to make a composition of the two clauses. This operation is similar to that used in Explanation-Based Generalization (EBG), in which the algorithm decides clauses to be composed by using explanation of a training example.

Instead of using explanation, we will use the following algorithm similar to FOIL:

Algorithm 2 Component-Based FOIL
Initialize $H \leftarrow \phi$
  $Remaining \leftarrow Positive(Examples)$
Repeat
  $C \leftarrow R(X1, X2, ...) : -$
    repeat
      $SClauses \leftarrow$ all possible subclauses in BK
        for all S in $SClauses$ do
          $C' \leftarrow$ compose S to the right-hand side of C
            calculate $Gain(C')$
        end for
      $C \leftarrow C'$ with the best $Gain$
    until $notCover(Negative(Examples),C)$
  $H \leftarrow H \cup C$
  $Remaining \leftarrow Remaining - Covered$
until $|Remaining|=0$
output H

In the case of *chords* predicate, by composing the clauses (1)-(4), the algorithm enumerates rules for chord sequences with an arbitrary length.

Example 1. By composing the clauses (1),(2) and (4), we obtain the following rule:

```
chords(A)  :-
          has_chord(A, B, C),
          key(C),
          moll-or-dur(C),
          chord(C),
          form(C),
          inversion(C),
          root_omission-or-not(C),
          semi_own-or-not(C),
          vice_dominant(C),
          augment_chord-or-not(C),
          change(C),
          additional(C),
          function(C).
```

By replacing the literals from key(C) to function(C) by the right hand sides of clauses in the appendix, we obtain rules which represent a chord sequence with a length of 1.

The search space is comparable to attribute-based learning algorithms, since it does not search the space of assigning variables. According to the appendix, the number of alternatives of each feature is: key(C) : 15, moll-or-dur(C) : 4, chord(C) : 8, form(C) : 5, inversion(C) : 8, root_omission-or-not(C) : 3, semi_own-or-not(C) : 3, vice_dominant(C) : 8, augment_chord-or-not(C) : 3, change(C) : 6, additional(C) : 5, function(C) : 4. The number of these combinations is $15*4*8*5*8*3*3*8*3*6*5*4 = 497,664,000$, all of which can be searched, although we have to introduce some search strategies for a longer sequence.

Example 2. By composing the clauses (1),(2),(3),(2) and (4), we obtain the following rule:

```
chords(A)  :-
          has_chord(A, B, C),
          key(C),
          moll-or-dur(C),
          chord(C),
          form(C),
          inversion(C),
          root_omission-or-not(C),
          semi_own-or-not(C),
          vice_dominant(C),
          augment_chord-or-not(C),
```

```
          change(C),
          additional(C),
          function(C),
        next_to(A, B, D),
          has_chord(A, D, E),
          key(E),
          moll-or-dur(E),
          chord(E),
          form(E),
          inversion(E),
          root_omission-or-not(E),
          semi_own-or-not(E),
          vice_dominant(E),
          augment_chord-or-not(E),
          change(E),
          additional(E),
          function(E).
```

By replacing the literals from key(C) to function(C) and from key(E) to function(E) by the right hand sides of clauses in the appendix, we obtain rules which represent a chord sequence with a length of 2..

As such, our method quickly synthesizes a rule for a long chord sequence.

5 Conclusion

We propose a method to learn rules based on components. To eliminate the search space, we have to give a component set as clauses. This component set decides the rule space and are similar to a syntax rule set in formal languages, which is described easily when we know the syntax. This will be an application-oriented project. The authors will test this method in the music domain and chemical structure formula[2].

In Ambient Intelligence, CAUI can be used as a tool to compose musical pieces dynamically. In this case, we need to extract structures in musical scores dynamically and incrementally. Our future work includes incremental extraction of structures in scores based on components.

References

[1] Legaspi, R., Hashimoto, Y., Moriyama, K., Kurihara, S., Numao, M.: Music compositional intelligence with an affective flavor. In: ACM International Conference on Intelligent User Interfaces, pp. 216–224 (2007)

[2] Nattee, C., Sinthupinyo, S., Numao, M., Okada, T.: Learning first-order rules from data with multiple parts: Applications on mining chemical compound data. In: Proceedings 21st International Conference on Machine Learning, pp. 606–614 (2004)

[3] Numao, M., Takagi, S., Nakamura, K.: Constructive adaptive user interfaces — composing music based on human feelings. In: Proc. Eighteenth National Conference on Artificial Intelligence (AAAI 2002), pp. 193–198. The AAAI Press / The MIT Press (2002)

[4] Quinlan, J.R.: Learning logical definitions from relations. Machine Learning 5, 239–266 (1990)

[5] Sugimoto, T., Legaspi, R., Ota, A., Moriyama, K., Kurihara, S., Numao, M.: Modelling affective-based music compositional intelligence with the aid of ANS analyses. Knowledge-Based Systems 21(3), 200–208 (2008)

A Components for Candidate Rules

```
key(C) :- key_c(C). key(C) :- key_cis(C). key(C) :- key_d(C).
key(C) :- key_e(C). key(C) :- key_f(C). key(C) :- key_fis(C).
key(C) :- key_g(C). key(C) :- key_a(C). key(C) :- key_h(C).
key(C) :- key_des(C). key(C) :- key_es(C). key(C) :- key_ges(C).
key(C) :- key_as(C). key(C) :- key_b(C).
key(C). % don't care

moll-or-dur(C) :- dur(C). moll-or-dur(C) :- moll(C).
moll-or-dur(C) :- moll_dur(C).
moll_dur(C). % don't care

chord(C) :- chord_I(C). chord(C) :- chord_II(C).
chord(C) :- chord_III(C). chord(C) :- chord_IV(C).
chord(C) :- chord_V(C). chord(C) :- chord_VI(C).
chord(C) :- chord_VII(C).
chord(C). % don't care

form(C) :- form_V(C).  form(C) :- form_VII(C).
form(C) :- form_IX(C). form(C) :- form_XI(C).
form(C). % don't care

inversion(C)      :-    inversion_Zero(C).    inversion(C)    :-
inversion_I(C).
inversion(C)      :-      inversion_I(C).     inversion(C)    :-
inversion_II(C).
inversion(C)      :-    inversion_III(C).     inversion(C)    :-
inversion_IV(C).
inversion(C) :- inversion_V(C).
inversion(C). % don't care

root_omission-or-not(C) :- root_omission(C).
root_omission-or-not(C) :- no_root_omission(C).
root_omission-or-not(C). % don't care

semi_own-or-not(C)    :-    semi_own(C).   semi_own-or-not(C)   :-
no_semi_own(C).
semi_own-or-not(C). % don't care

vice_dominant(C) :- vice_dominant_II(C).
vice_dominant(C) :- vice_dominant_III(C).
vice_dominant(C) :- vice_dominant_IV(C).
vice_dominant(C) :- double_dominant(C).
vice_dominant(C) :- vice_dominant_VI(C).
```

```
vice_dominant(C) :- vice_dominant_VII(C).
vice_dominant(C) :- no_vice_dominant(C).
vice_dominant(C). % don't care

augment_chord-or-not(C) :- augment_chord(C).
augment_chord-or-not(C) :- no_augment_chord(C).
augment_chord-or-not(C). % don't care

change(C) :- napori_VI(C). change(C) :- doria_IV(C).
change(C) :- displacement_up(C). change(C) :- sus4(C).
change(C) :- no_change(C).
change(C). % don't care

additional(C)      :-      additional_VI(C).      additional(C)      :-
additional_IV_VI(C).
    additional(C)      :-      additional_IX(C).      additional(C)      :-
no_additional(C).
    additional(C). % don't care

function(C) :- tonic(C). function(C) :- dominant(C).
function(C) :- subdominant(C).
function(C). % don't care
```

Development of Symbiotic Brain-Machine Interfaces Using a Neurophysiology Cyberworkstation

Justin C. Sanchez[1,2,3], Renato Figueiredo[4], Jose Fortes[4], and Jose C. Principe[3,4]

[1] Department of Pediatrics
[2] Department of Neuroscience
[3] Department of Biomedical Engineering
[4] Department of Electrical and Computer Engineering
University of Florida
Gainesville, Florida
jcs77@ufl.edu, fortes@ufl.edu, principe@cnel.ufl.edu

Abstract. We seek to develop a new generation of brain-machine interfaces (BMI) that enable both the user and the computer to engage in a symbiotic relationship where they must co-adapt to each other to solve goal-directed tasks. Such a framework would allow the possibility real-time understanding and modeling of brain behavior and adaptation to a changing environment, a major departure from either offline learning and static models or one-way adaptive models in conventional BMIs. To achieve a symbiotic architecture requires a computing infrastructure that can accommodate multiple neural systems, respond within the processing deadlines of sensorimotor information, and can provide powerful computational resources to design new modeling approaches. To address these issues we present or ongoing work in the development of a neurophysiology Cyberworkstation for BMI design.

Keywords: Brain-Machine Interface, Co-Adaptive, Cyberworkstation.

1 Introduction

Brain-machine interfaces (BMIs) offer tremendous promise as assistive systems for motor-impaired patients, as new paradigms for man-machine interaction, and as vehicles for the discovery and promotion of new computational principles for autonomous and intelligent systems. At the core of a motor BMI, is an embedded computer programmed with information processing models of the motor system to dialogue directly and in real-time with the user's sensori-motor commands derived directly from the nervous system. Thus, two key problems of BMI research are (1) to establish the proper experimental interactive paradigm between biological and machine intelligence and (2) to model how the brain plans and controls motion. Both the search for solutions to these problems and the solutions themselves require the development of new computational frameworks into *in-vivo* contexts.

Many groups have conducted research in BMIs and the approach has been strongly signal processing based without much concern to incorporate the design principles of the biologic system in the interface. The implementation path has either taken an

J.A. Jacko (Ed.): Human-Computer Interaction, Part II, HCII 2009, LNCS 5611, pp. 606–615, 2009.
© Springer-Verlag Berlin Heidelberg 2009

unsupervised approach by finding causal relationships in the data [1], a supervised approach using (functional) regression [2], or more sophisticated methods of sequential estimation [3] to minimize the error between predicted and known behavior. These approaches are primarily data-driven techniques that seek out correlation and structure between the spatio-temporal neural activation and behavior. Once the model is trained, the procedure is to *fix the model parameters* for use in a test set that assumes stationarity in the functional mapping. Some of the best known linear models that have used this architecture in the BMI literature are the Wiener filter (FIR) [4, 5] and Population Vector [6], generative models [7-9], and nonlinear dynamic neural networks (a time delay neural network or recurrent neural networks [10-12]) models that assume behavior can be captured by a static input-output model and that the spike train statistics do not change over time. While these models have been shown to work well in specific scenarios, they carry with them these strong assumptions and will likely not be feasible over the long term.

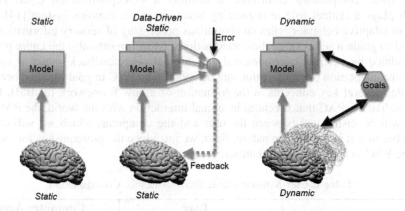

Fig. 1. Evolution of BMI modeling; (a) First generation BMIs with strong static assumptions for both the model and user; (b) Data-driven approach for relaxing static modeling assumptions though the use of multiple models trained with an error response; (c) Co-adaptive BMIs have a common goal for the user and model thus allowing for dynamic sharing of control

Figure 1 illustrates the ongoing evolution in BMI modeling. Conventional BMIs assume a static, single model to translate the spatio-temporal patterns of brain activity into a desired response available from an able user. In a test set, the model translates the intent of the user (also assumed to be static) into behavior without requiring body movements (Fig. 1a). BMIs of this type proved the possibility of translating thoughts into actions, but do not work reliably for multiple tasks in a clinical setting. To build upon these efforts in the past 3 years we considered a biologically plausible architecture with multiple models specialized for parts of the trajectory, thus improving both reliability and accuracy (Fig. 1b). Our research revealed an imbalance between the roles of the user and the BMI. When the desired response is used in training it simplifies model building, but also enforces a role of signal translator to the BMI which is incompatible with the dynamic nature of brain activity and the tasks in the environment. To create a BMI capable of capturing new and complex tasks with minimal training and accommodate the changing brain activity, a co-adaptive system is necessary. The externally imposed information should be kept at a minimum, i.e. the system should learn how to evaluate actions and learn from mistakes independently (Fig. 1c). This lead us to evaluate an alternate training paradigm.

We are particularly interested in developing an emergent system where the user and computer cooperatively seek to maximize goals while interacting with a complex, dynamical environment. Both the user and the computer are in a symbiotic relationship where they must co-adapt to each other to solve tasks. This behavior depends on a series of events or elemental procedures that promote specific brain or behavioral syntax, feedback, and repetition over time [13]; hence, the sequential evaluative process is always ongoing, adheres to strict timing and cooperative-competitive processes. With these processes, intelligent motor control and more importantly goal-directed behavior can be built with closed-loop mechanisms which continuously adapt internal and external antecedents of the world, express intent though behavior in the environment, and evaluate the consequences of those behaviors to promote learning. Collectively these components contribute to forming a Perception-Acton Cycle (PAC) which plays a critical role in organizing behavior in the nervous system [14]. This form of adaptive behavior relies on continuous processing of sensory information that is used to guide a series of goal-directed actions. Most importantly, the entire process is regulated by external environmental and internal neurofeedback, which is used to guide the adaptation of computation and behavior. The PAC in goal-directed behavior provides several key concepts in the formation of a new framework for BMI. However, unlike the PAC that is central in animal interaction with the world, the PAC in a BMI will be distributed between the user and the computer, which we will call an agent because it is assistive in nature. Next, we introduce the prerequisites for modifying the PAC to incorporate two entities.

Table 1. User-Neuroprosthetic Prerequisites for Co-Adaptation

	User	**Computer Agent**
Representation	Brain States	Environmental States
Valuation	Goal-Directed	Goal-Directed
Action Selection	Neuromodulation	Competition
Outcome Measures	Internal Reward Expectation	Predicted Error
Learning	Reinforcement Based	Reinforcement Based
Co-Adaptation	Dynamic Brain Organization	Optimization of Parameters

2   Minimal Prerequesites for Co-adaptation

In order to symbiotically link artificial intelligent tools with neural systems, a new set of protocols must be derived to enable and empower dialogue between two seemingly different entities. A minimal set of six prerequisites given in Table 1 describe the essential computation that is required to enact a symbiotic PAC. These prerequisites are based on concepts considered to be key in value-based decision making [15]. Unique to the development of intelligent BMIs is that the user and neuroprosthetic each have their own perspective and contribution to each prerequisite as described below.

Representation. Internal to the user, the spatio-temporal structure of neural activation forms a coding of intent for action in the external world. At any given moment, the neural code can be sampled as a brain state defined as the vector of values (from all recording electrodes) that describe the operating point within a space of all possible state values. The syntax or sequence of brain states must be able to support a sufficiently rich computational repertoire and must encode a range of values with sufficient accuracy and discriminability. These brain states could contain either a local or distributed representation depending on where the signals are being collected.

While the representation of brain states are embedded internally in the user, the representation of the BMI is embodied in the environment [16]. The BMI connection created from the brain state to the environment forms a channel for communication from the internal to external worlds. In the external world, the state representation of the neuroprosthetic includes the sequence of sensory information about the environment that is relevant to goal directed behavior. For example, environmental state could be action oriented and update the position or velocity of the BMI. It is important to note that the state need not contain all the details about the environment but a sufficiently rich sequence that summarizes the important information that lead to the current state. If the environmental state representation has this property, it could be considered to be Markov.

Valuation. Valuation is the process of how a system assigns value to actions and behavior outcomes. For goal-directed motor behavior, we seek systems that compute with action-outcome sequences and assign high value to outcomes that yield desirable rewards. In the design of BMIs, it is desirable for both the user to be highly responsive to each other through the immediate update of value as soon as an outcome changes. This approach is very different from habitual valuation which does not participate in continual self-analysis [17]. For BMI, one of the main computational goals is to develop real-time methods for coupling the valuation between the user and BMI for a variety of action-outcome associations.

Action Selection. To complete goal-directed behaviors, both the user and neuroprosthetic tool must perform actions in the environment. The method of precisely timing and triggering particular actions that support the task objective is dependent on if there are internal or external representations used. For the user, action selection is performed through the intentional and transient excitation or inhibition (neuromodulation) of neural activity that is capable of supporting a subset of actions. This functional relationship between neuromodulation and the signaling of actions defines the process of action selection. It is expected that under the influence of intelligent BMIs, the primary motor cortex will undergo functional reorganization during motor learning [18-20]. This reorganization in action selection is due in part to how the neuroprosthetic tool synergistically performs action selection in the external environment. Computationally, choosing one action from a set of actions can be implemented through competition, where actions compete with each other to be activated. Using a set of discriminant functions, the action or actions with the highest values can be declared the winner and selected for use in the goal-directed behavior.

Outcome Measures. To determine the success of the goal-directed behavior, both the user and neuroprosthetic tool have different measures of outcome. The prediction error, as its name implies, is the consequence of uncertainty in goal achievement and can be linked either directly to an inherent characteristic of the environment or to internal representations of reward in the user. Reward expectation of the user is expressed in reward centers of the brain [21] and evaluates the states of environment in terms of an increase or decrease in the probability of earning reward. During the cycles of the PAC the reward expectation of the user can be modulated by the novelty and type of environmental conditions encountered. Ideally, the goal of intelligent BMIs is to create synergies in both outcome measures so that the expectations are proportional to the prediction error of the neuroprosthetic tool.

Learning. Because of the rich interactions between the user and the neuroprosthtic, the way that the system learns cannot be a fixed input output mapper (as in conventional BMIs), but it has to be a state dependent system that utilize experience. Throughout this process it develops a model of the world, which in BMIs will include a model of the interaction with the user. Reinforcement Learning (RL) is a computational framework for goal based learning and decision-making. Learning through interaction with environment distinguishes this method from other learning paradigms. There have been many developments in the machine learning RL paradigm [22-25] which originated from the theory of optimal control in Markov Decision Processes [26]. One of its strengths is the ability to learn which control actions will maximize reward given the state of the environment [27]. Traditionally, RL is applied to design optimal controllers because it learns how a computer agent (CA) should provide control actions to its interface with an environment in order to maximize rewards earned over time [26]. The CA is initially naïve but learns through interactions, eventually developing an action selection strategy, which achieves goals to earn rewards. However, in symbiotic BMIs where computational models are conjoined with neurophysiology in real-time, it may be possible to acquire the knowledge to bring more realism into the theory of reinforcement learning [28].

Co-Adaptation. Here we make the distinction between adaptability and cooperative co-adaptation that refers to a much deeper symbiotic relationship between the user and the computational agent who share control to reach common goals, hence, enabling the possibility of continual evolution of the interactive process. This approach must go beyond the simple combination of neurobiological and computation models because this does not elucidate the relationship between the linked, heterogeneous responses of neural systems to behavioral outcomes. A co-adaptive BMI must also consider the interactions that influence the net benefits of behavioral, computational, and physiological strategies. First, adaptive responses in the co-adaptive BMI will likely occur at different spatial and temporal scales. Second, through feedback the expression of neural intent continuously shapes the computational model while the behavior of the BMI shapes the user. The challenge is to define appropriate BMI architectures to determine the mechanistic links between neurophysiologic levels of abstraction and behavior and understand the evolution of neuroprosthetic usage. The details of how co-adaptive BMIs are engineered through reinforcement learning will be presented next.

3 Development of a Cyberworkstation to Test Co-adaptive BMIs

With the prerequisites of co-adaptive BMIs defined, the computational and engineering design challenge becomes one of architectural choices and integrating both the user and computer into a cooperative structure. Toward this goal we have an ongoing collaboration to develop a Cyberworkstation (CW) which consolidates software and hardware resources across three collaborating labs (Neuroprosthetics Research Group (NRG), Advanced Computing and Information Systems (ACIS) Lab), and Computational NeuroEngineering Laboratory (CNEL) at the University of Florida [29]. This consolidation facilitates *local* hardware control via powerful *remote* processing. Figure 1 illustrates this concept with a closed loop BMI experiment where neural signals are sampled from behaving animals (at NRG) and sent across the network for computing. Then a variety of BMI models process these data on a pool of servers (at ACIS). Model results are aggregated and used to control robot movement (at NRG).

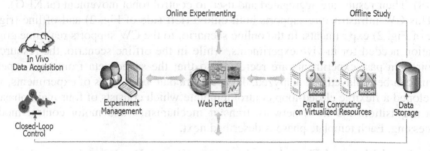

Fig. 2. Infrastructure for online and offline analysis

The CW was engineered to meet the following specifications for symbiotic BMI applications:

1. Real-time operation that scale with biological responses (<100ms)
2. Parallel processing capability for multi-input, multi-output models
3. Large memory for neurophysiologic data streams and model parameterization
4. Customizable signal processing models.
5. Integrated analysis platform for visualization of modeling and physiological parameters
6. Data warehousing
7. Simple user interfaces

The application-side requirements create information technology (IT) requirements:

1. High performance and real-time computation
2. Resource multiplexing (virtualization)
3. Real-time communication
4. Template-based framework-workflow
5. Data streaming and storage

Our research has been directed to developing middleware that can aggregate and reserve the necessary resources, create appropriate parallel execution environments, and guarantee the necessary Quality-of-Service (QoS) in computation and communication to meet response deadlines while provided the capabilities listed above. In effect, the middleware deploys an *on-demand* neuroscience research test-bed which consolidates distributed software and hardware resources to support time-critical and resource-demanding computing. Additionally, scientists are provided a powerful interface to dynamically manage and analyze experiments.

Online experimenting is based on a real-time, closed-loop system consisting of three key components: in vivo data acquisition from multielectrode arrays implanted in the brain, parallel computational modeling for neural decoding, and prosthetic control. Figure 2 shows the entire CW, including each of the three components. Neural signals are sampled from behaving animals (at NRG) and sent across the network for computing. A variety of BMI models (designed to investigate principles of neural coding) process these data in parallel on a pool of physical and virtual servers (at ACIS). Their results are aggregated and used to control robot movement (at NRG).

This CW infrastructure supports both online (left side of Fig. 2) and offline (right side of Fig. 2) experiments. In the online scenario, to the CW supports real-time computation needed for in-vivo experiments, while in the offline scenario, the resources required in past experiments are recreated so that the saved data from past experiments can be replayed and analyzed. To accommodate both types of experiments, we developed a flexible closed-loop control template which consists of four main phases: data acquisition and flow, network transfer mechanisms, and motor control model processing. Each template phase is described next.

Data Acquisition and Flow. A local program (PentusaData) samples neural signals from multi-channel digital signal processing (DSP) device. The DSP contains buffers which store estimated firing rates from electrodes implanted in behaving animals at the NRG laboratory. After acquiring neural activity from the brain, PentusaData generates an input data structure and sends it over the network to the ACIS processing cluster.

Once the data reaches ACIS, MPI processes are used to handle it. The master process (GlobalBMI) manages and distributes data to other worker processes (LocalBMI) that execute motor control models. These processes communicate locally to exchange data and determine the responsibilities of each motor control model toward the final output. The worker model implementation comprises both *computation* of motor commands from the neural signal and *continuous model adaptation*. Based on the responsibility assigned to each model [30], all of the worker model results are aggregated and sent to the GlobalBMI which creates the output data structure to send back to NRG. Then the local program (PentusaData) completes the robot motor task based on the motor command in the output data structure.

This CW sampled 32 electrodes (up to 96 neurons on the DSPs used in NRG) in 2.7ms with a standard deviation of 5.59ms. (To accomplish this required parallelization of the DSP). Expanding this to 192 neurons is now possible with the latest TDT software component (SortSpike3) - this would double amount of necessary sampling but should still be less than 10% of a 100ms computing budget. The theoretical maximum number of electrodes the CW could support involves a tradeoff between the other processes in the computation budget and network transfer speed.

Network Transfer. Communication and control of the CW will require the three subsystems (PentusaData, GlobalBMI, and LocalBMI) to perform all of their computation within the 100ms deadline for each behavioral action. Since the NRG and ACIS sites are approximately 500m apart, the overhead and limitations in network communication need to be addressed. Using TCP protocol to transfer data can achieve reliability via transport-layer timeout and retransmission, but it is difficult to control these mechanisms with the desired recovery policies and timing constraints [ref]. Instead, the CW implemented a custom reliability mechanism transfer upon the faster but less reliable UDP protocol. The middleware on the data acquisition server monitors the elapsed time after sending out the data. A timeout happens when it detects that it is unlikely to get the computation results back in time to meet the deadline. It then stores this failed data sample in a circular first-in-first-out (FIFO) buffer, and starts a new closed-loop cycle by polling for the next sample. Benchmarking of the closed loop communication protocol revealed that the round trip could be reliably completed within 5ms.

Model Computation. The possibility of concurrent execution of many BMI models in the CW will require a tremendous amount of computing power and storage capacity. Thus, the system needs to efficiently aggregate resources for model computation and integrate with onsite (local) signal sampling and robotic movement. The CW computes these models-sets in parallel using MPI. Parallel computation is conducted upon resources provided through virtualization to provide efficient utilization of resources. Virtualization allows many VMs to be created upon a single physical machine and transparently share its computing and storage resources. Each VM can be customized with the necessary execution environment, including operating system and libraries, to support seamless deployment of a BMI model. Multiple models can run concurrently with dedicated VMs, where resources are dynamically provisioned according to model demands and timing requirements.

For offline experiments, virtual machines allow the model computation to share resources with other jobs in an isolated manner. These jobs are managed via a cluster management system that provides queuing and scheduling of job executions on the virtual machines. Because online experiments have stricter timing requirements for the model computation, a set of physical resources must be reserved in advance to prepare a cluster of virtual machines for the online computation. The existing offline jobs on these reserved resources can be transparently suspended or relocated during the online experiment by suspending or migrating their VMs.

4 Conclusion

We have presented progress here towards a new framework to seamlessly bridge computational resources with *in vivo* experimentation in order to build symbiotic BMIs operating in dynamic environments. Online and offline BMI experiments can be performed on it in a closed-loop manner that includes *in vivo* data acquisition, reliable network transfer, and parallel model computation. With this computational infrastructure we seek to deploy next generation decoding algorithms that incorporate dynamics responses of both the brain and a computer agent working toward goals.

This solution for distributed BMIs could lay the ground for scalable middleware techniques that, in the long run, can support increasingly-elaborate neurophysiologic research test beds in which subjects can carry out more complex tasks. These advanced test beds will be essential for the development and optimization of the computational components that can be implemented on future workstations with multiple multi-core processors which, collectively, will be able to provide the necessary resources deeper study into BMI neural coding and function.

References

1. Buzsáki, G.: Rhythms of the Brain. Oxford University Press, New York (2006)
2. Kim, S.P., Sanchez, J.C., Rao, Y.N., Erdogmus, D., Principe, J.C., Carmena, J.M., Lebedev, M.A., Nicolelis, M.A.L.: A Comparison of Optimal MIMO Linear and Nonlinear Models for Brain-Machine Interfaces. J. Neural Engineering 3, 145–161 (2006)
3. Brown, E.N., Kass, R.E., Mitra, P.P.: Multiple Neural Spike Train Data Analysis: State-of-the-art and Future Challenges. Nature Neuroscience 7, 456–461 (2004)
4. Serruya, M.D., Hatsopoulos, N.G., Paninski, L., Fellows, M.R., Donoghue, J.P.: Brain-machine interface: Instant neural control of a movement signal. Nature 416, 141–142 (2002)
5. Wessberg, J., Stambaugh, C.R., Kralik, J.D., Beck, P.D., Laubach, M., Chapin, J.K., Kim, J., Biggs, S.J., Srinivasan, M.A., Nicolelis, M.A.L.: Real-time prediction of hand trajectory by ensembles of cortical neurons in primates. Nature 408, 361–365 (2000)
6. Helms Tillery, S.I., Taylor, D.M., Schwartz, A.B.: Training in cortical control of neuroprosthetic devices improves signal extraction from small neuronal ensembles. Reviews in the Neurosciences 14, 107–119 (2003)
7. Moran, D.W., Schwartz, A.B.: Motor cortical representation of speed and direction during reaching. Journal of Neurophysiology 82, 2676–2692 (1999)
8. Taylor, D.M., Tillery, S.I.H., Schwartz, A.B.: Direct cortical control of 3D neuroprosthetic devices. Science 296, 1829–1832 (2002)
9. Wu, W., Black, M.J., Gao, Y., Bienenstock, E., Serruya, M., Donoghue, J.P.: Inferring hand motion from multi-cell recordings in motor cortex using a Kalman filter. In: SAB Workshop on Motor Control in Humans and Robots: on the Interplay of Real Brains and Artificial Devices, University of Edinburgh, Scotland, pp. 66–73 (2002)
10. Chapin, J.K., Moxon, K.A., Markowitz, R.S., Nicolelis, M.A.: Real-time control of a robot arm using simultaneously recorded neurons in the motor cortex. Nature Neuroscience 2, 664–670 (1999)
11. Gao, Y., Black, M.J., Bienenstock, E., Wu, W., Donoghue, J.P.: A quantitative comparison of linear and non-linear models of motor cortical activity for the encoding and decoding of arm motions. In: The 1st International IEEE EMBS Conference on Neural Engineering, Capri, Italy (2003)
12. Sanchez, J.C., Kim, S.P., Erdogmus, D., Rao, Y.N., Principe, J.C., Wessberg, J., Nicolelis, M.A.L.: Input-output mapping performance of linear and nonlinear models for estimating hand trajectories from cortical neuronal firing patterns. In: International Work on Neural Networks for Signal Processing, Martigny, Switzerland, pp. 139–148 (2002)
13. Calvin, W.H.: The emergence of intelligence. Scientific American 9, 44–51 (1990)

14. Fuster, J.M.: Upper processing stages of the perception-action cycle. Trends in Cognitive Sciences 8, 143–145 (2004)
15. Rangel, A., Cramerer, C., Montague, P.R.: A framework for studying the neurobiology of value-based decision making. Nature Reviews Neuroscience 9, 545–556 (2008)
16. Edelman, G.M., Mountcastle, V.B.: Neurosciences Research Program. In: The mindful brain: cortical organization and the group-selective theory of higher brain function. MIT Press, Cambridge (1978)
17. Dayan, P., Niv, Y., Seymour, B., Daw, N.D.: The misbehavior of value and the discipline of the will. Neural Networks 19, 1153–1160 (2006)
18. Jackson, A., Mavoori, J., Fetz, E.E.: Long-term motor cortex plasticity induced by an electronic neural implant. Nature 444, 56–60 (2006)
19. Kleim, J.A., Barbay, S., Nudo, R.J.: Functional reorganization of the rat motor cortex following motor skill learning. Journal of Neurophysiology 80, 3321–3325 (1998)
20. Rioult-Pedotti, M.S., Friedman, D., Hess, G., Donoghue, J.P.: Strengthening of horizontal cortical connections following skill learning. Nature Neuroscience 1, 230–234 (1998)
21. Schultz, W.: Multiple reward signals in the brain. Nature Reviews Neuroscience 1, 199–207 (2000)
22. Sutton, R.S., Barto, A.G.: Reinforcement learning: an introduction. The MIT Press, Cambridge (1998)
23. Doya, K., Samejima, K., Katagiri, K., Kawato, M.: Multiple model-based reinforcement learning. Neural Computation 14, 1347–1369 (2002)
24. Rivest, F., Bengio, Y., Kalask, J.: Brain Inspired reinforcement learning, in NIPS, Vancouver, CA (2004)
25. Jong, N., Stone, P.: Kernel Based models for reinforcement learning. In: Proc. ICML Workshop on Kernel machines for Reinforcement Learning, Pittsburgh, PA (2006)
26. Sutton, R.S., Barto, A.G.: Reinforcement learning: an introduction. MIT Press, Cambridge (1998)
27. Worgotter, F., Porr, B.: Temporal sequence learning, prediction, and control: a review of different models and their relation to biological mechanisms. Neural Computation 17, 245–319 (2005)
28. DiGiovanna, J., Mahmoudi, B., Fortes, J., Principe, J.C., Sanchez, J.C.: Co-adaptive Brain Machine Interface via Reinforcement Learning. In: IEEE Transactions on Biomedical Engineering (Special issue on Hybrid Bionics) (2008) (in press)
29. Zhao, M., Rattanatamrong, P., DiGiovanna, J., Mahmoudi, B., Figueiredo, R.J., Sanchez, J.C., Principe, J.C., Fortes, J.C.: BMI Cyberworkstation: Enabling Dynamic Data-Driven Brain-Machine Interface Research through Cyberinfrastructure. In: IEEE International Conference of the Engineering in Medicine and Biology Society, Vancouver, Canada, pp. 646–649 (2008)
30. Wolpert, D., Kawato, M.: Multiple paired forward inverse models for motor control. Neural Networks 11, 1317–1329 (1998)

Sensor Modalities for Brain-Computer Interfacing

Gerwin Schalk[1,2,3,4,5]

[1] Wadsworth Center, New York State Department of Health
[2] Department of Neurology, Albany Medical College
[3] Department of Neurosurgery, Washington University in St. Louis
[4] Department of Biomedical Engineering, Rensselaer Polytechnic Institute
[5] Department of Biomedical Sciences, State University of New York at Albany

Abstract. Many people have neuromuscular conditions or disorders that impair the neural pathways that control muscles. Those most severely affected lose all voluntary muscle control and hence lose the ability to communicate. Brain-computer interfaces (BCIs) might be able to restore some communication or control functions for these people by creating a new communication channel – directly from the brain to an output device. Many studies over the past two decades have shown that such BCI communication is possible and that it can serve useful functions. This paper reviews the different sensor methodologies that have been explored in these studies.

Keywords: Brain-computer interface, BCI, Neural Engineering, Neural Prosthesis.

1 Introduction

Many neurological conditions can disrupt the information flow between the brain and its environment. These conditions include brain or spinal cord injury, amyotrophic lateral sclerosis (ALS), brain stem stroke, multiple sclerosis, etc. These conditions and other degenerative diseases impair the neural pathways that control muscles or impair the muscles themselves. Severe cases may result in loss of voluntary muscle control, including eye movements and respiration. Thus, affected individuals may become completely locked in to their bodies and unable to communicate in any way. Modern medical technologies can allow many of such extremely paralyzed individuals to live long lives, which exacerbates the personal, social, and economic burdens of their disabilities. Without any options for curing these disorders, three options for restoring functions remain [1, 2].

The first option is to increase the capabilities of remaining output options. In other words, muscles that are still under voluntary control can substitute for the paralyzed muscles. This substitution is often limited in practice, but may still be useful. For example, with appropriate technologies, severely paralyzed individuals can use eye movements to control computers [3]; or they may use hand movements to produce synthetic speech [4-9].

The second option is to restore function by detouring around the damaged communication pathways. For example, patients with spinal cord injury can use muscle activity above the level of the lesion to control electrical stimulation of paralyzed muscles,

J.A. Jacko (Ed.): Human-Computer Interaction, Part II, HCII 2009, LNCS 5611, pp. 616–622, 2009.
© Springer-Verlag Berlin Heidelberg 2009

and thereby restore useful movements. This possibility has been used to restore hand-grasp function to patients with cervical spinal cord injuries [10-13].

The final option for restoring function to people with severe motor disabilities is to directly interface the brain with an output device. This technology is called a direct brain-computer interface (BCI) for conveying messages and commands to the external world (see Fig. 1). Many different types of sensors for monitoring brain activity exist, and could in principle be used to realize a BCI. There is considerable debate in the literature about which of these sensors are most appropriate for BCI operation. The purpose of this review is to compare and contrast the most important characteristics of these sensors. Currently, most sensors measure electrical potentials on the scalp (electroencephalography (EEG)), on the surface of the brain (electrocorticography (ECoG)), or even within the brain (microelectrode recordings). In addition, other sensors can measure magnetic activity associated with electrical brain signal changes (magnetoencephalography (MEG)) or metabolic processes that are related to brain function (e.g., positron emission tomography (PET), functional magnetic resonance imaging (fMRI), and functional near infrared imaging (fNIR)) [14]. However, MEG, PET, fMRI, and fNIR are still technically demanding or expensive. Furthermore, PET, fMRI, and fNIR, which measure the increase of blood flow corresponding to increased brain activity, detect only relatively slow changes in brain function and thus are probably not ideal choices for rapid communication. Consequently, at present the only realistic sensor options for BCI research and application appear to be electrical sensors placed either on the scalp, the surface of the brain, or inside the brain. These are the only methods that use relatively simple and inexpensive equipment, can capture fast changes in brain activity, and can function in most environments. These methods are reviewed in the following sections and are illustrated in Fig. 2.

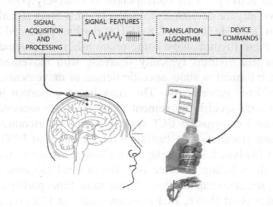

Fig. 1. Functional diagram of any BCI system. Signals from the brain are acquired by electrodes on the scalp, the cortical surface, or from within the cortex and processed to extract those features of brain signals that reflect the user's intent. These features are translated into device commands that control different output devices.

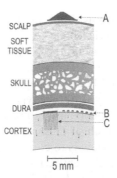

Fig. 2. Sensor methodologies used for BCI systems. Brain signals are detected by electrodes on the scalp (A), the surface of the brain (B), or from within the brain (C). Electrodes on the scalp (A) are noninvasive, but are relatively distant from the small signals produced by the brain. Electrodes on the surface of the brain (B) are much closer to the sources of signals within the brain, but do not actually penetrate the brain. Microelectrodes implanted within the brain (C) are closest to the origins of brain activity, but are more invasive and also face as yet unresolved issues with robustness. (From [15].)

2 Electroencephalography (EEG)

Non-invasive BCIs use electroencephalographic (EEG) activity recorded from the scalp [15-29]. This recording method is convenient, safe, and inexpensive. EEG electrodes are placed on the scalp and conductive gel is applied between each electrode and the scalp. EEG measures the electrical potential between the signal electrode and a reference electrode. It thereby measures the concerted activity of many millions of brain cells. Thus, in order to be detected by EEG sensors, a large brain area has to produce concurrent activity. This corresponds to relatively poor spatial resolution [16, 17] that allows only the detection of relatively gross brain signal changes, such as modulations of mu (8-12 Hz) or beta (18-25 Hz) rhythms produced by motor areas of the brain. While these rhythms have some relationship to movements or movement imagery (e.g., mu/beta rhythms typically decrease with movements), they are not thought to contain information about specific details of movements, such as the position or velocity of hand movements. This may be an important limitation because signals associated with specific movement parameters are successfully used as the basis for BCI control in invasive BCI systems. This shortcoming has often been pointed out by some scientists as a fundamental limitation of EEG for the BCI purpose. However, EEG-based BCIs have been shown to support higher performance than often assumed, including accurate two-dimensional movement control without [18] and with [19] selection capabilities. At the same time, perhaps as a consequence of the limitation discussed above, BCI systems based on EEG typically require substantial training to achieve accurate 1D or 2D device control (about 20 and 50 30-min training sessions, respectively). Furthermore, EEG recordings are susceptible to artifacts created by other sources, such as electromyographic (EMG) signals produced by muscle contractions, environmental noise, etc. These problems have thus far impeded the widespread clinical application of this safe and relatively inexpensive technology.

3 Electrocorticography (ECoG)

A different sensor method uses electrodes that are placed on the surface of the brain (electrocorticography (ECoG)). These sensors measure local field potential activity that captures brain signal changes on the order of millimeters (rather than a tenth of a millimeter captured by an implanted microelectrode). ECoG electrodes are in direct contact with the brain, and thus do not need the application of any conductive gel. This methodology could be a powerful but yet practical alternative EEG and microelectrode. ECoG has higher spatial resolution than EEG (i.e., millimeters vs. centimeters [17, 20-24], broader bandwidth (i.e., 0-200 Hz vs. 0-40 Hz), higher amplitude (i.e., 50-100 µV maximum vs. 10-20 µV), and far less vulnerability to artifacts such as EMG [16, 17]. At the same time, because ECoG electrodes do not penetrate the brain, they are likely to have greater long-term stability compared to implanted microelectrodes. These favorable features of fidelity and robustness have recently allowed for encouraging evidence that ECoG encodes substantial details of movements or actions [37-42]. Using ECoG signals, several recent studies demonstrated that people could rapidly acquire one-dimensional [25-28] or two-dimensional [29] control of a computer cursor.

4 Microelectrode Recordings

Microelectrode recordings from within the brain represent activity from one or multiple neurons. These recordings have been used as a basis for BCI systems [30-38]. These systems use firing rates of individual or multiple neurons, or the overall neuronal activity (local field potentials (LFPs)) of multiple neurons recorded within the brain. These signals have very high spatial resolution; and primarily in animal studies, they have been shown to encode signals that correspond to multiple degrees of freedom of movements [30, 37]. However, the stability of recordings from electrodes implanted within the brain is currently uncertain because electrodes are subject to different tissue responses that lead to encapsulation [39]. Also, tiny movements of the electrodes can move them away from individual neurons. Furthermore, effective operation of BCI systems depends of substantial initial and continual expert supervision. Thus, despite recent encouraging evidence that BCI technologies based on microelectrodes may be useful to people with paralysis [31], the difficulties described above currently impede widespread clinical implementation of such invasive BCI technologies [40].

5 Summary and Conclusions

In summary, an increasing body of evidence gathered over the past two decades has demonstrated that brain-computer interface technology does work and that it may serve useful functions. However, while a number of these studies are impressive, most systems have largely remained laboratory demonstrations. This is because the prevailing recording methodologies, EEG and microelectrode recordings, still face substantial issues of capability, practicality, and/or robustness. In the case of EEG,

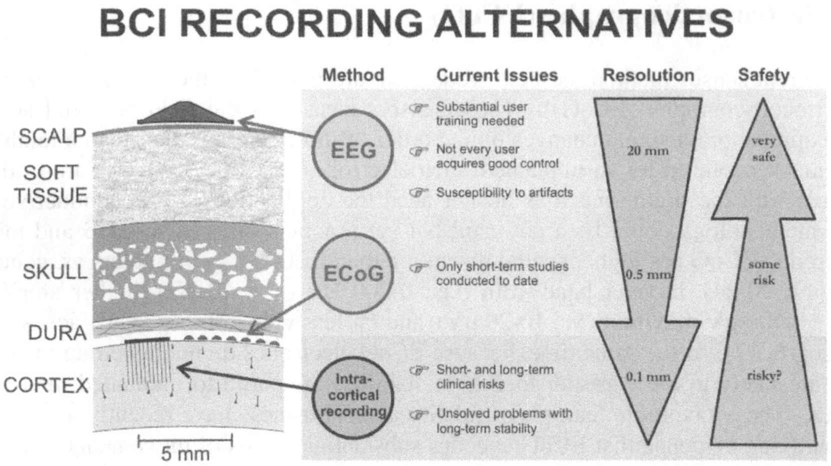

BCI RECORDING ALTERNATIVES

Fig. 3. Advantages and disadvantages of different recording methodologies

these are mainly the substantial training requirements, and susceptibility to artifacts, whereas for microelectrode recordings, these are mainly the unresolved problems with stability (Fig. 3). In consequence, ECoG-based BCI systems may emerge as an alternative recording methodology that combines the advantages of EEG and microelectrode recordings, and could thereby form the basis for BCI systems with major clinical implications.

Acknowledgement

This work was supported by the US Army Research Office (W911NF-07-1-0415 and W911NF-08-1-0216) and the NIH/NIBIB (EB006356 and EB00856).

References

1. Wolpaw, J.R., Birbaumer, N., McFarland, D.J., Pfurtscheller, G., Vaughan, T.M.: Brain-computer interfaces for communication and control. Clin. Neurophysiol. 113, 767–791 (2002)
2. Allison, B.Z., Wolpaw, E.W., Wolpaw, J.R.: Brain-computer interface systems: progress and prospects. Expert Rev. Med. Devices 4, 463–474 (2007)
3. Kumar, M., Paepcke, A., Winograd, T.: EyePoint: practical pointing and selection using gaze and keyboard. In: Proceedings of the SIGCHI conference on Human factors in computing systems. San Jose, CA, pp. 421–430 (2007)
4. Damper, R.I., Burnett, J.W., Gray, P.W., Straus, L.P., Symes, R.A.: Hand-Held Text-to-Speech Device for the Non-Vocal Disabled. J. Biomed. Eng. 9, 332–340 (1987)
5. Fels, S.S., Hinton, G.E.: Glove-TalkII-a neural-network interface which maps gestures to parallel formant speech synthesizer controls. IEEE Trans. Neural Netw. 9, 205–212 (1998)

6. Fels, S.S.: Using normalized RBF networks to map hand gestures to speech. In: Radial basis function networks 2: new advances in design, pp. 59–101. Physica-Verlag GmbH, Heidelberg (2001)

7. Kubota, M., Sakakihara, Y., Uchiyama, Y., Nara, A., Nagata, T., Nitta, H., Ishimoto, K., Oka, A., Horio, K., Yanagisawa, M.: New Ocular Movement Detector System As a Communication Tool in Ventilator-Assisted Werdnig-Hoffmann Disease. Dev. Med. Child Neurol. 42, 61–64 (2000)

8. Chen, Y.L., Tang, F.T., Chang, W.H., Wong, M.K., Shih, Y.Y., Kuo, T.S.: The New Design of an Infrared-Controlled Human-Computer Interface for the Disabled. IEEE Trans. Rehabil. Eng. 7, 474–481 (1999)

9. LaCourse, J.R., Hludik, F.C.: An Eye Movement Communication-Control System for the Disabled. IEEE Trans. Biomed. Eng. 37, 1215–1220 (1990)

10. Peckham, P.H., Keith, M.W., Kilgore, K.L., Grill, J.H., Wuolle, K.S., Thrope, G.B., Gorman, P., Hobby, J., Mulcahey, M.J., Carroll, S., Hentz, V.R., Wiegner, A.: Efficacy of an implanted neuroprosthesis for restoring hand grasp in tetraplegia: a multicenter study. Arch. Phys. Med. Rehabil. 82, 1380–1388 (2001)

11. Hoffer, J.A., Stein, R.B., Haugland, M.K., Sinkjaer, T., Durfee, W.K., Schwartz, A.B., Loeb, G.E., Kantor, C.: Neural Signals for Command Control and Feedback in Functional Neuromuscular Stimulation: a Review. J. Rehabil. Res. Dev. 33, 145–157 (1996)

12. Ferguson, K.A., Polando, G., Kobetic, R., Triolo, R.J., Marsolais, E.B.: Walking With a Hybrid Orthosis System. Spinal. Cord. 37, 800–804 (1999)

13. Kilgore, K.L., Peckham, P.H., Keith, M.W., Thrope, G.B., Wuolle, K.S., Bryden, A.M., Hart, R.L.: An Implanted Upper-Extremity Neuroprothesis: Follow-Up of Five Patients. J. Bone Joint Surg. 79-A, 533–541 (1997)

14. Wolpaw, J.R., Loeb, G.E., Allison, B.Z., Donchin, E., do Nascimento, O.F., Heetderks, W.J., Nijboer, F., Shain, W.G., Turner, J.N.: BCI Meeting 2005–workshop on signals and recording methods. IEEE Trans. Neural Syst. Rehabil. Eng. 14, 138–141 (2006)

15. Wolpaw, J.R., Birbaumer, N.: Brain-computer interfaces for communication and control. In: Selzer, M.E., Clarke, S., Cohen, L.G., Duncan, P., Gage, F.H. (eds.) Textbook of Neural Repair and Rehabilitation; Neural Repair and Plasticity, pp. 602–614. Cambridge University Press, Cambridge (2006)

16. Srinivasan, R., Nunez, P.L., Silberstein, R.B.: Spatial Filtering and Neocortical Dynamics: Estimates of EEG Coherence. IEEE Trans. Biomed. Eng. 45, 814–826 (1998)

17. Freeman, W.J., Holmes, M.D., Burke, B.C., Vanhatalo, S.: Spatial Spectra of Scalp EEG and EMG From Awake Humans. Clin. Neurophysiol. 114, 1053–1068 (2003)

18. Wolpaw, J.R., McFarland, D.J.: Control of a two-dimensional movement signal by a noninvasive brain-computer interface in humans. Proc. Natl. Acad. Sci. U.S.A. 101, 17849–17854 (2004)

19. McFarland, D., Krusienski, D., Sarnacki, W., Wolpaw, J.: Emulation of computer mouse control with a noninvasive brain–computer interface. J. Neural Eng. 5, 101–110 (2008)

20. Heetderks, W.J., Schmidt, E.M.: Chronic, Multiple Unit Recording of Neural Activity With Micromachined Silicon Electrodes (1995)

21. Ikeda, A., Shibasaki, H.: Invasive Recording of Movement-Related Cortical Potentials in Humans. J. Clin. Neurophysiol. 9, 509–520 (1992)

22. Schmidt, E.M.: Single Neuron Recording From Motor Cortex As a Possible Source of Signals for Control of External Devices. Ann. Biomed. Eng. 8, 339–349 (1980)

23. Levine, S.P., Huggins, J.E., BeMent, S.L., Kushwaha, R.K., Schuh, L.A., Rohde, M.M., Passaro, E.A., Ross, D.A., Elisevich, K.V., Smith, B.J.: A Direct Brain Interface Based on Event-Related Potentials. IEEE Trans. Rehabil. Eng. 8, 180–185 (2000)

24. Huggins, L., BeMent, K., Schuh, P., Rohde, R., Elisevich, S.: Detection of event-related potentials for development of a direct brain interface. J. Clin. Neurophysiol. 16, 448–455 (1999)
25. Wilson, J.A., Felton, E.A., Garell, P.C., Schalk, G., Williams, J.C.: ECoG factors underlying multimodal control of a brain-computer interface. IEEE transactions on neural systems and rehabilitation engineering: a publication of the IEEE Engineering in Medicine and Biology Society 14, 246–250 (2006)
26. Leuthardt, E.C., Miller, K.J., Schalk, G., Rao, R.P., Ojemann, J.G.: Electrocorticography-based brain computer interface–the Seattle experience. IEEE transactions on neural systems and rehabilitation engineering: a publication of the IEEE Engineering in Medicine and Biology Society 14, 194–198 (2006)
27. Leuthardt, E.C., Schalk, G., Wolpaw, J.R., Ojemann, J.G., Moran, D.W.: A brain-computer interface using electrocorticographic signals in humans. Journal of Neural Engineering 1, 63–71 (2004)
28. Felton, E.A., Wilson, J.A., Williams, J.C., Garell, P.C.: Electrocorticographically controlled brain-computer interfaces using motor and sensory imagery in patients with temporary subdural electrode implants. Report of four cases. J. Neurosurg. 106, 495–500 (2007)
29. Schalk, G., Miller, K., Anderson, N., Wilson, J., Smyth, M., Ojemann, J., Moran, D., Wolpaw, J., Leuthardt, E.: Two-dimensional movement control using electrocorticographic signals in humans. J. Neural Eng. 5, 75–84 (2008)
30. Velliste, M., Perel, S., Spalding, M.C., Whitford, A.S., Schwartz, A.B.: Cortical control of a prosthetic arm for self-feeding. Nature 453, 1098–1101 (2008)
31. Hochberg, L., Serruya, M., Friehs, G., Mukand, J., Saleh, C.A., Branner, C., Penn, R., Donoghue, J.: Neuronal ensemble control of prosthetic devices by a human with tetraplegia. Nature 442, 164–171 (2006)
32. Santhanam, G., Ryu, S.I., Yu, B.M., Afshar, A., Shenoy, K.V.: A high-performance brain-computer interface. Nature 442, 195–198 (2006)
33. Lebedev, M.A., Carmena, J.M., O'Doherty, J.E., Zacksenhouse, M., Henriquez, C.S., Principe, J.C., Nicolelis, M.A.: Cortical ensemble adaptation to represent velocity of an artificial actuator controlled by a brain-machine interface. J. Neurosci. 25, 4681–4693 (2005)
34. Andersen, R.A., Burdick, J.W., Musallam, S., Pesaran, B., Cham, J.G.: Cognitive neural prosthetics. Trends Cogn. Sci (Regul. Ed.) 8, 486–493 (2004)
35. Shenoy, K.V., Meeker, D., Cao, S., Kureshi, S.A., Pesaran, B., Buneo, C.A., Batista, A.P., Mitra, P.P., Burdick, J.W., Andersen, R.A.: Neural prosthetic control signals from plan activity. Neuroreport 14, 591–596 (2003)
36. Serruya, M., Hatsopoulos, N., Paninski, L., Fellows, M., Donoghue, J.: Instant neural control of a movement signal. Nature 416, 141–142 (2002)
37. Taylor, D.M., Tillery, S.I., Schwartz, A.B.: Direct cortical control of 3D neuroprosthetic devices. Science 296, 1829–1832 (2002)
38. Georgopoulos, A.P., Schwartz, A.B., Kettner, R.E.: Neuronal population coding of movement direction. Science 233, 1416–1419 (1986)
39. Shain, W., Spataro, L., Dilgen, J., Haverstick, K., Retterer, S., Isaacson, M., Saltzman, M., Turner, J.: Controlling Cellular Reactive Responses Around Neural Prosthetic Devices Using Peripheral and Local Intervention Strategies. IEEE Trans. Neural Syst. Rehabil. Eng. 11, 186–188 (2003)
40. Schalk, G.: Brain-computer symbiosis. J. Neural Eng. 15, P1–P15 (2008)

A Novel Dry Electrode for Brain-Computer Interface

Eric W. Sellers[1], Peter Turner[2], William A. Sarnacki[3], Tobin McManus[2],
Theresa M. Vaughan[3], and Robert Matthews[2]

[1] East Tennessee State University, PO Box 70649, Johnson City, TN 37614
sellers@etsu.edu
[2] QUASAR, 5764 Pacific Center Blvd. Suite 107, San Diego, CA 92121
peter@quasarusa.com, tobin@quasarusa.com, robm@quasarusa.com
[3] Wadsworth Center, NY State Dept. of Health, E1001 Empire State Plaza,
Albany, NY 12201
Sarnacki@wadsworth.org, vaugan@wadsworth.org

Abstract. A brain-computer interface is a device that uses signals recorded from the brain to directly control a computer. In the last few years, P300-based brain-computer interfaces (BCIs) have proven an effective and reliable means of communication for people with severe motor disabilities such as amyotrophic lateral sclerosis (ALS). Despite this fact, relatively few individuals have benefited from currently available BCI technology. Independent BCI use requires easily acquired, good-quality electroencephalographic (EEG) signals maintained over long periods in less-than-ideal electrical environments. Conventional, wet-sensor, electrodes require careful application. Faulty or inadequate preparation, noisy environments, or gel evaporation can result in poor signal quality. Poor signal quality produces poor user performance, system downtime, and user and caregiver frustration. This study demonstrates that a hybrid dry electrode sensor array (HESA) performs as well as traditional wet electrodes and may help propel BCI technology to a widely accepted alternative mode of communication.

Keywords: Brain-computer interface, P300 event-related potential, dry electrode, amyotrophic lateral sclerosis.

1 Introduction

Severe motor disabilities such as amyotrophic lateral sclerosis can reduce or eliminate neuromuscular control and deprive affected people of communication that is vital to their mental and physical health. Recent advances in noninvasive EEG-based brain-computer interfaces (BCIs) have given these patients new hope for communication and control of their environment [1], [2], [3], [4], [5], [6], [7]. BCIs can succeed where other devices fail because they use a control technology that depends directly on neuronal signals without any requirement for neuromuscular control [8]. In the last few years, the P300-based BCI has proven to be an effective and reliable means of communication for severely disabled individuals. However, limitations in the duration of each use, the need for extensive caregiver support and training, and technical support from trained researchers have made providing the technology to more than a few individuals impractical. An obvious impediment to widespread acceptance of BCI technology is the need for an improved wet electrolyte-based EEG sensor [9], or

J.A. Jacko (Ed.): Human-Computer Interaction, Part II, HCII 2009, LNCS 5611, pp. 623–631, 2009.
© Springer-Verlag Berlin Heidelberg 2009

a dry sensor. The current study provides data showing that a hybrid dry electrode array (HESA) can perform as well as a standard wet electrode array (WEA) in a P300-based BCI paradigm. HESA sensors have been tested in a variety of contexts and have been shown to record EEG signals with high fidelity [10], [11]. The hybrid sensors can be applied with light, comfortable pressure of approximately 2 psi and record EEG for practically unlimited times without the need for electrolytes or skin treatments of any kind.

The P300 component of the event-related potential (ERP) is a large, vertex-positive component with a latency of about 300 ms after a triggering event. It was discovered more than 40 years ago [12], and after intensive research the robust nature of the component has been well established [13], [14], [15]. A P300 is generated when a human observer detects a rare or meaningful event, especially among a series of other, more frequent events [16]. A stimulus presentation typically used to elicit a P300 is called the oddball paradigm. To qualify as an oddball paradigm the presentation must meet three requirements. First, the stimuli must be presented in a random order. Second, the subject must attend to the presentation sequence. Third, one category must

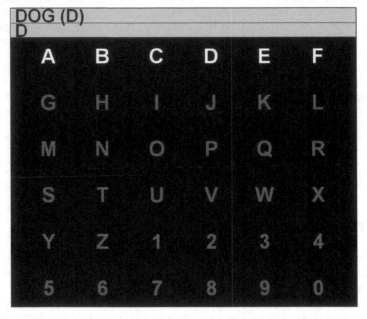

Fig. 1. An example of a 6x6 speller matrix configured for copy-spelling. At the top, the word DOG is presented. The letter in parentheses (D) is the current target letter. As rows and columns flash successively, the user is asked to count how many times the letter D (the target) flashes. This twelve-flash series is repeated a predetermined number of times. The responses for each row and column are averaged, and a classifier is applied. The intersection of the row and column with the highest classification values is selected. In this case, the target letter D flashing in either a column or a row elicits a P300 response and the a D is presented as feedback to the user on the line below the presented word DOG at the top of the matrix.

be presented infrequently. The P300 Speller meets these criteria because the rows and columns of the matrix flash randomly, the subject attends to one specific matrix character, and the attended character flashes one out of every six flashes.

The use of the P300 response for BCI control has been well documented [2], [17], [18], [19], [20], [21], [22]. The matrix speller version of the P300-based BCI flashes rows and columns of letters and numbers in rapid succession. Each flash of a row or a column is one stimulus. For a 6 x 6 alphanumeric matrix (Figure 1), each character flashes in only one of six rows, and in only one of six columns. The user is instructed to attend to only one character while it flashes in the matrix. This is the target character. Thus, two of 12 stimuli are targets and 10 of 12 stimuli are non-targets. A P300 response is produced when either the row or column containing the target item flashes. This sequence of flashing rows and columns is repeated a number of times. The BCI system recognizes the user's selection by detecting and averaging the P300 responses. Averaging is required as the P300 signal is smaller than the other components of the typical brain signal. Thus, improvements in signal recording and/or signal processing methods should increase the overall speed and accuracy of the P300-based BCI.

2 Methods

2.1 Hybrid EEG Sensor Technology

Measurement of the EEG for everyday use of a BCI requires the application of sensors through thicknesses of hair. To meet this requirement, QUASAR has developed a novel *hybrid biosensor* (Figure 2). This sensor measures EEG through hair and without any skin preparation. To accomplish this, the sensor uses a set of 'fingers' that are small enough to reach through the hair without trapping hair beneath the finger. Figure 3 shows the hybrid electrodes mounted in a headpiece along with the conventional wet electrodes.

In contrast to conventional EEG electrode technology, which relies on a low impedance contact to the scalp, these hybrid biosensors use a combination of high impedance resistive and capacitive contact to the scalp, and innovative processing electronics to reduce pickup and susceptibility to common-mode signals on the body. The hybrid biosensor consists of an electrode, an ultra-high input impedance amplifier circuit, a common-mode follower (CMF; a proprietary technology for reducing common mode signals), and a wireless node that contains a gain/filter module and a data acquisition/communications module. As the contact impedance between the scalp and each finger can be as high $10^7\Omega$, the amplifier electronics are shielded and integrated with the electrode in order to limit interference caused by the pickup of external signals. The hybrid sensors and wireless node data acquisition channels are closely phase and gain matched and can provide individual EEG signals or high common-mode rejection ratio difference signals (CMRR > 70dB between 1Hz – 50Hz) between biosensors.

Fig. 2. A) QUASAR hybrid EEG biosensor used in the current study. B) The sensor and housing with padding to fit the sensor into the headpiece.

The CMF is used to reduce the sensitivity of the hybrid biosensor to common mode signals on the body. The CMF is a separate hybrid biosensor on or near the scalp that measures the potential of the body relative to the ground of the amplifier system. Ultra-high input impedance for the CMF (~10^{12} Ω) ensures that the output of the CMF tracks the body-ground potential with a high degree of accuracy. The CMF output is used in the wireless node as a reference for the EEG measurement by the electrodes. In this way, the common-mode signal appearing on the body is dynamically removed from the EEG measurement. This typically achieves a CMRR of 50 to 70 dB.

2.2 Data Acquisition and Processing

The HESA and WEA sensors were mounted in the headpiece shown in Figure 3. Each array had four sensors or electrodes (Cz, Pz, PO7, PO8) and one reference sensor or electrode located on the right mastoid. The WEA had a ground electrode located on the left mastoid. The HESA had a biosensor reference on the right mastoid and common-mode follower on the left mastoid. The EEG signals were acquired, digitized at a rate of 256 Hz, digitally bandpass filtered 0.5–30, and stored using a g.USBamp. The HESA samples were buffered at the sensor by a trans-conductance amplifier with ultra high impedance, calibrated to provide data samples for the software in the same voltage range as those of the WEA, then digitized by the g.USBamp. Thus, four WEA channels and four HESA channels were simultaneously recorded. All aspects of data collection and experimental control will be performed by the BCI2000 system [23].

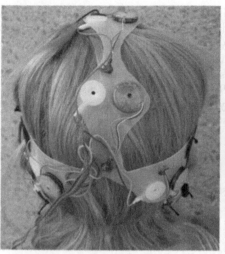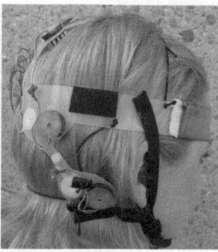

Fig. 3. Headpiece used to make simultaneous HESA and WEA electrode comparison measurements. Spring loaded clamps on the elastic pieces made for quick and convenient adjustment for head size and sensor loading. The smaller electrodes on the left (right panel) are the WEA electrodes, and the larger disk to the right is the HESA electrode.

2.3 Task, Procedure, Design, and Analysis

Participants sat in a reclining chair approximately 1.5 m from a CRT video monitor that presented the P300 spelling matrix (Figure 1), all were able-bodied. In each experimental session, the participant was asked to focus on each letter in the words "Wadsworth brain computer interface" between each word of the phrase a 1-min break was given. As Figure 1 illustrates, each word in the phrase appeared in sequence on the top line above the matrix. The participant was instructed to attend to the letter indicated with parenthesis while it flashed in the matrix and to silently count the number of times it flashed. Each row and column was flashed 15 times. Thus, the selected letter flashed 30 times out of 180 total flashes. The data collected during the first two words was used to train the SWLDA classifier (described in [20] and [24]). That classifier was then applied to the second two words. Thus, the training data set included 14 character presentations and the test data set included 17 character presentations.

The duration of each experimental session was approximately 30 minutes. Eight participants completed one session that concurrently recorded HESA and WEA data. Classification accuracy was the dependent variable used to examine system performance. We also compared the event-related potential data for the participants.

3   Results

The event-related potentials were similar for the HESA and WEA sensors. Figure 4 shows averaged waveforms for data collected concurrently from the HESA and WEA electrodes. It is reasonable to expect slight variability in the waveforms because the HESA and WEA sensors were located approximately 1.5 cm away from each other, center-to-center distance. The average signal strength for each sensor and each subject was also calculated. To calculate this quantity, the data from each electrode are plotted on a histogram (x-axis Signal, y-axis Number of Events at each voltage). Mean amplitude Vrms is then read to include 90% of the points. This gives a quantity that represents the amplitude that captures 90% of all the signals recorded. The mean rms amplitude for all subject's EEG was 9.10μV for the HESA sensor and 9.17μV for the WEA sensor. Thus, the wet and dry sensors variability is near identical, to be expected of sensors of equal fidelity measuring a common EEG signal.

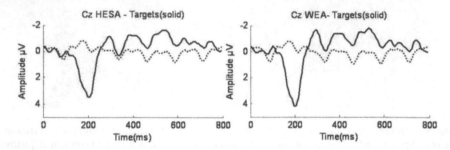

Fig. 4. Averaged ERP waveforms for target items (solid line) and non-target items (all other rows and columns) are graphed as a function of time after the flash, with positive voltage downward. The periodic signal in the non-target waveform corresponds to the frequency the flashes. These data are averaged across all trials in a session in which HESA and wet data was recorded concurrently for one representative participant.

Table 1. Mean classification accuracy for each participant

Participant	HESA % correct	WEA % correct
A	29	29
B	76	94
C	82	76
D	12	18
E	65	47
F	94	100
G	82	100
H	100	100
Mean	67.5	70.5

Mean percent correct classification accuracy for each of the eight participants is shown in Table 1. Overall, the classification accuracy was similar for the HESA and the WEA arrays when the EEG was collected in side-by-side concurrent recordings (paired t-test; p=.50). These initial results demonstrate the efficacy of the HESA system and provide confirmation that a HESA-based BCI system can perform as well as a wet electrode-based BCI system, when proper care is taken to ensure signal quality.

4 Discussion and Conclusions

These data show that the HESA and WEA sensors provide equivalent BCI classification accuracy while participants perform a copy spelling task, in a preliminary data set. In addition, the signal fidelity of the two EEG recording methods is very similar (as measured by root mean square and the event-related potentials). This initial success suggests that dry sensor technology may provide a more user friendly and more acceptable implementation of a P300-based BCI.

One common complaint among able-bodied and disabled BCI users is the necessity of the electrolyte based gel that needs to be washed out of the hair after each session. Obviously, the need to wash the hair is eliminated with HESA sensors and this can substantially reduce the burden associated with BCI use for the BCI user and also for the person assisting the BCI user. It is also not necessary to abrade the scalp when using the HESA sensors which makes them more comfortable to wear. Future work will focus on testing the HESA with a larger group of subjects who will participate in multiple experimental sessions and on developing a mounting system that can be comfortable to wear for severely disabled individuals who may be limited to a prone position.

Acknowledgement

This work was supported by grant 1R41NS060348-01 from the National Institute of Health/National Institute of Neurological Disease and Stroke.

References

1. Kübler, A., Nijboer, F., Mellinger, J., Vaughan, T.M., Pawelzik, H., Schalk, G., McFarland, D.J., Birbaumer, N., Wolpaw, J.R.: Patients with ALS can use sensorimotor rhythms to operate a brain-computer interface. Neurology 64, 1775–1777 (2005)
2. Nijboer, F., Sellers, E.W., Mellinger, J., Jordan, M.A., Matuz, T., Furdea, A., Mochty, U., Krusienski, D.J., Vaughan, T.M., Wolpaw, J.R., Birbaumer, N., Kübler, A.: A brain-computer interface for people with amyotrophic lateral sclerosis. Clinical Neurophysiology 119(8), 1909–1916 (2008) PMID: 18571984
3. Piccione, F., Giorgi, F., Tonin, P., Priftis, K., Giove, S., Silvoni, S., Palmas, G., Beverina, F.: P300-based brain computer interface: reliability and performance in healthy and paralysed participants. Clin. Neurophysiol. 117, 531–537 (2006)
4. Sellers, E.W., Donchin, E.: A P300-based brain-computer interface: Initial tests by ALS patients. Clin. Neurophysiol. 117, 538–548 (2006)
5. Sellers, E.W., Vaughan, T.M., McFarland, D.J., Krusienski, D.J., Mackler, S.A., Cardillo, R.A., Schalk, G., Binder-Macleod, S.A., Wolpaw, J.R.: Daily use of a brain-computer interface by a man with ALS. In: Society for Neuroscience annual meeting, Atlanta, GA (2006)

6. Sellers, E.W., Vaughan, T.M., McFarland, D.J., Carmack, C.S., Schalk, G., Cardillo, R.A., Mackler, S.A., Braun, E.M., Halder, S., Lee, S., Fudrea, A., Kübler, A., Wolpaw, J.R.: Brain-Computer Interface for people with ALS: long-term daily use in the home environment. Program No. 414.5, Abstract Viewer/Itinerary Planner, Washington, DC. Society for Neuroscience (2007) (Online)
7. Sellers, E.W., Townsend, G., Boulay, C., LaPallo, B.K., Vaughan, T.M., Wolpaw, J.R.: The P300 brain-computer interface: A new stimulus presentation paradigm. Program No. 778.21, Abstract Viewer/Itinerary Planner, Washington, DC. Society for Neuroscience (2008) (Online)
8. Wolpaw, J.R., Birbaumer, N., McFarland, D.J., Pfurtscheller, G., Vaughan, T.M.: Brain computer interfaces for communication and control. Clin. Neurophysiol. 113, 767–791 (2002)
9. Vaughan, T.M., McFarland, D.J., Schalk, G., Sarnacki, W.A., Krusienski, D.J., Sellers, E.W., Wolpaw, J.R.: The Wadsworth BCI research and development program: At home with BCI. IEEE Trans. Neural. Syst. Rehabil. Eng. 14, 229–233 (2006)
10. Matthews, R., McDonald, N.J., Hervieux, P., Turner, P.J., Steindorf, M.A.: A Wearable Physiological Sensor Suite for Unobtrusive Monitoring of Physiological and Cognitive State, in Engineering in Medicine and Biology Society, 2007. In: EMBC 2007, Proceedings of the 29th Annual International Conference of the IEEE, August 22-26, 2007, vol. 26, pp. 5276–5281 (2007)
11. Matthews, R., Turner, P.J., McDonald, N.J., Ermolaev, K., McManus, T., Shelby, R.A., Steindorf, M.A.: Real Time Workload Classification from an Ambulatory Wireless EEG System Using Hybrid EEG Electrodes, presented during the Invited Session. In: Towards Truly Wearable Electroencephalography at the 30th Annual International IEEE EMBS Conference, Vancouver, British Columbia, Canada, August 20-24 (2008)
12. Sutton, S., Braren, M., Zubin, J., John, E.R.: Evoked-potential correlates of stimulus uncertainty. Science 150, 1187–1188 (1965)
13. Donchin, E., Karis, D., Bashore, T.R., Coles, M.G.H., Gratton, G.: Cognitive psychophysiology and human information processing. In: Coles, M.G.H., Donchin, E., Porges, S.W. (eds.) Psychophysiology Systems, Processes and Applications, pp. 244–267. Guilford Press, New York (1986)
14. Fabiani, M., Gratton, G., Karis, D., Donchin, E.: Definition, identification, and reliability of measurement of the P300 component of the event-related brain potential. Advances in Psychophysiology 2, 1–78 (1987)
15. Pritchard, W.: The psychophysiology of P300. Psych. Bull. 89, 506–540 (1981)
16. Duncan Johnson, C., Donchin, E.: On quantifying surprise: The variation of event-related potentials with subjective probability. Psychophysiology 14, 456–467 (1977)
17. Donchin, E., Spencer, K.M., Wijesinghe, R.: The mental prosthesis: assessing the speed of a P300-based brain-computer interface. IEEE Trans. Rehab. Eng. 8, 174–179 (2000)
18. Farwell, L.A., Donchin, E.: Talking off the top of your head: toward a mental prosthesis utilizing event-related brain potentials. Electroencephalogr. clin. Neurophysiol. 70, 510–523 (1988)
19. Kaper, M., Meinicke, P., Grossekathoefer, U., Lingner, T., Ritter, H.: BCI Competition 2003- Data set IIb: Support vector machines for the P300 speller paradigm. IEEE Trans. Biomed. Eng. 51, 1073–1076 (2004)
20. Sellers, E.W., Krusienski, D.J., McFarland, D.J., Vaughan, T.M., Wolpaw, J.R.: A P300 event-related potential brain-computer interface (BCI): The effects of matrix size and inter stimulus interval on Performance. Biol. Psychol. 73, 242–252 (2006b)

21. Serby, H., Yom-Tov, E., Inbar, G.F.: An improved P300-based brain-computer interface. IEEE Trans. Neural Syst. Rehabil. Eng. 13, 89–98 (2005)
22. Lenhardt, A., Kaper, M., Ritter, H.J.: An adaptive P300-Based Online Brain-Computer Interface. IEEE Transactions on Neural Systems and Rehabilitation Engineering 16, 121–130 (2008)
23. Schalk, G., McFarland, D.J., Hinterberger, T., Birbaumer, N., Wolpaw, J.R.: BCI2000: A general-purpose brain-computer interface (BCI) system. IEEE Trans. Biomed. Eng. 51, 1034–1043 (2004)
24. Krusienski, D.J., Sellers, E.W., McFarland, D.J., Vaughan, T.M., Wolpaw, J.R.: Toward Enhanced P300 Speller Performance. Journal of Neuroscience Methods 167, 15–21 (2008) PMID: 17822777

Effect of Mental Training on BCI Performance

Lee-Fan Tan[1], Ashok Jansari[2], Shian-Ling Keng[3], and Sing-Yau Goh[1]

[1] Department of Mechatronics and BioMedical Engineering, Faculty of Engineering and
Science, Universiti Tunku Abdul Rahman, Kuala Lumpur, Malaysia
tanlf@utar.edu.my, gohsy@utar.edu.my
[2] School of Psychology, University of East London, London, UK
A.Jansari@uel.ac.uk
[3] Department of Psychology and Neuroscience, Duke University, North Carolina, USA
slk18@duke.edu

Abstract. This paper reports initial findings from a randomized controlled trial conducted on 9 subjects to investigate the effect of two mental training programs (a mindfulness meditation and learning to play a guitar) on their BCI performance. After 4 weeks of intervention, results show that subjects who had undergone a program of mindfulness meditation improved their BCI performance scores significantly compared to a no-treatment control group. Subjects who were learning to play a guitar also improved their BCI performance scores but not as much as the meditation group.

1 Introduction

Changes in EEG activity during imagery of motor actions have been used in Brain-Computer Interface (BCI) systems to operate devices such as a neuroprosthesis, wheelchair and switches to control home appliances [1-6]. A proper control of EEG activity ensures the success of BCI operation. However, the patterns of EEG activities rely on the mental stability of the user. Earlier studies have reported that the classification accuracy of a BCI system can improve if the subjects can maintain their interest and attention or degrade if the subject has insufficient attention and frustration [7]. Also, human factors such as fatigue, frustration and other variations of mental states are important considerations in BCI controls [8]. On the words, subjects may have a better performance if they can learn to control their mental states better and to be more focused during the BCI tests.

Our study investigated the effect of two forms of mental trainings - mindfulness meditation and learning to play a musical instrument. Mindfulness meditation is a practice of attention skill. Mindfulness has been defined as "the awareness that emerges through paying attention on purpose, in the present moment, and non-judgmentally to the unfolding of experience, moment to moment" [9]. Although there are different forms of mindfulness meditation, each of the practices involves bringing attention to the present moment. Learning to play a musical instrument such as a classical guitar is also a practice of attention where very often the beginners are required to focus their attention on their fingers' movements.

J.A. Jacko (Ed.): Human-Computer Interaction, Part II, HCII 2009, LNCS 5611, pp. 632–635, 2009.
© Springer-Verlag Berlin Heidelberg 2009

2 Method

A total of 30 healthy under-graduates age between 18 and 22 years old participated in the study. Because of limited time to analyze all the data, the present paper reports only initial findings from 9 randomly selected subjects. Prior to enrolment in the study, all subjects were screened through the use of a demographic form and a phone interview to ensure that they did not have previous experience in any formal mental practices that are related to our intervention programs.

The baseline assessment of the BCI performance tests was conducted on the subjects upon entry to the study (T0 = baseline). Following baseline testing, the subjects were randomized into Group A (mindfulness meditation), Group B (learning to play a guitar) and Group C (the control group).

The interventions consisted of the following programs. Subjects in Group A attended a mindfulness meditation lesson of 1 hour duration under the instruction of a professional meditation teacher twice a week. Subjects in Group B learned to play a classical guitar under the guidance of a professional instructor for 1 hour once a week. The subjects were required to fulfill at least 80% attendance of their intervention programs and spend at least 20 minutes each day for home practice. A post-intervention BCI performance tests was conducted after 4 weeks (T1) of the intervention programs.

During the assessment, each subject was required to complete an EEG experiment that was conducted using a Nicolet 64-channels EEG acquisition system prior to the BCI performance test. A total of 9 electrodes were placed over the sensorimotor cortex area to collect the EEG signals produced from three mental tasks: imaginary left hand movement (LEFT), imaginary right hand movement (RIGHT) and imaginary both feet movement (FOOT). The EEG signals of all possible combinations of bipolar EEG channels and mental tasks were analyzed offline by a 10x10 fold cross validation and a R^2 spectra analysis. The combination that gave the highest accuracy in the cross validation analysis was selected be used in the BCI tests.

In the BCI performance test, we used a BCI system that has previously been used to activate a prosthetic hand [3] and control a wheelchair in an indoor environment [5]. The BCI test starts with a 30-minute training phase. Raw EEG signals produced from two different mental tasks are filtered by using a 5 – 40 Hz elliptic filter and their AR coefficients determined. The LDA classifier is used to match the AR coefficients to different mental tasks. In the testing phase, a Graphical User Interface (GUI) is designed to allow selection of 4 options – "A", "B", "C", "D" (Figure 1) and a

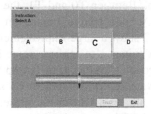

Fig. 1. A GUI for selection of the 4 options

"RESET" option. The options "A", "B'", "C" and "D" scrolls from left to right. Selection of the option is made when the desired letter enters the highlighted selection box. Instructions were displayed at the top left of the scrolling selection bar and the subjects were required to follow the instructions to select the options using motor imagery.

The BCI Performance was measured by the parameters including True Positive (TP), False Positive (FP), total time taken to complete a randomized sequence of selections (Tc), and accuracy that calculated based on the percentage of TP, percentage of FP generated during the duration of selection time (T_s) and non-activation time (T_{NA}) respectively as shown in Equation 1. Higher percentage of accuracy and shorter amount of time taken to complete the test cycle indicate a better BCI performance.

$$Accuracy = \frac{P(TP) \times T_S + (100 - P(FP)) \times T_{NA}}{T_{NA} + T_S} \, (\%) \tag{1}$$

Where,

P(TP) is the percentage of true positive (the correct decision made during T_S),

P(FP) is the percentage of the false positive (the incorrect decision made during T_{NA}),

T_S is the selection time (the duration of time in the test cycle when the subject could make a selection), and

T_{NA} is non-activation time (the duration of time in the test cycle when the subject is not supposed to make any selection)

The optimum time to complete the test sequence is 7 minutes. An example of a randomized sequence of selections is as follows:

```
Select A → Reset → Select D → Reset → Select C → Reset → Select B
→ Rest for 30 seconds → Reset → Select C → Reset → Select A → Re-
set → Select B → Reset → Select D → Rest for 30 seconds → Reset →
Select B → Reset → Select C → Reset → Select D → Reset → Select A
→ Rest for 30 seconds → Reset
```

3 Result and Discussion

The results of baseline assessment and post-intervention for 9 subjects after 4 weeks of intervention are shown in Table 1. The results show that BCI performance as reflected by the completion time, Tc of the BCI selection tests of the subjects varies from individual to individual. Between T0 and T1, the overall average BCI performance of subjects in Group A (with meditation training) has improved significantly. Notably, subjects A1 and A2 show a large improvement in the accuracy. Subjects in Group B (learning to play a guitar) also register some improvement but not as much as compared to those in Group A. Subjects in Group C (the control group) did not show any significant improvement. In fact subject C1 showed a significant reduction in BCI performance. All in all, results from the present study indicated that mental training programs such as mindfulness meditation show promising potential in terms of improving BCI performance, potentially through mechanisms such as improved the stabilities of mental states and produced more consistent EEG patterns.

This is a continuing study and future work will report on BCI performance measurements as well other psychological tests on concentration and attention over a longer period of intervention.

Table 1. Results of the BCI test in the baseline assessment (T0) and post-assessment (T1)

Subject	T0				T1				Comparison	
	%TP	%FP	Tc (minute)	Accuracy (%)	%TP	%FP	Tc (minute)	Accuracy (%)	Changes of Tc (minute)	Changes of Accuracy (%)
A1	47.55	43.52	38.17	51.31	47.79	4.26	19.17	67.39	-19.00	16.08
A2	30.74	21.16	41.50	49.00	83.08	33.96	9.83	75.42	-31.67	26.42
A3	24.05	10.19	72.17	59.82	54.05	37.55	40.25	58.59	-31.92	-1.23
B1	29.50	17.07	56.42	62.33	41.63	23.46	30.92	56.87	-25.50	-5.46
B2	62.14	26.52	19.58	68.51	72.06	13.33	10.67	78.91	-8.91	10.40
B3	46.26	18.77	35.33	69.10	34.73	21.50	51.50	56.47	16.17	-12.63
C1	81.08	36.36	11.67	72.86	37.45	22.47	53.33	60.31	41.66	-12.55
C2	43.95	26.82	42.42	58.94	62.40	49.10	40.00	57.08	-2.42	-1.86
C3	37.09	13.29	32.17	59.33	28.87	21.89	33.92	60.93	1.75	1.60

Acknowledgement. This work is supported by a Malaysian Ministry of Science Technology and Innovation (MOSTI) Science Fund Project No. 02-02-11-SF0011.

References

1. Wolpaw, J.R., Birbaumer, N., McFarland, D.J., Pfurtscheller, G., Vaughan, T.M.: Brain-Computer Interfaces for Communication and Control. Clin. Neurophysiol. 113, 767–791 (2002)
2. Birch, G.E., Mason, S.G., Borisoff, J.F.: Current Trends in Brain-Computer Interface Research at the Neil Square Foundation. IEEE Trans. on Neural Systems and Rehab. Eng. 11(2), 123–126 (2003)
3. Goh, S.Y., Ng, S.C., Phang, Y.M., Yong, X.Y., Lim, E., Yazed, A.M., Shuhaida, Y.: A Brain-Computer Interface for Control of a Prosthetic Hand. J. Science and Tech. in the Tropics 1, 35–41 (2005)
4. Lebb, R., Friedman, D., Muller-Putz, G.R., Scherer, R., Slator, M., Pfurtscheller, G.: Self-paced (Asynchronous) BCI Control of a Wheelchair in Virtual Environments: A Case Study with a Tetraplegic. Computational Intelligence and Neuroscience (2007) DOI 10.1155/2007/79642
5. Tan, L.F., Ng, C.S., Ng, J.Q., Goh, S.Y.: A Brain-Computer Interface with Intelligent Distributed Controller for Wheelchair. In: 4th Kuala Lumpur International Conference on Biomedical Engineering, IFMBE Proceedings, vol. 21, pp. 641–644 (2008)
6. Gao, X.R., Xu, D.F., Cheng, M., Gao, S.K.: A BCI-based Environmental Controller for Motion-Disabled. IEEE Trans. on Neural Systems and Rehab. Eng. 11(2), 137–140 (2003)
7. Guger, C., Edlinger, G., Harkam, W., Niedermayer, I., Pfurtscheller, G.: How Many People are Able to Operate an EEG-based Brain-Computer Interface (BCI)? IEEE Trans. on Neural System and Rehab. Eng. 11(2), 145–147 (2003)
8. Lo, P.C., Wu, S.D., Wu, Y.C.: Meditation Training Enhances the Efficacy of BCI System Control. In: Proceedings of the 2004 IEEE International Conference on Networking, Sensing and Control, vol. 2, pp. 825–828 (2004)
9. Kabat-Zinn, J.: Mindfulness-based Interventions in Context: Past, Present, and Future. Clin. Psychology: Science and Practice 10, 144–156 (2003)

The Research on EEG Coherence Around Central Area of Left Hemisphere According to Grab Movement of Right Hand

Mincheol Whang[1], Jincheol Woo[2], and Jongwha Kim[2]

[1] Dept. of Digital Media Technology, Sangmyung University,
7 Hongji-dong, Jongro-Ku, Seoul, Korea
whang@smu.ac.kr
[2] Dept. of Computer Science, Sangmyung University
7 Hongji-dong, Jongro-Ku, Seoul, Korea
{mcun,rmx2003}@naver.com

Abstract. This study is to find significant EEG coherence for predict movement. Eight students were asked to visuo-motor task and their EMG at flexor carpi radialis of right hand and EEG at C3 and 4 orthogonal points 2.5 cm away from C3 were measured. EEG coherence between non-motor area and motor area and between motor areas were analyzed based on movement duration calculated from EMG activation, movement delay and coherence delay. In the results, most participants showed significant coherence between sensory or frontal and motor area discriminating movement and non-movement. However, there were individual differences in areas and frequency band showing significant coherence.

Keywords: EEG Coherence, EMG, hand grab movement, movement delay .

1 Introduction

Brain has been tried to be connect directly to machine for providing with recovery from sensory and motor function injury or loss[1, 2]. EEG has become media of real-time interaction and been studied to determine significant parameters of brain function. One of the significant parameters was coherence.

EEG coherence represents integration of cortical activity among local areas of brain. There has been attempt to EEG coherence related to movement or task. EEG coherence has been shown to increase between sensory and motor areas in visuo-motor task which was visual triggering led to limb movement [3]. Since mental readiness of movement such as anticipation and attention has also been found to increase EEG coherence [4], it meant information process of movement from perception, recognition, execution and learning [5]. It has been shown over fronto-parietal area [5, 6] at all the frequency range [4]. Some findings showed that alpha coherence was more significant than the other frequency ranges[7-9]. Not only EEG coherence between motor area and nonmotor area of brain but one between different motor areas has been studied. Functional coupling along motor cortex resulted in EEG coherence showing increase at premovement and movement between multiple motor areas [10].

J.A. Jacko (Ed.): Human-Computer Interaction, Part II, HCII 2009, LNCS 5611, pp. 636–642, 2009.
© Springer-Verlag Berlin Heidelberg 2009

EEG coherence has not been influenced by task difficulty proving insignificant difference between simple and complex tasks [11]. Also, it has been shown to be developed with movement velocity but not with direction and mode coordination of movement [12]. Coherence between EEG and EMG has been observed to be significant with source localization of EEG correlated with specific frequency range of EMG [13, 14].

Researches of EEG coherence have successfully shown significant results from off-line analysis taking the disadvantage that it was not easy to consider individual difference of brain function. EEG could be volitionally controlled to accelerate rhythm for appropriate responding from perception to response [9]. Another disadvantage was measurement burden using many sensors on skin. It could not avoid from ergonomic problem of practical application beyond medical domain. For example, game industry has recently produced new functional game using BCI [15].

Therefore, this study is to construct on-line EEG coherence system considering individual difference for predicting movement using five electrodes around different motor and non-motor area.

2 Methods

Eight undergraduate students ranging in ages from 20 to 27 years participated in this study. They did not have any physical and mental problem and were paid for the participation. Measurement areas were newly defined as five areas consisting C3 in 10-20 international system and four points orthogonally directed 2.5 cm away from C3 as shown in Figure 1. C3 was denoted by CH1, vertical top point by CH2, vertical down point by CH4, horizontal left point by CH5 and horizontal right point by CH3. And this arrangement was determined according to correlation among cach movement areas or between movement area and non-movement area. Measurement points were determined to examine coherence between non-motor area and motor area such as between sensory area (CH4) and motor areas (C3, CH3, and CH5), and between sensory area (CH4) and frontal area (CH2). Measurement points also were for testing coherence between motor areas (C3, CH3 and CH5). Since the task was grab movement of right hand in this study, left hemisphere was observed.

EMG also measured at flexor carpi radialis of right hand for recognizing the moment and the duration of movement.

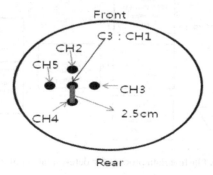

Fig. 1. Measurement Areas

The task was visuo-motor movement which was grabbing movement of right hand with performed when signal was flashed on and rest when signal off. Its velocity was two grabs per second.

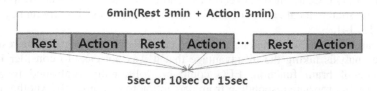

Fig. 2. Shown is data collecting time of sequential movement and rest

Data was collected at the sequential movement and rest as shown in Figure 2. Total time of data collecting was six minutes consisting of respective three minutes for movement and rest. Time intervals were randomly selected among five, ten and fifteen second per both movement and rest in order to avoid less attention of movement caused by anticipation of movement moment.

Since coherence was determined according to movement in this study, the parameters affecting it were delay and actual time of movement. Although visually signaled the moment and duration of movement, there was individually different in actual movement. Therefore, this study considered four parameters which were movement delay, coherence delay, actual duration of movement and the number of coherence. The movement delay was time between visual indication of movement and movement while the coherence delay was between one and coherence occurrence as shown Figure 4.

3 Analysis

Data has processed to obtain rule of coherence discriminating between movement and non-movement as shown in Figure 3. The rule included threshold value of four parameters. Both EEG and EMG were measured when participants performed grabbing movement. EMG measurement provided information of the movement duration and the movement delay as shown in Figure 4. Then the actual movement was calculated for EEG coherence.

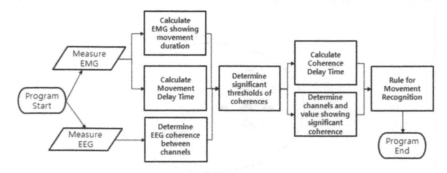

Fig. 3. On-line data process for determination of coherence

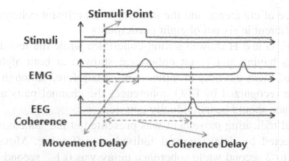

Fig. 4. Shown are movement delay and coherence delay

Significant EEG coherence discriminating between movement and non-movement was determined as shown in Figure 5. According to EMG activation, EEG coherences of movement and rest were respectively analyzed. EEG coherence was averaged for 336 repetitive movements and 412 repetitive rests. The significant coherence was determined at mean plus median between two times variance. It was individually determined for further analysis of four parameters.

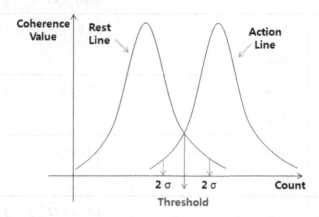

Fig. 5. Determination of significant coherence (threshold) discriminating between movement and rest

The pairs showing significant EEG coherence among five channels between movement and non-movement were determined by t-test. Then, coherences of alpha band and beta band of EEG at previously determined the pairs of channels were calculated and provided with constructing the rule which used later to recognize movement. Therefore, the rule included significant values of parameters such as delay time, movement duration, significant coherences and EEG channels.

4   Results

There were findings showing significant channel pairs and coherences in alpha and beta band discriminating movement and non-movement by t-test as shown in Table 1.

The significance of coherence and the number of significant coherence (p < 0.1) was individually different in six out of eight participants.

Participant F, G and H showed strong coherence while the rest did weak or none. All participants having significant coherence showed at both alpha band and beta band but one of them did only at alpha band. Therefore, although same movement was tried to be recognized by EEG coherence, the channel pairs and the frequency band of coherence should be individually counted.

Visual signal indicating movement was presented at the same condition but actual movement affected by delay showed individual difference. Movement delay was ranged from 1 to 2 second while coherence delay was 0.1-2 second more than movement delay.

Table 1. Individual difference of significant coherence, movement delay and coherence delay discriminating movement and non-movement

Participant	Frequency	No of Significant Channel	Movement Delay (sec)	Coherence Delay (sec)
A	Alpha	3	1 ± 0	1.83 ± 1.18
	Beta	1		
B	Alpha	1	1.9 ± 1.05	2 ± 1.32
	Beta	1		
C	Alpha	1	1.35 ± 0.24	2.78 ± 1.46
	Beta	1		
D	-	-	1.93 ± 1.32	3.12 ± 1.01
E	-	-	1.75 ± 1.22	1.78 ± 1.32
F	Alpha	2	1.3 ± 1.01	1.75 ± 1.55
	Beta	9		
G	Alpha	5	1.42 ± 0.35	2.19 ± 1.42
H	Alpha	3	1.86 ± 1.47	2.2 ± 0.71
	Beta	3		

Figure 6 showed areas showing significant coherence at alpha and beta band between movement and rest. Six participants showed significant coherence between sensory area and motor area. Therefore, coherence could recognize that task was visuo-motor movement. However, the pairs of coherence and their frequency band showed individual difference. The participants having lots of coherences showed coherence extended to frontal area from sensory area. The coherences between motor areas were observed in four participants out of eight participants.

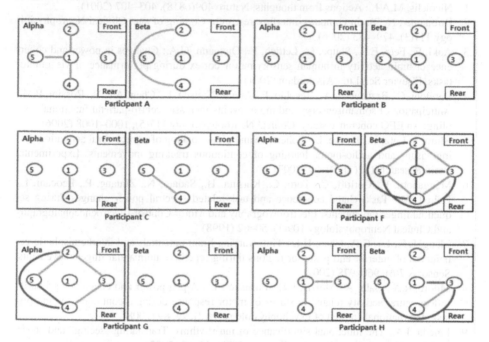

Fig. 6. Shown are areas showing significant coherence at alpha and beta band between movement and rest. (Light gray line: p < 0.1, Dark gray line: P <0.05).

5 Conclusion

This study was to find significant coherence discriminating movement and non-movement. Eight undergraduate students were asked to performed visuo-motor task of grab movement of right hand. EEG at C3 and 4 orthogonal points 2.5 cm away from C3 were measured for coherence and EMG at flexor carpi radialis of right hand for measure movement delay and movement duration.

The results of t-test showed there were areas of significant coherences although they were individually difference. There were delay between visual signal indicating movement and movement and one and coherence occurrence. This caused also, to individual difference of actual movement. These delays were considered in analysis of coherence and it was successful of finding significant coherence between sensory and motor area for movement recognition. Some participant showed strong coherence from sensory to frontal area while most participants maintained significant from sensory and motor area.

Therefore, EEG coherence was enabled to predict movement. Its accuracy may be enhanced in the consideration of individual pattern of coherence areas and coherence bands.

References

1. Nicolelis, M.A.L.: Actions from thoughts. Nature 409(6818), 403–407 (2001)
2. Birbaumer, N.: Brain-computer-interface research: Coming of age. Clinical Neurophysiology 117(3), 479–483 (2006)
3. Aoki, F., Fetz, E.E., Shupe, L., Lettich, E., Ojemann, G.A.: Changes in power and coherence of brain activity in human sensoryimotor cortex during performance of visuomotor tasks. Elsevier Sci. Ltd., Amsterdam (2001)
4. Babiloni, C., BrancucCi, A., Vecchio, F., Arendt-Nielsen, L., Chen, A.C.N., Rossini, P.M.: Anticipation of somatosensoryy and motor events increases centro-parietal functional coupling: An EEG coherence study. Clinical Neurophysiology 117(5), 1000–1008 (2006)
5. Blum, J., Lutz, K., Jancke, L.: Coherence and phase locking of intracerebral activation during visuo- and audio-motor learning of continuous tracking movements. Experimental Brain Research 182(1), 59–69 (2007)
6. Manganotti, P., Gerloff, C., Toro, C., Katsuta, H., Sadato, N., Zhuang, P., Leocani, L., Hallett, M.: Task-related coherence and task-related spectral power changes during sequential finger movements. Electromyography and Motor Control-Electroencephalography and Clinical Neurophysiology 109(1), 50–62 (1998)
7. Meng, L.F., Lu, C.P., Chan, H.L.: Time-varying brain potentials and interhemispheric coherences of anterior and posterior regions during repetitive unimanual finger movements. Sensorys 7(6), 960–978 (2007)
8. Moore, R.A., Gale, A., Morris, P.H., Forrester, D.: Alpha power and coherence primarily reflect neural activity related to stages of motor response during a continuous monitoring task. International Journal of Psychophysiology 69(2), 79–89 (2008)
9. Pineda, J.A.: The functional significance of mu rhythms: Translating "seeing" and "hearing" into "doing". Brain Research Reviews 50(1), 57–68 (2005)
10. Ohara, S., Mima, T., Baba, K., Ikeda, A., Kunieda, T., Matsumoto, R., Yamamoto, J., Matsuhashi, M., Nagamine, T., Hirasawa, K., Hori, T., Mihara, T., Hashimoto, N., Salenius, S., Shibasaki, H.: Increased synchronization of cortical oscillatory activities between human supplementary motor and primary sensoryimotor areas during voluntary movements. Journal of Neuroscience 21(23), 9377–9386 (2001)
11. Calmels, C., Hars, M., Holmes, P., Jarry, G., Stam, C.J.: Non-linear EEG synchronization during observation and execution of simple and complex sequential finger movements. Experimental Brain Research 190(4), 389–400 (2008)
12. Fuchs, A., Jirsa, V.K., Kelso, J.A.S.: Theory of the Relation between Human Brain Activity (MEG) and Hand Movements. NeuroImage 11(5), 359–369 (2000)
13. Mima, T., Hallett, M.: Electroencephalographic analysis of cortico-muscular coherence: reference effect, volume conduction and generator mechanism. Clinical Neurophysiology 110(11), 1892–1899 (1999)
14. Bortel, R., Sovka, P.: EEG-EMG coherence enhancement. Signal Processing 86(7), 1737–1751 (2006)
15. Krepki, R., Blankertz, B., Curio, G., Muller, K.R.: The Berlin Brain-Computer Interface (BBCI) - towards a new communication channel for online control in gaming applications. Springer, Heidelberg (2007)

Part VI

Language, Voice, Sound and Communication

A Speech-Act Oriented Approach for User-Interactive Editing and Regulation Processes Applied in Written and Spoken Technical Texts

Christina Alexandris

National University of Athens,
Athens, Greece
calexandris@gs.uoa.gr

Abstract. A speech-act oriented approach for Controlled Language specifications is presented for the implementation in a user-interactive HCI system for the editing process and for the regulation of written and, subsequently, spoken technical texts for Modern Greek. Sublanguage-specific and sublanguage independent parameters are used targeting to "Precision", "Directness" and "User-friendliness", based on the criteria of Moeller, 2005 for the success and efficiency of spoken Human-Computer Interaction, on the Utterance Level, the Functional Level and the Satisfaction Level.

Keywords: Controlled Language, Speech Act, Technical texts, Task-oriented dialog, prosodic modeling.

1 Introduction

The present study concerns a speech-act oriented approach for Controlled Language specifications in a user-interactive HCI system for the editing process and for the regulation of written and, subsequently, spoken technical texts. The language concerned is spoken and written Modern Greek, a language with a limited tradition in the production of technical texts and also a language into which a large number of technical texts are translated, the translation process often impacting the quality of the text produced. A basic problem that is addressed is the handling of ambiguity and difficulties in comprehensibility in instructive technical texts, especially when targets such as immediate and successful implementation, as well as security must be achieved.

The use of Controlled Languages has become a common approach for the efficient handling of the syntax and the lexicon of technical texts, with a tradition in languages such as English, German and French. In Controlled Languages, the identification of the functions of sentence types in the technical texts is data-driven and defined by the specific sublanguage of the technical text concerned, often in combination to the related speech act or speech acts expressed in the sentence.

J.A. Jacko (Ed.): Human-Computer Interaction, Part II, HCII 2009, LNCS 5611, pp. 645–653, 2009.

2 The Speech Act – Oriented Approach

The proposed strategy is based on an agent-oriented approach for the analysis of language [4] and targets to the success and efficiency of spoken Human-Computer Interaction, on the Utterance Level, the Functional Level and the Satisfaction Level, according to the criteria of Moeller, 2005.

The criteria on the Utterance Level (Question-Answer-Level) include informativeness, intelligibility and metacommunication handling [7]. The ease of use limits and/or functional limits, initiative and interaction control, processing speed/smoothness are classified as criteria concerning the Functional Level (System Capabilties) [7]. The criteria in respect to the Satisfaction Level include perceived task success, comparability of human partner and trustworthiness [7]. These principles and targets are summarized here as "Precision", "Directness" and "User-friendliness".

2.1 Speech Acts for Technical Texts and Task-Oriented Dialog

Here, the speech-act oriented approach for Controlled Language specifications is based on the (1) Task-oriented Dialog Speech Acts according to Heeman et al., 1998 and on the (2) Speech Acts for Technical Texts according to Lehrndorfer, 1996.

Specifically, the proposed speech-act oriented approach for Controlled Language specifications is based on the Speech Acts "Direction/Command", "Precaution/Safety" and "Description of Product/Device", defined as Speech Acts for Technical Texts [6].

For spoken technical texts constituting task-oriented dialogs, the Speech Acts for Technical Texts are combined with the Speech Acts for Task-oriented Dialogs [5], namely "Yes/No Question", "Request", "Check", "Confirm", "Inform", "Acknowledge" and "Filled-Pause".

2.2 Sublanguage-Specific and Sublanguage-Independent Parameters

The Speech Acts for Technical Texts define the type of action to be executed in respect to the sublanguage-specific and sublanguage-independent parameters of the Controlled Language. In a user-interactive system for editing technical texts with the use of a Controlled Language, the sublanguage-specific and sublanguage-independent parameters may be presented to the user in the form of questions and/or suggestions. In a Task-oriented Dialog system for spoken technical texts, the proposed sublanguage-specific and sublanguage-independent parameters can be used in the design phase of a Dialog System, in a user-interactive editing tool to be applied automatically in the implementation phase.

The scheme in which the General Guidelines can be described is characterized by the differentiation between rules that are (a) technical texts sublanguage-independent and (b) technical texts sublanguage-dependent parameters. An additional differentiation is the differentiation among General Guidelines related to (1) Syntax and (2) General Guidelines related to the Lexicon. In turn, the General Guidelines related to Syntax can be differentiated in (a) sublanguage-independent and (b) sublanguage-dependent rules. Similarly, the General Guidelines related to the Lexicon can be differentiated in (a) sublanguage-independent and (b) sublanguage-dependent rules.

For the language concerned, sublanguage-independent parameters concern sentence-length, order of information presented within a sentence, choice of verbs according to the speech-act indicated and the form of encoding information describing time, space (movement), quality and quantity. Sublanguage-specific parameters for Modern Greek involve the choice of processing or not processing "mixed categories" (for instance, participles), the choice of processing or not processing anaphora and the choice of verbs that are not related speech acts, but to the sublanguage-specific terminology.

3   The Sublanguage-Independent Parameters as a Controlled Language

3.1   Speech Acts for Technical Texts and Sentence Form

In respect to the sublanguage-independent parameters, sentence length is determined by the type of conjunction used for the breaking-down of the sentences into shorter units, to ensure clarity and intelligibility. The function of the conjunctions (for example, temporal, causative etc.) is linked to the Speech Act for Technical Texts related to each conjunction [6], a relation that is observed to be applicable in Modern Greek as well (Table 1). Specifically, it is observed that in Modern Greek the breaking-down process is determined by the conjunctions expressing the Speech Act "Direction/Command" [6]. In contrary, this process is seldom initiated by conjunctions linked to the Speech Act "Description of Product/Device" [6], since this process most often results to alterations in the information content of the original sentence.

Table 1. Relation of Sentence Content, Speech Act and "Breaking-Down" process (Modern Greek)

Sentence Content	Speech Act	Modification
Telicity	Direction/Command	breaking-down
Cause	Direction/Command	breaking-down
	Description of Product/Device	breaking-down
Condition	Direction/Command	breaking-down
	Description of Product/Device	no modification
Manner	Description of Product/Device	no modification
Contradiction	Description of Product/Device	no modification

Specifically, for the Speech Act Direction/Command, the breaking-down process is applied if the tasks to be performed are a serial sequence. For example, in the sentence "Deactivate the device and pull the plug", the sentence will be broken down into the following sentences: "Deactivate the device. Pull the plug". If the tasks are to be executed simultaneously, the sentence initiated by a temporal conjunction is preserved, as in the case of the sentence "While you press the green button, you can speak through the microphone" (translation from Modern Greek, with proximity to original syntactic structure). In the case of temporal overlapping of the tasks to be performed, the broken-down sentences are linked by the "and" conjunction, as in the example "Hold pieces B-4 and B-4 under the surface and screw them there" (translation from Modern Greek, with proximity to original syntactic structure).

Additionally, the Speech Acts for Technical Texts also determine the order of the elements appearing in the sentences (Table 2). For example, in sentences expressing the Speech Act "Direction/Command" the first element is the verb, as in the case of the utterance "Choose the Microsoft-Word file you wish to open and press the button Open" (translation from Modern Greek, with proximity to original syntactic structure). In this case, the verb is positioned in the beginning of the sentence, regardless of whether the verb constitutes sublanguage-specific terminology or also expresses a speech act. Typical variations of the verbal element include verbs with an infinitive and verbs with a temporal expression. In Speech Acts expressing Precaution/Safety, the first element is the negation, as in the case of the utterance "Don't push with force". Typical variations of the negation include negations followed by (or following) a temporal expression and negations following attention markers such as "Attention" and "Caution". A noun usually appears as the first element in sentences expressing the Speech Act "Description of Product/Device", as in the example "The small circular plug is located at the back of the unit".

Table 2. Relation of first element in sentence and Speech Act (Modern Greek)

First element	Variations:	Speech Act
Verb	Verbal expression Verb with infinitive Verb with temporal expression	Direction/Command
Negation	Negation with temporal expression Attention marker with negation	Precaution/Safety
Noun	-	Description of Product/Device

3.2 Speech Acts for Technical Texts and Lexicon

In respect to the lexicon, verbs that express a speech act in Technical Texts are defined as a specific sublanguage-independent group. In the domain of the Technical Texts, these verbs are identified as Directives, related to the Speech Acts "Command/Requirement", "Prohibition", "Permission", "Possibility" and "Recommendation" [6]. The recommended respective verbs for Modern Greek ensuring a one-to-one mapping to the respective Speech Act and discouraging ambiguity are the following: Command/Requirement is mapped to the verbs "pr´epi-na" ("must"-infinitive) or "xri´azete" ("needed"), Prohibition, Permission and Recommendation are explicitly stated in the verbs "apagor´evete" ("prohibited"), "epitr´epete" ("allowed") and "prot´inete" ("is recommended") respectively, whereas Possibility is mapped to the verbs "bor´i" ("can") or "´ine dinat´on" ("is possible"). In the previous examples, the transcriptions of the Greek expressions are purely phonological and are not based on morphological and orthographic criteria.

A similar preference strategy is applied to negations, where the particle "´mi" ("don't") as well as the negative expression with the temporal semantic content "po´te" ("never") are usually used to negate full sentences and are, therefore, preferred as opposed to the negative particle "ّ dhen" ("not", "does not"), mainly used to negate verbs. As an additional sublanguage-independent parameter, the achievement of precision and clarity in information describing time, space (movement), quality and quantity is targeted with the use of adverbial modifiers [2], as in the expressions "precisely under", "exactly before", "completely flat" and "exactly two".

The proposed parameters are oriented toward the targets of the criteria of informativeness, intelligibility and metacommunication handling on the Utterance Level [7], and may be expressed here as "Precision", and "Directness".

4   The Speech Act – Oriented Approach in Spoken Technical Texts

4.1   Relation of Speech Acts and Steps in Task-Oriented Dialog Structure

In spoken Technical Texts constituting task-oriented dialogs, the content of the utterances produced by the Conversational Agent is related to the Speech Acts for Task-oriented Dialogs [5], and modeled according to the above-described specifications for the written Technical Texts (Table 3). The Speech Acts for Task-oriented Dialogs involve speech acts related to user-input recognition ("Acknowledge"), confirmation of user-input "Confirm", checking task completion/task success requested or activated by user ("Check"), providing user with necessary information or informing user about data requested by user, task success/failure or current status of process/system ("Inform") and handling of waiting time ("Filled Pause") [5]. The System may ask the user to provide specific input ("Request") and expect the user's response ("Respond") [5]. For reasons of efficiency, in many dialog systems, a considerable percentage of the questions asked by the System constitute "Yes/No Questions" ("Yes/No Question") requiring a "Yes" or a "No" as an answer from the user ("Yes/No Answer") [5].

In dialog systems for spoken technical texts, steps in the dialog structure may be related to more than one Speech Act. Specifically, steps in the dialog structure involving the recognition of the user's answer and/or keyword recognition in user-input may be related to the "Acknowledge", "Request" or "Y/N Question" Speech Acts, as in the respective examples of utterances produced by the System (or System's Conversational Agent", namely "You have chosen the "Abort" option" ("Acknowledge"), "Please enter the requested date. Please press "1" ("Request") [8] and "Do you wish to execute the program?" ("Y/N Question").

Problems in the processing of user-input and/or errors in the keyword recognition in user-input may be related to the both the Speech Acts "Check" and "Request", as in the example of the produced utterance "Input cannot be processed", "Your input cannot be processed. Please repeat" ("Check")/("Request").

Input provided by the user that does not constitute a "Yes/No Answer" or is not related to keyword recognition (Free input) can be followed by the Speech Acts "Check", "Inform" or "Request" as in the respective examples of utterances produced by the System "We assume that you have completed the process" ("Check") [8], "You still have 30 seconds to file your complaint" ("Inform") and "Please add any further information you consider important" ("Request") [8].

The Speech Acts "Confirm" and "Inform" may concern the closing of the dialog between System and User, as shown in the respective examples "Your entry has been successfully registered" ("Confirm") [8] and "Your entry has been registered as No IE-6780923478" ("Inform"). Waiting time for the processing of user-input or for the completion of a process is handled by appropriate messages produced by the System such as "Please wait for two seconds" [8], identified as a "Filled Pause" Speech Act.

Table 3. Relation of Step in Task-oriented Dialog Structure and Speech Act

Step in Dialog Structure	Example	Speech Act
Answer / Keyword Recognition	Do you wish to execute the program?	Y/N Question
Problems or errors in Answer / Keyword Recognition	Your input cannot be processed.	Inform
Free Input	You still have 30 seconds to file your complaint	
Close Dialog	Your entry has been registered as No IE-6780923478.	
Answer / Keyword Recognition	Please enter the requested date Please press "1" Please choose "Confirm", "Repeat" or "Abort"	Request
Problems or errors in Answer / Keyword Recognition	Your input cannot be processed: Please repeat	
Free Input	Please add any further information you consider important	
Problems or errors in Answer / Keyword Recognition	Input cannot be processed.	Check
Free Input	We assume that you have completed the process	
Close Dialog	Your entry has been successfully registered	Confirm
All steps in Dialog Structure	Please wait for two seconds	Filled Pause
Answer / Keyword Recognition	You have chosen the "Abort" option	Acknowledge

4.2 Prosodic Modeling and Speech Acts for Task-Oriented Dialog

Prosodic modeling of the utterances related to the Speech Acts for Task-oriented Dialogs is based on the use of prosodic emphasis on the sublanguage-specific elements constituting the most important information in the sentence's semantic content, as well as sublanguage-independent elements such as negations and elements expressing time, space (movement), quality and quantity [1].

Specifically, prosodic emphasis on the negations and elements expressing time, space (movement), quality and quantity is used for the achievement of Precision [1], while prosodic emphasis on sublanguage-specific expressions and terminology is used for the achievement of comprehensibility resulting to Directness (Table 4).

Table 4. Relation of prosodic emphasis in Task-oriented Dialog Speech Acts and the purpose of utterance in spoken technical text (Modern Greek)

Parameter type	Elements receiving prosodic emphasis in Task-oriented Dialog Speech Acts	Purpose
Sublanguage-independent	spatial, temporal, quantitative expressions expressions related to manner and quality	Achievement of precision
Sublanguage-specific	Sublanguage-specific lexicon, expressions and terminology	Achievement of directness

For example, for the efficient handling of semantic content and/or for precision and directness in the interactions, the words "yes", "no", "packaging", "execute", "code", (sublanguage-specific expressions), "two minutes", "thirty seconds" (quantity - time), and "cannot" (negation) receive prosodic emphasis in the respective sentences: "SYSTEM: Please answer the following questions with a "yes" or a "no" Was there a problem with the packaging?", "SYSTEM: "Do you wish to execute the program?" (Speech Act: Yes/No Question), "SYSTEM: What is the code of the container?" (Speech Act: Request), "SYSTEM: Wait for two minutes" (Speech Act: Filled Pause), "SYSTEM: "You still have 30 seconds to file your complaint" (Speech Act: Inform), "SYSTEM: Your input cannot be processed" (Speech Act: Inform/Check).

Here, we note that all translations from Modern Greek are rendered with proximity to original syntactic structure.

4.3 Prosodic Modeling and Non Task-Oriented Speech Acts

Utterances produced by the Conversational Agent that are not directly related to the Speech Acts for Task-oriented Dialogs [3], such as the Speech Acts "Thank" or "Apologize", are not subjected to a sublanguage-independent strategy for prosodic modeling. In this case, prosodic modeling is sublanguage-specific, possibly empirical up to a certain extent, and also related to the style of communication chosen for the HCI system concerned.

The style of communication chosen is relate to the User-model of the Dialog System and targets to User-friendliness. For example, for the achievement of User-friendliness in the interactions [3], the words "sorry", "correctly", "thank" and "additional" receive prosodic emphasis in the respective sentences [1]: "SYSTEM: I'm sorry, I was not able to understand you correctly" (Speech Act "Apologize", followed by an error message) [8] and "I thank you for the additional input" ("Thank").

The speech-act oriented approach in the steps of the dialog structure for spoken technical texts are targeted to meet the requirements of "Precision", "Directness" and "User-friendliness", summarizing the criteria of informativeness, intelligibility and metacommunication handling on the Utterance Level (Question-Answer-Level) [7], the Functional Level (initiative and interaction control) [7] and the Satisfaction Level (perceived task success, comparability of human partner and trustworthiness) [7].

5 Applications

For the achievement of "Precision" and "Directness" in written technical texts, the above-presented sublanguage-independent parameters used as a Controlled Language may be applied automatically or in a user-interactive tool for editing technical texts. In the user-interactive tool, the proposed sublanguage-specific and sublanguage-independent parameters may be presented in the form of questions and/or suggestions to the user. Sublanguage-specific parameters allow the user to make decisions to meet the needs and requirements of the sublanguage concerned. These may occur in form of questions towards the user, or may be implemented automatically as a sublanguage-specific module interacting with the sublanguage-independent parameters.

For the achievement of "Precision", "Directness" and "User-friendliness" in spoken technical texts, the proposed sublanguage-specific and sublanguage-independent parameters can be used in design phase of the Dialog System. This can be achieved with or without a user-interactive editing tool, with the purpose of the application in the implementation phase.

6 Further Research

The efficiency of the sublanguage-independent parameters in the proposed speech act-oriented approach remains to be evaluated in a larger number of technical applications. The Speech Acts for Technical Texts according to Lehrndorfer, 1996, involving the German language and the Task-oriented Dialog Speech Acts according to Heeman et al., 1998, concerning the English language, the combination of which is proposed and described here, is observed to be compatible with the features of technical texts in Modern Greek. The compatibility of the above-described Speech Acts in respect to other languages or other language groups remains to be investigated.

Furthermore, the effect of the proposed sublanguage-independent parameters may also be tested in task-oriented but not technical applications, such as customer services and e-learning.

References

1. Alexandris, C.: Word Category and Prosodic Emphasis in Dialog Modules of Speech Technology Applications. In: Botinis, A. (ed.) Proceedings of the 2nd ISCA Workshop on Experimental Linguistics, ExLing 2008, Athens, Greece, August 2008, pp. 5–8 (2008)
2. Alexandris, C.: Show and Tell: Using Semantically Processable Prosodic Markers for Spatial Expressions in an HCI System for Consumer Complaints. In: Jacko, J.A. (ed.) Human-Computer Interaction. HCI Intelligent Multimodal Interaction Environment, vol. 4552, pp. 13–22. Springer, New York (2007)
3. Alexandris, C., Fotinea, S.-E.: Discourse Particles: Indicators of Positive and Non-Positive Politeness in the Discourse Structure of Dialog Systems for Modern Greek. International Journal for Language Data Processing "Sprache & Datenverarbeitung" 2004(1-2), 19–29 (2004)
4. Hausser, R.: A Computational Model of Natural Language Communication, Interpretation, Inference and Production in Database Semantics. Springer, Berlin (2006)

5. Heeman, R., Byron, D., Allen, J.F.: Identifying Discourse Markers in Spoken Dialog. In: Proceedings of the AAAI Spring Symposium on Applying Machine Learning to Discourse Processing, Stanford (March 1998)
6. Lehrndorfer, A.: Kontrolliertes Deutsch: Linguistische und Sprachpsychologische Leitlinien für eine (maschniell) kontrollierte Sprache in der technischen Dokumentation. Narr, Tuebingen (1996)
7. Moeller, S.: Quality of Telephone-Based Spoken Dialogue Systems. Springer, New York (2005)
8. Nottas, M., Alexandris, C., Tsopanoglou, A., Bakamidis, S.: A Hybrid Approach to Dialog Input in the CitzenShield Dialog System for Consumer Complaints. In: Proceedings of HCI 2007, Beijing China (2007)

Interacting with a Music Conducting System

Carlos Rene Argueta, Ching-Ju Ko, and Yi-Shin Chen

Institute Of Information Systems and Applications
Department of Computer Science
National Tsing Hua University
Hsin-Chu 300, Taiwan
{kid.a.rgueta,yishin,ichiro.hit.51}@gmail.com

Abstract. Music conducting is the art of directing musical ensembles with hand gestures to personalize and diversify a musical piece. The ability to successfully perform a musical piece demands intense training and coordination from the conductor, but preparing a practice session is an expensive and time-consuming task. Accordingly, there is a need for alternatives to provide adequate training to conductors at all skill levels; virtual reality technology holds promise for this application. The goal of this research was to study the mechanics of music conducting and develop a system capable of closely simulating the conducting experience. After extensive discussions with professional and nonprofessional conductors, as well as extensive research on music conducting material, we identified several key features of conducting. A set of lightweight algorithms exploring those features were developed to enable tempo control and instrument emphasis, two core components of conducting. By using position/orientation sensors and data gloves as the interface for human-computer interaction, we developed a functional version of the system. Evaluating the algorithms in real-world scenarios gave us promising results; most users of the final system expressed satisfaction with the virtual experience.

Keywords: music conducting, human-computer interaction, virtual reality, tempo control, instrument emphasis.

1 Introduction

Recently, numerous advances in multimedia and human-computer interaction (HCI) technology have opened new ways to enrich our lives in the future. Currently, these advances are most used in the video game industry; for example, using controllers to mimic pitching a baseball or playing a guitar. However, these impressive techniques can be applied to the real world as well as virtual reality.

In real life, there are many activities and professions that could benefit from multimedia and HCI systems. The music conducting profession is a good example. In this field, a music conducting system would be a helpful teaching tool in schools, and a cheap and practical solution for amateur conductors. Even professional conductors could use a conducting system for experimenting with the shape of musical pieces. Conducting systems could also help composers to experience their creations.

Motivated by all the benefits of a conducting system, we focused on developing this application. The system should be able to correctly interpret a conductor's

J.A. Jacko (Ed.): Human-Computer Interaction, Part II, HCII 2009, LNCS 5611, pp. 654–663, 2009.

commands from his/her body language to recognize the key elements such as beat, tempo, volume, and emphasis. Moreover, the system should make it possible for the user to conduct in a realistic way. The system should also satisfy practical application requirements: simple equipment, real-time response, and user independence.

Previous research efforts have failed to provide all these features. No system can simultaneously interpret beat, tempo, and the emphasis intentions of conductors; most either ignore some components or discard details. Calculating tempo from hand movement is the most-addressed issue. However, most works only calculate tempo from the hand/baton velocity [1, 2, 3], giving inaccurate results. Some well-known systems try to detect beat-points by up-down movements [4]; however, real beating is far more than up-and-down movements. Other systems are either user-dependent [5, 6] or physically uncomfortable [7]. Therefore, a robust, complete, and realistic conducting system is highly desirable.

To satisfy these requirements, we propose a method that analyzes the trajectory of the conductor's hand. By analyzing the structure of the shapes drawn in the vertical plane, we can extract a set of features allowing us to determine the beat patterns and adjust the tempo. Similarly, a set of features extracted from the horizontal plane help us determine whether the user has changed emphasis from one instrument to another. Our methods allow us to build a reliable user- and hardware-independent system. Thus, no prior knowledge or skill is needed to operate the system. Furthermore, our instrument emphasis module can be adapted to other applications of HCI requiring the function of pointing at any desired object.

We evaluated our tempo and emphasis control algorithms with both experienced and inexperienced conductors. To prove the user-independence of our methods, each user carefully assessed the system performance with different beat patterns. The experimental results clearly show the improved performance of our method. Furthermore, most conductors were satisfied with the system.

2 Overview of Conducting

Every human-computer interaction system needs adequate hardware for the interface between human and computer. In a Conducting System, the user interacts with a virtual orchestra by means of hand gestures. To facilitate interaction between the user and the system, we opted to use data gloves and motion sensing devices located on the user's hands and arms instead of cameras and computer vision techniques to trace the user's movements (Fig. 1). The sensor data (termed *conducting data*) received from the tracking hardware was interpreted, resulting in an adjustment of the performance of the virtual orchestra by either changing the behavior of an individual instrument or the orchestra as a whole. Besides the tracking devices, additional hardware to provide feedback from the system to the user include a screen in front of the user to display the virtual positions of the instruments and speakers to play the musical piece executed by the virtual orchestra (Fig. 1).

The *conducting data* is composed of points in 3-D space representing the hand position and Euler angles representing the forearm orientation throughout the whole conducting session. The points shape the *conducting trajectory*. For simplicity, we will divide the *conducting trajectory* into the *horizontal conducting trajectory* (*conducting trajectory* projected on the horizontal plane) and the *vertical conducting trajectory* (*conducting trajectory* projected on the vertical plane).

Fig. 1. Hardware setup for the Interactive Conducting System

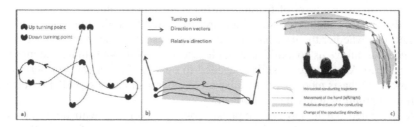

Fig. 2. a) 4-beat pattern in the vertical trajectory. b) Horizontal conducting trajectory. c) Horizontal trajectory during a change of instrument emphasis.

In the vertical plane, the *conducting trajectory* describes several gestures proper to the art of conducting. Among these gestures are the beat patterns, used in conducting to mark the tempo (example shown in Fig. 2a). Each beat pattern represents a music measure and is composed of a limited number of beat points. The portion of the *conducting trajectory* describing a single beat is called a *beat trajectory*. Since the arm has a direction of motion when drawing *beat trajectories* in the air, we call a *turning point* the 3-D point representing the hand position at which the direction of motion changes. There are several *turning points* in a single *beat trajectory* (Fig. 2a).

In the horizontal plane, the beat patterns mostly follow an oscillatory movement. This hand swing from side to side will incur changes of direction, resulting in *turning points* as in the *vertical trajectory* (Fig. 2b). When oscillating, the hand is usually directed towards a specific instrument.

3   Framework

3.1   Tempo Control

Several works [1, 2, 3] in this area try to monitor changes in velocity of the *conducting trajectory* in order to detect the tempo. These studies have a major premise: if tempo is not changed, the speed in a *beat trajectory* should be constant. However, it is hard for a conductor to keep a constant speed when conducting.[1] To avoid this problem, Lee et al. [8] examined the temporal properties of users' gestures to determine how the timing of the beat points related to the music beats. Nevertheless, maintaining the same speed at the beat level is not feasible and conductors instead concentrate on keeping a similar tempo at the measure level. Therefore, a measure-based tempo control approach is preferable.

The difficulty of measure-based recognition is to determine the boundaries of each measure within the *conducting trajectory,* more precisely, the *vertical conducting trajectory.* We find the first and last *beat trajectory* of each measure in order to count the beats per measure. This is a tremendous task as a conductor uses a wide variety of gestures ranging from our target beat patterns to idiosyncratic musical expression gestures.

After extensive observation and experimentation with conducting data, we grasped several properties of the *conducting trajectory* as the base for our tempo control algorithm. The details are given below. We first analyzed the structure of a *beat trajectory.* There are three important structural features in any *beat trajectory:* a *start point,* an *end point,* and a *beat point.* Both the *start point* and the *end point* are described by *up turning points,* but the *beat point,* representing the bouncing movements, is the *down turning point* at the bottom of the *beat trajectory* (Fig. 2a). In some studies [8], the tempo was calculated based on these three points; this beat-based approach performed better than the velocity approach. However, each *beat trajectory* within the same measure differs significantly in structure and hence in time duration, resulting in a very unstable tempo when the beat-based approach is used. In order to obtain a better tempo adjustment, we probed each detected *beat trajectory* to determine whether or not it terminated the current measure/beat pattern and later we extracted the tempo from the measure.

Depending on the pattern performed, some *beat trajectories* exhibit special movement characteristics. For instance, the last beat trajectory of classic beat patterns (2-, 3-, 4-, 6-beat patterns) describes a leftward movement. Hence, if the current *beat trajectory* moves to the left, a special flag indicating a candidate end of measure could be placed.

Another useful characteristic is the ratio of the incremented bounding box area of the trajectory. Except for the last beat in the measure, which moves leftward towards the center of the pattern, every beat increases the size of the bounding box area (Fig. 3a). Exceptions occur when the conductor wants to give a cue, inform the orchestra to play louder, or simply stress the new measure; in those cases, the last beat trajectory will be longer. To deal with this exception we consider the bounding box of the candidate last beat (determined by the flag). If this bounding box is near the upper right

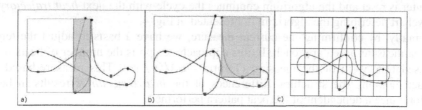

Fig. 3. a) Bounding box for 1st beat (gray) and 1st + 2nd beats (white) of the 4-beat pattern. b) Relative position of the last beat trajectory in the 4-beat pattern. c) Grid for the 4-beat pattern.

---

[1] In our experiments, even an experienced conductor could not maintain a constant tempo at all times. However, the average tempo was always similar.

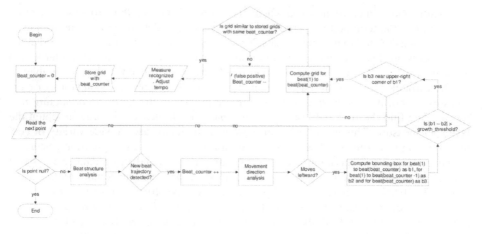

Fig. 4. Flowchart of the measure recognition algorithm

corner of the box for the whole pattern, then it is considered as the last beat in the current measure (shown in Fig. 3b).

By applying these three characteristics (beat structure, direction, and bounding box) we can find the last beat of the pattern and consequently determine the number of beats per measure. However, the conductor may mix beat patterns with gestures of his own to express his interpretation of the musical piece. This deformation of the beat patterns might result in detecting nonexistent beats (false positives). To tackle this issue we introduced the *grid of beat trajectory* to confirm the number of beats per measure.

The *beat trajectory grid* is an elaboration of the bounding box. The idea is to view the vertical plane as composed of grids or small rectangles. The total area of the set of grid cells traversed by the *conducting trajectory* is tightly related to the beat pattern (Fig. 3c). Moreover, different *beat trajectories* within the same beat pattern maintain a similar grid area. Mixing beat patterns with other gestures results in grid areas that are outside of the normal size range for a given pattern or *beat trajectory*. By recalling historical grid data from the current conducting session, we can eliminate false positives with abnormal grid sizes. After the measure is confirmed by the grids, the beat counter is reset and the algorithm continues the cycle with the next *beat trajectory*. A flowchart describing the algorithm in presented in Fig. 4.

Finally, by confirming the current measure, we have a basis to adjust the tempo with a measure-based approach. In this approach, tempo is the number of beats w per elapsed time v (s) of the measure (Tempo $= 60/(v/w)$). This measure-based approach ignoring the structural differences of the *beat trajectories* results in better performance independent of the beat pattern performed.

3.2 Instrument Emphasis

Volume control is a crucial component of a conducting system; however, it has been left out of this paper due to the simplicity of its implementation. Typically, the conductor will express his desire to change the volume with special gestures. A typical hand gesture to increase the volume is a palm up gesture. Similarly, a palm down gesture is a request to decrease the volume. The palm down and palm up gestures, along with other specific volume control gestures, are typically performed with the left hand. Using the data glove, which detects the level of flexure of the fingers, we can easily detect those hand gestures. What most previous research cannot do is allow the user to change the tempo or volume of individual instruments in the virtual orchestra. This capability requires the system to understand the user's intention to focus on a specific instrument. We call this intention the instrument emphasis. By incorporating the instrument emphasis during conducting, the conducting system can allow the user to truly personalize a musical piece, at the same time increasing the level of reality of the overall experience.

Recognizing instrument emphasis is not simple. Previous efforts tried to deal with this component by detecting a pointing gesture towards a certain instrument section [9]. The fact is that there is no such pointing gesture. Moreover, simply detecting the direction in which the arm points is insufficient because the arm is in constant motion. This inherent characteristic of conducting forces us to find a better feature describing the overall arm direction.

The tempo control module analyses the *vertical conducting trajectory* to retrieve its features. This trajectory often takes the shape of the different beat patterns (Fig. 2a). The instrument emphasis module, in contrast, mostly focuses on the horizontal trajectory which follows an oscillatory motion pattern (Fig. 2b-c). As in tempo control, we need to find *turning points* in the trajectory. A Finite State Machine (FSM) model was used to detect the changes in direction corresponding to the *turning points*. Since FSMs are well studied, we omit the details.

The *turning points* in the horizontal trajectory are not very useful by themselves. However, the vectors representing the pointing direction of the arm that passes through the *turning points* (termed *direction vectors*) bound the overall pointing direction (Fig. 2b). In most cases, two consecutive *direction vectors* crossing two consecutive *turning points* will intersect, producing what we call a *conducting angle*. The *conducting angle* describes the overall direction of the arm. The idea is simple: while the user is conducting towards the same instrument section, the oscillatory movement makes two consecutive *direction vectors* intersect, producing angles that have a similar magnitude. When the conductor changes her emphasis to another instrument section, the angle immediately produced will have a larger value (Fig. 2c). Finally, after the overall direction is set towards the new section, similar-valued angles will appear again. Detecting the larger angle is the key to detecting instrument emphasis changes.

It is important to mention that the *conducting angles,* extracted from the *horizontal trajectory,* work for virtual orchestras composed of a single level or row of instruments. To detect the proper instrument section in multilevel or multi-row orchestras, additional analysis of the *vertical conducting trajectory* is necessary. Clustering can be used to determine the specific row of the instrument. First we dynamically cluster the *start point* of each measure into k clusters according to their relative position in the vertical plane. Each cluster area should then map to one level (row) of the virtual orchestra. While the user is performing, the clustering approach dynamically divides the vertical plane into k zones (k is the number of levels of the orchestra) where higher zones correspond to higher levels within the orchestra. Some flexibility should be allowed by using a threshold for the clustering algorithm.

So far we have defined the *conducting angles* as a powerful feature to determine the instrument emphasis of the conducting. Only the "big" angles actually describe a change of emphasis. A way to detect the "big" outlier angles within the set of angles was developed. Outliers are commonly viewed as abnormal observations that can decrease the performance of a system. For our application, the outlier angle is a useful feature and we have defined a lightweight algorithm to detect it. The algorithm is simple; we compare the difference between the observed angle and the median of the set to a threshold. If the difference is bigger than the threshold then the angle is declared as an outlier and a change of emphasis is detected.

Predefined thresholds work well when we have prior knowledge of the system generating the data. For our application, the data generator is the user. In order to preserve user-independence, we need to dynamically compute the threshold from the data sequence. Although the standard deviation is a good estimate of variability, it is very sensitive to outliers and thus not suitable for our purpose [10]. A more robust estimate is the median absolute deviation (MAD). There is abundant information about MAD on the web so we omit the details.

The use of a dynamic threshold such as MAD guarantees that our instrument emphasis module remains user-independent, but there are still a couple of issues to consider. First, an additional requirement for our system is real-time response. As we add more and more angles to the set, the time required to process them increases. Second, the notion of "big" angles is relative since an angle may be "big" within a certain range but not so "big" within a larger range. Both problems are easily solved with one addition to the outlier algorithm. For the locality problem, defining outliers in the dynamic applications as violations of local variation patterns, we decided to add a sliding window mechanism to the algorithm. A sliding window of the proper size will not only keep the processing time small but also preserve the outlier property of the "big" angles. By experiment we found that the best window size is $n = b*2$, where b is the number of beats per measure.

4 Evaluation

Simulating a real-world activity in a virtual-reality environment is not a trivial task. Generally, the virtual system lacks certain elements, reducing the level of reality. Besides an evaluation of the virtual system, the key algorithms running behind the scenes should be evaluated under real-world conditions to guarantee the best possible experience. Accordingly, we designed two different scenarios to evaluate the system. First, we evaluated the measure recognition algorithm in a real-world *offline* scenario. Second, users were asked to play the Interactive Conducting System in an *online* scenario and evaluate it on a scale of 1 to 5.

4.1 Offline Scenario

The goal of the *offline scenario* was to examine our system under real-world conditions. This scenario evaluated the measure recognition algorithm, which is the heart of the tempo control module. The scenario consisted of two rehearsal sessions by real orchestras with professional conductors. Using real-world conducting sessions to test

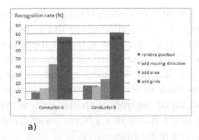

Criteria	Average	Standard Deviation
Accuracy	3.9	0.88
Response Time	3.7	0.67
Amusement	3.78	0.97
Overall performance	3.9	0.57

a)   b)

Fig. 5. a) Recognition rate of our measure recognition algorithm evaluated offline. b) Users' evaluation of the Interactive Conducting System in an online scenario.

our approach represented a big challenge since all the complexities of real conducting were present. The features included the beat patterns (our target), as well as many other complex gestures for volume control, musical expression, instrument emphasis, etc., making the *conducting trajectory* extremely complex and irregular.

During our experiment, the *conducting data* was collected using the sensing hardware and data gloves described in Section 2. Additionally, a video of the frontal view of the conductor was recorded to check and validate our output. The collected *conducting data* were input four times to the algorithm in an incremental setup. We start with a basic setup which only analyzed one characteristic of the trajectory. In each iteration, we added a new characteristic to the analysis and studied its impact on the overall performance. The output from the analysis included the number of recognized measures and the type of beat patterns performed. Once the measures were recognized, adjusting the tempo was trivial.

Fig. 4a shows that every new characteristic of the trajectory analyzed by the algorithm increased the recognition rate. However, the performance remained unsatisfactory before adding the final characteristic. This was due to the high complexity of the *conducting trajectory* in real life, resulting in many false positives. Nevertheless, after adding the grid characteristic, the performance increased dramatically. This increase proved that grids did what they were meant to: detect and reject gestures that did not correspond to beat patterns.

4.2 Online Scenario

In the *online scenario*, we wanted to test the fully functional interactive conducting system. This system comprised both tempo control and instrument emphasis modules. To evaluate the system, we asked the users to provide their feedback on how realistic their experience was while playing with the system. To measure the level of realism, we asked four questions to the user including how accurate, how fast (response time), how much fun the system was, and how good the overall performance was. The user was required to answer on a scale from 1 to 5 where 1 indicated very unsatisfactory and 5 represented very satisfactory.

To perform the experiment, we picked 10 users with different skill levels (from inexperienced to amateur). The users conducted using the hardware described in Section 2 and Fig. 1. While conducting, they were asked to perform different beat patterns and change the instrument emphasis at any time they wanted. After every emphasis change, they received feedback from the system through the screen displaying the virtual position of the instruments. Finally, after using the system they were required to fill out the questionnaire. Fig. 4b shows how satisfied the users were, on average, with all aspects of the system. The lowest score, 3.7, was for the response time. The low standard deviations suggest that all the users agreed on the good performance of the system in every evaluation criterion. Moreover, various positive comments were left in the comments section of the questionnaire, such as: "I think the feature of "instrument emphasis" really helps move this system away from dull, and the sensitivity performs pretty well, too. It's quite impressive."

5 Conclusions

This paper proposes a set of lightweight algorithms to analyze key characteristics of conducting and make a virtual conducting application possible. Our measure recognition approach performed well under extreme conditions, achieving a maximum recognition rate of 82%. This performance should allow smooth measure-based tempo control in the less complex virtual environment. Furthermore, users of the final system expressed their satisfaction with the interactive system. According to their evaluations, the system's accuracy and overall performance were good (with a score of 3.9 each). Users also reported that the instrument emphasis module increased the level of reality and enjoyment of the experience, making it less dull and more interactive.

Although volume control was not addressed in this paper, some techniques developed in this work can be used to tackle that component. For instance, we could use bounding boxes or grids to track the growth of patterns representing a request to increase the volume.

According to the requirements for a conducting system, such as ease of use, real-time response, and a realistic experience, our proposed interactive conducting system represents a significant HCI for the music profession. We hope to soon see our completed system in the classrooms of music academies or even in the home of a professional conductor.

References

1. Borchers, J., Lee, E., Nakra, T.M.: You're the Conductor: a Realistic Interactive Conducting System for Children. In: NIME 2004, pp. 68–73 (2004)
2. Murphy, D., Andersen, T.H., Jensen, K.: Conducting Audio Files Via Computer Vision. In: Gesture Workshop, pp. 529–540 (2003)
3. Borchers, J., Lee, E., Samminger, W., Muhlhauser, M.: Personal Orchestra: a Real-Time Audio/Video System for Interactive Conducting. Multimedia Syst. 9(6), 594–594 (2004)
4. Lee, E., Grull, I., Kiel, H., Borchers, J.: CONGA: a Framework for Adaptive Conducting Gesture Analysis. In: NIME 2006, pp. 260–265 (2006)
5. Usa, S., Mochida, Y.: A Multi-Modal Conducting Simulator. Journal of Japan Society for Fuzzy Theory and Systems 10(4), 127–136 (1998)
6. Kolesnik, P.: Conducting Gesture Recognition System. Master Thesis, McGill University (2004)

7. Marrin, T., Picard, R.W.: The Conductor's Jacket: A Device for Recording Expressive Musical Gestures. In: Proceedings of the International Computer Music Conference TR470 (1998)
8. Lee, E., Wolf, M., Borchers, J.: Improving Orchestral Conducting Systems in Public Spaces: Examining the Temporal Characteristics and Conceptual Models of Conducting Gestures. In: CHI 2005, pp. 731–740 (2005)
9. Morita, H., Hashimoto, S., Ohteru, S.: A Computer Music System that Follows a Human Conductor. Computer 24(7), 44–53 (1991)
10. Huber, P.: Robust Statistics. Wiley, New York (1981)

Hierarchical Structure: A Step for Jointly Designing Interactive Software Dialog and Task Model

Sybille Caffiau[1,2], Patrick Girard[1], Laurent Guittet[1], and Dominique L. Scapin[2]

[1] Laboratoire d'Informatique Scientifique et Industrielle, Téléport 2-1 avenue Clément Ader,
86961 Futuroscope Cedex, France
{sybille.caffiau,girard,guittet,sanou}@ensma.fr
[2] Institut National de Recherche en Informatique et en Automatique,
Domaine de Voluceau -Rocquencourt- B.P.105
78153, Le Chesnay, France
Dominique.Scapin@inria.fr

Abstract. In order to design interactive applications, the first step is usually the definition of user needs. While performing this step, activities may be modeled using task models. Some task model components express scheduling information that describes the task dynamics. According to a model-based approach, the dynamics of applications (i.e.: the dialog) can be formalized using a dialog model. Several approaches seek to exploit the task model information to perform the dialog model. This paper aims to show that the use of the hierarchical dialog model facilitates its design according to task model information during the whole iterative design process.

Keywords: task models, dialog, iterative design.

1 Introduction

According to a user-centered approach to design interactive applications, the starting point is to provide specifications in the form of task models. Some models were developed [1, 2]. They support the theory of action [3] that decomposes actions until they are atomic. Therefore, task models allow to express activity hierarchically from a high abstraction level to a more concrete level.

From the specification of the user needs expressed in the form of task models (and other specification information), the designer performs the other design steps that produce the implemented application. Each of these steps is the object of validation phases. Models were developed in order to support each design step. This paper is focused on one of these models, which specifies the dynamics of the application, named the dialog.

The use of task models to design dialog is mainly based on the exploitation of task scheduling. Task scheduling allows to temporally organize tasks. It is exploited when a task model is dynamically used (in the simulation tool, for example). Several approaches aim at exploiting task scheduling to automatically generate interactive applications from task models [4, 5]. However, some studies show that scheduling information on task models is not sufficient to generate complete interactive applications [6, 7]. In particular, this design method does not take into account the iterative aspect of the interactive application design.

J.A. Jacko (Ed.): Human-Computer Interaction, Part II, HCII 2009, LNCS 5611, pp. 664–673, 2009.
© Springer-Verlag Berlin Heidelberg 2009

In order to design task models, several methods were developed based on inter-views. Task modeling is an iterative process (initial interview, design of a first task model version, iteration on information gathering and assessment, update of the task model...) [8]. Task models that are used as a starting point to design interactive appli-cations are therefore iteratively modified several times in order to take into account new information. Thus, the design method process is repeated for each modification of task models. The dialog based on task models is similarly modified.

The next section (section 2) is focused on the dialog models and the approaches followed to design them. In this paper, we show that the use of hierarchically struc-tured dialog formalism facilitates the user-centered iterative design process. This statement will be illustrated by the design of the interactive application of a case study: the mastermind game (section 3). The application specifications are expressed in the form of task models. However, they are modified during all the design process (caused by user feedback taking into account new functionalities...). From this case study we highlight the main benefits of the use of a hierarchical structure to jointly design dialog and task models (section 4). Finally, we conclude and present future research avenues (section 5).

2 Related Work

In order to express the dynamics of interactive applications, dialog models were de-veloped. All formalisms [9] that exist in order to express dialog models are grouped into three sets: the event-based formalisms, the grammar-based formalisms and the state-based formalisms. The use of state-based dialog models enables verification of properties (such as the vivacity property [10]). Moreover, among all the dialog mod-els, few studies have been performed in order to allow their use in the interactive application design process. Therefore, by using developed tools or libraries, only four state-based models can be integrated in this process: the State Machines [11], the Interactive Cooperative Objects (ICO) [12], the Hierarchical Interactors [13] and the Hierarchical State Machine (HSM) [14].

All the state-based models are based on the **state machine** model. Dialog ex-pressed using state machines (automate) can be implemented using the *SwingStates* JAVA Library [15]. State machines (or State Transition Diagrams) are defined as sets of four elements: an initial state, a set of states, a set of transitions and a set of labels associated with transitions.

Transitions allow going from a state to another. Generally, when expressing dia-logue, transitions represent user actions, mainly on widgets. Implementations gener-ally use *events*. Each transition may be associated with guards and actions. The guard propriety, has to be true to enable the execution of the transition. The action is the code executed when the transition is fired.

When an event is performed, if there is a transition that corresponds to the current state with a guard property equals to true, then the *transition action* is executed. At the beginning, the current state is the initial state. State machine representations are represented by ellipses and transitions by arrows.

State machines are used to express the interactive application dialog [9]. However, they explicitly describe all states of the dialog. The design of interactive applications may imply a great number of states. In order to take into account the exponential number of states, several models split up the expression of the dialog.

The **Interactive Cooperative Object** (ICO) formalism deals with the expression of the interactive application dynamics. This formalism is composed of Cooperative Objects [16] and Petri nets. The PetShop tool [17] was developed in order to simulate and animate the interactive application dialog expressed using the ICO formalism. The ICO dialog composition does not imply an hierarchical organization.

At the end of the 80's, the **Hierarchical Interactors** were developed [18] in order to express the dialog of CAD systems. They structure the dialog and integrate its design into a complete architecture (H^4) [13]. State machines, which exchange information by the means of tokens, express the dialog hierarchically. The hierarchical division is based on the split of transitions of the hierarchically superior level.

The last dialog formalism, the **Hierarchical State Machines**, allows the expression of automate in states of another automate (as in the StateCharts formalism [19]). There is no tool that supports this model, but as for the automates, a toolkit was developed in order to implement Hierarchical State Machine: HsmTk [14].

These models are used in several approaches that explore the design of interactive application dialog models from specifications. All these approaches are based on specifications expressed as task models. First, model transformation approaches propose the generation of dialog from a task model [4, 5]. The resulting dialog corresponds to an application window chain and has some limitations [7]. From this observation, some approaches propose to perform verifications on the dialog model according to a task model. For example, Navarre in [20] describes the dialog validation (expressed using ICO) according to the task model (expressed using CTT [21]) through the use of scenarios.

However, dialog model verifications can be performed only once the complete dialog is designed without any intermediate verification. Moreover, for each task model modification, the designer has to perform all the dialog model validation process again. In order to integrate a systematic dialog model checking in the application design, we study the benefits of the use of a hierarchical model to express the dialog to perform its validation according to a task model.

3   Iterative Design of an Interactive Application

In order to illustrate the benefits of using hierarchical structure for dialog, we will describe a case study: the design of an interactive application supporting a game, Mastermind. During the design process, specifications are modified and thus, the dialog model needs to integrate the changes. This section is organized as a scenario of design modifications that corresponds to a real iterative application design.

The mastermind game is a code-breaking game for two players: the *codemaker* and the *codebreaker*. The *codemaker* chooses four color pegs (from six) composing the code that the *codebreaker* has to guess. The same color may appear several times on the code. To guess the code, the *codebreaker* composes color-propositions (at most eight). Once the proposition is submitted, the *codemaker* provides feedback indicating the number of pegs correct for both color and position and the number of pegs correct for color but placed in the wrong position.

3.1 Initial Specification

The first specification of the Mastermind game concerns its rules. However, this application game is a one-player game, the computer acting as *codemaker*. The user is the *codebreaker*. The composition of propositions is made by placing pegs from left to right. Once placed, a peg cannot be replaced or deleted.

Task model. To design the application corresponding to this specification, the first step is the task model design (presented in Figure 1 a). This task model was designed using the K-MAD formalism [22] and its associated tool K-MADe [23]. This task model formalism is hierarchically composed of tasks and allows formally taking into account the world objects in the scheduling specification. By using them, we can for example express the fact that a player can make at most eight propositions if he/she does not break the code before.

Playing a Mastermind game (*Play to Mastermind*) is sequentially composed of the definition of the code to break (*Generate secret code*) and its guess (*Guess code*). In order to guess the code, the first step is entering a code proposition (*Compose a code*). Next, this proposition is automatically evaluated (*Evaluate*) by the system. Allowing placing the fourth pegs (*Place peg 1*, *Place peg 2*, *Place peg 3* and *Place peg 4*), the system needs to initialize the proposition place (*Init proposition place*). As tasks *Init proposition place*, *Place peg 1*, *Place peg 2*, *Place peg 3* and *Place peg 4* are sequentially scheduled, the position of each peg depends on its number of placements (For example, the third placed peg is in the third position in the current proposition).

Tasks composing *Guess code* are performed several times as the user can make several propositions before breaking the code. *Guess code* is therefore an iterative task (indicated by "I:predicate"). It is performed while the code is not broken and eight propositions are not made.

Dialog model. In order to express the dialog of the Mastermind game application, we use a hierarchical dialog model. This model aims to extend the hierarchical interactor model in order to be able to express the dialog of all kinds of interactive applications. A library has been developed, which allows the implementation of this dialog model in JAVA applications. State machines of each dialog abstraction level have the same graphical representation as that described before. In addition, the transition execution is managed by tokens that are produced by user actions or other state machines. We chose to represent the transitions by the name of the token that triggered it. Moreover, each transition can produce a token (consumed by another state machines) therefore, we represent them in blue.

We can divide the dialog of the initial Mastermind game application into three hierarchical levels (Figure 1 b). Each level is expressed with a state machine. The higher abstraction level dialog is the global dialog of the game (*AGame*). The state machine is composed of two states and two transitions. From the initial state, the single transition is the game beginning transition. Once this transition is triggered, the current state becomes the *Set* state that expresses a current game state. From the second state, the game can be completed and the current state goes back to the *Init* state.

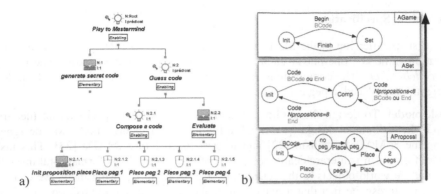

Fig. 1. a) Task model and b) Dialog model of initial specifications

A game is composed of several sets. The global dialog of a set is expressed by the middle abstraction level state machine (*ASet*). This state machine is composed of two states corresponding to the initial state and the guessing code state (*Comp*). The initial state expresses the current state when no code has been proposed. Once a code is proposed (*Code* transition), the current state becomes the second state (*Comp*).

Finally, making a code is expressed on the third state machine (*AProposal*). From the initial state, a transition expressing the beginning of a code making can be fired (*BCode*). The transition execution changes the current state that becomes the *1-peg* state. The next three states are successively reached by transitions triggered by the peg placing. Once the fourth peg is placed, the current state goes back to the *Init* state.

3.2 First Specification Modification

Placing the four pegs following this process (without any possibility of changing a placed peg) seems to be difficult for the player, who wants to change the game rules. The next specification version is performed for the user to be able to delete the last placed peg.

Task model. The specification modification corresponds to the execution of the task *Compose a code*. This task model part is modified as shown on Figure 2 a. Once the computer initializes the current proposition place (*Init proposition place*), the user can place pegs (*Place peg*). In order to place, players can place the next one (*Place next peg* (precondition: *there is at least one free position*)) or delete the last one (*Delete previous peg* (precondition: *there is at least one peg placed*)) as many times as he/she likes. Once the code is composed (four pegs compose the proposal), it can be submitted to evaluation.

Dialog model. This first specification modification concerns only the code making. The dialog corresponding to the code making is expressed in the *AProposal* dialog model. The state machine that expresses the dialog of the first specification modification is presented in Figure 2 b.

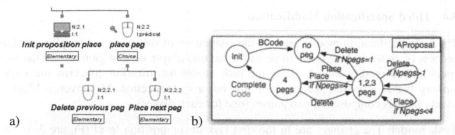

Fig. 2. Consequences of the first specification modification a)on task model b)on dialog model

The state machine is composed of four states and four transition types. As in the first specification modification dialog, only one transition can be triggered (*BCode*) from the initial state (*Init*) of the *AProposal* state machine. This transition expresses the beginning of a code making. The three next states represent the code making states. The first one expresses the state when no peg composes the current code; the second one expresses the state when one, two or three pegs are placed and the last state when the code is completed. The deletion of the previous peg (*Delete*) can be performed only in the *1,2,3-peg* and *4-peg* states, and the code evaluation (*Complete*) can be performed only from the *4-peg* state. The *Code* token is created by performing the *Complete* transition.

3.3 Second Specification Modification

The second specification modification also concerns the game rules. In order to add a more complex level, the user wishes to add the possibility that spaces compose a code. Moreover, the peg placing is without any order. In this third version, the interactions are based on direct manipulation techniques.

Task model. The task model that corresponds to this goal needs few modifications. Only the tasks to place peg are modified, the deletion and the placing of the pegs is not limited to the previous and the next peg but can be the deletion of any place pegs and the placing at any available place. Moreover, the *submit* task precondition condition is modified. While the submission can be performed in the second task model version only when the four pegs are placed, in the third task model version, there is no condition to submit.

Dialog model. As for the first specification modification, only one dialog model has to be modified: *Aproposal*. While in the first specification modification state machine, three states express the code making states (without any peg, with one, two or three pegs and with four pegs), in the second specification modification state machine, only one state is mandatory. From this state, a transition computes the end of the code making (*Complete*). This transition does not have any pre condition in order to authorize spaces in the codes.

In addition, in order to integrate direct manipulation techniques to place and delete the pegs, an abstract level is added under the *AProposal*. This abstraction level expresses the interaction technique level to perform *Place* and *Delete* transitions.

3.4   Third Specification Modification

The last specification modification is the adaptation of the game to two players. The process of *codebreaking* is the same as for the one player version game (after the two specification modifications). Here, the task model modification concerns the *code-making* that is a second player action and not a system action. Moreover, a Mastermind match is composed of two games (one for each player).

Task model. The changes are in the first task decomposition level (Figure 3a). The high abstraction level task is sequentially composed of the two iterations on the code composition task and on the guessing task. Last, a system task displays the marks of both players.

Dialog model. In order to express a two-player dialog model (Figure 3b), a state machine is added to the dialog. This (*ATwoPlayers*) state machine expresses the dialog of the higher abstraction level. From the initial state, a *BPlay* transition can be triggered. This transition expresses the start of the two-player game. From this state, the *Code* transition can be fired changing the current state. The *guess 1* state expresses the state when the second player is guessing the code. Once the first guessing part is performed (*Mark*), the same states and transitions are performed for the second player.

In order to take into account the communication between the abstraction levels, some token productions are added (such as *Mark* that is produced by the *End* transition in the *AGame* state machine and that triggers a transition in *ATwoPlayers*).

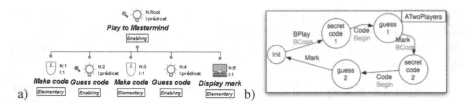

a)   b)

Fig. 3. Consequences of the third specification modification a)on task model b)on dialog model

4   Benefits of a Hierarchical Structure for the Iterative Design

The first benefit of the hierarchical structure for the dialog is its **modularization**. The benefits from this code division are similar to all other modularization techniques (focus on each specific part, reuse of parts…). For example, by using the architecture model to organize the application code, we can adapt methods for each part (such as the dialog part). Moreover, the modularization also allows the use of parts for several applications. For example, one of the Mastermind game dialog part is focused on the management of a game session (*AGame*). This dialog part is common with the majority of game applications (game beginning, playing state and game finishing). Thus, the corresponding machine states (and its implementation) can be used in the dialog design (and implementation) of all game applications.

The dialog modularization organizes the dialog according to the abstraction level. The abstraction level modularization highlights the second benefit of the use of hierarchical structure to express dialog: the **centralization of modification in order to integrate specification modifications**. This point was illustrated in our case study of designing the Mastermind game dialog. As we stated before, the user-centered design begins by the user needs specification in the form of task models. This design iteratively integrates modifications. By composing a dialog according to the different abstraction levels, we can associate the abstraction levels of the dialog model and the abstraction levels of the task models. Even if this association is not a bijective function, it allows the isolation of modifications that have to be made.

As the dialog abstraction level is associated with a task model abstraction level, from the modification brought into the task model, we can infer which dialog abstraction level will reflect this modification. As was shown in the third part, the isolation of a dialog part according to the position of specification modifications in the task tree minimizes the number of modifications. Moreover, these modifications are independently brought (without any repercussion on other levels). There are two types of integrations of modifications on a dialog model:
- the addition of another abstraction level (from one player to two players).
- the change of an existing state machine. For example, the first task model abstraction level is associated with the first dialog state machine (*AProposal*) (Figure 2).

Moreover, the expression of the dialog parts according to the abstraction level is **adapted to design refinements**. Task models are progressively designed according to the iterative information addition [24]. By using a hierarchical dialog model, we can follow this design process.

Finally, task models are defined in order to express activities from data gathering, which not necessarily imply the description of the interaction used. However, approaches that study the design of dialog from task models add the interaction information in order to link tasks and dialog transitions (such as [5]). The hierarchical dialog description integrates interaction techniques at a dialog abstraction level that does not depend on task models. For example, an abstraction dialog level was added in order to migrate from an interaction based on buttons to an interaction based on the use of a direct manipulation technique (the use of drag and drop to place or delete pegs). The added state machine manages the use of the direct manipulation technique. Thus, the **validation of the dialog models according to the task models does not depend on the used interaction type** (provided that the interaction allows to perform elementary tasks).

5   Conclusion and Prospects

Model-based design uses studies on the use of models (verification of properties, transformation of models...) in order to design interactive applications and to verify them. Among the used models in this approach, two contain elements linked to the application dynamics: task models and dialog models. Even if all the specifications required to design dialog models are not included in task models [6], dynamic information ought to be taken into account. This correspondence between both models implies making modifications on the dialog as soon as the task model is modified or completed. As the task model design is iterative, the dialog is thus iteratively modified as well.

We show in this paper that the taking into account of the implication of specification modifications in the dialog is facilitated when the dialog model is hierarchically structured. This hierarchical presentation allows the dialog model to follow the same structure (decomposition by abstraction level) as task models. Thanks to this similarity of composition on abstraction levels, for each modification on task models, the designer has only to update the associated dialog model parts.

The study presented in this paper is one step in a wider approach aiming to design interactive application dialog models. The goal is to allow designers to design the dialog part according to the specifications expressed in task models (i.e. verifying dialog models do not transgress task model scheduling information during all the design process). The division of dialog models into different abstraction level parts allows to combine a dialog design with a task model design. Each of these associations constitutes an independent module. The next step of our study is the comparison of elements of both module constituents (task model part and dialog model part). We plan to establish rules of check between models that constitute dynamic design recommendations. The verification of these recommendations will be ensured using model-driven engineering methods (http://planet-mde.org/).

References

1. Balbo, S., Ozkan, N., Paris, C.: Choosing the Right Task-modeling Notation: A Taxonomy. In: Diaper, D., Stanton, N.A. (eds.) The Handbook of Task Analysis for Human-Computer Interaction, pp. 445–466 (2004)
2. Limbourg, Q., Vanderdonckt, J.: Comparing Task Models for User Interface Design. In: Diaper, D., Stanton, N. (eds.) The Handbook of Task Analysis for Human-Computer Interaction, ch. 6, pp. 135–154 (2004)
3. Norman, D.A.: The Psychology of Everyday Things (1988)
4. Mori, G., Paternò, F., Santoro, C.: Design and Development of Multidevice User Interfaces through MultiplcLogical Dcscriptions. IEEE Transactions on Softwarc Enginccring, 507–520 (August 2004)
5. Luyten, K., Clerckx, T., Coninx, K., Vanderdonckt, J.: Derivation of a Dialog Model from a Task Model by Activity Chain Extraction. In: Jorge, J.A., Jardim Nunes, N., Falcão e Cunha, J. (eds.) DSV-IS 2003. LNCS, vol. 2844, pp. 203–217. Springer, Heidelberg (2003)
6. Palanque, P., Bastide, R., Winckler, M.: Automatic Generation of Interactive Systems: Why A Task Model is not Enough. In: Stephanidis, C., Jacko, J. (eds.) Human - Computer Interaction. Theory and Practive, vol. 1, Héraklion, Gréce, pp. 198–202 (2003)
7. Caffiau, S., Girard, P., Scapin, D., Guittet, L.: Generating Interactive Applications from Task Models: A Hard Challenge. In: Winckler, M., Johnson, H., Palanque, P. (eds.) TAMODIA 2007. LNCS, vol. 4849, pp. 267–272. Springer, Heidelberg (2007)
8. Couix, S.: Usages et construction des modèles de tâches dans la pratique de l'ergonomie: une étude exploratoire,
http://www.biomedicale.univ-paris5.fr/taskmodelsurvey/accueil/
9. Olsen, D.R.: User Interface Management Systems: Models and Algorithms. San Mateo (CA), USA (1992)

10. Aït-Ameur, Y., Baron, M.: Bridging the gap between formal and experimental validation approaches in HCI systems design: use of the event B proof based technique. In: Margaria, T., Steffen, B. (eds.) ISoLA 2004. LNCS, vol. 4313, pp. 74–81. Springer, Heidelberg (2006)

11. Jacob, R.J.K.: Using Formal Specification in the Design of Human-Computer Interface. In: Human Factors in computing systems, pp. 315–321 (1982)

12. Palanque, P., Bastide, R.: Petri-Net Based Design of User Interfaces using the Interactive Cooperative Objects Formalism. In: Interactive Systems: Design, Specification, and Verification (DSV-IS 1994), F. Paternò, Bocca di Magra, Italy, pp. 383–400 (1994)

13. Depaulis, F., Jambon, F., Girard, P., Guittet, L.: Le modèle d'architecture logicielle H4: Principes, usages, outils et retours d'expérience dans les applications de conception technique. Revue d'Interaction Homme-Machine 7(1), 93–129 (2006)

14. Blanch, R., Beaudouin-Lafon, M.: Programming Rich Interactions using the Hierarchical State Machine Toolkit. In: AVI 2006, Venice, Italy, pp. 51–58 (2006)

15. Appert, C., Beaudouin-Lafont, M.: SwingStates: Adding State Machines to the Swing Toolkit. In: UIST 2006, pp. 319–322 (2006)

16. Bastide, R.: Objets coopératifs: Un formalisme pour la modélisation des systèmes concurrents. Thesis. Université de Toulouse 1 (1992)

17. Bastide, R.: PetShop: a tool for the formal specification of CORBA systems. In: Conference on object Oriented Programming Systems Languages and Applications, Minneapolis, United States, vol. 167 (2000)

18. Texier, G.: Contribution à l'ingéniérie des systèmes interactifs: Un environnement de conception graphique d'applications spécialisées de conception. Thesis. Université de Poitiers, 230 (2000)

19. Harel, D.: Statecharts: a visual formalism for complex systems. Science of Computer Programming 8(3), 231–274 (1987)

20. Navarre, D., Palanque, P., Paterno, F., Santoro, C., Bastide, R.: A Tool Suite for Integrating Task and System Models through Scenarios. In: Johnson, C. (ed.) DSV-IS 2001. LNCS, vol. 2220, pp. 88–113. Springer, Heidelberg (2001)

21. Paternò, F., Mancini, C., Meniconi, S.: ConcurTaskTrees: A Diagrammatic Notation for Specifying Task Models. In: IFIP TC13 human-computer interaction conference (INTERACT 1997), Sydney, Australia, pp. 362–369 (1997)

22. Lucquiaud, V.: Sémantique et Outil pour la Modélisation des Tâches Utilisateur: N-MDA. Thesis. Poitiers, 285 (2005)

23. K-MADe electronic reference, http://kmade.sourceforge.net/

24. Sebillote, S.: Task analysis and formalization according to MAD: Hierarchical task analysis, method of data gathering and examples of task description

Breaking of the Interaction Cycle: Independent Interpretation and Generation for Advanced Dialogue Management

David del Valle-Agudo, Javier Calle-Gómez, Dolores Cuadra-Fernández,
and Jessica Rivero-Espinosa

Carlos III University of Madrid. Av. Universidad 30, 28911 Leganés, Spain
{dvalle,fcalle,dcuadra,jrivero}@inf.uc3m.es

Abstract. This paper presents an architecture for Natural Interaction Systems in order to make interpretation and generation processes independent, opposite to the traditional development of the interaction, typically called *Interaction Cycle*. With this aim a multi-agent platform is applied, together with a joint action Dialogue Manager based on the Threads Model [1] and an advanced Presentation Manager. The combination of these factors enables: a concurrent execution of all processed involved in the Natural Interaction; the capability of adjust on each moment new goals from both, user and system, into the state of interaction; and organizing both processes depending on the need, opportunity and obligation of generate new utterances, respectively.

Keywords: Natural Interaction Systems, Turn Taking, Grounding, Independent Interpretation and Generation, Threads Model.

1 Introduction

This work is outlined in the Human Computer Interaction (HCI) field, more specifically in Natural Interaction Systems which aim is to make accessible the technology by means of the same modalities, codes and procedures that humans use to interact one to each other, that is, through a Natural Interaction (NI).

An important effort has been achieved to develop this kind of systems over the last years, especially regarding global and local organization of interaction -links between different goals- and- the internal development of each goal-. However, the temporal organization of the interaction, called *Grounding*, has been barely put into practice up to this moment. Traditionally, the interactive process has been modelled as the pass of a baton in a relay race. According to this supposition, on each moment the floor of the interaction (turn) falls on one of the participants, and once he/she finish his/her turn execution (intervention), the floor pass to the next one, from one to another until the interaction ends. In this temporal organization, generation is supposed to be the consequence of the interpretation of a user intervention, and then the user is expected to perform a new one and so on, from the beginning to the end of the interaction.

Natural Interaction is a more complex process which grounding goes beyond these rules. In real human interactions neither the last of interventions, nor its relative position are defined beforehand. Actually, it is a joint process where each participant

J.A. Jacko (Ed.): Human-Computer Interaction, Part II, HCII 2009, LNCS 5611, pp. 674–683, 2009.

assesses at each moment the need, obligation and opportunity of taking part in, depending on the state of his goals, the ownership of the floor and the state of the different components of the system. Consequently, participants perform their interventions dynamically along the time, even overlapping or interrupting other participants.

In order to support this type of interaction, architectures which make the processes independent of the different components of the system, able of coordinate them, and capable of developing strategies for dialogue management based on the joint action theories are required.

This paper departs from a brief review of the state of the art, afterwards it discusses the need to make independent the interpretation and generation processes, and finally an architecture is proposed to solve this problem. Some conclusions complete the exposition.

2 State of the Art

Starting from Cohen's classification [2], and considering the structures and knowledge managed in the interaction, Mc Tear [3] classifies the Natural Interaction Systems in the categories shown in Table 1:

Table 1. Classification of Natural Interaction Systems

Category	Formalizes	Examples
Dialogue grammars	Sets of states and their transitions	VoiceXML [4]
Frames	Plans to be satisfied	VERBMOBIL [5]
Plans	Forms to be filled out	WITAS [6]
Intentional models	The development of the participants' initiatives	COLLAGEN TM [7]
Joint action models	Collaborative actions among participants in order to satisfy their own goals based on the joint action theories [8]	TRIPS [9] JASPIS [10] SOPAT [11]

Although from a theoretical point of view this last category lays the foundation of the natural representation of the interaction in all their organizational levels (global, local and temporal), interaction systems so far have been focused just on the management of the interaction from the global and local levels.

There exist some systems that propose architectures based on collaborative agents with the aim to improve the management of the temporal development of the interaction. Amongst others, SOPAT [11] and CHIL [12] are systems capable of incorporate pro-active behaviors as consequence of internal and external events (but without affecting their interventions dynamically with the changes produced simultaneously in the sociologic circumstances). Some others like INTEGRATV-4ALL [13] or HIGGINS [14] manage the commitment of the joint goals with the purpose of incorporate the feed back into the interaction (although not simultaneously with the speaker intervention).

Definitively, in spite of this approaches, the grounding has been restricted until now to a pass of baton, called Interaction Cycle, where the speaker constructs unilaterally its intervention, without considering neither the influence of the sociolinguistic circumstances nor the simultaneous backchannel offered by the listener once it has been formalized.

3 Breaking of the Interaction Cycle

The Interaction Cycle stems from traditional conception of interaction [15], according to any communication where there is an active element, the source, and a passive one, the receiver. Consequently, the dialogue is an action where participants play one of these roles, either the sender or receiver, and they cannot play both simultaneously. From this point of view, the interaction is considered an action achieved from the speaker to the listener, without additional flows of information emitted on the opposite direction. Furthermore, it is considered that the interaction ground passes from one to another participant alternatively, like a baton, in a predefined and fixed order. The result is an interaction consisting of a unique process, with a cyclical structure that involves the succession of five steps: acquisition, interpretation, operation, generation and synthesis. In some parts of the cycle the system plays the role of listener (acquisition and interpretation); in some others the role of speaker (generation and synthesis); and in the intermediate step (operation) it performs the operations that users want to access by means of the interaction.

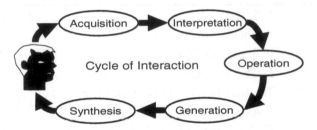

Fig. 1. Traditional Interaction Cycle in Natural Interaction Systems

Theoretically, the aforementioned temporal organization is suitable to develop very accurate and natural interactions with real users, mainly in transactional or information retrieval oriented domains. The example 1 shows a particular scenario of interaction that follows this modality of grounding.

This example is structured in segments [16] a, aa and ab, each of them composed of some interventions (a by a_1, aa by aa_1 and aa_2, and ab by ab_1 and ab_2). In spite of having a correct local and global organization (the relations between interventions of each segment and between different segments, respectively), the traditional cycle of interaction is characterized by an excessive inflexibility in the turn taking and construction of interventions, compared with a real exchange produced by humans in the real use of language [10]. In fact, some issues, such as overlook that listeners co-participate in the production of the speaker interventions or not to adapt messages content to the quantity of information required by a specific listener, are unnatural and sometimes aggressive practices in the human interaction.

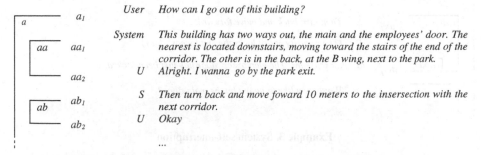

		User	How can I go out of this building?
a	a_1		
		System	This building has two ways out, the main and the employees' door. The
aa	aa_1		nearest is located downstairs, moving toward the stairs of the end of the
			corridor. The other is in the back, at the B wing, next to the park.
	aa_2	U	Alright. I wanna go by the park exit.
		S	Then turn back and move foward 10 meters to the insersection with the
ab	ab_1		next corridor.
	ab_2	U	Okay
			...

Example 1. Cycle of Interaction

A closer scenario to a real human-human interaction is example 2. In this interaction neither the duration nor the content of the intervention $aa_1 + aa_1' + aa_1''$ are fixed unilaterally by the speaker. It is built jointly by both participants based on a previous formalization of the speaker (the intervention aa_1 of the first example) and considering the backchannel emitted by the listener (in the interventions aaa_1, aab_1 and aac_1): aaa_1 provides evidences of excessive information (updating aa_1 into aa_1') and aab_1, expressed by different modes than speech, highlights leak of information (causing the reformulation of aa_1' into aa_1'').

		U	How can I go out of this building?
a	a_1		
		S	This building has two ways out, the main and the employees' door. The
aa	aa_1		nearest is located downstairs, moving [toward...]
aaa	aaa_1	U	[Oh!, ok]. Now I [get it]
	aa_1'	S	[Yep]. The other exit gives onto the park
aab	aab_1	U	(User is confused)
	aa_1''	S	...that is in the back, at the B wing
aac	aac_1	U	Okay, lets go by there.
ab	ab_1	S	Turn back and move foward 10 meters to the insersection with the next
			corridor.
	ab_2	U	Okay
			...

Example 2. Co-construction of system intervention

On the other hand, a change in the circumstances surrounding the interaction could alter the interaction cycle (Example 3) by introducing events during the system intervention that could triggers its reformulation.

The example 3 shows an interaction where the occurrence of an event meanwhile intervention ab_1 is in progress forces the system to introduce a cancellation goal over the just opened exchange ab. This represents a system self-interruption.

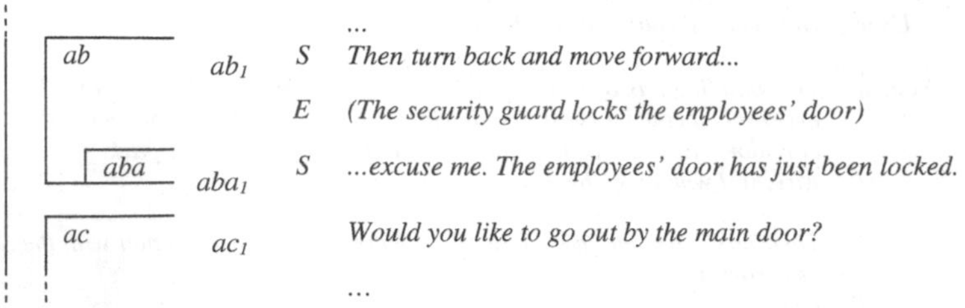
...
ab
ab_1
S Then turn back and move forward...
E (The security guard locks the employees' door)
aba
aba_1
S ...excuse me. The employees' door has just been locked.
ac
ac_1
Would you like to go out by the main door?
...

Example 3. System self-interruption

In the same way, it is possible to show similar examples of how evidences about the interest and attention, the increment of the urgency of some goals or their cancellation, amongst others factors, could have effects on the interaction development.

Definitely, against the traditional conception, the Natural Interaction is a collaborative action where each act is accomplished jointly by all participants [17]. The interaction is constructed both by speaker interventions and the evidences of closures that listeners provide him/her by means of their backchannel utterances. As result, neither the duration of interventions, nor their order or content are predefined previously, but emerge dynamically as participants evaluate the need and opportunity of taking the turn on the interaction, even overlapping or interrupting each others. A turn taking management restricted to the Interaction Cycle constitutes an important limitation of the natural interaction development. This fact becomes more striking as the interactive systems capabilities are improving in aspects such as pro-activity, adaptability, commitment management, etc.

In order to provide a more natural behavior in terms of temporal organization, Natural Interaction Systems should be supported by cognitive architectures based on the joint action theories and implemented through a multi-agent approach, thus enabling coordination and independence of the interpretative and generative processes. Furthermore, they should also observe advanced presentation mechanisms that deal with issues as turn taking management and grounding.

4 Framework

The current paper describes the system LaBDA-Interactor. This approach consists of a Natural Interaction System with an intentional dialogue management -based on the Threads Model- and an advanced presentation management which allows the independence of the interpretative and generative processes and their coordination.

In order to support the implementation of this system, a suitable blackboard-oriented multi-agent platform (Ecosystem) has been developed. This platform consists of a set of tools to implement autonomous, independent and cooperative agents; mechanisms for an efficient communication of the agents over a Database Management System (Oracle 10g); along with proper agents for ensuring a correct balance of the population of agents and the brokering of their request.

Knowledge models will be implemented into one or more agents (depending on the model design), performing on n the same or on different machines distributed in a LAN. Each component contains structured knowledge and reasoning mechanisms to provide a set of services. For solving such services they can apply several strategies, which could involve access to common resources and/or services requests to other models. Thus, any result comes from the collaboration of the whole. The influence of the different knowledge models in the interaction is simultaneous, that is, the system's interactive behavior is the result of their autonomous processing and utter cooperation. Consequently, their implementation must observe their concurrence and autonomy. Furthermore, each model abstraction could be fulfilled by placing different concurrent approaches for that model, competing for giving the best solution in less time. Moreover, it has to ensure services availability by destroying collapsed agents and creating new ones as required.

This work has been partially supported by the Regional Government of Madrid under the Research Network MAVIR (S-0505/TIC-0267); the SOPAT project supported by the Spanish Ministry of Education and Science (CIT-410000-2007-12), and the ongoing projects THUBAN and 'Access Channel to Digital Resources and Contents', supported by the Spanish Ministry of Education and Science (TIN2008-02711 and TSI-020501-2008-54, respectively).

5   Cognitive Architecture for an Independent Interpretation and Generation

This work presents a cognitive architecture for Natural Interaction Systems in order to solve problems related to the independence of the interpretation and generation processes. The architecture proposes specialized models to cover all knowledge used during the interaction. These models are: Interface Components, Presentation Manager and Dialogue Models (figure 2a).

The **Interface Components** are going to receive and express messages concurrently, so they require the intervention of a controlling component.

The **Presentation Manager** performs the following tasks: fusion of messages received from different input interface components; fission of system interventions into messages to be expressed by different output interface components; management of the continuity of the system and user interfaces; monitoring of floor; and coordination of the interpretation and generation processes.

Fusion and fission deal with those problems resulting from incorporate multimodality and multilingualism on interaction (in both directions). These functions make transparent for the core of the natural interaction system those modalities and languages that participants use during the development of the interaction. For this purpose, speech acts theories [18] are applied unifying the meaning into a common representation despite its modality or language. In order to make a difference between interpretation and generation processes, it is necessary to define some new functions connected with the *turns management*. These functions are turns continuity management, turns taking management and process coordination.

Turns continuity management: from the interpretation, there is a mandatory need of detect the continuity that underlies the performance of these independent extracts of expressions, checking units of expression with complete interpretative meanings – communicative acts- susceptible of mean changes in the state of interaction. Regarding to generation, system performance is sensible to new changes arising in the

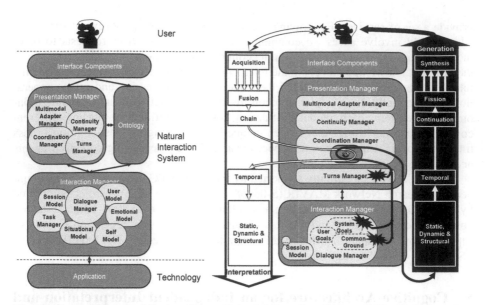

Fig. 2. a) Cognitive Architecture for a Natural Interaction System (left). b) Independent Generation and Interpretation Processes (right).

sociolinguistic circumstances that surrounds their production and to the interpretation of new user utterances. In consequence, system interventions can be reformulated, self-interrupted and corrected. This fact requires the ability to incorporate new extract of expression yielded by the system into the flow of expression on course.

Turn taking management: A more complex turn taking requires depicts the state of the turns that participants are yielding. It is important to consider issues as the track of each turn execution, the position of participants in face of future turns, etc... This information makes possible to estimate when it is possible, required or mandatory to produce new system interventions, according to human interactions [19].

Processes coordination: The independence between interpretation and generation processes requires monitoring and coordinate access to the resources shared by both processes. These processes require consulting and updating the information stored in the different components involved in the interaction. This is the case of the knowledge about the state of the joint goals, user, session, situation, emotions, self-knowledge about the system and the ontology.

The **Interaction Manager** is the component responsible for the interactive behavior of the system. It is organized in Dialogue Model, Task Model and some other sociolinguistic knowledge models involved in the interaction.

The core of the Interaction Manager is the Dialogue Manager, which represents the progress of the goals shared by the participants, as well as their discursive own goals (individual goals). The Dialogue Manager is a component of crucial importance to support a suitable independence between interpretative and generative processes.

The Task Model is the component of the Interaction Manager which is in charge of making technology accessible for users. Therefore, it represents the operative layer of Natural Interaction Systems. The interaction, as consequence of the interpretation of user utterances and the generation of system ones, reaches interactive states connected with the execution of certain task (which are the reason for what the user participates in the interaction).

Together with the dialogical and operative knowledge, and in order to enrich the interaction management, there exists additional sociolinguistic knowledge of influence on the interaction. This is the knowledge related to users, circumstances (situation), emotions, system, session and ontology.

In this work, a specific dialog model has been applied: Threads Model. This is an intentional joint-action dialog model which is based on the notion of dialogue threads. Threads are acquired as sub dialogue abstractions from the corpus, and instanced during the interaction with a set of features fixing the interaction state, context, attention, etc. Once any thread instance has been set, it can be developed, cancelled, or temporarily abandoned to be reopened later. This sub dialogue management is good for the advanced turn handling because it allows introducing and developing new thread instances anytime, thus enabling interlocutor's interruptions and even self-interruptions. However, attentional management becomes a delicate matter because of the risk of misunderstanding between participants in the interaction.

The threads commitment management is the solution applied by this model. Every thread instance is stored in a *common ground*, along with its features and a value for the belief of commitment. The commitment has three aspects: information (mutual knowledge), attention (focus), and interest (link to individual goals).

When the commitment value decreases some other threads are used to reinforce it (reinforcement and repair techniques). Anytime a thread is to be developed and its commitment (at any level) is found to be low, a reinforcement technique will be introduced to avoid confusion and provide fluency to dialog. The concrete technique will be chosen suited to the sort and the degree of commitment.

On the other hand, joint threads progress as a result of the need for any participant to develop his own goals. The system urgency to reach a goal is given by a criticism function, an expression dependent on some variables of the situation, session, state of threads, etc. These variables change either as consequence of interventions interpretation or generation or as effect of changes in the sociolinguistic circumstances. The criticism value of a system own goal could reach thresholds that trigger new generative processes. Then, the assessment of the interaction state and the turn taking management may, in case, give raise to new system actions.

As mentioned before, there exist two independent processes, interpretation and generation, developed simultaneously throughout the interaction. These processes use the functions and knowledge defined and updates their states as follows (figure 2b):

Interpretation Process: The input interface components acquire during the time fragments of user utterances, which are sent to the Adapter Manager in order to compose them in a unique data flow (modality and language independent). The Continuity Manager detects continuity between the fragments previously received and the new fragments, making possible to discover units endowed with a complete interactive meaning. These units, represented in terms of communicative acts, are interpreted from a temporal, structural, dynamic, and static point of view under the permission of the Coordinator Component.

Generation Process: The different knowledge models involved in the Natural Interaction updates their states of information as effect of both interpretation of new pieces of user utterances and changes produced in the sociolinguistic circumstances that surround the interaction. These changes could trigger new generation processes. During their courses, the Generator evaluates the need, opportunity and obligation of produce new pieces of contribution and formalize them as a sequence of communicative acts, with the permission of the Coordination Manager. Continuity Manager coordinates the continuation, rectification or reformulation of the previously formalized pieces of intervention and the Adapter Manager express in the adequate modalities and languages the new communicative acts.

8 Conclusions and Future Work

The proposed approach makes independent interpretation and generation processes, hence allowing an advanced and more natural grounding than the traditional Interaction Cycle. It is supported by a suited multi-agent platform, an intentional joint-action dialog model, and an advanced Presentation Manager able to deal with issues as the continuity management of interventions, the processes coordination and the turn taking management.

The improvement of the temporal organization of interventions in Natural Interaction Systems is an essential task insofar as their interactive capabilities improve (for example, their pro-active behavior and the incorporation of situational knowledge in the interaction), making clear the high rigidity and inflexibility of the temporal development of the Interaction Cycle. This approach is also able to develop the Interaction Cycle when the domain of interaction requires such type of grounding.

It is still pending the analysis, design and implementation of advanced strategies of turn taking, continuity management, processes coordination and goals management in order to exploit the goodness of the proposed architecture and reach a more natural temporal organization of the interaction. In the same way, it is an important issue the adaptation of current methodologies for evaluating Natural Interaction Systems [20] to provide a measurement of the benefits of these new abilities both in subjective and objective manners.

References

1. Calle, F.J.: Interacción Natural Mediante Procesamiento Intencional: Modelo de Hilos en diálogos (Spanish). PhD Thesis. Universidad Politécnica de Madrid (2004)
2. Cohen, P.R.: Dialogue Modeling. In: Cole, R., Mariani, J., Uszkoreit, H., Batista-Varile, G., Zaenen, A., Zampolli, A., Zue, V. (eds.) Survey of the State of the Art in Human Language Technology, pp. 234–240. Cambridge Uni. Press and Giardini (1997)
3. Mc Tear, M.: Spoken Dialogue Technology. Springer, Heidelberg (2004)
4. Larson, J.A.: VoiceXML: An Introduction to Developing Speech Applications. Prentice Hall, New York (2002)
5. Alexandersson, J., Reithinger, N., Maier, E.: Insights into the Dialogue Processing of Verbmobil. In: Fifth Conference on Applied Natural Language Processing, Washington D.C., pp. 33–40 (1997)

6. Lemon, O., Gruenstein, A., Peters, P.: Collaborative Activities and Multi-tasking in Dialogue Systems. Traitement Automatique des Langues (TAL) 43(2), 131–154 (2002); Special Issue on Dialogue
7. Rich, C., Sidner, C.L., Lesh, N.: COLLAGEN: Applying Collaborative Discourse Theory to Human-Computer Interaction. In: AI Magazine, Special Issue on Intelligent User Interfaces, vol. 22(4), pp. 15–25. AAAI Press, Menlo Park (2001)
8. Blaylock, N., Allen, J., Ferguson, G.: Managing Communicative Intentions with Collaborative Problem Solving. In: Kuppevelt, J., Smith, R.W. (eds.) Current and New Directions in Discourse and Dialogue, pp. 63–84. Kluwer A. Pubs, Dordrecht (2003)
9. Turunen, M., Hakulinen, J., Räihä, K.J., Salonen, E.P., Prusi, A.K., Prusi, P.: An Architecture and Applications for Speech-Based Accessibility Systems. IBM Systems Journal 44(3), 48–503 (2005)
10. Clark, H.H.: Using Language, p. 432. Cambridge University Press, Cambridge (1996)
11. Cuadra, D., Rivero, J., Valle, D., Calle, F.J.: Enhancing Natural Interaction with Circumstantial Knowledge. In: Richards, D. (ed.) International Transactions on Systems Science and Applications, vol. 4(2), pp. 122–129. Springer, Heidelberg (2008)
12. Edlund, J., Heldner, M., Gustafson, J.: Utterance Segmentation and Turn-Taking in Spoken Dialogue Systems. In: Schmitz, F., Wagner, S. (eds.) Sprachtechnologie, Mobile Kommunikation und Linguistische Ressourcen, Germany, pp. 576–587 (2005)
13. Calle, F.J., Martínez, P., Valle, D., Cuadra, D.: Towards the Achievement of Natural Interaction. In: Redondo, M., Bravo, C., Ortega, M. (eds.) Engineering the User Interface: from Research to Practice, vol. 12, pp. 63–79. Springer, Heidelberg (2009)
14. Skantze, G., Edlund, J., Carlson, R.: Talking with HIGGINS: Challenges in a Spoken Dialogue System for Pedestrian City Navigation. In: André, E., Dybkjær, L., Minker, W., Neumann, H., Weber, M. (eds.) PIT 2006. LNCS, vol. 4021, pp. 193–196. Springer, Heidelberg (2006)
15. Gallardo-Paúls, B.: Análisis Conversacional y Pragmática del Receptor (Spanish). Episteme, Valencia (1996)
16. Schegloff, E.A.: Sequence Organization in Interaction, 300 p. Cambridge Uni. Press, Cambridge (2007)
17. Roberts, G.L., Bavelas, J.B.: The Communicative Dictionary: A Collaborative Theory of Meaning. In: Stewart, J. (ed.) Beyond the Symbol Model, pp. 135–160. State University of New York Press, Albany (1996)
18. López-Cozar, R., Araki, M.: Spoken, Multilingual and Multimodal Dialogue Systems, p. 272. John Wiley & Sons, Chichester (2005)
19. Austin, J.L.: How to Do Things with Words. In: Urmson, J.O. (ed.) The William James Lectures delivered at Harvard University in 1955. Oxford Univ. Press, Oxford (1962)
20. Sacks, H., Schegloff, E.A., Jefferson, G.: A Simplest Systematics for the Organization of Turn-Taking for Conversation. Language 50, 696–735 (1974)
21. Calle, F.J., García-Serrano, A., Martínez, P.: Intentional Processing as a Key for Rational Behaviour Through Natural Interaction. Interacting with Computers 18, 1419–1446 (2006)

SimulSort: Multivariate Data Exploration through an Enhanced Sorting Technique

Inkyoung Hur and Ji Soo Yi

School of Industrial Engineering, Purdue University
315 N. Grant Street, West Lafayette, IN 47907-2023, USA
{ihur,yij}@purdue.edu

Abstract. Sorting is one of the well-understood and widely-used interaction techniques. Sorting has been adopted in many software applications and supports various cognitive tasks. However, when used in analyzing multi-attribute data in a table, sorting appears to be limited. When a table is sorted by a column, it rearranges the whole table, so the insights gained through the previous sorting arrangements of another column are often difficult to retain. Thus, this study proposed an alternative interaction technique, called "SimulSort." By sorting all of the columns simultaneously, SimulSort helps users see an overview of the data at a glance. Additional interaction techniques, such as highlighting and zooming, were also employed to alleviate the drawbacks of SimulSort. A within-subject controlled study with 15 participants was conducted to compare SimulSort and the typical sorting feature. The results showed typical sorting and SimulSort work with comparable efficiency and effectiveness for most of the tasks. Sorting more effectively supports understanding correlation and reading corresponding values, and SimulSort shows the potential to more effectively support tasks that need multi-attribute analyses. The implications of the results and planned future work are discussed as well.

Keywords: Sort, SimulSort, information visualization, multi-attribute data analysis, tabular information, and decision support system.

1 Introduction

Sorting, arranging items in an ordered sequence, is one of the well-understood and universally used interaction techniques in many software applications, such as spreadsheets, word processors, and even email clients (e.g., sorting emails by date). Many user interfaces that contain any kind of list or table of data employ the sorting feature. With sorting, people can accomplish various tasks, such as searching for a particular or extreme value, identifying the general patterns of values, or determining relationships between values in two or more different columns.

However, sorting does not appear to be ideal for supporting multi-attribute data analyses. For example, suppose a consumer tries to select a car. She then collects information about various cars and archives the information on a spreadsheet. While reviewing the cars, she may sort the spreadsheet by the "price" column to find the ten least expensive cars. Then, she might want to pick out the most fuel efficient car among the ten. However, by sorting the information with the "fuel efficiency"

J.A. Jacko (Ed.): Human-Computer Interaction, Part II, HCII 2009, LNCS 5611, pp. 684–693, 2009.

column, she loses insights gained through the previously sorted information. To avoid this, she should have marked the ten cars on the spreadsheet or somewhere else. However, even with this extra effort, she may run into problems in analyzing multi-attribute information if the number of considered attributes increases.

To resolve this issue, the present study proposed an interaction technique, called "SimulSort." When SimulSort is used on a table of data, all columns in a table are sorted simultaneously, so that the corresponding attributes of a data point (e.g., the price and fuel efficiency of a car) are no longer shown in the same row. Instead, when a mouse cursor hovers on a cell of the table, all corresponding cells (or different attributes of a record) in different columns are highlighted. This visual representation of tabular data may be perceived as somewhat unfamiliar, but it would help people compare two or more choices by considering multiple attributes simultaneously. An additional visualization technique, such as zooming, was also employed to overcome some drawbacks of SimulSort. To identify the advantages and disadvantages of SimulSort over the typical sorting feature, we also conducted a usage study.

The rest of this paper is organized as follows: Section 2 discusses relevant literature regarding sorting interaction techniques and information visualization. Section 3 introduces SimulSort and interaction techniques. Section 4 lists the research hypotheses used in comparing typical sorting and SimulSort. Section 5 details the design of the experiment. Sections 6 and 7 describe the results of the experiment and their implications. Lastly, section 8 discusses the conclusions of this study and some future work.

2   Background

2.1   Sorting

In spite of the ubiquity of sorting, we found little literature discussing how sorting has been used so far. In 1785, Priestley made an early breakthrough in visual sorting with the first timeline charts, which used individual bars to compare the life spans of persons [1]. In 1901, Hollerith developed a sorting machine, called a "card sorter," that was employed to sort US census data, saving more than two years [2]. In 1967, Bertin emphasized the importance of the correspondence between the act of sorting values and its representation in helping readers gain a meaningful understanding of the data and useful retention [3]. This visualization theory of Bertin became a discipline of sorting visualization [4]. Other than these, most of literature regarding sorting has been devoted to developing and evaluating different sorting algorithms in computer science, which is not the focus of this paper.

In spite of a dearth of literature regarding sorting, the universal adoption of the sorting feature by numerous software applications proves that it is a well-understood and useful interaction technique. We found that sorting could be helpful in various tasks, such as finding extreme values or outliers, finding a certain value, verifying the existence of a certain value, detecting patterns of data, understanding the relationships of data, and organizing or clustering data.

However, we also noticed when multiple attributes must be analyzed simultaneously, sorting appears to be limited. As described in the previous scenario, when a tabular data set is sorted by an attribute, the whole table is rearranged, making previous arrangement disappears, which limits the utility of the feature when multiple attributes should be considered together.

One might argue that the multi-column sorting feature, found in Microsoft Excel®, would help overcome this limitation because it sorts multiple columns at the same time. However, this sorting feature is only useful as a tie breaker. For example, if data are sorted by Columns A and B, the data are sorted by Column A first, and sorting by Column B only affects on the rows that have the same values in Column A. Other rows that have different values in Column A will stay the same. Thus, a different approach is necessary to deal with this issue.

2.2 Multivariate Information Visualization

The limitation of the currently available sorting has been remedied in various information visualization techniques. One would be parallel coordinates [5, 6], which layouts multiple axes in parallel and represents data points as multiple lines connecting these axes as shown in Fig. 1. By presenting multiple axes in parallel, a user can explore multiple attributes at a glance without changing sorting orders of different columns. Instead, lines connecting those axes represent a data point. Though various implementations of parallel coordinates have subtle differences in detailed interaction techniques, all of them share the same visual representation technique.

Another approach is parallel bargrams, which is more similar to tabular view. Each row represents an attribute and values in each row are sorted as shown in Fig. 2. Parallel bargrams has been implemented in different systems, such as MultiNAV [7], FOCUS [8] (which evolved into InfoZoom [9]) and EZChooser [10]. Again, different implementations have subtle differences in interaction techniques, such as how filtering works, but they essentially rely on the same visual representation.

As easily noticeable from Fig. 1 and 2, both visualization techniques are designed to deal with multi-attribute data. They help users understand general trends and interesting patterns at a glance without changing the arrangement of information. In other words, the data points are already sorted. In parallel coordinates,

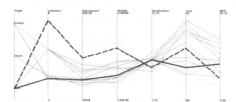
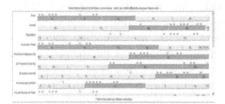

Fig. 1. Parallel coordinates (Parvis [6])   **Fig. 2.** Parallel bargrams (EZChooser [11])

each axis represents a sorted column. In parallel bargrams, each row is sorted horizontally.

However, they also have limitations. First, the novelty of techniques may cause them to be relatively difficult to learn and use. Both visual representations are quite different from a familiar tabular view, so, for novice users, these tools could be challenging to use. Second, visualizing a large data often hides the details of information. As shown in Fig. 1 and 2, detailed information about each individual data is generally hidden. In other implementations, detailed information could be shown upon requests using tooltip features, but we found that these could be generally problematic since users cannot see these details readily.

Table Lens [12], which was designed to handle a large table with a zooming interface, is inspiring. Though Table Lens does not specifically resolve the limitation of sorting, it is easy to learn and use since it is based on a traditional tabular view and shows the overview of large data and details using the zooming techniques. Table Lens also uses a horizontal bar graph on top of a numerical value in each cell to help a user quickly identify the trends in the data.

3 SimulSort

Thus, we propose an alternative visualization technique, called "SimulSort," which combines the strengths of the reviewed visualization techniques but still retains and leverages the well-understood sorting feature in a tabular view. Fig. 3 is a screenshot of SimulSort, and contains a data set of 70 used cars as an example. As shown in the figure, every column is sorted. The attributes of a car are no longer shown in a single row. Instead, in order to retrieve values of a certain car, the highlight feature should be used. When a mouse cursor hovers over the cell, Car No. 11, the corresponding cells are highlighted in yellow as shown in Fig. 3. This visualization supports the similar tasks that parallel coordinates and parallel bargrams support. Comparing Car No. 11 (highlighted in yellow) and Car No. 12 (highlighted in light blue) over multiple attributes becomes much easier. A user does not need to sort different columns multiple times to compare these two cars.

One might notice that some values are not shown in Fig. 3. For example, the mileage of Car No. 11 is not shown in the figure. Thus, a zooming feature is provided, so that a user can zoom out to show all of the rows at a glance as shown in Fig. 4 by selecting a radio button on the top left portion of the screen. Of course, due to the limitation of screen real estate, in the zoomed-out view, the detailed number for each cell cannot be shown. Instead, bar graphs provide information to help a user compare between values. When the user wants to have details, the screen can be changed back to the zoomed-in view.

SimulSort is implemented using Adobe Flex and flare, so that it can be interactive and accessible through most of the web-browsers in the market. The data source used in SimulSort is XML, so that any type of tabular data that is convertible to XML used by SimulSort.

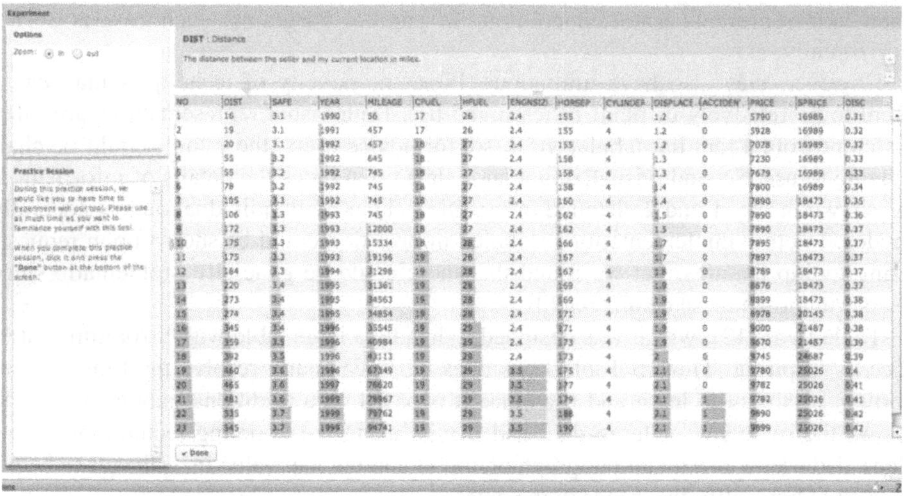

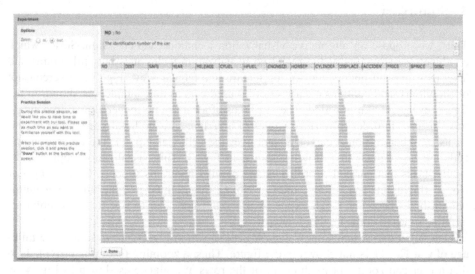

Fig. 3. A screenshot of a table using SimulSort with a zoomed in view

Fig. 4. A screenshot of a table using SimulSort with a zoomed out view

4   Hypotheses

After pilot studies with three participants, we found potential in SimulSort to support various tasks. To test this speculation, two sets of hypotheses were constructed. The first set of hypotheses is comparing the effects of two sorting techniques (typical sorting vs. SimulSort) on performance measures, such as a response time and accuracy, of various tasks. A sub set of tasks were selected from the low-level analytic activities for multivariate data surveyed by Amar et al. [13].

- H1-1: Participants retrieve values more quickly and correctly while using typical sorting than while using SimulSort.
- H1-2: Participants filter values more quickly and correctly while using typical sorting than while using SimulSort.
- H1-3: Participants sort values more quickly and correctly while using typical sorting than while using SimulSort.
- H1-4: Participants find a correlation more quickly and correctly while using typical sorting than while using SimulSort.

In addition, we would like to investigate the effect of different sorting techniques on the decision performances, such as response time and decision quality. We also hypothesized that the discrepancy will increase as the number of attributes to consider increases from three to seven.

- H2-1: Participants make a decision with the smaller number (three) of criteria more quickly and confidently while using SimulSort than while using typical sorting.
- H2-2: Participants make a decision with the larger number (seven) of criteria more quickly and confidently while using SimulSort than while using typical sorting.

5 Methods

5.1 Participants

Fifteen participants (7 males and 8 females; age: 21 – 31) at Purdue University were recruited for the experiment. The completed education level of these participants varied from high school to master's degree, but all had general, high-level computer experience. On average, they have used a computer about 13 years. Fourteen out of 15 participants reported that they are "comfortable" or "very comfortable" in using computers. At the end of experiment, they were compensated at the rate of eight US dollars per hour.

5.2 Datasets

Three artificial datasets of used cars were generated for the experiment. Each dataset has 70 used cars and 14 attributes. Random numbers were generated to make three datasets different enough to avoid any learning effects. At the same, to make complexities of the three datasets equivalent, the average of inter-attributes correlations were adjusted around zero (i.e., 0.0001, -0.0002, and 0.0003). This blocked the potential effects of inter-attributes correlations on decision quality [14].

5.3 Procedure

When a participant arrived at the lab, the pre-task survey was conducted to collect subject's demographic information, including education levels and computer literacy. After the pre-task survey, participants were asked to answer questions on paper in one baseline setting (i.e., without any sorting feature) and two experimental settings (i.e., with typical sorting and with SimulSort). The orders of the two experimental settings and used datasets were randomized. Whenever a new setting was introduced, an experimenter described how to use the interface, and participants had a chance to explore the interface without time limitation. After completion of each setting, the subjects were asked to answer questions regarding decision qualities. At the end, participants were interviewed before being compensated.

5.4 Measures

Response time, accuracy, and decision quality were used as performance measures. The response time was derived by taking the difference of the recorded times each task started and completed. Task accuracy is binary in conformity to the answer is correct or incorrect. Decision qualities of each decision were captured through the post-task questionnaire in terms of confidence of their decisions, using a five-level Likert scale:

$$Decision\ Quality = \frac{WeightedAdditiveValue\ Choice - WeightedAdditiveValue\ Worst}{WeightedAdditiveValue\ Best - WeightedAdditiveValue\ Worst} \quad (1)$$

6 Results

While analyzing data, t-tests, Mann-Whitney test and two proportions tests were employed for the quantitative measures (e.g., response times and decision qualities) and binary measures (e.g., accuracy), respectively. Table 1 summarizes the uncovered findings, the effects upon the tests gives the means, standard deviations (S.D.), and t value, W value, and p values for each question and hypothesis.

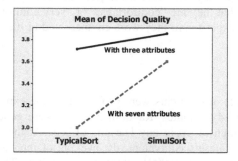

Fig. 5. Means of the decision quality for different settings and number of attributes

Participants while using SimulSort did not demonstrated significantly different performances in most of the activities (H1-1 and H1-2 were falsified) from while using typical sorting features except for two activities. For example, participants sorted values more quickly (H1-3 was partially supported) and found a correlation more correctly (H1-4 was partially supported) while using typical sorting than while using SimulSort, as shown in Table 1.

When considering the number of criteria in the decision making activity, we found slight differences in the mean scores of decision quality, as shown in Fig. 5. Simul-Sort and typical sorting features were not judged to be different on the response time and decision quality with three criteria (H2-1 was falsified). The mean of decision quality of SimulSort with seven attributes was 3.6, which was higher than the mean of decision quality of typical sorting features, 3.0, but the difference was not statistically significant at the error level of 0.05, though (H2-2 was falsified).

Table 1. Results of t-test, Mann-Whitney test, and two proportions test of using typical sorting and SimulSort

Question/ Artifact	Response time (seconds)		Accuracy (Decision Quality)	
	Mean (S.D.)	t(df)/W , p values	Mean (S.D)	t(df)/W , p values
Question 1	What is the government-tested safety rating of car #21? (H1-1)			
Sort	40 (35)	t(25) = -0.28	100%	Z = 0
SimulSort	43 (26)	p = 0.778	100%	p = 1
Question 2	Which used cars are made in 2008? (H1-2)			
Sort	21 (14)	t(21) = -1.41	100%	Z = 1.04
SimulSort	32 (27)	p = 0.173	93%	p = 0.301
Question 3	List the ten most closely located cars. (H1-3)			
Sort	**57 (34)**	**t(22) = -3.30**	93%	Z = 0
SimulSort	**113 (56)**	**p = 0.003***	93%	p = 1
Question 4	What attribute has the highest correlation with the year attribute? (H1-4)			
Sort	117 (111)	t(24) = -0.66	**73%**	**Z = 3.46**
SimulSort	140 (77)	p = 0.514	**20%**	**p = 0.001***
Question 5	Which cars are the two best if you have the following criteria (lower price, more recently manufactured, and lower mileage)? (H2-1)			
Sort	158 (108)	t(25) = -1.66	3.7(0.9)	W=196
SimulSort	227 (110)	p = 0.109	3.9(0.8)	p = 0.7336
Question 6	Which cars are the two best if you have the following more comprehensive criteria (Lower price, More recently manufactured, lower mileage, high city/highway fuel efficiency, high government tested safety rating, lower number of accidents, more closely located)? (H2-2)			
Sort	183 (128)	t(24) = 0.13	3.0(1.2)	W=199.5
SimulSort	176 (161)	p = 0.901	3.6(1.0)	p = 0.1569

*Statistically significant differences are found at the error level of 0.05.

7 Discussion

These results show that typical sorting features and SimulSort are generally compara-ble, but they potentially have different advantages and disadvantages related to the accomplishment of different tasks. These two sorting techniques provide comparable effectiveness in supporting most of the tasks except for sorting and finding correla-tions tasks, but SimulSort might potentially support decision making with large num-ber of criteria.

It took a significantly longer time to find ten minimum values when using Simul-Sort than when using typical sorting (H1-3). Based on our observation, this result was due to the fact that SimulSort required scrolling a bar to look up the values in high-lighted cells that were scattered, while typical sorting required seeing only one row in which related values existed. Finding correlations was challenging with use of Simul-Sort (H1-4) because the positions of many highlighted cells must be remembered, which caused errors. In the other hand, with typical sorting features, participants sim-ply sorted one column and compare other columns.

Although the results were not statistically significant, SimulSort can be regarded as helping users develop high confidence in the decisions made. In the post-task inter-views, many subjects reported that SimulSort was helpful when multiple attributes were considered at the same time, though subjects are no more likely to use SimulSort over typical sorting features for decision makings with the small number of criteria. Although SimulSort could be unfamiliar to the participants, some subjects quickly made a strategy for better decision making. One strategy was to find the item that had more factors of positive influence in the lower position and more factors of negative influence in the upper position, when data are in ascending order. We observed that, although subjects did not seem to know the accurate values, they did know what the strengths and weaknesses were. In addition, using zooming-out feature and SimulSort together in making decisions indicated that bar graphs in one screen delivered visual messages that allow users to understand data and possibly mental tradeoff.

8 Conclusions

This paper proposed a new multidimensional sorting technique, which was designed to help users make decisions based on multiple-attribute information. We empirically compared SimulSort with the typical sorting feature, which showed that these two interaction techniques are generally comparable in all except the two tasks tested.

One limitation of this study is the lack of participants. Some of non-significant dif-ferences could be due to the limited number of participants. In two decision tasks, some interesting patterns were found, but it could not be proven that these differences were statistically significant.

However, it was still encouraging to find that SimulSort was quickly understood and used to support various tasks effectively. Due to the unfamiliarity of SimulSort, we expected that some participants had troubles of understanding it. However, most of the participants used it properly and came up with some heuristics, amplifying the advantages of SimulSort. Further investigation will provide more clear evidence of the effectiveness of SimulSort.

However, many other questions remain unanswered. Is it possible to combine typi-cal sorting and SimulSort? Would the performance results be different if SimulSort had more flexibility to choose increasing order or decreasing order in each column? At what minimum number of attributes would SimulSort shows any statistically sig-nificant improvement of performances? How and where do users eyes move when using SimulSort? What is the subtle cognitive mechanism for sorting visualization regarding decision making? Those questions will be investigated in further research.

References

1. Priestley, J.: A description of a chart of biography; with a catalogue of all the names inserted in it, and the dates annexed to them. In: Eighteenth century collections online, London (1785)
2. Knuth, D.E.: The art of computer programming. Addison-Wiley, Reading (1968-1973)
3. Bertin, J.: Semiology of graphics: diagrams, networks, maps. University of Wisconsin Press, Madison (1983)
4. Mazza, R.: Introduction to Information Visualization (2004)
5. Hauser, H., Ledermann, F., Doleisch, H.: Angular Brushing of Extended Parallel Coordinates. In: IEEE Symposium on Information Visualization (2002)
6. Parvis, http://home.subnet.at/flo/mv/parvis/
7. Lanning, T., Wittenburg, K., Heinrichs, M., Fyock, C., Li, G.: Multidimensional Information Visualization through Sliding Rods. In: Proceedings of the working conference on Advanced visual interfaces table of contents, Palermo, Italy, pp. 173–180 (2000)
8. Spenke, M., Beilken, C., Berlage, T.: FOCUS: the interactive table for product comparison and selection. In: 9th annual ACM symposium on User interface software and technology, pp. 41–50. ACM, Seattle (1996)
9. Spenke, M., Beilken, C.: InfoZoom-Analysing Formula One racing results with an interactive data mining and visualisation tool. In: International Conference on Data Mining, Cambridge University, Cambridge (2000)
10. Wittenburg, K., Lanning, T., Heinrichs, M., Stanton, M.: Parallel bargrams for consumerbased information exploration and choice. In: 14th annual ACM symposium on User interface software and technology, pp. 51–60. ACM, Orlando (2001)
11. Verizon myEzchooser,
    http://brisa.merl.com:8080/myezchooser/index2.htm
12. Rao, R., Card, S.K.: The Table Lens: Merging Graphical and Symbolic Representations in an Interactive Focus + Context Visualization for Tabular Information. In: Proceedings of the SIGCHI conference on Human factors in computing systems: celebrating interdependence, pp. 318–322. ACM Press, New York (1994)
13. Amar, R., Eagan, J., Stasko, J.: Low-Level Components of Analytic Activity in Information Visualization. In: Proceedings of the IEEE Symposium on Information Visualization, pp. 111–117 (2005)
14. Lurie, N.H.: Decision Making in Information-Rich Environments: The Role of Information Structure. J. Consumer Research. 30, 473–486 (2004)

WeMe: Seamless Active and Passive Liquid Communication

Nicolas Masson and Wendy E. Mackay

INRIA & Université Paris-Sud 11
Bât. 490 Université Paris Sud, 91405 Orsay, France
{masson,mackay}@lri.fr

Abstract. WeMe is designed to help remote families stay in touch, providing peripheral awareness of each other combined with the possibility of more direct interaction. WeMe's ferrofluid bubbles move in response to ambient sounds, both local and distant. As many as three family members can generate patterns intentionally, by moving their hands around the surface. WeMe acts as a stand-alone sculpture, a passive indicator of remote activity and a source of shared interaction.

Keywords: Ambient display, peripheral awareness, communication appliances, presence.

1 Introduction

Today's families members are often separated from each other, in different cites, states or even countries, and require better ways to stay in contact. Despite the wide variety of communication technologies available, such as telephones, email and on-line chat, our studies [1, 2] show that these do not suffice: family members would like other, more subtle ways to stay in touch. For example, Brown and Weiser's [3] concept of 'calm technology' passes easily from the periphery of our attention, to the center and back again. Combining this peripheral engagement provides an interesting complement to communication devices designed for focused attention.

We are exploring how to support communication among remote family members that allows them to move seamlessly between active and passive interaction. Our work is based on the concept of a *communication appliance* [1], in which we provide a dedicated 'always on' communication channel between two or three households, using simple to use, aesthetically pleasing objects that convey information from each participant. This paper describes WeMe, a communication appliance designed to let family members shift smoothly between peripheral and engaged interaction. WeMe uses ambient sound and movement to display dynamic fluid patterns that are easy to interpret, based on the families' existing intimate knowledge of each other, while remaining ambiguous, providing subtle communication while protecting privacy.

2 Design Problem

Communication objects can act as vehicles for exchanging information or as representations of this information in and of themselves. Telephones, for example, are the

J.A. Jacko (Ed.): Human-Computer Interaction, Part II, HCII 2009, LNCS 5611, pp. 694–700, 2009.

former, remaining independent from the messages they transmit. An alternative is to augment everyday objects, tranforming them into communication devices. For example, pairs of LoversCups [4] vibrate when long-distance couples simultaneously sip their respective cups. Similarly, COMSlippers [5] relay patterns of light based on the movement of the other's feet. Both augment existing objects, e.g. by adding LEDs, and use these embedded features to transmit information.

We can also use the shape of the device as the basis of the comunication. For example, Itoh et al.'s 'Tsunagari communication' [6] transmits presence by moving and changing the color of optic fibers, simulating plant in a planter. Here the form of the object, in this case, the position and color of the Tsunagari 'plant', becomes the message. If the state of the communication channel has a physical representation, it helps participants interpret the message. For example, Lottridge et al.'s MissU [2] lets remote couples share background sounds and music. The volume level is embodied in the controls, providing partial information about each other's activities.

We argue that technology designed for the home should be aesthetically pleasing, not just functional. The above examples show how we can transform communication objects into sculpture or conversation pieces. If we use ambiguity, in Gaver's [7] sense of 'remaining open to multiple interpretations', we can encourage family members to co-interpret what is being communicated, maintaining interest in the object and taking advantage of family members' knowledge of each other. In this paper, our specific design challenge was to create a communication object that is both beautiful and subtly useful. Our goal is to design an object that merits a place in the living room even when there is no communication, while offering progressively more interest, as both local and remote participants become successively more engaged.

3   WeMe Design

We designed WeMe (Fig. 2) to provide shared awareness and distant interaction, reflected in the object's form. We chose a three-dimensional object containing a fluid that moves as the participants interact. Liquid movement is organic, with no noise or mechanical movement, and provides an unusual and diverse source of visual patterns. To fulfill these specifications, we used ferrofluid (Fig. 1), a liquid composed of oil and iron nanoparticles with magnetic properties: its shape moves in response to changes in the magnetic field.

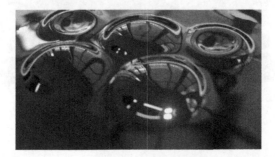

Fig. 1. Ferrofluid

WeMes are designed for use in pairs, one per household, with a continuously connected data channel (Circa [8]). Each WeMe 'display' integrates activity patterns from both local and remote households, which helps to maintain interest and encourages sharing and remote interaction. Seeing patterns generated directly from one's own activity helps participants interpret the activities of remote participants and reinforces relationships. Each household controls a different bubble area on the WeMe surface (Fig. 3): either the center (blue bubbles) or the outer ring (gold bubbles).

Appropriate interaction techniques for active and passive manipulation of liquid are not obvious. WeMes use sound levels and physical presence of family members to affect the liquid's shape, to foster awareness and distant interaction. Two aspects of the fluid can be manipulated: ambient audio levels drive the speed of vibrations in the liquid. The proximity of a hand or object is sensed with sensors, which affects certain zones in WeMes' overall shape.

WeMe responds to ambient sounds causing the bubbles to move up and down. The bubble size is increasing or decreasing on the liquid surface in order to produce the movement effect. When there is little sound, the movement is limited, rather like breathing. As the sound level increases, the movement speed increases as well. Local family members can see their own bubbles moving in response to local sounds, and at the same time, see the remote family's bubbles moving in response to the remote sounds.

Fig. 2. WeMe concept

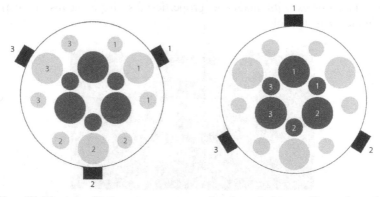

Fig. 3. Two WeMe units: Yellow areas correspond to household one, blue to household two. Each black sensor controls movement with the numbered bubbles.

Family members can also interact with WeMe directly, by moving their hands around its outer edges (Fig. 4). This stops the ambient movement of the bubbles and creates a different form of movement, directly related to the user's actions. Fig. 3 shows the configuration of two WeMe's: each has three zones, controlled by separate proximity sensors located around the side.

This permits one, two or three people to control the bubbles, inviting collaborative activity. Proximity sensors detect the position of the hands and WeMe generates bubbles in response, with larger bubbles appearing as the hands move closer. Moving one's hands up or down 'locks' the bubbles in place, allowing the user to preserve a particular bubble pattern. We used directional detection to improve the user's control and to prohibit mutual interference. This bubble modeling allows family members to develop their own ways of interpreting each other's actions, even to the level of simple messages. At the same time, the form is ambiguous, and open to multiple interpretations. The family members themselves must come to their own understandings of what each other's actions mean.

We were careful to ensure that ambient and user-created bubbles are easy to distinguish by the mapping with the movement or the shape. We also considered privacy issues: moving bubbles convey information about ambient sound levels, but not the exact nature of the sound. This provides a passive awareness of general noise levels (an indicator of presence and activity) to the remote family, without requiring any specific action on either family's part.

Fig. 4. WeMe's proximity sensor detects when the user places her hands next to one of the sensors, which affects the magnetic field and controls the bubbles

4   WeMe Offers a Range of Possible Uses

WeMe can stand alone, as a sculpture or a conversation piece. It displays a continually changing set of patterns, based on random ambient sounds in one or both households, even if nobody uses it explicitly. At this level, WeMe is a reflective object, of interest in its own right even if it is not currently connected. It provides an ever-changing reflection of the audio activity in the room, from very gentle abstract patterns when it is quiet, to more dynamic movement that reacts to the sound of people or other environmental sounds, such as the television.

When at least one person interacts with WeMe explicitly, it is transformed into a communication object. For example, if one moves one's hands back and forth in a regular fashion, the proximity detectors generate bubble patterns that are clearly distinguishable from either randomly generated sounds or even pulsing music. One can 'play' WeMe like a visual musical instrument, moving one's hands to affect the proximity sensors or making sounds to affect all the activators at once. Several people in the same room (as many as three) can interact with WeMe at the same time. They can collaborate, modifying each other's patterns or co-create a shared pattern.

When two WeMes are connected, participants gain peripheral awareness of what is happening in the other household. Family members gain a sense of each other's type and level of activity, even if remote family members are not interacting with WeMe explicitly at that moment. Their interpretations of those patterns are greatly enhanced by their existing knowledge of the other people and their daily activities.

Remote participants can decide to interact with each other, either by imitating or by moving in opposition to the other person's patterns. Of course, they can also create their own complementary patterns. Sudden changes in bubble activity can draw attention to changes in the other household. Remote family members can easily identify explicitly generated patterns and tell if one or more people are interacting with it.

Although WeMe is, on the surface, a very simple device, it is interesting across a number of different use dimensions. WeMe provides participants with a smooth transition between peripheral awareness of each other and focused communication. Whether stand-alone or interconnected, it provides a visually interesting object that encourages both reflection and communication. It generates diverse patterns, making it easy to distinguish between intentional and ambient activity.

WeMe never requires explicit action in order to be interesting, but it does encourage spontaneous interaction, offering a lightweight and amusing additional communication channel for people who know each other well. These quick and easy interactions, often only a few moments at a time, help to provide a sense of shared community and presence.

5   Example of Use

Family members who live together have a variety of ways to keep track of each others' activities. WeMe provides a novel approach for helping remote family members maintain awareness at a distance. For example, lets consider two households, Mary and her husband John who live in New York and Mary's father George, who lives in Boston. Mary comes home after work, bringing today's paper into the living room. She notes that the WeMe bubbles that represent her father's house are moving in a gentle low-level pattern, while her own bubbles move more rapidly as she places the magazine on the coffee table. She can tell that her father has not come home yet, but that during the day, he had played with WeMe, because the overall pattern has changed since that morning.

Mary begins to prepare dinner. 30 minutes later, after placing the lasagna in the oven, she goes over to play with the WeMe, making different waves in the bubbles. and leaving a new pattern for her father to see when he arrives. Later, she glances over and sees that the bubbles are moving rapidly; she goes over to the WeMe and starts to move in direct opposition to the bubbles made by her father, letting him know she's there and wordlessly interacting for a few minutes. Just then, her husband John comes over, and adds his movements, so that all three proximity sensors are activated. George can tell that he is playing with two people, not just one, and assumes that John has come home. Later that evening, members of both households retire to the living room, but remain aware of each other through the on-going gentle movements of the WeMe bubbles.

6 Implementation

WeMe consists of three components: the body, an electromagnetic wiring board and Ferrofluid. The body consists of a transparent bell, placed over the ferrofluid, and an attached opaque plastic module that hides the Wiring board and electromagnets. The Wiring board provides the power supply for the six sets of electro-magnets with several capacitors. Infrared proximity detectors detect the distances of hands from the body. The application software is loaded inside the Wiring microcontroller. WeMe is linked via a USB connection to a computer for the network communication with the other WeMe (Fig. 5).

Fig. 5. WeMe implementation

7 Conclusion

WeMe is an example of a communication appliance that provides remote family members with an extremely simple interface to support varying levels of engagement. WeMe's 'liquid communication' provides an aesthetically pleasing form of inter-family communication, that retains privacy, permits ambiguity, provides passive awareness and encourages playful interaction locally and at a distance.

Acknowledgments. Thanks to ENSCI for supporting the creation of this design, and to professor Jean-Louis Frechin for his feedback. Thanks to Caroline Journaux for her collaboration and design expertise. Thanks to Danielle Lottridge for her discussions and feedback .

References

1. Hutchinson, H., Mackay, W., Westerlund, B., Bederson, B.B., Druin, A., Plaisant, C., Beaudoin-Lafon, M., Conversy, S., Evans, H., Hansen, H., Roussel, N., Eiderbäck, B., Lindquist, S., Sundblad, Y.: Technology Probes: Inspiring Design for and with Families. In: Proceedings of the SIGCHI conference on Human factors in computing systems, pp. 17–24 (2003)

2. Lottridge, D., Masson, N., Mackay, W.: Sharing Empty Moments: Design for Remote Couples. In: Proceedings of the SIGCHI conference on Human factors in computing systems, pp. 2329–2338 (2009)
3. Weiser, M., Brown, J.S.: The Coming Age of Calm Technology. PowerGrid Journal, v.1.01 (July 1996)
4. Chung, H., Lee, C.J., Selker, T.: Lover's cups: drinking interfaces as new communication channels. In: CHI 2006 extended abstracts on Human factors in computing systems, pp. 375–380 (2006)
5. Chen, C., Forlizzi, J., Jennings, P.: ComSlipper: an expressive design to support awareness and availability. In: CHI 2006 extended abstracts on Human factors in computing systems, pp. 369–374 (2006)
6. Itoh, Y., Miyajima, A., Watanabe, T.: 'TSUNAGARI' Communication: Fostering a Feeling of Connection between Family Members. In: CHI 2002 extended abstracts on Human factors in computing systems, pp. 810–811 (2002)
7. Gaver, B., Beaver, J., Benford, S.: Ambiguity as a resource for design. In: Proceedings of the SIGCHI conference on Human factors in computing systems, pp. 233–240 (2003)
8. Nars, E.: Circa. Ph.D. Dissertation, U. Paris-Sud, France (2007)

Study of Feature Values for
Subjective Classification of Music

Masashi Murakami and Toshikazu Kato

Chuo University,
1-13-27, Kasuga, Bunkyo-ku, Tokyo, Japan
{masa_m,kato}@indsys.chuo-u.ac.jp

Abstract. In this research, we analyze how the sound and music relate to humans from the aspect of Kansei engineering. We analyze what features of the sound humans pay attention and how humans interpret sound. Therefore, we divide the signal processing of sound that humans do into four levels. At the physiological level, processing is done by the auditory characteristic. In this level, humans don't interpret the image of the sound yet. There is no subjectivity for the sound. By using auditory characteristic, we investigate the features which help in the case that sound and music is analyzed. We consider that the processing at early stage of auditory nervous system is to extract the change in power, which is obtained from the segmentation of the sound-signals which is divided by band of the frequency and time interval, and its contrast. We also consider the features obtained by that extraction. Moreover, in the cognitive level, we analyze the correlation of that features with the word of interpretation that humans do subjectively. By these modelings, we develop the method of retrieving the sound and music that having the similarity, or having the image that is expressed by any subjective words.

Keywords: Music, Hierarchical model of Kansei, Auditory characteristic.

1 Introduction

Various studies have been made of music retrieval due to the increase in multimedia technology and its contents of recent years [1, 2]. However, these retrievals are based on the metadata of music and there are few on the classification of music itself. As the similarity of music cannot be obtained by these studies, it can't be said that the listeners have been always satisfied with the result of the retrievals. Therefore, in this study, we attempted the analysis of music by the attributes of auditory perception from the viewpoint of the audiological psychology which recognizes the sound at a physiological level.

With this approach, it is possible to establish the feature values of music by the attribution of auditory perception at a physiological level, without using a complicated model.

2 Hierarchical Model of Kansei (Sensitivity)

We notice the individual difference of the standard of interpretation which appears through the process of human perception and we are seeking to conduct a further study

J.A. Jacko (Ed.): Human-Computer Interaction, Part II, HCII 2009, LNCS 5611, pp. 701–709, 2009.

of the engineering modeling of this phenomenon [3-7]. By the application of this way of thinking, a model of human beings and the sound is shown hierarchically (Fig.1.). This Model is divided in several levels. There are physical level, physiological level, psychological level, and cognitive level.

At first, we can find physical level. This level is based on the features (the intrinsic features as a frequency-based physical signal) of sound itself. This level deal in signals, but signals are not received humans yet. So, this level deal before a human being can perceive the sound.

At second, we can find physiological level. This level perceives sound based on the results of the extraction of various features. The sounds are implemented in the physiological response feature by the attribution of auditory perception and the nerve pathways, through the human senses.

Next, we find psychological level. This level expresses or interprets the features of sound or music by classifying the weight of the features. Features are obtained at the physiological level and by its subsequent grouping.

At last, cognitive level that interprets music by adopting a generic word (image word) for each of the groups classified at a psychological level.

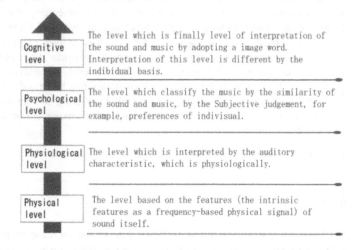

Fig. 1. Hierarchical model of Kansei for Auditory Information Processing

3   Sound as a Physical Signal

When conducting experiments on music, it is very important to consider the source of sound to be investigated. Taking recent automatic playing systems for examples, many of them re-create faithfully the contents of music written on scores [8, 9]. However, we receive a different impression of musical performances given by world-class musicians from that of the automatic playing system. This difference can be explained by tempo fluctuations in musical performance [10].

4 Auditory Feature Values at a Physiological Level [11]

It can be considered that human beings take notice of some features of sound at a physiological level and can evaluate those features. We take notice of the following three points as the above features and seek the amount of features for the purpose of the human classification of the sound.

Pitch of sound is not measured directly and it is given by the attributes of auditory perception which can perceive relatively the change of sound. Therefore, we consider it important to use the pitch of sound as feature values at a physiological level. And, Intensity of sound is difficult to measure directly the intensity of sound. Therefore, such a method is employed that measures relatively the intensity of sound by logarithmics, indicating a comparison of the intensity of two sounds. As the intensity of sound is one of the attributions of auditory perception, we consider it important to use it as feature values for the classification of the intensity of sound. Moreover, we take notice of the importance of time variation of sound. Most sounds have a time variation and it is important to perceive this time variation for the study of the auditory perception. As music is composed of the time variation of sound, we consider it important to use the time variation of sound as a feature value.

5 Experiment of Similarity Retrieval at a Physiological Level

For each feature value at a physiological level as mentioned in Section 4, for this study, analysis was made by changing the frequency data into the short-lasting Fourier transform. Additionally, we aim to model on a physiological level by conducting the retrieval experiment of similar music through the evaluation experiment of feature values.

5.1 Short-Lasting Fourier Transform of Music Data

A power spectrum can be obtained by the use of the short-lasting Fourier transform. In this study, we divided the result of the short-lasting Fourier transform into plural ranges by the following process in order to study the relationship between the time variation of sound and the attributes of auditory perception. The result of the division is shown in Fig. 2.

(i) The frequency, which represents the vertical axis of the power spectrum, is divided by the six ranges shown in Table. 1.

Table 1. Frequency spectrum per range

	range
Treble	5000~10000Hz
Middle Treble	2600~5000Hz
Mediant	320~2600Hz
Middle Bass	160~320Hz
Bass	40~160Hz
Bassy	20~40Hz

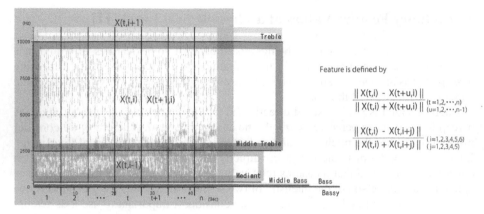

Fig. 2. Division of spectrum by range and time

(ii) The time period, which represents the horizontal axis of the power spectrum, is divided by "S" seconds.

Now, the value of "S" is established by the formula (1) with the following conditions;

(A) Sampling frequency of the data used is 22050Hz.

(B) Sampling frequency is halved in the process of the short-lasting Fourier transform.

(C) In order to implement the short-lasting Fourier transform, the number of data should be 2 multiplied by n.

$$s = \frac{2^n}{22050 \ / \ 2} = \frac{2^{12}}{11025} \approx 0.37 \ (n = 12) \cdot \tag{1}$$

As it is set as "n=12", the time period per divided range is equal to the time per note of a tune with tempo of BPM 160. It is considered that the value of "n= 12" is the most appropriate for the time period per divided range. By performing the following processing of the divided ranges, the amount statistics is sought from feature values. For the next step, evaluation is made of this statistics quantity.

(a) According to the Weber-Fechner Law, "The amount of perception is proportional to the logarithmic in the amount of stimulus," a logarithmic value (logPS) is sought of the power spectrum

(b) LogPS is sought of each of the six (6) ranges divided by (i).

(c) The contrast of logPS is sought between the different ranges at the same time, "t."

(d) The contrast of logPS is sought between the different ranges at different times, "t, t+1."

In order to evaluate the significance of feature values and its statistics quantity, a retrieval experiment of similar music was performed by the use of the statistics quantity which was sought, based on the proposed feature values.

5.2 Summary of the Experiment

The music data were collected from the 576 tunes of the Sound Material Collection [12], excluding recordings of sound effects and human voices. Fifty (50) tunes were selected at random among them, and the retrieval experiment of similar music was performed using these tunes as the key tunes. An evaluation was made of the proposed feature values by seeking the average relevance ratio of the top 5, 10, 15 and 20 similar music of the examination result. Further, in order to compare with the proposed feature values, the same experiment was performed using a power spectrum obtained from the fast Fourier transform as feature values.

5.3 Result of the Experiment

The relevance ratios are shown in Table. 2 of the result of the retrieval experiment of similar music, by the fast Fourier transform and by the proposed feature values.

Table 2. Relevance ratio of the top 20 similar music of the examination result

	5th	10th	15th	20th
Proposed feature values	72.8%	64.2%	56.4%	48.7%
Fast Fourier transform	59.1%	53.2%	47.5%	42.3%

The Wilcoxon rank-sum test was made using the results shown in Table. 2 and also an examination was performed of the significance of the difference of relevance ratios by the proposed feature values and by the use of the fast Fourier transform. As a result, at a significance level of 1%, the difference was recognized as significant between the two relevance ratios of the feature values.

6 Experiment of Similarity Retrieval at a Cognitive Level

In order to establish a Kansei model at a cognitive level, an experiment was conducted by the use of an adjective called an "image word" to combine the human Kansei and the physical features of music.

6.1 Selection of Image Words and the Summary of the Experiment

A questionnaire was carried out in advance on the subjects of "Image words frequently used for the evaluation of music." The following words were selected as the image words which are popularly used by the subjects to describe he images of the music (Table. 3.).

Table 3. Image words used in the experiment

Image words
vivid
fresh
tranquil
pleasant
monotonous
swinging

As the next step, a study was made on a five (5) grade evaluation to determine whether each image word was applicable or not for the 288 tunes which were selected at random among the music data base of 576 tunes, and then a model was formed of Kansei of auditory perception. Further, the two ways of analysis were performed using physical feature values at the dimension of 216 without any modification, and by the use of the stepwise selection.

6.2 Result of the Experiment

Table 4 show the Multiple Correlation Coefficients adjusted for degrees of freedom by the Multiple Regression Equation, which were sought as the result of the experiment.

In the case where variable selection was applied only for the image word "monotonous," it resulted in a low multiple correlation coefficient. Of the other image words, higher multiple correlation coefficients resulted when variable selection was performed. However, of the difference of the value of multiple correlation coefficients by variable selection, a Wilcoxon rank-sum test was conducted. As a result, no significance was recognized in the difference.

Table 4. Multiple correlation coefficients when variable selection performed and not performed

Image words	Variable selection performed	Variable selection not performed
vivid	0.5024	0.6534
fresh	0.6217	0.6516
tranquil	0.7997	0.8513
pleasant	0.5956	0.6842
monotonous	0.6661	0.5548
swinging	0.6817	0.7594

6.3 Evaluation Experiment of the Kansei Model of Auditory Perception

A retrieval experiment was performed about the Kansei of music by the use of the established Kansei model of auditory perception, and then by its retrieval precision, an evaluation was made of the established Kansei model of auditory perception.

Retrieval experiment of the music was performed by selecting 288 tunes out of the music data base of 576 tunes. An evaluation was performed about the established Kansei model of auditory perception, by seeking the relevance ratio of the top 20 estimated values per image word. Further, in the experiment in the Section 6.1, an experiment was carried out about the difference of the multiple correlation coefficients by variable selection.

6.4 Result of the Experiment

A retrieval experiment of Kansei was performed about music by the use of the Kansei model of auditory perception. As a result of the experiment, the relevance ratios of the top 20 tunes were found as shown in Table. 5, which were retrieved per image word.

Table 5. Relevance ratios of the top 20 tunes

Image words	Variable selection performed	Variable selection not performed
vivid	70.0%	80.0%
fresh	75.0%	75.0%
tranquil	80.0%	95.0%
pleasant	70.0%	80.0%
monotonous	80.0%	85.0%
swinging	80.0%	90.0%

Table. 5 show that the relevant ratio was higher in all the image words when variable selection was performed. A Wilcoxon rank-sum test was made using results of the difference of the relevance ratio. As a result, the difference of relevance ratio was recognized at a significant level of 1%. Additionally, a retrieval experiment of Kansei was performed about the difference by variable selection. As a result, the difference of the relevant ratio was recognized. Table 7 illustrates that extremely high accuracy can be obtained of each image word as the result of a retrieval experiment of the Kansei of music, using a hearing Kansei model, which was established based on the proposed feature values and which underwent variable selection.

7 Improvement of Feature Values

As the number of the dimensions of the proposed feature values decreased by 1/10 when variable selection was performed, it is considered that the proposed feature values are redundant. Additionally, it is necessary to seek the feature values necessary for each image word. In order to seek the feature values necessary for each image word, the authors sought the standard partial regression coefficient by the multiple regression of the Kansei model of auditory perception. The feature values were sought of the top five (5) most important. Table. 6 shows one example of the variety of the said feature values.

Table 6. Top 5 of the level of importance of "Vivid"

Image word	Vivid
1st	Whole of midrange
2nd	Contrast between middle treble and midrange
3rd	Contrast between treble and bass
4th	Contrast between middle bass and treble
5th	Contrast between middle treble and treble

The following can be considered from the result of Table. 6. "Vivid" - As the contrasts between various ranges of sound are ranked high on the axis of the "whole of midrange," it can be considered that both features are important in a wide range, of the whole of tune and of a short time. Table.7 shows the importance of the features for "Fresh". Similar features to "Vivid" are shown in Table. 7. But Whole of midrange is shown in 3rd and 4th. Therefore, whole of the music is importance for features. Table. 8 shows the importance of the features for "Tranquil". In this table, bassy range appears and treble range disappears. Therefore, bass range of the whole of tune is important for the features.

Table 7. Top 5 of the level of importance of "Fresh"

Image terms	Fresh
1st	Contrast between treble and bass
2nd	Contrast between middle treble and midrange
3rd	Whole of midrange
4th	Whole of midrange
5th	Contrast between middle and treble

Table 8. Top 5 of the level of importance of "Tranquil"

Image terms	Tranquil
1st	Contrast between bass and midrange
2nd	Whole of bassy
3rd	Contrast between middle and middle treble
4th	Contrast between middle bass and middle treble
5th	Contrast between bass and middle bass

8 Challenge and Perspective

In this study, we proposed the feature values of sound from the viewpoint of human attributes of auditory perception at a physiological level. With the results of the evaluation experiment of statistics quantity which was obtained from the proposed feature values, we have obtained the possibility of classification not depending on the name of tunes or composers, but by the use of the feature values which we proposed for this study, As a future policy, we will seek the improvement of statistics quantity, the most appropriate division of sound range, the increase in experiment data and others. Furthermore, by the use of the established auditory perception model, we are attempting the quantification / classification, by audio comparison experiment, of musical performances given by master musicians and by machines.

References

1. Yuya, H., Kenichi, F., Kouichi, M., Satosi, K., Masayuki, N.: Acquisition Mechanism of Personal Sensitivity in Musical Composition Mechanism. In: National Convention of Japanese Society for Artificial Intelligence (20th)
2. Yuya, I., Tetsuji, T., Satoru, H.: Recommendation System of Musical Composition by the Use of the Grouping of Impression Words. In: National Convention of Japanese Society for Artificial Intelligence (20th)
3. Syunichi, K., Katsumasa, S.: Research and Development of Sensitivity Agent and Human Media Data Base—Sensitivity Work Shop. System/Information/Control 42(5), 253–259 (1998)
4. Kato, T.: Trans-category Retrieval Based on Subjective Perception Process Models. In: Proc. IEEE Multimedia and Expo ICME 2004, vol. TP9-5 (2004)
5. Kouta, H., Tosikazu, K.: Design Approach of the Retrieval System of Sensitivity; Sensitivity System Modeling. Journal of the Information Processing Society of Japan; Data Base 46(SIG19(TOD 29)) (2005)
6. Masahiro, T., Tosikazu, K.: Modeling of the Sensitivity of Auditory Perception by the Use of Hierarchical Classification and Application for the Retrieval of Similar Image. Journal of the Information Processing Society of Japan Data 44(SIG8(TOD 18)), 37–45 (2003)
7. Yasuhiko, T., Tosikazu, K.: Feature Analysis of the Range of Similar Images and the Modeling of the Sensitivity of Auditory Perception. Journal of the Institute of Electronics, Information and Communication Engineers; D-II J87-D-II(10), 1983–1995 (2004)
8. Yasuhiko, O., Kenichi, S., Yutaka, M., Yosinobu, K., Yasuo, N.: Establishment of an Automatic Playing System for Piano, adding the Information of Musicians/Extraction of the Features of Performance in Topical Parts? by Neutral Network. Study Report, Information Processing Society of Japan
9. Takayuki, H., Susumu, H.: Automatic Playing of Music for Piano by use of Standard Performance Data. Study Report, Information Processing Society of Japan
10. Tetsuya, O.: Base of the Style of Musical Performance, pp. 158–165. Shunjusha Co., Ltd. (1998)
11. Moor, B.C.J., Kengo, O. (translation supervisor): Survey of Audiological Psychology. Seisinshobo Co., Ltd. (1994)
12. On-Man-Tan, D.: E-Frontier Co., Ltd
13. Tsuyoshi, T., Yosuke, M., Tomotada, I., Tetsunori, K.: A Conversational Robot utilizing Facial and Body Expressions. In: 2000 IEEE International Conference on System, Man and Cybernetics, pp. 858–863. IEEE Press, New York (2000)

Development of Speech Input Method for Interactive VoiceWeb Systems

Ryuichi Nisimura[1], Jumpei Miyake[2], Hideki Kawahara[1], and Toshio Irino[1]

[1] Wakayama University, 930 Sakaedani, Wakayama-shi, Wakayama, Japan
[2] Nara Institute of Science and Technology, 8916-5 Takayama-cho, Ikoma-shi, Nara, Japan
nisimura@sys.wakayama-u.ac.jp

Abstract. We have developed a speech input method called "w3voice" to build practical and handy voice-enabled Web applications. It is constructed using a simple Java applet and CGI programs comprising free software. In our website (http://w3voice.jp/), we have released automatic speech recognition and spoken dialogue applications that are suitable for practical use. The mechanism of voice-based interaction is developed on the basis of raw audio signal transmissions via the POST method and the redirection response of HTTP. The system also aims at organizing a voice database collected from home and office environments over the Internet. The purpose of the work is to observe actual voice interactions of human-machine and human-human. We have succeeded in acquiring 8,412 inputs (47.9 inputs per day) captured by using normal PCs over a period of seven months. The experiments confirmed the user-friendliness of our system in human-machine dialogues with trial users.

Keywords: Voice-enabled Web, Spoken interface, Voice collection.

1 Introduction

We have developed a speech input method for interactive voice-enabled Web system. The proposed system is constructed using a simple Java applet and CGI programs. It would serve as a practical speech interface system comprising only free software.

The World Wide Web has become an increasingly more popular system for finding information on the Internet. At present, nearly every computer-based communication service is developed on the Web framework. Further, Internet citizens have begun to benefit significantly from transmitting multimedia data over Web 2.0, which refers to second-generation Internet-based Web services such as video upload sites, social networking sites, and Wiki tools. To increase the use of speech interface technologies in everyday life, it is necessary to use a speech input method for Web systems.

A large-scale collection of voice database is indispensable for the study of voice interfaces. We have been collecting voices in cases such as simulated scenarios, WOZ (Wizard of Oz) dialogue tests[1], telephone-based system[2,3], and public space tests[4]. However, an evaluation of voices captured by normal PCs is still insufficient to organize a voice database. To develop and utilize the speech interface further, it is important to know the recording conditions prevalent in home and office environments [5]. Further, it is also important to know the configurations of the PCs used for

J.A. Jacko (Ed.): Human-Computer Interaction, Part II, HCII 2009, LNCS 5611, pp. 710–719, 2009.

recording voices through the use of field tests. The proposed system is designed to collect actual voices in homes and offices through the Internet.

2 Related Works

Advanced Web systems that enable voice-based interactions have been proposed, such as the MIT WebGalaxy system[6][7]. Voice Extensible Markup Language (VoiceXML)[1], which is the W3C[2] standard XML format, can be used to develop a spoken dialogue interface with a voice browser[8]. SALT (Speech Application Language Tags) is an other extension of HTML (Hypertext Markup Language) that adds a speech interface to Web systems[9]. They require special add-on programs or customized Web browsers: therefore, users must preinstall a speech recognition and synthesis engine and prepare nonstandard programs for voice recording. However, complicated setups make it difficult for users to access voice-enabled websites.

Adobe Flash, which is a popular animation player for the Web environment, can be used for voice recording using generic Web browsers. However, a rich development tool that is not freely available is required to produce Flash objects containing a voice recording function. Moreover, the system might require a custom-built Web server to serve websites with a voice recording facility. Hence, developments of a voice-enabled Web system by Flash are not necessarily an easy process.

3 Overview

Figure 1 shows a screen shot of the proposed Web system. The website features an online fruit shop. In this site, users can use our spoken dialogue interface.

The Web browser displays normal HTML documents, Flash movies, and a recording panel. An HTML document that contains text, images, etc., provides instructions on how to use this Web site. One of the HTML documents also presents the results of an

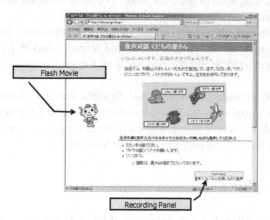

Fig. 1. Screen shot of voice-enabled website

---

[1] http://www.voicexml.org/
[2] http://www.w3.org/

order placed by a user. The Flash movie provides an animated agent to realize significant visual interactions between the system and the user. The synthetic voice of the agent produced by dialogue processing would be sounded by embedding a Flash movie.

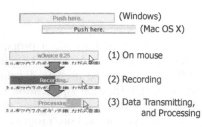

Fig. 2. Recording panel

Figure 2 shows a close-up of the recording panel in the Web interface. The recording panel is the most important component of our voice-enabled Web framework. It is a pure Java applet (using Java Sound API of standard Java APIs) that records the voice of a user and transmits it to a Web server.

When the recording panel is activated by pressing the button, the voice of the user is recorded through the microphone of the client PC. After the button is released, the panel begins to upload the recorded signals to the Web server.

The recording panel also provides visual feedback to the user, as shown in Figure2. During voice recording, a bar of the panel acts as a power-level meter. Users can monitor their voice signal level by observing the red bar (Figure 2 - 2). The message "under processing now" is displayed on the bar while the recorded signals are transmitted to the Web server and processed in a dialogue sequence (Figure 2 -3). Subsequently, browser shows processing a result after the transmission is completed.

We designed the proposed w3voice system to actualize the following concepts:

1. Users can use our voice-enabled web system with easy setup procedures without any add-on program pre-installations on the client PC.
2. Web developers can develop their original voice-enabled web pages by using our free development tool kits with existing technologies (CGI programs and standard Web protocols), and open-source software. We have released the development tool kits in our website, http://w3voice.jp/skeleton/.
3. Our system can run identically on all supported platforms, including all major operating systems such as Windows (XP and Vista), MacOS X, and Linux. Users can use their preferred Web browsers such as Internet Explorer, Mozilla, Firefox, and Safari.
4. Our system can provide practicable and flexible framework that enables a wide variety of speech applications. To realize them, we have adopted server-side architecture in which the major processing sequences (speech recognition, speech synthesis, contents output) are performed on the Web server.

4   Program Modules

Figure 3 shows an outline of the architecture of the w3voice system. The system consists of two program modules – a client PC module and a Web server module.

4.1 Client PC Module

As mentioned earlier, the client PC module is a Java applet that is launched automatically by HTML codes as follows.

```
<applet code="w3voice.class" code-
base="http://w3voice.jp/" archive="w3voice.jar">
<param name="SamplingRate" value="44100">
<param name="UploadURL"
value="http://w3voice.jp/shop/upload.cgi">
</applet>
```

Fig. 3.

The applet runs on the Java VM of the Web browser and it records the user's voice and transmits the signals to the Web server. The POST method of HTTP is used as the signal transmission protocol. The applet has been implemented such that it functions as an upload routine similar to a Web browser program. Thus, our system can operate on broadband networks developed for Web browsing because the POST method is a standard protocol used to upload images and movie files.

In this HTML code, Website developer can specify the sampling rate for recording voice by assigning a value to the parameter "SamplingRate." The URL address of the site to which the signals must be uploaded must be defined in "UploadURL."

4.2 Web Server Module

We have designed a server-side architecture in which the processing sequence of the system is performed on the Web server.

As shown in Figure 4, the CGI program forked from a Web server program (httpd) comprises two parts. One part receives the signals from the applet and stores them in a file. The other part consists of the main program that processes the signals, recognizes voices, and produces outputs.

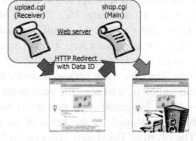

Fig. 4. CGI processes

The recorded signals transmitted by the applet are captured in "upload.cgi," which is assigned in UploadURL (Section 4.1). It creates a unique ID number for the stored data.

Then, the main program, e.g., "shop.cgi" in the case of the online fruit shop, is called by the Web browser. The address (URL) of the main program is provided to the browser through the HTTP redirect response outputted by upload.cgi as follows.

```
HTTP/1.1 302
Date: Sun, 18 Mar 2007 13:15:42 GMT
Server: Apache/1.3.33 (Debian GNU/Linux)
Location: http://w3voice.jp/shop/shop.cgi?q=ID
Connection: close
Content-Type: application/x-perl
```

The "Location:" field contains the URL of the main program identifying the stored data by its ID number.

Thus, our system does not require any special protocol to realize a practical voice-enabled Web interface. The CGI programs can be written in any programming language such as C/C++, Perl, PHP, Ruby, and Shell script.

5 Applications

Original and novel voice-enabled Web applications using the w3voice system have been released. In this section, we would like to make a brief presentation of these applications. They are readily available at the following Web site[3]:

http://w3voice.jp/

5.1 Speech Recognition and Dialogue (Figure 5)

As shown in Section 3 (online fruit shop), the w3voice system can provide speech recognition and dialogue services.

Web Julius is a Web-based front-end interface for Julius[4], which is an open source speech recognition engine[10]. This application realizes quick-access interface for a dictation system without requiring the installation of any speech recognition programs on the client PC. The HTML text shows the recognized results outputted by Julius for an input voice. Users can quickly

Fig. 5. Left: Speech Recognizer Web Julius. Right: Web Takemaru-kun, Japanese spoken dialogue system.

change the decoding parameters of N-best and a beam search through a Web-based interface. We have prepared many built-in language and acoustic models to adapt to the linguistic and acoustic parameters of the input voice.

Web Takemaru-kun system is our Japanese spoken dialogue system, which has been developed on the basis of an existing system[4, 11] with the w3voice system. The original Takemaru-kun system has been permanently installed in the entrance hall of the Ikoma Community Center in order to provide visitors with information on the center and Ikoma City. The authors have been examining the spoken dialogue interface with a friendly animated agent through a long-term field test that commenced in November 2002. Our analysis of user voices recorded during this test shows that many citizens approve of the Takemaru-kun agent. The w3voice system allows users to readily interact with the Takemaru-kun agent through the Internet and also makes the interaction a pleasant experience.

---

[3] It should be noted that the content on our website is currently in Japanese because our speech recognition program can accept inputs only in Japanese. However the proposed framework of w3voice system does not depend on the language of the speaker.

[4] http://julius.sourceforge.jp/

5.2 Speech Analysis and Synthesis

Because the w3voice system processes raw audio signals transmitted by the client PC, any post signal processing technique can be adopted.

The spectrogram analyzer (Figure 6) is a simple signal analyzer that shows a sound spectrogram produced by MATLAB, which is a numerical computing environment distributed by The MathWorks[5]. The analyzer is beneficial to students learning about signal processing, although this content is very simple.

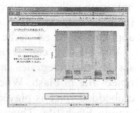

Fig. 6. Web-base sound spectrogram analyzer

w3voice.jp provides a voice-changer application to ensure user privacy (Figure 7). An uploaded signal is

Fig. 7. Screen shot of the STRAIGHT voice changer. A synthesized voice would be played by clicking a point on the grid. User can control the pitch stretch of changed voices by the x-coordinate of mouse cursor. The spectrum stretch is represented by the y-coordinate.

decomposed into source information and resonator information by STRAIGHT[12]. In addition, the users can also reset the vocal parameters. By applying dynamic Web programming techniques using Ajax (Asynchronous JavaScript and XML), a synthesized voice is reproduced by a single click in real time. The vocal parameters are preserved as HTTP cookies by the Web browser, which are referred by the voice conversion routines of other applications.

5.3 Web Communication

Our system can be used to build new Web-based communication tools using which the uploaded voices can be shared by many users.

As for an example, we have introduced a speech-oriented interface onto a Web-based online forum system[6]. Anchor tags linking to transmitted voice files are

---

[5] http://www.mathworks.com/
[6] http://w3voice.jp/keijiban/

provided by the forum system to users who enjoy chatting using natural voices. A conventional online forum system allows users to use text-based information to communicate with each other. The source code of the voice-enabled forum system, which includes only 235 lines of the Perl script, demonstrates the ease with which voice applications based on the w3voice system can be developed.

Voice Photo[7] can be used to create speaking photo albums on the Web. It is a free service that integrates uploaded voice recordings with JPEG files and generates an object file in Flash. When the user moves the mouse cursor over the Flash file, the embedded voice is played. The file generated by this service can be downloaded as a simple Flash file. Thus, webmasters can easily place them on their blogs or home-pages.

6 Experiments

6.1 Data Collection

The operation of "w3voice.jp" began on March 9, 2007. Internet users can browse to our site and try out our voice-enabled Web at anytime and from anywhere.

All voices transmitted from the client PC are stored on our Web server. We are investigating access logs containing recorded user voices and their PC configurations.

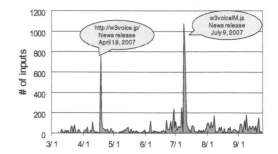

Fig. 8. Number of inputs per day without zero length inputs (March 9, 2007 – September 24)

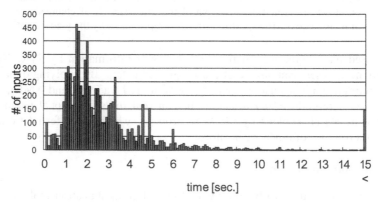

Fig. 9. Distributions of input lengths (displaying 0 < sec. < 15)

We have succeeded in acquiring 9,758 inputs from March 9 to September 24, 2007 (7 months). Figure 8 shows the number of collected voice recordings per day. The

---

[7] http://w3voice.jp/VoicePhoto/

number of the averaged input per day was 47.6 since August when the access became regular. They were obtained from 1,179 unique IP addresses. We have acquired informative successes by public testing the system with consecutive and extensive uses from users.

Figure 9 shows distributions of utterance lengths, where the horizontal axis indicates the lengths of the inputs (sec.). There were 1,346 (13.8%) inputs of zero length, which occurred due to a single click of the recording panel. The majority were performed to check the responses against the click of the panel. Although some users had misconceptions regarding the use of the panel in recording voices, they recorded their voices correctly after the second attempt. Meanwhile, the longest recorded input was a discourse speech with 6286.3 s.

Table 1. Configurations of computing environments in the experiments

Operating system	Web browser	#
Windows XP	Internet Explorer	8
Windows XP	FireFox	1
MacOS X	Safari	3
Total		12

6.2 Evaluation

An evaluation was conducted to investigate the user-friendliness of our system with regard to human-machine dialogues. Our aim was to observe the occurrences of problems caused by programming bugs and human error.

Twelve students from our laboratory served as the trial users. Their task was to access the Web Takemaru-kun system and have conversations by using their office PCs. Ten trials were conducted by each user. Table 1 shows the computing environments of each user who evaluated our system.

The results revealed that all but one trial user could interact with the Takemaru-kun agent. The operating system of the user who could not interact was MacOS X. His Macintosh computer contained more than one audio device. He had changed a setting for the microphone lines in the control panel of MacOS X before testing the system. However, the Web browser was not restarted after changing the microphone line. Hence, silent signals were captured in his trials.

7 Conclusions

This paper proposes a speech input method to develop practical and handy voice-enabled Web applications. It is constructed using a simple Java applet and CGI programs based on free software. The proposed system does not require the installation of any special add-on programs, which can be a difficult process, for using spoken interface applications. We have named this system "w3voice."

This paper explains the mechanism of voice-based interactions based on the HTTP POST method and the HTTP redirect response in detail.

Examples of voice-enabled Web applications such as a speech recognizer, spoken dialogue system, spectrogram analyzer, voice changer, and an online forum are introduced in this paper. Indeed, all users having an Internet connection can use these applications on our Web site.

Further, web developers can build voice applications easily by using the w3voice system. To induce the Web developers to start voice Web systems, we have begun to distribute a set of sample source codes of the w3voice system under an open-source license. It also contains key-signed Java applet and short English documents. You can download it from our website[8].

The system also aims at organizing a voice database using the voices recorded in home and office environments. We have succeeded in acquiring 8,412 inputs (47.9 inputs per day) captured by normal PCs over a period of seven months.

The user-friendliness of our system in human-machine dialogues is confirmed by the results of experiments in which several students evaluated the system as trial users.

7.1 Future Work

Technical improvements for the next version of the w3voice system are planned. To reduce the network load, it is important to compress the data stream transmitted from the applet to the Web server. Further, it is necessary to investigate the robustness of our system against simultaneous multiple access. We are also considering the examination of automatic speech segmentation without requiring mouse operations. However, the introduction of automatic recording involves some awkward problems that involve securing user privacy. In the feedback we received for our users, the uneasiness of an electrical interception in using an automatic voice recording program was pointed out. The tapping act without careful consideration might lack the reliability of the users.

We consider that the most important element in our work is the continuation of testing the system. We have been performing detailed analysis of the collected voice recordings. This project would contribute to improving the human-machine and human-human communications.

References

1. Kawaguchi, N., et al.: Multimedia Corpus of In-Car Speech Communication. Journal of VLSI Signal Processing-Systems for Signal, Image, and Video Technology 36, 153–159 (2004)
2. Raux, A., et al.: Doing Research on a Deployed Spoken Dialogue System: One Year of Let's Go! Experience. In: Proc. Interspeec 2006, pp. 65–68 (2006)
3. Turunen, M., et al.: Evaluation of a Spoken Dialogue System with Usability Tests and Long-term Pilot Studies: Similarities and Differences. In: Proc. Interspeec 2006, pp. 1057–1060 (2006)
4. Nisimura, R., et al.: Operating a Public Spoken Guidance System in Real Environment. In: Proc. Interspeec 2005, pp. 845–848 (2005)
5. Hara, S., et al.: An online customizable music retrieval system with a spoken dialogue interface. The Journal of the Acoustical Society of America (4th Joint Meeting of ASA/ASJ) 120(5) Pt. 2, 3378–3379 (2006)

---

[8] http://w3voice.jp/skeleton/

6. Lau, R., et al.: WebGalaxy - Integrating Spoken Language and Hypertext Navigation. In: Proc. EUROSPEEC 1997, pp. 883–886 (1997)
7. Gruenstein, A., et al.: Scalable and Portable Web-Based Multimodal Dialogue Interaction with Geographical Database. In: Proc. Interspeech 2006, pp. 453–456 (2006)
8. Oshry, M., et al.: Voice Extensible Markup Language (VoiceXML) Version 2.1, W3C Recommendation, W3C (2007)
9. The SALT Forum, SALT: Speech Application Tags (SALT) 1.0 Specification (2002)
10. Lee, A., et al.: Julius – An Open Source Real-Time Large Vocabulary Recognition Engine. In: Proc. EUROSPEEC 2001, pp. 1691–1694 (2001)
11. Nisimura, R., et al.: Public Speech-Oriented Guidance System with Adult and Child Discrimination Capability. In: Proc. ICASSP 2004, vol. 1, pp. 433–436 (2004)
12. Banno, H., et al.: Implementatioin of realtime STRAIGHT speech manipulation system: Report on its first implementation. Acoustic Science and Technology 28(3), 140–146 (2007)

Non-verbal Communication System Using Pictograms

Makiko Okita[1], Yuki Nakaura[1], and Hidetsugu Suto[2]

[1] Hokkaido University of Education
2-34, Midorigaoka, Iwamizawa-shi, Hokkaido, 068-8642 Japan
okita@iwa.hokkyodai.ac.jp
[2] Muroran Institute of Technology
7-1, Mizumotocho, Muroran-shi, Hokkaido, 050-8585 Japan
suto@csse.muroran-it.ac.jp

Abstract. A system is described that uses pictograms to support interactive non-verbal communication. While pictograms are typically used with objects, this system uses them for events as well. Moreover, whereas communication systems using pictograms are generally designed for people with disabilities, this system is designed for people in general. It can thus be used between a non-disabled person and a person with a disability, between an adult and a child, between a Japanese person and an American person, and so on.

1 Introduction

Pictograms (picture signs) are widely used to visually display information such as the function of a device or the purpose of a facility [1]. For example, a pictogram representing a man or a woman is typically found outside a restroom. Another example is a pictogram representing a fleeing person on a fire exit door (Fig. 1). Pictograms are commonly displayed in public areas at international events such as the Olympics and world expositions. In short, they are widely used because they enable communication across cultures and across generations [2].

Fig. 1. Example pictogram

Pictograms can also be used for interactive communication. For instance, people with a speech disability can use pictograms to communicate with others. The pictograms are used as a type of language. Systems using pictograms for this purpose are thus constructed on the basis of a linguistic system from the standpoint of communication = transmitting meaning. Hence, they do not reflect the feelings of the people who are communicating. However, pictograms inherently have a high non-verbal nature, and we should use this non-verbal nature when using pictograms for communication in order to represent our feelings.

J.A. Jacko (Ed.): Human-Computer Interaction, Part II, HCII 2009, LNCS 5611, pp. 720–724, 2009.

We previously proposed the use of pictograms for non-verbal communication [3]. In this paper, a concrete communication system with pictogram is proposed. In addition the proposed system is analyzed by comparing with previous works.

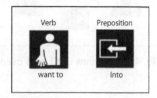

Fig. 2. Example of PIC symbols

2 Background

2.1 Communicating Using PIC System

The PIC system [4] is a well developed system for interactive communication using pictograms. It was designed for people with a speaking disability, and several devices have been developed to support it [5]. In this system, a user points to a PIC symbol (a picture sign corresponding to a word) displayed on a screen in order to represent his/her intentions. Each symbol corresponds to one word. The words represented include verbs and prepositions as well as nouns and adjectives. Example verb and preposition PIC symbols are shown in Fig. 2. The sequential presentation of PIC symbols thus corresponds to translating ideas into picture signs. A PIC system is usually implemented using cards or a touch panel.

There are 3,000–5,000 PIC symbols, and users have to wield these symbols in order to communicate. About 3,000 of them are necessary for normal communication, and memorizing that many is not easy. The effort involved is comparable to that of learning a foreign language.

2.2 Pictograms Used with Objects and Events

Pictograms are most commonly placed in a fixed location. Such pictograms represent the relationship between that place and a person, so they can be called "pictograms used with objects (*mono*)." That is, they are media for one-way communication, as illustrated in Fig. 3. In contrast, interactivity is required for pictograms used for communication between people. Such pictograms represent a user's intention and state, so can be called "pictograms used with events (*koto*)." That is, they are media for interactive communication, as illustrated in Fig. 4.

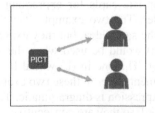

Fig. 3. Pictogram used with objects

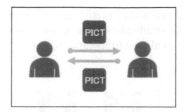

Fig. 4. Pictograms used with events

3 Proposed System

3.1 "Pict Script"

As mentioned in the Introduction, we previously proposed the use of pictograms for non-verbal communication. The Pict Script system we developed is based on the background described above and has the following features.

1. It has high flexibility. It can be used for not only consecutive expressions but also diagrammatic expressions.
2. It is usable by not only people with disabilities but also people in general. It can be used for various styles of communication.
3. Its output can indicate the user's feelings.
4. It promotes communication.

Fig. 5. Example Pict Scripts: (a) "looking for a book store"; (b) "looking for the book department"

3.2 "Handy Pict"

Handy Pict is the tool we have now developed for nonverbal communication. It is based on the concept of Pict Script. Pictograms are printed on small cards. They are classified into four categories: "Act," "One," "State," and "Other."

A user selects the appropriate cards for expressing his/her intention and places them in the appropriate order. The two example Pict Scripts shown in Fig. 5 were constructed on the basis of the same idea, but they express it differently to match the situation. The example in (a) would be used when the user is searching for a book-store along a shopping street. The one in (b) would be used when searching for the book department in a department store. In these two examples, a picture is constructed by arranging cards, so the expression is diagrammatic. The examples shown in Figs. 6 and 7 treat each card as a word, so they are consecutive expressions.

Fig. 6. Example Pict Script: "I want to buy these books"

Fig. 7. Example Pict Script: "Where are the books?"

In short, a person can use Handy Pict to generate expressions that match his/her intention and the situation.

4 Discussion

4.1 Communication Using Handy Pict

The features of Handy Pict are as follows.

- Because Handy Pict does not need either syntax or parts of speech, learning to use it is relatively easy.
- Users can generate expressions that match the situation.
- Users can represent their intentions in a straight-forward manner.
- Users have to append words and pictures when describing specific things, e.g., things that are referred to using proper nouns.
- The signs used are commonly known, e.g., the question mark.
- The pictures on the cards should be updated when the shapes of the corresponding objects change.
- There is no expression corresponding to "Why."

Accordingly, devices that implement Pict Script do more than apply pictograms to a language they support communication using prepared pictograms.

4.2 Preliminary Evaluation

The proposed system is still in the early stages of development, and formal experiments have not yet been carried out. However, a number of people have used the prototype system, so we have some preliminary findings.

Many users used Handy Pict to express an intention like, "I want to buy these books" (Fig. 8(a)). Several added a card at the beginning to express their feeling, like "I'm sad because I can't find the books" (Fig. 8(b)). This "feelings" card could mean sad or embarrassed. In this case, the cards order does not correspond to the word order. We are focusing on the use of "feelings" cards and will evaluate our proposed system on the basis of the functions of the cards representing feelings.

Fig. 8. User Pict Scripts: (a) "Where are the books?"; (b) "I'm sad because I can't find the books"

5 Conclusion

We have implemented our Pict Script concept, i.e., the use of pictograms for non-verbal communication, in a tool we call "Handy Pict." It is important that one's intentions should be stated clearly, and we expect accuracy and speed in communication by ear. Moreover, communication should include sufficient time for the two parties to gain an understanding of each other. Although some may feel that this is a waste of time from the viewpoint of technology, we feel that understanding one another is one of the most important factors in communication. While the proposed system was developed for non-verbal communications, it can also support verbal communications. For example, it could be used to support the care of senior citizens and the education of students.

References

1. Kyoto University of Art and Design: Information Society and Communications, Kadokawa Shoten (2000) (Japanese)
2. Ota, Y.: Pictogram Design, Kashiwa Shobo (1987) (Japanese)
3. Okita, M., Nakaura, Y., Suto, H.: A design for non-verbal communication by using pictograms, Kansei Forum in Sapporo (2009) (Japanese)
4. Pictogram and Communication, http://www.pic-com.jp
5. Fujiwara, K.: Communication by Visual Symbols, Brain Shuppan (2001) (Japanese)
6. Shimizu, H. (ed.): Psychology of Visual Symbols, Brain Shuppan (2003) (Japanese)

Modeling Word Selection in Predictive Text Entry

Hamed H. Sad and Franck Poirier

VALORIA lab., Université de Bretagne-Sud, Vannes, France
{sad,poirier}@univ-ubs.fr

Abstract. Although word, or short phrase, selection from a list is an extensively used task on different types of interfaces, there is no accepted model for its execution time in the literature. We present a Keystroke Level Model (KLM) adapted for this task on both desktop and handheld interfaces. The model is built from the results of an empirical study for exploring the effect of the list sorting and the number of words displayed to the user on the selection time of a word at a specified position in the list. The resulting model is integrated into an existing model for predicting the text entry speed of word-disambiguation entry methods. The predicted text entry speed is then compared to the published empirical results and to the theoretical results of the model that doesn't take into account word selection search time. The error between prediction and empirical-results is effectively reduced using the modified model.

Keywords: User interface, modeling, word selection, text entry, evaluation.

1 Introduction

Word lists are commonly used in graphical user interface. By word list interface, we mean any list of words or short phrases presented to the user for selection. Words proposed by a text editor as a correction for an incorrectly typed word, word lists appearing after entering an ambiguous code in word disambiguation text entry techniques on mobile devices, and country selection lists are some examples of typical word list interfaces. In this work, we study user performance when she/he interacts with such lists, focusing on their use in mobile text entry.

The theoretical evaluation of interfaces requires Human Computer Interaction (HCI) models for the task under evaluation. In the context of our work, which is the evaluation of entry methods on mobile devices, there are some well-established models and method for predicting user performance. One of the extensively used models is Fitts' law, which models rapid aimed pointing tasks [1-3]. Another well known law is the Hick-Hyman law for modeling the choice time required for a user to choose one alternative among n [4]. If we have the necessary models for all tasks on a given interface, we need an organized systematic analysis method, or framework, to put these models in action. Keystroke Level Model (KLM) [5] is a widely used method of analysis in the domain of HCI. KLM is a simplified variation of GOMS, and is based on the Model Human Processor (MHP) [6] which is a highly simplified architecture for human perception, cognition and motor activities. Simple modeling using KLM and GOMS can be not just easier to use, but also avoid not-yet-resolved scientific puzzles that distract from practical modeler's goal [7]. For this reason and due to the success-

J.A. Jacko (Ed.): Human-Computer Interaction, Part II, HCII 2009, LNCS 5611, pp. 725–734, 2009.
© Springer-Verlag Berlin Heidelberg 2009

ful application of KLM in many user interface evaluations [8, 9], we decided to base our modeling of the word selection on it.

2 Related Works

Up to our knowledge, the execution time of the task of selecting a word from a list has not yet modeled. Theoretically, the task can be analyzed using existing sophisticated cognitive architecture. According to cognitive architecture, a task is studied by considering human processors and memories involved during its execution which requires deep knowledge in psychology. The appealing architecture in the domain of HCI is EPIC, see [10] for a brief description of EPIC and an application example. However, applying EPIC to a particular task situation is extremely complex, involving programming the cognitive processor in its own language [11, 12]. In practical modeling for interface design, more approximate and coarser-grained architectures can be not just easier to use, but also avoid not-yet-resolved scientific puzzles that distract from the practical modeler's goals [7].

Another area of related work is menu search modeling which is well studied in the literature. Word selection from a list is different from menu search because the contents of the list are not static. Hence, word selection is mainly visual scanning rather than response choice, even for the expert user. In an empirical study [13], menu search was found to be well modeled by the Hick-Hyman law for response choice, then by Fitts's law for pointing time. This result supports that expert users doesn't visually inspect each element of the menu. We think that for a word list with continuously changing contents, she/he needs more time to search a word. In this case, menu search modeling can't be directly applied for word selection task.

The low-level perceptual, cognitive, and motor processing that people use when they select a known target item from a menu have been modeled in [14]. The author proposed several user strategies that may be applied in menu search. Assuming a given strategy, the selection time is calculated and the results are compared to the actual user test results to validate or refuse the proposed strategy.

3 Empirical Study

The objective of our empirical study is getting the information we need to model the selection time of a word from a list. In case of random word order in the list, our hypothesis is that selection time is related linearly to the position of the required word in the list. We expect that the relation will not be greatly affected by whether scrolling is needed to reach the desired word or not. In the case of a sorted list, we expect that the user will apply the strategy of binary search, and that selection time will be related in a log relation to the chosen word index, with no significant effect for scrolling. We build our belief about the absence of significant effect for scrolling on the parallel processing of motor activity required for scrolling the list, with the visual search for the desired word. We think that the whole operation will be dominated by the visual search.

We carried out two separate studies. The first experiment was an exploration of word selection task on desktop interfaces. We interested in the desktop interfaces where the mouse is used on large non-touch screen for two reasons. The first is, up to our knowledge, there is no a published model for the task. The second reason is that empirical results have been already published about user performance on a text entry method [15] where words were entered by selecting them from a list. The interface of that method was implemented on the desktop. We planned to test our model against these results hence it was necessary to have desktop model for word selection. The second experiment was for modeling word selection on handheld interfaces where the stylus is used on a small touch screen. Since much handheld text entry methods have appeared in the literature where word selection is an essential task in their operation. We need a word selection model on handheld interfaces to evaluate such methods.

3.1 Word Selection on Desktop Interface

Method. The experiment principal interface is shown in Fig. 1. The contents of the list were always 20 words, loaded from a total of 1,000 words each time a user started a test. Before beginning, the user was given an explanation on how to use the interface. When the user started the test, the 20 words were loaded in either alphabetical or random order. The user was then notified of the order in which the words appear to him. The number of words displayed to the user was randomly chosen between 4 and 10 words for each test.

Fig. 1. Word selection interface

A word is presented to the user, who has all the time he wished to memorize it. Once memorized, he signals that she/he is ready by clicking the "Select" button. At this moment, the list contents are displayed, the selection-time timer is started, and the button "Select" is disabled. The user searches the list, scrolls it if necessary, and selects the memorized word by clicking on it. At this moment, the Timer is stopped, another word is presented, and the result for the previous word is stored. The process continues until the user complete the selection of 10 words, then the test ends. The input from the keyboard was disabled during the test, so that the user uses only the mouse for selecting and scrolling.

The test was done online, using the web, with a test page written using the dynamic HTML so that all the processing required during the test was done by the participant's machine. In this way, the selection time of a word was not affected by any data transmission time.

Participants. The participants were from the university's community: researchers and students. Each participant was invited to participate to the test online. The number of trials was left to the participant's choice. We considered they were all experts in selecting a word from a list, since it is a common task in their every-day work. It was assumed that the practice factor did not affect the results much, since the contents of the list were different for each test. We obtained over 40 participants (some preferred to participate anonymously hence the exact number in unknown), most did two or three trials, and some did more than three. We collected the data for about 300 trials, or about 3000 word selection operations.

Results. Since the data was collected online, it was expected to find some data points that didn't represent the task – for example, the participant was interrupted during the test. For this reason, we filtered the data and removed the samples which were clearly outside task time (very far from the average of similar data points). We also excluded the data samples where a mouse wheel was used. About 100 data points were removed. Fig. 2 and Fig. 3 show the selection time versus word index relationship for alphabetical and randomly ordered word lists. The two figures show that the relationship can be approximated by a lincar graph with a relatively smaller slope for the case of alphabetically arranged words. For alphabetically arranged words, the selection time is related to the index of the selected word by the relationship: $T=142.287 \, n + 2857$ ms with $R^2=0.953$. For the randomly arranged words, the relationships were $T=186.19 \, n + 3266$ ms, $R^2=0.95$.

The above relationships are for words where scrolling was needed to make a selection. Fig. 2 and Fig. 3 slow also the selection time word-index data points for words that didn't require scrolling in either case, alphabetically and randomly ordered lists respectively. In the case of random order, the selection time and word-index data point was well represented by a linear graph: $T=81.178 \, n + 2336$ ms, see Fig. 3. We highlight that in the alphabetical order case (Fig. 2), we were not able to discover the relationship. Note also that there is a marked change in the relationships between the words that need scrolling and those that do not. We will return to these issues and others in the result discussion section.

Results Discussion. It was expected that the selection time would increase in a logarithmic relationship with the index of the alphabetically ordered words, since the user is expected to use the order evidence to search the list. The results don't agree with our hypothesis, the empirical data is well fitted by a linear graph rather than logarithmic one. Our explanation of this result is that the list was too short to force the user to call upon the order evidence in searching it. We think that for relatively long lists, the user will switch his search strategy from linearly investigating words to a binary search strategy hence a logarithmic selection time.

We note also that the word selection time increases suddenly in the transition from words that don't need scrolling for selection to those that need it. We consider this is normal, as it represents the time required by the user to make the decision for scrolling and to locate the scroll bars to begin using it. The increase was about one second in both alphabetical and randomly sorted lists.

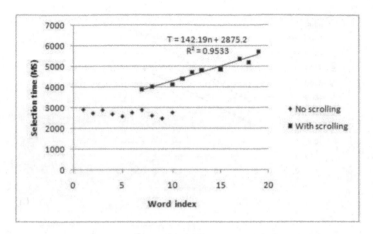

Fig. 2. Selection time (ms) versus word index for alphabetically arranged words

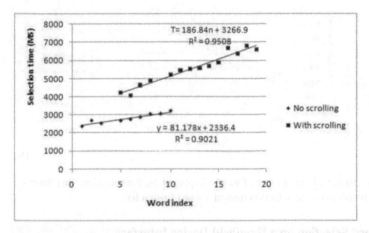

Fig. 3. Selection time (ms) versus word index for randomly arranged words

Since the size of the list, 20 words, was the same for all trials, few words presented meant a significant scrolling scale (words scrolled to scroll-movement ratio). We investigated the effect of the number of words displayed to the user on the selection time (see Fig. 4-a). The results showed an increase in the selection time of about 1.1 seconds in the case of 4 words displayed to the user, compared to 8 words.

Fig. 4-b shows the effect of learning on the selection time of a word. It shows the selection time-word index relation, for all the participants who did at least five sessions, during the first and fifth sessions of the test. We found a small effect for the learning, which supports our assumption that the task is common.

We found that the assumption that the scrolling doesn't affect the word selection time is false. Figure 3 shows that there is a significant difference between the slopes of the linear fitting line for the two cases: selection with scroll and without scroll. This indicates that the process is not completely dominated by the visual search, and the motor movement has a non-negligible effect of the selection time.

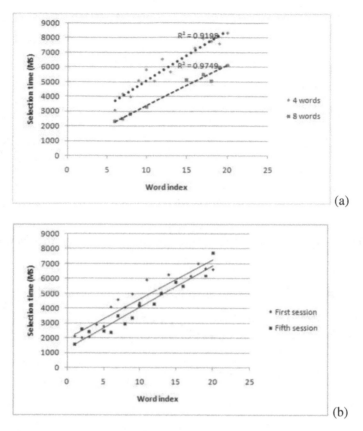

(a)

(b)

Fig. 4. (a): Effect of the number of words displayed on the selection time from a word list; (b): Effect of learning on the selection time of a word from a list

3.2 Word Selection on a Handheld Device Interface

Method. The interface is the same as for the desktop study, but implemented on the DELL AXIM X51-v personal digital assistant (PDA). The software to collect word selection data was written in C# using the .NET framework class library.

The participant is provided with a short explanation of the experiment, and then she/he starts doing consecutive short sessions, 10 word selections for each. The stages of selecting the word and the characteristics of the list are the same as in the desktop interface mentioned above, except that the number of words displayed to the user is the same for all trials – 6 words – and only the randomly ordered list are used. These choices were based on the objective of the experiment, which is the modeling of word disambiguation text entry methods. These methods use frequency ordering (random order from the research point of view), and display words for the user to choose. A survey on the number of words presented in the prediction lists indicated that 6 words represent the currently available prediction lists on these devices.

Participants. Eight researchers from the VALORIA laboratory (http://www-valoria.univ-ubs.fr) participated in the study, and each accomplished 10 sessions. They all use the computer regularly in their work, and some of them own a handheld device with a touch screen. Their ages were between 25 and 50 years.

Results. Fig. 5 shows the selection time versus word index relation. The same linear relationship as the desktop interface is reproduced for the handheld interface with a touch screen and stylus, with different slopes and constants. We also studied the effect of learning between sessions, and found it didn't have a significant effect on the results.

4 Modeling the Word Selection Task

Returning to the problem of modeling the word selection task, now we search for an adapted KLM model that could be used for modeling selection time. We need such a model in the evaluation of ambiguous text entry methods where a word-list is presented to the user to select the desired one. The model is limited to only the random order of the words in the list because it represents, at least from the user point of view, the order of the prediction list on these methods. Considering the empirical results, modeling the task as an expert-user menu selection search, i.e. logarithmic selection time, does not work.

Selection without scrolling: A simple model for word selection can be given as: selection time $T = s\,n + W$ ms, where n is the index of the selected word, s is a word scanning slope of about 80, (see Figures 3, 5) and W is a constant which is task-dependent. This constant is 1,026 in the case of a stylus and touch screen, and 2,336 when using a mouse and the normal desktop screen. It includes the keystroke operator K of 0.2 seconds of clicking on the desired word. This model should be applied to short lists of unexpected contents, requiring no scrolling to reach its contents.

Selection with scrolling: If the required word is hidden and requires scrolling along the list to be reached, the model depends on the task and the interface. It is $T = 202\,n + 1{,}463$ ms and $T = 187\,n + 3{,}267$ ms for the handheld and the desktop interfaces respectively. Although we did not examine long disordered lists, we expect the model will apply. For long ordered lists, we assume that the user will switch to a binary search strategy, and the selection time will be in logarithmic relation with the word index.

These equations are used to calculate the time required to select a word from a list in the context of KLM. We can put a symbol S (Selection), for the task and the time is calculated from the above equations. The operator S is applied the same way the operator P is applied in the KLM model, but instead of using Fitts' law to calculate the pointing time, the given equations are used to calculate the word selection time.

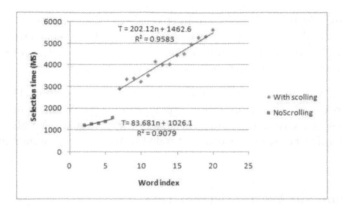

Fig. 5. Selection time in ms versus word index for a handheld device interface

5 Application of the Word-Selection Model in Text Entry Speed Evaluation

In a theoretical prediction of the text-entry speed, based on motor and linguistics components, T9 entry method was found to have 40.6 words per minute(WPM) for the expert user [16]. In a user study using the same entry method, expert user entry speed was found to be from 15.05 to 25.68 WPM, depending on the text to be typed [17]. In the case of TouchMeKey4 [15], the same theoretical model will give higher speeds than it gives for T9, because it uses only 4 keys instead of 8 keys. However, after five hours of learning, the average entry-speed was found to be 12 WPM on TouchMeKey4 [15]. It is clear that there is a big difference between the empirical and the predicted results. In this section, we integrate the word selection time model into the Soukoreff and Mackenzie model [18] that gives the above theoretical results. The purpose of this integration is to increase the entry-speed prediction accuracy for the entry methods employing word selection.

The model of Soukoreff and Mackenzie calculates the time taken by an expert user to move from one key to another to type a character. The average time for typing a character (T_c) is calculated by weighting each possible digram by its frequency in the language. Knowing the average length of a word in a given language, the model calculates the word average entry time as the average number of character per word multiplied by the average character entry time.

Instead of basing the entry speed only on the character average entry time as in the Soukoreff and Mackenzie model, we integrated the word selection model discussed before. For each word in our corpus, we calculated the entry time with the equation:

$$T_{word} = \{N\, T_c + (80n + 1{,}026)\}\ ms, \qquad \text{no scrolling}$$

$$T_{word} = \{N\, T_c + (202n + 1{,}463)\}\ ms, \qquad \text{with scrolling}$$

Where: N is the word length, n is the index of the word in the disambiguation word list, and the linear time part is the word selection and confirmation time resulting from the empirical study. Knowing the time for entering every word, we calculated the word average time:

$$T_{word_{average}} = \sum_{all\ words} P_{word} T_{word}\ ms$$

Where: P_{word} is the word probability calculated as the word frequency divided by the sum of all words frequencies. The entry speed is then calculated as:

$$WPM = \frac{60}{(T_{word_{average}}/1000)}$$

We now apply the modified model to TouchMeKey4. We used the Fitts' law parameters calculated empirically in [19] (a=83, b=127 for the stylus and touch screen interface), the parameters from [18] are used for the desktop interfaces . We used the first 10,000 words from the American National Corpus word frequency list available (http://americannationalcorpus.org/SecondRelease/frequency2.html). The predicted entry speed of the modified model was 18.3 and 13 WPM for the PDA and the desktop respectively. Considering the empirically measured entry speed of 12 WPM on a desktop interface [15], the results of our modified model is very conclusive.

6 Conclusion

We presented a model for the word selection task. It predicts the time necessary to select a word from a word-list, including the time to visually search the list and if necessary to scroll it. To validate our model, we applied it to predict the text entry speed of a published text entry method. The speed we got using our modified model and the parameter the desktop interaction, the calculated entry speed was 13 WPM, which is very eloquent considering the empirically evaluated entry speed found to be 12 WPM on the desktop interface. By applying the original model which doesn't take word selection time into account, the predicted entry speed was 28 WPM. Thus, our modified model significantly reduced the error gap between the predicted and empirical results compared to the original model.

References

1. MacKenzie, I.S., Buxton, W.: Extending Fitts' law to two-dimensional tasks. In: Proceedings of the SIGCHI conference on Human factors in computing systems. ACM Press, Monterey (1992)
2. MacKenzie, I.S., Soukoreff, R.W.: A model of two-thumb text entry. Graphics Interface 2002. In: Canadian Information Processing Society, Toronto, Canada, pp. 117–124 (2002)
3. Zhai, S., Hunter, M., Smith, B.A.: The metropolis keyboard - an exploration of quantitative techniques for virtual keyboard design. In: Proceedings of the 13th annual ACM symposium on User interface software and technology. ACM Press, San Diego (2000)
4. MacKenzie, I.S., Zhang, S.X.: An empirical investigation of the novice experience with soft keyboards. Behaviour & Information Technology 20, 411–418 (2001)
5. Card, S.K., Moran, T.P., Newell, A.: The keystroke-level model for user performance time with interactive systems. Commun. ACM 23, 396–410 (1980)

6. Card, S.K., Moran, T.P., Newell, A.: The Psychology of Human-Computer Interaction. L. Erlbaum Associates Inc., Mahwah (1983)
7. Kieras, D.E.: Fidelity Issues In Cognitive Architectures For HCI Modelling: Be Careful What You Wish For. In: 11th International Conference On Human Computer Interaction (HCII 2005), Las Vegas (2005)
8. Luo, L., John, B.E.: Predicting task execution time on handheld devices using the keystroke-level model. In: CHI 2005 extended abstracts on Human factors in computing systems. ACM Press, Portland (2005)
9. Holleis, P., Otto, F., Hussmann, H., Schmidt, A.: Keystroke-level model for advanced mobile phone interaction. In: Proceedings of the SIGCHI conference on Human factors in computing systems. ACM, San Jose (2007)
10. Kieras, D.E., Wood, S.D., Meyer, D.E.: Predictive engineering models using the EPIC architecture for a high-performance task. In: Proceedings of the SIGCHI conference on Human factors in computing systems. ACM Press/Addison-Wesley Publishing Co., Denver (1995)
11. Crystal, A., Ellington, B.: Task analysis and human-computer interaction: approaches, techniques, and levels of analysis. In: Tenth Americas Conference on Information Systems (AMCIS 2004), New York (2004)
12. Salvucci, D.D., Lee, F.J.: Simple cognitive modeling in a complex cognitive architecture. In: Proceedings of the SIGCHI conference on Human factors in computing systems. ACM, Ft. Lauderdale (2003)
13. Landauer, T.K., Nachbar, D.W.: Selection from alphabetic and numeric menu trees using a touch screen: breadth, depth, and width. SIGCHI Bull. 16, 73–78 (1985)
14. Hornof, A.J., Kieras, D.E.: Cognitive modeling reveals menu search in both random and systematic. In: Proceedings of the SIGCHI conference on Human factors in computing systems. ACM, Atlanta (1997)
15. Tanaka-Ishii, K., Inutsuka, Y., Takeichi, M.: Entering text with a four-button device. In: Proceedings of the 19th international conference on Computational linguistics, Taipei, Taiwan. Association for Computational Linguistics, vol. 1, pp. 988–994 (2002)
16. Silfverberg, M., MacKenzie, I.S., Korhonen, P.: Predicting text entry speed on mobile phones. In: Proceedings of the SIGCHI conference on Human factors in computing systems, pp. 9–16. ACM Press, The Hague (2000)
17. James, C.L., Reischel, K.M.: Text input for mobile devices: comparing model prediction to actual performance. In: Proceedings of the SIGCHI conference on Human factors in computing systems. ACM Press, Seattle (2001)
18. Soukoreff, R.W., MacKenzie, I.S.: Theoretical upper and lower bounds on typing speed using a stylus and soft keyboard. Behaviour & Information Technology 14, 370–379 (1995)
19. Zhai, S., Sue, A., Accot, J.: Movement model, hits distribution and learning in virtual keyboarding. In: Proceedings of the SIGCHI conference on Human factors in computing systems: Changing our world, changing ourselves. ACM Press, Minneapolis (2002)

Using Pictographic Representation, Syntactic Information and Gestures in Text Entry

Hamed H. Sad and Franck Poirier

VALORIA lab., Université de Bretagne-Sud, Vannes, France
{sad,poirier}@univ-ubs.fr

Abstract. With the increasing popularity of touch screen mobile devices, it is becoming increasingly important to design fast and reliable methods for text input on such devices. In this work, we exploit the capabilities of those devices and a specific language model to enhance the efficiency of text entry tasks. We will distribute the roles between the user and the device in a way that allocates the tasks to the side where they can be efficiently done. The user is not a good processor of syntactic and memory retrieval operations but she/he is a highly efficient processor for handling semantic and pattern recognition operations. The reverse is true for computational devices. These facts are exploited in two designs for the entry of common words which represent a high percentage of our written and spoken materials. A common word is typed in two or three clicks, with or without a gesture on a touch screen.

Keywords: mobile text entry, pictographs, pen gestures, syntactic information.

1 Introduction

Currently, the design of a usable text entry method for mobile devices is an active research area. As the device size shrinks, text entry becomes slower and error-prone [1]. In this section, we discuss the relevant characteristics of the three entities involved in the text entry activity: the user, the written text and the device. Clarifying these characteristics helps us to synthesis efficient and easy to use entry methods.

1.1 Text and Human Communication

For humans, text is not an object in itself, but it is a mean for representing and communicating knowledge and messages. What is mainly stored in our memory is not text but knowledge in terms of concepts, objects, scenes, functions, colors, etc. This is clear if we consider people who don't know any writing system, they still able to store knowledge and directly communicate it. When humans communicate knowledge and information, they need some sort of coding. In the following, we discuss direct and indirect human communication and how they are related to text.

By direct communication we mean person to person dialog. In our early days, we learned about our environment: objects, functions, and other semantics. For communicating these meanings, a representation was needed. The early representation we learned was an isolated utterance for each meaning (word) without any

J.A. Jacko (Ed.): Human-Computer Interaction, Part II, HCII 2009, LNCS 5611, pp. 735–744, 2009.
© Springer-Verlag Berlin Heidelberg 2009

decompositions into letters. Even with our limited capabilities as children, before learning reading and writing, we were able to store and manipulate a large number of such utterances, thanks to our inherently efficient pattern matching and semantic processing systems[2].

Information representation is strongly influenced by the media of indirect communication. Stones and paper appeared as a media for indirect communication a long time ago. Since papers and stones can't convey word pronunciation employed in early human direct communication, a new coding system was needed. The paper can only store drawing which human gesture on them. It was difficult for him to manage a unique drawing for each meaning (word). The code used and continued to nowadays is the decomposition of words to letters. The coding process of letters and group of letters to indicate meanings was suitable to the media used: paper. Humans have been used this system for communication for very long time, the result is that they default to it even the media has been changed. Now we use computing devices to persist our messages and ideas. The devices have the following characteristics which do not exist with the paper.

- Receiving pen gestures
- Detect sounds
- Detect movement
- See scenes through camera
- Do processing.

The last capability is important. In addition to being like a paper in receiving pen gestures, and due to its processing power, the device can determine the beginning, direction and velocity of the gestures. Then it can process this information.

1.2 Text Characteristics

Grammatical Classification of Words. Human beings use words in a more or less fixed order to communicate a message. Each word has a grammatical identity that determines its position in a group of words. We have the knowledge that enables us to determine and use the grammatical identity of a word in an efficient and fast way. We may remember the grammatical category of a word but not its spelling. Although this information seems to be very relevant to text entry, it is rarely used.

Frequent Words. Although a relatively large number of words are used for human communication, some are used very often and others are rarely used. Our analysis of English (http://americannationalcorpus.org) and French (http://www.lexique.org) corpora shows that only about 150 and 400 words make up half of the communication in the American English and French languages respectively. Most currently used text entry methods don't exploit this fact. Prediction-based methods use the word frequency for sorting the prediction results, but practically no method processes them specifically in the word coding stage. For example, in keyboard based methods, the same coding is used for both frequent and non-frequent words: tapping a key sequence according to the word's letters.

Context. Another relevant characteristic of our written text is the *context*. Our use of words is affected by the context of the message we need to communicate. We already know the context of our message before writing it. The current designs of text entry systems rarely consider this fact. Such designs should enable the user to select the context of her/his message and make the typing of words related to that context faster than others.

In this work, we show how to manage task assignment between the user and the machine in text entry system design. The principle is to assign tasks the human can do in efficient, pleasant and fast ways to the user. In the same time, tasks that require remembering fine details and fast processing are assigned to the machine.

Why should we base our entry system designs on the process used for the paper era? Why not change the process stages themselves by removing the letter coding stage and directly input meaning, at least for the frequent words? In other words, letter encoding was not an objective but a means in text typing tasks. We think that by using the new capabilities of the modern interactive devices, we can avoid the mean and reach directly to the objective. In the next sections, we will introduce an example that demonstrates bypassing letter encoding and enables the user to choose the context of her/his message. We also present a keyboard that uses the grammatical identity of the word as a shortcut for reaching it.

2 Related Works

Many text entry methods has been proposed in the literature of HCI, see [3]for a survey. The methods related to this work are mainly in two kinds: pen-gesture and soft-keyboard. There are many proposed pen gesture-based text entry methods [4-7]. All these method are character based. To enter a word, the user types it character by character. Each character requires a separate pen gesture. In some methods[8, 9], the entry may be continuous (without lifting up the stylus) but it still connected character by character gestures. Some text entry methods are designed to help the gradual transition from character-level gestures to word-level gestures. *SHARK2*, now called *ShapeWriter*, is an example of these methods where users can draw word-level gestures on a keyboard to enter words directly[10].

Many soft keyboards are proposed with different key-letter layouts. Almost all these layout are revisited and evaluated in a paper specially dedicated to the performance of the soft keyboard[11]. Another type of keyboards commonly used on mobile devices are the ambiguous keyboards. They use less number of keys and usually are based on a language model for disambiguation and predictions [12, 13].

Using pictographs to enter text is not common on mobile devices because it requires huge resources. Desktop systems are used to help peoples with some disabilities to enter text using pictographs. Axelia (www.axelia.com) is an example of such systems. In general, semantic and syntactic information is rarely used in text entry. They may be used to refine prediction[14], but we can't find any previous work where they are used to code or indicate the words to be entered.

3 Entering Text Using Pictographs

We propose an interface to enter text that bypasses letter encoding. It's based on the mental models of meanings already existing in the human mind, and can be processed at very high speed. On the device side, we will exploit what the machine can do efficiently: storing large amounts of data and efficiently processing them. On the human side, we will exploit pattern recognition, which user does fast and efficiently.

3.1 Design

The system uses simple graphical elements with gestures designed to reach directly to the desired meaning, and consequently the word. The symbol suggests a set of desired meanings based on the knowledge we have about our everyday life. A symbol may be simple or complex. A complex symbol contain many distinct regions, each of which suggests a group of meanings. Figure (1-a) shows a possible design for the common words symbols. The person symbol is a complex one that contains many regions. The head, for example, suggests meaning such as *think, head, hair imagine,* and *brain* while the foot region suggests meanings such as *walk, run, foot, boot, footwear, shoes,* and *go.* The small home symbol to the right of the person symbol is a simple one. It suggests the common words related to the home and family domains. The circle to the right of the person represents the sun and suggests the common words related to the nature.

The symbol set at the right is designed to suggest the common tool words. The group of vertical and horizontal lines with an arrow at the middle is a metaphor for pronouns. At the right of the group, the upper vertical line suggests all the pronouns related to the singular first (speaker) person like: *I, my, mine,* etc. The triple line below suggests the first (speaker) plural pronouns like: *we, us, our,* etc. The lines to the right represent the same pronouns as those to the left but for the second (listener) person. The vertical lines at the bottom suggest the pronouns for the third person. Finally the horizontal line in the group is assigned to other pronouns such as *another, other, one,* etc.

The set of rectangles in the upper-right region suggests the common conjunctions, prepositions articles and demonstrative adjectives. The positive, negative and equal signs suggest positive, negative, and equivalence common words. The question, exclamation, negation marks are allocated to the related words. The clock symbol and the line strips after and before it suggest the time-related words such as *yesterday, today, tomorrow,* etc. The set of rectangles to the left of the letters is used to suggest the positional words such as *up, down, middle, right, inside,* etc. For common words which can't easily be related to one of the symbols on the page, letter groups are used to suggest them by them initial letter.

Since a symbol can refer to many meanings, we use the pen gesture (flick) to disambiguate them. The first point of the pen gesture on a symbol determines the region within it. The last point determines the direction of the gesture. If the gesture consists only of one point, no direction is assigned to the gesture, in this case the system returns all the meaning related to the region, otherwise gesture direction disambiguation is used.

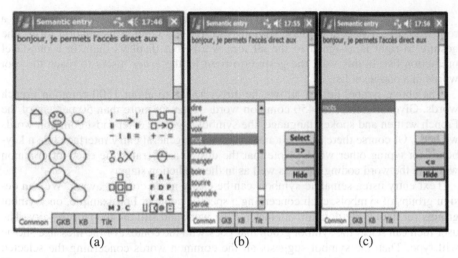

(a)   (b)   (c)

Fig. 1. (a) The common words symbol page, (b) the two levels prediction list with the first level displayed, and (c) the two levels prediction list with the second level displayed

In fact, many designs of gesture disambiguation can be used. In our test prototype, the following grammatical gestures are used:

- Down-right: verbs in the future tense
- Down: verbs in the present tense
- Down-left: verbs in the past tense
- Left: delete the last typed word
- Up-right: adjectives
- Up: nouns
- Up-left other parts of speech or grammatical categories
- Right: one-level prediction list (explained later)

Our test prototype is built upon a corpus of the French language. When using the down gestures for the verbs, the list is very long because a verb has many conjugations in French. For example, when we need to type the verb "*monte*" which means *to walk up*, we use the metaphor of the foot and the gesture down for the present tense. The verb "*aller, sortir, passer*, etc" (*go, exit, pass*, etc) are also assigned to the foot but they are more frequent and so come before the desired verb. Given that each verb has many conjugations for different persons and modes, the desired verb comes far down in the list. To overcome this problem, the no-gesture simple tap is assigned to the root words related to the metaphor symbol.

The no-gesture simple tap produces all the root words in a two levels prediction list, figure (1-b) shows the list associated to the mouse region on the person symbol. The user can select one of them, to enter it or to get the related words. In the case of the verb "*monte*" (to go up), she/he selects the root verb:"*monter*", then he chooses to display sub-words which include all the conjugations of the verb. Figure (1-c) shows the sub-words for the selected root words "mot" (word) in Figure (1-b). Since the no-gesture is assigned to only the root words, it gets a limited length list, but it is a two-level list and thus requires one or two steps before selecting a word, compared to the one-level.

All other gestures give one-level prediction lists. Sometimes, we need to enter a root word like a verb in the base (infinitive) form or a noun in its citation form. The gesture to right is assigned to the all root words, but displays them in a one-level prediction list. In this way, the gesture to right let the *expert* users to reach the root words in a one-level list.

The above symbol design allows the direct access to about 1500 common French words. Given that the first 450 common words represent more than 50 percent of the French written and spoken language, the symbol page can enter most common words we need. Of course there will be a need for another general entry interface like a keyboard for typing other words. Note that the design accelerates the entry of common words in the word coding stage as well as in the prediction stage.

Text entry using semantic symbols can be easily made context aware. We can design groups of symbols, each concerning a specific context. For example, one symbol groups for the family domain, another for the work and still another for the city. The user then can select the symbol group that goes with the context of the message she/he will type. Then the symbol suggests all the common words concerning the selected context.

In conclusion, using pictographic symbols allows the direct access to about 1500 frequent words using some symbols that appear on half of the PDA screen. Using a model for word selection from a list [15] we have developed in another work, a novice can enter words using the system at a rate of 40.5 wpm on a PDA which is very fast compared to existing entry methods on PDAs.

4 Grammatical Shortcuts for Frequent Words on Keyboard

In this section we show how the grammatical information can be used as shortcuts for rapid access, bypassing most of the letter coding stage for common words. Figure (2-a) shows the usual French keyboard that exploits both text characteristics and the grammatical identity of words. With respect to text characteristics, when the keyboard is used in word mode and after typing at least one letter, it disables all the keys holding any invalid following character and presents the most common words that start with the typed letters so far (see figure 2-a). Disabling invalid keys reduces the chance of clicking an incorrect key, especially on mobile devices where the size of the soft keys is relatively small and clicking an incorrect key is the most frequent error.

Instead of predicting all possible completion words, the user can use simple grammatical gesture to specify the grammatical identity of the desired words. Figure (2-b) shows the two prediction lists when the user has specified that the next word is a noun by starting his gesture on the key L then moving upwards. The upper list is the completion list, and the lower list is the list of all common nouns starting with the selected letter. We note that the completion list doesn't contain the French word "lettre"(*letter*) because there are many other more common words start with "l". To reach the desired word "lettre" the user has to specify more letters as in figure (2-a). Limiting the list by filtering only the nouns allowed the desired word to be in the contents of the grammatical prediction list by specifying only the first letter.

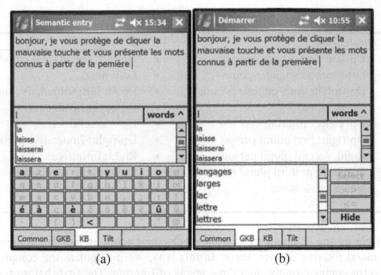

Fig. 2. (a) the keyboard after clicking the key "l" for entering the French word "lettre"(letter). All invalid keys are deactivated and the common completion words starting with L are displayed (b) the state of the entry after gesturing up starting from the key "l". The two prediction list: completion and grammatical lists are displayed

As in the case of pictographs entry described above, we can imagine many designs for the grammatical gestures. In our testing prototype, we used the same gesture assignments as used in the pictographs entry, except for the gesture to the right. On the keyboard, the simple click without any gesture is reserved for the normal operation of the keyboard. Since it can't be used for displaying all common root words as in the case of pictographs entry, we used the gesture to the right for this purpose on the keyboard.

5 Filtering Gestures

In some cases, using the semantic or grammatical keyboards produces a long prediction word list. This problem is very clear for French language verbs, since a verb has many conjugations. For example, when gesturing downward starting from the foot region of the human symbol (Figure 1-a) for typing the French verb "*monte*" (to go up), the suggested list includes all the present-tense conjugations of all related verbs, for all moods and persons. The same is also true when gesturing down on a key on the grammatical keyboard (Figure (2-a). Searching a long prediction list is a time and resource-consuming task [15]. We can assign this tedious (for the user task) to the machine by using simple gestures.

The user commands the machine to do the required filtering by using a gesture. The idea of employing gestures for executing a second-stage filtering can be extended to other word types and situations. For the French language verbs lists, we assigned the person and mode filtering gestures in analogy to the French language conjugation as shown in table 1.

Table 1. Filtering gestures for person and mood

Person filtering	Mood filtering
• Up-left: first singular person • Left: second singular person • Down-left: third singular person • Down: none • Up: cancel filtering • Up-right: first plural person • Right: second plural person • Down-right: third plural person • No gestures: none	• Up-left: conditional mood • Left: none • Down-left: subjunctive mood • Down: indicative mood • Up: cancel filtering • Up-right: Imperative mood • Right: infinitive • Down-right: participant • No gestures: none

The filtering can be applied on two levels by first applying the person then apply-ing the mood filtering or vice versa. In this way, we manipulate the complexity of French verbs conjugation through three levels of filtering. The first- before accessing the prediction list,- is choosing the tense, the second and the third –during the predic-tion list investigation- are the person and mood filtering on the prediction list. Filter-ing allows fast access to words, as well as promoting choosing over remembering complex syntax.

6 Text Prediction Infrastructure

A special data structure is used as an infrastructure for prediction. It's a letter tree constructed from a corpus of word-frequency pairs. Each node in the tree represents a letter and contains a list of pointers to all valid continuation letters nodes from it, each with its associated frequency. It also contains one backward pointer to the node pre-ceding it. The tree has the following characteristics:
- Given a letter sequence, it provides all possible valid letters continuation sorted by their frequency.
- Given a letter sequence, it provides all valid continuation words, up to a specified number, sorted by their frequency
- Any possible letter sequence exists only once, so it optimizes the storage space compared to word dictionary.
- Each node in the tree can be intermediate or final. Final nodes are leaves in the tree. An intermediate or final node can be the last node for a word. In this case it contains the meaning identifiers (semantic and syntactic information) that word represents.
- Each distinct word has a grammatical identity encoded in a 16 binary bits
- The meaning identifier indicates whether the meaning is root or sub-meaning. Given the root meaning all possible sub-meaning can be accessed directly from the tree.

- All the tree is indexed by the meaning identifier, i.e. given the meaning ID we can reach directly to the last node in the word for that meaning, consequently all the information concerning the meaning and its syntactic data.

Although the data structure includes additional data other than the words, using the letter tree makes the size of the structure reasonable so that it can be used on mobile devices.

7 Conclusion and Future work

We presented two designs to type frequent words on mobile devices with touch screen. The first design employed pictographs and word lists to enable rapid and easy access to common words. The second one exploited the syntactic information and the redundancy in the language to provide rapid entry and to minimize the errors by preventing them.

The idea of allocating tasks between the device and the user can be further extended. Sentences could be entered in terms of root nouns and infinitive verbs. The user then sets some adjustments by making symbol-based choices. A possible extension is to specify the sentence tense on a time line. In a similar way we can express the mood, number, and gender, etc. Based on this information and language model the device can reformulate the sentence in the correct way.

References

1. Sears, A., Revis, D., Swatski, J., Shneiderman, B.: Investigating touchscreen typing: the effect of keyboard size on typing speed. Behaviour & Information Technology 12, 17–22 (1993)
2. Kim, S., Jang, G.-j., Lee, W.-H., Kweon, I.S.: How Human Visual Systems Recognize Objects - A Novel Computational Model. In: Proceedings of the Pattern Recognition, 17th International Conference on (ICPR 2004), vol. 3-03. IEEE Computer Society Press, Los Alamitos (2004)
3. MacKenzie, S., Soukoreff, R.W.: Text Entry for Mobile Computing: Models and Methods. Theory and Practice Human-Computer Interaction 17, 147–198 (2002)
4. Cechanowicz, J., Dawson, S., Victor, M., Subramanian, S.: Stylus based text input using expanding CIRRIN. In: Proceedings of the working conference on Advanced visual interfaces. ACM, Venezia (2006)
5. Perlin, K.: Quikwriting: continuous stylus-based text entry. In: Proceedings of the 11th annual ACM symposium on User interface software and technology, pp. 215–216. ACM Press, San Francisco (1998)
6. Venolia, D., Neiberg, F.: T-cube: a fast, self-disclosing pen-based alphabet. In: Conference companion on Human factors in computing systems, p. 218. ACM Press, Boston (1994)
7. Goldberg, D.: Unistrokes for computerized interpretation od handwriting. In: Patent, U. (ed.) Xerox corporation, stamford, conn., US, vol. 41 (1995)
8. Mankoff, J., Abowd, G.D.: Cirrin: a word-level unistroke keyboard for pen input. In: Proceedings of the 11th annual ACM symposium on User interface software and technology, pp. 213–214. ACM Press, San Francisco (1998)

9. Isokoski, P., Raisamo, R.: Quikwriting as a multi-device text entry method. In: Proceedings of the third Nordic conference on Human-computer interaction, pp. 105–108. ACM Press, Tampere (2004)
10. Kristensson, P.-O., Zhai, S.: SHARK2: a large vocabulary shorthand writing system for pen-based computers. In: Proceedings of the 17th annual ACM symposium on User interface software and technology. ACM Press, Santa Fe (2004)
11. Zhai, S., Hunter, M., Smith, B.A.: Performance optimization of virtual keyboards Human-Computer Interaction, vol. 17, pp. 89–129 (2002)
12. Tanaka-Ishii, K., Inutsuka, Y., Takeichi, M.: Entering text with a four-button device. In: Proceedings of the 19th international conference on Computational linguistics, vol. 1, pp. 988–994. Association for Computational Linguistics, Taipei (2002)
13. Poirier, F., Belatar, M.: Évaluation d'analogies scripturales pour la conception d'une méthode de saisie en mobilité – Uni-Glyph. In: Ergo-IA, pp. 333–336. Technopole Izarbel, Bidart/Biaritz, France (2006)
14. Gong, J.: Semantic \& syntactic context-aware text entry methods. In: Proceedings of the 9th international ACM SIGACCESS conference on Computers and accessibility, ACM, Tempe Arizona (2007)
15. Sad, H.H., Poirier, F.: Modeling word selection in predictive text entry. In: 13th International Conference on Human-Computer Interaction (HCII 2009), San Diego, USA (2009)

Embodied Sound Media Technology for the Enhancement of the Sound Presence

Kenji Suzuki

Dept. of Intelligent Interaction Technologies, University of Tsukuba
305-8573 Tsukuba, Japan
kenji@ieee.org

Abstract. In this paper, the paradigms of Embodied Sound Media (ESM) technology are described with several case studies. The ESM is designed to formalize a musical sound-space based on the conversion of free human movement into sounds. This technology includes the measurement of human motion, processing, acoustic conversion and output. The first idea was to introduce direct and intuitive sound feedbacks within the context of not only embodied interaction between humans and devices but also social interaction among humans. The developed system is a sort of active aid for an embodied performance that allows the users to get feedback for emotional stimuli in terms of sound surrounding the users. The overviews of several devices developed in this scenario and the potential applications to physical fitness, exercise, entertainment, assistive technology and rehabilitation are also addressed.

Keywords: Embodied sound media, wearable device, sound interface, sound conversion, social-musical interaction.

1 Introduction

Sound is a typical and important channel of non-verbal communication that humans often use to express their feelings. In addition to that, sound plays a key role for humans to transmit information to others. It is essentially a mode of expression and a mode of emotion and affection among people. So far the paradigms of the embodied interaction between humans and devices in the framework of *Embodied Sound Media* (ESM) have been exploring [1]. Since humans often accompany music with body motion, a number of studies have reported wearable systems and sensing technologies for a musical performance. Bahn et al. [2] focused on the human body itself in the musical performance, and addressed that musical performance has been inextricably linked to the human body. For increasing the degrees of freedom of musical expression, a number of researchers and musicians have explored new types of musical system that overcomes the physical limitations of musical instruments and the human vocal cords [3], [4], [5]. Various types of sensing techniques have been used to detect human motion, and the measured body movements are mapped to music or sound.

These developed instruments provide the ESM environment where everyone can enjoy it for playing the sounds and also can interact with others through collaborative musical experiences. In the interactive environment, people can communicates with each other by means of sound, music and his/her own body motion.

J.A. Jacko (Ed.): Human-Computer Interaction, Part II, HCII 2009, LNCS 5611, pp. 745–751, 2009.
© Springer-Verlag Berlin Heidelberg 2009

In this paper, the paradigms of Embodied Sound Media technology are described with several case studies such as (i) an interface for socio-musical interaction, (ii) a wearable device designed to some musical pieces by a simple and intuitive manipulations, and (iii) another wearable device to convert human bioelectrical signals caused by human movement or muscles activity. The ESM is designed to formalize a musical sound-space based on the conversion of free human movement into sounds. Performances in these three applications followed by the discussed concept.

2 MusicGlove

This research aims to develop a wearable musical interface which enables to control audio and video signals by using hand gestures and human body motions. An audio-visual manipulation system has been developed, which realizes tracks control, time-based operations and searching for tracks from massive music library. It aims to build an emotional and affecting musical interaction, and will provide a better method of music listening to people. A sophisticated glove-like device with an acceleration sensor and several strain sensors has been developed. A realtime signal processing and musical control are executed as a result of gesture recognition. A stand-alone device is developed in order to perform as a musical controller and player at the same time. The development of a compact and sophisticated sensor device, and the performance of audio and video signals control are described in this session.

In this case study, a sophisticated interface that enables users to control the sound and music in intuitive and efficient manners is investigated. The glove-like input device is one of the conventional interfaces for human-computer interaction. The developed system, *MusicGlove*, has a role of interactive music player and explorer, which performs tracks control, time-stretching of audio and video signals, and information retrieval from massive music library as a result of hand gestures and body motion recognition [6].

Hardware Configuration. The overview of the developed glove-like sensing device is shown in figure 1. The device consists of one 3-axis acceleration sensor, 4 strain sensors, 1 microprocessor for signal processing and control, Bluetooth wireless module, a portable music player and a battery. The measurement range of the acceleration sensor is from ±10[g]. As the sensor is fixed on external side of the wrist part, X, Y, Z-axis are also fixed at a given position. Four strain sensors are mounted at upside of index finger and mid finger, and also inner and exterior side of wrist. The strain sensors provide analog value of bending of each position. The glove like device has lightweight and is designed to satisfy the minimum requirement for musical control. The arrangement of sensors is determined as a result of preliminary experiments. The microprocessor is used to obtain sensor data, to perform gesture recognition, and then to transmit processed data to the wireless module. The device communicates with the host computer via Bluetooth. The music player can be connected to the microprocessor via dock connector port. In the all-in-one application, the microprocessor generates control signals for the music player.

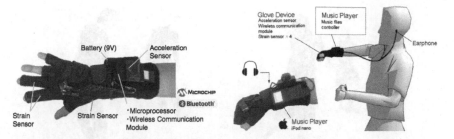

Fig. 1. MusicGlove - a wearable interface for sound/music manipulation. The glove-shape device allows the users to explore music pieces. Human gesture and body motion are measured by the developed wearable device capable to control the tracks, audio and also video signals.

Interaction Style. A portable music player can be attached with the glove device, and the users are able to control music player by his/her gestures. This enables the system to be stand-alone, and users can listen to music via headphone or earphones that are directly connected to the developed device without any other equipments. The embedded microprocessor produces a control signal to the player such as: play or stop tracks, skip to the next or previous music, fast forward and rewind, and volume control by means of acceleration and strain sensors.

The control of tracks is done according to the hand posture, which includes the following functions: play, stop, skip to the next music, back to the previous music, and volume control. This mode is initiated when the user stretches index finger, and the hand is then shaped like pointing to the air. In addition, the user is able to search audio tracks by grasping gesture at the air. In this mode, audio tracks presented to the user in a successive manner. Search for audio tracks is regarded as repetition of trial and error to choose a music (or album) from massive libraries. The system will present the first part of a track in a music library at each step of search successively according to the user's searching motion. The searching motion is regarded as a simple hand motion which is detected based on the accumulated value of the acceleration sensors in all-axes. The user listens to audio data, and acts a grasping motion of playing music when she/he finds a desired track or library. Grasping motion is detected based on the strain sensors. In addition, waving user's hand is regarded as "shuffle search." The user is able to choose a media library or tracks in a random manner. These manipulations provide users with intuitive search like grasping a music at the air.

3   Beacon: An Interface for Socio-musical Interaction

Beacon is a novel instrument for socio-musical interaction where a number of participants can produce sounds by feet in collaboration with each other. The developed instrument will provide an interactive environment around it. The *beacon* produces laser beams lying on the ground and rotating. Audio sounds are then produced when the beams pass individual performer's foot. As the performers are able to control the pitch and sound length according to the foot location and angles facing the instrument, the performer's body motion and foot behavior can be translated into sound and music in an intuitive manner. A number of line laser modules are installed around the

Fig. 2. Performance with *beacon* - an interface for socio-musical interaction. The battery operated device with cylindrical shape, 75[cm] height and 15 [cm] diameter, performs the sensing the movement of surrounding humans, music processing and audio output.

top of the interface, and the laser beams are produced and rotated around the interface. The beam performs like a moving string because sounds are generated every time the beam lying on the ground passes the performers' feet. A real-time motion capture technique and pattern recognition of users' feet are used in order to create a new style of musical interaction.

Hardware Configuration. The developed instrument consists of a loudspeaker, a small-size computer, 60 line laser modules, 2 laser range finders, dial and buttons interface, and battery. All equipments are installed in a cylinder shaped interface as illustrated in figure 2. This instrument is a kind of small lighthouse sending out line laser beams. The beams are used not only to mark the current location to produce the sound but also to assist musical interaction. In the current implementation, up to 4 laser beams with equiangularly-spaced directions are lying on the ground and rotating during musical performance. The rotation speed of laser beams can be set from 40bpm to 100bpm. At the bottom of the instrument, two laser range-finders are installed and used for the distance measurement to performers, in particular those foot positions and its angles every 100 ms at the height of 1 cm from the ground. The installed range-finder has 4[m] measuring range with 99% range accuracy, and also has a 240 degree angle of view for each. Two range-finders are used in order to obtain omni-directional distance map every time.

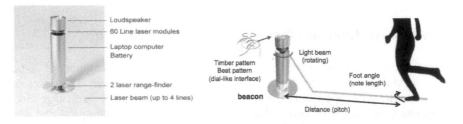

Fig. 3. Performance with *beacon* - an interface for socio-musical interaction. The battery operated device with cylindrical shape, 75[cm] height and 15 [cm] diameter, performs the sensing the movement of surrounding humans, music processing and audio output.

Motion-to-sound Mapping. The performer is regarded as a musical note. *beacon* generates sounds when the beams passed individual performers as if the rotating laser beams could detect them. However, in reality, the performers around by *beacon* are detected at all times by the equipped omini-directional laser range-finder. A number of performers, therefore, can participate in a musical session, and individual performers is able to change the pitch in accordance with the distance from the center of the instrument to the foot. The sound lengths, on the other hand, are determined based on the foot angles. When the performer points his/her toes toward the *beacon*, shorter sounds are produced. The performer put the entire length of the foot facing beacon, longer sounds are played. The attack and decay of each note are predetermined, and the sound volume is fixed in this work. The timbre, tone colors and major/minor keys can be selected, even during the performance, by using buttons and a dial interface that are equipped at the top of instrument.

The relationship between the facing angle to the instrument and measured angular area with different distances is also investigated. The measured data are collected with facing foot angles every 22.5 [deg]. A clear difference can be seen according to the facing angles of foot at the distance of 500-1000 [mm]. However, there are small differences over the distance of 1500 [mm]. Based on this result, the foot angles are used for control of sound length within the area less then 1500 [mm] radius from the instrument.

Here a novel interface *beacon* for socio-musical interaction is introduced. This instrument allows performers not only to communicate with each other via music and motion, but also to improve the quality of sound production by training and devising various types of behavior. This novel instrument thus can be used for the physical exercise or recreation with fun. Moreover, by arranging small objects around the instrument, a variety of sound will be produced like an environmental music box. Sounds are generated when the laser beam passes the objects as well as human performers. This installation provides a new artistic expression for spatial designers. This round-shape interface does not have any directional characteristics and plays a key role of gathering people for affective communication.

4 BioTones

In order to convert directly human movement to sound, a wearable device to generate sounds based on bioelectrical signals, especially surface electromyogram(EMG) is developed. In the proposed method, salient features of EMG signal are mapped into sound features by a wearable device that is capable to obtain the EMG signal and also to create audio signal. This device allows people to get auditory feedback from muscle tension while preserving the property of original signal. The proposed approach is suitable for several applications such as biofeedback treatment, sport training, and entertainment. In particular, an application to biofeedback treatment for migraine headache and tension headache is considered.

The electromyogram monitor is used to monitor human's neuromuscular function as visualization of muscular activities. The monitor is widely used for not only the medical purpose but also the analysis of muscular activities in exercise and sports science. However, there are several critical problems in terms of visual feedback i) people are forced to stay in front of the monitor, and ii) showing multiple EMG

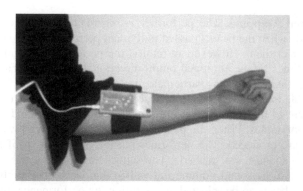

Fig. 4. BioTones: a wearable device to convert his/her bioelectrical signals based on electromyogram signals into audio sounds. The device is capable to extract the signals and also to generate audio sounds. The users simply can listen to sound by using normal headphones.

signals by using the traditional monitors due to the complexity of the signal features although the principle feature is the activity level. On the other hand, the auditory feedback is also effective to show the change and characteristics of bioelectrical signals caused by the muscular activity. Sound has three basic characteristics: loudness, pitch, and timbre. Not only the control of loudness and pitch but also the timbre control is capable to represent a variety of muscular activity.

Hardware Configuration. The *bioTones* consists of a pair of disposable electrodes, bioelectric amplifier, microprocessor, digital signal processor, and audio amplifier. This enables to extract bioelectrical signals and also generate audio signals. The user is able to listen to sounds simply through the normal headphone system. The developed prototype is designed to measure the bioelectrical signals on the surface of the flexor carpi radialis muscle. This is a muscle of the human forearm that is used to flex and abduct the hand. The device is fixed to the forearm with a tightened belt.

Motion-to-sound Mapping. There are several mapping rules in accordance with the target application. There are two features of bioelectrical signals: level and frequency characteristics as well as sound features. Direct mapping is regarded as the direct correspondence between bioelectrical and audio signals in terms of the level and frequency. On the other hand, cross mapping is regarded as alternation of the level and frequency characteristics between bioelectrical and audio signals. This device does not aim to extract salient features of bioelectrical signals but to preserve the original features as much as possible. The purpose of these mapping is to represent a variety of the muscular activity by a variety of sound features.

This is a novel method of sonification that is an alternative to visualization technique. It should be noted that the temporal and pressure resolution is higher than the visual perception due to the characteristics of auditory perception. The wearable device benefits a wide range of users because people can get auditory feedback solely by wearing it and listing to sound at any time and place, even in transit or on the walking.

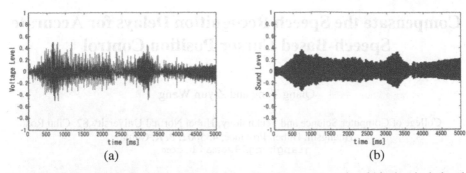

Fig. 5. Examples of bioelectrical and audio signals: (a) is an example of bioelectrical signal, and (b) is the converted audio signal. The signal conversion is performed by two types of mappings: direct mapping and cross mapping.

5 Conclusions

In this paper, the paradigms of *Embodied Sound Media* (ESM) technology are described with several case studies. This media technology is designed to formalize a musical sound-space based on the conversion of free human movement into sounds. Three case studies, (i) MusicGlove, (ii) beacon and (iii) bioTones, have different perspectives of ESM, and all devices are designed to provide direct and intuitive sound feedbacks within the context of not only embodied interaction between humans and devices but also social interaction among humans. The developed system is a sort of active aid for an embodied performance that allows the users to get feedback for emotional stimuli in terms of sound surrounding the users. The potential applications include physical fitness, exercise, edutainment (education and entertainment), assistive technology and rehabilitation.

Acknowledgments. This work is supported in part by CREST project "Generation and Control Technology of Human-entrained embodied Media" of the Japan Science and Technology Agency (JST), and the Global COE Program on "Cybernics: fusion of human, machine, and information systems," MEXT, Japan.

References

1. Suzuki, K., Hashimoto, S.: Robotic Interface for Embodied Interaction via Dance And Musical Performance. Proceedings of the IEEE 92(4), 656–671 (2004)
2. Bahn, C., Hahn, T., Trueman, D.: Physicality and feedback: A focus on the body in the performance of electronic music. In: International Computer Music Conference, pp. 44–51 (2001)
3. Wanderley, M., Baffier, M.: Trends in Gestural Control of Music. IRCAM, Paris (2000)
4. Camurri, A., et al.: EyesWeb - toward gesture and affect recognition in dance/music interactive systems. Computer Music J. 24(1), 57–69 (2000)
5. Paradiso, J.: The Brain Opera Technology: New instruments and gestural sensors for musical interaction and performance. J. New Music Research 28(2), 130–149 (1999)
6. Hayafuchi, K., Suzuki, K.: MusicGlove: A Wearable Musical Controller for Massive Media Library. In: 8th International Conference on New Interfaces for Musical Expression, Genoa, Italy (2008)

Compensate the Speech Recognition Delays for Accurate Speech-Based Cursor Position Control

Qiang Tong and Ziyun Wang

College of Computer Science and Technology, Hubei Normal University,82, Cihu Road,
Huangshi, Hubei Province, 435002, P. R. China
qiangtong99@gmail.com

Abstract. In this paper, we describe a back-compensate mechanism to improve the precision of speech-based cursor control. Using this mechanism we can control the cursor more easily to move to small on-screen targets during continuous direction-based navigation despite the processing delays associated with speech recognition. In comparison, using traditional speech-recognition systems, it is difficult to move the cursor precisely to a desired position because of the processing delays introduced by speech recognition. We also describe an experiment in which we evaluated the two alternative solutions, one using the traditional speech-based cursor control, and the other using the back-compensate mechanism. We present the encouraging evaluation results at the end of this paper and discuss future work.

Keywords: Speech recognition, delays, navigation, mouse, cursor control.

1   Introduction

With the development of practical speech recognition systems and tools such as IBM ViaVoice and Microsoft Speech SDK, a user can operate a computer and use computer applications with only voice without traditional input devices such as keyboards and mice. This is important for individuals with physical disabilities and limited abilities to use keyboards and mice. Speech-recognition enabled computer applications can also help users who need hand-free solutions when their hands are engaged in other tasks.

Computer mouse has been one of the most important computer input devices since the 1960s. Modern computer operating systems, such as Windows, Mac OS and Linux, all provide WIMP (Windows, Icons, Menus and pointing devices) style interfaces. Almost every computer has a mouse and a keyboard as standard input devices.

Combining speech recognition with WIMP style interfaces to create speech-based cursor control is very useful. It can help individuals with physical disabilities to use any existing windows-based applications normally as opposed to only use special applications designed for persons with disabilities.

One crucial problem with speech-based cursor control application is that speech recognition always has delays during it works; the user must complete the utterance of a word and wait for the recognition results. The speech-recognition result is only

J.A. Jacko (Ed.): Human-Computer Interaction, Part II, HCII 2009, LNCS 5611, pp. 752–760, 2009.

available at the end of the utterance, not at the start; this shortcoming limited the use of speech based-applications especially for the continuous direction-based navigation of speech-based cursor control. For example, the user specifies "Move Left" and the cursor begins to move to left, when the cursor gets to the target the user says "Stop" intending to have the cursor stop at the target. In speech-based systems, the cursor often misses the target because the speech-recognition delays effect. The delay effect becomes unacceptable when the user's speech speed is slow ("stooooop"), the cursor will stop farther away from the target.

This paper proposes the use of a compensate mechanism to help speech-based cursor control to remedy against the delay effects with speech-recognition.

2 Related Work

Sears, Lin, and Karimullah [5] provided a detailed analysis of the delays associated with the execution of speech-based commands, and they designed a predictive cursor to help user to estimate where to issue the "Stop" command before the actual cursor got to the target, but it failed to prove beneficial. This is because they hypothesized that the predictive distance for a user is constant. They calibrated the offset used for the predictive cursor for each individual user before they conducted the tests, but a user can't always issue the same commands using the same amount of time. The research, however, found that cursor speed, target size, and speech recognition delays and errors are the most critical factors in achieving precision using speech-based cursor control.

Dai, Goldman, Sear, Lozier [2] presented a grid-based cursor control method. In this grid-based system, the screen was divided into a 3x3 grid numbered one through nine in row-major order. The user spoke aloud the number of the grid that contained the target, and then the chosen grid was recursively divided into a smaller 3x3 grid, and the user continued to speak out the number of the target grid, fine-tuning the target position to move the cursor to reach the proper location eventually. Additional commands were provided to move the whole 3x3 grid in four directions or back up a recursion level if the user made a mistake. This grid-based approach can be efficient in moving the cursor to a point on the screen, but it does not allow the user to move the cursor continuously like in a normal WIMP environment. Further more, this approach works in applications where the cursor is only used for picking targets on the screen; it doesn't help in applications that require the use of the continuous motion of the cursor, such as drawing a line in a painting program.

Igarashi, Hughes [3] showed how nonverbal voice can be used for interaction control, where the user controlled the application directly using continuous voice command, and the system provided immediate feed back. For example, one could say "Cursor up, ahhhhhh...", and the cursor would continually move up while the "ahhh" sound continued, it will stop at once when the "ahhh" sound ended. Subsequent systems have used similar non-verbal voices for continuous input [1][2][6][7], primarily for mouse pointer control. The limitation of these techniques is that it requires an unnatural way of using the human voice.

3 Backward Compensate Cursor Control

We focus on speech-based cursor control for continuous directional navigation. Because of the delay associated with spoken commands, a moving cursor will not stop immediately when the "Stop" command is issued; it will pass the target for some additional distance before it stops, assuming the beginning of the utterance is when the cursor SHOULD stop. Our solution is to make cursor jump back an appropriate distance to compensate the additional distance the cursor travels after the "Stop" command is issued, therefore the cursor will stop at the desired position after the compensation.

Sears, Lin, and Karimullah [5] have mentioned a compensate solution. In that solution, the compensated distance is calculated by determining the average delays from historical usage data. Because true delay for each command never remains a constant, the compensated delay feels artificial and inaccurate.

In fact, the length of command utterance not only varies from person to person, it also varies for the same person from time to time, for example, when a person's speech speed changes due to fatigue or excitement. Therefore the compensate distance should not be a constant value.

In our solution, we detect the delay associated with spoken command such as "Stop" every time when it is issued. Because the speed of the cursor is known, we can calculate the extra distance the cursor travels every time, we then make the cursor jump backwards this additional distance to the correct position when the command is issued. The process is illustrated in Fig.1.

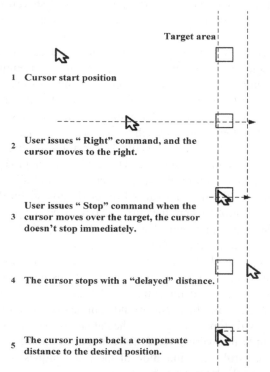

Fig. 1. Illustration of the compensate cursor control

The key contribution of this solution is that the compensate distance is not a constant value, but it is calculated with the actual delay based on when the spoken command is issued and when it is recognized. For example, when the user issues the command STOP as "Stop" (speaking normal speed) and "S-t-o-p" (speaking slowly), the delays are very different, therefore the compensate distances are very different too, the second one is a bigger compensation whereas the first one is smaller.

We implemented the speech-based cursor control with compensate cursor solution as follows:

Our application supports 4 directional voice commands: Left (Move left), Right (Move right), Up (Move up), Down (Move down), and two action commands Stop and Click (mouse left click). Of curse we can add other commands such as Double Click, Drag and other directional commands if necessary.

The cursor moves at a rate of 100 pixels per second.

When the cursor is not moving, if any directional command is issued, the cursor begins to move; when the "Stop" command is issued, the cursor stops and jumps back a compensated distance (as shown in Figure 1); when the cursor is moving, if a different directional command is issued, the cursor does a 3-step adjustment: the first step is to stop, the second step is to jump back a compensate distance, and then the third step is to begin a new direction movement according to the new directional command.

4 Experiment

4.1 Participants

Sixteen HBNU students (8 females and 8 males) volunteered to participate in a usability study. They all speak Chinese and have no hearing, speech, or cognitive impairments. Their average age was 21. They were divided into two groups with one group using a compensate speech-based cursor application and the other group using a normal voice-controlled cursor application.

4.2 Equipment

An IBM ThinkPad running Windows XP was used. The LCD screen had a diagonal size of 14.1 inches and the display resolution was set to 960x600 pixels; Our speech cursor control applications were developed using Delphi 7.0 and Microsoft speech recognition engine 5.1 through Microsoft Speech API. All participants used a headset mounted microphone when testing the application. A set of custom applications were developed using Delphi, presenting 3 different sizes of targets. The applications all automatically recorded the voice command events, and various timing such as selection time used to pick the target.

4.3 Experiment Design

The purpose of this experiment is to determine the benefits of our compensate mechanism in speech-based cursor control systems. The two sets of test applications are only different in whether the delay is processed when stop or change direction command is issued. For accuracy, we designed a script for every test subject to follow in

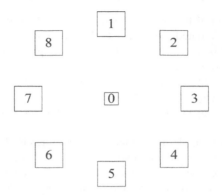

Fig. 2. Target direction relative to the cursor start position

using both applications to complete the same list of tasks in the same order on a screen layout illustrated in Fig. 2:

- use speech command to click the center button 0 to start the task, control the cursor to move to button 1, stop the cursor and click. If the cursor does not stop in the button's click-able area, adjust it's position using speech command before clicking the button,
- repeat the clicking task from button 1 to button.8;
- at last click button 1.

All the steps are controlled by speech-based cursor in both types of applications. The application programs automatically record the time, number of stop commands and total number of speech commands issued.

In order to obtain valid data, we give the participants enough time to train the voice recognition engine to ensure it can recognize their speech commands. Before the formal usability test, every participant trained at least 30 tasks to get complete familiarity with the speech-based control solution they would use.

Sears concluded that users had little difficulty accurately select large targets [5], therefore it is only meaningful to measure performance using realistic sized target. There are four sizes for Windows icons: 48 × 48, 32 × 32, 24 × 24, and 16 × 16 pixels[8]. The Windows toolbar displays two sizes for icons: 24 × 24 and 16 × 16 pixels. We chose 3 kinds of square targets measuring 16x16, 24x24 , and 32x32 pixels (referred to as D16,D24,D32). If our speech-based cursor system can work in such testing environment, it will provide an indication of its usefulness for normal windows applications. These three target sizes were tested separately. For each target size, the buttons are arranged the same way as depicted in Figure.2.

During the execution of every task, our test application recorded the number of "Stop" commands, total number of speech commands except "click", and the time to finish a task.

4.4 Hypotheses

We expect the delay-compensated speech-cursor control to have a significant impact on the user's performance. The user's performance is measured by total number of speech commands to finish a task, the selection time and number of "stop" commands used. The hypotheses for this experiment were:

H0a: The compensate cursor will not have a significant effect on the total number of speech commands and the time required to finish the test tasks compared to a standard speech controlled cursor.

H0b: The compensate cursor will have a significant effect on the total number of speech commands and the times required to finish the test tasks compared to a standard speech controlled cursor.

H1a: The target size will not have a significant effect on compensate cursor control.

H1b: The target size will have a significant effect on compensate cursor control.

(Note, as reported in [5], target size's effect is significant in normal speech-controlled cursor applications.).

4.5 Results

Means and standard deviations for the tasks including number of "stop" commands, total number of commands (including directional commands) and selection time using compensate and standard cursor control solutions are reported in Table 1.

Table 1. Means and standard deviations (in parentheses) of number of "Stop" commands , number of all voice commands, and selection time(in seconds) for tasks completed using two types of cursor controls and 3 types target sizes

	Compensate cursor			Normal cursor		
	Number of "stop"	Number of all commands	Selection time	Number of "stop"	Number of all commands	Selection time
D16	11.23	30.46	40.84	21	60.38	66.29
	(1.59)	(3.18)	(2.48)	(3.87)	(10.57)	(10.80)
D24	9.08	26.46	37.45	14.77	40.38	46.50
	(0.28)	(0.88)	(1.11)	(2.62)	(5.01)	(5.89)
D32	9	26	35.39	12.15	33.38	38.06
	(0)	(0)	(1.06)	(1.52)	(3.60)	(3.93)

For the total number of speech commands, a one-way analysis of variance (ANOVA) with repeated measures for target size was utilized to assess the effect of cursor type. As we expected, the type of cursor control has a significant effect on the total number of commands required to finish the task ($F (1, 76) = 60.12$, $p < 0.001$), and from figure 3, we can see the total number of commands increased a lot using the normal cursor control when the target size is reduced from D32 to D16, but for delay-compensated cursor control solution the number only increased a little.

For selection time, another ANOVA with repeated measures for target size was utilized to assess the effect of cursor type. The result indicated a significant effect for delay-compensated cursor control type ($F (1, 76) = 29.31$, $p < 0.001$). From figure.4, we can see that when the target size is reduced from D32 to D16, the selection time increased a lot using non-compensate solution, and the compensate solution only increased a little at the same time.

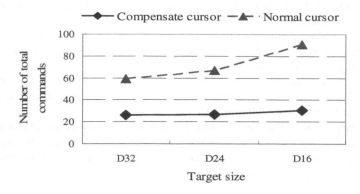

Fig. 3. Means of total commands using compensate and non-compensate solutions

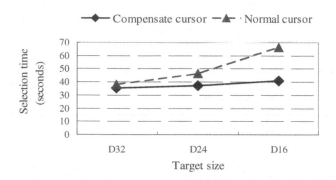

Fig. 4. Means of target selection time using compensate and non-compensate solutions

In addition, the target size has a significant effect on the on the total number required to finish the task for compensate type (F (2, 36) =21.59, p<0.001), the result also indicated that the target size has a significant effect on the selection time for compensate type (F (2, 36) =34.57, p<0.001). But from Fig.3 and Fig.4 can see that the delay-compensated approach fares better: that the size of the target doesn't have as much impact on delay-compensated approach than on normal approach.

H0b and H1b were supported by the data analysis.

5 Discussion

As expected, the delay-compensated cursor control solution provided significant benefits compared with the standard speech-based cursor control solution. When the target size is small the delay-compensated cursor control solution has even more advantage, the total number of commands is only the half of the that of non-compensated solution.

Though target size has a significant effect on the tasks, the effect is far less significant on delay-compensated cursor control solution compared with standard solution.

This is illustrated in Figure.3 and Figure.4, especially when the target size changed from D32 to D24, the target size has no significant effect on total number of commands (F (1,24)=3.6, p>0.05) for delay-compensated cursor control solution.

For D32 and D24 target sizes, the delay-compensated solution has recorded the least total number of speech commands: 26 times and stop number: 9 times..

We observed that out of the total time to finish the tasks (denoted as Selection Time), the time the cursor took to travel the distance between targets was significant. This time cursor moving time was also constant for different target sizes. Therefore, we considered the number of total speech commands as a more important performance measure that the Selection Time.

Finish the same task uses less time and fewer speech commands means the delay-compensated cursor control solution gives user more efficiency and confidence to use speech-based cursor control.

6 Future Work

Theoretically our solution can compensate the main delays associated with speech recognition, namely speaking time and processing delays. But this approach still can not compensate the reaction delays, for example, the delay introduced when the cursor moves into the target area but the user hasn't reacted immediately, just like a unfocused 100-meter dash athlete hesitates to start to run after the starting gun shot.

We plan to conduct additional future work to investigate the relationship between cursor speed and the reaction delays, and study the way to compensate the reaction delays, or the way to help user to reduce the reaction delays.

Another area for further study is around variable cursor speed. In our current implementation the cursor's speed is constant. We plan to add speed control to the application, so we can control the cursor to move faster when it needs to travel longer distances, and move slower for shorter distances or when it near the targets. We believe such variable cursor speed controls will improve usability and are more realistic.

7 Conclusion

We presented a new delay-compensated solution for speech-based cursor control, where the cursor movement is reversed at the end of the speech command recognition to compensate speech delay. We conducted preliminary usability tests to show that delay-compensated cursor control provides the expected benefits. The result is encouraging, compared with the normal speech-based cursor, our solution allows users to finish the same task faster and use fewer commands.

Using delay-compensated cursor control solution can help speech-based cursor control systems to overcome the limitation of accurately positioning control associated introduced by the recognition delay. At the same time the user can control the cursor by a natural way of using the voice.

Acknowledgements.   This material is based upon work supported by the Science Foundation of Technology Bureau of HuangShi, Hubei Province in P.R. China (Grant No: HZT [2007]40), Any opinions, findings and conclusions, or recommendations expressed in this material are those of the authors and do not necessarily reflect the views of Technology Bureau of HuangShi. We also supported by the plan for scientific and technological innovation team of excellent young and middle-aged in institute of high learning of Hubei Province in P.R. China (Grant No:T200806).

References

1. Olwal, A., Feiner, S.: Interaction techniques using prosodic features of speech and audio localization. In: IUI 2005: Proc. 10th Int. Conf. on Intelligent User Interfaces, pp. 284–286. ACM Press, New York (2005)
2. Harada, S., Landay, J.A., Malkin, J., Li, X., Bilmes, J.A.: The vocal joystick: evaluation of voice-based cursor control techniques. In: Proc. Assets 2006, pp. 197–204. ACM Press, New York (2006)
3. Dai, L., Goldman, R., Sears, A., Lozier, J.: Speech-based cursor control: a study of grid-based solutions. In: Proceedings of the 6th international ACM SIGACCESS conference on Computers and accessibility, vol. (77-78), pp. 94–101. ACM Press, New York (2004)
4. Igarashi, T., Hughes, J.F.: Voice as sound: using non-verbal voice input for interactive control. In: UIST 2001: Proceedings of the 14th annual ACM symposium on User interface software and technology, pp. 155–156. ACM Press, New York (2001)
5. Sears, A., Lin, M., Karimullah, A.S.: Speech-Based Cursor Control: Understanding the effects of target size, cursor speed, and command selection. Universal Access in the Information Society 2(1), 30–43 (2002)
6. Mihara, Y., Shibayama, E., Takahashi, S.: The migratory cursor: accurate speech-based cursor movement by moving multiple ghost cursors using non-verbal vocalizations. In: Assets 2005: Proceedings of the 7th international ACM SIGACCESS conference on Computers and accessibility, pp. 76–83. ACM Press, New York (2005)
7. Sporka, A.J., Kurniawan, S.H., Slavík, P.: Whistling user interface (U3I). In: User Interfaces for All, p. 472 (2004)
8. Windows User Experience Team Microsoft Corporation (July 2001). Creating Windows XP Icons, http://msdn.microsoft.com/en-us/library/ms997636.aspx (visited, July 2008)

Effectiveness of the Text Display in
Bilingual Presentation of JSL/JT
for Emergency Information

Shunichi Yonemura, Shin-ichiro Eitoku, and Kazuo Kamata

Hikarinooka Yokosuka-Shi Kanagawa 239-0847 Japan
yonemura.syunichi@lab.ntt.co.jp

Abstract. This paper describes an experiment on the message transmission effectiveness achieved by adding Japanese text (JT) to a Japanese sign language (JSL) video. The transmission efficiency of information and the understanding of information are quantitatively measured. The situation assumed is that information about a vehicle accident is to be displayed in a railroad carriage to deaf people. Three information methods are examined JT, JSL, and JT+JSL. We show that JT and JT+JSL yield high correct answer rates; JSL yields low rates. Furthermore, the subjects' impressions of the three methods show that they responded favorably to JT.

1 Introduction

The demand to the information presentation by a universal design is becoming high in recent years. One of the public space for which universal design is needed is a railroad vehicle. For example, when disasters such as an earthquake and a railroad accident occur, it is necessary to transmit urgent information to a passenger quickly and certainly. In order to achieve the reliable transmission of information to deaf people, the process of prompting the awareness to information presentation first and then assisting an understanding to information is required. It is effective to use tactile interactions, such as a vibrator, at the awareness achievement to information presentation. With support of information understanding, it has been said that what is necessary is just to perform information presentation by sign language. However, in an emergency, there is very little research on which information presentation method is suitable for deaf people.

This paper describes an experiment on the message transmission effectiveness achieved by adding Japanese text (JT) to a Japanese sign language (JSL) video. The transmission efficiency of information and the understanding of information are quantitatively measured. The situation assumed is that information about a vehicle accident is to be displayed in a railroad carriage to deaf people. Three information methods are examined JT, JSL, and JT+JSL. We show that JT and JT+JSL yield high correct answer rates; JSL yields low rates. Furthermore, the subjects' impressions of the three methods show that they responded favorably to JT.

J.A. Jacko (Ed.): Human-Computer Interaction, Part II, HCII 2009, LNCS 5611, pp. 761–769, 2009.
© Springer-Verlag Berlin Heidelberg 2009

2 Experiment

2.1 Subjects

The subjects were 20 men and women aged from 20 to 60. All had lost their hearing before 9 years old and used JSL in everyday life.

2.2 Procedure

The subject was guided in the room in which the experimental device was installed, and was given about the outline of an experiment task and the assumed situation. On the desk of a laboratory, the 21-inch display for an experiment (ProLite H540S / II-YAMA) was installed, and the experimenter took a seat on the chair next to the desk. The sizes of the display were 324mm long and 432mm wide, and resolution was vertical 1200dot and width 1600dot. The distance of a subject and a display was adjusted by about 50cm.

Fig. 1 shows the example of a message display used in the experiment task. The experiment challenged each subject with 30 unique messages; after reading each message, the subject was asked to answer a series of questions about the message's content. Ten messages were shown using each method and the combinations of message and display method were randomly selected.

Fig. 2 shows the example of a display of a reconfirmation test. In the reconfirmation test, the question sentence was displayed by both a Japanese text and sign language, and the choice for a reply was shown by only the Japanese text. In the message display screen, the text was displayed on the left-hand side of the screen, and sign

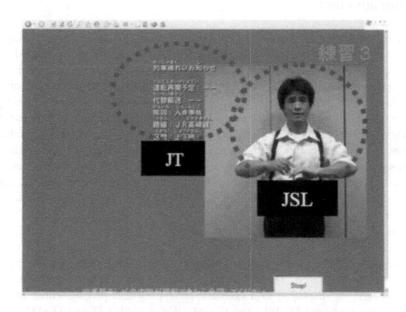

Fig. 1. An example of message display in the experiment

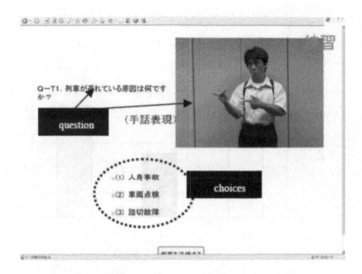

Fig. 2. An example of a display of a reconfirmation test

language video was displayed on right-hand side. The length of a text box is ten characters per line, and it was adjusted so that it might start a new line within a text box, in exceeding ten characters by one line. The Gothic character (27 points) was used for the font for a text display. Each subject read the message displayed on a liquid crystal display on a desk in a laboratory, and responded to the recognition test displayed immediately after that. In the experiment, the time taken to "read" the message and the percentage of correct answers to the questions were recorded. The subject was told to assume the situation where the train in which the subject was riding stopped suddenly and the message was shown on the display in the carriage. Before beginning the experiment, a list of the words used to make the messages was shown to the subject; they were explained until the subject understood them.

3 Results

3.1 Message Reading Time

Fig. 3 shows average message read time. 3. A vertical axis shows time (second), and a horizontal axis shows each message displaying method. Average message read time was 32.1 seconds (SD=7.0) with JSL, 13.0 seconds (SD=5.7) with JT, and 22.5 seconds (SD=10.8) with JT+JSL. The message read time was JT < JSL + JT < JSL. The difference was significant ($F(2, 57) = 27.65$, $p= 0.000 < 0.01$) at the 1% level as indicated by the ANOVA test. The result indicates that message reading is quickened up by text display in the JSL/JT bilingual presentation.

Message reading time

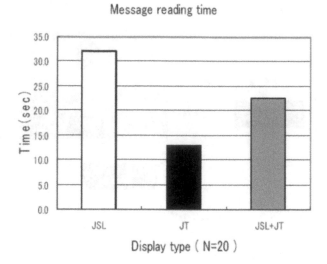

Display type (N=20)

Fig. 3. Message read time

3.2 Percentage of Correct Answers

Fig. 4 shows the percentage of correct answers to the recognition test questions. In Fig. 4, vertical axis is a percentage of correct answers, and horizontal axis is each message displaying method. As shown in Fig. 4, the correct answer rates were 0.79 (SD=0.14) for JSL, 0.88 (SD=0.08) for JT, and 0.89 (SD=0.12) for JT+JSL. The difference was significant ($F(2, 57) = 4.29$, p= 0.018<0.05) at the 5% level as indicated by the ANOVA test. A multiple comparison using the method of Tukey showed that there was a significant tendency with regard to JSL versus JT (p= 0.063>0.05, <0.1), and a significant difference at the level 5% between JSL and JT+JSL (p= 0.023<0.05). The results show that the using text display raised the level of message understanding.

3.3 Subjective Evaluation

The subjects' impressions of the three methods were collected at the end of the performance measurement using a questionnaire. The questionnaires consist of five items as following:

1. Accuracy: I think that a message is transmitted correctly.
2. Quickness: I think that a message is transmitted quickly.
3. Easy understanding: I think that it is easy to understand a message.
4. Conformity in an emergency: I think that this displaying method is suitable for an urgent message like this time.
5. Sense of security: I think that this display method has sense of security.

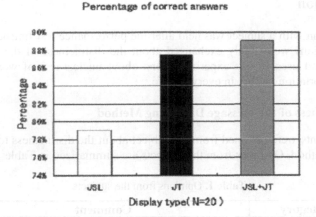

Fig. 4. Percentage of correct answers of the recognition test

Fig. 5 shows the results of the subjects' impressions of the three different methods. Vertical axis is a rating value, and horizontal axis is each questionnaire. In the figure, white stick express JSL, a black stick express JT, and the gray stick expresses JSL+JT, respectively. As shown in the figure, the JSL was scored remarkably low by all subjects in all questionnaire areas. As a result of performing a Kruskal Wallis test about each evaluation criteria, the significant difference of the 1% level was detected with all the questions (accuracy, quickness, understanding ease, conformity in an emergency, sense of security). This confirms that message presentation is improved by using text display.

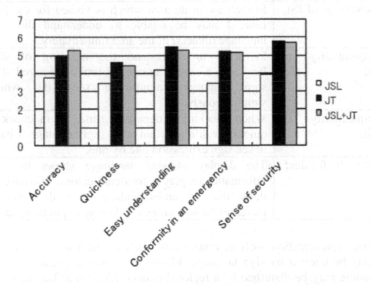

Fig. 5. Impression evaluation to the three message displaying methods

4 Discussion

Free discussion with a subject was held after the performance test finished. In the discussion, opinions were freely exchanged about the distinctness of the message displaying method used in this experiment, and about unclearness of words used in a public transportation facility in everyday life.

4.1 Distinctness of the Message Displaying Method

Some comments were obtained from the subject about the distinctness to the message displaying method. Opinions from the subjects are summarized in Table 1.

Table 1. Opinions from the subjects

Category	Comment
Expression of JSL	A name of the station, a name of a place, etc. may be unclear by sign language.
Expression of JSL	The translator who is appearing on sign language video seemed to have been hard to do sign language, in order that there might be no reaction of a partner (the camera was a conversation partner). Therefore, possibly there was an unclear portion by sign language expression. Reactions, such as a partner's expression, are required of the conversation in usual sign language. However, I think that it was the sign language different from usually since there was no reaction of a partner this time.
Expression of JSL	In the case of an area which is visited for the first time, I may be unable to understand the sign language (dialect) of the area immediately.
Sequentiality of JSL	In order to understand the meaning of sign language, a certain amount of time is required. The sign language cannot be seen the whole simultaneously.
Sequentiality of JSL	When checking a departure time, I can check it quickly with a text, but with sign language, I have to see sign expression one by one.
Symbolic for deaf	The display of sign language shows that an information display is for deaf persons. Moreover, I think that an understanding of a deaf person increases by sign language display in public space.

Numeric representation such as time, nouns such as the name of a place and a station may be unclear by sign language. Moreover, it was suggested that message understanding may be disturbed by a regional dialect. Since sign language was a sequential language on condition of a dialog with a partner, in an urgent scene which was assumed in this experiment, the subject felt a feeling of irritation, and impatience.

It was suggested from the experimental result that the text display in a Japanese text can cover the minus aspects of sign language especially in an emergency.

4.2 Difficult Japanese Words for a Deaf Person

Various opinions were obtained when a question was asked about "whether there are any difficult words when you use a public transportation facility usually." The words indicated to be difficult for understanding are special terms which a railroad contractor uses, and are not generally used in daily life. There were some subjects who claim that such words need the additional explanation for using transportation facilities.

4.3 Gaze Analysis of Message Reading

Fig. 6 shows an average gaze duration of message reading in JSL/JT bilingual presentation. Vertical axis is duration time, and horizontal axis is the degree of advance of reading which divided message reading time into three stages. As shown in Fig. 6, subject's gaze is distributed almost equally to both JSL area and JT area. This means that visual comparison of JSL and JT is frequently performed in every three stage. When a message cannot understand enough only by sign language, a subject is supposed to compensate an understanding with reference to a text. Since the information acquisition by glance is possible by text reading, they can read alternatively only the portion which was hard to understand by JSL.

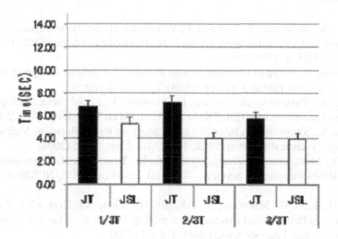

Fig. 6. Average gaze duration in message reading

5 Conclusion

An experiment was conducted on the effect of adding text to emergency messages displayed in sign language. The transmission efficiency of information and the understanding of information are quantitatively measured. The situation assumed is that information about a vehicle accident is to be displayed in a railroad carriage to deaf people. Three information methods are examined JT, JSL, and JT+JSL. We show that JT and JT+JSL yield high correct answer rates; JSL yields low rates. Furthermore, the subjects' impressions of the three methods show that they responded favorably to JT. The results confirm that adding the text equivalent of the emergency message is very effective in decreasing the time taken to capture the message and raising the level of understanding.

The text display was effective as a result of carrying out measurement of information reading performance, and impression evaluation. However, as a result of conducting gaze analysis of the information reading process by a subject, the subject's information reading strategy was proved to be a continued comparison of both sign language and a text. This result may have been influenced by that the message expression was restrictive and that the lexical level was controlled by presentation of the word list. Although there may be individual difference, comparison of sign language and a text certainly occurs in bilingual presentation of urgent information. Therefore, in presentation of the urgent information to deaf people, just presentation of text messages is insufficient, and it is required to use presentation of sign language together. Smooth cooperation of the awareness to information and information reading is the most important at the information presentation in an emergency. The navigation in an emergency by the cooperation of attention in a tactile sense and information reading should be improved by the further research.

References

1. Kamata, K., Shionome, T., Yuyama, I., Yamamoto, H.: Study on Universal Design for Information and Communication Services. In: Proceedings of the IEICE General Conference, vol. 2005, p. 202 (2005)
2. Nagashima, Y.: Support to elderly people and disabled persons – Support for hearing impaired. Journal of Human Interface Society 7(1), 33–40 (2005)
3. Kamata, K., Yamamoto, H., Yuyama, I., Shionome, T.: Focial Factors in Signed Language Communication Services. IEICE technical report, SITE 2005-2, pp. 7–12 (2005)
4. Kamata, K., Shionome, T., Inoue, T.: Basic Study on Public Relations Magazine in Signed Language. Technical report of IEICE, HCS 2004-3, pp. 11–16 (2004)
5. Yano, Y., Matsumoto, Y., Zhang, L., Kamata, K., Yamamoto, H.: Universalisation of Public Relations Information Services. Technical report of IEICE, HCS2005-57, pp. 13–16 (2006)
6. Naito, N., Kato, H., Murakami, Y., Ishihara, H.: Minagawa: Evaluation of the Visual Information in Remote Sign Language Interpreting System for a Lecture Scene. The Transaction of Human Interface Society 5(4), 475–482 (2003)
7. Igi, S., Watanabe, R., Lu, S.: Synthesis and Editing Tool for Japanese Sign Language Animation. The transactions of the IEICE D-I J84-D-I(6), 987–995 (2001)
8. Sakiyama, T., Oohira, E., Sagawa, H., Ooki, M., Ikeda, H.: A Generation Method for Real-Time Sign Language Animation. The transactions of the IEICE D-II J79-D-II (2), 182–190 (1996)
9. Abe, M., Sakou, H., Sagawa, H.: Sign Language Translation Based on Syntactic and Semantic Analysis. The transactions of the IEICE D-II J76-D-II(9), 2023–2030 (1993)

10. Kamata, K., Satoh, T., Yamamoto, H., Fischer, S.: Effect of Signing Rate on Temporal Structures in Japanese Sign Language Sentences. The journal of the Institute of Image Information and Television Engineers 56(5), 872–876 (2002)
11. Nishikawa, S., Takahashi, H., Kobayashi, M., Ishihara, Y., Shibata, K.: Real-Time Japanese Captioning System for the Hearing Impaired Persons. The transactions of the IEICE D-II J78-D-II(11), 1589–1597 (1995)
12. Monma, T., Sawamura, E., Fukushima, T., Maruyama, I., Ehara, T., Shirai, K.: Automatic Closed-Caption Production System on TV Programs for Hearing-Impaired People. The transactions of the IEICE D-II J84-D-II(6), 888–897 (2001)
13. JIS X8341-2: Guidelines for older persons and persons with disabilities – Information and communications equipment, software and services – Part 2: Information processing equipment, Japanese Standards Association (2004)
14. ISO 9241-12: 1998 Ergonomic requirements for office work with visual display terminals (VDTs) - Part 12: Presentation of information (1998)

Part VII

Visualisation, Images, and Pictures

Specifying the Representation of Non-geometric Information in 3D Virtual Environments

Kaveh Bazargan and Gilles Falquet

CUI - University of Geneva
7, route de Drize, CH-1227 Carouge, Switzerland
{kaveh.bazargan,gilles.falquet}@unige.ch

Abstract. In 3D virtual environments (3DVE), we need to know what an object looks like (i.e. geometric information) and what the object is, what are its properties and characteristics and how it relates to other objects (i.e. non-geometric information). Several interactive presentation techniques have been devised to incorporate non-geometric information into 3DVEs. The relevance of a technique depends on the context. Therefore, the choice of an appropriate representation technique cannot be done once for all and must be adapted to the context. In this paper, we first present a preliminary classification of representation techniques for non-geometric information in 3DVE. Then we propose a formalism, based on description logics, to describe the usability of a technique in a given context. We show how these descriptions can be processed to select appropriate techniques when automatically or semi-automatically generating a 3DVE.

Keywords: Information-rich virtual environments, 3D interaction techniques, Human computer interaction, Usability.

1 Introduction

3D virtual environments (3DVE) are 3D user interfaces that are intended to represent geometric objects, like buildings, roads, trees, engine parts, etc. In order to perform a task in 3DVE, a user generally needs more knowledge than what is represented by 3D objects. For instance, he or she needs to know not only what an object looks like, but also what the object is, what are its properties and characteristics and how an object relates to other objects. Therefore, in addition to 3D geometry, these applications must integrate non-geometric information in the virtual environment. These environments are frequently referred to as semantically enriched virtual environments. Many types of non-geometric information can appear in such environments: simple numeric values associated to 3D objects (e.g. the heat of a part); semantic relationships between objects (e.g. "this parking lot belongs to that building"); or abstract concepts (e.g. safety instructions for operating a device).

Several interactive presentation techniques have been devised to incorporate these types of information into 3DVE: Illustrative Shadows [1], Virtual PDA [2], Croquet 3D Windows [3] & Interactors [4], Interactive 2D Media Layers [5], Sidebar [6], 3D labels [7] and many more. Obviously, none of them is intrinsically better than the

J.A. Jacko (Ed.): Human-Computer Interaction, Part II, HCII 2009, LNCS 5611, pp. 773–782, 2009.

others in all situations. Indeed, the suitability of a technique depends on several factors such as the user profile, the current task the user is performing, the location in the 3D environment, or the characteristics of the information to display (size, semantic links to other information and so on). Thus, the choice of an appropriate representation technique cannot be done once for all; it must be constantly adapted to the context. Our research is limited to the usability study of selected abstract information representation techniques in 3DVE dedicated to performing two main tasks: *consulting information* and *visualising relations*.

When considering user interface (UI) generation this means that the UI designer must be provided with adequate tools to specify which representation techniques to use in which context. UI designers should be able to specify the adaptation of the presentation, for each kind of non-geometric information. In order to obtain usable interfaces, with enhanced usability, the UI designer should also be provided with ergonomic guidelines, as design patterns, to help her or him to select appropriate representation techniques. In this paper, we propose a model and language to specify the adaptive choice of representation techniques.

2   Interaction Techniques in 3D Virtual Environments

Interaction techniques provide the user with means to execute different types of task in 3D space. Therefore, interaction techniques are classified according to the tasks that they support. Bowman [8] proposed three basic interaction tasks in 3D user interfaces: the *object selection* and the *object manipulation* to handle 3D objects inside the 3D scene and the *navigation* to explore the 3D scene.

Existing 3D interaction techniques are divided into two groups: *Selection-Manipulation* and *Navigation*. 3D widgets [9] can be used to put controls on objects. Both *perceptual* information and *abstract* information are subjected to *selection* and *manipulation*. Examples of *perceptual* information are position, shape, color, texture etc. of 3D object. *Abstract information* is information that is not normally directly perceptible in the physical world. For example, information about the visual appearance or surface texture of a table is directly *perceptible*, while information about its date and place of manufacture is not (this information is thus *abstract*) [10]. Several selection and manipulation techniques have been created and several classifications [11] of interaction techniques have also been proposed.

Navigation in 3D environments is made of two components: the motor component and the decision-making component. In the literature, the motor component is called by different names such as *motion, locomotion, travel* or *viewpoint motion control* [8]. The decision-making component is usually known as *wayfinding*. The interaction techniques for navigation include travel techniques and way finding aids. Travel techniques support exploration and manoeuvring tasks while wayfinding aids are helpful for search tasks. Navigation is composed of *exploration, search* and *manoeuvering* tasks. Travel techniques such as physical movement, manual viewpoint manipulation, direction specification (steering), destination specification (target-based travel) and path specification (route planning) support the exploration and the manoeuvering tasks. Wayfinding aids such as map, artificial landmark [12] etc. support search tasks.

Other ways of interaction are related with tasks that involve issuing commands to the application in order to change system mode or activate some functionality. Techniques that support system control tasks in three-dimensions are graphical menus, voice commands, gestural interaction and virtual tools [13] with specific functions. A survey of existing 3D menus along with a taxonomy considering their hierarchical nature is provided in [14].

3 Representation Techniques for Non-geometric Information

In this section we present and classify selected techniques that have been devised and used to represent non-geometric information in 3DVE. This classification is based on the following criteria:

Layout space and placement. Polys [15] has revised the design space originally proposed in [10] to more accurately capture the nuances regarding where the abstract information is located and how it is associated to the perceptual information. Five types of layout spaces have been identified. In the *Object Space* layout, abstract information is always linked to the object it describes, even if the object is moved. The *World Space* layout is relative to a fixed area, region, or location in the environment. The *User Space* layout is relative to the user's location but not their viewing angle. The *Viewport Space* layout is related to the superimposed image plane where overlays and layers are located. In the *Display Space* layout space abstract visualizations are located outside the rendered view in some additional screen area.

Type of media. Integrating rich media types in 3DVE improves how users perceive, understand, and interact with visual representations of abstract information. Each presentation technique is designed to handle a specific type of media or a specific information structure. This can range from mere numbers and strings to sets textual information, multimedia documents, tables or graph structures.

Size of media or information density. To achieve usable results for users to understand and interpret the 3DVE, each technique must ensure that a fragment of abstract information is visible and unambiguously associated with an object located in the 3D scene. For instance, in dense or crowded scenes with a large number of annotation panels, users can be quickly overwhelmed or confused as annotations consume the visual space. This visibility issue sets a number of constraints on the size of the media. For instance, if the media is text, the size can range from a short label composed of few words to several paragraphs.

Our review of related work shows that labeling of 3DVE are well studied, but, representation techniques for integrating abstract information in 3DVE have not yet been systematically classified and studied. Table 1 provides a selected list of interactive representation techniques for non-geometric information in 3DVE.

Illustrative Shadows. [1] are projections onto a flat plane that enables schematic illustrations which are focused on specific information extraction tasks and facilitates the integration of generated textual information that leads to further meaning. Illustrative Shadows provide an intuitive visual link and a level of integration between interactive 3D graphics and supplemental 2D information displays that is hard to achieve with other concepts (see Figure 1).

Table 1. Selected list of interactive representation techniques for non-geometric information in 3DVE

Technique \ Attribute	Layout space	Type of media	Size of media	Typical application domain	Ref.
Illustrative Shadows	object & viewport space	short text, image	1 paragraph, small image	3D medical education & training	[1]
Virtual PDA	world space	multimedia	any size	3D science education	[2]
Croquet 3D Windows	user space	multimedia	any size	collaborative 3D platform	[3]
Croquet 3D Interactor	object space	text label, thumbnail	few words, small image	collaborative 3D platform	[4]
2D Media Layer	viewport space	multimedia	any size	virtual museum visit	[5]
Sidebar	display space	short text, list, thumbnail	few para-graphs, small image	interactive training & simulation	[6]
3D labels	object space	text label	few words	virtual city visit	[7]

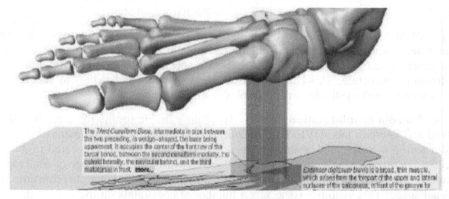

Fig. 1. Illustrative Shadows

Virtual PDAs. [2] are intended to display information not directly related to a particular object but more general information about the scene. For instance, one of the PDA's buttons can display a 2D map of the scene, while another button shows messages coming from an automated agent that sends suggestions to the scene visitor (see Figure 2).

Croquet 3D windows. [3] are general windows that live within the 3D scene. They can display any type of information: texts, graphs, spreadsheets, images, etc. They also serve as portals to jump to other worlds (scenes). In addition they are equipped with 3D

Fig. 2. 2D map displayed by a Virtual PDA

(a)	(b)

Fig. 3. Croquet 3D windows (a) and 3D buttons details (b)

buttons that sit on top of them. A particularly interesting feature is the downward arrow button that is intended to move the user from her current location to some place in front of the window, from where the window's content is easy to see. Thus, it saves the user the effort to walk to a suitable viewpoint (see Figure 3(a) and 3(b)).

Croquet 3D interactors [4] are similar to magic lenses that, when pointed at a particular object, reveal annotations attached to this object. Interactors act selectively, meaning that they reveal only annotations made through the same interactor. Thus an interactor is a kind of viewpoint related 3D generalization lens [16]. Interactors can be combined to simultaneously show annotations belonging to several viewpoints (see Figure 4).

The interactive 2D media layer technique [5] is a kind of 2D menu composed of elements in form of icons. When activated, by clicking, the 2D layer displays a panel, the elements of which are icons arranged in rows and columns. Clicking on an icon displays the related document (a image, a text, or a video). The 2D layer is not strongly connected to one scene object, but its location indicates that it contains information about the surrounding objects (see Figure 5).

Fig. 4. Croquet 3D interactors

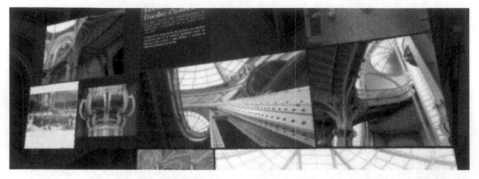

Fig. 5. Interactive 2D media layer

The sidebar technique [6] is designed to let the user interact with objects within the 3D scene and navigate from one component to another via textual description listed in a vertical sidebar menu (see Figure 6).

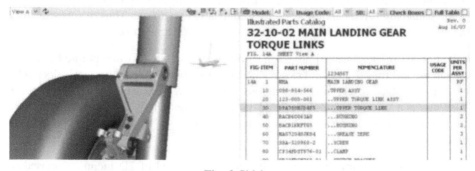

Fig. 6. Sidebar

The 3D labels technique [7] is based on the automated, dynamic placement of labels attached to objects of 3D scenes. These labels are seamlessly integrated into the 3D scene by textured polygons aligned to parameterized hulls, which generalize an object's geometry (see Figure 7).

Fig. 7. 3D labels

4 Model for the Formal Analysis of Representation Techniques

In order to explain our model, we concentrate on a single generic task that is acquiring information about an object or a part of the scene. In what follows we consider techniques for presenting information related to a focal object, which can be geometric or non-geometric. When analyzing the usability of a display technique several factors must be taken into account:
- the number and type of information objects to display
- the semantic relations to display and the types of the related objects
- the geometric context of the focus object

It is obvious that certain techniques are not appropriate for some type of information. For instance, a 3D label [7] can only be used to display relatively short texts or icons. It is certainly inappropriate for displaying a long text document. In addition, a label placed on or close to the referenced object cannot be read if it is surrounded by large objects.

Our goal is not only to describe the usability of the techniques but also to formally specify 3D interfaces and use these specifications to automatically or semi-automatically generate the interfaces. Thus we need a formal framework to express usability of the techniques. For this purpose we will use of an information model that is close to usual object-oriented models and we will express the above-defined factors in description logics [17].

4.1 Information Model

The information model we consider is a classes-property model. Each object of the semantically enriched 3D scene is an instance of a class. It may be linked to other objects through properties, which are binary relations. We distinguish two main categories of classes:

Geometric classes: these are classes of objects that have a geometric representation but also non-geometric properties (e.g. a room has a geometry but it may also have a capacity, a name, a temperature, etc.). The representation of a geometric object in a scene is given either by its geometry and position or by the geometry and position of its components.

Non-geometric (or abstract) classes: these are concepts that do not have a direct geometric representation in this environment (e.g. an emergency procedure or a building permit). Non-geometric classes include basic datatype classes (Integer, String, etc.), generic document classes such as Image, Sound, Movie, Text, or Multimedia_document, and **associations**. Associations (as in UML) serve to materialize semantic relations between geometric or non-geometric objects.

Display situation. A display situation is relative to a *focal object* and it is comprised of a *display set*, and a *geometric context*. The focal object is the geometric object is currently observing or analyzing. The display set is set of non-geometric objects that must be displayed to describe the focal object. These object may be simple data (integer, strings, …), documents (images, sounds, …), or semantic associations connecting the focal object to other objects. The geometric context is made of the scene objects that lie in some neighborhood of the focal object.

We propose to use description logics expressions to describe display situations. For this purpose we define the following logical vocabulary:

- the basic concepts are the classes of the information model (Geometric_object, Non_geometric_oject, Integer, String, Image, Association, …)
- the display role is intended to connect focal object to each object of the display set
- if an object to display is an association, the target role connects it to the object(s) it associates to the focus object. An association may also bear one or more labels (connected through the label role).
- there are roles corresponding to the usual geometric and topological relations such as (above, below, within-radius-*k*, …, proper-part, intersects, disjoint, …). These roles typically link the focus object to the objects that form its geometric context.

A display situation applies to a focal object if this object belongs to the concept defined by the situation expression. For example, the following expression defines a situation where all the objects to display are strings and the focal object is not below any geometric object.

S1 = **forall** display . String **and** (not **exists** below . Geometric_Object)

In this second example, we specify that the display set is made of associations to geometric objects that are not contained in any other geometric object

S2 = **forall** display . (Association **and forall** target (Geometric **and not exists** proper_part_of . Geometric_Object))

4.2 Description of Usability of a Technique and Technique Selection

A usability descriptor is a 4-tuple $<T, A, S, U>$ meaning that technique T, when used to perform task A in situation S has usability U. The value U would typically be obtained as the result of usability tests carried out with a panel of users.

For example, the tuple

UD1 = <Top3DLabel, "identify object", S1, high>

would represent the fact that the Top3DLabel (imaginary) technique has usability value high for the task "identify object" in situation S1 (defined here-above).

Technique selection. These usability descriptors can be used to select the most appropriate display technique in a 3D virtual environment. In fact, this selection problem reduces to subsumption and instance checking problems in description logics.

Given an object o in a 3DVE and a display set attached to o (through a display role), a usability descriptor $<T, A, S, U>$ applies to o if o is an instance of S, i.e. if o belongs to the situation described by the DL expression S.

If we have a set $\mathbf{U}$ of usability descriptors (obtained through usability tests), finding appropriate display techniques for performing task A on o amounts to find descriptors $d = <T, A, S, U>$ in $\mathbf{U}$ such that d applies to o and the usability U of d is maximal. Similarly, if V is a situation expression, it is possible to find the best techniques for all occurrences of V by finding the descriptors $<T, A, S, U>$ such that V is subsumed by S and U is maximal.

Since the subsumption and instance checking problems are computable, even in very expressive description logics, this provides an effective procedure for selecting display technique in 3DVE. This selection procedure can be employed as part of a process that automatically generates 3DVE from specifications. It can also be integrated in an interactive 3DVE design tool to help the designer choose appropriate techniques.

5 Conclusion and Perspectives

This paper presents the first steps toward the creation of a specification framework for semantically enriched 3DVE. These environments are characterized by the presence of non-geometric information connected to the geometric objects of the scene.

We have shown that there already exists a range of presentation techniques for non-geometric information, but they haven't been thoroughly studied in a usability perspective. In order to carry out such a study it is necessary to define characteristic factors such as the type and quantity of information relation to display.

We have proposed to use description logic expression to formally define these factors. Since reasoning in description logics is decidable (and sometimes tractable), the usability results are directly usable to automatically select the most appropriate display technique in a given context. And thus, to generate adaptive 3D interfaces.

Our ongoing research agenda includes work to acquire usability measure for the techniques presented in this paper and to build an ontology of presentation techniques coupled with a specification system.

References

1. Ritter, F., Sonnet, H., Hartmann, K., Strothotte, T.: Illustrative shadows: integrating 3D and 2D information displays. In: Proceedings of the 8th international Conference on intelligent User interfaces IUI 2003, pp. 166–173. ACM, New York (2003)
2. Science Alberta Foundation, http://www.wonderville.ca/
3. The Croquet Consortium, http://www.opencroquet.org/
4. Kadobayashi, R., Lombardi, J., McCahill, M.P., Stearns, H., Tanaka, K., Kay, A.: 3D Model Annotation from Multiple Viewpoints for Croquet. In: Proceedings of the 4th International C5 Conference, pp. 10–15. IEEE Computer Society, Washington (2006)

5. Interactive tour of the Grand Palais, http://www.grandpalais.fr/visite/fr/
6. Parallel Graphics. Cortona3D, http://www.cortona3d.com/try/demos.php
7. Maass, S., Döllner, J.: Seamless Integration of Labels into Interactive Virtual 3D Environments Using Parameterized Hulls. In: Proceedings of the 4th International Symposium on Computational Aesthetics in Graphics, Visualization, and Imaging, pp. 33–40. Eurographics Association, Lisbon (2008)
8. Bowman, D., Kruijff, E., LaViola, J., Mine, M., Poupyrev, I.: 3D User Interfaces: Theory and Practice. Addison Wesley, Reading (2004)
9. Dachselt, R., Hinz, M.: Three-dimensional widgets revisited - towards future standardization. In: Bowman, D., Froehlich, B., Kitamura, Y., Stuerzlinger, W. (eds.) New directions in 3D user interfaces, pp. 89–92. Shaker Verlag, Aachen (2005)
10. Bowman, D., North, C., Chen, J., Polys, N., Pyla, P., Yilmaz, U.: Information-Rich Virtual Environments: Theory, Tools, and Research Agenda. In: Proceedings of ACM Virtual Reality Software and Technology, Osaka, Japan (2003)
11. Poupyrev, I., Billinghurst, M., Weghorst, S., Ichikawa, T.: Go-Go Interaction Technique: Non-Linear Mapping for Direct Manipulation in VR. In: Proceedings of the ACM Symposium on User Interface Software and Technology (1996)
12. Parush, A., Berman, D.: Navigation and orientation in 3D user interfaces: the impact of navigation aids and landmarks. Int. J. Hum.-Comput. Stud. 61(3), 375–395 (2004)
13. Reyes-Lecuona, A., Diaz-Estrella, A.: New interaction paradigms in virtual environments. In: Electrotechnical Conference, MELECON 2006, pp. 449–452. IEEE, Los Alamitos (2006)
14. Dachselt, R., Hübner, A.: Three-dimensional menus: a survey and taxonomy. Computers and Graphics 31(1), 53–65 (2007)
15. Polys, N.F.: Display Techniques in Information-Rich Virtual Environments. Doctoral Thesis. UMI Order Number: AAI3241161. Virginia Polytechnic Institute & State University (2006)
16. Trapp, M., Glander, T., Buchholz, H., Döllner, J.: 3D Generalization Lenses for Interactive Focus + Context Visualization of Virtual City Models. In: Proceedings of the 2008 12th international Conference information Visualisation, vol. 00, IV, pp. 356–361. IEEE Computer Society, Washington (2008)
17. Borgida, A., Brachman, R.J.: Conceptual modeling with description logics. In: Baader, F., Calvanese, D., McGuinness, D.L., Nardi, D., Patel-Schneider, P.F. (eds.) The Description Logic Handbook: theory, Implementation, and Applications, pp. 349–372. Cambridge University Press, New York (2003)

Prompter "●" Based Creating Thinking Support Communication System That Allows Hand-Drawing

Li Jen Chen[1], Jun Ohya[1], Shunichi Yonemura[2], Sven Forstmann[1],
and Yukio Tokunaga[3]

[1] GITS Waseda University, 1-3-10 Nishiwaseda, Shinjuku-ku,
Tokyo, 135-8548, Japan
[2] NTT Cyber Solution Laboratories, 3-7-5, Toyosu, Koutou-ku,
Kanagawa, 239-0847, Japan
[3] Shibaura Institute of Technology, 1-1 Hikari-no-Oka, Yokosuka-shi,
Tokyo, 169-0051, Japan

Abstract. Research into creative thinking-support tools and communication is commonly focused on how to develop and share ideas between participants or with others. In this paper, we proposes a creative thinking support method that utilizes randomly generated visual prompter (black circle) image patterns (VP-patterns) and free hand-drawing and writing functions. Concepts and ideas of the research have been explained together with the development of the systems (CSP1 and CSP2). Experiments have been conducted in order to evaluate the potentials and effectiveness of the system. From the results, a tendency towards inspiring creative ideas by participants has been observed.

Keywords: Creative communication, visual stimuli, idea generation, creative thinking support, self-expression, learn and develop creative ability.

1   Introduction

Researchers and educators have shown great interest in the fields of creative processes, thinking-support methods and educations. There has been numerous research into creative thinking-support tools, creative process and communications (e.g. [1][2][3][4][5][6]). However, it is always difficult to investigate and evaluate those processes and methods since development of human creativity is a very complex activity (both consciously and unconsciously), and requires knowledge from several different domains, such as psychology, physiology, sociology and cognition computer science and linguistics etc. Past researches of the creative thinking-support methods and tools tended to focus on developing thought processes towards an existing idea or generate idea for certain groups or fields, instead of supporting the generation of ideas. In this paper, the authors try to approach creative thinking support from different point of views, and propose a creative thinking (idea generation and creativity education) support method that utilizes randomly generated visual prompter (black circle) image patterns (VP-patterns) and free hand-drawing and writing functions.

J.A. Jacko (Ed.): Human-Computer Interaction, Part II, HCII 2009, LNCS 5611, pp. 783–790, 2009.
© Springer-Verlag Berlin Heidelberg 2009

2 Background, Concept, Purpose of Research

The authors have been researching a visual tele-communication method between two
or more participants for inspiring ideas and supporting creative thinking processes.
More specifically, our first Communication System with Prompter (CSP1), as shown
in Fig 1, was built and analyzed [7]. The CSP1 randomly encloses VP-patterns within
the background frame of "Creation Window," as cognitive stimuli to participant in
order to encourage cognitive discovery. The participant then associates the idea with
other information, including personal experiences and knowledge, and creates the
"message" by inputting texts (character-type data) into the "Creation Window." During the creation process, the inspired ideas and associated information are combined
together and transferred into visual forms, which appear to the participant as visual
stimuli and lead to encourage cognitive discovery. Then, the participant sends the
"message" to the opponent participant via the network. The sent "message" can be a
source of stimuli for the ideas and creations for the opponent participant: i.e., the sent
"message" supports the opponent's creative thinking process as the presentational
interpretative stimuli.

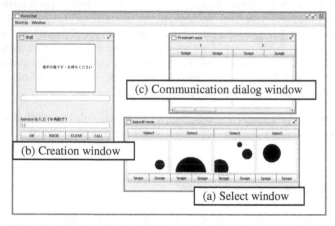

Fig. 1. Interface of Communication System with Prompter (CSP1)

Although the prototype CSP1 has shown a considerable tendency toward the inspiration of creative ideas by the participants, a main limitation of CSP1 is that it only
allows text input. If arbitrary hand-drawing input is also allowed, creative thinking
process might be more enhanced. To confirm this, we conducted paper based simulation, in which the participants can hand-draw arbitrary figures in a paper in which VP-
patterns are printed [8]. The simulation results suggested that we should develop our
second networked system, CSP2, which allows the participants' hand-drawing.

The authors actually built a CSP2 system. As shown in Fig 2a and 2b, CSP2 has
not only all the functions present in CSP1 but also handwriting and drawing functions. The CSP2 system is designed so that the participants can express their ideas,
inspirations and thoughts more easily, freely and rapidly than CSP1.

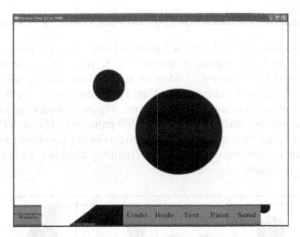

Fig. 2a. Paint module (Creation Window) interface of CSP2 (Functions are located on the bottom of the Creation Window, which allows user to "undo" and "Redo" the actions, create message in "Text" mode through hardware or software keyboards, or "Paint" mode with free hand writing or drawing. The "Send" allows user to send the message to sever and display in the "Conversation Window".)

Fig. 2b. Display module (Conversation Window) interface of CSP2 (User can enlarge the message by point on the message, as shown on the Fig 2b. The "Paint" on the left corner allows user to go back to "Paint module (Creation Window).)

The CSP2 system is implemented as a client-server application, where the client consists of three basic components, (1) Paint module (Creation Window), Fig 2a, which allows participant to input handwritings and drawings, (2) Conversation display module (Conversation Window), Fig 2b, which shows the recent messages, and (3) Network module, which handles the communication between participants. The paint module and the conversation display module are realized in two screens, where the participants can easily switch between the two at any time.

2.1 The Concept of Communication System with Visual "●" Prompter (CSP)

The research hint was inspired from a Japanese book, "Ehon-Zukuri training [9]", in English as "Picture book making Training" by S. Hasegawa, a comic writer. The CSP1 was inspired by Hasegawa's idea on using black circles which then further motivated and developed into a visual tele-communication method and system between two participants using the VP-patterns. Figure 3 shows examples of the VP-patterns (There are 50 different types of VP-patterns). Those VP-patterns were designed and analyzed through several experiments in our previous research and were selected in order to stimulate participants' creativity thinking without hindrance or interference the processes.

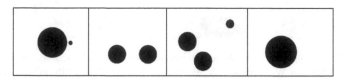

Fig. 3. Examples of VP-Patterns embedded within CSP1 and CSP2

2.2 Inspiration by Visual "●" Prompter Image Patterns

Visual expression usually interacts with viewers' cognitive processes to convey or deliver information or messages. The expression brings up viewers' attention to its individual properties and also stimulates and affects viewers' imaginary associations. Urban[10] has suggested two main groups of components of creativity, the cognitive, such as divergent thinking and doing, general knowledge and thinking base, and specific knowledge base and skills; the personality components, focusing and task commitment, motives and motivation, and openness and tolerance of ambiguity. In authors' previous research, we have researched and analyzed into the creative thinking support method and discovered an important and interesting feature: the "Fortuitous Effect." The "Fortuitous Effect" is based on the theory of surrealism[11], which suggests that a random, fortuitous prompt, while free of conscious control, can be a source of inspiration. This "Fortuitous Effect" results from the process of randomly generating VP-patterns within the "Creation Window" interface of the CSP2, those VP-patterns also can be seen as visual stimuli which encourage divergent thinking process and cognitively foster creative thinking processes.

Another important feature of the system is that the VP- pattern is polysemous and ambiguous; it can refer to any other objects or feelings, either abstract or concrete. As the stimuli mentioned in one of the first stimulation for design from the additional subtest of the Heidelberger Intelligenztest (HIT) [12][13], in the form of figural elements or fragments, were intentionally designed in an incomplete and irregular fashion in order to achieve maximum flexibility as an imperative for creativity. The circle shape and fragments of the circle shapes grouped together within the square frame gives the form of partially complete shapes and some incompletes position in an irregular fashion, which gives flexibility and suggestibility to trigger or evoke creative thinking. On the other hand, circle shape is the most common shape, which gives the advantage that users can see it as other things or objects, and the black color, when considered in another way, is a mixture of all colors, which allows user to see it as any color.

There are three key features in CSP2 which aims to stimulate, encourage, or provoke creative thinking process and idea generation:

1. Inspiration through the "Fortuitous Effect": The positions, sizes, and numbers of the VP- patterns were preset beforehand; therefore, users have to consider the contents together with image patterns' features and properties, which might stimulate imaginary associations and encourage divergent thinking which leads to affects on the expression, and go beyond the imaginations and thoughts of the users.

2. Inspiration through sketching: The definition for "sketch" in this paper is drawing processes by a participant through his or her own hands. While the participant sketches an unclear or abstract idea on paper, they are able to view the idea from third person points of view, which might rouse the imaginary or emotional associations and inspire new ideas [14].

3. Inspiration through the messages created by other users or opponents. Users can learn or imitate expressions from messages create by other users, which cannot only inspire new ideas in the users, but can also enrich users' expressions, and learn and develop creative abilities.

3   Experiment and Results and Discussion

3.1 Purpose of the Experiment

It is thought that the "Fortuitous Effect" and VP-patterns encourage and stimulate participants to gain inspiration, foster to generate new idea, provoke and establish creative and imaginative thinking, enrich self-expression, learn and develop creative ability while creating and receiving messages. Therefore, experiments of system with blank background of "Creation Window", Communication System with Blank background (CSB), and system with randomly VP-patterns, CSP2, have been conducted in order to compare the differences of how VP-patterns affect, influent and inspire participants.

3.2 Experimental Method

In the experiments, participants were divided into pairs; each pair participated in two experiments: Experiment CSB and Experiment CSP2. In each experiment, the instructions of the experiments were explained, and an imaginative question (eg. What if...) was given to the participants as a creative domain and focus in order to compare the results between different pairs. Experiment's procedures were as follow:

1. Participant A started to create message according to his/her thoughts or feelings about the imaginative question by hand-writing or drawing freely on the "Creation Window".

2. After receiving the "Message" from Participant A, Participant B started to create "Message" according to his/her thoughts or feelings toward the imaginative question or in response to Participant A's "Message".

3. The above processes repeated till participants completed ten (10) messages. (Approx. one (1) hour duration)

4. After each experiment, each participant was separately interviewed and questioned about his/her thoughts and feelings toward each messages created during the experiments.
5. Each participant has also been requested to give a degree to his own created messages, from zero (0) to ten (10), and also give evaluations to the opponent participant's messages.
6. Lastly, the pair of participants has been requested to talk or share their thoughts about those created "messages" to ensure and gain more understanding about each other's meanings, feelings and thoughts.

3.3 Experimental Results and Discussion

The results of Experiment CSB were mostly created by participant's own wills and thoughts, which strongly refer to the general information and knowledge or backgrounds of their knowledge and specialties. Although the results seem quite interesting and creative, but most of them were referring to what has been already imaged or created. The unconventionality of those messages was somehow missing. Some message results of Experiment CSB are shown as Fig 4 and Fig 5 below.

Fig. 4. And Fig 5. "Message" created by Participant using CSB (Fig. 5, Japanese words' translations are: left: "Future", right: "Can be seen")

The results of Experiment CSP2 were mostly created or started creation process from VP-patterns. Some of the messages have shown some tendencies that VP-patterns do encourage, influence or provoke towards creative thinking and inspirations. Although it is difficult to describe the results messages of CSP2 full of unconventionality, but some messages do shown tendency towards original, surrealistic and fictional imaginations. The followings are some examples of message results by using CSP2. Messages shown in Fig 6a and 6b have shown encourage towards cognitive discovery, where both messages were created by Participant A using the same VP-Pattern. While Participant A was creating message Fig 6b, Participant A has reinterpreted Fig 6a and seen Fig 6a as a visual stimuli and was inspired by Fig 6a, which then created Fig 6b using the same VP-Pattern. Messages shown in Fig 7a and 7b have shown tendency towards conceptual discovery, where Fig 7a was created by Participant A, and Fig 7b was created by Participant B after seen the Fig 7a. Obviously, Participant B was so inspired by Participant A's message (Fig 7a) that Participant B drew the same element (robot) as Participant A.

Fig. 5a. and Fig. 6b. "Messages" created by Participant A using same VP-patterns. (Fig. 6a, Japanese words' translations are: upper left: "huh!", upper right: "Justice□", middle: "I will stop the bomb.", and low right: "The bomb". Fig. 6b, Japanese words' translations are: upper: "Oh!!", middle: "robot", and lower right: " The bomb".)

Fig. 6. and Fig 8. "Messages" created by Participant A(Fig. 7) and Participant B(Fig. 8). (Fig. 7, Japanese words' translations are: upper: "AD 2208 Robot is breaking out", 2nd upper left "hello hello", 3 black circles: Earth, Venus and Mars, lower right: "What the robot in the justice side will do?". In Fig. 8, Japanese words' translations are: upper: "Oh!!", middle: "the robot", right: "the bomb".)

The interview data have shown that most participants refer themselves as conventional and not a creative type of person who merely draw, paint or involve in any sort of creative activities in their daily occasions, and were pretty surprised and amazed about the outcomes of their own creations. Participants' evaluations towards messages have shown interesting results that most participants evaluated his/her own creations higher than or equal to opponents' through all participated experiments. From the interview, we also understand that participants often started creation with an "unclear" idea or images, then while sketching the idea or imagine, the sketching somehow associates to other imaginations or ideas and form the final "message". This have proved that participants have been inspired through sketching, which allows participants to view the idea from third person points of view, and rouse the imaginary or emotional associations and inspire new ideas and creative thinking.

4 Conclusion

This paper has approached creative thinking support from different point of views and has proposed a new Communication System with Prompter, which allows the participants' hand-drawing. From the results of the experiments, the tendency towards cognitive discovery has been observed, and the encouragement towards conceptual discovery has been recognized. Influence and stimulation by VP-patterns, stimulations through sketching and influence by other's messages have also been approved. In order to obtain more solid conclusion, we should collect experimental data of a larger number of participants.

References

1. Hori, K.: Visualization of Mind. Journal of Visualization 19(72), 2–6 (1999)
2. Kawakita, J.: Keijeiho to Miraigaku. Tokyo Chuokoronsha, Tokyo (1996)
3. Sumi, Y.: Visual Displays as Stimuli to Cognitive Processes. Journal of Visualization 19(72), 17–22 (1999)
4. Suwa, M.: Visual Displays as Stimuli to Cognitive Processes. Journal of Visualization 19(72), 13–18 (1999)
5. Suwa, M.: The Act of Creation: A cognitive Coupling of External Representation, Dynamic Perception, the Construction of Self and Meta Cognitive Practice. Journal of Cognitive Studies 11(1), 26–36 (2004)
6. Tan, A.-G.: Creativity: A Handbook for Teachers. World Scientific Publishing Co. Pre. Ltd., USA (2007)
7. Chen, L.J., Harada, N., Yonemura, S., Ohya, J., Tokunaga, Y.: A study of a Computer Mediated Communication via the prompt system. In: IEEE International Conference on Multimedia Expo., Beijing (2007)
8. Chen, L.J., Yonemura, S., Ohya, J., Tokunaga, Y.: A study of a Computer Mediated Communication via the prompt system: Analysis of the affects on the stimulation of thought processes and the inspiration of creative ideas. In: IADIS Interfaces and Human Computer Interaction, Amsterdam (2008)
9. Hasegawa, S.: Ehon-Zukuri Training. Chikumashobo, Tokyo (1988)
10. Urban, K.K.: Different models in describing, exploring, explaining and nurturing creativity in society. European Journal for High Ability 6, 143–159 (1995)
11. Tythacott, L.: Surrealism and the exotic. Routledge, London (2003)
12. Kratzmeier, H.: Heidelberger Intelligenztest. HIT 1-2. Weinheim, Beltz (1977)
13. Urban, K.K.: Assessing Creativity: The Test for Creative Thinking – Drawing Production (TCT-DP). International Education Journal 6(2), 272–280 (2005)
14. Nakajima, Y.: Eizo no shinrigaku: maruchimedia no kiso. Tokyo Science co. (1996)

A Zoomable User Interface for Presenting Hierarchical Diagrams on Large Screens

C. Geiger[1], H. Reckter[2], R. Dumitrescu[3], S. Kahl[3], and J. Berssenbrügge[3]

[1] Düsseldorf University of Applied Sciences, Düsseldorf, Germany
geiger@fh-duesseldorf.de
[2] Harz University of Applied Sciences, Wernigerode, Germany
hreckter@hs-hsrz.de
[3] Heinz Nixdorf Institute / University Paderborn, Paderborn, Germany
{Roman.Dumitrescu,Sascha.Kahl,
Jan.Berssenbruegge}@hni.uni-paderborn.de

Abstract. We present the design, implementation and initial evaluation of a zoomable interface dedicated to present a large hierarchical design model of a complex mechatronic system. The large hierarchical structure of the model is illustrated by means of a visual notation and consists of over 800 elements. An efficient presentation of this complex model is realized by means of a zoomable user interface that is rendered on a large Virtual Reality wall with a high resolution (3860 x 2160). We assume that this visualization set-up combined with dedicated interaction techniques for selection and navigation reduces the cognitive workload of a passive audience and supports the understanding of complex hierarchical structures. To validate this assumption we have designed a small experiment that compares the traditional visualization techniques PowerPoint and paper sheets with this new presentation form.

1 Introduction

Zoomable User Interfaces (ZUIs) organize information in space and scale, and use zooming and panning as main interaction techniques. A number of projects already presented the successful application of ZUIs in domains like web browsing, story telling or image viewing. User studies examined navigation patterns and the usability of interaction techniques of zoomable user interfaces. These are mainly based on zooming and panning techniques because these interactions seem to be very intuitive for exploring complex information spaces. Colin Ware observed in [12] that users in real life typically make use of zooming by moving their bodies and thus their views mostly forward and backward and seldom sideward. Panning is mostly achieved by head rotation sideways and up/down. Thus, ZUIs seem to support an intuitive and reality-based interaction style. While significant research on this topic exists and first commercial / open-source applications have been released, most ZUIs concentrate on information visualization tasks following Shneiderman's InfoVis mantra „Overview, Zoom, Filter, Details on Demand". These tasks have been largely examined for users that actively explore the information space. On the other hand, there are fewer results how the design of ZUIs affects a passive audience. In this research project, we are mainly interested how a group of people can understand a complex information

J.A. Jacko (Ed.): Human-Computer Interaction, Part II, HCII 2009, LNCS 5611, pp. 791–800, 2009.

structure if it is presented by large hierarchical diagrams in a guided presentation. Our approach to visualize the huge information space is two-folded: a large screen set-up with a 4*HD resolution (3840x2160) and the use of zoomable interaction techniques for selection and navigation within the diagrams. In this paper we present the effect of dedicated zoomable interaction techniques on a large screen for the presentation of large hierarchical information spaces. We visualized a diagram comprising of very large number of elements used to model the design of an innovative railway system. This 2D-diagram was visualized on a Virtual Reality Power Wall and used during a presentation for a passive audience and a presenter who interacts with the diagram.

2 Zoomable Interfaces: Basics and Related Work

In 2000, Raskin proposed that "The zooming interface paradigm can replace the browser, the desktop metaphor, and the traditional operating system..." [8] . Over the past thirty years the WIMP paradigm dominated the 2D graphical user interface world. Today, the advent of next generation user interfaces employing large multi-screen, multi-touch, multi-view or mobile 2D interfaces calls for new emerging interface paradigms. Among them, the Zoomable User Interface (ZUI) approach, sometimes called multi-scale user interfaces, is of particular interest when the user needs to visualize large information spaces. ZUIs use the metaphor of an infinite two-dimensional plane to represent the user's workspace and the ability to view this plane at an infinite high level of detail. In practice, the metaphor's infiniteness is often re-stricted by technical and conceptual constraints limiting the implemented zoom and pan interactions techniques to a suitable degree of resolution. The user is able to change the view of her workspace with these techniques. Advanced interaction is provided by semantic zooming, which introduces different kinds of representation based on the level of zooming. For example zooming into a hierarchical information structure (e.g. a system model of a complete car) presents details of each subsystem (e.g. the motor engine). The first ZUI system, Pad, is credited to Perlin and Fox, who published their work in 1993 [6]. The Pad system embodied a single shared work-space, where any part could be visible at any time. Pad used semantic zooming as a novel concept and featured a magic lens metaphor, a concept that allows multiple focus points with different representations within a single application. Objects are positioned and scaled on a plane and the user navigates using zooming and panning. ZUIs since then use these techniques and propose that this approach is close to the user's cognitive abilities. Furnas and Bederson worked on formal aspects of multi-scale interfaces and developed a visualization technique called space-scale diagrams [5]. These represent a spatial world and its different magnifications and allow the direct visualization and analysis of important scale-related issues of user interfaces. Scale is explicitly described using the vertical axis of the diagram, thus an object is represented at different scales. Perlin and Meyer combined ZUIs with nested UI wid-gets and developed recursively nested user interfaces [7]. The major goal of this approach was to present an easy-to-navigate user interface by a layered structure of controls. With zoomable nested GUIs, widgets can be hierarchically arranged at arbi-trary depth. Bederson developed the most prominent ZUI framework approach, the Jazz toolkit [3]. It builds on ideas of PAD and its successor PAD++, and adds scene graph structure to simplify the design of non-trivial ZUIs. Jazz was written in Java and Swing and allowed embedding a ZUI component inside regular Java program code. This way, 2.5D-space applications could be created easily. A number of applications were built using Jazz and its successor Piccolo [10]. The image browser PhotoMesa provides the user with a zoomable view into a directory structure containing images [1]. Using the concept of treemaps, an automated screen space management was implemented. Bederson also developed CounterPoint, a presentation tool that enhances PowerPoint by new ZUI features like slide sorting and multiple paths. With CounterPoint it was possible to present one single presentation to different audiences or within different time constraints [9]. While many ZUI systems focus on domain specific applications, ORRIL is a framework that aids the design of ZUIs in general. Based on a set of requirements for ZUI design that is structured in four groups (display, data, interaction, results), ORRIL implements a component-based approach using objects, regions, relations and interface logic as basic building block types of a each ZUI. The authors presented an example that used ORRIL to design a ZUI for a media player[11]. ZUIs for representing abstract graph structures like UML charts have presented by Frisch et al [15]. They address the problem of visualizing the global structure of complex UML diagrams and the detailed relationships of individual UML elements and propose the usage of semantic zooming and other intuitive interactions techniques to ease the navigation between different diagrams. Beside a number of ZUI toolkits and dedicated ZUI applications some authors have studied the design and usability of zoomable interaction techniques in general. Hornbaek et al designed and evaluated navigation patterns and usability of ZUIs with and without overview [16]. Subjects preferred the overview interface and scored this significantly higher. On the other hand the work showed that ZUIs might eliminate the need for overviews in some cases. Recently, Jetter ct al have introduced the ZOIL user interface paradigm [14]. This approach is aimed at unifying all types of local and remote information objects with their functionality and their mutual relations in a single workspace. ZOIL, the zoomable object-oriented information landscape paradigm is based on five design principles: (1) object-oriented user interface, (2) Semantic Zooming, (3) Nested Information Visualization, (4) information space as information landscape, and nomadic cross-platform user interfaces. The presented UI paradigm was applied to personal information management tasks.

3 Application: System Design in Mechanical Engineering

Modern mechanical engineering products are affected by a high degree of information and communication technology. This is aptly expressed by the term "mechatronics" and denotes the symbiotic cooperation of mechanics, electronics, control engineering and software engineering to improve the behaviour of a technical system. Modern automobiles, machine tools or airplanes are prominent examples of mechatronic systems. The conceivable development of communication and information technology opens up new perspectives, which move far beyond current standards of mechatronics: today mechatronic systems have an inherent partial intelligence. The behaviour of these systems is characterized by the communication and cooperation of intelligent subsystems that can optimize themselves. This new feature enables advanced mechatronic systems that have the ability to react autonomously and flexibly on changing operation conditions [17]. The functionality of self-optimizing systems leads to an increased design complexity and requires an effective cooperation and communication between developers from different domains throughout the development process. Established design methodologies laid the foundation to meet these challenges, but need to be fundamentally extended and supported by domain-spanning methods and tools. The development of self-optimizing systems can be basically divided into two main phases: the domain-spanning conceptual design and the domain-specific "concretization". Within the conceptual design, the basic structure and the operation mode of the system are defined and the system is also structured into modules that form logical and functional units. These units can be independently developed, tested, maintained and, if later on necessary, exchanged. All results of the conceptual design are specified in the so-called "principal solution". Based upon the principle solution the subsequent domain-specific "concretization" is planned and realized. The term "concretization" describes the domain-specific design of the technical system. The aim of the concretization is the complete description of the system by using the construction structure and the component structure. This results in fairly complex system models. Communication and cooperation between all stakeholders involved is essential for a successful and efficient development of mechatronic and self-optimizing systems. Within the conceptual design phase domain-spanning development tasks and their results have to be visualized, so that developers can further elaborate the system design in a cooperative way. In the concretization phase, developers work independently from others on modules in different domains. Their specific development tasks need to be synchronized with those of other domains or modules. Therefore domain- and module-spanning coordination processes need to be defined and communicated between developers by means of appropriate visual tools.

We identified the following user tasks. **Overview and Details:** Developers have to synchronize their work with other activities in the development process and need to identify which process steps relate to others and which can be refined and executed independently. This requires a visual overview of the complete development process as well as a focus on specific and detailed information of individual development tasks and their results. **Search, Filter and Results**: The large number of process steps requires an efficient search mechanism. Arbitrary types of process elements should be selectable by filter operations and results should be represented and accessed efficiently. **Interactive Navigation and Presentation:** Communication between stakeholders is best realized by means of an interactive visualization of the complete system model. Users must be able to efficiently navigate through the complex model and present selected elements at an arbitrary level of detail. Moreover, it should be possible to present a sequence of user-defined views of the system model, for example to discuss a specific workflow.

We chose a complex application example by selecting the complete design model of an innovative railway prototype called "Neue Bahntechnik Paderborn/RailCab" (http://www-nbp.uni-paderborn.de). The system model defines an autonomous vehicle (RailCabs) that supplies transport for both passengers and cargo. RailCabs drive on demand and reduce energy by forming convoys pro-actively. The complete development process of the RailCab comprises of 850 development steps including about 900 development objects, e.g. kinematic models, dynamic models, controller models, state charts, list of requirements, test results etc.

4   Visualization Techniques

Previous visualizations of the railcab prototype model have been presented using a very large paper sheet (3.5m x 1.5 m) or a large PowerPoint presentation. Thus, this design model is a suitable test case for a zoomable user interface application. We defined a presentation use case for this scenario: A group of 7 to 20 people participates in a presentation meeting. The presenter illustrates central ideas of the system model by zooming and panning through the model at different levels of detail. After 10 minutes of presentation the audience can ask questions which the presenter answers interactively by navigating through the model. The complete model was too large to fit on the VR screen (4.7 x 2.4 m, see the next section about the VR set up). Therefore, we implemented a ZUI interface with zoom, pan, overview, and animated transitions to arbitrary model positions. Semantic zooming with different abstraction layers was used to cope with the complexity of the diagram during presentation. The implemented ZUI in figure 1 shows details of the selected diagram.

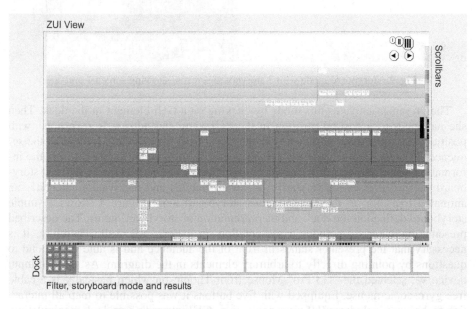

Fig. 1. ZUI and GUI of the presentation application

Coloured scrollbars indicate the maximum size in horizontal and vertical direction and provide an interactive overview. The position of the detailed ZUI view can be easily changed with classical zoom and pan operations as well as with the GUI scrollbars. The presenter can modify the diagram's level of abstraction by zooming in or out or by means of the GUI elements at the top right. Clicking on a diagram element will center it and focus at the selected element. A focus rectangle can alternatively be used to select and focus on a group of elements. Each interaction that results in a movement is automatically calculated with correct transitions between abstract levels and implements a semantic level of detail. Ease-In and Ease-Out at the beginning and end of each animation reduce the cognitive load of the audience when following fast movements through the diagram. The dock in the lower UI area can be switched off to focus only on the ZUI view. For filter operations the dock provides filter types at the lower left side. Clicking on an icon filters out all positions where the selected element type exists in the diagram. It is possible to pan through the results and select one of them. The ZUI view will automatically perform an animated transition to the selected point and adjust the zoom level. To further support the presenter we integrated a storyboard that allows creating and viewing a simplified linear tour through the diagram. There are two modes when this feature is used. The editor mode allows creating a sequence of positions that are visited in linear order.

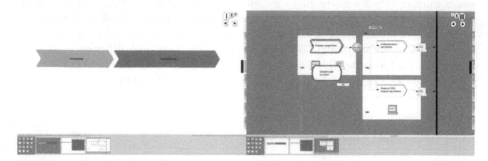

Fig. 2. Storyboard mode with 3 storyboard screens, showing screen 1 and 3

The presenter activates this mode by clicking on a GUI element in the dock. Then she navigates to a desired position in the ZUI view and adds a "screenshots" with position and zoom level parameters to the storyboard list or delete screens in the sequence. In presentation mode the presenter is able to navigate freely through the information space. However, if she wants to proceed with the previously defined storyboard she just presses the forward / backward buttons and the system calculates an animated transition to the next/previous storyboard item. Figure 4 shows a simple storyboard defined in the dock and its presentation of storyboard items. The described presentation scenario includes a presentation on a large VR wall. Therefore, it is necessary that the presenter stands in front of the audience and is able to respond to questions by pointing directly to arbitrary elements in the diagram. As suitable input device we selected the "Go Pro"-Mouse from Thompson which basically is a cable free gyroscopic mouse. Equipped with five buttons it was possible to map all interaction techniques including ZUI view navigation, GUI interaction or dock manipulation. The system model was created by mechatronic engineers using Microsoft Visio and dedicated shape palettes. The presentation engine imports the XML-based Visio file and automatically creates a suitable screen layout. A semantic level of detail is provided, i. e., system elements are rendered with three different levels of complexity (see figure 3). Based on the user-defined zoom level the presentation engine selects the appropriate abstraction details. The layout is computed in real-time and it is possible to switch to a 3D view that presented the diagram in a perspective view (see figure 4, right). For each diagram element it is possible to link a Full-HD resolution image, a HD movie file or a transition to another diagram element. The application was implemented in OpenGL and .net with C# as programming language.

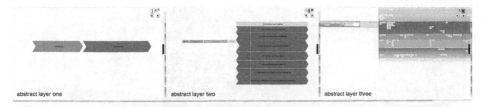

Fig. 3. The three abstract levels of the VR ZUI application

5 Information Visualization on a Virtual Reality Power Wall

We run our ZUI prototype on a high resolution multi-channel projection system consisting of 4 projection screens, where left, right, and floor projections provide a resolution of 1920 x 2160 pixel, and the center projection provides 3840 x 2160 pixel. The center screen has dimensions of 4.7 m by 2.64 m. The system can display images in mono or passive stereo. Floor, left, and right projection each use 4 Full HD beamers for display, while the center screen is fired by 2 special beamers that provide a resolution of 4 x Full HD each. This results in a resolution of roughly 20 million pixels in total for all projection screens. All 14 projectors are driven by in total 5 PCs. Each PC is connected to an Nvidia Quadro Plex graphics system that feeds 4 Full HD channels. So we have one PC-Quadro Plex unit for center left eye, center screen right eye, left screen, right screen, and floor projection. The high-resolution projection system is used to visualize engineering data like very complex 3D-CAD models. Due to the high resolution of the system, engineers can focus on small parts and sub components, while, at the same time, do not loose the overview of the whole assembly. This allows more efficient design review processes in product development. Other applications, e.g. a night driving simulation, provide a highly detailed visualisation of the lighting characteristics of the virtual prototypes of automotive headlights. Here, engineers can evaluate even small details in the illumination of the road ahead of a vehicle. More research-oriented applications focus on efficient randomized rendering techniques that are capable of displaying very large polygon datasets of up to 60 GB or 10^{14} triangles. To display the ZUI prototype, presented in this paper, we use the center projection screen of the system in monoscopic projection (see figure 6, left). To drive this screen, we use one PC, connected to one Quadro Plex systems, which fires the 4 segments (each in Full HD resolution) of the center screen. With 3840 x 2160 pixels that are projected onto the 4.7 m by 2.64 m center screen, we end up with a pixel size of 1.2 mm by 1.2 mm. For our projection screen dimensions this means, at 5 m viewing distance in the middle of the centre screen, the viewer's field of accurate colour perception covers the whole projection screen, while the human eye still is capable of resolving every pixel on the projection screen. There is enough room in front of the projection screen, to group a small number of users in front of the screen and provide optimal viewing for all.

The material of the projection screen itself provides a large viewing angle, which ensures a good colour and contrast reproduction even under less optimal viewing angles from viewing positions outside the sweet spot. So all users are capable of overlooking the whole projection area, while also being able to enjoy the full resolution

Fig. 4. User presenting the ZUI on a VR wall

the system provides for displaying graphical items within the ZUI. This is very important when it comes to reading small text or detecting small graphical pictograms within the ZUI. There is no need for the user to move closer to or away from the projection screen, in order to have a better view onto the screen. Interaction and navigation within the ZUI is done using a wireless gyro mouse. The user stands in front of the projection screen, acting as a demonstrator for the audience, and navigates through the hierarchical diagrams using the ZUI. When standing in the sweet spot, the audience has an optimal view onto the screen, so zooming-interaction is only needed to show more details within the hierarchical diagrams that are to be presented within our application context.

6   Test Design and Preliminary Evaluation Results

We designed a small experiment to validate our hypothesis that a zoomable user interface helps users to understand the presentation of a complex system model on a VR wall and reduces the cognitive effort. However, due to the prototypical state of our current system the preliminary results of the experiment should help to guide the iterative development process and validate the overall evaluation design rather than to confirm our hypothesis. The confirmative evaluation and analysis is left to future work. In the experiment, a presenter explained details of the complex railcab system model introduced in section 2. The presenter used three alternative visualizations. A large paper sheet model illustrated the complete system design. The sheet is 3.0m times 1.5m large and mounted on a wall. The second variant is a PowerPoint presentation that was successfully used during lectures and project meetings. The third variant is the ZUI presentation with the implemented interaction techniques described in previous sections. The audience, mechanical engineering students in their final year, is split up into six groups and each group is assigned one of the six possible visualization sequences. The presenter is always the same and explains the model using the available presentation techniques of each type of illustration. After each presentation students are asked to fill out a questionnaire. This includes a short test with questions about the system model and evaluates if the subjects have understood the technical content of presentation. Additionally, the students filled out a short qualitative review with questions on the suitability of each medium to present complex information, the presentation style of the teacher and their opinion about the best way to present the model. We selected 6 groups each with 2 students, (11m+1f), bachelor of mechanical engineering, aged between 23 and 35. The experiment was designed as "within groups"-experiment and each group participated in all three presentations but in a different order. After each presentation the subjects answered the qualitative test questions and filled out a qualitative review. Although not statistical significant, we observed that test results were better (= number of correct answers) if subjects participates earlier in the ZUI Power Wall presentation. The qualitative review showed that participants had some problems to follow the unusual, non-linear presentation with animated transitions. However, the ZUI Power Wall presentation was rated as best medium and the amount of provided detailed information was significantly larger than the other presentation variants. The presenter's style was equally rated as "good" in all treatments. From the preliminary results we significantly refined our test design and extended it. Summarizing, the preliminary results indicated that even with a reduced data set as used in this test, the new presentation medium VR wall performed similar to the well-known presentation forms of PowerPoint and paper sheet. Given the fact that the VR Wall is designed to present large information spaces with deep hierarchical structures, we expect to validate our hypothesis in future experiments.

7 Conclusion, Future Work, Acknowledgement

The use of a zoomable user interface and dedicated interaction techniques helped to present an overview of a complex system model, zoom to different detail levels with additional support for semantic abstraction and filter and retrieve interesting elements. A "storyboard"-mode allows to define a sequential presentation path through the complete model. The application has been implemented on a VR wall and runs efficiently in real-time. We have designed an experiment that should validate our hypothesis that ZUI interaction provides benefits for presenting complex hierarchical information. Future work will complete the prototypical implementation and conduct a full usability study to evaluate the hypothesis about the suitability of ZUIs for complex system design.

We thank Stefanie Müller, Brian Schimmel, Stefan Schulze and Peter Weinreich for their excellent work on the implementation of the ZUI project. This contribution was partially developed and published in the course of the Collaborative Research Centre 614 "Self-Optimizing Concepts and Structures in Mechanical Engineering" funded by the German Research Foundation (DFG) under grant number SFB 614. One author is supported by the International Graduate School of Dynamic Intelligent Systems.

References

1. Bederson, B.B.: PhotoMesa: A Zoomable Image Browser Using Quantum Treemaps and Bubblemaps. In: Proceedings of User Interface Software and Technology (UIST 2001), pp. 71–80. ACM Press, New York (2001)
2. Bederson, B.B., Hollan, J.D., Perlin, K., Meyer, J., Bacon, D., Furnas, G.W.: Pad++: A Zoomable Graphical Sketchpad for Exploring Alternate Interface Physics. Journal of Visual Languages and Computing 7, 3–31 (1996)
3. Bederson, B.B., Meyer, J., Good, L.: Jazz: An Extensible Zoomable User Interface Graphics Toolkit in Java. In: Proceedings of User Interface Software and Technology (UIST 2000), pp. 171–180. ACM Press, New York (2000)

4. Bier, E., Stone, M., Pier, K., Buxton, W., DeRose, T.: Toolglass and Magic Lenses:The See-Through Interface. In: Proceedings of Computer Graphics (SIGGRAPH 1993), pp. 73–80. ACM Press, New York (1993)
5. Furnas, G.W., Bederson, B.B.: Space-Scale Diagrams: Understanding Multiscale Interfaces. In: Proceedings of Human Factors in Computing Systems (CHI 1995), pp. 234–241. ACM Press, New York (1995)
6. Perlin, K., Fox, D.: Pad: An Alternative Approach to the Computer Interface. In: Proceedings of Computer Graphics (SIGGRAPH 1993). ACM Press, New York (1993)
7. Perlin, K., Meyer, J.: Nested User Interface Components. In: Proceedings of User Interface Software and Technology (UIST 1999), pp. 11–18. ACM Press, New York (1999)
8. Raskin, J.: The Humane Interface. In: New Directions for Designing Interactive Systems. Addison-Wesley, Reading (2000)
9. Good, L., Bederson, B.B.: Zoomable user interfaces as a medium for slide show presentations. In: IEEE Int. Symposium on Information Visualization, p. 1 (2002)
10. Bederson, B.B., Grosjean, J., Meyer, J.: Toolkit Design for Interactive Structured Graphics. IEEE Transactions on Software Engineering 30(8) (2004)
11. Bennet, M., Cummins, F.: ORRIL: A Simple Building Block Approach to Zoomable User Interfaces. In: 8th Conf. on Information Visualisation, IV (2004)
12. Ware, Colin: Information Visualization. In: Perception for Design. Morgan Kaufmann, San Francisco (2004)
13. Gundelsweiler, F., Memmel, T., Reiterer, H.: ZEUS - Zoomable Explorative User Interface for Searching and Object Presentation. In: HCI International, Beijing (2007)
14. Jetter, H.-C., König, W.A., Gerken, J., Reiterer, H.: ZOIL - A Cross-Platform User Interface Paradigm for Personal Information Management. In: PIM 2008, Personal Information Management, CHI 2008 Workshop, Florence, Italy (2008)
15. Frisch, M., Dachselt, R., Brückmann, T.: Towards seamless semantic zooming techniques for UML diagrams. In: Proceedings of the 4th ACM Symposium on Software Visuallization SoftVis 2008. ACM, New York (2008)
16. Hornbaek, K., Bederson, B.B., Plaisant, C.: Navigation Patterns and Usability of Zoomable User Interfaces with and without an Overview. ACM Transactions on Computer-Human Interaction 9(4) (2002)
17. Henkler, S., Hirsch, M., Kahl, S., Schmidt, A.: Development of Self-optimizing Systems: Domain-spanning and Domain-specific Models exemplified by an Air Gap Adjustment System for Autonomous Vehicles. In: ASME Int. Design Engineering Technical Conferences and Computers and Information in Engineering Conference, New York, USA, ASME, August 3-6 (2008)

Phorigami: A Photo Browser Based on Meta-categorization and Origami Visualization

Shuo-Hsiu Hsu[1], Pierre Cubaud[2], and Sylvie Jumpertz[1]

[1] Orange Labs, 4, rue de Clos Courtel BP91226,
35512 Cesson Sévigné Cedex, France
{shuohsiu.hsu,sylvie.jumpertz}@orange-ftgroup.com
[2] CNAM-CEDRIC, 55 rue du Turbigo, 75003 Paris, France
cubaud@cnam.fr

Abstract. Phorigami is a photo browser whose meta-interface visualizes photos by groups according to the analysis of photo contexts. At the core of Phorigami, we proposed a meta-categorization for photo regrouping. This categorization method encompasses the scope of current or expected recognition technologies. Two experiments are conducted by manual classification tasks to study the pertinence of proposed categorization method. We then outline our meta-interface by applying different interaction technique to feature each photo group.

Keywords: Categorization, digital photo collections, content management, interface design.

1 Introduction

For people in this age of digital explosion, building digital personal photo collections becomes indispensable due to the availability of image capturing devices and various free services on the internet. The drastic growth of digital photos either in public shared space or personal collections becomes a "black hole" from the viewpoint of management and has stressed the conventional, WIMP-based, management interfaces. Organizing the collections through categories or themes is an evident way of reducing/filtering the information flux to the user. A posteriori categorization via content analysis techniques is a very promising approach, since the production of metadata is time consuming and inefficient for large public applications. In the work of Rodden, two basic interface features are required to facilitate photo browsing [4]. The first feature is the task-free management technique such as clustering photos by chronological order that add-on camera metadata is utilized. The other feature is the capacity of presenting maximal content by the interface. In [5], low level content-based analysis is applied to present the result of image search which is clustered by similarity; however, photo clustering by similarity may not enhance the efficiency in browsing when users do not have a clear idea about the target in mind. *PhotoTOC* is integrated with time-based and content-based clustering to automatically organize digital photos according to their events [10]. The result of their experiment confirms positive feedback about using an automatic organization technique for the management of digital photo collection. Besides, *FotoFile* [9] and *EasyAlbum* [11] are applied with an annotation and content-based analysis technique to manage people by face recognition.

J.A. Jacko (Ed.): Human-Computer Interaction, Part II, HCII 2009, LNCS 5611, pp. 801–810, 2009.

The problem of establishing a relative viewpoint from unordered digital photos is investigated with content-based analysis in [7]. In addition, Jaimes et al. raise the issue of detecting non-identical duplicate photos in consumer photo collections [6]. They propose a content-based analysis algorithm and conduct an experiment by manual classification to observe the performance of proposed algorithm, but no concrete interface is addressed in their study.

Photoware based on content analysis techniques mostly focus on specifying queries and enhancing its performance, but their visualization and interaction techniques still rely on traditionnal, WIMP interface [1]. Some studies such as PhotoMesa [2], Photo tourism [8], Face Bubble [15] and the work of Porta [3] have tried to make up for this shortcoming by integrating unconventional visualization and interaction technique into the photo browser, however appropriate visualization and interaction techniques are still in search. Moreover, the conventional photo management applications for the end user are, to this day, only used to deal with a specific situation of use. The relevance of these specific situations with respect to "everyman" photo collection is rarely addressed in the literature.

2 A Meta-categorization for Everyman Photographs

To date, digital cameras provide more automatic "scene-adapted" functions to enhance photo quality and to facilitate shooting photos. For example, the camera interface in Sony Ericsson K800i provides the "shoot mode" and "scenes selection" as illustrated in Fig.1. The shoot mode offers four shooting statuses while six options are configured in scene selection. Apparently, such digital camera interfaces tend to automatically "categorize" digital photos by different contexts. It is to be noted that the metadata of digital photo has been explored to enhance the efficiency of photo retrieval, yet no interface has mentioned the use of this kind of metadata for photo management. We consider that the metadata from those camera modes can be useful for digital photo management and photos taken by different modes from digital cameras can be pre-categorized in the camera metadata. Such automatic categorization can potentially benefit the management of photo collections.

The previously presented camera modes reveal clues for digital photo management and such camera modes can be traced back form user's photo shooting behavior. Therefore we propose a meta-categorization method based on the analysis of the relation between the viewpoint of the photographer and the focused targets. The objective of categorization is to perform an automatic organization of photo contents and to highlight different contexts in the photo collection. This proposed method can

Fig. 1. Interface of Shoot Mode(SM) and Scenes Selection(SS) in Sony Ericsson K800i

potentially be implemented by the state of the art in content-based image analysis algorithm and camera metadata. Therefore, we analyze the photo shooting in terms of two parameters: the movement of the camera and the focused targets in two states (static and mobile). A similar idea of analyzing photos by camera and photographer has been used in Jaimes et al. [6] in terms of camera, scene and parameters of image to detect duplicate digital photos. In our definition, we add a third dimension called "groups" for targets, in order to include the user experience in taking group photos in a reunion. The Table 1 presents the distribution of parameters and associated dimensions.

In Table 1, six classifications are generated as A, B, C, D, E, F and we explain each classification with associated photo scenarios in Table 2. Type A refers to a scenario of a simple static view point where each single photo is focused on a static object from the same environment; for example, a user takes photos of several artworks on an exhibition and the scenario of "multi-view" in type B describes how the photographer changes the position to take a photo of each face of a static object, especially for buildings. Associated examples are illustrated in Fig. 2. Types C and D belong to the motion-capturing scenario where the photographer takes photos of a moving object. The difference between C and D depends on the status of the camera. An example of type C is presented in Fig. 3 where the photographer stays motionless to take photos of walking pedestrians with a bird's-eye view. Type D presents where the photographer moves the camera to trace an object in motion. Likewise, types E and F in Fig. 4 are the group photos in a reunion. It is to be noted that type E refers to photos of a static group while photos concerning the subject replacement [6] or changes in movement are classified as type F. In addition, the double-shot or multishot of a digital camera on the same target are what have caused the problems in managing digital photo collections [6]. In our categorization, such double-shot photos in the same context will be possibly categorized in type B, C, D, F while the intention of photographer is merely to take a "better" photo.

Table 1. Movement of camera and focused targets.

Target of photographer \ Camera	Fixed	Mobile
Fixed	A	B
Mobile	C	D
Groups(subject replacement)	E	F

Table 2. Classifications with associated contexts and interaction techniques

Type	Intention of Photographer	Photo Context	Interaction Technique
A	Simple static view	Panorama	Panoramic Presentation
B	Multi-view		
C	Motion capturing	Action	Animated Photo Presentation
D	Motion capturing		
E	Groups	Social Relation	Simple Folding Presentation
F	Groups in motion and subject replacement		

Fig. 2. Type A: Simple static view(left), Type B: Multi-view (right)

Fig. 3. Type C: Motion capturing with fixed camera (left) Type D: Motion capturing with mobile camera (right)

Fig. 4. Type E: Groups (left), Type F: Groups in motion(right)

3 Pilot Study and Findings

3.1 Objective and Procedure

We have conducted two experiments with manual classification to study the relevance of our meta-categorization for personal photo collections. These preliminary results will be used as the reference for implementing the future prototype. The first experiment (E1) aims to discover how many photos can actually be classified from different personal photo collections. Our hypothesis for E1 was that our proposed categorization method could achieve at least a 50% classification rate in each personal photo collection. We conducted a second experiment (E2) to study the variation of personal judgment in the classification result. In E2, ten participants use our method to classify the same photo album. The objective of the second experiment is not only to obtain an average error rate (variation rate) of manual classification but also to examine how subjects execute tasks in terms of personal judgment toward unknown photo albums.

The samples of photo collections are provided by volunteers and the criterion is to collect "everyman" photo album from novices and amateurs. Our sample collection contains twenty personal albums from ten female and ten male photographers, with an age range of 24-34. Participant profiles are university students, junior high school teachers, university administrative staff, engineers, marketing assistant and stewardesses. The size of volunteers' photo collections ranges from 1149 to 14297 digital photos. To lower the size of our collection samples, we choose photos according to the chronological order of their albums to construct a collection with around 1000 items. The final collection size of 20 volunteers ranges from 973 to 1333 photos. The core of our experiments is the manual classification task by participants in which they group photos by highlighting them on printed material according to our proposed method. The procedure of E1 is conducted by the same participant who manually classified 20 personal photo collections. Our participant ran tasks for two collections per day and each photo collection took around 2 hours for classification task. For E2, one photo collection with a size of 973 photos was chosen as our sample. We invited 10 volunteers to manually classify the sample collection. The description of our proposed categorization is presented before each classification task starts. A hard copy of Table 1 is offered to the participant during each task. The volunteers are Masters students from the Universities of Rennes, unlinked with the owners of our sample collection. The duration of the task in E2 is also around 2 hours.

3.2 Results

We counted the number of classified photos by their categories in each experiment and featured the results by pie charts and sequential bars. The pie charts in Fig. 5 present the distribution of each photo type by color and a category G in black is added to present the unclassified photos. The classification rate in E1 is 57% (std. dev. = 7.9%). In E2, the classification rate is 83% (std. dev = 1.3%). These results confirmed our hypothesis that our meta-categorization can classify more than 50% photos in "everyman" photo collection. The result of E1 for the 20 photo albums is illustrated in Fig. 6. Since the subjectivity of participants affects the classification tasks, the rate of E2 is higher than that of E1. Another reason to the high rate in E2 is that two participants thoroughly classified all the photos. For these two experiments, photos are generally unclassified when they are considered as belonging to different contexts. Where photographers may probably only take one photo of a scene, such a situation will result in unclassified photos. We also discovered that some photos belonging to one of the six photo types were not classified due to their wrong chronological order by the original photographer.

To study the variation of participants, we applied the method of matrix permutation [14] to analyze participants' classification flow in sequential bar chart (Fig. 7). The horizontal axis in the bar chart represents the number of photos ranging from 1 to 973 and the vertical axis represents each participant. We selected four overlap areas as illustrated in Fig. 8 and trace back to the associated photo contents. Firstly, the turns of classification flow are related to photo contents; which means that the more different themes the collection has, the more turns it will get. In our sample photo

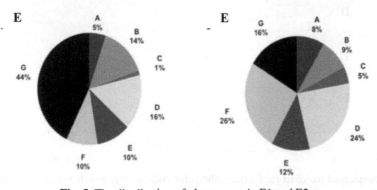

Fig. 5. The distribution of photo types in E1 and E2

collection, photos in areas A, B, C and D include fewer themes than those in other areas; thus participants can have a clear idea about the photo context. That is why participants have more consistency in classification of photos in these four areas. A contrasted classification result occurs in the area B. Some participants classify photos into category B while the result of most participants' is category D. Such contrast can be explained either as participants' errors or as the variation by the subjective judgment of participants. The sequential bar chart can also be used to study the frequency

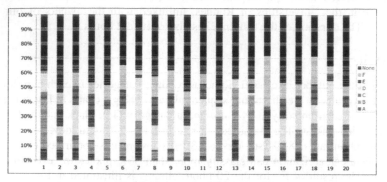

Fig. 6. The result of E1 in detail

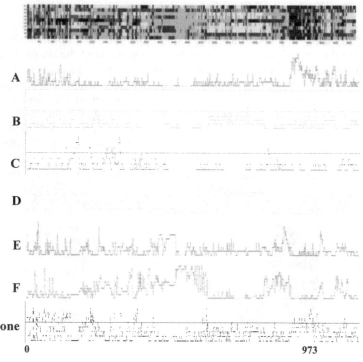

Fig. 7. Sequential bar chart for E2.(top), the color-coding corresponds to Fig.5 Plot chart for E2 (bottom)

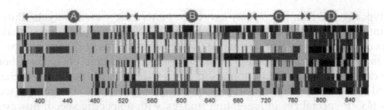

Fig. 8. Overlap areas in the sequential bar chart

of the same classification result for each photo. The classification result is visualized in Fig. 7 by seven plot charts according to the photo type. The axis Y of the plot chart represents the number of participants who have the same classification result for the same photo and the axis X represents the number of photos. We obtained a consistent result for the overlap areas of classification results both from the sequential bar chart and the plot chart. We found that the frequency of unclassified photos was more intensive during the first 120 photos where either participants have not yet got used to the classification method or photos are considered unclassified due to various photo themes. Various themes in the photo collection may probably burden the loading in participants' classification tasks. While participants are not the original photographer, they try to reconstruct the context for photos according to their own visual experiences. Participants who have no emotional feedback for the photos can merely categorize photos by visual content analysis and this is basically the same method that a computer algorithm uses for image analysis. Other participants, whose emotional feedback is triggered by photos, tend to establish the photo context more easily. One participant expressed that photos were much easier to classify if he had already been in the scene where the photographer was. In general, the subjectivity effects participants' decisions as to whether or not their emotional cues are triggered by photo contexts. Furthermore, the result also reveals that some participants have difficulties in detecting changes both in the movement of camera and targets; they can only deal with one factor in classification tasks.

4   Origami Visualization

To embody the characteristics of each photo category, we explore appropriate mappings of metaphor for our interaction techniques in terms of two directions: human experience in interacting with paper–like objects and the art of origami. The law of folding in origami art has been applied to solve problems in engineering, industrial design and scientific work [12]. The folding technique of origami art functions in order to represent an object via a minimal presentation. To achieve the maximal content visualization mentioned by Roden [4], the folding mechanism of origami benefits to minimize the space in visualizing a large collection. Similarly, a folding technique is proposed in the work of [16] to space folding for multi-focus interaction. Potentially, the space-saving of the folding technique may be an alternative when visualizing large multimedia contents on small screen devices [17]. In general, we outline our interface, Phorigami, with different origami visualization in Table 2.

For types A and B in Fig. 9, they express a panoramic view of targets; thus the potential interaction technique can be an interactive panoramic photo presentation such as an accordion-like folding technique which compresses the space of panoramic photos into a folding mode and presents an entire panoramic photo by a horizontal photo extension. For motion by frames in types C and D, the potential mechanism is supposed to manipulate motion frames like a GIF animation. The related technique such as RSVP specializes in presenting images with a specific speed; however, such preset browsing speed fails to be adapted in different contexts and may limit the user behavior in browsing images. Therefore, we propose a "manual" Rolodex technique that users can customize the browsing speed to render the original scenario of motion photos. In addition, a pile-like presentation is used to visualize types E and F.

An interface prototype is currently being developed using the Processing environment, in order to simulate the visualization and the interaction techniques. The three types of origami visualization will be implemented with tactile technology to enhance

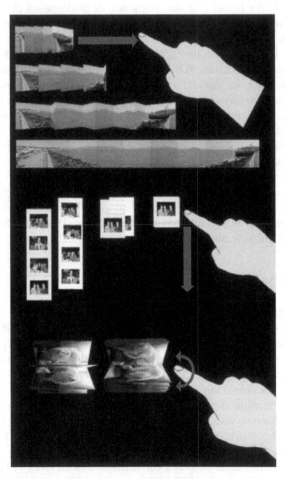

Fig. 9. Panoramic Presentation (top) Group photos (middle) Animated photo presentation (bottom)

Fig. 10. Visualization of 537 photos with Phorigami

the sense of manipulation toward virtual objects. Fig.10 shows a snapshot of Phorigami visualizing 561 photos (half of the E2 sample collection, as classified by one of the subjects). In this example, the screen space used by Phorigami is more than three times less than that used by a conventional thumbnail interface. In general, photo albums presented by Phorigami display rich visualization results; however, the usability of the different interaction techniques and related metaphor mapping still need to be examined.

5 Conclusion and Future Work

Photos as a medium convey contextual messages and render the original scenes by viewpoints of photographers. Defending the flood of digital photos necessitates a novel meta-interface whose visualization and interaction techniques are capable of dealing with varied photo types and embodying the characteristic of each category. While conventional interfaces focus on specifying queries for image retrieval, they fail to satisfy users by customizing functions for varied demand of photo works in browsing. Our proposed meta-categorization and meta-interface are a first step for dealing with every-man photo albums. Our future work will focus on conducting deeper user studies on comparing Phorigami with conventional thumbnail image browsers. The issue of serendipitous browsing will also be considered in the next work steps.

Acknowledgments. We would like to thank our participants at University of Rennes1 and Rennes2 for their participation in the experiment and thanks also goes to Chia-yi Shy, Yi-wen Chen, Po-Wei Huang, Hau-chen Wang, Irene Chen, Pieter-Jan Vandormael and other volunteers for the sharing of their digital photo albums.

References

1. Kirk, D., Sellen, A., Rother, C., Wood, K.R.: Understanding photowork. In: ACM CHI 2006, pp. 761–770 (2006)
2. Bederson, B.B.: PhotoMesa: a zoomable image browser using quantum treemaps and bubblemaps. In: ACM UIST 2001, pp. 71–80 (2001)

3. Porta, M.: Browsing large collections of images through unconventional visualization techniques. In: ACM AVI 2006, pp. 440–444 (2006)
4. Rodden, K.: How Do People Organise Their Photographs? In: BCS-IRSG Annual Colloquium on IR Research (1999)
5. Rodden, K., Basalaj, W., Sinclair, D., Wood, K.R.: Does organization by similarity assist image browsing ? In: ACM CHI 2001, pp. 190–197 (2001)
6. Jaimes, A., Chang, S.F., Loui, A.: Detection of non-identical duplicate consumer photographs. In: Pacific Rim conference on Multimedia, pp.16–20 (2003)
7. Schaffalitzky, F., Zisserman, A.: Multi-view Matching for Unordered Image Sets, or How Do I Organize My Holiday Snaps? In: Heyden, A., Sparr, G., Nielsen, M., Johansen, P. (eds.) ECCV 2002. LNCS, vol. 2350, pp. 414–431. Springer, Heidelberg (2002)
8. Snavely, N., Seitz, S.M., Szeliski, R.: Photo tourism: exploring photo collections in 3D. ACM Trans. Graph. 25(3), 835–846 (2006)
9. Kuchinsky, A., Pering, C., Creech, M.L., Freeze, D.F., Serra, B., Gwizdka, J.: FotoFile: A Consumer Multimedia Organization and Retrieval System. In: ACM CHI 1999, pp. 496–503 (1999)
10. Platt, J., Czerwinski, M., Field, B.: PhotoTOC: Automatic Clustering for Browsing Personal Photographs. In: Fourth IEEE Pacific Rim Conference on Multimedia, vol. 1, pp. 6–10 (2003)
11. Cui, J., Wen, F., Xiao, R., Tian, Y., Tang, X.: EasyAlbum: an interactive photo annotation system based on face clustering and re-ranking. In: ACM CHI 2007, pp. 367–376 (2007)
12. Robert Lang. Idea + Square = Origami,
    http://www.ted.com/index.php/talks/
    robert_lang_folds_way_new_origami.html
13. Cooper, K., Bruijn, O., Spence, R., Witkowski, M.: A comparison of static and moving presentation modes for image collections. In: ACM AVI 2006, pp. 381–388 (2006)
14. Bertin, J.: La graphique et le traitement graphique de l'information. Flammarion, Paris (1977)
15. Xiao, J., Zhang, T.: Face Bubble: photo browsing by faces. In: ACM AVI 2008, pp. 343–346 (2008)
16. Elmqvist, N., Henry, N., Riche, Y., Fekete, J.D.: Melange: space folding for multi-focus interaction. In: ACM CHI 2008, pp. 1333–1342 (2008)
17. Hsu, S.H., Jumpertz, S., Cubaud, P.: A tangible interface for browsing digital photo collections. In: ACM TEI 2008. pp. 31–32 (2008)

Sphere Anchored Map: A Visualization Technique for Bipartite Graphs in 3D

Takao Ito, Kazuo Misue, and Jiro Tanaka

Department of Computer Science, University of Tsukuba,
Tennodai, Tsukuba, 305-8577 Ibaraki, Japan
ito@iplab.cs.tsukuba.ac.jp,
{misue,jiro}@cs.tsukuba.ac.jp

Abstract. Circular anchored maps have been proposed as a drawing technique to acquire knowledge from bipartite graphs, where nodes in one set are arranged on a circumference. However, the readability decreases when large-scale graphs are drawn. To maintain the readability in drawing large-scale graphs, we developed "sphere anchored maps," in which nodes in one set are arranged on a sphere. We describe the layout method for sphere anchored maps and the results of our user study. The results of our study revealed that more clusters of free nodes can be found using sphere anchored maps than using circular anchored maps. Thus, our maps have high readability, particularly around anchors.

1 Introduction

Information with bipartite graph structures can be seen in various real-world areas, for example, customers and products, web pages and visitors, or papers and authors. This information often has a large-scale graph structure. Visualizing this information is an efficient method of analysis. However, conventional visualization techniques for bipartite graphs [1-5] do not provide enough readability for drawing large-scale graphs.

"Anchored maps [1,2]" have been proposed as an effective drawing technique to acquire the knowledge from bipartite graphs. Nodes in one set are called "anchors," and nodes in another set are called "free nodes" (They can be exchanged).Anchors are arranged on a circumference, and free nodes are arranged at suitable positions in relation to adjacent anchors. For convenience, we call this visualization technique "circular anchored maps (CAMs)" in this paper.

When large-scale graphs are drawn, the readability particularly around the anchors is low on the CAMs (Fig. 1). We think that arranging anchors on the circumference causes low readability in the CAMs. Thus, to increase the readability, we extend them by arranging anchors on a sphere that has 2D layout space while keeping their features. We call this visualization technique "sphere anchored maps (SAMs)."

In this paper, we describe the features of SAMs and a layout method developed to satisfy their aesthetic criteria. Additionally, we show the results of a user study to evaluate the readability around anchors.

J.A. Jacko (Ed.): Human-Computer Interaction, Part II, HCII 2009, LNCS 5611, pp. 811–820, 2009.
© Springer-Verlag Berlin Heidelberg 2009

2 Related Work

Zheng et al. [3] proposed two layout models for bipartite graphs and proved theorems of edge crossing for these models. Giacomo et al. [4] proposed drawing bipartite graphs on two curves so that the edges do not cross. Newton et al. [5] proposed new heuristics for two-sided bipartite graph drawing. We describe a new visualization technique for large-scale bipartite graphs to maintain high readability.

Related work on 3D visualization includes a study in which Munzner et al. [6] developed H3, which lays out trees on 3D hyperbolic space with high readability. Ho et al. [7] developed drawing techniques that lay out clustered graphs in which each cluster is arranged on a 2D plane and in which a parent graph of clusters is laid out in 3D. We developed a drawing technique for bipartite graphs in 3D.

3 Circular Anchored Maps and Existing Problems

CAMs have been proposed as a drawing technique of anchored maps for bipartite graphs [1]. CAMs arrange anchors on the circumference at equal intervals and free nodes by spring embedding [8]. CAMs have the following features:

- **The positions of free nodes are understandable in relation to the anchors.** The anchors are fixed on the circumference at equal intervals, which produces an effect like the coordinate system.
- **Clusters of free nodes can be discerned based on their relation to the anchors.** The free nodes are divided into clusters by the connective relationships with adjacent anchors. This illustrates what kinds of clusters exist and which anchor subset is responsible for constructing each cluster.

The readability of CAMs is low when large-scale graphs are drawn. Fig. 1 shows an example where a graph that has 52 anchors and 1137 free nodes was drawn as a CAM.

We focus particularly on problems where the readability around anchors is low. Anchors are arranged in CAMs on the circumference that has only 1D layout space. Thus, only two anchors can be adjacent to a certain anchor spatially, and the anchors'

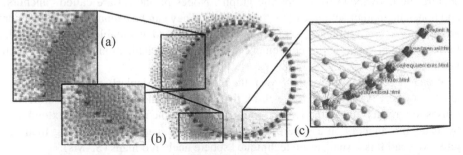

Fig. 1. Drawn example of circular anchored map (CAM). Anchors are represented by rectangles (cubes). Free nodes are represented by circles (spheres).

arrangement tends to become a straight line as the number of anchors increases. Therefore, free nodes adjacent to anchors arranged closely are arranged on the circumference, and edges connected to these nodes become difficult to read (Fig. 1(c)). Additionally, clusters of free nodes around anchors are often mixed with other clusters (Fig. 1 (a) and (b)).

4 Sphere Anchored Maps

We think that arranging anchors on a circumference that has a 1D layout space causes these problems. Thus, we arrange anchors on a sphere that has 2D layout space and free nodes in 3D space. In SAMs, anchors are arranged on the sphere, free nodes do not receive the restriction of the position, and edges are drawn using straight lines.

An example of a SAM is shown in Fig. 2. The same graph that is in Fig. 1 is drawn. This graph represents the relationships between a web page and visitors. Anchors drawn by cubes mean web pages, and free nodes drawn by spheres mean visitors. The readability around anchors increases by extending anchors' layout space to 2D. Mixtures among clusters of free nodes are not caused because the layout space broadens. For example, Fig. 2 (b) has three large clusters of free nodes that are mixed in Fig. 1. It indicates that many visitors accessed pages A, B, and C, pages A and B, and pages A and C, but few visitors accessed pages B and C. Additionally, we can see that a cluster of free nodes in the center of Fig. 2 (c) connects to six anchors. We know that visitors that accessed one of the pages represented by these anchors tend to access others.

The occlusion of nodes in 3D visualization is a problem. We address this problem by rotating the drawn graph [9] based on the research by Ware et al. [10]. Sample videos are available from the first author's web site[1].

We use the following aesthetic criteria to develop layout methods for SAMs. These aesthetic criteria are extensions of aesthetic criteria of CAMs [1] and are important to keep their features.

- **(R1)** Nodes adjacent to each other are laid out as closely as possible.
- **(R2)** Anchors adjacent to common free nodes are laid out as closely as possible.
- **(R3)** Anchors are distributed on the sphere as evenly as possible.

We describe formal expressions for R1 and R2 because these are used later in this paper. Suppose that A is the set of anchors, F is the set of free nodes, $P(n)$ is a 3D vector expressing a position of node n, and $A(f)$ is the set of anchors adjacent to free node f, that is, $A(f) = \{a \in A | (a, f) \in E\}$. Here, we assume that $A(f) = \{a_1, a_2, a_3, ..., a_m\}$. Moreover, suppose that r is the radius of the sphere, and $d(n_1, n_2)$ is a Euclid distance between node n_1 and node n_2.

- R1 is to minimize $l(E)$ expressed by:

$$l(E) = \sum_{(a,f) \in E} d(a, f)$$ (1)

---

[1] http://www.iplab.cs.tsukuba.ac.jp/~ito/

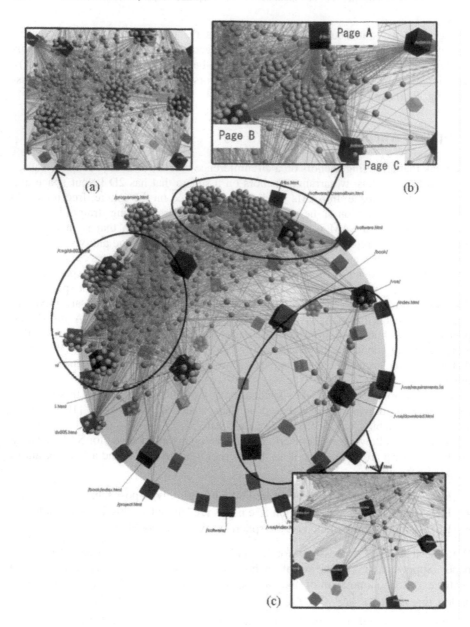

Fig. 2. Drawn example of sphere anchored map (SAM). In this figure, (a), (b), and (c) correspond with (a), (b), and (c) in Fig. 1.

- R2 is to minimize $g(F)$ expressed by:

$$g(F) = \sum_{f \in F} \left(\sum_{a_i, a_j \in A(f), i < j} \cos^{-1}\left(\frac{P(a_i) \bullet P(a_j)}{r^2} \right) \right) \tag{2}$$

In exp(1), $l(E)$ indicates the total length of the edges. In exp(2), $g(F)$ indicates the total length of the arc between anchors adjacent to the common free node. If the value of $g(F)$ is small, the anchors adjacent to the common free node are laid out closely.

5 Layout Method

The layout method of anchors is important because the layout of anchors influences the readability of SAMs. In CAMs or two-sided graphs [5], we only consider the order of nodes. CAMs decide the order of anchors on the circumference (in other words, on the vertices of a regular polygon) by running an algorithm. However, the layout space of anchors in SAM is 2D. Therefore, deciding the position of the anchors is difficult.

We extended the *layout-explore algorithm* used in CAMs, in which the map is laid out according to the following three steps.

1. Candidate positions for anchors to satisfy aesthetic criterion R3 are obtained by considering anchors to be electrons and by simulating their behavior on the sphere.
2. The layout of anchors to satisfy aesthetic criteria R1 and R2 are explored using the layout-explore algorithm.
3. Free nodes are arranged using force-directed placement.

5.1 Candidate Positions for Anchors

In the first step, candidate positions for anchors to satisfy aesthetic criterion R3 are obtained. It is a hard problem called the "sphere packing problem [11,12]." However, our purpose was not to resolve this problem but to acquire a high-readability layout. Thus, we obtained candidate positions for anchors by simulating "the behavior of electrons on the sphere."

5.2 Layout-Explore Algorithm

In the second step, the layout-explore algorithm used in the CAMs computes a quasi-optimal order of anchors for the *penalty* [1]. This algorithm repeatedly chooses two anchors and exchanges them if the penalty decreases by doing so. It starts the comparison by choosing anchors far from each other, then shortens the distance between compared anchors, and finally compares adjoined anchors at the end. If the penalty does not decrease at a certain distance, the distance is cut in half. The algorithm continues until the distance becomes zero.

In the layout-explore algorithm used in the SAMs, the order near to a certain anchor is used as the distance.

We use $l(E)$ or $g(F)$ as the penalty. However, $l(E)$ can be evaluated only after the position of free nodes has been decided. Therefore, we approximate the position of free nodes using the barycenter of adjacent anchors.

The layout-explore algorithm used in the SAMs is shown in Algorithm 1. Here, A is a set of anchors, *currentPenalty* is the function that returns the value of the current penalty, and *NearFromA(a,d)* is the function that returns the nearest d-th anchor from anchor a.

Algorithm 1

```
 1 : double p0 = currentPenalty;
 2 : int d = |A| - 1;
 3 : while (d > 0) {
 4 :     boolean c = false;
 5 :     do {
 6 :         c = false;
 7 :         for (int i = 0; i < |A|; i++) {
 8 :             Swap A[i] for NearFromA(A[i],d);
 9 :             double p1 = currentPenalty;
10 :             if (p1 < p0) {
11 :                 p0 = p1; c = true;
12 :             } else {
13 :                 Swap A[i] for earFromA(A[i],d);
14 :             }
15 :         }
16 :     } while (c);
17 :     d = d / 2;
18 : }
```

Algorithm 1 will definitely stop at some point because the penalty cannot keep decreasing infinitely, that is, the patterns of the layout of the anchors are finite.

5.3 Efficacy of our Layout Method

The efficacy of our layout method is illustrated in Fig. 3. Fig. 3(a) shows a state where the anchor's arrangement candidate has been obtained (anchors are arranged at random). Fig. 3(b) shows the results of the layout-explore algorithm. In the random layout, most of the free nodes are arranged around the center of the sphere. As a result, free nodes that have no relationship with each other gather in the central part of the sphere. Fig. 3(b), wherein free nodes are arranged around the surface of the sphere, is an overview of the graph.

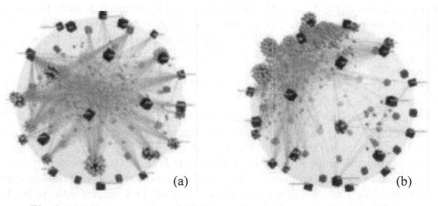

(a)   (b)

Fig. 3. (a) laid out at random. (b) laid out using the layout-explorer algorithm.

6 User Study

We implemented our technique in C#+Managed DirectX and performed a user study to evaluate the readability of the SAMs, particularly around anchors. The study included six participants.

We asked the participants to perform tasks using both a SAM and a CAM. A cluster of free nodes (F-cluster) is a set of free nodes that connect to the same anchors. In this task, participants looked for all "target F-clusters," which constituted five or more free nodes and were connected to two or more anchors, from a graph in a limited amount of time. When the participants found a F-cluster, they selected one of the free nodes in the F-cluster by right-clicking it, thereby highlighting the F-cluster. Selected (highlighted) F-clusters could be unselected by right-clicking them again. Participants translated anchored maps by middle-dragging, rotating them by right-dragging, zooming in/out using the mouse wheel, and controlling the edge opacity, size of anchors, and size of the free nodes using the left panel. The number of target F-clusters and selected F-clusters and the time remaining were shown at the upper left of the screen. When the number of target F-clusters equaled the number of selected F-clusters, a beep sounded. The time given was limited to $7 \times$ the number of target F-clusters in seconds. After the participants found all the target F-clusters, they clicked a button, and the task was over. Fig. 4 shows screenshots of the test program.

Participants performed two tasks using the CAM and two tasks using the SAM as training. Then, they performed ten tasks each using the CAM and SAM. Three participants performed tasks using the previous CAM, and the others performed tasks using the previous SAM. The same graphs were used in both anchored maps.

Ten bipartite graphs used in the ten tasks were generated using the following procedure.

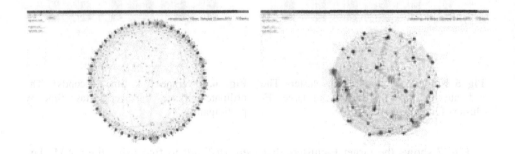

Fig. 4. Screenshots of test program. The left image shows the test of the CAM, and the right image shows the test of the SAM. F-Clusters highlighted in green are F-clusters selected by the participants. The participants controlled the edge opacity, size of the anchors, and the size of the free nodes using the left panel.

1. Generate 50 nodes laid out as anchors.
2. All anchors connect to 16 anchors through a node laid out as a free node. All anchors are 16 degrees, and all free nodes are 2 degrees.
3. Edges are replaced from 30 to 70 times at random.
4. From 30 to 60 free nodes are added at random. They connect to two anchors.
5. From 20 to 80 edges are added at random.
6. From 10 to 25 F-clusters are added at random. They have from 5 to 10 free nodes.
7. From 3 to 10 F-clusters are added at random. They have from 10 to 30 free nodes.
8. From 3 to 10 F-clusters are added at random. They have from 2 to 3 free nodes.

The generated graphs had 50 anchors, about 650 free nodes, about 1400 edges, and about 17 target F-clusters. F-clusters in these graphs tended to be arranged around anchors. The order of tasks was random.

6.1 Results

Fig. 5 shows the number of target F-clusters found in the time provided. The ten tasks had a total of 165 target F-clusters. While 160.8 target F-clusters were found using the CAM, 164.8 target F-clusters were found using the SAM. Five participants found all of the target F-clusters using the SAM. A paired t-test revealed a significant difference ($p < 0.05$, $t=5.66$).

Fig. 6 shows the task time. Five participants finished on time using the SAM, while all participants failed to finish on time using the CAM. We found a significant difference in a paired t-test ($p < 0.05$, $t= -3.08$).

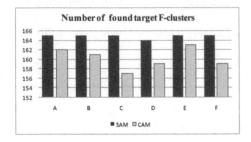 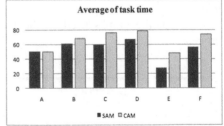

Fig. 5. Number of found target F-clusters. The ordinate indicates the number of target F-clusters found by participants.

Fig. 6. Average task time (seconds). The ordinate indicates the average task time by participants.

Fig. 7 shows the target F-clusters that were difficult to find using the CAM. The upper and lower images show the same F-cluster, and the left and right images show drawn results of the CAM and SAM respectively. In (a), a target F-cluster highlighted in light blue was mixed with other F-clusters and overlapped an anchor. A target F-cluster highlighted in light blue in (b) resolved these problems. A target F-cluster in (c) also overlapped an anchor. In (d), the overlap did not occur, and we can see that this F-cluster clearly connects to three anchors.

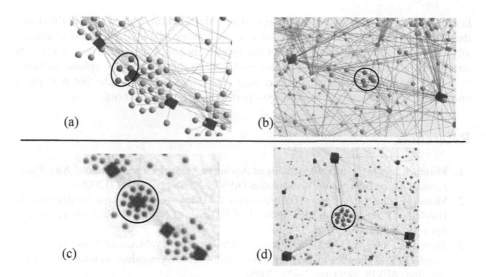

Fig. 7. Target F-clusters highlighted in light blue that were difficult to find. Upper images and lower images show the same F-cluster.

7 Discussion

Using the SAM, the participants found target F-clusters that were mixed or arranged around anchors in the CAM because they were separated in the SAM. Thus, more target F-clusters were found using the SAM than the CAM.

Most participants also performed tasks more quickly using the SAM. Therefore, we think that SAMs increase the readability. However, one participant performed tasks more quickly using the CAM. We think the reason for this is that rotating took more time in the SAM.

In Fig. 7(c), a target F-cluster consisted of many free nodes, but finding this was difficult. We think the reason for this is that the participants misunderstood that this F-cluster connected to a single anchor because it was arranged on an anchor. In the CAM, free nodes that connected to a few anchors tended to be arranged on an anchor as the number of anchors increased. However, in the SAM, free nodes connected to a few anchors tended to be arranged at a position that did not overlap anchors than with the CAM. Thus, the SAM enables us to find F-clusters and understand their features more easily.

The results of our user study demonstrate that SAMs have higher readability, particularly around anchors, than CAMs. In anchored maps, a large F-cluster tends to be arranged around anchors. Thus, we conclude that SAMs are quite useful.

8 Conclusions

We developed a new visualization technique for large-scale bipartite graphs, called sphere anchored maps. In this technique, anchors are arranged on a sphere that has 2D layout space while keeping the features of circular anchored maps. We defined aesthetic criteria for the sphere anchored maps and developed a layout method. Additionally, we evaluated the effectiveness of the sphere anchored maps in a user study. The study showed that more clusters of free nodes were found using the sphere anchored map than using the circular anchored map. Therefore, we conclude that the sphere anchored maps increase the readability—particularly around anchors.

References

1. Misue, K.: Drawing Bipartite Graphs as Anchored Maps. In: Proceedings of Asia-Pacific Symposium on Information Visualization (APVIS 2006), pp. 169–177 (2006)
2. Misue, K.: Overview of Network Information by Using Anchored Maps. In: Apolloni, B., Howlett, R.J., Jain, L. (eds.) KES 2007, Part II. LNCS (LNAI), vol. 4693, pp. 1269–1276. Springer, Heidelberg (2007)
3. Zheng, L., Song, L., Eades, P.: Crossing Minimization Problems of Drawing Bipartite Graphs in Two Clusters. In: Proceedings of Asia-Pacific Symposium on Information Visualization (APVIS 2005), pp. 33–38 (2005)
4. Giacomo, E.D., Grilli, L., Liotta, G.: Drawing Bipartite Graphs on Two Curves. In: Kaufmann, M., Wagner, D. (eds.) GD 2006. LNCS, vol. 4372, pp. 380–385. Springer, Heidelberg (2007)
5. Newton, M., Sykora, O., Vrto, I.: Two New Heuristics for Two-Sided Bipartite Graph Drawing. In: Goodrich, M.T., Kobourov, S.G. (eds.) GD 2002. LNCS, vol. 2528, pp. 312–319. Springer, Heidelberg (2002)
6. Munzner, T.: H3: Laying out large directed graphs in 3d hyperbolic space. In: Proceedings of the 1997 IEEE Symposium on Information Visualization, pp. 2–10 (1997)
7. Ho, J., Hong, S.H.: Drawing Clustered Graphs in Three imensions. In: Healy, P., Nikolov, N.S. (eds.) GD 2005. LNCS, vol. 3843, pp. 492–502. Springer, Heidelberg (2006)
8. Eades, P.: A heuristic for graph drawing. Congressus Numeranitium 42, 149–160 (1984)
9. Ito, T., Misue, K., Tanaka, J.: Drawing of Spherical Anchored Map in 3D Space for Bipartite Graphs and Interactive Browsing Techniques. In: Proc. 70th Conf. Inf. Proc. Soc. Jpn, pp. 4-317–4-318 (2008) (in Japanese)
10. Ware, C., Franck, G.: Evaluating Stereo and Motion Cues for Visualizing Information Nets in Three Dimensions. In: ACM Transactions on Graphics, pp. 121–140 (1996)
11. Saff, E.B., Kuijlaars, A.B.J.: Distributing many points on the sphere. Mathematical Intelligencer 19(1), 5–11 (1997)
12. Katanforoush, A., Shahshahani, M.: Distributing Points on the Sphere. I. Experiment. Math. 12(2), 199–209 (2003)

Motion Stroke-A Tablet-Based Interface for Motion Design Tool Using Drawing

Haruki Kouda[1], Ichiroh Kanaya[2], and Kosuke Sato[1]

[1] Graduate School of Engineering Science, Osaka University, Japan
{kouda-h,sato}@sens.sys.es.osaka-u.ac.jp
[2] Graduate School of Engineering, Osaka University, Japan
kanaya@design.frc.eng.osaka-u.ac.jp

Abstract. Conventional animation tools provide users with complicated operations which require them to adjust too much variables to design a virtual model's 3D motion. In the proposed system, "Motion Stroke", users can control these variables only by their 2D drawings on a tablet surface. The proposed interface allows users to create new motions through a trial-and-error process which is nature in drawing of a picture on a paper. It offers a familiar form for designing of a virtual object's motion. We conducted several evaluations and confirmed that the proposed system allows users to explore their desired motions flexibly.

Keywords: Motion deign, Drawing, User interface.

1 Introduction and Motivation

A 3D motion design of a CG model is a cumbersome and complicated task since motions of all vertices of the model have to be controlled in each frame. The Keyframing is the most general method where a user only has to assign vertices' positions in several discrete frames, and then these positions are automatically interpolated and consequently the entire motion is created. However the simple interpolation of the Keyframing is not suitable for designing of a motion whose velocity gradually changes. In such a case, a lot of keyframes have to be prepared. The user also has to take multiple vertices' motions into account at the same time. Furthermore, when preparing keyframes, theq user cannot check a generated motion. Therefore, motion design with the Keyframing assumes a well skilled user.

In this paper, we propose a motion design system called "Motion Stroke" where a user can design 3D motions of a CG model with a 2D drawing on a tablet surface. The proposed method is suitable in the early stage of motion design since the user can perform a number of 2D drawings through a trial-and-error process to explore his/her desired motions. This is similar to a case that visual artists or designers perform rough sketches in early stages of their creative activities. A velocity of a user's drawing motion is not constant but gradually changes in a similar way to a basic animation motion which is known as "Slow In and Slow Out" [3]. Therefore, in the proposed method a user easily designs such a natural motion which could not been obtained easily by Keyframing technique. Furthermore, the user can change only the artistic impression of the motion by controlling a spatial frequency of a drawing.

J.A. Jacko (Ed.): Human-Computer Interaction, Part II, HCII 2009, LNCS 5611, pp. 821–829, 2009.
© Springer-Verlag Berlin Heidelberg 2009

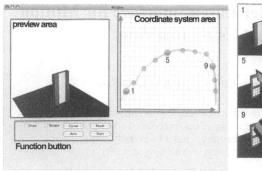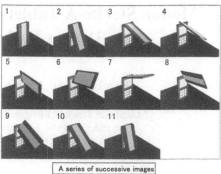

Fig. 1. System overview and design of motion (left) The system consists of simple GUI parts; preview area, function buttons, and coordinate system area. In the coordinate system area, two motion control parameters are assigned to each axis. (right) A new motion combined two simple motions arbitrarily is generated with the drawing in coordinate system area and result is continuously displayed in preview area.

The remainder of the paper is organized as follows: in the next section we briefly describe related works. Following this, Sec.3 presents the detailed principle and implementation of our proposed motion design method. In Sec.4, we describe the evaluations. We conclude with a direction for further work in Sec.5.

2 Related Works

A lot of approaches in making motion such as motion capture and physically based simulation have been developed. For example, performance-driven motion and puppeteering usually rely on a specialized input device or a motion-capture system [8]. The direct mapping that they assign between the character's DOFs and the device's DOFs requires a significant learning for the system. Shin et al. [7] proposed a motion capture methods for assigning a performer's full body motion to virtual characters of different sizes. Dontcheva et al. [2] proposed layered acting method that the user designs complex motions by multiple acting passes. These techniques are expensive to use and are not suitable for use of designing imaginary motions. An intuitive motion interfaces for novice users without special devices has been studied for many years.

To help novice users create motions easily, many new interfaces have been proposed. K-sketch [1] is a pen-based system that relies on users' intuitive sense of space and time while still supporting a wide range of uses. K-sketch enables users to create 2D animations, informal, for general purpose. Motion Doodles[10] is an interface for sketching a character motion. Users' drawings such as lines, arcs, and loops are parsed and mapped to a parameterized output motions that further reflect the location and timing of the input sketch. These two tools are produced with an aim of building working surroundings in which users' labor effectiveness have been reduced. But, with their system, because of use with motion library or interpolating technique, the range of motions that are made by is restricted and fine adjustment is so lazy work.

Performance timing for keyframe animation [9] is an interface to time keyframes using gestures without changing the motion itself. The system allows users to do act-out the timing information using a simple 2D input device such as a mouse or pen-tablet. Because of design limitation in the system, setting keyframe process and preview process is separated.

Ngo et al. [5] used an interpolation technique for manipulating 2D vector graphics. Key poses are embedded in a special structure called a simplicial configuration complex. Rademacher [6] used an interpolation for controlling the view-dependent geometry. Key geometries are associated with specific view directions and are blended according to the current view direction. Laszlo et al. [4] combined interactive character control with physics-based simulations. They showed an example in which the horizontal and vertical motions of the mouse were directly mapped to the character's individual DOFs.

3 "Motion Stroke" System

The proposed system "Motion Stroke" consists of a pen tablet (WACOM; Cintiq) and a computer (MacBook: Intel Core2Duo 2.1GHz, memory 2GB) as shown in Fig.2. Left figure of Fig.1 shows the outlook of the implemented software which consists of "preview area" where generated motions are displayed, a few "function buttons" and "coordinate system area" where users perform 2D drawings.

In the "coordinate system" area, two motion variables such as translation along x-axis or rotation around y-axis are assigned to horizontal and vertical axes respectively (Fig.3). Each point in the coordinate system represents a position and pose of a manipulated model, and thus a set of points on a user's drawing line represents a motion sequence. Users can control the two motion variables at the same time only by drawing a line in the "coordinate system area". Generated motions can be checked in the "preview area" while drawing lines. Therefore users can easily explore their desired motions through a simple trial-and-error process where they just draw-and-erase lines in the "coordinate system area". Furthermore, users can easily change the velocity of the motion only by controlling their drawing speeds. Right figure of Fig.1 shows an example of a generated motion with the proposed method. In this case, two different rotations around a hinge of a mobile phone model are assigned to the axes of the "coordinate system area". It is confirmed that a complicated 3D motion can be designed with a single 2D drawing line.

To combine more than three motion parameters, we propose to assign drawing parameter to the horizontal axis in a new coordinate system area. Fig. 4 shows the concept of the process. Drawing a line, users combine two motion parameters a and b.

The line is fitted to approximated curve $L(s)$, and a new coordinate system area which s is assigned to horizontal axis is generated. After assigning additional motion parameter c to the other axis, user can combine motions. Fig.4 shows the concept diagram of this process.

To adjust artistic features of an input drawing, we implemented two types of modification functions. First one is to adjust the strength of drawing fluctuation. In the system, according to the position of "Smoothness" slidebar controlled by a user, the strength is changed as post processing. We assume that the fluctuation mainly appears in the middle components ($\pm24{\sim}48$ components) of P-type Fourier descriptor. The position of the slidebar indexes the weight of the middle components.

824   H. Kouda, I. Kanaya, and K. Sato

Fig. 2. Outlook of the system

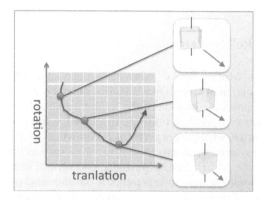

Fig. 3. Concept diagram of coordinate system view. A point in the view indicates a certain position and posture of the object. By changing the shape of drawing, user can combine two motions arbitrarily. By changing the speed of drawing user can adjust the timing of motion.

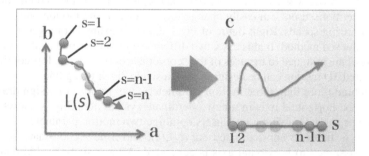

Fig. 4. Assigning motion to parameterized axis. Drawing parameter *s* was assigned to horizontal axis in new coordinate system area. Additional motion parameter *c* is assigned to vertical axis.

Another adjusting function is to regulate drawing velocity. "Constant" button fixes to a certain constant velocity in drawing, although the user may change the velocity of pen in input area. Once the user pushes the button, the smoothness of the drawing is normalized in time domain.

4 Evaluation

We conducted three kinds of experiments to evaluate how accurate users can reproduce their desired motions, how users use the proposed system when controlling more than two motion variables, and how an impression of a motion is changed when the spatial frequency of a drawing is changed.

4.1 Accuracy of Motion Reproduction

The first experiment was conducted to evaluate how accurate users can reproduce their desired motions. We prepared four sample 3D motions (i.e. four sample corresponding 2D lines shown in Fig.5). In the experiment, we let participants to watch sample motions and estimate the corresponding 2D lines. They could watch the samples anytime they wanted and drew lines in the "coordinate system area" and checked motions in the "preview area" until they thought they could draw correct lines. After that, we calculated the similarity between two drawing lines: a sample drawing line and a line drawn by a participant. We applied P-type Fourier descriptor for the line similarity calculation. Using P-type Fourier descriptor, a line is expressed as Fourier components. In the experiment, feature vector of each line is defined as a vector composed with 11 components that are the lowest of Fourier components (DC component and $\pm 1\sim 5$ components). The line similarity is defined as Euclidean distance between two feature vectors.

We recruited four participants from the local university. We explained all the system features to each participant, but did not show any demonstrations. Each participant practiced to use the system for ten minutes. Fig.5 shows the results of the estimated lines and Table.1 shows the calculated line similarities between sample lines and estimated lines. Note that a participant couldn't estimate any lines in sample 3 and 4.

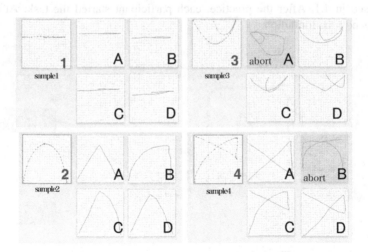

Fig. 5. Sample drawings and subjects input drawings

Table 1. Index of line similarity between sample lines and estimated lines

Subjects \ Sample	Sample1	Sample2	Sample3	Sample4
A	66.2	146.4	(×)	222.1
B	58.4	141.1	158.4	(×)
C	41.2	103.2	136.1	81.8
D	78.8	114.0	324.4	139.5

The results show that though participants could estimate correct lines in case of simple motions such as sample 1 and 2, it was difficult to estimate the correct lines in case of complicated motions. Therefore, a user of our system can reproduce the desired motion correctly when the motion is simple.

4.2 Observation of Motion Design Process

The second experiment was conducted to observe how users use the proposed system when controlling more than two motion variables. In the experiment, we used human–type object that contains four movable components; leg, hip, arm and shoulder. Combining four motions of these components, participants were asked to make walking motion. Fig.6 shows the overview of application used in the task. Selecting *checkbox* placed each sides of axis of coordinate system area, participants can select motions that should be combined by drawing. Pushing *Axis button*, a new coordinate system area in which parameter of drawing is assigned to horizontal axis is generated. Pushing *Play button*, participants can replay the motion.

We recruited three participants from the local university. We explained all the system features to each participant, but did not show any demonstrations. Each participant practiced to use the system for ten minutes with same model as mobile phone object used in 4.1. After the practice, each participant started the task. At the task, there was no time limitation.

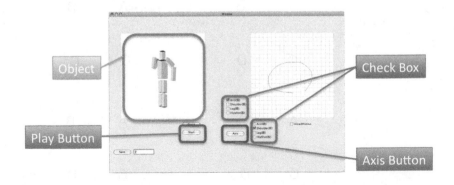

Fig. 6. Application overview used in the task

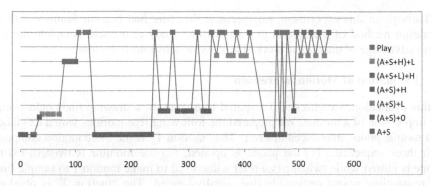

Fig. 7. Proceed history of the task by user A Horizontal axis shows time [sec], and vertical axis shows category of motion combined (A:arm, S:shoulder, L:leg, H:Hip)

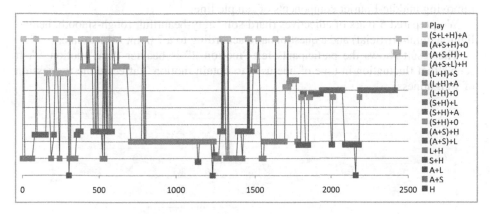

Fig. 8. Proceed History of the task by user B

Fig.7 shows the history of the task by user A. X-axis of graph shows time [sec] and Y-axis shows category of combining motion. For example, from 120[s] to 240[s], user A combined arm and shoulder motion, and after that, she pushed "*Play button*" once to replay the motion and start further combining hip motion. From the history, user A could combine four motions in first two minutes at the task. She also rarely used "Play button" to replay the motion in the early stage of the task. It may be said that these behavior are caused by familiarity or work efficiency of the proposed system. From the interview with user A after the experimental task, she said that she could draw lines without watching coordinate system area, but with preview area. It seemed that she could combine motions since with physical activities of hand drawing. Using the system, she could draw lines and check generated motions simultaneously.

On the other hand, Fig.8 shows the history of task by user B. This participant tried to create variety new motions by changing the order of combining motions. From the interview with user B, same as user A, he could understand the way to use of application in short time, and explored his desired motion flexibly.

Throughout this experiment, we speculate that user had become familiar with the operation method of the system in a short time. They also could complete the task using advantage of drawing in work efficiency or sensuous operation.

4.3 Evaluation of Motion Impression

In this evaluation, we checked if a spatial frequency of a drawing line could control the impression of a motion. We prepared the following five motions with a CG model of a mobile phone introduced in Fig.1. The "motion 1" is the basic motion composed with three sequences; (1) the phone is opened, (2) the monitor is twisted, (3) the phone is closed while twisting (we refer a line used to make motion 1 to sample line). By resampling points on sample line equally-spaced, The "motion 2" is obtained. Motion 3(motion 4) is obtained with a line that is made by multiplying middle-Fourier components of sample line by 4(8). Motion 5 is obtained with a line that is made by removing middle-Fourier components of sample line.

We prepared 5 pairs of adjectives (hard-soft, ugly-beautiful, rough-smooth, heavy-light, natural-artificial) and a questionnaire according to a 7 point Likert scale.

The result shows the participants felt "motion 2" is heavier than "motion 1". It seems that fluctuation in time of line used to obtain motion 2 affected the impression of weightiness.

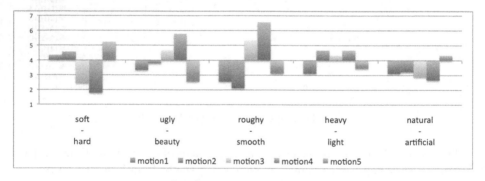

Fig. 9. Result of questionnaire

Moreover, the participants felt "motion 3 or 4" is harder, uglier, heavier and rougher than "motion 1". On the other hand, "motion 5" is more natural than "motion 1". It seems that fluctuation in space of line used to obtain motion 3, 4 or 5 affected the impression of refinement.

5 Conclusion

In this paper, we proposed a novel motion design system "Motion Stroke" where users can create a wide range of 3D motions with simple 2D hand drawings. Three types of experiments show the proposed system is sensuous for creating simple motions in the early stage of the motion design, where it allows users to control impressions of designed motions.

For future work, it is necessary to design the interface considered not only the variable adjustment process but also the shape design process or the variable definition process.

References

1. Davis, R.C., Colwell, B., Launda, J.A.: K-sketch: A" Kinetic "Sketch Pad for Novice Animators. In: CHI 2008 Proceedings, pp. 413–422 (2008)
2. Dontcheva, M., Yngve, G., Popovic, Z.: Layered Acting for Character Animation. ACM Transactions on Graphics 22(3), 409–416 (2003)
3. Lasseter, J.: Principles of Traditional Animation Applied to 3 Computer Animation. Computer Graphics 21(4), 35–44 (1987)
4. Laszlo, J., van de Panne, M., Fumie, E.: Interactive Control for Physically-based Animation. In: Proceedings of ACM SIGGRAPH 2000, ACM Press / ACM SIGGRAPH, Ed., Computer Graphics Proceedings. Annual Conference Series, pp. 201–208. ACM, New York (2000)
5. Ngo, T., Cutrell, D., Dana, J., Donald, B., Loeb, L., Zhu, S.: Accessible Animation and Customizable Graphics via Simplicial Configuration Modeling. In: Proceedings of ACM SIGGRAPH 2000, ACM Press / ACM SIGGRAPH, Computer Graphics Proceedings. Annual Conference Series, pp. 403–410. ACM, New York (2000)
6. Rose, C., Bodenheimer, B., Cohen, M.: Verbs and Adverbs: Multidimensional Motion Interpolation Using Radial Basis Functions. IEEE Computer Graphics and Applications 18(5), 32–40 (1998)
7. Shin, H.J., Lee, J., Gleicher, M., Shin, S.Y.: Computer Puppetry: An Importance-Based Approach. ACM Transactions on Graphics 20(2), 67–94 (2001)
8. Sturman, D.J.: Computer Puppetry. IEEE Computer Graphics and Applications 18(1), 38–45 (1998)
9. Terra, S.C.L., Metoyer, R.A.: Performance Timing for Keyframe Animation. In: Eurographics/ACM SIGGRAPH Symposium on Computer Animation (2004)
10. Thorne, M., Burke, D., Van de Panne, M.: Motion Doodles: An interface for sketching Character Motion. ACM Transactions on Graphics, TOG (2004)

Tooling the Dynamic Behavior Models of Graphical DSLs

Tihamér Levendovszky and Tamás Mészáros

Budapest University of Technology and Economics,
Department of Automation and Applied Informatics,
Goldmann György tér 3, H-1111 Budapest, Hungary
{tihamer,mesztam}@aut.bme.hu
http://www.aut.bme.hu

Abstract. Domain-specific modeling is a powerful technique to describe complex systems in a precise but still understandable way. Rapid creation of graphical Domain-Specific Languages (DSLs) has been focused for many years. Research efforts have proven that metamodeling is a promising way of defining the abstract syntax of the language. It is also clear that DSLs can be developed to describe the concrete syntax and the dynamic behavior. Previous research has contributed a set of graphical DSLs to model the behavior ("animation") of arbitrary graphical DSLs. This paper contributes practical techniques to simplify our message handling method, automate the integration process, and show where domain-specific model patterns can help to accelerate the simulation modeling process.

Keywords: Domain-Specific Modeling Languages, Metamodeling, Simulation.

1 Introduction

Domain-specific modeling is a powerful technique to describe complex systems in a precise but still understandable way. The strength of domain-specific modeling lies in the application of domain-specific languages to describe a system. Domain-specific languages are specialized to a concrete application domain; therefore, they are particularly efficient in their problem area compared to general purpose languages. Rapid creation of graphical Domain-Specific Languages (DSLs) has been focused for many years. Research efforts have proven that metamodeling is a promising way of defining the abstract syntax of the language. It is also clear that DSLs can be developed to describe the concrete syntax.

VMTS [1] is a general purpose metamodeling and model transformation environment. The visualization of models is supported by the VMTS Presentation Framework (VPF) [2]. VPF is a highly customizable presentation layer built on domain-specific plugins that can be defined in a declarative manner. The VMTS Animation Framework (VAF) [3] is a flexible framework supporting the real-time animation of models both in their visualized and modeled properties.

J.A. Jacko (Ed.): Human-Computer Interaction, Part II, HCII 2009, LNCS 5611, pp. 830–839, 2009.

When we started using VAF, we encountered several simplification and support opportunities that make VMTS a more efficient and user-friendly tool that is able to visualize the simulation of third party tools with metamodeling techniques. This paper contributes practical techniques to simplify our message handling method, automate the integration process, and show where domain-specific model patterns can help to accelerate the modeling process.

1.1 VMTS Animation Framework

VAF separates the animation from the domain-dependent knowledge of the dynamic behavior. For instance, a dynamic behavior of a graphically simulated statechart is really different from that of a simulated continuous control system model. In our approach, the domain knowledge can be considered a black-box whose integration is supported with visual modeling techniques. Using this approach, we can integrate various simulation frameworks or self-written components with event-based communication. The architecture of VAF is illustrated in Fig. 1.

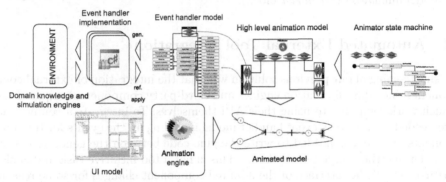

Fig. 1. Architecture of the VMTS Animation Framework

The animation framework provides three visual languages to describe the dynamic behavior of a metamodeled model and their processing via an event-based concept. The key elements in our approach are the events. Events are parameterizable messages that connect the components in our environment. The services of the Presentation Framework, the domain-specific extensions, possible external simulation engines (*ENVIRONMENT* block in Fig. 1) are wrapped with event handlers, which provide an event-base interface. Communication with event handlers can be established using events. The definition of event handlers for custom components is supported with a visual language (*Event handler model* block). The visual language defines the event handler, its parameters, the possible events, and the parameters of the events - called *entities*. Based on the model, the skeleton of the event handler can be generated (*Event handler implementation* block). We have already implemented the elementary event handlers to wrap the functions of the modeling environment, however, in case of integrating a third-party component, the glue code between the component and the skeleton has to be written manually.

The animation logic can be described using an event-based state machine, called *Animator*. We have designed another visual language to define these state machines (*Animator state machine* block). The state machine consumes and produces events. The transitions of the state machine are guarded by conditions testing the input events and may fire other events after performing the transition. The input (output) events of the state machine are created in (sent to) another state machine or an event handler. The events produced by the event handlers and the state machines are scheduled and processed by a DEVS-based [4] simulator engine (*Animation engine* block). The event handlers and the state machines can be connected in a high-level model (*High level animation model* block). The communication between components is established through ports. Ports can be considered labeled buffers, which have a configurable size. On executing an animation, both the high-level model and the low-level state machines are converted into source code, which is executed after an automated compilation phase. In addition to model animation, another visual language is provided to design the layout of the user interface, which can be applied when executing a model animation (*UI model* block).

2   Automated External Tool Integration

A shortcoming of our previous solution was that the integration of external components (including simulation engines and third-party components) required too much work compared to using their API themselves. To integrate a component, we needed to create the event handler model including all the events for the components and we also needed to write the glue-code between the generated event handler and the component by hand. This is not a too intuitive task and is also error-prone. If the interface of the adapted component changes for some reason, the changes had to be propagated to the event handler model by hand, and the glue-code also had to be updated. To address this issue we decided to use reflection to load the metainformation of the component and to generate the event handler classes automatically, including both the event implementations and the glue code. There are several types of .NET class-members we can assign events to. The most trivial one is the .NET *event*. .NET events are language-supported solutions to implement some kind of notification service. One can subscribe delegates (roughly: function pointers) to the published events of an object, and they can be called by the publisher object using the Observer design pattern [5]. If a .NET event is fired, the event handler should catch it, and fire the appropriate animation event with the right parameters (received from the .NET event) through a port. If we consider the *MouseClicked* event of the *Control* object in the .NET Base Class Library, it has two parameters: the first is called *sender* and has a type of *object* – this parameter identifies the sender of the event –, the second one is called *e* and is of type *MouseEventArgs* – it identifies the location of the click, the pressed button etc. To wrap this .NET event we need to (i) create a modeled event with the same type of properties as the parameters of the event has (*object*, (ii) subscribe to the appropriate event of the inspected object with a callback method, (iii) instantiate the modeled event and fire it through a port if the callback method is called. A simple member method can also be considered both an event source and a sink as well: a method call can be initiated by firing an event to the event handler, the parameters of the event should correspond to the parameters of the called method. The possible return value of the method call can be propagated towards the animation logic using an event as well. For example we assume a *GetMatrix* method having a parameter of type *string* and a return value of type *double[,]*. The method can be wrapped with two events: *GetMatrix* and *GetMatrix_*. The *GetMatrix* event has a property of type *string* (as the corresponding method also has such a similar parameter), while *GetMatrix_* – the response event sent by the event handler – has a property of type *double[,]*, which corresponds to the return value of the wrapped method. .NET *properties* can be considered getter/setter methods for private fields or calculated data. However, instead of function calls, we usually access the hidden data with the syntax of accessing member fields. In fact, properties are implemented with special methods in the background, but the language hides them to the programmer. Thus, properties require three events to be created: (i) one to set the value of the property (similar to a method call without return value), (ii) one to query its value (sent to the event handler component) and (iii) another one to return the value in response to the query (sent by the event handler component).

Instead of modeling the necessary events to wrap a component, we provide tools to automate the wrapping. In addition to define events in the event handler model manually, one can extend the event handler by adding *fields* to it. A field can be considered a member variable of the event handler, and the type of the field can be defined in an arbitrary external .NET assembly. Each field has the following attributes: *name, type, initField* and *members*. Setting the *initField* attribute to true indicates the instantiation of the field together with the instantiation of the event handler. The *members* attribute of the field defines the members of the field-type we would like to generate events and default event handlers for. Members are identified by name (*memberName* attribute), overloaded method names are distinguished with an order-id postfix. Each modeled member corresponds to an existing member of the type of the parent field. If a member is selected for generation, one, two or three events (depending on its type) are generated with parameters to wrap the properties of the wrapped member. The *portId* attribute of a *Member* identifies the port the generated events are sent or received through. Furthermore, we can also specify whether to generate the send/receive events using the *send* and *receive* attributes. This feature is useful if we do not want to take care of the return value of a method call, or, for example we would like to get the value of a property, but we would never like to set it directly. For example, if we would like to wrap a *Form* control, especially for its *ShowDialog* method and *MouseClicked* event, we need to add a *Field* of type *Form* to an event handler, add two *Members* called *MouseClicked* and *ShowDialog* to the *Field*, set their *PortId* attribute to an existing port, and set their *Send* and *Receive* attributes to true – in fact, the *Send* attribute of members for .NET events is omitted. The presented procedure is also supported by a graphical user interface which automatically provides available type members and ports to create *Member* attributes

2.1   Integration of the MATLAB-Simulink Simulator

To illustrate the usage of our approach, we have integrated the MATLAB [6] API into VMTS, and we simulated a Simulink model and presented its results in VMTS. MATLAB does not have an official .NET-based interface, so we have used a free class library which wraps the most important MATLAB operations with a .NET class. The name of the component is *EngMATLib* [7]. The event handler model for *EngMATLib* contains a single *EventHandler* node which has a field called *matlab*, and its *type* is set to *EngMATLib*. We selected the *Execute* and *GetMatrix* methods of *EngMATLib* to generate events for. The *Execute* method is used to execute an arbitrary MATLAB command using its interpreter. It does not have a return value, and expects a single string parameter, thus the generator produces an event class called *Execute*, which has a string attribute. The *GetMatrix* method returns a floating point matrix identified by its *name* parameter. As the *GetMatrix* method has a return value, we generate both a *query* event (called *GetMatrix*) which has a *name* attribute, and a *response* event (called *GetMatrix_*) for the return value of the method call. Based on the performed settings the event handler implementation can be generated.

The simulated Simulink model (called *sldemo_autotrans*, Fig. 2 c) is shipped with the MATLAB installation, and models an automatic transmission controller. If we execute the simulation in Simulink, we can inspect the parameters of the car (including speed, engine rotation-per-minute, and throttle state) at different conditions. In the following example, we present these parameters on diagrams and also on monitors in VMTS. For this purpose, we have created a very simple visual language which can model indicators: numeric and stripe (Fig. 2 d). Each indicator has a *name* a *range* and a *value*, the modeled indicators are animated according to the results received from MATLAB.

Fig. 2 a and b present the high-and low-level (state machine) animation models. As it can be seen on the high-level animation model, the animator is connected to (i) the UI event handler (*EH_UI*), (ii) to the generated *EngMATLib* event handler and (iii) to a *Timer* which schedules the animation by sending a *Tick* event every 0.1 secs. The state machine model consists of the following steps: (1) query the active diagram, which contains the indicators to be animated (Fig. 2 e); (2) execute the simulation by sending an *Execute* event with a *"sim('sldemo_autotrans')"* command to MATLAB; (3) query the time, speed, RPM and throttle state vectors using *GetMatrix* on the signal logging structure called *sldemo_autotrans_output*; (4) obtain a reference to the indicators using their names; (5) present the data-vectors on a diagram; (6) animate the indicators by iterating through the vectors, and updating the *Value* property of the indicators based on the data-vectors. Note, that the loop is controlled by the *Ticks* of the timer event handler.

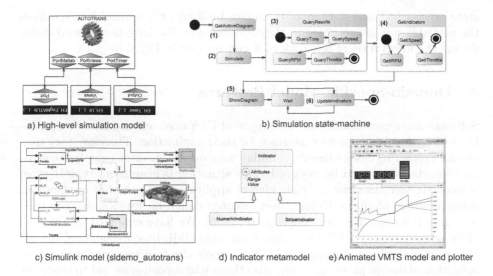

a) High-level simulation model

b) Simulation state-machine

c) Simulink model (sldemo_autotrans)

d) Indicator metamodel

e) Animated VMTS model and plotter

Fig. 2. Integrating Simulink simulations into VMTS

3   Hierarchical State Machines

Another shortcoming of our original solution was that in case of complex animation logics, the state machine became too large to be easily understood and
to be modified. To overcome this drawback, we have extended the state machine
formalism to support the modeling of hierarchical state machines. Fig. 3 depicts
the metamodel of the actual state machine language. The containment loop-edge
on the *State* node expresses the capability of building compound states. The execution of the extended state-machine is modified as follows: if a compound state
becomes active, (i) its *Action* script is executed, (ii) the *Start* state of its internal
state machine is activated, (iii) the internal state machine is executed, (iv) when
reaching a *Stop* state in the internal state machine, the container state becomes
active. If a nested state is active, both its and the container state's transitions
are checked when the state machine is activated. If a nested state does not have
any transitions which trigger the actual input, the transitions of the container

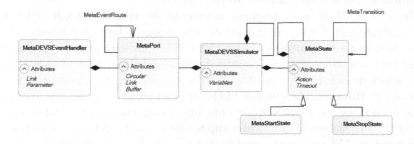

Fig. 3. State machine metamodel

state are verified, and - if any of them can be fired - the control is taken from the nested state, and returned to the container one. We have used nested states during the integration of Simulink as it can be seen in Fig. 2 b.

4   Domain-Specific Model Patterns

Software developers usually use a widespread UI framework and follow its guidelines when designing the user interface for their application. Therefore they usually met recurring cases when very similar components, or often exactly the same user interfaces, have to be designed. This situation is even more typical when someone is specialized for a certain kind of applications, e.g. mobile applications using a special platform. Using object oriented design techniques, one can handle these cases by applying design patterns [5]. We have extended [8] the idea of design patterns in VMTS to support not only UML based languages, but arbitrary metamodeled languages. VMTS also provides tool support for the rapid definition of design patterns, to organize them into repositories and to configure and insert patterns into an edited model. We have examined whether we can discover often recurring patterns in animation models and define them as animation design patterns. After creating numerous simulation models, we found that animation state machines are not quite appropriate sources to find patterns. This fact can be attributed to the language itself as well: the constraints of the transitions have to be defined in a textual way, and the firing of the events is also performed with action scripts. Furthermore, the integrated external components have their own type of events, and the specific state machines operate on these events. Instead of general patterns, one may discover recurring patterns during the animation of a specific domain.

The other two animation languages (the high-level animation language and the UI designer language - introduced in [3]) are better sources for pattern definition. Here we present only an outline of them. Two often recurring patterns for high-level animation models are presented in Fig. 4 a and b. The pattern in 4 a is the most elementary pattern which occurs in every animation model which provides visualization. The pattern contains an *Animator* and an *EventHandler* element, and their *Model* and *View* ports are connected with bi-directional *EventRoute* edges. Fig. 4 b can be considered the extension of 4 a with the notion of time by adding a *Timer* event handler to the model.

The VMTS UI designer language is used to describe the layout of the modeling environment during an animation. The designer language is very strict in the sense that most elements (windows in VMTS) have a maximal cardinality of 1. The two exceptions are the *DiagramWindow* and the *CustomWindow* components which model the presentation of a diagram or a custom edit control in the application. However, the number of the applied windows is limited by the size of the screen, as the more windows are presented, the smaller and less usable they are. Thus, the set of practically applicable layouts can be considered a small finite number. The two most common layouts are depicted in Fig. 4 c and d. In Fig. 4 c the most common windows (browser and property setter) are placed on the screen and one diagram is open. In Fig. 4 d the full screen is utilized: a diagram and the standard output windows are open. The usual scenario is that one can inspect the animation on the diagram, while the standard output presents trace information.

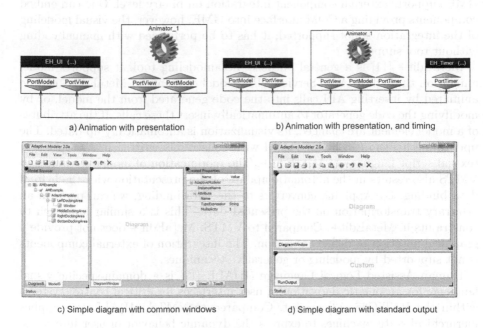

a) Animation with presentation   b) Animation with presentation, and timing

c) Simple diagram with common windows   d) Simple diagram with standard output

Fig. 4. Animation design patterns

5   Related Work

AToM3 [9] is a general purpose metamodeling environment with simulation and model animation features. AToM3 models can be animated either by handling predefined events fired during the editing of the model or by executing model transformation on the model and updating the visualization. Model elements in VMTS can also react to events similar to the ones defined in AToM3, but we do not define these event handlers in the metamodel but in the plugin which defines the concrete syntax. Our approach also focuses on the visualization and modeling of the animation logic, instead of implementing it by hand. AToM3 provides language-level support for the integration of external components which can be called from Python. The main benefit of our approach is its flexibility and extensibility: external components can be adapted to the animation framework, the integration of external components and frameworks can be modeled, and they are wrapped into a unified event-based interface.

The Generic Modeling Environment (GME) [10] is a general purpose metamodeling and program synthesis environment. GME provides two ways to animate models: (i) with the help of executing graph rewriting-based model transformations or (ii) by transforming models with custom traversing processors. Both approaches build on the fact that on updating model elements in the object space (MGA-MultiGraph Architecture) of GME, the presentation layer is notified about the changes, and the visualization of elements also updates. GME supports external component integration on binary level. One can embed components providing a COM interface into GME, however, the visual modeling of the integration is not supported, it has to be performed with manual coding without tool support.

MetaEdit+ [11] is a general purpose metamodeling tool. It supports model animation through its Web Service API. Model elements in MetaEdit+ can be animated by inserting API calls into the code generated from the model, or by modifying the code generator to automatically insert these calls. If the attributes of a model element are changed, its visualization is automatically up-dated. The update mechanism can be influenced with constraints written in a proprietary textual script language of MetaEdit+. The modification of model attributes in VMTS also results in the automatic update of the presentation with the help of data binding. By Applying converters to the data binding, we can perform an arbitrary transformation on the presented data. This is a similar approach to constraints in MetaEdit+. Compared to VMTS, MetaEdit+ does not provide a graphical notation to define animation. The integration of external components is not supported by modeling or generative techniques.

Human Assisted Logical Language (H)ALL [12] is a domain-specific visual language for automatic derivation of user interfaces for critical control systems within the BATIC3S [13] project. Compared to VMTS, (H)ALL also applies hierarchical state machines to express the dynamic behavior of user interfaces. The state machines communicate via messages. The semantics of (H)ALL models is defined with Concurrent Object-Oriented Petri-Nets [14] (CO-OPN). The conversion between (H)ALL and CO-OPN is described with QVT [15] transformations. Compared to VMTS, (H)ALL does not deal with the integration of external components, it needs proprietary integration of components to the coordination engine.

6   Conclusion

The focus of our contribution is how to simplify the handling of complex messages, how to support the automatic integration to external tools, and how to optimize use of the existing DSLs with domain-specific model patterns. We found that the use of hierarchical state machines to describe the message handling simplifies the models to a great extent. The automation of the integration process accelerates the development time significantly. We outlined a few design patterns that can help reusing existing high-level animation and user interface models. In our experience, using these practical techniques helps to make the graphical DSL-based approach more efficient than manual coding. Future work includes creating more applications, optimizing the generators, enriching the DSLs, and identifying more specific model patterns for the animation paradigm.

Acknowledgments. The fund of Mobile Innovation Centre has supported, in part, the activities described in this paper. This paper was supported by the János Bolyai Research Scholarship of the Hungarian Academy of Sciences.

References

1. VMTS homepage, http://vmts.aut.bme.hu
2. Mészáros, T., Mezei, G., Levendovszky, T.: A flexible, declarative presentation framework for domain-specific modeling. In: Proceedings of the working conference on Advanced visual interfaces (AVI 2008), Naples, Italy, pp. 309–312 (2008)
3. Mészáros, T., Mezei, G., Charaf, H.: Engineering the Dynamic Behavior of Meta-modeled Languages, Simulation, Special Issue on Multi-paradigm Modeling (2008) (accepted)
4. Zeigler, B.P., Praehofer, H., Kim, T.G.: Theory of Modeling and Simulation, 2nd edn. Academic Press, London (2000)
5. Gamma, E., et al.: Design Patterns: Elements of Reusable Object-Oriented Software. Addison-Wesley Professional, Reading (1994)
6. MATLAB homepage, http://www.mathworks.com
7. EngMATLib homepage, http://www.thecodeproject.com
8. Levendovszky, T., et al.: Supporting Domain-Specific Model Patterns with Meta-modeling, System Special Issue on Metamodeling (submitted)
9. de Lara, J., Vangheluwe, H.: AToM3: A Tool for Multi-Formalism and Meta-modeling. In: Kutsche, R.-D., Weber, H. (eds.) FASE 2002. LNCS, vol. 2306, pp. 174–188. Springer, Heidelberg (2002)
10. Lédeczi, Á., et al.: Composing Domain-Specific Design Environments. IEEE Computer 34(11), 44–51 (2001)
11. Tolvanen, J.-P.: MetaEdit+: integrated modeling and metamodeling environment for domain-specific languages. In: Companion to the 21st ACM SIGPLAN conference on Object-oriented programming systems, languages, and applications, Portland, USA, pp. 690–691 (2006)
12. Barroca, B., Amaral, V. (H)ALL: a DSVL for designing user interfaces for Control Systems. In: Proceedings of the 5th Nordic Workshop on Model Driven Engineering, Göteborg, Sweden (2007)
13. BATIC3S homepage, http://smv.unige.ch/tiki-index.php?page=BATICS
14. Buchs, B., Guelfi, N.: A formal specification framework for object-oriented distributed systems. IEEE Trans. Software Eng. 26(7), 635–652 (2000)
15. MOF QVT Final adopted specification, http://www.omg.org/docs/ptc/05-11-01.pdf

Pattern Recognition Strategies
for Interactive Sketch Composition

Sébastien Macé and Eric Anquetil

INSA de Rennes, Avenue des Buttes de Coësmes, F-35043 Rennes
CNRS, UMR IRISA, Campus de Beaulieu, F-35042 Rennes
Université Européenne de Bretagne, France
{sebastien.mace,eric.anquetil}@irisa.fr

Abstract. The design of industrial pen-based systems for sketch composition
and interpretation is still a challenging problem when dealing with complex
domains. In this paper, we present a method that is based on an eager interpretation of the user strokes, i.e. on an incremental process with visual feedback to
the user. We present the benefits of using such an interactive approach in order
to design efficient and robust sketch recognition. We focus more specifically on
the requirements in order to avoid as much as possible to disturb the user. We
show how we exploit pattern recognition strategies, for instance the evaluation
of adequacy measures thanks to the fuzzy set theory, the exploitation of reject
options, etc., to deal with each of these difficulties. The DALI method that we
present in this paper has been used to design an industrial system for the composition of electrical sketches. We show how the presented techniques are used
in this system.

Keywords: Hand-drawn shape recognition, pen-based interaction, visual languages and grammars, fuzzy set theory, reject options.

1 Introduction

Tablet PC and pen-based interaction are well adapted to the composition of documents in a mobility context. For example, workers on building sites could benefit
from this natural paradigm to draw sketches, such as electrical sketches, plans, tables,
etc., directly on computer systems while standing in front of installations.

Unfortunately, there is a lack of software taking advantage of pen-based interaction
to compose and edit such sketches on an intuitive way. This is because the interpretation of the strokes (i.e. the sequences of points captured by the sensitive screen between a pen-down and a pen-up) constituting a sketch is a complex problem of pattern
recognition. Therefore, many pen-based software are still based on WIMP interaction,
which is not well adapted for the composition of sketches in constrained environments. The goal of our works is to present a method for the interpretation of sketches
that is robust enough to design pen-based software usable in industrial circumstances
and constrained environments.

For such purpose, sketch interpretation strategies require good performances in
terms of pattern recognition. Several strategies have been proposed in the literature. In

J.A. Jacko (Ed.): Human-Computer Interaction, Part II, HCII 2009, LNCS 5611, pp. 840–849, 2009.
© Springer-Verlag Berlin Heidelberg 2009

fact, we can observe that their performances are often strongly linked with the constraints they impose to the user. As a consequence, it is necessary to find a balance between these constraints and the performances in terms of pattern recognition.

Nevertheless, it is also admitted that good pattern recognition performances are not enough to ensure the acceptance of sketch based software [5,11]: it is necessary to propose intuitive interaction with the user, easiness of error correction, etc.

Existing approaches can be separated into two main categories depending on the moment in which the user is involved in the interpretation process. *Lazy interpretation* consists in interpreting a sketch after all the strokes have been drawn. Lazy interaction is theoretically ideal from a human-computer interaction point of view, because no constraint is imposed to the user in the composition process and there is no intrusion into his creative process. Nevertheless, in practice, existing approaches generally offer weak recognition performances for the interpretation of sketches from complex domains. This is mainly due to a propagating error phenomenon: a stroke that is wrongly interpreted will often have dramatic impact on the interpretation of its surrounding strokes. As a consequence, lazy interpretation requires a strong integration of the user in a fastidious verification process for the correction of interpretation errors.

Eager interpretation consists in interpreting the sketch directly during its drawing. Basically, the idea is that if the user must be integrated to correct errors, it should rather be progressively, leading to an interactive sketch composition process. Thus, by eager interpretation, we not only refer to the incremental interpretation of the strokes, but also to the associated visual feedback. This way, the user can be integrated in the analysis process: he knows how his strokes are interpreted and can incrementally validate or correct these interpretations. The main impact is that the propagating error phenomenon disappears, because the system can rely on the interpretations that have been validated by the user to better interpret their surrounding strokes. As a consequence, the interpretation is more robust, which makes it possible to consider more ambitious applicative domains.

Even though eager interpretation strongly relies on the integration of the user, it is essential to avoid as much as possible to disturbing him and to break his creative process. The goal of this paper is to show how pattern recognition strategies can be exploited for such purpose. In the second section of this paper, we focus on eager interpretation and the impact of such process on pattern recognition and human-document interaction. Then, we informally present the general concepts of the generic *DALI method* that is the heart of our works. In section 4, we show how various pattern recognition techniques are used in this method to respond to the requirements of eager sketch interpretation. In the following section, we present a system, based on the DALI method, that is commercialized and used daily by a hundred of technicians, directly on building site.

2   Eager Interpretation and Human - Document Interaction

Eager interpretation has many impacts on the way hand-drawn strokes must be interpreted. The first and most essential requirement is to be able to interpret the strokes in real-time: it is not pertinent to make users wait for a feedback between each of their strokes. As a consequence, it is necessary to make a decision as quickly as possible.

This can be a tough problem because many methods are based on high combinatory algorithms [1].

The second requirement involves the quality of the feedback, i.e. of the interpretation process: it is necessary to make the right decision to avoid the user to have to correct an interpretation error. For instance, the interpretation process should detect the strokes that can't be interpreted with high confidence. This can be either because they are outliers, i.e. can't be interpreted as a symbol, or because they are ambiguous, i.e. can be interpreted in several ways. In consequence of both situations, many alternatives are possible (e.g. explicitly ask the user for the right interpretation, reject the stroke and implicitly ask the user to re-draw it, etc.).

Eager interpretation also requires making a decision at the right time, i.e. being able to decide whether or not there is enough information to make a decision and provide a visual feedback: it is sometimes necessary to wait for forthcoming strokes to interpret another one (e.g. with multi-stroke symbols or with one symbol that can be the prefix of another).

In the next section, we informally present the generic DALI method that we have designed for the composition and the interpretation of sketches. In section 4, we focus more specifically on the pattern recognition strategies that we use to overcome the problems presented in this section.

3 Presentation of the DALI Method

The goal of this paper is not to present the DALI method in details. Interested readers can refer to [7,8] for more information. In this section, we only present the concepts that are essential in the context of this paper.

The DALI method is based on two main components, which are respectively a visual grammar formalism that makes it possible to model knowledge about visual languages such as sketches, as well as a hand-drawn stroke analyzer, that exploits this knowledge to interpret strokes as efficiently as possible. We present both components and illustrate their originalities on the domain of electrical sketches.

3.1 Context-Driven Constraint Multiset Grammars

We have designed an extension of *constraint multiset grammars* (or *CMG*) [3,9], a well-formalized two-dimensional grammar, and proposed *context-driven constraint multiset grammars* (or *CD-CMG*). This extension has two main originalities: an externalization of contextual knowledge and an ability to model the imprecision of hand-drawn strokes. In this paper, we do not present the syntax of CD-CMG but focus on their theoretical concepts.

The first contribution of CD-CMG is an original modeling of the contextual knowledge. It is based on the definition of *document structural contexts* (DSC), which are locations in the sketch where we know, due to its structure, that some specific symbols can exist. In fact, a CD-CMG grammatical production extends a CMG production with:

- A *precondition block* that models the DSC in which the elements involved in the production must be located;
- A *postcondition block* that models the DSC that have to be created due to the interpretation of a specific symbol.

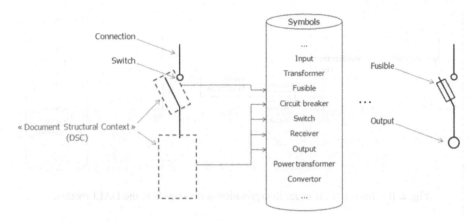

Fig. 1. The creation of a switch implies the creation of two new DSC that associate locations in the document to specific symbols

Figure 1 illustrates this on the switch electrical component: once it is created, new DSC that associate locations to potential symbols are created (a fusible can be drawn on the top left of a switch, and below a switch, we can find for instance another switch or an output, as presented on the right of the figure).

Thus, a sketch is not only modeled in terms of its elements but also by the DSC that constitute it. We will see in the next section how these DSC actually drive the analysis process on an efficient way.

Generally, sketch recognition strategies first involve a segmentation of each hand-drawn stroke of the sketch into graphical primitives, such as lines, circles, arcs, etc. [1,3,6]. Thus, grammatical productions model each symbol in terms of such primitives and of the structural constraint they must satisfy (their graphical arrangement). On the contrary, CD-CMG use the hand-drawn stroke as a graphical primitives, which means that each symbol is described in terms of the strokes that constitute it and of the constraints they satisfy (for instance, a switch is modeled as two strokes satisfying some constraints). The first consequence is that a stroke does not need to be system-atically segmented, which reduces potential errors. The second one is that we can use statistical recognition techniques, for instance based on neural networks (NN), hidden Markov models (HMM) or support vector machines (SVM), which are well adapted for dealing with imprecise data such as hand-drawn strokes.

3.2 Eager Interpretation of Hand-Drawn Strokes

The analysis process associated to CD-CMG exploits the formalized knowledge to interpret a stroke as efficiently as possible. This process is illustrated by figure 2. When the user draws a stroke, the analyzer detects the DSC in which it is located and triggers the grammatical productions that are associated to it: this is a *prediction process*, because only contextually coherent productions are considered (on figure 2, only electrical components can be drawn below a connection). This significantly reduces the complexity of the analysis process. Then, the *verification process* consists in evaluating each of these productions and finding the appropriate one. Once chosen,

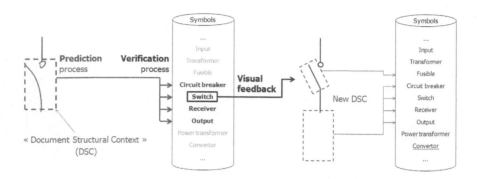

Fig. 2. Illustration of the eager interpretation process used in the DALI method

the interpretation is presented to the user thanks to a visual feedback (on figure 2, the strokes are interpreted as a switch). The interpretation of a new symbol implies the creation of new DSC which will help to interpret the following strokes.

The DALI method exploits the fuzzy set theory in order to evaluate an interpretation on a qualitative way. For that purpose, we associate a degree (between 0 and 1) to each constraint that has to be satisfied for an interpretation, and use fuzzy conjunction operators to compute a global adequacy measure of this interpretation. Thus, the decision making process consists basically in choosing the interpretation with the highest adequacy measure.

The authors would like to remind the importance of the integration of the user in the interpretation process: he is expected to implicitly validate (by continuing the composition of the document) or explicitly reject (by correcting or undoing) the results of the interpretation. Thus, the system should not question a decision that has been validated by the user; on the contrary, it should rather lean on these certainties to better interpret the following strokes. This once again limits the complexity of the process and makes it possible to analyze hand-drawn strokes in real-time.

4   Pattern Recognition Strategies for Eager Interpretation

In the previous section, we have presented the principle of the DALI method. In this section, we focus more specifically on the solutions we propose to avoid as much as possible disturbing the user.

4.1   Detecting Outlier Strokes

As introduced in section 2, a first requirement of eager interpretation is to detect strokes that can't be interpreted with high confidence. This first concerns the strokes that are meaningless or whose shapes are too far from the symbols of the sketch domain. Figure 3 presents an example of a stroke that has no meaning in the context of electrical sketches (in a musical score, this stroke should be interpreted as a G-key): the interpretation process should not try to find an interpretation at all cost, but should rather reject it and for instance ask the user to re-draw it.

Fig. 3. A stroke that should not be interpreted if drawn in an electrical sketch

Associated with the fuzzy set theory and the computing of interpretation adequacy measures, we exploit reject options and more specifically *outlier reject* [10]. This enables the system to detect when an interpretation is satisfying. The principle is quite intuitive: if the adequacy measure is not high enough (i.e. is below a given threshold) then this interpretation should not be considered any longer. This way, we can detect *outlier strokes*, which are strokes that can't be interpreted as a symbol of the sketch domain. This way, the system can have a special treatment for such strokes instead of displaying an interpretation that will probably be wrong.

4.2 Detecting Ambiguities

It is also necessary to detect strokes that are ambiguous, i.e. that can be interpreted as different symbols. Figure 3 presents the example of a stroke that can be interpreted either as a self-transformer or as an output in an electrical sketch.

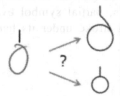

Fig. 4. A stroke that is ambiguous in an electrical sketch

To detect such situations, we once again exploit reject options and more specifically *ambiguity reject* [10]. The principle is to compare the adequacy measure of the two best interpretations and to compute a *confidence measure* that models the trust in the best interpretation; if this measure is below a given threshold, an ambiguity is detected. Once again, the system can have a specific treatment for ambiguous strokes instead of displaying an interpretation that has a high probability of being wrong.

4.3 Detecting Partial Symbol Strokes

In previous sections, we have implicitly assumed that symbols are drawn with one stroke; this is not the case in general. Thus, it is necessary to detect when a stroke can't be considered without the following ones and to postpone decision making. Note that we ask users to finish one symbol before drawing another one (but do not constraint the order in which the strokes constituting one symbol should be drawn). We believe that this constraint permits to limit combinatory problems. Figure 5 presents an example: on the left, the user draws a stroke that has no meaning but that should not be rejected, because it is only one part of a switch that will be finished with the following stroke (see on the right of figure 5).

Fig. 5. Necessity to postpone the decision-making process: the first stroke can't be interpreted but must not be rejected

In order to propose a robust eager interpretation process and a coherent visual feedback, we would like to detect these partial symbols, i.e. symbols that will be "finished" with following strokes. For that purpose, we evaluate the adequacy measures of partial symbols, i.e. of partial grammatical productions. This way, we can detect that the stroke on the left of figure 5 can be the first stroke of a switch (in fact, it can also be the first stroke of several other electrical components) and thus that it should not be rejected. In fact, we also use outlier reject to invalidate partial symbols.

The detection of partial symbols is not only necessary to avoid rejecting one stroke but also to detect a potential ambiguity that will require the following strokes in order to make a decision. Figure 6 presents an example: a small circle drawn below a connection can be the first stroke of a switch, but it can also be a "complete" output. Once again, partial symbol evaluation makes it possible to detect this and thus to keep a stroke under its hand-drawn aspect until another stroke is added.

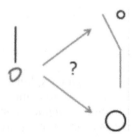

Fig. 6. The stroke on the left can be either the first stroke of a switch or an output

4.4 Detecting Multi Symbol Strokes

In previous section, we have shown how to detect a stroke that is a subpart of a symbol. In this section, we present how we detect the strokes that constitute several symbols. Figure 7 presents an example: the stroke on the left can't be interpreted as one electrical component or a part of one: this stroke is a sequence of three connections.

In order to interpret this stroke correctly, it is necessary to segment it. As presented in section 0, the DALI method is not based on a systematic segmentation process, which means that it is necessary to detect the need to segment punctually. For that purpose, we consider all outlier strokes as segmentation candidates: a stroke that can not be interpreted may need to be segmented. After the segmentation

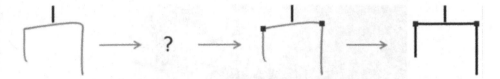

Fig. 7. One stroke that should be interpreted as a sequence of three connections

process, the system tries to analyze the resulting strokes: if they can all be interpreted, then the initial stroke was actually containing several symbols, otherwise it is an outlier stroke.

5 Design of "Script and Go Electrical Sketches"

In this section, we show how the DALI method has been used to design a system for the interactive composition of electrical sketches. As this system is addressed to technicians working in constrained environments such as building sites, it is essential to limit as much as possible to disturb the user with interpretation errors. Moreover, technicians are often standing in front of installations, which is not comfortable: our goal was thus to design a system to draw sketches as quickly as possible.

In this context, we have chosen to reject outlier strokes as well as ambiguous strokes. This means that each time the system is not able to interpret a stroke, it is deleted and must be re-drawn by the user; we have found it more adapted than asking explicitly for the correct interpretation, possibly between a subset of symbols. In fact, we even give an advantage to rejection with regards to errors, because it is much less constraining to only have to redraw a stroke than to also have to delete a misunderstood symbol.

"Script&Go Electrical Sketches" has been designed in collaboration with Evodia [4], a company that spreads out pen-based solutions. The statistical recognizers are based on fuzzy inference systems [2]. It is commercialized and used daily by a hundred of technicians, directly on building sites. Figure 8 presents a picture of a technician using "Script&Go Electrical Sketches". Videos are available at [4].

In [8], we have presented some evaluations of "Script&Go Electrical Sketches". We have first shown that the system performs interpretation in real-time (the median stroke processing time is always less than 0.4 seconds even when sketches become very complex). The experiments have also emphasized the good performances of the system in terms of pattern recognition: only 4.6% of the strokes are misunderstood and 3.6% are rejected (either because they are considered as outlier or ambiguous). We have also analyzed the performances in terms of segmentation and shown that it is consistent to only consider outlier strokes as candidates for the segmentation; this way, 91.8% of the strokes that need to be segmented are detected.

848   S. Macé and E. Anquetil

© Stéphane Texier

Fig. 8. A technician using "Script&Go Electrical Sketches"

6 Conclusion

The main thematic of this paper was *eager interpretation* of hand-drawn sketches, i.e. the incremental interpretation of the user strokes and the associated visual feedback. We have shown how it makes it possible to design a robust and efficient analysis process that exploits implicit validation and explicit correction from the user to make the most coherent decision. We have focused on the requirements of eager interpretation in order to design an intuitive human-computer interaction and shown how we overcome each of them thanks to pattern recognition techniques (for instance reject options to detect outlier and ambiguous strokes). All these techniques make it possible to design an interactive sketch composition process.

The DALI method that integrates the concepts presented in this article has been validated in an industrial context: it has been used to design a system for the composition of electrical sketches that is commercialized.

Future work will aim at quantifying the usability of the systems designed with the DALI method. For that purpose, we will work in collaboration with specialists from the experimental psychology community and end-users of these systems.

Acknowledgments. The authors would like to thank Guy Lorette, for his precious advices, as well as Stéphane Texier for letting us use the picture in figure 8.

References

1. Alvarado, C., Davis, R.: Dynamically Constructed Bayes Nets for Multi-Domain Sketch Understanding. In: Proceedings of the Nineteenth International Joint Conference on Artificial Intelligence (IJCAI 2005), pp. 1407–1412 (2005)
2. Anquetil, E., Bouchereau, E.: Integration of an on-line handwriting recognition system in a smart phone device. In: Proceedings of the Sixteenth International Conference on Pattern Recognition (ICPR 2002), pp. 192–195 (2002)
3. Chok, S., Marriott, K.: Automatic generation of intelligent diagram editors. ACM Transactions on Computer-Human Interaction 10(3), 244–276 (2003)
4. Evodia, http://www.evodia.fr
5. Frankish, C., Hull, R., Morgan, P.: Recognition accuracy and user acceptance of pen interfaces. In: Proceedings of the SIGCHI conference on Human factors in computing systems (CHI 1995), pp. 503–510 (1995)
6. Hammond, T., Davis, R.: LADDER, a sketching language for user interface developers. Computers & Graphics 29(4), 518–532 (2005)
7. Macé, S., Anquetil, E.: Design of a Pen-Based Electric Diagram Editor Based on Context-Driven Constraint Multiset Grammars. In: Jacko, J.A. (ed.) HCI 2007. LNCS, vol. 4551, pp. 418–428. Springer, Heidelberg (2007)
8. Macé, S., Anquetil, E.: Eager Interpretation of On-Line Hand-Drawn Structured Documents: The DALI Methodology. Pattern Recognition (2009)
9. Marriott, K.: Constraint multiset grammars. In: Proceedings of the IEEE Symposium on Visual Languages (VL 1994), pp. 118–125 (1994)
10. Mouchère, H., Anquetil, E.: A Unified Strategy to Deal with Different Natures of Reject. In: Proceedings of the International Conference on Pattern Recognition (ICPR 2006), pp. 792–795 (2006)
11. Zanibbi, R., Novins, K., Arvo, J., Zanibbi, K.: Aiding manipulation of handwritten mathematical expressions through style-preserving morphs. In: Proceedings of Graphics Interface (GI 2001), pp. 127–134 (2001)

Specification of a Drawing Facility for Diagram Editors

Sonja Maier and Mark Minas

Universität der Bundeswehr München, Germany
{sonja.maier,mark.minas}@unibw.de

Abstract. The purpose of this paper is to give an overview of a drawing approach for the visualization of diagrams. The approach is tailored to editors for visual languages, which support structured editing as well as free-hand editing. In this approach, the editor developer visually specifies layout behavior. From this specification a drawing facility is generated. With the generated editor, the user may perform incremental diagram drawing at any time. When visualizing components, taking into account geometric dependencies between different components for layout computation is a challenging task. Therefore, we choose the visual languages Petri nets and GUI forms as running examples. Based on these examples, we show the applicability of our approach to graph-based and hierarchical visual languages.

1 Introduction

When implementing an editor for a visual language, layout is a challenging task. The drawing approach should produce a good-looking result and should support the user. Additionally, the layout specification should be very easy. In the following, we introduce an approach that aims at achieving these concurrent goals.

The approach supports incremental layout computation, which is triggered by user input. As a consequence, layout needs to be computed at runtime. It is tailored to this requirement, which is best known in the graph drawing context as *online layout computation* [10].

With our generic approach, it is possible to compute an initial layout. E.g. for a Petri net editor, a simple graph layout is implemented. In addition, the approach is best suited for incremental layout [7, 8], which starts with an initial layout and performs minor changes to improve it while still preserving the mental map of the original layout.

Our approach succeeds in the context of editors that support *structured editing* as well as *free-hand editing*. Structured editors offer the user some operations that transform correct diagrams into (other) correct diagrams. Free-hand editors allow arranging diagram components on the screen without any restrictions.

It was implemented and tested in DıaMETa [4], an editor generation framework. With this tool an *editor developer* may create an editor for a specific visual language, e.g. Petri nets. The result is an editor that can be utilized by the *editor user* to create Petri nets. With DıaMETa, not only editors for graph-based visual languages like Petri nets, but also editors for other visual languages like GUI forms can be created (see Figure 1).

J.A. Jacko (Ed.): Human-Computer Interaction, Part II, HCII 2009, LNCS 5611, pp. 850–859, 2009.
© Springer-Verlag Berlin Heidelberg 2009

In Section 2 we introduce two visual editors that serve as running examples in this paper. Section 3 gives an overview of the functionality our approach offers to the editor user. The layout algorithm, which is applied after user interaction, is described in Section 4. Section 5 provides an overview of the possibilities the editor developer has when he creates a layout specification. Some details about the implementation of the approach are shown in Section 6. Especially DIAMETa is introduced in this section. In Section 7 future work is summarized and the paper is concluded.

2 Running Examples

In general, we distinguish two categories of visual languages: graph-like visual languages and non-graph-like visual languages. Examples for the first category are Petri nets, mindmaps or business process models. Examples for the second category are Nassi-Shneiderman diagrams, VEX diagrams [3] or GUI forms. In the following we shortly introduce the two visual languages that will serve as running examples.

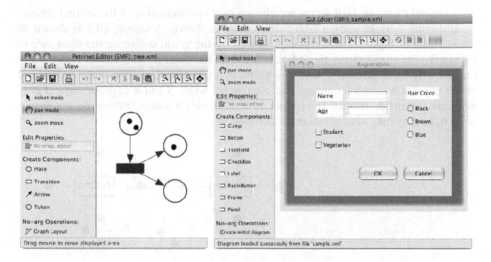

Fig. 1. Petri net editor & GUI forms editor

2.1 Petri Net Editor

As a representative of the first category, we choose Petri nets. In Figure 1 (left side), a Petri net editor, which was created with DIAMETa, is shown. Internally, the concrete syntax of the visual language is represented by a graph. More precisely, it is represented by a hypergraph [4], a generalization of graphs. In contrast to graphs, edges of hypergraphs may visit more than two nodes. E.g., a Petri net, as shown on the left side of Figure 2, is represented by the graph shown on the right side of Figure 2. Here, nodes are visualized as circles, *and edges are visualized as arrows and as rectangles*. Places and transitions have one attachment area (the edge "connects" one node), whereas arrows have two attachment areas (the edge "connects" two nodes).

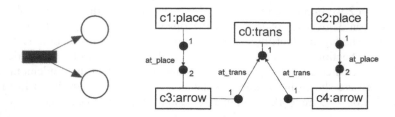

Fig. 2. A Petri net consisting of a transition and two places, and its graph model

In the graph, the edges that are visualized as rectangles represent the components contained in the diagram: one transition, two places and two arrows. The edges `at_place` and `at_trans` represent connections between arrow and place and connections between arrow and transition.

2.2 GUI Forms Editor

As a second example, GUI forms are chosen as a representative of the second category. In Figure 1 (right side), a GUI forms editor is shown. A sample GUI is shown on the left side of Figure 3, which is represented by the graph shown on the right side of Figure 3. The graph stores the information that the diagram consists of two buttons that are aligned horizontally, and of a panel that contains these two buttons. Nodes 1 and 2 express horizontal connections. Similarly, nodes 3 and 4 express vertical connections. An inside relation is expressed by the nodes 5 and 6. Buttons do not have a node 6, as they may not contain other components.

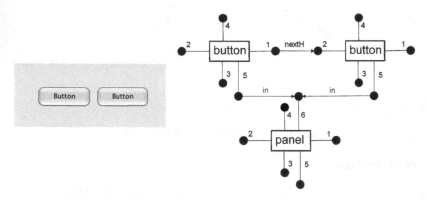

Fig. 3. A GUI consisting of two buttons and a panel, and its graph model

3 Layout Modes

After introducing the running examples, we now present an overview of the functionality our approach offers to the editor user.

The layout engine may either be called automatically each time the diagram is changed by the user, or the layout engine may be called explicitly, e.g. by clicking a

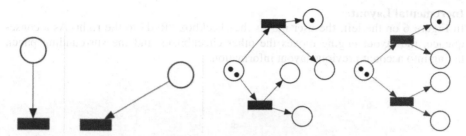

Fig. 4. Automatic & static layout

button. The first strategy is called *automatic layout* in the following, and the second strategy *static layout*. Furthermore, it may either be that a diagram is visualized the first time, or that a diagram was visualized already. The first usually happens in structured editing mode, the second in free-hand editing mode. In the first case, the layout engine does not take into account any previous layout information, and hence computes an *initial layout*. In the second case, the layout engine takes into account previous layout information, which means that an *incremental layout* is computed. In the next paragraph, we give an example of each of the four categories.

Automatic Layout
On the left side of Figure 4, a place is moved to the right. During movement, the arrow stays attached to the outlines of the components at any time.

Static Layout
After creating the diagram in image 3 of Figure 4, the user may click the button "Graph Layout" (see Figure 1). The layout engine considers the previous layout information, and draws the diagram as shown in image 4.

Initial Layout
For the GUI forms editor, we defined a structured editing operation that creates the graph shown on the left side of Figure 5. From this graph, the visualization that is shown on the right side of Figure 5 is automatically created.

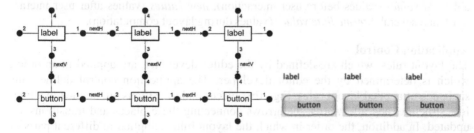

Fig. 5. Initial layout

Incremental Layout
In Figure 6 on the left, the user moves the checkbox "Red" to the right. As a consequence, the layout engine moves the other checkboxes and the surrounding panel, taking into account previous layout information.

Fig. 6. Incremental layout

4 Layout Algorithm

After describing the different layout modes, we now explain what happens if the layout engine is called. Roughly speaking, several *layout rules* are applied, following an application recipe (called *application control*).

The algorithm is based on ideas described in [1, 2]. In the new approach, layout rules are defined on the concrete syntax level, whereas the application control is described on the abstract syntax level. As layout rules are defined on the concrete syntax level, it is now possible to specify them visually in the application domain.

Layout Rule
The layout algorithm consists of several layout rules. Examples for layout rules are "align buttons horizontally" or "keep arrows attached to places". For each rule, one diagram component is given as input. This is usually a component, the user changed, or a component the layout engine changed. E.g., for the rule "keep arrows attached to places", this is the place. Then other components that are necessary for the layout rule are identified. In case of the rule "keep arrows attached to places", this is the arrow. The set of required components is called *pattern*. Then, if a certain *condition* is fulfilled, a particular *action* is applied. For the example rule, the condition checks if the "arrow is correctly attached", and the action executes "attach arrow correctly". This means that one (or more) layout attribute(s) of one (ore more) component(s) is (are) changed. In conditions and actions, attribute values may be accessed. Here, several values are available: *old values* (values before user interaction), *new values* (values after user interaction), and several *intermediate values* (values during layout computation).

Application Control
The layout rules, which are defined by the editor developer, are applied in an order, which is determined by the editor developer. The application control defines this sequence of applied layout rules. E.g., first places and transitions are aligned in a tree-like structure, and afterwards, the arrows connecting these places and transitions are updated. In addition, the order in which the layout rule is applied to different parts of the diagram usually follows an exact plan. For instance, buttons are aligned

horizontally from left to right. The layout creator can choose whether a rule is applied once, or iteratively until a certain condition is fulfilled. Besides, a rule may either be applied to just one match, or to all matches that occur.

5 Layouter Definition

In this section we will describe, how layout rules may be defined, and what concepts are used when implementing the application control. Rules are defined visually, whereas the application control has to be written by hand. From the visual specification of rules, Java classes are generated. The generated classes, together with some handwritten classes and some framework classes form the desired layout engine, which may be included in the editor.

5.1 Definition of Layout Rule

To allow a more intuitive description of layout, we introduced a visual language for layout rule definition, which is based on the concrete syntax of the diagram language.

A generic editor for specifying these rules is provided. This language-specific editor is based on a diagram editor for a certain visual language, which does not support layout yet (as shown in Figure 10).

In Figure 7, a screenshot of such an editor for GUI forms is shown. In order to create a layout rule, the editor developer draws a pattern, and enters the pattern name, a condition and a rule in the middle of the editor (from top to bottom). For specifying the pattern, he may use the components available on the left side of the editor. In the

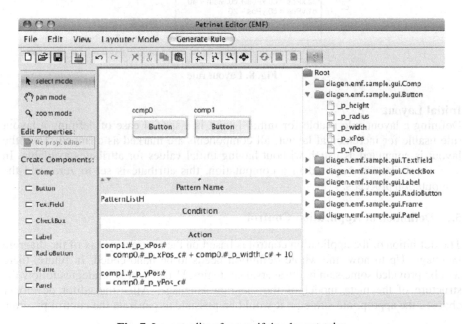

Fig. 7. Layout editor for specifying layout rules

example, he uses the component button twice. For specifying conditions and rules, he may access the attributes shown on the right side of the editor. In the example, he uses the attributes xPos, yPos and width.

Incremental Layout

To define a layout rule usable for incremental layout, we need to proceed as follows: He has to provide a pattern, a condition (which is optional) and a rule. In the example (Figure 7), the pattern consists of two buttons. The left button (comp0) is the component that was changed by the user. In the example, no condition is provided, which means that the rule is applied each time. The rule that is defined here updates the attributes xPos and yPos of the right component (comp1). Here, the new values of the attributes are used. ("_c" stands for changed.) If we want to use old values, we may access an attribute via #_p_xPos#.

Figure 8 shows another rule that modifies attributes. On the right side of Figure 8, a Petri net before and after applying a rule that updates the attributes xPos and yPos of the places c1 and c2 is shown. On the left side of Figure 8, the pattern is presented. Here, component c0 is the component, which the user has changed. A simplified version of the condition as well as the rule is shown in the middle of Figure 8. The rule introduces a (rather simple) tree-like structure to Petri nets.

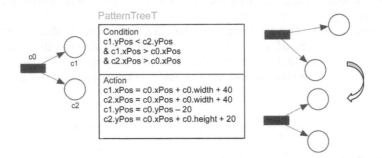

Fig. 8. Layout rule

Initial Layout

Defining a layout rule usable for initial layout is a special case of defining a layout rule usable for incremental layout: all components are marked as changed. Then the layout is computed as usual, without having initial values for attributes available. In case an attribute is required in a computation, this attribute is set to zero, and the computation proceeds.

5.2 Definition of Application Control

The definition of the application control is based on the abstract syntax of the diagram language. Up to now, the whole definition needs to be hand-coded. In future, there will be provided some standard traversal strategies. Usually these strategies follow the structure of the meta model of the diagram language. After the editor developer chooses the appropriate strategy, it would be possible to generate the control program automatically. Then, only the choice which action is applied to what part of the diagram needs to be defined.

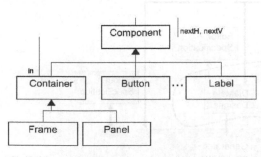

For instance, an excerpt of the meta model of GUI forms is shown in Figure 9. If a button is resized, we follow the links nextH and nextV. Following the link nextH, the next components are moved and resized. When following the link nextV, the next components are also moved and resized.

Fig. 9. Excerpt of the meta model of GUI forms

Another example is moving a panel. Then, the components, which are contained in the surrounding panel, are moved. Surrounding components (e.g. another panel or a frame) are also moved, if the moved panel would leave the surrounding component, otherwise.

6 Implementation

The approach was implemented and tested in DIAMETa [4], an editor generation framework. The editor generation framework DIAMETa provides an environment for rapidly developing diagram editors based on meta modeling. Figure 1, for instance, shows a DIAMETa editor for Petri nets (left) and a DIAMETa editor for GUI forms (right). Each DIAMETa editor is based on the same editor architecture, which is adjusted to the specific diagram language. DIAMETa's tool support for specification and code generation, primarily the DIAMETa Designer is described in this section.

6.1 DIAMETa Framework

The DIAMETa environment consists of a framework (consisting of layout editor framework and editor framework) and the DIAMETa Designer (Figure 10). The framework is basically a collection of Java classes and provides the dynamic editor functionality, necessary for editing and analyzing diagrams.

In order to create an editor for a specific diagram language, the editor developer has to enter two specifications: First, the *ECore Specification* [5], and second the *Editor Specification*. Besides, the editor developer has to provide a *Layout Specification*, which was described in Section 5.

A language's class diagram is defined by an ECore specification. The EMF compiler is used to create Java code that represents this model. The editor developer uses the DIAMETa Designer for specifying the concrete syntax and the visual appearance of diagram components, e.g., places (Petri nets) are drawn as circles. The DIAMETa Designer generates Java code from this specification.

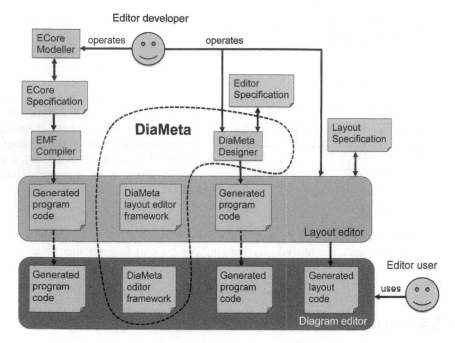

Fig. 10. DiaMeta framework

The Java code generated by the DiaMeta Designer, the Java code created by the EMF compiler, and the layout editor framework, implement a *Layout Editor* for the specified diagram language. The editor developer uses this Layout Editor for specifying the layout engine. From this specification, Java code is generated.

The Java code generated by the DiaMeta Designer, the Java code created by the EMF compiler, the Java code generated by the Layout Editor and the editor framework, finally implement a *Diagram Editor* for the specified diagram language.

7   Future Work and Conclusions

In this paper, we gave an overview of a drawing approach for the visualization of diagrams. The approach is tailored to an editor for visual languages, which supports structured editing as well as free-hand editing. Here, the editor developer visually specifies layout behavior. From this specification a drawing facility is generated. With the generated editor, the user may perform incremental diagram drawing at any time. As running examples, we chose the visual languages Petri nets and GUI forms, as representatives for graph-like and non-graph-like visual languages.

An open issue is the reusability of layout rules and application controls. At the moment, they are rewritten each time they are needed. To cope with this challenge, we plan to apply the concepts used in [11].

In this regard, we also plan to provide a way of integrating hand-written graph drawing algorithms. Right now, we are developing the graph drawing algorithms tree layout, force-directed layout, edge routing and layered drawing [6], which are tailored to the special needs of dynamic graph drawing.

Currently, we also work on a three-dimensional visualization of visual languages. In this context, we extend our layouting approach to a third dimension.

Up to now, we primarily focus on achieving "nice" results. In future, we also plan to take care of easy diagram manipulation. In this context, some user studies will need to be performed. To evaluate the "degree of mental map preservation", some metrics will be helpful [9].

References

1. Maier, S., Minas, M.: A Static Layout Algorithm for DiaMeta. In: Proc. of the 7th Intl. Workshop on Graph Transformation and Visual Modeling Techniques (GT-VMT 2008). ECEASST (2008)
2. Maier, S., Mazanek, S., Minas, M.: Layout Specification on the Concrete and Abstract Syntax Level of a Diagram Language. In: Proc. of the 2nd Intl. Workshop on Layout of (Software) Engineering Diagrams (LED 2008). ECEASST (2008)
3. Citrin, W., Hall, R., Zorn, B.: Programming with visual expressions. In: Proc. of IEEE Symposium on Visual Languages (VL 1995). IEEE Computer Society Press, Los Alamitos (1995)
4. Minas, M.: Generating Meta-Model-Based Freehand Editors. In: Proc. of 3rd Intl. Workshop on Graph Based Tools. ECEASST (2006)
5. Budinsky, F., Brodsky, S.A., Merks, E.: Eclipse Modeling Framework. Pearson Education, London (2003)
6. Di Battista, G., Eades, P., Tamassia, R., Tollis, I.G.: Graph Drawing. Prentice Hall, Englewood Cliffs (1999)
7. Purchase, H.C., Samra, A.: Extremes are better: Investigating mental map preservation in dynamic graphs. In: Proceedings Diagrams. LNCS(LNAI) (2008)
8. Misue, K., Eades, P., Lai, W., Sugiyama, K.: Layout adjustment and the mental map. Journal of Visual Languages and Computing (1995)
9. Bridgeman, S., Tamassia, R.: Difference metrics for interactive orthogonal graph drawing algorithms. In: Whitesides, S.H. (ed.) GD 1998. LNCS, vol. 1547, p. 57. Springer, Heidelberg (1999)
10. Branke, J.: Dynamic Graph Drawing. In: Drawing Graphs (1999)
11. Schmidt, C., Cramer, B., Kastens, U.: Usability Evaluation of a System for Implementation of Visual Languages. In: Proceedings VL/HCC 2007 (2007)

A Basic Study on a Drawing-Learning Support System in the Networked Environment

Takashi Nagai[1], Mizue Kayama[2], and Kazunori Itoh[2]

[1] Graduate School of Science and Technology, Shinshu University
nagai@ngi644.net
[2] Faculty of Engineering, Shinshu University
4-17-1 Wakasato, Nagano 380-8553 Japan
{kayama,itoh}@cs.shinshu-u.ac.jp

Abstract. The purpose of this study is to develop a support system in drawing-learning within a networked environment. In this paper, we describe the results of potential assessment for our system. Two assessment approaches are shown. One is the possibility of a digital pen as a drawing-tool. The other approach is the effectiveness of the drawing-learning support in the networked environment, based on the reuse of the learner's and/or expert's drawing process. The drawing process model for supporting individual drawing-learning is also discussed.

Keywords: Drawing-learning, Learning Support System, On-line Class, Drawing Process, Digital Pen.

1 Introduction

Drawing is one of the basic skills in art education, and all beginners in art must acquire drawing skills first [7,8]. This type of learning requires repeated practice with a trial-and-error process [2,5,6], so to learn drawing; it is categorized as skill-learning [4]. Recently, art education has been given in the networked environment; however, there is a limited range of functions and content for basic skill-learning like drawing [3,10,11]. In this type of learning, as the individual learner, especially for the beginner, recognizing drawing habits that need to be corrected, or what inappropriate drawing expressions are, is hard [9]. So their learning is a slow process.

The purpose of this study is to explore a support system for beginners in drawing within a networked environment. In this system, learners can receive the advice and assessments from art experts without time and/or place constraints. We investigate the possibility of supporting drawing-learning. In this paper, at first, the possibility of the digital pen as a writing tool [1], and the effectiveness of the drawing-learning support in the networked environment are discussed. Then, developing the drawing process model and its application as individual learning support are considered.

J.A. Jacko (Ed.): Human-Computer Interaction, Part II, HCII 2009, LNCS 5611, pp. 860–868, 2009.
© Springer-Verlag Berlin Heidelberg 2009

2 Drawing-Learning in Networked Environment

2.1 Learning Process

Drawing is the technique of looking carefully a motif, comprehending the figure, and portraying the motif with writing tools. The major difference between the off-line class and the on-line class is the availability of instruction during drawing. This type of instruction is more important than giving only a review for the finished work. Therefore, asking quick and personalized feedback from a tutor is an indispensable function for the networked learning environment. In this study, the learner's drawing process is recorded and reused in order to implement immediate and adaptive instruction.

The following is an ideal learning process in the proposed learning environment.

1. The tutor gives learners task/exercise.
2. Learners create a motif which fits a given task, draw it, and then send their drawing process data and finished work to the tutor.
3. Tutors replay the learner's drawing process, and then give guidance and correction to his process and work. Then, tutors send the assessment to each learner.
4. Learners review the returned assessment via the annotated drawing process and/or revised work.

2.2 Drawing-Learning Support in the Networked Environment

To clarify the effectiveness of the drawing-learning support, we interviewed five experts involved in the off-line drawing class. Before this investigation, all experts tried using the prototype model of our system. On our specific occasion, the drawing processes of some learners, having the same motif, utilizing pencils and digital pens, were used. (See Figure 1) All experts replayed and reviewed the learners' process data by using our system. The following are some feedback comments from those experts.

- Tutors are able to review the learner's drawing process and work after they finish their work; therefore, tutors can give adequate and appropriate guidance on the learner's need. Since tutors can check the whole drawing process and finished work, they can avoid unfair and/or misguided assessment.
- As tutors can present the specific assessment directly to learners; learners are able to confirm what tutors corrected repeatedly; learners would not forget, or miss, what was discussed in their class.
- Learners are able to recognize their incorrect behaviors when they replay their own drawing.

The learner's drawing processes were replayed and reused for detailed analysis of all experts. That is to say, the efficiency of the reviewing function for the learner's drawing process and drawing-learning support in a networked environment are shown.

Fig. 1. An example of drawing exercise with a pencil (left) and digital-pen (right)

2.3   The Possibility of a Digital Pen for Writing Tool

A general digital pen [1] as a drawing tool is applied to record the learner's drawing processes. To evaluate the possibility of a digital pen as a drawing-tool, four items were examined. The checked items were: 1) the maximum opening time, 2) the minimum writing pressure, 3) the maximum drawing density, and 4) the angle limit for the inclination. Table 1 shows these results.

Table 1. Some Specifications of the Digital Pen

Evaluated Item	Content	Result
The maximum operating time.	Continuable drawing time; how long a fully-charged battery takes to run out of power.	210 min. (Avg., 5 trials) Max 218 min., Min 199min.
The minimum writing pressure.	Gradually touch the pen tip to the paper; measure the alteration of pen pressure and the consistency of drawn lines on the paper.	The thin and weak line (but visible) is not able to record. Meanwhile, some lines, when pen pressure is zero, are possible to record.
The maximum drawing density.	To check the limit consistency, some lines are drawn to make a crosshatch in the specific field.	The digital pen can reach the upper limit of the density as a ballpoint pen.
The limit angle for the inclination.	Tilting the digital pen right and left, in a horizontal way.	Limit angle : $43° \leq \theta \leq 137°$

Five experts were shown these results and tried to express some drawings with this pen. After that, we conducted interviews with these experts about the possibilities of the digital pen. All the experts accepted the fundamental capability of this writing tool. At the same time, they also pointed out the need of adequate drawing tasks to suit those limitations shown in Table 1. Moreover, the following demerits, in comparing the digital pen and the pencil, were discussed:

- Not able to erase once learner draws.
- The width of line is fixed.
- The ways of expression is limited.

As a result, all experts agree this pen could be used as a wring tool in the drawing-learning, if the users of this system are limited to beginners. The demerits mentioned above would work well in beginner-level lessons. So, the possibility of the digital pen as a drawing tool is shown.

3 Considering the Drawing Process

In this study, the learner's drawing process is reused in two evaluations. One is the tutors' process evaluation, and the other is an individual learning support system's process evaluation. For the latter, we propose the automated assessment function based on the drawing process model.

3.1 Steps of Drawing Process

To clarify the drawing process of the art experts, we interviewed five experts. The steps and their contents of the drawing process are shown in Table 2.

Table 2. Steps and Contents of Drawing Process

Steps	Contents
1	Looking carefully at the motif.
2	Interpreting where the motif is located.
3	Fixing the composition with regard to the balance of the motif and picture plane.
4	Capturing the motif as a composition of simple configuration (i.e., rectangular solids).
5	Analyzing the architecture of the motif and capturing the shape.
6	Adding the texture of the motif.
7	Giving final lines/curves in detail.

3.2   Relation between Drawing Process and Finished Work

From the quantitative investigation of the drawing processes, mentioned in 2.3, the time variation of strokes and the pen-pressures show three different phases in the drawing process. Figure 2 presents the features of strokes and pen-pressures in these phases.

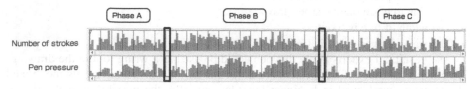

Fig. 2. The Example of Drawing Process

To divide each phase, two criterions must be fulfilled at the same time. The first one is the occurrence the number of strokes and pen-pressure become zero. These are shown in the squared areas in Figure 2. The second is the number of strokes, or average pen-pressure that must be different in-between continuing phases, which divided in the first criterion.

The drawing results of each phase are shown in Figure 3. According to the quantitative features of the drawing process shown in Figure 2 and the drawing results shown in Figure 3, the features of each phase are able to be described.

Phase A: Learners interpret picture composition, then fix naive lines. And they capture perspectives.

Phase B: Learners draw the motif totally, and the drawing becomes assessable.

Phase C: Learners add the texture and every detail of the motif. Then, they fix the balance of motif in the picture plane.

The learners drew until they were fully satisfied with the enhanced content of the drawing and then the drawing became their final work.

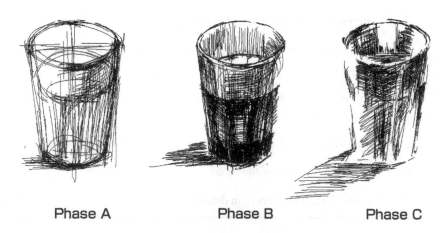

Fig. 3. The Drawing Results of Each Phase

3.3 Drawing Process and Drawing Phases

To identify the three phases of drawing data, we have to define the concrete and objective features of each phase.

Table 3 shows the quantitative features of these three phases. In this table, stroke pressure / number / line types; degree of assembled strokes size / dispersion; and the areas of drawing are presented. Pen pressure and number of strokes are relative values in the drawing process. Size and dispersion on the stroke sets are relative values in the drawing paper, or whole area, with composition. Each item is distinguished in two or three levels. Pen pressure is in low, medium, and high. Number of strokes is in light, medium, and superior. Line types are in straight-line, simple curve-line, and multiplicity. Simple curve-line means that when a line is changed to a Bezier curve, the control point is on the side against the line aspect. Multiplicity lines are made up with all kinds of lines. The size of stroke sets is large or small; dispersion is even or unequal; areas of drawing are in broad or narrow.

Table 4 is the connection of the drawing phase with the drawing steps. Phase A corresponds to steps 1, 2, 3, and 4; Phase B comprises steps 1 and 5; Phase C covers steps 1, 6 and 7. Phase A tends to appear in the beginning of whole drawing process. Phase B appears after Phase A and/or before Phase C. This phase commonly does not occur in the beginning and ending; Phase C often appears in the end of the drawing process.

Our drawing process model is developed by an inference engine which is able to detect the appearance of those three drawing phases based on their geometrical features shown in Table 2, 3 and 4.

Table 3. Features of Drawing Phases

Phase	Stroke			Stroke sets		Width of drawing
	Pressure	Number	Line types	Size	Dispersion	
A	Low	Light, Medium	Straight-line, simple curve-line	Large	Unequal	Broad
B	Medium, high	Superior	Multiplicity	Small	Even	Narrow
C	Low, Medium, High	Medium	Multiplicity	Small	Unequal	Narrow

Table 4. Connection of Drawing Steps with Drawing Phases

Phase	Steps	Timing
A	1, 2, 3, 4	Not end
B	1, 5	After A, Ahead of C
C	1, 6, 7	Not beginning

4   Individual Learning Support

The learner's drawing processes were arranged by the features in Table 3 , then divided into the three phases. Based on these results and the drawing process model mentioned in 3.3, we were able to provide some functions of the individual learning support for learners. For instance, if a given exercise is to draw a glass on a table, many beginners will start drawing the configuration of a glass. A cure for this action is to train beginners to draw a simple rectangular solid in order to understand the third dimension. This technique is for beginners to draw complicated configuration objects easily. In addition, the lines of a simple rectangular solid are auxiliary lines, so tutors should instruct learners not to draw those lines thickly. If learners draw incorrect lines with less pen pressure, the final work has a very small effect on the draft.

Considering the learner's drawing processes, the strokes are strong; line types are multiplicity; assembled strokes are small; and drawing areas are not broad. It is understandable that these features are not included in Phase A. Learners obtained the following advice from the support system; "observe the motif carefully, capture the motif as a simple configuration and start drawing it, control pen pressure in low, and use straight lines or simple curves to draw the motif. " At the same time, this serves experts and others for references.

Reusing experts and others' drawing processes help learners understand advice more clearly and easily. Moreover, comparing one's drawing process with others

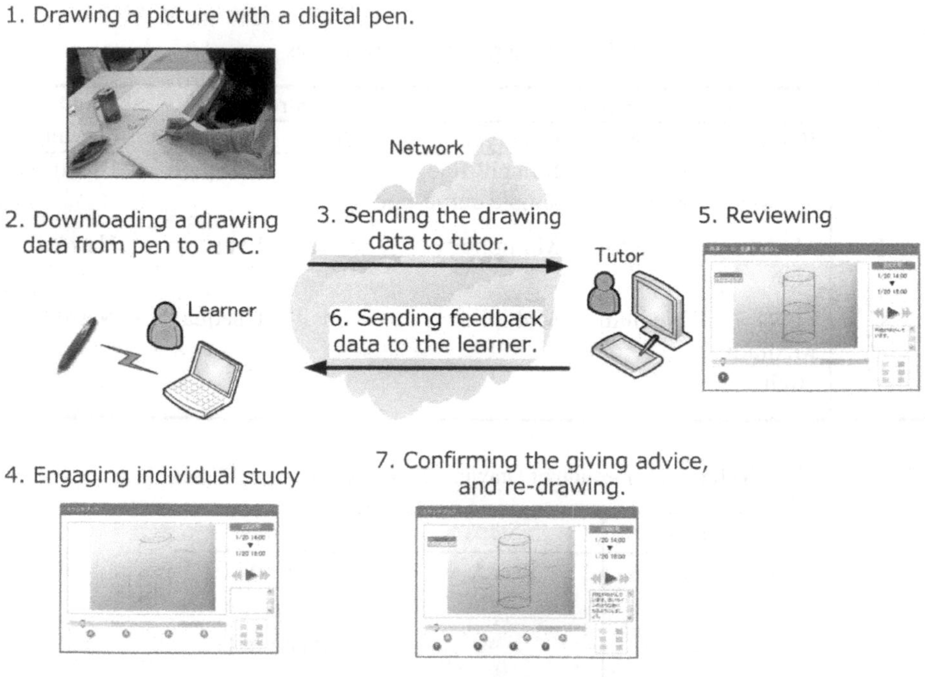

Fig. 4. Learning Flow with the Proposed System

could help them find new techniques and/or methods in drawing. This flow of learning is situated so that when learners hand in their drawing processes and then they obtain the tutors' feedback as individual learning support tools (See Figure 4). This system is able to detect the learner's drawing habits and then give advice to revise them; therefore, the expected merits of the system are fulfillments of automated individual learning and an improvement in learning efficiency.

5 Conclusion

In this paper, we describe the effectiveness of the digital pen as a drawing tool and the possibility and benefit of a drawing support system in a networked environment. As a result, the digital pen has high potentiality as a writing tool. Drawing-learning in a networked environment is also useful and available if the uses of the system are limited to the beginners of drawing. Moreover, we find the need for adequate drawing tasks to suit constraints and limitations of the digital pen. Additionally, we discussed a drawing process and its application for the individual learning support.

For future work, we will complete the implementation of the drawing process model and this learning support system. In addition, we have to extract the expertise, which is related to teaching a drawing method in a networked environment.

Acknowledgments

We give special thanks to Dai Nippon Printing Co., Ltd. who supported this research.

References

1. Anoto Group AB: Digital pen & paper, http://www.anoto.com/the-pen.aspx (accessed, 2009/2/1)
2. Bernstein, N.: The Co-ordination and Regulation of Movements. Pergamon Press, New York (1967)
3. Ferraris, C., Martel, C.: Regulation in Groupware: The Example of a Collaborative Drawing Tool for Young Children. In: Proc. of the 6th Int. Workshop on Groupware, pp. 119–127 (2000)
4. Furukawa, K.: Skill Science. Journal of Japanese Society for Artificial Intelligence 19(3), 355–364 (2004) (in Japanese)
5. Latash, M.L.: Progress in Motor Control. In: Bernstein's Traditions in Movement Studies, vol. 1. Human Kinetics, Urbana (1998)
6. Latash, M.L.: Progress in Motor Control. In: Structure-Function Relation in Voluntary Movement, vol. 2. Human Kinetics, Urbana (2002)
7. Sato, K.: Developmental Trial in Drawing Instruction at Art/Design Universities. Shizuoka University of Art and Culture bulletin 4, 153–162 (2004) (in Japanese)
8. Sekine, E.: A Trial to develop the ART SYSTEM. Art Education (6), 89–100 (1984) (in Japanese)

9. Takagi, S., Matsuda, N., Soga, M., Taki, H., Shima, T., Yashimoto, F.: A learning support system for beginners in pencil drawing. In: Proc. of the 1st Int. Conf. on Computer Graphics and Interactive Techniques in Australasia and South East Asia, pp. 281–282 (2003)
10. Tweddle, L.K.: Reinventing Papert's Constructionism - Boosting Young Children's Writing Skills with e-Learning Designed for Dyslexics. The Electronic Journal of e-Learning 6(3), 227–234 (2008)
11. University of the Arts London: MA Visual Arts (Digital Arts Online), http://www.wimbledon.arts.ac.uk/ (accessed, 2009/2/1)

Benefit and Evaluation of Interactive 3D Process Data Visualization for the Presentation of Complex Problems

Dorothea Pantförder[1], Birgit Vogel-Heuser[1], and Karin Schweizer[2]

[1] Chair of Embedded Systems, Faculty of Electrical Engineering/Computer Science,
University of Kassel, Wilhelmshöher Allee 73, 34121 Kassel, Germany
{pantfoerder,vogel-heuser}@uni-kassel.de
[2] Faculty of Social Sciences, University of Mannheim,
Schloss, Ehrenhof Ost, 68131 Mannheim, Germany
kschweiz@t-online.de

Abstract. The increasing complexity of industrial plants and more intelligent equipment technology lead to a growing amount of process data. The approach of interactive 3D process data visualization and associated training concepts for processes without a process model can assists operators to analyze complex processes. This paper describes a set of experiments that analyzed the benefits of a 3D data presentation as part of an HMI in combination with different types of operator training in process control.

Keywords: 3D visualization, operator training.

1 Motivation

One of the main questions in industry in the recent years is how to support the operator in monitoring and to controlling processes that are getting more and more complex. If the information is not preprocessed, more intelligent equipment technology may lead to an overload of information. Centralized control rooms and the reduction of operating personal increases the operator's work load. Finally, this can result in a rising error rate. Common 2D concepts in HMI and training may not support the operator sufficiently. The 3D process data visualization approach can support the operator in handling large amounts of data. By coding the data, e.g. through color or surface design, the information content of the visualization can be increased. By means of coloring and surface design it is possible to show more data in one view and to visualize potential coherences. Previous works showed the reduction of the number of visualization screens when using 3D [1].

3D data visualization can also be applied in training to support the operator in developing process knowledge. A 3D data player, a so called 3D slider, can be used to teach process dynamic to the operator on basis of real process data for processes without a process model. The operator is able to learn the process behavior in critical situations during the training phase and to identify similar situations in the operating phase.

Up to date, there are no detailed evaluation for 3D process data visualization in process control and operator training. This paper describes an empirical evaluation

J.A. Jacko (Ed.): Human-Computer Interaction, Part II, HCII 2009, LNCS 5611, pp. 869–878, 2009.
© Springer-Verlag Berlin Heidelberg 2009

that was conducted within the project PAST-P[1] to show the benefits of 3D visualization in process control.

2   State of the Art

In the following we describe the state of the art in 3D process data visualization and operator training.

2.1   3D in Process Data Visualization and the Psychological Background

Current HMI systems in process control use 2D representations like line diagrams and tables to visualize process data. These visualization elements are available in libraries and can be integrated into the process screen and be connected with process variables in a simple way. HMI systems also offer 3D representations of tanks and piping but this kind of representation has no additional benefit. Beuthel [2] and Hoppe [3] proved the advantages of 3D process data visualizations for special applications. Both studies measured the reaction time and the processing time to handle problem situations in 2D as compared with 3D visualizations. The results showed an advantage for 3D representation.

3D data visualization, like it is common in e.g. Matlab or Excel, is rarely used in process control. The time consuming development could be a reason for this. Each 3D scene has to be programmed step by step. For this reason, we developed a prototype library with 3D objects, so called 3D pattern [4]. These 3D patterns use standard interfaces like OPC or ActiveX and can be integrated in most state-of-the art HMI systems as easy as 2D visualization objects. The library was developed based on real application examples from industry and has been evaluated by experts.

In a pilot test the authors evaluated 2D and 3D visualization comparatively to reach a more reliable answer regarding the advance of 3D [5]. The results showed significant faster reaction time in the 3D environment if the problem situation was complex. This result corresponds with Wickens' "proximity-Compatibility"- principle [6]. This principle states that tasks that require the integration of information, benefit from a perceptual proximity of the display or visualization. The integration of information is necessary in particular for the detection of complex problems. These problems require the combination of three or more process values for the analysis of the system status. However, in the pilot test only one out of five problem situations disclose this benefit. One reason for the missing significance for the other problems could be the lack of complexity. The problem situations had to be simplified because subjects, which have no prior knowledge about the process, had to be trained adequately. Compared to real control rooms in industry, the experimental environment also had to be simplified. In the pretest the subjects had to observe only one diagram and could completely concentrate on this task. The task of an operator in a real control room is more complex as he has to observe a few monitors with different kinds of diagrams and tables. Furthermore, he has to attend to additional tasks that will distract him from his main task and by that reduces his attention to the process monitoring task.

---

[1] The project is funded by DFG (German Research Foundation under VO 937/7-1 and SCHW 736/3-1 from 5/2007 to 4/2009.

As 3D visualization is displayed on 2D screens the topic of interaction also has to be taken into account. Only by means of interactions like translation or rotation of elements can the 3D effect be perceived completely. Schönhage's [7] approach is based on the DIVA Java 3D-collection and implements five different kinds of interactions, so called behaviors. Amongst others, Schönhage provides interaction that enables to display additional information by mouse clicks / keystrokes or actions that move or rotate the 3D elements.

According to Witmer and Singer [8] interaction with a 3D scene also increases the sense of presence. Presence is defined as the sense of being present in a virtual environment, i.e. effects that influence the cognition of a state, the bonding to an event or the immersion into the virtual environment also influence the feeling of presence. Witmer and Singer specify four main factors. Two of them can be recognized as relevant for the task of monitoring process data:

- *Control factors:* degree of control, immediacy of control, anticipation of events, and mode of control and modifiability of physical environment.
- *Sensory factors:* sensory modality, environmental richness, multimodal presentation, consistency of multimodal information, degree of movement perception, active search.

The results of the pretest as well as the studies of Wickens on the complexity and Witmer and Singer on presence are the basis for our further experiments. These experiments have to be more realistic and therefore will be more complex.

2.2 Operator Training –Learning of Process Behavior

Increasing complexity of the experiment also takes up new training strategies. The pretest training is no longer sufficient to train the subjects for the more complex situations. In chemistry or pharmaceutical industry an operator is often trained by means of an operator training system (OTS) where a model based description of the process is available [9]. To learn process knowledge, the process dynamics need to be modeled in the OTS. The OTS systems use the original HMI interface of the process, which have to be learned, to display the system status and allow the operator to interact with the process. A simulation of the process calculates the new system status based on the actual state and the operators' intervention.

However, for a lot of processes it is not possible to identify the process model with an acceptable effort. In this cases operator training is often realized as training on the job. Novice operators are either trained by the start-up personnel or by an experienced operator based on their own mental model of the process. The 3D slider that was developed by the authors could be an alternative approach to teach the operator. Klein [11] showed that engineers often use knowledge from similar and familiar situations to solve a new problem instead of making time-consuming analysis. The 3D slider uses real scenarios and real process data from similar plants for a "scenario-based training" [12]. With the functionality of the slider it is possible to analyze historical data in an adjustable temporal scaling. In doing so the operator learns the process dynamic in familiar situations and can build up a mental model of the process. The training with the 3D slider requires real data of the process of a comparable plant. Some OTS use the approach by means of a slider in combination with simulated data but not with a 3D visualization. In the experiment we describe in the following three different types of training were evaluated in combination with 2D and 3D visualization.

3 Hypotheses

The main task of an operator in process control is the analysis of the actual process status. He has to differentiate between error and error free conditions and to identify the appropriate solution. Two different cases can be defined:
- **hit:** right identification of error conditions.
- **miss:** no identification or false identification of an error condition.

The following hypotheses were deduced:

(H1) 3D visualization leads to better error detection in complex problem situations than 2D visualization.

According to Wickens a 3D representation is beneficial for the detection of errors on complex problems, i.e. if it is necessary to combine at least three process values for the identification of the system state. Hence, for the error detection of complex problems, subjects that use 3D visualization will have more hits as compared to subjects that use 2D visualization.

(H2) 3D visualization with interaction leads to better error detection in complex problem situations compared with 3D visualization without interaction.

Interaction is a basic control factor that increases the presence. A 3D visualization with interaction leads to a higher control over the visualization environment and should facilitate the operators' task of error detection. Hence, subjects that use 3D with interaction will have more hits than subjects that use 3D without interaction.

4 Experiment

By analyzing the tasks in the control room of a continuous hydraulic press, the subjects' tasks in the experiment as well as the implementation of the HMI were designed.

4.1 Application Example

For the empirical evaluation of the described hypotheses an appropriate application example that is appropriate for 3D has to be identified. Due to the experiences of the authors the case study of the continuous hydraulic press (Fig. 1) was selected [13]. The hydraulic press is used to produce different kinds of fiber boards. A glued material mat runs into the continuous press where it is pressed between two moving steel belts. The heat, that is necessary for the technological process, is transferred by roller rods from the heating plate to the steel belt. Hydraulic cylinders generate the pressure to press the material mat to the set values of distance. The cylinders are located equally spaced along the whole length and width of the press. The thickness of the mat is measured by means of distance transducers at the outer edges of the steel belts and is controlled by increasing or reducing the pressure. Important data, like

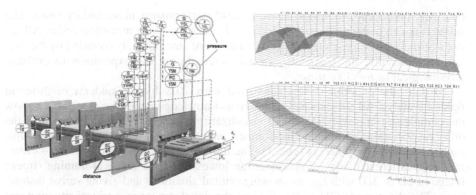

Fig. 1. P&ID of the continuous hydraulic press and associated 3D visualization of pressure and distance

temperature of the heating plate, thickness and pressure are continuously measured and displayed for the operator in the control room. Based on the actual process date and his knowledge about the process the operator decides how to take corrective actions on the process.

In the described application example multiple dependencies exist between different process factors, e.g. pressure and distance. The material has to be pressed to the set distance without exceeding the maximum pressure. For decision-making the operator has to observe both process values and set into correlation across and along the press. For the experiment five problem situations from the real application example were chosen: two simple and three complex ones.

4.2 Design of the Experiment

The subjects' task in the experiment was to monitor the press. The experiment was divided into three phases: audio-visual training, exploration phase and operation phase.

In the audio-visual phase the subjects were shown a video that explained the application process. The relevant process factors and their interrelations were explained. The critical process situations and their symptoms were described. Furthermore, the video gave an introduction to the process visualization and the options of taking corrective actions.

Next, the subjects enter into the exploration phase. Firstly, the subjects reconstruct the information from the video and comprehend the process behavior and the scenario based on simulated process data. In the second step, the subjects verify the obtained knowledge in the testing phase where they had to operate the process and attain feedback concerning the correctness of their interventions in the experimental environment.

In the operation phase, the subjects had to control the process. They had to decide whether they were confronted with normal or with critical process conditions. In case of a critical situation they had to take an appropriate corrective action. During the observation and control of the process they had to execute two additional tasks, i.e. hand writing product data on a protocol data sheet and communicating with colleagues in a chat instead of a walkie-talkie in a real plant (referring to Wicken's theory a second task was introduced, indicates the work load performance in secondary task). The subjects had to undergo the same selection of situations twice in random order. All actions of the subjects, e.g. error response time, were automatically recorded by the system. Additionally, the heart rate was measured during the experiment to evaluate physiological factors like stress.

To date, the experiment was conducted with 70 subjects (students of different fields of study). All subjects had no previous knowledge about the process. To allow the comparison between 2D and 3D visualizations as well as the comparison of the different variations of training, the subjects were divided randomly into five groups, each group with 14 subjects (Table 1). The training conditions were derived to examine three different modes of presence, the lowest mode: a classical training (freeze image in 2D or 3D) with figures showing critical situations and giving verbal instructions. The slider mode (2D or 3D) displays the development of a critical situation and should by that give more information to detect the critical situation. Training with slider and interaction (only 3D) should generate the highest presence because the interaction gives subjects the opportunity to feel more involved in the process. The training with slider and interaction was evaluated only in 3D because 2D does not allow comparable interaction features.

Table 1. Experimental Design (training options and dimension)

Dimension of HMI	Training with freeze image	Training with slider	Training with slider and interaction
2D	group 1	group 2	---
3D	group 3	group 4	group 5

Additionally, different questionnaires were included to examine attentiveness, self-assessment and feedback on presence etc. After the operation phase an interview was conducted to analyze the individual mental models.

4.3 Experimental Environment

For the evaluation an experimental environment, which is as realistic as possible, was developed. The main challenge was to find an optimum between the approximation to reality and an environment that does not overstrain novice subjects.

The environment is based on a PC with two monitors displaying four different diagrams. Depending on the provided scenario the subjects had to combine the information displayed in these diagrams to identify the problem and to deduce an appropriate input reaction. On an adjoining tablet PC they had to execute additional tasks, hand writing production protocol. Both PCs were connected and all relevant actions of the subjects on both systems were recorded in one database according to their timeline (more details to the environment are given in [14]).

5   Results of the Experiment

The following results refer to the evaluation of 70 subjects. Due to technical problems the results of one subject in group 5 could only be recorded in the first trail; however these results were included in the analysis. Table 2 gives an overview of the quantity of subjects in the five groups.

Table 2. Assignment of subjects to training variations

group	1	2	3	4	5
subjects	14	14	14	14	13,5

(H1)   *3D visualization leads to better error detection in complex problem situations than 2D visualization.*

For the evaluation of hypothesis 1, group 1 and group 2 were joined and represent an overall 2D group. In the same way, group 3 and group 4 were joined and represent the 3D group. Group 5 was not taken into consideration for this analysis. Table 3 shows the total number of errors depending on the experimental group (2D and 3D). The analysis of the results show no significant differences (Fisher test p=0.5) that can be ascribed to the dimension of the visualization.

Table 3. Hits and misses of complex problems depending on the dimension of the HMI

group	misses	hits	hits [%]
joined 2D	159	121	43.21
joined 3D	158	122	43.57

As the analysis shows no significant results, instead of joined group, each group will be analyzed individually. In the analysis, two aspects can be observed (Table 4). The group "2D freeze image" shows better results than the group "2D slider". In contrast the group "3D freeze image" obtains poorer results than the "3D slider" group.

Table 4. Frequency distribution of hits and misses of complex problems in different dimensions

group	misses	Hits	hits [%]
2D freeze image	72	68	48.57
2D slider	87	53	37.86
3D freeze image	86	54	38.57
3D slider	72	68	48.57

The evaluation shows that hypothesis 1 is false.

(H2)   *3D visualization with interaction leads to better error detection in complex problem situations than 3D visualization without interaction.*

For the evaluation of hypothesis 2 the five groups were compared. The analysis of table 5 shows that the group "3D slider with interaction" achieves the best result. Actually, this is the only group that obtains more hits than misses.

Table 5. Hits and misses of complex problems depending on different groups

group	misses	hits	hits [%]
2D freeze image	72	68	48.57
2D slider	87	53	37.86
3D freeze image	86	54	38.57
3D slider	72	68	48.57
3D slider with interaction	62	73	52.14

As the results show significance (chi-square = 11.08, df = 4, p < 0.05), hypothesis 2 can be proven.

6   Discussion of the Results

The analysis of the error rates on complex problems showed that a 3D visualization achieves the best results if the subject is given the opportunity to interact with the 3D scene. Group 5 was significantly better in error detection. A representation of data in 3D without interaction showed no advantage in the experiment. Contrary to the expectation, in several cases subjects of group 1 showed even better results than the subjects of group 3 or the same results like group 4.

The following reasons can be given for these results:

- The representation of data in a 2D diagram is always still the most well-known and widely-used type of data visualization. Therefore the handling of data representation is intuitive because of user's experience. A 2D visualization in combination with the slider in the exploration phase does not seem to be intuitive for the subjects. In the operating phase the groups 1 and 2 did not differ.
- The groups 3 and 4 also differ only in the exploration phase and not in the operating phase. Nevertheless in 3D the slider group was better in error recognition. The use of the 3D sliders in the exploration phase seems to be more intuitive for the user. This confirms Wickens' theory.
- Group 3 and 4 had a quasi 3D representation, meaning that it is only a predefined 2D projection of a 3D object. Only the interaction generates the real 3D effect that increases the subject's feeling of having control over the visualization, which refers to the presence phenomenon.

The analysis of hits and misses generally shows a high error rate. On top of that group 5 (3D slider with interaction), which was significantly better than the other groups, shows a number of hits that is barely more than 50 percent. This result leads to the assumption that the training phase has to be improved. The present design of the experiment permits no conclusion whether the subjects understood the process which they had to observe and to control, before they enter into the exploration and the operating phase.

7   Summary and Future Prospect

In this paper an experiment that evaluates the influence of different types of visualization (2D, 3D/ interaction) and training on error detection in process control was described. It was shown that training with the classical 2D freeze image seems to be very intuitive to the user and leads to good results in the operation phase. Referring to 3D visualization it was shown that interaction is an important factor. Only the combination of 3D with interaction leads to significantly better results in error detection.

Based on the presented results, it seems to be necessary to evaluate the influence of different kinds of interaction with 3D scenes. Besides the already analyzed behavior , namely "rotation", other types of interaction like "translation", "zoom" or "brushing" (context-sensitive display of additional data) have to be evaluated (with prerequisite if they are useful for the operator's task in this application).

For the development of further experiments, the process knowledge of the subjects has to be tested before they enter into the exploration and the operation phase. It must be ensured that the subjects have understood the process and the process intervention. If the subject achieves a certain level of process knowledge the experiment can be continued. Otherwise, the subject has to be trained and be tested again. Finally, if the subject does not improve, the experiment has to be aborted. This adaption of the experimental design should considerably decrease the error rate.

For a more realistic experimental design, it is necessary to examine more complex technical scenarios because the current results show positive correlation from complexity of the scenario to the benefit of 3D presentation. A more realistic scenario, i.e. a more complex scenario, will highlight the benefit of 3D with interaction as compared to the other training conditions in regards to the reaction time and identification of errors. Additionally a subsequent experiment focusing on elderly operators will be conducted. We expect that elderly people will profit from an adaptable interface, e.g. adaptable interaction etc.

The gained results will lead to the implementation of new functionalities in operator training systems and an improved operator training as well as a guideline for application engineers, who develop these systems.

References

1. Vogel-Heuser, B., Zeipelt, R.: Nutzen der 3D-Prozessdatenvisualisierung in der industriellen Prozessführung. atp - Automatisierungstechnische Praxis 45(3), 45–50 (2003)
2. Beuthel, C.: Dreidimensionale Prozessvisualisierung zum Führen technischer Anlagen am Beispiel eines Kohlekraftwerkes. PhD Thesis University of Clausthal-Zellerfeld. Papierflieger Verlag, Clausthal-Zellerfeld (1997)
3. Hoppe, S.M., Essenberg, G.R., Wiegmann, D.A., Overbye, T.J.: Three-dimensional displays as an effective visualization technique for power systems monitoring and control. Technical Report. University of Illinois, US (2004)
4. Friedrich, D., Moritz, S., Pantförder, D., Vogel-Heuser, B.: 3D-Patterns for the Data Analysis and Operation of Process Plant. In: International Association of Science and Technology for Development- Human Computer Interaction (IASTED-HCI), Phoenix (2005)

5. Vogel-Heuser, B., Schweizer, K., van Burgeler, A., Fuchs, Y., Pantförder, D.: Auswirkungen einer dreidimensionalen Prozessdatenvisualisierung auf die Fehlererkennung. Zeitschrift für Arbeitswissenschaft 61(1), 23–34 (2007)
6. Wickens, C.D., Andre, A.D.: Proximity Compatibility and Information Display: Effects of Color, Space, and Objectness on Information Integration. Human Factors 32(1), 61–77 (1990)
7. Schönhage, B., van Ballegooij, A., Eliëns, A.: 3D Gadgets for Business Process Visualization –a case study. In: Proceedings of the 5th symposium on Virtual Reality modelling language (web3D-VRML), Monterey CA, pp. 131–138 (2000)
8. Witmer, B.G., Singer, M.J.: Measuring Presence in Virtual Environments: A Presence Questionnaire. Presence 7(3), 225–240 (1998)
9. Kroll, A.: Status and perspectives of operator training simulation for the process industries. In: atp international, vol. 1(1), pp. 24–36 (2003)
10. Urbas, L.: Entwicklung und Realisierung einer Trainings- und Ausbildungsumgebung zur Schulung der Prozeßdynamik und des Anlagenbetriebs im Internet. Fortschr. -Ber. VDI-Reihe 810 Nr. 614. VDI-Verlag, Düsseldorf (1999)
11. Klein, G.A.: A Recognition-Primed Decision (RPD) Model of Rapid Decision Making. In: Klein, G.A., Oresanu, J., Calderwood, R., Zsambok, C.E. (eds.) Decision Making in Action: Models and Methods, pp. 138–147. Ablex Publishing, Norwood (1992)
12. Salas, E., Wilson, K.A., Priest, H.A., Guthrie, J.W.: Design, Delivery, and Evaluation of training systems. In: Salvendy, G. (ed.) Handbook of human factors and ergonomics, 3rd edn., pp. 472–512. John Wiley & Sons, New Jersy (2006)
13. Vogel-Heuser, B.: Automation in wood and paper industry. In: Nof, S.Y. (ed.) Handbook of Automation. Springer, New York (2008)
14. Pantförder, D., Vogel-Heuser, B.: Versuchsdesign für eine vergleichende Evaluation des Operator-Trainings bei der Visualisierung von Prozessdaten in einer 2D- und 3D-Umgebung. In: Useware, Verfahrens- und Produktionstechnik, Engineering, Informationspräsentation und Interaktionskonzepte, VDI/VDE-Berichte 2041, pp. 143–154. VDI-Verlag, Düsseldorf (2008)
15. Bortz, J.: Statistik für Sozialwissenschaftler. Springer, Berlin (1999)

Modeling the Difficulty for Centering Rectangles in One and Two Dimensions

Robert Pastel

Computer Science Department,
Michigan Technological University
Houghton, Michigan, USA
rpastel@mtu.edu

Abstract. Centering, positioning an object within specified bounds, is a common computer task, for example making selections using a standard mouse or on a touch screen using a finger. These experiments measured times for participants ($n = 131$) to position a rectangular cursor with various widths, p (10 px $\leq$ $p \leq$ 160 px), completely within rectangular targets with various widths, w, and tolerances, $t = w\text{-}p$ (4 px $\leq t \leq$ 160 px) in one and two dimensions. The analysis divides the movement time into two phases, the transport time and the centering time. Centering times are modeled well by $1/t$. All models have high correlation, $r^2 \geq 0.95$.

1 Introduction

Centering is positioning an object with a finite extent within specified bounds. Centering is a common task in many computer applications. Computer users perform centering whenever they make selections using a pointing device. The centering task is easy if the cursor size is small compared to the target size, but when the target size becomes small and only slightly larger than the cursor size then centering becomes difficult. Computer users instinctively understand that making selections using the standard cursor only requires locating the cursor's "hot spot" over the target. The cursor hot spot is a single pixel at the point of the cursor's arrow, so generally centering is easy, but when the target is less than 16 pixels in width, for example a window's exit button at the upper right hand corner, positioning the cursor's hot spot becomes difficult and requires a concerted effort. Centering becomes difficult when the pointer becomes large, for example using a finger to make selections on a touch screen. A lightly pressed finger tip is approximately 10 mm [3], or approximately 40 pixels (px) wide, so buttons on a touch screen must be larger than on a standard graphical user interfaces. Although touch screen drivers reduce the finger pressure region to the region's centroid, the location of the centroid is ambiguous to users, so to reduce error, touch screen users center their finger completely inside button.

Centering is also an important task in graphical applications, such as drawing software and other software where users position graphical objects relative to each other. A common task while using drawing software is to position an object adjacent to or over another object; this is a centering task. The task can be difficult if the tolerance is small. Users of drawing software learn to use "snap to" guidelines to increase the

J.A. Jacko (Ed.): Human-Computer Interaction, Part II, HCII 2009, LNCS 5611, pp. 879–888, 2009.
© Springer-Verlag Berlin Heidelberg 2009

perceived centering tolerance and to separate the degrees of freedom during the centering task.

Centering is often preceded by another manipulation task, such as transporting the object to the centering region, so previous centering experiments have included centering with repetitive selection tasks, mimicking Fitts's experiments [2] and analysis. In one experiment, Wiker et al. [8] studied the time for participants to manually position pins with various weights and sizes into holes in plates at various inclinations. Four practiced participants positioned pins of three sizes ($p = 1.00$ cm, 1.20 cm, 1.25 cm) repetitively into holes with diameter $w = 1.27$ cm separated by two distances ($A = 15.24$ cm, 30.48 cm). Wicker et al. initially modeled the total movement time (MT) for transporting and positioning the pins into holes with Fitts's law [2]

$$MT = a + b \log_2(2A/w) , \qquad (1)$$

where a and b are regression coefficients and $ID_F = \log_2(2A/w)$ is called the Fitts index of difficulty for transporting a infinitesimal probe a distance A with accuracy w. For the various probe weights and plate inclinations, they found slightly differing regression slopes and correlation coefficients, $0.71 \le r^2 \le 0.83$. The relatively poor correlations with respect to previous Fitts like experiments motivated Wicker et al. [8] to include an additional term in the model

$$MT = a + b \log_2(A/w) + c \log_2(w/t) , \qquad (2)$$

where c is an additional regression slope and $t = w\text{-}p$ is the pin-to-hole tolerance. The model separates the movement time "into a series of submovements or IDs; one for the rapid ballistic element and another for the slower, more precise positioning element"[8]. Wicker et al. found that modeling the total movement time with Eqn. (2) yielded much better correlations, $0.97 \le r^2 \le 0.99$.

In an *inverted* Fitts experiment, Hoffmann et al. [4] studied repetitive key pressing for keys with various widths ($w = 5$ mm, 10 mm, 15 mm) and various inter-key spacing ($C = 1$ mm, 5 mm, 10 mm, 15 mm, 20 mm). "An inverted Fitts task is defined as one in which the subject moves a probe of larger width to a target that may be smaller in width than the probe."[2] For inter-key separations greater than the finger width ($F \approx 7.1$ mm) [4], pressing the key only requires the finger to overlap with the key, so the tolerance is $t = w+2F\text{-}F = w+F$. For inter-key separations less than the finger width, pressing the key requires avoiding the adjacent keys, so the tolerance is $t = w+2C\text{-}F$. In an experiment which ten participants repetitively tapped unmarked keys separated by several keys (NKEY $= 1, 2, 3, 4, 5$ keys) on a keyboard with three rows of eight keys. Modeling the total movement time to press keys using Fitts's law

$$MT = a + b \log_2(A/t) \qquad (3)$$

yielded correlation $r^2 = 0.82$. The finger width was determined by minimizing the variance in the regression, so F represents a non-linear coefficient in the model. The relatively poor correlation motivated Hoffmann et al. to model repetitive key pressing with an additional term

$$MT = a + b \log_2(A/t) + c A , \qquad (4)$$

where c is an additional regression slope. The additional term was added to separate movement "carried out ballistically" [4] for tapping nearby keys (NKEY $= 1, 2, 3$)

from tapping distant keys (NKEY = 4, 5) "made under visual control" [4]. The correlation improved $r^2 = 0.91$, but the best fit model required adding a quadratic term, $\log_2^2(A/t)$, yielded correlation $r^2 = 0.95$.

Pastel [7] studied centering in the context of computer use. Participants ($n = 155$) repetitively clicked on circular targets with various diameters ($w = $ 44 px, 46 px, 50 px, 60 px, 80 px, 120 px, 140 px) using a circular cursor ($p = 40$ px diameter) separated by random distances, A. The circular cursor had to be completely within the target for a successful click. Modeling the total movement time, MT, using binned Fitts index of difficulty, $ID_F = \log_2(A/w + 1)$, yielded a fit with correlation $r^2 = 0.92$, but with a definite trend in the residuals. Pastel separated the transport and centering phases by defining a touch time (TT) and centering time (CT). TT is the time from initial cursor movement to the last time that the cursor just touches the target circle. CT is the time difference from just after the last cursor-target touch time and the time that the participant successfully acquires the target by clicking on the mouse button. So, $MT = TT + CT$. Touch time modeled using binned ID_F yielded a correlation $r^2 = 0.95$, but the model using binned A fitted TT better, $r^2 = 0.99$. Two models for centering time were considered. The model

$$CT = a + b \log_2(p/t + 1) \qquad (5)$$

was derived from information theory. The correlation using this model was good $r^2 = 0.92$. The other model

$$CT = a + b \, p/t \qquad (6)$$

was derived considering only the behavior of CT at the limiting cases, meaning as $t \rightarrow 0$ and ∞ and $p \rightarrow 0$. The correlation using this model was better, $r^2 = 0.99$.

All of the above experiments suffer from the weakness that they investigated centering using either a single probe or target size. Nevertheless, all the studies agree that using only Fitts's law to model repetitive positioning of probes with finite extent is insufficient and must include an additional term representing either the centering or transport portion of the task.

This paper seeks to address the deficiencies of the previous experiments by studying centering with various probe sizes and tolerances. Two experiments explore the difficulty of centering rectangles in one and two dimensions by measuring the time for participants to position rectangular cursors over larger rectangular targets. The experiments are a variation of two dimensional target acquisitions, using a computer mouse to make selections on targets at random initial target-cursor separations. This paper extends the work of Pastel [7] and seeks to separate the centering task from the preceding task of transporting the cursor to the target and illustrate when centering becomes difficult.

2 Experimental and Analytical Methods

Participants sat a comfortable distance (18 inches to 24 inches) from a 20-inch widescreen LCD monitor (1680x1050 resolution) to performed two experiments in a single sitting. In both experiments, participants repeatedly positioned a dark blue rectangular cursor over a randomly located larger light orange rectangular target on a mid grey computer screen using a computer mouse. The cursor acceleration was turned off during the experiments so that the cursor moved at a constant rate with respect to the mouse. The participants indicated when they perceived that the cursor was completely inside the target by clicking the mouse. After a successful click, the target rectangle would randomly reappear at another screen location, and the participant would continue with the next experimental trial by again positioning the cursor over the target and clicking. If the participant should click when the cursor was outside of the target or only partially overlapping the target, the experimental software would record an error. The target would not move, and the participants would have to continue with the trial until they had successfully positioned the cursor completely inside the target and clicked. Participants performed 10 trials with the same target and cursor size. The total movement time begun when the cursor started moving after the prior correct click and ended when the participant successfully positioned the cursor and clicked. If the participant performed errors, these were included in the total movement time.

The 131 participants were sophomore, junior, or senior students in computer science, computer engineering or introductory psychology courses. Their ages ranged from 18 to 42 years, the mean age was 20 years. Nearly all participants reported having between 5 and 20 years experience using the computer mouse, the mean experience was 12 years. Twenty two participants were females, and only five participants reported using their left hand to manipulate the mouse.

All 131 Participants performed one or two sessions (depending on the experiment) with 10 trials for each combination of target and cursor size, so a large quantity of data was collected. Consequently, the experimental and analytical powers in this paper are large and many factors are significant, so this paper uses partial η^2 for effect size [5] to determine the effectiveness of factors on the dependent variable and correlation, r^2, for comparing linear models.

3 One Dimensional Centering

Participants positioned large aspect rectangular cursors with various widths ($p = 10$ px, 20 px, 40 px, 80 px, 160 px) on large aspect targets with various tolerances ($t = w-p = 4$ px, 8 px, 16 px, 32 px, 64 px, 128 px). The experimental software constrained the cursor to move in only one dimension depending on the test orientation, vertical or horizontal. The length of the cursor was one half of the screen height for horizontal tests and one half of the screen width for vertical tests. The experiment consisted of 10 trials for each combination of cursor width, target tolerance and test orientation. The order of cursor width, target tolerance and test orientation was random for each participant.

All factors, inverse tolerance ($1/t$), initial separation (A), cursor width (p), test orientation, test number (N_{test}), and trial number were significant for MT (total movement time) [p-value < 0.006, $df = 75916$]. The larger partial η^2 are 0.5 for $1/t$, 0.05 for A, 0.02 for N_{test}, 0.015 for p. The large effect size for test number suggests that some learning did occur, as participants improve their performance in later tests. Nevertheless, we will ignore the effect of learning in the remaining analyses.

We modeled the mean total movement time using Fitts index of difficulty, $ID_F = \log_2(A/t + 1)$. Fig. 1 shows the regression plot for MT against binned ID_F. The 50 bins of ID_F had approximately 1500 data points each. The slope, 238 ms/bits, was significant [$F(1,48) = 1596$, p-value $< 2.2e\text{-}16$]. A typical value for the slope reported in the literature, 160 ms/bits [1, 6] is outside the 95% confidence interval, (233, 246) ms/bits. Although the correlation is high, $r^2 = 0.97$, the residuals show a trend that suggests that the slope increases with larger ID_F, which are more often associated with the small tolerances, and decreases with smaller ID_F, which are more often associated with the large tolerances.

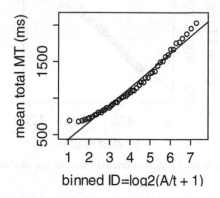

Fig. 1. Regression plot for mean total MT against binned by $ID_F = \log_2(A/t + 1)$ for the one dimensional centering experiment

Inspired by the suggestion of Wiker *et al.* [8] that the total movement time is composed of two submovements and following the analysis of Pastel [7], we divide the total movement time into a touch time (TT) and a centering time (CT). All factors and interaction terms were significant for TT [p-value $< 4.5e\text{-}06$, $df = 75972$], while only the factors $1/t$ and p and interaction of $1/t$ with p and A were significant for CT. Table 2 compares the effect size of factors and interactions for TT and CT. The factors A and p have larger effect size than $1/t$ for TT, The roles are reversed for CT; $1/t$ has a larger effect size than A and p. This exchange of effect size suggests that TT should be modeled by A, and CT should be modeled by $1/t$.

Table 1. Partial η^2 effect size for factors and interactions of TT and CT in 1d centering

Dependent Variable	Factor			Interaction		
	$1/t$	A	p	$A{:}1/t$	$p{:}1/t$	$A{:}p$
TT	0.03	0.2	0.1	0.005	0.006	0.0002
CT	0.5	0.0002	0.1	0.0003	0.01	0.000003

The linear model for the mean TT binned by $ID_F = \log_2(A/t + 1)$ (50 bins with 1500 data points each) has a lower correlation, $r^2 = 0.89$, than the correlation for the linear model of the total MT, and the data is slightly concaved up as in the MT plot. Modeling TT by binned A (50 bins with 1500 data points each) has a higher correlation, $r^2 = 0.93$, but Fig. 2 shows that the residual is anomalous for $A < 200$ px. For trials with initial cursor-target separation less than 200 px, the participants may be anticipating centering and the initial submovement may not be completely ballistic. The correlation modeling only binned $A > 200$ px (50 bins with 1220 data points each) is $r^2 = 0.98$. The regression slope and intercept for $A > 200$ px are 0.44 ms/px and 214 ms, respectively.

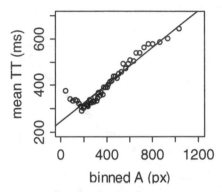

Fig. 2. Regression plot for mean *TT* against binned by *A* for the one dimensional centering experiment

Modeling the mean *CT* using Eqn. 5 (the modeled derived from information theory) yields correlation $r^2 = 0.87$, while the modeling using Eqn. 6 (the model considering only limit cases) has correlation $r^2 = 0.71$. Although the model based on information theory has higher correlation than the model based on limiting cases, both models have relatively low correlation. Recall from Table 1 that both factors $1/t$ and p have a large effect size for *CT*, this suggests that the appropriate model is

$$CT = a + b/t + c\,p/t + d\,p \tag{7}$$

where a, b, c and d are coefficients determined by the regression. Using this model the coefficients are $a = 285$ ms, $b = 3666$ ms•px, $c = 10.5$ ms, $d = 1.94$ ms/px, and the correlation is $r^2 = 0.98$. Although the correlation is high, the model is not very satisfying because it has four undetermined coefficients. Also, Fig. 3(a) clearly shows there is curvature in the *CT*s.

Consider the definition of centering time, the time between the last cursor-target touch and the time that the participant successfully clicks on the target. This definition implies that for each cursor width, p, the participant must first move the cursor a distance p for the cursor to be completely inside the target. *CT* could be separated into two parts, an entering time (*ET*) and a new centering time (*CT**). *CT** is the time for the participant to successfully click on the target after the cursor is complete inside the target. *ET* is the time between the last cursor-target touch and the succeeding first time that the cursor is completely inside the target, so $CT = ET + CT^*$. We expect that *ET* will be proportional to p because it is primarily a transport time. Modeling *CT** using

$$CT^* = a + b/t + c\,p/t \tag{8}$$

yields regression coefficients $a = 296$ ms, $b = 2608$ ms•px, $c = 7.4$ ms, and correlation $r^2 = 0.99$. The interaction term, p/t, would appear as the divergence of the regressions for each cursor width, p. Comparing Fig 3(a) and (b), the divergence of the CT^* data is nearly half that for the CT data. Fig. 3(b) shows the linear regression on CT^* using only the first two terms of Eqn. 8. The regression coefficients are $a = 295$ ms, $b = 3069$ ms•px and the correlation is $r^2 = 0.96$. The 95% confidence interval of the regression slope (2811, 3328) ms•px contains the approximate mid range slope, at $1/t = 0.125$ px^{-1}, for the CT^* complete model (Eqn. 8), 2986 ms•px.

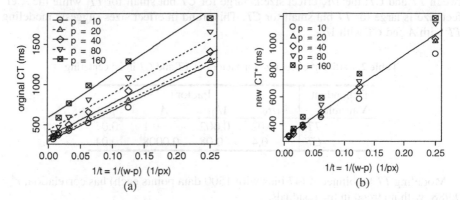

Fig. 3. Regression plots for centering time vs. centering tolerance. (a) Original centering time based on last time cursor just touches target. (b) New centering time based on last time cursor enters the target.

4 Two Dimensional Centering

Participants positioned square rectangular cursors with various widths ($p = 20$ px, 40 px, 80 px) on larger rectangular targets with various tolerances in the vertical ($t_V = w_{height}-p = 4$ px, 16 px, 32 px) and horizontal ($t_H = w_{width} - p = 4$ px, 16 px, 32 px) directions. Only horizontal targets were tested, meaning $t_V \leq t_H$. In this experiment, the participant moved the cursor in both directions using a USB mouse. The experiment consisted of two sessions with 10 trials for each combination of cursor width, and target tolerance. The order of cursor width and target tolerance was random for each participant.

All factors, inverse tolerances ($1/t_V$ and $1/t_H$), initial separation (A), cursor width (p), session number ($N_{session}$), test number, and trial number were significant for MT (total movement time) [p-value $< 2.2e-08$, $df = 70612$]. The larger partial η^2 are 0.4 for $1/t_V$, 0.07 for $1/t_H$, 0.03 for A, 0.003 for $N_{session}$, and 0.002 for p. The large effect size for session number suggests that some learning did occur, as participants improve their performance in the later session. Nevertheless, we will ignore the effect of learning in the remaining analyses.

Because the MT effect size for $1/t_V$ is much larger than that for $1/t_H$, we model the mean total MT using 47 binned $ID_F = \log_2(A/t_V + 1)$ with 1500 data points each. The slope, 259 ms/bits, was significant [$F(1,45) = 1127$, p-value $< 2.2e-16$], and the typical value for the slope, 160 ms/bits [1, 6], is outside the 95% confidence interval, (243, 274) ms/bits. Although the correlation is high, $r^2 = 0.96$, the residuals show an "S-shape" trend.

Again, we separate the $MT = TT + CT$ and analyze the effect sizes. All factors and first order interaction terms are significant for TT and CT except the interaction of A with p for CT [p-value < 0.03, $df = 70724$]. Table 2 gives the effect size for the factors of CT and TT. The effect size for the interaction $1/t_V{:}p$ was 0.005; all other interaction terms had effect size less then 0.005. The low $1/t_H$ effect size for both CT and TT implies that $1/t_H$ has little effect. Note the exchange of $1/t_V$ and A effect sizes between TT and CT; the $1/t_V$ effect size is large for CT but small for TT, while the A effect size is large for TT but small for CT. This trend in effect sizes suggests modeling TT with A and CT with $1/t_V$.

Table 2. Partial η^2 effect size for factors of TT and CT in 2d centering

Dependent Vairable	Factor			
	$1/t_V$	$1/t_H$	A	p
TT	0.02	0.002	0.1	0.07
CT	0.4	0.08	0.0008	0.04

Modeling TT by binned A (47 bins with 1500 data points each) has correlation, $r^2 = 0.988$, with no trend in the residuals.

We forego analyzing CT and investigate marginal regressions of CT^*, the center time after completely entering the target. The widest targets, $t_H = 32$ px, should be similar to the one dimensional (1d) centering experiments. Fig. 4(a) shows the regression of CT^* against t_V. The regression coefficients are $a = 234$ ms, $b = 3069$ ms•px and the correlation is $r^2 = 0.99$. The slope is outside the 95% confidence interval for the 1d centering regression slope. Also evident from Fig 4(a) is that for all tolerances participants performed the two dimensional (2d) centering faster than 1d centering. This could be because the 2d centering experiments were performed after the 1d experiments, and participants have learned to perform better. It also suggests that 2d centering is not more difficult then 1d centering. Fig. 4(b) shows that CT^* for the shortest targets, $t_V = 4$ px, is a constant 800 ms, and approximately equal to CT^* for the widest target at $t_V = 4$ px. The two models suggest that 2d centering time is dominated by the most constraining direction, t_V in this experiment.

Using $t = t_V$ in Eqn. 7 to model all the 2d CT^* data shows that the factors $1/t_V$ [F(1, 14) = 383, p-value = 1.4e-11] and p [F(1, 14) = 6.1, p-value = 0.2] are significant, but the interaction term p/t_V is not significant. The effect sizes are 0.96 for $1/t_V$ and 0.3 for p. Modeling CT^* using only the first two and fourth terms in Eqn. 7 yielded regression coefficients $a = 195$ ms, $b = 2180$ ms•px, $d = 1.91$ ms/px, and the correlation is $r^2 = 0.95$. The value of the coefficient for p, d, is small, and the effect size for p is less than half of that for $1/t_V$, so we model CT^* using only the first two terms of Eqn. 8. The regression coefficients are $a = 247$ ms, $b = 2180$ ms•px and the correlation is

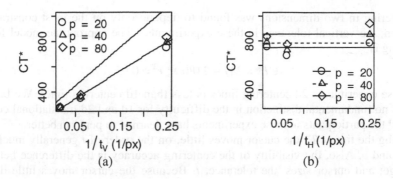

Fig. 4. Marginal regression plots of CT^* vs. tolerances. (a) For $t_H = 32$ px, the upper line is the 1d regression. (b) For $t_V = 4$ px, the regressions are constants for each cursor size, p.

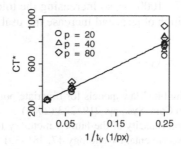

Fig. 5. Regression plot for all the 2 dimensional centering data, CT^* vs. $1/t_V$, the line is the regression of CT^* by $1/t_V$

$r^2 = 0.95$. The inclusion of the term in p improves the correlations only a little. Fig. 5 shows the entire 2 dimensional CT^* data and the regression using only $1/t_V$.

5 Conclusions

This paper agrees with the basic results of Wicker et al. [8] and Hoffmann [4] that positioning objects with finite extent within specified tolerances requires at least two terms, a term representing transport and a term representing centering. Two alternative definitions for centering time were studied. CT is defined as the time to successfully click on the target after just touching the target for the last time. CT^* is defined as the time to successfully click on the target after entering the target completely. So CT^* is always less than CT for any trial, and is less dependent on the cursor size, p. Appropriate models for 1d centering in a computer applications are

$$CT = 285 + 3666/t + 10.5p/t + 1.94\, p \; ; \; r^2 = 0.98 \; ,$$

$$CT^* = 296 + 2608/t + 7.4\, p/t \; ; \; r^2 = 0.99 \; ,$$

$$CT^* = 295 + 3069/t \; ; \; r^2 = 0.96 \; ,$$

where t is the centering tolerance and p is the probe size.

Centering in two dimensions was found to depend only on the most constraining direction, the vertical tolerance in these experiments. The appropriate model for 2d centering is

$$CT^* = 247 + 2180/t \; ; \; r^2 = 0.95 \; .$$

For these experiments 2d centering times is less than 1d centering times. We believe there is no fundamental distinction in the difficulty for 1d and 2d translational centering, and the participants in these experiments have learned to perform better.

During the time CT^* the cursor moves little, on the order of t generally much less than A and p. Also, the visibility of the centering accuracy is the difference between the target and cursor sizes, the tolerance, t. Because the cursor moves little during CT^*, and CT^* is inversely proportional to a possible stimuli strength, CT^* may be a reaction time rather than a movement time. CT^* is a significant portion of the time to position objects within specified bounds, 200 ms$\leq CT^* \leq$1000 ms, approximately half the total time, 500 ms$\leq MT \leq$1000 ms, so increasing the tolerance visibility could decrease the total time to position objects and increase the usability of pointing devices.

References

1. Accot, J., Zhai, S.: Refining Fitts' law models for bivariate pointing. In: Proc. of CHI 1992 Conf. on Human Factors in Com. Sys., pp. 219–223 (2003)
2. Fitts, P.M.: The information capacity of the human motor system in controlling the amplitude of movement. J. of Experimental Psychology 47, 381–391 (1954)
3. Hoffmann, E.R.: Effective target tolerance in an inverted Fitts task. Ergonomics 38, 828–836 (1995)
4. Hoffmann, E.R., Tsang, K.K., Mu, A.: Data-entry keyboard geometry and keying movement times. Ergonomics 38, 940–950 (1995)
5. Keppel, G.: Design and analysis: A researcher's handbook. Prentice Hall, Englewood Cliffs (1991)
6. MacKenzie, S.I., Buxton, W.: Extending Fitts' law to two-dimensional tasks. In: Proc. of CHI 1992 Conf. on Human Factors in Com. Sys., pp. 219–223 (1992)
7. Pastel, R.: The difficulty of centering circular discs. In: Proc. of the Human Factors and Ergonomics Society, vol. 52, pp. 1312–1316 (2008)
8. Wiker, S.F., Langolf, G.D., Caffin, D.B.: Arm posture and human movement capability. Human Factors 31, 421–441 (1989)

Composing Visual Syntax for Domain Specific Languages

Luis Pedro[1], Matteo Risoldi[1], Didier Buchs[1],
Bruno Barroca[2], and Vasco Amaral[2]

[1] Centre Universitaire d'Informatique
Université de Genève, Switzerland
{Didier.Buchs,Luis.Pedro,Matteo.Risoldi}@unige.ch
[2] Departamento de Informática, Faculdade de Ciências e Tecnologia
Universidade Nova de Lisboa, Portugal
{Bruno.Barroca,Vasco.Amaral}@di.fct.unl.pt

Abstract. With the increasing interest in metamodeling techniques for Domain Specific Modeling Languages (DSML) definition, there is a strong need to improve the language modeling process. One of the problems to solve is language evolution. Possible solutions include maximizing the reuse of metamodel patterns, composing them to form new, more expressive DSMLs.

In this paper we improve the process of rapid prototyping of DSML graphical editors in meta-modeling tools, by defining composition rules for the graphical syntax layer. The goal is to provide formally defined operators to specify what happens to graphical mappings when their respective metamodels are composed. This improves reuse of Domain Specific Modeling Languages definitions and reduces development time.

1 Introduction

With increasing reports of success stories both in industry and academy, Software Languages Engineering is becoming a more mature field. It is supported today by proper conceptual and practical tools. Several domains of application are now receiving benefit from the clarity and flexibility of specification that a Domain Specific Modeling Language (DSML) approach provides.

Among supporting tools, some allow providing a DSML with a graphical syntax and an editor, based on the DSML's metamodel. However, providing a graphical syntax to a DSML is still a very time consuming task. The main reasons are that it is a task with a very low level of reusability and that integration with the supporting tools is difficult. This is particularly relevant in the DSML prototyping phase where modifications are performed very often.

Our motivation is improving the state of the art in what concerns rapid development of graphical editors for DSMLs. In previous work, we defined what happens to the semantic mappings of DSMLs (expressed by model transformations) when two DSML metamodels are composed. This work goes further in defining a layer for graphical syntax composition. Operators are defined for the

J.A. Jacko (Ed.): Human-Computer Interaction, Part II, HCII 2009, LNCS 5611, pp. 889–898, 2009.
© Springer-Verlag Berlin Heidelberg 2009

composition of metamodels. We explore the consequences of metamodel composition on graphical syntax and on the generation of graphical editors. We use an example to illustrate the technique.

Section 2 will introduce some domain concepts we will use for composition examples. A metamodel and a graphical syntax will be given for each domain concept. Section 3 will define the composition operators and show how to compose the example metamodels and their associated graphical syntax. Section 4 will reference related work. Section 5 will resume the article and discuss limits and future work.

2   Case Study

Fig. 1 shows three simple metamodels. They represent very simple DSMLs, each of which can be used to model a different concept. The first (a) allows the specification of hierarchies of Objects. An Object may have one or more children Objects. The second metamodel (b) allows the specification of finite state machines (FSMs). A State may have outgoing Transitions, each one with a destination State. A State has an attribute initial (a boolean). The third metamodel (c) allows the specification of an event trigger. A Trigger is associated to one or more Events, which are triggered when the Trigger is activated.

Each of these metamodels has an associated graphical syntax, shown in Fig. 2. The graphical syntax for objects (a) represents an Object as a rounded box, and the children relationship as the containment of boxes (children are inside parents). The graphical syntax for FSMs (b) represents a State as a box, and a Transition as an arrow linking boxes. The direction of the arrow is given by the relationships. The initial attribute of states is represented by a dot in a corner of a state box (dot=true; no dot=false). The graphical syntax for triggers

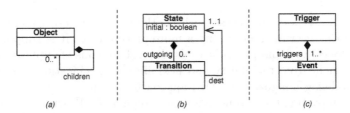

Fig. 1. Object, FSM and Trigger metamodels

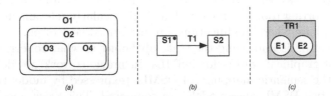

Fig. 2. Object, FSM and Trigger graphical syntax

(c) represents a `Trigger` as a gray box, containing a circle for each triggered `Event`. In all cases, visual elements are labeled with the elements ID.

In the following section we will show how, given these metamodels, a developer can define DSMLs to address each of the following example requirements:

1. Each object must contain an FSM.
2. Each object must be associated to an FSM. Several objects can be associated to the same FSM.
3. In an FSM, reaching a state may trigger events.
4. An FSM can be hierarchical; a state can contain an FSM. Getting to that state leads to the initial state of the internal FSM. From each internal state it is always possible to leave the external state.

3 Composition Approach

The composition approach extends previous work [13] on composition operators for DSML metamodel blocks. This work perceives DSML definition as an incremental task: a DSML's metamodel is created by composing several sub-metamodels, or *domain concepts*. Each concept is associated to one or more concrete graphical syntaxes. The semantic aspects of composition have been tackled in [13]. The work presented in this article goes further in exploring the syntactic aspects of composition at the graphical layer.

We use four composition operators [7] to compose metamodels and reuse graphical definitions. We assume that a domain concept is a metamodel with an associated graphical syntax and that in the process of developing a DSML several concepts are going to be composed. This section will give details about what happens to graphical syntax when these composition operators are used on metamodels. For all the examples and definitions that follow it is also assumed that there are three metamodels: a left metamodel mm_{left}; a right metamodel mm_{right}; and a resulting composed metamodel mm'. A composition of metamodels $Comp$ is defined by a mapping function $\varphi_{operator}$ as

$$mm' = Comp(mm_{left}, mm_{right}, \varphi_{operator})$$

where *operator* stands for the name of the composition operator to be specified. The metamodels used as an example are those presented in Fig. 1. Their associated graphical syntax is shown in Fig. 2.

3.1 Containment

This operator allows to create containment relations to provide hierarchical constructs. The hierarchy is defined by an aggregation relationship from one class of the left metamodel to a set of classes of the right metamodel. The containment operator is defined by $\varphi_{containment}$, a total function creating a map between elements of mm_{left} and mm_{right}:

$$\varphi_{containment} : mm_{left} \rightarrow mm_{right}, C$$

where C stands for the cardinality of the aggregation relationship between the metaclass of the mm_{left} metamodel and the metaclass(es) of the mm_{right} metamodel.

As an example, let mm_{left} be the Object metamodel in Fig. 1 (a) and as mm_{right} the State metamodel in Fig. 1 (b). Let us assume that the developer wants to define a language to specify an FSM inside each modeled object. The mapping function is defined as:

$$\varphi_{containment} = \{\langle Object, \{\langle State, 1..1 \rangle\}\rangle\}$$

The containment operator is applied to obtain a composed metamodel, shown in Fig. 3. The composition produced a state relationship which aggregates the State class inside the Object class.

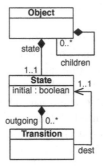

Fig. 3. Result of application of $\varphi_{containment} = \{\langle Object, \{\langle State, 1..1 \rangle\}\rangle\}$

The pattern produced by the composition (the state aggregation) is reflected in the graphical syntax by the possibility of defining states inside objects, as shown in Fig. 4. The graphical symbols for objects, states and transitions do not change.

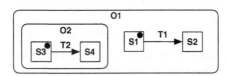

Fig. 4. Composed visual syntax for containment between Object and State

3.2 Association

The association operator is very similar to the containment operator in what concerns metamodel composition. However, instead of creating an aggregation, this operator creates a reference between a class of the mm_{left} metamodel and a class of the mm_{right} metamodel. The association operator is defined by the $\varphi_{association}$ mapping function:

$$\varphi_{association} : mm_{left} \rightarrow mm_{right}, C$$

where C is the cardinality of the reference between the metaclass of the mm_{left} metamodel and the metaclass of the mm_{right} metamodel.

As an example, let mm_{left} be the Object metamodel in Fig. 1 (a) and as mm_{right} the State metamodel in Fig. 1 (b). The developer wants to define a language to specify an FSM for each object; however, rather than defining the FSM inside the object, he just wants objects to reference an FSM, so that the same FSM can be used for several objects. The mapping function is defined as:

$$\varphi_{association} = \{\langle Object, \{\langle State, 1..1\rangle\}\rangle\}$$

Fig. 5 shows the result of applying the association operator. The composition produced a state reference, which relates the Object and State classes.

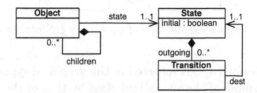

Fig. 5. Result of application of $\varphi_{association} = \{\langle Object, \{\langle State, 1..1\rangle\}\rangle\}$

The pattern produced by the composition (the state reference) is reflected in the graphical syntax by the possibility of creating a dashed arrow from an object to a state, as shown in Fig. 6. In this case too, graphical symbols for objects, states and transitions do not change.

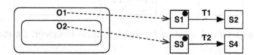

Fig. 6. Composed visual syntax for association between Object and State

3.3 Inheritance

The inheritance operator allows to compose metamodels with a UML-like inheritance concept. It specifies that a class of the left metamodel is specialized by a class of the right metamodel. The inheritance operator is defined by the $\varphi_{inherit}$ mapping function:

$$\varphi_{inherit} : mm_{left} \rightarrow mm_{right}$$

where the metaclass in mm_{left} is the specialized class and the metaclass in mm_{right} is the specialization class.

As an example, let mm_{left} be the Object metamodel in Fig. 1 (a) and as mm_{right} the Trigger metamodel in Fig. 1 (c). The developer wants to define a language for specifying FSMs, in which reaching a certain state triggers events. The mapping function is defined as:

$$\varphi_{inherit} = \{\langle State, Trigger \rangle\}$$

Fig. 7 shows the result of applying the inheritance operator. The `Trigger` class specializes the `State` class.

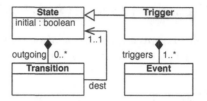

Fig. 7. Result of application of $\varphi_{inherit} = \{\langle State, Trigger \rangle\}$

The specialization pattern is reflected in the graphical syntax by substitution of the graphical symbol of the specialized class by that of the specializing class, as shown in Fig. 8. This allows defining FSMs in which a transition has a trigger – instead of a state – as source and/or destination. The graphical symbol for a trigger can be used in place of the graphical symbol for a state. Triggers and states keep their original graphical definition (e.g. one can still define events inside triggers, but not inside states).

Fig. 8. Composed visual syntax for inheritance between `State` and `Trigger`

3.4 Parameterized Merge

This operator is used as "join point" to compose two DSMLs. Originally, package merge was specified in the MOF specification [12]. Package merge allows the merging of packages to specialize metamodel classes having matching names. The necessity for metamodel classes to have matching names is however a strong limitation, which is not always satisfied.

In a more practical approach we defined the parameterized merge operation. φ_{merge} is a total function that creates a map between elements of mm_{left} and mm_{right}

$$\varphi_{merge} : mm_{left} \rightarrow mm_{right}$$

The merge between mm_{left} and mm_{right} is not performed on metamodel classes with matching names, but rather by defining a mapping fuction between classes:

– φ_{merge} is a function that maps metaclasses of the left and right metamodels;
– the merge is done on mm_{right} meaning that the element of mm_{right} defined in the φ_{merge} function keeps its name.

As an example, let mm_{left} be the Object metamodel in Fig. 1 (a) and as mm_{right} the State metamodel in Fig. 1 (b). Let us say that the developer wants to define a language to specify hierarchical finite state machines [3]. The mapping function is defined as:

$$\varphi_{merge} = \{\langle Object, State\rangle\}$$

The merge operator is applied to obtain a composed metamodel, shown in Fig. 9. The new State class has all attributes and relationships from the old State and Object classes, including the child aggregation.

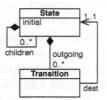

Fig. 9. Result of application of $\varphi_{merge} = \{\langle Object, State\rangle\}$

Here, the pattern is a graphical representation of a class having features of both merged classes. At the graphical syntax layer, it means that the graphical symbol for the State class keeps its graphical notation; however the newly added child aggregation makes it possible to define states inside other states (just like objects of the Object metamodel could be defined inside other objects). The resulting graphical syntax is shown in Fig. 10.

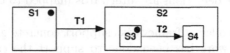

Fig. 10. Composed visual syntax for parameterized merge between Object and State

4   Related Work

Several tools can be found which are able to generate graphical editors from the metamodel of a language. These tools have different approaches to specify the concrete graphical syntax for DSMLs.

The Graphical Modeling Framework (GMF) [4] is an Eclipse project, with which a DSML's graphical editor can be generated. The resources for editor generation are the EMF metamodel of the language and several additional presentation models (gmfgraph, gmftool, gmfmap) mapped to the EMF metamodel.

The presentation models define the DSML's concrete syntax (diagram elements, toolbar options, etc).

The Generic Modeling Environment (GME) [6] is a highly configurable meta-modeling tool. Instead of having external descriptions for the concrete syntax, GME gives the ability to decorate the DSML's metamodel with special entities called *views*. For each element of the metamodel the designer can define a concrete visual syntax in the generated DSML's graphical editor.

Meta-CASE editors (e.g. MetaEdit+ [9]) are environments capable of generating CASE tools. They allow creating tool definitions in a high-level graphical environment. However, the user interface is coded manually. These environments store concrete syntax definitions directly in the metamodel properties.

Another framework is the Diagram Editor Generator (DiaGen) [11], which is an efficient solution to create visual editors for DSMLs. DiaGen is not based on metamodeling techniques; it uses its own specification language for defining the structure of diagrams. DiaGen supports editing of the concrete syntax in a graphical context, but in a tree control-based form only, where there is no support to define the graphical shape of elements. Concrete syntax in DiaGen is based on properties. DiaGen can generate an editor based on the specification using hypergraph grammars and transformations.

AToM3 (A Tool for Multi-formalism and Meta-Modelling) [1]) is a flexible modeling tool. It employs an appearance editor to define the graphical shape of model elements. It uses model properties to store the concrete syntax (model definitions are extended with visualization-based attributes). AToM3 can generate plug-ins that use the defined syntax, but the code generation is not based on a presentation DSL. Model views are generated with triple graph grammars.

Visual Modeling and Transformation System (VMTS) [10] is an n-layer meta-modeling environment that unifies the metamodeling techniques used by the common modeling tools. It employs model transformation applying graph rewriting as the underlying mechanism. Concrete syntax definitions are created by instantiating VMTS's Presentation DSL (VPD) and they define how model items are visualized. These definitions are afterwards mapped to the DSML's abstract syntax.

Although these modeling frameworks support concrete graphical syntax definitions, very little work has been done to support the composition of these definitions.

In [8] and [5], the first steps of DSML composition in GME are presented. In these works the composition operators (e.g. metamodel interfacing, class refinement) only affect the metamodel elements referring to the DSML's abstract syntax. The corresponding effects on the visual concrete syntax are left implicit, as part of the composition operator's semantics. In [7] an overview over the several composition operators for metamodel composition is provided, on which our work is based.

In [2], a new composition operator was introduced: template instantiation, in the context of GME. Again this composition operator does not focus on the visual concrete syntax, but only on the abstract syntax.

In [13] several new metamodel composition methods were presented, both at the syntactic and semantic level. These methods can be parameterized to specify what are the consequences of metamodel composition at the semantic level of a DSML (expressed as a model transformations to a target platform).

5 Conclusions

We presented a proposal for automatically mapping composition patterns to graphical syntax. A limitation of the presented work is that the composition operators might not cover all possible compositions. We might have a case in which we want to apply the metamodel composition operator and not have the composition of the graphical syntax. For example, we might want to define instances of class **State** inside class **Object**, but at the same time be able to have instances of **State** which are not contained in any object. This would require either manual composition, or identification of more complex composition patterns. Also, there are cases in which the proposed graphical representations for patterns might create ambiguity with pre-existing graphical notations of the composed metamodels. For example, if a metamodels already uses dashed arrows in its graphical syntax, then applying the Association operator to it might introduce more dashed arrows with a different meaning than the pre-existing ones. However, based on mentioned related work, we think the presented operators cover a large number of use cases.

Future work includes the identification of more complex patterns based on case studies. In order to do this, we have to explore the implementation of the proposed approaches using standardized tools. Our current point of view is that the most viable frameworks for implementation are GEF and GMF. Implementation in GEF might be easier to develop as the graphical syntax definition is at a lower level. The level of abstraction of definitions in GMF could make implementation more difficult; however, from the end user point of view it might be more usable.

Although further investigation is needed, we think that this approach is relevant in the context of defining the graphical layer of DSMLs. This task is usually non-trivial in current language development environments. Being able to reuse previously defined graphical patterns can boost DSML development productivity.

References

1. de Lara, J., Vangheluwe, H.: Using AToM3 as a Meta-CASE tool. In: 4th International Conference on Enterprise Information Systems, pp. 642–649 (2002)
2. Emerson, M., Sztipanovits, J.: Techniques for Metamodel Composition. In: OOP-SLA 6th Workshop on Domain Specific Modeling, pp. 123–139 (2006)
3. Girault, A., Lee, B., Lee, E.: Hierarchical finite state machines with multiple concurrency models. IEEE Transactions on Computer-Aided Design of Integrated Circuits and Systems 18(6), 742–760 (1999)

4. GMF Team. Eclipse graphical modeling framework,
   http://www.eclipse.org/modeling/gmf/ (visited in 2008).
5. Karsai, G., Maroti, M., Lédeczi, Á., Gray, J., Sztipanovits, J.: Composition and cloning in modeling and meta-modeling. IEEE Transactions on Control System Technology (special issue on Computer Automated Multi-Paradigm Modeling 12, 263–278 (2004)
6. Lédeczi, Á., Bakay, Á., Maróti, M., Völgyesi, P., Nordstrom, G., Sprinkle, J., Karsai, G.: Composing domain-specific design environments. IEEE Computer 34(11), 4451 (2001)
7. Lédeczi, Á., Nordstrom, G., Karsai, G., Völgyesi, P., Maróti, M.: On metamodel composition. In: Proceedings of the 2001 IEEE International Conference on Control Applications, 2001 (CCA 2001), Mexico City, Mexico, pp. 756–760. IEEE Computer Society Press, Los Alamitos (2001)
8. Lédeczi, Á., Vólgyesi, P., Karsai, G.: Metamodel composition in the Generic Modeling Environment. In: Communications at workshop on Adaptive Object- Models and Metamodeling Techniques, ECOOP 2001 (2001)
9. MetaCase Consulting. Metaedit, http://www.metacase.com (visited in 2008)
10. Mezei, G., Levendovszky, T., Charaf, H.: A model transformation for automated concrete syntax definitions of metamodeled visual languages. In: Proc. of 2nd InternationalWorkshop on Graph and Model Transformation 2006, Electronic Communications of the EASST, vol. 4 (2006)
11. Minas, M.: Specifying graph-like diagrams with DiaGen. Electronic Notes in Theoretical Computer Science 72(2), 102–111 (2002); GraBaTs 2002, Graph-Based Tools (First International Conference on Graph Transformation)
12. Object Management Group members. Meta-Object Facility 2.0 core specification. Technical report, OMG (January 2007),
    http://www.omg.org/cgi-bin/doc?formal/2006-01-01
13. Pedro, L., Amaral, V., Buchs, D.: Foundations for a domain specific modeling language prototyping environmen: A compositional approach. In: Proc. 8th OOPSLA ACM-SIGPLAN Workshop on Domain-Specific Modeling (DSM), University of Jyvaskylan (October 2008)

The Effectiveness of Interactivity in Computer-Based Instructional Diagrams

Lisa Whitman

North Carolina State University, Raleigh, NC 27695
Lisa_Whitman@ncsu.edu

Abstract. This study investigates if interaction between a student and instructional diagrams displayed on a computer can be effective in significantly improving understanding of the concepts the diagrams represent over viewing animated or static instructional diagrams. Participants viewed either interactive, animated, or static versions of multimedia tutorials that taught how a simple mechanical system, a lock, worked and how a complex mechanical system, an automobile clutch, worked. Participants were tested on recall and comprehension to determine which presentation style; static, animated, or interactive; greater impacts learning, and whether that impact is mediated by the complexity of the mechanical system. Participants who studied from interactive multimedia presentations demonstrating how simple and complex mechanical systems work performed significantly better on comprehension tests for both mechanical systems than those who studied from static or animated presentations. However, all participants performed similarly on recall tests. Research on the effectiveness of computer learning environments and how to optimize their potential for effective instruction through improved multimedia design is important as computers are increasingly being used for training and education.

1 Introduction

Discovering ways to improve teaching effectiveness is an important area of research. Traditional instructional delivery methods, such as lecture and textbooks, are still popular choices for instruction, but they may not be the best methods for teaching students about systems with interacting components, such as mechanical systems. Computer-based learning tools have the potential to instruct students in a way that other materials cannot. Computers can provide multimedia instruction, engaging different senses with audio, visual displays, and physical interaction. Computers also allow for animation so that students can see objects moving on a display. For example, diagrams can be animated and drawn step-by-step for students as if a teacher was drawing the diagrams for them. In contrast to other forms of study aids, such as textbooks or guides, computers have the potential to offer unique capabilities and opportunities for interaction between the student and the subject matter, giving students the ability to manipulate objects on the display and see the subsequent outcomes. For example, students can learn how an automobile clutch works by dragging and dropping pictures of automobile clutch parts on a computer screen to assemble the entire clutch and see how the parts interact. In addition, the computer can provide feedback on the

J.A. Jacko (Ed.): Human-Computer Interaction, Part II, HCII 2009, LNCS 5611, pp. 899–908, 2009.
© Springer-Verlag Berlin Heidelberg 2009

student's accuracy and level of understanding of the material in response to the student's interactions with the computer program. The effects of the capabilities of computers on instruction have yet to be fully explored and studied. Knowing more about how the capabilities of computers affect learning will allow the computer to be utilized to its greatest potential as a learning environment. The purpose of this current study is to determine if interactivity aids learning in computer-based instruction.

The results of this present study could have implications for the use of computers in instruction and training. Computers are quickly becoming a popular medium for instruction through the use of computer courseware, websites to supplement instruction and research, simulations to provide practice for training, and software applications that function as study aids. As computers continue to augment or replace classrooms and training facilities, research is needed on how to optimize the potential of computers as an instructional medium.

1.1 The Need for Computer-Based Instruction

Universities do not always have the capacity to accommodate all of the students who apply, or the flexibility to meet the needs of students who have other demands on their lives besides education. However, with developing technology, widespread access to computers and the Internet, and the use of electronic communication, computers present a potential solution [19]. With distance learning technology, universities can now expand to accommodate students who want to earn a degree, but cannot, or choose not, to attend traditional classroom sessions due to disabilities, traveling, or demands of work or family [6]. These universities can provide computer courseware accompanied with interaction from the professor through electronic mail, online chat sessions, bulletin boards, or in-class meetings. Distance learning is also utilized as a form of curriculum enrichment for elementary through high school students. Research has shown that these multimedia enhanced instructional programs are effective in motivating students and increasing their interest in learning [20].

Learning is no longer restricted to a traditional classroom setting. According to the National Science Board [16], the number of students taking courses and training, certificate, and degree programs online is escalating. From 1997 to 2001, enrollment in for-credit distance education courses more than doubled from 1.3 million to 2.9 million. During that time, the number of for-credit distance education courses also more than doubled from 47,500 to 118,000. With the demand for distance education courses and multimedia web-based instructional materials continuously rising, it is imperative that instructors know which forms of multimedia are optimal for teaching their students.

1.2 Multimedia Design in Computer-Based Learning

The human-computer interaction is unique in distance learning since the computer is assigned the role of instructor, while the user assumes the role of learner. The goal of this relationship is to allow the computer and user to interact in a way that will provide the most effective and efficient way of presenting and teaching the subject material to the user [10]. The design of multimedia instructional materials must be based on research that shows what types and uses of multimedia are beneficial for learning. The instructional effectiveness of a multimedia lesson should always be the design focus.

Research has shown that dual-mode presentation (audio and visual) of instructional information is more effective than single-mode presentation (visual alone) in teaching with static graphics [15] and animated graphics [13]. The authors concluded that these results were due to a reduction in cognitive load. Students do not experience cognitive overload in viewing verbal instruction with simultaneous audio because visual working memory and auditory working memory process independently of one another. However, visual working memory can become overloaded if there is competing visual stimuli, such as an animation and verbal instruction. In this situation, the student is forced to choose relevant pieces of information instead of being able to view and process all of it. This was demonstrated by Moreno and Mayer [14] who tested the effects of different narrated presentations of a multimedia scientific explanation of lightning formation. They found that learning comprehension was increased when verbal instruction was presented in both visual and audio formats, providing that the animation was not presented at the same time as the verbal information, and thus, not competing for processing in visual working memory. In addition, Czarkowski [5] found that students prefer audio and animation to static graphics and instructional materials without audio. Based on research on multimedia design for computer-based instruction, the instructional materials used in this current study presented verbal information about the systems visually with simultaneous auditory narration, preceded or followed by the diagram's animated demonstration or interactive mode.

Studies have shown graphical computer aids to enhance comprehension of complex subject matter [18], sparking further research studies in the effectiveness of computer-based instruction. Animated diagrams were found to be more effective than text alone in a study based on the instruction of tree diagrams [4]. Animated diagrams have been found to be more effective than static diagrams in a study that analyzed the effectiveness of instruction of computer algorithms [3]. Therefore, in the present study, it is predicted that students who view animated lessons about mechanical systems will outperform those who view static lessons on tests of recall and comprehension. However, Hegarty et al. [9] found that an animation did not facilitate comprehension of a mechanical system, a toilet, more than a static diagram. The authors proposed that this could be due to the nature of the mechanical system in the diagram. It was suggested that since the toilet consisted of two simultaneous causal chains it was more beneficial for the participants to comprehend the diagram by repeatedly mentally animating different sections of the toilet system at a time. It was proposed that animated diagrams might be more beneficial for learning comprehension of mechanical systems if the animations showed portions of the system and could be repeated. Thus, the diagrams used for this current study demonstrated the mechanical systems in both their entirety, as well as in segments, and the participants were allowed to view the diagrams and animations as much as they needed within a given period of time.

1.3 The Potential of Interactive Multimedia

A new question is whether the unique capabilities of interactive diagrams will provide increased effectiveness in instruction over animated and static diagrams that represent the same concepts. While animated diagrams have the capability to demonstrate instructional content in a way that facilitates learning through the illustration of life-like moving parts, interactive diagrams go beyond animated by enabling students to choose what they will learn. For example, students can choose when they want to see what happens when a clutch engages or disengages by clicking button by a diagram of a clutch. An interactive presentation can give students the most control over how they view the materials, allowing them to select when they view animations, what animations they want to see, and if they want to replay an accompanying audio narration. By being able to interact with the instructional presentation, a student is able to design the presentation based on how they want to study and their learning pace and preferences. The computer acts as a guide or tutor by showing the student what choices they have for material presentation modes, and allowing the student opportunities to enhance and customize their learning experience through the manipulation of their study materials.

Interactive diagrams may also help a user maintain interest in the subject, as well as provide motivation by discouraging passive learning and allowing the student to take a more involved and hands-on approach to grasping a concept. Research shows that active interaction with instructional materials is important to learning, and a valuable method for keeping students cognitively engaged in the instruction [12]. While the impact of interactive diagrams on learning have not been empirically tested in previous research, it has been predicted that they will be able to expand on the instructional potential of animated diagrams by allowing students to manipulate and control the animations in order to better perceive and comprehend them [22].

With interaction, students also have the opportunity to practice what they are learning since, through manipulation of objects on the display, they can reinforce concepts, such as dragging and dropping parts of a clutch to assemble it on the screen. The diagram can then be used and manipulated as many times as the user feels they need to practice in order to practice applying their knowledge and achieve mastery of the concept. In problem solving, more practice has been found to increase the long-term understanding of a subject matter [21].

Interactive diagrams also have the advantage of being able to offer feedback on the student's level of mastery of the concepts presented, and the application of their knowledge. Students receive immediate feedback on their progress by seeing the results of their manipulations and having the computer check if the outcome is correct. For example, students can assemble an automobile clutch diagram themselves by dragging the clutch's parts into place while learning about the individual parts and their roles in the functioning of the clutch. The computer gives the student immediate feedback if they are assembling the parts in the correct order or not. Feedback given by an instructional computer program in response to a user's manipulation of the display allows the user to determine their progress in acquiring knowledge and achieving mastery of a concept.

Thus, previous research supports the idea that interactive diagrams may facilitate learning like a tutor, guiding the student and allowing them to choose what they learn, practice what they learn, and receive feedback on their learning progress, unlike static and animated diagrams that simply present information. Based on these ideas, interactive lessons should prove helpful for students who are learning about simple mechanical systems, defined as having 10 or fewer moving parts, such as a common door lock mechanism, and complex mechanical systems, defined as having 11 or more moving parts, such as an automobile clutch. Previous studies have shown the effectiveness of actively engaging students in the learning process and how computers can assist in this capacity, but empirical research has not been previously conducted on interactive computer-based diagrams and their effectiveness in instruction. This present study expands upon previous research findings by exploring the instructional effectiveness of static, animated, and interactive presentations of instructional diagrams that represent simple and complex concepts. This study explores the effects of interactivity on recall and comprehension of mechanical systems. If interactivity lives up to its potential, then participants should have higher performance levels of recall and comprehension after studying from interactive instructional materials over static or animated instructional materials. To test these hypotheses, college students were given either interactive, animated or static lessons about a simple door lock and an automobile clutch. They were then tested on recall and comprehension.

2 Method

Participants were 90 undergraduate students from California State University, Northridge who received class credit for participating. The participants were screened to ensure that they did not have high levels of prior knowledge of the concepts represented in the instructional diagrams. All participants had at least a minimal level of experience with using a computer so that they knew how to point and click a mouse and drag objects on the display using a mouse. After being screened for color blindness [7], none of the participants were found to have deficient color vision. The participants were also given a spatial reasoning test that consisted of 20 questions of varying difficulty [2].

This study used a 3 X 2 mixed factorial design. Diagram presentation style (static, animated, and interactive) was the between-subjects factor, and complexity (simple, complex) was the within-subjects factor. The dependent variables were recall and comprehension.

Participants were randomly assigned to view either the static, animated, or interactive version of the tutorials for the simple and complex systems. The order of presentation for the two systems was counterbalanced to minimize order effects. Participants were allowed to spend ten minutes studying the simple system and fifteen minutes studying the complex system. The participants were able to repeat the audio in the static presentations, repeat animations in the animated presentations, and interact multiple times with the interactive diagrams as they saw fit to properly study the material, but they were limited in the amount of time that they could spend viewing the entire presentation.

After studying the presentation of the first system, the participants received the tests for recall and comprehension on the system that they just learned. The participants were told to complete the test to the best of their ability, to be as thorough and detailed in answering the questions as possible, and to write down as many facts, solutions, and reasoning behind their answers that they could. The participants were allowed to spend as much time as they needed to complete the tests. When a participant completed the tests, they were collected by the researcher and the participants then viewed the instructional materials for the other system of the same presentation style (static, animated, or interactive). After studying the materials for that system, the participants were again tested for recall and comprehension using the same proce-dures as for the first system.

Simple system. All three versions of the instructional presentations of the simple sys-tem; static, animated, and interactive; consisted of five slides that each included a dia-gram of the basic cylinder lock, verbal information describing the diagram and how the 6 different parts of the lock work and interact with each other, navigation buttons on the bottom of the screen that allowed the participants to return to the previous slide and advance to the next slide, and another button that, in the static presentation, re-played the audio for the current slide or, in the animated and interactive presentations, replayed the animation on the current slide. The descriptions of the diagrams were presented beside the diagrams so that they could be read, and the participants could also hear the descriptions being read through headphones to assist in reading or to al-low the participant to look at a diagram while listening to the descriptions.

Complex system. There were static, animated, and interactive versions of the complex system presentation, including diagrams of the 11 different parts of an auto-mobile clutch, their functions and relationships, and the purpose of the clutch in the operation of an automobile. Descriptions of the diagrams were presented beside the diagrams so that they could be read easily. The participants could hear audio re-cordings of the descriptions to assist in reading or to allow the participant to look at a diagram while listening to the descriptions. The instructional presentation of the sim-ple system consisted of thirteen slides that each included a diagram of part of the automobile clutch, written and auditory information describing the diagram, and but-tons on the bottom of the screen that allowed the participants to return to the previous slide, advance to the next slide, and replay the audio for the current slide in the static presentation or replay the animation in the animated presentation.

Recall tests. The recall tests included an open-ended question that prompted the par-ticipants to recall and write as much information and detail that they could remember about the system that they learned. Students received 1 point for each concept that they wrote down that was presented in the tutorial on that system. The recall tests also included a picture of a diagram of the system presented with blank labels for the par-ticipants to fill in the appropriate names of each of the system's parts. For the recall test on the simple system, participants received 1 point for labeling each of 6 parts of a lock discussed in the instructional presentation. For the recall test on the complex system, participants received 1 point for labeling each of 11 parts of a clutch dis-cussed in the instructional presentation. The overall recall test score was the total number of points earned from the open-ended question answers and the labels for the diagram.

Comprehension tests. For the comprehension tests, the participants were presented with four problems, and asked to provide plausible solutions based on the knowledge of the systems that they gained from the tutorials. The comprehension tests were scored by assigning 1 point for each acceptable solution to the trouble-shooting prob-lems that could have been inferred from the instructional presentation. The total points collected were used as an overall score to compare problem-solving testing performance across conditions.

3   Results

Removing cases due to prior knowledge of the mechanical systems or spending insufficient time to view the presentations reduced the usable sample size to 74 for the simple system and 72 for the complex system.

It was hypothesized that participants would recall more information about both simple and complex mechanical systems after studying interactive instructional multimedia presentations than after studying animated or static presentations. It was also hypothesized that participants who studied from animated presentations would recall more items than those who studied from static presentations. A 2-way mixed design analysis of variance (ANOVA), with recall as the dependent variable, indicated no significant interaction for performance on the recall tests between the simple and complex mechanical systems, $F(2, 68) = 0.165$, $p < 0.05$. No significant main effect on recall was found for presentation style, $F(2, 68) = 0.011$, $p > 0.05$. The analysis also indicated no significant main effects for complexity, $F(1, 68) = 0.593$, $p > 0.05$. Participants recalled a similar number of items about the simple mechanical system and the complex mechanical system whether they studied from the interactive presentation, the animated presentation, or static presentation.

It was also hypothesized that participants' performance in tests of comprehension of both simple and complex mechanical systems would be significantly better after studying interactive instructional multimedia presentations over animated or static presentations since the interactive diagrams provide practice in manipulating the diagrams and encourage active processing of relationships between the parts of the systems represented in the diagrams. A 2-way mixed design ANOVA, with comprehension as the dependent variable, found no interaction between presentation styles and complexity, $F(2, 68) = 0.298$, $p > 0.05$. The analysis indicated a significant main effect for presentation style, $F(2, 68) = 4.453$, $p < 0.05$. A Tukey HSD post-hoc analysis showed that comprehension test performance was significantly better for participants who studied the simple and complex mechanical systems from the interactive presentations ($M = 5.738$, $SD = 0.374$), over both the animated ($M = 4.442$, $SD = 0.336$), $p < .05$, and static presentations ($M = 4.375$, $SD = 0.350$), $p < .05$.

The spatial reasoning ability of participants did not have a significant effect on the effects that presentation style had on comprehension or recall test performance. Students who studied the mechanical systems from the animated presentations did perform better on the comprehension tests than those that studied from the static presentations, but not by a significant amount. The 2-way mixed design ANOVA indicated a significant main effect for complexity, $F(1, 68) = 23.389$, $p < 0.05$. Students performed significantly better on the comprehension tests for the simple system ($M = 5.604$) than the comprehension tests for the complex system ($M = 4.100$). Table 1 shows the means and standard deviations for comprehension test performance on the simple mechanical system and the complex mechanical system.

Table 1. Comprehension Test Performance

Presentation Style	Simple System		Complex System	
	M	SD	M	SD
Static	5.259	2.551	3.500	1.445
Animated	5.039	2.358	3.963	1.911
Interactive	6.524	2.400	4.952	2.224

4 Discussion

This study was designed to investigate if interaction between a student and computer-based instructional diagrams results in improved performance on recall and comprehension tests over studying from animated and static diagrams that represent the same concepts. No significant interaction was found between recall or comprehension test performance and complexity of the mechanical system being taught. Students performed significantly better on the comprehension tests for the simple system than the comprehension tests for the complex system. Participants performed similarly on recall tests after studying from static, animated, and interactive instructional presentations of simple and complex mechanical systems. Participants who studied from animated presentations did not perform significantly better on the tests than students who studied from static presentations. However, as hypothesized, participants who studied from interactive presentations performed significantly better on tests of comprehension for both simple and complex mechanical systems than participants who studied from animated or static presentations.

Past research has shown that animated diagrams can be more effective than static diagrams for teaching some subject material [3]. However, in a study conducted by Hegarty et al. [9], participants who viewed animated diagrams of a mechanical system did not show significantly better comprehension over those who viewed static diagrams. Similarly, the results of this present study demonstrated that animated presentations did not facilitate comprehension or recall of the mechanical systems more than static presentations. However, results of this study did show that interactive presentations were effective in significantly improving comprehension of simple and complex mechanical systems over static and animated presentations. This suggests that animated diagrams are not as beneficial for teaching mechanical systems as they are for teaching other subject matter, but interactive diagrams are an effective method for teaching mechanical systems.

Participants who viewed the interactive presentations showed significantly better comprehension of the mechanical systems over those who viewed static or animated instructional presentations, supporting previous research that predicted interactivity would be able to help students perceive and comprehend diagrams better than animation by providing students with the ability to manipulate and control the diagram [22] and allowing students to be more actively engaged in the instructional material through interactivity [12], thus engaging students in deep-level cognitive processing through behavioral processes [11].

The results of this study could have implications for many applications of computer- and web-based instruction. Computers are quickly becoming a popular medium for instruction through the use of computer courseware, websites to supplement instruction and research, simulations to provide practice for training, and software applications that function as study aids. As computers continue to augment or replace classrooms and training facilities, it is imperative to conduct research on how to optimize the potential of computers as an instructional medium. With the demand for distance education courses and multimedia web-based instructional materials continuously rising, it is helpful for instructors to know which forms of multimedia design are optimal for teaching their students before they invest resources and time in training and materials.

Further research is needed to discover the best methods for designing instructional multimedia presentations that increase comprehension of various subjects other than mechanical systems. This study showed that for the purpose of teaching mechanical systems, it is worth the time, resources, and effort of instructors to offer multimedia presentations that include interactive diagrams for maximum learning comprehension of the subject matter. Interactive diagrams may also be the most effective method for teaching other subject material, including topics similar to mechanical systems, such as physics and engineering. Further research is needed to show how interactivity can improve comprehension of other instructional content.

Further research can also expand on the findings of this study by exploring optimal ways of designing interactive diagrams. This present study utilized interactions that included controlling, selecting, and repeating animations, as well as hovering the mouse over objects to reveal labels, and dragging and dropping parts of an automobile clutch in the proper order to assemble the entire system. Further research can explore different types of interaction with diagrams that may improve recall as well as comprehension, or that are most beneficial for teaching certain subject matter.

Students can benefit significantly from interacting with diagrams, which improves comprehension by allowing students to choose what they want to learn, practice what they learn, and receive feedback on their learning progress. If the goal of an educational multimedia presentation is to promote comprehension of mechanical systems, then interactivity holds exciting promise.

References

1. Bennett, G.K., Seashore, H.G., Wesman, A.G.: Manual for the Differential Aptitude Tests, Forms S and T, 5th edn., p. 9. The Psychological Corporation, New York (1973)
2. Bennett, G.K., Seashore, H.G., Wesman, A.G.: Differential Aptitude Tests, Form S, pp. 42–47. The Psychological Corporation, New York (1973)
3. Catrambone, R., Seay, A.F.: Using animation to help students learn computer algorithms. Human Factors 44(3), 495–512 (2002, Fall)
4. Cox, R., McKendree, J., Tobin, R., Lee, J., Mayes, T.: Vicarious learning from dialogue and discourse – a controlled comparison. Instructional Science 27(6), 431–457 (1999)
5. Czarkowski, S.: The effects of animation, audio, and educational Content on recall and comprehension. Unpublished master's thesis, California State University, Northridge (1996)
6. Enghagen, L.: Technology and Higher Education. National Education Association, Washington (1997)
7. Hardy, L.H., Rand, G., Rittler, M.C.: AO H-R-R Pseudoisochromatic Plates, 2nd edn. American Optical Company, U.S.A (1957)
8. Harris, T., Brain, M.: How lock picking works. How Stuff Works (2001), http://science.howstuffworks.com/lock-picking3.htm
9. Hegarty, M., Quilici, J., Narayanan, N.H., Holmquist, S., Moreno, R.: Multimedia instruction: lessons from evaluation of theory-based design. Journal of Educational Multimedia and Hypermedia 8(2), 119–150 (1999)
10. Keller, A.: When Machines Teach: Designing Computer Courseware. Harper & Row, New York (1987)

11. Kennedy, G.E.: Promoting cognition in multimedia interactivity research. Journal of Interactive Learning Research 15(1), 43–61 (2004)
12. Kozielska, M.: Educational computer programs in learning of physics by action. In: Education Media International, pp. 161–166 (2000)
13. Mayer, R.E., Moreno, R.: A split-attention effect in multimedia learning: evidence for dual processing systems in working memory. Journal of Educational Psychology 90, 312–320 (1998)
14. Mayer, R.E., Moreno, R.: Verbal redundancy in multimedia learning: when reading helps listening. Journal of Educational Psychology 94(1), 156–163 (2002)
15. Mousavi, S.Y., Low, R., Sweller, J.: Reducing cognitive load by mixing auditory and visual presentation modes. Journal of Educational Psychology 87, 319–334 (1995)
16. National Science Board, Science and Engineering Indicators (vol. 1, NSB 04-1). National Science Foundation, Arlington (2004)
17. Nice, K.: How clutches work. How Stuff Works (2000),
    http://auto.howstuffworks.com/clutch.htm
18. Rigney, J., Lutz, K.A.: Effect of graphic analogies of concepts in chemistry on learning and attitude. Journal of Educational Psychology 68, 305–311 (1976)
19. Schrum, L.: Online teaching and learning: essential conditions for success! In: Distance Learning Technologies: Issues, Trends, and Opportunities, Idea Group, Hershey (2000)
20. Sherry, L.: Issues in distance learning. International Journal of Educational Telecommunications 1(4), 337–365 (1996)
21. Shute, V.J., Gawlick, L.A., Gluck, K.A.: Effects of practice and learner control on short- and long-term gain and efficiency. Human Factors 40(2), 296–311 (1998)
22. Tversky, B., Morrison, J.B.: Animation: can it facilitate? International Journal of Human-Computer Studies 57, 247–262 (2002)

Author Index

Printed in the United States
by Bookmasters

Printed in the United States
By Bookmasters